The Investment Advisor Body of Knowledge

Readings for the CIMA® Certification

**IMCA® INVESTMENT MANAGEMENT
CONSULTANTS ASSOCIATION**

WILEY

(Credits continued on page 1135)

ISBN 978-1-118-91232-4 (Paperback)
ISBN 978-1-118-91241-6 (ePDF)
ISBN 978-1-118-91234-8 (ePub)

SKY10074655_050824

Dedicated to My Family:
Sandi, Tyler, Erika, Dylan, and Drew
Mom and Dad: Sue and Curt
Brothers: Mike and Ken

Contents

Acknowledgments

IMCA Board of Directors

John Nersesian, CIMA, CFP, CPWA (Chair)
Scott Thayer, CIMA (Vice Chair)
Kevin Sanchez, CIMA, CFP, CPWA (Treasurer)
David Koulish, CPWA, CFP (Secretary)
Betsy Piper/Bach, JD, CIMA, CFP, CTFA (Past Chair)
David Archer, CIMA, AIFA
Dorothy Bossung, CIMA, CFP, CPWA
Bruce Curwood, CIMA, CFA
Tony Davidow, CIMA
Stewart Koesten, CIMA, CFP, AIF
John Moninger, CIMA, CPWA, AIF
Margaret Towle, PhD, CIMA, CPWA
Brett Wright, CIMA, CPWA
Keith Clemens, CIMA, CPWA
Todd Wagenberg, CIMA

CIMA Certification Commission

Jay Shein, PhD, CIMA, CFP (Chair)
David Archer, CIMA, AIFA
Lewis Assaley, PhD, CIMA
David Cordell, PhD, CFP, CFA
Alfred Eaton, CIMA, CFP
Phil Fazio, DBA, CFP, CIMA
Todd Wagenberg, CIMA
Ellen Walsh, CIMA
Deidre Spurlin Waltz, CIMA, CPWA, CFP
Frederick Weiss, CIMA
Grace Wellerts, CIMA, CFP

IMCA Technical Advisory Board

Bruce Curwood, CIMA, CFA
Phil Fazio, DBA, CFP, CIMA
Jonathan Golub, CFA
Nigel Lewis, PhD
Rex Macey, CIMA, CFA, CFP

Ash Rajan, MBA
Jay Shein, PhD, CIMA, CFP
Scott Thayer, CIMA
Margaret Towle, PhD, CIMA, CPWA

IMCA Staff

Sean Walters, CAE (Executive Director)
Ian MacKenzie (Chief Operations Officer)
Gary Diffendaffer, CFP (Chief Certification Officer)
Theresa Bartlett (Director of Certification)
Angie Lutterman, CPA (Chief Financial Officer)
Ceil Oetting, PHR (Senior Director, Human Resources)
Stephanie Lasser, CAE, CMP (Director of Education and Conferences)
Jamie Lewis (Education & Product Development Manager)
Cheryl Brandes (Education Programs Manager)
Tricia Fleming (Education Programs Coordinator and Administrator)
Jill Ladouceur (Director of Creative Services)
Ryan Hoffman (Director of Communications)
Debbie Nochlin (Managing Editor, *Investments & Wealth Monitor* and *Journal of Investment Consulting*)

A special thanks goes to Jamie Lewis for organizing and managing this project. Your patience and persistence were critical. This would never have come together without your tireless work. Thank you, Jamie!

Contributing Authors

M.J. Alhabeeb, PhD
Noel Amenc, PhD
Howard J. Atkinson, CIMA, CFA
Mark J. Anson, PhD, JD, CPA, CFA, CAIA
Kris Boudt, PhD
Alistair Bryne, PhD, CFA
Gerald W. Buetow Jr., PhD, CFA
Roger G. Clarke, PhD
W. Sean Cleary, PhD, CFA
Bruce M. Collins, PhD
Robert M. Conroy, DBA, CFA
Garry B. Crowder, JD
Christopher L. Culp, PhD
Joakim Darras
Pamela P. Drake, PhD, CFA
Frank J. Fabozzi, PhD, CFA, CPA
Ryan C. Fuhrmann, CFA
Khalid Ghayur, CFA
Felix Goltz
Larry Harris, PhD
Ronan G. Heaney

IMCA
David Iverson
Robert R. Johnson, PhD, CFA
David M. Jones, PhD
Paul D. Kaplan, CFA
Hossein Kazemi, PhD, CFA
Dorothy C. Kelly, CFA
Stephan A. Komon, CFA
Mark Kritzman, CFA
Asjeet S. Lamba, CFA
Veronique Le Sourd
Richard C. Marston, PhD
Lionel Martellini, PhD
Ron Mensink, CFA
Michael B. Miller
Benedict Peeters
Stephen C. Platt, CFA
Michael Pompian, CFA, CFP, CAIA
Ellen J. Rachlin
Bernd Scherer, PhD
Thomas Schneeweis, PhD, CAIA
Shani Shamah
Barry M. Sine, CFA
Vijay Singal, PhD, CFA
Frank E. Smudde, CFA
Robert A. Strong, CFA
Jarrod W. Wilcox, PhD
Richard Yamarone

Subject Matter Experts and Colleagues (who directly or indirectly influenced the development of this text)

Yacine Ait-Sahalia, PhD
Andrew Ang, PhD
Garry Bridgeman, CIMA
Jean Brunel, CFA
Mike Gallmeyer, PhD
Chris Geczy, PhD
Roger Gibson, CFA, CFP
John Granzow, CIMA
Mark Harbour, CFA, CIMA
Michael Kitces, MTAX, CFP
Jeff Jaffe, PhD
Richard Joyner, CPA, PFS, CFP, CIMA, CPWA
Greg LaBlanc, JD
Pierre Liang, PhD, CPA
Wai Lee, PhD
Andrew Lo, PhD

Arthur Lyons
Craig MacKinlay, PhD
Toby Moskowitz, PhD
Dede Pahl
Raghuram Rajan, PhD
Tarun Ramadorai, PhD
Doug Rogers, CFA
Geert Rouwenhorst, PhD
Shashin Shah, CFA, CFP
Ron Surz, CIMA
Jeff Thomas, JD, CIMA, CPWA
Vijay Vaidyanathan, PhD
Pietro Veronesi, PhD
Scott Welch, CIMA

Introduction

The Purpose of This Textbook

This textbook has been developed with two objectives in mind: Consolidate the key concepts, research, theories, and application that form the critical knowledge and skills of investment advisors and consultants into one volume; and offer CIMA certification candidates a comprehensive resource to help them in their studies as they proceed through their candidacy.

The Layout and Structure of This Textbook

We have leveraged works from some of the best minds in academia and industry to present a unified body of text that encompasses the CIMA Core Topics List. While the readings in the textbook follow the CIMA exam content blueprint by domain and section, not all of the (525) line items found on that list are covered in this book. That being said, you will find that most of those topics are reviewed in this text, and just as important, each is covered at a level of depth and cognitive skill as is appropriate.

In addition to following the order of the CIMA Core Topics List, we have woven readings together in a way that is logical and should be easy to follow. Some of the concepts found early in this textbook should be considered building blocks for content and application that will appear later in the text. Consequently you will see some repetition of concepts and calculations that we feel form a critical foundation for understanding more advanced application.

IMCA® is a registered trademark and Investment Management Consultants Association[SM] and Certified Investment Management Analyst[SM] are service marks of Investment Management Consultants Association Inc. and denote the highest quality of standards and education for financial professionals. CIMA®, CIMC®, and CPWA® are registered certification marks of Investment Management Consultants Association Inc. Certified Private Wealth Advisor is a pending certification mark of Investment Management Consultants Association Inc. Investment Management Consultants Association Inc. does not discriminate in educational opportunities or practices on the basis of race, color, religion, gender, national origin, age, disability, or any other characteristic protected by law.

For the most part we were able to use complete chapters and readings to explore various topics adequately, but there are cases in which we removed sub-sections of various works as they did not directly address CIMA curriculum; thus you may notice that some readings appear to jump around a bit. Suffice it to say, we've reduced the readings down to what we believe are the most critical components for candidates studying for the CIMA exams.

It is also important to note that not all of the readings are in agreement. For example, some authors prefer passive over active investment strategies; some authors prefer extensive use of alternative investments while others do not; and many authors disagree on the level of efficiency in the markets. We thought it best to include dissenting opinions, as it should be useful for readers to learn where debate lies in our industry and to explore different analyses and conclusions.

Another reason for incorporating the work of different authors is the value that each brings based on his or her own unique communication style. By introducing different writing styles, we help ensure that numerous learning styles are addressed, which should benefit the readers of this textbook. Therefore keep in mind that some authors will be "speaking your language" while others will not.

How to Use This Text

Each chapter begins with a brief introduction highlighting key concepts as they relate to investment advisors and consultants. These short intros build a framework for the readings found in each chapter, particularly since some chapters contain readings from different authors as described earlier. A list of learning objectives that tie directly to the CIMA Core Topics List is provided for each reading in the chapter. This list of objectives should help you focus on what is most important in each reading as it pertains to CIMA content and your exams.

We recommend that you become a proactive learner. Don't just read the text but interact with it: Take notes; make a list of key concepts and calculations; make a list of topics that you'll need to come back to and review again; make a list of questions concerning things you don't understand; work through the examples, problems, and quiz questions—then go back and do them again.

You should use the CIMA Core Topics List, found in the CIMA Candidate Handbook, as your road map for what you'll be responsible for on your exams. Self-assess your own strengths and weaknesses as you work through this textbook. Review the quiz databank as you continue to assess your competency. If you struggle with any subject matter in this textbook, we recommend you pursue additional resources in those areas as you continue to study and prepare to take the exams. You might consider other university level textbooks or web content and exam prep material from qualified and reliable sources. We do not, however, recommend that you consider this textbook as an "exam prep" resource or guide that covers exactly what you'll see on your exams, as that is not the purpose of this work. The text is, however, organized as a comprehensive resource designed to cover key concepts and applications found in the CIMA Core Topics List at an appropriate level of depth.

The CIMA Content

The content found in the following readings defines, discusses, and explains the core topics and learning objectives found in the CIMA Core Topics List used as a blueprint for the CIMA qualification and certification exams.

The CIMA Core Topics List includes content divided into six domains, including:

I. Governance

   IMCA's Code of Professional Responsibility and industry regulation are reviewed.

II. Fundamentals

   Key concepts and applications in statistics, the time value of money, economics, and global financial markets are described and explained.

III. Portfolio Performance and Risk Measurements

   Authors define and discuss risk attributes, risk measurements, performance measurement, and attribution. Concepts are explained and mathematical formulae are used to walk readers through quantitative methods and analysis.

IV. Traditional and Alternative Investments

   These readings include descriptions of various equity and fixed income investments such as stocks and bonds, various fund structures (such as mutual funds, exchange-traded funds, and hedge funds), foreign exchange, alternative investments, options, futures, and other derivatives. This section also includes a chapter covering technical analysis.

V. Portfolio Theory and Behavioral Finance

   Modern Portfolio Theory (MPT), and research and theories considered Post-MPT are explored and debated. Key concepts such as mean variance optimization (MVO), the efficient frontier, the Capital Allocation Line (CAL), diversification, the Capital Asset Pricing Model (CAPM), and the Arbitrage Pricing Theory (APT) are all discussed in detail.

VI. Investment Consulting Process

   The last section of this textbook reviews client discovery, the investment policy statement (IPS), portfolio construction methodology, risk management, and manager search and selection for those employing active managers and/or strategies. Tax-aware (tax-efficient) investment strategies are also explored.

This textbook is organized using these six domains and the 21 chapters to line up directly with the 21 sections that can be found under the six domains in the CIMA Candidate Handbook. There are approximately 111 core topics and 525 line items, per the CIMA exam content blueprint.

Disclaimer: The CIMA Qualification and Certification Exam topics and exam weightings are taken from the CIMA Candidate Handbook as approved by the CIMA Certification Commission. IMCA's education department and the authors and editors of this manuscript have no knowledge of actual exam content. The material and content published in this manuscript are for educational review purposes only, and do not guarantee an exhaustive compendium of exam questions covered on the exams. The CIMA Certification Commission neither endorses nor recommends this material.

Please note that IMCA-specific documents found in this text (e.g., CIMA Core Topics List, IMCA Code of Professional Responsibility, IMCA Standards of Practice, IMCA Performance Reporting Standards, IMCA Disciplinary Rules and Procedures, and IMCA Guidelines Regarding the Acceptance of Benefits from Third Parties) are subject to change; therefore we recommend candidates check IMCA's website at www.imca.org for the most recent version of these documents before testing.

The CIMA Exams

At the time of publication of this textbook, the CIMA qualification exam includes 60 multiple-choice questions given over a two-hour time period. The CIMA certification exam includes 110 multiple-choice questions given over a four-hour time period. Based on the core topics list, content from each of the six domains and each of the 21 subsections (chapters in this text) are tested on both exams. The primary differences in the two exams are in overall length, the topic coverage for each exam per the weightings identified in the core topics list, and in the cognitive level at which specific topics are tested. The certification exam should include questions that demand a higher level of cognitive skill and knowledge to answer correctly.

Candidates should be familiar with IMCA's "Sample Formula Sheet for CIMA Certification" which may be downloaded from IMCA's website. All candidates will be given a copy of the formula sheet during the qualification and certification exams. Note however that each university may use a different formula sheet, or possibly no formula sheet, for their exam. Candidates should be familiar with all of the terms and formulas on this sheet, but keep in mind that some of these calculations may be expressed differently (e.g., ordering of figures may be different, different symbols may be used, etc.). Therefore, candidates should know each well enough to be able to make the necessary adjustments if any formula is expressed differently in readings or on their exams. In other words, learn how to use the formulas; do not simply memorize them.

Candidates who report studying 100+ hours for the CIMA qualification exam and an additional 100+ hours for the certification exam demonstrate higher rates of success. Of course, the time needed to successfully comprehend and retain a sufficient amount of the material depends on several factors, including a candidate's existing knowledge and experience, study habits, focus, and determination.

Good luck to all of you who are studying for your exams. We wish every success to all investment advisors and consultants in the field who are placing the needs of their clients first, constantly working to improve their own skills, and seeking to provide the best services possible. All the best.

Additional Resources

The following resource is available online at (www.wiley.com) to further assist CIMA candidates in their studies:

- Quiz questions for each section

Helpful Web Links

IMCA—CIMA certification homepage: www.imca.org/cima

CIMA certification process: www.imca.org/cima-certification-process

CIMA study resources: www.imca.org/cima-study-resources

CIMA registered education providers: www.imca.org/pages/registered-education
-providers

CIMA core topics: www.imca.org/pages/2014-CIMA-Core-Topics

CHAPTER 1

IMCA Code of Professional Responsibility and Standards of Practice

I nvestment advisors and consultants are responsible for following laws and standards enforced by numerous government agencies, industry self-regulatory bodies, and the firms at which they are employed. As a professional certification body, the Investment Management Consultants Association (IMCA) prescribes and enforces its own code of ethics and standards as is described through its Code of Professional Responsibility ("code") and Standards of Practice ("standards").

The seven elements listed in IMCA's code serve as the core of IMCA's code of ethics. These seven code elements are designed to outline the key principles of IMCA's code. The code elements are listed in IMCA's standards under standard number one. Subsequent standards provide further explanation of code elements along with additional details of specific requirements and guidelines, further application of code elements, and numerous examples. In other words, the standards describe various code items in greater detail.

The concepts of fiduciary responsibility, disclosure, conflicts of interest, confidentiality, compliance, and competence are all described and explained in the readings found in this chapter.

Part I IMCA Code of Professional Responsibility

Learning Objectives
- List and explain the seven elements of IMCA's Code of Professional Responsibility.
- Apply the seven code elements appropriately when given a set of facts or circumstances.

Part II IMCA Standards of Practice

Learning Objectives
- Use IMCA's Standards of Practice to provide detailed explanations of the seven elements of IMCA's Code of Professional Responsibility.
- Determine the ramifications based on IMCA's Standards of Practice when given a set of facts or circumstances.

Part III IMCA Performance Reporting Standards

Learning Objective
- Differentiate between performance standards that must be observed (are required) and best practices.

Part IV IMCA Disciplinary Rules and Procedures

Learning Objectives
- Describe the disciplinary rules and procedures that apply to CIMA® designees.
- Apply IMCA's disciplinary rules and procedures when given a set of facts or circumstances.

Part V IMCA Guidelines Regarding the Acceptance of Benefits from Third Parties

Learning Objectives
- Describe IMCA's guidelines regarding a CIMA® designee's acceptance of benefits from third parties.
- Describe a CIMA® designee's responsibilities for disclosing third-party benefits.

Part I IMCA Code of Professional Responsibility

This Code has been adopted to promote and maintain a high standard of professional conduct in the investment management consulting profession. All members of IMCA are expected to subscribe to the Code, which serves to ensure public confidence in the integrity and service offered by professional investment management consultants. Adherence to the Code is required of all IMCA designation holders.

Each financial professional shall:

1. Serve the financial interests of clients. Each professional shall always place the financial interests of the client first. All recommendations to clients and decisions on behalf of clients shall be solely in the best interest of the client.
2. Disclose fully to clients services provided and compensation received. All financial relationships, direct or indirect, between consultants and investment managers, plan officials, beneficiaries, sponsors, or any other potential conflicts of interest shall be fully disclosed on a timely basis.
3. Provide to clients all material information related to the investment decision-making process as well as other information they may need to make informed decisions based on realistic expectations. All client inquiries shall be answered promptly, completely, and truthfully.
4. Maintain the confidentiality of all information entrusted by the client, to the fullest extent permitted by regulatory and legal entities in conjunction with the professional's firm/company policy.

5. Comply fully with all statutory and regulatory requirements affecting the delivery of investment consulting services to clients.
6. Maintain competency in investment management consulting and financial services through education and training to better serve clients and enhance investment management consulting.
7. Maintain a high level of professional ethical conduct.

Part II IMCA Standards of Practice

Standard 1: The IMCA Code of Professional Responsibility

See the IMCA Code of Professional Responsibility on previous page.

Standard 2: Responsibilities to the Client

STANDARD 2A—A CONSULTANT'S RESPONSIBILITY TO ASSIST IN ACHIEVEMENT OF CLIENT'S FINANCIAL GOALS Consultants have a responsibility to make the client's financial goals their highest priority. All recommendations must be made solely in the client's interests and intended to assist clients in reaching their financial goals.

Explanation Each client, whether institutional or individual, must have full confidence that the consultant will make objective, well-researched recommendations based on the client's goals and best interests.

Procedures for Compliance All consultants shall notify clients of their intent to provide unbiased, candid, informed recommendations intended solely to assist clients in reaching their financial goals and to promote the clients' best interests.

First and foremost, in order to determine the client's goals, the consultant shall profile each client to determine rate-of-return objectives, risk tolerance, time horizons, and tax status. Initial and ongoing recommendations shall be based upon the client's goals, both as originally determined and as they change over time. When conflicts or the potential for conflicts arise, the client must be fully advised of the situation. Without full disclosure of the consultant's role or the firm's role in any potential conflict of interest, the client's best interests may be compromised.

In addition to the IMCA Standards of Practice (Standards) and IMCA Code of Professional Responsibility (Code), consultants shall adhere to the firm's code of conduct and compliance. If at any time consultants believe that they cannot comply with these standards, they should resign the contract with the client.

Impact of the Standard The professional responsibility implied by this standard is the very basis for clients engaging a consultant on their behalf. Continual understanding, conveyance, and adherence to this standard enhance the stature of the client/consultant relationship and that of the investment consulting profession. Without compliance, trust—the most important aspect of the client/consultant relationship—cannot exist, and the balance of these standards becomes irrelevant.

STANDARD 2B—A CONSULTANT'S RESPONSIBILITY TO DISCLOSE ALL COMPENSATION Consultants have a responsibility to disclose to clients all compensation in all forms and amounts received for consulting services provided.

Explanation Client knowledge of compensation received for services rendered by the consultant establishes a relationship of trust between the parties. The disclosure of compensation as well as disclosure of any financial relationships between the consultant and service providers builds an ethical bridge in the relationship. Disclosure of all compensation, and the sources of such compensation, also eliminates the potential for conflicts of interest between the client and consultant.

Procedures for Compliance Consultants shall annually review all compensation received for consulting services rendered and report to the client any additional compensation beyond that which the client may reasonably be expected to know.

Impact of the Standard By eliminating the potential for conflicts of interest through the disclosure of compensation and its sources, the consultant enhances the reputation of the consulting profession and IMCA.

STANDARD 2C—A CONSULTANT'S RESPONSIBILITY TO PROVIDE ALL PERTINENT INFORMATION It is the responsibility of the consultant to provide each client with all requested information as well as all information available to the consultant that enables the client to make informed decisions.

Explanation In a world where huge amounts of information are easily available via the Internet, clients can access data that may or may not be relevant to their situations or that may be biased or incorrect. Even if relevant, correct, and unbiased, information and data do not translate to experience and knowledge. The consultant is responsible for fully researching all available information, determining the implications of that information for the client's situation, and providing full and objective comments.

Procedures for Compliance Consultants have a professional responsibility to research every relevant and applicable situation presented to them by clients to the fullest extent possible. In all instances, the consultant must inform the client of all aspects known to be relevant to a particular situation, positive or negative. Information shall be presented in an objective and unbiased manner to assist clients in understanding progress toward their goals. This information also shall be made available with a frequency that ensures meaningful communication between the consultant and client. Such information shall relate directly to the client's goals and financial situations.

Impact of the Standard By complying with this standard and presenting all information known to the consultant regarding the client's situation, consultants can help clients weigh the impact of their decisions in the light of full disclosure. This enhances the reputation of the investment consulting profession and IMCA as the professional sources of information, applicability, and objectivity.

STANDARD 2D—A CONSULTANT'S RESPONSIBILITY TO MAINTAIN CLIENT CONFIDENTIALITY AND PRIVACY Consultants have a responsibility to maintain the full privacy and confidentiality of all information provided to them by both institutional and individual clients.

Explanation   Institutions, including public funds, and individuals not only have the right to but the need for highly professional, candid, and confidential relationships with their consultants. In order to provide informed professional advice, a consultant must have access to all relevant information involving a client's financial situation, investment status, and goals. By acknowledging the privacy policy relating to the confidentiality of client information and the client/consultant relationship, the consultant will be more likely to obtain a full and candid disclosure of the required information.

Procedures for Compliance   Consultants shall advise clients of the privacy policy that applies to their relationship and assure them that all information gathered is of a strictly confidential nature. In addition, the compliance officer at the consultant's firm shall be notified of Standard 2d and the consultant's code of confidentiality.

All client records and information relating to financial situations and goals shall be kept private and confidential by the consultant. Even the disclosure of a client's name without obtaining prior permission from the client is prohibited. The use of client lists that may influence a potential client's decision relative to a consultant's capability is discouraged.

If professional references are requested by new or potential clients, consultants must obtain approval from existing clients in similar industries and situations prior to disclosing the names of these clients.

On no occasion shall the consultant disclose the financial status, goals, structure, or other information relating to any client to any other person or body unless legally required to do so. While certain situations may have similar structures and resolutions, any disclosure of a client's situation disenfranchises the privacy of the client/consultant relationship.

Regarding public funds, consultants may provide, if requested, information that exists in the public domain regarding public fund clients.

Impact of the Standard   Adherence to this standard improves the disclosure of information between the consultant and client and heightens the professionalism of the relationship.

STANDARD 2E—A CONSULTANT'S RESPONSIBILITY TO MAINTAIN COMPETENCE   Consultants have a responsibility to maintain competence through the highest ethical, professional, and ongoing educational practices within their means.

Explanation   The ability to render advice in a knowledgeable, professional, candid, and objective fashion is a basic requirement for establishing client trust. In order to have confidence in the advice being rendered, the client must have reason to fully trust the consultant's competencies and capabilities.

Procedures for Compliance   Consultants shall advise clients, partners, and their firms of their commitment to upholding professionalism through compliance with this standard.

Impact of the Standard   By adhering to this standard, the consultant assures clients that their consulting needs will be met competently and professionally.

Standard 3: Responsibilities to the Public

STANDARD 3A—A CONSULTANT'S RESPONSIBILITY TO ABSTAIN FROM USE OF MATERIAL NONPUBLIC INFORMATION Consultants who receive material nonpublic information in confidence have a responsibility to abstain from disclosure or use of that information, whether or not such use would cause harm to a client.

Explanation By nature of their profession, consultants hold a unique position of trust and are bound by rules of professional confidentiality. Unless required by law, they may not disclose private information revealed by reason of that profession or position.

Procedures for Compliance Consultants shall not disclose any confidential client information without the specific consent of the client unless in response to proper legal or regulatory processes. The use of client information for personal benefit is improper, even if it does not cause harm to the client.

Consultants who possess material nonpublic information related to the value of a security shall not trade or cause others to trade in that security if such trading would breach a duty or if the information was misappropriated or relates to a tender offer. If material nonpublic information is disclosed in breach of a duty, the consultant shall make all reasonable efforts to achieve public dissemination of such information.

Impact of the Standard Adherence to this standard enhances the reputation of consultants, both professionally and personally, and helps to ensure that CIMA® and CIMC® certificants and IMCA members are recognized as maintaining the highest standards of conduct.

STANDARD 3B—A CONSULTANT'S RESPONSIBILITY TO MAKE PROPER USE OF CERTIFIED INVESTMENT MANAGEMENT ANALYST® AND CERTIFIED INVESTMENT MANAGEMENT CONSULTANT® CERTIFICATIONS Consultants have a responsibility to ensure that the CIMA and CIMC certifications are used only by those who meet IMCA requirements. Specifications for proper use of the certifications have been established by IMCA.

Explanation The CIMA and CIMC certifications are intended to enhance public awareness of the investment management consulting profession and reflect the high standards set by IMCA. To protect the status of these certifications, their use has been regulated by IMCA, and CIMA and CIMC licensees are to use these certifications only in ways approved by IMCA.

Procedures for Compliance Only those individuals who meet IMCA requirements may use the CIMA or CIMC marks. These individuals are encouraged to use these references, but only in a proper, dignified, and judicious manner.

Qualified individuals may use the proper references verbally, in print, in advertisements, on business cards, on letterhead, and in marketing brochures. CIMA and CIMC licensees must obtain authorization as required from their firm's compliance department for use of the certification on business cards, letterhead, and other printed forms. When using the CIMA or CIMC logo or certification in printed materials, only IMCA-approved artwork, fonts, and positioning may be used, as specified in the Guide to Use of the IMCA Marks. Neither reference may be used as any part of a business name. The certification may not be used in any form that does not comply with current IMCA guidelines without the express written approval of IMCA prior to any such use.

The use of either reference may be accompanied by an explanation of the requirements that have been met in order to earn the CIMA or CIMC certification. Any explanation of the certification must be quoted directly in the approved form and language as outlined in the Guide to Use of the IMCA Marks.

Continued use of the CIMA or CIMC certification is dependent upon meeting continuing education requirements, as determined by IMCA, as well as strict adherence to the IMCA Standards of Practice and IMCA Code of Professional Responsibility.

Impact of the Standard   As the public's understanding of investment management consulting is broadened, adherence to this standard and standardized usage of the CIMA and CIMC certifications enhance recognition of CIMA and CIMC certifications as representing the highest standard in investment consulting expertise.

STANDARD 3C—A CONSULTANT'S RESPONSIBILITY TO BE FAIR AND ACCURATE IN ADVERTISING AND COMMUNICATIONS   It is the responsibility of the consultant to act with integrity, dignity, and honesty and to maintain the highest standards of ethics in all forms of communication.

Explanation   Consultants are prohibited from using communications, written or oral, in conjunction with professional services that contain false, fraudulent, misleading, deceptive, or unfair statements or claims. This includes, but is not limited to, a statement or claim that:

- Contains a misrepresentation of fact
- Fails to make full disclosure of relevant facts in a way that is likely to mislead or deceive
- Creates false or unjustified expectations of favorable results
- Implies educational or professional attainments or licensing recognition not supported in fact
- Represents that professional services can or will be competently performed for a stated fee when this is not the case or makes representations with respect to fees for professional services that do not disclose all variables that may reasonably be expected to affect the fees that will in fact be charged
- Contains other representations or implications that in reasonable probability will cause a person of ordinary prudence to misunderstand or be deceived

Consultants shall maintain the highest standards of ethics when using the media in any manner, whether for advertising or in interviews, scheduled or unscheduled.

Procedures for Compliance   Consultants shall not copy or use material in substantially the same form as the original prepared by another without acknowledging and identifying the name of the author, publisher, or source of such material. Consultants may use, without acknowledgment, factual information published by recognized financial and statistical reporting services or similar sources.

Any use of performance track records must not be misleading or deceptive. Returns shall be computed and communicated in compliance with the IMCA Performance Reporting Guidelines.

Communications shall make a clear distinction between fact and opinion. Clear distinction also shall be made between a consultant's personal standards, positions, and/or opinions and the standards, positions, and/or opinions of IMCA, the consultant's employer or firm, and associated brokers/dealers/agencies, should there be any variation.

CIMA and CIMC licensees may not use their certifications in any form of advertising or communication, written or oral, unless their continuing education requirement has been fulfilled. IMCA membership or CIMA and CIMC certifications may be referenced only in a dignified and judicious manner. The reference to the CIMA and CIMC certifications may be accompanied by an accurate explanation of the requirements, competency, and professional application that are associated with the right to use such certification. The use of any statement misrepresenting the nature of membership in IMCA or the CIMA and CIMC certifications is forbidden.

Impact of the Standard   Adherence to this standard ensures that IMCA and the CIMA and CIMC certifications are associated with honesty, accuracy, and fairness. This, in turn, ensures that IMCA members and especially CIMA and CIMC licensees continue to be held in high regard.

STANDARD 3D—A CONSULTANT'S RESPONSIBILITY TO MAINTAIN THE HIGHEST STANDARDS IN COMMENTING BEFORE REGULATORY ORGANIZATIONS   The consultant has a responsibility to act with integrity, dignity, and competence, maintaining the highest standards of ethics, when appearing before or submitting comment to a regulatory body or organization.

Explanation   To uphold the high standards set by IMCA and protect the reputation of the consulting profession, consultants may not engage in any comment, testimony, or act that would compromise the integrity of IMCA, the CIMA and CIMC certifications, or the profession as a whole.

Procedures for Compliance   Consultants must exercise due diligence and thoroughness in making all public comments, testimony, recommendations, or actions. Consultants shall ensure that their comment, testimony, recommendation, or action is appropriate, judicial, accurate, and reasonable to the highest extent possible and have a reasonable and adequate basis, supportable through proper research and investigation, for any position put forth. Consultants shall not hold forth any comment or act involving a dishonest, fraudulent, deceitful, or misrepresentative position. Consultants shall disclose all matters relevant to their intended comment, testimony, or action. This disclosure includes, but is not limited to:

- Conflicts of interest concerning clients, prospects, employers, firms, or individuals
- Beneficial compensation, fees, or ownership
- The inclusion or exclusion of material or relevant factors in the preparation of comment, testimony, recommendations, or actions

In presenting their comments, consultants shall make a clear distinction between fact and opinion. Consultants also shall make a clear distinction between their personal standards, positions, and/or opinions and the standards, positions, or opinions of IMCA, their employers or firms, and/or associated brokers/dealers/agencies, should there be any variation.

IMCA membership may be referenced only in a dignified and judicious manner. Consultants who have earned and maintained the right to use the CIMA or CIMC certification may, and are encouraged to, refer to their certification, but only in a proper, judicious, and dignified manner. The use of this reference may be accompanied by an accurate explanation of the requirements, competency, and professional application that are associated with the right to use such certification. Consultants may not make any statement misrepresenting the nature of membership in IMCA or the CIMA and CIMC certifications.

Impact of the Standard   By following these standards, consultants ensure that the best interests of the public are served while helping to maintain the highest regard for membership in IMCA and the CIMA and CIMC certifications.

STANDARD 3E—A CONSULTANT'S RESPONSIBILITY TO DISCLOSE THIRD-PARTY AFFILIATIONS

Consultants have a responsibility to fully disclose the nature and amount of any and all compensation, direct and indirect, paid to a nonaffiliated third party who refers, solicits, or otherwise assists the consultant in obtaining clients.

Explanation   Subject to the law and/or regulations of any governmental or regulatory body, nothing in these standards precludes consultants from compensating a nonaffiliated third party for referring, soliciting, or otherwise assisting the consultant in obtaining clients. IMCA believes, however, that it is in the best interests of the public that all financial arrangements, direct and indirect, associated with the relationship between the consultant and clients or prospective clients be fully disclosed. Disclosure of financial arrangements between consultants and third-party solicitors also is consistent with the spirit of the disclosure provisions of the IMCA Code of Professional Responsibility.

Procedures for Compliance   In addition to the disclosure that may be required by federal or state law and regulation, the amount and nature of the compensation paid or payable to the third-party solicitor must be fully disclosed in the written contract and/or written services agreement between the consultant and client.

Impact of the Standard   This standard ensures that all clients and prospective clients can be confident that a full disclosure will be made of all financial arrangements between consultants and third parties, including third-party solicitors, associated with the relationship between the client and consultant.

STANDARD 3F—A CONSULTANT'S PERFORMANCE REPORTING GUIDELINES RESPONSIBILITY TO COMPLY WITH IMCA

Consultants have a responsibility to use their best efforts to comply with the mandatory requirements and disclosures of IMCA Performance Reporting Guidelines and to use reasonable efforts to comply with the recommended requirements and disclosures of those guidelines.

Explanation IMCA believes that the best interests of the public are served by the adoption of a uniform and consistent approach to the analysis and reporting of performance information for manager search and analysis and performance measurement reporting. Therefore, the IMCA Performance Reporting Guidelines cover the collection, analysis, and reporting of performance information for manager search and analysis and performance reporting.

These guidelines stress the importance of providing accurate and comparable investment performance information and appropriate disclosures to clients during manager search and analysis and performance measurement reporting. The mandatory and recommended disclosures relate to the preparation of information provided to the client or prospective client as well as to the disclosure of potential conflicts of interest, relevant business relationships, and other pertinent items.

Procedures for Compliance IMCA recognizes that the terms "best efforts" and "reasonable efforts" are subject to interpretation. IMCA further recognizes that the employment status of consultants includes individuals who control the policies of their firms as well as persons who have little or no influence or control over the policies of their firms.

For consultants who control the policies of their firms, the term "best efforts" shall mean that the consultant must comply with the mandatory requirements and disclosures of the IMCA Performance Reporting Guidelines. For those consultants who do not control the policies of their firms, the term "best efforts" shall mean that if the firm does not comply with the mandatory requirements and disclosures of the IMCA Performance Reporting Guidelines, the consultant must submit a written request for compliance to those persons who control firm policies. Further, to the extent that consultants who do not control the policies of their firms can reasonably comply with the mandatory requirements, and such compliance is not in conflict with the policies of their firms, the consultant must comply.

All consultants also must take reasonable efforts to comply with the recommended requirements and disclosures of the guidelines. In determining whether efforts to comply are reasonable, consultants should take into consideration, among other things, their position with the firm and their ability to influence and/or control firm policy, available personnel and technological resources, and the time and costs that are required to comply with the recommended requirements.

Impact of the Standard Compliance with the IMCA Performance Reporting Guidelines instills confidence in the public that manager search information and client performance reporting are being presented fairly and accurately. Compliance with the guidelines also enables clients to make informed investment manager-selection decisions and manager-performance evaluations.

Standard 4: Responsibilities to the Profession

STANDARD 4A—A CONSULTANT'S RESPONSIBILITY TO MAKE PROPER USE OF PROFESSIONAL CERTIFICATIONS Consultants have a responsibility to use care in promoting their professional certifications, including the CIMA® and CIMC® certifications.

Explanation To maintain the status implied by a professional designation, consultants who have earned such certifications should display their accomplishments in a proper and dignified manner.

Procedures for Compliance Holders of professional certifications must present the mark correctly, e.g., Certified Investment Management Analyst or CIMA licensees, and Certified Investment Management Consultant or CIMC licensees, and may use the marks only if currently entitled to do so. On signage, business cards, or stationery, the mark may not be listed in words larger than the certificant's name. Marks may not be misrepresented in any way.

Impact of the Standard Compliance with this standard conveys professional courtesy and fairness and promotes respect for professional certifications.

STANDARD 4B—A CONSULTANT'S RESPONSIBILITY TO ABIDE BY REGULATIONS AND PRINCIPLES Consultants have a responsibility to make every effort to understand and comply with regulations and rules that are applicable to their specific positions and duties.

Explanation In addition to the standards presented in this booklet, consultants are governed by various rules, including fiduciary obligations, statutes of government regulatory agencies, and rules of self-regulatory organizations. These rules and standards should be followed at all times.

Procedures for Compliance Consultants must maintain knowledge of all rules and regulations that govern their profession. They must abide by these rules or obtain exceptions from the appropriate authority as necessary.

Impact of the Standard Compliance with all applicable rules and regulations ensures that the integrity of the consulting profession is upheld, competition is fair, and clients are well served.

STANDARD 4C—A CONSULTANT'S RESPONSIBILITY TO MAINTAIN KNOWLEDGE BASE THROUGH CONTINUING EDUCATION Consultants have a responsibility to stay current with changes in their field and to expand their knowledge beyond the formal coursework taught in the pursuit of a designation. This is achieved primarily through continuing education.

Explanation As times change, new ideas, investments, and laws are introduced constantly. To ensure that clients are well served, consultants must stay abreast of these changes and maintain competency in their profession.

Procedures for Compliance At a minimum, a consultant who holds a professional certification shall fulfill the continuing education requirements established for that designation. Consultants also should keep informed about broader issues involving the fields of investment management and investment consulting. Fulfilling this obligation may require more than attending the minimum number of classes needed to maintain a professional designation. A consultant could fulfill this responsibility by additional means, e.g., reading journals, undertaking self-study, or attending appropriate study groups.

Consultants shall not accept engagements unless they are competent in the specific area of expertise involved. If offered an engagement in an area where they are not competent, consultants shall either not accept the client, until and unless they have been able to obtain the appropriate level of competence, or seek the advice of qualified professionals and/or refer clients to those professionals.

Impact of the Standard   Compliance with this standard ensures that consultants fulfill their obligation to maintain a certain level of competence through continuing education and thereby continue to serve the best interests of the client.

STANDARD 4D—A CONSULTANT'S RESPONSIBILITY TO AVOID PLAGIARISM AND OTHER FORMS OF THEFT   It is the responsibility of the consultant to avoid using or copying materials prepared by another without proper authorization and acknowledgement.

Explanation   In addition to being unprofessional, plagiarism and other forms of theft are illegal.

Procedures for Compliance   If consultants wish to use the work of others, they must obtain the necessary permissions and include appropriate acknowledgments. Such acknowledgement includes, but is not limited to, identifying the author, publisher, and/or source of the material. While factual information such as that published by recognized financial and statistical reporting services may be used without acknowledgement, credit must be given to conclusions made by others that have been derived from the factual information.

Acknowledgement is to be made regardless of the medium used for communication (e.g., print, verbal, electronic). Acknowledgement may be made in the body of the communication or in a reference made in the body of the communication to a footnote that is easily available.

Impact of the Standard   Compliance with this standard promotes continued research and analytical efforts in the areas of investment management, performance, and investment consulting. Those who contribute to the investment consulting profession in this way may reconsider their efforts if their work is plagiarized.

STANDARD 4E—A CONSULTANT'S RESPONSIBILITY TO CONDUCT BUSINESS AND PERSONAL AFFAIRS PROFESSIONALLY AND ETHICALLY   Consultants have a responsibility to avoid conduct, in both their business and personal lives, that exhibits a lack of honesty, trustworthiness, or fitness to practice as a consulting professional.

Explanation   This standard goes beyond the requirements for technical compliance with rules and regulations and focuses on the integrity of consultants by prohibiting any professional or personal behavior that discredits the profession as a whole.

Procedures for Compliance   In all professional and personal activities, consultants shall abide by applicable laws and regulations, including those of IMCA. Consultants shall not engage in any acts of dishonesty, fraud, or misrepresentation that reflect negatively on professional competence or acts that indicate a general disrespect for the law.

Examples of such acts can include, but are not limited to:

- Acts resulting in conviction of a felony
- Acts resulting in conviction of a misdemeanor involving moral turpitude (e.g., lying, cheating, stealing)
- Conduct that compromises the integrity of the CIMA or CIMC certification or the consulting profession as a whole

In addition to self-regulatory agencies such as the Financial Industry Regulatory Authority (FINRA), the investment industry is regulated by government agencies, including the Securities and Exchange Commission (SEC), and the Department of Labor, that monitor conduct and take disciplinary action in cases of unethical behavior. IMCA procedures for investigating complaints against CIMA and CIMC licensees and implementing disciplinary action, if required, are outlined in the IMCA Disciplinary Rules and Procedures.

On the whole, however, compliance with Standard 4e is a matter of a consultant's own personal integrity and moral character. Each consultant must be aware of the implications of all professional and personal actions. Any conduct that reflects poorly on the individual, the employer or firm, or the profession as a whole should not be tolerated. General compliance with this standard can be enhanced by strict observation of the following broad guidelines:

- Abide by all statutory and regulatory requirements involving the delivery of consulting services.
- Establish and maintain a standard of excellence in all aspects of investment management consulting.
- Participate in IMCA activities designed to improve the consulting profession and uphold its reputation.
- Maintain the highest standard of personal conduct at all times.

Impact of the Standard   In conjunction with the IMCA Code of Professional Responsibility, compliance with this standard helps to promote and maintain the highest standard of personal and professional conduct in the investment management consulting profession. This, in turn, serves to ensure public confidence in the integrity and services offered by professional investment management consultants.

Standard 5: Responsibilities to the Employer

STANDARD 5A—A CONSULTANT'S RESPONSIBILITY TO INFORM EMPLOYER OF THE IMCA CODE AND STANDARDS   Consultants shall make employers aware of the IMCA Code of Professional Responsibility and Standards of Practice.

Explanation   Informing employers about the IMCA Code and Standards promotes awareness of professional responsibility and ethical practices and thereby increases consultants' adherence to these rules of conduct. In addition, the Standards may serve as the basis of employee programs within the consultant's Standards designed to enhance ethical awareness and advocate honesty in interactions with clients.

Procedures for Compliance   Consultants shall provide copies of the IMCA Code of Professional Responsibility and IMCA Standards of Practice to the appropriate persons within their organizations, typically their supervisors and/or compliance officers.

Impact of the Standard   By ensuring the dissemination of the IMCA Code and Standards to supervisory individuals responsible for overseeing consultant practices, Standard 5a assists the employer in supervision of the consultant's interaction with clients and adherence to professional standards.

STANDARD 5B—A CONSULTANT'S RESPONSIBILITY TO DISCLOSE CONFLICTS OF INTEREST

Consultants shall disclose to employers all situations, ownership of securities, and/or memberships on boards or in organizations that could reasonably interfere with their duty to employers or their ability to make unbiased and objective recommendations and decisions regarding their consulting clients.

Explanation   This standard protects employers and, indirectly, clients by requiring consultants to disclose those situations and actions that may result in a conflict of interest. Examples of these disclosures include the following:

- Recommending that clients invest in companies that use the consultant's services
- Holding a seat on the board of an organization that employs them as a consultant
- Maintaining a relationship with an investment advisor that could result in a conflict of interest

Procedures for Compliance   Consultants should notify their employers in writing of any situation that could lead to a conflict of interest, as outlined above. The consultant should retain copies of such notification.

Impact of the Standard   Adherence to this standard ensures that potential conflicts of interest are identified and addressed in a proactive, rather than reactive, manner, thereby minimizing potential loss of business and/or credibility.

STANDARD 5C—A CONSULTANT'S RESPONSIBILITY TO DISCLOSE ADDITIONAL COMPENSATION

It is the responsibility of consultants to disclose and obtain written approval from employers prior to accepting any compensation and/or benefits from clients or third parties that are in addition to compensation and benefits provided by employers.

Explanation   The purpose of this standard is to avert conflicts of interest and ensure objectivity in the delivery of consulting-related services to clients. Adherence to this standard should prevent the consultant from providing nonobjective advice or preferential treatment to any client. Under this standard, the consultant is barred from receiving compensation from outside sources or third parties without the approval of the employer. This includes payments to vendors by third parties for services that are for the benefit of the consultant.

Procedures for Compliance   Before entering into any compensation arrangement that has not been authorized or granted by the consultant's employer, the consultant must first disclose and obtain approval for the arrangement in writing. Additionally, the consultant may only provide services offered by the firm at the firm's stated fee schedules. The provision of additional services or the charging of fees not approved by the employer is prohibited.

Impact of the Standard   Adherence to this standard prevents the consultant from entering into compensation arrangements that could impair the consultant's ability to render objective and unbiased advice to each client.

STANDARD 5D—A CONSULTANT'S RESPONSIBILITY TO EXERCISE REASONABLE SUPERVISION

Consultants acting in a supervisory capacity (responsibility and authority over others) have a responsibility to exercise reasonable supervision to prevent, detect, and correct violations of the IMCA Standards of Practice.

Explanation   This standard helps to ensure that the IMCA Standards of Practice are carried out in a uniform and ethical manner by all employees in their relationships with consulting clients. To achieve this goal, supervisors should have a thorough and current understanding of the Standards and establish and implement compliance guidelines and procedures for employees to follow.

Procedures for Compliance   Through knowledge and periodic review of the Standards, supervisors are responsible for making a reasonable effort to detect violations. Once aware of any violation of the Standards, the supervisor must initiate a prompt and thorough investigation of the violation according to established compliance guidelines and procedures. Failure to supervise or to take prompt and thorough steps to assess, investigate, and correct violations of the Standards will be a breach of Standard 5d. However, if the supervisor implements steps to reasonably supervise but is not aware of a violation, the supervisor will not be in violation of this standard.

Supervisors must report to their employers any knowledge of procedures and guidelines that are not being followed. If, after the passage of a reasonable amount of time from the date of notification, the employer fails to take any action to correct the violation of the Standards, the consultant shall notify IMCA. Supervisors also should report to their employer and to IMCA any inadequacies they perceive in the IMCA Standards of Practice or in the procedures designed to detect violations of the Standards.

Impact of the Standard   Establishing guidelines for the supervisor's responsibility under the IMCA Standards of Practice increases the likelihood that violations will be detected and that procedures for corrective action can be implemented in a timely manner.

Part III IMCA Performance Reporting Standards

Section 1: Introduction

I. ENDORSEMENT Investment Management Consultants Association (IMCA) has established the following standards for investment performance reporting. Specifically, these standards cover the collection, analysis, and reporting of performance information related to manager search and analysis and the reporting of performance results to clients.

II. PHILOSOPHY The IMCA Performance Reporting Guidelines stress the importance of consultants providing accurate and comparable investment performance information and appropriate disclosures to clients during manager search and analysis and performance measurement reporting. Disclosure in this context is used in a broad sense. It includes disclosures relating to preparation of the information provided as well as to potential conflicts of interest, relevant business relationships, and other pertinent considerations.

III. PARTIES AFFECTED The IMCA Performance Reporting Guidelines are for investment management consultants. Consultants are encouraged to follow the Performance Reporting Guidelines in the course of conducting investment manager searches and monitoring performance.

Because of the nature of the consultant, client, and investment manager relationship, these guidelines may also affect parties outside the consulting profession. IMCA believes that these parties—clients, investment managers, custodians, and others—will benefit from the guidelines. The intent of the Performance Reporting Guidelines is not to create unnecessary burdens on third parties but rather to enable consultants to fulfill their professional responsibilities while assisting clients.

IV. CFA INSTITUTE PERFORMANCE PRESENTATION STANDARDS The IMCA Performance Reporting Guidelines were designed to complement the Global Investment Performance Standards (GIPS) of the CFA Institute.

GIPS cover items detailed primarily in Section 2 of this document (Manager Search and Analysis—methodologies for managers to compile and construct performance composites). IMCA believes the CFA Institute has contributed a valuable service to the investment community and endorses GIPS.

In their current form, GIPS apply mostly to the presentation of performance composites by investment managers to prospective clients. The IMCA Performance Reporting Guidelines, designed to complement GIPS, are applicable to the collection and analysis of performance data obtained from investment managers, as well as the consultant's reporting, monitoring, and analysis of performance results for the client.

V. COMPLIANCE Like GIPS, IMCA's Performance Reporting Guidelines are voluntary. No one is required to comply. The consultant may represent to clients, managers, and others that specific reports are in compliance with these standards by meeting all items and disclosures as listed in Section 4 of this document. When a manager search or performance report meets all of the Section 4 recommendations, the following written statement may be added to the report:

This report has been prepared and presented in compliance with the IMCA Performance Reporting Guidelines. IMCA has not been involved with the preparation or review of the report.

Section 2: Manager Search and Analysis

This section details standards to be followed by the consultant when assisting clients in selecting investment managers.

I. SOURCES OF DATA

A. Typically, the data used in providing manager search and analysis information is an investment manager's performance composite(s). Investment managers usually prepare these composites themselves. When this is the case, the consultant should disclose that the data were prepared by the investment manager and represent the average performance of actual portfolios. In other cases, the source and definition of the data should be disclosed.

B. The consultant should obtain performance composites that best represent the investment performance the client might have experienced as a client of the investment manager during the period being evaluated. For each investment manager who is to be evaluated, the consultant should review all composites within a firm or product group before selecting the appropriate composite(s) to be presented to a client. The intent is to ensure that a "select" composite is not presented to the client.

C. In order to ensure that the performance results presented accurately reflect the actual results achieved by a particular investment firm or product, the consultant should obtain information from the investment manager to support the performance composite calculations. Requested information could include the aggregate market values and cash flows of the performance composite, the returns for individual portfolios in the performance composites, or the underlying individual portfolio performance accounting data.

II. COMPOSITE CONSTRUCTION

A. Investment management consultants should use composites from firms that are in compliance with GIPS. If a consultant chooses to use a firm that is not in compliance with CFA Institute standards, the noncompliance must be disclosed to the client. The individual composites presented should also be prepared in compliance with GIPS, and noncompliance should be disclosed. For noncompliant firms and composites, the reasons for noncompliance should be disclosed to the client. Supplemental information should not be presented on a stand-alone basis.

B. Consultants, at a minimum, should use quarterly rate-of-return data in calculations. Monthly rate-of-return data are preferable.

C. Consultants are encouraged to obtain additional quantitative information about the performance composite—for example, equal-weighted results, the median, range, standard deviation, and other information necessary to effectively assess that a composite is representative of the investment product. This additional information includes required GIPS disclosures.

D. Model (simulated) portfolio: The consultant may present model portfolio results to a client as supplemental information, subject to the following constraints:

1. The consultant should provide the client with full disclosure concerning the methodology used and assumptions made. A statement that no assets were actually managed using the model must be included.

2. Model portfolio results should not be linked with actual results.

3. The investment manager should be encouraged to continue to calculate model portfolio results after actual implementation of the investment product to facilitate analysis and comparison by the consultant.

E. Hypothetical portfolio: The consultant may use hypothetical portfolio results to analyze an investment product and process, subject to the following constraints:

1. The consultant should provide the client with full disclosure concerning the weighting methodology used and assumptions made.

2. The firm must be in compliance with GIPS and the underlying composites used to construct the hypothetical portfolio must be constructed according to GIPS.

3. Disclosures for all underlying composites should be presented in accordance with the IMCA Performance Reporting Guidelines.

4. An example of a hypothetical portfolio is a balanced composite that combines stock and bond composites because the manager may not have managed balanced accounts in the past.

F. Transferability of historical record:

1. Past investment results belong to the investment firm (as defined by CFA Institute) that achieved those results, not to any single individual(s), and should not be altered to reflect personnel or other organizational changes. The consultant should disclose any significant changes in the personnel or organizational structure of the investment management firm that, in the consultant's opinion, might affect future performance.

2. Performance results achieved by key investment personnel while employed with another investment firm may be used by the new firm if the consultant determines that these professionals are implementing the same investment process with similar resources and disciplines at the new firm. The prior historical record may be linked with results achieved at the new firm to provide a long-term investment record. Disclosure of these circumstances to the client is mandatory, as is any SEC ruling on the ownership of the track record.

G. Special cases

In the absence of IMCA Guidelines or CFA Institute standards for an investment product, the manager and/or consultant should prepare performance results in accordance with appropriate, recognized industry standards such as the American Institute of Certified Public Accountants Standards. The goal should always be to have an accurate representation of the product's performance.

H. Additional information

The consultant should review the following information for each performance composite being presented (from the inception of the firm, the inception date of the investment product, or 10 years—whichever is shorter).

1. CFA Institute disclosure(s)
2. The total number and market value of portfolios included in the performance composite
3. The total number and market value of discretionary portfolios managed in a similar manner but not included in the composite
4. The total number and market value of nondiscretionary portfolios managed in a similar manner but not included in the composite
5. The average, median, smallest, and largest portfolios in the performance composite
6. The average asset allocation of the performance composite
7. An explanation of the criteria by which portfolios are excluded, deleted, or added to the performance composite
8. The standard deviation of individual portfolio returns included in the performance composite return
9. The range of returns (and the median return) within the performance composite
10. Quarterly, annual, and cumulative returns as well as the risk associated with the composite returns

I. The IMCA Performance Reporting Guidelines encourage investment management firms to obtain third-party verification that a performance composite is in compliance with GIPS.

III. DISCLOSURE AND PRESENTATION OF COMPOSITE RESULTS TO CLIENTS

A. Sources of data and definitions relating to these data should be disclosed.
B. Whenever investment results containing leverage are presented to a client, the details regarding the leverage should be disclosed.
C. For comparative purposes, the consultant should present the performance composite on both a gross basis (before deduction of the investment management fee) and a net basis (after deduction of the investment management fee). If only gross return information is presented to the client, additional information should be provided to enable the client to determine the impact of the manager's fee. The consultant must be consistent when using gross or net data. The manager's fee must also be presented.
D. The consultant should use "best efforts" to ensure that any rate-of-return comparisons are reasonable and appropriate.
E. The consultant should present annual and cumulative returns for each performance composite to clients in a format that facilitates the objective comparison of one manager with another. At a minimum, each year and each longest common time period should be included in the report. Returns for client-requested time periods, market cycles, or other time periods should be presented when needed. At a minimum, the returns for each composite should be presented from the inception of the firm, the inception of the investment product, or 10 years—whichever is shorter.

F. Rates of return for periods longer than one year should be presented in annualized form. Returns for periods shorter than one year should never be annualized.

G. Statistical measures of risk
   1. In addition to rates of return, measures of risk should be presented to give the client a more complete picture of the investment manager's results. The consultant should determine the number of observations that are sufficient for risk calculations.
   2. At a minimum, portfolio risk should be measured by calculation of an annualized standard deviation derived from monthly or quarterly total rates of return for a meaningful reporting period (as determined by the consultant).
   3. Measures of beta, residual standard deviation, correlation, covariance, semivariance, or other measures may be presented when appropriate.
   4. Presentation of fundamental portfolio characteristics such as price-earnings ratio, duration, yield, or quality is encouraged.

H. Benchmarks
   1. The intent in including benchmark comparisons is to provide the client with a means of comparing the investment managers being evaluated.
   2. The consultant should ensure that benchmarks are appropriate.
   3. Comparisons should be made for any time periods for which performance composite results are being presented. At a minimum, annual and cumulative returns should be compared. The inclusion of other time periods (e.g., quarterly, market cycles) is encouraged.
   4. Comparisons must include the presentation of appropriate measures of risk over time; these measures might include standard deviation of return and beta.

I. Sample peer comparisons
   1. The consultant should determine the appropriate investment product sample or grouping, based on information analyzed by the consultant.
   2. The consultant should disclose to the client the composition of any investment product sample used, including the treatment of fees.
   3. The consultant should disclose to the client that biases appear in all peer group samples, such as survivor, back-fill, classification, and composition biases.

J. Information provided to the client directly by the investment manager(s) should be in compliance with GIPS. The consultant is responsible for providing the client with appropriate disclosures regarding potential conflicts of interest, relevant business relationships, and other pertinent considerations.

IV. NONTRADITIONAL ASSET CLASSES

A. Types of assets
      These asset classes would include, but would not be limited to, derivative securities, municipal bonds, private investments, commodities, and real estate.

B. Treatment
      Nontraditional assets should generally be handled in accordance with GIPS.

C. Disclosure

Because many nontraditional asset classes involve complex investment strategies, complete disclosure of the nature and consequences of the investment strategies being used is essential.

Section 3: Reporting Performance Results to Clients

This section presents guidelines to be followed by the consultant in monitoring the historical and ongoing investment performance results of a client's existing investment managers.

I. SOURCES OF DATA

A. The data obtained for performance measurement purposes should consist of security market values and transactions.

B. The sources of data used in monitoring the historical and ongoing investment performance of a client's investment managers should be independent of the investment manager being evaluated. The consultant should avoid using data obtained directly from the manager unless these data are the sole available source of information. In this case, the consultant should substantiate the data whenever possible and must disclose their use to the client.

C. The preferred source of data is the custodian (bank, brokerage firm, insurance company, or others providing custodial services) that provides independent valuation of all security holdings and all portfolio transactions. Performance results, where possible, should be reconciled with the manager's reported performance.

D. Whenever summary market valuations, cash flows, or returns obtained from another consultant, the custodian, or the client are used instead of the original data, the consultant should use "best efforts" to confirm the validity and accuracy of the aggregation process. Additionally, the consultant should obtain information regarding the basis of the aggregated data—for example, cash versus accrual, trade date versus settlement date, gross basis (before deduction of fees) versus net basis (after deduction of fees).

E. The client should be informed regarding the source(s) of data used for performance reporting, particularly the use of noncustodial sources.

F. For mutual funds, the consultant may use data obtained from a third-party provider. The source of the data must be disclosed to the client.

G. There are special considerations regarding the collection of historical data for a new client or portfolio:

1. For reasons such as lack of original statements or client cost constraints, historical data sometimes may have to be obtained in compiled form from a consultant, the custodian, or the client.

2. If historical data are obtained from several different sources, the consultant should use best efforts to confirm that all data being used are consistent. The consultant should avoid mixing dissimilar data and should note the potential impact to the client when historical data are obtained from more than one source.

3. If dissimilar data must be used, the consultant should ensure that adjustments are made as necessary to ensure that discrepancies or discontinuities are not introduced into the performance results.

    4. The amount of historical data obtained should be consistent with the reporting goal of providing the client an accurate assessment of past performance.

H. Composite, model, or hypothetical returns should not be used for monitoring the historical and ongoing investment performance results of a client's existing investment managers.

 I. Frequency of data collection

    1. The interval of valuation data should be monthly; the minimum frequency should be quarterly.

    2. The interval for aggregation of transaction data should be daily; the minimum frequency should be monthly.

 J. Data obtained must always be checked for completeness and accuracy. The consultant should not assume that the custodial statements are complete and without error. Typical items that should be checked include missing or inaccurate pricing, transactions, or corporate actions, as well as posting in an incorrect period. When missing or incorrect information is discovered, it should be adjusted. In all cases, adjustments should be made in accordance with the goal of providing the client a performance report that is an accurate representation of portfolio results.

II. PERFORMANCE ANALYSIS

A. Calculations

    1. The reporting start date should be the date that represents the appropriate starting point for monitoring the investment manager's results, which is generally the month following inception.

    2. When portfolio performance is segregated, cash and equivalents should be treated as a distinct asset class.

    3. Portfolio data should be calculated on the basis of trade date. When trade-date accounting is not possible, settlement-date accounting may be used.

    4. Switching between trade-date and settlement date calculations is not permitted unless required for reasons such as a change in the accounting basis of the underlying custodial reports.

    5. Interest income should be calculated on an accrual basis. The use of dividend receivables is strongly recommended.

    6. Estimates of accrued income are permissible and should be disclosed to the client when used in lieu of actual accrued income.

    7. Convertible securities should be treated as a separate asset class or equity asset.

    8. Total rate of return, including capital appreciation plus income, is strongly recommended for judging overall investment results.

    9. A time-weighted rate-of-return calculation that minimizes the impact of cash flows should be used for any comparisons of the investment manager with appropriate indices or other managers.

  10. A dollar-weighted (internal) rate-of-return calculation should be used for comparisons with "dollar-" or "value-based" investment objective(s) such as actuarial rates of return or inflation. Dollar-weighted returns should also be used for some alternative investments where the manager controls cash flows.

11. When cash flow in excess of 10 percent of the market value of the portfolio or portfolio segment occurs, and the interim market value is available, an interim time-weighted calculation should be performed.
12. Gross returns (before deduction of fees) and net returns (after deduction of fees) should be calculated.
13. Returns should always be calculated after deduction of brokerage commissions.
14. Vehicle-specific considerations:
    a. Wrap-fee performance should be presented after deduction of all bundled fees. Gross performance (before all bundled fees) may also be shown.
    b. Net performance calculations for pooled private investment vehicles should reflect all fees and commissions both inside and outside of the vehicle.
    c. Mutual fund performance should be presented after deduction of all expenses, including loads.

B. Client composites
    1. Individual portfolios should be aggregated into a composite portfolio to enable the client to evaluate the performance of an overall pool of assets (e.g., the performance of the salaried employees' plan or the equity-oriented investment managers).
    2. Composites should be aggregated by combining the market values and cash flows of the individual portfolios.
    3. For client-reporting purposes, composites should not be created by averaging the returns of the individual portfolios.

C. Statistical measures of risk
    1. Measures of risk should be presented in addition to rates of return to give the client a more complete picture of the investment manager's results. The consultant should determine the number of observations that are sufficient for risk calculations.
    2. At a minimum, portfolio risk should be measured by calculating an annualized standard deviation derived from monthly or quarterly total rates of return for a meaningful reporting period (as determined by the consultant).
    3. Beta, residual standard deviation, correlation, covariance, semivariance, or other measures may be presented when appropriate.
    4. Presentation of fundamental portfolio characteristics such as yield, price-earnings ratio, duration, or quality is encouraged.

D. Benchmarks
    1. Benchmarks that represent the portfolio's investment style, strategy, and level of risk should be selected.
    2. Benchmarks should be constructed on the basis of total return.
    3. Balanced benchmarks should be constructed when necessary. Appropriate rebalancing techniques should be used.
    4. The benchmarks used as comparisons for a portfolio segment should reflect as accurately as possible the type of investment assets held in that segment.
    5. Benchmark comparisons should be applied consistently over time, and any substantial changes in their composition should be disclosed to the client.
    6. Composite results should be presented with their own set of benchmarks that reflect the asset mix and investment objective of the combined pool of assets.

7. The return for an individual manager should be contrasted to the manager's composite return for the appropriate mandate.

E. Comparative sample peer construction

1. If a manager's performance is compared with that of a peer group of managers, the peer group should be of similar style.

2. Time-weighted total rates of return should be used for construction of and comparisons with peer group samples.

3. Returns should be calculated either before or after deduction of investment management fees to ensure consistency and to allow comparison with the client portfolio.

4. Cash and equivalents for portfolios in the comparative sample should be treated in a manner consistent with the management of the client's portfolio.

5. The consultant should disclose to the client the construction and composition of any sample used for comparative purposes.

6. Sample comparisons should remain consistent over time unless material changes have occurred in the client's portfolio.

7. If measures of risk are presented for the portfolios in the comparative sample, a consistent method for calculating these measures should be used for all component portfolios.

8. If balanced-portfolio comparative samples are constructed from the returns for equity, fixed income, cash and equivalents, and other types of portfolios, returns for the balanced portfolio should be calculated with the assumption of at least annual rebalancing.

9. The consultant should disclose to the client that biases appear in all peer group samples, such as, survivor, back-fill, classification, and composition biases.

III. DISCLOSURE AND PRESENTATION OF RESULTS TO CLIENTS

A. General

1. The format of the performance report should clearly show the client what the investment results were, how the results compare with those of various benchmarks, and how much risk was incurred to achieve the investment results.

2. Any nonconformity with the IMCA Performance Reporting Guidelines should be disclosed to the client.

3. The consultant is responsible for providing the client with appropriate disclosure regarding potential conflicts of interest, relevant business relationships, and other pertinent considerations.

B. Time periods

1. Time periods presented should include quarterly, annual, and cumulative periods, market cycles, and any other time periods necessary to present an accurate and objective assessment of the investment manager's performance.

2. To minimize time-period bias, the consultant should normally focus on longer time periods and trends, while also being mindful of short-run trends, in judging the performance of the investment manager.

IV. NONTRADITIONAL ASSET CLASSES

A. These asset classes would include but not be limited to: derivative securities, municipal bonds, private investments, and real estate.
B. Performance reporting for nontraditional assets should be handled in a manner that provides the client with a reasonable and objective assessment of the portfolio's performance.
C. Because many nontraditional asset classes involve complex investment strategies, complete disclosure of the nature and consequences of the investment strategies being used is essential.

Section 4: Recommended Reporting and Disclosures

I. MINIMUM RECOMMENDED REPORTING AND DISCLOSURES—MANAGER SEARCH AND ANALYSIS   Listed below are the minimum recommended reporting and disclosures for compliance with the IMCA Performance Reporting Guidelines regarding manager search and analysis.

A. Performance composites presented to clients should be obtained from firms that state they are in compliance with GIPS.
B. The investment manager should provide individual performance composites that have been prepared in accordance with GIPS. The consultant should present GIPS-compliant performance composites to clients.
C. Supplemental performance information should be identified and disclosed. At least one GIPS compliant performance composite should accompany the supplemental information.
D. Model portfolio results should not be linked with performance composites of actual accounts for presentation to a client.
E. A statement should be included indicating that because a performance composite is an average of two or more accounts, it does not represent the performance of an actual portfolio.
F. When the investment manager has compiled the performance composite, this should be disclosed.
G. Cumulative returns for the longest common term should be shown for each manager.
H. Annual returns for each year presented should be shown for every manager.
I. Rates of return for periods longer than one year should be presented on an annualized basis. Returns for periods shorter than one year should not be annualized.
J. If only gross return information is presented to the client, information should be provided to enable the client to determine the impact of the manager's fee.
K. The manager's fees should be presented.
L. At least one appropriate risk measure should be presented.
M. At least one appropriate market index or custom benchmark should be presented as a basis for comparison.
N. The consultant should disclose potential conflicts of interest, relevant business relationships, or other pertinent information that might cause the consultant to have a conflict of interest.

II. MINIMUM RECOMMENDED REPORTING AND DISCLOSURES—REPORTING PERFORMANCE RESULTS TO CLIENTS   Listed below are the minimum recommended reporting and disclosures for compliance with the IMCA Performance Reporting Guidelines regarding reporting performance results to clients.

A. Time-weighted total rates of return should be calculated on at least a quarterly basis, using quarterly asset valuations and monthly transactions.

B. If the investment manager is the source of the portfolio accounting data, this should be disclosed to the client.

C. Annual rates of return for each year should be presented for 10 years or for the period from inception of the firm or inception of the investment product—whichever is shorter.

D. A cumulative return for the period from inception of the firm or inception of the investment product to date should be shown.

E. Rates of return for periods longer than one year should be presented on an annualized basis. Returns for periods of less than one year should not be annualized.

F. Information should be provided to enable the client to determine the impact of the manager's fees.

G. At least one appropriate risk measure should be presented.

H. At least one appropriate market index or custom benchmark should be presented as a basis for comparison.

 I. The consultant should disclose potential conflicts of interest, relevant business relationships, or other pertinent information that might cause the consultant to have a conflict of interest.

III. RECOMMENDED ADDITIONAL REPORTING AND DISCLOSURES—MANAGER SEARCH AND ANALYSIS   Listed below are recommended additional reporting and disclosures for compliance with the IMCA Performance Reporting Guidelines regarding manager search and analysis.

A. If sufficient history exists, one-, five-, and ten-year cumulative returns should be presented.

B. Cumulative returns should be shown for each manager from inception of the firm, inception of the investment product, or 10 years—whichever is shorter.

C. Performance composites presented to clients should be shown on both a gross basis (before deduction of the investment manager's fee) and a net basis (after deduction of the investment manager's fee).

IV. RECOMMENDED ADDITIONAL REPORTING AND DISCLOSURES—REPORTING PERFORMANCE RESULTS TO CLIENTS   Listed below are recommended additional reporting and disclosures for compliance with the IMCA Performance Reporting Guidelines regarding reporting performance results to clients.

A. Time-weighted total rates of return should be calculated on at least a monthly basis, using monthly asset valuations and daily transactions.

B. When cash flow in excess of 10 percent of the market value of a portfolio or portfolio segment occurs, and the interim market value is available or can be obtained, interim time-weighted calculations should be performed.

C. Trade-date accounting using accrued interest should be used to calculate returns and valuations.

D. If sufficient history exists, one-, five-, and ten-year cumulative returns should be presented.

E. An internal or dollar-weighted rate of return should be shown for the period from inception of the firm or inception of the investment product to date.

F. Comparative samples should contain portfolios whose performance has been calculated on the same fee basis as the portfolio(s) being analyzed.

G. Gross and net performance should be shown.

Part IV IMCA Disciplinary Rules and Procedures

Glossary

Candidate Individual who has been admitted to an IMCA program that may lead to an IMCA Designation.

Client Person or entity who receives professional services from an IMCA Licensee.

CIMA Certified Investment Management Analyst.

CIMC Certified Investment Management Consultant.

Code of Professional Responsibility (Code) A set of statements adopted by IMCA to promote and maintain the highest standards of personal and professional conduct in the investment management consultant profession.

CPWA Certified Private Wealth Advisor.

Disciplinary Rules and Procedures (Rules) A set of rules adopted by IMCA to enforce the IMCA Code of Professional Responsibility and Standards of Practice in order to maintain the integrity and goodwill of IMCA designations among members of the financial services industry and the public. The Rules may be amended from time to time.

Good Standing The status of an IMCA Designation that indicates the Licensee has met and continues to meet all requirements set by IMCA to maintain a license for the IMCA Designation.

Hearing Panel A panel appointed by the Professional Review Board (PRB) to hear a disciplinary case as more fully described herein. A Hearing Panel shall be composed of three individuals, all of whom hold an IMCA Designation, are IMCA members in good standing, and have held an IMCA Designation for at least two (2) years.

IMCA Investment Management Consultants Association.

IMCA Appeals Board Five (5) person board appointed by the IMCA Board of Directors to review and consider appeals from a final order issued by the PRB.

IMCA designation CIMA, CIMC, or CPWA license.

Licensee Person who is licensed by IMCA to use an IMCA Designation.

Legal Counsel A licensed attorney who is retained by IMCA for the purposes of assisting IMCA staff, the PRB, Hearing Panels, IMCA Appeals Board, and the

IMCA Board of Directors in implementing the Code, Standards of Practice, and Rules.

Professional Loss or Suspension Loss or suspension of a professional license, designation, or certification to offer services to the public as a registered securities representative, broker–dealer, insurance agent, real estate sales person or broker, attorney, accountant, investment advisor, or similar professional license, designation, or certification.

Professional Review Board (PRB) A Board established by IMCA to review, investigate, and rule on any Licensee's alleged infractions of the Code, Standards of Practice, and/or Rules.

Respondent An IMCA Licensee or a Candidate for an IMCA Designation who is the subject of a disciplinary petition.

Serious Crime (1) any felony; (2) any lesser crime, a necessary element of which as determined by its statutory or common law definition involves misrepresentation, fraud, extortion, misappropriation, or theft; and/or (3) an attempt or conspiracy to commit such crime, or solicitation of another to commit such crime.

Standards of Practice A set of statements adopted by IMCA, which sets forth the standards of conduct for Licensees and Candidates.

Disciplinary Rules and Procedures

ARTICLE 1: INTRODUCTION IMCA has adopted a Code and Standards of Practice, which set forth the standards of conduct for Licensees and Candidates. IMCA may amend the Code and Standards of Practice from time to time in its sole discretion. The Code and Standards of Practice define professional conduct by Licensees and Candidates. IMCA enforces the Code and Standards of Practice in order to protect and maintain the integrity and goodwill of the IMCA Designations among members of the financial services industry and the public. Licensees and Candidates are required to adhere to the Code and the Standards of Practice. Failure to do so may result in disciplinary action including termination or suspension of the right to use an IMCA Designation or termination of the right to pursue an IMCA Designation.

ARTICLE 2: PROFESSIONAL REVIEW BOARD

2.1 Jurisdiction IMCA has established a PRB to review, investigate, and rule on violations of the Code, Standards, or Rules by Licensees and Candidates and to conduct other activities as described in these Rules. The PRB shall be composed of at least six (6) Licensees in good standing who have held an IMCA Designation for at least two years. One of the PRB members shall serve as chair. The members of PRB shall be nominated by the IMCA President and ratified by the IMCA Board of Directors (IMCA Board). Each member of the PRB shall serve a three-year term on a staggered basis. Appointments to the PRB shall be made in a manner to ensure that the terms are staggered. For example, two of the appointees may have an initial term of one year; two appointees may have an initial term of two years; and two appointees may have an initial term of three years. As set forth herein, the PRB shall have exclusive jurisdiction over matters arising under the Code, Standards, and Rules.

2.2 Powers and Duties of the Professional Review Board and IMCA Staff The PRB is empowered to:

a. Investigate alleged infractions of the Code, Standards of Practice, and Rules and issue orders regarding private or public censure, the suspension or termination of the right to use an IMCA Designation by Licensees, or termination of Candidates who are found to have violated the Code, Standards of Practice, Rules, or other orders as may be appropriate.

b. Report to the IMCA Board with respect to the operations of the PRB.

c. Consider and propose amendments to the Code, Standards of Practice, and Rules for action by the IMCA Board.

d. Develop and adopt procedures for the fair and expeditious hearing of matters that come before it.

IMCA staff shall be responsible for:

a. Receiving and maintaining the confidentiality of complaints and other information received by IMCA from Clients or other parties with respect to Licensees' alleged violations of the Code, Standards of Practice, and/or Rules.

b. Providing periodic summaries to the PRB of all such complaints.

c. Conducting investigations of complaints at the direction of the PRB.

d. Preparing and submitting disciplinary petitions to the PRB after review by Legal Counsel.

e. Preparing and submitting disciplinary recommendations by a Hearing Panel to the PRB.

f. Preparing draft orders for review and approval by a Hearing Panel, the PRB, the IMCA Appeals Board, and/or any member of any of the aforementioned bodies.

g. Obtaining all necessary confidentiality and/or conflict of interest agreements by members of the PRB, the IMCA Appeals Board, and/or Hearing Panel members.

ARTICLE 3: GROUNDS FOR DISCIPLINE The following acts or omissions committed by a Licensee or Candidate individually or in concert with others shall constitute grounds for the filing of a disciplinary petition, initiation of disciplinary proceedings, and imposition of discipline:

a. Violation of the Code, Standards of Practice, or Rules.

b. Violation of federal or state statutes or regulations or rules of self-regulating bodies in respect to the financial services industry.

c. Violation of the criminal statutes of any state or the United States for commission of a Serious Crime. Conviction of a crime shall not be a prerequisite for the filing of a disciplinary petition.

d. Any act or omission that results in a Professional Loss or Suspension and/or the suspension or termination of a professional license, designation, or certification by a local, state, federal, or private licensing, designation or certification authority or organization.

e. Violation of the rules of FINRA or other financial services self-regulatory organization.

   f. Failure to respond to a disciplinary petition or a request of the Hearing Panel,
      or failure to comply with an order of a Hearing Panel, the PRB, and/or the
      IMCA Appeals Board
   g. The submission of false or misleading statements to IMCA, a Hearing Panel,
      the PRB, and/or the IMCA Appeals Board.
   h. Violation of the License Agreement between IMCA and the Licensee.

   The foregoing constitutes a nonexclusive list of grounds for discipline. Other
acts or omissions that constitute unprofessional conduct or that bring an IMCA Designation into disrepute or impair the goodwill of the IMCA Designation also may
constitute grounds for discipline.

ARTICLE 4: DISCIPLINARY PROCEEDINGS

4.1 Initiation of Disciplinary Proceedings

4.1.1   Once IMCA is notified in writing of a complaint against a Licensee or Candidate, IMCA staff shall have sixty (60) days from that date to research the complaint.
Within the sixty (60) day period, IMCA staff shall prepare and send a draft petition
to Legal Counsel for review and approval. Legal Counsel shall have sixty (60) days
to review the petition and determine if IMCA staff should forward the petition to the
PRB for initial review. Any of these time periods may be extended by the PRB upon
good cause shown.

4.1.2   The PRB shall undertake an initial review of each disciplinary petition for-
warded by IMCA staff. In cases in which a petition does not set forth sufficient facts
to show good cause for discipline, the PRB may either dismiss the petition in its
entirety or return the petition to IMCA staff for further research and leave to amend.
The PRB has sixty (60) days from receipt of the petition to make its determination.
This time period may be extended by the PRB upon good cause shown.

4.1.3   If the PRB finds a disciplinary petition establishes good cause for discipline,
it shall either: (a) in the event the PRB determines that the petition and supporting exhibits establish, without any reasonable grounds for dispute, that grounds for
discipline exist and that the appropriate remedy is a private censure, then the PRB
may authorize the issuance of a private letter informing the Respondent of these
conclusions and that a private censure would be the remedy. The Respondent shall
be offered the opportunity to have a hearing in lieu of the summary private censure;
or (b) appoint a three-member Hearing Panel to hear and review evidence with
respect to the petition. No member of the PRB or the IMCA Board may serve on a
Hearing Panel. The PRB chair shall appoint a Hearing Panel that shall be composed
of IMCA Designation holders in good standing who hold the same IMCA Designation
as the Respondent. The Hearing Panel chair, who is selected by the members of the
Hearing Panel, shall rule on all motions and objections and may grant extensions of
time concerning the deadlines provided by these Rules. No member of the Hearing
Panel shall participate in any proceeding in which the member or any member of
their immediate family or firm or employer has any financial or other interest, or
where such participation would involve a conflict of interest.

4.1.4 The Hearing Panel shall commence proceedings concerning a disciplinary petition by serving the disciplinary petition on the Respondent by certified mail to the Respondent's last known address and issuing a scheduling order setting the following dates:

    a. An answer to the disciplinary petition shall be filed with IMCA staff no later than thirty (30) days after the mailing date of the disciplinary petition to Respondent. The answer shall respond to the allegations set forth in the disciplinary petition and either request or waive the right to participate in a hearing before the Hearing Panel.

    b. During the period beginning thirty (30) days after the mailing date of the disciplinary petition to Respondent and ending ninety (90) days thereafter, the Hearing Panel may request that the Respondent produce documents concerning the alleged infraction and any facts, claims, or defenses asserted in the answer. The Respondent may request IMCA to produce its records relating to the Respondent as well as any documents that support the allegations contained in the disciplinary petition (Document Production Period). Any party who fails to produce documents requested by the other party during the Document Production Period shall not be permitted to use said documents for any purpose in proceedings governed by these Rules.

    c. The hearing date shall be set no later than ninety (90) days after the last day of the Document Production Period.

4.2 Failure to Respond to the Petition Failure to respond to the disciplinary petition within the period provided in paragraph 4.1.4 shall be deemed a default by the Respondent. Upon entry of an order of default by the Hearing Panel, the Respondent's license to use his or her IMCA Designation shall be immediately terminated and, in the case of a Candidate, the Respondent shall be terminated from the appropriate IMCA program. A notice of termination shall be sent to Respondent via certified mail.

    A Licensee must immediately cease all use of the IMCA Designation upon receipt of the notice of termination or other notification of termination from IMCA. Upon good cause shown at any time, a Respondent may move to set aside the default.

4.3 Hearing A Respondent who has filed an answer to a petition shall be entitled to a hearing before the Hearing Panel and may personally, or through an attorney (at Respondent's own expense), respond to the allegations contained in the disciplinary petition. The hearing shall take place at the location specified by the Hearing Panel, via video conference at Respondent's sole expense, or via teleconference. For the purposes of preservation of testimony, the proceedings may be recorded by IMCA staff, in which case the recording of the proceedings will be maintained at IMCA offices.

    At the hearing, the Respondent may present documentary evidence and testimony of witnesses in support of Respondent's answer; provided, however, that to be admissible, all such documentary evidence and the substance of all such witness testimony must have been disclosed to the Hearing Panel during the Document Production Period. The Hearing Panel shall set its own rules regarding the conduct of the hearing and the admission of evidence. Hearings may be conducted before a court reporter at the Respondent's option and cost, but if the Respondent intends to use a court reporter, Respondent shall notify IMCA of said intent and IMCA shall procure the court reporter. Respondent shall be responsible to pay for all costs associated with said court reporter, including, without limitation, production of a copy of the transcript for IMCA. All testimony presented shall be under oath.

Within sixty (60) days of the last day of the hearing, the Hearing Panel shall issue a report of its findings of fact and conclusions with respect to the allegations contained in the disciplinary petition, together with a proposed order setting forth the action recommended to the PRB.

The PRB shall review the Hearing Panel's report and proposed order and issue a final order within thirty (30) days after receiving the report and proposed order. The PRB's final order shall be sent to Respondent by certified mail within ten (10) business days of issuance.

In the event that the PRB finds that the Hearing Panel has abused its discretion or has made clearly erroneous findings of fact, the PRB may dismiss the disciplinary petition or remand it with instructions to the Hearing Panel to conduct further fact-finding or take other action consistent with the direction of the PRB.

4.4 Remedial Action The PRB has discretion to take any and/or all of the following action(s) in the event that a preponderance of the evidence submitted at the hearing establishes that grounds for disciplinary action exist:

a. Private censure. A private censure is a letter from the PRB to the Respondent advising the Respondent the PRB has determined private censure is the appropriate discipline. The fact of private censure shall not be made public. Other than through publication of anonymous decisions, the facts and circumstances supporting the private censure shall also not be made public. Although not publicly disseminated, the private censure letter shall be a permanent portion of Respondent's record, and a copy of the private censure letter shall be maintained in the Respondent's file at IMCA.

b. Public censure. The fact of and the facts and circumstances supporting the public censure shall be made public in any venues IMCA deems appropriate, including, but not limited to, IMCA's website, media alerts, and/or notification to FINRA or other financial services organizations and may be made available to others upon request.

c. Suspension of the right to use the IMCA Designation for a specific period of time. The fact of and the facts and circumstances supporting the suspension shall be made public in any venues IMCA deems appropriate, including, but not limited, to IMCA's website, media alerts, and/or notification to FINRA or other financial services organizations and may be made available to others upon request.

d. Termination of the right to use the IMCA Designation. The fact of and the facts and circumstances supporting the termination shall be made public in any venues IMCA deems appropriate, including, but not limited to,

IMCA's website, media alerts, and/or notification to FINRA or other financial services organizations and may be made available to others upon request.

e. Other action determined to be appropriate to remedy the conduct.

All remedial action, including private censures, shall be a permanent portion of the Respondent's record and shall be maintained in the Respondent's file at IMCA.

ARTICLE 5: APPEALS   A final order of the PRB is subject to review by the IMCA Appeals Board. Any discipline imposed by the PRB is stayed during the pendency of a timely filed appeal.

An appeal from a final order of the PRB must be filed within sixty (60) days of the date of the order. In the event a timely appeal is not filed, the PRB order shall become final and nonappealable, and any discipline ordered by the PRB shall apply from the date the order becomes final and nonappealable.

The IMCA Appeals Board will review an appeal within sixty (60) days after receipt of the appeal. The IMCA Appeals Board shall only review the record of the hearing and shall not conduct any de novo review of the matter. The decision of the IMCA Appeals Board is final and shall be transmitted to Respondent via certified mail within thirty (30) days after the date on which the IMCA Appeals Board makes its decision. Any discipline ordered by the PRB and/or the IMCA Appeals Board after an appeal shall apply from the date the PRB's or IMCA Appeals Board's decision becomes final and nonappealable.

A Respondent's failure to comply with any final and nonappealable orders of the PRB and/or the IMCA Appeals Board may be grounds for additional discipline, which may include the suspension or termination of the Respondent's IMCA Designation as provided in Rule 4.4.

ARTICLE 6: REPORTABLE EVENTS

6.1   Upon receipt of written notification by the Licensee or Candidate of being a defendant or respondent in any self-regulatory organization (e.g., FINRA), government agency, criminal, and/or civil complaint, investigation, mediation, or arbitration, every Licensee or Candidate must notify IMCA in writing of such action within sixty (60) days.

6.2   Every Licensee or Candidate, upon being convicted of a Serious Crime or being the subject of a Professional Loss or Suspension must notify IMCA in writing of such conviction, loss, or suspension within sixty (60) days after receipt of notification by the Licensee or Candidate of such conviction, loss, or suspension. Upon becoming aware of a Licensee's or Candidate's conviction for a Serious Crime or Professional Loss or Suspension, the PRB may, in its discretion, issue an order to show cause why the Licensee's license to use an IMCA Designation should not be immediately suspended or the Candidate should not immediately be terminated from the applicable IMCA program. Failure to respond to the order to show cause within ten (10) days of receipt may result in immediate suspension or termination of the Licensee or Candidate.

Responses to orders to show cause shall be referred to the PRB for further action under these Rules.

ARTICLE 7: REINSTATEMENT AFTER DISCIPLINE

7.1 Reinstatement after Termination   Termination shall be permanent and there shall be no grounds upon which a terminated Licensee or Candidate may seek reinstatement.

7.2 Reinstatement after Suspension   Unless otherwise provided by a PRB order or order of the IMCA Appeals Board issued after an appeal, within thirty (30) days of the expiration of the suspension term, a Respondent may file a petition for reinstatement. The petition for reinstatement must be accompanied by an affidavit of compliance signed by the Respondent reporting compliance with the order and setting forth the steps taken by the Respondent during the suspension period to rehabilitate himself or herself, and make amends to clients, colleagues, and others adversely affected by his/her actions. The Respondent also must verify in the petition for reinstatement that he or she has complied with IMCA's continuing education requirements throughout the suspension period.

7.3 Reinstatement by PRB   The PRB, upon review of the petition for reinstatement and the Respondent's affidavit, may, in its discretion, grant reinstatement or require the Respondent to attend a reinstatement hearing. All costs of the reinstatement hearing shall be borne by the Respondent. Reinstatement is within the sole discretion of the PRB and shall not be granted in the absence of clear and convincing evidence of compliance with the order, the Code, Standards of Practice, Rules, and IMCA's continuing education requirements. Upon or in conjunction with the PRB's grant or acceptance of a petition for reinstatement after disciplinary suspension, the Respondent, in order to be eligible to reactivate his or her license to use the IMCA Designation, shall comply with IMCA's rules regarding reactivation after disciplinary suspension.

7.4 Appeal from Reinstatement Decision   Any order by the PRB concerning reinstatement may be appealed to the IMCA Appeals Board using the same procedures as provided in Article 5 of these Rules.

Part V IMCA Guidelines for Consultants Regarding the Acceptance of Benefits from Third Parties

In General

The consultant always should remain objective. The acceptance of benefits of any kind, such as cash, gifts, products, services, expense-paid trips, lodging, special events, and so forth, from investment managers or vendors other than the consultant's employer or client may have an impact on a consultant's objectivity. Even when a consultant's objectivity has not in fact been impaired, the possibility of conflicting interest that arises from the acceptance of third-party benefits weakens a client's confidence in the consultant's objectivity and is therefore detrimental to the consultant/client relationship. Acceptance of any material benefit by a consultant from a third party is therefore discouraged.

The guidelines that follow do not supersede any more stringent guidelines or rules established by employers or government agencies.

Definitions

1. THIRD-PARTY BENEFIT A third-party benefit is any benefit received by a consultant or by any member of his family or household from any person or firm other than the consultant's employer or the consultant's client as a result of, or in the expectation or hope of generating professional relationships with the consultant, his employer, or his client. A third-party benefit may be cash or a noncash item or service that has value to the consultant. Gifts, merchandise, meals, tickets to events, trips, lodging, and outings are examples of noncash benefits.

2. MATERIAL Any third-party benefit with a fair-market value in excess of $100 is considered material.

3. OCCASIONS A third-party benefit is considered "occasional" if it occurs no more frequently than once a year.

Applicable Guidelines

1. A consultant should not solicit any third-party benefit under any circumstances.
2. A consultant should not accept any third-party benefit if its source is not identified.
3. A consultant should not under any circumstances accept any third-party benefit that is directly or indirectly linked to a manager or vendor's receipt of business from a client of the consultant.
4. No material third-party benefit should be accepted without the written approval of the consultant's employer.
5. A consultant should disclose to the client in writing any material third-party benefit he or she receives from a manager or vendor who also services that client. Disclosure is required if the consultant has, in fact or theory, any responsibility for the selection, monitoring, or evaluation of that manager or vendor for that client. Client disclosure in writing is not required if the client is present as a guest of the manager or vendor at the same event attended by the consultant, or if the client is present at the time the third-party benefit is delivered to the consultant.
6. A consultant should maintain a written record of all material third-party benefits received; this record should be open to inspection by the consultant's employer and client upon request.
7. Occasional meals, event tickets, or similar entertainment of a consultant and his or her guest need not be disclosed.

8. Reimbursement for the costs or expenses incurred when traveling to the offices of an investment manager for the purpose of conducting a due diligence inspection are considered to be a third-party benefit and should be treated accordingly.

9. A consultant may accept reimbursement for the reasonable cost or expense incurred in attendance at a training or educational meeting held by an investment manager or vendor, provided that his or her attendance at the meeting is approved in writing, in advance, by the consultant's employer and that it does in fact provide legitimate educational content. This reimbursement is, however, considered to be a third-party benefit and should be treated accordingly.

10. Attendance at industry-wide meetings or conferences, sponsored by multiple, totally unaffiliated investment managers or vendors or special events at such conferences, sponsored by a single manager or vendor, need not be disclosed, provided that the participation in sponsored events is open to all conference attendees.

CHAPTER 2

Regulatory Considerations

Investment advisors and consultants are subject to numerous laws and regulations that apply to the activities in which they engage, the products and services they provide, and the relationships they have with specific clientele they serve. Depending on these activities, products and services, relationships, and the jurisdictions in which they work, investment professionals may be subject to oversight by the following regulators: the SEC (Securities and Exchange Commission), FINRA (Financial Industry Regulatory Authority), and state securities boards or agencies among others.

This chapter explores fiduciary responsibilities, direct and indirect relationships, the principal-agent relationship, disqualified persons, prohibited transactions, and various laws and regulations that apply to investment advisors and consultants.

Learning Objectives
- Define the term "fiduciary" and describe the fiduciary responsibility of CIMA® designees.
- Describe the principal-agent relationship between investment professionals and individuals, trusts, foundations, endowments, and ERISA plan clients.
- Identify circumstances that may cause a person to be identified as a fiduciary.
- Describe laws that apply to investment advisors and consultants, including:
  ERISA (Employee Retirement Income Security Act)
  UPIA (Uniform Prudent Investor Act)
  UMIFA (Uniform Management of Institutional Funds Act)
  UPMIFA (Uniform Prudent Management of Institutional Funds Act)
  Other international, federal, and state laws
- Identify prohibited transactions.

In the client relationship, a consultant often is identified as a fiduciary or is said to have a fiduciary duty owed to the client. The term fiduciary can have a variety of meanings to clients and consultants. In general, a fiduciary duty, or capacity, can be defined as an ethical relationship between a consultant and a client in which the consultant is to act on behalf of and always in the best interest of the client. In turn, the client places trust and good faith in the consultant. The sole purpose of this relationship must be to safeguard the interests of the client at all times. Additionally, a fiduciary must adhere to a process that is deemed to be prudent.

The fiduciary relationship for a consultant and client can be established with individuals, trusts, foundations, endowments, ERISA plans, and many other circumstances. In each case, certain duties are expected to be performed at a minimum on behalf of the client or clients.

For individuals and trusts, the fiduciary has a responsibility to manage investments prudently. The Prudent Man Rule or the Prudent Investor Rule may apply in such cases. Although the rule is almost 200 years old and based on the *Harvard College v. Amory* case of 1830, it still is considered the foundation for most fiduciary relationships.

The rule states that trustees are directed to "observe how men of prudence, discretion, and intelligence manage their own affairs, not in regard to speculation, but in regard to the permanent disposition of their funds, considering the probable income, as well as the probable safety of the capital to be invested." Trustees are to exercise care and skill in the selection of investments.

The initial Prudent Man Rule focused primarily on the merits of the individual investments, did not allow for risky investments, and focused on investments in government securities. Over time, interpretation of the rule evolved, with large steps taking place after the Great Depression and after World War II.

The more modern Prudent Investment Rule incorporates the theory of diversification and allows for overall portfolio management as the guiding principle for astute investment management.

Trustees are considered to be fiduciaries to the beneficiaries. Legally, an account or property is committed to the trustee. A beneficiary has no legal title to the trust, but has a beneficial use or interest. In this relationship, the trustee must only act in the interest of the beneficiary, and can in no way act in his or her own best interest.

With foundations, endowments, and ERISA plans, a board of directors may be held to the same fiduciary standards as a trustee. A major difference is the board's capacity to act in the interest of an entity, or in some cases, a large group of individuals. In many cases, the entities or individuals have legal title or claim to assets that the board is managing on their behalf. The decisions may be on a different scale, but the core principal of the fiduciary relationship remains intact.

Another term for the relationship is the principal-agent relationship. In a trustee relationship, the principal is the beneficiary, the person who is owed the duty, while the agent would be the trustee, the person who is the fiduciary. Other examples of the principal-agent relationship include company-board of directors, client-consultant, and heirs-executors.

A consultant may be considered a fiduciary under a number of different circumstances. In most cases, as a fiduciary, the consultant must apply fiduciary standards and exercise those standards with care. Some cases are obvious and others are by default.

Direct Relationships

In many cases, the consultant should be aware of the direct fiduciary relationship. These cases include becoming a trustee and sitting on the board of directors of a foundation.

If a consultant is named as a trustee, the consultant must be prepared to act in a fiduciary capacity on behalf of the client. The foundational case for trustee fiduciary standards was *Keech v. Sandford* in 1726. The law ultimately states that the trustee has a strict duty and that there never should be a conflict of interest in the relationship. Consultants agreeing to become trustees must realize that they are expected to be fiduciaries.

A consultant who holds himself or herself out as a fiduciary for ERISA plans and pensions may be held to fiduciary standards. In these cases, consultants must be prepared to define the scope and nature of their relationship with the entity for which they are consulting.

Sitting on the board of directors for a company, foundation, or endowment also may make the consultant a fiduciary. The duties owed to the individuals or entities should be examined by the consultant prior to making the commitment to sit on a board.

Indirect Relationships

In some cases, the consultant may be held out as a fiduciary without realizing that he or she is being held to a fiduciary standard. Sitting on the board of directors, as described above, may be one of those cases. Another situation is in the case of discretionary accounts. If a consultant manages a discretionary account on behalf of a client, he or she may be considered a fiduciary. In most cases, if there is a question of the nature of the relationship, the consultant may be held to the high standards of fiduciary care.

Under current legislation, prohibited transactions for ERISA plans are specific. According to IRS Publication 560 and www.irs.gov, ERISA prohibited transactions including the following six:

1. A transfer of plan income or assets to, or use of them by or for the benefit of, a disqualified person
2. Any act of a fiduciary by which plan income or assets are used for his or her own interest
3. The receipt of consideration by a fiduciary for his or her own account from any party dealing with the plan in a transaction that involves plan income or assets
4. The sale, exchange, or lease of property between a plan and a disqualified person
5. Lending money or extending credit between a plan and a disqualified person
6. Furnishing goods, services, or facilities between a plan and a disqualified person

According to Publication 560, disqualified individuals include the following 10 types:

1. A fiduciary of the plan
2. A person providing services to the plan
3. An employer, any of whose employees are covered by the plan
4. An employee organization, any of whose members are covered by the plan
5. Any direct or indirect owner of 50 percent or more of any of the following:
   a. The combined voting power of all classes of stock entitled to vote, or the total value of shares of all classes of stock of a corporation
   b. that is an employer or employee organization described in (3) or (4)

    c. the capital interest or profits interest of a partnership that is an employer or employee organization described in (3) or (4)

    d. the beneficial interest of a trust or unincorporated enterprise that is an employer or an employee organization described in (3) or (4)

6. A member of the family of any individual described in (1), (2), (3), or (4) (i.e., the individual's spouse, ancestor, lineal descendant, or any spouse of a lineal descendant)

7. A corporation, partnership, trust, or estate of which (or in which) any direct or indirect owner described in (1) through (5) holds 50 percent or more of any of the following:

    a. The combined voting power of all classes of stock entitled to vote or the total value of shares of all classes of stock of a corporation

    b. The capital interest or profits interest of a partnership

    c. The beneficial interest of a trust or estate

8. An officer, director (or an individual having powers or responsibilities similar to those of officers or directors), a 10 percent or more shareholder, or highly compensated employee (earning 10 percent or more of the yearly wages of an employer) of a person described in (3), (4), (5), or (7)

9. A 10-percent or more (in capital or profits) partner or joint venture of a person described in (3), (4), (5), or (7)

10. Any disqualified person, as described in (1) through (9) above, who is a disqualified person with respect to any plan to which a multiemployer plan trust is permitted to make payments under section 4223 of ERISA

Consultants should pay particular attention to items (1) and (2). In general, as a disqualified individual, the consultant should not benefit from the relationship as the guidelines describe above.

Laws and Regulations

Consultants must be aware of different laws and the application of those laws for their clients. The laws serve as a basis of rules that ultimately are designed to protect the beneficiaries and plan participants that are covered.

ERISA

ERISA stands for the Employee Retirement Income Security Act of 1974.

This act established the standards for employee retirement, health, and other benefit plans. The act applies to nongovernment employers that offer these benefits. ERISA establishes the general rules for conduct, reporting, disclosures, procedures, and protection. Consolidated Omnibus Budget Reconciliation Act (COBRA) of 1985 and Health Insurance Portability and Accountability Act (HIPAA) of 1996 also are covered under ERISA.

The Department of Labor, Internal Revenue Service (IRS), and the Pension Benefit Guarantee Corporation (PBGC) each have responsibilities under ERISA.

The Department of Labor is responsible for the fiduciary and reporting requirements for company-sponsored ERISA plans such as 401(k)s, profit sharing plans, and defined benefit plans. Companies that sponsor these plans must disclose to their employees information about the financial health of the plan, how to participate, and other information that can allow employees to make informed decisions. Business owners and investment advisors can be sued by plan participants for breach of this fiduciary duty.

Though not a requirement, section 404(c) of ERISA provides minimum responsibilities and disclosures that plan participants should be provided with to lessen (but not eliminate) fiduciary liability. If the plan is intended to be compliant with section 404(c), plan participants must be explicitly made aware.

Minimum standards for participation, vesting, benefit accrual, and funding are provided for under ERISA and administered by the IRS. Certain standards must be met for these plans to receive favorable tax treatment; otherwise the IRS can disqualify the plans and assess penalties. The rules that plans must follow to maintain tax benefits include the following: pension plans must offer joint and survivor options and any ERISA plan cannot discriminate in favor of highly compensated employees or officers.

The Pension Protection Act of 2006 (PPA) specified two vesting options for any defined contribution plan offered by an employer. Participants can either become 100-percent vested in employer contributions after three years (cliff vesting) or gradually vest by 20 percent annually until 100-percent vested.

Employee contributions to a defined contribution plan are always 100-percent vested. Defined benefit plan vesting schedules differ slightly. Instead of a three-year lump vesting schedule, defined benefit plans can vest at 100 percent for up to five years of service. Alternatively, 20 percent of the plan can vest each year starting in year three.

Minimum funding rules established by ERISA and the PPA are meant to keep defined benefit plans properly funded for their beneficiaries. The PBGC provides a form of insurance for defined benefit plans only and does not provide protection for defined contribution plans such as 401(k) plans. If a pension plan cannot meet its obligations to its beneficiaries, the PBGC takes over the plan and provides some amount of pension benefit up to a guaranteed maximum that is adjusted annually.

A defined benefit plan sponsor may terminate a plan in either of two ways:

(1) a plan may undergo a standard termination when assets exist to provide benefits promised to the participants; (2) a distress termination occurs if the plan sponsor voluntarily terminates the plan, but there are either not enough assets to fund each participant's benefit or providing the benefits could potentially put the sponsor out of business. The PBGC also can initiate a plan's takeover on its own if it determines that a plan is unsustainable.

In addition to employer plans, ERISA also gave rise to the individual retirement account (IRA) or individual retirement arrangement, allowing individuals to defer taxes on some savings without necessitating an employer-sponsored plan.

Because ERISA covers all employer-sponsored benefit programs, the Consolidated Omnibus Budget Reconciliation Act (COBRA) of 1985 and Health Insurance Portability and Accountability Act (HIPAA) of 1996 also are part of ERISA. COBRA is most widely known for allowing a participant to continue under employer-provided health coverage for a limited period of time under certain conditions after separation from employment. COBRA also prohibits employers from limiting partic-ipation in retirement plans for new employees close to retirement age and freezing benefits for participants 65 or older.

HIPAA intended to make health insurance more portable by eliminating pre-existing conditions as the basis for an employer to refuse coverage in some cases. HIPAA also prevents the refusal of coverage due to health status, genetic information, or disability.

Uniform Prudent Investor Act (UPIA)

UPIA was adopted in 1992 and essentially updates the Prudent Man Rule.

UPIA makes it possible for investment managers and fiduciaries to manage a portfolio using methodologies from modern portfolio theory. Measurement of a port-folio's performance is based on the entire portfolio and not each individual under-lying asset. Individual securities, once considered too risky to include in a portfolio, such as commodities, futures, and derivatives, now are acceptable, based on the concept of managing a portfolio's overall risk.

Because UPIA now puts greater emphasis on the total return of a portfolio, fiduciaries should consider the impact on the portfolio caused by general economic conditions, inflation or deflation, tax consequences, the purpose of each individual investment within the total portfolio, other resources available to the beneficiaries, liquidity needs, and any special value or relationship any beneficiary or beneficiaries have with an asset.

One of the major complaints of the previous Prudent Investor Rule was that it did not specifically allow trustees to delegate investment management. UPIA corrects this oversight, allowing for professional investment management when this better fulfills the purpose of the trust.

Uniform Management of Institutional Funds Act (UMIFA) and Uniform Prudent Management of Institutional Funds Act (UPMIFA)

UPMIFA was designed to replace UMIFA. Both UMIFA and UPMIFA are at the core of law for endowments and charities. They provide rules regarding the guidelines for amounts a charity or endowment can spend and on what they can spend the funds. They also provide rules for the investment of funds.

UMIFA and UPMIFA differ based on the historical dollar value rule.

UMIFA considered the historical dollar, while UPMIFA states that institutions "may appropriate for expenditure or accumulate so much of an endowment fund as the institution determines to be prudent for the uses, benefits, purposes, and duration for which the endowment fund is established." In general, it is believed that the UPMIFA rules brought UMIFA up to date.

UPMIFA updated UMIFA in four key areas: investment conduct, expenditure of funds, delegation of management, and release or modification of restrictions.

To perform their fiduciary duty, charities are expected to manage the costs of their portfolio management prudently, consider the total portfolio when making individual investment decisions, and are specifically required to diversify and balance their portfolio in consideration of their risk tolerance.

UPMIFA also provides the following seven specific guidelines for amounts a charity or endowment can spend and on what they can spend the funds:

1. Duration and preservation of the endowment fund
2. The purposes of the institution and the endowment fund
3. General economic conditions
4. Effect of inflation or deflation
5. The expected total return from income and the appreciation of investments
6. Other resources of the institution
7. The investment policy of the institution

UMIFA updated the legal constraint that trusts can spend only income, subject to a floor defined by the historical dollar value. The historical dollar value is the sum of the original gift plus any additions required by the donor or by law. UPMIFA eliminated this rule and instead states that institutions "may appropriate for expenditure or accumulate so much of an endowment fund as the institution determines to be prudent for the uses, benefits, purposes, and duration for which the endowment fund is established."

For individual state governments that prefer more specific guidelines, they can amend the act to allow an initial assumption of imprudence if an organization spends more than 7 percent of the fund's fair market value over a three-year period using an averaging formula.

UPMIFA also clarifies the procedures for releasing or modifying restrictions on charitable funds. If notice is given to the state's attorney general and the changes are still consistent with the donor's intent, a court can allow modifications if it determines the funds are either unlawful or not practical to retain or the fund's purpose is impossible to achieve or is wasteful.

Additionally, if the amount of the donation in question is less than $25,000 and more than 20 years old, the charity may modify the fund's restrictions without going to court. Again, the state's attorney general must be notified, but if the charity receives no objections after 60 days, restrictions can be changed as long as the result is consistent with the original intent of the gift.

Federal Regulatory Agencies

The two core agencies for federal regulation in investment management are the Securities and Exchange Commission (SEC) and the Financial Industry Regulatory Agency (FINRA).

SEC

The mission of the U.S. Securities and Exchange Commission is to protect investors, maintain fair, orderly, and efficient markets, and facilitate capital formation. Though it is the primary overseer and regulator of the U.S. securities markets, the SEC works closely with many other institutions, including Congress, other federal departments and agencies, the self-regulatory organizations (e.g., the stock exchanges), state securities regulators, and various private sector organizations.

The Securities Exchange Act of 1934 created the SEC to interpret securities law, to provide rules regarding the disclosure of information by public companies, and to enforce those rules. Market participants, including securities exchanges, brokers and dealers, self-regulatory organizations, clearing agencies, and others are required to register with the SEC. These entities are required to disclose information regarding their financial condition and business practices, including the registration of new securities, annual shareholder reports, and mergers and acquisitions. The SEC requires also that investments such as mutual funds, exchanged-traded funds, and others disclose information useful to investors so that they can make informed investment decisions.

To determine standards for what information should be disclosed by these various organizations and public companies and how that information should be presented, the SEC works closely with self-regulatory organizations such as the Financial Accounting Standards Board. The SEC also oversees securities exchanges, self-regulatory organizations, and credit rating agencies.

In a single statement, the SEC exists to provide investors with rules for the fair execution of trades and to enforce those rules. To that end, several major violations of fair trading are prohibited by the SEC. The SEC prohibits the use of insider or nonpublic information to place trades. For example, wash sales can be used either to create artificial tax losses or, when used by very large shareholders, to mislead investors by manipulating the share price. Wash sales occur when investors sell shares only to almost immediately buy back those same or similar shares, usually within 30 days. Churning, whereby an advisor creates multiple transactions, typically over a short period of time, that generates commissions or other income and increases the costs to a client's invested assets without a clear benefit to the client, is also prohibited.

In order to provide investment professionals with the information they need to follow these rules and maintain the integrity of the securities industry, the SEC administers the examination and inspection programs for all registered self-regulatory agencies, investment companies, broker–dealers, and advisors, among others in the securities business.

The SEC also has jurisdiction over the private, nonprofit Securities Investor Protection Corporation (SIPC) that insures customer accounts at member brokerage firms against the failure of those same firms. Unlike Federal Deposit Insurance Corporation (FDIC) coverage, SIPC insurance does not insure accounts against loss due to market movements.

Financial Industry Regulatory Authority (FINRA)

FINRA is the largest independent, nonprofit self-regulatory organization (SRO) registered under the SEC for all securities firms doing business in the United States. It writes and enforces rules related to federal securities law to protect and educate investors. FINRA examines firms and can punish individuals and firms through fines, suspensions, and up to and including expulsion from the securities industry.

All brokers must be licensed and registered by FINRA, pass qualification exams, and satisfy continuing-education requirements. For the public's protection, FINRA also discloses any disciplinary action it takes against registered advisors.

Most advertisements and marketing material used by members must be filed with FINRA before an advisor or firm can distribute them to the public. Further, FINRA requires not only that the sales material be truthful, but that the security sold is suitable to the individual investor and that the investor receives complete disclosure about an investment before purchase. When problems arise, FINRA also administers the arbitration typically required as the starting point to begin to resolve disputes among investors and its members.

FINRA replaced the National Association of Securities Dealers (NASD) when its rulemaking and enforcement activities were consolidated with those of the enforcement division of the New York Stock Exchange in 2007.

Thus, FINRA also monitors securities exchanges for suspicious activities and provides educational materials freely available to the public.

State Agencies

Each state has its own state security administrator responsible for regulating the securities industry in that state. The state security administrator also can register securities offered or sold in their state and oversee the firms and individuals selling securities or providing investment advice to their citizens.

Although similar in scope to the SEC, investment advisors managing less than $100 million must register and file Form ADV with the state securities agency in their principal location.

The National Securities Markets Improvement Act of 1996 amended the Securities Act of 1933 to exempt securities traded nationwide and registered with the SEC from registering with a state individually. Each state's securities law or "blue sky laws," a name taken from a fraudulent rainmaking scheme against drought-stricken farmers, still provide the state with the authority to prosecute over securities fraud.

The North American Securities Administrators Association (NASAA) is the membership organization for each state's securities administrator as well as for U.S. territories, Canada, and Mexico.

CHAPTER 3

Statistics and Methods

S tatistical concepts and calculations form an important foundation for understanding applied financial methods and formulae. Investment advisors and consultants should have a firm grasp on quantitative concepts in order to analyze historical data, calculate and analyze investment risk and returns, draw accurate conclusions, and make appropriate recommendations to clients. This chapter provides explanations of key elementary statistical concepts.

Understanding and applying familiar concepts like compounding, discount factors, averages, measures of dispersion, and confidence intervals should come easily to investment advisors and consultants. More advanced statistical concepts and calculations however may take additional study to master. In practice, simply understanding the intuition of more advanced concepts and applications like multicollinearity and multivariate regression models is often sufficient. The readings in the chapter explain each concept from a mathematical framework and apply them to common financial and investment challenges to help one better understand and apply each tool in a more meaningful way.

Part I *Mathematics and Statistics for Financial Risk Management:* Some Basic Math

Learning Objectives
- Describe the concept of compounding and compute compound returns.
- Discuss the concept of limited liability.
- Graph log returns and discuss how logarithms are useful for charting times series that grow exponentially.
- Explain continuously compounded returns and convert the nominal rate into an annualized rate.
- Discuss the significance of discount factors.
- Describe the concept of an infinite series and determine the present value of a perpetuity that pays a stated coupon payment annually.

■ Describe the concept of a finite series and determine the present value of a newly issued bond that matures at a time certain and pays a stated coupon payment annually.

Part II *Mathematics and Statistics for Financial Risk Management:* Probabilities

Learning Objectives
■ Define and explain discrete random variables.
■ Define and explain continuous random variables.
■ Describe the concept of mutually exclusive events and calculate the probability that an investment will fall within a given range of returns.
■ Describe the concept of independent events and determine the probability that an investment will earn a return above a stated figure.
■ Explain probability matrices.

Part III *Mathematics and Statistics for Financial Risk Management:* Basic Statistics

Learning Objectives
■ Describe a population and sample data, and calculate the mean, median, and mode of a data set.
■ Describe discrete random variables and calculate the mean, median, and mode of a year-end portfolio value based on facts given, including default probabilities.
■ Describe continuous random variables.
■ Determine the price of a newly issued bond based on facts given including default probabilities.
■ Explain and calculate variance and standard deviation.
■ Describe and calculate variance and correlation.
■ Explain the concept of moments in statistical analysis.
■ Describe and illustrate skewness and kurtosis graphically.

Part IV *Mathematics and Statistics for Financial Risk Management:* Distributions

Learning Objectives
■ Describe a normal distribution and its implications for measuring returns and risk.
■ Explain the concept and application of Monte Carlo simulations for investment advisors and consultants.

Part V *Mathematics and Statistics for Financial Risk Management:* Hypothesis Testing and Confidence Intervals

Learning Objectives

- Review and calculate sample mean.
- Review and calculate sample variance.
- Explain the concept of confidence intervals and discuss the terms: *t*-distribution, *t*-statistic, and *t*-stat.
- Discuss hypothesis testing and confirm or reject a hypothesis based on various confidence levels.
- Discuss and calculate value-at-risk (VaR) and illustrate VaR graphically.
- Describe back-testing.
- Explain expected shortfall.

Part VI *Mathematics and Statistics for Financial Risk Management:* Linear Regression Analysis

Learning Objectives

- Describe linear regression and explain the formula (y = a + bx).
- Define coefficient of determination (R-squared) and explain how it is used.
- Explain the difference between univariate and multivariate regression models.
- Describe multicollinearity and discuss how increasingly integrated global financial markets cause challenges in managing risk.

Part VII *Mathematics and Statistics for Financial Risk Management:* Time Series Models

Learning Objectives

- Describe the concept of "random walks" and how it might apply to investment markets.
- Explain autocorrelation as it relates to measuring risk/return and random walks.
- Discuss why over-estimations and under-estimations of risk occur based on the assumptions a) that variance is linear in time and b) that no serial correlation exists.

Part I Some Basic Math

Compounding

Log returns might seem more complex than simple returns, but they have a number of advantages over simple returns in financial applications. One of the most useful features of log returns has to do with compounding returns. To get the return of a security for two periods using simple returns, we have to do something that is not very intuitive, namely adding one to each of the returns, multiplying, and then subtracting one:

$$R_{2,t} = \frac{P_t - P_{t-2}}{P_{t-2}} = (1 + R_{1,t})(1 + R_{1,t-1}) - 1 \tag{3.1}$$

Here the first subscript on R denotes the length of the return, and the second subscript is the traditional time subscript. With log returns, calculating multiperiod returns is much simpler; we simply add:

$$r_{2,t} = r_{1,t} + r_{1,t-1} \tag{3.2}$$

It is fairly straightforward to generalize this notation to any return length.

Sample Problem

Question:
Using Equation 3.1, generalize Equation 3.2 to returns of any length.

Answer:

$$R_{n,t} = \frac{P_t - P_{t-n}}{P_{t-n}} = \frac{P_t}{P_{t-n}} - 1 = \frac{P_t}{P_{t-1}} \frac{P_{t-1}}{P_{t-2}} \ldots \frac{P_{t-n+1}}{P_{t-n}} - 1$$

$$R_{n,t} = (1 + R_{1,t})(1 + R_{1,t-1}) \ldots (1 + R_{1,t-n+1}) - 1$$

$$(1 + R_{n,t}) = (1 + R_{1,t})(1 + R_{1,t-1}) \ldots (1 + R_{1,t-n+1})$$

$$r_{n,t} = r_{1,t} + r_{1,t-1} + \ldots + r_{1,t-n+1}$$

Note that to get to the last line, we took the logs of both sides of the previous equation, using the fact that the log of the product of any two variables is equal to the sum of their logs.

Limited Liability

Another useful feature of log returns relates to limited liability. For many financial assets, including equities and bonds, the most that you can lose is the amount that you've put into them. For example, if you purchase a share of XYZ Corporation for $100, the most you can lose is that $100. This is known as limited liability. Today, limited liability is such a common feature of financial instruments that it is easy to take it for granted, but this was not always the case. Indeed, the widespread adoption of limited liability in the nineteenth century made possible the large publicly traded companies that are so important to our modern economy, and the vast financial markets that accompany them.

That you can lose only your initial investment is equivalent to saying that the minimum possible return on your investment is –100 percent. At the other end of the spectrum, there is no upper limit to the amount you can make in an investment. The maximum possible return is, in theory, infinite. This range for simple returns,

−100 percent to infinity, translates to a range of negative infinity to positive infinity for log returns.

$$R_{min} = -100\% \Rightarrow r_{min} = -\infty$$
$$R_{max} = +\infty \Rightarrow r_{max} = +\infty$$
(3.3)

As we will see in the following sections, when it comes to mathematical and computer models in finance, it is often much easier to work with variables that are unbounded, that is, variables that can range from negative infinity to positive infinity.

Graphing Log Returns

Another useful feature of log returns is how they relate to log prices. By rearranging Equation 3.1 and taking logs, it is easy to see that:

$$r_t = p_t - p_{t-1}$$
(3.4)

where p_t is the log of P_t, the price at time t. To calculate log returns, rather than taking the log of one plus the simple return, we can simply calculate the logs of the prices and subtract.

Logarithms are also useful for charting time series that grow exponentially. Many computer applications allow you to chart data on a logarithmic scale. For an asset whose price grows exponentially, a logarithmic scale prevents the compression of data at low levels. Also, by rearranging Equation 3.4, we can easily see that the change in the log price over time is equal to the log return:

$$\Delta p_t = p_t - p_{t-1} = r_t$$
(3.5)

It follows that, for an asset whose return is constant, the change in the log price will also be constant over time. On a chart, this constant rate of change over time will translate into a constant slope. Figures 3.1 and 3.2 both show an asset whose price is increasing by 20 percent each year. The y-axis for the first chart shows the price; the y-axis for the second chart displays the log price.

For the chart in Figure 3.1, it is hard to tell if the rate of return is increasing or decreasing over time. For the chart in Figure 3.2, the fact that the line is straight is equivalent to saying that the line has a constant slope. From Equation 3.5 we know that this constant slope is equivalent to a constant rate of return.

In the first chart, the y-axis could just have easily been the actual price (on a log scale), but having the log prices allows us to do something else. Using Equation 3.4, we can easily estimate the log return. Over 10 periods, the log price increases from approximately 4.6 to 6.4. Subtracting and dividing gives us $(6.4 - 4.6)/10 = 18$ percent. So the log return is 18 percent per period, which—because log returns and simple returns are very close for small values—is very close to the actual simple return of 20 percent.

Continuously Compounded Returns

Another topic related to the idea of log returns is continuously compounded returns. For many financial products, including bonds, mortgages, and credit cards, interest

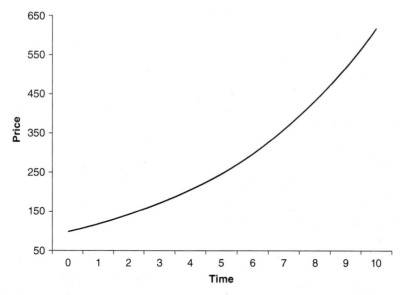

FIGURE 3.1   Normal Prices

rates are often quoted on an annualized periodic or nominal basis. At each payment date, the amount to be paid is equal to this nominal rate, divided by the number of periods, multiplied by some notional amount. For example, a bond with monthly coupon payments, a nominal rate of 6%, and a notional value of $1,000, would pay a coupon of $5 each month: (6% × $1,000)/12 = $5.

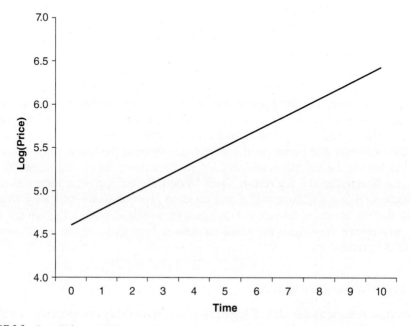

FIGURE 3.2   Log Prices

How do we compare two instruments with different payment frequencies? Are you better off paying 5 percent on an annual basis or 4.5 percent on a monthly basis? One solution is to turn the nominal rate into an annualized rate:

$$R_{\text{Annual}} = \left(1 + \frac{R_{\text{Nominal}}}{n}\right)^n - 1 \tag{3.6}$$

where n is the number of periods per year for the instrument.

If we hold R_{Annual} constant as n increases, R_{Nominal} gets smaller, but at a decreasing rate. Though the proof is omitted here, using L'Hôpital's rule, we can prove that, at the limit, as n approaches infinity, R_{Nominal} converges to the log rate. As n approaches infinity, it is as if the instrument is making infinitesimal payments on a continuous basis. Because of this, when used to define interest rates the log rate is often referred to as the continuously compounded rate, or simply the continuous rate. We can also compare two financial products with different payment periods by comparing their continuous rates.

Sample Problem

Question:
You are presented with two bonds. The first has a nominal rate of 20 percent paid on a semiannual basis. The second has a nominal rate of 19 percent paid on a monthly basis. Calculate the equivalent continuously compounded rate for each bond. Assuming both bonds have the same credit quality and are the same in all other respects, which is the better investment?

Answer:
First we compute the annual yield for both bonds:

$$R_{1,\text{Annual}} = \left(1 + \frac{20\%}{2}\right)^2 - 1 = 21.00\%$$

$$R_{2,\text{Annual}} = \left(1 + \frac{19\%}{12}\right)^{12} - 1 = 20.75\%$$

Next we convert these annualized returns into continuously compounded returns:

$$r_1 = \ln(1 + R_{1,\text{Annual}}) = 19.06\%$$
$$r_2 = \ln(1 + R_{2,\text{Annual}}) = 18.85\%$$

All other things being equal, the first bond is a better investment. We could base this on a comparison of either the annual or the continuously compounded rates.

Discount Factors

Most people have a preference for present income over future income. They would rather have a dollar today than a dollar one year from now. This is why banks charge interest on loans, and why investors expect positive returns on their investments.

Even in the absence of inflation, a rational person should prefer a dollar today to a dollar tomorrow. Looked at another way, we should require more than one dollar in the future to replace one dollar today.

In finance we often talk of discounting cash flows or future values. If we are discounting at a fixed rate, R, then the present value and future value are related as follows:

$$V_t = \frac{V_{t+n}}{(1+R)^n} \qquad (3.7)$$

where V_t is the value of the asset at time t and V_{t+n} is the value of the asset at time $t + n$. Because R is positive, V_t will necessarily be less than V_{t+n}. All else being equal, a higher discount rate will lead to a lower present value. Similarly, if the cash flow is further in the future—that is, n is greater—then the present value will also be lower.

Rather than work with the discount rate, R, it is sometimes easier to work with a discount factor. In order to obtain the present value, we simply multiply the future value by the discount factor:

$$V_t = \left(\frac{1}{1+R}\right)^n V_{t+n} = \delta^n V_{t+n} \qquad (3.8)$$

Because δ is less than one, V_t will necessarily be less than V_{t+n}. Different authors refer to δ or δ^n as the discount factor. The concept is the same, and which convention to use should be clear from the context.

Geometric Series

In the following two subsections we introduce geometric series. We start with series of infinite length. It may seem counterintuitive, but it is often easier to work with series of infinite length. With results in hand, we then move on to series of finite length in the second subsection.

INFINITE SERIES   The ancient Greek philosopher Zeno, in one of his famous paradoxes, tried to prove that motion was an illusion. He reasoned that, in order to get anywhere, you first had to travel half the distance to your ultimate destination. Once you made it to the halfway point, though, you would still have to travel half the remaining distance. No matter how many of these half journeys you completed, there would always be another half journey left. You could never possibly reach your destination.

While Zeno's reasoning turned out to be wrong, he was wrong in a very profound way. The infinitely decreasing distances that Zeno struggled with foreshadowed calculus, with its concept of change on an infinitesimal scale. Also, an infinite series of a variety of types turn up in any number of fields. In finance, we are often faced with series that can be treated as infinite. Even when the series is long, but clearly finite, the same basic tools that we develop to handle infinite series can be deployed.

In the case of the original paradox, we are basically trying to calculate the following summation:

$$S = \frac{1}{2} + \frac{1}{4} + \frac{1}{8} + \dots \tag{3.9}$$

What is S equal to? If we tried the brute force approach, adding up all the terms, we would literally be working on the problem forever. Luckily, there is an easier way. The trick is to notice that multiplying both sides of the equation by $\frac{1}{2}$ has the exact same effect as subtracting $\frac{1}{2}$ from both sides:

Multiply Both Sides by $\frac{1}{2}$	Subtract $\frac{1}{2}$ from Both Sides
$S = \frac{1}{2} + \frac{1}{4} + \frac{1}{8} + \dots$	$S = \frac{1}{2} + \frac{1}{4} + \frac{1}{8} + \dots$
$\frac{1}{2}S = \frac{1}{4} + \frac{1}{8} + \frac{1}{16} + \dots$	$S - \frac{1}{2} = \frac{1}{4} + \frac{1}{8} + \frac{1}{16} + \dots$

The right-hand sides of the final line of both equations are the same, so the left-hand sides of both equations must be equal. Taking the left-hand sides of both equations, and solving:

$$\frac{1}{2}S = S - \frac{1}{2}$$

$$\frac{1}{2}S = \frac{1}{2} \tag{3.10}$$

$$S = 1$$

The fact that the infinite series adds up to one tells us that Zeno was wrong. If we keep covering half the distance, but do it an infinite number of times, eventually we will cover the entire distance. The sum of all the half trips equals one full trip.

To generalize Zeno's paradox, assume we have the following series:

$$S = \sum_{i=1}^{\infty} \delta^i \tag{3.11}$$

In Zeno's case, δ was $\frac{1}{2}$. Because the members of the series are all powers of the same constant, we refer to these types of series as geometric series. As long as $|\delta|$ is less than one, the sum will be finite and we can employ the same basic strategy as before, this time multiplying both sides by δ.

$$\delta S = \sum_{i=1}^{\infty} \delta^{i+1}$$

$$\delta S = S - \delta^1 = S - \delta \tag{3.12}$$

$$S(1 - \delta) = \delta$$

$$S = \frac{\delta}{1 - \delta}$$

Substituting $\frac{1}{2}$ for δ, we see that the general equation agrees with our previously obtained result for Zeno's paradox.

Before deriving Equation 3.12, we stipulated that $|\delta|$ had to be less than one. The reason that $|\delta|$ has to be less than one may not be obvious. If δ is equal to one, we are simply adding together an infinite number of ones, and the sum is infinite. In this case, even though it requires us to divide by zero, Equation 3.12 will produce the correct answer.

If δ is greater than one, the sum is also infinite, but Equation 3.12 will give you the wrong answer. The reason is subtle. If δ is less than one, then δ^∞ converges to zero. When we multiplied both sides of the original equation by δ, in effect we added a $\delta^{\infty+1}$ term to the end of the original equation. If $|\delta|$ is less than one, this term is also zero, and the sum is unaltered. If $|\delta|$ is greater than one, however, this final term is itself infinitely large, and we can no longer assume that the sum is unaltered. If this is at all unclear, wait until the end of the following section on finite series, where we will revisit the issue. If δ is less than -1, the series will oscillate between increasingly large negative and positive values and will not converge. Finally, if δ equals -1, the series will flip back and forth between -1 and $+1$, and the sum will oscillate between -1 and 0.

One note of caution: In certain financial problems, you will come across geometric series that are very similar to Equation 3.11 except the first term is one, not δ. This is equivalent to setting the starting index of the summation to zero ($\delta^0 = 1$). Adding one to our previous result, we obtain the following equation:

$$S = \sum_{i=0}^{\infty} \delta^i = \frac{1}{1-\delta} \qquad (3.13)$$

As you can see, the change from $i = 0$ to $i = 1$ is very subtle, but has a very real impact.

Sample Problem

Question:
A perpetuity is a security that pays a fixed coupon for eternity. Determine the present value of a perpetuity, which pays a $5 coupon annually. Assume a constant 4 percent discount rate.

Answer:

$$V = \sum_{i=1}^{\infty} \frac{\$5}{(1.04)^i}$$

$$V = \$5 \sum_{i=1}^{\infty} \left(\frac{1}{1.04}\right)^i = \$5 \sum_{i=1}^{\infty} 0.96^i = \$5 \frac{0.96}{1-0.96} = \$5 \cdot 25$$

$$V = \$125$$

FINITE SERIES In many financial scenarios—including perpetuities and discount models for stocks and real estate—it is often convenient to treat an extremely long series of payments as if it were infinite. In other circumstances we are faced with very long but clearly finite series. In these circumstances the infinite series solution might give us a good approximation, but ultimately we will want a more precise answer.

The basic technique for summing a long but finite geometric series is the same as for an infinite geometric series. The only difference is that the terminal terms no longer converge to zero.

$$S = \sum_{i=0}^{n-1} \delta^i$$

$$\delta S = \sum_{i=0}^{n-1} \delta^{i+1} = S - \delta^0 + \delta^n \tag{3.14}$$

$$S = \frac{1 - \delta^n}{1 - \delta}$$

We can see that for $|\delta|$ less than 1, as n approaches infinity δ^n goes to zero and Equation 3.14 converges to Equation 3.12.

In finance, we will mostly be interested in situations where $|\delta|$ is less than one, but Equation 3.14, unlike Equation 3.12, is still valid for values of $|\delta|$ greater than one (check this for yourself). We did not need to rely on the final term converging to zero this time. If δ is greater than one, and we substitute infinity for n, we get:

$$S = \frac{1 - \delta^\infty}{1 - \delta} = \frac{1 - \infty}{1 - \delta} = \frac{-\infty}{1 - \delta} = \infty \tag{3.15}$$

For the last step, we rely on the fact that $(1 - \delta)$ is negative for δ greater than one. As promised in the preceding subsection, for δ greater than one, the sum of the infinite geometric series is indeed infinite.

Sample Problem

Question:
What is the present value of a newly issued 20-year bond, with a notional value of $100, and a 5 percent annual coupon? Assume a constant 4 percent discount rate, and no risk of default.

Answer:
This question utilizes discount factors and finite geometric series.

The bond will pay 20 coupons of $5, starting in a year's time. In addition, the notional value of the bond will be returned with the final coupon payment in 20 years. The present value, V, is then:

$$V = \sum_{i=1}^{20} \frac{\$5}{(1.04)^i} + \frac{\$100}{(1.04)^{20}} = \$5 \sum_{i=1}^{20} \frac{1}{(1.04)^i} + \frac{\$100}{(1.04)^{20}}$$

We start by evaluating the summation, using a discount factor of $\delta = \frac{1}{1.04} \approx$ 0.96:

$$S = \sum_{i=1}^{20} \frac{1}{(1.04)^i} = \sum_{i=1}^{20} \left(\frac{1}{1.04}\right)^i = \sum_{i=1}^{20} \delta^i = \delta + \delta^2 + \cdots + \delta^{19} + \delta^{20}$$

$$\delta S = \delta^2 + \delta^3 + \cdots + \delta^{20} + \delta^{21} = S - \delta + \delta^{21}$$

$$S(1 - \delta) = \delta - \delta^{21}$$

$$S = \frac{\delta - \delta^{21}}{1 - \delta} = 13.59$$

Inserting this result into the initial equation we obtain our final result:

$$V = \$5 \times 13.59 + \frac{\$100}{(1.04)^{20}} = \$113.59$$

Note that the present value of the bond, $113.59, is greater than the notional value of the bond, $100. In general, if there is no risk of default, and the coupon rate on the bond is higher than the discount rate, then the present value of the bond will be greater than the notional value of the bond.

When the price of a bond is less than the notional value of the bond, we say that the bond is selling at a discount. When the price of the bond is greater than the notional value, as in this example, we say that it is selling at a premium. When the price is exactly the same as the notional value, we say that it is selling at par.

Part II Probabilities

Discrete Random Variables

The concept of probability is central to risk management. Many concepts associated with probability are deceptively simple. The basics are easy, but there are many potential pitfalls.

In this chapter, we will be working with both discrete and continuous random variables. Discrete random variables can take on only a countable number of values—for example, a coin, which can only be heads or tails, or a bond, which can only have one of several letter ratings (AAA, AA, A, BBB, etc.). Assume we have a discrete random variable X, which can take various values, x_i. Further assume that the probability of any given x_i occurring is p_i. We write:

$$P[X = x_i] = p_i \text{ s.t. } x_i \in \{x_1, x_2, \ldots, x_n\} \tag{3.16}$$

where $P[\cdot]$ is our probability operator.

An important property of a random variable is that the sum of all the probabilities must equal one. In other words, the probability of any event occurring must equal one. Something has to happen. Using our current notation, we have:

$$\sum_{i=i}^{n} p_i = 1 \tag{3.17}$$

Continuous Random Variables

In contrast to a discrete random variable, a continuous random variable can take on any value within a given range. A good example of a continuous random variable is the return of a stock index. If the level of the index can be any real number between zero and infinity, then the return of the index can be any real number greater than −1.

Even if the range that the continuous variable occupies is finite, the number of values that it can take is infinite. For this reason, for a continuous variable, the probability of any *specific* value occurring is zero.

Even though we cannot talk about the probability of a specific value occurring, we can talk about the probability of a variable being within a certain range. Take, for example, the return on a stock market index over the next year. We can talk about the probability of the index return being between 6 percent and 7 percent, but talking about the probability of the return being exactly 6.001 percent or exactly 6.002 percent is meaningless. Even between 6.001 percent and 6.002 percent there are literally an infinite number of possible values. The probability of any one of those infinite values occurring is zero.

For a continuous random variable X, then, we can write:

$$P[r_1 < X < r_2] = p \tag{3.18}$$

which states that the probability of our random variable, X, being between r_1 and r_2 is equal to p.

Mutually Exclusive Events

For a given random variable, the probability of any of two mutually exclusive events occurring is just the sum of their individual probabilities. In statistics notation, we can write:

$$P[A \cup B] = P[A] + P[B] \tag{3.19}$$

where $A \cup B$ is the union of A and B. This is the probability of either A *or* B occurring. This is true only of mutually exclusive events.

This is a very simple rule, but, as mentioned previously, probability can be deceptively simple, and this property is easy to confuse. The confusion stems from the fact that *and* is synonymous with addition. If you say it this way, then the probability that A or B occurs is equal to the probability of A *and* the probability of B. It is not terribly difficult, but you can see where this could lead to a mistake.

This property of mutually exclusive events can be extended to any number of events. The probability that any of n mutually exclusive events occurs is simply the sum of the probabilities of those n events.

Sample Problem

Question:
Calculate the probability that a stock return is either below −10 percent or above 10 percent, given:

$$P[R < -10\%] = 14\%$$

$$P[R > +10\%] = 17\%$$

Answer:
Note that the two events are mutually exclusive; the return cannot be below −10 percent and above 10 percent at the same time. The answer is: 14 percent + 17 percent = 31 percent.

Independent Events

In the preceding example, we were talking about one random variable and two mutually exclusive events, but what happens when we have more than one random variable? What is the probability that it rains tomorrow *and* the return on stock XYZ is greater than 5 percent? The answer depends crucially on whether the two random variables influence each other or not. If the outcome of one random variable is not influenced by the outcome of the other random variable, then we say those variables are independent. *If* stock market returns are independent of the weather, then the stock market should be just as likely to be up on rainy days as it is on sunny days.

Assuming that the stock market and the weather are independent random variables, then the probability of the market being up and rain is just the product of the probabilities of the two events occurring individually. We can write this as follows:

$$P[rain\ and\ market\ up] = P[\text{rain} \cap market\ up] = P[\text{rain}] \cdot P[market\ up] \quad (3.20)$$

We often refer to the probability of two events occurring together as their joint probability.

Sample Problem

Question:
According to the most recent weather forecast, there is a 20 percent chance of rain tomorrow. The probability that stock XYZ returns more than 5 percent on any given day is 40 percent. The two events are independent. What is the probability that it rains and stock XYZ returns more than 5 percent tomorrow?

Answer:
Since the two events are independent, the probability that it rains and stock XYZ returns more than 5 percent is just the product of the two probabilities. The answer is: 20 percent × 40 percent = 8 percent.

TABLE 3.1

		Stocks		
		Outperform	Underperform	
Bonds	Upgrade	15%	5%	20%
	No Change	30%	25%	55%
	Downgrade	5%	20%	35%
		50%	50%	100%

Probability Matrices

When dealing with the joint probabilities of two variables, it is often convenient to summarize the various probabilities in a probability matrix or probability table. For example, pretend we are investigating a company that has issued both bonds and stock. The bonds can either be downgraded, be upgraded, or have no change in rating. The stock can either outperform the market or underperform the market.

In Table 3.1, the probability of both the company's stock outperforming the market *and* the bonds being upgraded is 15 percent. Similarly, the probability of the stock underperforming the market *and* the bonds having no change in rating is 25 percent. We can also see the unconditional probabilities, by adding across a row or down a column. The probability of the bonds being upgraded, irrespective of the stock's performance, is: 15 percent + 5 percent = 20 percent. Similarly, the probability of the equity outperforming the market is: 15 percent + 30 percent + 5 percent = 50 percent. Importantly, all of the joint probabilities add to 100 percent. Given all the possible events, one of them must happen.

Sample Problem

Question:
You are investigating a second company. As with our previous example, the company has issued both bonds and stock. The bonds can either be downgraded, be upgraded, or have no change in rating. The stock can either outperform the market or underperform the market. You are given the following probability matrix, which is missing three probabilities: X, Y, and Z. Calculate values for the missing probabilities.

Answer:
All of the values in the first column must add to 50 percent, the probability of the equity outperforming the market; therefore, we have:

$$5\% + 40\% + X = 50\%$$

$$X = 5\%$$

We can check our answer for X by summing across the third row: 5 percent + 30 percent = 35 percent.

Looking down the second column, we see that Y is equal to 20 percent:

$$0\% + Y + 30\% = 50\%$$

$$Y = 20\%$$

Finally, knowing that $Y = 20$ percent, we can sum across the second row to get Z:

$$40\% + Y = 40\% + 20\% = Z$$

$$Z = 60\%$$

Part III Basic Statistics

In this section we will learn how to describe a collection of data in precise statistical terms. Many of the concepts will be familiar, but the notation and terminology might be new. This notation and terminology will be used throughout the rest of the book.

Averages

Everybody knows what an average is. We come across averages every day, whether they are earned-run averages in baseball or grade point averages in school. In statistics there are actually three different types of averages: means, modes, and medians. By far the most commonly used average in risk management is the mean.

POPULATION AND SAMPLE DATA   If you wanted to know the mean age of people working in your firm, you would simply ask every person in the firm his or her age, add the ages together, and divide by the number of people in the firm. Assuming there are n employees and a_i is the age of the ith employee, then the mean, μ, is simply:

$$\mu = \frac{1}{n} \sum_{i=1}^{n} a_i = \frac{1}{n}(a_1 + a_2 + \cdots + a_{n-1} + a_n) \tag{3.21}$$

It is important at this stage to differentiate between population statistics and sample statistics. In this example, μ is the population mean. Assuming nobody lied about his or her age, and forgetting about rounding errors and other trivial details, we know the mean age of people in your firm *exactly*. We have a complete data set of everybody in your firm; we've surveyed the entire population.

This state of absolute certainty is, unfortunately, quite rare in finance. More often, we are faced with a situation such as this: estimate the mean return of stock ABC, given the most recent year of daily returns. In a situation like this, we assume there is some underlying data generating process, whose statistical properties are constant over time. The underlying process still has a true mean, but we cannot observe it directly. We can only estimate that mean based on our limited data sample. In our example, assuming n returns, we estimate the mean using the same formula as before:

$$\hat{\mu} = \frac{1}{n} \sum_{i=1}^{n} r_i = \frac{1}{n}(r_1 + r_2 + \ldots + r_{n-1} + r_n) \qquad (3.22)$$

where $\hat{\mu}$ (pronounced "mu hat") is our *estimate* of the true mean based on our sample of n returns. We call this the sample mean.

The median and mode are also types of averages. They are used less frequently in finance, but both can be useful. The median represents the center of a group of data; within the group, half the data points will be less than the median, and half will be greater. The mode is the value that occurs most frequently.

Sample Problem

Question:
Calculate the mean, median, and mode of the following data set:

$$-20\%, -10\%, -5\%, -5\%, 0\%, 10\%, 10\%, 10\%, 19\%$$

Answer:

$$\text{Mean} = \frac{1}{9}(-20\% - 10\% - 5\% - 5\% + 0\% + 10\% + 10\% + 10\% + 19\%) = 1\%$$

$$\text{Mode} = 10\%$$

$$\text{Median} = 0\%$$

If there is an even number of data points, the median is found by averaging the two center-most points. In the following series:

$$5\%, 10\%, 20\%, 25\%$$

the median is 15 percent. The median can be useful for summarizing data that is asymmetrical or contains significant outliers.

A data set can also have more than one mode. If the maximum frequency is shared by two or more values, all of those values are considered modes. In the following example, the modes are 10 percent and 20 percent:

$$5\%, 10\%, 10\%, 10\%, 14\%, 16\%, 20\%, 20\%, 20\%, 24\%$$

In calculating the mean in Equation 3.21 and Equation 3.22, each data point was counted exactly once. In certain situations, we might want to give more or less weight to certain data points. In calculating the average return of stocks in an equity index, we might want to give more weight to larger firms, perhaps weighting their returns in proportion to their market capitalization. Given n data points,

$x_i = x_1, x_2, \ldots, x_n$, with corresponding weights, w_i, we can define the weighted mean, μ_w, as:

$$\mu_w = \frac{\sum_{i=1}^{n} w_i x_i}{\sum_{i=1}^{n} w_i} \tag{3.23}$$

The standard mean from Equation 3.21 can be viewed as a special case of the weighted mean, where all the values have equal weight.

DISCRETE RANDOM VARIABLES   For a discrete random variable, we can also calculate the mean, median, and mode. For a random variable, X, with possible values, x_i, and corresponding probabilities, p_i, we define the mean, μ, as:

$$\mu = \sum_{i=1}^{n} p_i x_i \tag{3.24}$$

The equation for the mean of a discrete random variable is a special case of the weighted mean, where the outcomes are weighted by their probabilities, and the sum of the weights is equal to one.

The median of a discrete random variable is the value such that the probability that a value is less than or equal to the median is equal to 50 percent. Working from the other end of the distribution, we can also define the median such that 50 percent of the values are greater than or equal to the median. For a random variable, X, if we denote the median as m, we have:

$$P[X \geq m] = P[X \leq m] = 0.50 \tag{3.25}$$

For a discrete random variable, the mode is the value associated with the highest probability. As with population and sample data sets, the mode of a discrete random variable need not be unique.

Sample Problem

Question:
At the start of the year, a bond portfolio consists of two bonds, each worth $100. At the end of the year, if a bond defaults, it will be worth $20. If it does not default, the bond will be worth $100. The probability that both bonds default is 20 percent. The probability that neither bond defaults is 45 percent. What are the mean, median, and mode of the year-end portfolio value?

Answer:
We are given the probability for two outcomes:

$$P[V = \$40] = 20\%$$

$$P[V = \$200] = 45\%$$

At year-end, the value of the portfolio, V, can only have one of three values, and the sum of all the probabilities must sum to 100 percent. This allows us to calculate the final probability:

$$P[V = \$120] = 100\% - 20\% - 45\% = 35\%$$

The mean of V is then $140:

$$\mu = 0.20 \cdot \$40 + 0.35 \cdot \$120 + 0.45 \cdot \$200 = \$140$$

The mode of the distribution is $200; this is the most likely single outcome. The median of the distribution is $120; half of the outcomes are less than or equal to $120.

CONTINUOUS RANDOM VARIABLES We can also define the mean, median, and mode for a continuous random variable. To find the mean of a continuous random variable, we simply integrate the product of the variable and its probability density function (PDF). In the limit, this is equivalent to our approach to calculating the mean of a discrete random variable. For a continuous random variable, X, with a PDF, $f(x)$, the mean, μ, is then:

$$\mu = \int_{x_{min}}^{x_{max}} xf(x)dx \tag{3.26}$$

The median of a continuous random variable is defined exactly as it is for a discrete random variable, such that there is a 50 percent probability that values are less than or equal to, or greater than or equal to, the median. If we define the median as m, then:

$$\int_{x_{min}}^{m} f(x)dx = \int_{m}^{x_{max}} f(x)dx = 0.50 \tag{3.27}$$

Alternatively, we can define the median in terms of the cumulative distribution function. Given the cumulative distribution function, $F(x)$, and the median, m, we have:

$$F(m) = 0.50 \tag{3.28}$$

The mode of a continuous random variable corresponds to the maximum of the density function. As before, the mode need not be unique.

Sample Problem

Question:
Using the now-familiar probability density function discussed previously:

$$f(x) = \frac{x}{50} \text{ s.t. } 0 \leq x \leq 10$$

What are the mean, median, and mode of x?

Answer:

As we saw in a previous example, this probability density function is a triangle, between $x = 0$ and $x = 10$, and zero everywhere else.

Probability Density Function

For a continuous distribution, the mode corresponds to the maximum of the PDF. By inspection of the graph, we can see that the mode of $f(x)$ is equal to 10.

To calculate the median, we need to find m, such that the integral of $f(x)$ from the lower bound of $f(x)$, zero, to m is equal to 0.50. That is, we need to find:

$$\int_0^m \frac{x}{50} dx = 0.50$$

First we solve the left-hand side of the equation:

$$\int_0^m \frac{x}{50} dx = \frac{1}{50} \int_0^m x \, dx = \frac{1}{50} \left[\frac{1}{2} x^2 \right]_0^m = \frac{1}{100}(m^2 - 0) = \frac{m^2}{100}$$

Setting this result equal to 0.50 and solving for m, we obtain our final answer:

$$\frac{m^2}{100} = 0.50$$

$$m^2 = 50$$

$$m = \sqrt{50} = 7.07$$

In the last step we can ignore the negative root. If we hadn't calculated the median, looking at the graph it might be tempting to guess that the median is 5, the midpoint of the range of the distribution. This is a common mistake. Because lower values have less weight, the median ends up being greater than 5.

The mean is approximately 6.67:

$$\mu = \int_0^{10} x \frac{x}{50} dx = \frac{1}{50} \int_0^{10} x^2 dx = \frac{1}{50} \left[\frac{1}{3} x^3 \right]_0^{10} = \frac{1,000}{150} = \frac{20}{3} = 6.67$$

As with the median, it is a common mistake, based on inspection of the PDF, to guess that the mean is 5. However, what the PDF is telling us is that outcomes between 5 and 10 are much more likely than values between 0 and 5 (the PDF is higher between 5 and 10 than between 0 and 5). This is why the mean is greater than 5.

Expectations

On January 15, 2005, the Huygens space probe landed on the surface of Titan, the largest moon of Saturn. This was the culmination of a seven-year-long mission. During its descent and for over an hour after touching down on the surface, Huygens sent back detailed images, scientific readings, and even sounds from a strange world. There are liquid oceans on Titan, the landing site was littered with "rocks" composed of water ice, and weather on the moon includes methane rain. The Huygens probe was named after Christiaan Huygens, a Dutch polymath who first discovered Titan in 1655. In addition to astronomy and physics, Huygens had more prosaic interests, including probability theory. Originally published in Latin in 1657, *De Ratiociniis in Ludo Aleae*, or *The Value of All Chances in Games of Fortune*, was one of the first texts to formally explore one of the most important concepts in probability theory, namely expectations.

Like many of his contemporaries, Huygens was interested in games of chance. As he described it, if a game has a 50 percent probability of paying $3 and a 50 percent probability of paying $7, then this is, in a way, equivalent to having $5 with certainty. This is because we *expect*, on average, to win $5 in this game:

$$50\% \cdot \$3 + 50\% \cdot \$7 = \$5 \tag{3.29}$$

As one can already see, the concepts of expectations and averages are very closely linked. In the current example, if we play the game only once, there is no chance of winning exactly $5; we can win only $3 or $7. Still, even if we play the game only once, we say that the expected value of the game is $5. That we are talking about the mean of all the potential payouts is understood.

We can express the concept of expectation more formally using the expectations operator. We could state that the random variable, X, has an expected value of $5 as follows:

$$E[X] = 0.50 \cdot \$3 + 0.50 \cdot \$7 = \$5 \tag{3.30}$$

where $E[\cdot]$ is the expectation operator.[1]

In this example, the mean and the expected value have the same numeric value, $5. The same is true for discrete and continuous random variables. The expected value of a random variable is equal to the mean of the random variable.

While the value of the mean and the expected value may be the same in many situations, the two concepts are not exactly the same. In many situations in finance and risk management the terms can be used interchangeably. The difference is often subtle.

As the name suggests, expectations are often thought of as being forward-looking. Pretend we have a financial asset for which the mean annual return is equal to 15 percent. This is not an estimate; in this case, we *know* that the mean *is* 15 percent. We say that the expected value of the return next year is 15 percent. We expect the return to be 15 percent, because the probability-weighted mean of all the possible outcomes is 15 percent.

---

[1] Those of you with a background in physics might be more familiar with the term *expectation value* and the notation $\_X\_$ rather than $E[X]$. This is a matter of convention. Throughout this book we use the term *expected value* and $E[\cdot]$, which is currently more popular in finance and econometrics. Risk managers should be familiar with both conventions.

Now pretend that we don't actually *know* what the mean return of the asset is, but we have 10 years' worth of historical data, for which the sample mean is 15 percent. In this case the expected value may or may not be 15 percent. In most cases if we say that the expected value is equal to 15 percent, we are making two assumptions: first, we are assuming that the returns in our sample were generated by the same random process over the entire sample period; second, we are assuming that the returns will continue to be generated by this same process in the future. These are very strong assumptions. In finance and risk management, we often assume that the data we are interested in are being generated by a consistent, unchanging process. Testing the validity of this assumption can be an important part of risk management in practice.

The concept of expectations is also a much more general concept than the concept of the mean. Using the expectations operator, we can derive the expected value of functions of random variables. As we will see in subsequent sections, the concept of expectations underpins the definitions of other population statistics (variance, skew, kurtosis), and is important in understanding regression analysis and time series analysis. In these cases, even when we could use the mean to describe a calculation, in practice we tend to talk exclusively in terms of expectations.

Sample Problem

Question:
At the start of the year, you are asked to price a newly issued zero-coupon bond. The bond has a notional value of $100. You believe there is a 20 percent chance that the bond will default, in which case it will be worth $40 at the end of the year. There is also a 30 percent chance that the bond will be downgraded, in which case it will be worth $90 in a year's time. If the bond does not default and is not downgraded, it will be worth $100. Use a continuous interest rate of 5 percent to determine the current price of the bond.

Answer:
We first need to determine the expected future value of the bond, that is, the expected value of the bond in one year's time. We are given the following:

$$P[V_{t+1} = \$40] = 0.20$$
$$P[V_{t+1} = \$90] = 0.30$$

Because there are only three possible outcomes, the probability of no downgrades and no default must be 50 percent:

$$P[V_{t+1} = \$100] = 1 - 0.20 - 0.30 = 0.50$$

The expected value of the bond in one year is then:

$$E[V_{t+1}] = 0.20 \cdot \$40 + 0.30 \cdot \$90 + 0.50 \cdot \$100 = \$85$$

To get the current price of the bond we then discount this expected future value:

$$E[V_t] = e^{-0.5}E[V_{t+1}] = e^{-0.5}\$85 = \$80.85$$

The current price of the bond, in this case $80.85, is often referred to as the present value or fair value of the bond. The price is considered fair because the discounted expected value of the bond is the rational price to pay for the bond, given our knowledge of the world.

The expectations operator is linear. That is, for two random variables, X and Y, and a constant, c, the following two equations are true:

$$E[X + Y] = E[X] + E[Y]$$
$$E[cX] = cE[X] \tag{3.31}$$

If the expected value of one option, A, is $10, and the expected value of option B is $20, then the expected value of a portfolio containing A and B is $30, and the expected value of a portfolio containing five contracts of option A is $50.

Be very careful, though; the expectations operator is not multiplicative. The expected value of the product of two random variables is not necessarily the same as the product of their expected values:

$$E[XY] \neq E[X]E[Y] \tag{3.32}$$

Imagine we have two binary options. Each pays either $100 or nothing, depending on the value of some underlying asset at expiration. The probability of receiving $100 is 50 percent for both options. Further, assume that it is always the case that if the first option pays $100, the second pays $0, and vice versa. The expected value of each option separately is clearly $50. If we denote the payout of the first option as X and the payout of the second as Y, we have:

$$E[X] = E[Y] = 0.50 \cdot \$100 + 0.50 \cdot \$0 = \$50 \tag{3.33}$$

It follows that $E[X]E[Y] = \$50 \times \$50 = \$2,500$. In each scenario, though, one option is valued at zero, so the product of the payouts is always zero: $\$100 \cdot \$0 = \$0 \cdot \$100 = \$0$. The expected value of the product of the two option payouts is:

$$E[XY] = 0.50 \cdot \$100 \cdot \$0 + 0.50 \cdot \$0 \cdot \$100 = \$0 \tag{3.34}$$

In this case, the product of the expected values and the expected value of the products are clearly not equal. In the special case where $E[XY] = E[X]E[Y]$, we say that X and Y are independent.

If the expected value of the product of two variables does not necessarily equal the product of the expectations of those variables, it follows that the expected value of the product of a variable with itself does not necessarily equal the product of the expectations of that variable with itself; that is:

$$E[X^2] \neq E[X]^2 \tag{3.35}$$

Imagine we have a fair coin. Assign heads a value of +1 and tails a value of –1. We can write the probabilities of the outcomes as follows:

$$P[X = +1] = P[X = -1] = 0.50 \tag{3.36}$$

The expected value of any coin flip is zero, but the expected value of X^2 is +1, not zero:

$$E[X] = 0.50 \cdot (+1) + 0.50 \cdot (-1) = 0$$
$$E[X]^2 = 0^2 = 0 \tag{3.37}$$
$$E[X^2] = 0.50 \cdot (+1^2) + 0.50 \cdot (-1^2) = 1$$

As simple as this example is, this distinction is very important. As we will see, the difference between $E[X^2]$ and $E[X]^2$ is central to our definition of variance and standard deviation.

Sample Problem

Question:
Given the following equation:

$$y = (x + 5)^3 + x^2 + 10x$$

What is the expected value of y? Assume the following:

$$E[x] = 4$$
$$E[x^2] = 9$$
$$E[x^3] = 12$$

Answer:
Note that $E[x^2]$ and $E[x^3]$ cannot be derived from knowledge of $E[x]$. In this problem, $E[x^2] \neq E[x]^2$. As forewarned, the expectations operator is not necessarily multiplicative. To find the expected value of y, then, we first expand the term $(x + 5)^3$ within the expectations operator:

$$E[y] = E[(x + 5)^3 + x^2 + 10x] = E[x^3 + 16x^2 + 85x + 125]$$

Because the expectations operator is linear, we can separate the terms in the summation and move the constants outside the expectations operator. We do this in two steps:

$$E[y] = E[x^3] + E[16x^2] + E[85x] + E[125]$$
$$= E[x^3] + 16E[x^2] + 85E[x] + 125$$

At this point, we can substitute in the values for $E[x]$, $E[x^2]$, and $E[x^3]$, which we were given at the start of the exercise:

$$E[y] = 12 + 16 \cdot 9 + 85 \cdot 4 + 125 = 741$$

This gives us the final answer, 741.

Variance and Standard Deviation

The variance of a random variable measures how noisy or unpredictable that random variable is. Variance is defined as the expected value of the difference between the variable and its mean squared:

$$\sigma^2 = E[(X - \mu)^2] \tag{3.38}$$

where σ^2 is the variance of the random variable X with mean μ.

The square root of variance, typically denoted by σ, is called standard deviation. In finance we often refer to standard deviation as volatility. This is analogous to referring to the mean as the average. Standard deviation is a mathematically precise term, whereas volatility is a more general concept.

Sample Problem

Question:
A derivative has a 50/50 chance of being worth either +10 or −10 at expiry. What is the standard deviation of the derivative's value?

Answer:

$$\mu = 0.50 \cdot 10 + 0.50 \cdot (-10) = 0$$

$$\sigma^2 = 0.50 \cdot (10 - 0)^2 + 0.50 \cdot (-10 - 0)^2 = 0.5 \cdot 100 + 0.5 \cdot 100 = 100$$

$$\sigma = 10$$

In the previous example, we were calculating the population variance and standard deviation. *All* of the possible outcomes for the derivative were known.

To calculate the sample variance of a random variable X based on n observations, $x_1, x_2, \ldots, x_n$, we can use the following formula:

$$E\left[\sigma_x^2\right] = \hat{\sigma}_x^2 = \frac{1}{n-1} \sum_{i=1}^{n} (x_i - \hat{\mu}_x)^2 \tag{3.39}$$

where $\hat{\mu}_x$ is the sample mean from Equation 3.22. Given that we have n data points, it might seem odd that we are dividing the sum by $(n - 1)$ and not n. The reason has to do with the fact that $\hat{\mu}_x$ itself is an estimate of the true mean, which also contains a fraction of each x_i. We leave the proof for a problem at the end of the chapter, but it turns out that dividing by $(n - 1)$, not n, produces an unbiased estimate of σ^2. If the mean is known or we are calculating the population variance, then we divide by n. If instead the mean is also being estimated, then we divide by $n - 1$.

Equation 3.38 can easily be rearranged as follows (we leave the proof of this for an exercise, too):

$$\sigma^2 = E[X^2] - \mu^2 = E[X^2] - E[X]^2 \tag{3.40}$$

Note that variance can be nonzero only if $E[X^2] \neq E[X]^2$.

When writing computer programs, this last version of the variance formula is often useful, since it allows you to calculate the mean and the variance in the same loop. Also, in finance it is often convenient to assume that the mean of a random variable is close to zero. For example, based on theory, we might expect the spread between two equity indexes to have a mean of zero in the long run. In this case, the variance is simply the mean of the squared returns.

Sample Problem

Question:
Assume that the mean of daily Standard & Poor's (S&P) 500 returns is zero. You observe the following returns over the course of 10 days:

7%	−4%	11%	8%	3%	9%	−21%	10%	−9%	−1%

Estimate the standard deviation of daily S&P 500 returns.

Answer:
The sample mean is not exactly zero, but we are told to assume that the population mean *is* zero; therefore:

$$E\left[\sigma_r^2\right] = \hat{\sigma}_r^2 = \frac{1}{n}\sum_{i=1}^{n}\left(r_i^2 - 0^2\right) = \frac{1}{n}\sum_{i=1}^{n}r_i^2 = \frac{1}{10}0.0963 = 0.00963$$

$$\hat{\sigma}_r = 9.8\%$$

Note, because we were told to assume the mean was known, we divide by $n = 10$, not $(n - 1) = 9$.

As with the mean, for a continuous random variable we can calculate the variance by integrating with the probability density function. For a continuous random variable, X, with a probability density function, $f(x)$, the variance can be calculated as:

$$\sigma^2 = \int_{x_{min}}^{x_{max}} (x - \mu)^2 f(x)dx \tag{3.41}$$

It is not difficult to prove that, for either a discrete or a continuous random variable, multiplying by a constant will increase the standard deviation by the same factor:

$$\sigma[cX] = c\sigma[X] \tag{3.42}$$

In other words, if you own $10 of an equity with a standard deviation of $2, then $100 of the same equity will have a standard deviation of $20.

Adding a constant to a random variable, however, does not alter the standard deviation or the variance:

$$\sigma[X + c] = \sigma[X] \tag{3.43}$$

This is because the impact on the mean is the same as the impact on any draw of the random variable, leaving the deviation from the mean unchanged. If you own a portfolio with a standard deviation of $20, and then you add $1,000 of cash to that portfolio, the standard deviation of the portfolio will still be $20.

Standardized Variables

It is often convenient to work with variables where the mean is zero and the standard deviation is one. From the preceding section it is not difficult to prove that, given a random variable X with mean μ and standard deviation σ, we can define a second random variable Y:

$$Y = \frac{X - \mu}{\sigma} \tag{3.44}$$

such that Y will have a mean of zero and a standard deviation of one. We say that X has been standardized, or that Y is a standard random variable. In practice, if we have a data set and we want to standardize it, we first compute the sample mean and the standard deviation. Then, for each data point, we subtract the mean and divide by the standard deviation.

The inverse transformation can also be very useful when it comes to creating computer simulations. Simulations often begin with standardized variables, which need to be transformed into variables with a specific mean and standard deviation. In this case, we simply take the output from the standardized variable, multiply by the desired standard deviation, and then add the desired mean. The order is important. Adding a constant to a random variable will not change the standard deviation, but multiplying a non-mean-zero variable by a constant will change the mean.

Covariance

Up until now we have mostly been looking at statistics that summarize one variable. In risk management, we often want to describe the relationship between two random variables. For example, is there a relationship between the returns of an equity and the returns of a market index?

Covariance is analogous to variance, but instead of looking at the deviation from the mean of one variable, we are going to look at the relationship between the deviations of two variables:

$$\sigma_{XY} = E[(X - \mu_X)(Y - \mu_Y)] \tag{3.45}$$

where σ_{XY} is the covariance between two random variables, X and Y, with means μ_X and μ_Y, respectively. As you can see from the definition, variance is just a special case of covariance. Variance is the covariance of a variable with itself.

If X tends to be above μ_X when Y is above μ_Y (both deviations are positive), and X tends to be below μ_X when Y is below μ_Y (both deviations are negative), then the covariance will be positive (a positive number multiplied by a positive number is positive; likewise, for two negative numbers). If the opposite is true and the deviations tend to be of opposite sign, then the covariance will be negative. If the deviations have no discernible relationship, then the covariance will be zero.

Earlier in this chapter, we cautioned that the expectations operator is not generally multiplicative. This fact turns out to be closely related to the concept of covariance. Just as we rewrote our variance equation earlier, we can rewrite Equation 3.45 as follows:

$$\sigma_{XY} = E[(X - \mu_X)(Y - \mu_Y)] = E[XY] - \mu_X\mu_Y = E[XY] - E[X]E[Y] \qquad (3.46)$$

In the special case where the covariance between X and Y is zero, the expected value of XY is equal to the expected value of X multiplied by the expected value of Y:

$$\sigma_{XY} = 0 \Rightarrow E[XY] = E[X]E[Y] \qquad (3.47)$$

If the covariance is anything other than zero, then the two sides of this equation cannot be equal. Unless we know that the covariance between two variables is zero, we cannot assume that the expectations operator is multiplicative.

In order to calculate the covariance between two random variables, X and Y, assuming the means of both variables are known, we can use the following formula:

$$\hat{\sigma}_{X,Y} = \frac{1}{n} \sum_{i=1}^{n} (x_i - \mu_X)(y_i - \mu_Y)$$

If the means are unknown and must also be estimated, we replace n with $(n - 1)$:

$$\hat{\sigma}_{X,Y} = \frac{1}{n - 1} \sum_{i=1}^{n} (x_i - \hat{\mu}_X)(y_i - \hat{\mu}_Y)$$

If we replaced y_i in these formulas with x_i, calculating the covariance of X with itself, the resulting equations would be the same as the equations for calculating variance from the previous section.

Correlation

Closely related to the concept of covariance is correlation. To get the correlation of two variables, we simply divide their covariance by their respective standard deviations:

$$\rho_{XY} = \frac{\sigma_{XY}}{\sigma_X\sigma_Y} \qquad (3.48)$$

Correlation has the nice property that it varies between –1 and +1. If two variables have a correlation of +1, then we say they are perfectly correlated. If the ratio of one variable to another is always the same and positive then the two variables will be perfectly correlated.

If two variables are highly correlated, it is often the case that one variable *causes* the other variable, or that both variables share a common underlying driver. We will see later, though, that it is very easy for two random variables with no causal link to be highly correlated. *Correlation does not prove causation.* Similarly, if two variables are uncorrelated, it does not necessarily follow that they are unrelated. For example, a random variable that is symmetrical around zero and the square of that variable will have zero correlation.

Sample Problem

Question:
X is a random variable. X has an equal probability of being -1, 0, or $+1$. What is the correlation between X and Y if $Y = X^2$?

Answer:
We have:

$$P[X = -1] = P[X = 0] = P[X = 1] = \frac{1}{3}$$

$$Y = X^2$$

First we calculate the mean of both variables:

$$E[X] = \frac{1}{3}(-1) + \frac{1}{3}(0) + \frac{1}{3}(1) = 0$$

$$E[Y] = \frac{1}{3}(-1^2) + \frac{1}{3}(0^2) + \frac{1}{3}(1^2) = \frac{1}{3}(1) + \frac{1}{3}(0) + \frac{1}{3}(1) = \frac{2}{3}$$

The covariance can be found as:

$$\text{Cov}[X, Y] = E[(X - E[X])(Y - E[Y])]$$

$$\text{Cov}[X, Y] = \frac{1}{3}(-1 - 0)\left(1 - \frac{2}{3}\right) + \frac{1}{3}(0 - 0)\left(0 - \frac{2}{3}\right) + \frac{1}{3}(1 - 0)\left(1 - \frac{2}{3}\right) = 0$$

Because the covariance is zero, the correlation is also zero. There is no need to calculate the variances or standard deviations.

As forewarned, even though X and Y are clearly related, the correlation is zero.

Application: Portfolio Variance and Hedging

If we have a portfolio of securities and we wish to determine the variance of that portfolio, all we need to know is the variance of the underlying securities and their respective correlations.

For example, if we have two securities with random returns X_A and X_B, with means μ_A and μ_B and standard deviations σ_A and σ_B, respectively, we can calculate the variance of X_A plus X_B as follows:

$$\sigma_{A+B}^2 = \sigma_A^2 + \sigma_B^2 + 2\rho_{AB}\sigma_A\sigma_B \tag{3.49}$$

where ρ_{AB} is the correlation between X_A and X_B. The proof is left as an exercise. Notice that the last term can either increase or decrease the total variance. Both standard deviations must be positive; therefore, if the correlation is positive, the overall variance will be higher compared to the case where the correlation is negative.

If the variance of both securities is equal, then Equation 3.49 simplifies to:

$$\sigma^2_{A+B} = 2\sigma^2(1 + \rho_{AB}) \text{ where } \sigma^2_A = \sigma^2_B = \sigma^2 \tag{3.50}$$

Now we know that the correlation can vary between -1 and $+1$, so, substituting into our new equation, the portfolio variance must be bound by 0 and $4\sigma^2$. If we take the square root of both sides of the equation, we see that the standard deviation is bound by 0 and 2σ. Intuitively this should make sense. If, on the one hand, we own one share of an equity with a standard deviation of \$10 and then purchase another share of the *same* equity, then the standard deviation of our two-share portfolio must be \$20 (trivially, the correlation of a random variable with itself must be one). On the other hand, if we own one share of this equity and then purchase another security that always generates the exact opposite return, the portfolio is perfectly balanced. The returns are always zero, which implies a standard deviation of zero.

In the special case where the correlation between the two securities is zero, we can further simplify our equation. For the standard deviation:

$$\rho_{AB} = 0 \Rightarrow \sigma_{A+B} = \sqrt{2}\sigma \tag{3.51}$$

We can extend Equation 3.49 to any number of variables:

$$Y = \sum_{i=1}^{n} X_i$$

$$\tag{3.52}$$

$$\sigma^2_Y = \sum_{i=1}^{n} \sum_{j=1}^{n} \rho_{ij}\sigma_i\sigma_j$$

In the case where all of the X_i's are uncorrelated and all the variances are equal to σ, Equation 3.50 simplifies to:

$$\sigma_Y = \sqrt{n}\sigma \text{ iff } \rho_{ij} = 0 \forall i \neq j \tag{3.53}$$

This is the famous square root rule for the addition of uncorrelated variables. There are many situations in statistics in which we come across collections of random variables that are independent and have the same statistical properties. We term these variables independent and identically distributed (i.i.d.). In risk management we might have a large portfolio of securities, which can be approximated as a collection of i.i.d. variables. As we will see, this i.i.d. assumption also plays an important role in estimating the uncertainty inherent in statistics derived from sampling, and in the analysis of time series. In each of these situations, we will come back to this square root rule.

By combining Equation 3.49 with Equation 3.42, we arrive at an equation for calculating the variance of a linear combination of variables. If Y is a linear combination of X_A and X_B, such that:

$$Y = aX_A + bX_B \tag{3.54}$$

then, using our standard notation, we have:

$$\sigma^2_Y = a^2\sigma^2_A + b^2\sigma^2_B + 2ab\rho_{AB}\sigma_A\sigma_B \tag{3.55}$$

Correlation is central to the problem of hedging. Using the same notation as before, imagine we have \$1 of Security A, and we wish to hedge it with \$$b$ of Security

B (if h is positive, we are buying the security; if h is negative, we are shorting the security). In other words, h is the hedge ratio. We introduce the random variable P for our hedged portfolio. We can easily compute the variance of the hedge portfolio using Equation 3.55:

$$P = X_A + hX_B$$
$$\sigma_P^2 = \sigma_A^2 + h^2\sigma_B^2 + 2h\rho_{AB}\sigma_A\sigma_B \tag{3.56}$$

As a risk manager, we might be interested to know what hedge ratio would achieve the portfolio with the least variance. To find this minimum variance hedge ratio, we simply take the derivative of our equation for the portfolio variance with respect to h, and set it equal to zero:

$$\frac{d\sigma_P^2}{dh} = 2h\sigma_B^2 + 2\rho_{AB}\sigma_A\sigma_B$$
$$h^* = -\rho_{AB}\frac{\sigma_A}{\sigma_B} \tag{3.57}$$

You can check that this is indeed a minimum by calculating the second derivative. Substituting h^* back into our original equation, we see that the smallest variance we can achieve is:

$$\min\left[\sigma_P^2\right] = \sigma_A^2\left(1 - \rho_{AB}^2\right) \tag{3.58}$$

At the extremes, where ρ_{AB} equals -1 or $+1$, we can reduce the portfolio volatility to zero by buying or selling the hedge asset in proportion to the standard deviation of the assets. In between these two extremes we will always be left with some positive portfolio variance. This risk that we cannot hedge is referred to as idiosyncratic risk.

If the two securities in the portfolio are positively correlated, then selling \$$h$ of Security B will reduce the portfolio's volatility to the minimum possible level. Sell any less and the portfolio will be underhedged. Sell any more and the portfolio will be overhedged. In risk management it is possible to have too much of a good thing. A common mistake made by portfolio managers is to overhedge with a low-correlation instrument.

Notice that when ρ_{AB} equals zero (i.e., when the two securities are uncorrelated), the optimal hedge ratio is zero. You cannot hedge one security with another security if they are uncorrelated. Adding an uncorrelated security to a portfolio will always increase its volatility.

This last statement is not an argument against diversification. If your entire portfolio consists of \$100 invested in Security A and you *add* any amount of an uncorrelated Security B to the portfolio, the dollar standard deviation of the portfolio will increase. Alternatively, if Security A and Security B are uncorrelated and have the same standard deviation, then *replacing* some of Security A with Security B will decrease the dollar standard deviation of the portfolio. For example, \$80 of Security A plus \$20 of Security B will have a lower standard deviation than \$100 of Security A, but \$100 of Security A *plus* \$20 of Security B will have a higher standard deviation—again, assuming Security A and Security B are uncorrelated and have the same standard deviation.

Moments

Previously, we defined the mean of a variable X as:

$$\mu = E[X]$$

It turns out that we can generalize this concept as follows:

$$m_k = E[X^k] \qquad (3.59)$$

We refer to m_k as the kth moment of X. The mean of X is also the first moment of X.

Similarly, we can generalize the concept of variance as follows:

$$\mu_k = E[(X - \mu)^k] \qquad (3.60)$$

We refer to μ_k as the kth central moment of X. We say that the moment is central because it is central around the mean. Variance is simply the second central moment.

While we can easily calculate any central moment, in risk management it is very rare that we are interested in anything beyond the fourth central moment.

Skewness

The second central moment, variance, tells us how spread-out a random variable is around the mean. The third central moment tells us how symmetrical the distribution is around the mean. Rather than working with the third central moment directly, by convention we first standardize the statistic. This standardized third central moment is known as skewness:

$$\text{Skewness} = \frac{E[(X - \mu)^3]}{\sigma^3} \qquad (3.61)$$

where σ is the standard deviation of X.

By standardizing the central moment, it is much easier to compare two random variables. Multiplying a random variable by a constant will not change the skewness.

A random variable that is symmetrical about its mean will have zero skewness. If the skewness of the random variable is positive, we say that the random variable exhibits positive skew. Figures 3.3 and 3.4 show examples of positive and negative skewness.

Skewness is a very important concept in risk management. If the distributions of returns of two investments are the same in all respects, with the same mean and standard deviation but different skews, then the investment with more negative skew is generally considered to be more risky. Historical data suggest that many financial assets exhibit negative skew.

As with variance, the equation for skewness differs depending on whether we are calculating the population skewness or the sample skewness. For the population statistic, the skewness of a random variable X, based on n observations, $x_1, x_2, \ldots, x_n$, can be calculated as:

$$\hat{s} = \sum_{i=1}^{n} \left(\frac{x_i - \mu}{\sigma} \right)^3 \qquad (3.62)$$

where μ is the population mean and σ is the population standard deviation. Similar to our calculation of sample variance, if we are calculating the sample skewness, there is

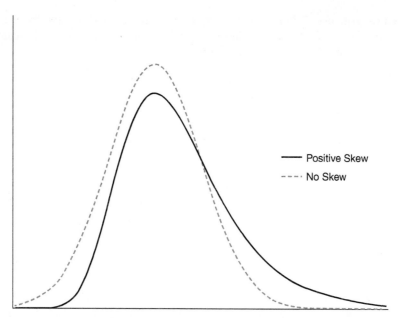

FIGURE 3.3   Positive Skew

going to be an overlap with the calculation of the sample mean and sample standard deviation. We need to correct for that. The sample skewness can be calculated as:

$$\tilde{s} = \frac{n}{(n-1)(n-2)} \sum_{i=1}^{n} \left(\frac{x_i - \hat{\mu}}{\hat{\sigma}} \right)^3 \tag{3.63}$$

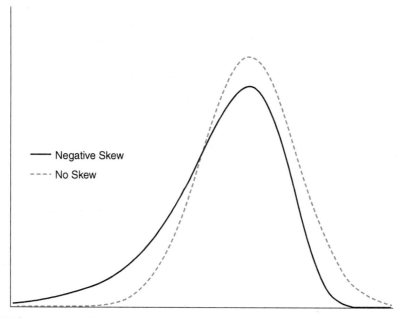

FIGURE 3.4   Negative Skew

Based on Equation 3.40 for variance, it is tempting to guess that the formula for the third central moment can be written simply in terms of $E[X^3]$ and μ. Be careful, as the two sides of this equation are not equal:

$$E[(X - \mu)^k] \neq E[X^3] - \mu^3 \tag{3.64}$$

The correct equation is:

$$E[(X - \mu)^3] = E[X^3] - 3\mu\sigma^2 - \mu^3 \tag{3.65}$$

Sample Problem

Question:
Prove that the left-hand side of Equation 3.65 is indeed equal to the right-hand side of the equation.

Answer:
We start by multiplying out the terms inside the expectation. This is not too difficult to do, but, as a shortcut, we could use the binomial theorem as mentioned previously:

$$E[(X - \mu)^3] = E[X^3 - 3\mu X^2 + 3\mu^2 X - \mu^3]$$

Next we separate the terms inside the expectations operator and move any constants, namely μ, outside the operator:

$$E[x^3 - 3\mu X^2 + 3\mu^2 X - 3\mu^3] = E[X^3] - 3\mu E[X^2] + 3\mu^2 E[X] - \mu^3$$

$E[X]$ is simply the mean, μ. For $E[X^2]$, we reorganize our equation for variance, Equation 3.40, as follows:

$$\sigma^2 = E[X^2] - \mu^2$$
$$E[X^2] = \sigma^2 + \mu^2$$

Substituting these results into our equation and collecting terms, we arrive at the final equation:

$$E[(X - \mu)^3] = E[X^3] - 3\mu(\sigma^2 + \mu^2) + 3\mu^2\mu - \mu^3$$
$$E[(X - \mu)^3] = E[X^3] - 3\mu\sigma^2 - \mu^3$$

For many symmetrical continuous distributions, the mean, median, and mode all have the same value. Many continuous distributions with negative skew have a mean that is less than the median, which is less than the mode. For example, it might be that a certain derivative is just as likely to produce positive returns as it is to produce negative returns (the median is zero), but there are more big negative returns than big positive returns (the distribution is skewed), so the mean is less than zero. As a risk manager, understanding the impact of skew on the mean relative to the median and mode can be useful. Be careful, though, as this rule of thumb does not always work. Many practitioners mistakenly believe that this rule of thumb is in fact always true. It is not, and it is very easy to produce a distribution that violates the rule.

Kurtosis

The fourth central moment is similar to the second central moment, in that it tells us how spread-out a random variable is, but it puts more weight on extreme points. As with skewness, rather than working with the central moment directly, we typically work with a standardized statistic. This standardized fourth central moment is known as the kurtosis. For a random variable X, we can define the kurtosis as K, where:

$$K = \frac{E[(X - \mu)^4]}{\sigma^4} \tag{3.66}$$

where σ is the standard deviation of X, and μ is its mean.

By standardizing the central moment, it is much easier to compare two random variables. As with skewness, multiplying a random variable by a constant will not change the kurtosis.

The following two populations have the same mean, variance, and skewness. The second population has a higher kurtosis.

Population 1: $\{-17, -17, 17, 17\}$

Population 2: $\{-23, -7, 7, 23\}$

Notice, to balance out the variance, when we moved the outer two points out six units, we had to move the inner two points in 10 units. Because the random variable with higher kurtosis has points further from the mean, we often refer to distribution with high kurtosis as fat-tailed. Figures 3.5 and 3.6 show examples of continuous distributions with high and low kurtosis.

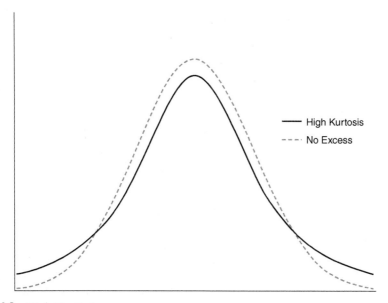

FIGURE 3.5　High Kurtosis

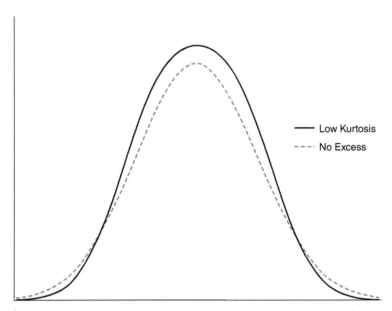

FIGURE 3.6 Low Kurtosis

Like skewness, kurtosis is an important concept in risk management. Many financial assets exhibit high levels of kurtosis. If the distribution of returns of two assets have the same mean, variance, and skewness, but different kurtosis, then the distribution with the higher kurtosis will tend to have more extreme points, and be considered more risky.

As with variance and skewness, the equation for kurtosis differs depending on whether we are calculating the population kurtosis or the sample kurtosis. For the population statistic, the kurtosis of a random variable X can be calculated as:

$$\hat{K} = \sum_{i=1}^{n} \left(\frac{x_i - \mu}{\sigma} \right)^4 \tag{3.67}$$

where μ is the population mean and σ is the population standard deviation. Similar to our calculation of sample variance, if we are calculating the sample kurtosis, there is going to be an overlap with the calculation of the sample mean and sample standard deviation. We need to correct for that. The sample kurtosis can be calculated as:

$$\tilde{K} = \frac{n(n+1)}{(n-1)(n-2)(n-3)} \sum_{i=1}^{n} \left(\frac{x_i - \hat{\mu}}{\hat{\sigma}} \right)^4 \tag{3.68}$$

Later we will study the normal distribution, which has a kurtosis of 3. Because normal distributions are so common, many people refer to "excess kurtosis," which is simply the kurtosis minus 3.

$$K_{\text{excess}} = K - 3 \tag{3.69}$$

In this way, the normal distribution has an excess kurtosis of 0. Distributions with positive excess kurtosis are termed leptokurtotic. Distributions with negative excess kurtosis are termed platykurtotic. Be careful; by default, many applications calculate excess kurtosis.

When we are also estimating the mean and variance, calculating the sample excess kurtosis is somewhat more complicated than just subtracting 3. The correct formula is:

$$\tilde{K}_{excess} = \tilde{K} - 3\frac{(n-1)^2}{(n-2)(n-3)}$$ (3.70)

where $\tilde{K}$ is the sample kurtosis from Equation 3.68. As n increases, the last term on the right-hand side converges to 3.

Part IV Distributions

Normal Distribution

The normal distribution is probably the most widely used distribution in statistics, and is extremely popular in finance. The normal distribution occurs in a large number of settings, and is extremely easy to work with.

In popular literature, the normal distribution is often referred to as the bell curve because of the shape of its probability density function (see Figure 3.7).

The probability density function of the normal distribution is symmetrical, with the mean and median coinciding with the highest point of the PDF. Because it is symmetrical, the skew of a normal distribution is always zero. The kurtosis of a normal distribution is always 3. By definition, the excess kurtosis of a normal distribution is zero.

In some fields it is more common to refer to the normal distribution as the Gaussian distribution, after the famous German mathematician Johann Gauss, who is credited with some of the earliest work with the distribution. It is not the case that one name is more precise than the other as with mean and average. Both normal distribution and Gaussian distribution are acceptable terms.

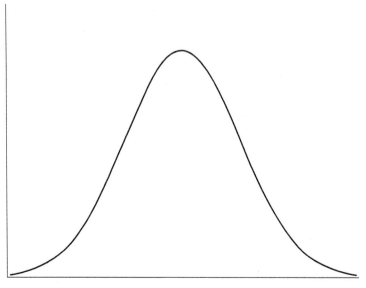

FIGURE 3.7 Normal Distribution Probability Density Function

TABLE 3.2   Normal Distribution Confidence Intervals

	One-Tailed	Two-Tailed
1.0%	−2.33	−2.58
2.5%	−1.96	−2.24
5.0%	−1.64	−1.96
10.0%	−1.28	−1.64
90.0%	1.28	1.64
95.0%	1.64	1.96
97.5%	1.96	2.24
99.0%	2.33	2.58

Normal distributions are used throughout finance and risk management. Previously, we suggested that log returns are extremely useful in financial modeling. One attribute that makes log returns particularly attractive is that they can be modeled using normal distributions. Normal distributions can generate numbers from negative infinity to positive infinity. For a particular normal distribution, the most extreme values might be extremely unlikely, but they can occur. This poses a problem for standard returns, which typically cannot be less than –100 percent. For log returns, though, there is no such constraint. Log returns also can range from negative to positive infinity.

Normally distributed log returns are widely used in financial simulations, and form the basis of a number of financial models, including the Black-Scholes option pricing model. As we will see, while this normal assumption is often a convenient starting point, much of risk management is focused on addressing departures from this normality assumption.

Because the normal distribution is so widely used, most practitioners are expected to have at least a rough idea of how much of the distribution falls within one, two, or three standard deviations. In risk management it is also useful to know how many standard deviations are needed to encompass 95 percent or 99 percent of outcomes. Table 3.2 lists some common values. Notice that for each row in the table, there is a "one-tailed" and "two-tailed" column. If we want to know how far we have to go to encompass 95 percent of the mass in the density function, the one-tailed value tells us that 95 percent of the values are less than 1.64 standard deviations above the mean. Because the normal distribution is symmetrical, it follows that 5 percent of the values are less than 1.64 standard deviations below the mean. The two-tailed value, in turn, tells us that 95 percent of the mass is within +/− 1.96 standard deviations of the mean. It follows that 2.5 percent of the outcomes are less than −1.96 standard deviations from the mean, and 2.5 percent are greater than +1.96 standard deviations from the mean. Rather than one-tailed and two-tailed, some authors refer to "one-sided" and "two-sided" values.

Application: Monte Carlo Simulations: Creating Normal Random Variables

While some problems in risk management have explicit analytic solutions, many problems have no exact mathematical solution. In these cases, we can often approximate a solution by creating a Monte Carlo simulation. A Monte Carlo simulation consists of a number of trials. For each trial we feed random inputs into a system of equations. By collecting the outputs from the system of equations for a large number of trials, we can estimate the statistical properties of the output variables.

Even in cases where explicit solutions might exist, a Monte Carlo solution might be preferable in practice if the explicit solution is difficult to derive or extremely complex. In some cases a simple Monte Carlo simulation can be easier to understand, thereby reducing operational risk.

In this chapter we will explore two closely related topics, confidence intervals and hypothesis testing. At the end of the chapter, we will explore applications, including value at risk (VaR).

Part V Hypothesis Testing and Confidence Intervals

The Sample Mean Revisited

Imagine we take the output from a standard random number generator on a computer, and multiply it by 100. The resulting data generating process (DGP) is a uniform random variable, which ranges between 0 and 100, with a mean of 50. If we generate 20 draws from this DGP and calculate the sample mean of those 20 draws, it is unlikely that the sample mean will be exactly 50. The sample mean might round to 50, say 50.03906724, but exactly 50 is next to impossible. In fact, given that we have only 20 data points, the sample mean might not even be close to the true mean.

The sample mean is actually a random variable itself. If we continue to repeat the experiment—generating 20 data points and calculating the sample mean each time—the calculated sample mean will be different every time. As we proved, even though we never get exactly 50, the expected value of each sample mean is in fact 50. It might sound strange to say it, but the mean of our sample mean is the true mean of the distribution. Using our standard notation:

$$E[\hat{\mu}] = \mu \tag{3.71}$$

Instead of 20 data points, what if we generate 1,000 data points? With 1,000 data points, the expected value of our sample mean is still 50, just as it was with 20 data points. While we still don't expect our sample mean to be exactly 50, we expect our sample mean will tend to be closer when we are using 1,000 data points. The reason is simple: a single outlier won't have nearly the impact in a pool of 1,000 data points that it will in a pool of 20. If we continue to generate sets of 1,000 data points, it stands to reason that the standard deviation of our sample mean will be lower with 1,000 data points than it would be if our sets contained only 20 data points.

It turns out that the variance of our sample mean doesn't just decrease with the sample size; it decreases in a predictable way, in proportion to the sample size. In other words, if our sample size is n and the true variance of our DGP is σ^2, then the variance of the sample mean is:

$$\sigma_{\hat{\mu}}^2 = \frac{\sigma^2}{n} \tag{3.72}$$

It follows that the standard deviation of the sample mean decreases with the square root of n. This square root is important. In order to reduce the standard deviation of the mean by a factor of 2, we need four times as many data points. To reduce it by a factor of 10, we need 100 times as much data. This is yet another example of the famous square root rule for independent and identically distributed (i.i.d.) variables.

In our current example, because the DGP follows a uniform distribution, we can easily calculate the variance of each data point. The variance of each data point is 833.33, $(100 - 1)^2/12 = 833.33$. This is equivalent to a standard deviation of approximately 28.87. For 20 data points, the standard deviation of the mean will then be $28.87/\sqrt{20} = 6.45$, and for 1,000 data points, the standard deviation will be $28.87/\sqrt{1,000} = 0.91$.

We have the mean and the standard deviation of our sample mean, but what about the shape of the distribution? You might think that the shape of the distribution would depend on the shape of the underlying distribution of the DGP. If we recast our formula for the sample mean slightly, though:

$$\hat{\mu} = \frac{1}{n}\sum_{i=1}^{n} x_i = \sum_{i=1}^{n} \frac{1}{n}x_i \qquad (3.73)$$

and regard each of the $(\frac{1}{n})x_i$'s as a random variable in its own right, we see that our sample mean is equivalent to the sum of n i.i.d. random variables, each with a mean of μ/n and a standard deviation of σ/n. Using the central limit theorem, we claim that the distribution of the sample mean converges to a normal distribution. For large values of n, the distribution of the sample mean will be extremely close to a normal distribution. Practitioners will often assume that the sample mean *is* normally distributed.

Sample Problem

Question:
You are given 10 years of monthly returns for a portfolio manager. The mean monthly return is 2.3 percent, and the standard deviation of the returns series is 3.6 percent. What is the standard deviation of the mean?

The portfolio manager is being compared against a benchmark with a mean monthly return of 1.5 percent. What is the probability that the portfolio manager's mean return exceeds the benchmark? Assume the sample mean is normally distributed.

Answer:
There are a total of 120 data points in the sample (10 years × 12 months per year). The standard deviation of the mean is then 0.33 percent:

$$\sigma_{\hat{\mu}} = \frac{\sigma}{\sqrt{n}} = \frac{3.6\%}{\sqrt{120}} = 0.33\%$$

The distance between the portfolio manager's mean return and the benchmark is –2.43 standard deviations: (1.50 percent – 2.30 percent)/0.33 percent = –2.43. For a normal distribution, 99.25 percent of the distribution lies above –2.43 standard deviations, and only 0.75 percent lies below. The difference between the portfolio manager and the benchmark is highly significant.

Sample Variance Revisited

Just as with the sample mean, we can treat the sample variance as a random variable. For a given DGP if we repeatedly calculate the sample variance, the expected value of the sample variance will equal the true variance, and the variance of the sample variance will equal:

$$E[(\hat{\sigma}^2 - \sigma^2)^2] = \sigma^4 \left(\frac{2}{n-1} + \frac{\kappa}{n} \right) \tag{3.74}$$

where n is the sample size, and κ is the excess kurtosis.

If the DGP has a normal distribution, then we can also say something about the shape of the distribution of the sample variance. If we have n sample points and $\hat{\sigma}^2$ is the sample variance, then our estimator will follow a chi-squared distribution with $(n-1)$ degrees of freedom:

$$(n-1)\frac{\hat{\sigma}^2}{\sigma^2} \sim \chi^2_{n-1} \tag{3.75}$$

where σ^2 is the population variance. Note that this is true only when the DGP has a normal distribution. Unfortunately, unlike the case of the sample mean, we cannot apply the central limit theorem here. Even when the sample size is large, if the underlying distribution is nonnormal, the statistic in Equation 3.75 can vary significantly from a chi-squared distribution.

Confidence Intervals

In our discussion of the sample mean, we assumed that the standard deviation of the underlying distribution was known. In practice, the true standard deviation is likely to be unknown. At the same time we are measuring our sample mean, we will typically be measuring a sample variance as well.

It turns out that if we first standardize our estimate of the sample mean using the sample standard deviation, the new random variable follows a Student's t-distribution with $(n-1)$ degrees of freedom:

$$t = \frac{\hat{\mu} - \mu}{\hat{\sigma}/\sqrt{n}} \tag{3.76}$$

Here the numerator is simply the difference between the sample mean and the population mean, while the denominator is the sample standard deviation divided by the square root of the sample size. To see why this new variable follows a t-distribution, we simply need to divide both the numerator and the denominator by the population standard deviation. This creates a standard normal variable in the numerator, and the square root of a chi-square variable in the denominator with the appropriate constant. We know from discussions on distributions that this combination of random variables follows a t-distribution. This standardized version of the population mean is so frequently used that it is referred to as a t-statistic, or simply a t-stat.

Technically, this result requires that the underlying distribution be normally distributed. As was the case with the sample variance, the denominator may not follow a chi-squared distribution if the underlying distribution is nonnormal. Oddly enough, for large sample sizes the overall t-statistic still converges to a t-distribution. If the sample size is small and the data distribution is nonnormal, be aware that the t-statistic, as defined here, may not be well approximated by a t-distribution.

By looking up the appropriate values for the t-distribution, we can establish the probability that our t-statistic is contained within a certain range:

$$P\left[x_L \leq \frac{\hat{\mu} - \mu}{\hat{\sigma}/\sqrt{n}} \leq x_U\right] = 1 - \alpha \qquad (3.77)$$

where x_L and x_U are constants, which, respectively, define the lower and upper bounds of the range within the t-distribution, and $(1 - \alpha)$ is the probability that our t-statistic will be found within that range. The right-hand side may seem a bit awkward, but, by convention, $(1 - \alpha)$ is called the confidence level, while α by itself is known as the significance level.

In practice, the population mean, μ, is often unknown. By rearranging the previous equation we come to an equation with a more interesting form:

$$P\left[\hat{\mu} - \frac{x_L \hat{\sigma}}{\sqrt{n}} \leq \mu \leq \hat{\mu} + \frac{x_U \hat{\sigma}}{\sqrt{n}}\right] = 1 - \alpha \qquad (3.78)$$

Looked at this way, we are now giving the probability that the population mean will be contained within the defined range. When it is formulated this way, we call this range the confidence interval for the population mean. Confidence intervals are not limited to the population mean. Though it may not be as simple, in theory we can define a confidence level for any distribution parameter.

Hypothesis Testing

One problem with confidence intervals is that they require us to settle on an arbitrary confidence level. While 95 percent and 99 percent are common choices for the confidence level in risk management, there is nothing sacred about these numbers. It would be perfectly legitimate to construct a 74.92 percent confidence interval. At the same time, we are often concerned with the probability that a certain variable exceeds a threshold. For example, given the observed returns of a mutual fund, what is the probability that the standard deviation of those returns is less than 20 percent?

In a sense, we want to turn the confidence interval around. Rather than saying there is an x percent probability that the population mean is contained within a given interval, we want to know what the probability is that the population mean is greater than y. When we pose the question this way, we are in the realm of hypothesis testing.

Traditionally the question is put in the form of a null hypothesis. If we are interested in knowing if the expected return of a portfolio manager is greater than 10 percent, we would write:

$$H_0 : \mu_r > 10\% \qquad (3.79)$$

where H_0 is known as the null hypothesis. Even though the true population mean is unknown, for the hypothesis test we assume the population mean *is* 10 percent. In effect, we are asking, *if* the true population mean *is* 10 percent, what is the probability that we would see a given sample mean? With our null hypothesis in hand, we gather our data, calculate the sample mean, and form the appropriate *t*-statistic. In this case, the appropriate *t*-statistic is:

$$t = \frac{\hat{\mu} - 10\%}{\sigma/\sqrt{n}} \qquad (3.80)$$

We can then look up the corresponding probability from the *t*-distribution.

In addition to the null hypothesis, we can offer an alternative hypothesis. In the previous example, where our null hypothesis is that the expected return is greater than 10 percent, the logical alternative would be that the expected return is less than or equal to 10 percent:

$$H_1 : \mu_r \leq 10\% \qquad (3.81)$$

In principle, we could test any number of hypotheses. In practice, as long as the alternative is trivial, we tend to limit ourselves to stating the null hypothesis.

WHICH WAY TO TEST? If we want to know if the expected return of a portfolio manager is greater than 10 percent, the obvious statement of the null hypothesis might seem to be $\mu_r > 10$ percent. But there is no reason that we couldn't have started with the alternative hypothesis, that $\mu_r \leq 10$ percent. Finding that the first is true and finding that the second is false are logically equivalent.

Many practitioners construct the null hypothesis so that the desired result is false. If we are an investor trying to find good portfolio managers, then we would make the null hypothesis $\mu_r \leq 10$ percent. That we want the expected return to be greater than 10 percent but we are testing for the opposite makes us seem objective. Unfortunately, in the case where there is a high probability that the manager's expected return is greater than 10 percent (a good result), we have to say, "We reject the null hypothesis that the manager's returns are less than or equal to 10 percent at the x percent level." This is very close to a double negative. Like a medical test where the good outcome is negative and the bad outcome is positive, we often find that the good outcome for a null hypothesis is rejection.

To make matters more complicated, what happens if the portfolio manager doesn't seem to be that good? If we *rejected* the null hypothesis when there was a high probability that the portfolio manager's expected return was greater than 10 percent, should we *accept* the null hypothesis when there is a high probability that the returns are less than 10 percent? In the realm of statistics, outright acceptance seems too certain. In practice, we can do two things. First, we can state that the probability of rejecting the null hypothesis is low (e.g., "The probability of rejecting the null hypothesis is only 4.2 percent"). More often we say that we *fail to reject* the null hypothesis (e.g., "We fail to reject the null hypothesis at the 95.8 percent level").

Sample Problem

Question:
At the start of the year, you believed that the annualized volatility of XYZ Corporation's equity was 45 percent. At the end of the year, you have collected a year of daily returns, 256 business days' worth. You calculate the standard deviation, annualize it, and come up with a value of 48 percent. Can you reject the null hypothesis, H_0: σ = 45 percent, at the 95 percent confidence level?

Answer:
The appropriate test statistic is:

$$(n-1)\frac{\hat{\sigma}^2}{\sigma^2} = (256-1)\frac{0.48^2}{0.45^2} = 290.13 \sim \chi^2_{255}$$

Notice that annualizing the standard deviation has no impact on the test statistic. The same factor would appear in the numerator and the denominator, leaving the ratio unchanged. For a chi-squared distribution with 255 degrees of freedom, 290.13 corresponds to a probability of 6.44 percent. We fail to reject the null hypothesis at the 95 percent confidence level.

Application: VaR

Value at risk (VaR) is one of the most widely used risk measures in finance. VaR was popularized by J.P. Morgan in the 1990s. The executives at J.P. Morgan wanted their risk managers to generate one statistic at the end of each day, which summarized the risk of the firm's entire portfolio. What they came up with was VaR.

Figure 3.8 provides a graphical representation of VaR. If the 95 percent VaR of a portfolio is $100, then we expect the portfolio will lose $100 or less in 95 percent of the scenarios, and lose $100 or more in 5 percent of the scenarios. We can define VaR for any level of confidence, but 95 percent has become an extremely popular choice in finance. The time horizon also needs to be specified for VaR. On trading desks, with liquid portfolios, it is common to measure the one-day 95 percent VaR. In other settings, in which less liquid assets may be involved, time frames of up to one year are not uncommon. VaR is decidedly a one-tailed confidence interval.

For a given confidence level, $1 - \alpha$, we can define value at risk more formally as:

$$P[L \leq VaR_\alpha] = 1 - \alpha \qquad (3.82)$$

where the random variable L is our loss.

Value at risk is often described as a confidence interval. As we saw earlier in this chapter, the term *confidence interval* is generally applied to the estimation of distribution parameters. In practice, when calculating VaR, the distribution is often taken as a given. Either way, the tools, concepts, and vocabulary are the same. So even though VaR may not technically be a confidence interval, we still refer to the *confidence level* of VaR.

Most practitioners reverse the sign of L when quoting VaR numbers. By this convention, a 95 percent VaR of $400 implies that there is a 5 percent probability

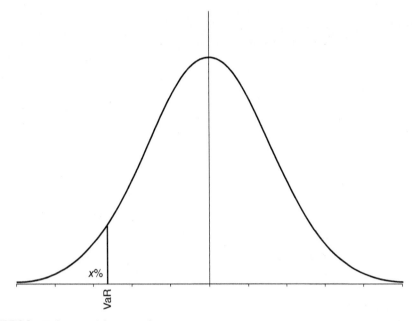

FIGURE 3.8 Value at Risk Example

that the portfolio will *lose* $400 or more. Because this represents a loss, others would say that the VaR is –$400. The former is more popular, and is the convention used throughout the rest of the book. In practice, it is often best to avoid any ambiguity by, for example, stating that the VaR is equal to a loss of $400.

   If an actual loss exceeds the predicted VaR threshold, that event is known as an exceedance. Another assumption of VaR models is that exceedance events are uncorrelated with each other. In other words, if our VaR measure is set at a one-day 95 percent confidence level, and there is an exceedance event today, then the probability of an exceedance event tomorrow is still 5 percent. An exceedance event today has no impact on the probability of future exceedance events.

Sample Problem

Question:
The probability density function (PDF) for daily profits at Triangle Asset Management can be described by the following function:

$$p = \frac{1}{10} + \frac{1}{100}\pi \quad -10 \le \pi \le 0$$

$$p = \frac{1}{10} - \frac{1}{100}\pi \quad 0 < \pi \le 10$$

Triangular Probability Density Function
What is the one-day 95 percent VaR for Triangle Asset Management?

Answer:
To find the 95 percent VaR, we need to find a, such that:

$$\int_{-10}^{a} pd\pi = 0.05$$

By inspection, half the distribution is below zero, so we need only bother with the first half of the function:

$$\int_{-10}^{a} \left(\frac{1}{10} + \frac{1}{100}\pi\right) d\pi = \left[\frac{1}{10}\pi + \frac{1}{200}\pi^2\right]_{-10}^{a}$$

$$= \frac{1}{10}a + \frac{1}{200}a^2 + 0.50 = 0.05$$

$$a^2 + 20a + 90 = 0$$

Using the quadratic formula, we can solve for a:

$$a = \frac{-20 \pm \sqrt{400 - 4 \cdot 90}}{2} = -10 \pm \sqrt{10}$$

Because the distribution is not defined for $\pi < -10$, we can ignore the negative, giving us the final answer:

$$a = -10 + \sqrt{10} = -6.84$$

The one-day 95 percent VaR for Triangle Asset Management is a loss of approximately 6.84.

BACK-TESTING   An obvious concern when using VaR is choosing the appropriate confidence interval. As mentioned, 95 percent has become a very popular choice in risk management. In some settings there may be a natural choice for the confidence level, but most of the time the exact choice is arbitrary.

A common mistake for newcomers is to choose a confidence level that is too high. Naturally, a higher confidence level sounds more conservative. A risk manager who measures one-day VaR at the 95 percent confidence level will, on average, experience an exceedance event every 20 days. A risk manager who measures VaR at the 99.9 percent confidence level expects to see an exceedance only once every 1,000 days. Is an event that happens once every 20 days really something that we need to worry about? It is tempting to believe that the risk manager using the 99.9 percent confidence level is concerned with more serious, riskier outcomes, and is therefore doing a better job.

The problem is that, as we go further and further out into the tail of the distribution, we become less and less certain of the shape of the distribution. In most cases, the assumed distribution of returns for our portfolio will be based on historical data. If we have 1,000 data points, then there are 50 data points to back up our 95 percent confidence level, but only one to back up our 99.9 percent confidence level. As with any distribution parameter, the variance of our estimate of the parameter decreases with the sample size. One data point is hardly a good sample size on which to base a parameter estimate.

A related problem has to do with back-testing. Good risk managers should regularly back-test their models. Back-testing entails checking the predicted outcome of a model against actual data. Any model parameter can be back-tested.

In the case of VaR, back-testing is easy. Each period can be viewed as a Bernoulli trial. In the case of one-day 95 percent VaR, there is a 5 percent chance of an exceedance event each day, and a 95 percent chance that there is no exceedance. Because exceedance events are independent, over the course of n days, the distribution of exceedances follows a binomial distribution:

$$P[K = k] = \binom{n}{k} p^k (1 - p)^{n-k} \tag{3.83}$$

In this case, n is the number of periods that we are using to back-test, k is the number of exceedances, and $(1 - p)$ is our confidence level.

Sample Problem

Question:
As a risk manager, you are tasked with calculating a daily 95 percent VaR statistic for a large fixed income portfolio. Over the past 100 days, there have been four exceedances. How many exceedances should you have expected? What was the probability of exactly four exceedances during this time? Four or less? Four or more?

Answer:
The probability of exactly four exceedances is 17.81 percent:

$$P[K = 4] = \binom{100}{4} 0.05^4 (1 - 0.05)^{100-4} = 0.1781$$

Remember, by convention, for a 95 percent VaR the probability of an exceedance is 5 percent, not 95 percent.

The probability of four or fewer exceedances is 43.60 percent. Here we simply do the same calculation as in the first part of the problem, but for zero, one, two, three, and four exceedances. It's important not to forget zero:

$$P[K \leq 4] = \sum_{k=0}^{4} \binom{100}{k} 0.05^k (1 - 0.05)^{100-k}$$

$$= 0.0059 + 0.0312 + 0.0812 + 0.1396 + 0.1781 = 0.4360$$

For the final result, we could use the brute force approach and calculate the probability for $k = 4, 5, 6, \ldots, 99, 100$, a total of 97 calculations. Instead we realize that the sum of all probabilities from 0 to 100 must be 100 percent; therefore, if the probability of $K \leq 4$ is 43.60 percent, then the probability of

$K > 4$ must be 100 percent $-$ 43.60 percent $=$ 56.40 percent. Be careful, though, as what we want is the probability for $K \geq 4$. To get this, we simply add the probability that $K = 4$, from the first part of our question, to get the final answer, 74.21 percent:

$$P[K \geq 4] = 0.5640 + 0.1781 = 0.7421$$

EXPECTED SHORTFALL   Another criticism of VaR is that it does not tell us anything about the tail of the distribution. Two portfolios could have the exact same 95 percent VaR, but very different distributions beyond the 95 percent confidence level.

More than VaR, then, what we really want to know is how big the loss will be when we have an exceedance event. Using the concept of conditional probability, we can define the expected value of a loss, given an exceedance, as follows:

$$E[L|L > \mathrm{VaR}_\alpha] = S \tag{3.84}$$

we refer to this conditional expected loss, S, as the expected shortfall.

If the profit function has a probability density function given by $f(x)$, and VaR is the VaR at the α confidence level, we can find the expected shortfall as:

$$S = \frac{1}{1-\alpha} \int_{-\infty}^{\mathrm{VaR}} x f(x)\, dx \tag{3.85}$$

In most cases the VaR for a portfolio will correspond to a loss, and Equation 3.85 will produce a negative value. As with VaR, it is common to reverse the sign when speaking about the expected shortfall.

Expected shortfall does answer an important question. What's more, expected shortfall turns out to be subadditive, thereby avoiding one of the major criticisms of VaR. As our discussion on back-testing suggests, though, the reliability of our expected shortfall measure may be difficult to gauge.

Sample Problem

Question:
In a previous example, the probability density function of Triangle Asset Management's daily profits could be described by the following function:

$$p = \frac{1}{10} + \frac{1}{100}\pi \quad -10 \leq \pi \leq 0$$

$$p = \frac{1}{10} - \frac{1}{100}\pi \quad 0 < \pi \leq 10$$

We calculated Triangle's one-day 95 percent VaR as a loss of $(10 - \sqrt{10}) =$ 6.84. For the same confidence level and time horizon, what is the expected shortfall?

Answer:

Because the VaR occurs in the region where $\pi < 0$, we need to utilize only the first half of the function. Using Equation 3.85, we have:

$$S = \frac{1}{0.05} \int\limits_{-10}^{\text{VaR}} \pi p d\pi = 20 \int\limits_{-10}^{\text{VaR}} \pi \left(\frac{1}{10} + \frac{1}{100}\pi\right) d\pi$$

$$= \int\limits_{-10}^{\text{VaR}} \left(2\pi + \frac{\pi^2}{5}\right) d\pi = \left[\pi^2 + \frac{1}{15}\pi^3\right]_{-10}^{\text{VaR}}$$

$$S = \left((-10 + \sqrt{10})^2 + \frac{1}{15}(-10 + \sqrt{10})^3\right) - \left((-10)^2 + \frac{1}{15}(-10)^3\right)$$

$$S = -10 + \frac{2}{3}\sqrt{10} = -7.89$$

Thus, the expected shortfall is a loss of 7.89. Intuitively this should make sense. The expected shortfall must be greater than the VaR, 6.84, but less than the minimum loss of 10. Because extreme events are less likely (the height of the PDF decreases away from the center), it also makes sense that the expected shortfall is closer to the VaR than it is to the maximum loss.

Part VI Linear Regression Analysis

Linear Regression (One Regressor)

One of the most popular models in statistics is the linear regression model. Given two constants, α and β, and a random error term, ε, in its simplest form the model posits a relationship between two variables, X and Y:

$$Y = \alpha + \beta X + \varepsilon \tag{3.86}$$

As specified, X is known as the regressor or independent variable. Similarly, Y is known as the regressand or dependent variable. As *dependent* implies, traditionally we think of X as *causing* Y. This relationship is not necessary, and in practice, especially in finance, this cause-and-effect relationship is either ambiguous or entirely absent. In finance, it is often the case that both X and Y are being driven by a common underlying factor.

The linear regression relationship is often represented graphically as a plot of Y against X, as shown in Figure 3.9. The solid line in the chart represents the deterministic portion of the linear regression equation, $Y = \alpha + \beta X$. For any particular point, the distance above or below the line is the error, ε, for that point.

Because there is only one regressor, this model is often referred to as a univariate regression. Mainly, this is to differentiate it from the multivariate model, with more than one regressor, which we will explore later in this chapter. While everybody agrees that a model with two or more regressors is multivariate, not everybody agrees

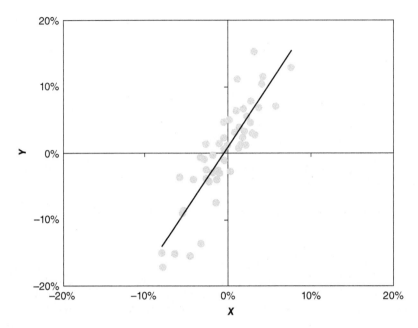

FIGURE 3.9   Linear Regression Example

that a model with one regressor is univariate. Even though the univariate model has one regressor, X, it has two variables, X and Y, which has led some people to refer to Equation 3.86 as a bivariate model. From here on out, however, we will refer to Equation 3.86 as a univariate model.

In Equation 3.86, α and β are constants. In the univariate model, α is typically referred to as the intercept, and β is often referred to as the slope. β is referred to as the slope because it measures the slope of the solid line when Y is plotted against X. We can see this by taking the derivative of Y with respect to X:

$$\frac{dY}{dX} = \beta \tag{3.87}$$

The final term in Equation 3.86, ε, represents a random error, or residual. The error term allows us to specify a relationship between X and Y, even when that relationship is not exact. In effect, the model is incomplete, it is an approximation. Changes in X may drive changes in Y, but there are other variables, which we are not modeling, which also impact Y. These unmodeled variables cause X and Y to deviate from a purely deterministic relationship. That deviation is captured by ε, our residual.

In risk management this division of the world into two parts, a part that can be explained by the model and a part that cannot, is a common dichotomy. We refer to risk that can be explained by our model as systematic risk, and to the part that cannot be explained by the model as idiosyncratic risk. In our regression model, Y is divided into a systematic component, $\alpha + \beta X$, and an idiosyncratic component, ε.

$$Y = \underbrace{\alpha + \beta X}_{\text{systematic}} + \underbrace{\varepsilon}_{\text{idiosyncratic}} \tag{3.88}$$

Which component of the overall risk is more important? It depends on what our objective is. As we will see, portfolio managers who wish to hedge certain risks in their portfolios are basically trying to reduce or eliminate systematic risk. Portfolio managers who try to mimic the returns of an index, on the other hand, can be viewed as trying to minimize idiosyncratic risk.

EVALUATING THE REGRESSION   Unlike a controlled laboratory experiment, the real world is a very noisy and complicated place. In finance it is rare that a simple univariate regression model is going to completely explain a large data set. In many cases, the data are so noisy that we must ask ourselves if the model is explaining anything at all. Even when a relationship appears to exist, we are likely to want some quantitative measure of just how strong that relationship is.

Probably the most popular statistic for describing linear regressions is the coefficient of determination, commonly known as R-squared, or just R^2. R^2 is often described as the goodness of fit of the linear regression. When R^2 is one, the regression model completely explains the data. If R^2 is one, all the residuals are zero, and the residual sum of squares, RSS, is zero. At the other end of the spectrum, if R^2 is zero, the model does not explain any variation in the observed data. In other words, Y does not vary with X, and β is zero.

To calculate the coefficient of determination, we need to define two additional terms: TSS, the total sum of squares, and ESS, the explained sum of squares. They are defined as:

$$\text{TSS} = \sum_{i=1}^{n} y_i^2$$

$$\text{ESS} = \sum_{i=1}^{n} \hat{y}_i^2 = \sum_{i=1}^{n} (\alpha + \beta x_i)^2$$

(3.89)

These two sums are related to the previously encountered residual sum of squares, as follows:

$$\text{TSS} = \text{ESS} + \text{RSS} \qquad (3.90)$$

In other words, the total variation in our regressand, TSS, can be broken down into two components, the part the model can explain, ESS, and the part the model cannot, RSS. These sums can be used to compute R^2:

$$R^2 = \frac{\text{ESS}}{\text{TSS}} = 1 - \frac{\text{RSS}}{\text{TSS}} \qquad (3.91)$$

As promised, when there are no residual errors, when RSS is zero, R^2 is one. Also, when ESS is zero, or when the variation in the errors is equal to TSS, R^2 is zero. It turns out that for the univariate linear regression model, R^2 is also equal to the correlation between X and Y squared. If X and Y are perfectly correlated, $\rho_{xy} = 1$, or perfectly negatively correlated, $\rho_{xy} = -1$, then R^2 will equal one.

Estimates of the regression parameters are just like the parameter estimates we examined earlier, and subject to hypothesis testing. In regression analysis, the most common null hypothesis is that the slope parameter, β, is zero. If β is zero, then the regression model does not explain any variation in the regressand.

In finance, we often want to know if α is significantly different from zero, but for different reasons. In modern finance, *alpha* has become synonymous with the ability of a portfolio manager to generate excess returns. This is because, in a regression equation modeling the returns of a portfolio manager, after we remove all the randomness, ε, and the influence of the explanatory variable, X, if α is still positive, then it is suggested that the portfolio manager is producing positive excess returns, something that should be very difficult in efficient markets. Of course, it's not just enough that the α is positive; we require that the α be positive *and* statistically significant.

Sample Problem

Question:
As a risk manager and expert on statistics, you are asked to evaluate the performance of a long/short equity portfolio manager. You are given 10 years of monthly return data. You regress the log returns of the portfolio manager against the log returns of a market index.

$$r_{\text{portfolio\_manager}} = \alpha + \beta r_{\text{market}} + \varepsilon$$

Assume both series are normally distributed and homoscedastic. From this analysis, you obtain the following regression results:

	Constant	Beta
Value	1.13%	20.39%
Std. dev.	0.48%	9.71%
R2	8.11%	

What can we say about the performance of the portfolio manager?

Answer:
The R^2 for the regression is low. Only 8.11 percent of the variation in the portfolio manager's returns can be explained by the constant, beta, and variation in the market. The rest is idiosyncratic risk, and is unexplained by the model.

That said, both the constant and the beta seem to be statistically significant (i.e., they are statistically different from zero). We can get the t-statistic by dividing the value of the coefficient by its standard deviation. For the constant, we have:

$$\frac{\hat{\alpha} - \alpha}{\hat{\sigma}_\alpha} = \frac{1.13\% - 0\%}{0.48\%} = 2.36$$

Similarly, for beta we have a t-statistic of 2.10. Using a statistical package, we calculate the corresponding probability associated with each t-statistic. This should be a two-tailed test with 118 degrees of freedom (10 years × 12 months per year − 2 parameters). We can reject the hypothesis that the constant and slope are zero at the 2 percent level and 4 percent level, respectively. In other words, there seems to be a significant market component to the fund manager's return, but the manager is also generating statistically significant excess returns.

Linear Regression (Multivariate)

Univariate regression models are extremely common in finance and risk management, but sometimes we require a slightly more complicated model. In these cases, we might use a multivariate regression model. The basic idea is the same, but instead of one regressand and one regressor, we have one regressand and multiple regressors. Our basic equation will look something like:

$$Y = \beta_1 + \beta_2 X_2 + \beta_3 X_3 + \ldots + \beta_n X_n \qquad (3.92)$$

Notice that rather than denoting the first constant with α, we chose to go with β_1. This is the more common convention in multivariate regression. To make the equation even more regular, we can assume that there is an X_1, which, unlike the other X's, is constant and always equal to one. This convention allows us to easily express a set of observations in matrix form. For t observations and n regressands, we could write:

$$
\begin{bmatrix} y_1 \\ y_2 \\ \vdots \\ y_t \end{bmatrix} =
\begin{bmatrix} x_{11} & x_{12} & \cdots & x_{1n} \\ x_{21} & x_{22} & \cdots & x_{2n} \\ \vdots & \vdots & \ddots & \\ x_{t1} & x_{t2} & \cdots & x_{tn} \end{bmatrix}
\begin{bmatrix} \beta_1 \\ \beta_2 \\ \vdots \\ \beta_n \end{bmatrix} +
\begin{bmatrix} \varepsilon_1 \\ \varepsilon_2 \\ \vdots \\ \varepsilon_t \end{bmatrix}
\qquad (3.93)
$$

where the first column of the **X** matrix—$x_{11}, x_{21}, \ldots, x_{t1}$—is understood to consist entirely of ones. The entire equation can be written more succinctly as:

$$\mathbf{Y} = \mathbf{X}\beta + \varepsilon \qquad (3.94)$$

where, as before, we have used bold letters to denote matrices.

MULTICOLLINEARITY   In order to determine the parameters of the multivariate regression, we again turn to our OLS assumptions. In the multivariate case, the assumptions are the same as before, but with one addition. In the multivariate case, we require that all of the independent variables be linearly independent of each other. We say that the independent variables must lack multicollinearity:

(A7) The independent variables have no multicollinearity.

To say that the independent variables lack multicollinearity means that it is impossible to express one of the independent variables as a linear combination of the others.

This additional assumption is required to remove ambiguity. To see why this is the case, imagine that we attempt a regression with two independent variables where the second independent variable, X_3, can be expressed as a linear function of the first independent variable, X_2:

$$
\begin{aligned}
Y &= \beta_1 + \beta_2 X_2 + \beta_3 X_3 + \varepsilon_1 \\
X_3 &= \lambda_1 + \lambda_2 X_2 + \varepsilon_2
\end{aligned}
\qquad (3.95)
$$

If we substitute the second line of Equation 3.95 into the first, we get:

$$Y = (\beta_1 + \beta_3\lambda_1) + (\beta_2 + \beta_3\lambda_2)X_2 + (\beta_3\varepsilon_2 + \varepsilon_1)$$
$$Y = \beta_4 + \beta_5 X_2 + \varepsilon_3 \tag{3.96}$$

In the second line, we have simplified by introducing new constants and a new error term. We have replaced $(\beta_1 + \beta_3\lambda_1)$ with β_4, replaced $(\beta_2 + \beta_3\lambda_2)$ with β_5, and replaced $(\beta_3\varepsilon_2 + \varepsilon_1)$ with ε_3. β_5 can be uniquely determined in a univariate regression, but there is an infinite number of combinations of β_2, β_3, and λ_2 that we could choose to equal β_5. If $\beta_5 = 10$, any of the following combinations would work:

$$\beta_2 = 10, \quad \beta_3 = 0, \quad \lambda_2 = 100$$
$$\beta_2 = 0, \quad \beta_3 = 10, \quad \lambda_2 = 1 \tag{3.97}$$
$$\beta_2 = 500, \quad \beta_3 = -49, \quad \lambda_2 = 10$$

This is why we say that β_2 and β_3 are ambiguous in the initial equation.

Even in the presence of multicollinearity, the regression model still works in a sense. In the preceding example, even though β_2 and β_3 are ambiguous, any combination where $(\beta_2 + \beta_3\lambda_2)$ equals β_5 will produce the same value of Y for a given set of X's. If our only objective is to predict Y, then the regression model still works. The problem is that the value of the parameters will be unstable. A slightly different data set can cause wild swings in the value of the parameter estimates, and may even flip the signs of the parameters. A variable that we expect to be positively correlated with the regressand may end up with a large negative beta. This makes interpreting the model difficult. Parameter instability is often a sign of multicollinearity.

There is no well-accepted procedure for dealing with multicollinearity. The easiest course of action is often simply to eliminate a variable from the regression. While easy, this is hardly satisfactory.

Another possibility is to transform the variables, to create uncorrelated variables out of linear combinations of the existing variables. In the previous example, even though X_3 is correlated with X_2, $X_3 - \lambda_2 X_2$ *is* uncorrelated with X_2.

$$X_3 - \lambda_2 X_2 = \lambda_1 + \varepsilon_3$$
$$\text{Cov}[X_2, X_3 - \lambda_2 X_2] = \text{Cov}[X_2, \lambda_1 + \varepsilon_3] = \text{Cov}[X_2, \varepsilon_3] = 0 \tag{3.98}$$

One potential problem with this approach is similar to what we saw with principal component analysis (which is really just another method for creating uncorrelated variables from linear combinations of correlated variables). If we are lucky, a linear combination of variables will have a simple economic interpretation. For example, if X_2 and X_3 are two equity indexes, then their difference might correspond to a familiar spread. Similarly, if the two variables are interest rates, their difference might bear some relation to the shape of the yield curve. Other linear combinations might be difficult to interpret, and if the relationship is not readily identifiable, then the relationship is more likely to be unstable or spurious.

Global financial markets are becoming increasingly integrated. More now than ever before, multicollinearity is a problem that risk managers need to be aware of.

Part VII Time Series Models

Time series describe how random variables evolve over time and form the basis of many financial models.

Random Walks

A time series is an equation or set of equations describing how a random variable or variables evolves over time. Probably the most basic time series is the random walk. For a random variable X, with a realization x_t at time t, the following conditions describe a random walk:

$$x_t = x_{t-1} + \varepsilon_t$$
$$E[\varepsilon_t] = 0$$
$$E\left[\varepsilon_t^2\right] = \sigma^2 \qquad (3.99)$$
$$E[\varepsilon_s \varepsilon_t] = 0 \ \forall s \neq t$$

In other words, X is equal to its value from the previous period, plus a random disturbance, is mean zero, with a constant variance. The last assumption, combined with the fact that ε_t is mean zero, tells us that the ε's from different periods will be uncorrelated with each other. In time series analysis, we typically refer to x_{t-1} as the first lagged value of x_t, or just the first lag of x_t. By this convention, x_{t-2} would be the second lag, x_{t-3} the third, and so on.

We can also think in terms of changes in X. Subtracting x_{t-1} from both sides of our initial equation:

$$\Delta x_t = x_t - x_{t-1} = \varepsilon_t \qquad (3.100)$$

In this basic random walk, Δ_{x_t} has all of the properties of our stochastic term, ε_t. Both are mean zero. Both have a constant variance, σ^2. Most importantly, the error terms are uncorrelated with each other. This system is not affected by its past. This is the defining feature of a random walk.

How does the system evolve over time? Note that Equation 3.99 is true for all time periods. All of the following equations are valid:

$$x_t = x_{t-1} + \varepsilon_t$$
$$x_{t-1} = x_{t-2} + \varepsilon_{t-1}$$
$$\vdots \qquad (3.101)$$
$$x_{t-i} = x_{t-i-1} + \varepsilon_{t-i}$$

By substituting the equation into itself, we can see how the equation evolves over multiple periods:

$$x_t = x_{t-1} + \varepsilon_t = x_{t-2} + \varepsilon_{t-1} + \varepsilon_t = x_0 + \sum_{i=1}^{t} \varepsilon_i \qquad (3.102)$$

At time t, X is simply the sum of its initial value, x_0, plus a series of random steps. Using this formula, it is easy to calculate the conditional mean and variance of x_t:

$$E[x_t \mid x_0] = x_0$$
$$\text{Var}[x_t \mid x_0] = t\sigma^2$$

(3.103)

If the variance increases proportionally with t, then the standard deviation increases with the square root of t. This is our familiar square root rule for independent and identically distributed (i.i.d.) variables. For a random walk, our best guess for the future value of the variable is simply the current value, but the probability of finding it near the current value becomes increasingly small.

Though the proof is omitted here, it is not difficult to show that, for a random walk, skewness is proportional to $t^{-0.5}$ and kurtosis is proportional to t^{-1}. In other words, while the mean, variance, and standard deviation increase over longer time spans, skewness and kurtosis become smaller.

The simple random walk is not a great model for equities, where we expect prices to increase over time, or for interest rates, which cannot be negative. With some rather trivial modification, though, we can accommodate both of these requirements.

Variance and Autocorrelation

Autocorrelation has a very important impact on variance as we look at longer and longer time periods. For our random walk, as we look at longer and longer periods, the variance grows in proportion to the length of time.

Assume returns follow a random walk:

$$r_t = \varepsilon_t$$

(3.104)

where ε_t is an i.i.d. disturbance term. Now define $y_{n,t}$ as an n period return; that is:

$$y_{n,t} = \sum_{i=0}^{n-1} r_{t-i} = \sum_{i=0}^{n-1} \varepsilon_{t-i}$$

(3.105)

As stated before, the variance of $y_{n,t}$ is proportional to n:

$$\text{Var}[y_{n,t}] = n\sigma_\varepsilon^2$$

(3.106)

and the standard deviation of $y_{n,t}$ is proportional to the square root of n. In other words, if the daily standard deviation of an equity index is 1 percent and the returns of the index follow a random walk, then the standard deviation of 25-day returns will be 5 percent, and the standard deviation of 100-day returns will be 10 percent.

When we introduce autocorrelation, this square root rule no longer holds. If instead of a random walk we start with an AR(1) series:

$$r_t = \alpha + \lambda r_{t-1} + \varepsilon_t = \frac{\alpha}{1 - \lambda} + \sum_{i=0}^{\infty} \lambda^i \varepsilon_{t-i}$$

(3.107)

Now define a two-period return:

$$y_{2,t} = r_t + r_{t-1} = \frac{2\alpha}{1 - \lambda} + \varepsilon_t + \sum_{i=0}^{\infty} \lambda^i (1 + \lambda)\varepsilon_{t-i-1} \qquad (3.108)$$

With just two periods, the introduction of autocorrelation has already made the description of our multiperiod return noticeably more complicated. The variance of this series is now:

$$\text{Var}[y_{2,t}] = \frac{2}{1 - \lambda}\sigma_\varepsilon^2 \qquad (3.109)$$

If λ is zero, then our time series is equivalent to a random walk and our new variance formula gives the correct answer: that the variance is still proportional to the length of our multiperiod return. If λ is greater than zero, and serial correlation is positive, then the two-period variance will be more than twice as great as the single-period variance. If λ is less than zero, and the serial correlation is negative, then the two-period variance will be less than twice the single-period variance. This makes sense. For series with negative serial correlation, a large positive return will tend to be followed by a negative return, pulling the series back toward its mean, thereby reducing the multiperiod volatility. The opposite is true for series with positive serial correlation.

Time series with slightly positive or negative serial correlation abound in finance. It is a common mistake to assume that variance is linear in time, when in fact it is not. Assuming no serial correlation when it does exist can lead to a serious overestimation or underestimation of risk.

CHAPTER 4

Applied Finance and Economics

This chapter is laid out in two sections: applied finance (the time value of money) and economics. The readings that follow offer a thorough review of time value of money (TVM) concepts and an overview of macroeconomic principles and analysis.

Section I: Time Value of Money

Investment advisors and consultants must understand the mathematics behind the concepts in the area of time value of money. They should be able to perform calculations by hand or with the help of a spreadsheet, computer program, or on their financial calculator. Simply understanding the intuition is not enough…the ability to calculate and apply are essential. The readings in this chapter explain each concept and provide numerous mathematical examples. Exercises and questions will help readers apply these formulae to solve practical problems in finance.

Part I *Foundations and Applications of the Time Value of Money:* The Basics of the Time Value of Money

Learning Objectives
- Explain the concept of the time value of money; and describe compounding, discounting, present value, and future value.
- Express present value and future value in an equation, and calculate each when given a fact pattern or problem to solve.
- Discuss frequency of compounding and explain the annual percentage rate (APR).
- Solve problems converting and comparing interest rates based on monthly, quarterly, semiannual, and annual interest payments.

Part II *Foundations and Applications of the Time Value of Money:* Don't Discount Discounting

Learning Objectives
- Describe discounting and express through a formula solving for present value (PV).

■ Solve for present value using various inputs for future value, time, and discount rate.

■ Solve for present value using different compounding periods.

Part III *Foundations and Applications of the Time Value of Money:* Cash Happens

Learning Objectives
■ Calculate the value of a stream of future cash flows.
■ Define and calculate the value of a perpetuity.
■ Differentiate between an ordinary annuity, an annuity due, and a deferred annuity.
■ Calculate the value of an ordinary annuity and an annuity due.

Part IV *Foundations and Applications of the Time Value of Money:* Yielding for Yields

Learning Objectives
■ Describe annual percentage rate (APR).
■ Solve problems converting different rates and compounding periods into APR.
■ Describe effective annual rate (EAR).
■ Solve problems by calculating the EAR.
■ Solve for the unknown interest rate (i).
■ Solve for the time-weighted return and money-weighted return.
■ Explain the Rule of 72 and the Rule of 69 and apply either to solve problems.

Part V *Foundations and Applications of the Time Value of Money:* Using Financial Calculators

Learning Objectives
■ Adjust the number of digits displayed.
■ Adjust the frequency of payments as appropriate.
■ Clear the function registers after each problem.
■ Identify the time value of money keys including: *n, i, PV, PMT,* and FV.
■ Solve for: *n, i, PV, PMT,* and FV.
■ Identify the cash flow keys including: *CF, I, NPV,* and *IRR.*
■ Solve for: *CF, I, NPV,* and *IRR.*
■ Check the timing of the cash flows using the beginning and end functions.

Part VI *Foundations and Applications of the Time Value of Money:* Formulas

Learning Objectives
■ Describe the concept, notation, and application of various formulas.
■ Solve problems by calculating (using) various formulas.

Section II: Economics

Investment advisors and consultants should not only understand basic economic principles, but they should possess the skills necessary to analyze economic data. Using this knowledge they may revise investment recommendations and/or make appropriate portfolio adjustments if applicable. While drawing definitive conclusions from this analysis is often difficult, investment professionals should benefit by considering possible implications and overlaying this new filter of information over a fundamental, technical, or behavioral framework for constructing and managing investment portfolios.

The readings that follow discuss economic concepts and principles, the U.S. monetary system and the Federal Reserve System, business and economic cycles, and analysis of measurements designed to reflect or predict economic activity.

Part I *Handbook of Finance:* Monetary Policy—How the Fed Sets, Implements, and Measures Policy Choices

Learning Objectives

- Explain the purpose and structure of the U.S. Federal Reserve System (the "Fed").
- Describe the mandated goals of the Fed.
- List and describe key economic influences on Fed policy including: nonfarm payrolls, industrial production, housing starts, motor vehicle sales, commodity prices, the employment cost index, and nonfarm productivity growth.
- Define monetary policy and differentiate from fiscal policy.
- Describe and explain how monetary policy is implemented.
- Discuss the impact of monetary policy and its influence on the economy and financial markets.
- Discuss the issue of global credibility and confidence in central banks worldwide.

Part II *The Trader's Guide to Key Economic Indicators:* Introduction

Learning Objectives

- Describe the business cycle and discuss the history of U.S. business cycle durations.
- Discuss the history and relationship between gross domestic product (GDP) and recessions in the U.S.

Part III *The Trader's Guide to Key Economic Indicators:* Gross Domestic Product

Learning Objectives

- Define and describe gross domestic product (GDP).
- Compare and contrast GDP to gross national product (GNP).

- Discuss the composition of U.S. GDP.
- Describe implicit price deflators and solve for annualized inflation.
- Describe the impact of inflation on GDP and discuss real and nominal GDP throughout history.
- Discuss the history and explain the importance of consumption expenditures on the economy.
- Discuss the history and explain the importance of investment spending on the economy.
- Discuss the history and explain the importance of government spending on the economy.
- Discuss the history and explain the importance of net exports on the economy.
- Discuss the history and explain the importance of final sales on the economy.
- Discuss the history and explain the importance of corporate profits on the economy.
- Describe the output gap and how it impacts an economy's growth and productivity.

Part IV *The Trader's Guide to Key Economic Indicators:* Indexes of Leading, Lagging, and Coincident Indictors

Learning Objectives
- Discuss the historical timing of indexes relative to cyclical turning points.
- List and describe the four components of the Conference Board's coincident index including: number of employees on nonagricultural payrolls; personal income less transfer payments; industrial production index; and manufacturing and trade sales.
- List and describe the 10 components of the leading index including: average workweek, production workers, and manufacturing; average weekly initial claims for unemployment insurance; manufacturers' new orders for consumer goods and materials; ISM new orders index; manufacturers' new orders for nondefense capital goods, excluding aircraft; monthly building permits for new private housing; stock prices; leading Credit Index, M2 money supply prior to 1990; the interest rate spread between the 10-year Treasury bond and the federal funds rate; and the average consumer expectations for economic conditions.
- List and describe the seven components of the lagging index including: average duration of unemployment; ratio of manufacturing and trade inventories to sales; manufacturing labor cost per unit of output; average prime rate; commercial and industrial loans outstanding; ratio of consumer installment credit to personal income; and change in the consumer price index for services.
- Explain how each set of indicators are used to analyze the economy and discuss how each may be used by investment advisors and consultants to manage portfolios more effectively.

Section I: Time Value of Money

Part I The Basics of the Time Value of Money

Remember that time is money.

—Benjamin Franklin, *Advice to a Young Tradesman* (1748)

Most people are familiar with the Seven Wonders of the World: the Great Pyramid of Giza, the Hanging Gardens of Babylon, the Statue of Zeus at Olympia, the Temple of Artemis at Ephesus, the Mausoleum of Maussollos at Halicarnassus, the Colossus of Rhodes, and the Lighthouse of Alexandria. Supposedly, when Baron von Rothschild was asked if he could list the Seven Wonders, he said he could not. However, he did respond by saying that he could name the Eighth Wonder of the World: compound interest. Actually, labeling compound interest as the Eighth Wonder of the World has been attributed to other notable figures: Benjamin Franklin, Bernard Baruch, and Albert Einstein. Regardless of to whom we attribute this label, as you will see in this chapter, the label is appropriate.

One of the most important tools in personal finance and investing is the time value of money. Evaluating financial transactions requires valuing uncertain future cash flows; that is, determining what uncertain cash flows are worth at different points in time. We are often concerned about what a future cash flow or a set of future cash flows are worth today, though there are applications in which we are concerned about the value of a cash flow at a future point in time.

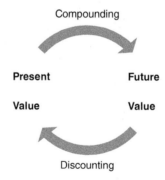

One complication is the *time value of money*: A dollar today is not worth a dollar tomorrow or next year. Another complication is that any amount of money promised in the future is uncertain, some riskier than others.

Moving money through time—that is, finding the equivalent value to money at different points in time—involves translating values from one period to another. Translating money from one period involves interest, which is how the time value of money and risk enter into the process.

Interest is the compensation for the opportunity cost of funds and the uncertainty of repayment of the amount borrowed; that is, it represents both the price of time and the price of risk. The price of time is compensation for the opportunity cost of funds—what someone could have done with the money elsewhere—and the price of risk is compensation for bearing risk. That is, the riskier the investment, the higher the interest rate.

Interest is *compound interest* if interest is paid on both the principal—the amount borrowed—and any accumulated interest. In other words, if you borrow $1,000 today for two years and the interest is 5 percent compound interest, at the end of two years you must repay the $1,000, plus interest on the $1,000 for two years and interest on the interest. The amount you repay at the end of two years is $1,102.50:

Repayment of principal		$1,000.00
Payment of interest on the principal—first year	5% of $1,000	50.00
Payment of interest on the principal—second year	5% of $1,000	50.00
Payment of interest in the second year on the interest from the first year	5% of $50	2.50
Total amount repaid at the end of the second year		$1,102.50

You can see the accumulation of values in Figure 4.1. The $2.50 in the second year is the interest on the first period's interest.

We refer to translating a value today into a value in the future as *compounding*, whereas *discounting* is translating a future value into the present.

The future value is the sum of the present value and interest:

$$\text{Future value} = \text{Present value} + \text{Interest}$$

Most financial transactions involve compound interest, though there are a few consumer transactions that use *simple interest*. Simple interest is the financing

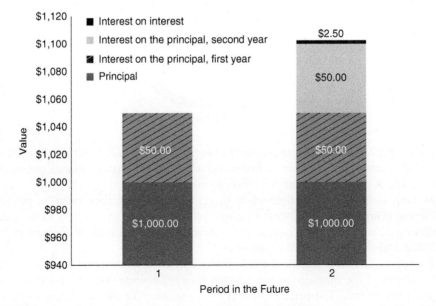

FIGURE 4.1   Components of the Future Value of $1,000 Invested at 5 Percent for Two Years

arrangement in which the amount repaid is the principal amount and interest on the principal amount. That is, interest is paid only on the principal or amount borrowed. For example, if you borrow $10,000 at 5 percent simple interest and repay the loan after two years, you must repay the $10,000, plus two periods interest at 5 percent:

$$\text{Repayment with simple interest} = \$10,000 + [\$10,000 \times 2 \times 0.05]$$

$$= \$11,000$$

In the case of compound interest, the amount repaid has three components:

1. The amount borrowed
2. The interest on the amount borrowed
3. The interest on interest

The *basic valuation equation* is the foundation of all the financial mathematics that involves compounding, and if you understand this equation, you understand most everything in financial mathematics:

$$FV = PV(1 + i)^n$$

where:

FV = the future value
PV = the present value
i = the rate of interest
n = is the number of compounding periods

The term $(1 + i)^n$ is the *compound factor*. When you multiply the value today—the present value—by the compound factor, you get the future value.

We can rearrange the basic valuation equation to solve for the present value, PV:

$$PV = FV \left[\frac{1}{(1 + i)^n} \right] = \frac{FV}{(1 + i)^n}$$

$$\uparrow$$
$$\text{Discount factor}$$

where $1 \div (1 + i)^n$ is the *discount factor*. When you multiply the value in the future by the discount factor, you get the present value.

In sum,

$$\frac{\text{Future}}{\text{value}} = \frac{\text{Present}}{\text{value}} \times \frac{\text{Compound}}{\text{factor}}$$

$$\frac{\text{Present}}{\text{value}} = \frac{\text{Future}}{\text{value}} \times \frac{\text{Discount}}{\text{value}}$$

Of Interest

The word *interest* is from the Latin word *intereo,* which means "to be lost." Interest developed from the concept that lending goods or money results in a loss to the lender because he or she did not have the use of the goods or money that is loaned.

In the English language, the word *usury* is associated with lending at excessive or illegal interest rates. In earlier times, however, usury (from the Latin *usura,* meaning "to use") was the price paid for the use of money or goods.

Compounding

We begin with compounding because this is the most straightforward way of demonstrating the effects of compound interest. Consider the following example: You invest $1,000 in an account today that pays 6 percent interest, compounded annually. How much will you have in the account at the end of one year if you make no withdrawals? Using the subscript to indicate the year the future value is associated with, after one year you will have

$$FV_1 = \$1{,}000(1 + 0.06) = \$1{,}060$$

After two years, the balance is

$$FV_2 = \$1{,}000(1 + 0.06)(1 + 0.06) = \$1{,}000(1 + 0.06)^2$$
$$= \$1{,}000(1.1236) = \$1{,}123.60$$

After five years, the balance is

$$FV_5 = \$1{,}000(1 + 0.06)^5 = \$1{,}000(1.3382) = \$1{,}338.23$$

After 10 years, the balance is

$$FV_{10} = \$1{,}000(1 + 0.06)^{10} = \$1{,}000(1.7908) = \$1{,}790.85$$

You can see the accumulation of interest from interest on the principal and interest on interest over time in Figure 4.2.

If you invest $1,000 today and receive $1,790.85 at the end of 10 years, we say that you have a return of 6 percent on your investment. This return is an average annual return, considering compounding.

Try It! 4.1: Savings

Suppose you deposit $1,000 in an account that earns 5 percent interest per year. If you do not make any withdrawals, how much will you have in the account at the end of 20 years?

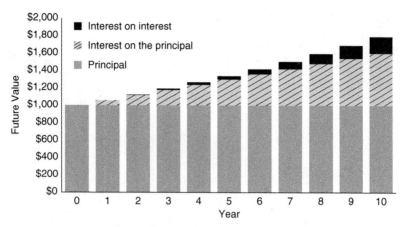

FIGURE 4.2   The Accumulation of Interest and Interest on Interest of a $1,000 Deposit with 6 Percent Compound Annual Interest

What if interest was not compounded interest, but rather simple interest? Then we would have a somewhat lower balance in the account after the first year. At the end of one year, with simple interest, you will have:

$$FV_1 = \$1,000 + [\$1,000(0.06)] = \$1,060$$

After two years:

$$FV_2 = \$1,000 + [\$1,000(0.06)] + [\$1,000(0.06)]$$
$$= \$1,000 + [\$1,000(0.06)(2)] = \$1,120$$

Financial Math in Action

Analysts often come up with estimates of growth in revenues and earnings for publicly traded companies. We can use these estimates to make projections.

Consider the Walt Disney Company. At the end of fiscal year 2008, analysts expected Disney's earnings to grow at a rate of 12.19 percent per year, in the long-term.* If Disney's earnings for fiscal year 2008 were $2.2788 per share and if we concur with the analysts, we can estimate the earnings per share for fiscal years into the future. For example, the estimate for the earnings per share for 2009 is

$$\$2.2788(1 + 0.1219) = \$2.5566 \text{ per share}$$

The estimate for 2010's earnings are

$$\$2.2788(1 + 0.1219)^2 = \$2.8682 \text{ per share}$$

The estimate for 2011's earnings are

$$\$2.2788 \times (1 + 0.1219)^3 = \$3.2179 \text{ per share}$$

*Estimates from Reuters.com/finance, accessed December 25, 2008.

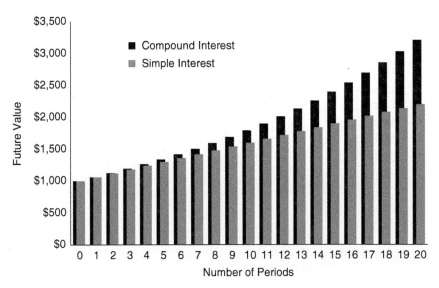

FIGURE 4.3   Future Value of $1,000 at a 6 Percent Interest Rate

After five years:

$$FV_5 = \$1,000 + [\$1,000\ (0.06)\ (5)] = \$1,300$$

And after 10 years:

$$FV_{10} = \$1,000 + [\$1,000\ (0.06)\ (10)] = \$1,600$$

You can see the difference between compounded and simple interest in Figure 4.3, in which we show the growth of $1,000 at 6 percent using both types of interest.

The difference between the future value with compounded interest and that with simple interest is the interest-on-interest. For example, at the end of 10 years the interest on interest is

Future value with compound interest	$1,790.85
Less future value with simple interest	$1,600.00
Interest on interest	$190.85

Most financial transactions involve compound interest. If the method of calculating interest is not stated, you should assume that the interest is compound interest.

EXAMPLE 4.1   Suppose that you invest $100,000 today in an investment that produces a return of 5 percent per year. What will the investment be worth in two years? Answer: **$110,250**.

We calculate the future value at the end of the second year, FV_2, as

$$FV_2 = \$100,000\,(1 + 0.05)^2 = \$100,000\,(1.1025) = \$110,250$$

EXAMPLE 4.2 Suppose you have a choice between two accounts, Account A and Account B. Account A provides 5 percent interest, compounded annually and Account B provides 5.25 percent simple interest. Which account provides the highest balance at the end of four years? Answer: Account A provides the higher balance at the end of four years. Consider a deposit of $10,000 today (though it really doesn't matter what the beginning balance is). What is the difference in the values of the two accounts? Answer: **$55.06**.

$$\text{Account A: } FV_4 = \$10,000 \times (1 + 0.05)^4 = \$12,155.06$$
$$\text{Account B: } FV_4 = \$10,000 + (\$10,000 \times 0.0525 \times 4) = \$12,100.00$$

The difference, $55.06, is the interest on interest.

Try It! 4.2: Loan Repayment

If you borrow $10,000 and the interest on the loan is 8 percent per year, all payable at the end of the loan, what is the amount that you must repay if the loan is for four years?

Calculator and Spreadsheet Solutions

The calculations are easier with the help of a financial calculator or a spreadsheet program. The calculator's financial functions assume compound interest. If you want to perform a calculation with simple interest, you must rely on the mathematical programs of your calculator.

The future value of $1,000, invested for 10 years at 6 percent, is $1,790.85, which we can calculate using a financial calculator or a spreadsheet with the following key strokes:

TI-83/84 (Using TVM Solver)	HP10B	Microsoft Excel
N = 10	1000 +/− PV	=FV(0.06,10,0,−1000)
I% = 6	10 N	
PV = −1000	6 I/YR	
PMT = 0	FV	
FV = *Solve*		

Calculation Tip

You will notice that we changed the sign on the PV when we put this information into the calculator. This is because of the way the calculator manufacturers program the financial function: assuming that the present value is the outflow. The changing of the sign for the present value is required in most (but not all) financial calculators and spreadsheets.

In the calculators, PV is the present value, N is the number of compound periods, I% or I/YR is the interest rate per period, and FV is the future value.

In Microsoft Excel®, the future value calculation uses the worksheet function FV:

$$=FV(\text{rate per period, number of periods, periodic payment,}$$
$$\text{present value, type})$$

Where "type" is 0 (indicating cash flows and values occur at the end of the period).* Using notation similar to that found on calculators, this command becomes

$$=FV(i,N,PMT,PV,0)$$

Because there are no other cash flows in this problem, PMT (which represents periodic cash flows, such as a mortgage payment) is zero. To calculate the FV, the function requires the following inputs:

$$=FV(.06,10,0,-1000,0)$$

---

*If we leave off the 0, this is assumed to be an end of period value.

Calculation Tip

In the financial functions of your calculator, the interest rate is represented as a whole number (that is, 6 for 6 percent), whereas in the math functions of your calculator and in spreadsheet functions, the interest rate is input in decimal form (that is, 0.06 for 6 percent).

If we want to use the math functions instead of the financial program of a calculator, you would need to use a power key, such as y^x or $\wedge$ and input the interest in decimal form:

TI-83/84	HP10B	Microsoft Excel
$(1+.06)\perp10$	$1+.06=$	$=1000*(1.06^{\wedge}10)$
ENTER	N y^x	
X1000	10 y^x	
ENTER	X1000	
	ENTER	

Why Can't I Calculate the Future Value with Simple Interest Using My Calculator Functions?

Calculators' time value of money programs are set up to perform calculations involving compound interest. If you want to calculate the future value using simple interest, you must resort to old-fashioned mathematics:

Simple interest = Principal amount × interest rate per period × number of periods

or

$$\text{Simple interest} = PV\,in$$

The future value of a lump-sum if interest is computed using simple interest is, therefore

$$FV_{\text{simple}} = PV + PV\,in = PV\,(1 + in)$$

If the present value is $1,000 and interest is simple interest at 5 percent per year, the future value after four periods is

$$FV_{\text{simple}} = \$1,000 + \$1,000\,(0.05)\,(4)$$

$$FV_{\text{simple}} = \$1,000\,(1 + 0.2) = \$1,200$$

The interest paid on interest in compounding is the difference between the future values with compound and simple interest.

Why not always use the financial functions in your calculator or spreadsheet? Because not every financial math problem fits neatly in the standard program and you may have to resort to the basic financial math.

Frequency of Compounding

If interest compounds more frequently than once per year, you need to consider this in any valuation problem involving compounded interest. Consider the following scenario.

You deposit $1,000 in an account at the beginning of the period, and interest is 12 percent per year, compounded quarterly.

This means that at the end of the first quarter, the account has a balance of

$$FV_{1\text{st quarter}} = \$1,000\left(1 + {0.12}\big/{4}\right) = \$1,000\,(1 + 0.03) = \$1,030$$

We calculate the quarters' balances in a like manner, with interest paid on the balance in the account:

$$FV_{2\text{nd quarter}} = \$1,030.00\,(1 + 0.03) = \$1,060.90$$
$$\Downarrow$$
$$FV_{3\text{rd quarter}} = \$1,060.90\,(1 + 0.03) = \$1,092.73$$
$$\Downarrow$$
$$FV_{4\text{th quarter}} = \$1,092.73\,(1 + 0.03) = \$1,125.51$$

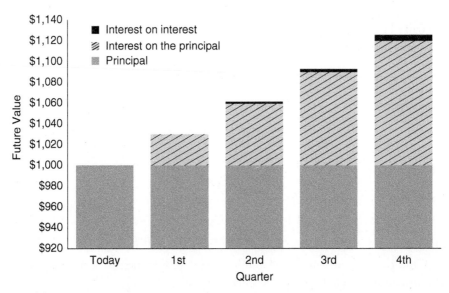

FIGURE 4.4   Growth of $1,000 in an Account with 12 Percent Interest per Year, Compounding Quarterly

Therefore, at the end of one year, there is a balance of $1,000 $(1 + 0.03)^4 =$ $1,125.51.

We show the growth of the funds in Figure 4.4.

When an interest rate is stated in terms of a rate per year, but interest is compounded more frequently than once per year, the stated annual rate is referred to as the *annual percentage rate* (APR), but the actual calculation requires using the rate per compound period and the number of compound periods. For example, if a loan of $5,000 for three years has an APR of 10 percent and interest compounds semiannually, the calculation of the future value at the end of three years uses:

$$i = \text{rate per compound period}$$
$$= 10\% \div 2 = 5\% \text{ per six months}$$
$$n = \text{number of compounding periods}$$
$$= 2 \text{ per year} \times 3 \text{ years} = 6 \text{ periods}$$

and, therefore,

$$FV_3 = \$5,000 \ (1 + 0.05)^6 = \$6,700.48$$

Notice that this future value is more than if we had ignored compounding of interest within a year, which would have produced a future value of $5,000 $(1 + 0.10)^3 = \$6,655$.

EXAMPLE 4.3   Suppose you invest $20,000 in an account that pays 12 percent interest, compounded monthly. How much do you have in the account at the end of five years? Answer: **$36,333.93**.

The number of periods is 60:

$$n = 5 \text{ years} \times 12 \text{ months per year} = 60 \text{ months}$$

and the rate per period is 1%:

$$i = \text{Rate per period} = 12\% \div 12 = 1\%$$

Therefore, the future value is $36,333.93. Using the math,

$$FV = \$20,000\,(1 + 0.01)^{60} = \$20,000\,(1.8167) = \$36,333.93$$

Using the financial calculator or spreadsheet time value of money functions:

TI-83/84	HP10B	Excel
PV −20000	20000 +/− PV	=FV(.01,60,0,−20000,0)
I 1	1 I/YR	
N 60	60 N	
FV Solve	FV	

Try It! 4.3: Frequency

Suppose you have a choice of borrowing $1 million with the following terms, with interest paid at the end of the loan:

10% APR, quarterly interest
10.5% APR, semi-annual interest
11% APR, annual interest

Under which loan terms would you have the largest payment at the end of four years?

Financial Math in Action

Credit card companies allow customers with balances to pay a minimum amount, instead of the full amount each month. What remains unpaid accumulates interest at sometimes quite high interest rates. Suppose you have charged $1,000 and choose to pay the minimum balance of 2 percent at the end of each month. And suppose your credit card company charges 29.99 percent APR interest, with monthly compounding.

How much will you owe after using the strategy of paying the minimum? Interest on unpaid balances is 29.99% ÷ 12 = 2.4992% per month:

Month from Now	Starting Balance	Interest for the Month	Balance Owed	Minimum Payment	Ending Balance
1	$1,000.00			$20.00	$980.00
2	$980.00	$24.49	$1,004.49	$20.09	$984.40
3	$984.40	$24.60	$1,009.00	$20.18	$988.82
4	$988.82	$24.71	$1,013.54	$20.27	$993.27
5	$993.27	$24.82	$1,018.09	$20.36	$997.73
6	$997.73	$24.93	$1,022.66	$20.45	$1,002.21
7	$1,002.21	$25.05	$1,027.26	$20.55	$1,006.71
8	$1,006.71	$25.16	$1,031.87	$20.64	$1,011.23
9	$1,011.23	$25.27	$1,036.50	$20.73	$1,015.77
10	$1,015.77	$25.39	$1,041.16	$20.82	$1,020.34
11	$1,020.34	$25.50	$1,045.84	$20.92	$1,024.92
12	$1,024.92	$25.61	$1,050.53	$21.01	$1,029.52

In other words, you will end up owing more at the end of the month.

What we have seen so far with respect to compounding is discrete or periodic compounding. However, many financial transactions, including credit card financing, involve *continuous compounding*. This is the extreme of the frequency of compounding, because interest compounds instantaneously. If interest compounds continuously, the compound factor uses the exponential function, e, which is the inverse of the natural logarithm.[1] The compound factor for continuous compounding requires the stated rate per year (that is, the APR) and the number of years:

$$e^{(\text{Annual interest rate}) \times (\text{Number of years})} = e^{\text{APR } n}$$

If annual interest is 10 percent, continuously compounded, the compound factor for one year is

$$e^{0.10} = 1.1052$$

For two years, the factor is

$$e^{0.10 \times 2} = e^{0.20} = 1.2214$$

For 10 years, the factor is

$$e^{0.10 \times 10} = e^{1} = 2.7183$$

The formula for the future value of an amount with continuous compounding is:

$$FV = PV\left[e^{APR\,n}\right]$$

The compound factor is $e^{\text{APR}\,n}$.

You can view continuous compounding as the limit of compounding frequency. Consider $1 million deposited in an account for five years, where this account pays 10 percent interest. With annual compounding, this deposit grows to

$$FV_{5,\text{ annual compounding}} = \$1,610,510$$

With continuous compounding, this deposit grows to

$$FV_{5,\text{ continuous compounding}} = \$1,648,721$$

You can see the difference between annual compounding and continuous compounding in Figure 4.5. At the end of 40 years, the difference between continuous compounding and annual compounding is over $9 million.

Using a calculator, you can find e^x in the math functions. For example, suppose you want to calculate the future value of $1,000 invested five years at 4 percent, with interest compounded continuously. The future value is:

$$FV_5 = \$1,000\ e^{0.04 \times 5} = \$1,000\ e^{0.2} = \$1,000\ (1.2214) = \$1,221.40$$

Using Microsoft Excel, you use the exponential worksheet function, EXP:

$$=1000 * EXP(0.04 * 5)$$

where the value in parentheses is the exponent.

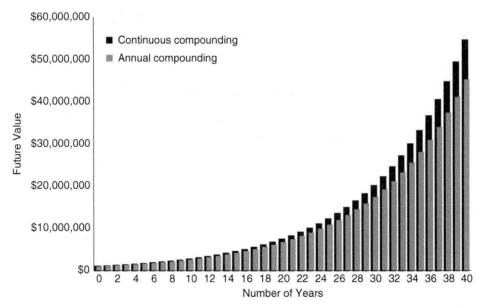

FIGURE 4.5 The Value of $1 Million at 10 Percent Interest, Compounded Annually vs. Continuously

---

Calculation Tip

The programmers of financial calculator and spreadsheet financial functions set these up for discrete compounding. You will need to use the math functions of the calculator or the spreadsheet to perform calculations for continuous compounding.

EXAMPLE 4.4 Suppose you invest $1,000 today in an account that pays 9 percent interest, compounded continuously. What will be the value in this account at the end of 10 years? Answer: **$2,459.60**.

The future value is $2,459.60:

$$FV = \$1,000 \; e^{0.09 \times 10} = \$1,000 \; e^{0.9}$$

$$= \$1,000 \,(2.4596) = \$2,459.60$$

EXAMPLE 4.5 Suppose you invest $5,000 in an account that earns 10 percent interest. How much more would you have after 20 years if interest compounds continuously instead of compounded semiannually? Answer: **$1,745.34**.

You would have $1,745.34 more:

$$FV_{continuously} = \$5,000 \; e^{0.1 \times 20}$$

$$= \$5,000 \,(7.3891) = \$36,945.28$$

$$FV_{semiannually} = \$5,000 \,(1 + 0.05)^{40}$$

$$= \$5,000 \,(7.0400) = \$35,199.94$$

$$Difference = \$36,945.28 - 35,199.94 = \$1,745.34$$

Try It! 4.4: Continuous Compounding

If you borrow $10,000 and the interest on the loan is 8 percent per year, compounded continuously, what is the amount that you must repay at the end of four years?

Summary

Understanding how compounding works helps you understand financial transactions, including how investments grow in value over time. The basic valuation equation, $FV = PV \,(1 + i)^n$, is the foundation of all of the financial math that you'll encounter in finance. What we will do in the following chapters is to build upon this basic valuation equation, and help you to understand how to translate future values to the present, calculate the yield or return on investments, calculate effective interest rates, amortize a loan, and value stocks and bonds.

While calculators and spreadsheets are very helpful, it is also important to understand the underlying math—because you might just encounter a financial transaction that doesn't fit neatly into one of these functions.

"Try It!" Solutions

4.1 Savings

$$\text{Amount on deposit} = \$1,000\,(1+0.05)^{20} = \$2,653.30$$

4.2 Loan Repayment

$$\text{Amount of repayment} = \$10,000\,(1+0.08)^{4} = \$13,604.89$$

Using a financial calculator: $PV = -10,000$; $i\% = 8$, $n = 4$. Solve for FV

4.3 Frequency of Compounding

The 10.5 percent with semiannual compounding requires the largest repayment:

$$FV_{\text{10\% APR, quarterly compounding}} = \$1,000,000\,(1+0.025)^{16} = \$1,484,505$$

$$FV_{\text{10.5\% APR, semiannual compounding}} = \$1,000,000\,(1+0.0525)^{8} = \$1,505,833$$

$$FV_{\text{10.75\% APR, annual compounding}} = \$1,000,000\,(1+0.1075)^{4} = \$1,504,440$$

4.4 Continuous Compounding

$$\text{Amount of repayment} = \$10,000\,e^{(0.08)(4)} = \$10,000\,e^{0.32} = \$13,771.28$$

Note

1. The "e" in the exponential function is also referred to as Euler's e, or the base of the natural logarithm. The numerical value of e truncated to 10 decimal places is 2.7182818284.

Part II Don't Discount Discounting

Remember, that money is of the prolific, generating nature. Money can beget money, and its offspring can beget more, and so on.

—Benjamin Franklin, *Advice to a Young Tradesman* (1748)

Much of what is done in valuing an asset, a company, a share of stock, or a bond, involves translating a future value to the present. We refer to translating a value back in time as *discounting*, which requires determining what a future amount or cash flow is worth today. Discounting is used in valuation because we often want to determine the value today of some future value or cash flow (e.g., what a bond is worth today if it promised interest and principal repayment in the future).

Discounting

The equation for the present value is a rearrangement of the basic valuation equation that we saw earlier:

$$PV = \frac{FV}{(1 + i)^n}$$

where

>   PV = the present value (today's value)
>   FV = the future value (a value or cash flow sometime in the future)
> i = the interest rate per period
> n = the number of compounding periods

From this formula for the present value we know that:

>   As the number of discount periods, n, becomes larger, the discount factor becomes smaller and the present value becomes less.
>   As the interest rate per period, i, becomes larger, the discount factor becomes smaller and the present value becomes less.

The discount rate is similar in concept to the interest rate in compounding values into the future—but with discounting, we are bringing values from the future to the present. For example, if you have some funds you want to put into an account today so that you have a specific balance in an account at a given time in the future, the discount rate is the interest rate that you would have to earn on the funds you set aside today so that you reach this goal.

In investing, the discount rate represents the *opportunity cost of funds*—that is, what you could have earned for the same level of risk. In other words, what else could you have done with the money?

i, r, k ...What's the Difference?

In this book, we use the lowercase "i" to indicate the interest rate. If you look at other books and website documents related to our topic, you will see other notations for the interest rate, including r for return or the required rate of return, and k for the cost of capital. These really represent the same concept: the time value of money.

We use "i" (despite our word processor's attempt to turn every lowercase i into the first-person singular pronoun, "I") to keep it simple and to remind you that it means interest. When we refer to the calculator functions, we use the notation that is closest to what appears on the calculator key, which is often I/YR.

We represent the time value of money by different notations, and by different names, depending on the application. For example:

Name	Common Application
Interest rate	Compounding
Discount rate	Discounting
Required rate of return	Return expected by investors, used in valuing securities, such as stocks and bonds
Cost of capital	Evaluating capital investments (e.g., buying a new plant), reflecting the cost of funds provided by bondholders and shareholders
Opportunity cost of funds	Evaluating competing investment opportunities

EXAMPLE 4.6   Suppose that you wish to have $20,000 saved by the end of six years. And suppose you deposit funds today in an account that pays 3 percent interest, compounded annually. How much must you deposit today to meet your goal?

You are given: FV = $20,000; $n = 6$; $i = 3\%$

Solve for the present value, PV:

$$PV = \$20,000 \div (1 + 0.03)^6 = \$20,000 \div 1.1941 = \$16,749.69$$

EXAMPLE 4.7   Suppose that you wish to have $1 million forty years from now. If you deposit funds today in an account that pays 5 percent interest, compounded annually, what amount must you deposit today to reach your goal? You are given the following data inputs:

$$FV = \$1,000,000$$
$$n = 40$$
$$i = 5\%$$

The present value is

$$PV = \$1,000,000 \div (1 + 0.05)^{40} = \$142,045.68$$

Looking at this same concept in terms of the opportunities, consider the type of problem in which you are promised a specific amount of funds at some future point in time. How much would you be willing to pay now for this investment considering what you could otherwise do with these funds in terms of investing? For example, suppose someone offered you an investment that would pay a lump sum of $10,000 five years from today. If your opportunity cost of funds is 5 percent, you should be willing to pay

$$PV = €10,000 \div (1 + 0.05)^5 = €10,000 \div 1.2763 = €7,835.26$$

To check this, consider the investment of $7.835.26 for five years in an account that pays 5 percent interest. The future value is

$$FV = €7,835.26 \times (1 + 0.05)^5 = €10,000$$

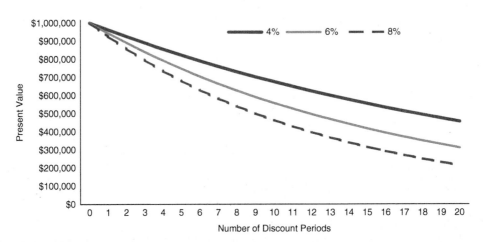

FIGURE 4.6 Present Value of $1 Million for a Different Number of Discount Periods and Different Discount Rates

If instead of 5 percent, your opportunity cost is 10 percent, the present value of this investment is

$$PV = €10,000 \div (1 + 0.10)^5 = €10,000 \div 1.6105 = €6,209.21$$

The discount rate affects the present value: the greater the discount rate, the lower the present value. The number of periods also affects the present value: the greater the number of discount periods, the lower the present value. (See Figure 4.6.)

Consider another problem. Suppose we discount $1 million to the present. If we discount this $1 million for five periods at 4 percent, the present value is

$$PV = \frac{\$1,000,000}{(1 + 0.04)^5} = \frac{\$1,000,000}{1.2167} = \$821,927.11$$

Discounting this same future value 10 periods at 4 percent produces a smaller present value:

$$PV = \frac{\$1,000,000}{(1 + 0.04)^{10}} = \frac{\$1,000,000}{1.4802} = \$675,564.17$$

We graph the present value of $1 million for different numbers of discount periods in Figure 4.6. As you can see in this graph, the slope of the relation between the present value and the number of discount periods is steeper, the greater the discount rate

We also graph the present value of $1 million for a different number of periods in Figure 4.7. As you can see in this Figure 4.7, the greater the number of discount periods, the more sensitive is the present value to the discount rate.

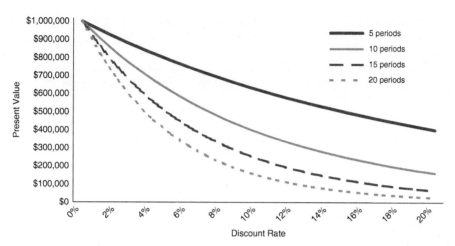

FIGURE 4.7   Present Value of $1 Million for a Different Number of Discount Periods and Different Discount Rates

Calculator and Spreadsheet Solutions

Calculate the present value of $6,000 to be received in eight years if the interest rate is 5 percent per year:

$$PV = \frac{\$6,000}{(1.05)^8} = \$4,061.04$$

The present value is $4,061.04. Using a financial calculator or spreadsheet, we need to input the number of periods, the interest rate, and the future value. In Microsoft Excel® we use the present value function:

=PV(RATE,NPER,PMT,FV,type)

where

RATE = the interest rate, stated in decimal form
NPER = the number of periods
PMT = 0 in this case because we are assuming no other cash flows.
FV   = the future value
type = reflects the timing (0 or end of period, the usual assumption, and 1 for the beginning of the period)

The last argument in the function, *type*, is optional. If you leave this off the list of arguments, the program assumes that the cash flows occur at the end of the period instead of the beginning of the period.

When you use a calculator, the order in which you enter the known values of PV, *i, n,* and so on, does not matter. However, when using a spreadsheet function, it is important to enter the arguments (the rate, the number of periods, etc.), in order. Providing the inputs in the wrong order will guarantee a wrong answer.

Using our notation, the present value function in Microsoft Excel is

=PV(i,n,PMT,FV,type)

Using financial calculators or a spreadsheet, the calculation of the present value of $6,000 discounted eight periods at 5 percent is the following:

TI-83/84 (Using TVM Solver)	HP10B	Microsoft Excel
N = 8	8 N	=PV(.05,8,0,60000,0)
I% = 5	5 I/YR	
FV = 6000	6000 FV	
PMT = 0	PV	
PV = Solve		

If you are using a financial calculator or spreadsheet, you will notice that the calculated present value is displayed as a negative number. This has to do with the way the program is written for the calculator; it is written such that $0 = FV - PV(1 + i)^n$. Think of the calculation in the following way: If you invest $4,061.04 (which is a cash outflow) today, you get $6,000 in the future (which is a cash inflow). We will refer to values in the positive, but if you are using a calculator or spreadsheet, you will need to mentally or actually multiply the resulting present value by negative one for a cleaner interpretation.

Calculation Tip

If you want to take a value to power (e.g., 1.05^8), you generally key in the base (e.g., 1.05) and then use the key marked as ^ or y^x: $(1 + 0.05)^8 = 1.4775$. To invert a value (e.g., $1 \div 1.4775$), use the key marked 1/x: $1 \div 1.4775 = 0.6768$.

Try It! 4.5: Discounting

What is the value today of $500,000 to be received in 10 years, with an interest rate of 7 percent?

Frequency of Compounding

Suppose that interest compounds more frequently than annually. We must therefore adjust both i and n to reflect this more frequent compounding. Consider an example: calculate the present value of $10,000 due at the end of five years if the annual interest rate is 6 percent, compounded semiannually. If the annual rate is 6 percent, the semiannual rate is $6\% \div 2 = 3\%$. The number of semiannual periods is five years × 2 times per year = 10. Therefore, the present value of this $10,000 is

$$PV = \$10{,}000 \div (1 + 0.03)^{10} = \$10{,}000 \div 1.3439 = \$10{,}000 \times 0.7441 = \$7{,}440.94$$

Try It! 4.6: Discounting and Frequency of Compounding

Which of the following requires the least amount of a deposit today?

A balance of $10,000, four years from today that has grown from a sum deposited in an account that pays 8 percent interest, compounded quarterly.

A balance of $10,000, five years from today that has grown from a sum deposited in an account that pays 7 percent interest, compounded annually.

A balance of $10,000, 10 years from today that has grown from a sum deposited in an account that pays 4 percent interest, compounded continuously.

A balance of $10,000, eight years from today that has grown from a sum deposited in an account that pays 4 percent interest, compounded semi-annually.

If interest compounds continuously, the present value is

$$PV = \frac{FV}{e^{APR\ n}}$$

where APR is the annual percentage rate, n is the number of years, and e is the base of the natural logarithm. For example, what is the present value of $10,000 due at the end of five years if the interest rate is 6 percent, compounded continuously? The answer is $7,408.18, that is,

$$PV = \$10{,}000 \div e^{0.06 \times 5} = \$10{,}000 \div e^{0.30}$$

$$= \$10{,}000 \div 1.3499 = \$10{,}000 \times 0.7408 = \$7{,}408.18$$

We can see the difference the frequency of compounding makes in Figure 4.8, in which we expand this last example to include quarterly and continuous compounding. For a given annual percentage rate, the greater the frequency of compounding, the greater is the effective interest rate and the smaller is the present value. But as you can also see in Figure 4.8 the difference may be quite small.

EXAMPLE 4.8 How much would you have to deposit today in an account that pays 4 percent annual interest, compounded quarterly, if you wish to have a balance of $100,000 at the end of 10 years? You are given the following data inputs:

$FV = \$100{,}000,$

$i = 4\% \div 4 = 1\%$

$n = 10 \times 4 = 40$ quarters

$PV = \$100{,}000 \div (1 + 0.01)^{40} = \$100{,}000(0.6717) = \$67{,}165.31$

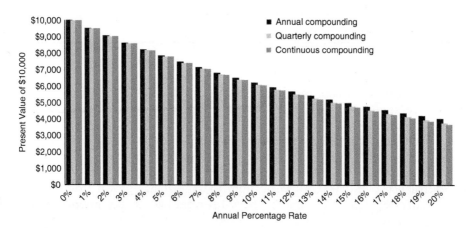

FIGURE 4.8   Discounting $10,000 for Five Years for Different Annual Percentage Rates and Different Frequencies of Compounding

EXAMPLE 4.9   How much would you have to deposit today in an account that pays 4 percent annual interest, compounded continuously, if you wish to have a balance of $100,000 at the end of 10 years? You are given the following information:

$$FV = \$100,000$$

$$i = 4\%$$

$$n = 10 \text{ years}$$

$$PV = \$100,000 \div e^{0.04 \times 10} = \$100,000 \, (0.67032) = \$67,032$$

EXAMPLE 4.10   Suppose you have two investment opportunities that promise $1 million in 20 years:

Investment A: A return of 6 percent per year, compounded monthly.
Investment B: A return of 5.8 percent per year, compounded continuously.

Which investment requires a larger investment today to reach your goal? Answer: **Investment B.**

$$PV_A = \$1,000,000 \div (1 + (0.06/12))240 = \$302,096.14$$
$$PV_B = \$1,000,000 \times (e^{0.058 \times 20}) = \$313,486.18$$

Try It! 4.7: Discounting with Continuous Compounding

Consider an investment, Investment X, which is a promise to pay $10,000 five years from now. You are comparing this investment with another investment, Investment Y, of similar risk, that is a promised yield of 6 percent per year, compounded continuously, over the same time. What would you be willing to pay for Investment X so that you are indifferent between Investment X and Y? In other words, what would the present value of Investment X have to be to have equivalent value to Investment Y?

Discounting More Than One Future Value

In many cases, we need to discount more than one future amount to determine the value of some investment. For example, in the case of a stock, the value of the stock depends on the expected future dividends. As another example, the value of a bond is the present value of the interest and repayment of bond principal expected in the future.

Consider an investment that promises $1,000 at the end of one year, $2,000 at the end of two years, and $3,000 at the end of three years. If the discount rate is 5 percent, what is the value of this investment today?

Diagramming these cash flows, we see the following:

Today	1	2	3	*Period*
	|	|	|	
	$1,000	$2,000	$3,000	*Cash flow*

Discounting each the cash flows for the appropriate number of periods results in a value today for the investment of $5,357.95:

Today	1	2	3
	|	|	|
	$1,000	$2,000	$3,000
$952.38 ⇐1000(1.05)1	⇏		
$1,814.06		⇐2000(1.05)2 ⇏	
$2,591.51			⇐3000(1.05)3 ⇏
$5,357.95			

To check our work, we could recognize that discounting these cash flows to the present is equivalent to first determining what these cash flows are worth at the end of three years—similar to a savings problem—and then discounting this value to the present. The future value of the cash flows in this example is:

Cash Flow	Future Value
$1,000	$1,102.50
$2,000	2,100.00
$3,000	3,000.00
Total	$6,202.50

Discounting the $6,202.50 three periods at 5 percent produces a present value of $5,357.95. What this check on our work shows is that implicit in the discounting calculation is an assumption that when you receive cash flows from an investment, we are assuming that we reinvest these cash flows into another investment that yields the same return—in this case 5 percent.

EXAMPLE 4.11   Suppose a friend wants to borrow some money from you and is willing to pay you back $5,000 two years from now and then $7,000 four years from today. If your opportunity cost of funds is 5 percent (that is, what you could have earned on the money in an investment with similar risk to a loan to your friend), how much are you willing to lend your friend? Answer: **$10,194.07**.

Period	Cash Flow	Calculation	Present Value
1	$0		$0
2	$5,000	$5,000(1+0.05)2	4,435.15
3	$0		0
4	$7,000	$7,000(1+0.05)4	5,758.92
Total			$10,194.07
Total		$6,202.50	

Calculator Solutions

The calculation of the present value of more than one cash flow is easier with built-in programs. The present value of more than one future cash flow is the net present value.

Using the calculator to determine the value today of a series of future cash flows is straightforward. In a calculator, this requires identifying the cash flows in the future in chronological order. If there are periods in the future in which there are no cash flows, then this needs to be included in the series of cash flows.

Consider the following series of cash flows:

End of Period	Cash Flow
1	$1,000
2	$0
3	$5,000
4	$0
5	$6,000

TEXAS INSTRUMENTS TI 83/84   In the TI-83/84 calculators, you create a series consisting of the set of cash flows. Once you save these in the calculator, you then apply the NPV function. What you enter in the NPV function is the following:

NPV(5, 0, {1000, 0, 500, 0, 6000})

where the first argument is the whole percentage interest rate, the next argument is the cash flow today (which is zero in this example), and the last argument is the list of cash flows. Alternatively to creating the list using the {} and STO, you can use the LIST function and enter the cash flows as a list and then use the NPV function that resides in the APPS.

HEWLETT-PACKARD HP10B   In the HP10B, you need to input these cash flows one at a time, including the zero cash flows, and then use the NPV function to solve for the present value. Note that we must enter the initial cash flow, that is, today's cash flow, first, followed by each successive period's cash flows.

MICROSOFT EXCEL   In Microsoft Excel, the function is similar to that used in the TI83/84. You type the values of the cash flows into adjacent cells, then use the NPV function, including the discount rate as the first argument, followed by the list of the cash flows or the reference to the cells that contain the cash flows.[1]

TI-83/84 Using NPV function	HP10B	Microsoft Excel		
2nd {1000,0,5000,0,6000}	0 CF_j		A	B
STO 2nd L1	1000 CF_j	1	Period	Cash flow
ENTER	0 CF_j	2	1	$1,000
APPS	5000 CF_j	3	2	$0
1:Finance ENTER	0 CF_j	4	3	$5,000
7:NPV ENTER	6000 CF_j	5	4	$0
(5, 2nd L1)	5 i	6	5	$6,000
ENTER	NPV	7	NPV	← = NPV(.05,B3:b7)

Try It! 4.8: Discounting with More Than One Cash Flow

Joe says that he can pay you $1,000 after one year and $2,000 after three years. If your opportunity cost of funds is 5 percent, how much are you willing to lend to Joe?

Determining the Number of Compounding Periods

Let's say that you place $1,000 in a savings account that pays 10 percent compounded interest per year. How long would it take the savings account balance to reach $5,000? In this case, we know the present value (PV = $1,000), the future value (FV = $5,000), and the interest rate (i = 10 percent per year). What we need to determine is the number of compounding periods.

Start with the basic valuation equation and insert the known values of PV, FV, and i:

$$FV = PV\,(1 + i)^n$$

$$\$5{,}000 = \$1{,}000\,(1 + 0.10)^n$$

Rearranging,

$$(1 + 0.10)^n = 5.000$$

Therefore, the compound factor is 5.0000.

We can determine the number of periods either mathematically or by using a financial calculator.[2] Solving the equation mathematically, we start with the following:

$$5 = (1 + 0.10)^n$$

We must somehow rearrange this equation so that the unknown value, n, is on one side of the equation and all the known values are on the other. To do this, we must use logarithms and a bit of algebra. Taking the natural log of both sides,

$$\ln 5 = n \times \ln(1 + 0.10)$$

or

$$\ln 5 = n \times \ln 1.10$$

where "ln" indicates the natural log. Substituting the values of the natural logs of 5 and 1.10, which we can calculate using most any calculator, we arrive at

$$1.6094 = n \times 0.0953.$$

Rearranging and solving for n,

$$n = 16.8877$$

which means 17 whole compound periods.

Because the last interest payment is at the end of the last year, the number of periods is 17—it would take 17 years for your $1,000 investment to grow to $5,000 if interest is compounded at 10 percent per year.

We can develop an equation for determining the number of periods, beginning with the valuation formula:

$$FV = PV\,(1 + i)^n$$

Using algebra and principles of logarithms,

$$n = \frac{\ln FV - \ln PV}{\ln(1 + i)}$$

Suppose that the present value of an investment is $100 and you wish to determine how long it will take for the investment to double in value if the investment earns 6 percent per year, compounded annually:

$$n = \frac{\ln 200 - \ln 100}{\ln(1 + 0.06)} = 11.8885 \Rightarrow 12 \text{ years}$$

Notice that we round off to the next whole period. To see why, consider this last example. After 11.8885 years, we have doubled our money if interest were paid 88.85 percent all the way through the twelfth year. But, we stated earlier that interest is paid at the end of each period—not part of the way through. At the end of the eleventh year, our investment is worth $189.93, and at the end of the twelfth year, our investment is worth $201.22. So our investment's value doubles by the twelfth period—with a little extra, $1.22.

But, of course, we could resort to using our financial calculator or spreadsheet functions to arrive at the number of periods:

TI-83/84 Using TVM Solver	HP10B	Microsoft Excel
PV = −100	100 +/− PV	=NPER(.06,0,−100,200,0)
PMT = 0	200 FV	
FV = 200	6 *i*/YR	
I% = 6	N	
N = Solve		

EXAMPLE 4.12 How long does it take to double your money if the interest rate is 5 percent per year, compounded annually? Answer: **15 years**.

$$\textit{Inputs: } PV = \$1; \ FV = \$2; \ i = 5\%$$

Solving for *n*:

$$n = (\ln \ 2 - \ln \ 1) \div \ln \ 1.05$$
$$= (0.6931 - 0) \div 0.0488$$
$$= 14.2029 \Rightarrow 15 \text{ years}$$

EXAMPLE 4.13 How long does it take to triple your money if the interest rate is 5 percent per year, compounded annually? Answer: **23 years**.

$$\textit{Inputs: } PV = \$1; \ FV = \$3; \ i \ = 5\%$$

Solving for *n*:

$$n = (\ln \ 3 - \ln \ 1) \div \ln \ 1.05$$
$$= (1.0986 - 0) \div 0.0488$$
$$= 22.5123 \text{ years} \Rightarrow 23 \text{ years}$$

EXAMPLE 4.14 How long does it take to double your money if the interest rate is 12 percent per year, compounded quarterly? Answer: **6 years**.

$$\textit{Inputs: } PV = \$1; \ FV = \$2; \ i = 12\% \div 4 = 3\%$$

Solving for n:

$$n = (0.6931 - 0) \div 0.0296$$

$$= 23.4155 \text{ quarters} \Rightarrow 24 \text{ quarters} = 6 \text{ years}$$

Try It! 4.9: Are We There Yet?

Suppose you deposit $1,000 in an account paying 9 percent APR interest, with monthly compounding. How long will it take this deposit to grow, with interest, to reach $10,000?

Summary

The discounting of future values is the foundation of valuation. We use discounting to determine how much we are willing to pay to receive a future amount or how much we need to deposit in an account today to achieve some savings goal. The rate at which we discount relates to the opportunity cost of funds. The greater this opportunity cost, the lower the present value. If the discount rate involves compounding of interest more than once within an annual period, the present value must reflect this compounding.

"Try It!" Solutions

4.5 Discounting

Inputs: $i = 7\%$, $n = 10$; $FV = 500,000$. Solve for the present value:

$$PV = \$254,174.65$$

4.6 Discounting and the Frequency of Compounding
        The continuous compounding arrangement has the smallest present value:
(a) $PV_a = \$10,000 \div (1 + 0.02)^{16} = \$7,284.46$
(b) $PV_b = \$10,000 \div (1 + 0.07)^5 = \$7,129.86$
(c) $PV_c = \$10,000 \div e^{(0.04)(10)} = \$6,703.20$
(d) $PV_d = \$10,000 \div (1 + 0.02)^{16} = \$7,284.46$

4.7 Discounting with Continuous Compounding

$$PV \text{ of Investment } X = \$10,000 \div e^{0.06 \times 5} = \$10,000 \div 1.34986 = \$7,409.18$$

4.8 Discounting with More Than One Cash Flow

$$PV = [\$1,000 \div 1.05] + [\$3,000 \times (1.05)^3] = \$952.38 + 2,591.51 = \$3,543.89$$

4.9 Are We There Yet?

$$PV = \$1,000; i = 9\% \div 12 = 0.75\%; \ FV = \$10,000$$

$$n = [\ln(10,000) - \ln(1000)] \div \ln(1 + 0.0075)$$

$$= [9.21034 - 6.90776] \div 0.007472 = 308.16 \text{ months} \rightarrow 309 \text{ months}$$

$$= \textbf{25 years, 9 months}$$

Notes

1. If there is an initial cash flow (that is, one today), we subtract it after the NPV calculation. For example, if this investment requires a $5,000 initial investment, the net present value would be calculated as: =NPV(0.05,B3:B7) − 5,000.
2. In the "olden" days, we used a table of factors to approximate the number of periods. We would look at the discount factors and find the factor for 10 percent interest that is closest to the factor of 5.

Part III Cash Happens

Price is what you pay. Value is what you get.

—Warren Buffett

When you value an investment, you compare the benefits of the investment with its cost. The process of valuation involves estimating future cash inflows and outflows, and discounting these future cash flows to the present at a discount rate that reflects the uncertainty of these cash flows. Another way of evaluating investments is to answer the question: Given its cost and its expected future benefits, what return will a particular investment provide? We will look at how to calculate the value and the return on investments, focusing on stocks in this reading.

Suppose your investment advisor suggests the following investment opportunity: Invest $900 today, and you will receive $1,000 one year from today. Whether or not this is a good deal depends on:

What you could have done with the $900 instead of investing it with the investment advisor.

How uncertain are you that the investment advisor will pay the $1,000 in one year.

If your other opportunities with the same amount of uncertainty provide a return of 10 percent, is this loan a good investment? There are two ways to evaluate this. First, you can figure out what you could have wound up with after one year, investing your $900 at 10 percent:

Value at end of one year = $900 + (10% of $900)
Value at end of one year = $900 (1 + 0.10)
Value at end of one year = $990

Because the $1,000 promised is more than $990, you are better off with the investment the advisor offers you.

Another way of looking at this is to figure out what the $1,000 promised in the future is worth today. To calculate its present value, we must discount the $1,000 at some rate. The rate we'll use is our opportunity cost of funds, which in this case is 10 percent:

$$\text{Value today of \$1,000 in one year} = \frac{\$1,000}{(1+0.10)^1} = \$909.09$$

This means that you consider $909.09 today to be worth the same as $1,000 in one year. In other words, if you invested $909.09 today in an investment that yields 10 percent, you end up with $1,000 in one year. Since today's value of the receipt of $1,000 in the future is $909.09 and it costs only $900 to get into this deal, the investment is attractive: It costs less than what you have determined it is worth.

Because there are two ways to look at this, through its future value or through its present value, which way should you go? While both approaches get you to the same decision, it is usually easier in terms of the present value of the investment.

Valuing a Stream of Future Cash Flows

We can generalize this relationship a bit more. Let CF_t represent the cash flow from the investment in period t, so that CF_1 is the cash flow at the end of period 1, CF_2 is the cash flow at the end of period 2, and so on, until the last cash flow at the end of period n, CFN. If the investment produces cash flows for a finite number of periods, n, and the discount rate is i, the value of the investment, the present value, is

$$\text{Present value of investment} = \frac{CF_1}{(1+i)^1} + \frac{CF_2}{(1+i)^2} + \frac{CF_3}{(1+i)^3} + \cdots + \frac{CF_n}{(1+i)^n}$$

which we can write more compactly as

$$PV = \sum_{t=1}^{n} \frac{CF_t}{(1+i)^t}$$

Suppose you have an opportunity to buy an asset expected to give you $500 in one year and $600 in two years. If your other investment opportunities with the same amount of risk give you a return of 5 percent a year, how much are you willing to pay today to get these two future receipts?

We can figure this out by discounting the $500 one period at 5 percent and the second $600 two periods at 5 percent:

$$\text{Present value of investment} = \frac{\$500}{(1+0.05)^1} + \frac{\$600}{(1+0.05)^2}$$

$$\text{Present value of investment} = \$476.19 + \$544.22 = \$1,020.41$$

Using a financial calculator's or spreadsheet's net present value (NPV) function, we can arrive at the same present value.[1] The NPV program requires you to input all cash flow, beginning with the cash flow in the next period, in order, and specifying the interest rate:

TI-83/84	HP10B	Microsoft Excel
{500,600} STO	0 CF$_j$	=NPV(.05,500,600)
listname	500 CF$_j$	
NPV(5,0, *listname*)	600 CF$_j$	
	5 I/YR	
	NPV	

Why didn't we use the spreadsheet or financial calculator time value of money functions and solve for PV? Because we are not dealing with a single cash flow in the future or a series of cash flows that are the same, rather, we have two cash flows and they are of different amounts. We need to use the calculator or spreadsheet's net present value function to solve this problem. Therefore, the present value of these flows is $1,020.41.[2]

In cases in which you require a present value of uneven cash flows, you can use a program in your financial calculator, the *net present value,* or *NPV,* program.

This investment is worth $1,020.41 today, so you will be willing to pay $1,020.41 or less for this investment:

If you pay more than $1,020.41, you get a return less than 5 percent.
If you pay less than $1,020.41 you get a return more than 5 percent.
If you pay $1,020.41 you get a return of 5 percent.

We can look at this problem from a different perspective, solving for the return on the investment. Suppose you pay $1,000 for the investment that produces $500 at the end of one period and $600 at the end of two periods. What is the return on this investment? Solving for the return involves trial and error; that is, trying different interest rates to find the one in which the cost of the investment (the $1,000) is equal to the present value of the two cash flows.

Try 4 percent:

$$\$1,000 = ?\frac{\$500}{(1+0.04)^1} + \frac{\$600}{(1+0.04)^2}$$

$$\$1,000 = ?\$480.77 + \$554.73$$

$$\$1,000 \neq \$1,035.50$$

This tells us that we have not discounted enough (that is, 4 percent is too low a rate). We know that the present value of these cash flows using a 5 percent discount rate is $1,020.41 (from our work above), so we should try an even higher rate of 6 percent.

Try 6 percent:

$$\$1,000 = ?\frac{\$500}{(1 + 0.06)^1} + \frac{\$600}{(1 + 0.06)^2}$$

$$\$1,000 = ?\$471.70 + \$534.00$$

$$\$1,000 \neq \$1,005.70$$

Repeating this same procedure using 7 percent gives us a value of the right-hand side of this equation of $991.35. Because $991.35 is less than the $1,000, this means that the rate that equates the cost of the investment (the $1,000) with the future cash flows is between 6 percent and 7 percent.

But thank goodness for financial calculators and the financial functions in spreadsheets so that we don't have to use trial and error every time we want to solve for a return based on an uneven cash flow stream. Using a spreadsheet or financial calculator's internal rate of return, IRR, function, we can determine this precisely—and without having to do all the iterations ourselves. Why do we use an IRR function? Because the return on investment, once we consider all the cash flows associated with the investment and the timing of these cash flows, is the investment's *internal rate of return* (IRR).

TI-83/84	HP10B	Microsoft Excel		
{500,600} STO *listname* IRR(−1000, *listname*)	−1000 CF_j 500 CF_j 600 CF_j IRR		A	
		1	−1000	
		2	500	
		3	600	
		4		← = IRR(A1:A3)

The interest rate that equates the $1,000 investment with the present value of the two cash flows is 6.39 percent. This means that if you buy this investment for $1,000 and hold it for two years, and receive the $500 and $600 as promised, you will have a return of 6.39 percent on your investment.

We can demonstrate this point by looking at this problem from a different angle. Suppose you invest $1,000 and can earn 6.39 percent on your investment. At the end of the first period, you will have $1,000 × (1 + 0.0639) = $1,063.90. At the end of the second period, you will have $1,063.90 × (1 + 0.0639) = $1,131.883. Your return on this investment is

$$PV = \$1,000$$

$$FV = \$1,131.883$$

$$n = 2$$

Solving for i using a calculator or spreadsheet, we find $i = 6.39\%$.

Now let's look at the benefit of receiving the $500 and the $600. At the end of the first period, you have $500. At the end of the second period, you have $600 + $500 × (1 + 0.0639) = $1,131.95. Therefore, these are equivalent investments because they have equivalent returns. What is happening here to make this true? The internal rate of return of 6.39 percent assumes that when there are cash flows from the investment (such as the $500 in this example), these cash flows are reinvested at the internal rate of 6.39 percent.

Financial Math in Action

For years, companies have been taking out life insurance policies on their employees. Sometimes these policies are insurance on key personnel—so-called key-man insurance. Other times these policies are insurance on personnel en masse (often dubbed janitors' insurance). Many of these policies are single-premium insurance—that is, one payment for the lifetime of the insured, so these policies are often in effect after the employee leaves the employer. Under current law, employers must have the employees' written permission to take out these policies, which may reduce their popularity among employees.

Suppose your employer bought a single-pay insurance policy on your life for $8,000 that pays a death benefit of $150,000. If you are 40 years old and your life expectancy is 80 years old, was this a good investment if the company's cost of capital is 8 percent? The future value of this investment is $150,000, but the present value is $150,000 ÷ (1 + 0.08)40 = $150,000 ÷ 21.7245 = $6,904.65. This was not a good investment, because the company spent $8,000 to get something with a value of $6,904.65. If you are 40 years old and you die when you are 50, was this a good investment? Yes, because the present value of the payoff of the policy is $150,000 ÷ (1 + 0.08)10 = $69,479.02, which is more than the company paid for the policy.

Bottom line? The sooner you die, the more valuable the life insurance is to your beneficiary.

Try It! 4.10: What's It Worth?

Consider the following cash inflows from an investment today:

Years from Today	End of Period Cash Flow
1	$3,000
2	$0
3	$2,500

If your opportunity cost of funds is 5 percent, what is this investment worth today?

Moving Values through Time

Consider the following: You plan to deposit $10,000 in one year, $20,000 in two years, and $30,000 in three years. If the interest earned on your deposits is 10 percent:

What is the value today of these deposits?
What will be the balance in the account at the end of the third year?

What is the value of the deposits today? We calculate the value of these deposits today as the sum of the present values, or $48,159.28:

Today 0	1	2	3
	|	|	|
$ 9,090.91	$10,000	$20,000	$30,000
16,528.93			
22,539.44			
$48,159.28 = PV			

Instead of calculating the individual present values and adding them, you can calculate the present value of this series of cash flows using spreadsheet and calculator functions:

TI-83/84	HP10B	Microsoft Excel
Create the list and store it in a list $\{CF_1,CF_2,CF_3\}$ STO listname $\{10000,20000,30000\}$ STO L1 Use the NPV program in the TVM Solver, NPV(interest rate, CF_0, listname) NPV(10,0,L1) ENTER	0 CF 10000 CF 20000 CF 30000 CF 10 I/YR NPV	A 1 10000 2 20000 3 30000 4 ← = NPV(.1,A1:A3)

Looking into the future, we can calculate the balance in the account at the end of the third year as the sum of the future values, or $$64,100:

Today 0	1	2	3
	|	|	|
	$10,000	$20,000	$30,000
			22,000
			12,000
			FV = $64,100

Note that there is no shortcut in most calculators and spreadsheets for the future value of an uneven series of cash flows.[3] In most cases, you need to calculate the future value of each of the individual cash flows and then sum these future values to arrive at the future value of the series.

Why would we want to know the future value of a series? Suppose you are setting aside funds for your retirement. What you may want to know is how much you will have available at the time you retire. You'll have to assume a specific return on your funds—that is, how much interest you can earn on your savings—but you can calculate how much you'll have at some future point in time.

Why would we want to know the present value of a series? Suppose you are considering investing in a project that will produce cash flows in the future. If you know what you can earn on similar projects, what is this project worth to you today? How much would you be willing to pay for this investment? We can calculate the present value of the future cash flows to determine the value today of these future cash flows.

EXAMPLE 4.15 Suppose you deposit $100 today, $200 one year from today, and $300 two years from today, in an account that pays 10 percent interest, compounded annually.

What is the balance in the account at the end of two years? Answer: **$641**.

$$FV = \left[\$100 \times (1.10)^2\right] + \left[\$200 \times 1.10\right] + \$300 = \$641$$

What is the balance in the account at the end of three years? Answer: **$705.10**.

$$FV = \left[\$100 \times (1.10)^3\right] + \left[\$200 \times (1.10)^2\right] + \left[\$300 \times 1.10\right]$$
$$= \$133.1 + 242 + 330 = \$641 \times 1.10 = \$705.10$$

What is the present value of these deposits? Answer: **$569.68**.

$$PV = \$100 + \left[\$200 \div 1.10\right] + \left[\$300 \div (1.10)^2\right]$$
$$= \$100 + 192.31 + 277.37 = \$569.68$$

EXAMPLE 4.16 Consider three cash flows:

Period	End of Period Cash Flow
20X1	$2,000
20X2	$4,000
20X3	$3,000

If the interest rate is 5 percent, what is the value of these cash flows at the end of 20X1? Answer: **$8,530.61**.

Period	End of Period Cash Flow	Calculation	Value at the End of 20X1
20X1	$2,000		$2,000.00
20X2	$4,000	$4,000 ÷ (1 + 0.05)	3,809.52
20X3	$3,000	$3,000 ÷ (1 + 0.05)^2	2,721.09
Total			$8,530.61

What is the value of these cash flows at the end of 20X3? Answer: **$9,405**.

Period	End of Period Cash Flow	Calculation	Value at the End of 20X3
20X1	$2,000	$2,000 \times (1 + 0.05)^2$	$2,205
20X2	$4,000	$4,000 \times (1 + 0.05)$	4,200
20X3	$3,000		3,000
Total			$9,405

We can check out work by comparing the present value and future value:

$$FV = PV \times (1 + 0.05)^2$$

$$\$9405 = \$8530.61 \times (\text{discount factor for two years at 5\%})$$

$$\$9405 \div 8530.61 = (1 + 0.05)^2$$

Check It Out

You can apply some commonsense checks to your work to make sure that you are at least in the ballpark. Consider the cash flows:

Period	End of Period Cash Flow
1	$10,000
2	$25,000
3	$15,000

If there was no interest (that is, $i = 0\%$), what would be the present value, at the end of period 0, of these cash flows?

$$PV = \frac{\$10,000}{(1 + 0.00)^1} + \frac{\$25,000}{(1 + 0.00)^2} + \frac{\$15,000}{(1 + 0.00)^3}$$

$$= \frac{\$10,000}{1} + \frac{\$25,000}{1} + \frac{\$15,000}{1} = \$50,000$$

In other words, the present value is the sum of the cash flow, or $50,000. If the interest rate is anything above 0 percent, the present value would be less than $50,000. Therefore, you can think of the sum of the cash flows as being the ceiling for the present value of the cash flows. The present value cannot be greater than this sum.

If there was no interest, what would be the future value, as of the end of period 3, of these cash flows?

$$FV = \$10,000 (1 + 0.00)^1 + \$25,000 (1 + 0.00)^2 + \$15,000 (1 + 0.00)^3 = \$50,000$$

In other words, the future value with interest at 0 percent is $50,000. If interest is above 0 percent—as it usually is—the future value will be more than the $50,000. Therefore, the sum of the cash flows is a floor for the future value—the future value will not be less than the sum of the cash flows.

Valuing a Perpetuity

Let's look at still another example. Suppose you are evaluating an investment that promises $10 every year forever. This type of cash flow stream is referred to as a *perpetuity*. The value of this investment is the present value of the stream of $10s to be received each year to infinity where each $10 is discounted the appropriate number of periods at some annual rate i:

$$\text{Present value of investment} = \frac{\$10}{(1+i)^1} + \frac{\$10}{(1+i)^2} + \frac{\$10}{(1+i)^3} + \cdots + \frac{\$10}{(1+i)^\infty}$$

which we can write in shorthand notation using summation notation as:

$$PV = \sum_{t=1}^{\infty} \frac{\$10}{(1+i)^t} = \$10 \sum_{t=1}^{\infty} \frac{1}{(1+i)^t}$$

As the number of discounting periods approaches infinity, the summation approaches $1 \div i$. To see why, consider the present value annuity factor for an interest rate of 10 percent, as the number of payments goes from 1 to 200:

Number of Payments in the Annuity	Present Value Annuity Discount Factor
1	0.0909
10	6.1446
50	9.9148
100	9.9993
1000	10.0000

That is,

$$\sum_{t=1}^{\infty} \frac{1}{(1+i)^t} \Rightarrow \frac{1}{i}$$

If the interest rate is 10 percent, as the number of payments increases, the factor approaches 10, or $1 \div 0.10$. Therefore, the present value of a perpetual annuity is very close to $1 \div i$.

We can rewrite the present value of the perpetual stream of $10 as

$$PV = \frac{CF}{i} \$10 \left(\frac{1}{i}\right) = \frac{\$10}{i}$$

If the discount rate to translate this future stream into a present value is 10 percent, the value of the investment is $100:

$$PV = \frac{\$10}{0.10} = \$100$$

The 10 percent is the discount rate, also referred to as the *capitalization rate*, for the future cash flows comprising this stream. Looking at this investment from another angle, if you consider the investment to be worth $100 today, you are capitalizing—translating future flows into a present value—the future cash flows at

10 percent per year. As you see from these examples, the value of an investment depends on:

The amount and timing of the future cash flows.
The discount rate used to translate these future cash flows into a value today.

This discount rate represents how much an investor is willing to pay today for the right to receive a future cash flow. Or, to put it another way, the discount rate is the rate of return the investor requires on an investment, given the price he or she is willing to pay for its expected future cash flow.

Let's consider another example. Suppose you are considering an investment that promises to pay $100 each period forever, and the interest rate you can earn on alternative investments of similar risk is 5 percent per period. What are you willing to pay today for this investment?

$$PV = \$100 \div 0.05 = \$2,000$$

Therefore, you would be willing to pay $2,000 today for this investment to receive, in return, the promise of $100 each period forever.

Financial Math in Action

The government of the United Kingdom has had bonds outstanding that never mature. These bonds are referred to as *consolidated stock*, or *consols*, that are part of the government debt. The bonds currently pay interest at a rate of 2.5 percent per year, paid four times a year. What is the value of one Consolidated Stock if the appropriate discount rate is 4 percent? For £100 face value consol, the periodic cash flow is £2.5 ÷ 4 = £0.625 every four months. The discount rate per period is 4% ÷ 4 = 1%. The value of a 100 face value consol is £0.625 ÷ 0.01 = £62.5.

Let's look at the value of a perpetuity from a different angle. Suppose that you have the opportunity to purchase an investment for $5,000 that promises to pay $50 at the end of every period forever. What is the periodic interest per period (that is, the return) on this investment?

We know that the present value is PV = $5,000 and the periodic, perpetual payment is CF = $50. Inserting these values into the formula for the present value of a perpetuity:

$$PV = \$5,000 = \$50 \div i$$

Solving for i, $i = \$50 \div \$5,000 = 0.01$ or 1% per period.

Therefore, an investment of $5,000 that generates $50 per period provides 1 percent compound interest per period.

EXAMPLE 4.17 Suppose you buy a share of stock that has a $2 dividend, paid at the end of each year. If you expect the dividend to be constant and paid each year, forever, what are you willing to pay for this share of stock if the opportunity cost of funds considering the risk of the stock, is 8 percent? Answer: **$25**.

$$PV = \frac{\$2}{0.08} = \$25$$

EXAMPLE 4.18   You observe that a share of stock is currently selling for $30 per share. If this stock has a constant dividend of $3 per year, paid at the end of each year, forever, what is the required rate of return on this stock? Answer: **10 percent**.

$$i = \frac{\$3}{\$30} = 10\%$$

Annuities

An *annuity* is a series of even cash flows. Because the cash flows are the same amount, the math is simpler. Suppose you have a series of three cash flows, each of $1,000. The first cash flow occurs one year from today, the second occurs two years from today, and the third occurs three years from today. The present value of this series is

$$PV = \frac{\$1,000}{(1+i)^1} + \frac{\$1,000}{(1+i)^2} + \frac{\$1,000}{(1+i)^3} = \sum_{t=1}^{3} \frac{\$1,000}{(1+i)^t} = \$1,000 \sum_{t=1}^{3} \frac{1}{(1+i)^t}$$

Using the notation CF to represent the periodic cash flow, we can represent this as

$$PV = \sum_{t=1}^{N} \frac{CF}{(1+i)^t} = CF \sum_{t=1}^{N} \frac{1}{(1+i)^t}$$

The term $\sum_{t=1}^{N} \frac{1}{(1+i)^t}$ is the annuity discount factor.

There are different types of annuities in financial transactions, which differ in terms of the timing of the first cash flow:

An *ordinary annuity* is an annuity in which the first cash flow is one period in the future.
An *annuity due* is an annuity in which the first cash flow occurs today.
A *deferred annuity* is an annuity in which the first cash flow occurs beyond one period from today.

The example that we just completed is an example of an ordinary annuity. You can see the timing issue when comparing the time lines associated with each. Consider the following three-cash-flow annuities: the ordinary annuity, an annuity due, and a deferred annuity with a deferral of three periods.

End of Period	Today	1	2	3	4	5
Ordinary annuity	PV	CF	CF	CF FV		
Annuity due	CF PV	CF	CF	FV		
Deferred annuity	PV			CF	CF	CF FV

CF represents the periodic cash flow amount. In the case of an annuity, this amount is the same each period. Because of the time value of money, the valuation of these annuities, whether we are referring to the present value or the future value, will be different.

Valuing an Ordinary Annuity

The ordinary annuity is the most common annuity that we encounter, although deferred annuities and annuities due do occur with some frequency as well. The future value of an ordinary annuity is simply the sum of the future values of the individual cash flows. Consider a three-payment ordinary annuity that has payments of $1,000 each and a 5 percent interest rate.

The future value of this annuity is

Today	1	2	3
	$1,000	$1,000	$1,000.0 1,102.5 1,050.0 FV = $3,152.5

The present value of this annuity is

Today	1	2	3
$952.381 907.029 863.838 PV = $2,723.248	$1,000	$1,000	$1,000

We can represent the value of the annuity in more general terms. Let t indicate a time period, CF represent the individual cash flow, and let n indicate the number of cash flows. The future value is the sum of the future values of the cash flows:

$$FV = CF(1 + i)^{N-1} + CF(1 + i)^{N-2} + \cdots + CF(1 + i)^0 = CF\left(\sum_{t=0}^{N-1}(1 + i)^t\right)$$

We can represent the present value of an ordinary annuity in mathematical terms as

$$PV = \sum_{t=1}^{N} \frac{CF}{(1+i)^t} = CF \sum_{t=1}^{N} \frac{1}{(1+i)^t} = CF \left(1 - \frac{(1+i)^N)}{i} \right)$$

We used the notation CF to indicate a cash flow. In the case of an annuity, this cash flow is the same each period. The term

$$\left(\sum_{t=0}^{N-1} (1+i)^t \right)$$

is referred to as the *future value annuity factor* and the term, whereas

$$\sum_{t=1}^{N} \frac{1}{(1+i)^t}$$

is referred to as the *present value annuity factor*. In financial calculator applications, we refer to the cash flow associated with an annuity as a payment, or PMT.[4]

Consider another example. Suppose you wish to calculate the present value of a four-payment ordinary annuity that has annual payments of $5,000 each. If the interest rate is 5 percent, the present value is $17,729.75. Using a calculator, we input the known values (i.e., *n, i,* PMT) and solve for PV.[5]

TI-83/84 Using TVM Solver	HP10B	Microsoft Excel
N = 4	4 N	=PV(0.05,4,5000,0)*−1
I% = 5	5 I/YR	
FV = 0	5000 PMT	
PMT = 5000	PV	
PV = *Solve*		

Referring to the timeline above, you can see that the value you calculated occurs one period before the first cash flow (i.e., today).

Now suppose you wish to calculate the future value. You use the same inputs, but simply solve for the future value instead of the present value, resulting in a value of $21,550.63. Referring to the previous time line, you can see that the value you calculated occurs at the same time as the last cash flow, which in this example is at the end of the fourth year.

TI-83/84 (Using TVM Solver)	HP10B	Microsoft Excel
N = 4	4 N	=FV(0.05,4,5000,0)*−1
I% = 5	5 I/YR	
PV = 0	5000 PMT	
PMT = 5000	FV	
FV = *Solve*		

EXAMPLE 4.19   What is the value of an investment that provides cash flows of $2,000 at the end of each year for the next four years if you have determined that the appropriate discount rate on this investment is 6 percent? Answer: **$6.930.21.**

Because these cash flows are the same amount and occur at regular intervals of time, we can solve this using an ordinary annuity, which means we can use the calculator or spreadsheet shortcut involving the PMT—the periodic, even cash flow. We are given the following data inputs:

$$PMT = \$2,000$$
$$N = 4$$
$$i = 6\%$$

Solving for the present value of an annuity, the value of this investment is $6,930.21.

Try It! 4.11: Back and Forth with Annuities

Consider a four-payment annuity in which the payment is $2,500 and the interest rate is 6 percent.

What is the present value of this annuity?
What is the future value of this annuity?

Valuing an Annuity Due

An annuity due is like an ordinary annuity, yet the *first cash flow occurs immediately,* instead of one period from today. This means that each cash flow is discounted one period less than each cash flow in a similar payment ordinary annuity:

$$FV = CF(1 + i)^1 + CF(1 + i)^2 + \cdots + CF(1 + i)^{N+1} = CF\left(\sum_{t=0}^{N}(1 + i)^{t+1}\right)$$

$$PV = \sum_{t=1}^{N}\frac{CF}{(1 + i)^{t-1}} = CF\sum_{t=1}^{N}\frac{1}{(1 + i)^{t-1}}$$

Consider the example of a three-payment annuity due with payments of $1,000 each and the interest rate is 5 percent. The future value of this annuity due is $3,310.125:

Today	1	2	3	
|	|	|	|	
$1,000	$1,000	$1,000		$1,157.625
⇨	⇨	⇨		1,102.500
				1,050.000
				FV= $3,310.125

The present value of this three-payment annuity due is

Today	1	2	3
$1,000.000	$1,000	$1,000	
$952.381	➚	➚	
907.029			
PV = $2,859.410			

Comparing the values of the ordinary annuity with those of the annuity due, you'll see that the values differ by a factor of $(1 + i)$:

	Value of Ordinary Annuity	Value of Annuity Due	Value of Annuity Due / Value of Ordinary Annuity
Present value	$2,723.248	$2,859.410	1.05
Future value	$3,152.500	$3,310.125	1.05

This factor represents the difference in the timing of the cash flows: the cash flows of the annuity due occur one period prior to the cash flows for a similar-payment ordinary annuity.

Calculation Tip

Using a financial calculator to value an annuity due requires changing the mode from END to BEG or BEGIN. Once in the BEG or BEGIN mode, you can input the values as you did with the ordinary annuity. A common mistake is to leave the calculator in the annuity due mode when calculating other, nondue problems.

Consider a five-payment annuity due with an annual payment of $3,000 and an interest rate of 6 percent. The present value of this annuity due is $13,395.317.

TI-83/84 (Using TVM Solver)	HP10B	Microsoft Excel
Set BEGIN	Set BEG	=PV(0.06,5,3000,0,1)*−1
N = 5	5 N	
I% = 6	6 I/YR	
FV = 0	3000 PMT	
PMT = 3000	PV	
PV = *Solve*		

The future value of this annuity due is $17,925.956:

TI-83/84 (Using TVM Solver)	HP10B	Microsoft Excel
Set BEGIN	Set BEG	=FV(0.06,5,3000,0,1)*−1
N = 5	5 N	
I% = 6	6 I/YR	
PV = 0	3000 PMT	
PMT = 3000	FV	
FV = *Solve*		

EXAMPLE 4.20   Suppose you have just won a $1 million lottery. When you win the lottery, you generally receive payments of the lottery jackpot over 20 years, with the first payment immediately. Therefore, your $1 million lottery winnings consist of 20 annual payments of $50,000 each, beginning when you claim your prize.[6] But wait! Don't forget about taxes. The IRS will take 28 percent of each check, so you are left with $36,000 each year.

So what is the $1 million lottery jackpot worth to you today? If you can invest your funds to produce a return of 3 percent, that $1 million jackpot, valuing the winnings as an annuity due, is worth $551,656.77 today:[7]

$$PMT = \$36,000$$

$$n = 20$$

$$i = 3\%$$

Solve for the present value of the annuity due, PV = $551,656.77.

So, if someone offered you a lump-sum of $500,000 for your lottery winnings, would you take it? No. If someone offered you $600,000 for your lottery winnings, would you take it? Yes.

Try It! 4.12: What Would You Take?

Suppose you win a lawsuit and the lawsuit settlement will be paid in 10 annual installments of $400,000 each, with the first payment today. If you can earn 6 percent on your investments and if someone offers you $3 million in exchange for your settlement, would you take it? Why?

Summary

Valuing an investment requires first identifying the type, amount, and timing of the cash flows associated with the investment. Once we estimate the amount and timing of the security's cash flows, the valuation of these cash flows requires the application of the time value of money mathematics to determine the present value of these future cash flows.

We can use a financial calculator or spreadsheet's built-in functions to calculate the present value of a series, the present value of uneven cash flows, or the present value of a series of even cash flows forever. When we want to calculate the value of a series of uneven cash flows out into the future, we must first determine the future value of each cash flow and then sum.

"Try It!" Solutions

4.10 What's It Worth?
  We are given the following data inputs:

$$CF_1 = \$3,000$$
$$CF_2 = \$0$$
$$CF_3 = \$2,500$$
$$i = 5\%$$

   Solving for the net present value, the value of this investment is $5,016.7369.

4.11 Back and Forth with Annuities
  The present value is $8,662.76, whereas the future value is $10,936.54.

  (a) Inputs: PMT = $2,500; $n = 4$; $i = 6\%$.
  (b) Solve for the present value. PV = $8,662.76.
  (c) Inputs: PMT = $2,500; $n = 4$; $i = 6\%$.
  (d) Solve for the future value. FV = $10,936.54.

4.12 What Would You Take?
  No, because the value of the settlement annuity is $3,120,677:

   Annuity due: PMT = $400,000; $n = 10$; $i = 6\%$. Solve for the present value.

Notes

1. Because we do not have a cash flow that occurs today in this scenario, we need to indicate the fact that today's cash flow is zero in the financial calculators; zero as the second element in the NPV function, and 0 for the initial CF_j for the HP10B calculator. If there is no cash flow you must input a "0" to hold the time period's place in the program—otherwise, the cash flow will receive an incorrect time value of money.

2. The *net present value* is the present value of all cash flows, whether they are positive or negative, discounted at the appropriate discount rate. We add the word "net" to "present value" because we are often using these calculations to determine how much value is added, on net, once you consider how much the investment costs and how much value you will get from the investment. Therefore, if this investment cost you $1,000, its net present value is $20.41.

3. Exceptions include the Hewlett-Packard 17B and 19B model calculators and the more recent Texas Instruments BA II models.

4. If we can use financial calculators or spreadsheets to solve these problems, why worry about the math? Because by laying the foundation of what consists of these mathematical relationships, you may be able to approach a problem that doesn't

fit into the simple, conventional type of problem if you understand the math behind it.

5. Be sure that your calculator is set for one payment per period and in the END mode.

6. This is an annuity due pattern of cash flows. It would be lousy public relations for a lottery commission to say, "Congratulations, you'll get your first check in one year," so most lotteries begin payments immediately.

7. In mathematical terms, this is $PV = CF \left(\sum_{t=1}^{N} \frac{1}{(1+i)^{t-1}} \right) = \$36,000 \left(\sum_{t=1}^{N} \frac{1}{(1+i)^{t-1}} \right) = \$551,656.77$.

Part IV Yielding for Yields

It has been my experience that competency in mathematics, both in numerical manipulations and in understanding its conceptual foundations, enhances a person's ability to handle the more ambiguous and qualitative relationships that dominate our day-to-day financial decision-making.

—Alan Greenspan

The basic concept underlying the time value of money is that when you invest, you are compensated for the time value of money and risk, and when you borrow, you must pay enough to compensate the lender for the time value of money and risk. Situations arise often in which we wish to determine the interest rate that is implied from an advertised or stated rate. There are also cases in which we wish to determine the rate of interest implied from a set of payments in a loan arrangement.

Annualized Rates of Interest

A common problem in finance is comparing alternative financing or investment opportunities when the interest rates are stated in a way that makes it difficult to compare terms. One lending source may offer terms that specify 9.25 percent annual percentage rate (APR), with interest compounding annually, whereas another lending source may offer terms of 9 percent APR with interest compounding continuously. How do you begin to compare these rates to determine which is a lower cost of borrowing? Ideally, we would like to translate these interest rates into some comparable form.

One obvious way to represent rates stated in various time intervals on a common basis is to express them in the same unit of time—so we annualize them. To annualize a rate is to put it on an annual basis. Supposedly, if you put all the terms on the same annual basis, they should be comparable. Right? Wrong.

There are two approaches to annualizing rates: the simple way, resulting in an APR, and the more complex way, resulting in an *effective annual rate* (EAR). These are both annualized rates, but they provide different information.

ANNUAL PERCENTAGE RATE   In Parts I and II, we showed you how we use the APR for compounding and discounting when interest compounds more frequently than annually. We look at the APR here to set the stage for determining the EAR, the effective annual rate.

Suppose a bank is willing to lend to you at the rate of 12 percent APR, with interest compounded monthly. What does this really mean in terms of what you end up paying? It means that you are paying $12\% \div 12 = 1\%$ each month and that interest compounds 12 times a year. Let's put this into an equation. Let i be the rate of interest per period and let n be the number of compounding periods in a year. The annualized rate, also referred to as the *nominal interest rate* or the APR, is

$$\text{APR} = i \times n$$

$$\text{APR} = 0.01 \times 12 = 12\%$$

A compound period may be a day, a week, a month, a three-month period, or any other portion of a year. The key to understanding interest rates, and in particular APRs, is to understand how frequently interest compounds within a year.

EXAMPLE 4.21 Suppose a bank offers you lending rates at 6 percent APR, with interest compounded monthly.

What is the compounding period? Answer: **A month**.

What is the rate per compounding period? Answer: **6 percent**.

The APR is 6 percent and there are 12 compound periods in a year. Therefore,

$$6\% \div 12 = 0.5\%$$

To check our work, $0.5\% \times 12 = 6\%$.

EXAMPLE 4.22 Suppose your credit card states that interest on unpaid balances is 24 percent APR, with interest compounded monthly. What is the interest rate per month for this credit card? Answer: **2 percent**.

The APR is 24 percent and there are 12 months in a year. Therefore, the rate per month is 24 percent $\div$ 12 = 2 percent.

Suppose you borrow $10,000 with the terms of interest at 12 percent APR, compounded monthly. If you repay the loan at the end of the year, how much interest do you have to pay? It's a bit more than 12 percent of the $10,000:

$$\text{FV} = \$10,000 \times (1 + 0.01)^{12} = \$11,268.25$$

The interest that you pay is $11,268.25 - $10,000 = $1,268.25, which is more than 12 percent of $10,000 (which would be $1,200). That additional $68.25 is because interest compounds monthly, even though you don't end up paying for it until the end of the year. Effectively, you are paying $1,268.25 $\div$ $10,000 = 12.6825 percent on the monthly compounding 12 percent APR loan.

So why do banks and other lenders report the APR? This is because the Federal Truth in Lending Act requires lenders to disclose the annual percentage rate on consumer loans.[1] But because the annual percentage rate ignores compounding and, therefore, understates the true cost of borrowing, savvy consumers need to take the extra step to figure out the effective rate. To make matters worse, the APR does not consider some other costs associated with lending transactions, as pointed out in the Report to Congress by the Board of Governors of the Federal Reserve System.[2]

To see how the APR works, let's consider the Lucky Break Loan Company. Lucky's loan terms are simple: Pay back the amount borrowed, plus 50 percent, in six months. Suppose you borrow $10,000 from Lucky. After six months, you must pay back the $10,000, plus $5,000. The annual percentage rate on financing with Lucky is the interest rate per period (50 percent for six months) multiplied by the number of compound periods in a year (two six-month periods in a year). For the Lucky Break financing arrangement,

$$\text{APR} = 0.50 \times 2 = 1.00 \text{ or } 100\% \text{ per year}$$

But what if you cannot pay Lucky back after six months? Lucky will let you off this time, but you must pay back the following at the end of the next six months:

The $10,000 borrowed.
The $5,000 interest from the first six months.
50 percent interest on both the unpaid $10,000 and the unpaid $5,000 interest ($15,000 × 0.50 = $7,500).

So, at the end of the year, knowing what is good for you, you pay off Lucky:

Amount of original loan	$10,000
Interest from first six months	5,000
Interest on second six months	7,500
Total payment at end of year	$22,500

It is unreasonable to assume that, after six months, Lucky would let you forget about paying interest on the $5,000 interest from the first six months. If Lucky would forget about the interest on interest, you would pay $20,000 at the end of the year—$10,000 repayment of principal and $10,000 interest—which is a 100 percent interest rate.

But Lucky doesn't forget. Using the Lucky Break method of financing, you have to pay $12,500 interest to borrow $10,000 for one year's time—or else. Because you have to pay $12,500 interest to borrow $10,000 over one year's time, you pay not 100 percent interest, but rather 125 percent interest per year:

$$\text{Annual interest rate on a Lucky Break loan} = \$12,500 \div \$10,000 = 125\%$$

What's going on here? It looks like the APR in the Lucky Break example ignores the compounding (interest on interest) that takes place after the first six months.

And that's the way it is with *all* APRs: the APR ignores the effect of compounding. The APR understates the true annual rate of interest if interest compounds at any time prior to the end of the year. Nevertheless, APR is viewed as an acceptable method of disclosing interest on many lending arrangements because it is easy to understand and simple to compute. However, because it ignores compounding, it is not the best way to evaluate financing terms.

Try It! 4.13: APR

Suppose you borrow $1,000 using a payday loan that has finance charges of 17.5 percent of the loan for a 10-day period. What is the APR on this loan?

First, identify the compounding period and the number of these periods in a year.
The compounding period is 10 days.
In a year period, there are 36.5 of these 10-day periods, so n is 36.5.
Second, identify the rate period compounding period. The interest per period, i, is 0.175.

The APR is therefore: APR = $i \times n$ = 0.175 × 36.5 = 6.3875 or **638.75%**.

EFFECTIVE ANNUAL RATE   As we've demonstrated, the APR ignores any compounding within a year. As a result, a loan with an APR of 6 percent and compounding monthly looks no different than a loan with an APR of 6 percent and annual compounding. But these loans are different—we just would never know it by looking at the APR. Consider a simple example. Suppose you want to borrow $10,000 and have three choices of financing:

A: APR of 6%, with monthly compounding.
B: APR of 6%, with quarterly compounding.
C: APR of 6%, with annual compounding.

If you pay off the loan at the end of the year, how much must you pay under each set of terms?

A: $10,000 × (1 + 0.005)12 = $10,616.78
B: $10,000 × (1 + 0.015)4 = $10,613.64
C: $10,000 × (1 + 0.06) = $10,600.00

Instead of having to work through financing terms and amounts owed, we can convert a stated interest rate into an effective rate of interest rate, which considers compounding. We can then compare effective rates to figure out the best financing terms.

The effective annual rate is the *true* economic return for a given time period because it takes into account the compounding of interest. The EAR is sometimes referred to as the *effective rate of interest*. Using our Lucky Break example, we see that we must pay $12,500 interest on the loan of $10,000 for one year. Effectively, we are paying 125 percent annual interest. Thus, 125 percent is the effective annual rate of interest.

The Federal Truth in Savings Act requires institutions to provide the APY for savings accounts, which is a rate that considers the effects of compound interest.[3] The APY is simply another name for the EAR. As a result of this law, consumers can compare the yields on different savings arrangements. Unfortunately, this law does not apply beyond savings accounts and, therefore, consumers and businesses must be able to calculate this yield on their own.

In the Lucky Break example, we can easily work through the calculation of interest and interest on interest. But for situations where interest is compounded more frequently, we need a direct way to calculate the effective annual rate. We can calculate it by resorting once again to our basic valuation equation:

$$FV = PV(1 + i)^n$$

Next, we consider that a return is the change in the value of an investment over a period and an annual return is the change in value over a year.

Suppose you invest $100 today in an account, which pays 6 percent annual interest, but interest compounds every four months. This means that 2 percent is paid every four months.

After four months, you have $100 \times 1.2 = $102.

After eight months you have $102 \times 1.02 = $104.04.

After one year you have $104.04 \times 1.02 = 106.1208$, or, $100 \times 1.02^3 = 106.1208.

The effective annual rate of interest is $6.1208 paid on $100, or 6.1208 percent. We can arrive at that interest by rearranging the basic valuation formula based on a one-year period:

$$\$106.1208 = \$100 \times (1 + 0.02)^3$$

$$\$106.1208 \div \$100 = (1 + 0.02)^3$$

$$1.061208 = (1 + 0.02)^3$$

$$EAR = (1 + 0.02)^3 - 1 = 0.061208 \text{ or } 6.1208\%$$

In more general terms, the effective interest rate, EAR, is

$$EAR = (1 + i)^n - 1$$

The effective rate of interest—the EAR—is therefore an annual rate that takes into consideration any compounding that occurs during the year.

Let's look at how the EAR is affected by the compounding. Suppose that the Safe Savings and Loan promises to pay 6 percent interest on accounts, compounded annually. Because interest is paid once, at the end of the year, the effective annual return, EAR, is 6 percent. If the 6 percent interest is paid on a semiannual basis— 3 percent every six months—the effective annual return is larger than 6 percent because interest is earned on the 3 percent interest earned at the end of the first six months. In this case, to calculate the EAR, the interest rate per compounding period—six months—is 0.03 (that is, $0.06 \div 2$) and the number of compounding periods in an annual period is 2:

$$EAR = (1 + i)^n - 1$$

$$EAR = (1 + 0.03)^2 - 1 = 1.0609 - 1 = 0.0609 \text{ or } 6.09\%$$

Extending this example to the case of quarterly compounding with a nominal interest rate of 6 percent we first calculate the interest rate per period, i, and the number of compounding periods in a year, n:

$$i = 0.06 \div 4 = 0.015 \text{ per quarter}$$

$$n = 12 \text{ months} \div 3 \text{ months} = 4 \text{ quarters in a year}$$

The EAR is

$$\text{EAR} = (1 + 0.015)^4 - 1 = 1.0614 - 1 = 0.0614 \text{ or } 6.14\%$$

Let's see how this math will help you compare investments. Suppose there are two banks: Bank A, paying 12 percent interest compounded semiannually, and Bank B, paying 11.9 percent interest compounded monthly. Which bank offers you the best return on your money? Comparing APRs, Bank A provides the higher return. But what about compound interest? We calculate the EAR for each account as

Bank A:

$$\text{EAR} = (1 + (0.12 \div 2))^2 - 1$$
$$= (1 + 0.06)^2 = 1.1236 - 1$$
$$= 0.1236 \text{ or } 12.36\%$$

Bank B:

$$\text{EAR} = (1 + (0.119 \div 12))^{12} - 1$$
$$= (1 + 0.0099)^{12} - 1 = 1.1257 - 1$$
$$= 0.1257 \text{ or } 12.57\%$$

Bank B offers the better return on your money, even though it advertises a lower APR. If you deposit $1,000 in Bank A for one year, you will have $1,123.60 at the end of the year. If you deposit $1,000 in Bank B for one year, you will have $1,125.70 at the end of the year, providing the better return on your savings.

You can see the effect on the EAR of the frequency of compounding within the year in Figure 4.9. In this figure, we graph the EAR that is equivalent to an APR of 12 percent for different frequencies of compounding, ranging from one compounding period a year (and, therefore, APR is equal to EAR), to compounding 52 times in a year (in other words, weekly). With weekly compounding, the EAR is 12.734 percent.

EXAMPLE 4.23 Suppose a bank offers you lending rates at 6 percent APR, with interest compounded monthly. What is the effective rate of interest on this lending?

The EAR is 6.168%: $\text{EAR} = (1 + 0.005)^{12} - 1 = 6.168\%$

EXAMPLE 4.24 Suppose your credit card states that interest on unpaid balances is 24 percent APR, with interest compounded monthly. What is the effective annual rate of interest on unpaid balances?

The EAR is 26.824%: $\text{EAR} = (1 + 0.02)^{12} - 1 = 26.824\%$

EXAMPLE 4.25 The ABC Credit Card Company offers you a credit card with an APR of 19.5%. If interest compounds daily, what is the effective annual rate of interest on

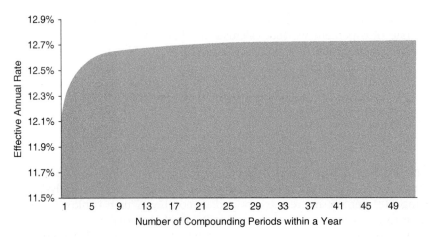

FIGURE 4.9   Effective Interest Rates for 12 Percent APR with Different Frequencies of Compounding

this credit card? You know the following: APR = 19.5%, n = 365, and i = 0.195 ÷ 365 = 0.00534247. The EAR is therefore 21.525%: EAR = $(1 + 0.00534247)^{365} - 1$ = 0.21525 or **21.525%**.

EXAMPLE 4.26   A payday loan is a short-term loan with very high interest rates. In a typical payday loan, if you want to borrow $100 you write a check for $125. The lender holds onto your check during the loan period. At the end of the loan period, usually 10 to 14 days, the lender deposits your check. If you want to extend your loan, you pay the minimum of $25 cash and then enter into a new contract to pay. If you do not pay off the loan or pay the fee to roll over the loan, the lender will deposit your check and you risk being charged with writing bad checks.

What is the APR for this payday loan?

$$APR = 0.25 \,(365/14) = \mathbf{651.79\%}$$

What is the EAR for this payday loan?

$$EAR = (1 + 0.25)^{365/14} - 1 = \mathbf{3{,}351.86\%}$$

The regulations pertaining to payday loans vary among states, but most states allow very generous lending terms—generous, that is, to the lenders.[4]

Try It! 4.14: Effective Interest Rates

A credit card offers a rate of 19.4 percent on unpaid balances. Interest compounds daily. What is the effective annual rate on this credit card?

Continuous Compounding

The extreme frequency of compounding is continuous compounding. Continuous compounding is when interest compounds at the smallest possible increment of time (that is, instantaneously, if you can imagine that). In continuous compounding, the rate per period becomes extremely small, which you can conclude if you divided the APR by infinity:

$$i = \text{APR} \div \infty$$

Along with this strange result, the number of compounding periods in a year, n, is infinite. As the rate of interest, i, gets smaller and the number of compounding periods approaches infinity, the EAR is

$$\text{EAR} = (1 + {}^{\text{APR}}/_{n})^{n} - 1$$

where the APR is the annual percentage rate. What does all this mean? It means that the interest rate per period approaches 0 and the number of compounding periods approaches infinity—at the same time! In the 1730s, a mathematician, Leonhard Euler, who was working on a string of mathematical issues that originated in the 1600s, noticed that for a given nominal interest rate under continuous compounding, the relationship between the nominal interest rate and the effective rate hinged on e:

$$\text{EAR} = e^{\text{APR}} - 1$$

e is the mathematical representation for the base of the natural logarithm. While much of that is beyond what we need for our purposes, the use of e does help us figure out the effective rate.

Financial Math in Action

Euler's e, which we use when interest compounds continuously, came out of work on logarithms. So why is e so useful? Because, in addition to compound interest, we can use e to describe phenomena such as radioactive decay and astronomical functions.

Want to learn more about e? Check out *e: The Story of a Number* by Eli Maop (Princeton University Press, 1994).

For the stated 6% annual interest rate compounded continuously, the EAR is

$$\text{EAR} = e^{0.06} - 1 = 1.0618 - 1 \quad \text{EAR} = 0.0618 \text{ or } 6.18\%$$

The relation between the frequency of compounding, for a given stated rate, and the effective annual rate of interest for this example indicates that the greater the frequency of compounding, the greater the EAR.

EXAMPLE 4.27   Which of the following terms represents the lowest cost of credit on an effective annual interest rate basis?

A: 10% APR, interest compounded semiannually.
B: 9.75% APR, interest compounded continuously.

C: 10.5% APR, interest compounded annually.
D: 9.8% APR, interest compounded quarterly.

Answer: **D**.

EAR $= (1 + 0.05)^2 - 1 = 10.25\%$
EAR $= e^{0.0975} - 1 = 10.241\%$
EAR $= 10.5\%$
EAR $= (1 + 0.0245)^4 - 1 = 10.166\%$

CALCULATOR AND SPREADSHEET APPLICATIONS   Financial calculators typically have a built-in program to help you go from APRs to EARs and vice versa. For example, using the financial calculator, we can calculate the EAR that corresponds to a 10% APR with quarterly compounding.[5] The result is an EAR of 10.3813%.

TI-83/84 (Using TVM Solver)	HP10B
EFF(10,4)	10 NOM%
ENTER	4 P/Y
	EFF%

In a similar manner, we can calculate the nominal (i.e., APR) rate that corresponds to a given EAR. Suppose we want to find the nominal rate with quarterly compounding that is equivalent to an effective rate of 10%. The equivalent APR is 9.6455%. In other words, if a lender charges 9.6455% APR, it will earn, effectively, 10% on the loan.

TI-83/84 (Using TVM Solver)	HP10B
NOM(10,4)	10 EFF%
ENTER	4 P/Y
	NOM%

Continuous compounding calculations cannot be done using the built-in finance programs. However, most calculators—whether financial or not—have a program that allows you to perform calculations using e, the base of natural logarithms. The EAR corresponding to an APR with continuous compounding is 10.52%, which you can calculate as $e^{0.1} - 1$.

TI-83/84	HP10B
$e^x(.1) - 1$ ENTER	.1
	$e^x - 1 =$

We can also use spreadsheet functions to calculate either the nominal rate or the effective rate. In Microsoft Excel, for example, you can calculate the effective rate that is equivalent to an APR of 10% with monthly compounding as

$$=\text{EFFECT}(.10,12)$$

which produces an answer of 10.471%.

Similarly, finding the nominal rate with monthly compounding that is equivalent to an EAR of 10%,

$$=\text{NOMINAL}(.10,12)$$

which produces an answer of 9.569%.

Suppose you have a loan of $100,000 that requires payments of $3,874.81 per month for 30 months. What is the effective annual rate? We can represent this problem in the mathematical relationship as

$$\$100,000 = \sum_{t=1}^{30} \frac{\$3,874.81}{(1 + i)^t}$$

The effective annual rate, EAR, is still calculated as

$$\text{EAR} = (1 + i)^{12} - 1$$

but we first have to determine the monthly rate. Using a financial calculator or spreadsheet to solve for the i, we have a monthly rate of 1%:

TI-83/84	HP10B	Microsoft Excel
N = 30	30 N	=RATE(30,3874.81,−100000,0)
PMT = 3874.81	3874.81 PMT	
PV = −100000	100000 +/− PV	
FV = 0	I/YR	
Solve for I		

Therefore, the EAR is $(1 + 0.01)^{12} - 1 = 12.683\%$. The APR of this loan (that is, what is advertised) is 12%: APR = 1% × 12 = 12%.

The calculation of the effective annual rate depends on the information that the lender provides. Some lenders will quote the loan amount, the payments, and the number of payments. Other lenders simply provide the APR and the frequency of payments.

DETERMINING THE UNKNOWN INTEREST RATE   Let's say that you have $1,000 to invest today and in five years you would like the investment to be worth $2,000. What interest rate would satisfy your investment objective? We know the present value (PV = $1,000), the future value (FV = $2,000), and the number of compounding periods ($n = 5$). Using the basic valuation equation,

$$\text{FV} = \text{PV}(1 + i)^n$$

and substituting the known values of FV, PV, and n,

$$\$2,000 = \$1,000 \, (1 + i)^5$$

Rearranging, we see that the ratio of the future value to the present value is equal to the compound factor for five periods at some unknown rate:

$$\$2,000 \div \$1,000 = (1 + i)^5 \text{ or } 2.000 = (1 + i)^5$$

where 2.000 is the compound factor.

Therefore, we have one equation with one unknown, i. We can determine the unknown interest rate either mathematically or by using a financial calculator.

We can determine the interest rate more precisely, however, by solving for i mathematically:

$$2 = (1 + i)^5$$

Taking the fifth root of both sides, and representing this operation in several equivalent ways,

$$1 + i = 2^{1/5} = 20^{0.20}$$

You'll need a calculator to figure out the fifth root:

$$2^{0.20} = 1.1487 = (1 + i)$$

$$i = 1.1487 - 1 = 0.1487 \text{ or } 14.87\%$$

Calculation Tip

Want to take the root of a value that is not the square root? To take the nth root, you take the base to the power of $1/n$. Consider the following examples of taking roots of 100:

Root	Calculation	Value
3rd root	$\sqrt[3]{100} = 100^{1/3} = 100^{0.333}$	4.6416
4th root	$\sqrt[4]{100} = 100^{1/4} = 100^{0.25}$	3.1623
5th root	$\sqrt[5]{100} = 100^{1/5} = 100^{0.2}$	2.5119
10th root	$\sqrt[10]{100} = 100^{1/10} = 100^{0.1}$	1.5849

In the TI-83/84 calculator, use $\wedge$ for the power. In the HP 10B calculator, use y^x.

Therefore, if you invested $1,000 in an investment that pays 14.87 percent compounded interest per year, for five years, you would have $2,000 at the end of the fifth year. We can formalize an equation for finding the interest rate when we know PV, FV, and n from the valuation equation and notation: FV = PV $(1 + i)^n$. Thus, using algebra,

$$i = (\sqrt[n]{\text{FV/PV}}) - 1$$

As an example, suppose that the value of an investment today is $100 and we expect the value of the investment in five years to be $150. What is the annual rate of appreciation in value of this investment over the five-year period?

We can use the math or financial programs in a calculator to solve for *i*, which is 8.447 percent.

TI-83/84 (Using TVM Solver)	HP10B	Microsoft Excel
N = 5	100 +/− PV	=RATE(5,0,−100,150,0,.10)
I% = Solve	5 N	
PV = −100	150 FV	
PMT = 0	I/YR	
FV = 150		

EXAMPLE 4.28 Suppose you borrow $1,000, with terms that you will repay in a lump sum of $1,750 at the end of three years. What is the effective interest rate on this loan? The inputs are: PV = $1,000; FV = $1,750; and $n = 3$. Solving, $i = (\$1,750 \div \$1,000)^{1/3} - 1 = \textbf{20.51\%}$.

APPLICATION: TIME-WEIGHTED RETURN There are many applications in which we need to determine the rate of change in values over time. To accomplish this, we calculate the time-weighted return. Examples include the growth in a savings account over time if interest rates change periodically and the growth in an investment portfolio over time. If values are changing over time, we refer to the rate of change as the *growth rate* if it is increasing over time, or the *rate of decline* or a *negative growth rate* if values are decreasing over time.

To make comparisons easier, we usually specify the growth rate as a rate per year. We can use the information about the starting value (the PV), the ending value (the FV), and the number of periods to determine the rate of growth of values over this time. To make comparisons among investments, we typically need to determine the average annual growth rate.

For example, consider an investment that has a value of $100 in year 0, a value of $150 at the end of the first year and a value of $200 at the end of two periods. What is this investment's annual growth rate?

$$PV = \$100$$

$$FV = \$200$$

$$n = 2$$

We know from the basic valuation equation that $FV = PV \, (1 + i)^n$. Rearranging and solving for *i*, we can see that

$$i = \sqrt[n]{\frac{FV}{PV}} - 1$$

Inserting the known values into this equation to solve for i, we conclude that the growth was 41.42 percent:

$$i = (\$200 \div \$100)^{1/2} - 1 = 20.5 - 1 = 1.4142 - 1 = 41.42\%$$

We could have easily used our spreadsheet program or financial calculator to perform this calculation as well.[6] Checking our work,

$$\$100 \, (1 + 0.4142) \times (1 + 0.4142) = \$200$$

Therefore, $100 grows to $200 at the rate of 41.42 percent per year.

This rate is the geometric average of the annual growth rates. To see this, consider the two annual growth rates for this example. The growth rate in the first year is ($150 – 100) ÷ $100 = $150 ÷ $100 = 50%. The growth rate for the second year is ($200 – 150) ÷ $150 = 33.3333%. We calculate the *geometric average return* (or *geometric mean return*) as

$$\text{Geometric average return} = [(1 + i_1) \times (1 + i_2) \times (1 + i_n)]^{1/n} - 1$$

where the subscript on i indicates the period. For this example is

$$\text{Geometric average return} = [(1 + 0.50) \times (1 + 0.3333)]^{1/2} - 1 = 41.42\%$$

This is different from the arithmetic average rate of (0.50 + 0.3333) ÷ 2 = 41.67%. The arithmetic average is not appropriate because it does not consider the effects of compounding. When we are dealing with returns on investments, we often refer to the geometric average of returns as simply the time-weighted return.

We can apply this return calculation to investments. Consider the returns on the S&P 500 Index for the following years:[7]

Year	Return
2001	−11.89%
2002	−11.20%
2003	28.69%
2004	10.88%
2005	4.91%
2006	15.79%
2007	5.49%

Over the years 2005 through 2007, the average annual return on the S&P 500 index was

$$\text{Return 2005–2007} = [(1 + 0.0491) \times (1 + 0.1579) \times (1 + 0.0549)]^{1/3} - 1$$

$$= 8.6175\%$$

Over the years 2001 through 2007, the average annual return on the S&P 500 index was 5.2493 percent:

Year	1 + Return
2001	0.8811
2002	× 0.8880
2003	× 1.2869
2004	× 1.1088
2005	× 1.0491
2006	× 1.1579
2007	× 1.0549
Product	1.052493
Less	1.000000
Return	0.052493

EXAMPLE 4.29   Walt Disney Company paid the following annual dividends from 2004 through 2008:

Year	Dividends Paid (in millions)	Dividends per Share
2004	$430	$0.21
2005	$490	$0.24
2006	$519	$0.27
2007	$637	$0.31
2008	$664	$0.35

1. What has been the growth in dividends paid between 2004 and 2008?
2. What has been the growth in dividends per share between 2004 and 2008?[8]

Answer:

1. PV = $430; FV = $664; $n = 4$; Solve for i. $i = $ **11.4743%**.
2. PV = $0.21; FV = $0.35; $n = 4$; Solve for i. $i = $ **13.6219%**.

Why four periods, instead of five? Because we are looking at growth from 2004 through 2008, so therefore from 2004 to 2005 is one period, 2005 to 2006 is the second period, and so on.

The dividends per share grew at a faster rate than the total dollar of dividends paid because the company bought back some shares of stock, which reduces the number of shares outstanding.

Finance Math in Action

The Office of Federal Housing Enterprise and Oversight maintains an index of home values for the United States, regions, and metropolitan statistical areas

(MSA).* We can use the financial math to determine the average annual growth in the value of homes, based on index values:

End of Year	Miami–Miami Beach, Florida MSA	Champaign–Urbana, Illinois MSA
1985	67.62	78.95
2000	127.97	127.58
2007	338.31	179.36

1985 through 2007

There are 22 years of growth from the end of 1985 to the end of 2007. The calculation for the Miami–Miami Beach MSA home price index indicates a growth of 7.583 percent:

$$\text{growth} = \sqrt[22]{\frac{338.31}{67.62}} - 1 = 7.583\% \text{ per year}$$

We could have also used a calculator or spreadsheet with the inputs of PV = 67.62, FV = 338.31, and n = 22.

The Champaign–Urbana MSA home price growth over the same period was 3.8 percent:

$$\text{growth} = \sqrt[22]{\frac{179.36}{78.95}} - 1 = 3800\% \text{ per year}$$

2000 through 2007

$$\text{Miami–Miami Beach MSA: growth} = \sqrt[7]{\frac{338.31}{127.97}} - 1 = 14.899\% \text{ per year}$$

$$\text{Champaign–Urbana MSA: growth} = \sqrt[7]{\frac{179.36}{127.58}} - 1 = 4.987\% \text{ per year}$$

*You can find the value of the indexes for all MSA at the Office of Federal Housing Enterprise Oversight (OFHEO) website, www.ofheo.gov.

APPLICATION: THE MONEY-WEIGHTED RETURN   The time-weighted return is useful in situations when you want to determine returns when there are no cash flows going in or out of the investment during its life. However, if you do have cash inflows or outflows during the investment's life, a better measure of return is the money-weighted return.

The *money-weighted return*, also known as the internal rate of return or the *dollar-weighted return*, considers the money flowing in and out of the investment. Suppose you have an investment with the following cash flows:

End of Year	Cash Flow
2011	−$100,000
2012	+20,000
2013	+30,000
2014	+40,000
2015	+50,000

The money-weighted return is the return that equates the present value of the cash inflows—the $20,000, $30,000, $40,000, and $50,000—with the cash outflow—the $100,000.

Representing this in an equation,

$$CF_0 = \sum_{t=1}^{N} \frac{CF_t}{(1 + IRR)^t}$$

and inserting the cash flows for the problem at hand:

$$-\$100,000 = \frac{\$10,000}{(1 + IRR)^1} + \frac{\$20,000}{(1 + IRR)^2} + \frac{\$30,000}{(1 + IRR)^3} + \frac{\$40,000}{(1 + IRR)^4}$$

We can solve this by using trial and error (which is usually no fun), the IRR function in a financial calculator, or the IRR function in a spreadsheet:

TI-83/84 Using TVM Solver	HP10B	Microsoft Excel
List:	100000 +/− CF$_j$	
{20000,30000,40000,50000}	20000 CF$_j$	
STO L1	30000 CF$_j$	
IRR(-100000,L1)	40000 CF$_j$	
	50000 CF$_j$	
	IRR	

	A	B	
1	2011	−100,000	
2	2012	20,000	
3	2013	30,000	
4	2014	40,000	
5	2015	50,000	
6			
7	IRR		←=IRR(B1:B5)

The internal rate of return for this series of cash flows is 12.826 percent.

TIME- VERSUS MONEY-WEIGHTED RETURNS To see the difference between the time-weighted and money-weighted returns, let's compare these methods of calculation on the following investment. Suppose you buy the stock on January 1, 2010, and sell the stock on January 1, 2012, receiving dividends at the beginning of 2011 and 2012:

Date	Stock Value	Dividend
December 31, 2010	$20	
December 31, 2011	$25	$1
December 31, 2012	$20	$1

The time-weighted return requires you to calculate the return for each period. We refer to this return as the holding period return (HPR). For a given period, the HPR is

$$\text{HPR for one period} = \frac{\text{Ending value} + \text{Dividend} - \text{Beginning value}}{\text{Beginning value}}$$

In our example, we must calculate the HPR for two periods: the year ending December 31, 2011, and the year ending December 31, 2012:[9]

Date	Stock Value	Dividend	HPR for the Year
December 31, 2010	$20		
December 31, 2011	$22	$1	$\frac{\$25 - 20 + 1}{\$20} = 0.30$
December 31, 2012	$20	$1	$\frac{\$20 - 25 + 1}{\$25} = -0.16$

Using these HPR, the time-weighted return is

$$\text{Time-weighted return} = [(1 + 0.30) \times (1 - 0.16)]^{1/2} - 1 = 4.5\%$$

We have to first identify the cash inflows and outflows in order to calculate the money-weighted return:

Date	Cash Flow
December 31, 2010	−$20
December 31, 2011	$1
December 31, 2012	$21

The money-weighted return is 5 percent. So which return do you use? The money-weighted return is the true return on the investment and is therefore preferred.

When do you use the time-weighted return?

The time-weighted return on investment is useful when you want to determine a return from one point in time to another, such as when you want to check the return on your portfolio between specific years. However, if you invested additional money or withdrew funds from the portfolio within this time, the time-weighted return is not accurate.

When do you use the money-weighted return?

The money-weighted return on investment is useful when you want to compare investments that require different size investments. And money-weighted returns are useful in determining the return on an investment when there are deposits and/or withdrawals during the lifetime of the investment.

Mathematically, there is a problem when using the money-weighted return in certain circumstances. If the cash flows change sign—from positive to negative or negative to positive—more than once during the life of the investment, there is no unique, mathematical solution to the problem and therefore whatever return that the calculator or spreadsheet calculates is not useful.[10]

Try It! 4.15: Return on Investment

Suppose you bought a stock today for $45. If the stock does not pay dividends, but you expect this stock to increase by 5 percent in the first year and 7 percent in the second year, what is your anticipated annual return on investment?

Financial Math in Action

The Beardstown Business and Professional Women's Investment Club—more familiarly known as the Beardstown Ladies—was an investment group of women in Illinois who reported returns on their investments that were simply too good to be true.

Started in 1983, the Ladies pooled their funds and invested these funds. They reported returns that exceeded the return on the market for the same period, which led to television appearances and book deals.

What was the key to their success? As it turns out, their apparent success came from ignoring additional contributions to the investment funds. By calculating returns incorrectly—by looking at the growth in the total funds, while ignoring investors' additional contributions into the fund, they were able to report that they beat the market. Once the problem with return calculations was exposed in the press in 1998, the Ladies retreated from the limelight.* *Bottom line?* If it looks too good to be true, it probably is.

---

*This was exposed by Shane Tritsch, "Bull Marketing," *Chicago Magazine*, March 1998.

Rules

THE RULE OF 72 The *Rule of 72* is a quick and approximate method of determining the combination of interest rate and number of periods needed to double your money. For example, if the interest rate is 6 percent, the approximate number of periods is $72 \div 6 = 12$. Using a calculator or spreadsheet, it takes 11.8957 periods.[11]

We could also use this rule to determine the interest rate for a given number of periods. For example, what would the interest rate have to be for you to double your money in 12 years? According to the Rule of 72, the rate is 6 percent, and using a calculator the rate is 5.9463 percent.[12]

The Rule of 72 is a good approximation for the number of periods:

Interest Rate	Approximate Number of Periods	Accurate Number of Periods
3%	24.00	23.45
4%	18.00	17.67
5%	14.40	14.25
6%	12.00	11.90
7%	10.29	10.24
8%	9.00	9.01
9%	8.00	8.04
10%	7.20	7.27

Looking at this from the perspective of estimating the interest rate:

Number of Periods	Approximate Interest Rate	Accurate Interest Rate
3	24.00%	25.99%
4	18.00%	18.92%
5	14.40%	14.87%
6	12.00%	12.25%
7	10.29%	10.41%
8	9.00%	9.05%
9	8.00%	8.01%
10	7.20%	7.18%

The rule tends to be more accurate when solving for an interest rate when the number of periods is around 10 periods, and more accurate when solving for the number of periods when the interest rate is around 7.85 percent, but it is a good rule of thumb no matter the rate or number of periods.

THE RULE OF 69   The *Rule of 69* is a quick and approximate method of determining the combination of interest rate and number of years needed to double your money if interest is continuously compounded. For example, if the interest rate is 6 percent, continuously compounded, the number of years needed to double your money is $69 \div 6 = 11.5$ years. Solving directly, the number of periods is 11.55245.[13]

Why do we refer to this rule as the Rule of 69? Because the natural logarithm of 2 is 0.693147, which, in percentage terms, is 69 percent. This rule is often "rounded up" and referred to as the *Rule of 70*, but as a Rule of 69, it's pretty accurate.

OTHER RULES   We can use other rules for simple approximations of interest rates and number of periods. The Rule of 114 is similar to the Rule of 72, but involves the tripling of values, whereas the Rule of 144 is the approximation for quadrupling values. You should note, however, that these are rules of thumb and that using a calculator or a spreadsheet will produce values that are more accurate.

Summary

Understanding how to calculate effective interest rates and yields enables you to make better choices, whether you are involved in borrowing or in lending. One of the most useful mathematical tools in finance is the effective annual rate formula, which enables you to put different financing terms on a common, annual basis.

In addition to calculating effective annual rates, we also looked at calculating returns on investments. There are different types of returns that you can calculate to evaluate an investment, but the two most common are the time-weighted return and the money-weighted return. If you want to evaluate the success of a particular investment over time, you can evaluate this using the time-weighted return, which is a geometric mean of the individual periods' returns. If the investment requires you to make additional investments or you intend to make withdrawals during the life of the investment, you will want to use the money-weighted return on investment to get the best reading of the return on your investment.

"Try It!" Solutions

4.13 APR

First, identify the compounding period and the number of these periods in a year.

The compounding period is 10 days.

In a year period, there are 36.5 of these 10-day periods, so n is 36.5.

Second, identify the rate period compounding period. The interest per period, i, is 0.175.

The APR is therefore: APR $= i \times n = 0.175 \times 36.5 = 6.3875$ or **638.75%**

4.14 Effective Annual Rate of Interest

$$\text{EAR} = (1 + 0.194/365)^{365} - 1 = 21.4034\%$$

4.15 Return on Investment

The average annual return on investment is $[(1 + 0.05) \times (1 + 0.07)]^{1/2} - 1 = 5.995\%$

Another way of looking at this is that you are anticipating that the stock will be worth $\$45 \times (1 + 0.05) \times (1 + 0.07) = \$50.5575$ two years from now. Solving for i,

Notes

1. 15 U.S.C. §§ 1601–1666j; and Federal Reserve System Regulation Z, 1968.
2. Board of Governors of the Federal Reserve System, Report to Congress, *Finance Charges for Consumer Credit under the Truth in Lending Act*, April 1996.
3. Federal Reserve System Regulation DD, 199.
4. For a list of state limits on payday loans, see the Bankrate Monitor at Bankrate.com.
5. Because these calculations require changing the payments per period settings (i.e., P/YR) in some calculator models, be sure to change these back to one payment per period following the calculations—otherwise all subsequent financial calculations may be incorrect.

6. Remember, though the inputs are PV = 100, FV = 200, and n = 22, you need to actually enter the present value as a negative value to use the built-in programs for solving for I/YR or RATE, for your financial calculator or spreadsheet functions, respectively.

7. We downloaded the total returns on the S&P 500 index from the Standard & Poor's website, www2.standardandpoors/spf/xls/MONTHLY.xls. These returns include not only the change in the value of the index, but also the dividends paid on the index's stocks.

8. Dividends per share are dividends paid divided by the number of shares outstanding.

9. So if this is the HPR, why don't we just calculate the return over the two years as the ratio of (1) the difference in the stock value (which is $0 in this example), plus the $2 of dividends, to (2) the beginning stock value? First, because there are two periods and we need to consider this fact, and second, because we can't just add the two dividend payments because they are received at different points in time and, hence, have different time values.

10. In this last problem, there was only one sign change in the cash flows (from −$20 to $1), so there is no problem.

11. You can solve for the number of periods directly using the basic equation, FV = PV $(1 + i)^n$. To solve for n, you need to take logs, rearrange, and solve for n: n = (ln 2 − ln1) / ln(1 + i); n = 11.89566.

12. You can solve directly for the interest rate by rearranging the basic equation FV = PV $(1 + i)^n$, and considering that the ratio of the future value to the present value, FV ÷ PV, is 2: $i = {}^{12}\sqrt{2} - 1 = 5.9463\%$.

13. Solving this directly, $e^{\mathrm{APR} \times n} = 2$; APR × n = ln 2; 0.06 × n = 0.693147; n = 11.55245.

Part V Using Financial Calculators

Financial calculators can save you lots of time and trouble in performing the mathematics described in this book. However, there are some basics that you need to know before becoming reliant upon the calculators for financial transactions. In this appendix, we cover the basic set-up and use of the financial functions in several popular financial calculators, as well as a versatile scientific calculator. If we do not cover the particular calculator that you have, don't worry. Most financial calculators follow similar programming and keys to the ones we discuss, so you just need to find your closest match.

The financial calculators that we cover in this part are the following:

- Hewlett-Packard 10B (HP10B)
- Texas Instruments BAII Plus (TI-BAII)
- Hewlett-Packard 12C (HP12C)

The Hewlett-Packard 17B and 19B calculators (HP17B and HP19B, respectively) have similar functions to the HP10B, so we don't perform each calculation with these calculators. (Refer to the instructions for the HP10B as needed.) However, where there are some differences, we will note these briefly.

In the part, we simplify our presentation by presenting the calculations for the HP10B. The HP10B is the simplest financial calculator to set up and use and its financial functions are very similar to those of the TI-BAII, HP12C, HP17B, and HP19B.

The scientific calculator that we cover is the Texas Instruments TI-83, whose financial calculations are identical to the more recent model, the TI-84. In referring to these calculators, we simply designate the calculator as TI-83/84.

Preparing the Calculator

Your calculator may come from the factory with certain display and calculation settings. For example, the HP10B comes ready to perform calculations using two decimal places (a display setting) and 12 payments per year (a calculation setting). If you need more precision, you need to adjust the display. Also, if you require one payment per period, as in most of our calculations, you need to adjust the payments per year.

ADJUST THE NUMBER OF DIGITS DISPLAYED Because financial transactions often use interest rates and compounding, use at least four places to the right of the decimal place for all calculations. You can set your calculator's display program to display a specified number of decimal places. To change the setting to display four decimal places, for example:

HP10B ■ DISP 4
HP12C f 4
HP17B DSP FIX 4 INPUT

You can adjust the number of decimal places that your calculator displays, but this adjustment does not affect the precision of the calculation within the calculator. As long as you perform the calculation within the calculator, the model determines the precision of the calculation. You may be displaying only four decimal places, but the calculation may use 14 decimal places.

Bottom line? Display at least four decimal places.

CHECK THE FREQUENCY OF PAYMENTS Most calculations require one interest compounding per period, and, in the case of annuities, one payment per period. However, some calculators come from the factory set up for mortgages and the settings are 12 payments per period.

For most calculations, we need to make sure that the calculator program we are using considers only one payment per period and one compounding per period.

HP10B	1 ■ P/YR
TI-BAII	P/Y 1 ENTER
HP12C	*Frequency of payments are not programmed.*
HP17B	FIN TVM OTHER P/YR 1 INPUT
TI-83/84	P/Y = 1

For simple lump sum problems, when you are calculating a present value given a future value or vice versa, the setting of the frequency of payments does not matter because there is no payment (PMT) specified—so it is set at the default setting of zero. But if you are working with a payment, as is the case with any annuity, you risk altering the valuation (in other words, making an error) if you do not set the payment frequency correctly.

There are some applications, such as mortgage payments, when you may want to set the payment frequency (e.g., 12 for mortgages). This works well as long as you specify the other parameters—the number of years and the interest rate—appropriately.

We do not recommend that you set the payment frequency to anything other than one per period. The reason? When you clear the time value of money registers (e.g., CLR TVM in the TI-BAII calculator), you don't clear or change this setting. In other words, a change in the P/Y remains until you reset it to the next value.[1] Therefore, you may get subsequent calculations incorrectly—and not realize it.

Bottom line? Set the P/Y to 1 no matter what the problem.

TI-83/84: P/Y and C/Y

The TI-83/84 financial program has both a P/Y and a C/Y key.

The P/Y setting is the number of payments per year.

The C/Y setting is for the number of times interest compounds in a year.

This is different than the HP10B, TABAII, and HP12C calculators that have only a P/Y setting. In these calculators, if the P/Y setting is 12 but the periodic payment is set to zero, the P/Y key acts as the equivalent to the C/Y key in the TI-83/84.

CLEAR THE FINANCIAL FUNCTION'S REGISTERS AFTER EACH PROBLEM   The information you input and the results of the calculations you perform are stored in the computer's registers (its memory for the bits and pieces of information). Clear your registers before starting a new calculation. If you fail to clear the registers in your calculator, you will find that the next problem you do will use data left over from the last problem, even if you had turned off your calculator since the last problem. To clear your calculator:

Calculator	Clearing Operation
HP10B	CLEAR ALL
TI-BAII	CLR WORK
HP12C	f REG
HP17B	CLEAR DATA

Each calculator has its own set of programs and clearing the registers that use these programs will differ. Some examples:

- *TI-BA II* has a specific clearing function for the time value of money registers, CLR TVM. However, this clearing does not clear the cash flow registers that we use in the NPV and IRR calculations; you will need to perform the more general CLEAR WORK to clear these registers.

■ *TI-83/84* You are filling in a screen and will change all entries to the appropriate values, so if the calculation has no payment, you will set the payment to zero: PMT = 0.

■ *HP17B* allows storage of individual cash flow data; you need to clear the cash flow information separately: ■ CLEAR DATA YES

A couple of warnings:

■ Keep in mind that clearing the display window on a calculator does not clear any registers.

■ Turning off the calculator does not clear any registers. The calculator will remember the last calculation you performed. You can turn off your calculator today and then turn it back on, assuming the batteries are still good, in two years and the calculator will remember your last calculation.

Bottom line? Learn how to clear your calculator's registers.

The Basics

The manufacturers design most calculators so that many keys serve double or triple duty to keep hand-held calculators small, but useful, for many different types of calculations. For example, in the HP10B calculator the key labeled y^x is used for both multiplication ($\times$) and raising a value to a power (y^x). How do you raise some value to a power? You first strike second-level key, and then y^x.[2] The second-level key tells the computer to use the second function (y^x) of this key, much like a Shift key on a keyboard.

Access to the double- or triple-level functions differs among calculators. For the HP10B, we access the alternate function of a key by using the colored key. In other models, the alternative function may be accessed through, for example, a 2nd key or a g key. You need to refer to the manual that came with your financial calculator to see how to access these second- or third-level functions.

In addition to access to different levels through a single key, some calculators, such as the Hewlett-Packard HP17B and HP19B models, have a set of unidentified keys (just below the display) that perform a function assigned to them based on the screen shown in the display. For example, if you select the time value of money screen (by striking the ■ key below the FIN in the display and then the ■ below the TVM in the display), these keys are assigned to represent PV, N, FV, and so on.

In the examples that follow, the keys are described by the label corresponding to the function you are using. For example, to calculate 3^4 on the HP10B, the key strokes are indicated as:

3 ■ y^x 4 y^x

which we represent as:

HP10B
1.05
■ y^x
4 y^x

The basic math calculations (such as addition, subtraction, multiplication, and division) are similar among the different brands and models. With the exception of the HP12C, the math is performed much like you would if you were doing it without the calculator. Consider the problem of multiplying 3 by 4:

All models except HP12C:

HP10B
3
×
4
=

You perform division, addition, and subtraction in a like manner.

The HP12C uses reverse-Polish notation, which is tough to get used to but becomes a time-saver in complex calculations.

HP12C
3
enter
4 ×

EXAMPLE   Solve the following using the calculator: 1.05 to the fourth power, or 1.05^4. The answer is 1.2155:

HP10B	TIBAII	HP12C	TI-83/84
1.05	1.05 y^x	1.05	1.05
∎ y^x	4 y^x	y^x	$\perp$
4 y^x		4	4
			enter

Solve the following using the calculator: fourth root of 1.05, or $\sqrt[4]{1.05} = 1.05^{1/4}$. The answer is 1.0123.

HP10B	TIBAII	HP12C	TI-83/84
1.05	1.05 y^x	1.05	1.05
∎ y^x	.25 y^x	y^x	$\perp$
.25 y^x		.25	.25
			enter

Financial Functions

In addition to the math functions, financial calculators provide two types of financial programs within the calculator.

TIME VALUE OF MONEY KEYS   A row of keys that we use to input the variables in a time value of money problem:

N	I/YR	PV	PMT	FV
↑	↑	↑	↑	↑
Number of compounding periods	Interest rate per compounding period	Present value	Periodic payment	Future value

We input values by typing in the value and then striking the appropriate TVM key. Once we input the known values, we then strike the value we seek to solve.

CASH FLOW KEYS   A set of keys or second-level keys to use to input cash flows to solve for the net present value (NPV) or the internal rate of return (IRR).

CF	I/YR	NPV	IRR
↑	↑	↑	↑
A period's cash flow	Interest rate per compounding period	Net present value	Internal rate of return

To use the cash flow program, we enter the cash flows in chronological order, and then either solve for the IRR or enter the interest rate and solve for the NPV.

TVM FUNCTIONS   Let's look closely at an example using the time value of money functions to solve a future value problem.

If an investor deposits $1,000 today in an account that pays 5 percent interest each year, how much will be in the account at the end of 10 years?

We are given the following in the problem description:

Present value, PV = $1,000
Interest rate per period, i = 5% per year
Number of periods, n = 10 years

and we want to solve for FV. The answer is $1,628.89.

In the financial calculators, the financial functions are on the face of the calculator. In the TI-83/84, you need to access the financial applications through its applications.

TI-83/84 Financial Applications

In the TI-83/84, you need to first enter the financial functions and then input the data into the screen. For example, TVM Solver screen on the TI-83/84 has everything set up and you simply enter in the values for n, etc.

Accessing the financial programs:

apps
1: Finance
enter
1: TVM Solver
enter
$n = 10$
$i\% = 5$
PV = −1000
PMT = 0
FV = alpha solve
P/Y = 1
C/Y = 1
PMT: end begin

When the cursor is at the FV = entry, use the ALPHA SOLVE to solve for the future value.

For presentation, we represent the inputs for the TI-83/84 for all the values that are necessary for the problem at hand.

The future value calculation is the following:

HP10B	TI-BAII	HP12C	TI-83/84
1000 +/−	1000 +/−	1000 CHS	N = 10
5 I/YR	5 I/YR	5 i	I% = 5
10 N	10 N	10 n	PV = −1000
FV	CPT	FV	*Solve for*
	FV		FV

Let's try another calculation.

Suppose you have a goal of saving $1,000 by three years from now. If you earn 6 percent on your savings, what is the amount you need to deposit today to reach this goal?

We have the following information:

FV = $1,000
n = 3
i = 6%

and want to solve for the present value, PV. The present value is $839.62.

Using the calculators,

HP10B	TIBAII	HP12C	TI-83/84
1000 FV	1000 FV	1000 FV	N = 10
6 I/YR	6 I/YR	6 i	I% = 6
3 N	3 N	3 n	FV = 1000
FV	CPT	FV	*Solve for*
	FV		FV

You will notice that the calculator reports the present value as a negative number, –839.62. This is the way the calculators are programmed. The correct answer is $829.62: if you invest $839.62 today, you will reach your goal of $1,000 at the end of three years.

CASH FLOW FUNCTIONS   The cash flow functions in financial calculators are separate from the TVM functions. We use the cash flow functions when we are valuing a set of uneven cash flows or determining a return, referred to as the internal rate of return, on a set of cash flows. In the case of these types of problems, the most challenging part of executing this on a calculator is inputting the cash flows correctly.

The basic idea is to enter all cash flows in chronological order. If there is a period that does not have a cash flow, you must enter a zero in the sequence; failure to include the zero will result in an incorrect valuation or return.

The calculators differ somewhat in terms of how you enter the initial cash flow, and some calculators allow or require you to indicate the frequency of the cash flow. How you enter the cash flows is what really sets the financial calculators apart.

Consider the following set of cash flows:

Period	Cash Flow
0	–$10,000
1	$1,000
2	$2,000
3	$12,000

And suppose we want to calculate the present value of these cash flows using a discount rate of 10 percent, as well as the internal rate of return. The net present value is $1,577.7611 and the internal rate of return is 16.1659 percent.

First, ignore the dollar signs. These cash flows may be dollars, yen, euros, or any other currency—it doesn't matter within the calculator. Second, ignore the commas that we typically use to help us view amounts; in other words, $1,000 is 1000 for calculator purposes.

We will treat the TI-83/84 separately because its method is quite different than the financial calculators. Using the three calculators, let's calculate the net present value and internal rate of return. We can see that the entry of the cash flows is different:

HP10B	TI-BAII	HP12C
10000 +/− CF$_j$	CF 10000 +/− ENTER	10000 CHS
1000 CF$_j$	↑ 1 enter	CF$_0$
2000 CF$_j$	↑ 1000 enter	1000 CF$_j$
12000 CF$_j$	↑ 1 enter	2000 CF$_j$
10 I/YR	↑ 2000 enter	12000 CF$_j$
■ NPV	↑ 1 enter	10 i
■ IRR	↑ 12000 enter	f NPV
	CPT NPV	f IRR
	10 enter	
	↑↑↑ *(to find NPV=)*	
	CPT	
	IRR CPT	

There are a few subtle differences among the methods of inputting data:

- The HP10B entry is the simplest.
- The TI-BAII requires indicating the frequency of each cash flow, which is rather tedious, and we must manage the data by using arrows; think of these arrows and changing cells in an imaginary spreadsheet, one that you cannot see.
- The HP12C has a different entry for the initial cash flow than the other cash flows, but otherwise it is similar to the HP10B.

The TI-83/84 requires us to input the cash flow by placing it in a list. Once these cash flows are in a list, we use the NPV and IRR programs with this list.

Option 1	Option 2
2nd {	STAT
1000,2000,12000	*Select* 1:EDIT enter
2nd {	*and then enter the cash flows in the list.*
STO L1	*To leave the list entry,* 2nd quit

Once you have cash flows saved in a list (using whatever list name you wish, including default names of L1, L2, etc.), you use the financial programs that you access through APPS and then selecting 1:Finance. There are two programs we use: 7:NPV and 8:IRR. In the NPV program, the interest rate (in whole numbers) is the first argument, the initial cash flow is the second argument, and the list is the third argument, each separated by commas:

TI-83/84
NPV(10,−10000,2nd L1
enter
enter

For the internal rate of return, there are two arguments: the initial cash flow and the list:

TI-83/84
IRR(−10000, 2nd L1
enter

Tips

USE SHORTCUTS WHENEVER POSSIBLE   Many calculators allow you to key in a value and then key in how many times that value is repeated. For example, if you have to input six consecutive cash flows of $1 each in your HP12C, for example, 1 g CF_j 6 g N_j, the sequence 6 g N_j tells the calculator's program that the one dollar cash flow is repeated six times.

Consider the following problem. We want to calculate the net present value, using a 10 percent interest rate, and the internal rate of return for the following cash flows:

Period	Cash Flow
0	−€10,000
1	€1,000
2	€1,000
3	€1,000
4	€12,000

The net present value is €683.0135 and the internal rate of return is 12.0896 percent. We can use the shortcuts for the series of three cash flows that are the same:[3]

HP10B	TI-BAII	HP12C
10000 +/− CF_j	CF 10000 +/− ENTER	10000 CHS
1000 CF_j	↑ 3 enter	CF_0
3 ■ Nj	↑ 1000 enter	1000 CF_j
12000 CF_j	↑ 1 enter	3 g N_j
10 I/YR	↑ 12000 enter	12000 CF_j
■ NPV	CPT NPV	10 i
■ IRR	10 enter	f NPV
	↑↑↑ *(to find NPV=)*	f IRR
	CPT	
	IRR CPT	

CHECK THE TIMING OF THE CASH FLOWS   Check to see whether your calculator is set up to assume cash flows at the end of the period or the beginning of the period.

Many calculator brands allow you to specify when cash flows occur (beginning or end of the period), which is useful for annuity due calculations. However, like most registers in the calculator, the calculator remembers the last way you specified the cash flows, so you must change this register if you, say, switch from an annuity due to an ordinary annuity calculation.

To change the setting from end-of-period to beginning-of-period, for example:

HP10B	■ BEG/END
TI-BAII	2nd format 4 enter
HP12C	g BEG
HP17B	fin tvm other beg exit

CHECK YOUR WORK   Always check for the reasonableness of your calculations; it's very easy to hit the wrong key—especially when taking tests. Learn to do your problem with your calculator and then check your answers using another method, such as with the basic math. Also, use commonsense checks for reasonableness. If the interest rate is greater than zero (which should be the case), then:

PV	<	FV
FV	>	PV
PV of a series of cash flows	<	Sum of series of cash flows
FV of a series of cash flows	>	Sum of series of cash flows

Troubleshooting Problems

1. I keep getting smaller present values and larger future values than what I should each time I try to replicate one of the examples.

    Check whether the calculator TVM settings are in the beginning of the period mode or the ending period mode.

    Check the P/Y setting to make sure it is equal to one.

    Check to make sure that you cleared the calculator before performing the calculation.

2. When I calculate the net present value of a series of cash flows, I sometimes (but not always) get a value less than what the value should be.

    Check to see whether you entered zero for periods in which the cash flows are zero.

3. When I calculate the internal rate of return for a series of cash flows, I sometimes (but not always) get a value less than what the value should be.

    Check to see whether you entered zero for periods in which the cash flows are zero.

4. When I calculate the net present value of a series of cash flows, I always get a value much larger than what the value should be.

    Check to see whether you entered the interest as a whole number instead of in decimal form. That is, if the interest rate is 10 percent, you should enter 10, not .1.

5. When I calculate the present value or the future value, I sometimes get an incorrect value, but there doesn't seem to be a pattern in these errors.

   Check to see whether you are clearing the calculator between each problem.

6. I get "no Solution" or "Error 5," or "ERR: NO SIGN CHNG" in the display window.

   Make sure that you have entered the present value as a negative value.

7. I am doing a simple lump sum problem (that is, converting a present value into a future value or vice versa), and the present value is equal to the future value.

   Check to see whether you entered the interest rate.

8. I use the HP12C and the values displayed have commas instead of decimal places.

   You have somehow changed the display to European notation. To change the display to U.S. display, first turn the calculator off and then turn it on while holding down the decimal point key.

9. I was performing a problem that required two steps, and my final answer is off by a few cents.

   If you calculate the first step in the calculator, write down the values, and then input these values in the calculator for the second step, you will have lost the precision from the first step. In other words, by using the displayed values in the first step as inputs to the second step, you did not consider that the displayed value is merely a few of the many decimal places that the calculator uses. Either tolerate the small imprecision, or figure out how to perform both steps sequentially in the calculator.

Notes

1. If you set P/YR to 12 and then turn off the calculator, the next time you pick it up and turn it on, the payment frequency is still 12.

2. The second-level keys in most calculators are indicated as colored (e.g., orange or blue), or simply 2nd.

3. In the case of the HP17B and the HP19B, the shortcut for cash flows is the prompt #TIMES that corresponds to a period's cash flow.

Part VI Formulas

Notation

APR	Annual percentage rate
CF	Cash flow
CIF_t	Cash inflow in period t
COF_t	Cash outflow in period t
D	Dividend per share
D_t	Dividend per share in period t
e	Euler's e
EAR	Effective annual rate
FV	Future value
g	Growth rate

HPR	Holding period return
i	Rate of interest
IRR	Internal rate of return
i_t	Interest rate in period t
M	Maturity or face value of a bond
n	Number of compounding periods
N	Number of payments
NPV	Net present value
P_0	Price per share of common stock
PI	Profitability index
PMT	Periodic, even payment
PV	Present value
r_d	Required rate of return on a bond
r_e	Required rate of return on equity
r_p	Required rate of return on a preferred stock
V	Value of a bond

Future value with discrete compounding:

$$FV = PV(1+i)^n$$

Future value with continuous compounding:

$$FV = PV\left[e^{APR\,n}\right]$$

Present value with discrete compounding:

$$PV = \frac{FV}{(1+i)^n}$$

Present value with continuous compounding:

$$PV = \frac{FV}{e^{APR n}}$$

Present value of a stream of cash flows:

$$PV = \sum_{t=1}^{N} \frac{CF_t}{(1+i)^t}$$

Present value of a perpetuity:

$$PV = \frac{CF}{i}$$

Present value of an ordinary annuity:

$$PV = \sum_{t=1}^{N} \frac{CF}{(1+i)^t} = CF \sum_{t=1}^{N} \frac{1}{(1+i)^t} = CF\left(1 - \frac{\left(1+i^N\right)}{i}\right)$$

Present value of an annuity due:

$$PV = \sum_{t=1}^{N} \frac{CF}{(1+i)^{t-1}} = CF \sum_{t=1}^{N} \frac{1}{(1+i)^{t-1}}$$

Annual percentage rate:

$$\text{APR} = i \times n$$

Effective annual rate, discrete compounding:

$$\text{EAR} = (1 + i)^n - 1$$

$$\text{EAR} = \left(1 + {}^{\text{APR}}\!/_n\right)^n - 1$$

Effective annual rate, continuous compounding:

$$\text{EAR} = e^{\text{APR}} - 1$$

Interest rate implied by PV, FV, and n:

$$i = \left(\sqrt[n]{{}^{\text{FV}}\!/_{\text{PV}}}\right) - 1$$

Geometric average return:

$$\text{Geometric average return} = [(1 + i_1) \times (1 + i_2) \times \ldots \times (1 + i_n)]^{1/n} - 1,$$

Holding period return for one period:

$$\text{HPR for one period} = \frac{\text{Ending value} + \text{Dividend} - \text{Beginning value}}{\text{Beginning value}}$$

Internal rate of return:

$$\text{CF}_0 = \sum_{t=1}^{N} \frac{\text{CF}_t}{(1 + \text{IRR})^t}$$

Loan valuation:

$$\text{PV} = \sum_{t=1}^{N} \frac{\text{PMT}}{\left(1 + \frac{\text{APR}}{12}\right)^t}$$

Bond equivalent yield:

$$\text{Bond equivalent yield} = \text{6-month yield} \times 2$$

Bond valuation:

$$V = \left[\sum_{t=1}^{N} \frac{\text{PMT}_t}{\left(1 + r_d\right)^t}\right] + \frac{M}{(1 + r_d)^N}$$

Value of a share of preferred stock:

$$P_0 = \frac{D}{r_p}$$

Value of a common stock:

$$P_0 = \sum_{t=1}^{\infty} \frac{D_t}{(1 + r_e)^t}$$

Value of a share of common stock if dividends grow at a constant rate:

$$P_0 = \frac{D_0(1+g)}{(r_e - g)} \qquad P_0 = \frac{D_1}{(r_e - g)}$$

Average annual return:

$$i = \sqrt[n]{\frac{FV}{PV}} - 1$$

Net present value:

$$NPV = \frac{\text{Present value}}{\text{of cash inflows}} - \frac{\text{Present value}}{\text{of cash outflows}} = \sum_{t=1}^{N} \frac{CF_t}{(1+i)^t}$$

Profitability index:

$$PI = \frac{\text{Present value}}{\text{of cash inflows}} \bigg/ \frac{\text{Present value}}{\text{of cash outflows}} = \frac{\sum_{t=1}^{N} \dfrac{CIF_t}{(1+i)^t}}{\sum_{t=1}^{N} \dfrac{COF_t}{(1+i)^t}}$$

Internal rate of return:

$$\$0 = \sum_{t=1}^{N} \frac{CF_t}{(1+IRR)^t}$$

Section II: Economics

Part I Monetary Policy: How the Fed Sets, Implements, and Measures Policy Choices

A significant element of competitive and successful equity and fixed income portfolio management is to understand and anticipate the effect of interest rate changes on asset prices. This chapter outlines the key components of the interest rate policy process undertaken by the Federal Reserve, the policy-making body that sets short-term interest rates. Although the Federal Reserve publicly announces its policy decisions, it is extremely useful for the portfolio manager to anticipate policy shifts. The portfolio manager who can anticipate policy shifts can more accurately anticipate changes in asset valuations. In order to anticipate policy shifts, the portfolio manager must not only understand the dynamics of the Fed's decision-making process but must watch the key economic indicators that the Fed watches.

Monetary policy is the U.S. government's most flexible policy tool. It is controlled by the Federal Reserve, which acts independently of government interference. The Federal Reserve, since early 1994, immediately announces policy decisions and communicates forthcoming policy intentions through venues such as Congressional testimony and public speeches. Other government policy instruments that influence economic activity include fiscal policy (taxes and spending), trade, foreign exchange, and other regulatory practices. But none of these government policy tools are as flexible as monetary policy.

Since the Federal Reserve's inception in 1913, it has had the primary task of ensuring that financial conditions are supportive of sustainable, noninflationary economic growth. The Fed has several tools it can employ to influence aggregate demand, output growth, and price behavior. But, as will be discussed later, all of the Fed policy tools directly influence short-term interest rates and only indirectly influence long-term rates.

The effectiveness of any Fed policy on achieving the goal of price stability is limited to the influence of that policy on both short- and long-term interest rates, real and nominal. Price stability is the primary prerequisite for steady long-term economic growth. Low inflation rates enable businesses to increase their investment in infrastructure, including new machinery and high-tech equipment. Therefore, a low inflationary environment brightens the prospects for future increases in productivity and an improved standard of living.

In the short term, the Fed must juggle the simultaneous objectives of stable prices and maximum employment (sustainable growth). Although the president appoints the Fed chairman by legislative decree, the Federal Reserve is an independent agency and is accountable to the public only through the legislative branch of the U.S. government. If the Fed were not an independent agency, it could be subject to political influences promoting economic growth over price stability.

Fed-induced price stability and the absence of consumer and business inflationary expectations are essential to containing speculation and allowing the capital markets to efficiently allocate funds in support of sustainable growth. Generally speaking, capital markets efficiently allocate funds to the sectors of the economy promising the highest risk-adjusted returns. This process is absolutely crucial to the wealth-creating success of modern capitalism. But, as we will discuss later, at times excesses of capital allocation can occur. Capital markets may allocate capital to countries where the risks of debt default or likely debt downgrades appears quite high, such as Mexico in 1995 and southeast Asia in 1997, as these participants have confidence central bankers will successfully stave off defaults. This exaggerated if not misplaced faith that somebody will bail them out of bad investments or lending decisions, called the moral hazard of central banking, is one of the few downside effects to the central bankers' role of lender of last resort.

Key Economic Influences on Fed Policy

Monetary policy is more art than science. In essence, Fed policy is a process of trial and error, observation, and adjustment. The Fed's policies are often countercyclical to the business cycle. At best, Fed policy makers can hope to smooth the peaks and troughs of business cycles. In pursuit of this countercyclical policy approach, when output is excessive relative to the economy's sustainable potential and is potentially inflationary, Fed officials will lean in the direction of more restraint in their policy stance. They will tend to increase interest rates, eventually slowing aggregate demand and output growth to a more sustainable and potentially less inflationary pace. Conversely, when output falters and falls below the economy's sustainable potential, recession threatens. Accordingly, Fed officials will tilt their policy stance in the direction of greater ease, and lower interest rates. Lower interest rates serve to

TABLE 4.1   Significant Economic Release

Payroll employment	Monthly—1st Friday
Housing starts	Monthly—3rd–4th week
Industrial production	Monthly—3rd week
ISM (supplier deliveries)	Monthly—1st business day
Motor vehicle sales	Monthly—1st–3rd business day
Durable goods orders	Monthly—4th week
Employment cost index	Quarterly
Nonfarm productivity growth	Quarterly
Commodity prices	Continuously released

boost aggregate demand and output growth, thereby lessening the threat of recession. A word of caution: Fed officials must feel their way along after implementing policy shifts because the effects from policy shifts are long, variable, and sometimes difficult to predict. The Fed enacts policy shifts based on economic forecasts. Economic forecasting is often an uncertain exercise.

One can develop an idea of the Fed's next policy objective by paying careful attention to various indicators of current economic activity. The key economic releases that serve as the Fed's intermediate policy indicators and that market participants should follow carefully include: nonfarm payrolls, ISM supplier deliveries, industrial production, housing starts, motor vehicle sales, durable goods orders, labor compensation, productivity growth, and commodity prices. Table 4.1 gives the release cycles of these economic indicators. Consistent and meaningful changes in these economic indicators will signal changes in the business cycle and in Fed policy.

- Nonfarm payrolls are released monthly and detail the previous month's changes in the complexion of the workforce including numbers employed, hourly pay changes, and hours worked. Supplier deliveries are part of the Institute for Supply Management's monthly survey. This report reflects survey results of the purchasing managers of hundreds of industrial corporations. The survey reports on the lead time between orders placed with suppliers and delivery of those orders. The greater the lead time, the stronger the economy and the lesser the lead time, the weaker the economy.
- Industrial production, released monthly, measures the collective output of factories, utilities, and mines. If final demand is high and inventory stockpiles are rapidly shrinking, future industrial production, employment, and income will be boosted as inventories are restocked, thereby stimulating economic activity. If, in contrast, final demand growth is slowing and inventory growth is excessive, future industrial production, employment, and income will weaken as inventories are trimmed, thereby depressing economic activity.
- Housing starts, published monthly, are the number of new single- and multifamily housing units begun for construction in the previous month. Housing starts, which are financed, are highly sensitive to interest rate changes. If housing starts slow dramatically, this signals that interest rates are high enough in the current economic environment to choke off demand. Conversely, if housing starts are increasing, this signals that interest rates are low enough in the current economic environment to promote demand.

- Motor vehicle sales, released monthly, are a key reflection of consumer confidence and income. Motor vehicle sales are strongly positively correlated to both income levels and consumer confidence.
- Durable goods orders, released monthly, are new orders placed by consumers with manufacturers of "large ticket" consumer goods, expected to last three or more years. These items may include appliances or business machinery.
- Commodity prices, for which the market receives continual input, are important indicators of future price rises in both producer and subsequently consumer prices. The most influential prices are those of raw goods and materials such as oil, lumber, metals, and agricultural commodities. Consistent, sympathetic, and significant price increases in these raw goods and materials will signal higher future prices in finished consumer goods.
- Employment cost index, which includes workers' wages, salaries, and benefits is released quarterly.
- Nonfarm-productivity growth, which is defined as output per hour and is released quarterly, is closely followed by Fed officials. In order to estimate the economy's sustainable potential, it is necessary to add productivity growth plus labor force growth. These are supply side factors.

It is extremely difficult to recognize meaningful and consistent changes in these economic variables: nonfarm payrolls, industrial production, housing starts, motor vehicle sales, durable good orders, commodity prices employment cost index, and productivity growth. Even if changes in these variables appear consistent and meaningful, it is difficult to predict whether the changes in the economic variables are temporary or if left unchecked will be longer lasting.

If the Fed believes the changes in key economic variables are consistent and potentially longer lasting, they will take measures to influence the availability of credit in the economy, which in turn influences aggregate demand and output growth. The Fed's most frequently employed policy tools include open market operations and changes to the discount rate. Less frequently, the Fed will employ changes in bank reserve requirements or verbal persuasion aimed at influencing bank behavior and capital market conditions with respect to the supply of credit to consumer and business borrowers, and even more rarely, the Fed may change margin requirements on stocks.

Through open market operations, the purchase or sale of U.S. government securities, the Fed either adds liquidity or funds into the market or subtracts liquidity or funds from the system. By changing the discount rate, the Fed changes the rate it charges depository institutions for the privilege of borrowing funds at the discount window. In January 2003, the Fed acted to tie the discount rate to the Federal funds rate. For financially sound member banks, the discount rate on primary borrowings at the discount window exceeds the Federal funds rate by 100 basis points. For secondary borrowings by less financially sound banks, the discount rate exceeds the Federal funds rate by 150 basis points. The combination of these tools can either make the cost of funds, that is, interest rates, cheaper or dearer. Open market operations work on the principles of supply and demand while changes in the discount rate directly alter the interest charged on funds. Discount rate changes are proposed by the board of directors of one or more district reserve banks for the approval by

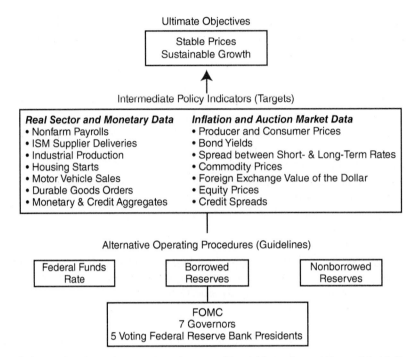

FIGURE 4.10   Fed Policy Objectives, Indicators (Targets), and Procedures (Guidelines)

the board of governors of the Federal Reserve. Open market operations are conducted by the Federal Open Market Committee (FOMC) in a manner consistent with decisions made at the periodic FOMC meetings. The FOMC consists of the seven members of the board of governors plus five voting bank presidents.

Two policy tools, changes in the reserve requirements and verbal persuasion, are tools infrequently used to reinforce stated Fed policy aims and they are used to complement policy changes already enacted through open market operations. Discount rate changes are more commonly used to put into effect Fed policy aims implemented through open market operations. These tools are employed by the Federal Reserve board of governors to underscore a policy of easing or tightening. Figure 4.10 attempts to simplify the decision-making and policy implementation process of the FOMC.

Historically, the Federal Reserve, under different chairmen, has introduced two contrasting techniques for implementing open market operations (see Figure 4.10). Initially, the Fed has used as its operating procedures (guidelines) a rigid federal fund rate target, generally in effect from the late 1920s through the late 1970s. More recently, Fed officials have introduced a more flexible Federal funds rate target. When the Fed uses a rigid Federal funds rate target, Fed open market operations tend to have procyclical results. That is, during economic expansions, the Fed's use of a rigid federal funds rate target, in the face of increasing money and credit demands, would result in the full accommodation of these demands, thereby triggering an acceleration in money and credit growth, excessive real growth, and the mounting threat of inflation. Conversely, during economic downturns, the Fed's use of a rigid Federal funds rate target, in the face of declining money and credit demands, would result in weakening money and credit growth, slowing real growth, and lessening inflation pressures. Fed chairman William McChesney Martin Jr., who was Fed chairman from 1951 to 1970, started the transition to a more flexible Federal funds rate target. He sought to achieve countercyclical effects when he introduced his "leaning against the wind" policy approach. Under this approach, if economic growth appears too strong relative to the economy's sustainable potential and consequently, potentially inflationary, the Fed would tighten its policy stance and increase its Federal funds rate target in order to restrain money and credit growth with the aim of slowing aggregate demand and output growth, thereby, lessening inflationary pressures. Conversely, if economic growth weakens, the Fed would "lean" toward an easier policy stance and lower its Federal funds target in order to stimulate economic growth. Under Fed chairmen Paul Volcker (1979–1987) and Alan Greenspan (1987–2006) still greater flexibility was introduced into the Fed's federal funds rate target in order to enhance countercyclical policy actions.

Regarding the intermediate policy indicators in Figure 4.10, Fed chairman Volcker tended to place primary policy emphasis on curtailing money and credit growth. In Volcker's own words in a statement before the Joint Economic Committee of the U.S. Congress on June 15, 1982, "[a] basic premise of monetary policy is that inflation cannot persist without excessive monetary growth, and it is our view that appropriately restrained growth of money and credit over the longer run is critical to achieving the ultimate objectives of reasonably stable prices and sustainable economic growth." Subsequently, however, Chairman Greenspan found it necessary to lessen the Fed's emphasis on monetary and credit growth in favor of greater policy emphasis on a wider range of intermediate indicators of the real sector, inflation, and auction (financial) markets. Greenspan feared that owing to globalization, securitization, and, most important, financial product innovation such as hedge funds, money, and credit growth was no longer a reliable predictor of economic activity and inflation. Greenspan also placed more emphasis on transparency and verbal persuasion in seeking to increase the effectiveness of monetary policy.

Implementing Monetary Policy: The Transmission Process

The *monetary policy transmission process* has always been a long and variable one. In the past the banking system, the conduit for monetary policy, was the dominant source of credit for consumers and businesses. Typically, it has taken from six to twelve months for a shift in monetary policy to work its way through the banking system and capital markets to impact aggregate demand and output. It takes even longer for a given policy shift to influent price behavior. Complicating this process in today's world, a decline in share of credit is supplied through the banking system and arising share of credit is supplied through globally integrated capital markets. As a result, the Federal Reserve today, more than in the past, must be highly attuned to financial market participants' perceptions of Fed intentions and potential market impact of the Fed's perceived intentions. The banking system remains the point of contact for the Fed when it initiates shifts in policy stance. However, Fed intentions and related market expectations of their intentions remain a critical concern in the transmission of Fed policy shifts. This process results in capital market asset price and interest rate adjustments that ultimately influence changes in aggregate demand, output growth, and inflation.

Friday, February 4, 1994 at 11:05 A.M.—FOMC meeting "Chairman Alan Greenspan announced today that/the Federal Open Market Committee decided to increase slightly the degree of pressure on reserve positions. The action is expected to be associated with a small increase in short-term money market interest rates.

The decision was taken to move toward a less accommodative stance in monetary policy in order to sustain and enhance the economic expansion.

Chairman Greenspan decided to announce this action immediately so as to avoid any misunderstanding of the committee's purposes, given the fact that this is the first firming of reserve market conditions by the committee since early 1989."

Tuesday, March 22, 1994 at 2:20 P.M.—FOMC meeting "Chairman Alan Greenspan announced today that the Federal Open Market Committee decided to increase slightly the degree of pressure on reserve positions. This action is expected to be associated with a small increase in short-term money market interest rates."

Monday, April 18, 1994 at 10:06 A.M.—FOMC telephone conference, call "Chairman Alan Greenspan announced today that the Federal Reserve will increase slightly the degree of pressure on reserve positions. This action is expected to be associated with a small increase in short-term, money market interest rates."

Tuesday, May 17, 1994 at 2:26 P.M.—FOMC meeting "The Federal Reserve today announced two actions designed to maintain favorable trends in inflation and thereby sustain the economic expansion. The Board approved an increase in the discount rate from 3 percent to 3.5 percent, effective immediately, and the Federal Open Market Committee agreed that this increase should be allowed to show through completely into interest rates in reserve markets. These actions, combined with the three adjustments initiated earlier this year by the FOMC, substantially remove the degree of monetary accommodation which prevailed throughout 1993. As always, the Federal Reserve will continue to monitor economic and financial developments to judge the appropriate stance of monetary policy. In taking the discount action, the Board approved requests submitted by the Boards of Directors of eleven Federal Reserve Banks—Boston, New York, Philadelphia, Richmond, Atlanta, Chicago, St. Louis, Minneapolis, Kansas City, Dallas, and San Francisco. The discount rate is the interest rate that is charged depository institutions when they borrow from their district Federal Reserve Bank."

Wednesday, July 6, 1994 at 2:18 P.M.—FOMC meeting "The meeting of the FOMC ended at 12:35 pm and there will be no further announcement."

FIGURE 4.11   Sampling of the Federal Reserve's Official Statements of FOMC Actions, First Half of 1994

Fed authorities began in February 1994 to immediately announce policy decisions. (See Figure 4.11 for policy statements following FOMC meetings.) Today's Fed monetary policy transmission process is a transparent one. Monetary policy transparency easily conveys Fed policy intentions. Typically, Fed officials, through speeches, interviews, and congressional testimony, will seek to prepare financial market participants for any policy shift that may be in store in upcoming policy meetings. Clear information on current Fed policy helps the monetary policy transmission process operate more effectively. Under former Fed chairman Greenspan, the Fed sought to be more transparent, and refined its methods of communication.

Historically, the Fed policy transmission process has worked largely by manipulating the cost of credit as supplied by the banking system. Specifically, to effect a policy shift, the Fed has traditionally begun by changing the composition of bank reserves. For example, more Fed restraint means the Fed manipulates a rising share of borrowed to total reserves, resulting in an increase in the cost of reserves. The increased cost of reserves is reflected in a higher Federal funds rate. (The Federal funds rate is the rate on bank reserve balances held at the Fed that are loaned and borrowed among banks, usually overnight.) Conversely, less Fed restraint (more ease) means the Fed manipulates a declining share of borrowed reserves to total reserves. This action results in a declining cost of reserves that is reflected in a lower Federal funds rate. Borrowed reserves are those reserves that banks borrow temporarily at the Fed's discount window for purposes of adjusting their reserve positions. Banks traditionally try to avoid borrowing at the Fed discount window. There is a perception that such borrowings are a sign of financial weakness. Banks that are forced to borrow temporarily at the discount window will, generally, first turn to other sources of loanable funds such as Federal funds or repo borrowings.

Banks, when faced with greater Fed restraint and a rising cost of loanable funds, find their net interest margins narrowing or their profits declining. In that case, the yield curve typically flattens or, when the Fed is tightening aggressively, inverts as short-term rates are pushed above longer-term rates. Under these circumstances, banks have less incentive to increase their investments and loans. This results in a decline in the availability of funds and an increase in the cost of bank credit to consumers and businesses. Therefore, consumers and businesses will cut back on their borrowing and spending. This in turn results in a declining rate of increase in real economic growth and eventually, a moderation in inflation pressures. Conversely, a Fed move toward an easier policy posture reduces banks' cost of funds. Banks find their net interest margins widening or profits increasing because the fed funds rate is far more elastic than long-term interest rates and the yield curve will steepen. Banks' incentive to increase the availability and reduce the cost of credit increases. This stimulates consumer and business borrowing and spending, thereby spurring real economic growth and eventually triggering a rise in inflationary pressures. The only exception to our converse case is in the environment of an inverted yield curve such as the U.S. government bond curve in the early 1980s. Despite the Fed's efforts to ease short-term rates in the initial stages, the reduction in the cost of funds to banks may not have a significant impact on potential profit margins if the yield curve is inverted enough. Long-term rates may be too low on a relative basis to short-term rates to make bank or other financial institutions' extensions of long-term credit profitable, at least initially.

To view this monetary transmission process from the investment side, Fed policy shifts set off a chain reaction. For example, in the case of a Fed shift towards a more restrictive policy posture, investors who hold short-term credit market instruments such as Treasury bills or money market mutual funds will find interest rates on their short-term investments moving up to higher and more attractive levels relative to yields on longer-term bonds. Accordingly, investors will shift their investments down the yield curve. They will sell longer-term bonds and place the proceeds in shorter-term money market investments. This process will result in rising longer-term interest rates. Rising longer-term interest rates will, in turn, make the returns on bonds more attractive relative to the returns on stocks. As a result, investors will sell stocks, place the proceeds in bonds, and stock prices will decline. As capital market expectations of future Fed restrictive intentions are formed, these portfolio asset adjustments between money market investments, bonds, and stocks will be hastened and intensified.

The Impact of Monetary Policy: Its Declining Direct Influence

Since the mid-1970s, there has been a sharp decline in the proportion of bank credit to total credit available. The bank share of total credit continues to fall. In mid-1970, it was 55 percent. By 2006, the banks' share of total credit was reduced to 25 percent. The main factors contributing to the declining bank share of total credit have been globalization of credit resources, securitization, and financial product innovation. The result has been a rising share of credit extended directly through the capital markets to consumers and businesses. Among the major new nonbank institutional suppliers of credit through the capital markets are mutual funds, hedge funds, pension funds, finance companies, and insurance companies. Currently, with the advent of the information revolution, these nonbank lenders are virtually in as good a position as bank lenders to assess market and credit risks.

Today, the Fed's policy transmission process works increasingly to a greater extent through capital market asset price adjustments and interest rates (that is, bonds, stocks, etc.) than through the availability of funds. As in the past, the Fed initiates a policy shift by changing the composition of bank reserves. As we have previously explained, there is a resulting change in the cost of funds as reflected in a change in the Federal funds rate. The Federal funds rate prompts positively correlated changes in short-term market rates. These changing costs of short-term credit include bank loans made at the prime rate and funds raised in the commercial paper market. The impact on capital market price adjustments work in the following manner: as short-term borrowing costs rise, borrowers find longer-term borrowing rates relatively more attractive. Eventually, corporate bond and fixed-rate mortgage offerings increase, driving up longer-term interest rates. This impact of Fed policy shifts on short-term and long-term market interest rates is magnified as Fed intentions are recognized by capital market participants. The participants form expectations of further Fed tightening (easing) moves, thereby affecting longer-term interest rates. Longer-term interest rates are influenced by the average of expected short-term rates plus a term premium that includes inflation expectations. The effect of capital market participants is reflected in the changing shapes of the yield curve as the Fed funds rate changes.

Rising longer-term interest rates and declining stock prices will increase the cost of capital. Increasing the cost of capital decreases business investment. Also, higher longer-term rates depress housing activity. In addition, declining financial asset prices depress consumer wealth and consumer spending, resulting in a decline in the pace of real economic activity. This process serves to moderate inflationary pressures. Commodity prices are likely to be falling in such an environment. Moreover, increasing interest rates will generally cause the value of the U.S. dollar to appreciate in the foreign exchange markets relative to other currencies. A stronger U.S. dollar will cause a decline in exports and a rise in imports, all other factors being equal. This rising trade deficit also serves to dampen economic activity.

Global Credibility: The Central Banker's Responsibility

Important influences on the global financial environment include: market deregulation or regulation, financial innovation, integrated global financial markets, and advanced information processing and communications technology. There is a massive pool of mobile capital that relentlessly seeks out countries where business activity generates the highest possible return for a given amount of risk. In order to compete effectively for capital from global investors, countries must pursue disciplined macroeconomic policies and probusiness microeconomic policies including deregulation and privatization. Countries competing for capital must aim for balanced and sustained noninflationary growth.

A more sobering lesson for modern-day central bankers is their reduced effectiveness in controlling massive global capital flows and related financial asset price bubbles. At times this has been manifested in capital market participants' overly optimistic view of central bankers' abilities and desire to stave off debt defaults. This may be particularly true in the case of staving off sovereign and quasi-sovereign debt where there is a history of central bankers providing meaningful amounts of liquidity. The legacy was underscored in the Mexican financial crisis in 1995. The U.S. government provided amounts up to US\$50 billion to the Mexican government, staving off a debt default. The benefits of staving off the Mexican default were not without drawbacks. This lesson can be found in the Asian financial crisis that began in mid-1997. The Asian financial turmoil began in the rapidly growing economy of Thailand and spread to the other Southeastern Asian countries of Malaysia, Indonesia, and the Philippines. These developing countries had benefited from an abundance of foreign liquidity. But the heavy capital inflows eventually resulted in excessive growth, mounting trade deficits, and speculative financial bubbles typically manifested in frenzied local bank-financed speculation in equities and real estate. The currency crisis in these Southeast Asian countries was triggered as escalating trade deficits scared away global money managers, triggering a rapid depreciation in their currencies, with interest rates rising sharply in response. As the bubble burst, real estate and equity prices plummeted. This unforeseen instability posed a major threat to the affected countries' banking systems, as bad debts mounted.

It was not until equity market selling pressures spread to Hong Kong that the rest of the world began to take serious notice. With the return of Hong Kong to Mainland China, the Chinese government kept the Hong Kong dollar pegged to the U.S. dollar as a matter of political principle. Nevertheless, speculators continued to attack the Hong Kong dollar on the assumption that it had to fall in line with other southeastern Asian currencies in order for Hong Kong to remain competitive. In its effort to fight off the speculative attack on the Hong Kong dollar, the Hong Kong Monetary Authority was forced to sharply increase interest rates, thereby weakening the Hong Kong real estate market and threatening Hong Kong banks with mounting bad debts.

Next, the Asian currency crisis spread to the larger South Korean economy, where the heavily indebted financial system was vulnerable, and ultimately to the huge Japanese economy, which was still attempting to recover from the bursting of its own 1980s financial bubble. Then, like a rapidly spreading contagion, the Asian currency depreciation and equity market plunge spread to Latin America and

TABLE 4.2 Changing Values in Asian Equities, Bonds, and Currencies

Country	Currency Levels		Equity Index—6-Month Return Local Currency Terms	Fixed Income Yield Benchmark	
	7/07/97	1/07/98	7/07/97/1/07/98	07/07/97	1/07/98
Malaysia	2.53	4.06	−50.87	T10+63	T10+260
Indonesia	2432.00	8000.00	−46.58	T10+118	T10+650
South Korea	883.00	1650.00	−47.7	T10+86	T10+525
Philippines	26.41	45.00	−36.53	T30+221	T30+440
Thailand	28.63	52.88	−41.5	T10+82	T10+500
Hong Kong	7.74	7.74	−35.8	T10+73	T10+160
Japan	112.78	131.73	−23.74	T10−371	T10−364

even Eastern Europe and Russia where previously high-performing debt and equity markets registered extremely disorderly declines, and ultimately to declines in the western European and U.S. stock markets. Table 4.2 illustrates the magnitude of these Asian market declines.

The importance of the Asian financial crisis is that it illustrates the lessening influence that central bankers have on today's globally integrated capital market flows, apart from serving as last-resort lenders of liquidity. The role of last-resort lender, however, should not be minimized. The central bank and supra-led package of loans to Mexico in 1995 staved off a dramatic currency crisis that could have led to a debt default. With the stunning advances in information processing and communications technology, global money managers can move capital around the world at virtually the speed of light. This capital, as already noted, seeks out opportunities offering the highest risk-adjusted returns, but it flees from turmoil. The point is that the increasingly efficient global capital markets are linked more tightly than ever before. Apart from maintaining anti-inflation credibility and serving as lenders of last resort, central bankers, including the U.S. Fed chairman, may in the future have only a marginal influence on these massive global capital market flows and related financial asset price bubbles.

Moreover, since the Asian currency turmoil, it is the stark power of the global capital markets themselves rather than domestic politicians or central bankers that are forcing major financial system changes in the affected countries, including the desirable privatization of public corporations and large-scale banking reform. The only means by which governments (or the IMF) can stabilize market forces is to respond by offering larger or more effective financial reform packages than global capital market participants expect. For example, global money managers are demanding that bank reform include provisions for allowing insolvent banks to fail and for the weaker banks to be acquired by healthy domestic or foreign financial institutions. In addition, taxpayer funds, along with deposit insurance, must be used to pay off depositors in failed banks. Also, most important, bank reform must make provisions for transparency, including full disclosure of bad loans and off-balance-sheet items by banks and securities firms.

Huge, global pools of mobile capital may serve to actually discipline national and global macroeconomics policies. If, for example, any developed or emerging country tries to boost growth through overly stimulative macroeconomic policies that are potentially inflationary for political reasons, its trade deficit will worsen and its currency will depreciate. Global institutional investors and money managers will become fearful of the increased inflationary threat and sell bonds, thus pushing long-term interest rates higher and helping to choke off growth in that developing or emerging country.

Former Fed chairman Greenspan was faced by a "conundrum" when he and his fellow policy makers began a prolonged series of rate-firming actions mid-2004. Specifically, despite an impressive series of short-term rate hikes, long-term rates actually declined, reducing the effects of Fed's firming actions. Eventually, Fed officials concluded that this atypical situation in which Fed policy was becoming less accommodative as the capital markets were becoming more accommodative, reflected a unique combination of low inflation expectations, a global savings glut, heavy global carry trades by hedge funds and other large institutional investors, and currency interventions, especially by Japan and China.

Accordingly, the best that any country can do for its citizens is to create a favorable economic climate for participation in the world economy. There are many important economic building blocks for positive participation in the world economy. These building blocks include deregulation, privatization, free markets, minimal government interference, longer-term productivity-enhancing measures (investment in education, job training, research as well as the implementation of technological innovations, and rewards for savings and investment), and, above all, central bank anti-inflation credibility and consistency. Longer-term price stability creates steady, predictable levels of economic growth. These are the rewards of pursuing a monetary policy that seeks price stability and, thereby, sets the stage for enhanced productivity.

In sum, while central bankers still play a key stabilization role in the effort to ensure that financial conditions are supportive of sustainable economic growth, the ability of central banks to influence massive global flows of mobile capital and related asset price bubbles is diminishing. This raises the specter of additional currency crises from time to time, not unlike those in Mexico in 1995 and in Southeast Asia in 1997. To be sure, central bankers can help limit the private sector's speculative tendencies by maintaining a high level of anti-inflation credibility. Moreover, central banks can help contain the damage when asset price bubbles break by serving as last-resort lenders of liquidity. But in the final analysis, these central bank influences are marginal compared with today's sheer power of global capital market forces.

Summary

In general, central bankers have the mandate to create an investment environment, which results in attractive risk-adjusted return on capital and stable capital flows. The Federal Reserve's policy transmission process influences the expectations of capital markets participants. While the Federal Reserve alters short-term borrowing rates, all lenders of capital adjust their cost of capital in response.

The Federal Reserve's policy shifts are countercyclical and affect the forward economic environment. Evident several months after the fact, the impact of these policy shifts is designed to enhance the economic environment. A positive economic environment attracts stable capital flows, which ultimately aid stable, noninflationary economic growth. This is the ultimate goal of a central banker.

References

Chang, K. H. 2003. *Appointing Central Bankers: The Politics of Monetary Policy in the United States and the European Monetary Union (Political Economy of Institutions and Decisions)*. Cambridge: Cambridge University Press.

Chappell, H. W., Jr., R. R. McGregor, and T. A. Vermilyea. 2005. *Committee Decisions on Monetary Policy: Evidence from Historical Records of the Federal Open Market Committee*. Boston: MIT Press.

Federal Reserve Bank of Minneapolis. 2001. *A Prescription for Monetary Policy: Proceedings from a Seminar Series*. Toronto: Books for Business.

Friedman, M., and Schwartz, A. J. 1971. *Monetary History of the United States, 1867–1960*. Princeton: Princeton University Press.

Gruben, W. 1997. *Exchange Rates, Capital Flows, and Monetary Policy in a Changing World Economy* (The Federal Reserve Bank of Dallas). Germany: Springer.

Greenspan, A. 2004. *Monetary Policy and Uncertainty: Adapting to a Changing Economy*. Federal Reserve Bank of Kansas City. University Press of the Pacific.

Jones, D. M. 1989. *Fed Watching and Interest Rate Projections: A Practical Guide*. New York: New York Institute of Finance.

Jones, D. M. 1992. "The Only Game in Town (Monetary Policy of the Federal Reserve System under Chairman Alan Greenspan)." *Mortgage Banking* 53, 1: 35–38.

Jones, D. M. 1996. *The Buck Stops Here: How the Federal Reserve Can Make or Break Your Financial Future*. New York: Prentice Hall Trade.

Jones, D. M. 2002. *Unlocking the Secrets of the Fed: How Monetary Policy Affects the Economy and Your Wealth-Creation Potential*. Hoboken, NJ: John Wiley & Sons.

Kettl, D. 1986. *Leadership at the Fed*. New Haven, CT: Yale University Press.

Kindleberger, C. P. 1978. *Manics, Panics, and Crashes*. New York: John Wiley & Sons.

Meltzer, A. H. 2004. *History of the Federal Reserve, volume 1: 1913–1951*. Chicago: University of Chicago Press.

Meyer, L. H. 2004. *A Term at the Fed: An Insider's View*. New York: Harper Collins.

Wooley, J. T. 1986. *Monetary Politics: The Federal Reserve and the Politics of Monetary Policy*. London: Cambridge University Press.

Part II Introduction to Key Economic Indicators

Investing without understanding the economy is like taking a trip without knowing anything about the climate of your destination. Inclement weather can wreak havoc on a vacation, especially if it involves outdoor activities. Just so, putting hard-earned money into the stock or bond market when economic conditions are unfavorable can destroy financial plans for a comfortable retirement, a new house, or a child's college education.

Some of the dozen-plus indicators discussed in this book are constructed by U.S. government agencies such as the U.S. Department of Commerce's Census Bureau, the U.S. Department of Labor, and the Board of Governors of the Federal Reserve System. Others are the products of private organizations such as the Institute for Supply Management, the Conference Board, and the University of Michigan. Some have excellent predictive powers. Others reflect principally the current state of the economy, and still others highlight industries that might outperform and so help identify the likely path of economic activity. All have one thing in common, however: In one way or another, they all relate to the business cycle.

The Business Cycle

The business cycle is one of the central concepts in modern economics. It was defined by celebrated economists Arthur Burns and Wesley Mitchell in their pioneering 1946 study, Measuring Business Cycles, written for the National Bureau of Economic Research (NBER), which today is the official arbiter of the U.S. business cycle. According to Burns and Mitchell, the business cycle is "a type of fluctuation found in the aggregate economic activity of nations that organize their work mainly in business enterprises: a cycle consists of expansions occurring at about the same time in many economic activities, followed by similarly general recessions, contractions, and revivals, which merge into the expansion phase of the next cycle."

No two business cycles are the same. As illustrated in Table 4.3, during the relatively short time that people have been measuring the U.S. economy, the length of expansions, from economic trough to peak, and of contractions, from peak to trough, has varied widely—although expansions, especially recently, generally have been longer and steadier than contractions. Expansions have ranged from 120 months (April 1991 to March 2001) to 10 months (March 1919 to January 1920), and downturns from 43 months (August 1929 to March 1933) to 6 months (February 1980 to July 1980). The amplitude of the peaks and troughs has also differed significantly from cycle to cycle.

One way to think of the business cycle is as a graphical representation of the total economic activity of a country. Because the accepted benchmark for economic activity in the United States is currently gross domestic product (GDP), economists generally identify the business cycle with the alternating increases and declines in GDP. Rising GDP marks economic expansion; falling GDP, a contraction (see Figure 4.12). That said, the business cycle, as defined by Burns and Mitchell, can't be fully captured by one indicator, even the nation's GDP. Rather, it is a compendium of indicators that reflects various aspects of the economy.

Economic indicators are classified according to how they relate to the business cycle. Those that reflect the current state of the economy are coincident; those that predict future conditions are leading; and those that confirm that a turning occurred are lagging.

TABLE 4.3   U.S. Business Cycle Durations

| Business Cycle Reference Dates (Quarterly Dates Are in Parentheses) | | Duration in Months | | | |
| | | Contraction | Expansion | Cycle | |
Peak	Trough	Peak to Trough	Previous Trough to This Peak	Trough from Previous Trough	Peak from Previous Peak
	December 1854 (IV)	–	–	–	–
June 1857 (II)	December 1858 (IV)	18	30	48	–
October 1860 (III)	June 1861 (III)	8	22	30	40
April 1865 (I)	December 1867 (I)	32	46	78	54
June 1869 (II)	December 1870 (IV)	18	18	36	50
October 1873 (III)	March 1879 (I)	65	34	99	52
March 1882 (I)	May 1885 (II)	38	36	74	101
March 1887 (II)	April 1888 (I)	13	22	35	60
July 1890 (III)	May 1891 (II)	10	27	37	40
January 1893 (I)	June 1894 (II)	17	20	37	30
December 1895 (IV)	June 1897 (II)	18	18	36	35
June 1899 (III)	December 1900 (IV)	18	24	42	42
September 1902 (IV)	August 1904 (III)	23	21	44	39
May 1907 (II)	June 1908 (II)	13	33	46	56
January 1910 (I)	January 1912 (IV)	24	19	43	32
January 1913 (I)	December 1914 (IV)	23	12	35	36
August 1918 (III)	March 1919 (I)	7	44	51	67
January 1920 (I)	July 1921 (III)	18	10	28	17
May 1923 (II)	July 1924 (III)	14	22	36	40
October 1926 (III)	November 1927 (IV)	13	27	40	41
August 1929 (III)	March 1933 (I)	43	21	64	34
May 1937 (II)	June 1938 (II)	13	50	63	93
February 1945 (I)	October 1945 (IV)	8	80	88	93
November 1948 (IV)	October 1949 (IV)	11	37	48	45
July 1953 (II)	May 1954 (II)	10	45	55	56
August 1957 (III)	April 1958 (II)	8	39	47	49
April 1960 (II)	February 1961 (I)	10	24	34	32
December 1969 (IV)	November 1970 (IV)	11	106	117	116
November 1973 (IV)	March 1975 (I)	16	36	52	47
January 1980 (I)	July 1980 (III)	6	58	64	74
July 1981 (III)	November 1982 (IV)	16	12	28	18
July 1990 (III)	March 1991 (I)	8	92	100	108
March 2001 (I)	November 2001 (IV)	8	120	128	128
December 2007 (IV)	June 2009 (II)	18	73	91	81
Average, all cycles:					
1854–2009 (33 cycles)		16	42	56	55*
1854–1919 (16 cycles)		22	27	48	49**
1919–1945 (6 cycles)		18	35	53	53
1945–2009 (11 cycles)		11	59	73	66

*32 cycles

**15 cycles

Source: National Bureau of Economic Research.

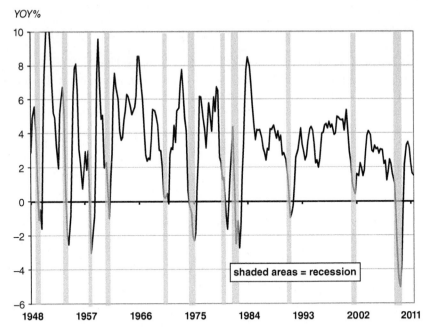

FIGURE 4.12   GDP and Highlighted Recessions

Source: U.S. Department of Commerce, Bureau of Economic Analysis; National Bureau of Economic Research.

Part III   Gross Domestic Product

Economics has received a bad rap. In the mid-nineteenth century, the great Scottish historian Thomas Carlyle dubbed this discipline "the dismal science," and jokes abound on Wall Street about economists being more boring than accountants. But truth be told, there is nothing more exciting than watching the newswire on a trading floor of a money-center bank minutes ahead of the release of a major market-moving economic report. One of the top excitement generators is the report on gross domestic product (GDP)—an indicator that is a combination of economics and accounting.

GDP is a more relevant measure of U.S. economic conditions than GNP, because the resources that are utilized in the production process are predominantly domestic. There are strong parallels between the GDP data and other U.S. economic indicators, such as industrial production and the Conference Board's index of coincident indicators (the coincident index).

The GDP is calculated and reported on a quarterly basis as part of the national income and product accounts (NIPAs). The NIPAs, which were developed and are maintained today by the Commerce Department's Bureau of Economic Analysis (BEA), are the most comprehensive data available regarding U.S. national output, production, and the distribution of income. Each GDP report contains data on the following:

■ Personal income and consumption expenditures
■ Corporate profits

■ National income
■ Inflation

These data tell the story of how the economy performed—whether it expanded or contracted—during a specific period, usually the preceding quarter. By looking at changes in the GDP's components and subcomponents and comparing these with changes that have occurred in the past, economists can draw inferences about the direction the economy might take in the future.

Of all the tasks market economists perform, generating a forecast for overall economic performance as measured by the GDP data is the one to which they dedicate the most time. In fact, the latest report on GDP is within arm's reach of most Wall Street economists. Because several departments in a trading institution rely on the economist's forecasts, this indicator has emerged as the foundation for all research and trading activity and usually sets the tone for all of Wall Street's financial prognostications.

GDP versus GNP

The NIPAs contain figures for both gross domestic product and gross national product. Before 1991, GNP was the benchmark for all economic activity in commentaries, reports, articles, and texts. GDP became the official barometer when the BEA decided that the measure was a better fit with the United Nations system of national accounts used by other nations, and so made international comparisons of economic growth easier.

GDP differs from GNP in what economists call *net factor income from foreign sources*: the difference between the value of receipts from foreign sources and the payments made to foreign sources.

The difference between the value of GDP and GNP is typically minuscule, usually less than 0.5 percent. (See Figure 4.13.)

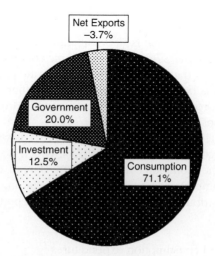

FIGURE 4.13   Composition of GDP

Source: U.S. Department of Commerce, Bureau of Economic Analysis.

Services constitute by far the largest category of consumer purchases. They account today for roughly 66 percent of all consumer spending, up from a mere third in 1950. No wonder the United States is said to have a service-based economy. Spending on goods comprises the remaining 34 percent.

Nondurable goods is the second-largest category of expenditures, representing about 23 percent of the total. Durable goods expenditures, the most volatile component, account for the remaining 11 percent.

Deflators

The difference between nominal GDP and real GDP is essentially inflation. It is thus possible to compute an economy's inflation rate from this difference. The result of the computation is called an *implicit price deflator.*

Every GDP report contains implicit price deflators for the headline GDP number and also for many of its subcomponents, such as consumption expenditures, government spending, and gross private domestic investment. Economists at the BEA calculate the GDP implicit price deflator using the following formula:

Implicit deflator = (Nominal value)/(Real value) × 100

For example, using data from the 2011 third-quarter GDP report, the GDP deflator for that period would be

($15.1809/$13.3378) × 100 = 113.81

The annualized inflation rate for a period can be derived using the formula:

Annualized inflation = (Current-period deflator/Previous-period deflator)^4 − 1

To compute the annualized inflation rate for third quarter 2011, for example, the third quarter 2011 GDP deflator computed above and the second quarter 2011 deflator of 113.11 would be plugged into the formula, to give

$$\text{Annualized inflation rate} = (113.81/113.11)^4 - 1$$

$$= (1.006189)^4 - 1 = 1.024985 - 1 = 0.024985,$$

$$\text{or approximately } 2.5\%$$

A similar formula is used to calculate the annualized quarterly growth rate of GDP as a whole, as well as each of its components and subcomponents:

Annualized quarterly growth rate = (Current quarter/Previous quarter)^4 − 1

For example, to compute the third quarter 2011 annualized growth rate, the second and third quarter 2011 GDP figures would be plugged into the formula, giving

$$\text{Annualized quarterly growth rate}$$

$$= [\text{QIII 2011 GDP/QII2011 GDP}]^4 - 1$$

$$= [13,337.8/13,271.8]^4 - 1$$

$$= [1.020041] - 1$$

$$= 0.02004, \text{ or approximately } 2.00\%$$

What Does It All Mean?

The GDP report contains a wealth of information about the nation's economy. Each of its components tells a different story about a particular group, sector, industry, or activity. Not surprisingly, then, different market participants look at different sections and draw different inferences. Retail analysts, for instance, focus mostly on consumer spending. Those covering housing, construction, or real estate investment trusts (REITs) concentrate on the residential activity in investment spending. Defense-industry analysts focus on the national defense spending component of government consumption expenditures and gross investment. Fixed-income analysts and investors, ever wary of the eroding effects of inflation, concern themselves with the GDP deflators and GDP growth rate. Traders, who are always on the lookout for possible market movers, watch for numbers that contradict expectations, which they track carefully, often jotting them down in notebooks kept at their desks, for quick reference when the real figures are announced.

GDP Growth

The annualized quarterly growth rate of real GDP is the headline number of the GDP report. As with most economic figures, strong positive postings are generally good news for the economy, corporate profits, and stock valuations. Not so for bonds, however. Inflation erodes the value of fixed-income securities, and more torrid economic growth is usually associated with higher rates of inflation.

Market reactions—both positive and negative—are more pronounced when the announced numbers differ from the expected ones. The larger the difference, the greater the market move. Say the Street consensus for the third quarter was for an annualized GDP growth rate of 4.2 percent. On the one hand, a weak posting of between 1 and 2 percent would probably spark a sell-off in the stock market and boost the price of fixed-income securities, lowering yields. Stronger-than-expected growth of 5.5 to 6.5 percent, on the other hand, would be well received by equity traders and frowned upon by fixed-income dealers.

Although the annualized quarterly figure is important, many economists prefer to look at the year-over-year change in GDP. The longer perspective makes it easier to spot turning points in the economy, such as an approaching recession or an acceleration of activity. Figure 4.14 illustrates this predictive effect.

As the chart shows, in the past 30 years the U.S. economy has experienced three recessions—in 1990–1991, 2001, and 2007–2009—each of which was preceded by significant declines in the growth rates of real and nominal GDP. Note that during the 1990–1991 recession, the real GDP growth rate fell below zero, while the nominal rate declined but stayed out of negative territory—a common occurrence during most post–World War II downturns. This is because the nominal figure incorporates the effects of inflation, which is almost always rising. For the growth rate of nominal GDP to become negative, the inflation rate would have to be negative (reflecting a decline in prices)—a condition known as deflation—at the same time that the economy is contracting. Deflation is extremely rare in the United States and indeed has been recorded only a couple of times anywhere.

During the 2007–2009 recession, the real and nominal measures of GDP contracted—the steepest declines in economic output since the Great Depression. This slump was accompanied by a mild case of deflation.

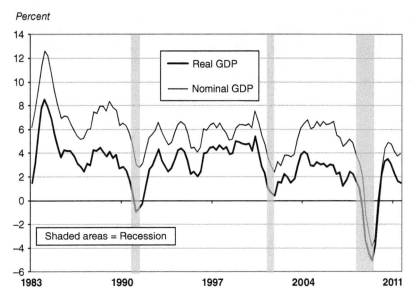

FIGURE 4.14   Real and Nominal GDP (Y/Y Percent)

On average, the year-over-year growth rate in GDP starts declining four to five quarters before a recession. Not all slowdowns, however, result in recession. By the time the warning signals appear, government policy makers have usually put in place measures to avert an economic downturn. The massive stimulus enacted at the onset of the financial crisis and recession in 2008 no doubt helped the U.S. economy avoid a deep depression.

Still, watching changes in year-over-year GDP growth can be useful for short-term forecasts: Very rarely do trends reverse immediately. It takes a great deal to knock a $15 trillion economy like that of the United States off-kilter. Luckily for those in the financial markets, several leading indicators usually send alerts when the behemoth is running out of energy.

To form a clearer picture of the economy, economists like to look at several indicators at once. This helps reduce the transmission of false signals. There are times when some individual indicators trend lower, suggesting a potential decline in activity. If several indicators are observed, and a majority point to positive activity, then it is possible to dismiss the weaker performing indicators as outliers, and draw the conclusion that the economy isn't in trouble.

Deflators

If GDP growth is the most important number in the release, the GDP deflators run a close second. As indicators of inflation, these deflators are preferred to the consumer price index (CPI), the producer price index (PPI), and other commodity price gauges by many traders and economists, including those at the Federal Reserve. Special favorites are the *headline deflator*, or *implicit GDP deflator*, the *personal consumption expenditure deflator*, and the *personal consumption expenditures less food and energy deflator*, also known as the *core PCED deflator*. The Street has adopted the last deflator as an unofficial benchmark for the core rate of inflation.

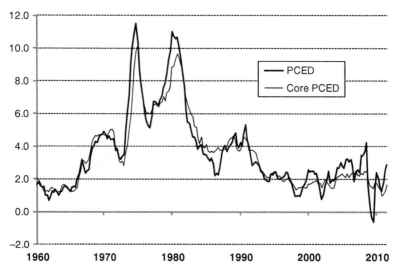

FIGURE 4.15   Personal Consumption Expenditure Deflators (Y/Y percent)

Bond traders in particular watch the deflators, knowing that greater-than-expected increases in these numbers usually depress fixed-income prices.

Why have the deflators superseded the other inflation measures? For starters, policy makers, traders, and investors in general want to see overarching economic trends, not smaller, more targeted ones. GDP deflators reflect price activity in the broader economy. The consumer price index, in contrast, is merely a "basket" of a few hundred goods and services, chosen by the Bureau of Labor Statistics. Traders focus on movements in the personal consumption expenditure excluding food and energy deflator, commonly referred to as the *core PCED*. This inflation measure is preferred to most of the others as it measures the core, excluding food and energy, rate of inflation that consumers face. Because prices of food and energy can fluctuate greatly during the month, economists like to view price trends without these noisy readings. Also, because private individuals are doing the overwhelming majority of the economy's consumption and this indicator contains all of the goods and services consumed, as opposed to a couple of hundred as in the case with the consumer price index, the core PCED has risen to the top of the list of most watched inflation gauges.

Figure 4.15 shows the 12-month trends in the personal consumption expenditure deflator (PCED) and the core PCED since 1960. The run-up in inflation from the mid-1970s through 1981 weighed heavily on the economy and made growth and hiring a difficult process. Since the Volcker Fed cracked down on inflation in 1979, the annual pace of price gains has been muted. The mild bout of deflation in 2009 can be seen by the sub-zero posting in the PCED.

Consumption Expenditures

As the consumer goes, so goes the U.S. economy. And this old saw may be more truthful than ever before. In the 1990s, it was believed that the consumer's utter resilience to disruptions such as war, attacks against the United States on U.S. soil, widespread corporate malfeasance, eight of the top 10 corporate bankruptcies in U.S.

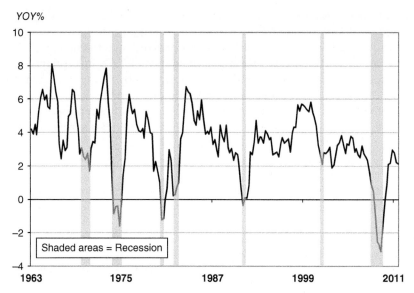

YOY%

FIGURE 4.16   Personal Consumption Expenditures

history, and presidential impeachment proceedings was the reason for the underlying strength of the economy. In previous decades, any single one of these disruptions likely would have upended the U.S. economy. Now it seems as though the consumer is capable of keeping the economy humming. It is the consumer who has prolonged expansion and made recessions shorter and milder.

In more recent years, consumers started to open their wallets relatively soon—about six months—after the end of the recession in June 2009. The pace of spending was somewhat subdued due to limited real income growth, poor employment prospects, and less access to credit cards, but their renewed spending is testament that American consumers can play Atlas and support macroeconomic recovery and expansion.

Generally, a drop in the growth rate of consumer spending is a surefire sign that the economy is on the verge of petering out. When people are feeling uneasy about the economic climate—perhaps unemployment is on the rise, or inflation is eroding the dollar's purchasing power, or individuals are just feeling tapped out—it shows in their spending habits. As the chart in Figure 4.16 shows, pronounced declines in the year-over-year growth in consumer expenditures have preceded each of the seven recessions in the United States since 1963. Traditionally, the first retrenchment occurs in purchases of big-ticket items, such as durable goods. So it is in that portion of consumer spending where you'll find early warnings of economic downturns.

Investment Spending

Capital equipment comprises all the industrial and technological items used to produce other goods and services for sale. The amount of money that companies invest in this equipment is thus a good predictor of future economic activity. It indicates whether corporate profitability is accelerating or decelerating, how managers view future economic conditions, and how strong or weak the economy is.

As explained earlier, the Street tends to focus on fixed investment—gross domestic investment minus inventories. Of the two categories of fixed investment, residential and nonresidential (or capital spending), the former is by far the smaller, accounting for just 20 to 25 percent of the total. One shouldn't underestimate the influence of residential business investment, however. Traditionally it has represented roughly 5 percent of total economic output, and housing construction has a tremendous multiplier effect on the economy: Once a house or apartment building has been built, personal consumption expenditures usually receive a big boost as owners head out to paint, decorate, and furnish their homes.

That said, analysts and economists tend to pay more attention to nonresidential investment. In part, this is because of the component's size—it accounts for almost three-quarters of total fixed investment. It also provides a great deal of insight into how the corporate sector views economic conditions. Finally, many equity traders, especially those active in the Nasdaq and on the lookout for the next Microsoft or Intel, are particularly interested in technology investment, which falls into the nonresidential category.

A certain amount of nonresidential fixed investment is always required, regardless of the overall state of the economy. Equipment and machinery, for example, constantly need to be refurbished, updated, and repaired. Every year the auto industry shuts down its plants for about two weeks to allow engineers to retool machinery for upcoming new car models. Weather, overuse, and just plain wear and tear cause capital equipment to break down. During booming periods of technological advances, some capital equipment becomes obsolete. Upgrades often help a business raise its level of productivity, which in turn helps the company's bottom line.

Rising capital spending is generally associated with periods of solid corporate profitability and economic prosperity. For businesses to invest in new capital equipment, they need sufficient profit growth. After all, they can't spend what they don't have. (Actually businesses can spend or invest by borrowing via issuance of bonds. But if the company doesn't have respected profit growth, then the ability to obtain the financing is hampered. With a poor financial history, companies are saddled with low credit ratings and are forced to pay higher returns for borrowing those needed funds.)

Management also needs to be positive about the economic outlook. If conditions are soft and consumer demand is unpromising, they will be less inclined to purchase new machinery and equipment. If, however, the economy is expanding at a respectable pace, economic fundamentals are conducive to continuing growth (low interest rates, low inflation, firm labor market growth), and consumers are spending, then businesses will be more likely to pick up the pace of their investment.

Capital equipment is generally very costly—think of the specialized machinery on automakers' assembly lines, the ovens and packaging systems in food-processing plants, the industrial-size kilns of cement manufacturers. Companies thus usually need to borrow to purchase such equipment. So the amount of business investment is closely related to the level of interest rates: Lower rates ease spending; higher rates make it more difficult. Accordingly, the Federal Reserve can influence capital spending by altering its target for the federal funds rate, the rate banks charge each other for overnight loans used to meet reserve requirements. If the Fed wants to spark capital spending, it lowers the overnight rate. Over time, yields on the entire maturity spectrum, from three-month Treasury bills to the 10-year Treasury note, decline as well, making it less expensive for businesses to finance costly investments such as new plants, factories, and equipment.

When investors realize that interest rates may be headed lower, whether as a result of slower inflation rates or the Federal Reserve's influence, they know that businesses are likely to pick up the pace of investment, because the financing of those products and services is going to be cheaper. To capitalize on such developments, traders might bid up the prices of those stocks that have their primary business in investment-related concerns like technology, machinery, tools, or capital equipment.

Government Spending

Wall Street doesn't generally pay much attention to government consumption expenditures and gross investment. One reason is that number's stability. Since 1947, government spending and investment has accounted for about 15 percent of total economic output. Only during periods of profound economic weakness or military conflict does the percentage rise, as the government picks up the pace of spending to boost economic growth or to support the war effort. In the post–World War II era, a peak of 24 percent was registered in 1953, at the end of the Korean War.

Within the government data, however, is one item to which some economists do pay attention, especially in recent times. That item is national defense spending. The long-term trend in national defense spending as a percentage of total government spending since the end of World War II has been consistently downward. Still, increases (in some instances, slight) have occurred when the government has ramped up purchases for military conflicts such as the Korean War in the early 1950s; Vietnam, in the mid-1960s to early 1970s; Desert Storm, in 1990; and most recently, the wars in Afghanistan and Iraq. Keep in mind that government spending on national defense isn't limited to the increased output of aircraft, electronic tracking devices, and missiles. Greater defense spending raises the level of employment—everything from engineering positions to manufacturing positions. And because of security reasons, those jobs tend to stay here in the United States and are not shipped abroad, as so many other manufacturing positions have been in recent years.

Net Exports

When the United States imports more than it exports—as has been the case for the better part of the past three decades—the net export balance is said to be in deficit. This reduces the level of GDP produced in a given period. Conversely, when exports outweigh imports, the trade balance is said to be in surplus. This results in an addition to economic activity. Such an outcome stands to reason, as U.S. export goods are produced by plants located in the United States, whereas imports are produced by foreign workers and sent to the United States. Figure 4.17 represents the value of net exports as a percentage of GDP. This percentage has been negative for a majority of the last 30 years, implying that the pace of imports is greater than that of exports, which reduces the level of domestic economic activity.

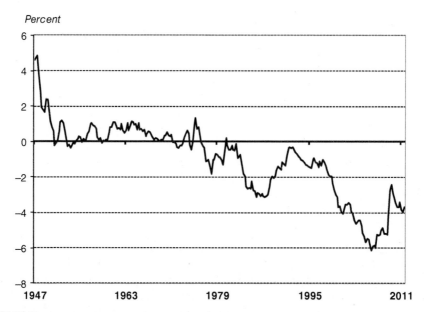

FIGURE 4.17   Net Exports as a Percentage of GDP

Imports needn't have a negative connotation, however. A number of resources are not as abundant in the United States as they are outside its borders. One obvious example is crude oil. The United States has domestic sources of oil but not enough to fuel its consumption. For that reason, it has to import about half its crude oil from foreign countries. Should we consider these imports disapprovingly? Probably not. The mere fact that the United States consumes so much crude is a testament to its economic vitality. Its plants and factories need a great deal of oil to produce what is the largest output in the world, employing millions of people and creating an economic climate that permits its citizens to prosper like no others on Earth. Spending on imports to heat our homes, run our transportation system, and conduct business should not be considered a drag on prosperity but an enhancement.

As with government expenditures, the trading community has little reason to get excited about the net export balance. It's true that the business community frowns on widening trade deficits because increasing imports slow U.S. GDP growth. But rising imports also mean that U.S. businesses and households are consuming more goods and services that they deem attractive. Nobody forces consumers to purchase Italian wine, Japanese cars, or Canadian lumber.

U.S. businesses and households purchase foreign-made goods for any number of reasons including price, quality, size, and taste. The primary force behind demand for foreign-produced goods is simply desirability.

Furthermore, foreign-produced goods tend to be cheaper. Because many countries in the world, particularly China, India, and several Asian-Pacific nations, have relatively low-cost labor, they are capable of producing goods at lower costs. These low-priced products are usually sent to the United States, which influences the prices of similar U.S.-produced goods. This globalization has led to a lower inflation rate here in the United States—especially since the mid-1990s.

Perhaps the major reason investors ignore the trade data is the data's minor influence on total economic activity. Over the past 55 years, the net export position has averaged a mere half a percentage point of total economic output.

Final Sales

Included in the addenda to Table 1 in the GDP report are three measures little noted by the financial media but closely scrutinized by the trading community because of the insights they provide into the underlying spending patterns in the GDP numbers. These three indicators are the final sales of domestic product, gross domestic purchases, and final sales to domestic purchasers.

Final sales of domestic product is a measure of the dollar value of goods produced in the United States in a particular period that are actually sold, rather than put into inventory. To calculate this figure, the BEA first computes the change in private inventories by comparing the current level of inventories with that of the previous period. This indicates how many goods have been added to businesses storage and thus how much of current production has remained unsold. This change in private inventories is then subtracted from GDP to give final sales. This is an important number, because it paints a more accurate picture than GDP of the current pace of spending in the economy. Economists say current pace because the quarterly figure excludes inventories that have been produced in previous quarters. Many times economists will compare the growth rates of GDP with those of final sales to determine whether economic growth is being driven by new production or by the consumption of goods that were previously produced and stored as inventories.

Gross domestic purchases measures all the goods U.S. residents have bought, no matter where the goods were produced. This figure is obtained by subtracting net exports from GDP. There is indeed a difference between GDP and gross domestic purchases. GDP is a measure of domestically produced goods and services, whereas gross domestic purchases is a measure of all the goods domestically purchased. Strong quarterly increases in gross domestic purchases generally imply solid demand by U.S. consumers, as only those purchases of domestic goods are calculated.

Final sales to domestic purchasers is the level of gross domestic purchases less the change in private inventories. It depicts the desire of Americans, both households and businesses, to spend, no matter where the goods or services are produced. Some economists consider it a good indicator of overall economic well-being. Slumping final sales to domestic purchasers suggests that U.S. consumers are tapped out.

Economists keep track of the year-over-year percentage change in final sales to domestic purchasers because of this measure's excellent record of foretelling periods of softer economic growth. As the chart in Figure 4.18 illustrates, each of the five recessions since 1980 was preceded by about a three-quarter-long decline in the year-over-year growth rate of final sales to domestic purchasers.

Corporate Profits

Market participants don't generally pay as much attention to the income side as to the expenditure side of GDP. That isn't to say the trends in wages and salaries aren't important to economists or to analysts who cover retail issues. What could be more telling about the future pace of spending, after all, than the amount of income

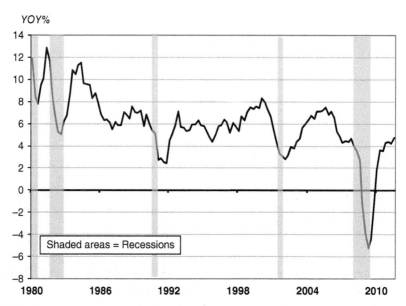

FIGURE 4.18   Final Sales to Domestic Puchasers

earned by would-be consumers? It's just that the trends of the expenditure side are accepted as being more accurate, because they aren't subject to inventory and capital consumption value adjustments, as the income-determined data are. Still, some income-side components can give valuable insights into economic trends. Among the most important of these are the measures of corporate profits.

As with most of the other measures discussed, a rise in corporate profits indicates a healthy business climate. The economy's growth cycle really starts with a lift in corporate profits. When businesses are successful, their incomes exceed costs, and they make profits. This permits them to invest in new capital equipment or employees.

Even more significant than pretax earnings are after-tax profits. From this figure, economists and analysts can judge how much money companies actually have to spend on new equipment or additional staff. As the chart in Figure 4.19 shows, businesses generally have shed workers when corporate profit growth contracts (below zero in the chart). The same holds true for business investment. After-tax corporate profits have generally declined approximately three quarters prior to periods of slowing economic growth or recessions.

The best measure of the funds that companies have available for spending and hiring, however, is the level of undistributed profits. Undistributed profits are a company's earnings after tax payments and dividend distributions. One striking feature of the chart in Figure 4.20 of the twentieth century and the first decade of the twenty-first century, is the paltry level of undistributed profits during the early 1970s, 1987, 2002, and in 2008 and 2009. All of these periods were associated with tumbling stock prices, high unemployment rates, and lackluster business investment.

The economic signals associated with corporate profits might not be as telling as they once were. As was noted earlier, in recent years the U.S. economy has

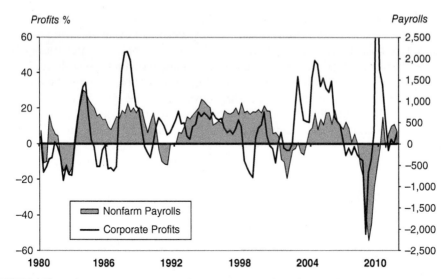

FIGURE 4.19   After-Tax Corporate Profits (Y/Y Percent) and Payroll Growth

become practically impervious to a whole host of negative influences that, if they had occurred in previous periods, would have resulted in recession and in some instances, quite possibly depression. Beginning in early 2001, the stock market bubble of the late 1990s burst, wiping out trillions of dollars in personal wealth. Widespread accounting scandals and egregious corporate impropriety also hammered investors' confidence, stalling the financial markets. For the first time in more than 50 years, the United States was attacked on its own soil, virtually paralyzing

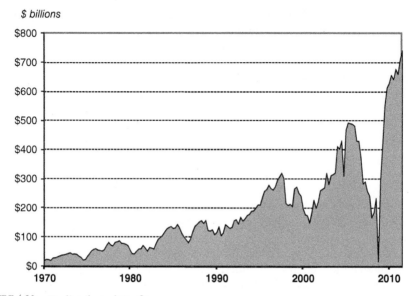

FIGURE 4.20   Undistributed Profits

the economy. Hundreds of thousands of businesses closed for weeks, and the borders were sealed. Fear of anthrax attacks was widespread. As if all of this weren't enough, U.S. armed forces became engaged in military conflicts in Afghanistan and Iraq. Yet despite all these profoundly negative influences in a relatively short period, the economy managed to avoid a deep or prolonged recession. Perhaps the ultimate sign of resiliency is that consumer spending never fell in the 2001 recession.

In 2007 through 2009, it took the rare combination of a recession, war, a global credit collapse, and a deep housing crisis to finally bring consumers to their knees.

Tricks from the Trenches

The *output gap* is the difference between the economy's actual and potential levels of production. This difference yields insight into important economic conditions, such as employment and inflation.

The economy's potential output is the amount of goods and services it would produce if it utilized all its resources. To determine this figure—the trend level— economists estimate the rate at which the economy can expand without sparking a rise in inflation. It is not an easy calculation, and it yields as many different answers as there are economists with different definitions for the maximum level of output, productivity, hours worked, and so on. Luckily, a widely accepted estimate of potential output is reported relatively frequently by the Congressional Budget Office (CBO). The CBO's website, www.cbo.gov, contains information about its methodology and underlying assumptions in computing the trend level, as well as a detailed historical data set.

A negative output gap exists when actual GDP growth is below its estimated potential. This suggests that the economy isn't utilizing all its labor and capital resources. Such periods of underutilization are usually characterized by high unemployment and low inflation, with plants and factories closing down, workers furloughed, and machinery idled. The chart in Figure 4.21 depicts periods of above- and below-potential trends in GDP over the past 20 years.

When GDP growth exceeds its calculated potential, creating a positive gap, the economy is pushed to its limit. All plants and factories are running at capacity, the labor force is fully employed, and economic output is skyrocketing. The chart in Figure 4.22 illustrates the relationship between a positive gap and falling unemployment. In periods of overutilization, such as 1997–2001, strains on the system develop, usually sparking inflation.

After the 1990–1991 recession, the jobs climate remained in the doldrums for several years. The economy started to accelerate in 1998, exceeding its potential in large part because of the surge in the stock market and the associated wealth effect. Then, after the dot-com bubble burst in 2000, the economy once again found itself in recession in 2001 with another jobless recovery.

It is easy to see the sizable collapse in economic output in 2008 and the cavernous gap between the economy's actual level of activity and its potential. It is unsurprising that the recovery continued to feel like an economy spinning its wheels despite the fact that the National Bureau of Economic Research called the end of the recession in June 2009.

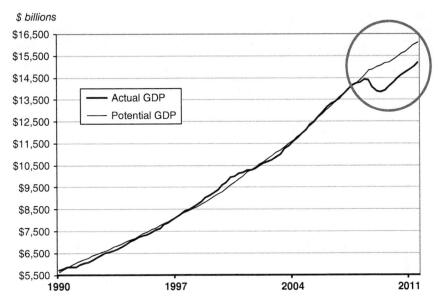

FIGURE 4.21   Actual and Potential GDP

Economists sometimes express the output gap in the form of a ratio derived by dividing the difference between actual output and potential output by potential output. When this ratio falls below zero, conditions are said to be soft, or sluggish; when it rises above zero, conditions are expansionary.

Because the output gap provides such telling economic insight into a whole host of economic relationships, it is a favorite of policy makers. The Federal Reserve, for

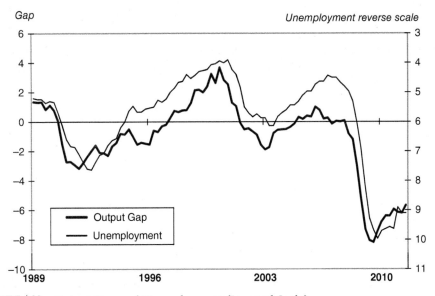

FIGURE 4.22   Output Gap and Unemployment (Inverted Scale)

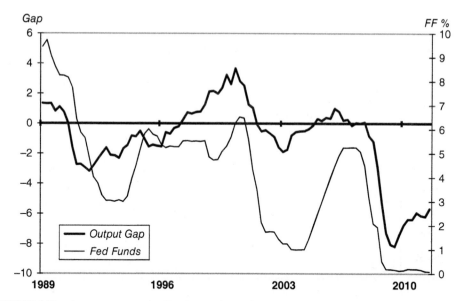

FIGURE 4.23   Output Gap and Effective Fed Fund Rate

example, considers it in determining where to set the federal funds rate. If the gap is negative, indicating that the economy is growing below its potential, the Fed may try to spark activity by lowering the overnight rate. This traditionally results in a decline all along the maturity spectrum, making it easier for companies to fund capital projects. It also spurs individuals' spending by rendering loans to purchase items such as automobiles and homes more affordable. Conversely, when the gap is positive, indicating that the economic party is getting a bit out of hand, the Fed may take away the punch bowl by increasing its overnight target rate, thus discouraging consumers and businesses from spending and investing. The chart in Figure 4.23 illustrates the tendency of the federal funds rate to follow the output gap.

The severe contraction in the output gap in the wake of the 2007–2009 recession was one of the many reasons the Fed continued to keep its benchmark overnight target rate at or near zero for such a sustained period.

References

Baumol, William J., and Alan S. Blinder. 1991. *Macroeconomics: Principles and Policy.* 5th ed. New York: Harcourt Brace Jovanovich.

Bernanke, Ben S., and Andrew B. Abel. 1998. *Macroeconomics.* 3rd ed. New York: Addison-Wesley.

Chow, Michael J., and William C. Dunkelberg. 2011. "The Small Business Sector in Recent Recoveries." *National Association for Business Economics Business Economics* 46, no. 4.

Congressional Budget Office. 2000. *The Budget and Economic Outlook: An Update.* Washington, DC. Also available online at www.cbo.gov/ftpdoc.cfm?index =2241&type=1.

———. 2001. *CBO's Method for Estimating Potential Output: An Update*. Washington, DC. Also available online at www.cbo.gov/ftpdoc.cfm?index=3020 &type=1.

Jones, Charles I. 2002. "Using Chain-Weighted NIPA Data." *Federal Reserve Bank of San Francisco Economic Letter* (August 2).

Landefeld, J. Steven. 1995. "BEA's Featured Measure of Output and Prices." National Association for Business Economics *NABE News*, no. 113 (September): 3–6, 26.

Landefeld, J. Steven, Eugene P. Seskin, and Barbara M. Fraumeni. 2008. "Taking the Pulse of the Economy: Measuring GDP." *Journal of Economic Perspectives* vol. 22, no. 2 (Spring): 193–216.

Mankiw, N. Gregory. 1998. *Principles of Macroeconomics*. Fort Worth, TX: Dryden Press.

Mitchell, Wesley C., ed. 1921. *Income in the United States: Its Amount and Distribution 1909–1919*. New York: Harcourt, Brace and Company.

Okun, Arthur M. 1962. "Potential GNP: Its Measurement and Significance." *Proceedings of the Business and Economic Statistics Section of the American Statistical Association*, 98–104.

Popkin, Joel. 2000. "The U.S. National Income and Product Accounts." *Journal of Economic Perspectives* 14, no. 2 (Spring): 214–24.

Prakken, Joel L., and Lisa T. Guirl. 1995. "Macro Modeling and Forecasting with Chain-Type Measures of GDP." National Association for Business Economics. *NABE News*, no. 113 (September): 7–13.

Rosenblum, Harvey, and Tyler Atkinson. 2010. "Gauging the Odds of a Double-Dip Recession Amid Signals and Slowdowns." *Federal Reserve Bank of Dallas Economic Letter* 5, no. 12 (December).

Ruggles, Nancy D., and Richard Ruggles. 1999. *National Accounting and Economic Policy*. Cheltenham, UK: Edward Elgar.

Steindel, Charles. 1995. "Chain-Weighting: The New Approach to Measuring GDP." *Federal Reserve Bank of New York Current Issues in Economics and Finance* 1, no. 9 (December).

U.S. Department of Commerce, Bureau of Economic Analysis. 1985. *An Introduction to National Economic Accounting*. Methodology Paper Series MP-1. Washington, DC: Government Printing Office. Also available online at www.bea.gov/methodologies/index.htm.

———. 1998. *National Income and Product Accounts of the United States*, 1929–94. 2 vols. Washington, DC: Government Printing Office.

———. 2000. "GDP: One of the Great Inventions of the 20th Century." *Survey of Current Business* (January): 6–4. Also available online at www.bea.gov/scb/toc/0100cont.htm.

———. 2002. *Corporate Profits: Profits Before Tax, Profits Tax Liability and Dividends*. Methodology Paper Series. Washington, DC: Government Printing Office. Also available online at www.bea.gov/methodologies/index.htm.

———. "Gross Domestic Product" (various releases). Also available online at www.bea.gov/newsreleases/relsarchivegdp.htm.

———. *Survey of Current Business* (various issues). Also available online at www.bea.gov/scb/date_guide.asp.

Whelan, Karl. 2000. *A Guide to the Use of Chain Aggregated NIPA Data*. Finance and Economics Discussion Series, 2000–35. Washington, DC: Federal Reserve Board of Governors.

Part IV Indexes of Leading, Lagging, and Coincident Indicators

If a market economist were given one wish, it might be for a single indicator that would consistently predict both the direction and the pace of the economy. Unfortunately, none has so far been discovered that fits the entire bill. Some indicators are wonderful at pinpointing levels of activity but fail to depict trends. Others excel at identifying particular areas of economic strength and weakness but can't measure broad-based performance.

Unable to find a single omnipotent indicator, economists have taken an assortment of those showing the most predictive accuracy and combined them into the index of leading economic indicators (LEI), or the leading index. This index is one of three composite indexes—along with the indexes of lagging and coincident indicators—that the Conference Board compiles and publishes in its monthly *Business Cycle Indicators* report. This report is usually released to the public at 10:00 A.M. (ET) four to five weeks after the end of the record month. It is available, together with historical data and explanations of the methodology behind the indexes, on the Conference Board's website, www.conferenceboard.org, or by subscription for a small annual fee.

Wall Streeters often refer to the entire *Business Cycle Indicators* report as the index of leading indicators, because that's the part to which they pay the most attention. In actuality, the charts, commentary, and data provided on all three indexes are extremely useful in identifying and explaining the different phases of the business cycle. Whereas the leading economic index points to future trends and turning points, the coincident index identifies those that are in the process of developing, and the lagging index confirms that these events have indeed occurred. Table 4.4 shows the number of months by which the three composite indicators led or lagged business cycle peaks or troughs, as defined by the National Bureau of Economic Research (NBER), from 1960 through 2001.

Because the components of the indexes are released earlier than the indexes themselves, the markets generally don't react strongly to the indicators report. Market participants, however, can still glean a great deal of information from the movements of the indexes and their components, not to mention the commentary and interpretation that the Conference Board's staff economists supply each month.

Evolution of an Indicator

The concept of composite economic indicators is not new, nor did it originate with the Conference Board. In the early 1930s, economists Arthur Burns and Wesley Mitchell at the NBER were already combining economic data series to identify trends and turning points in the economy. NBER first published the results of these efforts in 1938. By the 1960s, the U.S. Department of Commerce was releasing monthly reports containing the NBER's leading, lagging, and coincident indicators. The Commerce Department–NBER collaboration lasted until 1995, when the Conference Board— a private, not-for-profit, nonadvocacy research and business-membership group— assumed the responsibilities of calculating, reporting, and maintaining the composite indexes.

TABLE 4.4   Timing of the Indexes Relative to Cyclical Turning Points

	Composite Leading Index	Composite Coincident Index	Composite Lagging Index
Leads (−) or Lags (+) at business cycle peaks (months)*			
Apr 1960	−11	0	3
Dec 1969	−8	−2	3
Nov 1973	−9	0	13
Jan 1980	−15	0	3
Jul 1981	−8	0	2
Jul 1990	−18	−1	−12
Mar 2001	−11	−6	−4
Leads (−) or Lags (+) at business cycle troughs (months)			
Feb 1961	−11	0	9
Nov 1970	−7	0	15
Mar 1975	−2	1	17
Jul 1980	−2	0	3
Nov 1982	−10	1	6
Mar 1991	−2	0	21
Nov 2001	−7	17	28

*Business cycle peaks/troughs are determined by the NBER.
Source: Conference Board.

The leading, lagging, and coincident indexes all have undergone considerable revision in the course of their history. As the structure of the U.S. economy has changed, newer indicators have periodically replaced older ones that no longer accurately reflect the business cycle or that simply aren't calculated any more. As recently as November 1996, the Conference Board dropped two indicators—the price of sensitive materials and the volume of unfilled orders for manufactured durable goods—from the leading index, and added a new one: the yield spread.

In January 2012, another revision occurred when the Institute for Supply Management (ISM) supplier delivery index was replaced with the new orders index and a new Leading Credit Index was incorporated for the M2 component beginning in 1990. M2 remains in the leading index prior to 1990. This fine-tuning has kept the report an accurate tool for Wall Street economists and market participants.

Digging for the Data

The three indexes in the Conference Board's report are constructed from series of cyclical indicators, most of which are seasonally adjusted. Some of the components must be estimated; all are subject to later revision. The indexes themselves thus also need to be revised. The monthly release contains both initial values for the record month and revisions for the previous six months.

In constructing an index, the Conference Board calculates each component's month-over-month percentage change and then *standardizes* it—that is, adjusts it for volatility—so that indicators with more dramatic month-to-month movements won't dominate the index. The standardized percentage changes for all of the index's components are then added together. The sums derived for the leading and lagging indexes are adjusted again, so that their standard deviations equal that of the coincident index. Finally, the results for all three indexes are translated into levels representing changes from a base date, currently 2004, whose level is set at 100.

Because the composition of the three indexes is modified as the structure of the economy evolves, to remain in or be added to one of the indexes, a component must demonstrate consistency as a leading, coincident, or lagging indicator. It must also be the end product of a reliable data-collection process, adhere to a timely publication schedule, and be subject to only minor—or no—revisions.

Coincident Index

The four components of the Conference Board's coincident index are:

1. Number of employees on nonagricultural (that is, nonfarm) payrolls (in thousands),
2. Personal income less transfer payments (nominal rate in billions of chained 2005 dollars),
3. Industrial production index (2007 = 100), and
4. Manufacturing and trade sales (in millions of chained 2005 dollars).

The number of employees on nonagricultural payrolls is obtained from a survey of about 140,000 businesses conducted by the Bureau of Labor Statistics (BLS). The change in this number is one of the headline figures in the BLS's monthly *Employment Situation* report. The path followed by nonfarm payrolls has, in the main, paralleled that of growth in gross domestic product (GDP).

Personal income less transfer payments is derived from the *Personal Income and Outlays* report produced by the Bureau of Economic Analysis (BEA). The largest income source is wages and salaries, which account for about 55 percent of the total; transfer payments—government disbursements such as Social Security payments, veterans' benefits, and food stamps—usually constitute about 15 percent. Transfer payments are generally spent immediately on basic necessities, such as food or rent, not on durable goods and services. They thus have relatively little influence on macroeconomic activity. So income less transfer payments is generally considered a stronger, more representative economic indicator.

The total industrial production index is the headliner of the monthly *Industrial Production and Capacity Utilization* report published by the Federal Reserve Board. It is constructed of 312 components—representing the manufacturing, mining, and utilities industries—that are weighted according to the value they add during the production process. The index mirrors the general economy so closely that it is often used as a more timely proxy for the quarterly GDP report.

Manufacturing and trade sales data are collected as part of the national income and product accounts calculations. These data may be found in the *Manufacturing and Trade Inventories and Sales* (MTIS) report published by the Department of Commerce.

Leading Index

The 10 components of the leading index are the following:

1. Average workweek, production workers, manufacturing
2. Average weekly initial claims for unemployment insurance
3. Manufacturers' new orders for consumer goods and materials
4. ISM new orders index
5. Manufacturers' new orders for nondefense capital goods, excluding aircraft
6. Monthly building permits for new private housing
7. Stock prices
8. Leading Credit Index, M2 money supply prior to 1990
9. The interest-rate spread between the 10-year Treasury bond and the federal funds rate
10. Average consumer expectations for economic conditions

The rationale behind including some of these indicators is clear from their names: new "orders" and "expectations," for instance, are obviously forward-looking. The inclusion of others is less self-evident. All the components, however, were chosen because of their potency as predictors of economic activity.

The average weekly hours worked in manufacturing is derived from the same survey as the nonagricultural payroll figure described above and is also published in the BLS's *Employment Situation* report. Average weekly manufacturing hours constitute a good measure of future production levels and economic strength. Assuming workers maintain the same level of productivity, the more hours they put in on the job, the greater their output. When manufacturers foresee a softening in demand for their products, they tend to reduce workers' hours before cutting staff, which is more time-consuming and expensive to implement. It is also easier and cheaper to extend hours, should business seem poised to pick up, than to hire new employees. Substantial changes in the average hours worked thus reflect companies' pessimism or optimism about future economic conditions.

The average number of weekly initial claims for unemployment reflects the condition of the labor market. A rise in claims, as businesses lay off more and more employees, usually occurs in the early stages of economic downturns and thus can point to a coming recession. The correlation between jobless claims and the economy is not precise, however, in part because unemployment statistics are distorted by the differing eligibility requirements imposed by different states.

Manufacturers' new orders for consumer goods and materials and for nondefense capital goods, excluding aircraft, are excellent signs of how businesses regard the coming economic climate. Given the expenses involved in financing large purchases and in carrying inventory, wholesalers and retailers don't place orders for consumer goods unless they foresee a demand for these products. Similarly, companies don't invest in costly capital goods unless they believe they'll need the additional production capacity or efficiency created by such investments. Capital goods orders constitute a particularly powerful leading indicator, because business investment makes up approximately 15 percent of total GDP.

The new orders diffusion index is one of the five seasonally adjusted diffusion indexes that the ISM uses to construct the purchasing managers' index (PMI), the headline index of its monthly *Manufacturing ISM Report on Business*. The new orders index—which the ISM creates from responses to its survey of approximately 300 purchasing managers across the United States—measures expectations of future order demand. Readings above 50 percent indicate increased order growth, usually a sign of robust economic activity; readings below 50 percent indicate a contracting pace of demand and economic stagnation.

Statistics concerning building permits for new private housing are contained in the *New Residential Construction* report, released jointly by the U.S. Department of Housing and Urban Development and the U.S. Department of Commerce's Census Bureau. These data present insights into an element of the U.S. economy that both is crucial to its growth and signals its general well-being. Although new housing construction accounts directly for only a small percentage of GDP, it drives other activity, such as purchases of paint, home furnishings, and countless other consumer durables. Moreover, because buying a house is a huge undertaking for most individuals, it implies confidence in the stability of employment and earnings, as well as sound economic fundamentals.

The stock price component of the leading index is the monthly average for the Standard & Poor's 500 index, published in the S&P publication *The Outlook*. Inclusion of this has been questioned by some economists, who argue that stock prices are determined by speculation rather than by economic fundamentals and so should not be considered accurate gauges of future economic activity. The rationale for including stock prices is that they reflect the informed expectations of sophisticated traders and investors. To get ahead of the curve, these knowledgeable market participants make their trades before earnings are actually announced. Rising equity prices thus indicate expectations of greater corporate profitability, which in turn implies an expanding economy: When businesses are more profitable, they are better able to invest in new projects, plants, and factories, and to hire additional workers. Falling prices, conversely, indicate that investors expect lower profitability, which in turn means a slower economy.

The Conference Board created and adopted a new component to the LEI, the leading credit index. It is a compilation of several financial market indicators such as interest-rate swaps, credit default swaps, and the Federal Reserve's senior loan officer survey. Details of the new index are limited at the time of this book's publication.

Since most of those components have surfaced in the past 30 years, the Conference Board uses real M2 prior to 1990. Money supply is simply the amount of money in the economy. The Federal Reserve recognizes three types of monetary aggregates, which it labels M1, M2, and M3. The leading economic index uses M2, which, in addition to currency in circulation and deposits in savings and checking accounts, includes money market fund shares and other liquid assets, such as overnight repurchase agreements issued by commercial banks.

Economists commonly refer to money as the oil in the engine of economic activity. So it makes sense that the growth rate of the money supply is related to the growth rate of the economy. The relationship that associates money with economic activity is called the *quantity theory of money*, which may be summarized by the following expression:

$$M \times V = \text{Nominal GDP}$$

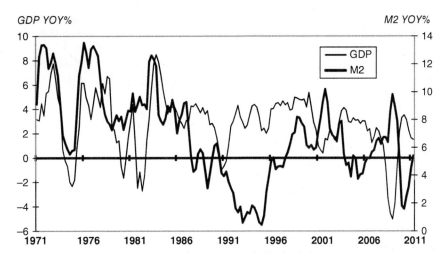

FIGURE 4.24   Changes in the Money Supply (M2) and in Real GDP

Source: Board of Governors of the Federal Reserve System; U.S. Department of Commerce, Bureau of Economic Analysis.

where M is the money supply and V is the velocity of money—how often a dollar changes hands in a given period. Economists have assumed that velocity changes slowly, if at all, over time. Given this assumption, any increase in the money supply would be mirrored by an increase in nominal GDP. Conversely, a contraction in money supply would be reflected in a contracting economy. This relationship is illustrated in the chart in Figure 4.24.

Economists have discovered, however, that the velocity of money has not been constant. Without V as a constant, the equation of exchange breaks down. Historically, velocity levels have varied for a number of reasons, including new regulations and innovations in banking such as the advent of ATM machines, direct-deposit banking, and e-banking. Still, the relationship between money and economic activity enjoys a long, successful association, as evidenced in the associated chart, and is therefore included in the index of leading economic indicators.

The interest-rate spread component of the leading index is the difference between the yield on the 10-year Treasury note and the federal funds rate—the rate banks charge one another on overnight loans needed to meet reserve requirements set by the Federal Reserve. For instance, if the federal funds rate is 3.25 percent and the 10-year Treasury is yielding 5.35 percent, the spread is 2.10 percent, or 210 basis points (a basis point is one-hundredth of a percent). The interest-rate spread is included among the leading indicators because interest-rate spreads determine the shape of the yield curve and the shape of the yield curve embodies fixed-income traders' expectations about the economy.

The yield curve shows the relationship between the yield on U.S. Treasury securities and their maturities. Longer-term rates are usually higher than shorter-term rates, because more things can affect the value of the bond in 10 years than in two, and lenders require greater rewards for undertaking these greater risks. Thus, under normal economically favorable conditions, interest-rate spreads are positive, and the

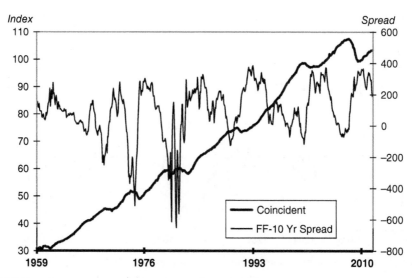

FIGURE 4.25   The Interest Rate Spread and the Coincident Index
Source: Board of Governors of the Federal Reserve System; Conference Board.

shape of the yield curve is gently convex—rising somewhat more steeply at the short end and leveling off a bit at the longer maturities.

Steep curves—large spreads—may temporarily be the result of current economic weakness. The Federal Reserve seeks to counter such weakness by reducing the overnight rate, thus lowering borrowing costs and encouraging business investment and consumer spending on interest rate–sensitive goods and services like housing and automobiles. This move stimulates the economy but can spark inflationary fears among the fixed-income community. Inflation erodes the value of future interest and principal payments. In anticipation, fixed-income investors sell off longer-term (more inflation-sensitive) bonds, depressing their prices and raising their yields. This, combined with the Fed's lowering of the short-term rate, steepens the yield curve. Conversely, when the economy seems to be running too hot, the Fed may seek to forestall a rise in inflation by raising its target overnight rate, discouraging spending and so slowing growth. The result is a flatter yield curve (smaller spreads).

The curve may also be inverted, with short-term rates higher than long-term rates and spreads below zero. This situation is generally associated with economic downturns, even recessions, as illustrated in Figure 4.25. The coincident index— which, because it reflects current economic conditions, may serve as a proxy for the business cycle—declines every time the spread between the federal funds rate and the 10-year Treasury becomes negative. This close correlation is one reason the Conference Board decided to include this gauge in its index of leading economic indicators.

Why does an inverted yield curve predict recessions? There is no definitive answer. Actually, one answer sometimes put forward is that an inverted curve may result from the Fed's overdoing it—raising rates so high that they not only cool but stifle growth (as well as any fears of inflation). What is clear is that expectations of weak economic conditions may encourage expectations of lower interest rates. This in turn leads to more purchases of longer-term bonds, pushing up their prices and lowering their yields. The result is an inverted curve.

In the aftermath of the credit crisis, recession, and collapse of Lehman Brothers in late 2008, the Federal Reserve lowered its benchmark target rate to a range of zero to 25 basis points. In August 2011, the central bank stated its intention to maintain the Fed funds rate at "exceptionally low levels…at least through mid-2013." This essentially kept an upward-sloping yield curve, since the short end was anchored at zero percent and longer-term rates can't fall below zero. This was somewhat of a distortion to the predictive nature of the LEI.

The index of consumer expectations is compiled monthly, along with the indexes of consumer sentiment and current economic conditions, by the University of Michigan's Survey Research Center, using responses to the university's *Survey of Consumers*. The survey asks consumers about their personal financial situations, overall economic conditions, and their buying attitudes, as well as various current issues and concerns. The index of consumer expectations summarizes the economic trends the respondents foresee.

Including this index among the leading indicators is a no-brainer. Consumer expectations about the economy are shaped mainly by consumers' experiences in the workplace. High confidence springs from expanding employment, increased production schedules, and rising wages, and thus points to a positive economic climate. It also helps foster that climate by encouraging spending, one of the major contributors to GDP. On the other hand, consumers are among the first to sense worsening economic conditions, reflected in slowdowns at their workplaces, and to retrench. This generally depresses the economy further. Not surprisingly, then, the index of consumer expectations has a good record of predicting turning points in both consumer spending and total economic activity.

Lagging Index

The lagging index has the following seven components:

1. Average duration of unemployment
2. Ratio of manufacturing and trade inventories to sales
3. Manufacturing labor cost per unit of output
4. Average prime rate
5. Commercial and industrial loans outstanding
6. Ratio of consumer installment credit to personal income
7. Change in the consumer price index for services

The average duration of unemployment is the average number of weeks that people are out of work. As this number rises, so does consumer frustration, which depresses spending and holds back economic growth. Decreases in the length of unemployment traditionally occur after a recovery is already under way. This is generally a function of businesses' reluctance to take on new workers until they are absolutely assured of recovery. Similarly, the steepest increases in the average duration of unemployment generally take place after a downturn has begun. That is why this is a lagging indicator.

The ratio of manufacturing and trade inventories to sales is calculated by the U.S. Department of Commerce's Census Bureau, using data from its *Manufacturers' Shipments, Inventories, and Orders* (M3) survey and its *Monthly Wholesale Trade* survey. The results are published in the Commerce Department's *Manufacturing and Trade Inventories and Sales* (MTIS) report. The ratio indicates how many months, given the current pace of sales, it will take for inventories to be entirely liquidated. A rising ratio means that businesses are unable to effect a steady reduction in their back stock, either because sales are too weak or because their inventories are accumulating too fast. In either case, this is a sign of economic weakness. A falling ratio, conversely, indicates that companies' shelves are emptying and that manufacturers may soon have to increase production to replenish their disappearing stocks—a bullish economic signal. Although economists watch the ratio for insight into future production activity, it is a lagging economic indicator. That's because, historically, inventories rise long after sales growth has halted. So the ratio reaches its peak in the middle of a recession.

The percentage change in manufacturing labor cost per unit of output is measured by an index constructed by the Conference Board from sources including the BEA's seasonally adjusted data on manufacturing employees' compensation and the Federal Reserve Board's data on manufacturing production. The index rises when manufacturers' labor costs increase faster than their output. Because monthly index movements are erratic, the percentage change used is measured over a six-month period. Peaks in the six-month rate of change are typically reached during recessions.

Data on the average monthly prime rate are compiled by the Fed. As the interest rate that banks charge their most creditworthy customers, such as blue-chip companies, the prime rate serves as a benchmark for loans to lesser quality borrowers. For instance, a smaller, younger company might have to pay two percentage points over prime. Because the prime rate moves with respect to changes in the federal funds overnight rate, periods of rising prime rates are usually the result of rate hikes instituted by the Federal Reserve in response to a potential overheating in the economy and possible mounting inflationary pressures. Falling prime rates are usually the result of the Fed's reductions in the overnight target rate, which are designed to stimulate economic activity. Banks tend to change the prime rate only after movements occur in the general economy.

The value of outstanding commercial and industrial loans is computed by the Fed and adjusted for inflation by the Conference Board. High commercial and industrial loan levels indicate that businesses have a favorable economic outlook and that they are willing to build and expand their operations and finance such growth with borrowed monies. Conversely, when the outlook is less encouraging and businesses are skeptical, loan growth is weaker. It tends to reach a peak after an expansion reaches its high-water mark and to bottom out more than a year after the end of a recession.

The ratio of consumer installment credit to personal income is computed using data from the Fed's monthly release detailing the amount of currently outstanding consumer credit, as well as from the BEA's monthly *Personal Income and Outlays* report. Consumer credit is not included in the BEA income figure, but for many Americans it is a critical income supplement. In times of financial insecurity, such as those that occur during downturns and recessions, people tend to reduce their personal borrowing and don't pick up the pace again until a trend of increasing income is firmly established. Accordingly, this ratio generally reaches its nadir a year or more after the end of a recession.

In the aftermath of the financial crisis and recession in 2007–2009, consumer revolving credit collapsed—banks weren't quick to lend since repayment wasn't likely. Consumers weren't exactly lining up for loans or credit card charges that they probably couldn't repay—unemployment rocketed above 10 percent—and the need for purchases was limited.

The change in the consumer price index for services measures the movement in the services component of the consumer price index, which is calculated monthly by the BLS. The month-to-month change in the consumer price index is the most popular measure of inflation. Service-sector inflation tends to increase after a recession has already begun and decrease even after it has ended. These tendencies result from what has been termed *recognition lags* and other such rigidities in the market.

What Does It All Mean?

The Conference Board's function in creating, refining, and maintaining the leading, lagging, and coincident indexes, which are presented monthly in its *Business Cycle Indicators* report, shouldn't be confused with what the National Bureau of Economic Research does. The NBER is the official arbiter of peaks and troughs in the business cycle. In pinpointing the dates of these crucial turning points, the bureau's economists consider many factors and consult several indicators, which include, but are not limited to, components of the coincident index. The Conference Board's *Business Cycle Indicators* report does not determine the official peaks and troughs of the U.S. economy. However, the turning points these indicators signal are remarkably similar to those the NBER designates.

Coincident Index

The coincident index is rarely mentioned in the business press. Still, it is very useful for assessing the current pace of economic activity. As Table 4.4 demonstrates, the coincident index closely tracks the turning points in the business cycles. It can thus serve as a benchmark in assessing the relationship of any economic statistic to the business cycle. One of the most commonly used representatives of this cycle is the GDP. A simple linear regression between the growth rates of real GDP and the coincident index yields an impressive correlation of around 86 percent. This close correlation, illustrated in Figure 4.26, makes the coincident index a useful and more timely proxy for the quarterly GDP.

The individual indicators composing the leading index differ considerably in their abilities to predict economic turning points. Some are very farsighted, others relatively nearsighted. The composite index combines these components in such a way that the whole outperforms any of its parts. The predictive accuracy of the composite is illustrated in Figure 4.27, which charts the quarterly year-over-year percentage change in the leading index against real GDP.

The chart clearly shows that hikes and dips in the leading index precede those in the economy by significant periods. According to the latest research, the index's

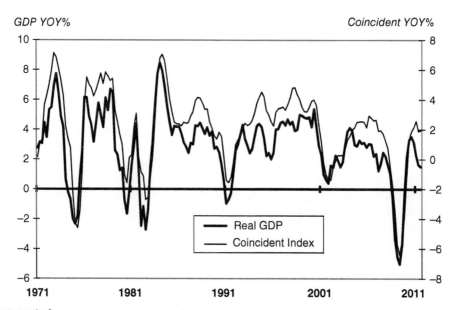

FIGURE 4.26   Index of Coincident Economic Indicators and Real GDP

Source: U.S. Department of Commerce, Bureau of Economic Analysis; Conference Board.

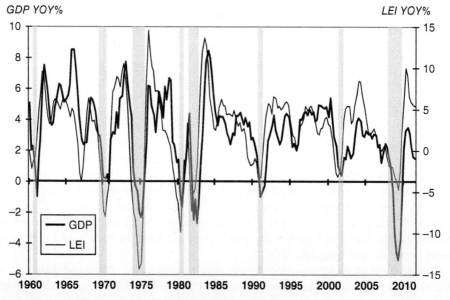

FIGURE 4.27   Index of Leading Economic Indicators and Real GDP

Source: U.S. Department of Commerce, Bureau of Economic Analysis; Conference Board; National Bureau of Economic Research.

average lead time is roughly nine months. The individual periods composing this average, however, vary considerably. This is in part because of the revisions that the index's components undergo, necessitating commensurate revisions in the composite. It also reflects the fact that every recession and every recovery is caused by different sets of circumstances. The ability of the leading index to foresee these turning points therefore also varies.

Lagging Index

The lagging index follows downturns in the business cycle (as represented by the coincident index) by about three months, and expansions by about fifteen. At first blush, this may seem to be pretty useless information—like driving a car by looking through the rearview mirror. Economists, however, argue that you can't know where you're going if you don't know where you've been. The index of lagging economic indicators confirms that turning points in economic activity that were identified by the leading and coincident indexes actually have occurred. It thus helps prevent the transmission of false signals.

How to Use What You See

Market participants generally don't pay a great deal of attention to the Conference Board's *Business Cycle Indicators* report because they've already had a chance to view and process for themselves the underlying data. Nevertheless, economists and businesses have traditionally looked for longer-term trends in the leading index to predict turning points in the economy.

The old rule of thumb was that three consecutive monthly declines in the index signaled a recession within a year, whereas three consecutive increases signaled a recovery. This rule was roughly accurate. It did predict several recessions that failed to materialize, however, and in the case of some correct calls, the lead times were negative—that is, the predictions came after the recession was already established. A reason for false recession predictions could be that although the index contains components representing the manufacturing, consumer, financial, employment, and business investment sectors, it has none that reflect demand for, or investment and employment in, the services industries that now dominate the economy. Moreover, the financial sectors that are represented often move in ways that don't parallel movement in the broader economy, generating both volatility and some of the false signals mentioned.

The leading index's record of predicting, as a popular quip has it, "seven of the last five recessions" has led some cynics to term it the "index of misleading indicators." That's not really fair. Still, to improve its predictive accuracy, economists often consider the index's moves in three dimensions—duration, depth, and diffusion—instead of just one—duration—as the three-month rule did. That is, in addition to requiring that changes extend over three months, the refined method looks at how large changes are and how many components are involved. For example, if nine of the index's 10 components show increases, but one—say, average weekly hours worked in manufacturing—falls, an expansion is more certain than if only four components increase, three decrease, and three are unchanged.

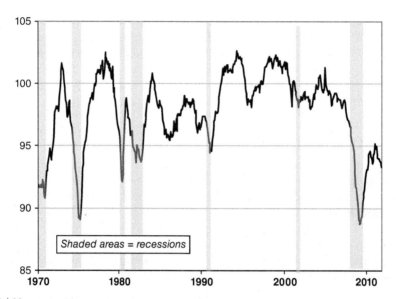

FIGURE 4.28   Coincident-to-Lagging Ratio and Recessions

Source: Conference Board; National Bureau of Economic Research.

Tricks from the Trenches

Wall Streeters, being innovators, have sought ways to improve even on the three-dimensional analysis. Their trick, with respect to the *Business Cycle Indicators* report, is to compute the ratio of the coincident index to the lagging index. The theory behind this ratio, informally referred to as the *coincident-to-lagging ratio*, is this: In the early stages of a recovery, coincident indicators are rising while lagging indicators, reflecting the conditions of earlier months, remain unchanged, resulting in a rising ratio. When an expansion is peaking, both sets of indicators will be rising, but the rate of increase for the coincident indicators will be slower, so the ratio will fall. Similarly, near the nadir of a recession, all the component indicators will again be moving in the same direction—this time, down—but the coincident indicators will fall more slowly, so the ratio will rise.

As you can see from the chart in Figure 4.28, the coincident-to-lagging ratio, like the leading index, has declined before every recession since 1970. But it has transmitted fewer false signals. One explanation for this relative success is that the coincident and lagging indexes do a better job of representing current and past economic performance, respectively, than the leading index does of assessing future activity.

References

Anderson, Gerald H., and John J. Erceg. 1989. "Forecasting Turning Points with Leading Indicators." Federal Reserve Bank of Cleveland Economic Commentary (October 1).

Burns, Arthur F., and Wesley Clair Mitchell. 1938. "Statistical Indicators of Cyclical Revivals." *NBER Bulletin* 69.

———. 1946. *Measuring Business Cycles*. New York: National Bureau of Economic Research.

Conference Board. *Business CycleIndicators*. New York: Conference Board (various issues).

———. *U.S. Leading Economic Indicators and Related Composite Indexes*. New York: Conference Board (various issues).

Diebold, Francis X., and Glenn D. Rudebusch. 1991. "Forecasting Output with the Composite Leading Index: A Real-Time Analysis." *Journal of the American Statistical Association* 86 (September): 603–610.

Dueker, Michael J. 1997. "Strengthening the Case for the Yield Curve as a Predictor of U.S. Recessions." *Federal Reserve Bank of St. Louis Review* 79, no. 2 (March/April): 41–51.

Duesenberry, James S. 1958. *Business Cycles and Economic Growth*. New York: McGraw-Hill.

Estrella, Arturo, and Frederic S. Mishkin. 1996. "The Yield Curve as a Predictor of U.S. Recessions." *Federal Reserve Bank of New York Current Issues in Economics and Finance* 2, no. 7 (June).

Gordon, Robert J., ed. 1986. *The American Business Cycle: Continuity and Change*. Chicago: University of Chicago Press.

Haubrich, Joseph G., and Ann M. Dombrosky. 1996. "Predicting Real Growth Using the Yield Curve." *Federal Reserve Bank of Cleveland Economic Review* 32, no. 1 (1st Quarter): 26–35.

Kozicki, Sharon. 1997. "Predicting Real Growth and Inflation with the Yield Spread." Federal Reserve Bank of Kansas City Economic Review (4th Quarter): 39–57.

Lee, Dara, and Ataman Ozyildirim. 2005. "Forthcoming Revisions to the Index of Leading Economic Indicators." Conference Board. www.conference-board.org/economics/bci/methodology.cfm.

Mankiw, N. Gregory. 1998. *Principles of Economics*. Fort Worth, TX: Dryden Press.

Mitchell, Wesley C. 1954. *Business Cycles: The Problem and Its Setting*. New York: National Bureau of Economic Research.

Moore, Geoffrey H. 1983. *Business Cycles: Inflation and Forecasting*, 2nd ed. Cambridge, MA: Ballinger Publishing.

———. 1990. *Leading Indicators for the 1990s*. Homewood, IL: Dow Jones-Irwin.

National Bureau of Economic Research. 1951. *Conference on Business Cycles*. New York: National Bureau of Economic Research.

———. 2003. "U.S. Business Cycle Expansions and Contractions." www.nber.org/cycles.html.

Sherman, Howard J. 1991. *The Business Cycle: Growth and Crisis under Capitalism*. Princeton, NJ: Princeton University Press.

Stock, James H., and Mark W. Watson. 1993. *Business Cycles: Indicators, and Forecasting*. Chicago: University of Chicago Press.

Zarnowitz, Victor. 1992. *Business Cycles: Theory, History, Indicators, and Forecasting*. Chicago: University of Chicago Press.

CHAPTER 5

Global Capital Markets

History and Valuation

I t is critical for investment advisors and consultants to know and understand the
history of global financial markets. This chapter looks back in time to review the
history of stocks, bonds, interest rates, and inflation. The readings explore U.S. stock
and bond markets as well as developed and emerging markets around the world.

The author introduces formulas and calculations as they pertain to measuring
risk and return, but the emphasis in these readings is on reviewing and interpreting
the history of the major fixed income and equities markets around the world over
the past century.

The first reading looks back at historical asset prices for stocks and bonds both in
the United States as well as in developed and emerging markets. The author explores
long-term annual average returns of stock and bonds and looks at those returns in
relation to risk and volatility. He also reviews the history of the equity premium and
real returns net of inflation over various periods of time.

The concept of valuation is also explored as the author considers various
arguments for traditional valuation measurements as well as alternative
approaches. The discussion over equity valuation includes evidence supporting key
drivers of valuation over time. This section also reviews historical inflation and
bond yields.

Part I *Portfolio Design: A Modern Approach to Asset Allocation:*
Long-Run Returns on Stocks and Bonds

Learning Objectives

- Discuss the history of stock and (Treasury) bond returns, standard deviations, and Sharpe ratios.
- Explain "risk premium" and discuss its history and variability over time.
- Describe and calculate real returns adjusting for inflation.
- Compare historical inflation rates and bond yields over time.
- Explain price-earnings ratios as a measure of value and discuss the history of stock market PE ratios over time.
- List and discuss alternative estimates of long-term stock market returns.
- Discuss potential upper and lower bounds for equity returns.

This reading reviews the various risks inherent in investing in global markets, from developed to emerging markets, and looks at each over different time periods. The author considers the benefits of international diversification, which have come under fire recently as correlations rose during the past financial crises. He then takes a look at stock prices in developed countries throughout time and argues that while valuation levels fluctuate, and sometimes significantly, the drivers of those asset prices are consistent despite the volatility.

This reading also looks at market returns on a risk-adjusted basis and reviews the history of price and return correlations between various markets. He then looks at the evolution of the development of various markets and current and past capitalization in the global equity marketplace. This reading also explores historical returns, valuation, and profitability of major international markets. Specific market and regional indexes will also be deconstructed.

Currency risk and opportunity are discussed, and the author considers strategies for hedging currency risk and capitalizing on currency opportunities within a portfolio.

Part II *Portfolio Design: A Modern Approach to Asset Allocation:* Foreign Stocks

Learning Objectives
- Describe the landscape of non–U.S. stock markets and their histories.
- Describe global equity market composition by investment capitalization.
- Discuss non–U.S. stock market returns, standard deviations, and Sharpe ratios.
- Explain and calculate currency capital gains and foreign stock returns.
- Describe strategies to manage currency risk in equity investments.
- Explain the diversification benefits of foreign stock investing.
- Discuss the methods and structures for owning foreign stocks including American Depository Receipts (ADRs).

This reading reviews common definitions and descriptions of "emerging markets" and discusses the rather short documented history of these financial markets. The author reviews historical returns and risk-adjusted metrics used to measure the performance of these investments and markets. He also explains additional risks taken when investing in these markets and reviews various ways to invest in less developed markets in terms of structures and strategies. The author then dissects the construction of common emerging markets indexes.

Part III *Portfolio Design: A Modern Approach to Asset Allocation:* Emerging Markets

Learning Objectives
- Define and describe the evolution of the term *emerging markets*.
- Compare emerging markets to the rest of the world in terms of Gross National Income (GNI).

- Explain the potential for growth in emerging markets relative to the rest of the world.
- Describe stock market capitalization of the emerging markets.
- Discuss the differences between actual market capitalization of emerging markets and their weightings in the MSCI emerging markets index.
- Describe the history of returns, standard deviations, and Sharpe ratios of emerging markets.
- List and describe the risks of investing in emerging markets.
- Discuss the history of stock market correlations between emerging markets and developed markets.
- Describe the history and returns of emerging market bonds.
- List and explain the unique opportunities and risks of investing in emerging market bonds.

This reading defines various types of fixed income investments and structures but also focuses on historical risk, returns, and variability based on changes in interest rates. One will witness how bond prices have moved over time, in both cyclical and secular markets, and in response to various economic and financial stimuli and political events. The author also explores real returns when accounting for inflation.

The reading begins by considering securities issued by the U.S. Treasury Department and expands into broader fixed income investments such as municipal bonds, corporate bonds, asset and mortgage backed bonds, high yield (junk) bonds and others. The author then explores fixed income investments outside of the United States, the risks involved, historical returns, and structures and products that offer access to these markets.

Part IV *Portfolio Design: A Modern Approach to Asset Allocation:* Bonds

Learning Objectives

- Describe U.S. Treasury bonds and discuss the relationship between inflation and bond yields over time.
- Describe the coupon yield, capital gain, total return, standard deviation, and Sharpe ratio of Treasury bonds by maturity over time.
- Describe the U.S. bond market in terms of investment representation among bond categories.
- Discuss the importance and implications of bond yield spreads.
- Compare various bond returns, standard deviations, and Sharpe ratios over time.
- Describe correlations between various bond categories over time.
- Describe world bond markets in terms of investment representation.
- Describe returns, standard deviations, and Sharpe ratios of various bonds in developed countries.
- Discuss correlations of bond markets in developed and developing countries over time.
- List and discuss the opportunities and risks of investing in various bond markets around the world.

Part I Long-Run Returns on Stocks and Bonds

Investors have a variety of assets in which they can invest, from private equity to mortgages to real estate. Yet it's best to begin a study of investments by focusing on the simplest of assets, stocks and bonds. The history of stock and bond returns extends much further back than any other assets. And the quality of the return data for stocks and bonds, at least government bonds, far exceeds the quality of return data for many alternative assets.

Most studies of U.S. markets rely on the well-known SBBI data set (© Morningstar) originally developed by Ibbotson Associates. The data set begins in 1926 when the University of Chicago's CRSP data set, on which it is based, also begins. The SBBI data set consists of six assets, large company and small company U.S. stocks, long-term and medium-term U.S. government bonds, U.S. corporate bonds, and U.S. Treasury bills. An inflation series based on the consumer price index is also reported. SBBI publishes an annual yearbook, Ibbotson SBBI, *Classic Yearbook— Market Results for Stocks, Bonds, Bills, and Inflation*, that contains valuable analyses of these six markets.

This chapter will use the SBBI data set, but will focus on the post-war period beginning in 1951 rather than the entire period extending back to 1926. Choosing an historical period over which to study returns involves a trade-off between two factors. On the one hand, the longer the data set, the more robust are any statistical inferences drawn from the data. On the other hand, the longer the data set, the more likely it is that structural changes will occur in the economy and in the investment markets. The early years of the SBBI data set from 1926 to 1950 includes a depression and a world war, two events that are unlikely to occur in the future.[1] Beginning in 1951 avoids the period after World War II when the U.S. Treasury followed a policy of pegging long-term interest rates. With the Treasury-Fed Accord of March 1951, interest rates could once again reflect market forces.

The period beginning in 1951 does include a variety of economic conditions. There are nine recessions during this period, so investment behavior over the business cycle can be studied in detail.[2] There is also a period of high inflation, in the 1970s, as well as two periods of relatively low inflation, in the 1950s and in the current decade. There are periods of rising interest rates and falling interest rates, so bond returns have fluctuated widely. And there are bull markets and bear markets for stocks.

Some observers might prefer to look at a much shorter sample period to make sure that any observations of past returns are relevant for today's markets. So, according to this reasoning, the past decade or past two decades might seem a better period to study. As will be shown below, the period since the early 1980s has been a very unusual one for both stocks and bonds. One of the biggest pitfalls for investors is to rely on this period to project future returns. Stocks and bonds do not always earn double-digit returns as they did in the 1980s and 1990s.

Stocks and Bonds since 1951

To study stock and bond returns, we will begin by focusing on two series, large company stocks and Treasury bonds. The large-cap series is from SBBI prior to 1974 and from Standard & Poor's from 1974 to present. Both series measure returns on

TABLE 5.1 Returns on Stocks and Bonds, 1951–2009

Asset	Geometric Average	Arithmetic Average	Standard Deviation	Sharpe Ratio
S&P 500	10.7%	11.3%	14.6%	0.45
Treasury bond	6.0%	6.3%	9.5%	0.17
Treasury bill	4.8%	4.7%	0.8%	

Prior to 1974, the SBBI Large Company Index (© Morningstar) is substituted for the S&P 500. The Treasury bond is the Long-Term Government Bond Index. It has an average maturity of 20 years. The Treasury bill is a one-month bill. Both are from 2010 SBBI Classic Yearbook.
Data Sources: © Morningstar and S&P.

the S&P Composite Index. The S&P Composite Index consists of 500 stocks from 1957 to present and a 90-stock S&P series prior to 1957. The Treasury bond is a 20-year Treasury bond also from SBBI.

Table 5.1 reports the average returns for these two assets. Also included is the one-month Treasury bill, the closest we can come to the risk-free rate of modern portfolio theory. Two averages are reported. The geometric (or compound) average return is the best estimate of the average return earned over this entire period. The arithmetic average is the best (i.e., least unbiased) estimate of next year's return. Also included in the table is the standard deviation. The averages and standard deviations are both expressed in annualized terms.

There are several notable features of these returns that should be emphasized. First, consider the Treasury bill and bond returns. There is a relatively small gap between the returns on these two series. As a reward for investing in a 20-year bond rather than a one-month Treasury bill, the investor earns an extra 1.2 percent. The 20-year bond has a large standard deviation of 9.5 percent. A one standard deviation band around the average return includes negative returns. Indeed, in 1999, there was a return of −9.0 percent on this series. And in 1994, following the Federal Reserve's dramatic reversal of interest rate policy, the return on this series was –7.8 percent.[3]

The return on the S&P 500 is 4.7 percent higher than the return on long-term Treasury bonds, and it is 5.9 percent higher than the risk-free return. The excess return of stocks over the risk-free return has been given a specific name, the *equity premium*. Using geometric averages, the equity premium is defined as

$$\text{Equity premium} = (1 + r_{SP})/(1 + r_F) - 1$$
$$= (1 + 0.107)/(1 + 0.048) - 1 = 5.6\%$$

where r_{SP} is the return on the S&P 500 and r_F is the risk-free Treasury bill return.[4] Sometimes the equity premium is defined by using the long-term bond rather than the risk-free return in which case the premium would be 4.4 percent rather than 5.6 percent. If the entire period from 1926 to present is studied, a period that includes the depression of the 1930s, the equity premium (defined relative to the risk-free return) is 5.9 percent. However it is defined, the equity premium is remarkably large.

This premium has provided equity investors with a rich reward for bearing the extra risk of owning equities. In a landmark study more than two decades ago, Mehra and Prescott (1985) showed that the equity premium is inconsistent with reasonable levels of risk aversion. They called the premium a puzzle. Since then, scores of finance researchers have set out to develop theoretical models of investor behavior that could explain the size of the premium.[5] Researchers have also studied the equity premium in other countries. A book by Dimson, Marsh, and Staunton (2002) estimates the equity premium for 16 industrial countries from 1900 to 2000 as ranging from 1.8 percent for Denmark to 7.4 percent for France, with an average equity premium of 4.9 percent. Wise investors don't spend too much time agonizing over the source of the premium. They simply take advantage of it by focusing on equities in their portfolios.

How Much More Attractive Are Stocks Than Bonds?

Many investors, though, see the equity premium as a necessary price for the extra risk of investing in stocks. After all, the standard deviation of the S&P 500 series is 14.6 percent in Table 5.1. But that explanation needs to be examined more closely because, as reported in Table 5.1, the standard deviation of the bond return is also quite high at 9.5 percent. To compare stocks and bonds, it's useful to ask the following question: If an investor were to choose between these two assets, which would be more attractive in risk-adjusted terms?[6]

To assess the return on stocks versus the return on bonds, the first step is to adjust each return for risk. The Sharpe ratio adjusts each return by first subtracting the risk-free rate, r_F, then dividing by the standard deviation. If r_j is the return on asset j and σ_j is its standard deviation, then the Sharpe ratio for asset j is

$$[r_j - r_F]/\sigma_j$$

To calculate the Sharpe ratio, we use the arithmetic returns and standard deviations in Table 5.1. It's possible to define a Sharpe ratio using geometric returns, but only if the standard deviation is defined over a similar long horizon.[7] Using the returns in Table 5.1, the Sharpe ratios are defined by

$$Stocks: [0.113 - 0.047]/0.146 = 0.45$$
$$Bonds: [0.063 - 0.047]/0.095 = 0.17$$

The Sharpe ratio for stocks is more than twice the size of the ratio for bonds. So, after adjusting for the higher risk of stocks, the (excess) return on stocks is much larger than bonds.

One way to view the relative returns on equity and bonds is to conduct an experiment. If an investor were to choose a portfolio consisting of the S&P 500 and the risk-free return with the same standard deviation as that of bonds, how much of an excess return would be earned on bonds? Figure 5.1 calculates the excess return on bonds as *negative* 2.7 percent. That is, the gap in Sharpe ratios shown above can be translated into an excess return of −2.7 percent at the level of risk of the bond. Viewed from this perspective, bonds are not very attractive.

How much difference does it make if we invest in medium-term bonds or if we study a longer period of time? If the medium-term bond is used instead of the long-term bond, the Sharpe ratio is 0.29 for the period since 1951, still much less than the Sharpe ratio for stocks. If stocks and bonds are compared over the entire period since 1926, the Sharpe ratio for stocks is 0.40, while that of long-term bonds

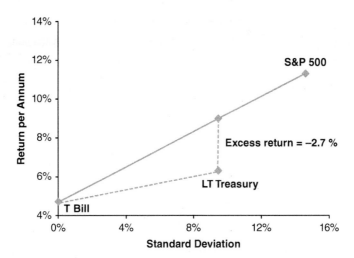

FIGURE 5.1   Comparing Stocks and Bonds, 1951–2009

is 0.22 and medium-term bonds is 0.32. So in both cases, the *risk-adjusted* return on stocks is substantially higher than that of bonds. Of course, no investor must choose between stocks and bonds. Later chapters will consider portfolios of stocks and bonds that will be more attractive than holdings of either asset alone.

Real Returns

Until this point, average returns have been measured without taking into account inflation. For a long-run investor, however, inflation can substantially reduce the real gain on a portfolio. Even modest inflation does a lot of damage. If inflation averages 2.5 percent per year, the cost of living rises by 28 percent in 10 years and by almost 64 percent in 20 years. Over time, moreover, inflation varies a great deal, so comparing nominal returns over different periods can be very misleading. In the 1970s, nominal stock returns (8.4 percent) were as high as in the 1960s (8.2 percent), but real returns were much lower in the 1970s (0.4 percent in the 1970s versus 5.1 percent in the 1960s).

To obtain real, or inflation-adjusted, returns, it's important to use a compound formula. If π is the inflation rate, then the real return on asset j can be written as

$$Real\ return = (1 + r_j)/(1 + \pi) - 1$$

Over the period from 1951 to 2009, the inflation rate has averaged 3.78 percent. So the real return on stocks and bonds is calculated as follows (using the geometric averages from Table 5.1).[8]

$$Real\ return\ on\ stocks = (1 + 0.1072)/(1 + 0.0378) - 1 = 0.067$$
$$Real\ return\ on\ bonds = (1 + 0.0602)/(1 + 0.0378) - 1 = 0.022$$

Inflation reduces bond returns proportionally much more than stock returns. A 2.2 percent real return on bonds seems small when earned by an asset with a 9.5 percent standard deviation.

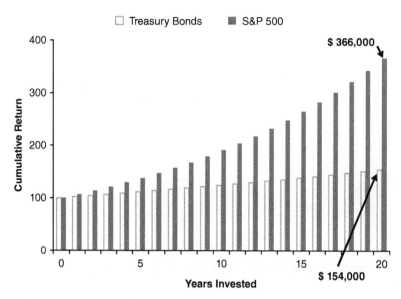

FIGURE 5.2 $100,000 Invested for 20 Years in Bonds versus Stocks (in 2009 Dollars)

The equity premium is seen in a new light once real returns are analyzed. Consider the following alternative investment strategies followed by a younger investor saving for retirement. If we assume that the investor has access to tax-deferred saving, the returns on the portfolio can be determined by simply calculating the accumulation of wealth based on real returns. The results are shown in Figure 5.2.

An investor who allocates all of a portfolio to bonds earns a real return of 2.2 percent over time. Over a 20-year period, for example, $100,000 turns into $154,000. It's important to note that this calculation has already taken inflation into account, so the investor can buy just as much with a dollar 20 years later. But a 54 percent cumulative return is not going to do much for retirement.

Contrast the bond return with the stock return. The same $100,000 invested at the 6.7 percent compound real return on stocks earned since 1951 increases to $366,000, or a 266 percent compound return. The equity premium may provide the extra return for a more comfortable retirement. Figure 5.2 shows the accumulation of (tax-deferred) wealth under the two alternative strategies.

Real returns are not just important to wealth accumulation. They are also vitally important to *spending*. Investors during their retirement years must base their spending plans on real returns, not nominal returns. So also must foundations, at least those that are unable to accumulate new funds to replace current spending.

Reconsidering Bond Returns

But what real returns can we expect in the future? As stated above, real compound returns on bonds since 1951 have averaged 2.2 percent. But many investors recall much higher returns over the past few decades. Huge capital gains enabled bond investors to earn equity-like returns. In fact, during the 1980s, bonds and stocks earned almost identical real returns of about 9 percent.

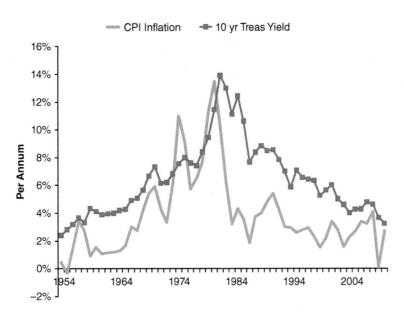

FIGURE 5.3   Inflation and Bond Yields, 1954–2009

Bonds had splendid returns in the 1980s and early 1990s for a very simple reason. Inflation and bond returns fell over this period. Soon after Paul Volcker was first named to lead the Federal Reserve in 1979, the inflation rate started to recede from historic highs. That's because Volcker and the Fed instituted a tough monetary regime aimed at sharply lowering the double-digit inflation that the country was experiencing.

Figure 5.3 shows the inflation rate and 10-year Treasury bond yield over the period since the early 1950s. After Volcker succeeded in driving inflation to low single digits, the bond yield stayed stubbornly high for a time. But eventually the bond market adjusted as inflationary expectations fell. As a result, bond returns soared. Investors in this market benefited whether they bought and held high coupon–paying bonds or sold out their bond positions after registering large capital gains.

Some investors are waiting patiently for high bond returns to resume. But the driving force for these record real returns was the reversal of the same inflation that had undermined the bond market in the late 1960s and 1970s. For the decade of the 1970s as a whole, in fact, the real average return on 20-year bonds was –3.8 percent! This was at a time when the stock market was at least breaking even in real terms. With bond yields in the 4 percent to 5 percent range (and recently even lower), we are clearly in a very different market setting than in the early 1980s. In this setting, bond returns may not be far different than they have been in the longer run.

Consider Table 5.2, which reports bond returns over five periods extending back to 1926. All of these returns have been adjusted for inflation, so they can be compared directly with one another. The period from 1981 to 2000 saw unusually high real returns on both medium-term and long-term bonds. An inflation-adjusted return of 8.1 percent per annum on a fixed income asset must be regarded as unusual!

TABLE 5.2   Real Returns on Medium-Term and Long-Term Treasury
Bonds and Large-Cap Stock Index

Period	Medium-Term Treasury Bond	Long-Term Treasury Bond	S&P 500 Stock Index
1981–2000	6.2%	8.1%	11.7%
1951–1980	−0.2%	−2.0%	6.4%
1951–2009	2.4%	2.2%	6.7%
1926–1950	1.9%	2.7%	6.3%
1926–2009	2.3%	2.3%	6.6%

The real returns are compound averages based on the CPI inflation rate. The
medium-term bond is a five-year Treasury bond and the long-term bond is
a 20-year Treasury bond. The stock index is described in the text.
Data Sources: © Morningstar and S&P.

Investors in the 1980s and 1990s were blessed with high bond returns as well as stock
returns. The longer period starting in 1951 witnessed much lower returns on bonds.[9]
That's because long-term bonds suffered such large losses in the high inflation period
of the 1970s. As Table 5.2 indicates, these losses lowered overall returns to −2.0
percent for the 30-year period ending in 1980.

Extending the bond series back to 1926 gives us returns that are very similar
to those over the whole period from 1951 to present, 2.3 percent returns for the
five-year medium-term bond and 2.3 percent for the 20-year long-term bond. The
table also reports real returns over the period prior to 1951, which are also much
lower than in the period from 1981 to 2000.

A reasonable way to interpret this historical record is that, in the long run, bonds
earn real returns in the neighborhood of 2 percent to 2.5 percent. Recall that bond
returns consist of a coupon plus a capital gain. In periods of rising inflation, there will
be sustained capital losses on bonds as yields rise to reflect inflation. This is what
we experienced in the 1970s. In periods of falling inflation, such as in the 1980s
and 1990s, there will be sustained capital gains on bonds as yields fall. But unless
inflation has a long-run trend to it, the capital gain element of the bond return should
be close to zero in the long run. Indeed, since 1951, the capital gain component of
the long-run bond return has been slightly negative at −0.4 percent.

On the basis of this historical record, how might we form expectations of future
bond returns? Forecasts of bond returns in the short run are best left to Wall Street
experts. They have about a 50 percent chance of being right in forecasting whether
interest rates will rise or fall. Forecasts for the longer run ought to be informed by
this long historical record. If real bond returns since 1926 have averaged around
2 percent to 2.5 percent, this seems like a prudent forecast for the future. The past
25 years were a great period to be an investor in bonds. But remember that these
returns simply reversed the disastrous losses of the preceding decades.

Reconsidering Stock Returns

The collapse of equity prices beginning in 2000 has led many investors to revise
their estimates of long-run equity returns. In place of the optimistic estimates of

high double-digit returns so characteristic of the late 1990s, some investors now envisage returns on equity equal to or even below those on fixed income.[10] If equity returns are this low in the future, there will have to be major revisions of long-run investment plans. Endowments and foundations will have to adopt significantly lower spending rules, and corporate pension funds will face increased funding costs. Individual investors will have to scale back their retirement plans.

As in the case of bond returns, it's instructive to look at historical returns, especially in periods prior to the bull market of the 1980s and 1990s. Table 5.2 reports average real compound returns over several past periods. The two-decade period from 1981 to 2000 saw unusually high real compound returns of 11.7 percent. No wonder that by the late 1990s, the expectations of investors had become so inflated.

Table 5.2 reports two sets of returns prior to the bull market. The first set of returns begins in 1951, like many estimates in this chapter, and ends in 1980. The second set of estimates begins in 1926 and ends in 1950. The two sets of estimates are remarkably similar, at least as far as the real returns are concerned. Without the bull market of the post-1980 period, the real return on stocks is 6.3 percent or 6.4 percent. An investor making plans in 1981 using historical averages to date would have assumed a much lower equity return than 20 years later.

The five years ending in 1999 saw the most incredible returns of the two decades. The real return on the S&P 500 index for these five years averaged 25.6 percent per year! These five years, moreover, had a dramatic effect on longer-term average returns even when returns are measured over a 50-year period. The average real return on the S&P 500 from 1951 to 1994 was only 7.2 percent. By the end of 1999, the average real return beginning in 1951 had risen to 8.9 percent. Figure 5.4 provides a graph of average real returns measured from 1951 to each year indicated on the graph starting with 1975. An investor measuring the real return on equity from 1951

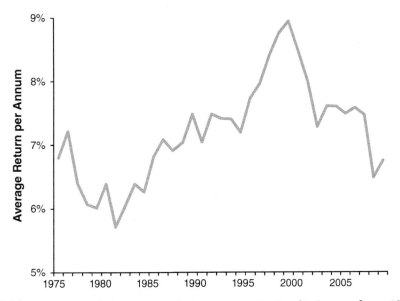

FIGURE 5.4   Estimates of Average Real Returns to Equity (Estimates from 1951 to Dates Shown)

to 1975 would have obtained a 6.8 percent average, but an investor measuring the return from 1951 to 1999 would have found an average 2.1 percent higher. The dramatic effects of 1995–1999 are evident in this figure.

Too many investors were misled by this bull market into believing that stock returns are always high. The most inflated expectations of future equity returns were adopted by investors who made the mistake of basing their estimates on the 1980s and 1990s only. But even investors who had the good judgment to look at longer spans of history ended up with inflated expectations because of the way that returns in the late 1990s temporarily inflated long-run averages. As Figure 5.4 shows, expectations based on data from 1951 to 1999 were inevitably inflated beyond what would have been reasonable just a few years earlier. The period since then has been one of retrenchment, culminating in the sharp downturn in stock prices during the financial crisis of 2007 and 2008. Figure 5.4 shows how even long-run averages vary widely depending on whether we have just experienced a dot-com boom or a financial crisis bust.

One reason why we might believe that average returns were being distorted by the 1980s and 1990s is that price-earnings (P-E) ratios rose so much over this period. Figure 5.5 shows the variation in P-E ratios for the S&P 500 index since 1951 as measured using the same methodology as Robert Shiller in his book, *Irrational Exuberance* (2000).[11] Shiller compares the S&P 500 index for a given year with the average reported earnings of the S&P companies over the previous 10 years. Both series are expressed in real terms using the CPI. The rise in P-Es during the 1990s, in particular, introduced an upward trend into the average real return on equity. Since P-Es remained relatively high (at least prior to the financial crisis), average historical returns that include the recent period may overestimate future returns. For that reason, several recent studies have adopted alternative approaches to estimating equity returns that rely on corporate fundamentals instead of market returns.

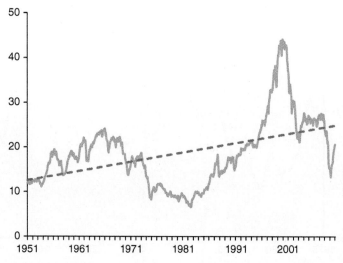

FIGURE 5.5   Price-Earnings Ratios for S&P 500, 1951–2009 (Current Real Price Relative to 10-Year Average Real Earnings)

Alternative Estimates of Long-Run Stock Returns

Returns on equity are based on two components, the dividend yield and the capital gain on the stock price. Rising valuations might inflate the capital gain component, so average historical returns on stocks may give an inflated estimate of future returns. For that reason, some experts have proposed basing estimates of stock returns on corporate earnings or dividends rather than market returns.

Fama and French's (2002) study of the equity premium provides alternative estimates of stock returns based on these corporate fundamentals. According to Fama and French, the average return on equity can be estimated in three alternative ways. The first measure simply calculates stock returns as we have already done using average dividend yields plus the average capital gains on the S&P 500 index. The second and third measures replace the capital gain on stocks with either the rate of growth of dividends or the rate of growth of earnings of the same firms in the S&P 500 index. The idea behind these measures is that capital gains cannot indefinitely outpace corporate fundamentals, so let's base long-run estimates of stock returns on corporate fundamentals themselves.

Investors in equities are ultimately interested in receiving a stream of dividends on their ownership shares. So it would seem that a measure of equity returns based on the growth of dividends should be preferred to a measure based on earnings. But as Figure 5.6 demonstrates, there has been a long-term decline in dividend yields in the United States, particularly in the past 20 years.[12] As a result, the growth rate of dividends is much lower than that of earnings. The decline in dividend yields may be due to tax policy, which favors retained over distributed earnings, but it may also be due to the belief by corporations that internal investment will give stockholders higher returns than their dividends can earn.[13] A measure that is free of variations

FIGURE 5.6   Dividend Yield for S&P 500, 1951–2009

TABLE 5.3   Average Real Returns on the S&P 500, Arithmetic Averages, 1951–2007

Averages Based on	Real Arithmetic Averages
Actual capital gain	8.6%
Dividend growth	5.0%
Earnings growth	6.9%

Note: Average returns are obtained by adding the average real dividend yield to the real capital gain as measured by the actual rise in stock prices, by the rate of growth of dividends, or the rate of growth of earnings of the S&P 500 firms.
Data Sources: The dividend and earnings data are from www.econ .yale.edu/~Shiller and the stock price data from Bloomberg.

in corporate dividend policy is one based on earnings growth rather than dividend growth. This third measure replaces the capital gain on the S&P index with the rate of growth of earnings for the firms in that same index.

Table 5.3 reports alternative estimates of average real returns for the S&P 500 based on the three methods for estimating the equity capital gain. Each estimate is obtained by adding to the real dividend yield some measure of the real capital gain on equity. The alternative estimates use actual capital gains, the growth of dividends replacing capital gains, and the growth of earnings replacing capital gains. All three measures are expressed in real terms using the consumer price index. Arithmetic averages rather than geometric averages are reported since the Fama-French methodology calculates arithmetic averages. The sample period used in Table 5.3 ends in 2007 rather than 2009 because reported earnings fluctuated so wildly during 2008 and 2009.[14]

Substituting dividend growth or earnings growth for the capital gain on stocks makes a huge difference. The substitution of dividend growth for the actual capital gains on stocks lowers the real arithmetic average return from 8.6 percent to 5.0 percent. Using earnings growth instead lowers the return to 6.9 percent. These alternative measures of average equity returns avoid reliance on the higher market valuations of the past two decades. But if they more accurately reflect future returns in the equity market, investors' expectations will have a large adjustment ahead.

Upper and Lower Bounds for Equity Returns

Investors making decisions about saving rates for retirement need to form estimates of future equity and bond returns. Investors already beginning retirement need to form such estimates in order to set spending rates in retirement. With such a wide variation between estimated returns, how are investors going to make informed decisions about future returns on their portfolio? Perhaps it is most sensible to use the estimates of real returns discussed above to set upper and lower bounds for expected equity returns.

Investment plans should be based on compound real returns, not arithmetic averages. That's because these plans are designed to last for decades or more. So

TABLE 5.4   Alternative Estimates of Long-Run Real and Nominal Stock Returns (Based on 2.5 percent Inflation Rate), 1951–2007

Averages Based on	Real Compound Averages	Nominal Compound Averages (Based on 2.5% Inflation)
Estimate based on actual capital gain	7.3%	10.0%
Alternative estimate based on earnings growth	5.3%	7.9%

The real compound averages are obtained from the real arithmetic averages in Table 5.3 by using the same methodology as in the Fama-French study (see text).
Data Sources: The dividend and earnings data are from www.econ.yale.edu/~Shiller and the stock price data from Bloomberg.

the averages reported in Table 5.3 must be converted into compound long-term equivalents. Fama and French develop what they call long-term estimates of real stock returns derived from arithmetic averages. Table 5.4 reports long-term estimates using the same methodology for the period from 1951 to 2007. Two estimates are provided, one based on actual capital gains and the other based on earnings growth.

Actual capital gains on stocks provide an upper bound for our estimates of future expected equity returns. In Table 5.4, that estimate is 7.3 percent. Figure 5.4 shows that a similar average real return would have been calculated if the sample period ended in the later 1980s or early 1990s. If it had ended in 2000, the real return estimate would have been quite a bit higher, but that would have reflected the high market valuations of the late 1990s.

The lower bound for an estimate of future returns could be based on the rate of growth of dividends or earnings rather than actual capital gains. Because dividend yields have fallen so much in the past two decades, it's probably better to focus on the earnings-based measures of stock returns. In that case, the real return would be estimated as in Table 5.4 at 5.3 percent using reported earnings. The lower bound would be preferred by investors who are wary of current market valuations.

How much difference does this alternative estimate of equity returns make? Consider a spending rule for a 50/50 portfolio split between stocks and bonds.[15] If stock returns are lowered by 2 percent as in Table 5.4, spending must be lowered by about 1 percent. This is a substantial reduction in spending whether the investor is a foundation (with an unlimited horizon) or a retiree (whose goal is to have the portfolio last through retirement).

To translate estimates into the nominal averages that most investors focus on, we must adopt an explicit forecast for inflation. Table 5.4 calculates the implied nominal stock returns based on a forecast of 2.5 percent for inflation. The estimates of nominal compound returns range from 7.9 percent to 10.0 percent. Some observers might regard even the lower bound as overly optimistic. With the lower bound estimates being based on corporate fundamentals, such observers have to explain why U.S. corporations should be expected to perform significantly worse than they have for the past 50-plus years.

In any case, if investors lower their expectations to these levels from the lofty returns of the 1980s and 1990s, they will have better prospects for reaching their long-run investment goals.

Alternative Estimates of Stock Returns

To understand alternative approaches to estimating equity returns, we need to begin with the basic components of a stock return. The stock return in any given year is equal to the dividend yield plus the capital gain:

$$R_t = D_t/P_{t-1} + (P_t - P_{t-1})/P_{t-1}$$

where P_t is the stock price at the end of year t and D_t is the dividend paid in year t. Estimates of future expected returns based on past historical data implicitly assume that capital gains in the past will repeat themselves. If past capital gains have been inflated as P-Es have risen, however, then past data may not be a good basis for future expectations. For that reason, some experts reject the use of past returns to predict future returns, and turn instead to more fundamental measures of corporate performance.

According to Fama and French 2002, the average return on equity can be estimated in three alternative ways. The first method simply measures the arithmetic average return over the sample period.

$$A(R_t) = A(D_t/P_{t-1}) + A(GP_t) \tag{5.1}$$

where $GP_t = (P_t - P_{t-1})/P_{t-1}$, the capital gain on the stock. If there is a rise in P-Es during the sample period, then the average capital gain will reflect this rise in P-Es, thereby inflating the estimate of future equity returns.

According to finance theory, the value of a stock should be based on expected future dividends. So an alternative measure of stock returns replaces the average capital gain by the average growth rate of dividends:

$$A(RD_t) = A(D_t/P_{t-1}) + A(GD_t) \tag{5.2}$$

where GD_t is the growth rate of dividends. Fama and French call this the *dividend growth* model of returns.

Finally, the third approach replaces the growth rate of dividends with the growth rate of earnings, GY_t:

$$A(RY_t) = A(D_t/P_{t-1}) + A(GY_t) \tag{5.3}$$

Fama and French call this model the *earnings growth* model.

In their study, Fama and French provided estimates of equity returns extending back into the nineteenth century. They report estimates of real equity returns for three periods, 1872 to 1950, 1951 to 2000, and 1872 to 2000. Their thesis is that the real return on equities over the past five decades is abnormally high not only when measured against either dividend or earnings growth (as discussed above), but also when compared with real returns in the earlier period, 1872–1950. The estimate of the real equity return using actual gains (Equation 5.1) is only 6.4 percent for the 1872 to 1950 period, in contrast to their estimate of 7.9 percent for the 1951 to 2000 period.[16] On the other hand, the estimates of real equity returns based on real dividend growth (Equation 5.2) are not much different in the earlier and later periods. Fama and French do not provide estimates of real equity returns based on earnings growth (as in Equation 5.3) prior to 1951 because of the dubious quality of the earnings data. Fama and French conclude that it is the average real return using Equation (5.1) measured over the past 50 years that is out of line.

Table 5.3 reports equity returns estimated for the 1951 to 2007 period using the Fama-French methodology. Arithmetic averages, expressed in real terms, are reported following the methodology in the Fama and French study. The equity returns reported in Table 5.3 are based on average annual returns for the S&P 500 generated as follows:

a. The data set consists of end-of-year price indexes (for the S&P 500) and annual totals (for dividends and earnings). The stock prices are from Bloomberg. The dividend and earnings series are provided by Robert Shiller on his website, www.econ.yale.edu/~shiller. Both series are updated using the Standard & Poor's website.

b. Real returns are calculated using the consumer price index from the IMF, International Financial Statistics

Equations 5.1 through 5.3 refer to arithmetic averages. Fama and French obtain long-term compound averages after adjusting for biases due to the higher volatility of earnings growth or stock price gains relative to dividend growth. Their procedure adjusts the arithmetic average of the RY_t series by subtracting 0.5 times the difference in the variances of the RY_t and RD_t series. They use a similar adjustment for the R_t series based on the actual capital gains on the stock index. When this procedure is applied to the arithmetic estimates of Table 5.3, we obtain the real compound averages reported in Table 5.4. These adjustments produce a long-term real return of 5.3 percent based on earnings growth compared with a long-term real return of 7.3 percent based on actual capital gains. The estimate of stock returns based on actual capital gains reported in Table 5.4 is about 1 percent lower than the estimate reported by Fama and French.[17] Their estimates ended in 2000 near the peak of the market. This underscores again the role of the stock market boom of the late 1990s in inflating long-term returns.

The estimates in Table 5.4 based on actual capital gains and earnings growth provide upper and lower bounds for stock market returns. With a gap of 2 percent, it makes a lot of difference whether long-run plans are based on the upper or lower estimates. In later chapters we will explore some of the implications of using these different estimates.

Notes

1. Unlikely is not the same as inconceivable. It doesn't make much sense to base future estimates of asset returns on a period that includes such unusual events. In any case, as will be shown below, the inclusion of years 1926 through 1950 does not change conclusions regarding long-term real returns or the equity premium.

2. Nine recessions is admittedly not a large statistical sample, but it is certainly a larger sample than can be found when we study emerging markets or alternative investments where data sets begin in the 1980s or later.

3. In February 1994, the Fed unexpectedly raised interest rates by 50 basis points. George Soros's hedge fund is said to have lost $600 million during this period, while Steinhardt Partners lost even more. (*New York Times*, March 4, 1994.)

4. When compound averages are involved, geometric differences between two asset classes are calculated using division rather than arithmetic subtraction. See the discussion in Chapter 4 of Ibbotson SBBI (2008).

5. A good survey of this research is provided by Kocherlakota (1996).

6. That is, the investor is choosing between these assets in an either-or framework. Later we will discuss how the investor would choose an optimal portfolio of stocks and bonds.

7. The arithmetic average is the least unbiased estimate of the return over a one-year horizon and the standard deviation is measured relative to the arithmetic average.

8. To avoid rounding errors, the returns are stated with more precision in this calculation.

9. Strangely enough, the real return on the medium-term series is actually higher than that of the long-term series. The arithmetic average for long-term bonds is higher than that of medium-term bonds.

10. Arnott and Bernstein (2002), for example, conclude that the equity premium over the risk-free rate is zero and that a sensible expectation for future real returns on stocks and bonds is 2 to 4 percent.

11. The stock price and earnings data are from www.econ.yale.edu/~shiller, which updates series reported in Shiller (2000).

12. The dividend data are also from www.econ.yale.edu/~shiller. The dividend yield is calculated by dividing the dividend for a given year by the S&P price on the last day of the preceding year. The S&P price is from Bloomberg.

13. The 2003 tax legislation lowering taxes on dividends significantly reduced these tax disadvantages.

14. Average reported earnings fluctuated from 66.2 in 2007 to 14.9 in 2007 and 51.0 in 2009. The real rate of growth of earnings was −77 percent in 2008 and +233 percent in 2009. Even though the estimates in Table 5.3 are based on almost 60 years of data, the arithmetic averages for the earnings measure fluctuate widely over the 2008 to 2009 period.

15. A 50/50 portfolio might be chosen by an investor early in retirement.

16. This is the compound real return based on Equation (5.1). The arithmetic average real return is 8.3 percent for 1872–1950.

17. Their estimate in Table IV of their paper is for the real equity premium, not the real equity return. But once the long-term equity premium is converted into a return, the estimate is about 8.3 percent for the real equity return based on actual capital gains.

References

Arnott, Robert D., and Peter L. Bernstein. 2002. "What risk premium is 'normal'?," *Financial Analyst Journal* (March–April).

Dimson, Elroy, Paul Marsh, and Mike Staunton. 2002. *Triumph of the optimists: 101 years of global investment returns.* Princeton: Princeton University Press.

Fama, Eugene F., and Kenneth R. French. 2002. "The equity premium." *The Journal of Finance* (April): 637–659.

Ibbotson® and SBBI®. 2008. Classic yearbook. © 2008 Morningstar.

Kocherlakota, Narayana R. 1996. "The equity premium: It's still a puzzle." *Journal of Economic Literature* (March): 42–47.

Mehra, Rajnish, and Edward C. Prescott. 1985. "The equity premium: A puzzle." *Journal of Monetary Economics* 15 (March): 145–161.

Shiller, Robert J. 2000. *Irrational exuberance.* Princeton: Princeton University Press.

Part II: Foreign Stocks

The world stock market had a capitalization of $35.0 trillion in 2008. Of that total, the U.S. stock market had a share of only 33.6 percent.[1] Another 39.9 percent consisted of stocks from the other industrial countries, with the remaining 26.5 percent being stocks of the so-called emerging markets. Many of the larger firms in these foreign markets are household names in the United States. In fact, many Americans may not even know that Nestlé, Unilever, and Philips are foreign firms. Yet American investors have only small proportions of foreign stocks in their portfolios. They often regard foreign stocks as too risky.

It's actually more complicated than that. International investing goes in and out of favor in the United States. In the 1980s and early 1990s, international stock returns were quite impressive, so U.S. investors flocked to international stock funds. Diversifying portfolios made sense to investors when returns were higher abroad. Then throughout the late 1990s, foreign stock returns lagged those in the high-flying U.S. markets. Arguments for international diversification fell on deaf ears when investors became caught up with the excitement of the fabulous returns on U.S. stocks in the late 1990s, particularly those in the technology industry. Why invest in London or Tokyo when Silicon Valley offers such superior returns? Then from 2002 to 2007, interest in foreign stocks picked up again. Why? A cynic would say that it was because foreign stock returns were surging ahead of U.S. stocks, propelled by the rebound of the Euro from its lows in early 2002.

There is a longer trend in international investing that is worth noting. International diversification has gone through three phases in the past 100 years or so. In the decades prior to the Depression of the 1930s and World War II, capital flowed freely around the world. London and Paris were the dominant financial centers for most of this period.[2] Bonds were issued in London and Paris to finance companies and projects around the world. For example, much of the financing for the building of the American railways originated in London. Other countries like South Africa, Australia, and Argentina benefited from ready access to European financial markets. Equity issues were less frequent than bond issues. But foreign investors had sizable stakes in many American companies.

The second phase began in the Great Depression of the 1930s when capital controls were imposed by most countries and when many previously issued foreign securities went into default. Private international investing almost ceased for three decades thereafter.[3] Many of the capital controls were left in place throughout the 1950s and 1960s, severely inhibiting international investing. During this period, financing was available primarily through loans from national governments and (in the postwar period) international agencies such as the World Bank. Even banks were wary of foreign lending.

The third phase began in the early 1970s when capital controls began to be lifted. It was in this period that the so-called Bretton Woods system of fixed exchange rates came to an end. In 1971, the Nixon Administration ended the dollar's tie to gold. Over the next few years, many industrial countries allowed their currencies to float vis-à-vis the dollar. With less need to defend their currencies, governments began to relax their capital controls. Some countries lagged behind in this process. Investors in Britain, for example, had to contend with controls until the late 1970s when the Thatcher government finally removed them. In the meantime, British residents were not allowed to take more than £50 out of the country! The French government had similar control limiting outflows by French residents.[4] By the late 1980s, however, there were virtually no limitations on foreign investing in any of the industrial countries.

The third phase of international investing saw the development of international stock indexes to track the performance of stocks around the world. In particular, beginning in 1970 the Morgan Stanley Capital International (MSCI) indexes provided a common methodology for measuring stocks in all of the industrial countries. Of course, it is possible to trace stock markets much earlier than 1970. Indeed, Dimson and colleagues (2002) report on the stock returns of many industrial countries for the century from 1900 to 2000. But the quality of national indexes varies widely during earlier periods. For example, how reliable do you think German stock indexes were during the hyperinflation of the 1920s or during the period of World War II? Hardly any emerging stock markets have data prior to the mid-1970s. Global emerging market stock market indexes begin in the mid to late 1980s.

This chapter will focus on the past four decades of stock market performance in the industrial countries using the MSCI indexes. The next part will address the emerging stock markets.

Returns on Foreign and U.S. Stocks

Figure 5.7 shows the stock market capitalization of the major regions of the world as reported in 2009 in the annual S&P *Global Stock Markets Factbook*.[5] As stated above, foreign industrial countries represent 39.9 percent of the world total, while emerging markets represent another 26.5 percent. Emerging markets are defined by S&P as countries with low per capita income.[6] The stocks of industrial countries other than the United States are often referred to as core foreign stocks.

The Morgan Stanley EAFE (Europe, Australasia, and the Far East) index is normally used to describe returns in these core countries even though this index excludes the Canadian market. The makeup of this index (as of 2009) is shown in Table 5.5. The European sub-index consisting of 16 countries has 64.4 percent of EAFE's market capitalization and the rest is in the five markets of the Pacific region. Japan's market is the largest in the index with a 25.1 percent weight. In the late 1980s, this market was even larger than that of the United States.

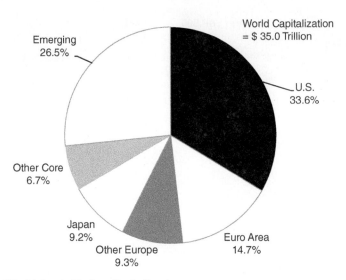

FIGURE 5.7   World Stock Market Capitalization

Figure 5.8 tracks the cumulative returns on the EAFE index compared with those of the S&P 500.[7] It's evident that after 40 years the two indexes have ended up very close to one another. EAFE's returns exceeded those of the United States throughout most of the 1970s and 1980s. The S&P 500 surged ahead in the 1990s with the huge boom in U.S. stocks. Then more recently EAFE has overtaken the lead. That it's a close horse race should not be surprising. After all, most industrial countries are at the same level of development. Individual countries may excel in one industry or

TABLE 5.5   Country Composition of MSCI EAFE Index

Europe Index	64.4%	Pacific Index	35.6%
Austria	0.6%	Australia	5.3%
Belgium	1.3%	Hong Kong	3.6%
Denmark	1.0%	Japan	25.1%
Finland	1.2%	New Zealand	0.2%
France	11.6%	Singapore	1.4%
Germany	8.6%		
Greece	0.7%		
Ireland	0.4%		
Italy	4.1%		
Netherlands	3.0%		
Norway	1.0%		
Portugal	0.5%		
Spain	7.4%		
Sweden	2.0%		
Switzerland	6.7%		
United Kingdom	14.4%		

Source for market capitalization: S&P *Global Stock Market Factbook,* 2009.

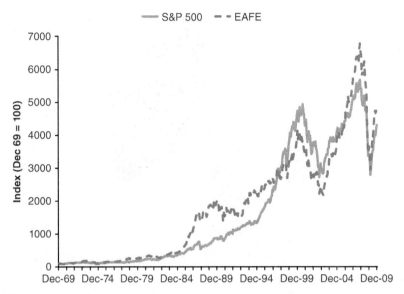

FIGURE 5.8   S&P 500 and EAFE Cumulative Returns, 1970–2009

another. The Japanese, for example, lead in autos and electronics, the Germans in machine tools, the French in luxury goods and nuclear technology, and the Americans in software and finance. But overall no country or region has a clear advantage in firm profitability and stock market performance.

Table 5.6 reports returns on the stocks of the industrial countries, measured in U.S. dollars, from 1970 (when the Morgan Stanley data set begins) to 2009. Three MSCI-developed country indexes are reported: the EAFE index, the European index (made up of the European component of the EAFE index), and the Pacific index (the Pacific component of that index). Two averages are presented, the compound (or geometric) average and the arithmetic average. All of the returns in this table are clustered near one another. The geometric return for the U.S. market is 0.1 percent above that of the Pacific market, but below those of the EAFE and European indexes. The arithmetic returns for the foreign markets are all somewhat higher than those of the United States. Table 5.6 also reports the Sharpe ratios for each index. The Sharpe ratios are also clustered around one another with ratios for the EAFE and S&P indexes exactly the same. So for the 40-year period as a whole, the returns on foreign and U.S. stock markets are remarkably similar.[8]

TABLE 5.6   World Stock Returns, 1970–2009

	Geometric Average	Arithmetic Average	Standard Deviation	Sharpe Ratio
S&P 500	9.9%	10.7%	15.6%	0.33
EAFE	10.2%	11.2%	17.2%	0.33
Europe	10.8%	11.9%	17.4%	0.36
Pacific	9.8%	11.5%	20.7%	0.29

Data Sources: © Morningstar, MSCI, and S&P.

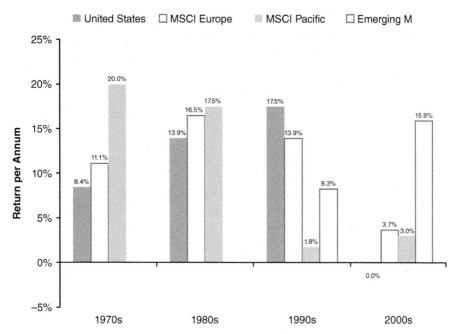

FIGURE 5.9   U.S. and Foreign Stock Returns by Decade, 1971–2009

Over shorter periods, however, there are wide variations in returns. It's instructive to look at returns by region from decade to decade. Figure 5.9 reports returns in dollars for four markets (with the emerging markets data beginning only in the 1990s). In the 1970s, 20 percent returns from the Pacific stock markets led the other markets, with the United States trailing Europe by 2.7 percent per year on average. In the 1980s, markets in the Pacific and Europe again outperformed the U.S. market with the gap between Europe and the United States averaging 2.6 percent. No wonder that American investors became enthusiastic about foreign stocks as these first two decades evolved. In the 1990s, tables were turned as the U.S. market outshone all the others. So far in the current decade, U.S. markets have lagged behind the others.

An investor examining this record of returns must focus on the following question. Which markets will outperform in coming decades? The sensible response is that investors do not know the answer to this question. That is the most cogent argument for diversifying abroad. Ignore correlations for the moment and focus on Figure 5.9. Should investors be concentrated in U.S. stocks if we could plausibly face decades more similar to the 1970s and 1980s than the 1990s?

To see to what extent markets can vary relative to one another, consider the EAFE and the S&P indexes over the 20-year period beginning in 1990. The gap in returns is an astonishingly large 3.8 percent per year. The main reason for EAFE's underperformance was the collapse of the Japanese market, which peaked in December 1989 before falling more than 75 percent. At its peak when the Nikkei index reached 38,900, the Japanese stock market was the largest in the world. In late 2009, it was still below 11,000. This helps to explain why the Pacific region did so well in the 1970s and 1980s, but then faltered so badly in the 1990s. An index of EAFE stocks *excluding Japan* outperforms the EAFE index as a whole by 4.0 percent per year! How much better off would Japanese investors have been if they had chosen a global rather than national portfolio?

Currency Capital Gains and Foreign Stock Returns

The returns reported in Table 5.6 and the accompanying figures are all measured in U.S. dollars in order to make them comparable to one another. Foreign stocks are denominated in their local currencies, but it's the return measured in dollars that matters to American investors. The return in dollars reflects both the return in local currency and the capital gain on the foreign currency.

Let R_L be the return on foreign stocks in local currency and R_X the capital gain on the foreign currency (measured in dollars per foreign currency). Then the return on foreign stocks measured in dollars, $R_\$$, is obtained as follows:

$$R_\$ = (1 + R_L)(1 + R_X) - 1$$

In 2003, for example, the return on Japanese stocks was 23.0 percent measured in yen, but the yen appreciated by 10.7 percent. So the return on Japanese stocks measured in dollars for the American investor was 36.2 percent:

$$R_\$ = (1 + 0.230)(1 + 0.107) - 1 = 0.362 \quad or \quad 36.2\%$$

The Japanese investor received the 23.0 percent return measured in yen, while the American investor received the higher 36.2 percent return that reflects the capital gain on the yen in 2003.

Figure 5.10 shows the average compound returns on foreign stocks measured in local currency and in dollars. In the case of the EAFE index as a whole, for example, the return in local currency from 1970 to 2009 was only 8.3 percent, but the return in dollars was 10.2 percent. The much higher return in dollars was due to an appreciation of 1.8 percent per year in the dollar value of foreign currencies (weighted by the size of each stock market in the EAFE index). The role of currency gains is particularly important in the case of the Japanese market. The average dollar return on Japanese stocks since 1970 is 9.7 percent per year, while the local currency return (in yen as viewed by a Japanese investor) is only 6.0 percent. The appreciation of the yen by an average of 3.5 percent accounted for the rest.[9] The country with the lowest return by far is Italy. Its return in local currency was a respectable 8.6 percent, but the depreciation of the lira lowered the return measured in dollars to 6.5 percent. The country with the highest return in dollars is Switzerland. Its relatively low return in Swiss francs was offset by a large appreciation of its currency relative to the dollar. The United Kingdom would have had as large a return as Switzerland if the pound had not depreciated against the dollar over this 35-year period.

In the short run, exchange rate movements can lead to much larger variations in stock returns measured in dollars. Consider the period of Ronald Reagan's presidency, 1981 to 1988. During Reagan's first term, the dollar rose sharply against the other major currencies. For example, the French franc price of the dollar rose from less than five FF per dollar in January 1981 to more than 10 FF per dollar in February 1985. As a result, the dollar returns on French stocks were severely depressed. As shown in Table 5.7, the return on French stocks in local currency was 19.4 percent per annum during the four-year period from 1981 to 1984, whereas the return on

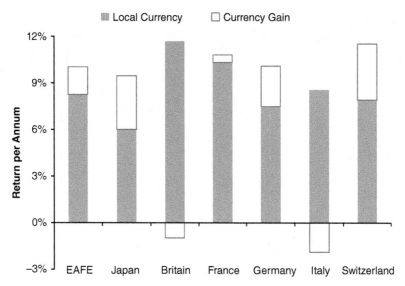

FIGURE 5.10   Foreign Stock Returns in Local Currency and Currency Gains, 1970–2009

these same stocks measured in dollars was a negative 1.1 percent. The gap between these returns was due to an average depreciation of the French franc of 17.2 percent from 1981 to 1984. During the same four years, the pound depreciated by 16.5 percent, the deutschmark by 10.2 percent, and the yen by 5.1 percent.

The Group of Five industrial countries are studied in Table 5.7 because they were the five countries taking part in the famous Plaza Accord meetings in September 1985. This meeting, held at the Plaza Hotel in New York City, was hosted by Secretary of the Treasury James Baker and included finance ministers and central bankers from the United States, Britain, France, Germany, and Japan. The Plaza Accord introduced a joint policy to drive the dollar down to more competitive levels. The Accord met with almost immediate success. The dollar had already fallen from its peak in March 1985 even before the Plaza meeting, but its fall accelerated after the meeting and kept falling until it had reached pre-Reagan levels against most major currencies.

The right side of Table 5.7 shows the effects of the dollar's fall (or the rise in foreign currencies) on stock returns. The right side of the table measures returns

TABLE 5.7   Average Returns on Group of Five Country Stocks during First and Second Reagan Administrations

Country	1981–1984 In Local Currency	In U.S. Dollars	1985–1988 In Local Currency	In U.S. Dollars
United States		10.9%		17.1%
Britain	25.7%	5.0%	15.6%	29.1%
France	19.4%	−1.1%	25.5%	40.9%
Germany	16.9%	5.0%	13.6%	31.1%
Japan	20.1%	14.0%	29.0%	53.5%

Data Source: MSCI.

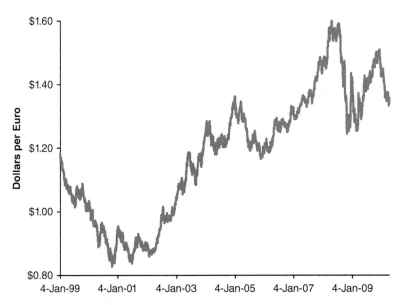

FIGURE 5.11   Exchange Rate for the Euro since 1999

during the second Reagan administration from 1985 to 1988. While foreign stock returns in local currency were impressive during this four-year period, the returns in dollars were from 13.5 percent to 24.5 percent higher than the local currency returns.

The period of the Reagan administration is not the only time that the dollar has varied sharply relative to other major currencies. A similar rise and fall in the dollar occurred soon after the new European currency, the Euro, replaced the currencies of 12 European countries. As shown in Figure 5.11, the Euro was introduced in 1999 at a price of $1.18 per Euro and proceeded to fall all the way to $0.83 per Euro in October 2000. Over the three years from January 1999 through December 2001, the fall in the Euro (and other European currencies) dragged down European stock returns by 7.2 percent. The Euro didn't reach its $1.18 price again until May 2003, but it kept soaring after that.

Figure 5.12 decomposes the dollar return on the MSCI European stock index into its two components. In the three years from 1999 to 2001, the dollar return on the European index averaged –5.0 percent per year because the currency loss of 7.2 percent more than offset the 2.3 percent stock return in local currency. The period after 2001 was very different. As shown in Figure 5.12, currency gains contributed 4.5 percent per year to European stock returns from 2002 through 2009. As a result, European stocks measured in dollars had positive returns of 7.0 percent per year, much higher than the 2.5 percent return in local currency during this period.

If currencies move this sharply, two natural questions arise. First, can such currency movements be forecasted? Second, if accurate forecasts are difficult, does currency hedging pay? Currency forecasting is too extensive a topic to cover adequately here. But investors should be skeptical if they see claims that forecasting is easy, particularly short-term forecasting. And they should also be skeptical if fund managers claim to know when to hedge and when not to.

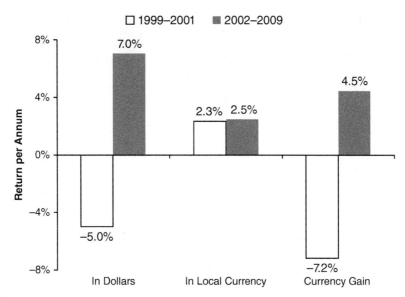

FIGURE 5.12   European Stock Returns since the Euro Was Introduced

What can be established is that in the long run a policy of hedging currencies has not had a major effect on overall returns, at least as far as the currencies of the major industrial countries are concerned. That's because currency futures contracts are fairly priced. In the long run, there is little profit or loss from selling currencies in the forward market (which an investor would do in order to hedge the currency risk). A policy of selling French francs to hedge the currency exposure on French stock investments, for example, made an average profit of minus 0.7 percent per year between 1979 and June 2009 ignoring transactions costs. The same policy applied to Deutschemarks made an average profit of only +0.5 percent per year.[10] It should not be surprising that returns are so small, since consistently high profits would be soon eliminated by additional speculators joining in the game.

A more surprising result is shown in Table 5.8. Currency hedging does not have much impact on risk. Table 5.8 compares the standard deviations of the country indexes when the stock returns are hedged and when they are left unhedged. In the case of the British stock index, hedging reduces the standard deviation from 19.9 percent to 17.1 percent, but in the case of the German stock index, the standard deviation of the hedged return is virtually identical to that of the unhedged return. More importantly, in no case does hedging make much of a difference. Why is that the case? Hedging has a marginal impact on risk because currency gains have a low correlation with foreign stock returns. This is in contrast to the case of foreign bonds where hedging makes a big difference. Because hedging has little effect on stock market risk, few investment managers choose to hedge their foreign stock portfolios.

A far more effective way to reduce the risk of foreign stock investments is to diversify the country risk. Figure 5.13 shows the standard deviations of MSCI country index returns measured in dollars and compares these with the standard deviation of the EAFE index as a whole. By diversifying across country stock markets, an

TABLE 5.8   Standard Deviations of Unhedged and Hedged Quarterly Returns on Stock Markets, January 1979–June 2009

Stock Market	Unhedged Dollar Return	Hedged Dollar Return
Britain	19.9%	17.1%
France	24.0%	23.1%
Germany	24.6%	24.5%
Japan	25.3%	22.0%
Switzerland	20.3%	20.4%

Data Sources: IMF, International Financial Statistics, and MSCI.

investment manager can reduce the standard deviation of foreign stocks from an average of about 22 percent per market to 17.2 percent for the EAFE index as a whole. Most active foreign stock managers do diversify country risk. That's true even of the bottom-up managers who base their portfolio choices on the performance of individual firms, not the markets in which they are listed.[11]

To summarize, currency effects add an extra dimension to investing in foreign stock markets. In the long run, returns on foreign stocks include a currency component that can either raise or lower the total return on these stocks as measured by an American investor. In the case of the EAFE index, for example, the return in dollars averaged 1.9 percent above the local currency return from 1970 through 2009. The higher return in dollars reflected the depreciation of the dollar that occurred over this period. At times, currency gains or losses can be a dominant factor, as in the first and second terms of Ronald Reagan's presidency. But there is little evidence that such currency gains or losses can be easily forecasted. An American investor must decide whether the total return on foreign stocks, including the currency component,

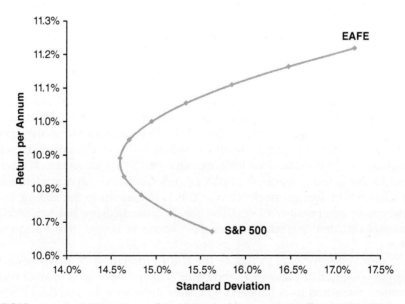

FIGURE 5.13   Standard Deviations of Stock Market Returns in Dollars, 1970–2009

is sufficiently attractive to warrant investment. As with all assets, returns have to be evaluated on a risk-adjusted basis, and the risk of foreign stocks is best evaluated in a portfolio context where their diversification benefits can be assessed.

Diversification Benefits of Foreign Stock Investing

A traditional argument in favor of diversification into foreign stocks was the relatively low correlation between foreign and domestic stocks. This low correlation meant that the risk of an internationally diversified portfolio could be lower than that of an all-U.S. portfolio. Over the period from 1970 (when the EAFE index begins) and 2009, for example, the correlation between EAFE and the S&P 500 index is only 0.60. The effects of this low correlation have often been illustrated using a horseshoe diagram like that found in Figure 5.13. The horseshoe shows various portfolios of U.S. and foreign stocks ranging from an all–S&P 500 portfolio (at the lower right end) to an all EAFE portfolio (at the higher right end). The powerful message of this chart is that diversified portfolios of foreign and domestic stocks have the dual benefit of *lower risk* and *higher return*. The horseshoe diagram was often used in the marketing materials of foreign stock mutual fund managers during the mid-1990s. Then for about 10 years, the horseshoe disappeared as a marketing device because EAFE was being outperformed so badly by the S&P that the horseshoe inverted. Diversified portfolios still lowered risk, but portfolios with high proportions of foreign stocks had lower returns than U.S.-only portfolios. With the surge in foreign stock returns since 2002, the horseshoe has become viable again. But notice that in Figure 5.13, the gap in returns between EAFE and the S&P 500 is only about 0.5 percent. It's the reduction in risk that matters for foreign diversification, not the increase in return.

To see how foreign diversification can improve the performance of a portfolio, see Figure 5.14, and consider Table 5.9, which compares portfolios with and without

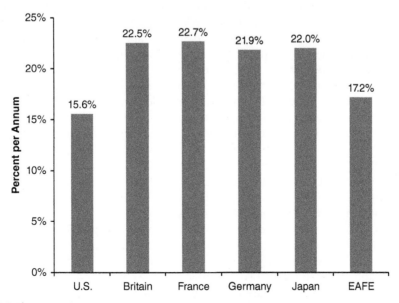

FIGURE 5.14   Portfolios of U.S. and Foreign Stocks, 1970–2009

TABLE 5.9   Performance of Portfolio with EAFE Added

	Geometric Average	Arithmetic Average	Standard Deviation	Sharpe Ratio
Portfolio A (1970–2009)				
Without EAFE	9.7%	10.0%	12.0%	0.37
25% EAFE	9.9%	10.1%	11.2%	0.41
Portfolio B (1979–2009)				
Without EAFE	11.0%	11.2%	12.2%	0.47
25% EAFE	10.8%	11.0%	11.6%	0.47

Portfolio A: Portfolio without EAFE consists of 25 percent in medium-term U.S. Treasuries and 75 percent in the S&P 500. When a 25 percent EAFE position is added, the S&P is reduced by 25 percent.
Portfolio B: Portfolio without EAFE consists of 25 percent in the Barclays Capital Aggregate, and 75 percent in the Russell 3000 all-cap stock index. The portfolio with EAFE has 25 percent in EAFE and 50 percent in the Russell 3000.
Data Sources: MSCI, © Morningstar, S&P, Barclays Capital, and Russell®.

the EAFE index. The first comparisons are for the period starting in 1970 when the EAFE index was introduced. There is an all-American portfolio consisting of 75 percent invested in the S&P 500 and 25 percent in the medium-term Treasury bond. The diversified portfolio replaces one third of the stock allocation, 25 percent of the whole portfolio, with foreign stocks. The portfolio containing EAFE has a higher return and lower standard deviation. So the Sharpe ratio is also higher at 0.41 as opposed to 0.37 for the all-American portfolio. That is not much of a difference, but it translates into 0.4 percent excess return for the diversified portfolio.[12]

The second set of portfolios is for a shorter period beginning in 1979. This set of portfolios replaces the S&P 500 with the Russell 3000 all-cap U.S. stock index and it replaces the medium-term Treasury with the Barclays Capital Aggregate Index (formerly the Lehman Aggregate index). Over the period beginning in 1979 (when the Russell indexes begin), the portfolio with 25 percent invested in EAFE has a lower return, but also has a lower risk. The Sharpe ratio of this diversified portfolio is exactly the same as that of the all-U.S. portfolio. So the benefits of international diversification disappear in this later period.[13]

One reason that the foreign diversification is less effective in more recent years is that the correlation between foreign and domestic stocks has increased markedly, so foreign diversification reduces risk less than it did in the past. Consider Table 5.10 where the correlations between the S&P 500 index and various foreign stock indexes are reported. For the full period beginning in 1970, EAFE has a correlation with the S&P 500 of only 0.60 and MSCI Pacific has an even lower correlation of 0.43. But for the past 10 years alone ending in 2009, the correlation between EAFE and the S&P rises to 0.87. There are correspondingly large increases in correlations between the S&P and the regional MSCI indexes.

When did this increase in correlations occur? Consider Figure 5.15, which shows five- and 10-year correlation coefficients between the EAFE and S&P 500 indexes. Since the EAFE index starts only in 1970, the graph begins in 1975 for the five-year correlation and in 1980 for the 10-year correlation. The figure is noteworthy in several respects. First, the correlations vary widely over time whether they are measured over five- or 10-year intervals. The five-year correlation begins above 60 percent and at

TABLE 5.10   Correlations between U.S. and Foreign Stocks

	Correlation with S&P 1970–2009	Correlation with S&P 2000–2009
EAFE	0.60	0.87
MSCI Europe	0.67	0.86
MSCI Pacific	0.43	0.72

Data Sources: MSCI, © Morningstar, and S&P.

times falls below 30 percent. The 10-year correlation shows less variability over time. But as late as 1997, the 10-year correlation is below 45 percent. Second, the sharp rise in correlation occurs relatively late in the sample period, in 1998 for five-year correlations and 2001 for 10-year correlations.

Most experts explain the recent rise of correlations on *increased integration of the world economy.* Over the past 20 or 30 years, international trade and international capital flows have both increased at rapid paces. There is such a contrast between the capital control world of the 1960s and today's world of free-flowing capital. There has also been a marked improvement in information flows. Information has always been transmitted almost instantly between countries, at least since the establishment of the worldwide telegraph system in the 1860s. But now there is much more information readily available about markets and companies than there was as recently as the 1970s. Databases of corporate performances, for example, are available for many foreign companies. And the web has provided instant access to annual reports and other corporate records.

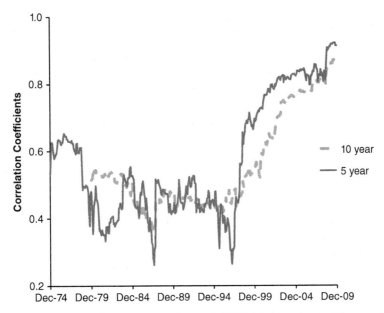

FIGURE 5.15   Correlations between S&P 500 and EAFE Measured over Five- and 10-Year Periods, 1970–2009

TABLE 5.11   Standard Deviations of Diversified Portfolios of
EAFE and S&P 500

Portfolio	Standard Deviation 1970–2009	Standard Deviation 2000–2009
EAFE alone	17.2%	18.1%
S&P 500 alone	15.6%	16.1%
20% EAFE	14.8%	16.2%
40% EAFE	14.6%	16.4%

20 percent (40 percent) portfolio consists of 20 percent (40 percent)
EAFE and the remainder in the S&P 500.
Data Sources: MSCI, © Morningstar, and S&P.

Nonetheless, it's hard to explain why this trend in integration should lead to an abrupt increase in correlations in the late 1990s. There is no evidence of an abrupt increase in international trade or capital flows around that time. Nor did instant communications become even more instantly available in the late 1990s.[14] However, without an alternative explanation of this phenomenon, all we can do is observe the change in correlations and study their impact on portfolios.

How much difference does the rise in correlations make to the case for international diversification? In Table 5.11, we compare the standard deviations of various portfolios for the full sample period of the EAFE index and for the past 10 years alone. For portfolios measured since 1970, a 20 percent allocation to EAFE lowers the risk of a stock portfolio by 0.8 percent. But for portfolios measured only over the past 10 years, a 20 percent allocation to EAFE actually raises risk marginally. So the gains from international diversification have disappeared.

So why should American investors go to the trouble of investing abroad? Those investors skeptical of international investing ought to think about turning the question around. Why should I keep all of my equity investments at home? Recall Figure 5.9, which shows the decade-by-decade performance of U.S. and foreign stocks. Returns vary a lot across regions over periods as long as a decade. Why would an American investor want to put all of his or her chips on one country? Betting on America alone paid off in the 1990s, but it wasn't as smart a strategy in the 1970s and 1980s. So far in this decade, no markets have done well except those of the emerging markets, but American markets have performed the worst of all.

Are There Shortcuts to Owning Foreign Stocks?

Investors have considered two shortcuts to owning foreign stocks that allow them to keep their money at home. The first shortcut involves investing in American Depository Receipts (or ADRs) instead of stocks of the same companies listed on foreign stock exchanges (foreign stocks). The second shortcut involves investing in the stocks of U.S. multinational firms that have extensive sales or production in foreign countries. The first shortcut represents a legitimate and convenient way to invest in foreign companies. The second shortcut fails to provide the foreign diversification that investors are seeking.

Consider first the ADR market. First developed in the 1920s, ADRs are negotiable certificates issued by a U.S. bank with rights to the underlying shares of stock held in trust at a custodian bank. These ADRs are sold, registered, and transferred within the United States like any share of stock in a U.S. company. Dividends are paid in foreign currency to the custodian bank that converts them to dollars. American investors find investing in ADRs very convenient compared with investing in shares in foreign stock markets. Investors do not have to worry about foreign currency transactions and custody remains in the United States.

To what extent is the American investor getting true foreign diversification by investing in ADRs? First, it's important to recognize that arbitrage will ensure that the returns on ADRs and on the underlying foreign stocks are identical except for transactions costs. Second, there are now almost 3,000 ADRs available in the U.S. market for firms from virtually every country that has an active stock market, so it's possible to invest in a wide variety of foreign stocks through ADRs.

To examine pricing of ADRs, consider first the case of liquid stocks that are widely traded by investors. If traders notice price discrepancies between the prices of ADRs and the underlying stocks, they will immediately jump on the opportunity to make an arbitrage (or riskless) profit. They will buy in the cheaper market and sell in the higher-priced market. Some investors believe that ADRs allow investors to avoid exchange risk because they are priced in dollars whereas foreign shares are priced in local currency. Arbitrage, however, will ensure that all gains and losses in currencies are reflected in ADR prices so that the return on the ADR (R_{ADR}) is aligned with the return on the underlying stock in the local market (R_{LStock}) as follows:

$$R_{ADR} = (1 + R_{L\,Stock})\,(1 + R_X) - 1$$

where R_X is the capital gain or loss on the local currency. ADRs and the shares of the same companies listed on their home exchanges should have the same prices and the same returns (when expressed in dollars) unless governments impose restrictions on the purchase and sale of the latter by foreigners.

Figure 5.16 illustrates how closely aligned are the prices of Toyota stock in Tokyo and Toyota's ADR in New York. Of course, the former is quoted in yen in the Japanese market, so Toyota's stock price must first be expressed in dollars to provide a meaningful comparison. In Figure 5.16, it's difficult to make out two distinct lines representing the ADR and Tokyo stock prices. The two lines will not be perfectly aligned because there are transactions costs in each market and, more importantly, because the two prices are recorded at the end of the trading day in each market (and there are 13 hours between the closing times of the Tokyo and New York markets).

Not all stocks are as liquid as Toyota. As with all financial assets, if trading is infrequent, price discrepancies may at times develop between the prices of the underlying foreign shares and those of the ADRs. In addition, some governments like Singapore put restrictions on foreign ownership of the underlying shares in the local market, so discrepancies between ADR prices and the prices of the underlying shares may remain persistently large. But that's because governments prevent arbitrage from working.

Table 5.12 gives a breakdown of ADRs by region and by the exchange on which they are traded in the United States. There are 1200 or so ADRs available from both Europe and Asia, and almost 300 from Latin America. So it is evident that an investor

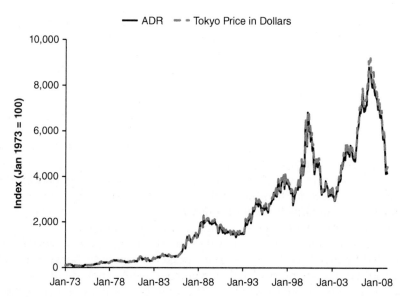

FIGURE 5.16   Toyota Tokyo Stock Price in Dollars and Toyota New York ADR Price in Dollars

can build a diversified portfolio of foreign stocks with ADRs alone. Indeed, some money managers offering foreign stock mutual funds only invest in ADRs. Some ADRs are listed on organized exchanges like the NYSE or NASDAQ, while others are sold only over the counter. Some ADRs are sponsored by the company involved, while others are offered to the American public without any formal sponsorship. ADRs are clearly an attractive alternative to the ownership of shares abroad.

While ADRs provide an effective way to diversify American portfolios, the stocks of American multinational firms do not. Many American multinational firms have

TABLE 5.12   Characteristics of ADRs, 2008

Region	Number of Stocks
Europe	1194
Asia	1296
Latin America	284
Africa	104
Other	56

Exchange Where Traded	Number of Stocks
NYSE	295
NASDAQ	114
AMEX	3
OTC	1434
Other	1088

Source: Bank of NY/Mellon.

extensive operations abroad. Their sales are multinational and, in many cases, so also is their production. Johnson & Johnson, for example, derives about 40 percent of its sales from foreign markets. And it has production facilities all over the world. Many investors believe that they can diversify their portfolios by investing in such American multinational companies.

In order for the stocks of these multinationals to provide effective foreign diversification, they must be correlated with the foreign stocks they are meant to replace in the portfolio. However, research has shown that the stocks of U.S. multinationals are much more highly correlated with the U.S. stock market than with foreign stock markets.[15] So replacing Nestlé with Hershey or Coca-Cola will lead to a portfolio that is not internationally diversified. There is no clear evidence why this is the case. Perhaps it's because U.S. multinational stocks are held predominantly by Americans, whereas European stocks are held predominantly by Europeans. It could also be because there is much more trading of foreign stocks on foreign exchanges than on U.S. exchanges.[16] Whatever the reason, the stocks of these multinationals can in no way substitute for the stocks of foreign firms represented in the foreign stock index.

Summary: Key Features of Foreign Stocks

In the long run, foreign stocks deliver comparable returns to those of U.S. stocks. From year to year and decade to decade, however, there are wide variations in performance across regions of the world. This provides a strong argument for diversification.

It has long been recognized that the relatively low correlation between foreign and U.S. stocks provides a portfolio diversification benefit. That correlation, however, has risen sharply since 1998. Most observers believe that the rising correlation is due to the increased integration of the world economy. There should be some doubts about this explanation if only because the rise in correlation occurred abruptly beginning in 1998 rather than in a continuous process over the past 20 years as integration occurred.

Currency movements influence stocks, particularly in the short run. The most dramatic example is found during the first and second terms of the Reagan administration when the dollar first soared, then fell back to earth. More recently, the dollar rose sharply against the Euro in the first three years of the latter's life only to fall back sharply since then. There is little evidence, however, that short-term currency movements can be accurately forecasted on a consistent basis.

Investors like to find shortcuts to investing in stocks listed on foreign exchanges. Buying ADRs instead of foreign stocks provides an effective way to diversify internationally because arbitrage keeps returns on ADRs closely aligned with those of the underlying stocks. Investing in U.S. multinational stocks, however, does not provide an effective means of diversification.

Perhaps the strongest argument for foreign stocks is that there is no reason to restrict a portfolio to the stocks of companies that happen to be headquartered in the United States. There is no way of knowing whether foreign stocks will outperform U.S. stocks in the decades ahead, so there is no reason to restrict investment to U.S. stocks.

Notes

1. These figures are derived from market capitalization statistics in the S&P *Global Stock Market Factbook*, 2009 edition.
2. Only in the 1920s did New York emerge as a major competitor.
3. That is, cross-border investments in stocks and bonds fell sharply. Multinational firms still found ways to expand across borders.
4. Successive French governments relaxed these controls during the 1970s, but the election of Francois Mitterand as French president in 1981 brought the reimposition of controls on outward flows of capital by French residents. These controls were finally lifted in the late 1980s.
5. The *Global Stock Markets Factbook* was developed by the International Finance Corporation, an arm of the World Bank. The division between industrial countries and emerging markets was determined by the IFC. Recently, the *Factbook* and the database for emerging markets stocks were sold by the IFC to the Standard & Poor's Corporation.
6. According to the S&P *Factbook*, any country with per capita income below Korea's is classified as an emerging market.
7. The EAFE index is from the MSCI database at www.mscibarra.com. The S&P index is from the SBBI database until 1973 and thereafter from the Zephyr database.
8. This is less the case for individual foreign countries (as will be seen in the following text), but it is true of the broad regional returns reported in Table 5.6.
9. The yen began the 1970s at its fixed rate of 360 ¥ per dollar (or $0.28 per hundred yen), while recently the yen has traded below 100 ¥ per dollar. Most of the appreciation of the yen occurred in the first 20 years.
10. The hedging policy consists of selling the French franc at the three-month forward rate quoted at the end of the preceding quarter, then closing the contract using the spot rate quoted at the end of the quarter. Beginning in 1999, the Euro exchange rate replaces the French franc and Deutschmark in these calculations.
11. Of course, managers must pay attention to the economies where the firms operate and must worry about overconcentration in any one economy or region.
12. That is, alpha* = 0.4 percent at the level of risk of the U.S.-foreign diversified portfolio.
13. If the S&P and MT Treasury bond is substituted for the R3000 and Barclays Aggregate bond index, the results are similar. So it is the shorter time period that leads to less gain from international diversification.
14. The Internet became important in the late 1990s, but just a little bit earlier, 1869 to be exact, a telegraph cable across the Atlantic linked New York markets with those in London and Paris.
15. If the returns on U.S. multinationals are regressed on both U.S. and foreign stock indexes (instead of just U.S. stock indexes as in a standard beta regression), the betas with respect to the foreign stock indexes are generally close to zero and statistically insignificant. See the discussion in Bodnar, Dumas, and Marston (2004).
16. There are exceptions to this pattern. Royal Dutch Shell, for example, has large trading on three exchanges, London, Amsterdam, and New York.

References

Bodnar, Gordon, Bernard Dumas, and Richard Marston. 2004. "Cross-Border Valuation: The International Cost of Equity Capital." In *Globalizing: Drivers, Consequences, and Implications*, edited by Hubert Gatignon and John Kimberly. INSEAD-Wharton Alliance.

Dimson, Elroy, Paul Marsh, and Mike Staunton. 2002. *Triumph of the Optimists: 101 Years of Global Investment Returns*. Princeton: Princeton University Press.

Part III Emerging Markets

Emerging markets—it may be one of the best marketing phrases ever devised. The phrase seems to describe markets that hold a lot of potential for future economic growth and the promise of future returns for investors. Since this phrase is usually attached to national markets where income is relatively low, a more accurate description would be the markets of less developed countries. Some countries will have great potential for growth and may actually be growing quite rapidly. Other countries, however, may have either little growth or actually be stumbling backwards. Naturally, few investors would want to invest in submerging markets, so all are labeled emerging.[1]

The World Bank champions the use of the term *emerging markets* through its affiliate, the International Finance Corporation (IFC). The IFC was created to foster private investment in developing countries. The IFC was the first organization to establish a database of stock market returns for the less developed countries, and it also started publishing an annual yearbook with extensive statistics describing the world's stock markets. (As discussed later, MSCI also has an extensive data set of emerging market stock returns.) In 2000, Standard & Poor's purchased the database and yearbook from the IFC, so the yearbook is now entitled the Standard & Poor's *Global Stock Markets Factbook*.

This chapter will show that emerging markets have provided handsome returns for international investors—at least over the past two decades since stock and bond returns first became available. Risks of investing in emerging markets, however, have also been quite sizable. Returns on emerging market stocks will be studied first. Then, because the bonds of emerging market countries are so closely related to the stocks of these countries, emerging market bonds will be studied.

What Is an Emerging Market?

How is an emerging market defined? The International Finance Corporation traditionally used one criterion, gross national income per capita.[2] Any country that was classified by the World Bank as a low income or middle income country was also classified as an emerging market. In 2008, China had a total gross national income of $3,899 billion, but a per capita income of only $2,940. Singapore, in contrast, had a gross national income of $168 billion, but a per capita income of $34,760.[3] So China

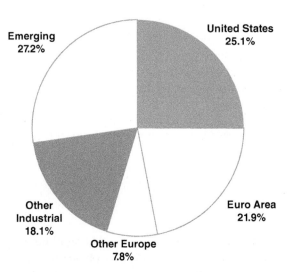

FIGURE 5.17   World Gross National Income in U.S. Dollars, 2008

is classified as an emerging market even though its total output was many times that of Singapore because its income per capita is so low.

The bulk of the world's income is earned by the high income countries. Figure 5.17 shows the division of the world's gross national income (GNI) in 2008. Only 27.2 percent of GNI is earned by the emerging market countries even though they represent 84 percent of the world's population. The developed countries dominate world output and world income. Western European countries (including the Euro area and other European industrial countries like the United Kingdom) produce almost 30 percent of world income and the United States another 25 percent, while the other developed countries of the world including Japan make up the rest.

Figure 5.18 breaks out the GNI of the six largest emerging market countries. China has the largest economy of any emerging market with a GNI larger than all but two of the developed countries (United States and Japan). With its rapid growth over the past two decades, China's economy is now larger than those of Germany, the United Kingdom, France, and Italy. China is one of the four BRIC countries highlighted in discussions of economic development, the others being Brazil, Russia, and India. All four of these countries are among the six economies shown in Figure 5.18. As shown later, the ranking of these six countries would be very different if adjusted for population size. China's huge GNI must be shared by a huge population.

When measuring national income, it's sensible to adjust for the cost of living. That is certainly true within a single country over time. If you want to measure the income of the average American today relative to decades ago, the only sensible way to measure income is to adjust for changes in the cost of living. So we might compare gross national income per capita in the year 1960 versus that of 2010 in terms of today's cost of living (2010 dollars). A similar approach might be used in comparing GNI per capita between countries at the same time since there might be substantial differences in the cost of living across countries. A basket of goods might be much less expensive in China than in Japan even if the basket itself were identical in both countries.

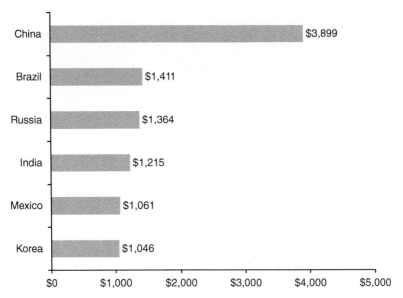

FIGURE 5.18   Gross National Income of Largest Emerging Market Countries, Billions of Dollars in 2008

Irving Kravis and his colleagues at the University of Pennsylvania developed a methodology for measuring the cost of living across countries.[4] This methodology, which has since been adopted by the World Bank and other international agencies, deflated gross national income using the cost of a common market basket to produce GNI adjusted for purchasing power parity or PPP. The results follow a consistent pattern. Less-developed countries have lower costs of living than industrial countries. So the GNI adjusted for PPP of the less-developed countries tends to be larger than the unadjusted GNI. In the case of the industrialized countries, the reverse is true. The GNI adjusted for PPP of these countries tends to be smaller than unadjusted GNI.

Figure 5.19 presents the GNI per capita of the six largest emerging market economies using two measures of national income. One measure, labeled unadjusted, simply converts the GNI per capita of a country into dollars using recent exchange rates.[5] The second measure, labeled PPP, adjusts for the cost of living using the Kravis methodology. The results are quite striking. China's GNI per capita is only $2,940 when measured at current exchange rates. But when it is adjusted for the low cost of living in China, GNI per capital rises above $6,000. Similarly, Mexico's GNI per capita is only $9,980 when measured using current exchange rates, but it rises to $14,270 when measured using PPP. Korea (by which we mean South Korea since the World Bank doesn't even have economic statistics for North Korea) is the richest of all emerging markets with a GNI per capita above $28,000 when using PPP.

To give some perspective on these GNI figures, consider the GNI per capita of some of the major industrial countries. The United States has a GNI per capita of $47,580 using current exchange rates and $46,970 using PPP. France has a GNI per capita of $42,250 at current exchange rates and $34,400 using PPP. The gap between the incomes of emerging markets and industrial economies is wide indeed.

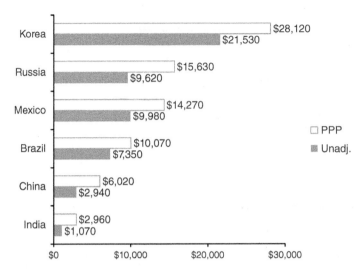

FIGURE 5.19   GNI Per Capita, Actual and PPP-Adjusted, 2008

Emerging Stock Market Indexes

Once definitions of emerging and developed countries are established, it's possible to divide the world's stock markets along the same lines. Emerging stock markets represent 26.5 percent of the world's stock markets of the total $35 trillion world stock market capitalization. So a block of countries with about 27 percent of the world's national income hosts about the same percentage of the world's stock market capitalization. The bulk of the market capitalization is found in the developed countries with the U.S. stock market representing almost 33.6 percent of the total (despite having only 25 percent of the world's gross national income).

The emerging stock markets are divided along regional lines in Figure 5.20. East Asia provides the largest block in terms of capitalization. This region consists of all markets between Indonesia and Korea except for Japan, Singapore, and Hong Kong (the latter being measured independently of China). South Asia includes India, which accounts for most of the region's market value. (East Asia and South Asia are combined in the Asia region in some of the statistics below.) The Middle East and Africa region includes two of the largest emerging stock markets, South Africa and Saudi Arabia.

These measures of market capitalizations may be misleading if we are interested in stocks that are actually available to the international investor. Not all shares issued by a firm are available to ordinary investors of that country, and even fewer are available to residents of other countries. There are several issues to sort through. First, some shares may be owned by the government or closely held by other investors. For example, firms in the same industrial group can cross-hold each others' shares. Second, some or all shares of a firm may be off-limits to foreign investors. Most foreign investment restrictions have been removed by developed countries, but such restrictions are widespread in the emerging countries.

To illustrate how different emerging markets look if we consider only investable indexes, consider Table 5.13, which compares actual (total) market capitalization for

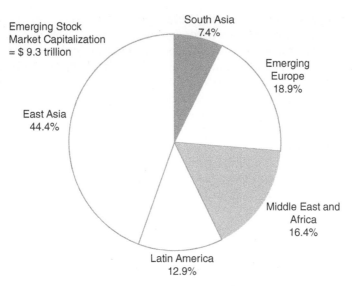

FIGURE 5.20   Stock Market Capitalization of the Emerging Markets

the emerging markets with the weights of the same regions or countries adopted by MSCI in its investable indexes. China has a 37.7 percent weight in the total market capitalization of the emerging markets, but only a 15.9 percent weight in the MSCI investable index. In contrast, Korea and Taiwan represent only 11.2 percent of the total market capitalization, but they represent 24.2 percent of the MSCI investable index. China has many stocks that are off-limits to foreigners or stocks that are only partially accessible to foreigners. Korea and Taiwan are much more open to foreign investors (even though their markets used to be subject to multiple restrictions).

MSCI has strict criteria for dividing countries in its three stock market categories, Developed, Emerging, and Frontier.[6] The criteria measure economic development, the size and liquidity of stock markets, and market accessibility. Developed countries are those that have country GNI per capita that is 25 percent above the World Bank's high-income threshold for three consecutive years and those that also satisfy high liquidity and accessibility requirements. (The GNI per capita threshold was $11,456,

TABLE 5.13   Emerging Market Capitalization Compared with MSCI Weights, 2007

Markets	Actual Market Capitalization	MSCI Weights
China	37.7%	15.9%
Korea and Taiwan	11.2%	24.2%
Rest of Asia	16.5%	14.5%
Brazil	8.3%	13.3%
Rest of Latin America	5.5%	7.0%
Europe, Middle East, and Africa	20.8%	25.1%

Sources: S&P *Factbook* for actual market capitalization, MSCI Barra for MSCI weights.

unadjusted for PPP, in 2007.) Emerging Markets are distinguished from Frontier Markets by having significant openness to foreign ownership and ease of capital inflows and outflows as well as having sufficient size and liquidity of its markets. Some countries shift between categories over time. Thus Israel was scheduled to be elevated to developed status in the spring of 2010, while Argentina has fallen to frontier status.

Because the investable universe is so different from the total emerging market universe, it's imperative for investors to use proper benchmarks for evaluating emerging market managers. Performance should be judged relative to the MSCI indexes, not relative to the broad stock market indexes of a country or region. Shanghai's stock market may have soared 20 percent over a particular period, but that does not mean that the investable indexes tracked by American investors have soared that much. They may have risen more or less than the Shanghai index.

Emerging Stock Market Returns

Emerging markets tend to be volatile and crisis-prone. But before examining the risks of investing in emerging markets, let's consider the returns earned in the past. The data sets for emerging market stocks do not extend back as far as those of developed countries. There are indexes for individual countries that extend back into the 1970s, but the broad indexes begin in the late 1980s. As in the case of the stocks of industrial countries, MSCI provides stock market indexes for the emerging markets that are widely used as benchmarks for emerging market funds. These indexes start in 1989.[7] There is a composite index for the emerging markets consisting of 22 emerging markets including five from Latin America, eight from Asia, and nine from Europe, the Middle East, and Africa. There are also regional indexes. The Latin American Emerging Market consists of Brazil, Chile, Colombia, Mexico, and Peru. The Asian index consists of China, Indonesia, India, Korea, Malaysia, Philippines, Taiwan, and Thailand. The Europe and Middle East index consists of Czech Republic, Hungary, Israel, Poland, Russia, and Turkey.[8]

Table 5.14 examines returns on the composite index for the emerging markets as a whole as well as regional emerging market indexes. The table compares emerging market returns with those of the S&P 500 and the MSCI EAFE developed country indexes.

TABLE 5.14 Emerging Market and Developed Market Stock Returns, 1989–2009

	Geometric Average	Arithmetic Average	Standard Deviation	Sharpe Ratio
Emerging Markets				
MSCI Composite	12.7%	15.1%	24.7%	0.46
Asia	7.7%	10.9%	26.1%	0.27
Latin America	20.0%	23.7%	32.1%	0.62
Europe and Middle East	11.5%	15.3%	29.8%	0.39
Developed Markets				
S&P 500	9.2%	10.0%	14.9%	0.41
MSCI EAFE	4.7%	6.2%	17.5%	0.13

Data Sources: MSCI and S&P.

Let's summarize the broad patterns:

1. Emerging market stock returns as a whole exceed those of the S&P 500 and far exceed those of the MSCI EAFE index. Recall that the EAFE index suffered badly from the collapse of Japan beginning in 1990. So any comparison that begins in the late 1980s is bound to show EAFE in a bad light.
2. Emerging market Asia has been a disappointment to investors. Returns beginning in 1989 fall far short of the emerging market index as a whole. The reason for this poor performance will be examined later in this chapter.
3. The Latin America index earned extraordinary returns during this period. No doubt the period studied matters here. Latin America suffered a lost decade in the 1980s because of the Latin American debt crisis that began in 1982. From low levels Latin American stock markets (as a whole) have risen sharply.
4. Europe and the Middle East have lagged behind Latin America.

As shown in Table 5.14, returns for the Asian region are much lower than those for the other regions as well as emerging markets as a whole. This is a true puzzle because Asia has grown faster than any other region in the world. The largest emerging market economy, China's, has had double-digit growth for much of the period. Shouldn't growth translate into high stock returns?

To answer this question, it is useful to correlate economic growth rates with stock returns. This is done in Figure 5.21 where the stock returns of 21 of the 25 largest emerging stock markets are regressed against the growth rates of these same economies.[9] The period studied is from 1990 to 2005 for economic growth and from 1990 to 2009 for stock market returns.[10] If economic growth is translated into stock returns, the regression line should be positively sloped. Higher economic growth

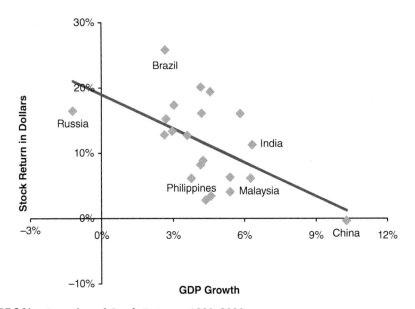

FIGURE 5.21   Growth and Stock Returns, 1990–2009

should generate higher stock returns. Instead, the regression line has a negative slope (–0.55). A country like Russia has had (slightly) negative economic growth, on average, over this period, but its stock return has been huge. China, on the other hand, has had very fast economic growth averaging almost 10 percent per year. But its stock return has been a little below zero, on average, since 1990. Note that if these two countries are omitted from the analysis, the correlation between economic growth and stock returns is still negative at –0.43.

Economists do not have a good explanation for why there is no positive relationship between economic growth and stock returns. The economic causation should go from high economic growth to high firm profits to high stock returns. There could be a break in the chain if high expected profits have already priced stocks in that country relatively high. Think of Japan in the 1980s when future growth and future profits appeared to have no upper limit, so Price-Earning Ratios (P/E) were sky high. There could also be a break between high growth and high profits. Certainly Soviet Russia had high growth (at least in the 1950s and 1960s), but were profits in this state-controlled economy high? (By profits we mean economic profits since all large enterprises were state owned.) In any case, the automatic assumption on Wall Street that a fast growing country or region will deliver high returns seems unwarranted at best.

To investigate the peculiar case of China in more detail, consider the returns on Chinese stocks beginning in December 1992 (when the MSCI China series begins) through 2009. The compound geometric return on China's investable index is –0.3 percent per year from 1993 through 2009 with a standard deviation of 38.5 percent. It is hard to believe that an economy growing as fast as China's could deliver such paltry returns. Figure 5.22 compares the return on the Chinese market with the return on the MSCI Asia index as a whole. The MSCI Asia index did not fare that well, but at least it had a positive return of 5.9 percent over the same period. It's

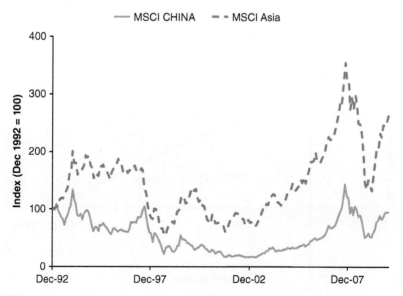

FIGURE 5.22   China and Emerging Asia Stock Markets Compared, 1992–2009

important to note that the returns just cited are investable returns, so they record what an average foreign investor would earn in these markets. Growth evidently does not reward all investors.

China, however, did have a terrific run late in the period. For the two years prior to the peak of its market in October 2007, the MSCI China index had a return of 306.4 percent! No wonder investors were rushing into this market. From that peak, the Chinese index fell 64.8 percent through October 2008. Through December 2009, it has again risen spectacularly by 87.9 percent. It has been quite a roller coaster ride. The key question is whether China's recent stock market performance is more indicative of the future than the full record of returns since 1992. China will no doubt remain volatile. But will it deliver more than the paltry returns seen *on average* since December 1992?

Risks of Investing in Emerging Stock Markets

Emerging markets are inherently risky. This is seen most simply by comparing the standard deviations of the emerging market indexes with those for the developed markets as in Table 5.14. But there are two features of emerging market risks that need to be explored in more detail. The first concerns the impact of emerging market stocks on portfolio risk. Emerging market stocks tend to be relatively low in correlation with developed country stocks, so their contribution to the overall risk of the portfolio may not be that great. The second feature concerns the volatility of emerging market stocks. The risks of emerging market stocks may be underestimated by conventional measures because they are prone to crises.

Table 5.15 reports correlations between emerging market stocks (MSCI Emerging Markets Composite Index) and the two developed country indexes, the S&P 500 and EAFE indexes. Two sets of correlations are shown, the first for the period beginning in 1989 when the investable indexes start and the second for the past 10 years alone, 2000 to 2009. For the period as a whole, the correlation between emerging market stocks and the S&P 500 is moderately lower than that found between the EAFE index and the S&P 500. A correlation of 0.66 is certainly lower than would be found between two types of U.S. stocks, like small-cap and large-cap stocks or value and growth stocks. So it shouldn't be surprising that diversification into emerging market stocks could lower the risk of an American stock portfolio. But, as shown

TABLE 5.15 Correlations between Emerging Market Stocks and Developed Market Stocks

	Correlation with S&P 500	Correlation with EAFE
1989–2009		
EAFE	0.71	
MSCI EM	0.66	0.68
2000–2009		
EAFE	0.88	
MSCI EM	0.79	0.88

Data Sources: MSCI and S&P.

in later chapters, emerging market stocks do not offer as much diversification as some alternative asset classes. This should not be that surprising given that many emerging market economies depend on exports to the developed countries, so their stock markets tend to boom at times when developed economies are doing well.

The previous part documented the rise in correlations between the EAFE index and U.S. stock market indexes in the past decade. A similar rise has occurred in the correlations between emerging market stocks and the developed country indexes. The correlation between the composite emerging market index and the S&P 500 has risen from 0.66 over the whole period to 0.79 over the past 10 years. No doubt the rise in correlation would have been even larger if the index had been available back through the 1970s and early 1980s. So whatever diversification benefits that were available over longer periods have been diminished, at least as long as correlations remain higher.

For American investors, the most important issue is how emerging markets fare within a portfolio because emerging markets are likely to be only a marginal asset within a portfolio dominated by American stocks and bonds. With the relatively low correlations reported in Table 5.15, it should not be surprising that a marginal allocation to emerging market stocks improves the performance of the portfolio.

Table 5.16 reports the results of two diversification experiments. In the first experiment, labeled Portfolio A in the table, an all-stock portfolio consisting of the S&P 500 index alone is diversified by adding a 10 percent allocation to emerging markets (using the MSCI EM index). In the second experiment, labeled Portfolio B in the table, a well-diversified portfolio of stocks and bonds is further diversified by adding 10 percent to emerging markets. This second portfolio consists of 25 percent in the Barclays Aggregate U.S. bond index, 50 percent in the S&P 500 index, and 25 percent in the EAFE index in the absence of emerging market stocks. When emerging market stocks are added to this portfolio, a 10 percent allocation to emerging market stocks reduces the S&P 500 allocation to 40 percent. The results are similar in both experiments. Emerging market stocks improve the risk-adjusted returns on both portfolios. The addition of a 10 percent allocation to

TABLE 5.16   Impact of Emerging Market Stocks on Portfolio Performance, 1989–2009

	Geometric Average	Arithmetic Average	Standard Deviation	Sharpe Ratio
Portfolio A				
Without Emerging Markets	9.2%	10.0%	14.9%	0.40
With 10% Emerging Markets	9.7%	10.5%	15.2%	0.43
Portfolio B				
Without Emerging Markets	8.0%	8.3%	11.2%	0.38
With 10% Emerging Markets	8.5%	8.8%	11.7%	0.41

Portfolio A consists of the S&P 500 alone or 90 percent S&P 500 with 10 percent in the MSCI Emerging Markets composite index.
Portfolio B is a diversified portfolio with 25 percent in the Barclays Aggregate index for U.S. bonds, 50 percent S&P 500, and 25 percent EAFE. The 10 percent in emerging markets reduces the S&P 500 weight to 40 percent.
Data Sources: Barclays Capital, MSCI, and S&P.

emerging market stocks raises the return on the portfolio but also raises the standard deviation of that portfolio. But the net effect is positive in that the Sharpe ratios of the portfolios with emerging markets are higher than those without emerging markets. In the case of the all-stock portfolios (labeled A in Table 5.16) adding emerging markets raises portfolio returns by 0.5 percent after adjusting for risk. That is, the Alpha* of the portfolio including emerging markets is 0.5 percent compared with the portfolio with the S&P 500 alone.[11] In the case of the stock/bond portfolios (labeled B in the table), the Alpha* of the portfolio including emerging markets is 0.4 percent. Diversification into emerging markets seems to pay, at least over the sample period for emerging market stocks beginning in 1989.

Another way to assess the contribution of emerging markets to a portfolio is to examine its systematic risk. Suppose that the emerging market index is to be added to an existing portfolio of stocks represented by the MSCI World index. The beta of the emerging market investable index, measured over the period from January 1989 through the end of 2009, is 1.17. The reason why the beta is so high is that the standard deviation of the emerging market series is 24.7 percent. So the relatively low correlation between emerging market stocks and this portfolio, 0.724, is not enough to keep the beta low.[12] On the other hand, the returns on the emerging market series are high enough to provide an excess return (or alpha) relative to the security market line of 7.1 percent! That is, the return on the investable index, 15.1 percent, exceeds the corresponding return on the security market line, 8.0 percent, by more than 7.1 percent over the period from 1989 to 2009. Diversification into emerging market stocks still pays despite the standard deviation and relatively high beta of these stocks. Note that if the S&P 500 is used as the market benchmark, then the risk-adjusted excess return on the Emerging Market Index (or alpha) shrinks to 4.6 percent because the S&P 500 return is 2.6 percent higher than the World Index return over this period.[13]

The indexes available for emerging market stocks extend back only to the late 1980s at best. With such a short history available, it's difficult to form judgments about how high returns will be in the future. Perhaps Asia, and China in particular, will provide much larger returns in the longer run. But, even more importantly, it's difficult to assess how risky emerging markets really are. Emerging stock markets are highly volatile and they are vulnerable to economic and financial crises.

Consider an investor trying to make decisions about emerging market stocks in early 1997. At that time, there were only eight years of data from the MSCI database. As shown in Figure 5.23, over the eight years ending in 1996, the compound return on the Asian Emerging Market Index was 14.8 percent per annum and the return on the composite index for all emerging markets was 19.9 percent per annum. It's true that over the same period, the S&P 500 offered hefty returns of 16.4 percent per year. But the correlations between emerging markets and U.S. stocks were low enough to justify large allocations to emerging market stocks.

In early 1997, few investors realized that Asian markets were about to be hit by a financial tsunami that would drive many markets down by 75 percent or more. The crisis first hit the Bangkok foreign exchange market in early July 1997 when the Thai central bank was forced to float the Thai baht. Speculation against Thailand's currency had been building up in the late spring, but few observers realized the extent of the speculation because the Thai central bank was secretly intervening in the foreign exchange market to keep forward exchange rates steady.[14] After the

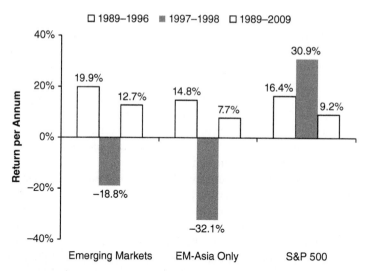

FIGURE 5.23   Emerging Market Stocks before and after the Asian Crisis Years of 1997–1998

Bank of Thailand had committed most of Thailand's foreign exchange reserves to these operations, the Thai Government was forced to float the Baht. The value of the baht was cut in half almost immediately (with the dollar initially rising against the Baht from Bt 25 per dollar to Bt 50 per dollar).

The collapse of the baht soon set off speculation against the Malaysian Ringgit, the Indonesian Rupiah, the Korean Won, and other Asian currencies. Why was there such widespread contagion? The most important reason is that firms in all of these countries had loaded up on dollar debt and other foreign currency debt. Once rumors of depreciation spread in the market, these firms rushed to hedge their foreign currency liabilities. If a fire breaks out in a ballroom, every one heads to the exits at the same time.

Stock market investors suffered grievously. Figure 5.23 shows that the Asian markets as a whole returned –32.1 percent per annum in 1997 and 1998. The stock markets of Thailand, Malaysia, and Korea all fell by 60 percent or more (in dollar terms). The contagion even spread to Latin America where markets fell 12.9 percent over the two-year period. Within a few years afterwards, emerging markets as a whole had recovered most of their lost ground. But in the case of the Asian stock markets, the index return per annum over the whole period from 1989 to 2009 is still more than 7 percent below what it was at the end of 1996!

The Asian crisis is not an isolated incident. Other markets have been prone to crisis. Consider three other important examples, Mexico in 1994, Russia in 1998, and Argentina in 2000 to 2002.

The Mexican crisis was precipitated by a currency collapse just as in the case of Thailand. In December 1994 following the inauguration of President Ernesto Zedillo, the peso depreciated from Ps 3.5 per dollar to Ps 7.0 per dollar. The depreciation led to widespread bankruptcies among Mexican firms (including major banks) because so much debt was denominated in dollars. The impact on the stock market was dramatic. The Mexican market fell by 60 percent (in dollar terms). It took several years for the Mexican economy to recover from this disaster.

The Russian crisis involved a default by the Russian government on its debt rather than currency depreciation. The Russian stock market began a dramatic decline a year before the actual default, which occurred in July 1998. Between September 1997 and a year later, the Russian stock market declined (in U.S. dollar terms) by more than 80 percent. The bond default itself precipitated a fall in many bond markets worldwide. Bond markets worldwide are not supposed to be very highly correlated. If you invest in Russian bonds and Brazilian bonds and Chinese bonds, it would seem that your portfolio is diversified. But when Russia defaulted on its bonds, there was a reassessment of risk worldwide. Spreads on bonds widened sharply both in the emerging bond markets and in the high-yield U.S. bond market (for so-called junk bonds). The most dramatic effect of this reassessment of risks was the collapse of Long-Term Capital Management, which had to be rescued by the major investment banks in September 1998.

The Argentine crisis began as early as 2000 when the long-established peg to the U.S. dollar began to be seriously questioned. In the early 1990s, the Argentine government had established a currency board to permanently fix the peso to the dollar.[15] Argentine inflation, which had soared more than 1,000 percent in the late 1980s, almost completely disappeared with this peg. Dollars and pesos became interchangeable in ordinary transactions as well as in financial contracts. By the late 1990s, however, the economy had slumped because of an overvalued exchange rate, especially after Brazil let its own currency depreciate against the dollar. In January 2002, Argentina was forced to float its currency and put controls on financial outflows. By that time, the stock market had already plummeted. From February 2000 until June 2002, a few months after the crisis, the Argentine market fell more than 80 percent in dollar terms.

Even in the absence of specific crises, these markets tend to be highly volatile. Consider the example of China once again. With a standard deviation of 38.5 percent, China's stock market is like a roller coaster. In the two years starting in December 1993, China's market fell 61 percent. It recovered most of this ground by 1997, but in August 1997 it fell sharply again as the Asian crisis hit. Within a year, the Chinese market had fallen by 80 percent (measured in dollar terms). Investors must be prepared for volatility if they invest in these markets.

Prior to the 2008 crisis, emerging markets' returns soared more than 85 percent from December 2005 to December 2007. So it has been hard to convince investors of the risks of investing in emerging market stocks. Of course, the plunge by 53 percent in 2008 may help.[16] It's even harder to remind investors that emerging market bonds have downside risk.

Emerging Market Bonds—A Brief History

Emerging market bonds have been around for two centuries at least. But most investors consider them a new asset class. The reason is that they almost entirely disappeared for more than 50 years. From the 1930s to the late 1980s, very few emerging market bonds were issued because investors had suffered too grievously from defaults in the 1930s.

There is a long tradition of defaults on emerging market bonds. The expectation has always been that some bonds will go into default because they had done so often in the past. In the late nineteenth century, emerging economies like those of

Argentina, Brazil, South Africa, and China regularly raised capital in London and Paris by issuing bonds. So did the emerging economy of the United States. Most of these bonds were denominated in pounds or French francs rather than in local currency. With fairly regular, but unpredictable frequency, these bonds would go into default. An example was the Argentina default that occurred during the Baring Brothers Crisis of 1890. The crisis began with a financial panic in Argentina, but soon affected the bond markets of other emerging economies such as the United States, and led to the collapse (and subsequent rescue by the Bank of England) of Barings Brothers itself, a long-established merchant bank in London.

When issuing bonds, most governments did not plan to default on their bonds. In fact, they often went to great lengths to avoid default. An example is the 1904 issue by the Chinese Imperial Railway, denominated in pounds and guaranteed by the Imperial Government of China. This bond continued to be serviced even after the Chinese revolution of 1911 under Sun Yat-sen for the simple reason that the revolutionary government wanted to retain access to the international capital markets. Only in the 1920s and 1930s did successor governments default on such bonds.[17] The 1930s saw many defaults by sovereign debtors. More than 70 percent of the foreign bonds issued in the U.S. market during the late 1920s (so-called Yankee bonds) went into default during the 1930s.[18]

After World War II, there was little eagerness to underwrite new bonds issued by the less developed countries. It was only in the 1970s that any sizable financing occurred outside of official channels such as the World Bank. But the new financing in the 1970s took the form of bank loans provided by the banks of the developed world rather than bonds. The innovation that occurred was that these loans were syndicated among a large group of banks so the originating bank or banks could place most of the loans and hence offload most of the default risk to other banks. Syndicated loans reached a peak in the early 1980s. It was then that the Latin American countries began to default on their loans. Technically, the loans were not in complete default, but the banks were eventually forced to reschedule the terms of these loans. Needless to say, syndicated loans ceased to be a major source of financing for emerging markets. With no sizable bond market financing available, emerging economies suffered from a lack of financing.

It was the American Treasury Secretary under President George H.W. Bush, Nicholas Brady, who resurrected the long-dormant international bond market. Brady did this by engineering the packaging of bank debt in the form of bonds that could be sold to nonbank investors. The resulting Brady bonds often contained Treasury bonds as partial collateral to make them more attractive to non-bank investors. The market for emerging market debt slowly revived.

RETURNS ON EMERGING MARKET BONDS   In the past decade, emerging market bonds have become an increasingly important source of finance for emerging economies and an attractive asset for investors seeking international diversification. Emerging economies have been able to expand financing through newly issued Eurobonds, bonds syndicated and sold internationally, and through bond issues in traditional national bond markets.[19] Most of these bonds are denominated in dollars, although bonds denominated in local currencies have become increasingly important.

The return series for emerging market bonds typically begin in the early 1990s after the Brady bonds were introduced. Table 5.17 reports the return on one such

TABLE 5.17   Emerging Market Bond Returns Compared with Other Returns, 1992–2009

	Geometric Average	Arithmetic Average	Standard Deviation	Sharpe Ratio
Bonds				
Emerging Market	12.2%	12.6%	14.3%	0.64
U.S.	6.4%	6.3%	3.8%	0.74
Stocks				
Emerging Market	9.6%	12.2%	24.2%	0.36
U.S.	7.7%	8.6%	14.8%	0.35

Emerging market bond index is the Merrill Lynch Emerging Market Sovereign Plus index. Other indexes are the Barclays Capital Aggregate U.S. bond index, MSCI Emerging Market stock index, and the S&P 500 U.S. stock index.
Data Sources: Barclays Capital, Merrill Lynch, MSCI, and S&P.

series, the Merrill Lynch Emerging Market Sovereign Plus index. This table compares emerging market bonds with U.S. dollar-denominated bonds, using the Barclays Capital Aggregate Bond Index (formerly the Lehman Aggregate Bond Index), and with two stock market indexes, the S&P 500 U.S. index and the MSCI emerging market stock index. The results are very surprising. Over this sample period, 1992 to 2009, emerging bonds deliver a 12.2 percent compound return. So these bonds deliver returns far above those of either stock index or the U.S. bond index. The standard deviation of 14.3 percent is very high for a bond index, but it appears that emerging market bonds deliver stock-like returns.

The surprising performance of emerging market bonds is explained by the reassessment of emerging market risks that has occurred since the early 1990s. Consider Figure 5.24, which shows the spread of emerging market bonds over U.S.

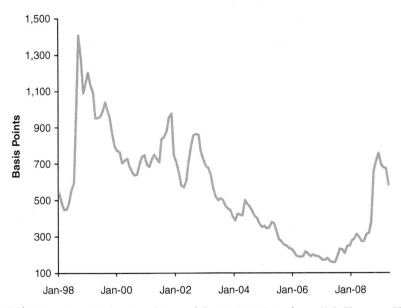

FIGURE 5.24   Emerging Market Bond Spread (in Basis Points above U.S. Treasury Yield)

TABLE 5.18   Correlations between Emerging Market Bonds and Other Assets, 1992–2009

	Merrill Lynch Emerging Market Bond Index	Barclays Aggregate Bond Index	MSCI Emerging Market Stock Index
EM Bonds	1.00		
Barclays Aggregate	0.32	1.00	
EM Stocks	0.66	−0.02	1.00
S&P 500	0.54	0.12	0.70

Data Sources: Emerging market bond index is the Merrill Lynch Emerging Market Sovereign Plus index. Other indexes are from Barclays Capital, MSCI, and S&P.

Treasuries (of the same maturity). Since reaching a peak of 1,400 basis points following the Russian bond default, emerging market spreads fell to 200 basis points or less prior to the 2007 and 2008 crisis. During this period of falling spreads, these bonds were increasingly viewed as almost like U.S. investment grade corporate debt. When interest spreads fall from 1,400 basis points to 200 basis points, investors thrive.

How should an investor interpret a spread of 200 basis points? A fair interpretation is that the market no longer foresees the possibility of Mexican-like devaluations or Russian-like defaults. The era of Argentine-like crises is forever behind us, or so it seems. For investors with a more skeptical attitude, the proper approach is to ask whether the returns shown in Table 5.17 are good indicators of future returns on emerging market bonds. The sensible answer is that there has been a once-for-all reassessment of emerging market risks. The reassessment may prove short-lived. But even if emerging market risks stay low, the investment gains from the reassessment have already been earned. The past returns on emerging market bonds should be viewed much like U.S. bonds were viewed in Part I of this chapter. Between the early 1980s and present, there has been a once-for-all reassessment of inflation risks in the U.S. market. This has led to a once-for-all reduction in U.S. bond yields and a temporary increase in U.S. bond returns. In the case of both types of bonds, the great returns are probably behind us.[20]

For the future, it's important to determine how emerging market bonds might fit in the portfolio. They are an odd bond series in that they are highly volatile, more like junk bonds in the United States than either U.S. or European conventional bonds. In Table 5.18, we report correlations between the emerging market bond index and the three other bond and stock indexes of Table 5.17. The highest correlation is not with other dollar bonds, but with the emerging market stock index. That's because both asset classes are subject to emerging market country risk.

Why are emerging market stocks and bonds so highly correlated? There is a common thread, emerging market country risk, tying these two asset classes together. If there is a crisis in Russia or East Asia or Latin America, emerging market bonds and emerging market stocks will both be reassessed. As an example, consider the markets for Argentine stocks and Brady bonds between January 1997 and January 2002. The Argentine stock index (measured in dollars) gave a return of −15.0 percent over this period. Argentine Brady bonds provided an annualized compound return of −12.7 percent. The reassessment of Argentine risks hit both markets very hard. The early success of the Argentine stabilization plan was followed by an accelerating slide into crisis culminating in the abandonment of the dollar peg in January 2002.

Emerging markets are risky. Emerging market stocks and bonds may still deserve a place in the portfolio. But the investor should be very aware of their volatility.

SUMMARY: KEY FEATURES OF EMERGING MARKET STOCKS AND BONDS   The world's stock and bond markets are divided into developed and emerging for a good reason— emerging markets are riskier. The dividing line between the countries themselves is somewhat arbitrary, but the division between the assets of these two sets of countries is a meaningful one. Standard deviations have been a step above those of developed stock markets. Consistent with higher risks, emerging market stocks have delivered stellar returns since the series began in the mid-1980s. And these stocks also provide diversification to a more traditional portfolio.

Unlike emerging market stocks, emerging market bonds seem too good to be true. The returns since the early 1990s have been better than stock returns with standard deviations below those of the S&P 500. This chapter has argued that the returns are due to a dramatic downward assessment of risks. This reassessment has provided once-for-all returns much like we have enjoyed from the reassessment of inflation in the U.S. bond market. Emerging market bonds, like their stock counterparts, are crisis-prone. But many investors will not believe this until the next crisis occurs. Caveat emptor.

Notes

1. The term *submerging markets* was coined by Goetzmann and Jorion (1999). These authors examine stock markets like those of Argentina and China that reemerged after decades of closure due to political instability. The term *frontier market* is given to a subset of emerging markets at lower stages of development.
2. More recently, the IFC (and Standard & Poor's after it took over the IFC database) refined the criteria used to distinguish emerging markets from developed markets. The criteria include the depth of the market, its lack of discriminatory controls on foreign investment, and its transparency.
3. All gross national income statistics are from the World Bank, World Development Indicators Database.
4. See Kravis, Kenessey, Heston, and Summers (1975). The International Comparison Project that Kravis and his coauthors pursued was financed under grants from the World Bank and other international agencies.
5. The unadjusted figure is obtained by using a moving average of the past three year's exchange rates. The World Bank calls this the Atlas method for calculating GNI.
6. See MSCI/Barra MSCI Market Classification Framework, June 2009.
7. As mentioned above, S&P also provides emerging stock market indexes including investable indexes begun by the International Finance Corporation and later sold to S&P. Those indexes give roughly similar results to the MSCI indexes.
8. The remaining countries in the composite index are from Africa: Egypt, Morocco, and South Africa.
9. This is an analysis updated from a similar one reported by Jeremy Siegel in his study of long-run returns on stock markets (Siegel 1998). The four countries

omitted either do not have GDP data available (Qatar) or have stock market data for only a few years (Kuwait, Saudi Arabia, and UAE).

10. Some countries have stock returns beginning later than 1990. Returns for China, for example, begin in 1992. If the stock returns are measured from 1990 to 2005 only, the correlation between growth and stock returns is even more negative.

11. Deriving Alpha* from the Sharpe ratios, $\alpha^* = (0.43 - 0.40) * 0.152 = 0.5\%$.

12. The high standard deviation of the emerging market series (relative to a standard deviation of 15.3 percent for the World Index) ensures that the beta is relatively large, $(0.724 * 0.247)/0.153 = 1.17$.

13. The World Index performs badly for the same reason that EAFE does over this period, the collapse of the Japanese market. Note that it is more appropriate to use the World Index to measure the beta of Emerging Markets than to use a U.S. index alone.

14. The Central Bank of Thailand was keeping the spot exchange rate fixed against a basket of currencies with a weight of 80 percent on the U.S. dollar. This was well understood by the foreign exchange market. What was less well known is that the supposedly market-determined forward exchange rate was also being held fixed by secret intervention. The Central Bank knew that a depreciating forward rate would alert investors worldwide to the weakness of the currency.

15. A currency board takes away the discretion over monetary policy that a traditional central bank always retains. The finance minister of the time, Domingo Cavallo, believed that only a currency board could establish credibility for an exchange rate peg.

16. That's compared with a 37 percent decline in the S&P 500 in 2008. In 2007 and 2008, the world learned that even industrial countries can suffer major financial crises!

17. Goetzmann et al. (2007) reviews some of the history of Chinese government debt issues and their subsequent defaults.

18. The U.S. bond market had become the primary source of international funding for emerging economies in the 1920s. The 70 percent excludes issues by Canadian borrowers.

19. Eurobonds were first issued in the 1960s long before the European currency, the Euro, was introduced. The term *Euro* reflects the European origin of the market, although Eurobonds can be issued by borrowers from anywhere in the world and are often sold to non-European investors.

20. This is not to deny that returns can be sizable for a short period following a crisis. In the case of the 2007 and 2008 crisis, spreads rose more than 7 percent, thus creating a short-term opportunity for investors once the crisis passed.

References

Goetzmann, William N., and Philippe Jorion. 1999. "Re-emerging markets." *Journal of Financial and Quantitative Analysis* (March): 1–32.

Goetzmann, William N., Andrey D. Ukhov, and Ning Zhu. 2007. "China and the world financial markets 1870–1939: Modern lessons from historical globalization." *Economic History Review* (May): 267–312.

Kravis, Irving B., Z. Kenessey, Allan Heston, and Robert Summers. 1975. *A system of international comparisons of gross product and purchasing power.* Baltimore: Johns Hopkins Press.

Siegel, Jeremy J. 1998. *Stocks for the Long Run,* 2nd Edition. New York: McGraw Hill.

MSCI/Barra. 2008. MSCI Barra emerging markets: A 20-year perspective. www .mscibarra.com/products/indices/em_20/EM_20_Anniversary.pdf.

Standard & Poor's, 2008, S&P *Global Stock Markets Factbook.*

Part IV Bonds

Stocks and bonds are the most important assets in most portfolios. Stocks and bonds provide the long-run appreciation necessary to sustain portfolios, while Part I showed that long-run bond returns, for U.S. Treasury bonds in particular, are so low that they hardly allow for any growth in wealth over time, at least after the returns have been adjusted for inflation. This part discusses three types of bonds, U.S. Treasury bonds, other bonds issued in the United States, and bonds issued in other industrial countries. The United States is the largest market for bonds in the world, but the bond markets of the other industrial countries are growing rapidly, particularly the markets in the Euro currency area. The returns on bonds have varied widely over the last few decades, so this part will investigate the main determinants of bond returns.

Bonds are often favored by investors because they provide fixed income in contrast to the variable returns offered by equities and by most other assets. A stream of fixed income payments is often viewed as essential to retirees as well as many institutional investors because of their need for continual income. Investors focusing only on yields, however, are too often disappointed by the overall performance of their investments. Bond yields represent part of the total return to fixed income assets, but the variation in yields over time leads to capital gains and losses that sometimes dominate the total return from holding bonds. That's especially true if the total return takes into account changes in the cost of living. In the 1970s, for example, bond yields were quite high relative to long-run averages. Yet bond returns were quite abysmal because of capital losses. As inflation and interest rates rose over the decade, existing bonds fell in value. So the total return on these bonds, including capital gains as well as coupons, was far lower than the coupons themselves. Returns on bonds in the 1970s were lower still when adjusted for inflation.

The fixed income of bond investments is illusory in countries with high inflation. It is also often illusory for securities with high default risk. So it's useful to begin with a discussion of what determines the interest rate on a bond. This discussion will help to explain why bond returns are so miserably low in some periods, particularly when adjusted for inflation, and why they are surprisingly high in other periods. Two important determinants of bond yields are (expected) inflation rates and (expected) default rates. The discussion of default risk will be postponed until later in this part by first focusing on U.S. government bonds with little if any default risk.

Treasury Bonds

How does inflation affect interest rates? In the short run, central banks often play a critical role in setting short-term interest rates. For example, the Federal Reserve

FIGURE 5.25   Inflation and U.S. Treasury Bond Yields, 1949–2009
Data Source: IMF, International Financial Statistics.

directly controls the Federal Funds interest rate, the rate at which banks borrow in the inter-bank market. And other short-term dollar interest rates, such as the commercial paper and Treasury bill interest rates in the United States or the LIBOR rate on dollar deposits in London, are loosely linked to the Fed Funds rate.[1] So if the Fed raises the Fed Funds rate by 25 basis points, or 0.25 percent, the commercial paper and Treasury bill rates and LIBOR are likely to rise by a similar amount (in normal times, at least). In the long-run, however, the role of the Federal Reserve is very different. In the long run, U.S. interest rates are primarily determined by inflation. And it is the Fed's role in helping to determine the inflation rate that matters.

Consider the history of U.S. interest rates since the late 1940s as shown in Figure 5.25. Except for a temporary bout of inflation during the Korean War, inflation remained low in the United States until the late 1960s and 1970s. Inflation peaked following two oil price shocks in 1973 and 1974 and 1979. Beginning in the late 1960s, interest rates slowly but surely responded to rising inflation as inflation expectations became imbedded in bond yields. The same inflation expectations led to rising wage demands and to downward pressure on the U.S. dollar. To lower interest yields from their highs in the late 1970s, it was necessary for the Federal Reserve to pursue a tight monetary policy. This shift in policy began with the appointment of Paul Volcker as Fed chair in 1979. The low interest rates that we experience today were made at the Fed. But in the long run, low interest rates result from low inflation, not from the Fed lowering the Fed Funds rate.

To provide further evidence of the link between inflation and interest rates, consider the bond *returns* earned on long-term Treasury bonds in each decade since 1950 as shown in Figure 5.26. This chart shows the nominal bond return, the inflation rate, and the real bond return. The latter is obtained by deflating the nominal

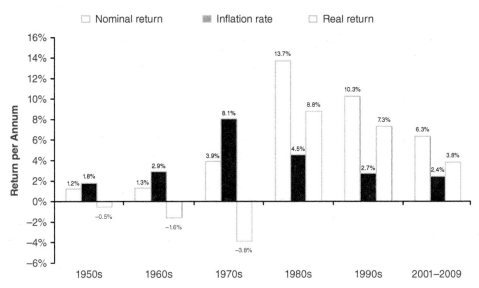

FIGURE 5.26 Nominal and Real Treasury Bond Returns by Decade
Data Source: ©Morningstar.

return by the inflation rate.[2] The low bond yields of the 1950s were matched by almost equally low inflation. The net result was a real bond return that was (slightly) negative. Over the next two decades, inflation expectations evidently lagged behind actual inflation so bond holders earned negative real bond returns of −1.6 percent and −3.8 percent, respectively! Fixed income earners were deceived by the steadiness of the coupons on their bonds. The real value of the bonds was being eroded by inflation, and the coupons themselves were being debased by rising price levels.

The terrific returns earned since 1981 are a direct result of the Fed's policy of fighting inflation. Over this period, bond yields and inflation expectations lagged behind actual inflation once again. But in this case, bond holders were surprised by falling inflation and they were rewarded with unusually large real returns on their bonds. In the decade from 1981 to 1990, the compound real return on the long-term (20-year) Treasury bond was 8.8 percent. That return was followed by a 7.3 percent compound return in the 1990s. Those returns are to be expected when inflation falls from 13.5 percent to its current level and when bond yields fall from almost 15 percent to less than 5 percent.

It's important for investors to realize how fundamental is the link between inflation and interest rates. Consider the experience of the major industrial countries over the last few decades. All of these countries have benefited from a decline in inflation and a decline in interest rates since 1980. So the triumph of the Federal Reserve over inflation was matched by similar victories in the other industrial countries. In Europe, the fight against inflation was spurred on by currency regimes that sought to limit exchange rate changes between European countries. In particular, the planned introduction of the Euro in 1999 forced countries to cut inflation in order to qualify for the currency union.[3] But despite these pressures, European countries differed widely in their inflation rates as did the other industrial countries. Between 1981

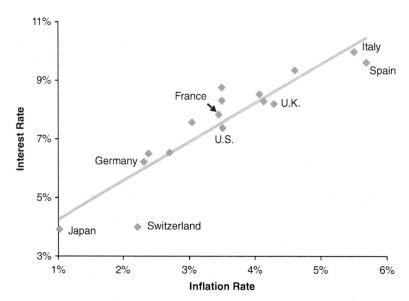

FIGURE 5.27   Interest Rates and Inflation Rates of the Major Industrial Countries, 1981–2008
Data Source: IMF, International Financial Statistics.

and 2008, inflation rates as measured by the consumer price index ranged from an average of 2.3 percent in Germany to 5.7 percent in Spain. Two countries outside the European Union, Japan and Switzerland, had even lower inflation rates than Germany, Japan's being only 1.0 percent.

The wide range of inflation rates was matched by an equally wide range of interest rates. Consider Figure 5.27, which shows the array of interest rates and inflation rates in 16 industrial countries between 1981 and 2008. If all of these countries maintained the same real interest rates throughout, they would all lie along a line. In practice, some countries have higher interest rates than their inflation rates justify, while others have lower interest rates.

The extreme case is that of Switzerland, which has an average inflation rate of 2.2 percent and an average interest rate of only 4.0 percent. The United States, in contrast, has an average inflation rate of 3.5 percent and an average interest rate of 7.4 percent. Despite these differences, Figure 5.27 shows a very clear link between inflation and interest rates in the long run. It's important to keep this in mind when considering bond returns earned over equally long periods.

Besides inflation, interest rates on Treasury bonds vary by maturity. In most periods, the term structure of interest rates is upward sloping. That is, longer maturity issues pay higher yields than those with shorter maturity. Consider Figure 5.28, which shows the term structure of yields on U.S. Treasury bonds in three different years, 1985, 1995, and 2005. In all three years the economy was growing, so the term structure of yields had its normal upward slope. (If a recession had occurred in one of these years, the term structure of yields could have been inverted temporarily.) Over the two decades shown in the figure, inflation and interest rates were dropping. So the whole term structure of yields fell over time. Thus the figure illustrates two

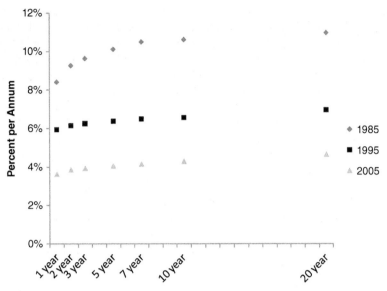

FIGURE 5.28   Term Structure of Treasury Bond Yields
Data Source: Federal Reserve Board.

of the three determinants of bond yields, inflation and the maturity of the bond. The third factor, default risk, is negligible in the case of Treasuries.

Bond yields are only one component of bond returns. Bond *returns* reflect both the coupon paid and the capital gain over the holding period of the return. If C is the coupon on a Treasury bond and B_{t-1} is the price of the bond at the end of the previous period, then the bond return during period t, R_t, is given by:

$$R_t = C/B_{t-1} + (B_t/B_{t-1} - 1)$$

The first term is the coupon price ratio and the second term is the capital gain on the bond during period t. Table 5.19 reports bond returns for two maturities of

TABLE 5.19   Treasury Bonds by Maturity

Maturity	Coupon Yield	Capital Gain	Total Return	Standard Deviation	Sharpe Ratio
1951–2009					
Long-term	6.3%	0.0%	6.3%	9.5%	0.17
Medium-term	5.9%	0.3%	6.2%	5.0%	0.29
1981–2009					
Long-term	7.4%	3.0%	10.4%	11.1%	0.47
Medium-term	6.6%	1.8%	8.4%	5.3%	0.60

The Treasury returns reported are for long-term 20-year bonds, and medium-term five-year bonds.
Data Source: ©Morningstar.

U.S. Treasuries. The long-term bond is a 20-year Treasury bond, while the medium-term is a five-year Treasury. First consider returns over the whole period since 1951. The long-term bond has higher volatility with a standard deviation of 9.5 percent compared with one of 5.0 percent for the medium-term issue. Over this long period, however, investors were not compensated for this higher volatility since the return on the long-term bond was only marginally higher than on the medium-term bond.

In periods of falling interest rates, such as those in the 1980s until present, long-term bonds should outperform medium-term bonds. That is indeed the case if performance is measured only in terms of returns. In Table 5.19, the return on the 20-year bond is 2.0 percent higher than on the 5-year bond during the period from 1981 to 2009. During this period, the capital gain component of the bond return contributed 3.0 percent to the total return. But the standard deviation of the 20-year bond is still substantially higher than that of the five-year bond, so the Sharpe ratio for the longer-term issue is still much lower than for the medium-term issue. So even in a period of falling interest rates, the 20-year bond seems to be dominated by the five-year bond. That's true at least if investors are focusing on one-year horizon returns. For investors with long-term liabilities, however, the 20-year bond may be the most attractive alternative. Such investors might be able to match long-term liabilities with long-term assets, thereby minimizing the volatility of their net asset positions.

The Wider U.S. Bond Market

At the end of 2008, the U.S. bond market encompassed securities with a total market value of $33.5 trillion (or $33,500 billion) according to the Securities Industry and Financial Markets Association.[4] Figure 5.29 shows the breakdown of fixed income securities as of the end of 2008. U.S. Treasury securities represent only 17.7 percent of the U.S. market. Municipal bonds (issued by local as well as state governments)

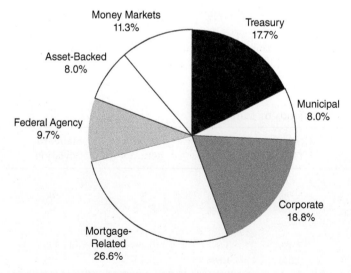

FIGURE 5.29   U.S. Bond Market in 2008

Source: Securities Industry and Financial Markets Association, 2009.

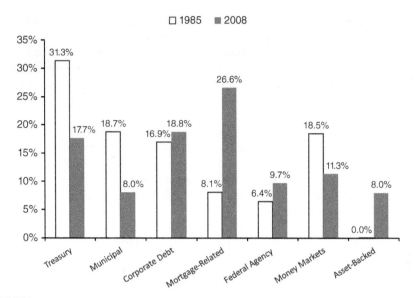

☐ 1985   ■ 2008

FIGURE 5.30   U.S. Bond Market in 1985 and 2008
Source: Securities Industry and Financial Markets Association, 2009.

represent 8.0 percent of the market, while corporate debt represents another 18.8 percent. Mortgage-related securities, 26.6 percent of the market, include those issued by the government agencies Fannie Mae and Freddie Mac as well as collateralized mortgage obligations (CMOs). Federal agency securities, 9.7 percent of the market, are nonmortgage obligations of agencies like the Federal Farm Loan Mortgage Corporation and the Student Loan Marketing Association. Money market securities and asset-backed bonds round out the rest.

The relative importance of Treasury bonds has declined over time because other bond markets have grown more rapidly. Part of this growth is due to financial innovation that has led to the securitization of assets that were previously held in bank balance sheets such as mortgages and commercial loans. Figure 5.30 shows how the bond market since 1985 has shifted away from Treasury securities toward other types of bonds that were relatively unimportant then. Thus Treasuries have shrunk from 31.3 percent of the U.S. bond market to only 17.7 percent as of 2008. Mortgage-related bonds have grown from 8.1 percent to 26.6 percent of the total. Asset-backed bonds, which didn't exist in 1985, are now 8.0 percent of the total.

Because most of the bonds shown in Figure 5.29 have higher default risk than U.S. Treasury bonds, their bond yields are correspondingly higher (adjusted for maturity). Consider the default premiums for investment grade corporate bonds. Both Standard & Poor's and Moody's rate the default risk on corporate bonds. According to the classification by Moody's, investment grade bonds are rated in four categories ranging from AAA to BAA. Over the period from 1980 to 2005, the 10-year Treasury bond had an average yield of 7.7 percent.[5] Over the same period, the yield on the highest rated of these corporate bonds, those with an AAA rating, averaged 8.8 percent for a premium of 1.1 percent over Treasuries.[6] The yields on the lowest-rated investment grade bonds, those with a BAA rating, had an average yield of 9.9 percent, so the premium over Treasuries was 2.2 percent and the premium over the highest grade corporate bonds was 1.1 percent. These premiums give some indication of the importance of default risk in the pricing of non-Treasury bonds.

Default risk is of utmost importance in pricing so-called high-yield bonds. Until the 1980s, the high-yield market consisted primarily of fallen angels, bonds that were originally issued as investment grade but had fallen below investment grade because of poor financial performance. It was only in the 1980s that investment banks such as Drexel Burnham saw the potential for issuing non-investment grade (or junk) bonds to provide financing for firms with weaker credit standing. Since then, the high-yield market has become an important part of the overall corporate bond market in the United States. According to Altman and Karlin (2008), the high-yield market at the end of 2007 totaled $1,090 billion in outstanding issues. SIFMA reports that total corporate debt outstanding in 2007 was $6,281 billion, so high yield represents about 17 percent of total corporate debt.

Figure 5.31 displays the default rates for high-yield bonds. The average default rate between 1984 and 2009 was 4.1 percent. This default rate varies widely over time, however, since recessions force many firms into financial distress. The effects of the Gulf War recession of 1990 to 1991 and the 2001 recession are evident in the high default rates shown on the graph. Notice that the recession that began in December 2007 saw only a modest rise in default rates in 2008 but then defaults rose to more than 10 percent in 2009.

The spreads of high-yield bonds over Treasury bonds also vary over time, through booms and busts. Figure 5.32 shows these spreads from 1985 through early 2009. The effects of the three recessions during this period are evident in the figure. During the Gulf War recession of 1991 to 1992 and during the 2001 recession, the

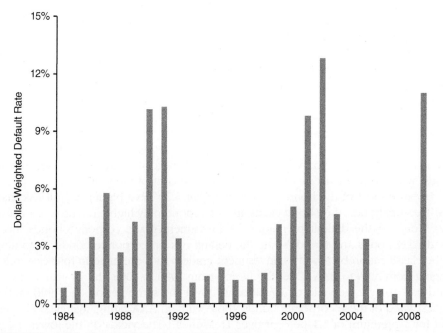

FIGURE 5.31   High-Yield Default Rates, 1984–2009

Data Source: JP Morgan.

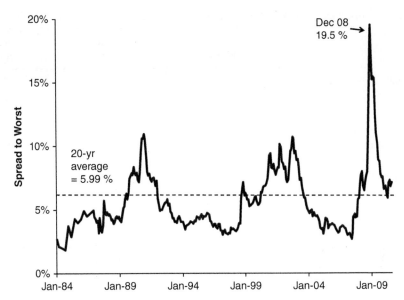

FIGURE 5.32   Spread of High-Yield Bonds over Treasuries
Data Source: JP Morgan.

spread rose more than 10 percent. In the recession beginning in December 2007, the spread reached almost 20 percent in late 2008 despite seeing relatively few defaults in that year. Such a high spread probably reflects as much the illiquidity of the high-yield market during the financial crisis as it does the expectation of future defaults.

High-yield spreads reflect the *ex ante* default risk of a bond, but do not indicate the *ex post* returns that the investor receives from investing in that bond. These ex post returns are measured using the Barclays Capital High-Yield index, which begins in July 1983. The returns on some of the other types of bonds shown in Figure 5.29 can be measured using indexes extending back into the 1980s or earlier. Corporate bond returns are one of the series provided in the SBBI Yearbooks with returns beginning in 1926 like the rest of the Morningstar series. Mortgage-backed bonds have a return series from Merrill Lynch beginning in 1976. Finally, there is a widely used investment-grade bond index called the Barclays Capital Aggregate Index (formerly the Lehman Aggregate Index).[7] This series also begins in 1976.

Returns on U.S. Bonds

The natural question to ask is: how well have non-Treasury bonds performed over time? Table 5.20 provides an analysis. Since bond returns begin at different times, each series is compared with the five-year medium term Treasury bond *over a common period*. In Table 5.20, there are three periods studied, each corresponding to the period over which a bond series is available:

1951–2009: Corporate Bond Index from Morningstar
1983–2009: Barclays Capital High-Yield Bond Index
1976–2009: Barclays Capital Aggregate Bond Index and Merrill Lynch Mortgage-backed Bond Index

TABLE 5.20   Comparisons between Medium-Term U.S. Treasuries and Other Bonds

Period	Average Return	Standard Deviation	Sharpe Ratio
1951-2009			
Medium-Term Treasury	6.2%	5.1%	0.29
Corporate Bond	6.5%	8.6%	0.21
July 1983–December 2009			
Medium-Term Treasury	7.7%	5.0%	0.62
High-Yield Bond	9.3%	8.8%	0.53
1976–2009			
Medium-Term Treasury	8.0%	5.8%	0.42
Mortgage-Backed Bond	8.6%	7.0%	0.44
Barclays Aggregate Bond	8.2%	5.7%	0.47

Data Sources: ©Morningstar for Medium-Term Treasuries and Corporate Bonds. Barclays Capital for the High-Yield and Aggregate Indexes and Merrill Lynch for the Mortgage-Backed Bond Index.

As shown in Table 5.20, non-Treasury bonds generally provide higher returns than Treasury bonds, at least over the long periods studied in the table. But risks (as measured by standard deviations) are also higher for these bonds. The last column of the table reports the Sharpe ratio for each series. The Sharpe ratios for corporate bonds and high-yield bonds are lower than that of the medium-term Treasury bond, while the Sharpe ratio for mortgage-backed bonds is a little higher.[8]

Bonds should also be evaluated in a portfolio setting just like any other asset. Table 5.21 reports the correlations between the major bond indexes and the medium-term Treasury bond. The last column of the table also reports the correlations with the S&P 500. Generally speaking, all of the U.S. bonds are highly correlated with Treasuries except for the high-yield series. The correlations are 0.70 or more for long-term Treasuries, (high-grade) corporate bonds, and mortgage-backed bonds. High-yield bonds have a near zero correlation of −0.02 with MT Treasuries because

TABLE 5.21   Correlations, 1985–2009

Bond Type	Correlation with Medium-Term Treasury Bond	Correlation with S&P 500
Medium-Term Treasuries	1.00	0.02
Long-Term Treasuries	0.84	0.11
Corporate Bonds	0.70	0.23
Mortgage-Backed	0.82	0.16
High-Yield	−0.02	0.56
Barclays Aggregate	0.88	0.21
Foreign Bonds	0.42	0.01

The bond indexes used are the Medium-Term and Long-Term Treasury Bond and Corporate Bond indexes from ©Morningstar, the High-Yield and Aggregate Bond indexes from Barclays Capital, the Mortgage-Backed Bond index from Merrill Lynch, and the Citigroup non-dollar World Bond Index.

the high-yield market is so cyclically sensitive. (We will postpone discussion of the foreign government series until the last section of this part.)

Bonds are often part of a larger portfolio with substantial allocations to stocks. So it's interesting to consider the correlations between the bond indexes and the S&P 500. It's clear from Table 5.21 that all of the bonds have relatively low correlation with stocks except for the high-yield series. The correlation between high-yield bonds and the S&P 500 is 0.56, so the diversification benefits of bonds in a portfolio heavily weighted toward stocks are certainly reduced when high-yield bonds are involved.

How much difference does it make if an investor diversifies a bond portfolio? This is an interesting question that an investment advisor often faces when the choice is between investing in a bond fund that is well diversified and investing in a narrow set of bonds directly. Consider the following experiment: An investor chooses between investment in the medium-term Treasury bond or the diversified Barclays Capital Aggregate Bond Index, the index described earlier that has only 23.9 percent in U.S. Treasuries. The Barclays Aggregate gives the investor exposure to corporate bonds (17.2 percent) as well as mortgage-backed bonds (44.8 percent) in addition to other investment-grade bonds. The comparison is shown in Table 5.20. Over the period from 1976 to 2009, the Barclays Aggregate has a return 0.2 percent higher than that of the medium-term U.S. Treasury bond, but the standard deviation is 0.1 percent lower. So the Sharpe ratio is higher. Alpha* allows us to compare the two bond investments after adjusting the Barclays Aggregate for the slightly higher level of risk associated with the Treasury bond. The investor gains an extra 0.3 percent excess return by investing in the Barclays Aggregate.[9] So the gains from diversification are evident even though most of these bonds are highly correlated.

Bond Markets Outside the United States

The world's bond markets have grown enormously in the last few decades. According to the Bank for International Settlements, the total value of all bonds outstanding as of September 2008 was $82.5 trillion.[10] This compares with a market capitalization of $54.2 trillion for the world's stock markets (at the end of 2007). The relative size of the world bond markets is shown in Figure 5.33. The U.S. bond market represents 31.3 percent of this total capitalization. But there are also major bond markets in the Euro area, Japan, and other industrial countries. All together, these national bond markets represent another 33.0 percent of the world market. The bond markets of the developing (or emerging market) countries add another 8.1 percent to the world's total. The remaining 27.6 percent are international bonds.

In addition to traditional national bond markets, there are parallel bond markets called international bond markets where most investors are offshore investors, but where borrowers can be from any country including the United States. Take the example of a U.S. dollar international bond issued in London by an American company with American and foreign underwriters and investors who are predominantly foreign. Twenty years ago, this bond would have been described as a Eurobond because it was underwritten in Europe, but today it is less confusing to call this dollar bond an international bond.[11] Since now there are no significant capital controls separating the U.S. bond market from the international bond market, an international bond issued by an American company will be almost identical in yield and

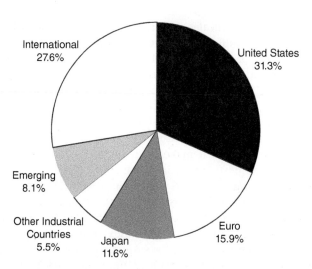

FIGURE 5.33   World Bond Markets, 2008 (Total Size of the World Bond Market in 2008 = $82.5 trillion)

Source: Bank for International Settlements, 2009.

price to a bond issued by the same company in the United States (as long as both bonds are denominated in dollars). The major difference between the two bonds is in ownership, since there are restrictions on sales of international bonds to U.S. residents. International bonds cannot be offered to Americans when they are first issued because these bonds have not been registered with the U.S. Securities and Exchange Commission. Some institutional investors buy these issues in the secondary market, but international bonds are primarily sold to foreign not American investors.[12]

This book is focused on investing, not borrowing, so the analysis to follow will ignore international bonds entirely. Instead, we will study investments in the national bond markets of foreign industrial countries.[13] These are the traditional national bond markets of countries like the United Kingdom and Japan. Many of these bonds are government bonds issued by the national governments of the countries involved, but there are also corporate bonds much like we find in the U.S. market. Almost all such national bonds are denominated in that country's currency. In Figure 5.33, these traditional national markets represent 33 percent of world bond markets or $27.2 trillion as of 2008.

The introduction of the Euro in 1999 led to consolidation of the bond markets of the 12 countries initially joining the European Union.[14] So instead of having separate bond markets (and separate trading centers) in countries like Germany and France, there was now a single market located in London with much-enhanced liquidity. As shown in Figure 5.33, the Euro area bond market is 15.9 percent of the world bond market, or roughly half the size of the U.S. national market.[15] Among foreign national bond markets, the Euro bond market is particularly attractive to Americans because it is the largest and most liquid foreign national bond market.

Interest rates on foreign bonds vary widely by country. First, interest rates are directly influenced by national inflation rates as shown earlier in Figure 5.27. These inflation rates vary widely by country depending upon the monetary policies of the central banks. Second, interest rates reflect the sovereign risk of the countries issuing the securities. For most of the sample period, the bonds of the industrial countries had little default risk. The government bonds of most of these countries carried AAA or AA ratings. That was true at least until the Greek crisis in 2010 when concerns about defaults in Europe led to default premiums for several national markets.

The returns on foreign bonds depend upon the currency in which they are measured. In their own local currencies, the returns are dependent on coupon yields and capital gains, just as in the case of U.S. bonds. But when measured in dollars, the returns on foreign bonds also depend on the capital gains or losses on the foreign currency itself. Thus the return on a foreign bond received by a U.S. domestic investor consists of two elements, the return expressed in foreign currency compounded by the capital gain on the currency. If $R_€$ is the return on a Euro-denominated bond *in Euros* and if R_X is the capital gain on the Euro, then the return on this bond as viewed by a dollar-based investor is given by

$$\text{Return in } \$ = \left(1 + R_€\right) * \left(1 + R_X\right) - 1$$

Returns on foreign bonds will be enhanced during periods when foreign currencies are rising against the dollar just as they benefit from rising bond prices within the Euro markets themselves.

Consider the returns on some of the major government bond markets as reported in Table 5.22. The bond indexes represented in the table are Citigroup indexes measured in dollars from 1987 through 2009. Also included in the table is a broader foreign bond index provided by Citigroup called the Non-U.S. Dollar World Government Bond Index. This index is a world-ex-U.S. government bond index representing the government bond markets of 21 industrial countries. All of the government bonds are denominated in domestic currency and each market represented has at least $20 billion in capitalization.[16] For comparison purposes, the returns on the two SBBI U.S. government bonds series, those for five-year medium-term bonds and 20-year long-term bonds, are also reported.

The first column of the table reports the average returns on each bond series, while the second column reports the standard deviations. All of the average returns

TABLE 5.22   Returns on Foreign and U.S. Government Bonds Measured in U.S. Dollars, 1987–2009

Bond Market	Average Return	Standard Deviation	Sharpe Ratio
France	9.3%	11.0%	0.47
Germany	8.1%	11.4%	0.35
Japan	7.1%	12.8%	0.23
Switzerland	7.2%	12.2%	0.25
United Kingdom	9.3%	11.4%	0.45
Non-Dollar World	8.1%	9.6%	0.41
U.S. Medium-Term	6.7%	4.8%	0.54
U.S. Long-Term	8.4%	9.9%	0.44

The foreign government bond series are all Citigroup indexes measured in dollars. The Non-Dollar World index is a 21-nation series. The U.S. government bond series are the Medium-Term (5-year) and Long-Term (20-year) indexes from Morningstar.
Data Sources: Citigroup and ©Morningstar.

for the foreign bond markets exceed those of the medium-term U.S. Treasury. The French and U.K. returns also exceed those of the long-term U.S. Treasury. But all of the standard deviations of the foreign bond indexes are much higher than those of medium-term U.S. bond and only the (non-dollar) World index has a lower standard deviation than the long-term U.S. Treasury. There is no doubt that the high volatility of the foreign bond returns is primarily caused by the volatility of the exchange rates used to translate local currency returns into dollars. Exchange rates are extremely volatile. In fact, the standard deviations for the foreign exchange gains and losses range from 10.0 percent for the dollar to pound exchange rate to 11.5 percent for the dollar to Swiss franc rate.[17] These foreign bonds may be too volatile to be attractive to an American investor as an *alternative* to U.S. Treasury bonds. That is even true of the diversified World Index, which has a return of 8.1 percent and a standard deviation of 9.6 percent. The Sharpe ratio for the World Index is much lower than that of the medium-term U.S. Treasury bond.

Yet foreign bonds are unlikely to be viewed as an *alternative* to U.S. bonds by any American investor. Instead, they might be considered as a *complement* to U.S. bonds in a well-diversified bond portfolio. How well do foreign bonds fare in a portfolio context? Table 5.21 indicates that the foreign bond index, which is the Non-U.S. Dollar World Government Bond index from Citigroup, has a relatively low correlation of 0.42 with the U.S. Treasury bond and a correlation of 0.01 with the S&P 500. Both correlations are attractive enough to consider adding foreign bonds to a U.S. portfolio.

Table 5.23 reports the gains from diversifying a U.S. bond portfolio by adding a 20 percent allocation to foreign bonds. The second row of the table reports the returns on a portfolio that has 20 percent in the Citigroup non-dollar World Government Bond Index and 80 percent in the Barclays Aggregate. The results are modest. The average return on the diversified U.S.-foreign bond portfolio is 0.4 percent higher than the portfolio based on the Barclays Aggregate Index alone, but the standard deviation is also higher. The net result is a Sharpe ratio of 0.84 for the diversified portfolio versus a Sharpe ratio of 0.81 for the Barclays Aggregate alone. This translates into an excess return, or alpha*, for the portfolio with foreign bonds of only 0.1 percent. A reasonable interpretation of this result is that investors have made most of their diversification gains by moving from U.S. Treasuries to the Barclays Aggregate mix of U.S. bonds. There is only a modest gain from diversifying further into foreign bonds.

TABLE 5.23   Effects of Diversifying a Bond Portfolio with Foreign Bonds, 1985–2009

	Average Return	Standard Deviation	Sharpe Ratio
Barclays Aggregate	7.9%	4.3%	0.81
Portfolio with Unhedged Foreign Bonds	8.3%	4.7%	0.84
Portfolio with Hedged Foreign Bonds	7.7%	3.9%	0.86

Notes: The diversified portfolios with foreign bonds consist of 80 percent in the Barclays Aggregate and 20 percent in the Citigroup non-dollar World Government Bond Index. The second row has the unhedged world index of foreign bonds and the third row has the hedged world index.
Data Sources: Barclays Capital and Citigroup.

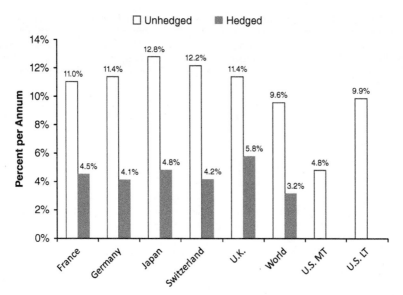

FIGURE 5.34 Standard Deviations of Government Bond Returns in Dollars, Hedged and Unhedged, 1987–2009

Data Sources: Citigroup, ©Morningstar, and IMF (for foreign exchange rates).

If foreign currency capital gains and losses raise the standard deviation of the foreign bond return, perhaps there is a case for hedging the currency risk. We will consider the simplest type of currency hedge where the foreign currency value of the bond investment at the beginning of the period is hedged using a forward contract. In that case, the hedged return consists of the return on the bond in local currency plus the forward premium on the hedge.

How much does the hedge reduce the risk of the foreign bond investment? Figure 5.34 compares the standard deviations of the Citigroup foreign government bond indexes before and after hedging. Hedging has a dramatic effect on the risk of a foreign bond investment. In the case of French bonds, for example, the standard deviation falls from 11.1 percent to 4.5 percent. For the Citigroup non-dollar World Government Bond Index, the standard deviation is cut by two-thirds.[18] All but two of the standard deviations of the hedged foreign bond series are below that of even the U.S. medium-term bond. So, unlike in the case of foreign stocks, hedging foreign bonds greatly reduces the risk faced by an American investor. Since currencies are highly correlated with the returns on foreign bonds *expressed in dollars,* hedging the currency risk sharply reduces the risk of the foreign bond investment.

Table 5.24 reports the returns on the hedged investments in foreign bonds. For all foreign bonds studied, returns on the hedged investments are lower than those on the unhedged investments because the dollar fell against many currencies over this time period. Hedge positions should not necessarily provide gains or losses in the long run (unless there are risk premiums on one currency or another). But over a particular sample period, a hedge may provide either gains or losses for an investor based in any particular currency. Over the 23 years ending in 2009, a dollar-based investor *selling* foreign currencies to hedge bond investments lost money on hedges

TABLE 5.24   Hedged Returns on Foreign and U.S. Government Bonds, 1987–2009

Bond Market	Average Return	Standard Deviation	Sharpe Ratio
France	6.7%	4.5%	0.56
Germany	6.3%	4.1%	0.52
Japan	7.0%	4.8%	0.59
Switzerland	6.2%	4.2%	0.50
United Kingdom	6.2%	5.8%	0.36
Non-Dollar World	6.8%	3.2%	0.86
U.S. Medium-Term	6.7%	4.8%	0.54
U.S. Long-Term	8.4%	9.9%	0.44

Notes: The hedged return is obtained by selling an equivalent amount of foreign currency in the forward market at the beginning of each period. In the case of the Citigroup world index, the hedge adjusts for any cash flows expected during the period.
Data Sources: Citigroup, ©Morningstar, and IMF (for foreign exchange rates).

involving the major currencies. The hedge for the world index lost 1.3 percent per year on average over this period.

Table 5.24 also reports the standard deviations and Sharpe ratios of the hedged investments. With standard deviations so low, the foreign bond returns generally have Sharpe ratios higher than that of the unhedged foreign bond series. In some cases, these Sharpe ratios are also higher than those of the U.S. Treasury bond indexes. Consider the world index hedged for exchange risk. By hedging, the return falls from 8.1 percent to 6.8 percent, but the standard deviation falls from 9.6 percent to 3.2 percent. The Sharpe ratio rises sharply to 0.86, far above that of the U.S. bond indexes.

Hedging the currency risk does raise the correlation between the foreign bond and U.S. bonds and stocks. The correlation with the medium-term Treasury bond rises from 0.42 to 0.61. That should not be surprising since a lot of the advantage of the foreign bond as a diversifier stems from the foreign currency component of the bond return, and hedging all but eliminates this factor from the bond investment. Consider the portfolio experiment again reported in Table 5.23 where foreign bonds are mixed with the Barclays Aggregate. If the foreign bond index is hedged, the resulting portfolio has a smaller standard deviation (3.9 percent rather than 4.3 percent for the Barclays Aggregate alone). The Sharpe ratio of the portfolio containing hedged foreign bonds is 0.86 versus 0.81 for the Barclays portfolio alone. The diversified portfolio delivers an excess return, or alpha*, of only 0.2 percent compared with the Barclays Aggregate alone. That is a very modest gain for international diversification of the bond portfolio!

What is the conclusion of all of this evidence regarding foreign bonds? The answer has to be that it is probably worthwhile to include bonds from foreign industrial countries in a diversified bond portfolio. Foreign bonds won't dramatically alter the performance of such a portfolio, but there is a marginal improvement in risk-adjusted returns. There is a strong case for hedging the foreign bonds if the investor is concerned about the *volatility* of foreign bond investments, since hedging reduces that volatility quite dramatically. The case for hedging is less compelling if foreign bonds are viewed as a component of an otherwise well-diversified portfolio.

Summary—Key Features of Bonds

Above all else, bond returns depend upon inflation. In the long run, inflation affects the yield offered on bonds. This link can be illustrated by studying the variation over time of interest rates and inflation in the United States or by studying the close link between average interest rates and average inflation rates in the industrial countries. Inflation also profoundly affects the real returns on bonds, especially in periods when inflation is rising or falling significantly as in the 1970s and 1980s. Real bond returns were unusually low in the 1970s (and even earlier) because bond yields failed to keep pace with inflation expectations. Similarly, the sharp downturn in inflation since the early 1980s has led to unusually high real bond returns.

Bond returns in the United States vary by type of bond. Over the last few decades, the bond market has evolved extensively as new classes of securities have emerged. The introduction of mortgage-backed bonds in the 1970s, high-yield debt in the 1980s, and other securitized debt in the 1980s and 1990s has greatly expanded the scope of the U.S. bond market. The returns on these new classes of bonds have fallen in line with those of the existing Treasury and corporate issues, at least when measured on a risk-adjusted basis. But their introduction has allowed investors to further diversify their portfolios. The gains from diversification are reasonably large.

Diversification into foreign bonds also makes some sense. The bonds of foreign industrial countries share many of the same characteristics as U.S. bonds, but their returns vary widely because of their (foreign) currency denomination. When these bonds are left unhedged, their standard deviations are very high (when measured in dollars for a U.S. investor). But hedging can reduce risk by almost two-thirds. And when these bonds are included in a diversified bond portfolio, even the unhedged bonds help to reduce risk, although only modestly.

Notes

1. LIBOR stands for the London Inter-bank Offer Rate in the dollar deposit market in London. The LIBOR market is one of the largest money markets in the world. The LIBOR rate serves as a benchmark for many interest rate contracts, including many floating rate mortgages in the United States.
2. The real return is defined as $(1 + \text{nominal return})/(1 + \text{inflation rate}) - 1$.
3. The European Monetary System (EMS), introduced in 1979, committed countries to maintaining their exchange rates within bands relative to fixed rates. But the EMS did not prevent countries from occasionally realigning their fixed rates by devaluing or revaluing their exchange rates with other partner countries, so inflation varied widely across the EMS countries. It was the Maastricht Treaty of 1991, setting Europe on a path toward monetary union in 1999, that spurred the high-inflation countries like Italy and Spain to reign in their monetary policies to qualify for the union.
4. SIFMA, Outstanding U.S. Bond Market Debt, SIFMA website table, March 2009.
5. The yields are reported in the IMF, International Financial Statistics (CD data set), May 2007.
6. The annual data for corporate yields are reported by www.bondmarkets.com. It would be misleading to attribute all of this gap of corporate yields over Treasury

yields to default risk since U.S. Treasuries have a state income tax advantage not afforded to corporate bonds. According to the U.S. Constitution, U.S. Treasuries are exempt from state and local taxes. If the marginal investor in U.S. Treasuries is a taxable U.S. resident, then the interest yield on Treasuries reflects this tax advantage.

7. As of the end of October 2008, this index had 23.9 percent in Treasuries, 13.5 percent in government-related bonds, 17.2 percent in corporate bonds, 44.8 percent in mortgage-backed bonds, and less than 1 percent in ABS. 81.4 percent of this index represented AAA-rated bonds. Source: www.barcap.com/indices.

8. Recall that the Treasury bond is free of state and local taxes, so the relative returns may reflect tax factors as well as default risk.

9. Alpha* = (0.47–0.42)*0.057 = 0.3%.

10. This figure is obtained by aggregating the national bond markets and international bond markets as reported on the Bank for International Settlements website (http://www.bis.org/statistics/secstats.htm).

11. The Eurobond or international bond market was initially developed to allow U.S. and foreign companies to raise debt financing in foreign markets to fund their foreign operations. Since many countries had capital controls inhibiting the flow of financing from their domestic markets, the international bond market offered a way to finance the multinational operations of these companies. Capital controls have largely been abolished in the industrial countries, so this market is now closely integrated with the national bond market in the same currency.

12. See Solnik and McLeavy (2004), Chapter 7.

13. Recall that Part III analyzed the bonds of emerging markets.

14. The countries adopting the Euro in 1999 included France, Germany, Belgium, Luxembourg, the Netherlands, Italy, Spain, Portugal, Ireland, Austria, and Finland. Greece joined in 2002. The 12 countries had only 11 bond markets because Belgium and Luxembourg shared a common currency even before the Union.

15. Both markets would be larger if international bonds issued in dollars and Euros, respectively, were included in the totals.

16. Most of the bonds have AAA or AA credit quality. The 21 countries represented in the index are Australia, Austria, Belgium, Canada, Denmark, Finland, France, Germany, Greece, Ireland, Italy, Japan, the Netherlands, Norway, Poland, Portugal, Singapore, Spain, Sweden, Switzerland, and the United Kingdom.

17. These standard deviations are measured for the capital gain/loss factor in the equation in the text, R_X.

18. Citigroup provides a hedged version of its 21-nation world (non-U.S.) government bond index. According to Citigroup (2006), the hedge is designed to offset not only the value of the investment at period $t-1$ but also any expected cash flows between $t-1$ and t.

References

Solnik, Bruno, and Dennis McLeavey. 2004. *International Investments*, 5th ed. Boston: Pearson Addison Wesley.

Citigroup. 2006. "Citigroup Global Fixed-Income Index Catalog—2006 Edition." August 31.

CHAPTER 6

Attributes of Risk

The concept of "risk" is defined in many different ways, is feared by most investors, and is often misunderstood. At a most basic level, risk can be described as the possibility of loss or that something unpleasant or bad will happen. Risk can also be described as the possibility that an expected outcome will not be achieved. Mathematically risk can be expressed as the "probability of loss" multiplied by "the expected loss," but investors often see risk simply as the chance that they will lose money. The concept and applications of risk are actually much more involved and complex, as one will see in this chapter.

It is the presence of risk that actually provides the potential or opportunity to gain in the financial markets. In a capitalistic or free-marketplace, risk is an essential component of growth, gain, and return. Without taking risk, investors should not experience the potential to gain anything other than some form of risk-free rate in a marketplace that is properly functioning. When looking at risk in this way, investors should see the positive side of risk (i.e., taking risk provides opportunity). Thus a critical responsibility of the investment advisor or consultant is to help clients understand, assess, and manage risk effectively.

The readings found in this chapter review the more common forms of risk. The authors also look at theoretical studies in risk, particularly as they pertain to financial markets and investments. The second reading looks at the probability of loss over different periods of time and provides mathematical examples to build a quantitative framework for better understanding risk.

Part I *Handbook of Finance:* Risks Associated with Investing

Learning Objectives

- Define "risk" and discuss the concept of "total risk" as it relates to measuring investment risk.
- Discuss the work of Harry Markowitz and the implications of diversification for managing risk.
- Define and differentiate between systematic and unsystematic risk.
- Describe inflation or purchasing power risk.
- Describe credit risk.
- Describe liquidity risk.

- Describe interest rate risk.
- Describe call/prepayment risk.
- Describe reinvestment risk.

Part II *The Handbook of Risk:* The Likelihood of Loss

Learning Objectives
- Discuss the concept and calculation of loss in a single period.
- Discuss the concept and calculation of a multiperiod annualized loss.
- Discuss the concept and calculation of a multiperiod cumulative loss.
- Discuss the concept and calculation of probability of at least one periodic loss.

Understanding the concept of risk and how it may be measured are however only the beginning of recommending appropriate investments and managing behavior. Investment advisors and consultants need to accurately assess the "risk tolerance" of their clients. There are many tools that may be used to determine an investor's ability to take risk and accurately identify one's sensitivity to risky outcomes. Such tools include volatility (or risk) tolerance questionnaires, investor profiles, and risk sensitivity simulations. Investment professionals therefore should be able to utilize tools and resources to help them better understand their clients' biases, sensitivity, and tolerance for risk.

An investor's history may also provide important insights to the financial professional. How did the investor react during periods of success in the past? Did he choose to take more risk (invest more aggressively) or did he sell some of his investment to capture gains (take money off the table)? How did the investor react during past periods of volatility and loss? Did he choose to sell everything when the investment did poorly (abandoning the long-term strategy), or did he choose to invest additional funds believing that he was buying at more favorable prices (double down)? An investor's history can often reveal the probability of behavior when he is faced with similar circumstances (positive and negative) in the future.

The field of behavioral economics/finance is another resource that investment advisors and consultants may use to better understand why investors think, feel, and behave the way that they do. To effectively manage risk, investment professionals should understand the various biases and mental heuristics individuals demonstrate and should learn to manage these behaviors in both themselves and their clients. This will be discussed in more detail in a later chapter.

An investment advisor or consultant may be skilled in recommending profitable investments, managing portfolios effectively, or consulting institutional clients prudently regarding the right asset allocation; but these activities may not be appropriate or even defendable if the advisor or consultant does not fully and accurately understand a client's understanding of and tolerance for risk.

Part I Risks Associated with Investing

There are various measures of risk. We will describe each of them here.

Total Risk

The dictionary defines risk as "hazard, peril, exposure to loss or injury." With respect to investments, investors have used a variety of definitions to describe risk. Today, the most commonly accepted definition of risk is one that involves a well-known statistical measure known as the variance. Specifically, investors quantify risk in terms of the variance of an asset's expected return. The variance of a random variable is a measure of the dispersion of the possible outcomes around the expected value. In the case of an asset's return, the variance is a measure of the dispersion of the possible outcomes for the return around the expected return.

There are two criticisms of the use of the variance as a measure of risk. The first criticism is that since the variance measures the dispersion of an asset's return around its expected value, it considers the possibility of returns above the expected return and below the expected return. Investors, however, do not view possible returns above the expected return as an unfavorable outcome. In fact, such outcomes are favorable. Because of this, some researchers have argued that measures of risk should not consider the possible returns above the expected return. Various measures of downside risk, such as risk of loss and value at risk, are currently being used by practitioners. The second criticism is that the variance is only one measure of how the returns vary around the expected return. When a probability distribution is not symmetrical around its expected return, then a statistical measure of the skewness of a distribution should be used in addition to the variance.

One way of reducing the risk associated with holding an individual security is by diversifying. Often, one hears investors talking about diversifying their portfolio. By this an investor means constructing a portfolio in such a way as to reduce portfolio risk without sacrificing return. This is certainly a goal that investors should seek. However, the question is, how does one do this in practice?

Some investors would say that a portfolio can be diversified by including assets across all asset classes. For example, one investor might argue that a portfolio should be diversified by investing in stocks, bonds, and real estate. While that might be reasonable, two questions must be addressed in order to construct a diversified portfolio. First, how much should be invested in each asset class? Should 40 percent of the portfolio be in stocks, 50 percent in bonds, and 10 percent in real estate, or is some other allocation more appropriate? Second, given the allocation, which specific stocks, bonds, and real estate should the investor select?

Some investors who focus only on one asset class such as common stock argue that such portfolios should also be diversified. By this they mean that an investor should not place all funds in the stock of one company, but rather should include stocks of many companies. Here, too, several questions must be answered in order to construct a diversified portfolio. First, which companies should be represented in the portfolio? Second, how much of the portfolio should be allocated to the stocks of each company?

Prior to the development of portfolio theory by Harry Markowitz (1952), while investors often talked about diversification in these general terms, they never provided the analytical tools by which to answer the questions posed here. Markowitz demonstrated that a diversification strategy should take into account the degree of covariance or correlation between asset returns in a portfolio. (The covariance or correlation of asset returns is a measure of the degree to which the returns on two assets vary or change together.) Indeed, a key contribution of what is now popularly referred to as "Markowitz diversification" or "mean-variance diversification" is the formulation of a security's risk in terms of a portfolio of securities, rather than the risk of an individual security. Markowitz diversification seeks to combine securities in a portfolio with returns that are less than perfectly positively correlated in an effort to lower portfolio risk (variance) without sacrificing return. It is the concern for maintaining return, while lowering risk through an analysis of the covariance between security returns, that separates Markowitz diversification from other approaches suggested for diversification and makes it more effective.

The principle of Markowitz diversification states that as the correlation (covariance) between the returns for assets that are combined in a portfolio decreases, so does the variance of the return for that portfolio. The good news is that investors can maintain expected portfolio return and lower portfolio risk by combining assets with lower (and preferably negative) correlations. However, the bad news is that very few assets have small to negative correlations with other assets. The problem, then, becomes one of searching among a large number of assets in an effort to discover the portfolio with the minimum risk at a given level of expected return or, equivalently, the highest expected return at a given level of risk.

Systematic versus Unsystematic Risk

The total risk of an asset or a portfolio can be divided into two types of risk: systematic risk and unsystematic risk. William Sharpe (1964) defined systematic risk as the portion of an asset's variability that can be attributed to a common factor. It is also called undiversifiable risk or market risk. Systematic risk is the minimum level of risk that can be attained for a portfolio by means of diversification across a large number of randomly chosen assets. As such, systematic risk is that which results from general market and economic conditions that cannot be diversified away.

Sharpe defined the portion of an asset's variability that can be diversified away as unsystematic risk. It is also called diversifiable risk, unique risk, residual risk, idiosyncratic risk, or company-specific risk. This is the risk that is unique to a company, such as a strike, the outcome of unfavorable litigation, or a natural catastrophe.

How diversification reduces unsystematic risk for portfolios is illustrated in Figure 6.1. The vertical axis shows the variance of a portfolio's return. This variance represents the total risk for the portfolio (systematic plus unsystematic). The horizontal axis shows the number of holdings of different assets (e.g., the number of common stock held of different issuers). As can be seen, as the number of asset holdings increases, the level of unsystematic risk is almost completely eliminated (that is, diversified away). Studies of different asset classes support this. For example, for common stock, several studies suggest that a portfolio size of about 20 randomly selected companies will completely eliminate unsystematic risk leaving only systematic risk. (The first study of this type was by Wagner and Lau 1971). In the case of corporate bonds, generally less than 40 corporate issues are needed to eliminate unsystematic risk.

The relationship between the movement in the price of an asset and the market can be estimated statistically. There are two products of the estimated relationship that investors use. The first is the beta of an asset. Beta measures the sensitivity of an asset's return to changes in the market's return. Hence, beta is referred to as an

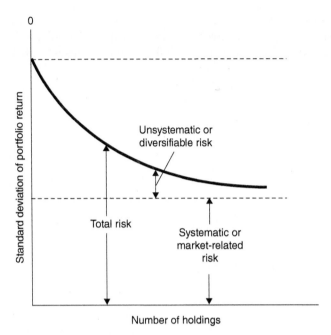

FIGURE 6.1 The Capital Market Line

index of systematic risk due to general market conditions that cannot be diversified away. For example, if an asset has a beta of 1.5, it means that, on average, if the market changes by 1 percent, the asset's return changes by about 1.5 percent. The beta for the market is 1. A beta greater than 1 means that the systematic risk is greater than that of the market; a beta less than 1 means that the systematic risk is less than that of the market. Brokerage firms, vendors such as Bloomberg, and online Internet services provide information on beta for common stock.

The second product is the ratio of the amount of systematic risk relative to the total risk. This ratio is called the coefficient of determination or R-squared. This ratio varies from 0 to 1. A value of 0.8 for a portfolio means that 80 percent of the variation in the return of the portfolio is explained by movements in the market. For individual assets, this ratio is typically low because there is a good deal of unsystematic risk. However, through diversification the ratio increases as unsystematic risk is reduced (see Figure 6.1).

Inflation or Purchasing Power Risk

Inflation risk, or purchasing power risk, arises because of the variation in the value of an asset's cash flows due to inflation, as measured in terms of purchasing power. For example, if an investor purchases an asset that produces an annual return of 5 percent and the rate of inflation is 3 percent, the purchasing power of the investor has not increased by 5 percent. Instead, the investor's purchasing power has increased by 2 percent. Inflation risk is the risk that the investor's return from the investment in an asset will be less than the rate of inflation.

Common stock is viewed by some as having little inflation risk. For all but inflation protection bonds, an investor is exposed to inflation risk by investing in fixed-rate bonds because the interest rate the issuer promises to make is fixed for the life of the issue.

Credit Risk

An investor who purchases a security not guaranteed by the U.S. government is viewed as being exposed to credit risk. There are several forms of credit risk: default risk, downgrade risk, and spread risk.

Default risk is defined as the risk that the issuer will fail to satisfy the terms of the obligation with respect to the timely payment of interest and repayment of the amount borrowed thereby forcing the issuer into bankruptcy. All investors in a bankrupt entity (common stockholders and bondholders) will realize a decline in the value of their security as a result of bankruptcy.

In the case of bonds, investors gauge the credit risk of an entity by looking at the credit ratings assigned to issues by rating companies, popularly referred to as rating agencies. There are three rating agencies in the United States: Moody's Investors Service, Standard & Poor's, and Fitch. When the credit rating of a bond is lowered by a rating agency, this action by a rating agency is referred to as the downgrading of a bond. The risk that a bond will be downgraded is called downgrade risk.

Credit spread risk is the risk that credit spreads in the market will increase resulting in poor performance of the bonds owned.

Liquidity Risk

When an investor wants to sell an asset, he or she is concerned whether the price that can be obtained from dealers is close to the true value of the asset. For example, if recent trades in the market for a particular asset have been between $40 and $40.50 and market conditions have not changed, an investor would expect to sell the asset in that range.

Liquidity risk is the risk that the investor will have to sell an asset below its true value where the true value is indicated by a recent transaction. The primary measure of liquidity is the size of the spread between the bid price (the price at which a dealer is willing to buy an asset) and the ask price (the price at which a dealer is willing to sell an asset). The wider the bid-ask spread, the greater the liquidity risk.

Liquidity risk is also important for portfolio managers that must mark to market positions periodically. For example, the manager of a mutual fund is required to report the market value of each holding at the end of each business day. This means accurate price information must be available. Some assets do not trade frequently and are therefore difficult to price.

Exchange Rate or Currency Risk

An asset whose payments are not in the domestic currency of the investor has unknown cash flows in the domestic currency. The cash flows in the investor's domestic currency are dependent on the exchange rate at the time the payments are received from the asset. For example, suppose an investor's domestic currency is the U.S. dollar and that the investor purchases an asset whose payments are in euros. If the euro depreciates relative to the U.S. dollar at the time a euro payment is received, then fewer U.S. dollars will be received.

The risk of receiving less of the domestic currency than is expected at the time of purchase when an asset makes payments in a currency other than the investor's domestic currency is called exchange rate risk or currency risk.

Risks for Bonds

There are systematic risks that affect bond returns in addition to those described above. They include interest rate risk, call/prepayment risk, and reinvestment risk.

Interest Rate Risk

The price of a bond changes as interest rates change. Specifically, price moves in the opposite direction to the change in interest rates. That is, if interest rates increase, the price of a bond will decline; if interest rates decrease, the price of a bond will increase. This is the reason a bond will sell above its par value (that is, sell at a premium) or below its par value (that is, sell at a discount). The risk that the price of a bond or bond portfolio will decline when interest rates increase is called interest rate risk.

The sensitivity of the price of a bond to changes in interest rates depends on the following factors:

- The bond's coupon rate
- The bond's maturity
- The level of interest rates

Specifically, the following relationships hold:

- All other factors being constant, the lower the coupon rate, the greater the price sensitivity of a bond for a given change in interest rates.
- All other factors being constant, the longer the maturity, the greater the price sensitivity of a bond for a given change in interest rates.
- All other factors being constant, the lower the level of interest rates, the greater the price volatility of a bond for a given change in interest rates.

Consequently, the price of a zero-coupon bond with a long maturity is highly sensitive to changes in interest rates. The price sensitivity is even greater in a low interest rate environment than in a high interest rate environment. For money market instruments, since their maturity is less than one year, the price is not very sensitive to changes in interest rates.

The price sensitivity of a bond to changes in interest rates can be estimated. This measure is called the duration of a bond. Duration is the approximate percentage change in the price of a bond for a 100-basis-point change in interest rates. For example, if a bond has a duration of 8, this means that for a 100-basis-point change in interest rates, the price will change by approximately 8 percent. For a 50-basis-point change in interest rates, the price of this bond would change by approximately 4 percent.

Given the price of a bond and its duration, the dollar price change can be estimated. For example if our bond with a duration of 8 has a price of $90,000, the price will change by about 8 percent for a 100-basis-point change in interest rates and therefore the dollar price change will be about $7,200 (8 percent times $90,000). For a 50-basis-point change, the price would change by about $3,600.

The concept of duration applies to a bond portfolio also. For example, if an investor has a bond portfolio with a duration of 6 and the market value of the portfolio is $1 million, this means that a change in interest rates of 100 basis points will change the value of the portfolio by approximately 6 percent and therefore the value of the portfolio will change by approximately $60,000. For a 25-basis-point change in interest rates, the portfolio's value will change by approximately 1.5 percent and the portfolio's value will change by approximately $15,000.

How is duration computed? First, two prices are computed. One is based on an increase in interest rates and the second is based on a decrease in interest rates. Duration is then computed as follows:

$$\text{Duration} = \frac{\text{Price rates decrease} - \text{Price rates increase}}{2 \times \text{Initial price} \times \text{Change in price in decimal form}}$$

Typically, interest rates fluctuate up and down by an amount less than 50 basis points. But regardless of the rate change used, the interpretation is still that it is the approximate percentage price change for a 100-basis-point change in rates.

There are limitations of duration that the investor should recognize. First, in calculating duration or using the duration provided by financial consultants or fund managers, it is assumed that the prices calculated in the numerator are done properly. This is not a problem for simple bonds. However, there are bonds where if interest rates are changed the estimated price must be estimated by complex pricing models. In turn, those models are based on several assumptions. So, for example, it is not surprising that two brokers providing information on duration for a complex bond could have materially different estimates. One broker could report a duration of four while another a duration of six! Moreover, mutual fund managers who manage a portfolio containing a large allocation to complex bonds could report a duration that is significantly different than the true price sensitivity of the fund to changes in interest rates due to improperly calculating the duration of the complex bonds.

The second limitation of duration is that it is a good approximation for small changes in interest rates (e.g., 50-basis-point change in rates) but the approximation is poorer for a larger change in interest rates. This does not mean that it is not useful for giving the investor a feel for the price sensitivity of a bond or a portfolio.

The third limitation has to do with the duration of a portfolio. In computing the duration of the portfolio, first the duration of each bond in the portfolio is computed. Then a weighted average of the duration of the bonds in the portfolio is computed to get the portfolio duration. The limitation comes about because it is assumed that the interest rate for all maturities change by the same number of basis points. So, if a portfolio has a 2-year, a 10-year, and a 20-year bond, when using a portfolio's duration it is assumed that the 2-year, 10-year, and 20-year bonds change by the same number of basis points. This assumption is commonly referred to as the "parallel yield curve assumption."

Call/Prepayment Risk

A bond may include a provision that allows the issuer to retire or call all or part of the issue before the maturity date. From the investor's perspective, there are three disadvantages to call provisions. First, the cash flow pattern of a callable bond is not known with certainty because it is not known when the bond will be called. Second, because the issuer is likely to call the bonds when interest rates have dropped below the bond's coupon rate, the investor is exposed to reinvestment risk; this is risk that the investor will have to reinvest the proceeds when the bond is called at interest rates lower than the bond's coupon rate. Finally, the price appreciation potential of a bond will be reduced relative to an otherwise comparable bond without a call provision. Because of these three disadvantages faced by the investor, a callable bond is said to expose the investor to call risk. The same disadvantages apply to mortgage-backed and asset-backed securities where the borrower can prepay. In this case the risk is referred to as prepayment risk.

Reinvestment Risk

Reinvestment risk is the risk that proceeds available for reinvestment must be reinvested at a lower interest rate than the instrument that generated the proceeds. In addition to reinvestment risk when investing in a callable or prepayable bond, reinvestment risk occurs when an investor purchases a bond and relies on the yield of that bond as a measure of return potential.

References

Markowitz, Harry. 1952. "Portfolio Selection." *Journal of Finance* 7(1): 77–91.
Sharpe, William F. 1964. "Capital Asset Prices." *Journal of Finance* 19(3): 425–442.
Wagner, W., and S. Lau. 1971. "The Effect of Diversification on Risk." *Financial Analyst Journal* 27(6): 48–53.

Part II The Likelihood of Loss

What is the likelihood that a particular investment strategy will lose money? This question seems rather straightforward and indeed is one of the most common standards against which alternative investment strategies are evaluated. It turns out upon reflection, however, that this question is surprisingly complex, and its answer may vary from one extreme to the other depending upon how the question is framed.

Let's begin with perhaps the most basic formulation of the question. What is the likelihood of a single period loss?

Single Period Loss

The value we wish to estimate is the probability that our investment will depreciate by some fraction from the beginning of the period to the end of the period after accounting for the income it generates. To get started, let's assume our investment has an expected return of 10 percent and a standard deviation of 20 percent and that we wish to estimate the likelihood of a 10 percent loss over the course of a year. Let's also simplify the analysis with the assumption that investment returns are normally distributed. Later we will consider the effect of compounding.

The assumption of a normal distribution arises from the belief that surprises are independent and come from the same underlying distribution. Statisticians refer to this notion as independent and identically distributed or "iid" for short. There is a simple thought experiment to illustrate the intuition of a normal distribution. Consider the potential outcomes for a single toss of a die. There is a 1/6 chance for each outcome—hardly a normal distribution. Now consider the distribution of the average of two tosses. There is only one way to average a one—by tossing a one on both tries, which has a likelihood of 1/36. There are five ways, however, to average a three: a three on both tosses, a two and a four, a four and a two, a one and a five, and a five and a one. Because each combination has a 1/36 likelihood, the probability of averaging a three equals the sum of the five probabilities, 5/36. It turns out that the distribution of the average of many tosses approaches a normal distribution even though the distribution of the potential outcomes for a single toss is distributed uniformly.

Now let's apply this insight to investment returns. Suppose there is an equal chance of a favorable or unfavorable surprise on any given day that influences the return of an investment. A long string of favorable or unfavorable surprises would be unusual. More likely, favorable and unfavorable surprises would tend to be offsetting. Therefore, we should expect to observe more returns that are closer to what we might consider average than extreme returns in either direction. As these surprises accumulate through time, the resultant distribution of returns will conform roughly to a normal distribution.

A normal distribution has several convenient properties. First of all, the mean, the median, and the mode are all the same; hence the distribution is symmetrical around these values. Second, we can infer the entire distribution from just two values, the mean and the standard deviation or its squared value, the variance. For example, 68 percent of a normal distribution's returns fall within the range of the mean plus and minus one standard deviation, and 95 percent of the returns are between the mean plus and minus two standard deviations. Based on our assumption of a 10 percent mean and a 20 percent standard deviation, 68 percent of the possible returns lie within a range of −10 percent to 30 percent, and 95 percent of the returns are between −30 percent and 50 percent. From these facts, we infer that the likelihood of at least a 10 percent loss equals 16 percent because 32 percent of the outcomes (16 percent on either side) lie outside the one standard deviation range.

This calculation works out very conveniently because a 10 percent loss is precisely one standard deviation below the mean. How do we estimate the probability of a 5 percent loss? This value is not located at a convenient distance from the mean for which the probabilities are commonly known. It lies somewhere between zero and one standard deviation below the mean. Precisely, it is 0.75 standard deviation units below the mean, which is found by dividing its distance from the mean by the standard deviation [(−5% −10%)/20% = −0.75]. The value −0.75 is referred to as a standardized variable normal deviate. Most spreadsheets have functions for converting standardized variables into probabilities, and statistics books have tables that map standardized variables onto probabilities. It turns out that 22.66 percent of a normal distribution is more than 0.75 standard deviations below the mean, which makes sense given that 16 percent of a normal distribution is more than one standard deviation below the mean. Thus an investment with a 10 percent expected return and a 20 percent standard deviation has a 22.66 percent chance of generating a 5 percent loss over the course of a year, *assuming its returns are normally distributed.*

Now let's consider the effect of compounding. Suppose we allocate $100,000 to an investment that has an equal chance of returning 30 percent or losing 10 percent each year. There are three possible values for our investment after two years. It can increase 30 percent per year to $169,000. It can increase 30 percent in the first year and fall 10 percent in the second year or reverse this performance, which in both cases will lead to an ending value of $117,000. Finally, it can lose 10 percent in both years resulting in a final value of $81,000. The expected annual return is equal to the average of the two possible returns, which is 10 percent, and the expected terminal value is the average of the three possible values, $121,000. (Remember to count $117,000 twice.) The distribution of the possible ending values is skewed in the sense that the high value is further above the middle value ($52,000) than the amount by which the low value is below the middle value ($36,000). Clearly, the distribution of ending wealth is asymmetric. If we were to extend this investment over many periods, the distribution of ending wealth would conform to a lognormal distribution, which simply means that the natural logarithms of the potential ending values are normally distributed. This result arises from the fact that compounding increases the impact of favorable surprises and reduces the impact of unfavorable surprises. The corresponding logarithms of the ending values are shown below:

Ending Values	Logarithm
169,000	12.038
117,000	11.670
81,000	11.302

Note that these logarithms are perfectly symmetric even though the corresponding wealth values are not. Because the logarithms of ending values are normally distributed, we calculate the probability of a loss by applying the normal distribution to logarithmic units. In order to calculate the probability of loss assuming a lognormal distribution, we start by converting the target return and the expected return into logarithmic units, which are commonly referred to as continuous returns. The target return of −10 percent corresponds to a continuous return of −10.5361 percent *ln*(0.90). The conversion of the 20 percent standard deviation of periodic returns into its continuous counterpart is more complicated. It equals the square root of the following quantity: $ln(0.20^2/(1.10)^2 + 1)$, which is 18.0342 percent. The conversion of the 10 percent periodic mean into a continuous mean is also tricky. It equals: $ln(1.10) - 0.180342^2/2$, which is 7.9049.

With these transformations the normal deviate of continuous returns equals -1.023, which corresponds to a 15.33 percent probability of a 10 percent loss over a single year. Now let's review how to estimate the likelihood of an average annual loss over a multiyear horizon.

Multiperiod Annualized Loss

The specific probability we wish to estimate is the likelihood that our investment will depreciate, on average, by 10 percent per year over several years. This particular standard does not require that our investment achieve a rate of return greater than -10 percent each and every year. It permits annual returns below -10 percent as long as they are offset by sufficiently high returns to produce an annualized return greater than -10 percent. Let's assume a 10-year horizon to illustrate the point. The relevant normal deviate is calculated by multiplying the annualized continuous returns by the number of years in our horizon and the standard deviation of continuous returns by the square root of the number of years, as shown below:

$$[(-0.105361 \times 10) - (0.079049 \times 10)] / (0.180342 \times \sqrt{10}) = -3.234$$

This normal deviate corresponds to a probability of 0.06 percent, which I imagine most investors would consider comfortably remote. If we shorten our horizon to five years the normal deviate increases to -2.286 and the probability rises to 1.11 percent, still not a particularly worrisome situation for most investors.

Now let's investigate the likelihood of a cumulative loss over a multiyear horizon.

Multiperiod Cumulative Loss

The likelihood that our investment will generate a 10 percent cumulative loss over 10 years corresponds to an annualized loss of 1.0481 percent. The only adjustment we need to make to our previous calculation of the normal deviate is to leave the target continuous return as -0.105361 instead of multiplying it by 10. In this case the normal deviate is -1.571, which corresponds to a 5.81 percent probability of occurrence. If we again shorten the horizon to five years the probability increases to 13.33 percent.

In general, if our investment's continuous return is expected to produce a gain or less of a loss than the loss we are focused on, a longer time horizon will reduce the probability of a multiperiod loss. Now let's explore the likelihood of experiencing a loss, not on average over our horizon, but in at least one of the years during our horizon.

At Least One Periodic Loss

The probability of a loss in one or more of the next 10 years is precisely equal to one minus the probability of not experiencing the loss in every one of the next 10 years.

In our earlier example of a single period loss, we estimated the probability of a 10 percent loss to equal 15.33 percent. It follows, therefore, that the likelihood of not experiencing a loss in a single year is 84.67 percent, and assuming year-to-year independence, the likelihood of avoiding a 10 percent, annual loss for 10 consecutive years equals 84.67 percent raised to the 10th power, which is 18.94 percent. Thus there is an 81.05 percent chance that our investment will lose 10 percent or more in at least one of the next 10 years. If we shorten our horizon to five years, the likelihood falls to 56.47 percent. In this case, the duration of our investment horizon has the opposite effect on the likelihood of loss. A shorter horizon reduces the number of opportunities for a single period loss.

This standard is much stricter than the earlier standards I described, but it is not unreasonable. A significant single period loss, even if it is likely to be reversed in time, may prompt an investor to react differently than had the investor focused only on the final result. It may be overly heroic to assume that we can ignore intermediate outcomes and stay focused on the long run. This line of reasoning leads to a final variation on the likelihood of loss—the probability that at some point an investment will fall to 90 percent of its original value, even if it subsequently recovers.

Likelihood of Reaching a Critical Value

In some cases, we wish to measure the likelihood of breaching a threshold at any point throughout our investment horizon and not just at its conclusion, irrespective of whether or not our investment subsequently recovers. In order to assess the likelihood of such an event, we apply a formula known as a first passage time probability. This formula is also quite messy. The probability that an investment will depreciate to a particular value over some horizon during which it is monitored continuously equals:

$$N[(ln(C/S) - \mu T)/(\sigma \sqrt{T})] + (C/S)^{2\mu/\sigma^2} N[ln(C/S) + \mu T)/(\sigma \sqrt{T})]$$

where

$N[]$ = cumulative normal distribution function
ln = natural logarithm
C = critical value
S = starting value
μ = continuous return
T = number of years in horizon
σ = continuous standard deviation

Our investment, which has a 7.9049 percent continuous return and an 18.0342 continuous standard deviation, has a 58.85 percent chance of falling to 90 percent or less of its initial value at some point during a 10-year horizon.

Summary

The likelihood of loss depends critically on how we frame the question. I have answered this question five different ways, all for the same investment, the same underlying distribution, and the same loss, and the answers range from 0.06 percent to 81.05 percent. These results are summarized in the following:

Likelihood of Loss	
Expected Return:	10%
Standard Deviation:	20%
Loss Amount:	10%
Likelihood of a single year loss:	15.33%
Likelihood of an average annual loss over 10 years:	0.06%
Likelihood of a cumulative loss over 10 years:	5.81%
Likelihood of a loss in one or more of the next 10 years:	81.05%
Likelihood of a cumulative loss at some point over the next 10 years (monitored continuously)	58.85%

It pays to know what you are asking.

CHAPTER 7

Risk Measurements

M easuring risk effectively should include both qualitative as well as quantitative analysis. This chapter focuses on fundamental quantitative metrics used to define and measure risk.

There is wide debate over the reliability of the various measures of investment risk. While each metric provides meaningful data, the interpretation of each varies greatly among investment professionals. Investment advisors and consultants should however be familiar with each measurement, how it is calculated, how each is different from the others, and how one may interpret the results of each. Understanding these measurements and their application help form a critical foundation for analyzing uncertainty, managing risk effectively, and communicating with clients appropriately.

Perhaps the most common way to measure investment risk today is by looking at asset or portfolio volatility. The industry's preferred method for calculating this uncertainty and dispersion from the average is to measure an investment's standard deviation. This chapter demonstrates how to calculate standard deviation (and variance) mathematically and discusses how to analyze and interpret the results.

Both readings introduce the concept of distribution as it relates to measuring the returns and volatility of investments and markets. The first reading discusses tracking error variance, probability shortfall, expected shortfall, and finally lower partial moments and semivariance. The second reading takes another look at the very important yet much maligned concept of normal distribution. It then addresses the realities of skewness and kurtosis by looking at the history of U.S. stock returns graphically.

Part I *Handbook of Risk:* Measuring and Managing Investment Risk

Learning Objectives
- List common measurements of investment risk.
- Describe and calculate variance and standard deviation.
- Explain normal distribution and skewness.
- Describe and explain the purpose and application of tracking error variance, probability of shortfall, expected shortfall, lower partial moments, and semivariance.

Part II *Investments: Principles of Portfolio and Equity Analysis*—Portfolio Risk and Return

Learning Objectives

- Describe the three main characteristics of and concept of normal distribution. List the appropriate percent of the observations within 1, 2, and 3 standard deviations of the mean.
- Explain skewness and illustrate (draw) positive and negative skewness graphically.
- Explain kurtosis and illustrate (draw) fat tails.
- Describe the history of U.S. stock price returns over time from a statistical perspective addressing skewness and kurtosis.

Part I Measuring and Managing Investment Risk

An essential component of effectively managing risk is the ability to measure it with relative precision. A conceptual understanding of the mathematical expressions of risk measurements is thus a necessary analytical tool for effective risk management. This part overviews the formulaic structure and applicable functions of some commonly used measures of risk.

One of the most common ways to describe investment risk is to relate it to the uncertainty or volatility of potential returns from an investment over time. For example, an investment whose returns could range between 4 and 6 percent is less volatile than an investment whose returns could range between −20 and +40 percent. The source of the uncertainty and the degree of its impact depend on the type of investment. The most common sources of investment risk are financial exposure to changes in interest rates, equity markets, inflation, foreign exchange rates, credit quality, and commodity prices. Effective risk management involves identifying the risk, estimating its magnitude, deciding how much risk will be assumed, and building structures to reduce unwanted risk. This chapter describes the commonly used measures of risk, reviews the most typical ways to describe risk in equity and fixed-income markets, and examines methods to manage risk in the financial markets.

Effective risk management requires a decision as to how much of the risk should be hedged and at what cost. Analytical tools are required if one wants to be most precise about measuring risk. As a result, we frequently resort to mathematical expressions to capture the central concepts. Understanding these concepts is critical if the investor wants to apply risk management techniques in practice. In fact, the rigor of the mathematics makes the subject easier to understand and apply, not more difficult. For readers who are less comfortable with the algebra, each important mathematical expression is followed by an explanation.

Reprinted from *Portable MBA in Investment*, John Wiley & Sons, 1994, 243–252.

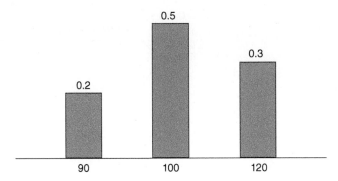

FIGURE 7.1   Probability of Security Price at Year End

Commonly Used Measures of Risk

The primary building block for discussing risk is the concept of a probability distribution of prices or returns. Figure 7.1 illustrates this concept. Figure 7.1 is a bar graph of the return possibilities for an investment. Suppose the investor purchases a security for $100. At the end of a year, the security could take on one of three values: $90, $100, or $120. The probability of each price occurring is given by the height of the bar in Figure 7.1. The *mean return* on the investment of $100 is calculated by multiplying the probability of each occurrence by the corresponding percentage return. Equation 7.1 shows the mathematical equivalent of the concept, indicating that the expected return is equal to the sum of the possible individual returns times the probability of each occurring:

$$E(R) = p_1 R_1 + p_2 R_2 + \cdots + p_n R_n$$

$$= \sum_{i=1}^{n} p_i R_i \tag{7.1}$$

where $E(R)$ equals the expected or mean return and R_i, represents the specific return outcome with probability p_i.[1] Table 7.1 shows that the mean return in the simple example illustrated in Figure 7.1 is equal to 4.0 percent.

TABLE 7.1   Expected Return and Risk for a Simple Investment

Price at Year End	Percentage Return on Original Investment	Probability	Probability-Weighted Return	Differential Return from the Mean	Probability-Weighted Differential Return Squared
90	−10.0	0.2	−2.0	−14.0	39.2
100	0.0	0.5	0.0	−4.0	8.0
120	20.0	0.3	6.0	16.0	76.8
Totals		1.0	4.0		124.0

Notes: Mean return = 4.0%, variance = 124.0%, standard deviation $\sqrt{124.0}$ = 11.1%.

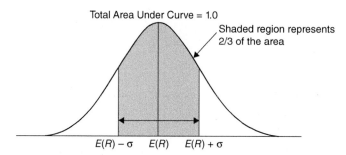

FIGURE 7.2   Normal Probability Distribution

STANDARD DEVIATION (VARIANCE)   One measure of risk is the variance of the probability distribution. The variance is calculated by squaring the deviation of each occurrence from the mean and multiplying each value by its associated probability. The sum of these values is equal to the variance of the distribution. The square root of the variance is referred to as the *standard deviation*. Equation 7.2 shows that the standard deviation is calculated by first summing the probability-weighted squared deviations of each outcome versus the mean and taking the square root of the sum:

$$\sigma = \sqrt{p_1[R_1 - E(R)]^2 + p_2[R_2 - E(R)]^2 + \ldots + p_n[R_n - E(R)]^2}$$

$$= \sqrt{\sum_{i=1}^{n} p_i[R_i - E(R)]^2} \tag{7.2}$$

Table 7.1 shows that the variance is equal to 124.0 (last column), whereas the standard deviation is equal to 11.1 percent. The variance or standard deviation is a common measure of risk and represents the variability of the returns around the mean. The higher the level of standard deviation, the more variability there is in the probability distribution.

A more complete probability distribution is shown in Figure 7.2, which shows its mean and standard deviation. If the distribution is normally distributed (producing the common bell-shaped curve), about two-thirds of the area will fall between the plus and minus one standard deviation from the mean. The shaded area in Figure 7.2 represents the probability of returns falling within the delineated range of returns.

Other things being equal, most investors prefer less volatile returns to more volatile returns. Other things, however, are usually not equal, which is when the deficiencies of standard deviation as a risk measure begin to appear. The first thing to note about the calculation of standard deviation is that the deviations above and below the mean return are given weights equal to their respective probability of occurring, yet most investors are more averse to negative deviations of the same probability than they are pleased with positive deviations of the same magnitude. Research in an area called *Prospect Theory* indicates that investors treat absolute gains and losses quite differently. (For example, see D. Kahneman and A. Tversky, "Prospect Theory: An Analysis of Decision under Risk," *Econometrica* [1979]: 263–291.) Consequently, if two investments have the same absolute deviations about the mean (giving the same standard deviation), but one has more negative returns, investors often view the distribution with the lower mean as riskier.

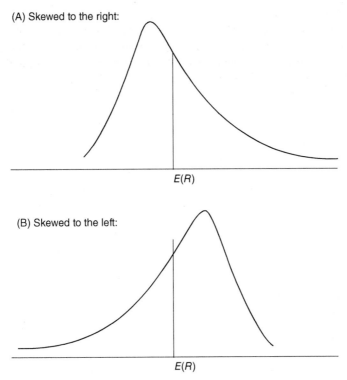

(A) Skewed to the right:

E(R)

(B) Skewed to the left:

E(R)

FIGURE 7.3   Skewed Probability Distributions: Equal Means and Variances but Different Downside Risk

Second, standard deviation as a measure of risk tends to work better when the probability distribution of returns is symmetric. If one distribution is skewed to one side or the other while another is symmetric around the mean, both might have the same standard deviation, but be perceived as having quite different levels of risk. This phenomenon is illustrated in Figure 7.3. Both distributions have identical means and variances. The variances are identical because the two distributions are mirror images of each other rotated around the mean. One of the important differences between the two is that the distribution skewed to the left (B) is characterized by less likely but larger losses and more likely but smaller gains than the distribution skewed to the right (A). Our intuitive notion of risk is often related to the possibility of *bad surprises*. The bad surprises in A are more likely but smaller and limited in magnitude, whereas the bad surprises in B are less likely but potentially much larger in magnitude. A risk-averse investor would generally prefer A to B on these grounds, although they have the same standard deviation.

The conceptual underpinning for the use of standard deviation (or variance) as a measure of risk is related to the theory of utility functions. *Expected utility* is a concept developed by Daniel Bernoulli, a famous Swiss mathematician in the 1700s, to explain the *St. Petersburg Paradox*. Bernoulli noted that a particular coin toss game led to an infinite expected payoff, but participants were willing to pay only a modest fee to play. He resolved the paradox by noting that participants do not assign the same value to each dollar of payoff. Larger payoffs resulting in more wealth are appreciated less and less, so that at the margin, players exhibit decreasing marginal utility as the payoff increases. The particular function that assigns a value to each level of payoff is referred to as the *investor's utility function.* Von Neumann and Morgenstern applied this approach to investment theory in 1944 in a volume that formed the basis for Markowitz's article in 1952 on how to form an efficient portfolio of securities using expected return and variance.

Consider an unspecified function, $U(R)$, which represents the utility of investment returns to a particular investor. Mathematicians have shown that the value of a particular function when its random input is close to its mean can be approximated by terms related to the expected value of the random input (called a *Taylor series expansion*). As a result, the expected utility of investment returns can be written as the desirability of the expected random return plus the rate of change in the utility of returns times the variance of returns plus some smaller-size terms, as shown in Equation 7.3.

$$E[U(R)] = U[E(R)] = U''[E(R)]\sigma^2/2 + Higher - Order\ Terms \qquad (7.3)$$

The term $U''[E(R)]$ represents the rate of change in the utility of investment returns when returns are about average. In mathematical terms, $U''[E(R)]$ represents the second derivative of $U(R)$ with respect to R.

If the returns are normally distributed, the higher-order terms are identically zero and the expected utility is

$$E[U(R)] = U[E(R)] + U''[E(R)]\sigma^2/2 \qquad (7.4)$$

Equation 7.4 indicates that the expected utility of an investment's returns is equal to the utility of the expected return plus a term related to the variance of returns.[2] It suggests that the investor would be concerned with only the mean and the variance of the investment return. It is this analysis that in part laid the foundation for the use of variance as a measure of risk in analyzing investment returns.

Equation 7.4 also serves to point out the weaknesses in using variance as a complete measure of risk. Students of mathematics know that a Taylor series expansion is only approximately true in the neighborhood of the expansion point (in our case, the mean return), and it is not in the neighborhood of the mean where investors' questions about risk usually lie. Investors are often concerned about downside returns, which may lie distant from the mean. Thus, investors are usually concerned about returns in a region where the expansion in Equation 7.4 is known to be less accurate. Using variance as the only measure of risk under these circumstances can lead to difficulties.

Furthermore, when returns are not normally distributed (because of the use of options or nonlinear trading strategies, for example), the higher-order terms in Equation 7.4 are nonzero, and overlooking this can distort the assessment of risk. Bookstaber and Clarke (in "Problems in Evaluating the Performance of Portfolios with Options," *Financial Analyst Journal* [January/February] 1985: 48–62) present examples where "if one used standard deviation or variance as a proxy for risk, it would appear that covered call writing is preferable [for reducing risk] to buying puts," and where "buying puts [for reducing risk] is inferior to the stock-only portfolio." Yet the purchase of puts eliminates most of the undesirable downside risk, whereas the sale of call options eliminates the desirable upside potential. Bookstaber and Clarke conclude that "variance is not a suitable proxy for risk in these cases because options strategies reduce variance asymmetrically." The asymmetric shape of the probability distribution distorts the conclusions that come from using variance as the only measure of risk.

In summary, variance or standard deviation is a commonly used measure of risk, but it can lead to misleading results under some circumstances:

- The probability distribution of returns is not symmetric. This could be inherent in the asset itself or could be induced by the use of options or nonlinear trading rules in the portfolio.
- A significant portion of the distribution lies in a range yielding negative returns. Investors often prefer to value gains differently from losses. This asymmetry is not reflected in the equal weighting treatment implicit in calculating standard deviation.

TRACKING ERROR VARIANCE   A modification of variance as a measure of risk is the calculation of tracking error variance relative to an underlying benchmark. Tracking error is defined as the difference between the investment return and a specified benchmark or target position, as shown in Equation 7.5. The tracking error is defined as

$$\Delta R = R - B \tag{7.5}$$

where B represents the benchmark or target return. The variance of the tracking error is sometimes used as a measure of risk when the investor is interested in seeing how closely a position tracks a particular desired result. In actuality, the variance of the total return can be thought of as a special case of the more general tracking error variance that results when the benchmark is equal to the expected return of the investment. In the example in Table 7.1, the standard deviation of the tracking error relative to the mean return is 11.1 percent and rises to 11.8 percent if zero is used as the target return.

In the more general case, the tracking error is calculated relative to a risky benchmark or index and represents how closely the investment tracks the desired result. Tracking error variance typically suffers from the same drawbacks as the normal variance, however. The tracking error variance calculation will treat deviations above the benchmark no differently from deviations below the benchmark return. If the consequences of deviations on the downside are more serious than the benefits of deviations on the upside, tracking error variance will not give a complete measure of risk.

PROBABILITY OF SHORTFALL   Another measure of risk proposed by Leslie A. Balzer (in "Measuring Investment Risk: A Review," *Journal of Investing* [Fall 1994]) among others is the probability of shortfall. The probability of shortfall measures the chance that returns from the investment may fall below some reference point. The reference point is often set at zero, but it could be set at any other meaningful level to reflect the minimum acceptable return. This measure of risk is captured in Equation 7.6.

$$\text{Shortfall probability} = \text{Probability} \ (R < B) \tag{7.6}$$

where R = the return on the investment and B = the benchmark or reference return.

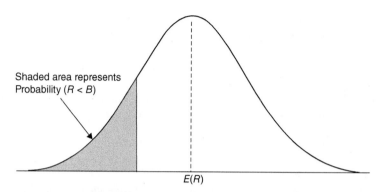

Shaded area represents
Probability $(R < B)$

$E(R)$

FIGURE 7.4   Shortfall Probability

In the case of the simple example in Table 7.1, the probability of shortfall below a return of 0 percent would be 20 percent. Figure 7.4 illustrates the probability of shortfall using a more general probability distribution. The shaded area to the left of the benchmark return represents the probability of shortfall. The benchmark return could also represent a risky asset or index return. In this case, the probability distribution would represent the distribution of tracking error relative to the index instead of the distribution of total return.

The risk measure in Equation 7.6 gives the probability that an undesirable event might occur, but gives no hint as to how severe it might be. For example, an investor might have two possible investment choices. In one case, the investor has a 10 percent probability of losing 20 percent, whereas in the other case, the investor has a 10 percent chance of losing 100 percent. The probability of shortfall ranks each investment as equivalent from a risk perspective, but most investors would clearly not be indifferent between the two. The second investment presents a much more serious loss if it does occur, even though the probability of losing is the same. Hence, even though the probability of shortfall may be of considerable interest, it is insufficient as a measure of risk.

EXPECTED SHORTFALL   An alternative to the probability of shortfall is the *expected shortfall*. This measure incorporates not only the probability of shortfall, but also the magnitude of the potential shortfall if it does occur. Equation 7.7 represents this notion, measuring the expected shortfall as the difference between the actual return and the benchmark over the range of returns when there is a shortfall.

$$\text{Expected shortfall} = E[R - B], \text{ over the range where } R - B < 0 \qquad (7.7)$$

In the simple example in Table 7.1, the expected shortfall below a 0 percent return is −2 percent. The expected shortfall represents the magnitude of the shortfall times the probability of it occurring. This measure is influenced by the entire downside portion of the probability distribution and is a more complete measure of downside risk than just the probability of shortfall itself.

A major problem with the expected shortfall measure is that it treats a large probability of a small shortfall as equivalent to a small probability of a large shortfall. We argued earlier, however, that investors tend to view losses differently from gains.

The expected shortfall measure has drawbacks if investors view the consequences of large losses per unit differently from small losses. This is often the case. Consider that most people insure their houses, but do not insure many minor items that may have a higher probability of loss than the house.

LOWER PARTIAL MOMENTS (LPMs) AND SEMIVARIANCE   Another class of risk measures is termed *lower partial moments* (LPMs) by Harlow (in "Asset Allocation in a Downside Risk Framework," *Financial Analysts Journal* [September/October 1991]). The term *partial* is used to reflect the fact that the measures relate to only one side of the return distribution relative to a target level. *Lower* indicates that the side of interest is the downside, where most investors are the most sensitive to volatility. The LPMs defined by Harlow can also be expanded to incorporate a risky benchmark as the target return in place of a fixed target return. This more general formulation enables these risk measures to incorporate the tracking error concept as well as the standard interpretation below a fixed return. A set of *relative* LPMs can be defined as the expected value of the tracking error raised to the power of

$$RLPM_n = E[R - B)^n], \text{ over the range where } R < B$$
$$= 0, \text{ over the range where } R \geq B \tag{7.8}$$

where n represents the order or ranking of the relative LPM.

This concept captures several of the measures referred to earlier. If $n = 0$, the relative LPM is equivalent to the probability of shortfall in Equation 7.6. If $n = 1$, the relative LPM is equal to the expected shortfall in Equation 7.7. Finally, if $n = 2$, the lower partial is equal to the relative lower partial variance. A special case of the lower partial variance when the benchmark is equal to the expected return of the distribution is termed the *semivariance* by Markowitz. The term *relative semivariance* (*relative semideviation* is the square root of the relative variance) is sometimes used in place of the term *lower partial moment* variance when the target return is not the mean of the distribution. In the example in Table 7.1, the *semideviation* is equal to 6.9 percent (calculated relative to the mean return), whereas the semideviation calculated relative to a 0 percent return is 4.5 percent.

Relative semivariance avoids many of the shortcomings that plague other measures of risk. It is an asymmetric measure that focuses on the downside of the probability distribution and avoids penalizing outperformance. It is a relatively complete measure in that it uses all values of the shortfall with their associated probabilities. It is also nonlinear in that it penalizes larger values more than smaller values because of the squaring of the tracking errors in the calculation. This is more consistent with observed investor behavior because most investors perceive infrequent but large losses as more risky than more frequent but small losses.

Nevertheless, there are some disadvantages in using relative semivariance as a measure of risk. Most are not so much conceptual as they are operational in nature. The first is a general lack of understanding of relative semivariance as a measure of risk. Variance and standard deviation are more well known and more integrated into the theoretical structure of investment decision making. Consequently, using semivariance as a measure of risk generally requires some additional education for the user. Second, mathematical optimizers used by most practitioners to make trade-offs between risk and return are generally not set up to construct portfolios of securities using semivariance as a measure of risk. This makes it more difficult to use relative semivariance as a practical tool without some changes in software. Third, there is no clear way to choose the target or benchmark return that is best to use when calculating the relative semivariance. A different benchmark will produce a different set of trade-offs between risk and return. Risk can be measured relative to any benchmark, but there are few guidelines in deciding which benchmark to use. Finally, the analytics for mixing individual securities in a portfolio are more difficult using relative semivariance than they are using variance as a measure of risk. That is, the interactions of securities are not easily decomposed into the individual securities risk measures as in the case of the calculation of variance. As a result, the portfolio has to be treated as a whole rather than building up the risk measures from its individual parts.

Part II Portfolio Risk and Return

Other Investment Characteristics

In evaluating investments using mean (expected return) and variance (risk), we make two important assumptions. First, we assume that the returns are normally distributed because a normal distribution can be fully characterized by its mean and variance. Second, we assume that markets are not only informationally efficient but that they are also operationally efficient. To the extent that these assumptions are violated, we need to consider additional investment characteristics. These are discussed next.

DISTRIBUTIONAL CHARACTERISTICS   As explained in an earlier chapter, a **normal distribution** has three main characteristics: its mean and median are equal; it is completely defined by two parameters, mean and variance; and it is symmetric around its mean with:

> 68 percent of the observations within $\pm 1\sigma$ of the mean.
> 95 percent of the observations within $\pm 2\sigma$ of the mean.
> 99 percent of the observations within $\pm 3\sigma$ of the mean.

Using only mean and variance would be appropriate to evaluate investments if returns were distributed normally. Returns, however, are not normally distributed; deviations from normality occur both because the returns are skewed, which means they are not symmetric around the mean, and because the probability of extreme events is significantly greater than what a normal distribution would suggest. The latter deviation is referred to as kurtosis or fat tails in a return distribution. The next sections discuss these deviations more in-depth.

Skewness   Skewness refers to asymmetry of the return distribution, that is, returns are not symmetric around the mean. A distribution is said to be left skewed or negatively skewed if most of the distribution is concentrated to the right, and right skewed or positively skewed if most is concentrated to the left. Figure 7.5 shows a typical

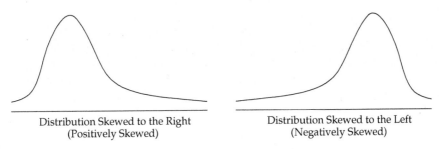

FIGURE 7.5   Skewness

Source: Reprinted from Fixed Income Readings for the Chartered Financial Analyst®
Program. Copyright CFA Institute.

representation of negative and positive skewness, whereas Figure 7.6 demonstrates
the negative skewness of stock returns by plotting a histogram of U.S. large company
stock returns for 1926–2008. Stock returns are usually negatively skewed because
there is a higher frequency of negative deviations from the mean, which also has
the effect of overestimating standard deviation.

Kurtosis   **Kurtosis** refers to fat tails or higher than normal probabilities for extreme
returns and has the effect of increasing an asset's risk that is not captured in a mean–
variance framework, as illustrated in Figure 7.7. Investors try to evaluate the effect
of kurtosis by using such statistical techniques as value at risk (VAR) and conditional
tail expectations.[3] Several market participants note that the probability and the magnitude of extreme events is underappreciated and was a primary contributing factor
to the financial crisis of 2008.[4] The higher probability of extreme negative outcomes
among stock returns can also be observed in Figure 7.6.

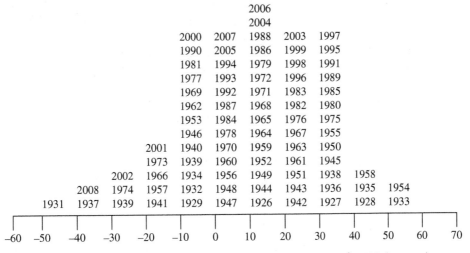

FIGURE 7.6   Histogram of U.S. Large Company Stock Returns, 1926–2008 (percent)

Source: 2009 Ibbotson SBBI Classic Yearbook (Table 2.2).

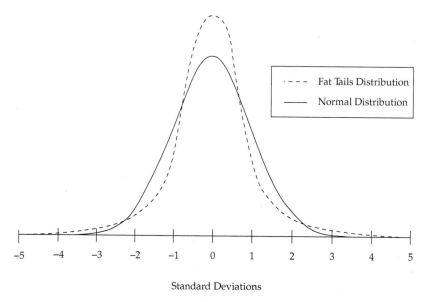

FIGURE 7.7   Kurtosis

Source: Reprinted from Fixed Income Readings for the Chartered Financial Analyst®
Program. Copyright CFA Institute.

Notes

1. The symbol $\sum\limits_{i}$ is a shorthand notation called a *summation,* which represents the
   sum of the terms following it.
2. The use of mean and variance can also be motivated by the use of a quadratic
   utility function. If quadratic utility describes how the investor evaluates the utility
   of wealth, the only measures that make a difference are the mean and variance of
   the distribution of wealth. Quadratic utility functions have some severe limitations,
   however, and don't describe the way people behave very well for extreme wealth
   values.
3. Value at risk (VAR) is a money measure of the minimum losses expected on
   a portfolio during a specified time period at a given level of probability. It is
   commonly used to measure the losses a portfolio can suffer under normal market
   conditions. For example, if a portfolio's one-day 10 percent VAR is d200,000, it
   implies that there is a 10 percent probability that the value of the portfolio will
   decrease by more than d200,000 over a single one-day period (under normal
   market conditions). This probability implies that the portfolio will experience a
   loss of at least d200,000 on one out of every ten days.
4. For example, see Bogle (2008) and Taleb (2007).

References

Bogle, John C. 2008. "Black Monday and Black Swans." *Financial Analysts Journal*
      64(2): 30–40.
Taleb, Nassim N. 2007. *The Black Swan: The Impact of the Highly Improbable.*
      New York: Random House.

CHAPTER 8

Performance Measurement
and Attribution

I nvestment advisors and consultants should be able to calculate numerous risk and performance metrics including: absolute and relative performance measurements, rolling period and annual returns, time-weighted and dollar-weighted returns, and arithmetic and geometric returns. They must also understand the application and implications of these tools and should be able to communicate such to their clients accurately and clearly.

Measuring and analyzing risk-adjusted performance is critical for understanding the effectiveness of individual investments and managers, and how their performance interacts with other investments within a portfolio. This chapter focuses on identifying useful risk and performance metrics, identifying appropriate benchmarks, and reviewing methods for measuring and analyzing specific determinants of individual and portfolio investment performance.

Investment professionals should have a solid understanding of various methods of analyzing and evaluating various investment strategies, styles, and managers. The readings in this chapter describe numerous quantitative methods for evaluating risk-adjusted performance and describe tools designed to show us the origins of both outperformance and underperformance. The authors discuss the concepts behind each measurement and walk through the math using numerous examples and formulae.

Part I *Investments: Principles of Portfolio and Equity Analysis*—Portfolio Risk and Return

Learning Objectives

- Calculate and interpret holding period return and describe its applicability.
- Calculate and interpret arithmetic or mean return and describe its applicability.
- Calculate and interpret geometric mean and describe its applicability.
- Calculate and interpret money-weighted (dollar-weighted) return or internal rate of return and describe its applicability.
- Calculate and interpret annualized return and describe its applicability.

- Calculate and interpret portfolio return and describe its applicability.
- Calculate and interpret gross and net returns and describe their applicability.
- Calculate and interpret pre-tax and after-tax returns and describe their applicability.
- Calculate and interpret real returns and describe their applicability.
- Calculate and interpret leveraged return and describe its applicability.

Part II *The Handbook of Risk:* Measuring Risk for Asset Allocation, Performance Evaluation, and Risk Control

Learning Objectives
- Differentiate between ex-ante risk and ex-post risk.
- Differentiate between idiosyncratic risk and systematic risk.
- Discuss and explain the concept of total risk and the use of volatility as a measure of risk.
- Describe the concepts of normal distribution, skewness, kurtosis, and downside risk.
- Explain the Capital Asset Pricing Model (CAPM).
- Calculate expected return based on CAPM.
- Calculate beta, covariance, and variance.
- Explain mean-variance optimization (MVO) and discuss its assumptions, conclusions, application, and weaknesses.
- Calculate and explain the application of the following risk-adjusted performance measurements: Sharpe ratio, tracking error, Sortino ratio, Jensen's alpha, Treynor ratio, and appraisal ratio.
- Describe the purpose for calculating value at risk (VaR) and calculate VaR using different assumptions.
- Discuss the implications of risk and performance measurement on portfolio construction and management.

Part III *Handbook of Finance:* Introduction to Performance Analysis

Learning Objectives
- Discuss the characteristics of an appropriate benchmark including: unambiguous, investable, measurable, appropriate, reflective of current investment opinions, and specified in advance.
- Explain the importance of published benchmark-centered disciplines and manager strategy disciplines.
- Discuss the debate on size and book-to-market factors.
- Describe the differences in structure and application between generic indices and custom benchmarks.
- Define and describe various methods of measuring alpha.

- Describe and differentiate between measuring relative performance to a peer group versus a benchmark.
- Explain the concept of performance attribution.
- Describe the Morningstar rating methodology.

Part IV IMCA—(excerpt from) *Math for Investment Consultants: Performance Measurement, Analysis, and Attribution*

Learning Objectives
- Determine how much of a manager's performance came from timing (active asset allocation) and how much came from security selection by performing attribution analysis.
  1. Calculate the normal position return.
  2. Calculate the value added for this fund.
  3. Determine the added performance due to the asset mix (timing) decision.
  4. Determine the added performance due to the asset selection decision.
- Calculate and discuss the application of Sharpe ratio.
- Calculate and discuss the application of Sortino ratio.
- Calculate and discuss the application of Modigliani squared (M-squared).
- Calculate and discuss the application of Treynor ratio.
- Calculate and discuss the application of Jensen's alpha.
- Calculate and discuss the application of Tracking error.
- Calculate and discuss the application of Information ratio.

Part I Portfolio Risk and Return

Return

Financial assets normally generate two types of return for investors. First, they may provide periodic income through cash dividends or interest payments. Second, the price of a financial asset can increase or decrease, leading to a capital gain or loss.

Certain financial assets, through design or choice, provide return through only one of these mechanisms. For example, investors in non-dividend-paying stocks, such as Google or Baidu, obtain their return from capital appreciation only. Similarly, you could also own or have a claim to assets that only generate periodic income. For example, defined benefit pension plans, retirement annuities, and reverse mortgages[1] make income payments as long as you live.

You should be aware that returns reported for stock indices are sometimes misleading because most index levels only capture price appreciation and do not adjust for cash dividends unless the stock index is labeled "total return" or "net dividends reinvested." For example, as reported by Yahoo! Finance, the S&P 500 Index of U.S. stocks was at 903.25 on December 31, 2008. Similarly, Yahoo! Finance reported that the index closed on July 30, 2002, at 902.78 implying a return of close to 0 percent over the approximately six-and-a-half-year period. The results are very different, however, if the total return S&P 500 Index is considered. The index was at 1283.62 on July 30, 2002, and had risen 13.2 percent to 1452.98 on December 31, 2008, giving an annual return of 1.9 percent. The difference in the two calculations arises from the fact that index levels reported by Yahoo! Finance and other reporting agencies do not include cash dividends, which are an important part of the total return. Thus, it is important to recognize and account for income from investments.

In the following subsection, we consider various types of returns, their computation, and their application.

HOLDING PERIOD RETURN   Returns can be measured over a single period or over multiple periods. Single period returns are straightforward because there is only one way to calculate them. Multiple period returns, however, can be calculated in various ways and it is important to be aware of these differences to avoid confusion.

A **holding period return** is the return earned from holding an asset for a single specified period of time. The period may be one day, one week, one month, five years, or any specified period. If the asset (bond, stock, etc.) is bought now, time $(t - 1)$, at a price of 100 and sold later, say at time t, at a price of 105 with no dividends or other income, then the holding period return is 5 percent [105 − (100/100)]. If the asset also pays an income of two units at time t, then the total return is 7 percent. This return can be generalized and shown as a mathematical expression:

$$R = \frac{P_t - P_{t-1} + D_t}{P_{t-1}} = \frac{P_t - P_{t-1}}{P_{t-1}} + \frac{D_t}{P_{t-1}} = \text{Capital gain} + \text{Dividend yield}$$
$$= \frac{P_T + D_T}{P_0} - 1$$

In the above expression, P is the price and D is the dividend. The subscript indicates the time of that price or dividend: $t - 1$ is the beginning of the period and t is the end of the period. The following two observations are important.

- We computed a capital gain of 5 percent and a dividend yield of 2 percent in the above example. For ease of illustration, we assumed that the dividend is paid at time t. If the dividend was received any time before t, our holding period return would have been higher because we would have earned a return by putting the dividend in the bank for the remainder of the period.
- Return can be expressed in decimals (0.07), fractions (7/100), or as a percent (7 percent). They are all equivalent.

The holding period return can be computed for a period longer than one year. For example, you may need to compute a three-year holding period return from three annual returns. In that case, the holding period return is computed by compounding the three annual returns: $R = [(1 + R_1) \times (1 + R_2) \times (1 + R_3)] - 1$, where R_1, R_2, and R_3 are the three annual returns.

In this and succeeding parts of this section, we consider the aggregation of several single period returns.

ARITHMETIC OR MEAN RETURN   When assets have returns for multiple holding periods, it is necessary to aggregate those returns into one overall return for ease of comparison and understanding. It is also possible to compute the return for a long or an unusual holding period. Such returns, however, may be difficult to interpret. For example, a return of 455 percent earned by AstraZeneca PLC over the past 16 years (1993 to 2008) may not be meaningful unless all other returns are computed for the same period. Therefore, most holding period returns are reported as daily, monthly, or annual returns.

Aggregating returns across several holding periods becomes a challenge and can lead to different conclusions depending on the method of aggregation. The remainder of this section is designed to present various ways of computing average returns as well as discussing their applicability.

The simplest way to compute the return is to take the simple average of all holding period returns. Thus, three annual returns of –50 percent, 35 percent, and 27 percent will give us an average of 4 percent per year $= \left(\dfrac{-50\% + 35\% + 27\%}{3} \right)$. The arithmetic return is easy to compute and has known statistical properties, such as standard deviation. We can calculate the arithmetic return and its standard deviation to determine how dispersed the observations are around the mean or if the mean return is statistically different from zero.

In general, the **arithmetic** or **mean return** is denoted by $\overline{R}_i$ and given by the following equation for asset i, where R_{it} is the return in period t and T is the total number of periods.

$$\overline{R}_i = \frac{R_{i1} + R_{i2} + \cdots + R_{i,T-1} + R_{iT}}{T} = \frac{1}{T} \sum_{t=1}^{T} R_{it}$$

GEOMETRIC MEAN RETURN   The arithmetic mean return is the average of the returns earned on a unit of investment at the beginning of each holding period. It assumes that the amount invested at the beginning of each period is the same, similar to the concept of calculating simple interest. However, because the base amount changes each year (the previous year's earnings needs to be added to or "compounded" to the beginning value of the investment), a holding or geometric period return may be quite different from the return implied by the arithmetic return. The geometric mean return assumes that the investment amount is not reset at the beginning of each year and, in effect, accounts for the compounding of returns. Basically, the geometric mean reflects a "buy-and-hold" strategy whereas arithmetic reflects a constant dollar investment at the beginning of each time period.[2]

A geometric mean return provides a more accurate representation of the return that an investor will earn than an arithmetic mean return, assuming that the investor holds the investment for the entire time. In general, the **geometric mean return** is denoted by $\overline{R}_{Gi}$ and given by the following equation for asset i,

$$\overline{R}_{Gi} = \sqrt[T]{(1 + R_{i1}) \times (1 + R_{i2}) \times \cdots \times (1 + R_{i,T-1}) \times (1 + R_{iT})} - 1 = \sqrt[T]{\prod_{t=1}^{T} (1 + R_{it})} - 1$$

where R_{it} is the return in period t and T is the total number of periods.

In the example in the previous section, we calculated the arithmetic mean to be 4 percent. Table 8.1 shows the actual return for each year and the actual amount at the end of each year using actual returns. Beginning with an initial investment

TABLE 8.1

	Actual Return for the Year	Year-End Actual Amount	Year-End Amount Using Arithmetic Return of 4 Percent	Year-End Amount Using Geometric Return of −5 Percent
Year 0		€1.0000	€1.0000	€1.0000
Year 1	−50%	€0.5000	€1.0400	€0.9500
Year 2	35%	€0.6750	€1.0816	€0.9025
Year 3	27%	€0.8573	€1.1249	€0.8574

of €1.0000, we will have €0.8573 at the end of the three-year period as shown in the third column. Note that we compounded the returns because, unless otherwise stated, we receive a return on the amount at the end of the prior year. That is, we will receive a return of 35 percent in the second year on the amount at the end of the first year, which is only €0.5000, not the initial amount of €1.0000. Let us compare the actual amount at the end of the three-year period, €0.8573, with the amount we get using an annual arithmetic mean return of 4 percent calculated above. The year-end amounts are shown in the fourth column using the arithmetic return of 4 percent. At the end of the three-year period, €1 will be worth €1.1249 (= 1.0000×1.04^3). This ending amount of €1.1249 is much larger than the actual amount of €0.8573. Clearly, the calculated arithmetic return is greater than the actual return. In general, the arithmetic return is biased upward unless the actual holding period returns are equal. The bias in arithmetic mean returns is particularly severe if holding period returns are a mix of both positive and negative returns, as in the example.

For our example and using the above formula, the geometric mean return per year is −5.0 percent, compared with an arithmetic mean return of 4.0 percent. The last column of Table 8.1 shows that using the geometric return of −5.0 percent generates a value of €0.8574 at the end of the three-year period, which is very close to the actual value of €0.8573. The small difference in ending values is the result of a slight approximation used in computing the geometric return of −5.0 percent. Because of the effect of compounding, the geometric mean return is always less than or equal to the arithmetic mean return, $\overline{R}_{Gi} \leq \overline{R}_i$, unless there is no variation in returns, in which case they are equal.

MONEY-WEIGHTED RETURN OR INTERNAL RATE OF RETURN   The above return computations do not account for the amount of money invested in different periods. It matters to an investor how much money was invested in each of the three years. If she had invested €10,000 in the first year, €1,000 in the second year, and €1,000 in the third year, then the return of −50 percent in the first year significantly hurts her. On the other hand, if she had invested only €100 in the first year, the effect of the −50 percent return is drastically reduced.

The **money-weighted return** accounts for the money invested and provides the investor with information on the return she earns on her actual investment. The money-weighted return and its calculation are similar to the **internal rate of return** and the yield to maturity. Just like the internal rate of return, amounts invested are

TABLE 8.2

Year	1	2	3
Balance from previous year	€0	€50	€1,000
New investment by the investor (cash inflow for the mutual fund) at the start of the year	100	950	0
Net balance at the beginning of year	100	1,000	1,000
Investment return for the year	−50%	35%	27%
Investment gain (loss)	−50	350	270
Withdrawal by the investor (cash outflow for the mutual fund) at the end of the year	0	−350	0
Balance at the end of year	€50	€1,000	€1,270

cash outflows from the investor's perspective and amounts returned or withdrawn by the investor, or the money that remains at the end of an investment cycle, is a cash inflow for the investor.

The money-weighted return can be illustrated most effectively with an example. In this example, we use the actual returns from the previous example. Assume that the investor invests €100 in a mutual fund at the beginning of the first year, adds another €950 at the beginning of the second year, and withdraws €350 at the end of the second year. The cash flows are shown in Table 8.2.

The internal rate of return is the discount rate at which the sum of present values of these cash flows will equal zero. In general, the equation may be expressed as follows, where T is the number of periods, CF_t is the cash flow at time t, and IRR is the internal rate of return or the money-weighted rate of return:

$$\sum_{t=0}^{T} \frac{CF_t}{(1 + \text{IRR})^t} = 0$$

A cash flow can be positive or negative; a positive cash flow is an inflow where money flows to the investor whereas a negative cash flow is an outflow where money flows away from the investor. We can compute the internal rate of return by using the above equation. The flows are expressed as follows, where each cash inflow or outflow occurs at the end of each year. Thus, CF_0 refers to the cash flow at the end of year 0 or beginning of year 1, and CF_3 refers to the cash flow at end of year 3 or beginning of year 4. Because cash flows are being discounted to the present—that is, end of year 0 or beginning of year 1—the period of discounting CF_0 is zero.

$CF_0 = -100$

$CF_1 = -950$

$CF_2 = +350$

$CF_3 = +1,270$

$$\frac{CF_0}{(1 + \text{IRR})^0} + \frac{CF_1}{(1 + \text{IRR})^1} + \frac{CF_2}{(1 + \text{IRR})^2} + \frac{CF_3}{(1 + \text{IRR})^3} = \frac{-100}{1} + \frac{-950}{(1 + \text{IRR})^1}$$

$$+ \frac{+350}{(1 + \text{IRR})^2} + \frac{+1270}{(1 + \text{IRR})^3} = 0$$

$\text{IRR} = 26.11\%$

IRR = 26.11 percent is the internal rate of return, or the money-weighted rate of return, which tells the investor what she earned on the actual euros invested for the entire period. This return is much greater than the arithmetic and geometric mean returns because only a small amount was invested when the mutual fund's return was −50 percent.

Although the money-weighted return is an accurate measure of what the investor actually earned on the money invested, it is limited in its applicability to other situations. For example, it does not allow for return comparison between different individuals or different investment opportunities. Two investors in the *same* mutual fund may have different money-weighted returns because they invested different amounts in different years.

COMPARISON OF RETURNS   The previous subsections have introduced a number of return measures. The following example illustrates the computation, comparison, and applicability of each measure.

EXAMPLE 8.1   Computation of Returns

Ulli Lohrmann and his wife, Suzanne Lohrmann, are planning for retirement and want to compare the past performance of a few mutual funds they are considering for investment. They believe that a comparison over a five-year period would be appropriate. They are given the following information about the Rhein Valley Superior Fund that they are considering.

Year	Assets under Management at the Beginning of Year	Net Return
1	€30 million	15%
2	€45 million	−5%
3	€20 million	10%
4	€25 million	15%
5	€35 million	3%

The Lohrmanns are interested in aggregating this information for ease of comparison with other funds.

1. Compute the holding period return for the five-year period.
2. Compute the arithmetic mean annual return.
3. Compute the geometric mean annual return. How does it compare with the arithmetic mean annual return?
4. The Lohrmanns want to earn a minimum annual return of 5 percent. Is the money-weighted annual return greater than 5 percent?

Solution to 1: The holding period return is $R = (1 + R_1)(1 + R_2)(1 + R_3)(1 + R_4)(1 + R_5) - 1 = (1.15)(0.95)(1.10)(1.15)(1.03) - 1 = 0.4235 = 42.35\%$ for the five-year period.

Solution to 2: The arithmetic mean annual return can be computed as an arithmetic mean of the returns given by this equation: $\overline{R}_i =$ $\dfrac{15\% - 5\% + 10\% + 15\% + 3\%}{5} = 7.60\%.$

Solution to 3: The geometric mean annual return can be computed using this equation:

$$\overline{R}_{Gi} = \sqrt[T]{(1+R_{i1}) \times (1+R_{i2}) \times \cdots \times (1+R_{i,T-1}) \times (1+R_{iT})} - 1$$

$$= \sqrt[5]{1.15 \times 0.95 \times 1.10 \times 1.15 \times 1.03} - 1$$

$$= \sqrt[5]{1.4235} - 1 = 0.0732 = 7.32\%$$

Thus, the geometric mean annual return is 7.32 percent, slightly less than the arithmetic mean return.

Solution to 4: To calculate the money-weighted rate of return, tabulate the annual returns and investment amounts to determine the cash flows, as shown in Table 8.3. All amounts are in millions of euros.

TABLE 8.3

Year	1	2	3	4	5
Balance from previous year	0	34.50	42.75	22.00	28.75
New investment by the investor (cash inflow for the Rhein fund)	30.00	10.50	0	3.00	6.25
Withdrawal by the investor (cash outflow for the Rhein fund)	0	0	−22.75	0	0
Net balance at the beginning of year	30.00	45.00	20.00	25.00	35.00
Investment return for the year	15%	−5%	10%	15%	3%
Investment gain (loss)	4.50	−2.25	2.00	3.75	1.05
Balance at the end of year	34.50	42.75	22.00	28.75	36.05

$CF_0 = -30.00, CF_1 = -10.50, CF_2 = +22.75, CF_3 = -3.00, CF_4 = -6.25,$
$CF_5 = +36.05$

For clarification, it may be appropriate to explain the notation for cash flows. Each cash inflow or outflow occurs at the end of each year. Thus, CF_0 refers to the cash flow at the end of year 0 or beginning of year 1, and CF_5 refers to the cash flow at end of year 5 or beginning of year 6. Because cash flows are being discounted to the present—that is, end of year 0 or beginning of year 1—the period of discounting CF_0 is zero whereas the period of discounting for CF_5 is five years.

To get the exact money-weighted rate of return (IRR), the following equation would be equal to zero. Instead of calculating, however, use the 5 percent return to see whether the value of the expression is positive or not. If it is positive, then the money-weighted rate of return is greater than 5 percent, because a 5 percent discount rate could not reduce the value to zero.

$$\frac{-30.00}{(1.05)^0} + \frac{-10.50}{(1.05)^1} + \frac{22.75}{(1.05)^2} + \frac{-3.00}{(1.05)^3} + \frac{-6.25}{(1.05)^4} + \frac{36.05}{(1.05)^5} = 1.1471$$

Because the value is positive, the money-weighted rate of return is greater than 5 percent. Using a financial calculator, the exact money-weighted rate of return is 5.86 percent.

ANNUALIZED RETURN   The period during which a return is earned or computed can vary and often we have to annualize a return that was calculated for a period that is shorter (or longer) than one year. You might buy a short-term treasury bill with a maturity of three months, or you might take a position in a futures contract that expires at the end of the next quarter. How can we compare these returns? In many cases, it is most convenient to annualize all available returns. Thus, daily, weekly, monthly, and quarterly returns are converted to an annual return. In addition, many formulas used for calculating certain values or prices may require all returns and periods to be expressed as annualized rates of return. For example, the most common version of the Black–Scholes option-pricing model requires annualized returns and periods to be in years.

To annualize any return for a period shorter than one year, the return for the period must be compounded by the number of periods in a year. A monthly return is compounded 12 times, a weekly return is compounded 52 times, and a quarterly return is compounded 4 times. Daily returns are normally compounded 365 times. For an uncommon number of days, we compound by the ratio of 365 to the number of days.

If the weekly return is 0.2 percent, then the compound annual return is computed as shown because there are 52 weeks in a year:

$$r_{annual} = (1 + r_{weekly})^{52} - 1 = (1 + 0.2\%)^{52} - 1$$
$$= (1.002)^{52} - 1 = 0.1095 = 10.95\%$$

If the return for 15 days is 0.4 percent, the annualized return is computed assuming 365 days in a year. Thus,

$$r_{annual} = (1 + r_{15})^{365/15} - 1 = (1 + 0.4\%)^{365/15} - 1$$
$$= (1.004)^{365/15} - 1 = 0.1020 = 10.20\%$$

A general equation to annualize returns is given, where c is the number of periods in a year. For a quarter, $c = 4$ and for a month, $c = 12$:

$$r_{annual} = (1 + r_{period})^c - 1$$

How can we annualize a return when the holding period return is more than one year? For example, how do we annualize an 18-month holding period return? Because one year contains two-thirds of 18-month periods, $c = 2/3$ in the above equation. An 18-month return of 20 percent can be annualized, as shown:

$$r_{annual} = (1 + r_{18\,month})^{2/3} - 1 = (1 + 0.20)^{2/3} - 1 = 0.1292 = 12.92\%$$

Similar expressions can be constructed when quarterly or weekly returns are needed for comparison instead of annual returns. In such cases, c is equal to the number of holding periods in a quarter or in a week. For example, assume that you want to convert daily returns to weekly returns or annual returns to weekly returns for comparison between weekly returns. For converting daily returns to weekly returns, $c = 5$, assuming that there are five trading days in a week. For converting annual returns to weekly returns, $c = 1/52$. The expressions for annual returns can then be rewritten as expressions for weekly returns, as shown:

$$r_{weekly} = (1 + r_{daily})^5 - 1; \qquad r_{weekly} = (1 + r_{annual})^{1/52} - 1$$

One major limitation of annualizing returns is the implicit assumption that returns can be repeated precisely; that is, money can be reinvested repeatedly while earning a similar return. This type of return is not always possible. An investor may earn a return of 5 percent during a week because the market went up that week or he got lucky with his stock, but it is highly unlikely that he will earn a return of 5 percent every week for the next 51 weeks, resulting in an annualized return of 1,164.3 percent ($= 1.05^{52} - 1$). Therefore, it is important to annualize short-term returns with this limitation in mind. Annualizing returns, however, allows for comparison among different assets and over different time periods.

EXAMPLE 8.2   Annualized Returns

London Arbitrageurs, PLC employs many analysts who devise and implement trading strategies. Mr. Brown is trying to evaluate three trading strategies that have been used for different periods of time.

- Keith believes that he can predict share price movements based on earnings announcements. In the past 100 days he has earned a return of 6.2 percent.
- Thomas has been very successful in predicting daily movements of the Australian dollar and the Japanese yen based on the carry trade. In the past four weeks, he has earned 2 percent after accounting for all transactions costs.
- Lisa follows the fashion industry and luxury retailers. She has been investing in these companies for the past three months. Her return is 5 percent.

Mr. Brown wants to give a prize to the best performer but is somewhat confused by the returns earned over different periods. Annualize returns in all three cases and advise Mr. Brown.

Solution:

Annualized return for Keith: $R_{Keith} = (1 + 0.062)^{365/100} - 1 = 0.2455 = 24.55\%$
Annualized return for Thomas: $R_{Thomas} = (1 + 0.02)^{52/4} - 1 = 0.2936 = 29.36\%$
Annualized return for Lisa: $R_{Lisa} = (1 + 0.05)^4 - 1 = 0.2155 = 21.55\%$

Thomas earned the highest return and deserves the reward, assuming the performance of all traders is representative of what they can achieve over the year.

PORTFOLIO RETURN   When several individual assets are combined into a portfolio, we can compute the portfolio return as a weighted average of the returns in the portfolio. The portfolio return is simply a weighted average of the returns of the individual investments, or assets. If asset 1 has a return of 20 percent and constitutes 25 percent of the portfolio's investment, then the contribution to the portfolio return is 5 percent (= 25% of 20%). In general, if asset i has a return of R_i and has a weight of w_i in the portfolio, then the portfolio return, R_P, is given as:

$$R_P = \sum_{i=1}^{N} w_i R_i, \ \sum_{i=1}^{N} w_i = 1$$

Note that the weights must add up to 1 because the assets in a portfolio, including cash, must account for 100 percent of the investment. Also, note that these are single period returns, so there are no cash flows during the period and the weights remain constant.

A two-asset portfolio is easier to work with, so we will use only two assets to illustrate most concepts. Extending the analysis to multiple assets, however, is easily achieved and covered in later sections. With only two assets in the portfolio, the portfolio return can be written as shown, where w_1 and w_2 are weights in assets 1 and 2.

$$R_P = w_1 R_1 + w_2 R_2$$

Because the portfolio consists of only two assets, the sum of the two weights should equal 100 percent. Therefore, $w_1 + w_2 = 1$ or $w_2 = (1 - w_1)$. By substituting, we can rewrite the above equation as follows:

$$R_P = w_1 R_1 + (1 - w_1) R_2$$

Other Major Return Measures and Their Applications

The statistical measures of return discussed in the previous section are generally applicable across a wide range of assets and time periods. Special assets, however, such as mutual funds, and other considerations, such as taxes or inflation, may require return measures that are specific to a particular application.

Although it is not possible to consider all types of special applications, we will discuss the effect of fees (gross versus net returns), taxes (pre-tax and after-tax returns), inflation (nominal and real returns), and leverage. Many investors use mutual funds or other external entities (i.e., investment vehicles) for investment. In those cases, funds charge management fees and expenses to the investors. Consequently, gross and net-of-fund-expense returns should also be considered. Of course, an investor may be interested in the net-of-expenses after-tax real return, which is in fact what an investor truly receives. We consider these additional return measures in the following sections.

GROSS AND NET RETURN   A **gross return** is the return earned by an asset manager prior to deductions for management expenses, custodial fees, taxes, or any other expenses that are not directly related to the generation of returns but rather related to the management and administration of an investment. These expenses are not deducted from the gross return because they may vary with the amount of assets under management or may vary because of the tax status of the investor. Trading expenses, however, such as commissions, are accounted for in (i.e., deducted from) the computation of gross return because trading expenses contribute directly to the return earned by the manager. Thus, gross return is an appropriate measure for evaluating and comparing the investment skill of asset managers because it does not include any fees related to the management and administration of an investment.

Net return is a measure of what the investment vehicle (mutual fund, etc.) has earned for the investor. Net return accounts for (i.e., deducts) all managerial and administrative expenses that reduce an investor's return. Because individual investors are most concerned about the net return (i.e., what they actually receive), small mutual funds with a limited amount of assets under management are at a disadvantage compared with the larger funds that can spread their largely fixed administrative expenses over a larger asset base. As a result, many small-sized mutual funds waive part of the expenses to keep the funds competitive.

PRE-TAX AND AFTER-TAX NOMINAL RETURN   All return measures discussed previously are pre-tax nominal returns—that is, no adjustment has been made for taxes or inflation. In general, all returns are pre-tax nominal returns unless they are otherwise designated.

Investors are concerned about the tax liability of their returns because taxes reduce the actual return that they receive. The two types of returns, capital gains (change in price) and income (such as dividends or interest), are usually taxed differently. Capital gains come in two forms, short-term capital gains and long-term capital gains. Long-term capital gains typically receive preferential tax treatment in a number of countries. Interest income is taxed as ordinary income in most countries. Dividend income may be taxed as ordinary income, may have a lower tax rate, or may be exempt from taxes depending on the country and the type of investor. The after-tax nominal return is computed as the total return minus any allowance for taxes on realized gains.[3]

Because taxes are paid on realized capital gains and income, the investment manager can minimize the tax liability by selecting appropriate securities (e.g., those subject to more favorable taxation, all other investment considerations equal) and reducing trading turnover. Therefore, many investors evaluate investment managers based on the after-tax nominal return.

REAL RETURNS   A nominal return (r) consists of three components: a real risk-free return as compensation for postponing consumption (r_{rF}), inflation as compensation for loss of purchasing power (π), and a risk premium for assuming risk (RP). Thus, nominal return and real return can be expressed as:

$$(1 + r) = (1 + r_{rF}) \times (1 + \pi) \times (1 + RP)$$
$$(1 + r_{real}) = (1 + r_{rF}) \times (1 + RP) \text{ or}$$
$$(1 + r_{real}) = (1 + r) \div (1 + \pi)$$

Often the real risk-free return and the risk premium are combined to arrive at the real "risky" rate as given in the second equation above, simply referred to as the *real return*. Real returns are particularly useful in comparing returns across time periods because inflation rates may vary over time. Real returns are also useful in comparing returns among countries when returns are expressed in local currencies instead of a constant investor currency in which inflation rates vary between countries (which are usually the case). Finally, the after-tax real return is what the investor receives as compensation for postponing consumption and assuming risk after paying taxes on investment returns. As a result, the after-tax real return becomes a reliable benchmark for making investment decisions. Although it is a measure of an investor's benchmark return, it is not commonly calculated by asset managers because it is difficult to estimate a general tax component applicable to all investors. For example, the tax component depends on an investor's specific taxation rate (marginal tax rate), how long the investor holds an investment (long-term versus short-term), and the type of account the asset is held in (tax-exempt, tax-deferred, or normal).

LEVERAGED RETURN In the previous calculations, we have assumed that the investor's position in an asset is equal to the total investment made by an investor using his or her own money. This section differs in that the investor creates a **leveraged** position. There are two ways of creating a claim on asset returns that are greater than the investment of one's own money. First, an investor may trade futures contracts in which the money required to take a position may be as little as 10 percent of the notional value of the asset. In this case, the leveraged return, the return on the investor's own money, is 10 times the actual return of the underlying security. Note that both the gains and losses are amplified by a factor of 10.

Investors can also invest more than their own money by borrowing money to purchase the asset. This approach is easily done in stocks and bonds, and very common when investing in real estate. If half (50 percent) of the money invested is borrowed, then the asset return to the investor is doubled, but the investor must account for interest to be paid on borrowed money.

EXAMPLE 8.3 Computation of Special Returns

Let's return to Example 8.1. After reading this section, Mr. Lohrmann decided that he was not being fair to the fund manager by including the asset management fee and other expenses because the small size of the fund would put it at a competitive disadvantage. He learns that the fund spends a fixed amount of €500,000 every year on expenses that are unrelated to the manager's performance.

Mr. Lohrmann has become concerned that both taxes and inflation may reduce his return. Based on the current tax code, he expects to pay 20 percent tax on the return he earns from his investment. Historically, inflation has been around 2 percent and he expects the same rate of inflation to be maintained.

1. Estimate the annual gross return for the first year by adding back the fixed expenses.
2. What is the net return that investors in the Rhein Valley Superior Fund earned during the five-year period?

3. What is the after-tax net return for the first year that investors earned from the Rhein Valley Superior Fund? Assume that all gains are realized at the end of the year and the taxes are paid immediately at that time.
4. What is the anticipated after-tax real return that investors would have earned in the fifth year?

Solution to 1: The gross return for the first year is higher by 1.67 percent (= €500,000/€30,000,000) than the investor return reported by the fund. Thus, the gross return is 16.67 percent (= 15% + 1.67%).

Solution to 2: The investor return reported by the mutual fund is the net return of the fund after accounting for all direct and indirect expenses. The net return is also the pre-tax nominal return because it has not been adjusted for taxes or inflation. The net return for the five-year holding period was 42.35 percent.

Solution to 3: The net return earned by investors during the first year was 15 percent. Applying a 20 percent tax rate, the after-tax return that accrues to the investors is 12 percent [= 15% – (0.20 × 15%)].

Solution to 4: As in Part 3, the after-tax return earned by investors in the fifth year is 2.4 percent [= 3% – (0.20 × 3%)]. Inflation reduces the return by 2 percent so the after-tax real return earned by investors in the fifth year is 0.39 percent, as shown:

$$= \frac{(1 + 2.40\%)}{(1 + 2.00\%)} - 1 = \frac{(1 + 0.0240)}{(1 + 0.0200)} - 1 = 1.0039 - 1 = 0.0039 = 0.39\%$$

Note that taxes are paid before adjusting for inflation.

Notes

1. A reverse mortgage is a type of loan that allows individuals to convert part of their home equity into cash. The loan is usually disbursed in a stream of payments made to the homeowner by the lender. As long as the homeowner lives in the home, they need not be repaid during the lifetime of the homeowner. The loan, however, can be paid off at any time by the borrower not necessarily by selling the home.
2. A buy-and-hold strategy assumes that the money invested initially grows or declines with time depending on whether a particular period's return is positive or negative. On the one hand, a geometric return compounds the returns and captures changes in values of the initial amount invested. On the other hand, arithmetic return assumes that we start with the same amount of money every period without compounding the return earned in a prior period.
3. Bonds issued at a discount to the par value may be taxed based on accrued gains instead of realized gains.

Part II Measuring Risk for Asset Allocation, Performance Evaluation, and Risk Control

This part explores the many differences between *ex ante* risk (the measurement of risk before a market shock occurs) and *ex post* risk (the analysis after the event). The author argues that any estimate of risk using purely historical data may be appropriate for performance evaluation, but not for risk control. When evaluating risks going forward, managers should consider the characteristics of the financial instruments currently held, regardless of the performance of those utilizing them.

The Language of Risk

Risk measurement is easily one of the most confusing phrases in the finance lexicon. A main source of this confusion is the distinction between the identification and measurement of *ex ante* risk versus *ex post* risk. Ex ante risk measurement is the evaluation of risk *before* that risk is actually incurred, and ex post risk measurement is the analysis of risk *after* it has been taken, usually for the purpose of evaluating historical performance on a risk-adjusted basis. In this paper, we explore the similarities and differences between ex ante and ex post measures of investment risk.

Asset allocation, performance evaluation, and risk management (that is, the formal measurement and control of risk-taking activities) are three important—and distinct—components of the investment management process. The latter two are intended primarily to provide a diagnostic check and regular informational feedback mechanism for the refinement of the first. But all are important. As we discuss here, unless risk is measured in a manner appropriate to its specific application, investors can get into trouble—for example, legitimate asset allocation decisions may be called into question by poor estimates of risk for risk-management purposes and other similar problems.

We explain here that the basic building block definitions of risk are essentially the same for ex ante and ex post measures of risk, but the means by which risk is measured (and the data used to do so) depends on the application of the particular measure. In particular, we examine the means by which risk can be calculated and summarized for three purposes: the ex ante measurement of risk for allocating capital into distinct asset classes; the ex post measurement of risk for evaluating risk-adjusted performance; and the ex ante measurement of risk for the management and control of risk and risk-taking trading/investment decisions. These three applications of risk measurement are, of course, strongly interrelated. A poor measure of risk-adjusted performance ex post may result in a lower allocation of capital on the next round of ex ante asset allocations, as may a high ex ante measure of risk for risk-control purposes.

We begin by outlining the basic building blocks by which market risk can be measured. Then we explore how those basic definitions of risk are applied in the allocation of capital into asset classes. Next we show how the building block risk measures are used in measuring risk-adjusted performance ex post. We explore several summary measures of risk that are useful for ex ante risk-control decisions. We show that although these measures are also based on the same basic definitions of

Reprinted from *The Journal of Performance Management* (Fall 1999): 55–73. New York: Institutional Investor, Inc. Copyright © Institutional Investor, Inc. All rights reserved.

risk used for performance evaluation, their calculation and application are fundamentally different.

BUILDING BLOCK DEFINITIONS OF RISK Market risk is measured in essentially two distinct ways. The first approach rests mainly on the probability and statistics of returns on asset classes, securities, and/or managers. This approach does not distinguish between the types of risk borne by the manager and looks only at total risk. The second approach, by contrast, uses historical data to analyze the components of total risk—namely, *idiosyncratic risk* and *systematic risk*. The former is risk that is specific to the particular asset in question. The idiosyncratic risk of a share of common stock or a corporate bond, for example, is the specific risk that the financial performance of the security issuer will adversely impact the value of the security. By contrast, systematic risk is the risk that a security's value declines as a result of changes in some risk factor that affects all asset prices in some way.

As we will show in the heart of this paper, despite some popular misconceptions to the contrary, these basic building blocks of risk are essentially the same regardless what the application is. When it comes to differentiating between the risk used to calculate risk-adjusted returns for performance evaluation and the risk used to make risk-control decisions (for example, limits and limits administration), few theoretical and conceptual differences exist between the two. Rather, the distinction comes in how the various building block measures of risk discussed in this section are calculated and applied.

THE TOTAL RISK PERSPECTIVE The analysis of total risk—whether ex ante for risk measurement or ex post for performance evaluation—involves the quantification of any uncertainty that impacts the value of an asset or portfolio. Consider a single asset j whose return from month $t - 1$ through month t is denoted $R_{j,t}$.[1] This return is a *random variable*—that is, the realized return in any given month is driven by random factors in such a way that the return is unknown until prices are realized at month t. The total risk of holding the asset from time $t - 1$ to time t can be summarized in various ways, all of which involve the application of probability and statistics. The two most common ways of summarizing total risk are discussed in the next two sections.

Volatility By far the most popular measure of the total risk of asset j for month t is the volatility of the return on that asset during month t. If the return on asset j is drawn from some probability distribution, $f_{j,t}(R)$, the variance of that asset return reflects the possibility that the realized return may be above or below the expected (average) return. Asset or portfolio volatility is commonly measured using variance (or standard deviation, which is the square root of variance). The standard deviation reflects fluctuations below and above the average return. Mathematically, we define variance in terms of the underlying probability:

$$\text{Var}(R_{j,t}) = \sigma_{j,t}^2 = \int_{-\infty}^{\infty} (R - E(R))^2 f_{j,t}(R) dR \tag{8.1}$$

where $E(R)$ is the expected return on asset j in month t. The expected return is another probabilistic concept that summarizes the average return on the asset in month t:

$$E(R_{j,t}) = \int_{-\infty}^{\infty} R f_{j,t}(R) dR \tag{8.2}$$

The previous mathematical definitions of variance and expected returns assume that we know the probability distribution from which the random returns are drawn—that is, that $f_{j,t}(R)$ is known. In other words, we assume that we know the exact probability to associate with every possible realizable return. For example, if we know that $f_{j,t}(R)$ is a normal distribution, then we know that there is a 5 percent probability that the actual return in month t will be 1.65 standard deviations below the mean return. But that, in turn, requires that we know the mean and standard deviation of asset j's return in month t.

For practical purposes, we never know the true probability distribution from which an asset's return is drawn. Instead, we use statistics to draw inferences about that probability—in other words, we take observed, historical data and use that to approximate the probability distributions that we cannot directly observe.

A collection of historical data that has been observed over a particular period of time is called a *time series*. If asset j is a share of IBM common stock, for example, a time series of monthly returns on asset j might include the past five years of observed monthly returns on IBM common stock.[2] We then could measure the historical variance of returns using the following formula:

$$\sigma^2 = \frac{1}{N-1} \sum_{t=1}^{N} (R_t - \overline{R})^2 \tag{8.3}$$

where $\overline{R}$ is the sample mean over the time series. Because these statistics depend critically on the length of the time series chosen, the particular time period spanned by the time series, and the frequency of the returns (such as daily versus monthly), we refer to the previous process as *sample statistics*.

In practice, sample statistics like the previous one are used to measure the risk of an asset rather than the more mathematical probability-based definitions. Nevertheless, it is important to recognize that there is a direct correspondence between sample statistics and the probability-based definitions that underlie those statistics; the former are simply used as a method of inferring what cannot be directly observed in the latter.

Other Measures of Total Risk   Volatility is often used to measure the risk of an asset for one primary reason—it is easy to compute. In addition, volatility measures in finance are popular because of the way they relate to the normal or bell-shaped distribution. Specifically, the normal distribution is symmetric, which means that a return of –R percent below the mean is just as likely to occur as a return of +R percent above the mean. Thus, the variance of a normal distribution is a *sufficient statistic* to describe fully the risks of the asset or portfolio.

However, when the returns on an asset are not symmetric or normally distributed, variance can be an imprecise measure of risk. Indeed, volatility can actually be misleading in some cases. Consider the two probability distributions shown in Figure 8.1 for Portfolios C and D.[3] The probability that returns will fall below some arbitrarily chosen target is just the area under the curves to the left of the vertical line drawn for that target—such as the gray shaded area for Portfolio D. Portfolios C and D have identical mean returns and the same variance. However, as the figure illustrates, Portfolio D is riskier than Portfolio C because the likelihood of returns falling below the target is much higher for Portfolio D than for C. This results because

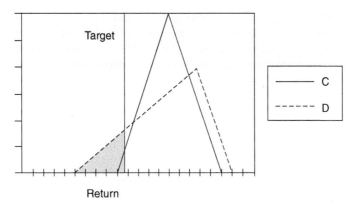

FIGURE 8.1   Probability Distribution of Portfolios C and D

Portfolio D has an asymmetric return distribution and Portfolio C does not. Specifically, Portfolio D has a return distribution that is negatively skewed—in other words, the probability of realizing a return of −R percent is greater than the probability of achieving a +R percent return.

When an asset's return distribution is asymmetric, variance is no longer a sufficient summary measure of the total risk of holding that asset. Instead, other summary statistics describing the presumed distribution of returns must be used to supplement variance.[4] The two most common such summary statistics are *skewness* and *kurtosis*. As noted previously, skewness measures the degree to which a return distribution is asymmetric. Kurtosis measures the *r*-fatness of the tails and the peakedness of the center of the distribution, usually relative to a normal distribution. If a distribution is *leptokurtic*, it has more probability in the tails and around the mean than in the middle. Common in markets like foreign exchange, leptokurtic returns are characteristic of markets that exhibit long periods of trending followed by short periods of volatile trend reversals and adjustments.

One popular measure of risk when portfolio returns are asymmetric is *downside risk*. This summary of the total risk of the portfolio is essentially the risk that portfolio returns will fall below some specific target return level. The general form for downside risk measures is written in terms of actual probability distributions:[5]

$$\int_{-\infty}^{T} (T - R)^z f_{j,t}(R)dR \tag{8.4}$$

where T is the prespecified target return and z is a parameter for the particular risk statistic chosen. When $z = 0$, the downside risk measure is called *below-target probability* (BTP) and is just

$$BTP = \int_{-\infty}^{T} f_{j,t}(R)dR \tag{8.5}$$

In other words, BTP simply measures the probability of a shortfall in returns below some target T.

BTP is often criticized because it reveals how likely returns are to fall below a chosen target, but it does not reveal the degree to which return shortfalls have occurred. A return 0.01 percent below target T is given just as much weight as a return 1,000 percent below target T. As a remedy for this problem, many focus instead on downside risk when parameter $z = 2$. This results in a measure of total risk called the *below-target variance* (BTV) or *downside semivariance*:

$$BTV = \int_{-\infty}^{T} (T - R)^2 f_{j,t}(R) dR \qquad (8.6)$$

BTV measures the risk of a return shortfall below the target and gives more weight in the calculation to larger shortfalls. The standard deviation of BTV is called the *below-target risk* (BTR). When the underlying return distribution is symmetric, BTV is equal to traditional portfolio variance.

Just as in the case of traditional variance, the link between probability and statistics requires using actual sample data to draw statistical inferences. The actual calculation of summary risk measures then requires using a sample statistic. The sample statistic for the BTV of a time series with N observations is:[6]

$$BTV = \frac{1}{N + 1} \sum_{t=1}^{N} (\max[T - R_t, 0])^2 \qquad (8.7)$$

Decomposing Total Risk into Its Components

The measures of total risk discussed in this section do not differentiate between the sources of risk—that is why some portfolios and assets are riskier than others. In that connection, the total risk of an asset also can be decomposed into idiosyncratic and systematic components. The former concerns those sources of risk in an asset that are particular to the asset in question, such as issuer-specific credit risk or earnings growth. The latter type of risk refers to movements in the price of an asset that are driven by movements in the market as a whole or by changes in some risk factor that affects all asset prices (for example, the inflation rate).

In order to allocate the total risk of an asset or portfolio into idiosyncratic and systematic components, some set of systematic risk factors must be defined. A systematic risk factor is any economic factor (such as aggregate consumption growth) whose changes drive *all* asset prices. The impact of a change in a risk factor on any particular asset price may be different depending on the asset, but if the risk factor is truly systematic, it affects all asset prices in some way.[7]

THE CAPITAL ASSET PRICING MODEL (CAPM)   The best way to understand systematic risk factors is by walking through the most common example—the Capital Asset Pricing Model (CAPM) of Sharpe, Lintner, Mossin, and Black. In the CAPM, the return on any asset j is related to a single risk factor—the return on the market portfolio. Specifically, the CAPM implies that the excess return on any asset j (for example, the return in excess of the risk-free rate) is proportional to the covariance of the return of that asset with returns on the market portfolio and to the excess return on the market portfolio. Although the model involves the true market portfolio of all invested wealth and the true risk-free rate, we usually measure these variables using a broad equity index (such as the S&P 500) and the U.S. Treasury bill rate, respectively.

Mathematically, the CAPM implies the following for any asset j:

$$E(R_j) - R_f = \beta_j[E(R_m) - R_f] \qquad (8.8)$$

where

$$
\begin{aligned}
E(R_j) &= \text{Expected return on asset } j \\
R_f &= \text{Risk-free rate (that is, Treasury bill rate)} \\
E(R_m) &= \text{Expected return on the market}
\end{aligned}
$$

where

$$
\beta_j = \frac{\text{Cov}(R_m, R_j)}{\text{Var}(R_m)} \tag{8.9}
$$

The parameter β_j measures the degree to which changes in the systematic risk factor (the market) impact changes in the expected asset returns. In other words, the expected excess return on the market portfolio is the risk factor, and β_j is the price of that risk factor in asset j. The price of market risk may be different for different assets, because both β_1 and $E(R_j)$ differ for different assets and portfolios. Nevertheless, the characterization of expected excess returns on the market as a systematic risk factor means that the excess return on the market always affects excess returns on assets somehow.

The CAPM is called a *single-factor model* because excess returns on all assets are systematically affected by only one factor—the excess return on the market portfolio. In the CAPM, all systematic risk is reflected in the relation between expected asset returns and expected market returns, and the price of this systematic risk—that is, the degree to which it affects returns on a particular asset—is reflected fully in beta.

Any particular asset also may be affected by idiosyncratic risk or market risk that is specific to the asset in question. To see the impact of systematic risk on the return on any asset j, we can rewrite the CAPM relation without using expected values:

$$
R_j - R_f = \beta_j[R_m - R_f] + \varepsilon_j \tag{8.10}
$$

where ε_j is a term that reflects the idiosyncratic risk of the asset. Equation 8.10 essentially says that the actual return on asset j is equal to the risk-free rate plus the asset's beta times the actual excess return on the market plus a random shock that reflects risk specific to asset j. If the expected value of ε_j is zero, Equation 8.10 becomes the CAPM equation in expected value terms. If R_j is the actual return on some well-diversified portfolio j rather than a single asset, the assumption that $E(\varepsilon_j) = 0$ is equivalent to presuming that the diversification effects of the portfolio cause all idiosyncratic risks to net out.

We can express the total risk of the portfolio (using variance as our measure of risk) in terms of its systematic and idiosyncratic components:

$$
\text{Var}(R_j) = \beta_j^2 \text{Var}(R_m) + \text{Var}(\varepsilon_j) + 2\beta_j \text{Cov}(R_m, \varepsilon_j) \tag{8.11}
$$

By definition, the idiosyncratic disturbance term is uncorrelated with returns on the market portfolio—otherwise, it would not be a truly idiosyncratic risk. This means that the last term in the previous equation is equal to zero, and we can express total risk as just the sum of the systematic and idiosyncratic risk:[8]

$$
\text{Var}(R_j) = \beta_j^2 \text{Var}(R_m) + \text{Var}(\varepsilon_j) \tag{8.12}
$$

MULTIFACTOR ASSET PRICING MODELS   The CAPM has been sharply criticized as an unrealistic representation of systematic risk. Specifically, significant academic work has shown that the excess return on the market is not the only factor that significantly affects all asset returns.[9] Other systematic risk factors known to affect all stock returns, for example, include leverage, market capitalization, dividend yields, and the ratio of book to market equity.

Numerous alternatives to the CAPM have been proposed that presume excess returns on any asset are a function of multiple systematic risk factors. The particular factors differ depending on the particular model in question, but the basic form of the relation is usually the same:[10]

$$R_j - R_F = \delta_1 \gamma_1 + \delta_2 \gamma_2 + \cdots + \delta_k \gamma_k + \varepsilon_j \qquad (8.13)$$

where γ_1, is the first systematic risk factor and δ_1 is the price of the first risk factor in asset j. In other words, δ_1 measures the sensitivity of returns on asset or portfolio j to changes in the first systematic risk factor and so on for the other risk factors through k. The number of risk factors, k, can be small or large depending on the particular model, all of which collectively reflect the systematic risk of asset j's returns. Like the CAPM, the term ε_j reflects the idiosyncratic risk of asset or portfolio j—in other words, the risk that is specific to asset or portfolio j.

Identifying systematic risk factors can be difficult, and the systematic risk factors usually need to have a few important characteristics. For one thing, the systematic risk factors should be mutually exclusive and uncorrelated with each other—that is, $\mathrm{Cov}(\gamma_m \gamma_{m+1}) = 0$ for all m. In addition, the idiosyncratic risk term should be uncorrelated with all the systematic risk factors—that is, $\mathrm{Cov}(\gamma_m \varepsilon_j) = 0$ for all m. Finally, the systematic risk factors should exhaustively span all of the possible sources of systematic risk impacting asset prices. Some factors that fall into these categories are macro-economic, such as *real consumption growth*. Other factors cannot be identified directly, so *factor-mimicking portfolios*—portfolios whose returns are perfectly correlated with the underlying risk factor—must be chosen as substitutes.

Under the previous assumptions about the idiosyncratic risk term and systematic risk factors, the total risk of asset or portfolio j can be decomposed using variance as the measure of risk:

$$\mathrm{Var}(R_j) = \delta_1^2 \mathrm{Var}(\gamma_1) + \delta_2^2 \mathrm{Var}(\gamma_2) + \ldots + \delta_k^2 \mathrm{Var}(\gamma_k) + \mathrm{Var}(\varepsilon_j)$$

Measures of Risk for Allocating Capital into Asset Classes

Perhaps the most important application of the measures of risk discussed in this section is facilitating ex ante decisions about how to allocate capital into asset classes on a risk-adjusted basis. The asset allocation decision first requires a plan sponsor or portfolio manager to identify the markets, as opposed to specific securities, in which to invest. Individual securities sharing common financial characteristics are grouped into those broader asset classes. Asset classes for potential investment are then selected based on several criteria: the ability to monitor performance, liquidity, and redundancy, and the ability to estimate risk, legal limitations, and diversification advantages. Once the asset classes have been identified, the weight of each asset class in the investment portfolio must be determined.

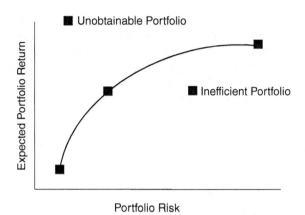

FIGURE 8.2   Efficient Frontier

MEAN-VARIANCE OPTIMIZATION   Nobel laureate Harry Markowitz first described the goal of portfolio theory as the process of identifying an *efficient set of portfolios*.[11] An efficient portfolio is a portfolio for which no greater expected return can be found without a corresponding increase in risk. Alternatively, efficient portfolios are those for which no greater certainty of returns can be achieved without a decrease in expected return. Once this efficient set of portfolios is identified at the asset class level, the investment manager chooses an actual allocation on that frontier that best conforms to the desired risk/return targets of the investors in the fund.[12]

The set of efficient portfolios is commonly called the *efficient frontier*. A typical set of such efficient portfolios is depicted in Figure 8.2. This plot associates the expected return on a portfolio with a given level of risk or, conversely, the risk of a portfolio with a given expected portfolio return.

The concave line depicted in the Figure 8.2 is the efficient frontier formed by tracing the boundary of all portfolios that are combinations of selected asset classes. Points inside the frontier are inefficient because less return for the risk is achieved. Points outside the line, by contrast, are more desirable, but are not obtainable (that is, infeasible). Portfolio 1 is the minimum risk portfolio and offers the least risk of any combination of asset classes, whereas Portfolio 3 is the maximum return/maximum risk portfolio. Although Portfolio 3 corresponds to 100 percent investment in the asset class with the greatest return, Portfolio 1, by contrast, usually will not be composed only of the least risky asset class owing to the risk-reducing effects of diversification across asset classes with different risks. For moderate return and risk, portfolios away from the endpoints, such as Portfolio 2, typically are chosen. Such portfolios usually consist of investments in many asset classes, thereby taking significant advantage of diversification effects.

The most common type of efficient frontier is the one popularized by Markowitz, which treats portfolio variance as a sufficient measure of risk. This frontier is called the *mean-variance-efficient frontier*, and portfolios on that frontier are called, not surprisingly, *mean-variance-efficient portfolios*. Figure 8.2 is an example of a mean-variance-efficient frontier when the *x*-axis indicating the portfolio risk is measured with standard deviation of the historical returns on each asset class.

Given a potential set of asset classes, the efficient frontier can be identified by *portfolio optimization*. Portfolio optimization involves a mathematical procedure called *quadratic programming* in which two objectives are considered: to maximize return and minimize risk. Portfolios on the mean-variance-efficient frontier are found by searching for the portfolio with the least variance given some minimum return. Repetition of this procedure for many return levels generates the efficient frontier.

One of the critical inputs into the portfolio optimization problem clearly is portfolio risk, which is measured as the variance or standard deviation of returns in a mean-variance portfolio optimization problem. The actual variance used as a measure for the risk of asset classes is the historical sample variance for each asset class over some sample period. The sample period is usually as historically long as possible (for example, 25+ years). Importantly, the historical variance of asset class returns is based solely on returns to the asset class itself and is not based on any actively managed portfolio involving that asset class.

MEAN-DOWNSIDE RISK PORTFOLIO OPTIMIZATION If the underlying distributions of asset and portfolio returns are not normally distributed, the asset class weights produced in solving the previous problem will not necessarily put the investor on the efficient frontier. Thus, minimizing variance for a given level of return will yield portfolio weights that do not compensate the investor for the risks of the portfolio with which the investor is concerned. To do that, we need to rely on a measure of downside risk as a proxy for total risk rather than just variance.

Once we have determined such a measure of downside risk, which considers all the higher-order moments with which we are concerned (such as the BTR), the problem becomes analogous to the simple mean-variance Markowitz model. The goal is to find a feasible portfolio that minimizes downside risk for some specified level of return.[13] Because higher-order moments are considered, no assumptions are being made about normally distributed returns or symmetric asset returns. The risk measure chosen (for example, the BTR or BTP) and the calculation of this measure is what distinguishes this type of model from the standard mean-variance Markowitz model.

Unfortunately, the mathematical technique used to solve the mean-variance portfolio optimization problem is not applicable in this case. The objective function—minimize downside risk—is nonlinear, and nonlinear optimization problems are a science unto themselves. Optimality in such models, in fact, is very difficult to determine.[14]

Finally, recognize that generating the efficient frontier with portfolio optimization techniques does not tell the plan manager the best portfolio actually to hold. The efficient frontier is a set of many portfolios, and a single optimal portfolio for the plan is not immediately obvious. The ultimate portfolio actually chosen should be the portfolio on the efficient frontier that best approximates the risk/return preferences of the residual claimants and/or sponsor of the fund.

Measures of Risk-Adjusted Performance

In addition to serving as the foundation for the allocation of capital into asset classes on a risk-adjusted basis, the measures of risk discussed earlier also provide the foundation for the measurement of performance. Specifically, when a portfolio manager's performance is evaluated, some measure of risk must be used to characterize and quantify the risk-adjusted returns of that manager—that is, how much risk was taken to generate some level of returns.

Performance evaluation is inherently backward-looking and ex post in nature. All measures of risk-adjusted performance are based on managers' past actual performance. True, inferences are sometimes drawn about how managers may perform in the future based on how they have performed in the past. But at its core, performance measurement relies solely on returns that have actually been realized in the past.

One important aspect of performance measurement involves the choice of an appropriate time series of historical return data—namely, the frequency and sample period. Reporting time periods are established by the Association for Investment Management and Research (AIMR) guidelines and other internal reporting instructions. To the extent that the choice of a time period over which to evaluate historical performance is left to the evaluator, there are no hard and fast rules except to choose a period that is long enough to yield good statistical estimates (at three years of monthly data or at least 30 observations) and that corresponds with any strategic directives the manager has been given. For example, a manager mandating to maximize the long-run value would suggest a longer evaluation time horizon, whereas a manager scalping initial public offerings (IPOs) might have a shorter sample data period for performance analysis purposes.

Measures of performance fall into two major categories, corresponding to the two perspectives on risk. Namely, risk-adjusted performance can be evaluated by examining either returns relative to various measures of total risk or returns relative to systematic and/or idiosyncratic risk. We discuss the major measures of performance in each of these categories in the next section.[15]

TOTAL RISK MEASURES OF PERFORMANCE Recall that total risk is a measure of the risk of a portfolio owing to systematic risk, idiosyncratic risk, or both. From the standpoint of the manager, both of these risks are important. Both affect compensation, peer evaluation, and other qualitative assessments of performance. But from the standpoint of the investors in the portfolio, what is of concern is how the risk of the portfolio impacts the investor's total invested wealth at risk. For example, an investor with all of his or her wealth invested in the portfolio being evaluated cares about both the systematic and idiosyncratic risk of the portfolio—any risk is relevant. However, an investor who has placed money into numerous different investment vehicles that are reasonably well diversified may care less about total portfolio risk and more about the portfolio's systematic risk. In the latter case, after all, idiosyncratic risk may be significant in a specific portfolio, but will have been almost completely diversified away by the investor.

Therefore, measures of risk-adjusted performance based on total risk are most appropriate when investors in the portfolio being evaluated have most of their wealth invested in the portfolio in question or when the portfolio in question is sufficiently diversified that it exhibits virtually no idiosyncratic risk on its own.

Return to Risk Ratio The Return to Risk Ratio is the ratio of average historical returns to the standard deviation of that manager's returns:[16]

$$\frac{\overline{R}_j}{\sigma_j} \tag{8.15}$$

where an overbar represents the sample average of the return on portfolio j and where σ_j is the standard deviation of portfolio j's returns over the chosen sample period. This is perhaps the simplest measure of return per unit of risk, where risk is defined as the standard deviation of actual returns. The Return to Risk Ratio thus quantifies the return per unit of total risk, where portfolio risk is presumed to be reflected entirely in the sample variance of the actual returns examined.

Sharpe Ratio   The Sharpe Ratio is quite similar to the Return to Risk Ratio and reveals a manager's excess returns per unit of risk, where risk is again defined as the historical standard deviation of returns. Specifically, the Sharpe Ratio is the ratio of the manager's average historical return minus the average Treasury bill (that is, risk-free) rate to the standard deviation of historical manager returns:[17]

$$\frac{R_j - T_F}{\sigma_j} \tag{8.16}$$

This measure can be viewed as the risk-adjusted return of assets acquired hypothetically assuming that Treasuries were used to finance the acquisition—in other words, the bang for the Treasury buck per unit of portfolio variability. Alternatively, by focusing on the cut performance of the actual manager vis-à-vis Treasury bills, the measure can be viewed as the benefit to holding risky assets relative to the opportunity cost of not holding riskless Treasuries.

Sharpe Ratios provide a way to compare and rank portfolios on a risk-adjusted basis, with higher Sharpe Ratios being more desirable. The Sharpe Ratio of a particular portfolio can be compared to the Sharpe Ratios of other benchmark portfolios or peer groups for risk-adjusted, comparative performance analysis. Thus, Sharpe Ratios can be used either to evaluate performance relative to the performance of other funds or indexes or to evaluate the return/risk profile of a manager in isolation as excess return per unit of risk.

Like the Return to Risk Ratio, the Sharpe Ratio is a performance measure based on the total risk of the portfolio. Variance, moreover, is presumed to be the only relevant summary statistic for capturing total risk. Therefore, the Sharpe Ratio makes two important implicit assumptions. First, because the measure is based on total risk, and thus aggregates systematic and idiosyncratic risk, this measure of performance is most appropriate when an investor has all or most of his or her wealth in the portfolio being evaluated. In other words, the Sharpe Ratio does not take into consideration that the investor may be holding other portfolios that result in the diversification of idiosyncratic risk across portfolios. Second, because standard deviation is used as a proxy for risk, the Sharpe Ratio assumes that the assets in the portfolio have return distributions that can be completely characterized by mean and variance. For portfolios including assets whose returns are not well described by a symmetric distribution, the Sharpe Ratio will reveal only part of the risk/return picture.

Tracking Error   Tracking error is defined as the standard deviation of excess returns (that is, the portfolio return less the returns on the relevant benchmark or index portfolio). The resulting statistic reveals the total risk of the portfolio in question, controlling for common factors influencing both the actual portfolio and the benchmark. In other words, the tracking error of a portfolio reveals the total risk in excess of the risk of the benchmark.

Consider the Sharpe Ratios for the portfolios j and m. The total risk of the two portfolios, which serves as the denominator for each Sharpe Ratio, is defined using the standard deviation of returns over some sample period $-\sigma_j$ and σ_m. Now suppose one wishes to compare the total risk of portfolio j in excess of portfolio m. In this case, total risk is the tracking error of portfolio j with respect to portfolio m. Using variance instead of standard deviation, the tracking error can be defined by the following equation:

$$\sigma_{j-m}2 = \text{Var}(R_j - R_m) = \text{Var}(R_m) - 2\text{Cov}(R_f R_m) \tag{8.17}$$

Note that tracking error takes into consideration the total risk of each portfolio and the co-movements between returns in the two portfolios.

Although Sharpe Ratios can be compared across managers and portfolios to gain insight into relative risk-adjusted performance, a simple comparison does not take into consideration the common factors that might be influencing both portfolios. We do not mean factors in the sense of asset pricing models, but are referring to anything that could cause two portfolio managers to have performance driven by similar decisions. Regardless what those factors are, it is important to take them into consideration. To see why, suppose one wanted to measure the risk of portfolio j relative to portfolio m and incorrectly attempted to do that by subtracting the denominator of the Sharpe Ratio for m from the denominator of the Sharpe Ratio for j. The result would simply be a subtraction of the two standard deviations, which would not take into consideration the covariance in the two portfolios.

Modified Sharpe Ratio The Modified Sharpe Ratio is a measure of excess portfolio returns to risk where both excess returns and risk are defined relative to a benchmark portfolio. Specifically, the Modified Sharpe Ratio measures the average portfolio returns less the average benchmark portfolio returns per unit of tracking error:

$$\frac{\overline{R}_j - \overline{R}_m}{\sigma_{j-m}} \tag{8.18}$$

This measure of risk offers a reasonably complete picture of the average benchmark-relative returns per unit of benchmark-relative total risk. It can be interpreted as the reward per unit of risk of investing in the actual portfolio rather than in the benchmark. Indeed, the traditional Sharpe Ratio is actually a special case of the Modified Sharpe Ratio where the benchmark portfolio is just a Treasury bill portfolio.

The Modified Sharpe Ratio can be extremely useful in comparing the performance of alternative investment portfolios. Unlike a simple comparison of two actual Sharpe Ratios, the Modified Sharpe Ratio takes into consideration the common factors that may be influencing risk and return in both portfolios. Like the Sharpe Ratio, however, the Modified Sharpe Ratio is a total risk performance measure. Because total risk includes both systematic and idiosyncratic risk, the Modified Sharpe Ratio may be less appropriate for investors who hold shares in a large number of different, diversified portfolios—that is, for investors whose idiosyncratic risks are largely diversified away. Also, like the Sharpe Ratio, variance remains the sole statistical summary of risk; asymmetric distributions and fat tails are therefore ignored.

It is worth noting the close similarity between the Modified Sharpe Ratio and the statistic commonly used for tests of significance—the *t-statistic*. If the denominator of the Modified Sharpe Ratio, the tracking error, is adjusted for (divided by) sample size, the result is the standard error or the mean:

$$s_{j-m} = \frac{\sigma_{j-m}}{\sqrt{N}} \qquad (8.19)$$

The *t*-statistic measures excess returns divided by the standard error of the mean:

$$t = \frac{\overline{R}_j - \overline{R}_m}{\frac{\sigma_{j-m}}{\sqrt{N}}} = \frac{\overline{R}_j - \overline{R}_m}{s_{j-m}} \qquad (8.20)$$

Although the original Sharpe Ratio can be used for an ex post risk-adjusted performance measure, the *t*-statistic also can be used as a test of the significance of excess returns earned. Further, it is a source, based on actual ex post historical manager data, for ex ante probabilistic inference of future excess returns.

Sortino Ratio   The Sortino Ratio is the average excess manager return per unit of downside risk—specifically, the BTR or downside semistandard deviation for a given return target T:

$$\frac{\overline{R}_j - \overline{R}_F}{BTR_j} \qquad (8.21)$$

As with the Sharpe Ratio, higher Sortino Ratios indicate more favorable risk/ return relations, and the Sortino Ratio of a particular fund is most useful when compared to Sortino Ratios of comparable funds or benchmarks.

The Sortino Ratio is essentially the same as the traditional Sharpe Ratio with one important difference—total risk is defined as downside risk rather than portfolio variance. For this reason, the Sortino Ratio is more attractive than the Sharpe Ratio when measuring the performance of portfolios whose returns are asymmetric. Unlike the Sharpe and Modified Sharpe Ratios, the Sortino Ratio is still a measure of total risk and thus is still inappropriate for investors whose total holdings are diversified and reflect no real idiosyncratic risks.

MEASURES OF IDIOSYNCRATIC AND SYSTEMATIC PERFORMANCE   In the case of investors in a portfolio with only a small fraction of their retirement assets or wealth invested in that portfolio, measures of risk based on either systematic or idiosyncratic risk may be of more interest than measures of total risk. For example, if a pension beneficiary invests in privately managed funds outside of his or her pension account in such a manner that his or her total investment portfolio is reasonably well diversified, he or she may prefer to evaluate alternative investments based on the return per unit of systematic risk rather than total risk. Several such performance measures are available—as well as measures based on idiosyncratic risk.

The particular means by which performance (returns) is adjusted for risk depends, of course, on the specific assumptions made about how risk is defined. Specifically, an asset pricing model must be assumed to hold in order to separate risk into its systematic and idiosyncratic components. Despite its lack of realism, the most common model used for such purposes is the CAPM. In addition, several performance measures based on multifactor risk also are available.

Jensen's Alpha One performance measure implied by the CAPM is *Jensen's alpha*, which measures the average excess return on a portfolio relative to the excess return predicted by the CAPM. To estimate this measure of performance, we need to run the following linear regression;

$$(R_p - R_f) = \alpha + \beta_p[R_m - R_f] + \varepsilon_p \tag{8.22}$$

where R_p is the time series of returns on the portfolio and where β_p is the covariance of portfolio returns and market returns divided by the variance of market returns.

If the CAPM holds, the estimated regression intercept should equal zero. We assume, moreover, that idiosyncratic risk is diversified away so that $E(\varepsilon_p) = 0$. As a result, the CAPM implies that the excess return on the portfolio exactly compensates investors for the systematic risk of the portfolio.

The estimated intercept indicates any positive excess returns above and beyond returns that are commensurate with the systematic risk of the position. In other words, Jensen's α measures the manager-specific returns in excess of those returns that are no more than a compensation for the systematic risk of the portfolio. A positive α indicates a value added by the portfolio manager, and negative α indicates that active management is penalizing investors in the fund.

However, if the CAPM is not the appropriate asset pricing model, Jensen's α can be a very biased measure of risk. Consider, for example, a portfolio of small-cap equities. One reason the CAPM may not be the best asset pricing model is that firm size is known to explain expected excess returns beyond those predicted by the CAPM relation. Specifically, small-cap firms tend to be riskier and have higher expected returns than large-cap firms. Consequently, the Jensen's α for a small-cap portfolio might be positive, suggesting at face value that returns to active management are positive. In reality, however, the positive estimate of α might simply reflect the greater systematic risk of the portfolio due to its small-cap concentration that is not reflected in the CAPM.

Treynor Ratio The Treynor Ratio is another measure of performance that assumes that the CAPM is the relevant means by which risk can be decomposed into systematic and idiosyncratic components. The Treynor Ratio is the analog of the Sharpe Ratio when only the price of systematic risk in the portfolio (the β of the portfolio) is deemed relevant to the investor. Specifically, the Treynor Ratio measures average excess returns over the chosen sample period relative to the portfolio's CAPM beta:

$$\frac{\overline{R}_j - \overline{R}_m}{\beta_j} \tag{8.23}$$

This summary measure of risk-adjusted performance yields an estimate of average excess returns per unit of systematic risk for portfolio j.

Appraisal Ratio The Appraisal Ratio is the third CAPM-based performance measure. The Appraisal Ratio is defined as $\alpha/\sigma_\varepsilon$ where α is Jensen's α and Σ_ε is the standard deviation of the residuals from the CAPM regression. The former is an estimate of the average excess return on a portfolio over and above the excess return that exactly compensates investors for the systematic risk of the portfolio, and the latter is a proxy for the idiosyncratic risk of the portfolio. The Appraisal Ratio thus reveals the average value added by managers (above the systematic risk-based excess return) per unit of idiosyncratic risk.

Market Risk Measurement for Risk Management Purposes

We have reviewed the various means by which risk can be defined conceptually. We have also examined the application of those risk measures to the ex ante allocation of capital into asset classes and the ex post analysis of risk-adjusted performance. In this section, we consider how the general measures of risk can be used to generate ex ante assessments of risk for the purpose of risk management and control.

Risk management is the process by which an organization tries to ensure that the risks to which it is exposed are those risks to which it thinks it is and needs to be exposed. In investment management, risk management therefore requires the investment manager to make an ongoing determination that the risks actually taken are commensurate with the risk/return target desired by investors. Performance evaluation plays a significant role in that process by enabling the plan to evaluate whether or not the risks that managers are taking are being commensurately reflected in realized returns. At the same time, market risk measurement can also be used for the purpose of risk control. Risk management and control is an ex ante process by which the plan tries to prevent excessive risks from being taken regardless of how they might impact returns. In other words, ex ante risk management tries to prevent large, unexpected losses arising from extremely risky investments by evaluating only the potential risk of those investments.

Fundamentally, market risk measures used for risk management and control trace to the same concepts of risk in probability and statistics on which performance measures rely. The critical distinction is that performance measures are based on the actual performance of a specific portfolio or manager, whereas market risk measures for risk management and control are based on the risk inherent to the instruments themselves. Whereas manager-specific data is used to estimate risk for performance evaluation purposes, instrument-specific data is used to estimate risk for monitoring and control purposes. The distinction will become clearer in the following section, where various risk measures and their relation to more traditional measures of investment risk are discussed.

VALUE AT RISK (VaR) Value at Risk (VaR) is a summary statistic that quantifies the exposure of a portfolio to market risk. Measuring risk using VaR allows the plan to make statements like the following: "We do not expect losses to exceed $1 million in more than 1 out of the next 20 months." VaR has a well-earned reputation as a useful summary measure of risk. It is comprehensive, enabling market risk to be examined at the instrument, fund, and aggregate portfolio levels. VaR also is consistent, facilitating the comparison of risk measures across different asset classes and securities. Because it summarizes market risk as a potential dollar loss, VaR is also an intelligible measure of risk that can easily be reported to plan managers and trustees.

In the context of the risk measures outlined in the section "Building Block Definitions of Risk," VaR also can be viewed as a way of summarizing a probability distribution or a sample distribution from which probabilistic inferences are drawn. Recall, for example, that variance is a way of summarizing a distribution of returns by describing how much dispersion those returns exhibit around the mean. Typically, VaR is used to summarize the point in the return distribution below which lies a certain amount of probability. VaR that is estimated at the 5 percent confidence level, for example, is a measure of the level below which returns are not expected to fall more than 5 percent of the time.

Distinctions between VaR and Measures of Risk for Performance   One of the main distinctions between VaR and measures of risk used for performance evaluation is that the latter uses actual portfolio returns data, whereas the former does not. VaR begins with the instruments in a portfolio at a particular time and then builds up to the estimate of risk from which ex ante inferences may be drawn. In other words, the statistics used to summarize risk are not particularly different in performance evaluation and VaR estimation; what differs is the probability or sampling distribution for which those statistics are calculated.

To measure performance, we simply looked at the distribution of historical portfolio returns and then chose a statistic like the mean or variance to summarize return and risk. To estimate the VaR of a portfolio, possible future values of that portfolio must be generated over a specific period of time called the *risk horizon*. The risk horizon is the interval over which the plan is concerned with changes in portfolio value (for example, monthly). The resulting distribution of possible portfolio changes is called the *VaR distribution*, which represents what the portfolio *might do* rather than what the portfolio *has done*. Once the VaR distribution is created for a chosen risk horizon, the VaR itself is just a number on the curve—that is, the change in the value of the portfolio leaving the specified amount of probability in the left-hand tail.

Creating a VaR distribution for a particular portfolio and a given risk horizon can be viewed as a two-step process. In the first step, the price or return distributions for each individual security or asset in the portfolio are generated. The instruments used as the basis for the portfolio VaR calculation are whatever instruments are in the portfolio at the time of the risk measurement. (This is quite distinct from performance measurement, which, focusing on portfolio-level returns, considers all instruments held in the portfolio over a specific period of time in the past.) The resulting VaR distributions for each instrument represent possible value changes in all the component assets over the risk horizon. Mathematically, for an asset whose per-period (for example, monthly) return distribution is known to be $f(R)$, the VaR at the x percent confidence level can be defined with the following equation:

$$0.05 = \int_{-\infty}^{\mathrm{Var}} f(R)dR \tag{8.24}$$

Next, the individual distributions somehow must be aggregated into a portfolio distribution using the appropriate measures of correlation. The resulting portfolio distribution then serves as the basis for the VaR summary measure.

An important assumption in almost all VaR calculations is that the portfolio whose risk is being evaluated does not change over the risk horizon.

This assumption of no turnover was not a major issue when VaR first arrived on the scene at derivative dealers. They were focused on 1- or 2-day—sometimes *intraday*—risk horizons and thus found VaR both easy to implement and relatively realistic. However, when it comes to generalizing VaR to a longer time horizon that is of more interest to institutional investors, the assumption of no portfolio changes becomes problematic. What does it mean, after all, to evaluate the 1-year VaR of a portfolio using only the portfolio's contents today if the turnover in the portfolio is 20 to 30 percent per day?

Methods for Calculating VaR   Methods for generating both the individual asset risk distributions and the portfolio risk distribution range from the simplistic to the indecipherably complex.[18] By far the easiest way to create the VaR distribution used in calculating the VaR statistic is just to assume that distribution is normal. Mean and variance are then sufficient statistics to fully characterize a normal distribution; they are all that is required to make probabilistic inferences about the distribution. For example, 5 percent of the probability in a normal distribution lies 1.65 standard deviations below the mean. So, a 5 percent VaR statistic for a portfolio of normally distributed returns can be computed by multiplying the current value (V) of the portfolio by its mean return minus 1.65 times its standard deviation:

$$VaR = V(\mu - 1.65\sigma) \qquad (8.25)$$

The variance used in the previous calculation is a neutral market estimate of the instrument's variance; this variance does not come from an actively managed position. For example, a moving average of the last 60 observed variances in the particular instrument in question may be used as the estimate for volatility.

In the case of two assets, the VaR of the portfolio can be computed in a similar manner using the variances of the two assets' returns. These variance-based risk measures then are combined using the correlation of the two assets' returns. The result is a VaR estimate for the portfolio.

The simplicity of the variance-based approach to VaR calculations lies in the assumption of normality. By assuming that returns on all financial instruments are normally distributed, the risk manager eliminates the need to come up with a VaR distribution using complicated modeling techniques. All that really must be done is to come up with the appropriate variances and correlations.

At the same time, however, by assuming normality, the risk manager has limited the VaR estimate. Normal distributions, as noted earlier, are symmetric. Therefore, any potential for skewness or fat tails in asset returns is totally ignored in the variance-only approach.

In addition to sacrificing the possibility that asset returns might not be normally distributed, the variance-only approach to calculating VaR also relies on the critical assumption that asset returns are totally independent across increments of time. A multiperiod VaR can be calculated only by calculating a single-period VaR from the available data and then extrapolating the multiday risk estimate. For example, suppose variances and correlations are available for historical returns measured at the daily frequency. To get from a 1-day VaR to a *T*-day VaR—where *T* is the risk horizon of interest—the variance-only approach requires that the 1-day VaR be multiplied by the square root of *T*.

For return variances and correlations measured at the monthly frequency or lower, this assumption might not be terribly implausible. For daily variances and correlations, however, serial independence is a very strong and usually an unrealistic assumption in most markets. The problem is less severe for short risk horizons, of course. So, using a 1-day VaR as the basis for a 5-day VaR might be acceptable, whereas a 1-day VaR extrapolated into a 1-year VaR would be highly problematic in most markets.

Despite the simplicity of most variance-based VaR measurement methods, many practitioners prefer to avoid the restrictive assumptions underlying that approach— that is, symmetric return distributions that are independent and stable over time. To avoid these assumptions, a risk manager must actually generate a full distribution of possible future portfolio values—a distribution that is neither necessarily normal nor symmetric.

Historical simulation is perhaps the easiest alternative to variance-based VaR. This approach generates VaR distributions merely by rearranging historical data— in other words, resampling time series data on the relevant asset prices or returns. This can be about as easy computationally as variance-based VaR, and it does not presuppose that everything in the world is normally distributed. Nevertheless, the approach is highly dependent on the availability of potentially massive amounts of historical data. In addition, the VaR resulting from a historical simulation is totally sample dependent.

More advanced approaches to VaR calculation usually involve some type of forward-looking simulation model, such as Monte Carlo. Implementing simulation methods typically is computationally intensive, expensive, and heavily dependent on personnel resources. For that reason, simulation has remained largely limited to active trading firms and institutional investors. Nevertheless, simulation does enable users to depart from normality assumptions about underlying asset returns without forcing them to rely on a single historical data sample. Simulation also eliminates the need to assume independence in returns over time—as a result, VaR calculations are no longer restricted to 1-day estimates that must be extrapolated over the total risk horizon.

Relations between VaR and Measures of Risk Used for Performance Evaluation As noted, the principal distinction between a market risk measurement used for risk management like VaR and risk measures used to calculate performance are the underlying distributions used to calculate the relevant summary statistics about risk. To see this, just suppose for a moment that we are working with the same probability distribution and that distribution is known.

With the same portfolio distribution used as the basis for calculating risk statistics, the close correspondence between risk measures used for performance evaluation and risk measures used for risk management and control becomes obvious. For example, assume that the common return distribution is a normal distribution. In that case, we can divide the average excess portfolio returns by the

5 percent variance-based VaR (expressed as a return) and multiply the result by 1.65 to get the Sharpe Ratio:

$$\left(\frac{\overline{R}_p - \overline{R}_f}{\text{VaR} - R_p} \right) 1.65 = \left(\frac{\overline{R}_p - \overline{R}_f}{1.65\sigma_p} \right) 1.65 = \left(\frac{\overline{R}_p - \overline{R}_f}{\sigma_p} \right) \qquad (8.26)$$

It should not be surprising that these two statistics are so closely related—variance-based VaR estimates and the Information Ratio are also related. In the Sharpe Ratio, standard deviation is the only measure of risk. In the VaR calculated when returns are normally distributed, 1.65 times the standard deviation subtracted from the mean is the only measure of risk. When both calculations are based on the same standard deviation, the fundamental result is the same. In short, we may be summarizing the information contained in the returns distribution differently using the Sharpe Ratio and VaR, but the information itself is the same because the distribution is the same.

It should be clear that unless the previous VaR statistic and Sharpe Ratio are calculated using exactly the same variance, the correspondence between the two statistics will break down. This should be the case. As noted, the variance used for the Sharpe Ratio is the variance of actual historical portfolio returns, whereas the variance used for the VaR calculation is a function of the variances and covariances of the instruments in the portfolio as of the date of the calculation and based not on actual performance, but rather on neutral market data.

Benchmark-Relative VaR   VaR can be calculated in an absolute sense for a specific portfolio or for a given portfolio relative to some index portfolio or benchmark. In an absolute VaR, only the distribution of actual portfolio returns is used to calculate the VaR statistic. In a benchmark-relative VaR, the distribution summarized with the VaR statistic is the distribution of the difference between returns on the target portfolio and returns on the benchmark. The resulting VaR statistic then measures the loss associated with the chosen confidence level and risk horizon relative to the benchmark loss. In other words, absolute VaR summarizes the absolute loss that is not expected to occur more than some percentage—say, 5 percent—of the time. A 5 percent benchmark-relative VaR, by contrast, summarizes the potential for a loss below the loss expected with the same probability on the benchmark portfolio. For example, suppose the monthly benchmark-relative VaR on an equity portfolio benchmarked to the S&P 500 is $1 million at the 5 percent confidence level. This means that with a 5 percent probability, the equity portfolio in question will underperform the S&P 500 by more than $1 million.

DOWNSIDE RISK MEASURES   As an alternative to VaR, some institutions summarize their risk for risk management and control purposes using downside risk measures rather than variance-based measures that assume symmetry in the underlying distribution. BTP and BTR were discussed as statistical measures of risk, and those statistics can be used directly for risk management and control purposes. In other words, if a pension plan's sole objective is to avoid a shortfall of assets below a liability target of, say, 5 percent, the BTP and/or BTR calculated with a target of $T = 5$ percent could serve as the basis for risk-control decisions.

As in the case of VaR, the primary distinction between applications of downside risk measures for performance evaluation and for risk control is the underlying return distribution being summarized by the statistic. When actual portfolio returns are the basis for the calculation, BTR can serve as the basis for risk-adjusted performance evaluation through the Sortino Ratio. When the downside semivariances of the instruments held in a portfolio on any given day are used to estimate future possible returns, the BTR summary measure reveals different information entirely.

REASONS FOR MEASURING MARKET RISK EX ANTE   In order for VaR or other measures of ex ante market risk to make sense, the investment policy and asset allocation decision must first be accepted as *sacrosanct*. VaR should compliment rather than compete with the primary investment management goals of the investment plan. It is a tool for helping the plan determine whether the risks to which it is exposed are those risks to which the plan thinks it is and wants/needs to be exposed. VaR will never tell the plan how much risk to take. It will only tell the plan manager how much risk is being taken.

Taking the investment policy as a given, a plan manager can apply VaR in at least four ways to the operation of his or her funds.[19] First, one of the primary benefits of VaR is that it facilitates the consistent and regular monitoring of market risk. The plan can calculate and monitor VaR on a variety of different levels. When calculated and monitored at the portfolio level, the risks taken by individual asset managers—whether they are internal traders and portfolio managers or external account managers—can be evaluated on an ongoing basis. Market risk can be tracked and monitored at the aggregate fund level, as well as by asset class, by issuer/counterparty, and the like.

Second, VaR can benefit the plan by helping to reduce any unnecessary transactional scrutiny by directors and trustees. In this way, VaR can actually help give portfolio managers more autonomy than they might otherwise have without a formalized, VaR-based risk management process.

A third application of VaR involves measuring and monitoring market risk using a formal system of predefined risk targets or thresholds. In essence, risk thresholds take ad hoc risk monitoring one step further and systematize the process by which VaR levels are evaluated and discussed for portfolios or managers—or in some cases, for the whole investment fund. A system of risk thresholds is tantamount to setting up a tripwire around an investment field, where the field is characterized by a fund's investment policy and risk tolerance. This tripwire is defined in terms of the maximum tolerable VaR allocated to a manager or portfolio and then is monitored by regularly (for example, weekly) comparing actual VaRs to these predefined targets. Investment managers are permitted to leave the field when they want, but the tripwire signals senior managers that they have done so. When a tripwire is hit (a VaR threshold is breached), an *exception report* is generated, and discussions and explanations are required.

The hallmark of a well-functioning risk target system is not that targets are never breached or that all executions are rectified through liquidating or hedging current holdings. Rather, the primary benefit of a risk target system is the formalization of a process by which exceptions are discussed, addressed, and analyzed. Therefore, risk thresholds are a useful means by which asset managers can systematically monitor and control their market risks without attenuating the autonomy of their portfolio managers. Because the primary purpose of risk limits is to systematize discussions about actual market risk exposures relative to defined risk tolerances, huge investments in VaR calculation systems, moreover, typically are not required. Even an imprecise measure of VaR will usually accomplish the desired result of formalizing the risk-monitoring process.

A more extreme version of risk targets and risk thresholds is a system of rigid risk limits. This application of VaR is also known as a *risk budget*. In a risk budget, the fund's total VaR is calculated and then allocated to asset classes and specific portfolios in terms of absolute and benchmark-relative VaR as well as Shortfall at Risk (SaR). Managers are then required to remain within their allocated risk budget along these risk dimensions. So, whereas risk targets resemble a tripwire around a field that managers must account ex post for crossing, a true risk budget acts as an electric fence around the field that managers simply cannot cross ex ante.

A total risk budget defined across all portfolios can create numerous problems for many institutional investors. First, risk budgeting relies at some level on the absolute VaR of a fund and its portfolios. To the extent that the measurement methodology is imperfect, the risk budget will be wrong. If the VaR measurement methodology is more biased for some asset classes or security types than others, some managers could be penalized or rewarded simply because of flaws in the measurement methodology. In the extreme, relatively riskier funds could be given a risk budget that is too high, whereas relatively safer funds could be allocated too little VaR.

Second, risk budgeting defined across both asset classes and portfolios can contradict and call into question the fund's asset allocation decision. This can be especially problematic if a board of trustees must approve changes in the asset allocation unless hitting a risk limit in the risk budget triggers the change. Because many institutional investors allocate capital into asset classes annually using traditional mean-variance asset allocation and portfolio optimization techniques, a VaR budget for asset classes and portfolios, where VaR is measured using a variance-based approach, would have to be enforced annually. If the risk budget is enforced more frequently than annually, the risk budget will call into question the asset allocation simply because volatility changes in the markets on a regular basis. Variance-induced changes in VaR, therefore, prompt a shift in the asset allocation through the risk budget. Even though the practical consequence is a change in the asset allocation itself, the actual trigger is the risk budget, so the board may never be consulted.

To avoid this problem, risk budgeting should be limited to rebalancing funds between portfolios within the same asset class. Even then, asset managers contemplating a risk budget will need to allocate a considerable sum of money for the VaR calculation system to ensure that the calculation method is not biased against particular managers or financial instruments.

RELATION TO ASSET ALLOCATION   Although risk measures used for performance evaluation purposes are clearly ex post measures of market risk, risk measures used for both asset allocation and risk-management purposes are both ex ante. The question naturally arises as to how the two are different.

Conceptually, the ex ante measurement of risk for asset allocation and risk management are not different at all. Both rely on the same basic building block definitions of risk, and both use tactics-neutral data about financial instruments rather than specific managers. Nevertheless, the applications are different in several important ways.

One distinction between the measurement of risk for asset allocation and risk management is the specific asset for which risk is being measured. Asset allocation focuses on risk measurement exclusively at the level of asset classes, whereas most applications of VaR or BTR involve portfolio-specific and often security-specific information. Returns on asset classes are usually sufficient to solve the asset allocation problem, whereas that is rarely adequate to engage in the monitoring of risk for risk-control purposes (for example, catching leveraged derivatives).

Another distinction lies in the frequency with which the evaluations are undertaken. Asset allocation and rebalancing are often extremely time consuming and costly. Large pension plans typically have an annual asset allocation with quarterly or monthly rebalancing horizons. When risk is measured to monitor trading activities, the time horizon is often much shorter, thus necessitating a different means by which risk is measured.

Finally, risk is defined solely as variance in most asset allocation problems because of the prevalence of the Markowitz mean-variance portfolio optimization paradigm. In principle, an efficient frontier can be generated based on other definitions of risk, such as BTR, but such exercises are significantly more cumbersome and resource intensive. Measures like VaR and BTR can, however, be calculated for risk control and monitoring purposes without the optimization. These measures, however, need not be variance based. Risk measurement for risk-management purposes thus provides the plan with additional insights about downside risks that may not be adequately captured in a variance statistic.

Because of the similarities between ex ante risk measures for asset allocation and risk management, variance-based VaR measures in particular can actually result in serious problems when the asset allocation is also undertaken using mean-variance optimization. If both measures of risk are based on the exact same variance, both the asset allocation and VaR will reveal equivalent information. But if the variance is different for the VaR because the frequency of VaR measurement is higher than the frequency of the asset allocation decision, the variance will change with market movements and could lead to rebalances in the asset allocation. On the one hand, this may be based on new, better information than the original asset allocation. On the other hand, that is what rebalancing targets are for, and frequent rebalancing triggered by VaR (or risk budgets) could become extraordinarily impractical and costly.

Conclusions

We have attempted to demonstrate how various measures of risk are related and can be used in different ways to measure risk for performance evaluation and for risk management and control. The various economic and statistical means by which risk itself is measured in finance do not really differ based on the application. However, the data and assumptions used in those applications do strongly influence the result.

In general, any measure of risk that is based on historical returns on an actively managed portfolio is appropriate for performance evaluation, but not risk measurement for risk control. Historical returns on an actual actively managed portfolio are ex post measures of risk and may have no bearing on the risk of a position held from today through tomorrow. True, the measures of risk used for risk management and control purposes are also based on historical data, which lies at the core of any statistical inference problem. However, that data, unlike data for performance evaluation, is tactics neutral. It should not and cannot depend on tactical management decisions, but rather should be confined to neutral market data about the risk inherent in instruments themselves.

The investment management process can be viewed as a cycle in which asset allocation leads to performance evaluation, performance evaluation leads to risk management, and risk management leads to asset allocation. When capital is first allocated into asset classes, ex ante measures of risk are required. Similarly, measuring risk ex ante for risk-control purposes facilitates the security selection process. Measuring risk ex post, in turn, helps determine how effective the other types of risk measures were based on actual data. Perhaps the best way to distinguish between measures of risk used for performance evaluation and those used for risk-control decisions, therefore, is to follow this rule: When evaluating performance, measure the risk of the manager based on his or her actual past performance; when evaluating risk going forward, measure the risk of the instruments currently held based on their actual past performance, regardless of who was trading them.

Note: The authors are grateful to Brian Heimsoth, Geoff Ihle, Andrea Neves, Kamaryn Tanner, and especially Pat Lipton for their helpful comments and their extensive work with us on this subject. The standard disclaimer applies, however, and we alone are responsible for any remaining errors or omissions. The views expressed herein are the views of the authors alone and do not necessarily represent the views of either the State of Wisconsin Investment Board or of CP Risk Management LLC and its clients.

Notes

1. We focus on monthly returns for simplicity. In reality, any frequency can be used.
2. Returns can be computed either arithmetically or using continuous compounding. We use the former because it enables us to consider explicitly any dividend payments.
3. See Christopher Culp, Kamaryn Tanner, and Ron Mensink, "Risk, Returns, and Retirement," *Risk* (October 1987). For a more detailed discussion, see Kamaryn T. Tanner, "An Asymmetric Distribution Model for Portfolio Optimization," manuscript, Graduate School of Business, The University of Chicago (1997).
4. Rarely are any of these statistics adequate in isolation. They usually must be considered together, as we will explain in more detail later.
5. We drop the subscript notation j for simplicity, noting that all statistics still refer to any asset or portfolio j.
6. The sum is often divided by N instead of $N + 1$, but for large samples, the results change little.

7. The most common means by which risk factors affect asset returns is through a relation that is presumed to be linear. Although this need not be the case, we confine our discussion to linear factor models. For a more general discussion, see John Cochrane, "Asset Pricing," manuscript (1999).

8. Readers may recognize the CAPM expression using actual returns as a type of linear regression. In a typical Ordinary Least Squares regression, we assume that $Cov(R_j, \varepsilon_j) = 0$. But this is a statistical assumption; whether it is actually true is an empirical matter.

9. See, for example, Eugene F. Fama and Kenneth R. French, "Common Risk Factors in the Returns on Stocks and Bonds," *Journal of Financial Economics* (February 1993).

10. This particular representation is linear. For a more general discussion, see Cochrane, "Asset Pricing."

11. See the reproduction in Harry Markowitz, *Portfolio Selection* (London: Blackwell, 1991).

12. Attempting to ascertain the true risk/return preferences of investors is admittedly difficult, but nevertheless plays an important part in the investment management process.

13. See Tanner, "An Asymmetric Distribution Model."

14. Ibid.

15. To keep this survey simple, we do not provide citations for the performance measures discussed. Most of these measures and their original sources can be found in any investments textbook. See, for example, Zvi Bodie, Alex Kane, and Alan J. Marcus, *Investments* (Chicago: Irwin Professional Publishing, 1993). A more advanced discussion and more recent literature survey can be found in Mark Grinblatt and Sheridan Titman, "Performance Evaluation," in *Handbooks in Operations Research & Management Science*, vol. 9, eds. R. Jarrow et al. (Amsterdam: Elsevier Science, 1995).

16. This is also sometimes called the Information Ratio. Many practitioners also refer to the Modified Sharpe Ratio, which is discussed later, as the Information Ratio. To avoid any confusion, we do not use the term *Information Ratio* to describe any performance measures in this document.

17. Strictly speaking, the ratio should be the average excess historical returns divided by the standard deviation of the *difference* between actual portfolio returns and the Treasury bill rate. In doing the actual calculation, most people simply calculate the standard deviation of portfolio returns as the denominator. If the risk-free rate is truly risk free, the variance of the risk-free rate is zero and the variance of the actual portfolio return less the risk-free rate should equal the variance of the actual return. Sometimes people actually do calculate the standard deviation of the residual because the Treasury bill rate does exhibit some positive variability.

18. Brief summaries of these methods are provided in Christopher L. Culp, Merton H. Miller, and Andrea M. P. Neves, "Value at Risk: Uses and Abuses," *Journal of Applied Corporate Finance* (Winter 1998), and Christopher L. Gulp, Ron Miller, and Andrea M. P. Neves, "Value at Risk for Asset Manager," *Derivatives Quarterly* (Winter 1998).

19. See Christopher L. Culp and Ron Mensink, "Use and Misuse of a Risk Management Tool," *Pensions & Investments* (August 1998).

Part III Introduction to Performance Analysis

Performance analysis, which is the final stage in the portfolio management process, is a major concern for both investors and portfolio managers. It provides an overall evaluation of the success of the investment process in reaching its objective. In so doing, it allows managers to evolve toward better control of the investment process and provides them with the means to improve it. Performance analysis covers all techniques, ranging from simple measure of the difference in the value of the portfolio between the beginning and the end of the evaluation period, to performance attribution of the contribution of each phase in the investment process to the overall portfolio performance, also including managers' skill evaluation.

Performance measurement is central to the management delegation process. Managers must respond to two of their clients' concerns. On the one hand, this involves showing that the performance obtained is satisfactory in comparison with the risk taken. On the other, it involves convincing them that the remuneration is justified and that the decisions made by the management firm on behalf of their client have produced additional return compared to that which would have been obtained had the client not employed the management firm's services.

International Performance Measurement Standardization Process

In view of the commercial importance of performance measurement, asset management firms have invested significantly in implementing it and making it reliable and sophisticated.

One of the first investments was to construct a standardized reporting, calculation, and presentation system that makes it easier to understand and compare managers' performances. This approach, promoted initially by the major U.S. managers and investors through the Association for Investment Management and Research Performance Presentation Standards (AIMR-PPS) standards, has progressed significantly in Europe since the middle of the 1990s, as a result of the adoption of a set of rules common to all countries (GIPS: Global Investment Performance Standards). For uniformity purposes, the IPC (Investment Performance Committee), which supervises and approves the national implementations of the GIPS standards, encourages professional organizations or national authorities to adopt the GIPS standards through their translated versions (TGs), without modifying them. To date, however, numerous countries have expressed a desire to implement specific adaptations.

While there has been progress in harmonizing performance measurement, it should be noted that the functional coverage of the GIPS remains limited. In fact, for management mandates, the GIPS provide information on fund returns that is equivalent in quality and accuracy to that of mutual funds through the concept of net asset value. The implementation of composites, which correspond to sorts of peer groups, the composition of which is controlled in order to forestall any manipulation, does not settle the matter of the benchmark that is truly representative of the asset allocation policy of the fund or mandate. The questions of risk-adjusted measurement or performance attribution, because they are less readily consensual, as a result of the large number of models and indicators available both in the academic literature and on the market, have not yet been the subject of standardization. Domestic or regional working groups may certainly issue recommendations, but we cannot truly consider that internationally recognized and accepted standards have emerged in this area.

In view of the sales and marketing importance of risk-adjusted return measurement or performance attribution, it is unlikely that this question will have a unanimous reply in the near future. Even if managers, plan sponsors, and consultants are greatly in favor of recommendations for performance attribution being implemented, the application of standards does not receive widespread support, including from consultants, who perhaps feel that one of their areas of expertise would become commonplace.

RISK-ADJUSTED MEASURE The risk-adjusted measure favored by professionals still relies to a large extent on the Sharpe ratio (Sharpe 1964), which compares the average excess return in relation to the risk-free rate to the volatility of the portfolio. This measure assumes that fund performance can be reduced to the first and second order moments of the return distribution (its mean and variance), which is only true in the Gaussian case (that is, the return distribution is normal). Unfortunately, normal distributions are rarely observed for asset returns in financial markets, even over the medium or long term, and even less in portfolios that integrate dynamic strategies or derivative instruments. More recently, a wide variety of indicators such as the Sortino ratio or the value at risk (VaR)–adjusted return have begun to be highlighted by managers to respond to the criticism aimed at reporting that was based on the Sharpe ratio alone.

While the risk-adjusted measure was being fine-tuned in order to evaluate the fair reward for the risks taken by the investor, the asset management industry also developed methods for evaluating the manager's outperformance. This involves justifying the choice of active management and, at the same time, the related management fees. This evaluation of the managers' outperformance (or alpha) has given rise to a significant amount of academic literature, which has provided the justification for the development of complex and costly software in recent years. Using multifactor models, researchers have tried to respond to criticism of the significance and stability of the alphas and betas drawn from the single-factor market model (that is, capital asset pricing model, CAPM). This approach is detailed in the section "Analysis of Alphas" later in this chapter.

INDICES AND BENCHMARKING The issue of the manager's outperformance or alpha raises the question of the choice of benchmark. The manager's performance is always presented in terms of and compared with that of a benchmark. The construction of a customized benchmark or "normal portfolio" using a historical or factor/style analysis of the portfolio composition is one of the major stages in performance analysis.

Bailey, Richards, and Tierney (1990) and Bailey (1992) set out rules that are commonly accepted today on what a valid benchmark should be:

1. Unambiguous
2. Investable
3. Measurable
4. Appropriate
5. Reflective of current investment opinions
6. Specified in advance

While rules 1, 2, 3, and 6 are unquestioned and are approached by professionals and researchers in the same way, rules 4 and 5 are more problematic. Bailey (1992) suggests that a benchmark is appropriate if "it is consistent with the manager's investment style" and that a benchmark is reflective of current investment opinion if "the manager has current investment knowledge of the securities that make up the benchmark."

In order to respect these conditions, managers must define a benchmark for which the securities are truly reflective of the neutral weight of the manager's universe. This benchmark approach, which is also called a "normal portfolio" and is intended to be representative of the risks taken over the analysis period, is not always compatible with the use of market indices.

Kuenzi (2003) highlighted the fact that two types of investment disciplines were observed on the market:

1. *Published benchmark-centered disciplines.* This involves the manager tracking published indices. The tracking does not exclude market timing and stock-picking practices in the case of active management, but over the period of analysis the published benchmark represents the "average" or neutral weight of the manager's portfolio.
2. *Manager strategy discipline.* This investment discipline assumes that the manager does not follow a market index, but has his own view on the risks and returns of the securities. This difference in viewpoint between the market and the manager leads the latter to construct an individual benchmark that is representative of his strategy.

In order to cope with the second approach, where the manager's style may be different from that of the benchmark, it is, of course, possible to turn to style indices or a combination of style indices, but this approach assumes that the style indices are themselves representative of the manager's views, which is not always the case.

The existence of published style indices does not presuppose that there is a consensus on the definition of the style and that the manager adheres to the index style. For example, a "growth" manager may not wish to take on the "technological" or "debt" bias of some "growth" style indices.

This lack of consensus is leading to an increasing number of style indices in the equity universe. It is also the consequence of an ongoing debate on the significance of the factors that are supposed to describe the style of the stocks. The use of benchmark is detailed in the next section.

Debate on Size and Book-to-Market Factors

Perhaps one of the most striking empirical findings in asset pricing over the past decade is the fact that a variety of empirical anomalies exist, which suggests that equity performance is not well described by standard capital market equilibrium models such as the CAPM. In particular, it has been reported (e.g., Fama and French, 1992) that both the market capitalization (size factor) and the ratio of book-to-market equity (B/M factor) explain a significant fraction of the cross-sectional difference in expected returns.

The existence and significance of a value and size premium are currently at the heart of a heated debate in asset-pricing research, as there is still no consensus over the economic interpretation of these empirical results. One interpretation is that the value premium is compensation for risks missed by the CAPM (e.g., Fama and French, 1992; Cochrane, 2001). In this interpretation, based on the fact that there seems to be common variation in distressed (value) firms' earnings that is not explained by market earnings, the book-to-market effect would be a proxy for some "distress" or "recession" factor. Fama and French (1992) suggest that multifactor models, justified through arbitrage arguments (arbitrage pricing theory developed by Ross [1976]) or equilibrium arguments—continuous-time CAPM—developed by Merton [1973]), have the potential to account for these differentials in style returns.

However, research has argued that the documented ability of size and B/M to explain the cross-section of stock returns is not necessarily inconsistent with a single-factor conditional CAPM. In particular, Jagannathan and Wang (1996) use a conditional CAPM framework to show that the beta-premium sensitivity, defined as the slope coefficient from a regression of conditional beta on expected risk premium, affects average returns along with the unconditional beta. In other words, that line of research promotes the argument that, while there is not much difference in unconditional betas between value and growth, there is evidence that the conditional market betas of value (growth) stocks covary positively (negatively) with the expected risk premium (see, e.g., Petkova and Zhang, 2002). Hence, the value premium would be explained by the fact that value stocks are more (less) risky than growth stocks in bad (good) times when marginal utility of consumption, and therefore expected risk premium, is high (low).

A completely different interpretation is that a behavioral bias would explain the value premium as naive investors irrationally undervalue distressed stocks and over-value growth stocks. In particular, Lakonishok, Shleifer, and Vishny (1994) argue that "value strategies yield higher returns because these strategies exploit the suboptimal behavior of the typical investor and not because these strategies are fundamentally riskier." A final interpretation is that the value premium is a sample-specific illusion (see, e.g., MacKinlay, 1995).

Whatever the explanation, rational (supported by a standard single-factor model or a suitable multifactor extension), behavioral, or data mining, it is certainly the case that this question has become a focal point of academic research in asset pricing theory. In parallel, the relevance of style (growth versus value, small cap versus large cap) has also become predominant in industry practice. Today, the concept of equity styles is widely accepted in the investment community and permeates the way most investors think about the stock markets and investment managers. The acceptance of equity style investing may in particular be gauged from the proliferation of style indices published by several vendors, including Russell, Wilshire Associates, BARRA/Standard & Poor's (S&P), Morgan Stanley Securities International (MSCI), Dow Jones, Prudential Securities International (PSI), among many others in the United States.

Amenc and Martellini (2003) report evidence of strong heterogeneity in the information conveyed by competing indices, and argue that this heterogeneity poses serious problems for modern portfolio analysis and empirical tests of asset pricing theory: if the true book-to-market and size factors are not observable, and if there is very little robustness with respect to the choice of the proxy used in empirical tests, then the relevance of these factors in asset pricing theory may never be empirically testable. This is somewhat reminiscent of Roll's (1977) critique of the CAPM.

Use of Benchmarks

Benchmarks constitute the reference portfolio and play a crucial role in evaluating performance in an accurate manner. As explained earlier in this chapter, the main quality of a benchmark is thus to properly reflect the risk exposure of the portfolio, that is, the assets contained and the strategy followed. It must follow the same calculation rules as the portfolio that is being evaluated. Problems in this context can arise from dividends that are sometimes excluded from the performance of an equity index (price index) or supposed to be directly reinvested (performance index), which does not necessarily correspond to the portfolio itself. The different kinds of benchmarks portfolio managers declare to use in performance measurement are discussed next.

GENERIC INDICES   While typically broad-market indices are used, some firms will use generic investment style indices. These include growth stock indices, value stock indices, small-cap stock indices, and large-cap stock indices, and provide a solution to the problem of selecting a benchmark portfolio that better reflects the characteristics of the managed portfolio. In particular, style indices avoid a situation where a manager following a particular style is rewarded for performance that is due to a favorable cycle for the investment style he adheres to. Proponents of style indices usually highlight this danger of evaluating style instead of skill.

We can, however, explain reservations with regard to generic style indices through the heterogeneity in the set of assets under consideration, as well as some heterogeneity in the index construction methods of different providers. As a consequence, return differences between competing equity style indices can be substantial. For example, for the month of February 2001 the return on the S&P 500 BARRA Growth Index was 11.75 percent while that of the Dow Jones for the same style was 18.36 percent. In addition, a generic index may not truly reflect the style followed by a particular manager, as generic indices exist only for some predefined categories. For the managers that do not fit into these categories, Sharpe benchmarks and normal portfolios (see below) provide a much better description of the manager's style.

CUSTOMIZED BENCHMARKS AND NORMAL PORTFOLIOS   There are several approaches to the construction of a benchmark that is truly representative of the asset allocation. The simple one consists of a simple combination of market indices. More sophisticated methods lead to the construction of "customized" benchmarks, referred to in the academic literature as the "normal portfolios" approach.

Normal portfolios are benchmarks that are tailor-made for each manager. They were developed from the principle that the portfolio manager's returns should be compared to the returns of a reference portfolio whose structure and composition are as similar as possible to those of the portfolio that is being evaluated. More often than not, portfolio managers are specialized in a single category of assets and therefore do not consider the complete universe of securities. Thus, broad indices are not suitable for evaluating their performance, because they contain securities that will not be included in the composition of the manager's portfolio. In addition, the proportions of each security in the indices are generally different from those chosen by the manager. The use of these indices as a benchmark could lead to an incorrect evaluation of the manager's performance. Managers could appear skillful if their style is favored by the market, or their result could be qualified as poor if their style is not favored by the market. We therefore prefer specialized benchmarks to broad indices.

A normal portfolio is defined by Christopherson (1989, p. 382) in the following way: "It is a portfolio that is made up of a set of securities that contains all the securities from which the manager is liable to make his choice, weighted in the same way as they are weighted in the manager's portfolio." A normal portfolio is therefore a specialized benchmark. It allows the manager's performance to be determined by evaluating his capacity to select the best securities and/or the best sectors in his normal universe. If the manager's performance is worse than that of the normal benchmark, one can conclude that the portfolio was managed poorly. This category of benchmark is therefore the one that allows for the most equitable evaluation of performance.

The objective in constructing a normal portfolio is to obtain an average characterization of the portfolio to be evaluated. The definition of a normal portfolio for a particular manager is not unique. Several methods enable normal portfolios to be built. The simplest and most commonly used technique for building a portfolio involves drawing up a list of securities, based on the historical composition of the portfolios held by the manager. A second approach involves basing the list of securities on exposure to risk factors. The manager's average exposure to different risk indices is analyzed to define the benchmark's exposures. A third method uses style indices to create a weighted combination of indices that corresponds to the manager's portfolio.

The first two approaches rely on the same principle: establishing a reduced list of securities from a broad universe by setting criteria that could relate to the price/earnings (P/E) ratio or exposure to certain factors. The portfolio is then constructed from the resulting list by attributing a weighting to each security. The first approach allows us to determine whether managers select the best securities within their normal universe. The second approach allows us to study the macro- or microeconomic sources of return and risk more precisely. The benchmark is based on the manager's portfolio risk factors. It is created by choosing securities similar to those selected by the manager and with an exposure to factors that is similar to the manager's average exposure. The benchmark therefore allows the manager's capacity to select securities from his universe to be evaluated, given his risk exposure profile. The third approach was developed by Sharpe and consists of performing multiple regressions on several specialized indices in order to obtain an index that is a linear combination of the different style indices available and corresponds best to the management style to be evaluated. The Sharpe benchmarks are therefore examples of normal benchmarks. The Sharpe benchmarks actually solve the problem of the investment style indices' being too specific since manager style is explained from a linear combination of the different indices. This third approach allows us to say whether the manager's performance can be better than that of a combination of style indices. The weightings assigned to each style index are based on the analysis of the manager's portfolio returns (returns-based analysis).

We can also mention the existence of complex benchmark construction methods that aim to create a benchmark truly representative of the historical allocation of the portfolio by using a factor approach or a probabilistic approach (portfolio opportunity distribution). These methods are widely discussed in the literature but do not seem to have a significant influence on actual practices.

Analysis of Alphas

Alpha is defined as the differential between the return on the portfolio in excess of the risk-free rate and some measure of normal return explained by an asset-pricing model and which represents the return of a passive portfolio with similar allocation. It is used to evaluate manager skill in doing active management. In essence, what differentiates the methods of analyzing alpha is the estimation of the normal return, that is, the part of return that represents the fair reward for the risk taken by the manager.

Apart from such an absolute performance measure, risk can be defined as the risk of deviating from a benchmark portfolio (tracking error). In this context, a skillful manager achieves returns above the benchmark with little tracking error. For asset management firms, identifying whether a manager's performance can be attributed to luck or skill is a crucial issue, as skill can be expected to have a favorable impact on future performance.

DIFFERENT MODELS FOR NORMAL RETURNS: ACADEMIC APPROACH

Market Models   Based on the CAPM, Jensen (1972) developed his alpha measure, which represents the additional return that is due to the manager's choices as opposed to the return that is due to the portfolio's exposure to market risk. Alpha analysis based on market models tends not to be widely used. This may be because of doubts about the validity of the CAPM and the CAPM's beta as a relevant measure of risk. This has been discussed in asset-pricing literature, notably by Fama and French (1992), who highlighted the importance of the size and book-to-market factors.

The result also depends on the choice of reference index. In addition, when managers practice a market timing strategy, beta varies according to anticipated movements in the market. As a consequence, the Jensen alpha often becomes negative, and does not then reflect the real performance of the manager.

Multifactor Models   The multifactor models contribute more information to alpha analysis than to CAPM-based measures. Asset returns can be decomposed linearly according to several risk factors common to all the assets, but with specific sensitivity to each. Once the model has been determined, the contribution of each factor to the overall portfolio performance can be attributed. Performance analysis then consists of evaluating whether the manager was able to orient the portfolio toward the most rewarding risk factors. *Ex post* observation of the level of returns compared to the consensus returns allows us to evaluate whether the manager was right or not to deviate from the benchmark by orienting the portfolio toward certain factors.

Analysis of portfolio performance with the help of a multifactor model should be applied to relatively homogenous asset classes because the factors identified depend on the type of assets under consideration. Despite the merits of such models, investors and portfolio managers may be reluctant to use multifactor models due to the risk of misspecification involved. Models that use implicit factors that have been extracted by means of inductive statistics, however, reduce model risk but increase sample risk, since the choice of a period conditions the extraction of the factors. In addition, implicit factor models render the interpretation and verification of the results difficult, as the model is often perceived as a "black box."

Style Analysis   Returns-based style analysis (RBSA), which was introduced by Sharpe (1988, 1992), consists of using the returns of asset classes as factors in the factor model. Asset class returns are estimated using returns on indices for distinct asset classes. In its strong form, RBSA uses a portfolio constraint (the coefficients are constrained to add up to one) and a positivity constraint (the coefficients are constrained to be positive). As a consequence, the factor loadings can be interpreted as portfolio weights for each asset class, for a portfolio that represents the risk exposure of the managed portfolio.

Firms may be reluctant to use this form of alpha analysis due to the fact that it has been promoted as a means of evaluating performance from an "outsider's perspective," when information on the effective asset mix is not available, a problem that does not arise for asset management firms when evaluating internal managers.

EVALUATING ALPHAS: PRACTITIONERS' APPROACH

Performance Relative to a Peer Group   While academic research has shown the limitations of a peer group approach in determining managers' alphas, this form of analysis of alpha appears to be popular. Performance analysis that is based on a comparison with a peer group supposes that the risk characteristics of the portfolio are well reflected by the peer group. A common practice is the use of a standardized Sharpe ratio in a peer group in order to evaluate investment funds.

However, in the United Kingdom, evaluation within a peer group has seen criticism in the recommendations made by the Myners report on institutional investment. The Myners report had criticized benchmarking against a peer group for not taking liability-related returns into account. Furthermore, the report argued that the peer group approach to performance measurement led to asset allocation decisions that often replicated average behavior in order to stick to the benchmark.

Performance Relative to a Benchmark   The *information ratio* is defined as the excess return compared to the benchmark per unit of tracking error. The excess return of a portfolio corresponds to the share of the return that is not explained by the benchmark. It results from the choices made by the manager to overweight securities that he hopes will have a return greater than that of the benchmark. The tracking error measures the variations in the residual return.

This form of analyzing alpha tends to be commonly used for relative performance to evaluate managers. Maximizing the information ratio, however, is often likely to generate strategies with very low tracking error (simply because the tracking error appears in the denominator of the information ratio, so that minimizing that quantity allows the information ratio to be increased significantly). Therefore, the maximization of returns subject to a tracking error constraint could be more useful than evaluating managers on the basis of the information ratio.

Performance Attribution

Performance attribution originated in the United States and is more recent in Europe. This can be explained by the longer tradition of delegating investment decisions to outside managers in the United States, namely, by pension funds and multimanagers. In addition, due to the large number of sophisticated institutional investors such as pension funds, advanced methods were used earlier. Performance attribution was first developed for equities and thus benefited from stock market–oriented investing in the United States.

Multifactor and arithmetic models are the most widespread in the area of performance attribution. Often, the multifactor approach, because it provides more information on the characteristics of the securities and enables those characteristics to be linked very accurately to the performance of the portfolio, is favored by the manager. It is the basis for the process of constructing the portfolio by decomposing the tracking error. We also note that multifactor analysis is used a lot more in performance attribution than in the analysis of alphas for manager evaluation, which can be explained by the fact that alpha is a rather academic notion. We note furthermore that multifactor models are used even more for portfolio risk analysis.

The *arithmetic approach*, due to Brinson, Hood, and Beebower (1986), attributes performance according to the stages in the investment management process. The portfolio performance is divided into asset allocation, stock picking, and the currency effect for international portfolios. An additional term, measuring the interaction between tactical asset allocation and stock picking, is sometimes explicitly formulated or integrated into either asset allocation or stock-picking term. These various terms are obtained by comparing the portfolio to be evaluated with a benchmark portfolio made of the same asset class with weightings corresponding to the portfolio long-term allocation. The tactical asset allocation component of performance is calculated by comparing the real portfolio to a portfolio having the benchmark asset classes return, but the real portfolio asset allocation. The stock-picking component is calculated by comparing the real portfolio to a portfolio having the real portfolio asset classes return, but the benchmark asset allocation. The excess portfolio return is therefore divided into a term that comes from an allocation between the asset classes that is different from that of the benchmark and correspond to a different level of risk; a term that comes from stock picking, which is different from that of the benchmark within each asset class; and a final term that represents the interaction between the two.

There is no dominant model or consensus for the moment in the area of performance attribution. In the area of equity investment, performance attribution is subject not only to an arithmetic portfolio return decomposition approach but also a more financial one using factor approaches. More specifically, it seems that when it involves performance attribution that is intended for the clientele, the arithmetic method is favored, but when it involves analyzing the exposure of the performance differential compared to the benchmark, the multifactor decomposition that was already used to estimate the tracking error is favored by the manager.

This observation of model and method heterogeneity is consistent with the study carried out on the subject by Spaulding (2002), who shows that even when we only consider the purely arithmetic performance attribution methods, it is rare for any model to represent more than 25 percent of the market share.

"Performance Is the Product"

The results of performance analysis have considerable consequences for managers, as the value added of an active strategy is judged by the performance in terms of returns over an alternative passive strategy with the same risk. The image factor that derives from good results in the past is decisive for asset managers as it determines possible fees and the capital inflows into its products.

As a report by Morgan states, in a difficult environment for the industry, "performance is the product." But while performance is a main driver of the asset management business, measurement of performance is still not very developed, with rather unsophisticated measures for risk-adjusted performance dominating reporting and manager rankings. In addition, the importance of performance has not necessarily convinced the majority of asset managers, because they tend to overestimate the importance of service and the client relationship while they underestimate the importance of past returns and risk in the investor's choice of an asset manager.

For institutional management, performance is also a key factor in the success of asset management firms. While the 1990s were marked by the significant influence of the qualitative rating of asset management firms, with investors expecting that their investment management process would guarantee control over the risks and benchmark tracking, since the year 2000 the quality of the organization of the investment management process has been played down in favor of performance.

We therefore observe an acceleration in mandate switches that is no longer due only to changes in the investor's allocation, but also linked to the performance and risk management offered by the asset management firm.

In the management of "retail" funds, it is clear that depending on whether the network is more or less captive, performance has a greater or lesser influence. In those countries that have a significant independent distribution network, the influence of the agencies that rate funds and the performance of funds is therefore considerable. This influence should be considered with care since there is awareness of the imperfections of the ranking methods, which are based more often than not on peer groups that are defined fairly arbitrarily and do not reflect the fund allocation policy. This fact has been highlighted by different studies of fund ratings. Del Guercio and Tkac (2001) found that in the United States a mutual fund's initial five-star rating yields a seven-month abnormal flow of $26 million, which is 53 percent above the flow that would normally be expected. In that context, managers are paying close attention to the quality of the rating.

The structural change in the asset management industry also plays its part in revealing the value of performance analysis. The industry is becoming increasingly specialized, which leads to a need for customized benchmark portfolios. The most visible development is specialization in investment styles, which has led to the creation of a number of style benchmarks that are more useful for taking into account specific characteristics than a global market index. In addition, the broad peer group comparison approach has been criticized, notably by the Myners report (2001), which was commissioned by the UK government and recommends using a customized benchmark.

Apart from the equity universe, benchmarks for other asset classes such as fixed income securities and alternative investments have been the object of industry initiatives such as the launch of an alternative to proprietary bond indices by third-party providers and more and more indices that cover the hedge fund universe (such as the indices launched by S&P and MSCI).

The increasing choice among rival indices has investors looking more than ever at the quality of benchmarks available on the market. What is more, with the proliferation of multimanager structures, there is an increasing need for methods that allow the contribution of each manager to be attributed individually.

FUND PERFORMANCE RATING   Quantitative ratings have been introduced by firms such as Standard & Poor's, Lipper, and Morningstar.

The S&P ratings use a measure of relative performance, the information ratio of a fund, as the rating criterion. The benchmark portfolio is represented by the funds in the same category (that is, its peer group).

Morningstar calculates a risk-adjusted return based on the fund's net return after annual fees and its three-year historical volatility. A measure of relative volatility is deduced from relative net performance in order to establish the Morningstar risk-adjusted return. This performance measure leads to a ranking that is consistent with that of an expected utility maximizing investor with constant relative risk aversion (see Sharpe, 1998).

Lipper takes a particular approach in attaching a double rating to each fund. The first rating concerns consistent return whereas the second judges the capital preservation offered by the fund. Ratings (Lipper Leader, 2, 3, 4, 5) are attributed separately for consistent return and capital preservation. The Lipper rating for consistent return uses an information ratio in a peer group (the fund's category) as well as the Hurst exponent H (see Hurst, 1951). The latter measures the persistence of a time series, that is, the regularity of the fund's returns over the past. A Hurst exponent of one-half actually corresponds to a typical random walk assumption stating that the fund returns have independent increments. A Hurst exponent between one-half and 1 means that the fund returns exhibit positive serial correlation: Past returns are not independent of each other, and good returns are more likely to follow good returns, meaning that the fund shows consistency in returns. The opposite holds for a fund with a Hurst exponent between 0 and one-half: the fund returns exhibit negative serial correlation, and therefore little consistency. Lipper classifies funds into three groups: those with an H above 0.55, those with H below 0.45, and those in between. In each group, investment funds are then ranked by their information ratios.

The rating for capital preservation uses lower partial moment analysis in order to measure downside risk. The target return is defined as 0 by Lipper so that only negative returns are taken into account when calculating risk. One problem investors are faced with is the comparability of ratings. In fact, even if S&P and Morningstar both use relative performance within a peer group, the attribution of stars (both ratings attribute one to five stars to investment funds) is based on different distributions. The number of stars does not therefore correspond to the same relative standing of a fund. A three-star rating from S&P, for example, means that the fund is within the top 31 percent to 50 percent, whereas the same number of stars from Morningstar means that the fund is in the middle third of ranked funds. A one-star rating from S&P corresponds to a position in the bottom quartile, whereas one star from Morningstar means that the fund is among the bottom decile of its category.

In addition, the methods of the large U.S. rating agencies rely on grouping funds into peer groups and calculating the return and risk in relation to the peer group. These techniques are relatively unsophisticated and pose a number of problems. As a result, the grouping of portfolios or managers into homogenous peer groups creates a true dilemma. As detailed information on the asset allocation policy of peers is hard to obtain (in the case of external peers), very broad peer groups that do not reflect the specifics of the portfolio that is being evaluated are formed. In that way, a "North American stocks" category does not account for style allocations, even though they are very popular in the American market. The definition of a relevant peer group poses a dilemma, as broad categories do not take into account a specialized manager's style, and narrow categories do not capture the characteristics of strategies that are based on diversification between multiple styles or asset classes.

In fact, the difficulties involved in prior categorization of portfolios according to their financial characteristics often lead professionals to challenge the classification of their fund when it is not favorable to them.

As to the predictive capability of fund ratings, a study on the Morningstar ratings (before the methodology revision done in 2002) by Blake and Morey (2000) found that low ratings indicate relatively poor future performance while there is little evidence that the highest-rated funds outperform the medium-rated funds. More important, the study finds that the ratings do not do better than the fund's past average monthly returns as a naive predictor of performance (see Amenc and Lesourd, 2005 for more details on the relative merits of various rating systems).

Summary

This chapter presents an overview of the various aspects involved in portfolio performance measurement, both from an academic standpoint and from the practitioner's perspective. It successively covers the subject of benchmark definition, alpha measurement, performance attribution, and managers' skill evaluation, to conclude with an introduction to performance ratings.

References

Amenc, N., and V. Lesourd. 2005. Rating the ratings. Working paper, EDHEC Risk and Asset Management Research Center.

Amenc, N., and L. Martellini. 2003. Desperately seeking pure style indexes. Working paper, EDHEC Risk and Asset Management Research Center.

Bailey, J. 1992. Are manager universes acceptable performance benchmarks? *Journal of Portfolio Management* 18, 3: 9–13.

Bailey, J., T. Richards, and D. Tierney. 1990. Benchmark portfolios and the manager/plan sponsor relationship. In *Current Topics in Investment Management*, ed. F. J. Fabozzi. New York: Harper Collins.

Blake, C., and M. Morey. 2000. Morningstar ratings and mutual fund performance. *Journal of Financial and Quantitative Analysis* 35, 3: 451–483.

Brinson, G. P., L. R. Hood, and G. L. Beebower. 1986. Determinants of portfolio performance. *Financial Analysts Journal* 42, July/August: 38–44.

Christopherson, J. 1989. Normal portfolios and their construction. In *Portfolio and Investment Management*, ed. F. J. Fabozzi. Chicago: Probus Publishing.

Cochrane, J. 2001. *Asset pricing*. Princeton, NJ: Princeton University Press.

Del Guercio, D., and P. A. Tkac. 2001. Star power: The effect of Morningstar ratings on mutual fund flows. Working Paper No 2001-15, Federal Reserve Bank of Atlanta.

Fama, E., and K. French. 1992. The cross-section of expected stock returns. *Journal of Finance* 47, 2: 442–465.

Hurst, H. E. 1951. Long-term storage of reservoirs. *Transactions of the American Society of Civil Engineers*, 116; formalized in *The Fractal Geometry of Nature* (1977), by B. Mandelbrot. New York: W.H. Freeman and Co.

Jagannathan, R., and Z. Wang. 1996. The conditional CAPM and the cross-section of expected returns. *Journal of Finance* 51, 1: 3–53.

Jensen, M. C. 1972. Optimal utilization of market forecasts and the evaluation of investment performance. In *Mathematical Methods in Investment and Finance*, eds. G. P. Szego and K. Shell. Amsterdam: North-Holland.

Kuenzi, D. E. 2003. Strategy benchmarks. *Journal of Portfolio Management* 29, 2: 46–56.

Lakonishok, J., A. Shleifer, and R. Vishny. 1994. Contrarian investment, extrapolation, and risk. *Journal of Finance* 49, 5: 1541–1578.

MacKinlay, C. 1995. Multifactor models do not explain deviations from the CAPM. *Journal of Financial Economics* 38, 1: 3–28.

Morgan Stanley Equity Research Europe. 2002. *Performance Is the Product: Outlook for UK Asset Managers.*

Merton, R. C. 1973. An intertemporal capital asset pricing model. *Econometrica* 41, 5: 867–888.

Myners, P. 2001. Institutional investment in the United Kingdom: A review. Report to the Chancellor of the Exchequer, HM Treasury, March.

Petkova, R., and L. Zhang. 2002. Is value riskier than growth? Working Paper, William E. Simon Graduate School of Business Administration, University of Rochester.

Roll, R. 1977. A critique of the asset pricing theory's tests, part 1: On past and potential testability of the theory. *Journal of Financial Economics* 4, 2: 129–176.

Ross, S. 1976. The arbitrage theory of capital asset pricing. *Journal of Economic Theory* 13, December: 341–360.

Sharpe, W. 1964. Capital asset prices: A theory of market equilibrium under conditions of risk. *Journal of Finance* 19, 3: 425–442.

Sharpe, W. 1988. Determining a fund's effective asset mix. *Investment Management Review* 2, December: 59–69.

Sharpe, W. 1992. Asset allocation: Management style and performance measurement. *Journal of Portfolio Management* 18, Winter: 7–19.

Sharpe, W. 1998. Morningstar's risk-adusted ratings. *Financial Analysts Journal* 54, July/August: 21–33.

Spaulding, D. 2002. Performance measurement attribution survey—detailed results. *The Spaulding Group.*

Part IV Performance Measurement, Analysis, and Attribution

Performance Measure and Evaluation

When evaluating a manager, the consultant may be interested in whether the value added by a manager can be attributed to market timing or to security selection. To perform this analysis, the consultant must have established a normal asset allocation for the portfolio.

Consider Table 8.4.

TABLE 8.4

Asset Class	Policy or Normal Weight	Actual Weight	Index Return
Stocks	57%	45%	6%
Bonds	37%	55%	3%
Cash	6%	0%	2%

The return on the managed portfolio was 5.1 percent.

Setting a Benchmark

If the manager had been invested in index funds according to the policy weights, the portfolio return would have been 0.57(6) + 0.37(3) + 0.06(2) = 4.65 percent. This is the sum of the products of the policy weights with the index returns. This is the benchmark return. However, the manager did better than the benchmark. The manager achieved an added 0.45 percent of value (5.1% − 4.65%).

Attribution

How much of the manager's overperformance came from timing (active asset allocation) and how much came from security selection? If the manager had been invested according to the actual allocation using index funds, the return would have been 0.45(6) + 0.55(3) = 4.35%. This is the sum of the products of the actual weights and the index returns. So the timing decisions had reduced the return from 4.65 percent to 4.35 percent. The effect from timing is (4.35% − 4.65%) = −0.30%. However, overall the manager earned 5.1 percent, which is 0.45 percent above the benchmark. The lost return was made up and surpassed so there must have been a much larger security selection effect. Security selection must be +0.75% (0.45% + 0.30%).

The 0.45% value added can be attributed to market timing (−0.30%) and security selection (0.75%). This is summarized as follows:

Benchmark Return = Policy Weights × Index Returns = 4.65%
Value Added by Manager = Manager Return − Benchmark Return = 0.45%
Manager Return Due to Allocation = Actual Weights × Index Returns = 4.35%
Value Added by Manager = Value Added by Timing + Value Added by Security
    Selection = 0.45%

TABLE 8.5   Hypothetical Mutual Fund Data

Asset Class	Fund Commitment	Normal Position	Fund Return for Class	Class Benchmark Return
Equity	0.70	0.60	7.28	5.81
Bonds	0.07	0.30	1.89	1.45
Cash	0.23	0.10	0.20	0.48

Value Added by Timing = Manager Return Due to Allocation – Benchmark Return = –0.30%

Value Added by Security Selection = Value Added by Manager – Value Added by Timing = 0.75%

This is a simple example of an attribution analysis.

Consider the data about a mutual fund in Table 8.5.

Calculate the following:

1. The normal position return
2. The value added for this fund
3. The added performance due to the asset mix (timing) decision
4. The added performance due to the asset selection decision

1. Normal Position Return = Σ [(Normal Position for Class) × (Class Benchmark Return)]

$$= \text{Normal Position Equity} \times \text{Benchmark Return Equity}$$
$$+ \text{Normal Position Bond} \times \text{Benchmark Return Bonds}$$
$$+ \text{Normal Position Cash} \times \text{Benchmark Return Cash}$$
$$= (0.60)(5.81) + (0.30)(1.45) + (0.10)(0.48) = 3.97$$

2. Value Added for This Fund = Σ [(Actual Return) – (Normal Position Return)]

Actual Return
$$= \text{Fund Commitment Equity} \times \text{Fund Return Equity}$$
$$+ \text{Fund Commitment Bonds} \times \text{Fund Return Bonds}$$
$$+ \text{Fund Commitment Cash} \times \text{Fund Return Cash}$$
$$= (0.70)(7.28) + (0.07)(1.89) + (0.23)(0.20) = 5.27$$
Value Added = 5.27 – 3.97 = 1.30

3. The added performance due to the asset mix (timing) decision

Value Added from Active Asset Allocation = Σ [Fund Weight for Class) – (Normal Position for Class)] × [(Class Benchmark Return) – (Normal Position Return)]

$$= (0.70 - 0.60) \times (5.81 - 3.97)$$
$$+ (0.07 - 0.30) \times (1.45 - 3.97)$$
$$+ (0.23 - 0.10) \times (0.48 - 3.97)$$
$$= 0.31$$

4. The added performance due to the asset selection decision

Value Added from Asset Selection Decision = Σ [Fund Weight for Class] $\times$ [(Fund Return for Class) $-$ (Class Benchmark Return)]

$$
\begin{aligned}
&= (0.70) \times (7.28 - 5.81) \\
&+ (0.07) \times (1.89 - 1.45) \\
&+ (0.23) \times (0.20 - 0.48) \\
&= 0.995
\end{aligned}
$$

Total Risk-Adjusted Measures

It is natural to try to represent performance with a single number that incorporates both the calculations of return and risk. This is risk-adjusted return. Since theory suggests that rate of return and risk are directly related, investors want to know if they are being compensated for the risk they have assumed. There are several ratios that attempt to do this.

SHARPE RATIO The Sharpe ratio measures the total risk of the portfolio by including standard deviation instead of only the systematic risk (i.e., beta). It does not implicitly assume that a portfolio is well diversifed. The foundation of the Sharpe ratio is Modern Portfolio Theory (MPT), and the idea is the higher the Sharpe ratio, the closer the portfolio is to the mean variance portfolio. This means that the Sharpe Index standardizes the return in excess of the risk-free rate by the variability of the returns. The formula for the Sharpe ratio is as follows:

$$
\text{Sharpe ratio} = \frac{\text{Average actual return} - \text{Average risk-free return}}{\text{Standard deviation of the portfolio}}
$$

$$
\text{Sharpe ratio} = \frac{\overline{R}_p - \overline{R}_f}{\sigma_p}
$$

The Sharpe ratio divides the excess return (actual return minus the risk-free return) of a portfolio by the standard deviation of the portfolio. Since standard deviation is in the denominator, the equation measures total risk. Technically, the Sharpe ratio should use the arithmetic average of the returns. In practice, the geometric mean is frequently used.

Consider that portfolio X earns a 13 percent return with a standard deviation of 30 percent, and portfolio Y earns 15 percent with a standard deviation of 20 percent. The risk-free rate is 5 percent. The Sharpe index is calculated for each portfolio as follows:

$$
S_x = \frac{13 - 5}{30} = 0.27\%
$$

$$
S_y = \frac{15 - 5}{20} = 0.50\%
$$

This indicates that portfolio Y outperformed portfolio X on a risk-adjusted basis.

SORTINO RATIO   The Sortino ratio is also based on MPT and is closely related to the Sharpe ratio except that it uses downside risk. The Sortino ratio gives the same ranking as the Sharpe ratio of portfolio performance.

$$\text{Sortino ratio} = \frac{\text{Average actual return} - \text{Average risk-free return}}{\text{Downside semistandard deviation}}$$

$$\text{Sortino ratio} = \frac{\overline{R}_p - \overline{R}_f}{\text{Downside } \sigma_p}$$

M-SQUARED   M-squared is a return measure that adjusts for total risk from the mix of funds or managers being evaluated. The weightings of the mix are selected to match the total risk of an index (e.g., S&P 500). The calculation is

$$M^2 = \left[1 - \frac{\sigma \text{ S\&P 500}}{\sigma \text{ Fund}}\right] \times [\text{T-bill return}] + \left[\frac{\sigma \text{ S\&P 500}}{\sigma \text{ Fund}}\right] \times [\text{Actual return}]$$

Consider the following:

	Return	Standard Deviation
Portfolio	10%	15%
S&P 500	11%	17%

Also assume that the risk-free rate of return on a T-Bill is 5 percent. M-squared can be found by:

$$M^2 = \left[1 - \frac{0.17}{0.15}\right] \times [0.05] + \left[\frac{0.17}{0.15}\right] \times [0.10] = 0.1067 \text{ or } 10.67\%$$

This implies that the portfolio underperformed the market when adjusting for total risk. The portfolio's total risk-adjusted return of 10.67 percent is less than the S&P 500's return of 11 percent. M-squared is directly related to the Sharpe ratio. Therefore, a higher Sharpe ratio implies a higher M-squared, and a lower Sharpe ratio implies a lower M-squared.

Market Risk Adjusted Measures

TREYNOR RATIO   The Treynor ratio is similar to the Sharpe ratio, except it uses the beta of the portfolio in the denominator. This means that it is using systematic risk instead of total risk. This measure assumes the portfolio is fully diversified.

$$\text{Treynor ratio} = \frac{\text{Average actual return} - \text{Average risk-free return}}{\text{Beta of the portfolio}}$$

$$\text{Treynor ratio} = \frac{\overline{R}_p - \overline{R}_f}{\beta_p}$$

Consider the following example to understand how to interpret the Treynor ratio. The S&P 500 earns 11 percent when a government T-Bill earns 5 percent. Portfolio X earns a 13 percent return with a beta of 1.3, and portfolio Y earns

15 percent with a beta of 2.0. Using the information, the Treynor ratio is calculated for the market portfolio and each portfolio as follows:

$$T_m = \frac{11 - 5}{1} = 6.00$$

$$T_x = \frac{13 - 5}{11.3} = 6.15$$

$$T_y = \frac{15 - 5}{21} = 5.00$$

This indicates that portfolio X outperformed the market and portfolio Y on a risk-adjusted basis. However, the results do not indicate by how much each portfolio outperformed the market. You will notice that when calculating the Sharpe ratio earlier, the results were the opposite. That is, portfolio Y outperformed portfolio X when using Sharpe ratio. The difference in ranking occurs because the measure of risk is different.

ALPHA (JENSEN'S PERFORMANCE INDEX) To explain Jensen's performance measure, it is necessary to first define alpha, but first let us take a step back. A further refinement that CAPM brings to Modern Portfolio Theory (MPT) is the graph of expected return versus standard deviation. It is linear with standard deviation on the *x*-axis and expected return of the *y*-axis. The standard deviation of the portfolio measures the total market and nonmarket risk of the portfolio. Interestingly, this graph makes the case for passive investing in the market portfolio rather than an actively managed account and here is why:

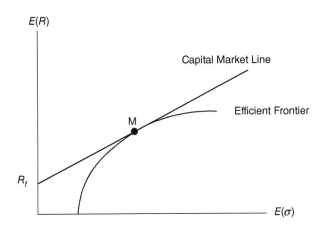

As mentioned before, the standard deviation of the portfolio measures the total market and nonmarket risk of the portfolio. Portfolio optimizer software is available that uses CAPM to graphically represent portfolios along the risk-return trade-off curve. This curve is the efficient frontier. The Capital Market Line (CML) represents the best combination of risky and risk-free assets. (Note the difference between the CML, which has an *x*-axis of σ_p, and the SML, which is β_p). Points below the CML offer too little return for the risk. Theoretically, no returns can be above the CML. The point at which the efficient frontier curve meets the straight line is the optimal market portfolio of risky assets. The market portfolio represents the ultimate or completely diversified portfolio. If, indeed, this is also the optimal risky portfolio, why should an investor choose an active investment strategy?

The answer lies in the fact that actual portfolio returns may exceed the CAPM equation:

$$E(R_p) = R_F + \beta_p(R_M - R_F)$$

In other words, there is a residual tacked on to the expected return. This residual is termed alpha (α). It measures the nonmarket return associated with the portfolio. Positive alpha means that the manager has added value through his or her security selection and timing. Negative alphas indicate value subtracted. Alpha is calculated as:

$$\text{Actual return} = \text{Expected return} + \text{Alpha}$$
$$\text{Actual return} = R_F + \beta_P(R_M - R_F) + \alpha$$

Typically this is written as:

$$R_P = \alpha + E(R_P)$$

So, we solve for α:

$$\alpha = E(R_p) - [R_f + \beta_p(R_m - R_f)]$$

Where, $E(R_p)$ is the expected return of the portfolio, R_f is the return on a risk-free asset, R_m is the return on the market, and β is the beta of an asset. The α (also referred to as Jensen's alpha) value indicates whether a portfolio manager is superior or inferior in market timing and stock selection.

For example, assume a return of 17 percent with a beta of 1.3 for manager X when the market return is 14.5 percent and the risk-free rate is 5 percent. Jensen's alpha is expressed as

$$J_a = 17 - [5 + (14.5 - 5)1.3] = -0.35\%$$

Nonmarket Risk Measure

TRACKING ERROR   Another statistic to consider is tracking error. Tracking error is the annualized standard deviation of monthly excess returns. You can generally assume the tracking error is normally distributed. To calculate an annual tracking error, multiply the observed tracking error by the square root of the number of periods in one year. If you use quarterly data, the annual tracking error is found by multiplying the observed tracking error by the square root of 4.

The following is a sample of quarterly returns (annualized) for portfolio A, portfolio B, and the index:

Portfolio A	Portfolio B	Index
3.5%	3.9%	4.5%
7.3%	7.1%	6.9%
6.5%	6.9%	7.4%
4.4%	4.3%	4.5%
5.3%	4.9%	5.3%

Which portfolio has the *least* tracking error to the index? The standard deviation of portfolio A is 1.53, for portfolio B is 1.49, and for the index is 1.36.

The portfolio with the least standard deviation ratio to the index has the least tracking error. The ratio of portfolio A to the index is 1.53/1.36 = 1.125. The ratio of portfolio B to the index is 1.49/1.36 = 1.096. Therefore, portfolio B exhibits the least tracking error to the index.

INFORMATION RATIO The information ratio is the average excess return of a portfolio over a benchmark divided by the standard deviation of the excess returns. This measures the ability to select securities relative to a benchmark. It captures both the size of the excess return and the ability to do so consistently.

Information Ratio = excess return/tracking error

Assume the following statistics for two small-cap portfolios:

Portfolio	Alpha (basis points)	Tracking Error (basis points)
1	345	607
2	455	935

Information ratio for portfolio 1 = 345/607 = 0.568

Information ratio for portfolio 2 = 455/935 = 0.487

The higher the information ratio, the more likely it is that a manager's performance is the result of skill rather than luck. A high information ratio will result from a positive alpha and low tracking error. However, the information ratio is of limited value in your decision if the information is based on relatively few years. It requires several years of gathering information for a high confidence ratio. If we do not know how many years the information is based on, we can state that if your risk profile is low, you might select portfolio 1; if high, you might select portfolio 2.

CHAPTER 9

Traditional Global Investments

Equity and Fixed Income

I nvestment advisors and consultants must be familiar with the numerous structures and characteristics of various global equity investments. The first reading in this chapter reviews market organization and structure as well as the more common forms of equity investments both in the United States and abroad and how each is classified. The second reading discusses the risk-reward trade-off of equity investments both theoretically and historically. Valuation is also discussed. The third reading reviews the concept and history of equity styles boxes. The fourth reading explains financial statement analysis with a specific review of the most common metrics and ratios used in fundamental analysis. The last reading reviews common benchmarks and indices used in performance evaluation and analysis.

Part I *Investments: Principles of Portfolio and Equity Analysis:* Market Organization and Structure

Learning Objectives
- Describe classifications of assets and markets.
- Describe the major types of securities, currencies, contracts, commodities, and real assets that trade in organized markets, including their distinguishing characteristics and major subtypes.

Part II *Investments: Principles of Portfolio and Equity Analysis:* Overview of Equity Securities

Learning Objectives
- Discuss the importance and relative performance of equity securities in global financial markets.
- Discuss the characteristics of various types of equity securities.
- Distinguish between public and private equity securities.
- Discuss the differences in voting rights and other ownership characteristics among various equity classes.

- Discuss the methods for investing in nondomestic equity securities.
- Compare and contrast the risk and return characteristics of various types of equity securities.
- Explain the role of equity securities in the financing of a company's assets and creating company value.
- Distinguish between the market value and book value of equity securities.
- Compare and contrast a company's cost of equity, its (accounting) return on equity, and investors' required rates of return

Part III *ActiveBeta Indexes: Capturing Systematic Sources of Active Equity Returns:* The Evolution of Equity Style Indexes

Learning Objectives

- Present different empirical challenges to financial theories such as the Capital Asset Pricing Model (CAPM) and the Efficient Market Hypothesis (EMH).
- Describe theoretical explanations for anomalies to financial theories.
- Describe the history of the establishment of equity styles including the works of Sharpe, Fama, and French.
- Draw and describe the traditional "equity style box."
- Explain the methodology of the equity style index, and list the strengths and weaknesses of using this methodology as a basis for portfolio construction.

Part IV *Mathematical Finance:* Cost of Capital and Ratio Analysis

Learning Objectives

- Define the concept of the cost of capital.
- Describe and calculate the weighted-average cost of capital.
- Describe and explain the importance of the following profitability ratios: gross profit margin, operating profit margin, net profit margin, return on investment, and return on equity.
- Describe and explain the importance of the following market-based ratios: price-earnings (P/E) ratio, price-earnings-growth ratio, earnings per share (EPS), dividend yield, cash flow per share, payout ratio, book value per share, price-book value ratio, price/sales ratio, and Tobin's Q ratio.
- Describe and explain the importance of the following operational ratios: inventory turnover ratio, accounts receivable turnover ratio, accounts payable turnover ratio, fixed asset turnover ratio, and total asset turnover ratio.
- Describe and explain the importance of the following liquidity ratios: current ratio, acid-test ratio, net working capital ratio, and cash-current liabilities ratio.
- Describe and explain the importance of the following debt ratios: debt-asset ratio, debt-equity ratio, solvency ratio, times interest earned ratio, and operating income-fixed payments ratio.
- Discuss the importance of financial statement analysis (ratio analysis), using both the balance sheet and the income-expense statement, to an integrated model such as the DuPont model.

Part V *Investments: Principles of Portfolio and Equity Analysis:* Security Market Indices

Learning Objectives

- Describe a security market index.
- Calculate and interpret the value, price return, and total return of an index.
- Discuss the choices and issues in index construction and management.
- Compare and contrast the different weighting methods used in index construction.
- Calculate and interpret the value and return of an index on the basis of its weighting method.
- Discuss rebalancing and reconstitution.
- Discuss uses of security market indices.
- Discuss types of equity indices.
- Compare and contrast the types of security market indices.

Part I Market Organization and Structure

Assets and Contracts

People, companies, and governments use many different assets and contracts to further their financial goals and to manage their risks. The most common assets include financial assets (such as bank deposits, certificates of deposit, loans, mortgages, corporate and government bonds and notes, common and preferred stocks, real estate investment trusts, master limited partnership interests, pooled investment products, and exchange-traded funds), currencies, certain commodities (such as gold and oil), and real assets (such as real estate). The most common contracts are option, futures, forward, swap, and insurance contracts. People, companies, and governments use these assets and contracts to raise funds, to invest, to profit from information-motivated trading, to hedge risks, and/or to transfer money from one form to another.

CLASSIFICATIONS OF ASSETS AND MARKETS Practitioners often classify assets and the markets in which they trade by various common characteristics to facilitate communications with their clients, with each other, and with regulators.

The most actively traded assets are securities, currencies, contracts, and commodities. In addition, real assets are traded. Securities generally include debt instruments, equities, and shares in pooled investment vehicles. Currencies are monies issued by national monetary authorities. Contracts are agreements to exchange securities, currencies, commodities, or other contracts in the future. Commodities include precious metals, energy products, industrial metals, and agricultural products. Real assets are tangible properties such as real estate, airplanes, or machinery. Securities, currencies, and contracts are classified as financial assets whereas commodities and real assets are classified as physical assets.

Securities are further classified as debt or equity. Debt instruments (also called fixed-income instruments) are promises to repay borrowed money. Equities represent ownership in companies. Pooled investment vehicle shares represent ownership of an undivided interest in an investment portfolio. The portfolio may include securities, currencies, contracts, commodities, or real assets. Pooled investment vehicles, such as exchange-traded funds, which exclusively own shares in other companies generally are also considered equities.

Securities are also classified by whether they are public or private securities. Public securities are those registered to trade in public markets, such as on exchanges or through dealers. In most jurisdictions, issuers must meet stringent minimum regulatory standards, including reporting and corporate governance standards, to issue publicly traded securities.

Private securities are all other securities. Often, only specially qualified investors can purchase private equities and private debt instruments. Investors may purchase them directly from the issuer or indirectly through an investment vehicle specifically formed to hold such securities. Issuers often issue private securities when they find public reporting standards too burdensome or when they do not want to conform to the regulatory standards associated with public equity. **Venture capital** is private equity that investors supply to companies when or shortly after they are founded. Private securities generally are illiquid. In contrast, many public securities trade in liquid markets in which sellers can easily find buyers for their securities.

Contracts are derivative contracts if their values depend on the prices of other underlying assets. Derivative contracts may be classified as physical or financial depending on whether the underlying instruments are physical products or financial securities. Equity derivatives are contracts whose values depend on equities or indices of equities. Fixed-income derivatives are contracts whose values depend on debt securities or indices of debt securities.

Practitioners classify markets by whether the markets trade instruments for immediate delivery or for future delivery. Markets that trade contracts that call for delivery in the future are forward or futures markets. Those that trade for immediate delivery are called spot markets to distinguish them from forward markets that trade contracts on the same underlying instruments. Options markets trade contracts that deliver in the future, but delivery takes place only if the holders of the options choose to exercise them.

When issuers sell securities to investors, practitioners say that they trade in the **primary market.** When investors sell those securities to others, they trade in the **secondary market.** In the primary market, funds flow to the issuer of the security from the purchaser. In the secondary market, funds flow between traders.

Practitioners classify financial markets as money markets or capital markets. Money markets trade debt instruments maturing in one year or less. The most common such instruments are repurchase agreements, negotiable certificates of deposit, government bills, and commercial paper. In contrast, capital markets trade instruments of longer duration, such as bonds and equities, whose values depend on the creditworthiness of the issuers and on payments of interest or dividends that will be made in the future and may be uncertain. Corporations generally finance their operations in the capital markets, but some also finance a portion of their operations by issuing short-term securities, such as commercial paper.

Finally, practitioners distinguish between traditional investment markets and alternative investment markets. Traditional investments include all publicly traded debts and equities and shares in pooled investment vehicles that hold publicly traded debts and/or equities. Alternative investments include hedge funds, private equities (including venture capital), commodities, real estate securities and real estate properties, securitized debts, operating leases, machinery, collectibles, and precious gems. Because these investments are often hard to trade and hard to value, they may sometimes trade at substantial deviations from their intrinsic values. The discounts compensate investors for the research that they must do to value these assets and for their inability to easily sell the assets if they need to liquidate a portion of their portfolios.

The remainder of this section describes the most common assets and contracts that people, companies, and governments trade.

EXAMPLE 9.1   Asset and Market Classification

The investment policy of a mutual fund permits the fund to invest only in public equities traded in secondary markets. Would the fund be able to purchase:

1. Common stock of a company that trades on a large stock exchange?
2. Common stock of a public company that trades only through dealers?
3. A government bond?
4. A single stock futures contract?
5. Common stock sold for the first time by a properly registered public company?
6. Shares in a privately held bank with €10 billion of capital?

Solutions:

1. Yes. Common stock is equity. Those common stocks that trade on large exchanges invariably are public equities that trade in secondary markets.
2. Yes. Dealer markets are secondary markets and the security is a public equity.
3. No. Although government bonds are public securities, they are not equities. They are debt securities.
4. No. Although the underlying instruments for single stock futures are invariably public equities, single stock futures are derivative contracts not equities.
5. No. The fund would not be able to buy these shares because a purchase from the issuer would be in the primary market. The fund would have to wait until it could buy the shares from someone other than the issuer.
6. No. These shares are private equities, not public equities. The public prominence of the company does not make its securities public securities unless they have been properly registered as public securities.

SECURITIES   People, companies, and governments sell securities to raise money. Securities include bonds, notes, commercial paper, mortgages, common stocks, preferred stocks, warrants, mutual fund shares, unit trusts, and depository receipts. These can be classified broadly as fixed-income instruments, equities, and shares in pooled investment vehicles. Note that the legal definition of a security varies by country and may or may not coincide with the usage here. Securities that are sold to the public or that can be resold to the public are called issues. Companies and governments are the most common issuers.

Fixed Income Fixed-income instruments contractually include predetermined payment schedules that usually include interest and principal payments. Fixed-income instruments generally are promises to repay borrowed money but may include other instruments with payment schedules, such as settlements of legal cases or prizes from lotteries. The payment amounts may be prespecified or they may vary according to a fixed formula that depends on the future values of an interest rate or a commodity price. Bonds, notes, bills, certificates of deposit, commercial paper, repurchase agreements, loan agreements, and mortgages are examples of promises to repay money in the future. People, companies, and governments create fixed-income instruments when they borrow money.

Corporations and governments issue bonds and notes. Fixed-income securities with shorter maturities are called "notes," those with longer maturities are called "bonds." The cutoff is usually at 10 years. In practice, however, the terms are generally used interchangeably. Both become short-term instruments when the remaining time until maturity is short, usually taken to be one year or less.

Some corporations issue convertible bonds, which are typically convertible into stock, usually at the option of the holder after some period. If stock prices are high so that conversion is likely, convertibles are valued like stock. Conversely, if stock prices are low so that conversion is unlikely, convertibles are valued like bonds.

Bills, certificates of deposit, and commercial paper are respectively issued by governments, banks, and corporations. They usually mature within a year of being issued; certificates of deposit sometimes have longer initial maturities.

Repurchase agreements (repos) are short-term lending instruments. The term can be as short as overnight. A borrower seeking funds will sell an instrument—typically a high-quality bond—to a lender with an agreement to repurchase it later at a slightly higher price based on an agreed-upon interest rate.

Practitioners distinguish between short-term, intermediate-term, and long-term fixed-income securities. No general consensus exists about the definition of short-term, intermediate-term, and long-term. Instruments that mature in less than one to two years are considered short-term instruments whereas those that mature in more than five to ten years are considered long-term instruments. In the middle are intermediate-term instruments.

Instruments trading in money markets are called money market instruments. Such instruments are traded debt instruments maturing in one year or less. Money market funds and corporations seeking a return on their short-term cash balances typically hold money market instruments.

Equities Equities represent ownership rights in companies. These include common and preferred shares. Common shareholders own residual rights to the assets of the company. They have the right to receive any dividends declared by the boards of directors, and in the event of liquidation, any assets remaining after all other claims are paid. Acting through the boards of directors that they elect, common shareholders usually can select the managers who run the corporations.

Preferred shares are equities that have preferred rights (relative to common shares) to the cash flows and assets of the company. Preferred shareholders generally have the right to receive a specific dividend on a regular basis. If the preferred share is a cumulative preferred equity, the company must pay the preferred shareholders any previously omitted dividends before it can pay dividends to the common shareholders. Preferred shareholders also have higher claims to assets relative to common shareholders in the event of corporate liquidation. For valuation purposes, financial analysts generally treat preferred stocks as fixed-income securities when the issuers will clearly be able to pay their promised dividends in the foreseeable future.

Warrants are securities issued by a corporation that allow the warrant holders to buy a security issued by that corporation, if they so desire, usually at any time before the warrants expire or, if not, upon expiration. The security that warrant holders can buy usually is the issuer's common stock, in which case the warrants are considered equities because the warrant holders can obtain equity in the company by exercising their warrants. The warrant exercise price is the price that the warrant holder must pay to buy the security.

EXAMPLE 9.2   Securities

What factors distinguish fixed-income securities from equities?

Solution: Fixed-income securities generate income on a regular schedule. They derive their value from the promise to pay a scheduled cash flow. The most common fixed-income securities are promises made by people, companies, and governments to repay loans.

Equities represent residual ownership in companies after all other claims—including any fixed-income liabilities of the company—have been satisfied. For corporations, the claims of preferred equities typically have priority over the claims of common equities. Common equities have the residual ownership in corporations.

Pooled Investments   Pooled investment vehicles are mutual funds, trusts, depositories, and hedge funds that issue securities that represent shared ownership in the assets that these entities hold. The securities created by mutual funds, trusts, depositories, and hedge funds are respectively called *shares, units, depository receipts,* and *limited partnership interests* but practitioners often use these terms interchangeably. People invest in pooled investment vehicles to benefit from the investment management services of their managers and from diversification opportunities that are not readily available to them on an individual basis.

Mutual funds are investment vehicles that pool money from many investors for investment in a portfolio of securities. They are often legally organized as investment trusts or as corporate investment companies. Pooled investment vehicles may be open-ended or closed-ended. Open-ended funds issue new shares and redeem existing shares on demand, usually on a daily basis. The price at which a fund redeems and sells the fund's shares is based on the net asset value of the fund's portfolio, which is the difference between the fund's assets and liabilities, expressed on a per share basis. Investors generally buy and sell open-ended mutual funds by trading with the mutual fund.

In contrast, closed-end funds issue shares in primary market offerings that the fund or its investment bankers arrange. Once issued, investors cannot sell their shares of the fund back to the fund by demanding redemption. Instead, investors in closed-end funds must sell their shares to other investors in the secondary market. The secondary market prices of closed-end funds may differ—sometimes quite significantly—from their net asset values. Closed-end funds generally trade at a discount to their net asset values. The discount reflects the expenses of running the fund and sometimes investor concerns about the quality of the management. Closed-end funds may also trade at a discount or a premium to net asset value when investors believe that the portfolio securities are overvalued or undervalued. Many financial analysts thus believe that discounts and premiums on closed-end funds measure market sentiment.

Exchange-traded funds (ETFs) and exchange-traded notes (ETNs) are open-ended funds that investors can trade among themselves in secondary markets. The prices at which ETFs trade rarely differ much from net asset values because a class of investors, known as authorized participants (APs), has the option of trading directly with the ETF. If the market price of an equity ETF is sufficiently below its net asset value, APs will buy shares in the secondary market at market price and redeem shares at net asset value with the fund. Conversely, if the price of an ETF is sufficiently above its net asset value, APs will buy shares from the fund at net asset value and sell shares in the secondary market at market price. As a result, the market price and net asset values of ETFs tend to converge.

Many ETFs permit only in-kind deposits and redemptions. Buyers who buy directly from such a fund pay for their shares with a portfolio of securities rather than with cash. Similarly, sellers receive a portfolio of securities. The transaction portfolio generally is very similar—often essentially identical—to the portfolio held by the fund. Practitioners sometimes call such funds "depositories" because they issue depository receipts for the portfolios that traders deposit with them. The traders then trade the receipts in the secondary market. Some warehouses holding industrial materials and precious metals also issue tradable warehouse receipts.

Asset-backed securities are securities whose values and income payments are derived from a pool of assets, such as mortgage bonds, credit card debt, or car loans. These securities typically pass interest and principal payments received from the pool of assets through to their holders on a monthly basis. These payments may depend on formulas that give some classes of securities—called tranches—backed by the pool more value than other classes.

Hedge funds are investment funds that generally organize as limited partnerships. The hedge fund managers are the general partners. The limited partners are qualified investors who are wealthy enough and well informed enough to tolerate and accept substantial losses, should they occur. The regulatory requirements to participate in a hedge fund and the regulatory restrictions on hedge funds vary by jurisdiction. Most hedge funds follow only one investment strategy, but no single investment strategy characterizes hedge funds as a group. Hedge funds exist that follow almost every imaginable strategy ranging from long–short arbitrage in the stock markets to direct investments in exotic alternative assets.

The primary distinguishing characteristic of hedge funds is their management compensation scheme. Almost all funds pay their managers with an annual fee that is proportional to their assets and with an additional performance fee that depends on the wealth that the funds generate for their shareholders. A secondary distinguishing characteristic of many hedge funds is the use of leverage to increase risk exposure and to hopefully increase returns.

CURRENCIES Currencies are monies issued by national monetary authorities. Approximately 175 currencies are currently in use throughout the world. Some of these currencies are regarded as reserve currencies. Reserve currencies are currencies that national central banks and other monetary authorities hold in significant quantities. The primary reserve currencies are the U.S. dollar and the euro. Secondary reserve currencies include the British pound, the Japanese yen, and the Swiss franc.

Currencies trade in foreign exchange markets. In spot currency transactions, one currency is immediately or almost immediately exchanged for another. The rate of exchange is called the spot exchange rate. Traders typically negotiate institutional trades in multiples of large quantities, such as US$1 million or ¥100 million. Institutional trades generally settle in two business days.

Retail currency trades most commonly take place through commercial banks when their customers exchange currencies at a location of the bank, use ATM machines when traveling to withdraw a different currency than the currency in which their bank accounts are denominated, or use credit cards to buy items priced in different currencies. Retail currency trades also take place at airport kiosks, at storefront currency exchanges, or on the street.

REAL ASSETS Real assets include such tangible properties as real estate, airplanes, machinery, or lumber stands. These assets normally are held by operating companies, such as real estate developers, airplane leasing companies, manufacturers, or loggers. Many institutional investment managers, however, have been adding real assets to their portfolios as direct investments (involving direct ownership of the real assets) and indirect investments (involving indirect ownership, for example, purchase of securities of companies that invest in real assets or real estate investment trusts). Investments in real assets are attractive to them because of the income and tax benefits that they often generate, and because changes in their values may have a low correlation with other investments that the managers hold.

Direct investments in real assets generally require substantial management to ensure that the assets are maintained and used efficiently. Investment managers investing in such assets must either hire personnel to manage them or hire outside management companies. Either way, management of real assets is quite costly.

Real assets are unique properties in the sense that no two assets are alike. An example of a unique property is a real estate parcel. No two parcels are the same because, if nothing else, they are located in different places. Real assets generally differ in their conditions, remaining useful lives, locations, and suitability for various purposes. These differences are very important to the people who use them, so the market for a given real asset may be very limited. Thus, real assets tend to trade in very illiquid markets.

The heterogeneity of real assets, their illiquidity, and the substantial costs of managing them are all factors that complicate the valuation of real assets and generally make them unsuitable for most investment portfolios. These same problems, however, often cause real assets to be misvalued in the market, so astute information-motivated traders may occasionally identify significantly undervalued assets. The benefits from purchasing such assets, however, are often offset by the substantial costs of searching for them and by the substantial costs of managing them.

Many financial intermediaries create entities, such as real estate investment trusts (REITs) and master limited partnerships (MLPs), to securitize real assets and to facilitate indirect investment in real assets. The financial intermediaries manage the assets and pass through the net benefits after management costs to the investors who hold these securities. Because these securities are much more homogenous and divisible than the real assets that they represent, they tend to trade in much more liquid markets. Thus, they are much more suitable as investments than the real assets themselves.

Of course, investors seeking exposure to real assets can also buy shares in corporations that hold and operate real assets. Although almost all corporations hold and operate real assets, many specialize in assets that particularly interest investors seeking exposure to specific real asset classes. For example, investors interested in owning aircraft can buy an aircraft leasing company such as Waha Capital (Abu Dhabi Securities Exchange) and Aircastle Limited (NYSE).

EXAMPLE 9.3   Assets and Contracts

Consider the following assets and contracts:

Bank deposits	Hedge funds
Certificates of deposit	Master limited partnership interests
Common stocks	Mortgages
Corporate bonds	Mutual funds
Currencies	Stock option contracts
Exchange-traded funds	Preferred stocks
Lumber forward contracts	Real estate parcels
Crude oil futures contracts	Interest rate swaps
Gold	Treasury notes

1. Which of these represent ownership in corporations?
2. Which of these are debt instruments?
3. Which of these are created by traders rather than by issuers?
4. Which of these are pooled investment vehicles?
5. Which of these are real assets?
6. Which of these would a home builder most likely use to hedge construction costs?
7. Which of these would a corporation trade when moving cash balances among various countries?

Solutions:

1. Common and preferred stocks represent ownership in corporations.
2. Bank deposits, certificates of deposit, corporate bonds, mortgages, and Treasury notes are all debt instruments. They respectively represent loans made to banks, corporations, mortgagees (typically real estate owners), and the Treasury.

3. Lumber forward contracts, crude oil futures contracts, stock option contracts, and interest rate swaps are created when the seller sells them to a buyer.
4. Exchange-traded funds, hedge funds, and mutual funds are pooled investment vehicles. They represent shared ownership in a portfolio of other assets.
5. Real estate parcels are real assets.
6. A builder would buy lumber forward contracts to lock in the price of lumber needed to build homes.
7. Corporations often trade currencies when moving cash from one country to another.

Part II Overview of Equity Securities

1. Introduction

Equity securities represent ownership claims on a company's net assets. As an asset class, equity plays a fundamental role in investment analysis and portfolio management because it represents a significant portion of many individual and institutional investment portfolios.

The study of equity securities is important for many reasons. First, the decision on how much of a client's portfolio to allocate to equities affects the risk and return characteristics of the entire portfolio. Second, different types of equity securities have different ownership claims on a company's net assets, which affect their risk and return characteristics in different ways. Finally, variations in the features of equity securities are reflected in their market prices, so it is important to understand the valuation implications of these features.

This part provides an overview of equity securities and their different features and establishes the background required to analyze and value equity securities in a global context. It addresses the following questions:

- What distinguishes common shares from preference shares, and what purposes do these securities serve in financing a company's operations?
- What are convertible preference shares, and why are they often used to raise equity for unseasoned or highly risky companies?
- What are private equity securities, and how do they differ from public equity securities?
- What are depository receipts and their various types, and what is the rationale for investing in them?
- What are the risk factors involved in investing in equity securities?
- How do equity securities create company value?
- What is the relationship between a company's cost of equity, its return on equity, and investors' required rate of return?

The remainder of this part is organized as follows. Section 2 provides an overview of global equity markets and their historical performance. Section 3 examines the different types and characteristics of equity securities, and Section 4 outlines the differences between public and private equity securities. Section 5 provides an overview of the various types of equity securities listed and traded in global markets.

Section 6 discusses the risk and return characteristics of equity securities. Section 7 examines the role of equity securities in creating company value and the relationship between a company's cost of equity, its return on equity, and investors' required rate of return. Section 8 concludes and summarizes this part.

2. Equity Securities in Global Financial Markets

This section highlights the relative importance and performance of equity securities as an asset class. We examine the total market capitalization and trading volume of global equity markets and the prevalence of equity ownership across various geographic regions. We also examine historical returns on equities and compare them to the returns on government bonds and bills.

Figure 9.1 summarizes the contributions of selected countries and geographic regions to global gross domestic product (GDP) and global equity market

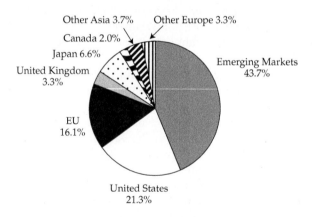

A. Contribution to World GDP

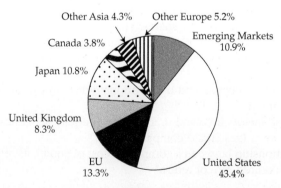

B. Contribution to Global Stock Market Capitalization

FIGURE 9.1   Country and Regional Contributions to Global GDP and Equity Market Capitalization (2007)

Sources: MacroMavens, *IMF World Economic Outlook 2008,* Standard & Poor's BMI Global Index weights.

TABLE 9.1   Equity Markets Ranked by Total Market Capitalization at the End of 2008 (billions of U.S. dollars)

Rank	Name of Market	Total U.S. Dollar Market Capitalization	Total U.S. Dollar Trading Volume	Number of Listed Companies
1	NYSE Euronext (U.S.)	$9,208.9	$33,638.9	3,011
2	Tokyo Stock Exchange Group	$3,115.8	$5,607.3	2,390
3	NASDAQ OMX	$2,396.3	$36,446.5	2,952
4	NYSE Euronext (Europe)	$2,101.7	$4,411.2	1,002
5	London Stock Exchange	$1,868.2	$6,271.5	3,096
6	Shanghai Stock Exchange	$1,425.4	$2,600.2	864
7	Hong Kong Exchanges	$1,328.8	$1,629.8	1,261
8	Deutsche Börse	$1,110.6	$4,678.8	832
9	TSX Group	$1,033.4	$1,716.2	3,841
10	BME Spanish Exchanges	$948.4	$2,410.7	3,576

Note that market capitalization by company is calculated by multiplying its stock price by the number of shares outstanding. The market's overall capitalization is the aggregate of the market capitalizations of all companies traded on that market. The number of listed companies includes both domestic and foreign companies whose shares trade on these markets.

Source: Adapted from the *World Federation of Exchanges 2008 Report* (see www.world-exchanges.org).

capitalization. Analysts can examine the relationship between equity market capitalization and GDP as an indicator of whether the global equity market (or a specific country or region's equity market) is under, over, or fairly valued. Global equity markets expanded at twice the rate of global GDP between 1993 and 2004. At the beginning of 2008, global GDP and equity market capitalization were nearly equal at approximately US$55 trillion.[1] This implies an equity market capitalization to GDP ratio of 100 percent, which was almost twice the long-run average of 50 percent and indicates that global equity markets were overvalued at that time.

Figure 9.1 illustrates the significant value that investors attach to publicly traded equities relative to the sum of goods and services produced globally every year. It shows the continued significance, and the potential overrepresentation, of U.S. equity markets relative to their contribution to global GDP. That is, while U.S. equity markets contribute around 43 percent to the total capitalization of global equity markets, their contribution to the global GDP is only around 21 percent. Following the stock market turmoil in 2008, however, the market capitalization to GDP ratio of the United States fell to 59 percent, which is significantly lower than its long-run average of 79 percent.[2]

As equity markets outside the United States develop and become increasingly global, their total capitalization levels are expected to grow closer to their respective world GDP contributions. Therefore, it is important to understand and analyze equity securities from a global perspective.

Table 9.1 lists the top 10 equity markets at the end of 2008 based on total market capitalization (in billions of U.S. dollars), trading volume, and the number of listed

---

[1] EconomyWatch.com, www.economywatch.com/gdp/world-gdp/.

[2] For further details, see Bary (2008).

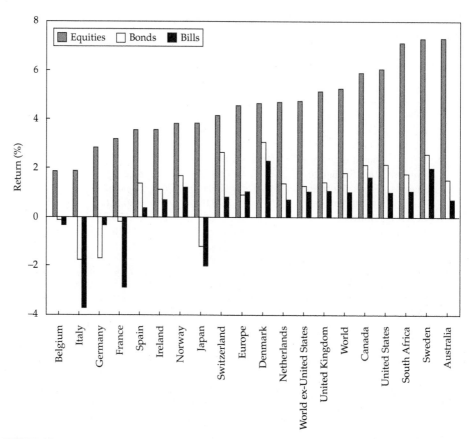

FIGURE 9.2   Real Returns on Global Equity Securities, Bonds, and Bills during 1900–2008
Source: Dimson, Marsh, and Staunton (2009).

companies.[3] Note that the rankings differ based on the criteria used. For example, the top three markets based on total market capitalization are the NYSE Euronext (U.S.), Tokyo Stock Exchange Group, and NASDAQ OMX; however, the top three markets based on total U.S. dollar trading volume are the Nasdaq OMX, NYSE Euronext (U.S.), and London Stock Exchange, respectively.[4] A relatively new entrant to this top 10 list is China's Shanghai Stock Exchange, which is the only emerging equity market represented on this list.

Figure 9.2 compares the *real* (or inflation-adjusted) compounded returns on government bonds, government bills, and equity securities in 17 countries during

---

[3] The market capitalization of an individual stock is computed as the share price multiplied by the number of shares outstanding. The total market capitalization of an equity market is the sum of the market capitalizations of each individual stock listed on that market. Similarly, the total trading volume of an equity market is computed by value weighting the total trading volume of each individual stock listed on that market. Total dollar trading volume is computed as the average share price multiplied by the number of shares traded.

[4] NASDAQ is the acronym for the National Association of Securities Dealers Automated Quotations.

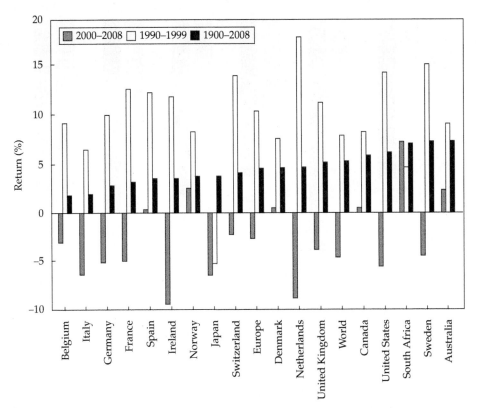

FIGURE 9.3 Real Returns on Global Equity Securities during 1900–2008, 1990–1999, and 2000–2008

Source: Dimson, Marsh, and Staunton (2009).

1900–2008.[5] In real terms, government bonds and bills have essentially kept pace with the inflation rate, earning annualized real returns of 1 percent to 2 percent in most countries.[6] By comparison, real returns in equity markets have generally been above 4 percent per year in most markets—with a world average return just over 5 percent and a world average return excluding the United States just under 5 percent. During this period, Australia and Sweden were the best performing markets followed by South Africa, the United States, and Canada.

Figure 9.3 focuses on the real compounded rates of return on equity securities in the same 17 countries during 1900–2008 as well as during the more recent time periods of 1990–1999 and 2000–2008. During 2000–2008, with the exception of Australia, Norway, and South Africa, real returns were negative or close to zero in all markets including the world average. This is in sharp contrast to the performance

---

[5] The real return for a country is computed by taking the nominal return and subtracting the observed inflation rate in that country.

[6] The exceptions are Belgium, Italy, Germany, France, and Japan—where the average real returns on government bonds have been negative. This is due to the very high inflation rates in these countries during the world war years.

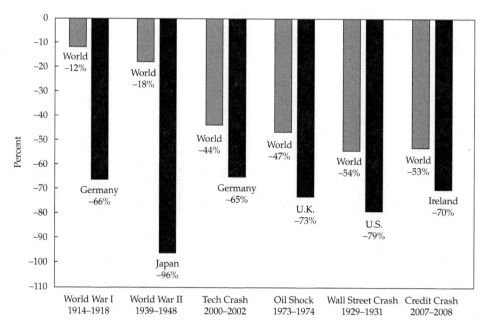

FIGURE 9.4   Extreme Losses in Global Equity Markets during 1900–2008
Source: Adapted from Dimson, Marsh, and Staunton (2009).

of these markets during 1990–1999, when inflation rates and interest rates were at record lows in most countries and growth in corporate profits was at record highs.[7]

The volatility in equity market returns is further highlighted in Figure 9.4, which shows the average performance of world equity markets and the worst performing equity market during World War I, World War II, the technology crash, the oil crisis, the Wall Street crash, and the more recent banking/credit crash. Note that in each period the losses suffered by the worst affected equity market were much larger than the average global losses. The data for the credit crash is as of the end of 2008 and thus does not fully capture the extent of its effects on world equity markets. It is more than likely that in the future, the credit crash of 2007–2008 will be viewed as being the worst of all the extreme market losses.

These observations and historical data are consistent with the concept that the return on securities is directly related to risk level. That is, equity securities have higher risk levels when compared with government bonds and bills, they earn higher rates of return to compensate investors for these higher risk levels, and they also tend to be more volatile over time.

Given the high risk levels associated with equity securities, it is reasonable to expect that investors' tolerance for risk will tend to differ across equity markets. This is illustrated in Table 9.2, which shows the results of a series of studies conducted by the Australian Securities Exchange on international differences in equity ownership. During the 2000–2008 period, equity ownership as a percentage

---

[7] The only exception to this was the Japanese equity market, which experienced negative real returns in the 1990s as well. Even in the case of Japan, however, the average real compounded return over the much longer 1900–2008 period has been around 4 percent per year.

TABLE 9.2   International Comparisons of Stock Ownership in Selected Countries: 2000–2008

	2000	2002	2004	2006	2008
Australia—Direct/Indirect	52%	50%	55%	46%	41%
Canada—Shares/Funds	49	46	49	N/A	N/A
Germany—Shares/Funds	19	18	16	16	14
Hong Kong—Shares	22	20	24	N/A	22
New Zealand	24	N/A	23	26	N/A
South Korea—Shares	7	8	8	7	N/A
Switzerland—Shares/Funds	34	25	21	21	21
Sweden—Shares	22	23	22	20	18
U.K.—Shares/Funds	26	25	22	20	18
U.S.—Direct/Indirect	N/A	50	49	N/A	45

The percentages reported in the table are based on samples of the adult population in each country who own equity securities either directly or indirectly through investment or retirement funds. For example, 41 percent of the adult population of Australia in 2008 (approximately 6.7 million people) owned equity securities either directly or indirectly. As noted in the study, it is not appropriate to make absolute comparisons across countries given the differences in methodology, sampling, timing, and definitions that have been used in different countries. However, trends across different countries can be identified.

Source: Adapted from the *2008 Australian Share Ownership Study* conducted by the Australian Securities Exchange (see www.asx.com.au). For Australia and the United States, the data pertain to direct and indirect ownership in equity markets; for other countries, the data pertain to direct ownership in shares and share funds. Data not available in specific years are shown as "N/A."

of the population was lowest in South Korea (averaging 7.5 percent), followed by Germany (16.6 percent) and Sweden (21 percent). In contrast, Australia, Canada, and the United States had the highest equity ownership as a percentage of the population (averaging almost 50 percent). In addition, there has been a relative decline in share ownership in several countries over recent years, which is not surprising given the recent overall uncertainty in global economies and the volatility in equity markets that this uncertainty has created.

An important implication from the above discussion is that equity securities represent a key asset class for global investors because of their unique return and risk characteristics. We next examine the various types of equity securities traded on global markets and their salient characteristics.

3. Types and Characteristics of Equity Securities

Companies finance their operations by issuing either debt or equity securities. A key difference between these securities is that debt is a liability of the issuing company, whereas equity is not. This means that when a company issues debt, it is contractually obligated to repay the amount it borrows (i.e., the principal or face value of the debt) at a specified future date. The cost of using these funds is called interest, which the company is contractually obligated to pay until the debt matures or is retired.

When the company issues equity securities, it is not contractually obligated to repay the amount it receives from shareholders, nor is it contractually obligated to make periodic payments to shareholders for the use of their funds. Instead, shareholders have a claim on the company's assets after all liabilities have been paid. Because of this residual claim, equity shareholders are considered to be owners of the company. Investors who purchase equity securities are seeking total return (i.e., capital or price appreciation and dividend income), whereas investors who purchase debt securities (and hold until maturity) are seeking interest income. As a result, equity investors expect the company's management to act in their best interest by making operating decisions that will maximize the market price of their shares (i.e., shareholder wealth).

In addition to common shares (also known as ordinary shares or common stock), companies may also issue preference shares (also known as preferred stock), the other type of equity security. The following sections discuss the different types and characteristics of common and preference securities.

COMMON SHARES   **Common shares** represent an ownership interest in a company and are the predominant type of equity security. As a result, investors share in the operating performance of the company, participate in the governance process through voting rights, and have a claim on the company's net assets in the case of liquidation. Companies may choose to pay out some, or all, of their net income in the form of cash dividends to common shareholders, but they are not contractually obligated to do so.[8]

Voting rights provide shareholders with the opportunity to participate in major corporate governance decisions, including the election of its board of directors, the decision to merge with or take over another company, and the selection of outside auditors. Shareholder voting generally takes place during a company's annual meeting. As a result of geographic limitations and the large number of shareholders, it is often not feasible for shareholders to attend the annual meeting in person. For this reason, shareholders may **vote by proxy,** which allows a designated party—such as another shareholder, a shareholder representative, or management—to vote on the shareholders' behalf.

Regular shareholder voting, where each share represents one vote, is referred to as **statutory voting.** Although it is the common method of voting, it is not always the most appropriate one to use to elect a board of directors. To better serve shareholders who own a small number of shares, **cumulative voting** is often used. Cumulative voting allows shareholders to direct their total voting rights to specific candidates, as opposed to having to allocate their voting rights evenly among all candidates. Total voting rights are based on the number of shares owned multiplied by the number of board directors being elected. For example, under cumulative voting, if four board directors are to be elected, a shareholder who owns 100 shares is entitled to 400 votes and can either cast all 400 votes in favor of a single candidate or spread them across the candidates in any proportion. In contrast, under statutory voting, a shareholder would be able to cast only a maximum of 100 votes for each candidate.

The key benefit to cumulative voting is that it allows shareholders with a small number of shares to apply all of their votes to one candidate, thus providing the opportunity for a higher level of representation on the board than would be allowed under statutory voting.

Table 9.3 describes the rights of Viacom Corporation's shareholders. In this case, a dual-share arrangement allows the founding chairman and his family to control

---

[8] It is also possible for companies to pay more than the current period's net income as dividends. Such payout policies are, however, generally not sustainable in the long run.

TABLE 9.3   Share Class Arrangements at Viacom Corporation

Viacom has two classes of common stock: Class A, which is the voting stock, and Class B, which is the nonvoting stock. There is no difference between the two classes except for voting rights; they generally trade within a close price range of each other. There are, however, far more shares of Class B outstanding, so most of the trading occurs in that class.

Voting Rights—Holders of Class A common stock are entitled to one vote per share. Holders of Class B common stock do not have any voting rights, except as required by Delaware law. Generally, all matters to be voted on by Viacom stockholders must be approved by a majority of the aggregate voting power of the shares of Class A common stock present in person or represented by proxy, except as required by Delaware law.

Dividends—Stockholders of Class A common stock and Class B common stock will share ratably in any cash dividend declared by the Board of Directors, subject to any preferential rights of any outstanding preferred stock. Viacom does not currently pay a cash dividend, and any decision to pay a cash dividend in the future will be at the discretion of the Board of Directors and will depend on many factors.

Conversion—So long as there are 5,000 shares of Class A common stock outstanding, each share of Class A common stock will be convertible at the option of the holder of such share into one share of Class B common stock.

Liquidation Rights—In the event of liquidation, dissolution, or winding-up of Viacom, all stockholders of common stock, regardless of class, will be entitled to share ratably in any assets available for distributions to stockholders of shares of Viacom common stock subject to the preferential rights of any outstanding preferred stock.

Split, Subdivisions, or Combination—In the event of a split, subdivision, or combination of the outstanding shares of Class A common stock or Class B common stock, the outstanding shares of the other class of common stock will be divided proportionally.

Preemptive Rights—Shares of Class A common stock and Class B common stock do not entitle a stockholder to any preemptive rights enabling a stockholder to subscribe for or receive shares of stock of any class or any other securities convertible into shares of stock of any class of Viacom.

This information has been adapted from Viacom's investor relations website and its 10-K filing with the U.S. Securities and Exchange Commission; see www.viacom.com.

more than 70 percent of the voting rights through the ownership of Class A shares. This arrangement gives them the ability to exert control over the board of director election process, corporate decision making, and other important aspects of managing the company. A cumulative voting arrangement for any minority shareholders of Class A shares would improve their board representation.

As seen in Table 9.3, companies can issue different classes of common shares (Class A and Class B shares), with each class offering different ownership rights.[9] For example, as shown in Table 9.4, the Ford Motor Company has Class A shares ("Common Stock"), which are owned by the investing public. It also has Class B shares, which are owned only by the Ford family. The exhibit contains an excerpt from Ford's *2008 Annual Report* (p. 115). Class A shareholders have 60 percent voting

---

[9] In some countries, including the United States, companies can issue different classes of shares, with Class A shares being the most common. The role and function of different classes of shares is described in more detail in Table 9.3.

TABLE 9.4   Share Class Arrangements at Ford Motor Company

NOTE 21. CAPITAL STOCK AND AMOUNTS PER SHARE

All general voting power is vested in the holders of Common Stock and Class B Stock.
   Holders of our Common Stock have 60% of the general voting power and holders of our
   Class B Stock are entitled to such number of votes per share as will give them the
   remaining 40%. Shares of Common Stock and Class B Stock share equally in dividends
   when and as paid, with stock dividends payable in shares of stock of the class held. As
   discussed in Note 16, we are prohibited from paying dividends (other than dividends
   payable in stock) under the terms of the Credit Agreement.
If liquidated, each share of Common Stock will be entitled to the first $0.50 available for
   distribution to holders of Common Stock and Class B Stock, each share of Class B Stock
   will be entitled to the next $1.00 so available, each share of Common Stock will be
   entitled to the next $0.50 so available and each share of Common and Class B Stock will
   be entitled to an equal amount thereafter.

Extracted from Ford Motor Company's *2008 Annual Report* (http://virtual.stivesonline.com/publication/
?i=14030).

rights, whereas Class B shareholders have 40 percent. In the case of liquidation,
however, Class B shareholders will not only receive the first US$0.50 per share that
is available for distribution (as will Class A shareholders), but they will also receive
the next US$1.00 per share that is available for distribution before Class A sharehold-
ers receive anything else. Thus, Class B shareholders have an opportunity to receive
a larger proportion of distributions upon liquidation than do Class A shareholders.[10]

Common shares may also be callable or putable. **Callable common shares** (also
known as redeemable common shares) give the issuing company the option (or
right), but not the obligation, to buy back shares from investors at a call price that is
specified when the shares are originally issued. It is most common for companies to
call (or redeem) their common shares when the market price is above the prespecified call price. The company benefits because it can buy back its shares below the
current market price and later resell them at a higher market price, and it can also
reduce dividend payments to preserve capital, if required. Investors benefit because
they receive a guaranteed return when their shares are called. Table 9.5 provides an
example of callable common shares issued by Genomic Solutions in the U.S. market. The exhibit provides details on the creation of callable common shares used to
consummate a strategic alliance between PerkinElmer and Genomic Solutions. The
arrangement contains provisions more favorable to PerkinElmer because at the time
it was a more established and better capitalized company than Genomic Solutions.

Putable common shares give investors the option or right to sell their shares
(i.e., "put" them) back to the issuing company at a price that is specified when
the shares are originally issued. Investors will generally sell their shares back to
the issuing company when the market price is below the prespecified put price.

---

[10] For example, if US$2.00 per share is available for distribution, the Common Stock (Class A)
shareholders will receive US$0.50 per share, while the Class B shareholders will receive
US$1.50 per share. However, if there is US$3.50 per share available for distribution, the Common Stock shareholders will receive a total of US$1.50 per share and the Class B shareholders
will receive a total of US$2.00 per share.

TABLE 9.5   Callable Stock Arrangement from Genomic Solutions

The following information assumes that the underwriters do not exercise the overallotment option granted by us to purchase additional shares in the offering:

Callable common stock offered by us:	7,000,000 shares
Callable common stock to be outstanding after the offering:	22,718,888 shares
Common stock to be outstanding after the offering:	1,269,841 shares
Proposed Nasdaq National Market symbol:	GNSL
Use of proceeds:	General corporate purposes and possible future acquisitions

For two years from the completion of this offering, we may require all holders of our callable common stock to sell their shares back to us. We must exercise this right at PerkinElmer's direction. The price for repurchase of our callable common stock generally will be 20% over the market price. PerkinElmer also has a right to match any third party offer for our callable common stock or our business that our board of directors is prepared to accept.

Genomic Solutions Form S-1 as filed with the U.S. SEC (14 May 2000); see www.edgar-online.com.

TABLE 9.6   Putable Stock Arrangement for Dreyer's Grand Ice Cream

Dreyer's Grand Ice Cream Holdings, Inc. ("Dreyer's") (NNM: DRYR) announced today that the period during which holders of shares of Dreyer's Class A Callable Putable Common Stock (the "Class A Shares") could require Dreyer's to purchase their Class A Shares (the "Put Right") for a cash payment of $83.10 per Class A Share (the "Purchase Price") expired at 5:00 p.m. New York City time on January 13, 2006 (the "Expiration Time"). According to the report of the depositary agent for the Put Right, holders of an aggregate of 30,518,885 Class A Shares (including 1,792,193 shares subject to guaranteed delivery procedures) properly exercised the Put Right.

"Dreyer's Announces Expiration of Put Period and Anticipated Merger with Nestle," *Business Wire* (14 January 2006): www.findarticles.com/p/articles/mi_m0EIN/is_2006_Jan_14/ai_n16001349.

Thus, the put option feature limits the potential loss for investors. From the issuing company's perspective, the put option facilitates raising capital because the shares are more appealing to investors.

Table 9.6 provides an example of putable common shares issued by Dreyer's, now a subsidiary of Switzerland-based Nestlé. In this case, shareholders had the right to sell their shares to Dreyer's for US $83.10, the prespecified put price.

PREFERENCE SHARES   **Preference shares** (or preferred stock) rank above common shares with respect to the payment of dividends and the distribution of the company's net assets upon liquidation.[11] However, preference shareholders do not share in the operating performance of the company and generally do not have any voting rights, unless explicitly allowed for at issuance. Preference shares have characteristics of both debt securities and common shares. Similar to the interest payments on debt

---

[11] Preference shares have a lower priority than debt in the case of liquidation. That is, debt holders have a higher claim on a firm's assets in the event of liquidation and will receive what is owed to them first, followed by preference shareholders and then common shareholders.

TABLE 9.7   Callable Stock Arrangement between Goldman Sachs and Berkshire Hathaway

New York, NY, September 23,2008—The Goldman Sachs Group, Inc. (NYSE: GS) announced today that it has reached an agreement to sell $5 billion of perpetual preferred stock to Berkshire Hathaway, Inc. in a private offering. The preferred stock has a dividend of 10 percent and is callable at any time at a 10 percent premium. In conjunction with this offering, Berkshire Hathaway will also receive warrants to purchase $5 billion of common stock with a strike price of $ 115 per share, which are exercisable at any time for a five year term. In addition, Goldman Sachs is raising at least $2.5 billion in common equity in a public offering.

Goldman Sachs, "Berkshire Hathaway to Invest $5 billion in Goldman Sachs," (23 September 2008): www.goldmansachs.com/our-firm/press/press-releases/archived/2008/berkshire-hathaway-invest.html.

securities, the dividends on preference shares are fixed and are generally higher than the dividends on common shares. However, unlike interest payments, preference dividends are not contractual obligations of the company. Similar to common shares, preference shares can be perpetual (i.e., no fixed maturity date), can pay dividends indefinitely, and can be callable or putable.

Table 9.7 provides an example of callable preference shares issued by Goldman Sachs to raise capital during the credit crisis of 2008. In this case, Berkshire Hathaway, the purchaser of the shares, will receive an ongoing dividend from Goldman Sachs. If Goldman Sachs chooses to buy back the shares, it must do so at a 10 percent premium above their par value.

Dividends on preference shares can be cumulative, noncumulative, participating, non-participating, or some combination thereof (i.e., cumulative participating, cumulative nonparticipating, noncumulative participating, noncumulative nonparticipating).

Dividends on **cumulative preference shares** accrue so that if the company decides not to pay a dividend in one or more periods, the unpaid dividends accrue and must be paid in full before dividends on common shares can be paid. In contrast, **noncumulative preference shares** have no such provision. This means that any dividends that are not paid in the current or subsequent periods are forfeited permanently and are not accrued over time to be paid at a later date. However, the company is still not permitted to pay any dividends to common shareholders in the current period unless preferred dividends have been paid first.

Participating preference shares entitle the shareholders to receive the standard preferred dividend plus the opportunity to receive an additional dividend if the company's profits exceed a prespecified level. In addition, participating preference shares can also contain provisions that entitle shareholders to an additional distribution of the company's assets upon liquidation, above the par (or face) value of the preference shares. **Nonparticipating preference shares** do not allow shareholders to share in the profits of the company. Instead, shareholders are entitled to receive only a fixed dividend payment and the par value of the shares in the event of liquidation. The use of participating preference shares is much more common for smaller, riskier companies where the possibility of future liquidation is more of a concern to investors.

Preference shares can also be convertible. **Convertible preference shares** entitle shareholders to convert their shares into a specified number of common shares.

TABLE 9.8   Examples of Preference Shares Issued by DBS Bank

SINGAPORE, MAY 12—DBS Bank said today it plans to offer S$700 million in preference shares and make it available to both retail and institutional investors in Singapore. Called the DBS Preferred Investment Issue, it will yield investors a fixed noncumulative gross dividend rate of 6% for the first ten years and a floating rate thereafter. The DBS Preferred Investment Issue will be offered in two tranches, consisting of a S$100 million tranche to retail investors via ATMs and a S$600 million placement tranche available to both retail and institutional investors. Depending on investor demand, DBS could increase the offering amount.

Jackson Tai, President and Chief Operating Officer of DBS Group Holdings, said that following the success of the hybrid Tier 1 issue in March, DBS decided to make this new issue available to the local retail investors. "We consider these issues as an important capital management tool. We were pleased with the success of our hybrid Tier 1 issue for institutional investors and wanted to introduce a capital instrument that would be available to retail investors as well."

DBS Preferred Investment Issues are perpetual securities, redeemable after ten years at the option of DBS Bank and at every dividend date thereafter subject to certain redemption conditions. They are issued by DBS Bank and are considered to be core Tier 1 capital under the Monetary Authority of Singapore and Bank of International Settlement's guidelines. They will be listed on the Singapore Exchange Securities Trading Limited and can be traded on the secondary market through a broker. Holders of the DBS Preferred Investment Issue will receive the dividend net of the 24.5% income tax. Investors may claim the tax credit in their tax returns.

DBS Bank, "DBS Follows US$850 Million Offering of Subordinated Notes to International Markets with Singapore Dollar Market Financing" (12 May 2001): www.dbs.com/newsroom/2001/Pages/press010512.aspx.

This conversion ratio is determined at issuance. Convertible preference shares have the following advantages:

- They allow investors to earn a higher dividend than if they invested in the company's common shares.
- They allow investors the opportunity to share in the profits of the company.
- They allow investors to benefit from a rise in the price of the common shares through the conversion option.
- Their price is less volatile than the underlying common shares because the dividend payments are known and more stable.

As a result, the use of convertible preference shares is a popular financing option in venture capital and private equity transactions in which the issuing companies are considered to be of higher risk and when it may be years before the issuing company "goes public" (i.e., issues common shares to the public).

Table 9.8 provides examples of the types and characteristics of preference shares as issued by DBS Bank of Singapore.

4. Private versus Public Equity Securities

Our discussion so far has focused on equity securities that are issued and traded in public markets and on exchanges. Equity securities can also be issued and traded in private equity markets. **Private equity securities** are issued primarily to institutional investors via nonpublic offerings, such as private placements. Because they are not listed on public exchanges, there is no active secondary market for these securities. As a result, private equity securities do not have "market determined" quoted prices, are highly illiquid, and require negotiations between investors in order to be traded. In addition, financial statements and other important information needed to determine the fair value of private equity securities may be difficult to obtain because the issuing companies are typically not required by regulatory authorities to publish this information.

There are three primary types of private equity investments: venture capital, leveraged buyouts, and private investment in public equity. **Venture capital** investments provide "seed" or start-up capital, early-stage financing, or mezzanine financing to companies that are in the early stages of development and require additional capital for expansion. These funds are then used to finance the company's product development and growth. Venture capitalists range from family and friends to wealthy individuals and private equity funds. Because the equity securities issued to venture capitalists are not publicly traded, they generally require a commitment of funds for a relatively long period of time; the opportunity to "exit" the investment is typically within 3 to 10 years from the initial start-up. The exit return earned by these private equity investors is based on the price that the securities can be sold for if and when the start-up company first goes public, either via an **initial public offering** (IPO) on the stock market or by being sold to other investors.

A **leveraged buyout** (LBO) occurs when a group of investors (such as the company's management or a private equity partnership) uses a large amount of debt to purchase all of the outstanding common shares of a publicly traded company. In cases where the group of investors acquiring the company is primarily comprised of the company's existing management, the transaction is referred to as a **management buyout** (MBO). After the shares are purchased, they cease to trade on an exchange and the investor group takes full control of the company. In other words, the company is taken "private" or has been privatized. Companies that are candidates for these types of transactions generally have large amounts of undervalued assets (which can be sold to reduce debt) and generate high levels of cash flows (which are used to make interest and principal payments on the debt). The ultimate objective of a buyout (LBO or MBO) is to restructure the acquired company and later take it "public" again by issuing new shares to the public in the primary market.

The third type of private investment is a **private investment in public equity**, or PIPE.[12] This type of investment is generally sought by a public company that is in need of additional capital quickly and is willing to sell a sizeable ownership position to a private investor or investor group. For example, a company may require a large investment of new equity funds in a short period of time because it has significant expansion opportunities, is facing high levels of indebtedness, or is experiencing a rapid deterioration in its operations. Depending on how urgent the need is and the size of the capital requirement, the private investor may be able to purchase shares in

---

[12] The term PIPE is widely used in the United States; it is referred to as a private finance initiative (PFI) in the United Kingdom. The more generic term of public–private partnership is used in other markets.

TABLE 9.9   Example of a PIPE Transaction

On July 20, 2009, hhgregg completed a public stock offering of 4,025,000 shares of its common stock at $16.50 per share. Concurrently with the public offering, investment funds affiliated with Freeman Spogli & Co. purchased an additional 1,000,000 shares of common stock, in a private placement transaction, at the price per share paid by the public in the offering. Proceeds, net of underwriting fees, from the public stock offering and private placement, totaled approximately $78.6 million. These proceeds will be used for general corporate purposes, including funding the Company's accelerated new store growth plans.

This information was obtained from hhgregg's first quarter fiscal 2009 earnings report (http://ir.hhgregg .com/releasedetail.cfm?ReleaseID=401980).

the company at a significant discount to the publicly quoted market price. Table 9.9 contains a recent PIPE transaction for the electronics retailer hhgregg, which also included the issuance of additional common shares to the public.

While the global private equity market is relatively small in comparison to the global public equity market, it has experienced considerable growth over the past three decades. According to a study of the private equity market sponsored by the *World Economic Forum* and spanning the period 1970–2007, approximately US$3.6 trillion in debt and equity were acquired in leveraged buyouts. Of this amount, approximately 75 percent or US$2.7 trillion worth of transactions occurred during 2001–2007.[13] While the U.S. and the U.K markets were the focus of most private equity investments during the 1980s and 1990s, private equity investments outside of these markets have grown substantially in recent years. In addition, the number of companies operating under private equity ownership has also grown. For example, during the mid-1990s, fewer than 2,000 companies were under LBO ownership compared to close to 14,000 companies that were under LBO ownership globally at the beginning of 2007. The holding period for private equity investments has also increased during this time period from three to five years (1980s and 1990s) to approximately 10 years.[14]

The move to longer holding periods has given private equity investors the opportunity to more effectively and patiently address any underlying operational issues facing the company and to better manage it for long-term value creation. Because of the longer holding periods, more private equity firms are issuing convertible preference shares because they provide investors with greater total return potential through their dividend payments and the ability to convert their shares into common shares during an IPO.

In operating a publicly traded company, management often feels pressured to focus on short-term results[15] (e.g., meeting quarterly sales and earnings targets from analysts biased toward near-term price performance) instead of operating the company to obtain long-term sustainable revenue and earnings growth. By "going private," management can adopt a more long-term focus and can eliminate certain costs

---

[13] Strömberg (2008).

[14] See, for example, Bailey, Wirth, and Zapol (2005).

[15] For further information, see "Overcoming Short-Termism: A Call for a More Responsible Approach to Investment and Business Management" (www.aspeninstitute.org/bsp/cvsg/ policy2009).

that are necessary to operate a publicly traded company—such as the cost of meeting regulatory and stock exchange filing requirements, the cost of maintaining investor relations departments to communicate with shareholders and the media, and the cost of holding quarterly analyst conference calls.

As described previously, public equity markets are much larger than private equity networks and allow companies more opportunities to raise capital that is subsequently actively traded in secondary markets. By operating under public scrutiny, companies are incentivized to be more open in terms of corporate governance and executive compensation to ensure that they are acting for the benefit of shareholders. In fact, some studies have shown that private equity firms score lower in terms of corporate governance effectiveness, which may be attributed to the fact that shareholders, analysts, and other stakeholders are able to influence management when corporate governance and other policies are public.

5. Investing in Nondomestic Equity Securities

Technological innovations and the growth of electronic information exchanges (electronic trading networks, the Internet, etc.) have accelerated the integration and growth of global financial markets. As detailed previously, global capital markets have expanded at a much more rapid rate than global GDP in recent years; both primary and secondary international markets have benefited from the enhanced ability to rapidly and openly exchange information. Increased integration of equity markets has made it easier and less expensive for companies to raise capital and to expand their shareholder base beyond their local market. Integration has also made it easier for investors to invest in companies that are located outside of their domestic markets. This has enabled investors to further diversify and improve the risk and return characteristics of their portfolios by adding a class of assets with lower correlations to local country assets.

One barrier to investing globally is that many countries still impose "foreign restrictions" on individuals and companies from other countries that want to invest in their domestic companies. There are three primary reasons for these restrictions. The first is to limit the amount of control that foreign investors can exert on domestic companies. For example, some countries prevent foreign investors from acquiring a majority interest in domestic companies. The second is to give domestic investors the opportunity to own shares in the foreign companies that are conducting business in their country. For example, the Swedish home furnishings retailer IKEA abandoned efforts to invest in parts of the Asia/Pacific region because local governments did not want IKEA to maintain complete ownership of its stores. The third reason is to reduce the volatility of capital flows into and out of domestic equity markets. For example, one of the main consequences of the Asian Financial Crisis in 1997–1998 was the large outflow of capital from such emerging market countries as Thailand, Indonesia, and South Korea. These outflows led to dramatic declines in the equity markets of these countries and significant currency devaluations and resulted in many governments placing restrictions on capital flows. Today, many of these same markets have built up currency reserves to better withstand capital outflows inherent in economic contractions and periods of financial market turmoil.

Studies have shown that reducing restrictions on foreign ownership has led to improved equity market performance over the long term.[16] Although restrictions vary widely, more countries are allowing increasing levels of foreign ownership. For example, Australia has sought tax reforms as a means to encourage international demand for its managed funds in order to increase its role as an international financial center. China recently announced plans to allow designated foreign institutional investors to invest up to US$1 billion in its domestic yuan-denominated A shares (up from a previous US$800 million) as it seeks to slowly liberalize its stock markets.

Over the past two decades, three trends have emerged: (1) an increasing number of companies have issued shares in markets outside of their home country; (2) the number of companies whose shares are traded in markets outside of their home has increased; and (3) an increasing number of companies are dual listed, which means that their shares are simultaneously issued and traded in two or more markets. Companies located in emerging markets have particularly benefited from these trends because they no longer have to be concerned with capital constraints or lack of liquidity in their domestic markets. These companies have found it easier to raise capital in the markets of developed countries because these markets generally have higher levels of liquidity and more stringent financial reporting requirements and accounting standards. Being listed on an international exchange has a number of benefits. It can increase investor awareness about the company's products and services, enhance the liquidity of the company's shares, and increase corporate transparency because of the additional market exposure and the need to meet a greater number of filing requirements.

Technological advancements have made it easier for investors to trade shares in foreign markets. The German insurance company Allianz SE recently delisted its shares from the NYSE and certain European markets because international investors increasingly traded its shares on the Frankfurt Stock Exchange. Figure 9.5 illustrates the extent to which the institutional shareholder base at BASF, a large German chemical corporation, has become increasingly global in nature.

DIRECT INVESTING Investors can use a variety of methods to invest in the equity of companies outside of their local market. The most obvious is to buy and sell securities directly in foreign markets. However, this means that all transactions—including the purchase and sale of shares, dividend payments, and capital gains—are in the company's, not the investor's, domestic currency. In addition, investors must be familiar with the trading, clearing, and settlement regulations and procedures of that market. Investing directly often results in less transparency and more volatility because audited financial information may not be provided on a regular basis and the market may be less liquid. Alternatively, investors can use such securities as depository receipts and global registered shares, which represent the equity of international companies and are traded on local exchanges and in the local currencies. With these securities, investors have to worry less about currency conversions (price quotations and dividend payments are in the investor's local currency), unfamiliar market practices, and differences in accounting standards. The sections that follow discuss various securities that investors can invest in outside of their home market.

---

[16] See, for example, Henry and Chari (2007).

BASF is one of the largest publicly owned companies with around 460,000 share-holders and a high free float. An analysis of the shareholder structure carried out in September 2008 showed that, at 22% of share capital, the United States and Canada made up the largest regional group of institutional investors. Institutional investors from Germany made up 13%. Shareholders from Great Britain and Ireland held 14% of BASF shares, while a further 14% are held by institutional investors from the rest of Europe. Around 28% of the company's share capital is held by private investors, most of whom are resident in Germany

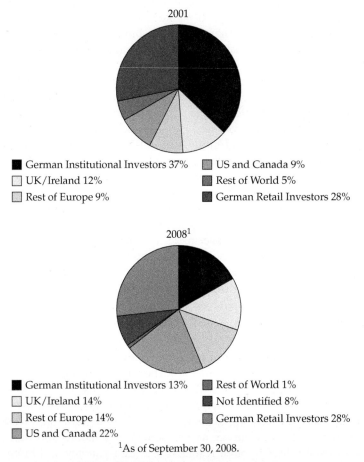

FIGURE 9.5   Example of Increased Globalization of Share Ownership

Adapted from BASF's investor relations web site (www.basf.com). *Free float* refers to the extent that shares are readily and freely tradable in the secondary market.

DEPOSITORY RECEIPTS   A depository[17] receipt (DR) is a security that trades like an ordinary share on a local exchange and represents an economic interest in a foreign

[17] Note that the spellings *depositary* and *depository* are used interchangeably in financial markets. In this part, we use the spelling *depository* throughout.

company. It allows the publicly listed shares of a foreign company to be traded on an exchange outside its domestic market. A depository receipt is created when the equity shares of a foreign company are deposited in a bank (i.e., the depository) in the country on whose exchange the shares will trade. The depository then issues receipts that represent the shares that were deposited. The number of receipts issued and the price of each DR is based on a ratio, which specifies the number of depository receipts to the underlying shares. Consequently, a DR may represent one share of the underlying stock, many shares of the underlying stock, or a fractional share of the underlying stock. The price of each DR will be affected by factors that affect the price of the underlying shares, such as company fundamentals, market conditions, analysts' recommendations, and exchange rate movements. In addition, any short-term valuation discrepancies between shares traded on multiple exchanges represent a quick arbitrage profit opportunity for astute traders to exploit. The responsibilities of the depository bank that issues the receipts include acting as custodian and as a registrar. This entails handling dividend payments, other taxable events, stock splits, and serving as the transfer agent for the foreign company whose securities the DR represents. The Bank of New York Mellon is the largest depository bank; however, Deutsche Bank, JPMorgan, and Citibank also offer depository services.[18]

A DR can be **sponsored** or **unsponsored**. A sponsored DR is when the foreign company whose shares are held by the depository has a direct involvement in the issuance of the receipts. Investors in sponsored DRs have the same rights as the direct owners of the common shares (e.g., the right to vote and the right to receive dividends). In contrast, with an unsponsored DR, the underlying foreign company has no involvement with the issuance of the receipts. Instead, the depository purchases the foreign company's shares in its domestic market and then issues the receipts through brokerage firms in the depository's local market. In this case, the depository bank, not the investors in the DR, retains the voting rights. Sponsored DRs are generally subject to greater reporting requirements than unsponsored DRs. In the United States, for example, sponsored DRs must be registered (meet the reporting requirements) with the U.S. Securities and Exchange Commission (SEC). Table 9.10 contains an example of a sponsored DR issued by Japan Airlines.

There are two types of depository receipts: Global depository receipts (GDRs) and American depository receipts (ADRs), which are described next.

Global Depository Receipts   A **global depository receipt** (GDR) is issued outside of the company's home country and outside of the United States. The depository bank that issues GDRs is generally located (or has branches) in the countries on whose exchanges the shares are traded. A key advantage of GDRs is that they are not subject to the foreign ownership and capital flow restrictions that may be imposed by the issuing company's home country because they are sold outside of that country. The issuing company selects the exchange where the GDR is to be traded based on such factors as investors' familiarity with the company or the existence of a large international investor base. The London and Luxembourg exchanges were the first ones to trade GDRs. Other stock exchanges trading GDRs are the Dubai International Financial Exchange, the Singapore Stock Exchange, and the Hong Kong Stock Exchange.

---

[18] Boubakri, Cosset, and Samet (2008).

TABLE 9.10   Sponsored versus Unsponsored Depository Receipts

The Japan Airlines (JAL) Group, Asia's biggest airline grouping, has picked the Bank of New York as the depository bank to make its previously unsponsored American depository receipts (ADRs) sponsored. By taking this action and by boosting investor relations activities in the U.S., the JAL group aims to increase the number of overseas shareholders. The JAL Group's sponsored ADRs became effective on August 19th, 2004 and dealing will start on August 25th. The JAL Group's American depository receipts had been previously issued in the U.S. as unsponsored ADRs by several U.S. depository banks since the 1970s. However, as unsponsored ADRs are issued without the involvement of the company itself, the company has difficulty in identifying ADR holders and controlling ADRs. From now, the JAL Group will be able to better serve its ADR holders and, at the same time, the JAL Group intends to increase its overseas investors.

Adapted from Japan Airlines Group's investor relations web site (www.jal.com/en/press/2004/082301/img/ADRS.pdf).

Currently, the London and Luxembourg exchanges are where most GDRs are traded because they can be issued in a more timely manner and at a lower cost. Regardless of the exchange they are traded on, the majority of GDRs are denominated in U.S. dollars, although the number of GDRs denominated in pound sterling and euros is increasing. Note that although GDRs cannot be listed on U.S. exchanges, they can be privately placed with institutional investors based in the United States.

American Depository Receipts   An **American depository receipt** (ADR) is a U.S. dollar-denominated security that trades like a common share on U.S. exchanges. First created in 1927, ADRs are the oldest type of depository receipts and are currently the most commonly traded depository receipts. They enable foreign companies to raise capital from U.S. investors. Note that an ADR is one form of a GDR; however, not all GDRs are ADRs because GDRs cannot be publicly traded in the United States. The term **American depository share** (ADS) is often used in tandem with the term ADR. A depository share is a security that is actually traded in the issuing company's domestic market. That is, while American depository receipts are the certificates that are traded on U.S. markets, American depository shares are the underlying shares on which these receipts are based.

There are four primary types of ADRs, with each type having different levels of corporate governance and filing requirements. Level I Sponsored ADRs trade in the over-the-counter (OTC) market and do not require full registration with the Securities and Exchange Commission (SEC). Level II and Level III Sponsored ADRs can trade on the New York Stock Exchange (NYSE), NASDAQ, and American Stock Exchange (AMEX). Level II and III ADRs allow companies to raise capital and make acquisitions using these securities. However, the issuing companies must fulfill all SEC requirements.

The fourth type of ADR, an SEC Rule 144A or a Regulation S depository receipt, does not require SEC registration. Instead, foreign companies are able to raise capital by privately placing these depository receipts with qualified institutional investors or to offshore non-U.S. investors. Table 9.11 summarizes the main features of ADRs.

More than 2,000 DRs, from over 80 countries, currently trade on U.S. exchanges. Based on current statistics, the total market value of DRs issued and traded is

TABLE 9.11   Summary of the Main Features of American Depository Receipts

	Level I (Unlisted)	Level II (Listed)	Level III (Listed)	Rule 144A (Unlisted)
Objectives	Develop and broaden U.S. investor base with existing shares	Develop and broaden U.S. investor base with existing shares	Develop and broaden U.S. investor base with existing/ new shares	Access qualified institutional buyers (QIBs)
Raising capital on U.S. markets?	No	No	Yes, through public offerings	Yes, through private placements to QIBs
SEC registration	Form F-6	Form F-6	Forms F-1 and F-6	None
Trading	Over the counter (OTC)	NYSE, NASDAQ, or AMEX	NYSE, NASDAQ, or AMEX	Private offerings, resales, and trading through automated linkages such as PORTAL
Listing fees	Low	High	High	Low
Size and earnings requirements	None	Yes	Yes	None

Source: Adapted from Boubakri, Cosset, and Samet (2008): Table 1.

estimated at approximately US$2 trillion, or 15 percent of the total dollar value of equities traded in U.S. markets.[19]

Global Registered Share   A **global registered share** (GRS) is a common share that is traded on different stock exchanges around the world in different currencies. Currency conversions are not needed to purchase or sell them, because identical shares are quoted and traded in different currencies. Thus, the same share purchased on the Swiss exchange in Swiss francs can be sold on the Tokyo exchange for Japanese yen. As a result, GRSs offer more flexibility than depository receipts because the shares represent an actual ownership interest in the company that can be traded anywhere and currency conversions are not needed to purchase or sell them. GRSs were created and issued by Daimler Chrysler in 1998.

Basket of Listed Depository Receipts   Another type of global security is a **basket of listed depository receipts** (BLDR), which is an exchange-traded fund (ETF) that represents a portfolio of depository receipts. An ETF is a security that tracks an index but trades like an individual share on an exchange. An equity-ETF is a security that contains a portfolio of equities that tracks an index. It trades throughout the day and can be bought, sold, or sold short, just like an individual share. Like ordinary shares, ETFs can also be purchased on margin and used in hedging or arbitrage strategies. The BLDR is a specific class of ETF security that consists of an underlying portfolio of

---

[19] JPMorgan Depositary Receipt Guide (2005):4.

DRs and is designed to track the price performance of an underlying DR index. For example, the Asia 50 ADR Index Fund is a capitalization-weighted ETF designed to track the performance of 50 Asian market-based ADRs.

6. Risk and Return Characteristics of Equity Securities

Different types of equity securities have different ownership claims on a company's net assets. The type of equity security and its features affect its risk and return characteristics. The following sections discuss the different return and risk characteristics of equity securities.

RETURN CHARACTERISTICS OF EQUITY SECURITIES There are two main sources of equity securities' total return: price change (or capital gain) and dividend income. The price change represents the difference between the purchase price (P_{t-1}) and the sale price (P_t) of a share at the end of time $t - 1$ and t, respectively. Cash or stock dividends (D_t) represent distributions that the company makes to its shareholders during period t. Therefore, an equity security's total return is calculated as:

$$\text{Total return, } R_t = (P_t - P_{t-1} + D_t)/P_{t-1} \qquad (9.1)$$

For non-dividend-paying stocks, the total return consists of price appreciation only. Companies that are in the early stages of their life cycle generally do not pay dividends because earnings and cash flows are reinvested to finance the company's growth. In contrast, companies that are in the mature phase of their life cycle may not have as many profitable growth opportunities; therefore, excess cash flows are often returned to investors via the payment of regular dividends or through share repurchases.

For investors who purchase depository receipts or foreign shares directly, there is a third source of return: **foreign exchange gains** (or losses). Foreign exchange gains arise because of the change in the exchange rate between the investor's currency and the currency that the foreign shares are denominated in. For example, U.S. investors who purchase the ADRs of a Japanese company will earn an additional return if the yen appreciates relative to the U.S. dollar. Conversely, these investors will earn a lower total return if the yen depreciates relative to the U.S. dollar. For example, if the total return for a Japanese company was 10 percent in Japan and the yen depreciated by 10 percent against the U.S. dollar, the total return of the ADR would be (approximately) 0 percent. If the yen had instead appreciated by 10 percent against the U.S. dollar, the total return of the ADR would be (approximately) 20 percent.

Investors who only consider price appreciation overlook an important source of return: the compounding that results from reinvested dividends. Reinvested dividends are cash dividends that the investor receives and uses to purchase additional shares. As Figure 9.6 shows, in the long run total returns on equity securities are dramatically influenced by the compounding effect of reinvested dividends. Between 1900 and 2008, US$1 invested in U.S. equities in 1900 would have grown in *real* terms to US$582 with dividends reinvested, but to just US$6 when taking only the price appreciation or capital gain into account. This corresponds to a real compounded return of 6 percent per year with dividends reinvested versus only 1.7 percent per year without dividends reinvested. As a comparison, Figure 9.6 shows the ending

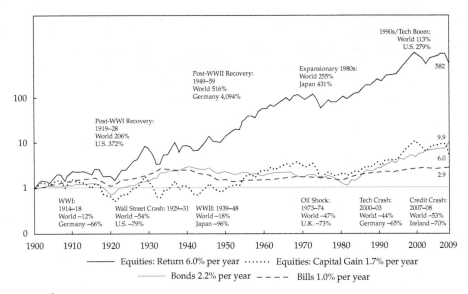

FIGURE 9.6 Impact of Reinvested Dividends on Cumulative Real Returns in the U.S. Equity Market: 1900–2008

Source: Dimson, Marsh, and Staunton (2009).

real wealth for bonds and bills, which are US$9.90 and US$2.90, respectively. These ending real wealth figures correspond to annualized real compounded returns of 2.1 percent on bonds and 1.0 percent on bills. This exhibit also shows the various bear markets (the lower boxes) over these periods, which were described in detail in Figure 9.4. In addition, it shows that each bear market was followed by a significant upward trend in the U.S. (and other) equity markets (the upper boxes).

RISK OF EQUITY SECURITIES The risk of any security is based on the uncertainty of its future cash flows. The greater the uncertainty of its future cash flows, the greater the risk and the more variable or volatile the security's price. As discussed previously, an equity security's total return is determined by its price change and dividends. Therefore, the risk of an equity security can be defined as the uncertainty of its expected (or future) total return. Risk is most often measured by calculating the standard deviation of the equity's expected total return.

A variety of different methods can be used to estimate an equity's expected total return and risk. One method uses the equity's average historical return and the standard deviation of this return as proxies for its expected future return and risk. Another method involves estimating a range of future returns over a specified period of time, assigning probabilities to those returns, and then calculating an expected return and a standard deviation of return based on this information.

The type of equity security, as well as its characteristics, affects the uncertainty of its future cash flows and therefore its risk. In general, preference shares are less risky than common shares for three main reasons:

1. Dividends on preference shares are known and fixed, and they account for a large portion of the preference shares' total return. Therefore, there is less uncertainty about future cash flows.

2. Preference shareholders receive dividends and other distributions before common shareholders.
3. The amount preference shareholders will receive if the company is liquidated is known and fixed as the par (or face) value of their shares. However, there is no guarantee that investors will receive that amount if the company experiences financial difficulty.

With common shares, however, a larger portion of shareholders' total return (or all of their total return for nondividend shares) is based on future price appreciation, and future dividends are unknown. If the company is liquidated, common shareholders will receive whatever amount (if any) is remaining after the company's creditors and preference shareholders have been paid. In summary, because the uncertainty surrounding the total return of preference shares is less than common shares, preference shares have lower risk and lower expected return than common shares.

It is important to note that some preference shares and common shares can be riskier than others because of their associated characteristics. For example, from an investor's point of view, putable common or preference shares are less risky than their callable or noncallable counterparts because they give the investor the option to sell the shares to the issuer at a predetermined price. This predetermined price establishes a minimum price that investors will receive and reduces the uncertainty associated with the security's future cash flow. As a result, putable shares generally pay a lower dividend than nonputable shares.

Because the major source of total return for preference shares is dividend income, the primary risk affecting all preference shares is the uncertainty of future dividend payments. Regardless of the preference shares' features (callable, putable, cumulative, etc.), the greater the uncertainty surrounding the issuer's ability to pay dividends, the greater the risk. Because the ability of a company to pay dividends is based on its future cash flows and net income, investors try to estimate these amounts by examining past trends or forecasting future amounts. The more earnings and the greater amount of cash flow that the company has had, or is expected to have, the lower the uncertainty and risk associated with its ability to pay future dividends.

Callable common or preference shares are riskier than their noncallable counterparts because the issuer has the option to redeem the shares at a predetermined price. Because the call price limits investors' potential future total return, callable shares generally pay a higher dividend to compensate investors for the risk that the shares could be called in the future. Similarly, putable preference shares have lower risk than nonputable preference shares. Cumulative preference shares have lower risk than noncumulative preference shares because the cumulative feature gives investors the right to receive any unpaid dividends before any dividends can be paid to common shareholders.

7. Equity Securities and Company Value

Companies issue equity securities on primary markets to raise capital and increase liquidity. This additional liquidity also provides the corporation an additional "currency" (its equity), which it can use to make acquisitions and provide stock option-based incentives to employees. The primary goal of raising capital is to finance the company's revenue-generating activities in order to increase its net income and maximize the wealth of its shareholders. In most cases, the capital that is raised is used to finance the purchase of long-lived assets, capital expansion projects, research and development, the entry into new product or geographic regions, and the acquisition of other companies. Alternatively, a company may be forced to raise capital to ensure that it continues to operate as a going concern. In these cases, capital is raised to fulfill regulatory requirements, improve capital adequacy ratios, or to ensure that debt covenants are met.

The ultimate goal of management is to increase the book value (shareholders' equity on a company's balance sheet) of the company and maximize the market value of its equity. Although management actions can directly affect the book value of the company (by increasing net income or by selling or purchasing its own shares), they can only indirectly affect the market value of its equity. The book value of a company's equity—the difference between its total assets and total liabilities—increases when the company retains its net income. The more net income that is earned and retained, the greater the company's book value of equity. Because management's decisions directly influence a company's net income, they also directly influence its book value of equity.

The market value of the company's equity, however, reflects the collective and differing expectations of investors concerning the amount, timing, and uncertainty of the company's future cash flows. Rarely will book value and market value be equal. Although management may be accomplishing its objective of increasing the company's book value, this increase may not be reflected in the market value of the company's equity because it does not affect investors' expectations about the company's future cash flows. A key measure that investors use to evaluate the effectiveness of management in increasing the company's book value is the accounting return on equity.

ACCOUNTING RETURN ON EQUITY **Return on equity** (ROE) is the primary measure that equity investors use to determine whether the management of a company is effectively and efficiently using the capital they have provided to generate profits. It measures the total amount of net income available to common shareholders generated by the total equity capital invested in the company. It is computed as net income available to ordinary shareholders (i.e., after preferred dividends have been deducted) divided by the average total book value of equity (BVE). That is:

$$\text{ROE}_t = \frac{\text{NI}_t}{\text{Average BVE}_t} = \frac{\text{NI}_t}{(\text{BVE}_t + \text{BVE}_{t-1})/2} \qquad (9.2)$$

where NI_t is the net income in year t and the average book value of equity is computed as the book values at the beginning and end of year t divided by 2. Return on equity assumes that the net income produced in the current year is generated by the equity existing at the beginning of the year and any new equity that was invested during the year. Note that some formulas only use shareholders' equity at the beginning of year t (that is, the end of year $t - 1$) in the denominator. This assumes that only the equity existing at the beginning of the year was used to generate the company's net income during the year. That is:

$$\text{ROE}_t = \frac{\text{NI}_t}{\text{BVE}_{t-1}} \qquad (9.3)$$

Both formulas are appropriate to use as long as they are applied consistently. For example, using beginning of the year book value is appropriate when book values

TABLE 9.12 Net Income and Book Value of Equity for Pfizer, Novartis AG, and GlaxoSmithKline (in thousands of U.S. dollars)

	Financial Year Ending		
	31 Dec 2008	31 Dec 2007	31 Dec 2006
Pfizer			
Net income	$8,104,000	$8,144,000	$19,337,000
Total stockholders' equity	$57,556,000	$65,010,000	$71,358,000
Novartis AG			
Net income	$8,233,000	$11,968,000	$5,264,000
Total stockholders' equity	$50,437,000	$49,396,000	$41,670,000
GlaxoSmithKline			
Net income	$6,822,505	$10,605,663	$8,747,382
Total stockholders' equity	$11,483,295	$19,180,072	$67,888,692

are relatively stable over time or when computing ROE for a company annually over a period of time. Average book value is more appropriate if a company experiences more volatile year-end book values or if the industry convention is to use average book values in calculating ROE.

One caveat to be aware of when computing and analyzing ROE is that net income and the book value of equity are directly affected by management's choice of accounting methods, such as those relating to depreciation (straight line versus accelerated methods) or inventories (first in, first out versus weighted average cost). Different accounting methods can make it difficult to compare the return on equity of companies even if they operate in the same industry. It may also be difficult to compare the ROE of the same company over time if its accounting methods have changed during that time.

Table 9.12 contains information on the net income and total book value of shareholders' equity for three **blue chip** (widely held large market capitalization companies that are considered financially sound and are leaders in their respective industry or local stock market) pharmaceutical companies: Pfizer, Novartis AG, and GlaxoSmithKline. The data are for their financial years ending December 2006 through December 2008.[20]

Using the average book value of equity, the return on equity for Pfizer for the years ending December 2007 and 2008 can be calculated as:

Return on equity for the year ending December 2007

$$\text{ROE}_{2007} = \frac{\text{NI}_{2007}}{(\text{BVE}_{2006} + \text{BVE}_{2007})/2} = \frac{8,144,000}{(71,358,000 + 65,010,000)/2} = 11.9\%$$

Return on equity for the year ending December 2008

$$\text{ROE}_{2008} = \frac{\text{NI}_{2008}}{(\text{BVE}_{2007} + \text{BVE}_{2008})/2} = \frac{8,104,000}{(65,010,000 + 57,556,000)/2} = 13.2\%$$

---

[20] Pfizer uses U.S. GAAP to prepare its financial statements; Novartis and GlaxoSmithKline use International Financial Reporting Standards. Therefore, it would be inappropriate to compare the ROE of Pfizer to that of Novartis or GlaxoSmithKline.

TABLE 9.13   Return on Equity for Pfizer, Novartis AG, and GlaxoSmithKline

	31 Dec 2008	31 Dec 2007
Pfizer	13.2%	11.9%
Novartis AG	16.5%	26.3%
GlaxoSmithKline	44.5%	24.4%

Table 9.13 summarizes the return on equity for Novartis and GlaxoSmithKline in addition to Pfizer for 2007 and 2008.

In the case of Novartis, the ROE of 26.3 percent in 2007 indicates that the company was able to generate a return (profit) of US$0.263 on every US$ 1.00 of capital invested by shareholders. In 2008, its operating performance deteriorated because it was only able to generate a 16.5 percent return on its equity. In contrast, GlaxoSmithKline almost doubled its return on equity over this period, from 24.4 percent to 44.5 percent. Pfizer's ROE remained relatively unchanged.

ROE can increase if net income increases at a faster rate than shareholders' equity or if net income decreases at a slower rate than shareholders' equity. In the case of Novartis, ROE fell in 2008 because its net income decreased by over 30 percent while shareholders' equity remained relatively stable. Stated differently, Novartis was less effective in using its equity capital to generate profits in 2008 than in 2007. In the case of GlaxoSmithKline, its ROE increased dramatically from 24.4 percent to 44.5 percent in 2007 versus 2008 even though its net income fell over 35 percent because its average shareholder equity decreased dramatically from 2006–2007 to 2007–2008.

An important question to ask is whether an increasing ROE is always good. The short answer is, "it depends." One reason ROE can increase is if net income decreases at a slower rate than shareholders' equity, which is not a positive sign. In addition, ROE can increase if the company issues debt and then uses the proceeds to repurchase some of its outstanding shares. This action will increase the company's leverage and make its equity riskier. Therefore, it is important to examine the source of changes in the company's net income *and* shareholders' equity over time. The DuPont formula can be used to analyze the sources of changes in a company's ROE.

The book value of a company's equity reflects the historical operating and financing decisions of its management. The market value of the company's equity reflects these decisions as well as investors' collective assessment and expectations about the company's future cash flows generated by its positive net present value investment opportunities. If investors believe that the company has a large number of these future cash flow-generating investment opportunities, the market value of the company's equity will exceed its book value. Table 9.14 shows the market price per share, the total number of shares outstanding, and the total book value of shareholders' equity for Pfizer, Novartis AG, and GlaxoSmithKline at the end of December 2008. This exhibit also shows the total market value of equity (or market capitalization) computed as the number of shares outstanding multiplied by the market price per share.

Note that in Table 9.14, the total market value of equity for Pfizer is computed as:

Market value of equity = Market price per share × Shares outstanding

Market value of equity = US$16.97 × 6,750,000 = US$114,547,500

TABLE 9.14 Market Information for Pfizer, Novartis AG, and GlaxoSmithKline (in thousands of U.S. dollars, except Market Price)

	Pfizer	Novartis AG	GlaxoSmithKline
Market price	$16.97	$47.64	$35.84
Total shares outstanding	6,750,000	2,260,000	2,530,000
Total shareholders' equity	$57,556,000	$50,437,000	$11,483,295
Total market value of equity	$114,547,500	$107,666,400	$90,675,200

The book value of equity per share for Pfizer can be computed as:

Book value of equity per share = Total shareholders' equity/Shares outstanding

Book value of equity per share = US$57,556,000/6,750,000 = US$8.53

A useful ratio to compute is a company's price-to-book ratio, which is also referred to as the market-to-book ratio. This ratio provides an indication of investors' expectations about a company's future investment and cash flow-generating opportunities. The larger the price-to-book ratio (i.e., the greater the divergence between market value per share and book value per share), the more favorably investors will view the company's future investment opportunities. For Pfizer the price-to-book ratio is:

Price-to-book ratio = Market price per share/Book value of equity per share

Price-to-book ratio = US$16.97/US$8.53 = 1.99

Table 9.15 contains the market price per share, book value of equity per share, and price-to-book ratios for Novartis and GlaxoSmithKline in addition to Pfizer.

The market price per share of all three companies exceeds their respective book values, so their price-to-book ratios are all greater than 1.00. However, there are significant differences in the sizes of their price-to-book ratios. GlaxoSmithKline has the largest price-to-book ratio, while the price-to-book ratios of Pfizer and Novartis are similar to each other. This suggests that investors believe that GlaxoSmithKline has substantially higher future growth opportunities than either Pfizer or Novartis.

It is not appropriate to compare the price-to-book ratios of companies in different industries because their price-to-book ratios also reflect investors' outlooks for the industry. Companies in high growth industries, such as technology, will generally have higher price-to-book ratios than companies in slower growth (i.e., mature) industries, such as heavy equipment. Therefore, it is more appropriate to compare the price-to-book ratios of companies in the same industry. A company with relatively

TABLE 9.15 Pfizer, Novartis AG, and GlaxoSmithKline

	Pfizer	Novartis AG	GlaxoSmithKline
Market price per share	$16.97	$47.64	$35.84
Book value of equity per share	$8.53	$22.32	$4.54
Price-to-book ratio	1.99	2.13	7.89

TABLE 9.16 Book Value versus Intrinsic Value

We regularly report our per-share book value, an easily calculable number, though one of limited use. Just as regularly, we tell you that what counts is intrinsic value, a number that is impossible to pinpoint but essential to estimate.

For example, in 1964, we could state with certitude that Berkshire's per-share book value was $19.46. However, that figure considerably overstated the stock's intrinsic value since all of the company's resources were tied up in a sub-profitable textile business. Our textile assets had neither going-concern nor liquidation values equal to their carrying values. In 1964, then, anyone inquiring into the soundness of Berkshire's balance sheet might well have deserved the answer once offered up by a Hollywood mogul of dubious reputation: "Don't worry, the liabilities are solid."

Today, Berkshire's situation has reversed: Many of the businesses we control are worth far more than their carrying value. (Those we don't control, such as Coca-Cola or Gillette, are carried at current market values.) We continue to give you book value figures, however, because they serve as a rough, understated, tracking measure for Berkshire's intrinsic value.

We define intrinsic value as the discounted value of the cash that can be taken out of a business during its remaining life. Anyone calculating intrinsic value necessarily comes up with a highly subjective figure that will change both as estimates of future cash flows are revised and as interest rates move. Despite its fuzziness, however, intrinsic value is all-important and is the only logical way to evaluate the relative attractiveness of investments and businesses.

To see how historical input (book value) and future output (intrinsic value) can diverge, let's look at another form of investment, a college education. Think of the education's cost as its "book value." If it is to be accurate, the cost should include the earnings that were foregone by the student because he chose college rather than a job.

For this exercise, we will ignore the important non-economic benefits of an education and focus strictly on its economic value. First, we must estimate the earnings that the graduate will receive over his lifetime and subtract from that figure an estimate of what he would have earned had he lacked his education. That gives us an excess earnings figure, which must then be discounted, at an appropriate interest rate, back to graduation day. The dollar result equals the intrinsic economic value of the education.

Extracts from Berkshire Hathaway's *2008 Annual Report* (www.berkshirehathaway.com).

high growth opportunities compared to its industry peers would likely have a higher price-to-book ratio than the average price-to-book ratio of the industry.

Book value and return on equity are useful in helping analysts determine value but can be limited as a primary means to estimate a company's true or intrinsic value, which is the present value of its future projected cash flows. In Table 9.16, Warren Buffett, one of the most successful investors in the world and CEO of Berkshire Hathaway, provides an explanation of the differences between the book value of a company and its intrinsic value in a letter to shareholders. As discussed previously, market value reflects the collective and differing expectations of investors concerning the amount, timing, and uncertainty of a company's future cash flows. A company's intrinsic value can only be estimated because it is impossible to predict the amount and timing of its future cash flows. However, astute investors—such as Buffett— have been able to profit from discrepancies between their estimates of a company's intrinsic value and the market value of its equity.

THE COST OF EQUITY AND INVESTORS' REQUIRED RATES OF RETURN   When companies issue debt (or borrow from a bank) or equity securities, there is a cost associated with the capital that is raised. In order to maximize profitability and shareholder wealth, companies attempt to raise capital efficiently so as to minimize these costs.

When a company issues debt, the cost it incurs for the use of these funds is called the cost of debt. The cost of debt is relatively easy to estimate because it reflects the periodic interest (or coupon) rate that the company is contractually obligated to pay to its bondholders (lenders). When a company raises capital by issuing equity, the cost it incurs is called the cost of equity. Unlike debt, however, the company is not contractually obligated to make any payments to its shareholders for the use of their funds. As a result, the cost of equity is more difficult to estimate.

Investors require a return on the funds they provide to the company. This return is called the investor's minimum required rate of return. When investors purchase the company's debt securities, their minimum required rate of return is the periodic rate of interest they charge the company for the use of their funds. Because all of the bondholders receive the same periodic rate of interest, their required rate of return is the same. Therefore, the company's cost of debt and the investors' minimum required rate of return on the debt are the same.

When investors purchase the company's equity securities, their minimum required rate of return is based on the future cash flows they expect to receive. Because these future cash flows are both uncertain and unknown, the investors' minimum required rate of return must be estimated. In addition, the minimum required return may differ across investors based on their expectations about the company's future cash flows. As a result, the company's cost of equity may be different from the investors' minimum required rate of return on equity.[21] Because companies try to raise capital at the lowest possible cost, the company's cost of equity is often used as a proxy for the investors' *minimum* required rate of return.

In other words, the cost of equity can be thought of as the minimum expected rate of return that a company must offer its investors to purchase its shares in the primary market and to maintain its share price in the secondary market. If this expected rate of return is not maintained in the secondary market, then the share price will adjust so that it meets the minimum required rate of return demanded by investors. For example, if investors require a higher rate of return on equity than the company's cost of equity, they would sell their shares and invest their funds elsewhere resulting in a decline in the company's share price. As the share price declined, the cost of equity would increase to reach the higher rate of return that investors require.

Two models commonly used to estimate a company's cost of equity (or investors' minimum required rate of return) are the dividend discount model (DDM) and the capital asset pricing model (CAPM).

The cost of debt (after tax) and the cost of equity (i.e., the minimum required rates of return on debt and equity) are integral components of the capital budgeting process because they are used to estimate a company's weighted average cost of

---

[21] Another important factor that can cause a firm's cost of equity to differ from investors' required rate of return on equity is the flotation cost associated with equity.

capital (WACC). Capital budgeting is the decision-making process that companies use to evaluate potential long-term investments. The WACC represents the minimum required rate of return that the company must earn on its long-term investments to satisfy all providers of capital. The company then chooses among those long-term investments with expected returns that are greater than its WACC.

8. Summary

Equity securities play a fundamental role in investment analysis and portfolio management. The importance of this asset class continues to grow on a global scale because of the need for equity capital in developed and emerging markets, technological innovation, and the growing sophistication of electronic information exchange. Given their absolute return potential and ability to impact the risk and return characteristics of portfolios, equity securities are of importance to both individual and institutional investors.

This part introduces equity securities and provides an overview of global equity markets. A detailed analysis of their historical performance shows that equity securities have offered average real annual returns superior to government bills and bonds, which have provided average real annual returns that have only kept pace with inflation. The different types and characteristics of common and preference equity securities are examined, and the primary differences between public and private equity securities are outlined. An overview of the various types of equity securities listed and traded in global markets is provided, including a discussion of their risk and return characteristics. Finally, the role of equity securities in creating company value is examined as well as the relationship between a company's cost of equity, its accounting return on equity, investors' required rate of return, and the company's intrinsic value.

We conclude with a summary of the key components of this part:

- Common shares represent an ownership interest in a company and give investors a claim on its operating performance, the opportunity to participate in the corporate decision-making process, and a claim on the company's net assets in the case of liquidation.
- Callable common shares give the issuer the right to buy back the shares from shareholders at a price determined when the shares are originally issued.
- Putable common shares give shareholders the right to sell the shares back to the issuer at a price specified when the shares are originally issued.
- Preference shares are a form of equity in which payments made to preference shareholders take precedence over any payments made to common stockholders.
- Cumulative preference shares are preference shares on which dividend payments are accrued so that any payments omitted by the company must be paid before another dividend can be paid to common shareholders. Noncumulative preference shares have no such provisions, implying that the dividend payments are at the company's discretion and are thus similar to payments made to common shareholders.

- Participating preference shares allow investors to receive the standard preferred dividend plus the opportunity to receive a share of corporate profits above a prespecified amount. Nonparticipating preference shares allow investors to simply receive the initial investment plus any accrued dividends in the event of liquidation.
- Callable and putable preference shares provide issuers and investors with the same rights and obligations as their common share counterparts.
- Private equity securities are issued primarily to institutional investors in private placements and do not trade in secondary equity markets. There are three types of private equity investments: venture capital, leveraged buyouts, and private investments in public equity (PIPEs).
- The objective of private equity investing is to increase the ability of the company's management to focus on its operating activities for long-term value creation. The strategy is to take the "private" company "public" after certain profit and other benchmarks have been met.
- Depository receipts are securities that trade like ordinary shares on a local exchange but which represent an economic interest in a foreign company. They allow the publicly listed shares of foreign companies to be traded on an exchange outside their domestic market.
- American depository receipts are U.S. dollar-denominated securities trading much like standard U.S. securities on U.S. markets. Global depository receipts are similar to ADRs but contain certain restrictions in terms of their ability to be resold among investors.
- Underlying characteristics of equity securities can greatly affect their risk and return.
- A company's accounting return on equity is the total return that it earns on shareholders' book equity.
- A company's cost of equity is the minimum rate of return that stockholders require the company to pay them for investing in its equity.

References

Bailey, E., M. Wirth, and D. Zapol. 2005. "Venture Capital and Global Health." *Financing Global Health Ventures*, Discussion Paper (September 2005). www.commonscapital.com/downloads/Venture_Capital_and_Global_Health .pdf.

Bary, A. 2008. "Does Extreme Stress Signal an Economic Snapback?" *Barron's* (24 November 2008): online.barrons.com/article/SB122732177515750213.html.

Boubakri, N., J.-C. Cosset, and A. Samet. 2008. "The Choice of ADRs." Finance International Meeting AFFI – EUROFIDAI, December 2007. http://ssrn .com/abstract51006839.

Dimson, E., P. Marsh, and M. Staunton. 2009. *Credit Suisse Global Investment Returns Sourcebook 2009*. Zurich, Switzerland: Credit Suisse Research Institute.

Henry, P. B., and A. Chari. 2007. "Risk Sharing and Asset Prices: Evidence from a Natural Experiment." Working Paper; Center on Democracy, Development, and the Rule of Law.

Strömberg, P. 2008. "The New Demography of Private Equity." *The Global Economic Impact of Private Equity Report 2008*, World Economic Forum.

Part III The Evolution of Equity Style Indexes

The advent and expansion of equity indexation has given investors some valuable tools. The market indexes fulfill many investor needs, such as:

- Asset class and asset allocation research and implementation
- Performance benchmarking of active core managers
- Vehicles for implementing passive replication strategies

Market indexes represent an important development in equity investing. However, questions still remain. Are core market indexes enough? What improvements can be made to better reflect active managers' investment processes? Do investors need more precise information upon which to base their decisions? Are core index returns easy for active managers to outperform, and, if so, why?

In this chapter, we consider these and other questions and analyze where the answers have taken the equity index industry. In particular, we look at the driving forces behind the development of more specific equity indexes, especially style-based equity indexes. We further discuss the pitfalls of the current index offerings and how these issues might be rectified.

Empirical Challenges to Financial Theories

The Capital Asset Pricing Model (CAPM) represents one of the central theories in the evolution of equity indexes. In the CAPM, since any idiosyncratic portfolio risk unrelated to the market can be eliminated by diversification, stock returns are defined by their exposure to a single risk factor, the market, which is called market beta.

Combining the CAPM with the Efficient Market Hypothesis (EMH) leads to certain conclusions. If markets are efficient, then trying to beat the market by finding new information or analyzing information better than others seems challenging, if not futile. Meanwhile, if all risk, except market risk, can be diversified away, then any risk taken other than market risk should not be rewarded with excess return. These ideas led to investing in the most diversified portfolio available, the market itself. This, in turn, encouraged the development of broad equity indexes and index funds for both investment and benchmark purposes.

Of course, as the CAPM and the EMH grew in acceptance and popularity, people began to search for holes in these ideas. Among the key questions were:

- How efficient are markets? Do markets fully incorporate all available information?
- Is market risk, or beta, the only risk that drives return? Do other systematic risks exist, beyond the market beta?

Economic researchers soon found empirical evidence of various "anomalies" left unexplainable, in their view, by the CAPM and the EMH. One of the first anomalies was discovered by Rolf Banz in 1979—the Size effect. Banz found that stocks with smaller market capitalizations outperformed stocks with larger market capitalizations. This result held true for these differing groups of stocks even after adjusting for their

Beta, or exposure to the overall market. In other words, the single-factor systematic risk, the market beta, did not account for the excess returns of small cap stocks.

Around the same time, a second critical anomaly was found—the Valuation effect. Detailed by Sanjoy Basu in 1977, this exception to the CAPM showed that stocks with lower price-earnings (P/E) ratios outperformed stocks with higher P/E ratios. That is, cheaper stocks provide better returns than expensive stocks, again after adjusting for market beta. Later studies confirmed this Valuation effect, including the use of other factors, such as price-book value.

The research into these various anomalies initially involved little *ex-ante* framework or hypothesis. Academics appeared more focused on testing the basic premise of the one-factor CAPM. The question seemed more "Does it work?," not "Why do exceptions exist?" The answers to the "why" question proved diverse, and the debate over which explanation is most correct continues to this day.

Theoretical Explanations of Anomalies

So, if markets are efficient and the CAPM, in some form, holds, what exactly are these anomalies? The first, and perhaps most obvious, explanation is that markets are not efficient, or at least not completely efficient. In this case, the Size and Valuation effects represent market inefficiencies. These effects arise from the inability of the market to correctly interpret and fully incorporate all available information. Thus, practitioners can tilt their portfolios toward smaller or cheaper stocks to beat the market without taking undue risk.

Economic theory offers a critique of the inefficiency explanation that is hard to refute. If the Size and Valuation effects exist solely due to the inability of market participants to price in information, and this situation is widely known and understood, why do these effects persist? Arbitrage (i.e., risk-free profit opportunity) should arise from this informational disconnect. Over time, and with enough arbitraging investors, these effects should become negligible and unprofitable in the face of transaction costs. However, the Size and Valuation effects remain, even after the publicized research of Banz, Basu, and others.

Another thought on these effects is that they are simply time-period-specific observations. This explanation suggests that researchers discovered anomalies like Size and Valuation by picking a particular time period and trying whatever factors they could find until they "fit" the data for that time period. Presumably, by using this data-mining approach, factors found to outperform in one period would have no reason to do so in another, independent time period. The long-term (out-of-sample) evidence of the power of Size and Valuation makes this explanation difficult to accept.

Behavioral finance also attempts to explain various anomalies, including Size and Valuation. In broad strokes, behavioral finance believes that investors can behave irrationally, not always as the rational operators portrayed by the EMH. As an example of this biased behavior, investors may favor buying stocks of companies they know, leading to the overpricing of larger, well-known stocks and underpricing of their smaller brethren. In another illustration, individuals may overestimate the rapid growth of certain companies, thus causing their stocks to become expensive on a P/E basis and to underperform when these extrapolated expectations are not met.

A fourth explanation of the Size and Valuation effects is that these factors represent some additional risk taken by investors. In essence, this idea suggests that the one-factor CAPM is incomplete and that factors beyond market exposure require consideration. Academics espousing the EMH prefer this explanation because it does not call into question market efficiency. Rather, this risk premium idea allows for a more robust version of the CAPM that better captures the systematic risks that are priced by the market.

Economic theorists and financial practitioners continue to debate the behavioral and risk premium explanations for the discovered anomalies, particularly Size and Valuation. We will consider how these effects, and the questions regarding why they exist, influenced the evolution of equity style indexes. If the one-factor CAPM is insufficient, then perhaps solely employing core market indexes is also insufficient. These findings led to the next steps in the development of equity indexes based on factors, or investment styles.

Establishing Equity Styles

Whether behavioral or risk premium, the idea that investors needed to consider more than market beta gained credence. Equity style management increased in popularity, with managers becoming classified according to size segment or value/growth, as growth emerged as the counterpart to value. Investment consultants began to advise clients to add small-cap and value- and growth-oriented strategies to their overall portfolios to increase diversification.

In the late 1980s, William Sharpe, the father of the CAPM, used regression analysis to determine the exposure of portfolios, such as mutual funds, to various style factors. He published his "returns-based style analysis" methodology in 1988, with further refinements being released in 1992. Sharpe focused on large cap, small cap, value, and growth as the style choices for his analysis, a key step in establishing the popular equity styles seen today in the marketplace.

Sharpe's approach took the returns over time of a given portfolio or fund and regressed these returns against the selected style benchmarks. In this way, returns-based style analysis can shed light on how a portfolio tilts in reality, whether intentionally or unintentionally. Generally, portfolios are combinations of the various styles, not purely one or two styles. Sharpe's analytical technique thus gave investors a clearer picture of how their investments actually were managed, not just what the fund description stated.

Sharpe's methodology also provided a basis for assessing a manager's ability to provide true alpha. By deriving a relevant combination of styles for comparison purposes, investors could evaluate whether active management returns came from manager skill or simply one or more styles that could be captured passively. This point is critical not only in manager selection but also in determining the appropriate nature of management fees, in light of potential passive style index alternatives.

Moving further down the equity style path, Eugene Fama and Kenneth French produced an influential paper in 1992. Fama and French considered the performance and power of Size and Valuation, determining that these factors are significant in the explanation of stock returns, as well as the prediction of these returns. In fact, the information found in Size and Valuation largely overwhelmed Beta as an explanatory factor. However, Beta still had power in certain time periods, leading Fama and French to retain it in their model. The Fama-French three-factor model thus incorporated Size, Valuation, and Beta to explain returns. The inclusion of Size and

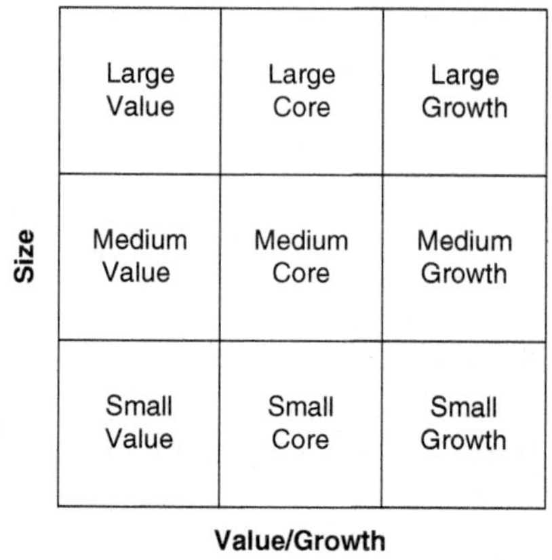

Large Value	Large Core	Large Growth
Medium Value	Medium Core	Medium Growth
Small Value	Small Core	Small Growth

Size (vertical axis label)

Value/Growth

FIGURE 9.7   Equity Style Box

Source: Westpeak.

Valuation built upon Sharpe's work and further solidified styles as an important part of equity investing.

Given the academic stature of the authors, the Fama-French three-factor model was quickly accepted in the marketplace. Mutual fund analysts and consultants, such as Morningstar, often categorize managers based on "style boxes" related to the Sharpe methodology or Fama-French three-factor model. A typical style box for equities is shown in Figure 9.7.

As one can see in this style box, large-cap stocks represent one end of the stock spectrum, with small-cap stocks representing the opposite end. By the same token, value stocks (based on high book value-price ratios, earnings-price ratios, etc.) find their mirror image in growth stocks.

With the advent of styles and style boxes, consultants and investors uncovered a tool to classify managers. Mutual funds, consequently, began to market themselves according to the best match of their investing methods and these styles. Equity style indexes achieved increased popularity as a more specific measure of performance for managers, as well as an investment alternative through passive-replication mutual funds.

Equity Style Index Methodology

In the mid-1980s, providers of core equity indexes moved into the style index arena. The Frank Russell Company and Wilshire Associates created the first of these styles indexes, with several competitors soon to follow. Long-time index standard-bearers Standard & Poor's, in conjunction with the factor model firm Barra, and Dow Jones also entered the style fray. These indexes became particularly popular in the United States, and investors soon had several equity style choices.

Size indexes were quite straightforward. Index providers took their broad universe of stocks, for example the Russell 3000 Index, and divided the constituents according to market capitalization. Thus, the Russell 3000 Index breaks down into the Russell 1000 Index of large cap stocks and the Russell 2000 Index of small cap stocks. While index providers have made adjustments to market capitalization, such as available shares or float, the Size indexes are basically reflective of the market value of stocks.

With Size classifications established, index providers initially took a similar tack to Sharpe and Fama-French when creating their value and growth style indexes. Early style indexation saw index providers divide the overall, or core, universe in half according to a single factor, such as book value-price. The high book value-price half became the value index. The other half became the growth index. Thus, the value and growth indexes are defined in terms of each other, and the combination of the two style halves equals the whole core index. This value/growth classification scheme was then applied to the various broad large cap and small cap equity indexes.

More recently, equity style index construction has become somewhat more sophisticated. The process has evolved to define growth more explicitly, in terms of long-term realized growth and/or expected growth, thus creating a two-dimensional process for dividing the core universe into growth and value. In addition, many index providers now establish both value and growth classifications using multiple descriptors, not just a single factor, such as book value-price. Today, the value nature of a stock may result from its scores on additional factors relating to earnings, sales, or dividend yield. Furthermore, stocks generally are not either value or growth, but rather can have characteristics of both styles. Still, the two style halves continue to be defined in terms of each other and together cover fully and exactly the market capitalization and constituents of the broader core index, in most cases.

Pitfalls of Current Equity Style Indexes

The development of styles in this fashion, particularly those pertaining to value or growth characteristics, has created a number of difficulties for the investment management industry. We will address some of these in more depth later in the book, but a brief overview is appropriate in this chapter to connect where indexes are to where indexes need to be.

The first challenge is the use of growth. As this factor initially emerged as the opposite of value, it may be more precise to call these style indexes non-value instead of growth. The usefulness of a non-value, or growth, equity index is questionable as a practical matter. Our research indicates that growth does not represent a systematic source of return, while value clearly does represent such a source. Also, while growth managers do exist, growth benchmarks do not appear to capture their investment methodologies. It is hard to imagine many managers explicitly or implicitly seeking out expensive non-value stocks for their own sake. Lastly, growth benchmarks, as currently and historically defined, have often trailed value and core indexes by significant margins. This performance makes tracking a growth index, or measuring managers against said index, a somewhat irrational decision.

A second question that arises in style index construction is coverage of the core index. Does the entire market capitalization and constituency of the core index need to be present in the combination of the value and growth indexes? While some "pure" style indexes exist, most index providers employ a complete coverage philosophy in their style index construction. This policy forces stocks that may have little or no real value or growth qualities into one camp or the other. While this method does account for all the stocks in the universe, it is not the most efficient way to obtain the returns to a core style. Yet, fullness of coverage continues to override purity of capture in the most popular equity style indexes.

Another test for style indexes is how to incorporate the most recent and relevant information in the index. A common belief of index providers is that indexes need to be as stable, and have as little turnover, as possible. While this idea makes some sense, it can cause a mismatch between indexes and higher-turnover active management strategies. More frequent rebalancing of equity style indexes can alleviate this problem if the transaction costs can be contained.

Conclusion

Academic research called into question the sole use of a single-factor CAPM and, consequently, the focus on only core equity indexes. Consultants rapidly picked up on this research, as they sought better ways to measure the performance of active equity managers. To meet this need, index providers built suites of equity style indexes based largely on Size and Valuation. The construction methodology of these style indexes has evolved over the years, bringing the industry to its current stage of development.

Still, improvements in the framework of equity style indexes seem necessary for the industry to take the next steps. Indexes need to better reflect the activities of portfolio managers in order to serve as appropriate benchmarks. This is especially true of the growth indexes, which essentially emerged only as a counterpart to value, not as a stand-alone systematic source of active equity returns.

References

Banz, R. W. 1981. "The Relationship between Return and Market Value of Common Stock." *Journal of Financial Economics* 9: 3–18.

Basu, S. 1977. "Investment Performance of Common Stocks in Relation to Their Price-Earnings Ratios: A Test of the Efficient Market Hypothesis." *Journal of Finance* 32, 3: 663–682.

Fama, Eugene, and Kenneth French. 1992. "The Cross-Section of Expected Stock Returns." *Journal of Finance* 47, 2: 427–466.

Sharpe, W. F. 1988. "Determining a Fund's Effective Asset Mix." *Investment Management Review* (December): 59–69.

Part IV Cost of Capital and Ratio Analysis

The **cost of capital** is a crucial concept in the context of financial decision making, especially in terms of being the accepted criteria by which a firm would decide whether an investment can or cannot potentially increase the firm's stock price. It is defined as:

1. The rate of return that the firm must earn on its investment to maintain a proper market value for its stock.
2. The rate of return that the investor must require to make its capital attractive for rewarding investment opportunities.

Before- and After-Tax Cost of Capital

If a firm uses a long-term debt such as selling bonds to finance its operation, a before-tax cost of debt can be calculated as

$$CC_b = \frac{I + [(M - NP)/n]}{(NP + M)/2}$$

where CC_b, is the cost of capital for bonds, I is the annual interest, M is the face value of bonds, NP is the net proceeds, which is the face value adjusted to the flotation cost, and n is the number of years to redemption.

Example 9.1 Suppose that a corporation is planning to collect a capital of $5 million by selling its bonds of $1,000, $8\frac{1}{2}\%$ coupon rate. Given that the firm is selling at a discount of $30 per bond and that the flotation cost is 2% per bond, calculate the 20-year and the before-tax cost of capital.

$$I = \$1,000(.085) = 85$$

$$B_d = M - D$$

$$= \$1,000 - \$30 = \$970$$

$$NP = \$970 - (\$970 \times .02) = \$950.60$$

$$CC_b = \frac{I + [(M - NP)/n]}{(NP + N)/2}$$

$$= \frac{85 + [(\$1,000 - \$950.60)/20]}{(\$950.60 + \$1,000)/2}$$

$$= \frac{87.47}{\$975.30} = .09 \quad \text{before-tax cost of capital is 9\%}$$

To get the after-tax cost of capital (CC_a), we use

$$CC_a = CC_b(1 - T)$$

where T is the corporate tax rate. Suppose that the corporate tax rate is 39%; then the after-tax cost of capital would be

$$CC_a = .09(1 - .39) = .055 \text{ or } 5.5\%$$

Weighted-Average Cost of Capital

A firms **capital structure** is the mix of debt and equity used to finance the firm's operation. The cost of many basic long-term sources of capital, such as stocks and bonds, have been detailed before. What remains is how these types of capital relate to the firm's capital structure and that is what the overall weighted-average cost of capital does. It is a method to determine the cohesiveness of the firm's capital structure by weighting the cost of each capital component based on its proportion as measured by the market value or book value.

$$CC_{wa} = \sum_{i=1}^{n} w_i k_i$$

where CC_{wa} is the cost of capital weighted average, w_i is the proportion of any type of capital in the firm's capital structure, and k_i is the cost of any type of capital.

Example 9.2   The components of a corporation's capital structure and their individual costs are outlined below and in Table 9.17.

1. Long-term debt takes 38% of capital structure and costs 5.59%.
2. Preferred stock represents 14% and costs 9.62%.
3. Common stock takes the remaining 48% and costs 12.35%.

Calculate the corporation's weighted-average cost of capital and explain what it means.

$$CC_{wa} = \sum_{i=1}^{3} w_i k_i = 9.4\%$$

The weighted-average cost of capital is 9.4%, which means that this corporation would be able to accept all investment projects that would potentially earn returns greater than or at least equal to 9.4%.

Ratio Analysis

Shareholders, creditors, and managers are all very interested in a firm's performance as expressed through its financial statements. Prospective investors as well as current stockholders wish to know more about the firm's trends in returns and potential risks, and ultimately, to have a better understanding of what affects the share price and their share of the firm's profits. Managers' main interest is in their capacity to control and monitor a firm's performance and to take it to the best possible level. All of this would establish the need to analyze the firm's financial statements by the way of constructing and calculating a variety of ratios that would serve as general indicators to assess the firm's performance. Ratio analysis also considers two points of view: the **cross-sectional,** where a comparison of those financial indicators is made at the same point in time, and the **time series,** where the indicators are analyzed as trends extending over a period of time. Most financial ratios are related to the investment, as they are related to the way in which the firm employs and manages its capital. Regarding the term of analysis, most financial ratios are related to short-run analysis, as they address specific aspects of performance, such as the ratios of profitability, liquidity, and operations. In long-run analysis, ratios of debt would be a typical example.

TABLE 9.17

Source of Capital	% of Capital Structure, w_i	Cost of Capital, k_i	$w_i k_i$
Long-term debt	.38	.0559	.0212
Preferred stock	.14	.0962	.0135
Common stock	.48	.1235	.0593
	100.00		$\sum_{1}^{3} w_i k_i = .094$

PROFITABILITY RATIOS   Profitability ratios are also called **efficiency ratios** since the major objective is to assess how efficiently firms utilize their assets and, ultimately, how they are able to attract investers and their capital.

Gross Profit Margin Ratio (GPMR)   This ratio shows how much gross profit, GP (sales after paying for the cost of goods sold), is generated by each dollar of net sales, NS (gross sales minus all goods returned).

$$GPMR = \frac{GP}{NS}$$

Example 9.3   If gross profit is \$83,420 and net sales is \$185,377, the GPMR would be

$$GPMR = \frac{\$83,420}{\$185,377} = .45$$

A gross profit margin of 45% means that out of each dollar of net sales, 45 cents would be gross profit.

Operating Profit Margin Ratis (OPMR)   Instead of the gross profit in the GPMR, the OPMR shows the operating profits as they are related to net sales. Operating profit is another term for operating income, which is the same as EBIT (earnings before income and taxes).

$$OPMR = \frac{OY}{NS}$$

Example 9.4   If the operating income is \$45,000 the and net sales is \$300,000, the OPMR is

$$OPMR = \frac{\$45,000}{\$300,000} = .15$$

which means that 19 cents out of each dollar of net sales in this firm goes to the operating income budget.

Net Profit Margin Ratio (NPMR)   This time, the net profit is related to the net sales. The NPMR states how much net profit the firm earns from its volume of sales.

$$NPMR = \frac{NP}{NS}$$

Example 9.5   Suppose that the net profit in one firm is \$35,287 and the net sales are \$298,971. The NPMR would be

$$NPMR = \frac{\$35,287}{\$298,971} = .118$$

or 11.8%, meaning that of each dollar of net sales, this firm would have a little less than 12 cents as net profit. This measure is important especially because it paints a picture of the profit after all expenses, including interest and taxes, have been paid for.

Return on Investment Ratio (ROIR)   The ROIR is also known as the ROA (return on assets). It relates net profit (i.e., after interest and taxes) to total assets (TA) of a firm.

$$\boxed{\text{ROIR} = \frac{\text{NP}}{\text{TA}}}$$

Example 9.6   Let's use the previous net profit figure of $35,287 against a total asset of $250,000. The ROIR would be

$$\text{ROIR} = \frac{\$35,287}{\$250,000} = 14\%$$

which says that each dollar of the total asset value would give 14 cents in net profit.

Return on Equity Ratio (ROER)   In this ratio, the net profit (NP) is related to the owner's equity (OE) in its format of both preferred and common stock. It basically tells stockholders a crucial piece of information: how much of their money a firm would turn into net profit:

$$\boxed{\text{ROER} = \frac{\text{NP}}{\text{OE}}}$$

Example 9.7   Suppose that the owner's equity is valued at $79,500. The net profit of $35,287 would be forming an ROER as

$$\text{ROER} = \frac{\$32,287}{\$79,500} = 44\%$$

which tells shareholders that this firm is able to turn 44 cents of each dollar of their investment into a net profit.

Sales–Asset Ratio (SAR)   The SAR is another efficiency ratio. It shows how efficient the use of resources is, as an important aspect of a firm's performance and its ability to generate profits. It relates sales to total assets.

$$\boxed{\text{SAR} = \frac{S}{\text{TA}}}$$

Example 9.8   Suppose that the volume of sales for a firm reached $46,890 and its records indicate that the value of its total assets at the beginning of the year was $60,522 and at the end of the year was $50,177. The firm's SAR would consist of dividing the sales (S) by the average value of assets since we have two readings:

$$\text{SAR} = \frac{\$46,890}{(\$60,522 + \$50,177)/2}$$
$$= .85$$

This ratio says that the firm is working hard to put its assets to use in producing and selling its products.

Sales to Net Working Capital Ratio (SNWCR)   This time we relate sales to the net working capital, which is basically the firm's short-run net worth or the difference between the current assets and the current liabilities. That current sense of measure is what gives this ratio its more important meanings:

$$SNWCR = \frac{S}{NWC}$$

Example 9.9   Suppose that the working capital in the firm of Example 9.8 is $3,590. Its SNWCR would be

$$SNWCR = \frac{\$46,890}{\$3,590} = 13.1$$

This ratio reflects how the volume of sales relates to the firm's current net worth: in other words, how the net working capital has been put to use.

MARKET-BASED RATIOS   Market-based ratios reflect a firm's performance as it is associated with the related market, and therefore the ratios would be looked at with great interest by current investors, potential investors, and managers.

Price–Earnings (P/E) Ratio   The P/E ratio is one of the most important and commonly used ratios. It relates the market price of a firm's common stock (MPS) to its earnings per share (EPS).

$$P/E = \frac{MPS}{EPS}$$

This ratio reflects investors' confidence in a firm's financial performance; therefore, the higher the P/E, the higher the appraisal given by the stock market.

Example 9.10   If a firm's market price per share of common stock is $65 and the firm has a $7.45 earnings per share, the firm's P/E is

$$P/E = \frac{\$65}{\$7.45} = 8.72$$

which means that this firm's common stock is selling in the stock market for nearly nine times its earnings.

Price–Earnings–Growth Ratio (PEGR)   This ratio employs the P/E ratio and relates it to a firm's expected growth rate per year (EGR). It reflects the firm's potential value of a share of stock.

$$PEGR = \frac{P/E}{EGR}$$

Example 9.11   Suppose that a firm with a P/E of 8.72 expects an annual growth rate of 8%. Its PEGR would be

$$PEGR = \frac{8.72}{8} = 1.09$$

It is theorized that PEGRs represent the following:

- If PEGR = 1 to 2: The firm's stock is in the normal range of value.
- If PEGR < 1: The firm's stock is undervalued.
- If PEGR > 2: The firm's stock is overvalued.

Earnings per Share (EPS)   The EPS is more important to common stockholders in particular because it is calculated by dividing the net profit (after subtracting the dividends for preferred stock) by the outstanding number of shares of common stock.

$$\text{EPS} = \frac{\text{NP} - D_p}{\text{no. shares}}$$

Example 9.12   Suppose that a firm has a net profit of $600,000. It pays 7% of its dividends to preferred stockholders and distributes the remainder among the 40,000 shares of common stock. Its EPS would be

$$\text{dividends for preferred stocks, } D_p = \$600,000 \times .07 = \$42,000$$

$$\text{EPS} = \frac{\$600,000 - \$42,000}{40,000} = \$13.95$$

This means that for each share of common stock that investors own, they earn $13.95.

Dividend Yield (DY)   The DY is obtained by dividing dividends of common stock per share (DPS) by the market price of stock (MPS):

$$\text{DY} = \frac{\text{DPS}}{\text{MPS}}$$

If the dividend per share is $1.95 and the stock price is $35, the dividend yield is

$$\text{DY} = \frac{\$1.95}{\$35} = 5.6\%$$

which says that common stockholders receive only 5.6% as a dividend for the price that each share of stock sells for in the market.

Cash Flow per Share (CFPS)   The CFPS is just like earnings per share (EPS) except that it uses cash flow instead of net profit. Some financial analysts believe that real operating cash flow (OCF) is a much more reliable measure than net profit, which includes a lot of accounts receivable. A measure of the cash available as related to the number of shares of common stock is a good indicator of a firm's financial health.

$$\text{CFPS} = \frac{\text{OCF}}{\text{no. shares}}$$

Example 9.13   Suppose that a firm has an operating cash flow of $65,000 and its shares of common stock reach 500,000 shares outstanding. Its CFPS would be

$$\text{CFPS} = \frac{\$65,000}{500,000} = \$.13$$

which means that the cash flow per share in this firm is 13 cents.

Payout Ratio (PYOR)   This ratio shows how much earnings per share would be paid out as cash dividends for common stockholders (D_c).

$$PYOR = \frac{D_c}{EPS}$$

Example 9.14   Let's suppose that for a firm with an EPS of $13.95, $3.10 is paid out as a cash dividend per share. The payout ratio would then be

$$PYOR = \frac{\$3.10}{\$13.95} = \$.22$$

which means that 22 cents out of each dollar earned per share is being paid out as a dividend.

Book Value per Share (BVPS)   This ratio shows the stockholder's equity or net worth (NW) for each share held.

$$BVPS = \frac{NW}{no.\ shares}$$

Example 9.15   Suppose that a firm's total assets are $747,000, and total liabilities are $517,000 and there are 20,000 shares outstanding. What would be the book value per share?

$$NW = A - L$$
$$= \$747,000 - \$517,000$$
$$= \$230,000$$
$$BVPS = \frac{230,000}{20,000} = \$11.50$$

This means that each share is worth $11.50 of the firm's net worth.

Price–Book Value Ratio (PBVR)   This ratio shows how the market price of a stock (MPS) is related to the book value per share (BVPS):

$$PBVR = \frac{MPS}{BVPS}$$

Example 9.16   Suppose that the stock of the firm in Example 9.16 is sold in the market for $20. The price–book value ratio would be

$$PBVR = \frac{\$20}{\$11.50} = \$1.74$$

A PBVR of $1.74 means that this firm is worth 74% more than the shareholders put into it.

Generally, the PBVR can be read like this:

- If PBVR > 1: The firm is utilizing assets efficiently.
- If PBVR < 1: The firm is utilizing assets inefficiently.
- If PBVR = 1: The firm is utilizing on the margin.

Price/Sales (P/S) Ratio   This ratio shows how many dollars it takes to buy a dollar's worth of a firm's revenue. It is calculated by dividing the market capitalization (MC), which is (stock price × no. shares) by the firm's revenue for the last year (TR).

$$MC = MPS \times no.\ shares$$

$$\boxed{P/S = \frac{MC}{TR}}$$

Example 9.17   If we take the stock price and the number of shares from the preceding examples: MPS = \$20 and the number of shares = 20,000, and if we suppose that the revenue of this firm last year was \$650,000, the market capitalization (MC) would be

$$MC = \$20 \times 20,000 = \$400,000$$

$$P/S = \frac{\$400,000}{\$650,000} = .62$$

A price/sales ratio of 62% is good; it describes a case in which the investors get more than they invest. Generally, market analysts have come up with the criterion that the P/S ratio should be less than if not equal to 75%:

$$\boxed{P/S \leq .75}$$

and investors should avoid firms with price/sales ratios above 150%.

Tobin's Q-Ratio   Tobin's Q-ratio is named after the economist James Tobin, who came up with this ratio as an improvement over the traditional price–book value ratio (PBVR). Tobin believes that both the debt and equity of a firm should be included in the top of the ratio, and instead of depending on the firm's book value the bottom should be the firm's entire assets in their replacement cost, which is adjusted for inflation. In this case, Tobin's Q would reflect accurately where the firm stands.

$$\boxed{Tobin's\ Q = \frac{TA_{mv}}{TA_{rv}}}$$

where TA_{mv} is the market value of the firm's total assets and TA_{rv} is the replacement value of total assets.

Example 9.18   If the market value of total assets of a firm is \$127 million and its replacement cost is \$150 million, its Tobin's Q value would be

$$Tobin's\ Q = \frac{127}{150} = 84.6\%$$

Tobin referred to the rule of thumb for this ratio:

- If Tobin's $Q > 1$: The firm would have the capacity and incentive to invest more.
- If Tobin's $Q < 1$: The firm cannot invest and may acquire assets through merger.

OPERATIONAL RATIOS   Members of this group of ratios are also called **activity ratios.** They deal with the extent to which the firm is able to convert various accounts into cash or sales. These accounts include inventory, accounts receivable, accounts payable, fixed assets, and total asset turnover.

Inventory Turnover Ratio (ITR)   This ratio relates the cost of goods sold (COGS) to the value of inventory (INY):

$$ITR = \frac{COGS}{INY}$$

Often, inventory is calculated as an average of the inventory at the beginning of the year and at the end of the year.

Example 9.19   If the cost of goods sold is $130,000 and the average value of inventory is $53,560, the ITR would be

$$ITR = \frac{\$130,000}{\$53,560} = 2.43$$

An ITR of 2.43 means that the firm moves its inventory 2.43 times a year. The ITR can also be expressed as the **average age of inventory** (AAINY), which is a measure of how many days the average inventory stays in stock. That would be done by dividing the number of days a year (365) by the ITR.

$$AAINY = \frac{365}{ITR}$$

So if we divide 365, by 2.43 we get

$$AAINY = \frac{365}{2.43} = 150$$

which means that it would take 150 days for this firm to carry its inventory.

Accounts Receivable Turnover (ART)   The ART is also called the **average collection period,** which shows the extent to which customers pay their credit bills. It is the account receivable (AR) divided by the average daily sales (DS):

$$ART = \frac{AR}{DS}$$

Example 9.20   If the account receivable has $550,000 and the annual sales are $3,650,000, we can get ART by first getting the daily sales by dividing the annual sales by 365:

$$\frac{\$3,650,000}{365} = 10,000$$

$$ART = \frac{\$550,000}{10,000} = 55$$

which means that it would take the firm 55 days to collect its bills. This is not good unless the firm has a 60-day collection standard, but it is usually 30 days.

Account Payable Turnover (APT)   The APT is also called the **average payment period.** It is similar to the accounts receivable turnover in that it divides the account payable (APY) by the average daily purchase (DP).

$$APT = \frac{APY}{DP}$$

Example 9.21   Suppose that a firm's accounts payable shows $480,000 and its daily purchases are estimated by $15,517. Its APT would be

$$APT = \frac{\$480,000}{\$15,517} = 31 \text{ days}$$

That means that on average the firm has 31 days to pay its bills, which would be a very good standard.

Fixed Asset Turnover (FAT)   The FAT relates the volume of sales (NS) to the firm's fixed assets (FA).

$$FAT = \frac{NS}{FA}$$

Example 9.22   Suppose that a firm has a total value of fixed assets of $79,365 and its net sales are estimated at $133,773. Its FAT value would be

$$FAT = \frac{\$133,773}{\$79,365} = 1.7$$

which means that this firm is able to generate a sales value 1.7 times that of the value of its fixed assets.

Total Asset Turnover (TAT)   The TAT is just like the FAT except that this time the net sales value is related to all assets in the firm instead of only the fixed assets.

$$TAT = \frac{NS}{TA}$$

Example 9.23   Suppose that all assets in Example 9.22 are $140,593; the total asset turnover TAT would then be

$$TAT = \frac{\$133,773}{\$140,593} = .95$$

A total asset turnover of 95% means that a firm is able to turn over 95% of its asset value in net sales.

LIQUIDITY RATIOS   Liquidity ratios show a firm's ability to handle and pay its short-term liabilities and obligations. The more liquid assets the firm can lay its hands on, the easier and smoother the entire performance will be. Liquidity ratios include the current ratio, the quick ratio, the net working capital ratio, and the cash ratio.

Current Ratio (CR)   This ratio is probably the most popular among financial ratios for its direct relevance. It simply describes how current assets (CA) are related to current liabilities (CL):

$$CR = \frac{CA}{CL}$$

Example 9.24   Suppose that a firm's current assets are valued at $1.5 million and its current liabilities are estimated at $980,711. The firm's current ratio would be

$$CR = \frac{\$1,500,000}{\$980,711} = \$1.53$$

A current ratio of 1.53 means that this firm has 1 dollar and 53 cents in its current asset value to meet each dollar of its current obligations. Generally, the current ratio is recommended by most financial analysts to be 2 or more, which means that for a firm to be robust, it has to own at least twice as much as it owes.

$$CR \geq 2$$

The firm here has to dedicate 65 cents out of each dollar of its current assets to pay its current creditor's claims (1/1.53) = .65.

Acid-Test Ratio (QR)   This ratio is also called the **quick ratio.** It is similar to the current ratio above except that the value of inventory is taken away from the current assets.

$$QR = \frac{CA - INY}{CL}$$

Example 9.25   If the entire inventory in the firm of Example 9.24 was estimated at $380,664, the quick ratio would be

$$QR = \frac{\$1,500,000 - \$380,664}{\$980,711} = 1.14$$

which means that the firm has a dollar and 14 cents for each dollar of its creditor's claims. It is noteworthy to mention here that if there are any prepaid items, they would also be subtracted from the current assets along the inventory value.

Net Working Capital Ratio (NWCR)   The net working capital is the short-run net worth of a firm. It is the difference between the current assets and the current liabilities. If we divide the net working capital (NWC) by the available total assets (TA), we get the net working capital ratio (NWCR), which shows the firm's potential cash capacity.

$$NWCR = \frac{NWC}{TA}$$

Example 9.26   Suppose that the total assets for the firm in Example 9.25 is $49,950,592 and that the current assets and liabilities stay at $1,500,000 and $980,771, respectively. The firm's net working capital would be

$$NWC = CA - CL$$

$$= \$1,500,000 - \$980,711$$

$$= \$519.289$$

and its net working capital ratio would be

$$NWCR = \frac{\$519{,}289}{\$4{,}950{,}592} = .10$$

which means that this firm has 10 cents in current net worth in each dollar of its total assets.

Cash–Current Liabilities Ratio (CCLR)   This ratio tracks down cash and marketable securities (C + MS) that are at hand and weighs them against the due current obligations and liabilities (CL).

$$\boxed{CCLR = \frac{C + MS}{CL}}$$

Example 9.27   If we keep the current liabilities of the last firm at $980,711 and assume that cash is counted as $27,500 and marketable securities estimated at $31,342, the firm's cash-to-current liabilities ratio (CCLR) would be

$$CCLR = \frac{\$27{,}500 + \$31{,}342}{\$980{,}711} = .06$$

which says that this firm holds some liquid assets in terms of cash and marketable securities equal to 6 cents to meet each dollar of its current liabilities.

Interval Ratio (InR)   This ratio is another expression of the cash-current liabilities ratio but in terms of time. It reveals how many days a firm is able to meet its short-term obligations. It is obtained by dividing not only cash and marketable securities, but also accounts receivable (AR), by the daily expenditures on current liabilities or current liabilities per day (CLPD).

$$\boxed{InR = \frac{C + MS + AR}{CLPD}}$$

Example 9.28   Let's consider $18,500 in accounts receivable in Example 9.27. Also consider that the average daily expenditures on obligations is calculated at $1,250.

$$InR = \frac{\$27{,}500 + \$31{,}342 + \$18{,}500}{\$1{,}250} = 62 \text{ days}$$

An interval ratio of 62 days means that the firm can continue to meet its average daily spending of $1,250 on obligations for 2 months, tapping its reserve of cash, marketable securities, and accounts receivable.

DEBT RATIOS Debt ratios are also called **leverage ratios.** Because of the increased financial leverage and risk that comes with using more debt in a firm's financing, debt ratios have more importance. These ratios indicate the extent to which a firm's assets are tied to a creditor's claims and therefore the firm's ability to meet the fixed payments that are due to pay off debt.

Debt–Asset (D/A) Ratio This is a direct measure of the percentage of a firm's total assets that belong to creditors: in other words, how much of other people's money is used to generate business profits. It is obtained simply by dividing total liabilities or debt (TD) by total assets (TA).

$$D/A = \frac{TD}{TA}$$

Example 9.29 If a firm has a total debt of $734,000 and its total assets are estimated at $1,930,570, its debt–asset ratio would be

$$D/A = \frac{\$734,000}{\$1,930,570} = .38$$

which means that 38% of the firm's assets is financed with debt.

Debt–Equity (D/E) Ratio This ratio weighs a firm's total debt (TD) to its owner's equity (*E*). It shows the percentage of owner's equity that is generated by debt.

$$D/E = \frac{TD}{E}$$

Example 9.30 If the firm in Example 9.29 has an equity estimated at $1,200,000, its D/E ratio would be

$$D/E = \frac{\$734,000}{\$1,200,000} = .61$$

A D/E of 61% means that for every dollar of owner's equity in the firm, 61 cents is owed to creditors.

Solvency Ratio (Sol) The solvency ratio is the opposite of the D/A ratio: It is obtained by dividing total assets by total debt. It shows to what extent a firm's total assets can handle its total liabilities or debt.

$$Sol = \frac{TA}{TD}$$

Example 9.31 Let's reverse the D/A ratio in Example 9.29, and see what kind of solvency ratio we get:

$$Sol = \frac{\$1,930,570}{\$734,000} = 2.6$$

This solvency ratio means that the firm actually owns 2.6 times more than it owes, and therefore it is solvent. Solvency criteria are:

- If Sol > 1: The firm is solvent.
- If Sol < 1: The firm is insolvent.
- If Sol = 1: The firm is on the margin when its total debt is equal its total assets.

Times Interest Earned Ratio (TIER)   This ratio measures the extent to which a firm is able to make its interest payments. It is obtained by dividing the firm's operating income (OY) (earnings before interest and taxes) by the annual amount of interest due to creditors.

$$\text{TIER} = \frac{\text{OY}}{I}$$

Example 9.32   Suppose that a firm's operating income is \$170,000 and its total annual interest payment is \$35,000. The times–interest earned ratio would be

$$\text{TIER} = \frac{\$170,000}{\$35,000} = 4.9$$

This means that this firm has an operating income almost five times larger than the interest payment due. We can also say that for every dollar of interest the firm pays to creditors, it has almost \$5 in the form of operating income. Still yet, we can say that the firm has enough of a paying capacity to be able to service its debt for about five years.

Operating Income–Fixed Payments Ratio (OYFPR)   This ratio is an expanded TIER. Instead of interest payments only in the denominator, all other fixed payments are added to the interest payments, such as payment for principal (P), payments for preferred stocks as dividends (D_{ps}), and scheduled lease payments (L).

$$\text{OYFPR} = \frac{\text{OY}}{I + P + D_{ps} + L}$$

Example 9.33   Consider the following fixed payments as additions to the interest payment in Example 9.32: P, \$22,000; D_{ps}, \$51,000; L, \$11,000. Then the (OYFPR) would be

$$\text{OYFPR} = \frac{\$170,000}{\$35,000 + \$22,000 + \$51,000 + \$11,000}$$
$$= 1.43$$

Still, this firm's operating income is 1.43 times more than all the fixed payments due.

Note that the principal payment, lease payment, and preferred stock payment have to be in before-tax status. If they are in after-tax status, they have to be converted to before-tax status by dividing them by ($I - T$).

$$(P + D_{ps} + L)_b = \frac{(P + D_{ps} + L)_a}{I - T}$$

where T is the corporate tax rate.

The DuPont Model

The **DuPont model** is a system of financial analysis that has been used by financial managers since its invention by financial analysts working at the DuPont Corporation in the 1920s. It can be described as a collective method of financial analysis, although it has been characterized by some analysts as a complete system of financial ratio utilization. The basic premise of this model is to combine the firm's two financial statements:

1. The income–expense statement
2. The balance sheet

and to incorporate the impact of three important elements:

- The profits on sales, represented by the net profit margin ratio
- The efficiency of asset utilization, represented by the total asset turnover ratio
- The leverage impact, represented by the equity multiplier

The model has two major objectives:

1. To analyze what determines the size of return that investors look forward to receiving from firms in which they invest. This objective is achieved by breaking the return on equity (ROE) into two components: the return on investment (ROI) and the equity multiplier (EM).

$$\boxed{\text{ROE} = \text{ROI} \cdot \text{EM}}$$

2. To break the elements of ROE into subelements: The return on investment is obtained by multiplying the net profit margin (NPM) by the total assets turnover (TAT):

$$\boxed{\text{ROI} = \text{NPM} \cdot \text{TAT}}$$

Furthermore, the net profit margin is obtained by dividing net profits by net sales, and total asset turnover is obtained by dividing net sales by total assets:

$$\text{NPM} = \frac{\text{NP}}{\text{NS}} \quad \text{and} \quad \text{TAT} = \frac{\text{NS}}{\text{TA}}$$

The equity multiplier (EM) is the ratio of total assets to owner's equity:

$$\text{EM} = \frac{\text{TA}}{\text{OE}}$$

To substitute all of the elements, we get

$$\text{ROE} = \frac{\text{NP}}{\text{NS}} \cdot \frac{\text{NS}}{\text{TA}} \cdot \frac{\text{TA}}{\text{OE}}$$

Canceling out NS and TA, we get:

$$\boxed{\text{ROE} = \frac{\text{NP}}{\text{OE}}}$$

Figure 9.8 shows how the various elements are taken from two financial statements, the balance sheet and the income–expense statement, to establish the return on equity.

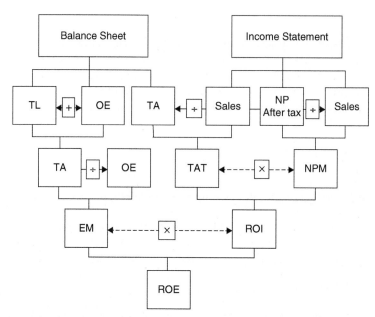

FIGURE 9.8   The DuPont Model.

A Final Word about Ratios

We have discussed a large number of ratios over five categories covering almost every possible aspect of business performance. These ratios are not to be memorized but to be understood and used and interpreted well. They are mathematical terms of one amount divided by another and therefore must be understood as such. The interpretation simply has to be focused on reading the numerator as part of the denominator or the denominator as the whole, including the numerator: simply how the part above the division line relates to the part below the line. Business performance has many aspects, and this is a reason to say that an analyst would be much wiser to use many ratios than only one or two. A comparison has to be consistent in terms of the time period, and requires consistency in size and line of product, among many other factors. A comparison can be made horizontally by the cross-section approach to compare the same ratio across firms, and vertically by the time-series approach to compare ratios of the same firm over the years. Data have to be from sources that were already checked and approved and should be from audited statements. Because of many overlaps, ratios for particular purposes of financial analysis have to be chosen carefully to prevent redundancy.

Part V Security Market Indices

Index Definition and Calculations of Value and Returns

A **security market index** represents a given security market, market segment, or asset class. Most indices are constructed as portfolios of marketable securities.

The value of an index is calculated on a regular basis using either the actual or estimated market prices of the individual securities, known as **constituent**

securities, within the index. For each security market index, investors may encounter two versions of the same index (i.e., an index with identical constituent securities and weights): one version based on price return and one version based on total return. As the name suggests, a **price return index,** also known as a **price index,** reflects *only* the prices of the constituent securities within the index. A **total return index,** in contrast, reflects not only the prices of the constituent securities but also the reinvestment of all income received since inception.

At inception, the values of the price and total return versions of an index are equal. As time passes, however, the value of the total return index, which includes the reinvestment of all dividends and/or interest received, will exceed the value of the price return index by an increasing amount. A look at how the values of each version are calculated over multiple periods illustrates why.

The value of a price return index is calculated as:

$$V_{PRI} = \frac{\sum_{i=1}^{N} n_i P_i}{D} \tag{9.4}$$

where

V_{PRI} = the value of the price return index
n_i = the number of units of constituent security i held in the index portfolio
N = the number of constituent securities in the index
P_i = the unit price of constituent security i
D = the value of the divisor

The **divisor** is a number initially chosen at inception. It is frequently chosen so that the price index has a convenient initial value, such as 1,000. The index provider then adjusts the value of the divisor as necessary to avoid changes in the index value that are unrelated to changes in the prices of its constituent securities. For example, when changing index constituents, the index provider may adjust the divisor so that the value of the index with the new constituents equals the value of the index prior to the changes.

Index return calculations, like calculations of investment portfolio returns, may measure price return or total return. **Price return** measures only price appreciation or percentage change in price. **Total return** measures price appreciation plus interest, dividends, and other distributions.

Index Construction and Management

Constructing and managing a security market index is similar to constructing and managing a portfolio of securities. Index providers must decide the following:

1. Which target market should the index represent?
2. Which securities should be selected from that target market?
3. How much weight should be allocated to each security in the index?
4. When should the index be rebalanced?
5. When should the security selection and weighting decision be reexamined?

TARGET MARKET AND SECURITY SELECTION   The first decision in index construction is identifying the target market, market segment, or asset class that the index is intended to represent. The target market may be defined very broadly or narrowly. It may be based on asset class (e.g., equities, fixed income, real estate, commodities, hedge funds); geographic region (e.g., Japan, South Africa, Latin America, Europe); the exchange on which the securities are traded (e.g., Shanghai, Toronto, Tokyo), and/or other characteristics (e.g., economic sector, company size, investment style, duration, or credit quality).

The target market determines the investment universe and the securities available for inclusion in the index. Once the investment universe is identified, the number of securities and the specific securities to include in the index must be determined. The constituent securities could be nearly all those in the target market or a representative sample of the target market. Some equity indices, such as the S&P 500 Index and the FTSE 100, fix the number of securities included in the index and indicate this number in the name of the index. Other indices allow the number of securities to vary to reflect changes in the target market or to maintain a certain percentage of the target market. For example, the Tokyo Stock Price Index (TOPIX) represents and includes all of the largest stocks, known as the First Section, listed on the Tokyo Stock Exchange. To be included in the First Section—and thus the TOPIX—stocks must meet certain criteria, such as the number of shares outstanding, the number of shareholders, and market capitalization. Stocks that no longer meet the criteria are removed from the First Section and also the TOPIX. Objective or mechanical rules determine the constituent securities of most, but not all, indices. The Sensex of Bombay and the S&P 500, for example, use a selection committee and more subjective decision-making rules to determine constituent securities.

INDEX WEIGHTING   The weighting decision determines how much of each security to include in the index and has a substantial impact on an index's value. Index providers use a number of methods to weight the constituent securities in an index. Indices can be price weighted, equal weighted, market-capitalization weighted, or fundamentally weighted. Each weighting method has its advantages and disadvantages.

Price Weighting   The simplest method to weight an index and the one used by Charles Dow to construct the Dow Jones Industrial Average is **price weighting**. In price weighting, the weight on each constituent security is determined by dividing its price by the sum of all the prices of the constituent securities. The weight is calculated using the following formula:

$$w_i^P = \frac{P_i}{\sum_{i=1}^{N} P_i} \tag{9.5}$$

Table 9.18 illustrates the values, weights, and single-period returns following inception of a price-weighted equity index with five constituent securities. The value of the price-weighted index is determined by dividing the sum of the security values (101.50) by the divisor, which is typically set at inception to equal the initial number of securities in the index. Thus, in our example, the divisor is 5 and the initial value of the index is calculated as $101.50 \div 5 = 20.30$.

TABLE 9.18 Example of a Price-Weighted Equity Index

Security	Shares in Index	BOP Price	Value (Shares × BOP Price)	BOP Weight %	EOP Price	Dividends per Share	Value (Shares × EOP Price)	Total Dividends	Price Return %	Total Return %	BOP Weight × Price Return %	BOP Weight × Total Return %	EOP Weight %
A	1	50.00	50.00	49.26	55.00	0.75	55.00	0.75	10.00	11.50	4.93	5.66	52.38
B	1	25.00	25.00	24.63	22.00	0.10	22.00	0.10	-12.00	-11.60	-2.96	-2.86	20.95
C	1	12.50	12.50	12.32	8.00	0.00	8.00	0.00	-36.00	-36.00	-4.43	-4.43	7.62
D	1	10.00	10.00	9.85	14.00	0.05	14.00	0.05	40.00	40.50	3.94	3.99	13.33
E	1	4.00	4.00	3.94	6.00	0.00	6.00	0.00	50.00	50.00	1.97	1.97	5.72
Total			101.50	100.00			105.00	0.90			3.45	4.33	100.00
Index Value			20.30				21.00	0.18	3.45	4.33			

Divisor = 5
BOP = Beginning of period
EOP = End of period

Type of Index	BOP Value	Return %	EOP Value
Price Return	20.30	3.45	21.00
Total Return	20.30	4.33	21.18

TABLE 9.19   Impact of 2-for-1 Split in Security A

Security	Price before Split	Weight before Split (%)	Price after Split	Weight after Split (%)
A	55.00	52.38	27.50	35.48
B	22.00	20.95	22.00	28.39
C	8.00	7.62	8.00	10.32
D	14.00	13.33	14.00	18.07
E	6.00	5.72	6.00	7.74
Total	105.00	100.00	77.50	100.00
Divisor	5.00		3.69	
Index Value	21.00		21.00	

As illustrated in this exhibit, Security A, which has the highest price, also has the highest weighting and thus will have the greatest impact on the return of the index. Note how both the price return and the total return of the index are calculated on the basis of the corresponding returns on the constituent securities.

A property unique to price-weighted indices is that a stock split on one constituent security changes the weights on all the securities in the index.[1] To prevent the stock split and the resulting new weights from changing the value of the index, the index provider must adjust the value of the divisor as illustrated in Table 9.19. Given a 2-for-1 split in Security A, the divisor is adjusted by dividing the sum of the constituent prices *after* the split (77.50) by the value of the index *before* the split (21.00). This adjustment results in changing the divisor from 5 to 3.69 so that the index value is maintained at 21.00.

The primary advantage of price weighting is its simplicity. The main disadvantage of price weighting is that it results in arbitrary weights for each security. In particular, a stock split in any one security causes arbitrary changes in the weights of all the constituents' securities.

Equal Weighting   Another simple index weighting method is **equal weighting**. This method assigns an equal weight to each constituent security at inception. The weights are calculated as:

$$w_i^E = \frac{1}{N} \tag{9.6}$$

where

  w_i = fraction of the portfolio that is allocated to security i or weight of security i
  N = number of securities in the index

To construct an equal-weighted index from the five securities in Table 9.18, the index provider allocates one-fifth (20 percent) of the value of the index (at

---

[1] A stock split is an increase in the number of shares outstanding and a proportionate decrease in the price per share such that the total market value of equity, as well as investors' proportionate ownership in the company, does not change.

the beginning of the period) to each security. Dividing the value allocated to each security by each security's individual share price determines the number of shares of each security to include in the index. Unlike a price-weighted index, where the weights are arbitrarily determined by the market prices, the weights in an equal-weighted index are arbitrarily assigned by the index provider.

Table 9.20 illustrates the values, weights, and single-period returns following inception of an equal-weighted index with the same constituent securities as those in Table 9.18. This example assumes a beginning index portfolio value of 10,000 (i.e., an investment of 2,000 in each security). To set the initial value of the index to 1,000, the divisor is set to 10 (10,000 ÷ 10 = 1,000).

Tables 9.18 and 9.20 demonstrate how different weighting methods result in different returns. The 10.4 percent price return of the equal-weighted index shown in Table 9.20 differs significantly from the 3.45 percent price return of the price-weighted index in Table 9.18.

Like price weighting, the primary advantage of equal weighting is its simplicity. Equal weighting, however, has a number of disadvantages. First, securities that constitute the largest fraction of the target market value are underrepresented, and securities that constitute a small fraction of the target market value are overrepresented. Second, after the index is constructed and the prices of constituent securities change, the index is no longer equally weighted. Therefore, maintaining equal weights requires frequent adjustments (rebalancing) to the index.

Market-Capitalization Weighting In **market-capitalization weighting,** or value weighting, the weight on each constituent security is determined by dividing its market capitalization by the total market capitalization (the sum of the market capitalization) of all the securities in the index. Market capitalization or value is calculated by multiplying the number of shares outstanding by the market price per share.

The market-capitalization weight of security i is:

$$w_i^M = \frac{Q_i P_i}{\sum_{j=1}^{N} Q_j P_j} \tag{9.7}$$

where

w_i = fraction of the portfolio that is allocated to security i or weight of security i

Q_i = number of shares outstanding of security i

P_i = share price of security i

N = number of securities in the index

Table 9.21 illustrates the values, weights, and single-period returns following inception of a market-capitalization-weighted index for the same five-security market. Security A, with 3,000 shares outstanding and a price of 50 per share, has a market capitalization of 150,000 or 26.29 percent (150,000/570,500) of the entire index portfolio. The resulting index weights in the exhibit reflect the relative value of each security as measured by its market capitalization.

TABLE 9.20 Example of an Equal-Weighted Equity Index

Security	Shares in Index	BOP Price	Value (Shares × BOP Price)	Weight %	EOP Price	Dividends per Share	Value (Shares × EOP Price)	Total Dividends	Price Return %	Total Return %	Weight × Price Return %	Weight × Total Return %	EOP Weight %
A	40	50.00	2,000	20.00	55.00	0.75	2,200	30	10.00	11.50	2.00	2.30	19.93
B	80	25.00	2,000	20.00	22.00	0.10	1,760	8	−12.00	−11.60	−2.40	−2.32	15.94
C	160	12.50	2,000	20.00	8.00	0.00	1,280	0	−36.00	−36.00	−7.20	−7.20	11.60
D	200	10.00	2,000	20.00	14.00	0.05	2,800	10	40.00	40.50	8.00	8.10	25.36
E	500	4.00	2,000	20.00	6.00	0.00	3,000	0	50.00	50.00	10.00	10.00	27.17
Total			10,000	100.00			11,040	48			10.40	10.88	100.00
Index Value			1,000				1,104	4.80	10.40	10.88			

Divisor = 10
BOP = Beginning of period
EOP = End of period

Type of Index	BOP Value	Return %	EOP Value
Price Return	1,000.00	10.40	1,104.00
Total Return	1,000.00	10.88	1,108.80

TABLE 9.21 Example of a Market-Capitalization-Weighted Equity Index

Stock	Shares Outstanding	BOP Price	BOP Market Cap	BOP Weight %	EOP Price	Dividends per Share	EOP Market Cap	Total Dividends	Price Return %	Total Return %	BOP Weight × Price Return %	BOP Weight × Total Return %	EOP Weight %
A	3,000	50.00	150,000	26.29	55.00	0.75	165,000	2,250	10.00	11.50	2.63	3.02	28.50
B	10,000	25.00	250,000	43.82	22.00	0.10	220,000	1,000	-12.00	-11.60	-5.26	-5.08	38.00
C	5,000	12.50	62,500	10.96	8.00	0.00	40,000	0	-36.00	-36.00	-3.95	-3.95	6.91
D	8,000	10.00	80,000	14.02	14.00	0.05	112,000	400	40.00	40.50	5.61	5.68	19.34
E	7,000	4.00	28,000	4.91	6.00	0.00	42,000	0	50.00	50.00	2.46	2.46	7.25
Total			570,500	100.00			579,000	3,650		2.13	1.49	2.13	100.00
Index Value			1,000				1,014.90	6.40	1.49				

Divisor = 570.50
BOP = Beginning of period
EOP = End of period

Type of Index	BOP Value	EOP Value	Return %
Price Return	1,000.00	1,014.90	1.49
Total Return	1,000.00	1,021.30	2.13

463

As shown in Tables 9.18, 9.20, and 9.21, the weighting method affects the index's returns. The price and total returns of the market-capitalization index in Table 9.21 (1.49 percent and 2.13 percent, respectively) differ significantly from those of the price-weighted (3.45 percent and 4.33 percent, respectively) and equal-weighted (10.40 percent and 10.88 percent, respectively) indices. To understand the source and magnitude of the difference, compare the weights and returns of each security under each of the weighting methods. The weight of Security A, for example, ranges from 49.26 percent in the price-weighted index to 20 percent in the equal-weighted index. With a price return of 10 percent, Security A contributes 4.93 percent to the price return of the price-weighted index, 2.00 percent to the price return of the equal-weighted index, and 2.63 percent to the price return of the market-capitalization-weighted index. With a total return of 11.50 percent, Security A contributes 5.66 percent to the total return of the price-weighted index, 2.30 percent to the total return of the equal-weighted index, and 3.02 percent to the total return of the market-capitalization-weighted index.

Fundamental Weighting   **Fundamental weighting** attempts to address the disadvantages of market-capitalization weighting by using measures of a company's size that are independent of its security price to determine the weight on each constituent security. These measures include book value, cash flow, revenues, earnings, dividends, and number of employees.

Some fundamental indices use a single measure, such as total dividends, to weight the constituent securities, whereas others combine the weights from several measures to form a composite value that is used for weighting.

Letting F_i denote a given fundamental size measure of company i, the fundamental weight on security i is

$$w_i^F = \frac{F_i}{\displaystyle\sum_{j=1}^{N} F_j} \tag{9.8}$$

Relative to a market-capitalization-weighted index, a fundamental index with weights based on such an item as earnings will result in greater weights on constituent securities with earnings yields (earnings divided by price) that are higher than the earnings yield of the overall market-weighted portfolio. Similarly, stocks with earnings yields less than the yield on the overall market-weighted portfolio will have lower weights. For example, suppose there are two stocks in an index. Stock A has a market capitalization of €200 million, Stock B has a market capitalization of €800 million, and their aggregate market capitalization is €1 billion (€1,000 million). Both companies have earnings of €20 million and aggregate earnings of €40 million. Thus, Stock A has an earnings yield of 10 percent (20/200) and Stock B has an earnings yield of 2.5 percent (20/800). The earnings weight of Stock A is 50 percent (20/40), which is higher than its market-capitalization weight of 20 percent (200/1,000). The earnings weight of Stock B is 50 percent (20/40), which is less than its market-capitalization weight of 80 percent (800/1,000). Relative to the market-cap-weighted index, the earnings-weighted index overweights the high-yield Stock A and underweights the low-yield Stock B.

The most important property of fundamental weighting is that it leads to indices that have a "value" tilt. That is, a fundamentally weighted index has ratios of book value, earnings, dividends, and so forth to market value that are higher than its market-capitalization-weighted counterpart. Also, in contrast to the momentum "effect" of market-capitalization-weighted indices, fundamentally weighted indices generally will have a contrarian "effect" in that the portfolio weights will shift away from securities that have increased in relative value and toward securities that have fallen in relative value whenever the portfolio is rebalanced.

Uses of Market Indices

Indices were initially created to give a sense of how a particular security market performed on a given day. With the development of modern financial theory, their uses in investment management have expanded significantly. Some of the major uses of indices include:

- Gauges of market sentiment.
- Proxies for measuring and modeling returns, systematic risk, and risk-adjusted performance.
- Proxies for asset classes in asset allocation models.
- Benchmarks for actively managed portfolios.
- Model portfolios for such investment products as index funds and exchange-traded funds (ETFs).

Investors using security market indices must be familiar with how various indices are constructed in order to select the index or indices most appropriate for their needs.

GAUGES OF MARKET SENTIMENT   The original purpose of stock market indices was to provide a gauge of investor confidence or market sentiment. As indicators of the collective opinion of market participants, indices reflect investor attitudes and behavior. The Dow Jones Industrial Average has a long history, is frequently quoted in the media, and remains a popular gauge of market sentiment. It may not accurately reflect the overall attitude of investors or the "market," however, because the index consists of only 30 of the thousands of U.S. stocks traded each day.

PROXIES FOR MEASURING AND MODELING RETURNS, SYSTEMATIC RISK, AND RISK-ADJUSTED PERFORMANCE   The capital asset pricing model (CAPM) defines beta as the systematic risk of a security with respect to the entire market. The market portfolio in the CAPM consists of all risky securities. To represent the performance of the market portfolio, investors use a broad index. For example, the Tokyo Stock Price Index (TOPIX) and the S&P 500 often serve as proxies for the market portfolio in Japan and the United States, respectively, and are used for measuring and modeling systematic risk and market returns.

Security market indices also serve as market proxies when measuring risk-adjusted performance. The beta of an actively managed portfolio allows investors to form a passive alternative with the same level of systematic risk. For example, if the beta of an actively managed portfolio of global stocks is 0.95 with respect to the MSCI World Index, investors can create a passive portfolio with the same systematic risk by investing 95 percent of their portfolio in a MSCI World Index fund and holding the remaining 5 percent in cash. Alpha, the difference between the return of the actively managed portfolio and the return of the passive portfolio, is a measure of risk-adjusted return or investment performance. Alpha can be the result of manager skill (or lack thereof), transaction costs, and fees.

PROXIES FOR ASSET CLASSES IN ASSET ALLOCATION MODELS   Because indices exhibit the risk and return profiles of select groups of securities, they play a critical role as proxies for asset classes in asset allocation models. They provide the historical data used to model the risks and returns of different asset classes.

BENCHMARKS FOR ACTIVELY MANAGED PORTFOLIOS   Investors often use indices as benchmarks to evaluate the performance of active portfolio managers. The index selected as the benchmark should reflect the investment strategy used by the manager. For example, an active manager investing in global small-capitalization stocks should be evaluated using a benchmark index, such as the FTSE Global Small Cap Index, which includes 4,600 small-capitalization stocks across 48 countries.

The choice of an index to use as a benchmark is important because an inappropriate index could lead to incorrect conclusions regarding an active manager's investment performance. Suppose that the small-cap manager underperformed the small-cap index but outperformed a broad equity market index. If investors use the broad market index as a benchmark, they might conclude that the small-cap manager is earning his or her fees and should be retained or given additional assets to invest. Using the small-cap index as a benchmark might lead to a very different conclusion.

MODEL PORTFOLIOS FOR INVESTMENT PRODUCTS   Indices also serve as the basis for the development of new investment products. Using indices as benchmarks for actively managed portfolios has led some investors to conclude that they should invest in the benchmarks instead. Based on the CAPM's conclusion that investors should hold the market portfolio, broad market index funds have been developed to function as proxies for the market portfolio.

Investment management firms initially developed and managed index portfolios for institutional investors. Eventually, mutual fund companies introduced index funds for individual investors. Subsequently, investment management firms introduced exchange-traded funds, which are managed the same way as index mutual funds but trade like stocks.

The first ETFs were based on existing indices. As the popularity of ETFs increased, index providers created new indices for the specific purpose of forming ETFs, leading to the creation of numerous narrowly defined indices with corresponding ETFs. The Market Vectors Vietnam ETF, for example, allows investors to invest in the equity market of Vietnam.

The choice of indices to meet the needs of investors is extensive. Index providers are constantly looking for opportunities to develop indices to meet the needs of investors.

Equity Indices

A wide variety of equity indices exist, including broad market, multimarket, sector, and style indices.

BROAD MARKET INDICES A broad equity market index, as its name suggests, represents an entire given equity market and typically includes securities representing more than 90 percent of the selected market. For example, the Shanghai Stock Exchange Composite Index (SSE) is a market-capitalization-weighted index of all shares that trade on the Shanghai Stock Exchange. In the United States, the Wilshire 5000 Total Market Index is a market-capitalization-weighted index that includes more than 6,000 equity securities and is designed to represent the entire U.S. equity market.[2] The Russell 3000, consisting of the largest 3,000 stocks by market capitalization, represents 99 percent of the U.S. equity market.

MULTIMARKET INDICES **Multimarket indices** usually comprise indices from different countries and are designed to represent multiple security markets. Multimarket indices may represent multiple national markets, geographic regions, economic development groups, and, in some cases, the entire world. World indices are of importance to investors who take a global approach to equity investing without any particular bias toward a particular country or region. A number of index providers publish families of multimarket equity indices.

MSCI Barra offers a number of multimarket indices. As shown in Table 9.22, MSCI Barra classifies countries along two dimensions: level of economic development and geographic region. Developmental groups, which MSCI Barra refers to as market classifications, include developed markets, emerging markets, and frontier markets. The geographic regions are largely divided by longitudinal lines of the globe: the Americas, Europe with Africa, and Asia with the Pacific. MSCI Barra provides country-specific indices for each of the developed and emerging market countries within its multimarket indices. MSCI Barra periodically reviews the market classifications of countries in its indices for movement from frontier markets to emerging markets and from emerging markets to developed markets and reconstitutes the indices accordingly.

Fundamental Weighting in Multimarket Indices

Some index providers weight the securities within each country by market capitalization and then weight each country in the overall index in proportion to its relative GDP, effectively creating fundamental weighting in multimarket indices. GDP-weighted indices were some of the first fundamentally weighted indices created. Introduced in 1987 by MSCI to address the 60 percent weight of Japanese equities in the market-capitalization-weighted MSCI EAFE Index at the time, GDP-weighted indices reduced the allocation to Japanese equities by half.[3]

SECTOR INDICES **Sector indices** represent and track different economic sectors—such as consumer goods, energy, finance, health care, and technology—on either a national, regional, or global basis. Because different sectors of the economy behave differently over the course of the business cycle, some investors may seek to overweight or underweight their exposure to particular sectors.

---

[2] Despite its name, the Wilshire 5000 has no constraint on the number of securities that can be included. It included approximately 5,000 securities at inception.

[3] Schoenfeld (2004), 220.

TABLE 9.22   MSCI International Equity Indices—Country and Market Coverage (as of June 2009)

Developed Markets		
Americas	Europe	Pacific
Canada, United States	Austria, Belgium, Denmark, Finland, France, Germany, Greece, Ireland, Italy, Netherlands, Norway, Portugal, Spain, Sweden, Switzerland, United Kingdom	Australia, Hong Kong, Japan, New Zealand, Singapore

Emerging Markets		
Americas	Europe, Middle East, Africa	Asia
Argentina,[a] Brazil, Chile, Colombia, Mexico, Peru	Czech Republic, Egypt, Hungary, Israel, Jordan, Morocco, Poland, Russia, South Africa, Turkey	China, India, Indonesia, South Korea, Malaysia, Pakistan,[b] Philippines, Taiwan, Thailand

Frontier Markets				
Americas	Central & Eastern Europe & CIS	Africa	Middle East	Asia
Jamaica,[c] Trinidad & Tobago[c]	Bulgaria, Croatia, Estonia, Lithuania, Kazakhstan, Romania, Serbia, Slovenia, Ukraine	Botswana,[d] Ghana,[d] Kenya, Mauritius, Nigeria, Tunisia	Lebanon, Bahrain, Kuwait, Oman, Qatar, United Arab Emirates, Saudi Arabia[e]	Sri Lanka, Vietnam

[a]The MSCI Argentina Index was reclassified from the MSCI Emerging Markets Index to the MSCI Frontier Markets Index at the end of May 2009 to coincide with the May 2009 Semi-Annual Index Review.
[b]The MSCI Pakistan Index was removed from the MSCI Emerging Markets Index as of the close of December 31, 2008, to reflect the deterioration of investability conditions in the Pakistani equity market. In May 2009, the MSCI Pakistan Index was added to the MSCI Frontier Markets Index to coincide with the May 2009 Semi-Annual Index Review.
[c]In May 2009, the MSCI Trinidad & Tobago Index was added to the MSCI Frontier Markets Index. However, the MSCI Jamaica Index continues to be maintained as a stand-alone country index because it does not meet the liquidity requirements of the Frontiers Market Index.
[d]Botswana and Ghana currently stand alone and are not included in the MSCI Frontier Markets Index. The addition of these two countries to the MSCI Frontier Market Index is under consideration.
[e]Saudi Arabia is currently not included in the MSCI Frontier Markets Index but is part of the MSCI GCC Countries Index.
Source: MSCI Barra (www.mscibarra.com/products/indices/equity/index.jsp), June 2009.

Sector indices are organized as families; each index within the family represents an economic sector. Typically, the aggregation of a sector index family is equivalent to a broad market index. Economic sector classification can be applied on a global, regional, or country-specific basis, but no universally agreed upon sector classification method exists.

Sector indices play an important role in performance analysis because they provide a means to determine whether a portfolio manager is more successful at stock selection or sector allocation. Sector indices also serve as model portfolios for sector-specific ETFs and other investment products.

STYLE INDICES Style indices represent groups of securities classified according to market capitalization, value, growth, or a combination of these characteristics. They are intended to reflect the investing styles of certain investors, such as the growth investor, value investor, and small-cap investor.

Market Capitalization Market-capitalization indices represent securities categorized according to the major capitalization categories: large cap, midcap, and small cap. With no universal definition of these categories, the indices differ on the distinctions between large cap and midcap and between midcap and small cap, as well as the minimum market-capitalization size required to be included in a small-cap index. Classification into categories can be based on absolute market capitalization (e.g., below €100 million) or relative market capitalization (e.g., the smallest 2,500 stocks).

Value/Growth Classification Some indices represent categories of stocks based on their classifications as either value or growth stocks. Different index providers use different factors and valuation ratios (low price-to-book ratios, low price-to-earnings ratios, high dividend yields, etc.) to distinguish between value and growth equities.

Market Capitalization and Value/Growth Classification Combining the three market-capitalization groups with value and growth classifications results in six basic style index categories:

Large-Cap Value	Large-Cap Growth
Mid-Cap Value	Mid-Cap Growth
Small-Cap Value	Small-Cap Growth

Because indices use different size and valuation classifications, the constituents of indices designed to represent a given style, such as small-cap value, may differ—sometimes substantially.

Because valuation ratios and market capitalizations change over time, stocks frequently migrate from one style index category to another on reconstitution dates. As a result, style indices generally have much higher turnover than do broad market indices.

Reference

Schoenfeld, S. A. 2004. *Active Index Investing*. Hoboken, NJ: John Wiley & Sons.

CHAPTER 10

Fixed-Income Vehicles

S tocks and stock markets get most of the attention among investors and their advisors, but fixed income securities and the funds invested through bond markets dwarf the amount of money invested in stocks worldwide. Investment advisors and consultants should understand bond basics such as the various types of fixed income investment structures and strategies, and their risks; but they should also be able to calculate or value these investments as well. This chapter takes a look at numerous fixed income investments in the United States and abroad, reviews the primary characteristics and risks of these investments, and calculates the values of these securities based on various events and circumstances.

Part I *Portfolio Design: A Modern Approach to Asset Allocation:* Bonds

Learning Objectives

- Explain the relationship between interest rates and inflation and discuss the history of inflation in the United States.
- Define and differentiate between nominal and real returns. Discuss the history of Treasury bond returns over time.
- Discuss the history of inflation and bond returns for developed countries over time.
- Discuss coupon yield, capital gain, total return, standard deviation, and the Sharpe Ratio of treasury bonds by maturity over time.
- Discuss default rates of U.S. bonds over time.
- Compare the returns and standard deviations of corporate bonds and treasury bonds over time.
- Describe and discuss the correlation of bonds and stocks over time.
- Describe the global bond market in terms of countries and regions that participate and the types of bonds they offer.
- Discuss global bond market returns and standard deviations over time.
- Explain the benefits of diversifying a bond portfolio with exposure to global markets.
- Discuss the concept of currency risk as it relates to bond portfolios and discuss strategies for managing this risk more effectively.

Part II *Handbook of Finance:* Bonds: Investment Features and Risks

Learning Objectives

- Describe the concept and purpose of a bond.
- List and describe the various sectors of the bond market.
- Explain the features of bonds including: maturity, par value, coupon rate, and accrued interest.
- List and describe the provisions for paying off bonds including: call and refunding provisions, prepayments, and sinking fund provisions.
- Describe and calculate the following yield measures: current yield, yield to maturity, yield to call, yield to put, yield to worst, and cash flow yield.
- List and explain the key risks associated with investing in bonds including: interest rate risk, call and prepayment risk, credit risk, liquidity risk, exchange rate or currency risk, and inflation or purchasing power risk.

Part III *Handbook of Finance:* Effective Duration and Convexity

Learning Objectives

- Explain the concepts of effective and modified duration.
- Explain the concept of convexity.
- Describe the impact of a call option (for a callable bond) on duration and convexity.
- Describe the impact of a put option (for a putable bond) on duration and convexity.
- Explain how investors should analyze duration and convexity and how they might use this information to build and manage bond portfolios more effectively.

Part IV *Foundations and Applications of the Time Value of Money:* Values Tied to Bonds

Learning Objectives

- Describe the concept of bonds and their basic features and risks.
- Explain the calculation of the present value of a bond.
- Calculate the value of a coupon bond.
- Discuss the importance and application of premiums and discounts.
- Calculate the value of a zero-coupon bond.
- Calculate yield to maturity.
- Discuss reinvestment and interest rate risk.
- Describe the yield curve and its significance.
- Discuss credit risk.

Part I Bonds

This chapter will discuss three types of bonds: U.S. Treasury bonds, other bonds issued in the United States, and bonds issued in other industrial countries. The United States is the largest market for bonds in the world, but the bond markets of the other industrial countries are growing rapidly, particularly the markets in the Euro currency area. The returns on bonds have varied widely over the last few decades, so the chapter will investigate the main determinants of bond returns.

Bonds are often favored by investors because they provide fixed income in contrast to the variable returns offered by equities and by most other assets. A stream of fixed income payments is often viewed as essential to retirees as well as many institutional investors because of their need for continual income. Investors focusing only on yields, however, are too often disappointed by the overall performance of their investments. Bond yields represent part of the total return to fixed income assets, but the variation in yields over time leads to capital gains and losses that sometimes dominate the total return from holding bonds. That's especially true if the total return takes into account changes in the cost of living. In the 1970s, for example, bond yields were quite high relative to long-run averages. Yet bond returns were quite abysmal because of capital losses. As inflation and interest rates rose over the decade, existing bonds fell in value. So the total return on these bonds, including capital gains as well as coupons, was far lower than the coupons themselves. Returns on bonds in the 1970s were lower still when adjusted for inflation.

The fixed income of bond investments is illusory in countries with high inflation. It is also often illusory for securities with high default risk. So it's useful to begin with a discussion of what determines the interest rate on a bond. This discussion will help to explain why bond returns are so miserably low in some periods, particularly when adjusted for inflation, and why they are surprisingly high in other periods. Two important determinants of bond yields are (expected) inflation rates and (expected) default rates. The discussion of default risk will be postponed until later in this chapter by first focusing on U.S. government bonds with little if any default risk.

Treasury Bonds

How does inflation affect interest rates? In the short run, central banks often play a critical role in setting short-term interest rates. For example, the Federal Reserve directly controls the Federal Funds interest rate, the rate at which banks borrow in the inter-bank market. And other short-term dollar interest rates, such as the commercial paper and Treasury bill interest rates in the United States or the LIBOR rate on dollar deposits in London, are loosely linked to the Fed Funds rate.[1] So if the Fed raises the Fed Funds rate by 25 basis points, or 0.25 percent, the commercial paper and Treasury bill rates and LIBOR are likely to rise by a similar amount (in normal times, at least). In the long-run, however, the role of the Federal Reserve is very different. In the long run, U.S. interest rates are primarily determined by inflation. And it is the Fed's role in helping to determine the inflation rate that matters.

Consider the history of U.S. interest rates since the late 1940s as shown in Figure 10.1. Except for a temporary bout of inflation during the Korean War, inflation remained low in the United States until the late 1960s and 1970s. Inflation

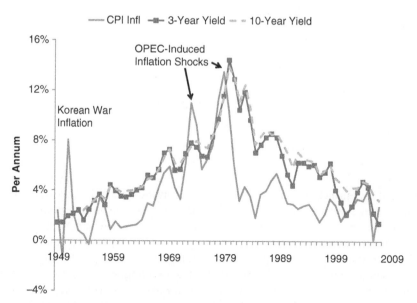

FIGURE 10.1   Inflation and U.S. Treasury Bond Yields, 1949–2009
Data Source: IMF, International Financial Statistics.

peaked following two oil price shocks in 1973 and 1974 and 1979. Beginning in the late 1960s, interest rates slowly but surely responded to rising inflation as inflation expectations became imbedded in bond yields. The same inflation expectations led to rising wage demands and to downward pressure on the U.S. dollar. To lower interest yields from their highs in the late 1970s, it was necessary for the Federal Reserve to pursue a tight monetary policy. This shift in policy began with the appointment of Paul Volcker as Fed chair in 1979. The low interest rates that we experience today were made at the Fed. But in the long run, low interest rates result from low inflation, not from the Fed lowering the Fed Funds rate.

   To provide further evidence of the link between inflation and interest rates, consider the bond *returns* earned on long-term Treasury bonds in each decade since 1950 as shown in Figure 10.2. This chart shows the nominal bond return, the inflation rate, and the real bond return. The latter is obtained by deflating the nominal return by the inflation rate.[2] The low bond yields of the 1950s were matched by almost equally low inflation. The net result was a real bond return that was (slightly) negative. Over the next two decades, inflation expectations evidently lagged behind actual inflation so bond holders earned negative real bond returns of −1.6 percent and −3.8 percent, respectively! Fixed income earners were deceived by the steadiness of the coupons on their bonds. The real value of the bonds was being eroded by inflation, and the coupons themselves were being debased by rising price levels.

   The terrific returns earned since 1981 are a direct result of the Fed's policy of fighting inflation. Over this period, bond yields and inflation expectations lagged behind actual inflation once again. But in this case, bond holders were surprised by falling inflation and they were rewarded with unusually large real returns on their bonds. In the decade from 1981 to 1990, the compound real return on the long-term (20-year) Treasury bond was 8.8 percent. That return was followed by a 7.3 percent

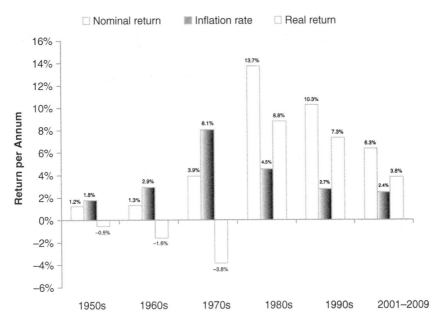

FIGURE 10.2   Nominal and Real Treasury Bond Returns by Decade
Data Source: © Morningstar.

compound return in the 1990s. Those returns are to be expected when inflation falls from 13.5 percent to its current level and when bond yields fall from almost 15 percent to less than 5 percent.

It's important for investors to realize how fundamental is the link between inflation and interest rates. Consider the experience of the major industrial countries over the past few decades. All of these countries have benefited from a decline in inflation and a decline in interest rates since 1980. So the triumph of the Federal Reserve over inflation was matched by similar victories in the other industrial countries. In Europe, the fight against inflation was spurred on by currency regimes that sought to limit exchange rate changes between European countries. In particular, the planned introduction of the Euro in 1999 forced countries to cut inflation in order to qualify for the currency union.[3] But despite these pressures, European countries differed widely in their inflation rates as did the other industrial countries. Between 1981 and 2008, inflation rates as measured by the consumer price index ranged from an average of 2.3 percent in Germany to 5.7 percent in Spain. Two countries outside the European Union, Japan and Switzerland, had even lower inflation rates than Germany, Japan's being only 1.0 percent.

The wide range of inflation rates was matched by an equally wide range of interest rates. Consider Figure 10.3 which shows the array of interest rates and inflation rates in 16 industrial countries between 1981 and 2008. If all of these countries maintained the same real interest rates throughout, they would all lie along a line. In practice, some countries have higher interest rates than their inflation rates justify, while others have lower interest rates.

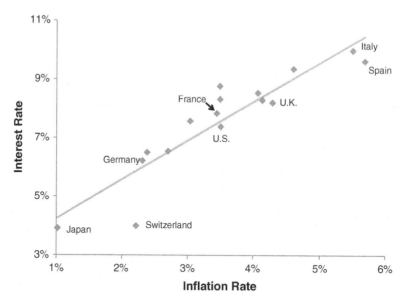

FIGURE 10.3   Interest Rates and Inflation Rates of the Major Industrial Countries, 1981–2008
Data Source: IMF, International Financial Statistics.

The extreme case is that of Switzerland, which has an average inflation rate of 2.2 percent and an average interest rate of only 4.0 percent. The United States, in contrast, has an average inflation rate of 3.5 percent and an average interest rate of 7.4 percent. Despite these differences, Figure 10.3 shows a very clear link between inflation and interest rates in the long run. It's important to keep this in mind when considering bond returns earned over equally long periods.

Besides inflation, interest rates on Treasury bonds vary by maturity. In most periods, the term structure of interest rates is upward sloping. That is, longer maturity issues pay higher yields than those with shorter maturity. Consider Figure 10.4, which shows the term structure of yields on U.S. Treasury bonds in three different years, 1985, 1995, and 2005. In all three years the economy was growing, so the term structure of yields had its normal upward slope. (If a recession had occurred in one of these years, the term structure of yields could have been inverted temporarily.) Over the two decades shown in the figure, inflation and interest rates were dropping. So the whole term structure of yields fell over time. Thus the figure illustrates two of the three determinants of bond yields, inflation and the maturity of the bond. The third factor, default risk, is negligible in the case of Treasuries.

Bond yields are only one component of bond returns. Bond *returns* reflect both the coupon paid and the capital gain over the holding period of the return. If C is the coupon on a Treasury bond and B_{t-1} is the price of the bond at the end of the previous period, then the bond return during period t, R_t, is given by:

$$R_t = C/B_{t-1} + (B_t/B_{t-1} - 1)$$

The first term is the coupon price ratio and the second term is the capital gain on the bond during period t. Table 10.1 reports bond returns for two maturities of

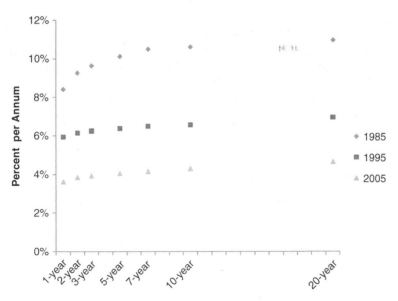

FIGURE 10.4   Term Structure of Treasury Bond Yields
Data Source: Federal Reserve Board.

U.S. Treasuries. The long-term bond is a 20-year Treasury bond, while the medium-term is a five-year Treasury. First consider returns over the whole period since 1951. The long-term bond has higher volatility with a standard deviation of 9.5 percent compared with one of 5.0 percent for the medium-term issue. Over this long period, however, investors were not compensated for this higher volatility since the return on the long-term bond was only marginally higher than on the medium-term bond.

In periods of falling interest rates, such as those in the 1980s until present, long-term bonds should outperform medium-term bonds. That is indeed the case if performance is measured only in terms of returns. In Table 10.1, the return on the 20-year bond is 2.0 percent higher than on the five-year bond during the period from 1981 to 2009. During this period, the capital gain component of the bond return contributed 3.0 percent to the total return. But the standard deviation of the 20-year

TABLE 10.1   Treasury Bonds by Maturity

Maturity	Coupon Yield	Capital Gain	Total Return	Standard Deviation	Sharpe Ratio
1951–2009					
Long-term	6.3%	0.0%	6.3%	9.5%	0.17
Medium-term	5.9%	0.3%	6.2%	5.0%	0.29
1981–2009					
Long-term	7.4%	3.0%	10.4%	11.1%	0.47
Medium-term	6.6%	1.8%	8.4%	5.3%	0.60

The Treasury returns reported are for long-term 20-year bonds, and medium-term five-year bonds.
Data Source: © Morningstar.

bond is still substantially higher than that of the five-year bond, so the Sharpe ratio for the longer-term issue is still much lower than for the medium-term issue. So even in a period of falling interest rates, the 20-year bond seems to be dominated by the five-year bond. That's true at least if investors are focusing on one-year horizon returns. For investors with long-term liabilities, however, the 20-year bond may be the most attractive alternative. Such investors might be able to match long-term liabilities with long-term assets, thereby minimizing the volatility of their net asset positions.

The Wider U.S. Bond Market

At the end of 2008, the U.S. bond market encompassed securities with a total market value of $33.5 trillion (or $33,500 billion) according to the Securities Industry and Financial Markets Association.[4] Figure 10.5 shows the breakdown of fixed income securities as of the end of 2008. U.S. Treasury securities represent only 17.7 percent of the U.S. market. Municipal bonds (issued by local as well as state governments) represent 8.0 percent of the market, while corporate debt represents another 18.8 percent. Mortgage-related securities, 26.6 percent of the market, include those issued by the government agencies Fannie Mae and Freddie Mac as well as collateralized mortgage obligations (CMOs). Federal agency securities, 9.7 percent of the market, are nonmortgage obligations of agencies like the Federal Farm Loan Mortgage Corporation and the Student Loan Marketing Association. Money market securities and asset-backed bonds round out the rest.

The relative importance of Treasury bonds has declined over time because other bond markets have grown more rapidly. Part of this growth is due to financial innovation that has led to the securitization of assets that were previously held in bank balance sheets such as mortgages and commercial loans. Figure 10.6 shows how

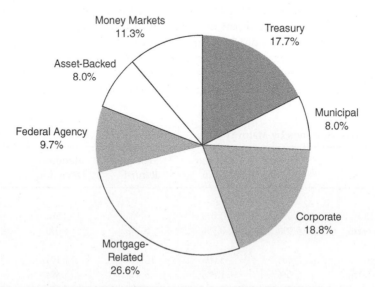

FIGURE 10.5   U.S. Bond Market in 2008

Source: Securities Industry and Financial Markets Association, 2009.

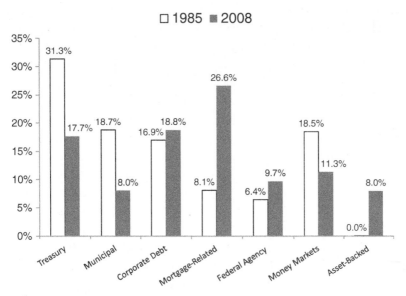

FIGURE 10.6   U.S. Bond Market in 1985 and 2008
Source: Securities Industry and Financial Markets Association, 2009.

the bond market since 1985 has shifted away from Treasury securities toward other types of bonds that were relatively unimportant then. Thus Treasuries have shrunk from 31.3 percent of the U.S. bond market to only 17.7 percent as of 2008. Mortgage-related bonds have grown from 8.1 percent to 26.6 percent of the total. Asset-backed bonds, which didn't exist in 1985, are now 8.0 percent of the total.

Because most of the bonds shown in Figure 10.5 have higher default risk than U.S. Treasury bonds, their bond yields are correspondingly higher (adjusted for maturity). Consider the default premiums for investment grade corporate bonds. Both Standard & Poor's and Moody's rate the default risk on corporate bonds. According to the classification by Moody's, investment grade bonds are rated in four categories ranging from AAA to BAA. Over the period from 1980 to 2005, the 10-year Treasury bond had an average yield of 7.7 percent.[5] Over the same period, the yield on the highest rated of these corporate bonds, those with an AAA rating, averaged 8.8 percent for a premium of 1.1 percent over Treasuries.[6] The yields on the lowest-rated investment grade bonds, those with a BAA rating, had an average yield of 9.9 percent, so the premium over Treasuries was 2.2 percent and the premium over the highest grade corporate bonds was 1.1 percent. These premiums give some indication of the importance of default risk in the pricing of non-Treasury bonds.

Default risk is of utmost importance in pricing so-called high-yield bonds. Until the 1980s, the high-yield market consisted primarily of fallen angels, bonds that were originally issued as investment grade, but that had fallen below investment grade because of poor financial performance. It was only in the 1980s that investment banks such as Drexel Burnham saw the potential for issuing noninvestment grade (or junk) bonds to provide financing for firms with weaker credit standing. Since then, the high-yield market has become an important part of the overall corporate

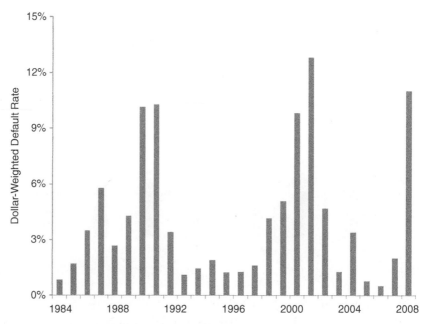

FIGURE 10.7   High-Yield Default Rates, 1984–2009

Data Source: JP Morgan.

bond market in the United States. According to Altman and Karlin (2008), the high-yield market at the end of 2007 totaled $1,090 billion in outstanding issues. SIFMA reports that total corporate debt outstanding in 2007 was $6,281 billion, so high yield represents about 17 percent of total corporate debt.

Figure 10.7 displays the default rates for high-yield bonds. The average default rate between 1984 and 2009 was 4.1 percent. This default rate varies widely over time, however, since recessions force many firms into financial distress. The effects of the Gulf War recession of 1990 to 1991 and the 2001 recession are evident in the high default rates shown on the graph. Notice that the recession that began in December 2007 saw only a modest rise in default rates in 2008 but then defaults rose to more than 10 percent in 2009.

The spreads of high-yield bonds over Treasury bonds also vary over time, through booms and busts. Figure 10.8 shows these spreads from 1985 through early 2009. The effects of the three recessions during this period are evident in the figure. During the Gulf War recession of 1991 to 1992 and during the 2001 recession, the spread rose more than 10 percent. In the recession beginning in December 2007, the spread reached almost 20 percent in late 2008 despite seeing relatively few defaults in that year. Such a high spread probably reflects as much the illiquidity of the high-yield market during the financial crisis as it does the expectation of future defaults.

High-yield spreads reflect the *ex ante* default risk of a bond, but do not indicate the *ex post* returns that the investor receives from investing in that bond. These ex post returns are measured using the Barclays Capital High-yield index which begins in July 1983. The returns on some of the other types of bonds shown in Figure 10.5 can be measured using indexes extending back into the 1980s or earlier. Corporate bond returns are one of the series provided in the SBBI Yearbooks with

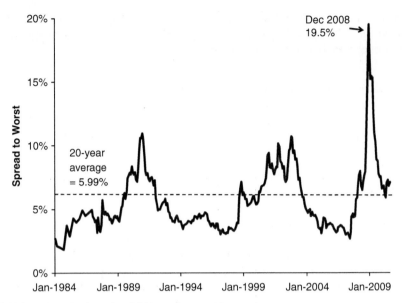

FIGURE 10.8   Spread of High-Yield Bonds over Treasuries
Data Source: JP Morgan.

returns beginning in 1926 like the rest of the Morningstar series. Mortgage-backed bonds have a return series from Merrill Lynch beginning in 1976. Finally, there is a widely used investment-grade bond index called the Barclays Capital Aggregate Index (formerly the Lehman Aggregate Index).[7] This series also begins in 1976.

Returns on U.S. Bonds

The natural question to ask is: How well have non-Treasury bonds performed over time? Table 10.2 provides an analysis. Since bond returns begin at different times,

TABLE 10.2   Comparisons between Medium-Term U.S. Treasuries and Other Bonds

Period	Average Return	Standard Deviation	Sharpe Ratio
1951–2009			
Medium-Term Treasury	6.2%	5.1%	0.29
Corporate Bond	6.5%	8.6%	0.21
July 1983–December 2009			
Medium-Term Treasury	7.7%	5.0%	0.62
High-Yield Bond	9.3%	8.8%	0.53
1976–2009			
Medium-Term Treasury	8.0%	5.8%	0.42
Mortgage-Backed Bond	8.6%	7.0%	0.44
Barclays Aggregate Bond	8.2%	5.7%	0.47

Data Sources: © Morningstar for Medium-Term Treasuries and Corporate Bonds. Barclays Capital for the High-Yield and Aggregate Indexes and Merrill Lynch for the Mortgage-Backed Bond Index.

each series is compared with the five-year medium term Treasury bond *over a common period*. In Table 10.2, there are three periods studied, each corresponding to the period over which a bond series is available:

1951–2009: Corporate Bond Index from Morningstar
1983–2009: Barclays Capital High Yield Bond Index
1976–2009: Barclays Capital Aggregate Bond Index and Merrill Lynch Mortgage-
         Backed Bond Index

As shown in Table 10.2, non-Treasury bonds generally provide higher returns than Treasury bonds, at least over the long periods studied in the table. But risks (as measured by standard deviations) are also higher for these bonds. The last column of the table reports the Sharpe ratio for each series. The Sharpe ratios for corporate bonds and high-yield bonds are lower than that of the medium-term Treasury bond, while the Sharpe ratio for mortgage-backed bonds is a little higher.[8]

Bonds should also be evaluated in a portfolio setting just like any other asset. Table 10.3 reports the correlations between the major bond indexes and the medium-term Treasury bond. The last column of the table also reports the correlations with the S&P 500. Generally speaking, all of the U.S. bonds are highly correlated with Treasuries except for the high-yield series. The correlations are 0.70 or more for long-term Treasuries, (high-grade) corporate bonds, and mortgage-backed bonds. High-yield bonds have a near zero correlation of −0.02 with MT Treasuries because the high-yield market is so cyclically sensitive.

Bonds are often part of a larger portfolio with substantial allocations to stocks. So it's interesting to consider the correlations between the bond indexes and the S&P 500. It's clear from Table 10.3 that all of the bonds have relatively low correlation with stocks except for the high-yield series. The correlation between high-yield bonds and the S&P 500 is 0.56, so the diversification benefits of bonds in a portfolio heavily weighted toward stocks are certainly reduced when high-yield bonds are involved.

How much difference does it make if an investor diversifies a bond portfolio? This is an interesting question that an investment advisor often faces when the choice

TABLE 10.3   Correlations, 1985–2009

Bond Type	Correlation with Medium-Term Treasury Bond	Correlation with S&P 500
Medium-Term Treasuries	1.00	0.02
Long-Term Treasuries	0.84	0.11
Corporate Bonds	0.70	0.23
Mortgage-Backed	0.82	0.16
High-Yield	−0.02	0.56
Barclays Aggregate	0.88	0.21
Foreign Bonds	0.42	0.01

The bond indexes used are the Medium-Term and Long-Term Treasury Bond and Corporate Bond indexes from © Morningstar, the High-Yield and Aggregate Bond indexes from Barclays Capital, the Mortgage-Backed Bond index from Merrill Lynch, and the Citigroup nondollar World Bond Index.

is between investing in a bond fund that is well diversified and investing in a narrow set of bonds directly. Consider the following experiment: An investor chooses between investment in the medium-term Treasury bond or the diversified Barclays Capital Aggregate Bond Index, the index described earlier that has only 23.9 percent in U.S. Treasuries. The Barclays Aggregate gives the investor exposure to corporate bonds (17.2 percent) as well as mortgage-backed bonds (44.8 percent) in addition to other investment-grade bonds. The comparison is shown in Table 10.2. Over the period from 1976 to 2009, the Barclays Aggregate has a return 0.2 percent higher than that of the medium-term U.S. Treasury bond, but the standard deviation is 0.1 percent lower. So the Sharpe ratio is higher. Alpha* allows us to compare the two bond investments after adjusting the Barclays Aggregate for the slightly higher level of risk associated with the Treasury bond. The investor gains an extra 0.3 percent excess return by investing in the Barclays Aggregate.[9] So the gains from diversification are evident even though most of these bonds are highly correlated.

Bond Markets outside the United States

The world's bond markets have grown enormously in the last few decades. According to the Bank for International Settlements, the total value of all bonds outstanding as of September 2008 was $82.5 trillion.[10] This compares with a market capitalization of $54.2 trillion for the world's stock markets (at the end of 2007). The relative size of the world bond markets is shown in Figure 10.9. The U.S. bond market represents 31.3 percent of this total capitalization. But there are also major bond markets in the Euro area, Japan, and other industrial countries. All together, these national bond markets represent another 33.0 percent of the world market. The bond markets of the developing (or emerging market) countries add another 8.1 percent to the world's total. The remaining 27.6 percent are international bonds.

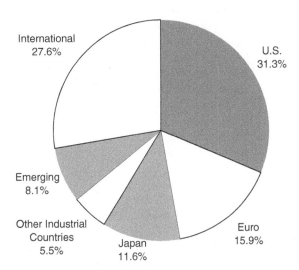

FIGURE 10.9 World Bond Markets, 2008 (Total Size of the World Bond Market in 2008 = $82.5 trillion)

Source: Bank for International Settlements, 2009.

In addition to traditional national bond markets, there are parallel bond markets called international bond markets where most investors are offshore investors, but where borrowers can be from any country including the United States. Take the example of a U.S. dollar international bond issued in London by an American company with American and foreign underwriters and investors who are predominantly foreign. Twenty years ago, this bond would have been described as a Eurobond because it was underwritten in Europe, but today it is less confusing to call this dollar bond an international bond.[11] Since now there are no significant capital controls separating the U.S. bond market from the international bond market, an international bond issued by an American company will be almost identical in yield and price to a bond issued by the same company in the United States (as long as both bonds are denominated in dollars). The major difference between the two bonds is in ownership, since there are restrictions on sales of international bonds to U.S. residents. International bonds cannot be offered to Americans when they are first issued because these bonds have not been registered with the U.S. Securities and Exchange Commission. Some institutional investors buy these issues in the secondary market, but international bonds are primarily sold to foreign not American investors.[12]

This book is focused on investing, not borrowing, so the analysis to follow will ignore international bonds entirely. Instead, we will study investments in the national bond markets of foreign industrial countries. These are the traditional national bond markets of countries like the United Kingdom and Japan. Many of these bonds are government bonds issued by the national governments of the countries involved, but there are also corporate bonds much like we find in the U.S. market. Almost all such national bonds are denominated in that country's currency. In Figure 10.9, these traditional national markets represent 33 percent of world bond markets or $27.2 trillion as of 2008.

The introduction of the euro in 1999 led to consolidation of the bond markets of the 12 countries initially joining the European Union.[13] So instead of having separate bond markets (and separate trading centers) in countries like Germany and France, there was now a single market located in London with much-enhanced liquidity. As shown in Figure 10.9, the euro area bond market is 15.9 percent of the world bond market, or roughly half the size of the U.S. national market.[14] Among foreign national bond markets, the Euro bond market is particularly attractive to Americans because it is the largest and most liquid foreign national bond market.

Interest rates on foreign bonds vary widely by country. First, interest rates are directly influenced by national inflation rates as shown earlier in Figure 10.3. These inflation rates vary widely by country depending upon the monetary policies of the central banks. Second, interest rates reflect the sovereign risk of the countries issuing the securities. For most of the sample period, the bonds of the industrial countries had little default risk. The government bonds of most of these countries carried AAA or AA ratings. That was true at least until the Greek crisis in 2010 when concerns about defaults in Europe led to default premiums for several national markets.

The returns on foreign bonds depend upon the currency in which they are measured. In their own local currencies, the returns are dependent on coupon yields and capital gains, just as in the case of U.S. bonds. But when measured in dollars, the returns on foreign bonds also depend on the capital gains or losses on the foreign currency itself. Thus the return on a foreign bond received by a U.S. domestic investor consists of two elements, the return expressed in foreign currency compounded by

TABLE 10.4 Returns on Foreign and U.S. Government Bonds Measured in U.S. Dollars, 1987–2009

Bond Market	Average Return	Standard Deviation	Sharpe Ratio
France	9.3%	11.0%	0.47
Germany	8.1%	11.4%	0.35
Japan	7.1%	12.8%	0.23
Switzerland	7.2%	12.2%	0.25
United Kingdom	9.3%	11.4%	0.45
Nondollar World	8.1%	9.6%	0.41
U.S. Medium-Term	6.7%	4.8%	0.54
U.S. Long-Term	8.4%	9.9%	0.44

The foreign government bond series are all Citigroup indexes measured in dollars. The Non-Dollar World index is a 21-nation series. The U.S. government bond series are the Medium-Term (5-year) and Long-Term (20-year) indexes from Morningstar.
Data Sources: Citigroup and © Morningstar.

the capital gain on the currency. If $R_{\in}$ is the return on a Euro-denominated bond *in Euros* and if R_X is the capital gain on the Euro, then the return on this bond as viewed by a dollar-based investor is given by

$$\text{Return in } \$ = (1 + R_{\in}) * (1 + R_X) - 1$$

Returns on foreign bonds will be enhanced during periods when foreign currencies are rising against the dollar just as they benefit from rising bond prices within the Euro markets themselves.

Consider the returns on some of the major government bond markets as reported in Table 10.4. The bond indexes represented in the table are Citigroup indexes measured in dollars from 1987 through 2009. Also included in the table is a broader foreign bond index provided by Citigroup called the Non-U.S. Dollar World Government Bond Index. This index is a world-ex-U.S. government bond index representing the government bond markets of 21 industrial countries. All of the government bonds are denominated in domestic currency and each market represented has at least $20 billion in capitalization.[15] For comparison purposes, the returns on the two SBBI U.S. government bonds series, those for five-year medium-term bonds and 20-year long-term bonds, are also reported.

The first column of the table reports the average returns on each bond series, while the second column reports the standard deviations. All of the average returns for the foreign bond markets exceed those of the medium-term U.S. Treasury. The French and U.K. returns also exceed those of the long-term U.S. Treasury. But all of the standard deviations of the foreign bond indexes are much higher than those of medium-term U.S. bond and only the (nondollar) World index has a lower standard deviation than the long-term U.S. Treasury. There is no doubt that the high volatility of the foreign bond returns is primarily caused by the volatility of the exchange rates used to translate local currency returns into dollars. Exchange rates are extremely volatile. In fact, the standard deviations for the foreign exchange gains and losses range from 10.0 percent for the dollar to pound exchange rate to 11.5 percent for the dollar to Swiss franc rate.[16] These foreign bonds may be too volatile to be attractive

TABLE 10.5   Effects of Diversifying a Bond Portfolio with Foreign Bonds, 1985–2009

	Average Return	Standard Deviation	Sharpe Ratio
Barclays Aggregate	7.9%	4.3%	0.81
Portfolio with Unhedged Foreign Bonds	8.3%	4.7%	0.84
Portfolio with Hedged Foreign Bonds	7.7%	3.9%	0.86

Notes: The diversified portfolios with foreign bonds consist of 80 percent in the Barclays Aggregate and 20 percent in the Citigroup nondollar World Government Bond Index. The second row has the unhedged world index of foreign bonds and the third row has the hedged world index.
Data Sources: Barclays Capital and Citigroup.

to an American investor as an *alternative* to U.S. Treasury bonds. That is even true of the diversified World Index, which has a return of 8.1 percent and a standard deviation of 9.6 percent. The Sharpe ratio for the World Index is much lower than that of the medium-term U.S. Treasury bond.

Yet foreign bonds are unlikely to be viewed as an *alternative* to U.S. bonds by any American investor. Instead, they might be considered as a *complement* to U.S. bonds in a well-diversified bond portfolio. How well do foreign bonds fare in a portfolio context? Table 10.3 indicates that the foreign bond index, which is the Non-U.S. Dollar World Government Bond index from Citigroup, has a relatively low correlation of 0.42 with the U.S. Treasury bond and a correlation of 0.01 with the S&P 500. Both correlations are attractive enough to consider adding foreign bonds to a U.S. portfolio.

Table 10.5 reports the gains from diversifying a U.S. bond portfolio by adding a 20 percent allocation to foreign bonds. The second row of the table reports the returns on a portfolio that has 20 percent in the Citigroup nondollar World Government Bond Index and 80 percent in the Barclays Aggregate. The results are modest. The average return on the diversified U.S.-foreign bond portfolio is 0.4 percent higher than the portfolio based on the Barclays Aggregate Index alone, but the standard deviation is also higher. The net result is a Sharpe ratio of 0.84 for the diversified portfolio versus a Sharpe ratio of 0.81 for the Barclays Aggregate alone. This translates into an excess return, or alpha*, for the portfolio with foreign bonds of only 0.1 percent. A reasonable interpretation of this result is that investors have made most of their diversification gains by moving from U.S. Treasuries to the Barclays Aggregate mix of U.S. bonds. There is only a modest gain from diversifying further into foreign bonds.

If foreign currency capital gains and losses raise the standard deviation of the foreign bond return, perhaps there is a case for hedging the currency risk. We will consider the simplest type of currency hedge where the foreign currency value of the bond investment at the beginning of the period is hedged using a forward contract. In that case, the hedged return consists of the return on the bond in local currency plus the forward premium on the hedge.

How much does the hedge reduce the risk of the foreign bond investment? Figure 10.10 compares the standard deviations of the Citigroup foreign government bond indexes before and after hedging. Hedging has a dramatic effect on the risk of a foreign bond investment. In the case of French bonds, for example, the standard deviation falls from 11.1 percent to 4.5 percent. For the Citigroup nondollar World

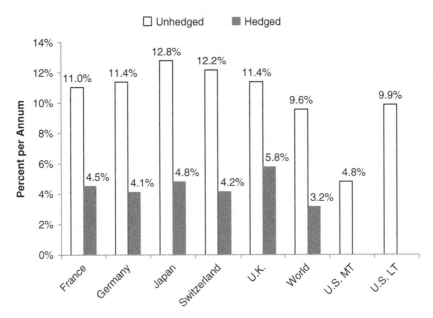

FIGURE 10.10 Standard Deviations of Government Bond Returns in Dollars, Hedged and Unhedged, 1987–2009

Data Sources: Citigroup, © Morningstar, and IMF (for foreign exchange rates).

Government Bond Index, the standard deviation is cut by two-thirds.[17] All but two of the standard deviations of the hedged foreign bond series are below that of even the U.S. medium-term bond. So, unlike in the case of foreign stocks, hedging foreign bonds greatly reduces the risk faced by an American investor. Since currencies are highly correlated with the returns on foreign bonds *expressed in dollars,* hedging the currency risk sharply reduces the risk of the foreign bond investment.

Table 10.6 reports the returns on the hedged investments in foreign bonds. For all foreign bonds studied, returns on the hedged investments are lower than those

TABLE 10.6 Hedged Returns on Foreign and U.S. Government Bonds, 1987–2009

Bond Market	Average Return	Standard Deviation	Sharpe Ratio
France	6.7%	4.5%	0.56
Germany	6.3%	4.1%	0.52
Japan	7.0%	4.8%	0.59
Switzerland	6.2%	4.2%	0.50
United Kingdom	6.2%	5.8%	0.36
Nondollar World	6.8%	3.2%	0.86
U.S. Medium-Term	6.7%	4.8%	0.54
U.S. Long-Term	8.4%	9.9%	0.44

Notes: The hedged return is obtained by selling an equivalent amount of foreign currency in the forward market at the beginning of each period. In the case of the Citigroup world index, the hedge adjusts for any cash flows expected during the period.

Data Sources: Citigroup, © Morningstar, and IMF (for foreign exchange rates).

on the unhedged investments because the dollar fell against many currencies over this time period. Hedge positions should not necessarily provide gains or losses in the long run (unless there are risk premiums on one currency or another). But over a particular sample period, a hedge may provide either gains or losses for an investor based in any particular currency. Over the 23 years ending in 2009, a dollar-based investor *selling* foreign currencies to hedge bond investments lost money on hedges involving the major currencies. The hedge for the world index lost 1.3 percent per year on average over this period.

Table 10.6 also reports the standard deviations and Sharpe ratios of the hedged investments. With standard deviations so low, the foreign bond returns generally have Sharpe ratios higher than that of the unhedged foreign bond series. In some cases, these Sharpe ratios are also higher than those of the U.S. Treasury bond indexes. Consider the world index hedged for exchange risk. By hedging, the return falls from 8.1 percent to 6.8 percent, but the standard deviation falls from 9.6 percent to 3.2 percent. The Sharpe ratio rises sharply to 0.86, far above that of the U.S. bond indexes.

Hedging the currency risk does raise the correlation between the foreign bond and U.S. bonds and stocks. The correlation with the medium-term Treasury bond rises from 0.42 to 0.61. That should not be surprising since a lot of the advantage of the foreign bond as a diversifier stems from the foreign currency component of the bond return, and hedging all but eliminates this factor from the bond investment. Consider the portfolio experiment again reported in Table 10.5 where foreign bonds are mixed with the Barclays Aggregate. If the foreign bond index is hedged, the resulting portfolio has a smaller standard deviation (3.9 percent rather than 4.3 percent for the Barclays Aggregate alone). The Sharpe ratio of the portfolio containing hedged foreign bonds is 0.86 versus 0.81 for the Barclays portfolio alone. The diversified portfolio delivers an excess return, or alpha*, of only 0.2 percent compared with the Barclays Aggregate alone. That is a very modest gain for international diversification of the bond portfolio!

What is the conclusion of all of this evidence regarding foreign bonds? The answer has to be that it is probably worthwhile to include bonds from foreign industrial countries in a diversified bond portfolio. Foreign bonds won't dramatically alter the performance of such a portfolio, but there is a marginal improvement in risk-adjusted returns. There is a strong case for hedging the foreign bonds if the investor is concerned about the *volatility* of foreign bond investments, since hedging reduces that volatility quite dramatically. The case for hedging is less compelling if foreign bonds are viewed as a component of an otherwise well-diversified portfolio.

Summary—Key Features of Bonds

Above all else, bond returns depend upon inflation. In the long run, inflation affects the yield offered on bonds. This link can be illustrated by studying the variation over time of interest rates and inflation in the United States or by studying the close link between average interest rates and average inflation rates in the industrial countries. Inflation also profoundly affects the real returns on bonds, especially in periods when inflation is rising or falling significantly as in the 1970s and 1980s. Real bond returns were unusually low in the 1970s (and even earlier) because bond yields failed to keep pace with inflation expectations. Similarly, the sharp downturn in inflation since the early 1980s has led to unusually high real bond returns.

Bond returns in the United States vary by type of bond. Over the past few decades, the bond market has evolved extensively as new classes of securities have emerged. The introduction of mortgage-backed bonds in the 1970s, high-yield debt in the 1980s, and other securitized debt in the 1980s and 1990s has greatly expanded the scope of the U.S. bond market. The returns on these new classes of bonds have fallen in line with those of the existing Treasury and corporate issues, at least when measured on a risk-adjusted basis. But their introduction has allowed investors to further diversify their portfolios. The gains from diversification are reasonably large.

Diversification into foreign bonds also makes some sense. The bonds of foreign industrial countries share many of the same characteristics as U.S. bonds, but their returns vary widely because of their (foreign) currency denomination. When these bonds are left unhedged, their standard deviations are very high (when measured in dollars for a U.S. investor). But hedging can reduce risk by almost two-thirds. And when these bonds are included in a diversified bond portfolio, even the unhedged bonds help to reduce risk, although only modestly.

Notes

1. LIBOR stands for the London Interbank Offer Rate in the dollar deposit market in London. The LIBOR market is one of the largest money markets in the world. The LIBOR rate serves as a benchmark for many interest rate contracts, including many floating rate mortgages in the United States.
2. The real return is defined as (1 + nominal return)/(1+ inflation rate) − 1.
3. The European Monetary System (EMS), introduced in 1979, committed countries to maintaining their exchange rates within bands relative to fixed rates. But the EMS did not prevent countries from occasionally realigning their fixed rates by devaluing or revaluing their exchange rates with other partner countries, so inflation varied widely across the EMS countries. It was the Maastricht Treaty of 1991, setting Europe on a path toward monetary union in 1999, that spurred the high-inflation countries like Italy and Spain to reign in their monetary policies to qualify for the union.
4. SIFMA, Outstanding U.S. Bond Market Debt, SIFMA website table, March 2009.
5. The yields are reported in the IMF, International Financial Statistics (CD dataset), May 2007.
6. The annual data for corporate yields are reported by www.bondmarkets.com. It would be misleading to attribute all of this gap of corporate yields over Treasury yields to default risk since U.S. Treasuries have a state income tax advantage not afforded to corporate bonds. According to the U.S. Constitution, U.S. Treasuries are exempt from state and local taxes. If the marginal investor in U.S. Treasuries is a taxable U.S. resident, then the interest yield on Treasuries reflects this tax advantage.
7. As of the end of October 2008, this index had 23.9 percent in Treasuries, 13.5 percent in government-related bonds, 17.2 percent in corporate bonds, 44.8 percent in mortgage-backed bonds, and less than 1 percent in ABS.81.4 percent of this index represented AAA-rated bonds. *Source:* www.barcap.com/indices.
8. Recall that the Treasury bond is free of state and local taxes, so the relative returns may reflect tax factors as well as default risk.
9. Alpha* = (0.47–0.42) ∗ 0.057 = 0.3%.

10. This figure is obtained by aggregating the national bond markets and international bond markets as reported on the Bank for International Settlements website (www.bis.org/statistics/secstats.htm).
11. The Eurobond or international bond market was initially developed to allow U.S. and foreign companies to raise debt financing in foreign markets to fund their foreign operations. Since many countries had capital controls inhibiting the flow of financing from their domestic markets, the international bond market offered a way to finance the multinational operations of these companies. Capital controls have largely been abolished in the industrial countries, so this market is now closely integrated with the national bond market in the same currency.
12. See Solnik and McLeavy (2004).
13. The countries adopting the Euro in 1999 included France, Germany, Belgium, Luxembourg, the Netherlands, Italy, Spain, Portugal, Ireland, Austria, and Finland. Greece joined in 2002. The 12 countries had only 11 bond markets because Belgium and Luxembourg shared a common currency even before the Union.
14. Both markets would be larger if international bonds issued in dollars and Euros, respectively, were included in the totals.
15. Most of the bonds have AAA or AA credit quality. The 21 countries represented in the index are Australia, Austria, Belgium, Canada, Denmark, Finland, France, Germany, Greece, Ireland, Italy, Japan, the Netherlands, Norway, Poland, Portugal, Singapore, Spain, Sweden, Switzerland, and the United Kingdom.
16. These standard deviations are measured for the capital gain/loss factor in the equation in the text, RX.
17. Citigroup provides a hedged version of its 21-nation world (non-U.S.) government bond index. According to Citigroup (2006), the hedge is designed to offset not only the value of the investment at period $t - 1$ but also any expected cash flows between $t - 1$ and t.

References

Altman, Edward I., and Brenda Karlin. 2008. "Defaults and Returns in the High-Yield Bond and Distressed Debt Market: The Year 2007 in Review and Outlook." New York University Salomon Center, Leonard N. Stern School of Business.
Solnik, Bruno, and Dennis McLeavey. 2004. *International Investments*. Boston: Pearson Addison Wesley. 5th edition.

Part II Bonds: Investment Features and Risks

In its simplest form, a bond is a financial obligation of an entity that promises to pay a specified sum of money at specified future dates. The entity that promises to make the payment is called the issuer of the security or the borrower. Some examples of issuers are the U.S. government or a foreign government, a state or local government entity, a domestic or foreign corporation, and a supranational government such as the World Bank. The investor who purchases a bond is said to be the lender or creditor. The promised payments that the issuer agrees to make at the specified dates consist of two components: interest payments and repayment of the amount borrowed.

The purpose of this chapter is to explain the investment features of bonds, the various measures of yield quoted for bonds, and the risks that investors face when investing in bonds.

Sectors of the Bond Market

There are many ways to classify the bond market. One way is in terms of the taxability of the interest at the federal income tax level. In the United States, most securities issued by state and local governments and by entities that they establish, referred to as municipal bonds or municipal securities, are exempt from federal income taxation. While there are reasons why some issuers of municipal bonds will issue taxable bonds, the municipal bond market is generally viewed as the market for tax-exempt securities. As such, the primary attraction to investors is this tax feature.

The largest part of the bond market is the taxable market. There are various ways to describe this sector. Investment banking firms that have developed bond market indexes use various classifications. The most popular indexes are those published by Lehman Brothers, and within the group of indexes it publishes, the one followed most closely by investors in the United States is the U.S. Aggregate Index. That index contains the six sectors shown in Table 10.7 along with the percentage of each sector in terms of market value as of July 20, 2007. We'll review each of the sectors later in this chapter.

Another way of classifying bond markets is in terms of the *global bond market*. One starts by partitioning a given country's bond market into a national bond market and an international bond market. In turn, a country's national bond market can be divided into a domestic bond market and a foreign bond market with the distinction being the domicile of the issuer. The *domestic bond market* is the market where bond issues of entities domiciled within that country are issued and then traded; the *foreign bond market* is the market where bond issues of nondomiciled entities of that country are issued and then subsequently traded within the country. Each country has a nickname for foreign bonds. For example, in the United States, "Yankee bonds" are bonds issued by non-U.S. entities and then traded in the U.S. market. In the United Kingdom, foreign bonds are called "bulldog bonds." The *international bond market*, also referred to as the *offshore bond market*, is the market where bonds are issued and then traded outside of the country and not regulated by the country.

TABLE 10.7 Sectors of the Lehman Brothers U.S. Aggregate Index

Sector	Percent of Market Value (as of July 20, 2007)
Treasury	23.49%
Agency	10.60
Mortgage Pass-Through	37.90
Commercial MBS	4.89
Asset-Backed Securities	1.12
Credit	22.02

Source: Data obtained from Lehman Brothers, *Global Relative Value,* Fixed Income Research, July 23, 2007.

An important sector of the international bond market is the market for bonds that are underwritten by an international syndicate, issued simultaneously to investors in a number of countries, and issued outside of the jurisdiction of any single country. This market is popularly referred to as the *Eurobond market* and the bonds are called *Eurobonds*. Unfortunately, the name is misleading. The currency in which Eurobonds are denominated can be any currency, not just euros. In fact, Eurobonds are classified according to the denomination of the currency (e.g., Eurodollar bonds and Euroyen bonds). Nor are Eurobonds traded in just Europe. *Global bonds* from the perspective of a country are bonds that are not only traded in that country's foreign bond market but also in the Eurobond market.

While the U.S. bond market is the largest bond market in the world, there are other bond markets in which U.S. investors participate.

Features of Bonds

The promises of the issuer and the rights of the bondholders are set forth in great detail in the indenture. Bondholders would have great difficulty in determining from time to time whether the issuer was keeping all the promises made in the indenture. This problem is resolved for the most part by bringing in a trustee as a third party to the contract. The indenture is made out to the trustee as a representative of the interests of the bondholders; that is, a trustee acts in a fiduciary capacity for bondholders. A trustee is a bond or trust company with a trust department whose officers are experts in performing the functions of a trustee.

MATURITY   Unlike common stock, which has a perpetual life, bonds have a date on which they mature. The number of years over which the issuer has promised to meet the conditions of the obligation is referred to as the *term to maturity*. The *maturity* of a bond refers to the date that the debt will cease to exist, at which time the issuer will redeem the bond by paying the amount borrowed. The maturity date of a bond is always identified when describing a bond. For example, a description of a bond might state "due 12/15/2025."

The practice in the bond market is to refer to the "term to maturity" of a bond as simply its "maturity" or "term." Despite sounding like a fixed date in which the bond matures, there are provisions that may be included in the indenture that grants either the issuer or bondholder the right to alter a bond's term to maturity. These provisions, which will be described later in this chapter, include call provisions, put provisions, conversion provisions, and accelerated sinking fund provisions.

The maturity of a debt instrument is used for classifying two sectors of the market. Debt instruments with a maturity of one year or less are referred to as *money market instruments* and trade in the *money market*. What we typically refer to as the "bond market" is debt instruments with a maturity greater than one year. The bond market is then categorized further based on the debt instrument's term to maturity: short-term, intermediate-term, and long-term. The classification is somewhat arbitrary and varies among market participants. A common classification is that short-term bonds have a maturity of from 1 to 5 years, intermediate-term bonds have a maturity from 5 to 12 years, and long-term bonds have a maturity that exceeds 12 years.

Typically, the maturity of a bond does not exceed 30 years. There are, of course, exceptions. For example, Walt Disney Company issued 100-year bonds in July 1993 and the Tennessee Valley Authority issued 50-year bonds in December 1993.

The term to maturity of a bond is important for two reasons in addition to indicating the time period over which the bondholder can expect to receive interest payments and the number of years before the principal will be paid in full. The first reason is that the yield on a bond depends on it. At any given point in time, the relationship between the yield and maturity of a bond (called the yield curve) indicates how bondholders are compensated for investing in bonds with different maturities. The second reason is that the price of a bond will fluctuate over its life as interest rates in the market change. The degree of price volatility of a bond is dependent on its maturity. More specifically, all other factors constant, the longer the maturity of a bond, the greater the price volatility resulting from a change in interest rates.

PAR VALUE   The *par value* of a bond is the amount that the issuer agrees to repay the bondholder by the maturity date. This amount is also referred to as the *principal, face value, redemption value,* or *maturity value.*

Because bonds can have a different par value, the practice is to quote the price of a bond as a percentage of its par value. A value of 100 means 100 percent of par value. So, for example, if a bond has a par value of $1,000 and is selling for $850, this bond would be said to be selling at 85. If a bond with a par value of $100,000 is selling for $106,000, the bond is said to be selling for 106.

COUPON RATE   The annual interest rate that the issuer agrees to pay each year is called the *coupon rate.* The annual amount of the interest payment made to bondholders during the term of the bond is called the *coupon* and is determined by multiplying the coupon rate by the par value of the bond. For example, a bond with a 6 percent coupon rate and a par value of $1,000 will pay annual interest of $60.

When describing a bond issue, the coupon rate is indicated along with the maturity date. For example, the expression "5.5s of 2/15/2024" means a bond with a 5.5 percent coupon rate maturing on 2/15/2024.

For bonds issued in the United States, the usual practice is for the issuer to pay the coupon in two semiannual installments. Mortgage-backed securities and asset-backed securities typically pay interest monthly. For bonds issued in some markets outside the United States, coupon payments are made only once per year.

In addition to indicating the coupon payments that the investor should expect to receive over the term of the bond, the coupon rate also affects the bond's price sensitivity to changes in market interest rates. All other factors constant, the higher the coupon rate, the less the price will change in response to a change in market interest rates.

There are securities that have a coupon rate that increases over time according to a specified schedule. These securities are called *step-up notes* because the coupon rate "steps up" over time. For example, a five-year step-up note might have a coupon rate that is 5 percent for the first two years and 6 percent for the last three years. Or, the step-up note could call for a 5 percent coupon rate for the first two years, 5.5 percent for the third and fourth years, and 6 percent for the fifth year. When there is only one change (or step up), as in our first example, the issue is referred to as a single step-up note. When there is more than one increase, as in our second example, the issue is referred to as a multiple step-up note.

Not all bonds make periodic coupon payments. *Zero-coupon bonds,* as the name indicates, do not make periodic coupon payments. Instead, the holder of a zero-coupon bond realizes interest at the maturity date. The aggregate interest earned is the difference between the maturity value and the purchase price. For example, if an investor purchases a zero-coupon bond for 63, the aggregate interest at the maturity date is 37, the difference between the par value (100) and the price paid (63). The reason why certain investors like zero-coupon bonds is that they eliminated one of the risks that we will discuss later, reinvestment risk. The disadvantage of a zero-coupon bond is that the accrued interest earned each year is taxed despite the fact that no actual cash payment is made.

There are issues whose coupon payment is deferred for a specified number of years. That is, there is no coupon payment for the deferred period and then a lump sum payment at some specified date and coupon payments until maturity. These securities are referred to as *deferred interest securities.*

A coupon-bearing security need not have a fixed interest rate over the term of the bond. These are bonds that have an interest rate that is as variable. These bonds are referred to as *floating-rate securities.* In fact, another way to classify bond markets is the *fixed-rate bond market* and the *floating-rate bond market.* Floating-rate securities appeal to institutional investors such as depository institutions (banks, savings and loan associations, and credit unions) because it provides a better match against their funding costs, which are typically floating-rate debt. Typically, the interest rate is adjusted on specific dates, referred to as the *coupon reset date.* There is typically a formula for the new coupon rate that has the following generic formula:

Reference rate + Quoted margin

The quoted margin is the additional amount that the issuer agrees to pay above the reference rate. The most common reference rate is the London Interbank Offered Rate (LIBOR). LIBOR is the interest rate at which major international banks offer each other on Eurodollar certificates of deposit with given maturities. The maturities range from overnight to five years. Suppose that the reference rate is one-month LIBOR and the index spread is 80 basis points. (A basis point is equal to 0.0001 or 0.01 percent. Thus, 100 basis points are equal to 1 percent.) Then the coupon reset formula is:

One-month LIBOR + 80 basis points

So, if one-month LIBOR on the coupon reset date is 4.6 percent, the coupon rate is reset for that period at 5.4 percent (4.6 percent plus 80 basis points).

The quoted margin need not be a positive value. It could be subtracted from the reference rate. For example, the reference rate could be the yield on a five-year Treasury security and the coupon rate could reset every six months based on the following coupon reset formula:

Five-year Treasury yield − 50 basis points

While the reference rate for most floating-rate securities is an interest rate or an interest rate index, there are some issues where this is not the case. Instead, the reference rate can be some financial index such as the return on the Standard &

Poor's 500 index or a nonfinancial index such as the price of a commodity or the consumer price index.

Typically, the coupon reset formula on floating-rate securities is such that the coupon rate increases when the reference rate increases, and decreases when the reference rate decreases. There are issues whose coupon rate moves in the opposite direction from the change in the reference rate. Such issues are called *inverse floaters* or *reverse floaters*. A general coupon reset formula for an inverse floater is:

$$K - L \times (\text{Reference rate})$$

For example, suppose that for a particular inverse floater K is 10 percent and L is 1. Then the coupon reset formula would be:

$$10\% - \text{Reference rate}$$

Suppose that the reference rate is one-month LIBOR, then the coupon reset formula would be:

$$10\% - \text{One-month LIBOR}$$

If in some month, one-month LIBOR at the coupon reset date is 5 percent, the coupon rate for the period is 5 percent. If in the next month, one-month LIBOR declines to 4.5 percent, the coupon rate increases to 5.5 percent.

A floating-rate security may have a restriction on the maximum coupon rate that will be paid at a reset date. The maximum coupon rate is called a *cap*. Because a cap restricts the coupon rate from increasing, a cap is an unattractive feature for the investor. In the case of an inverse floater, one can see from the general formula that the maximum interest rate would be K.

This occurs when the reference rate is zero. In contrast, there could be a *floor*, which is the minimum coupon rate specified and this is an attractive feature for the investor.

Not all floating-rate notes have the generic formula given above. Some have a coupon rate that depends on the range for a reference rate. This type of floating-rate security, called a *range note,* has a coupon rate equal to the reference rate as long as the reference rate is within a certain range at the reset date. If the reference rate is outside of the range, the coupon rate is zero for that period. For example, a three-year range note might specify that the reference rate is one-year LIBOR and that the coupon rate resets every year. The coupon rate for the year will be one-year LIBOR as long as one-year LIBOR at the coupon reset date falls within the range as specified below:

	Year 1	Year 2	Year 3
Lower limit of range	4.5%	5.25%	6.00%
Upper limit of range	5.5%	6.75%	7.50%

If one-year LIBOR is outside of the range, the coupon rate is zero. For example, if in year 1, one-year LIBOR is 5 percent at the coupon reset date, the coupon rate for the year is 5 percent. However, if one-year LIBOR is 6 percent, the coupon rate for the year is zero because one-year LIBOR is greater than the upper limit for year 1 of 5.5 percent.

ACCRUED INTEREST   In the United States, coupon interest is typically paid semiannual for government bonds and corporate, agency, and municipal bonds. In some countries, interest is paid annually. For mortgage-backed and asset-backed securities, interest is usually paid monthly. The coupon interest payment is made to the bondholder of record. Thus, if an investor sells a bond between coupon payments and the buyer holds it until the next coupon payment, then the entire coupon interest earned for the period will be paid to the buyer of the bond since the buyer will be the holder of record. The seller of the bond gives up the interest from the time of the last coupon payment to the time until the bond is sold. The amount of interest over this period that will be received by the buyer even though it was earned by the seller is called *accrued interest.*

In the United States and in many countries, the bond buyer must compensate the bond seller for the accrued interest. The amount that the buyer pays the seller is the agreed-upon price for the bond plus accrued interest. This amount is called the *full price.* The agreed-upon bond price without accrued interest is called the *clean price.*

A bond in which the buyer must pay the seller accrued interest is said to be trading *cum-coupon.* If the buyer forgoes the next coupon payment, the bond is said to be trading *ex-coupon.* In the United States, bonds are always traded cum-coupon. There are bond markets outside the United States where bonds are traded ex-coupon for a certain period before the coupon payment date.

There are exceptions to the rule that the bond buyer must pay the bond seller accrued interest. The most important exception is when the issuer has not fulfilled its promise to make the periodic payments. In this case, the issuer is said to be in default. In such instances, the bond's price is sold without accrued interest and is said to be *traded flat.*

When calculating accrued interest, three pieces of information are needed: (1) the number of days in the accrued interest period, (2) the number of days in the coupon period, and (3) the dollar amount of the coupon payment. The number of days in the accrued interest period represents the number of days over which the investor has earned interest. Given these values, the accrued interest (AI), assuming semiannual payments, is calculated as follows:

$$AI = \frac{\text{Annual coupon}}{2} \times \frac{\text{Days in AI period}}{\text{Days in coupon period}}$$

For example, suppose that (a) there are 50 days in the accrued interest period, (b) there are 183 days in a coupon period, and (c) the annual coupon per $100 of par value is $8. Then the accrued interest is:

$$AI = \frac{\$8}{2} \times \frac{50}{183} = \$1,029$$

It is not simple to determine the number of days in the accrued interest period and the number of days in the coupon period. The calculation begins with the determination of three key dates:

1. Trade date
2. Settlement date
3. Value date

The *trade date* is the date on which the transaction is executed. The *settlement date* is the date a transaction is completed. The settlement date varies by the type of bond. Unlike the settlement date, the *value date* is not constrained to fall on a business day.

Interest accrues on a bond from and including the date of the previous coupon up to but excluding the value date. (This is the definition used by the International Securities Market Association [ISMA].) However, this may differ slightly in some non-U.S. markets. For example, in some countries interest accrues up to and including the value date. For a newly issued security, there is no previous coupon payment. Instead, the interest accrues from a date called the dated date.

Day Count Conventions The number of days in the accrued interest period and the number of days in the coupon period may not be simply the actual number of calendar days between two dates. The reason is that there is a market convention for each type of security that specifies how to determine the number of days between two dates. These conventions are called *day count conventions.*

In calculating the number of days between two dates, the actual number of days is not always the same as the number of days that should be used in the accrued interest formula. The number of days used depends on the day count convention for the particular security. Specifically, there are different day count conventions for Treasury securities than for government agency securities, municipal bonds, and corporate bonds.

For coupon-bearing Treasury securities, the day count convention used is to determine the actual number of days between two dates. This is referred to as the "actual/actual day count convention." For example, consider a coupon-bearing Treasury security whose previous coupon payment was March 1. The next coupon payment would be on September 1. Suppose this Treasury security is purchased with a value date of July 17. The actual number of days between July 17 (the value date) and September 1 (the date of the next coupon payment is 46 days) is shown below:

July 17 to July 31	14 days
August	31 days
September 1	1 day
	46 days

The number of days in the coupon period is the actual number of days between March 1 and September 1, which is 184 days. The number of days between the last coupon payment (March 1) to July 17 is therefore 138 days (184 days – 46 days).

For coupon-bearing agency, municipal, and corporate bonds, a different day-count convention is used. It is assumed that every month has 30 days, that any six-month period has 180 days, and that there are 360 days in a year. This day-count convention is referred to as the "30/360 day count convention." For example, consider a security purchased with a value date of July 17, the previous coupon payment on March 1, and the next coupon payment on September 1. If the security is an agency, municipal, or corporate bond rather than a Treasury security, the number of days until the next coupon payment is 44 days as shown below:

July 17 to July 31	13 days
August	30 days
September 1	1 day
	44 days

The number of days from March 1 to July 17 is 136, which is the number of days in the accrued interest period.

PROVISIONS FOR PAYING OFF BONDS The issuer of a bond agrees to repay the principal by the stated maturity date. The issuer can agree to repay the entire amount borrowed in one lump sum payment at the maturity date. That is, the issuer is not required to make any principal repayments prior to the maturity date. Such bonds are said to have a *bullet maturity.*

There are bond issues that consist of a series of blocks of securities maturing in sequence. The blocks of securities are said to be *serial bonds.* The coupon rate for each block can be different. One type of corporate bond in which there are serial bonds is an equipment trust certificate. Municipal bonds are often issued as serial bonds.

Bonds backed by pools of loans (mortgage-backed securities and asset-backed securities) often have a schedule of principal repayments. Such bonds are said to be *amortizing securities.* For many loans, the payments are structured so that when the last loan payment is made, the entire amount owed is fully paid off. Another example of an amortizing feature is a bond that has a *sinking fund provision.* This provision for repayment of a bond may be designed to liquidate all of an issue by the maturity date, or it may be arranged to repay only a part of the total by the maturity date.

A bond issue may have a call provision granting the issuer an option to retire all or part of the issue prior to the stated maturity date. Some issues specify that the issuer must retire a predetermined amount of the issue periodically. Various types of call provisions are discussed below.

Call and Refunding Provisions An issuer generally wants the right to retire a bond issue prior to the stated maturity date because it recognizes that at some time in the future the general level of interest rates may fall sufficiently below the issue's coupon rate so that redeeming the issue and replacing it with another issue with a lower coupon rate would be economically beneficial. This right is a disadvantage to the bondholder since proceeds received must be reinvested at a lower interest rate. As a result, an issuer who wants to include this right as part of a bond offering must compensate the bondholder when the issue is sold by offering a higher coupon rate, or equivalently, accepting a lower price than if the right is not included.

The right of the issuer to retire the issue prior to the stated maturity date is referred to as a call option. If an issuer exercises this right, the issuer is said to "call the bond." The price that the issuer must pay to retire the issue is referred to as the call price. There may not be a call price but a call schedule, which sets forth a call price based on when the issuer can exercise the call option.

When a bond is issued, typically the issuer may not call the bond for a number of years. That is, the issue is said to have a *deferred call*. The date at which the bond may first be called is referred to as the *first call date*. However, not all issues have a deferred call. If a bond issue does not have any protection against early call, then it is said to be a currently callable issue. But most new bond issues, even if currently callable, usually have some restrictions against certain types of early redemption. The most common restriction is that of prohibiting the refunding of the bonds for a certain number of years. *Refunding* a bond issue means redeeming bonds with funds obtained through the sale of a new bond issue.

Call protection is much more absolute than refunding protection. While there may be certain exceptions to absolute or complete call protection in some cases, it still provides greater assurance against premature and unwanted redemption than does refunding protection. Refunding prohibition merely prevents redemption only from certain sources of funds, namely the proceeds of other debt issues sold at a lower cost of money. The bondholder is protected only if interest rates decline, and the borrower can obtain lower-cost money to pay off the debt.

Bonds can be called in whole (the entire issue) or in part (only a portion). When less than the entire issue is called, the specific bonds to be called are selected randomly or on a pro rata basis.

Generally, the call schedule is such that the call price at the first call date is a premium over the par value and scaled down to the par value over time. The date at which the issue is first callable at par value is referred to as the *first par call date*. However, not all issues have a call schedule in which the call price starts out as a premium over par. There are issues where the call price at the first call date and subsequent call dates is par value. In such cases, the first call date is the same as the first par call date.

For zero-coupon bonds, there are three types of call schedules that can be used. The first is a call schedule for which the call price is below par value at the first call date and scales up to par value over time. The second type is one in which the call price at the first call date is above par and scales down to par. The third type is a schedule in which the call price is par value at the first call date and any subsequent call date.

The call prices in a call schedule are referred to as the regular or general redemption prices. There are also special redemption prices for debt redeemed through the sinking fund and through other provisions, and the proceeds from the confiscation of property through the right of eminent domain. The special redemption price is usually par value, but in the case of some utility issues it initially may be the public offering price, which is amortized down to par value (if a premium) over the life of the bonds.

Prepayments   For amortizing securities backed by loans and with a schedule of principal repayments, individual borrowers typically have the option to pay off all or part of their loan prior to the scheduled date. Any principal repayment prior to the scheduled date is called a *prepayment*. The right of borrowers to prepay is called the *prepayment option*.

Basically, the prepayment option is the same as a call option. However, unlike a call option, there is not a call price that depends on when the borrower pays off the issue. Typically, the price at which a loan is prepaid is at par value.

Sinking Fund Provision A *sinking fund provision* included in a bond indenture requires the issuer to retire a specified portion of an issue each year. Usually, the periodic payments required for sinking fund purposes will be the same for each period. A few indentures might permit variable periodic payments, where payments change according to certain prescribed conditions set forth in the indenture. The alleged purpose of the sinking fund provision is to reduce credit risk. This kind of provision for repayment of debt may be designed to liquidate all of a bond issue by the maturity date, or it may be arranged to pay only a part of the total by the end of the term. If only a part is paid, the remainder is called a *balloon maturity*. Many indentures include a provision that grants the issuer the option to retire more than the amount stipulated for sinking fund retirement. This is referred to as an *accelerated sinking fund provision.*

To satisfy the sinking fund requirement, an issuer is typically granted one of the following choices: (1) make a cash payment of the face amount of the bonds to be retired to the trustee, who then calls the bonds for redemption using a lottery, or (2) deliver to the trustee bonds purchased in the open market that have a total par value equal to the amount that must be retired. If the bonds are retired using the first method, interest payments stop at the redemption date.

Usually the sinking fund call price is the par value if the bonds were originally sold at par. When issued at a price in excess of par, the call price generally starts at the issuance price and scales down to par as the issue approaches maturity.

There is a difference between the amortizing feature for a bond with a sinking fund provision and the regularly scheduled principal repayment for a mortgage-backed and an asset-backed security. The owner of a mortgage-backed security and an asset-backed security knows that, assuming no default, there will be principal repayments. In contrast, the owner of a bond with a sinking fund provision is not assured that his or her particular holding will be called to satisfy the sinking fund requirement.

OPTIONS GRANTED TO BONDHOLDERS A provision in the indenture could grant either the bondholder and/or the issuer an option to take some action against the other party. The most common type of option embedded in a bond is a call option, which we discussed above. This option is granted to the issuer. There are two options that can be granted to the bondholder: the right to put the issue and the right to convert the issue.

An issue with a put provision grants the bondholder the right to sell the issue (that is, force the issuer to redeem the issue) at a specified price on designated dates. The specified price is called the put price. Typically, a bond is puttable at par value if it is issued at or close to par value. For a zero-coupon bond, the put price is below par. The advantage of the put provision to the bondholder is that if after the issue date market rates rise above the issue's coupon rate, the bondholder can force the issuer to redeem the bond at the put price and then reinvest the proceeds at the prevailing higher rate.

A *convertible bond* is an issue giving the bondholder the right to exchange the bond for a specified number of shares of common stock. Such a feature allows the bondholder to take advantage of favorable movements in the price of the issuer's common stock. An *exchangeable bond* allows the bondholder to exchange the issue for a specified number of shares of common stock of a corporation different from the issuer of the bond.

CURRENCY DENOMINATION   The payments that the issuer makes to the bondholder can be in any currency. For bonds issued in the United States, the issuer typically makes both coupon payments and principal repayments in U.S. dollars. However, there is nothing that forces the issuer to make payments in U.S dollars. The indenture can specify that the issuer may make payments in some other specified currency. For example, payments may be made in euros or yen.

An issue in which payments to bondholders are in U.S. dollars is called a dollar-denominated issue. A non-dollar-denominated issue is one in which payments are not denominated in U.S. dollars. There are some issues whose coupon payments are in one currency and whose principal payment is in another currency. An issue with this characteristic is called a dual-currency issue.

Some issues allow either the issuer or the bondholder the right to select the currency in which a payment will be paid. This option effectively gives the party with the right to choose the currency the opportunity to benefit from a favorable exchange rate movement.

Yield Measures

When an investor purchases a bond, he or she can expect to receive a dollar return from one or more of the following three sources:

1. The coupon interest payments made by the issuer.
2. Any capital gain (or capital loss—a negative dollar return) when the security matures, is called, or is sold.
3. Income from reinvestment of the interim cash flows.

Any yield measure that purports to measure the potential return from a bond should consider all three sources of return described above.

The most obvious source of return is the periodic coupon interest payments. For zero-coupon instruments, the return from this source is zero, although the investor is effectively receiving interest by purchasing a security below its par value and realizing interest at the maturity date when the investor receives the par value.

When the proceeds received when a bond matures, is called, or is sold are greater than the purchase price, a capital gain results. For a bond held to maturity, there will be a capital gain if the bond is purchased below its par value. A bond purchased below its par value is said to be purchased at a discount. For example, a bond purchased for $94.17 with a par value of $100 will generate a capital gain of $5.83 ($100 − $94.17) if held to maturity. For a callable bond, a capital gain results if the price at which the bond is called (that is, the call price) is greater than the purchase price. For example, if the bond in our previous example is callable and subsequently called at $100.5, a capital gain of $6.33 ($100.5 − $94.17) will be realized. If the same bond is sold prior to its maturity or before it is called, a capital gain will result if the proceeds exceed the purchase price. So, if our hypothetical bond is sold prior to the maturity date for $103, the capital gain would be $8.83 ($103 − $94.17).

A capital loss is generated when the proceeds received when a bond matures, is called, or is sold are less than the purchase price. For a bond held to maturity, there will be a capital loss if the bond is purchased for more than its par value. A bond purchased for more than its par value is said to be purchased at a premium. For example, a bond purchased for $102.5 with a par value of $100 will generate a capital loss of $2.5 ($102.5 − $100) if held to maturity. For a callable bond, a capital loss results if the price at which the bond is called is less than the purchase price. For example, if the bond in our previous example is callable and subsequently called at $100.5, a capital loss of $2 ($102.5 − $100.5) will be realized. If the same bond is sold prior to its maturity or before it is called, a capital loss will result if the sale price is less than the purchase price. So, if our hypothetical bond is sold prior to the maturity date for $98.5, the capital loss would be $4 ($102.5 − $98.5).

With the exception of zero-coupon instruments, bonds make periodic payments of interest that can be reinvested until the security is removed from the portfolio. There are also instruments in which there are periodic principal repayments that can be reinvested until the security is removed from the portfolio. Repayment of principal prior to the maturity date occurs for amortizing instruments such as mortgage-backed securities and asset-backed securities. The interest earned from reinvesting the interim cash flows (interest and/or principal payments) until the security is removed from the portfolio is called reinvestment income.

There are several yield measures cited in the bond market. These include current yield, yield to maturity, yield to call, yield to put, yield to worst, and cash flow yield. Below we explain how each measure is calculated and its limitations.

CURRENT YIELD   The *current yield* relates the annual dollar coupon interest to the market price. The formula for the current yield is:

$$\text{Current yield} = \frac{\text{Annual dollar coupon interest}}{\text{Price}}$$

For example, the current yield for a 7 percent eight-year bond whose price is $94.17 is 7.43 percent as shown below:

$$\text{Current yield} = \frac{\$7}{\$94.17} = 0.0743 = 7.43\%$$

The current yield will be greater than the coupon rate when the bond sells at a discount; the reverse is true for a bond selling at a premium. For a bond selling at par, the current yield will be equal to the coupon rate.

The drawback of the current yield is that it considers only the coupon interest and no other source that will impact an investor's return. No consideration is given to the capital gain that the investor will realize when a bond is purchased at a discount and held to maturity; nor is there any recognition of the capital loss that the investor will realize if a bond purchased at a premium is held to maturity.

YIELD TO MATURITY   The most popular measure of yield in the bond market is the *yield to maturity*. The yield to maturity is the interest rate that will make the present value of the cash flows from a bond equal to its market price plus accrued interest. To find the yield to maturity, we first determine the cash flows. Then an iterative procedure is used to find the interest rate that will make the present value of the cash flows equal to the market price plus accrued interest. In the illustrations presented below, we assume that the next coupon payment will be six months from now so that there is no accrued interest.

To illustrate, consider a 7 percent eight-year bond selling for $94.17. The cash flows for this bond are (a) 16 payments every 6 months of $3.50 and (b) a payment

16 six-month periods from now of $100. The present value using various discount (interest) rates is:

Interest rate	3.5%	3.6%	3.7%	3.8%	3.9%	4.0%
Present value	100.00	98.80	97.62	96.45	95.30	94.17

When a 4.0 percent interest rate is used, the present value of the cash flows is equal to $94.17, which is the price of the bond. Hence, 4.0 percent is the semiannual yield to maturity.

The market convention adopted is to double the semiannual yield and call that yield to maturity. Thus, the yield to maturity for the above bond is 8 percent (2 times 4.0 percent). The yield to maturity computed using this convention— doubling the semiannual yield—is called a *bond-equivalent yield*.

The following relationships between the price of a bond, coupon rate, current yield, and yield to maturity hold:

Bond Selling at				Relationship		
Par	Coupon rate	=	Current yield	=	YTM
Discount	Coupon rate	<	Current yield	<	YTM
Premium	Coupon rate	>	Current yield	>	YTM

The yield to maturity considers not only the coupon income but also any capital gain or loss that the investor will realize by holding the bond to maturity. The yield to maturity also considers the timing of the cash flows. It does consider reinvestment income; however, it assumes that the coupon payments can be reinvested at an interest rate equal to the yield to maturity. So, if the yield to maturity for a bond is 8 percent, for example, to earn that yield the coupon payments must be reinvested at an interest rate equal to 8 percent. The following illustration clearly demonstrates this point.

Suppose an investor has $94.17 and places the funds in a certificate of deposit that pays 4 percent every six months for eight years or 8 percent per year (on a bond-equivalent basis). At the end of eight years, the $94.17 investment will grow to $176.38. Instead, suppose an investor buys the following bond: a 7 percent eight-year bond selling for $94.17. The yield to maturity for this bond is 8 percent. The investor would expect that at the end of eight years, the total dollars from the investment will be $176.38.

Let's look at what the investor will receive. There will be 16 semiannual interest payments of $3.50, which will total $56. When the bond matures, the investor will receive $100. Thus, the total dollars that the investor will receive is $156 by holding the bond to maturity. But this is less than the $176.38 necessary to produce a yield of 8 percent on a bond-equivalent basis by $20.38 ($176.38 minus $156). How is this deficiency supposed to be made up? If the investor reinvests the coupon payments at a semiannual interest rate of 4 percent (or 8 percent annual rate on a bond-equivalent basis), then the interest earned on the coupon payments will be $20.38. Consequently, of the $82.21 total dollar return ($176.38 minus $94.17) necessary to produce a yield of 8 percent, about 25 percent ($20.38 divided by $82.21) must be generated by reinvesting the coupon payments.

Clearly, the investor will only realize the yield to maturity that is stated at the time of purchase if (1) the coupon payments can be reinvested at the yield to maturity and (2) the bond is held to maturity. With respect to the first assumption, the risk that an investor faces is that future interest rates will be less than the yield to maturity at the time the bond is purchased. This risk is referred to as reinvestment risk—a risk we explain later in this chapter. If the bond is not held to maturity, it may have to be sold for less than its purchase price, resulting in a return that is less than the yield to maturity. The risk that a bond will have to be sold at a loss is referred to as interest rate risk, as explained later in this chapter.

There are two characteristics of a bond that determine the degree of reinvestment risk. First, for a given yield to maturity and a given coupon rate, the longer the maturity the more the bond's total dollar return is dependent on reinvestment income to realize the yield to maturity at the time of purchase (that is, the greater the reinvestment risk). The implication is that the yield to maturity measure for long-term coupon bonds tells little about the potential yield that an investor may realize if the bond is held to maturity. For long-term bonds, in high interest rate environments the reinvestment income component may be as high as 70 percent of the bond's potential total dollar return.

The second characteristic that determines the degree of reinvestment risk is the coupon rate. For a given maturity and a given yield to maturity, the higher the coupon rate, the more dependent the bond's total dollar return will be on the reinvestment of the coupon payments in order to produce the yield to maturity at the time of purchase. This means that holding maturity and yield to maturity constant, premium bonds will be more dependent on reinvestment income than bonds selling at par. In contrast, discount bonds will be less dependent on reinvestment income than bonds selling at par. For zero-coupon bonds, none of the bond's total dollar return is dependent on reinvestment income. So, a zero-coupon bond has no reinvestment risk if held to maturity.

YIELD TO CALL When a bond is callable, the practice has been to calculate a *yield to call* as well as a yield to maturity. As explained earlier, a callable bond may have a call schedule. The yield to call assumes that the issuer will call the bond at some assumed call date and the call price is then the call price specified in the call schedule.

Typically, investors calculate a yield to first call or yield to next call, a yield to first par call, and yield to refunding. The *yield to first call* is computed for an issue that is not currently callable, while the *yield to next call* is computed for an issue that is currently callable. *Yield to refunding* is used when bonds are currently callable but have some restrictions on the source of funds used to buy back the debt when a call is exercised. The refunding date is the first date the bond can be called using lower-cost debt.

The procedure for calculating any yield to call measure is the same as for any yield calculation: determine the interest rate that will make the present value of the expected cash flows equal to the price plus accrued interest. In the case of yield to first call, the expected cash flows are the coupon payments to the first call date and the call price. For the yield to first par call, the expected cash flows are the coupon payments to the first date at which the issuer can call the bond at par and the par value. For the yield to refunding, the expected cash flows are the coupon payments to the first refunding date and the call price at the first refunding date.

To illustrate the computation, consider a 7 percent eight-year bond with a maturity value of $100 selling for $106.36. Suppose that the first call date is three years from now and the call price is $103. The cash flows for this bond if it is called in three years are (a) six coupon payments of $3.50 and (b) $103 in six 6-month periods from now. The process for finding the yield to first call is the same as for finding the yield to maturity. It can be shown that a semiannual interest rate of 2.8 percent makes the present value of the cash flows equal to the price is 2.8 percent. Therefore, the yield to first call on a bond-equivalent basis is 5.6 percent.

Let's take a closer look at the yield to call as a measure of the potential return of a security. The yield to call does consider all three sources of potential return from owning a bond. However, as in the case of the yield to maturity, it assumes that all cash flows can be reinvested at the yield to call until the assumed call date. As we just demonstrated, this assumption may be inappropriate. Moreover, the yield to call assumes that (a) the investor will hold the bond to the assumed call date and (b) the issuer will call the bond on that date.

These assumptions underlying the yield to call are often unrealistic. They do not take into account how an investor will reinvest the proceeds if the issue is called. For example, consider two bonds, M and N. Suppose that the yield to maturity for bond M, a five-year noncallable bond, is 7.5 percent, while for bond N the yield to call assuming the bond will be called in three years is 7.8 percent. Which bond is better for an investor with a five-year investment horizon? It's not possible to tell for the yields cited. If the investor intends to hold the bond for five years and the issuer calls bond N after three years, the total dollars that will be available at the end of five years will depend on the interest rate that can be earned from investing funds from the call date to the end of the investment horizon.

YIELD TO PUT When a bond is puttable, the yield to the first put date is calculated. The yield to put is the interest rate that will make the present value of the cash flows to the first put date equal to the price plus accrued interest. As with all yield measures (except the current yield), yield to put assumes that any interim coupon payments can be reinvested at the yield calculated. Moreover, the yield to put assumes that the bond will be put on the first put date.

YIELD TO WORST A yield can be calculated for every possible call date and put date. In addition, a yield to maturity can be calculated. The lowest of all these possible yields is called the yield to worst. For example, suppose that there are only four possible call dates for a callable bond and that a yield to call assuming each possible call date is 6 percent, 6.2 percent, 5.8 percent, and 5.7 percent, and that the yield to maturity is 7.5 percent. Then the yield to worst is the minimum of these values, 5.7 percent in our example.

The yield to worst measure holds little meaning as a measure of potential return.

CASH FLOW YIELD Mortgage-backed securities and asset-backed securities are backed by a pool of loans. The cash flows for these securities include principal repayment as well as interest. The complication that arises is that the individual borrowers whose loans make up the pool typically can prepay their loan in whole or in part prior to the scheduled principal repayment date. Because of prepayments, in order to project the cash flows it is necessary to make an assumption about the rate at which prepayments will occur. This rate is called the prepayment rate or prepayment speed.

Given the cash flows based on the assumed prepayment rate, a yield can be calculated. The yield is the interest rate that will make the present value of the projected cash flows equal to the price plus accrued interest. A yield calculated in this way is called a *cash flow yield*.

Typically, the cash flows for mortgage-backed and asset-backed securities are monthly. Therefore, the interest rate that will make the present value of the projected principal repayment and interest payments equal to the market price plus accrued interest is a monthly rate. The bond-equivalent yield is found by calculating the effective six-month interest rate and then doubling it. That is:

$$\text{Cash flow yield on a bond-equivalent basis (if monthly pay)}$$
$$= 2[(1 + \text{Monthly yield})^6 - 1]$$

For example, if the monthly yield is 0.5 percent, then

$$\text{Cash flow yield on a bond-equivalent basis (if monthly pay)}$$
$$= 2[(1.005)^6 - 1] = 6.08\%$$

As we have noted, the yield to maturity has two shortcomings as a measure of a bond's potential return: (1) it is assumed that the coupon payments can be reinvested at a rate equal to the yield to maturity, and (2) it is assumed that the bond is held to maturity. These shortcomings are equally present in application of the cash flow yield measure: (a) the projected cash flows are assumed to be reinvested at the cash flow yield, and (b) the mortgage-backed or asset-backed security is assumed to be held until the final payoff of all the loans based on some prepayment assumption. The importance of reinvestment risk—the risk that the cash flows will be reinvested at a rate less than the cash flow yield—is particularly important for mortgage-backed and asset-backed securities since payments are typically monthly and include principal repayments (scheduled and prepayments), as well as interest. Moreover, the cash flow yield is dependent on realization of the projected cash flows according to some prepayment rate. If actual prepayments differ significantly from the prepayment rate assumed, the cash flow yield will not be realized.

Risks Associated with Investing in Bonds

Bonds expose an investor to one or more of the following six risks: (1) interest rate risk, (2) call and prepayment risk, (3) credit risk, (4) liquidity risk, (5) exchange rate or currency risk, and (6) inflation or purchasing power risk.

INTEREST RATE RISK   The price of a typical bond will change in the opposite direction from a change in interest rates. That is, when interest rates rise, a bond's price will fall; when interest rates fall, a bond's price will rise. For example, consider a 6 percent 20-year bond. If the yield investors require to buy this bond is 6 percent, the price of this bond would be $100. However, if the required yield increased to 6.5 percent, the price of this bond would decline to $94.4479. Thus, for a 50-basis-point increase in yield, the bond's price declines by 5.55 percent. If, instead, the yield declines from 6 percent to 5.5 percent, the bond's price will rise by 6.02 percent to $106.0195.

The reason for this inverse relationship between price and changes in interest rates or changes in market yields is as follows. Suppose investor X purchases our hypothetical 6 percent coupon 20-year bond at par value ($100). The yield for this bond is 6 percent. Suppose that immediately after the purchase of this bond two things happen. First, market interest rates rise to 6.50 percent so that if an investor wants to buy a similar 20-year bond, a 6.50 percent coupon rate would have to be paid by the bond issuer in order to offer the bond at par value. Second, suppose investor X wants to sell the bond. In attempting to sell the bond, investor X would not find an investor who would be willing to pay par value for a bond with a coupon rate of 6 percent. The reason is that any investor who wanted to purchase this bond could obtain a similar 20-year bond with a coupon rate 50 basis points higher, 6.5 percent. What can the investor do? The investor cannot force the issuer to change the coupon rate to 6.5 percent. Nor can the investor force the issuer to shorten the maturity of the bond to a point where a new investor would be willing to accept a 6 percent coupon rate. The only thing that the investor can do is adjust the price of the bond so that at the new price the buyer would realize a yield of 6.5 percent. This means that the price would have to be adjusted down to a price below par value. The new price must be $94.4469. While we assumed in our illustration an initial price of par value, the principle holds for any purchase price. Regardless of the price that an investor pays for a bond, an increase in market interest rates will result in a decline in a bond's price.

Suppose instead of a rise in market interest rates to 6.5 percent, they decline to 5.5 percent. Investors would be more than happy to purchase the 6 percent coupon 20-year bond for par value. However, investor X realizes that the market is only offering investors the opportunity to buy a similar bond at par value with a coupon rate of 5.5 percent. Consequently, investor X will increase the price of the bond until it offers a yield of 5.5 percent. That price is $106.0195.

Since the price of a bond fluctuates with market interest rates, the risk that an investor faces is that the price of a bond held in a portfolio will decline if market interest rates rise. This risk is referred to as *interest rate risk* and is a major risk faced by investors in the bond market.

Bond Features That Affect Interest Rate Risk The degree of sensitivity of a bond's price to changes in market interest rates depends on various characteristics of the issue, such as maturity and coupon rate. Consider first maturity. All other factors constant, the longer the maturity, the greater the bond's price sensitivity to changes in interest rates. For example, we know that for a 6 percent 20-year bond selling to yield 6 percent, a rise in the yield required by investors to 6.5 percent will cause the bond's price to decline from $100 to $94.4479, a 5.55 percent price decline. For a 6 percent five-year bond selling to yield 6 percent, the price is $100. A rise in the yield required by investors from 6 percent to 6.5 percent would decrease the price to $97.8944. The decline in the bond's price is only 2.11 percent.

Now let's turn to the coupon rate. A property of a bond is that all other factors constant, the lower the coupon rate, the greater the bond's price sensitivity to changes in interest rates. For example, consider a 9 percent 20-year bond selling to yield 6 percent. The price of this bond would be $112.7953. If the yield required by investors increases by 50 basis points to 6.5 percent, the price of this bond would fall by 2.01 percent to $110.5280. This decline is less than the 5.55 percent decline for the

6 percent 20-year bond selling to yield 6 percent. An implication is that zero-coupon bonds have greater price sensitivity to interest rate changes than same-maturity bonds bearing a coupon rate and trading at the same yield.

Because of default or credit risk (discussed later), different bonds trade at different yields, even if they have the same coupon rate and maturity. How, then, holding other factors constant, does the level of interest rates affect a bond's price sensitivity to changes in interest rates? As it turns out, the higher the level of interest rates that a bond trades at, the lower the price sensitivity.

To see this, we can compare a 6 percent 20-year bond initially selling at a yield of 6 percent, and a 6 percent 20-year bond initially selling at a yield of 10 percent. The former is initially at a price of $100, and the latter carries a price of $65.68. Now, if the yield on both bonds increases by 100 basis points, the first bond trades down by 10.68 points (10.68 percent). After the assumed increase in yield, the second bond will trade at a price of $59.88, for a price decline of only 5.80 points (or 8.83 percent). Thus, we see that the bond that trades at a lower yield is more volatile in both percentage price change and absolute price change, as long as the other bond characteristics are the same. An implication of this is that, for a given change in interest rates, price sensitivity is lower when the level of interest rates in the market is high, and price sensitivity is higher when the level of interest rates is low.

We can summarize these three characteristics that affect the bond's price sensitivity to changes in market interest rates as follows:

> *Characteristic 1:* For a given maturity and initial yield, the lower the coupon rate the greater the bond's price sensitivity to changes in market interest rates.
> *Characteristic 2:* For a given coupon rate and initial yield, the longer the maturity of a bond the greater the bond's price sensitivity to changes in market interest rates.
> *Characteristic 3:* For a given coupon rate and maturity, the lower the level of interest rates the greater the bond's price sensitivity to changes in market interest rates.

A bond's price sensitivity bond will also depend on any options embedded in the issue. This is explained below when we discuss call risk.

Interest Rate Risk for Floating-Rate Securities   The change in the price of a fixed-rate coupon bond when market interest rates change is due to the fact that the bond's coupon rate differs from the prevailing market interest rate. For a floating-rate security, the coupon rate is reset periodically based on the prevailing value for the reference rate plus the contractually specified index spread. The index spread is set for the life of the security. The price of a floating-rate security will fluctuate depending on the following three factors.

First, the longer the time to the next coupon reset date, the greater the potential price fluctuation. For example, consider a floating-rate security whose coupon resets every six months and the coupon formula is six-month LIBOR plus 20 basis points. Suppose that on the coupon reset date six-month LIBOR is 5.8 percent. If the next day after the coupon is reset, six-month LIBOR rises to 6.1 percent, this means that this security is offering a six-month coupon rate that is less than the prevailing six-month rate for the remaining six months. The price of the security must decline to reflect this. Suppose instead that the coupon resets every month at one-month LIBOR and that this rate rises right after a coupon rate is reset. Then, while the investor would be realizing a submarket one-month coupon rate, it is for only a month. The price decline will be less than for the security that resets every six months.

The second reason why a floating-rate security's price will fluctuate is that the index spread that investors want in the market changes. For example, consider once again the security whose coupon reset formula is six-month LIBOR plus 20 basis points. If market conditions change such that investors want an index spread of 30 basis points rather than 20 basis points, this security would be offering a coupon rate that is 10 basis points below the market rate. As a result, the security's price will decline.

Finally, as noted earlier, a floating-rate security may have a cap. Once the coupon rate as specified by the coupon reset formula rises above the cap rate, the security offers a below market coupon rate and its price will decline. In fact, once the cap is reached, the security's price will react much the same way to changes in market interest rates as that of a fixed-rate coupon security.

Measuring Interest Rate Risk   Investors are interested in estimating the price sensitivity of a bond to changes in market interest rates. The measure commonly used to approximate the percentage price change is duration. Duration gives the approximate percentage price change for a 100-basis-point change in interest rates.

The duration for the 6 percent coupon five-year bond trading at par to yield 6 percent is 4.27. Thus, the price of this bond will change by approximately 4.27 percent if interest rates change by 100 basis points. For a 50 basis point change, this bond's price will change by approximately 2.14 percent (4.27 percent divided by 2). As explained above, this bond's price would actually change by 2.11 percent. Thus, duration does a good job of approximating the percentage price change. It turns out that the approximation is good the smaller the change in interest rates. The approximation is not as good for a large change in interest rates.

CALL AND PREPAYMENT RISK   As explained earlier, a bond may include a provision that allows the issuer to retire or call all or part of the issue before the maturity date. From the investor's perspective, there are three disadvantages to call provisions. First, the cash flow pattern of a callable bond is not known with certainty. Second, because the issuer will call the bonds when interest rates have dropped, the investor is exposed to reinvestment risk; that is, the investor will have to reinvest the proceeds when the bond is called at relatively lower interest rates. Finally, the capital appreciation potential of a bond will be reduced, because the price of a callable bond may not rise much above the price at which the issuer will call the bond. Because of these disadvantages faced by the investor, a callable bond is said to expose the investor to *call risk*. The same disadvantages apply to bonds that can prepay. In this case the risk is referred to as *prepayment risk*.

CREDIT RISK   In general, one thinks of credit risk as the risk that the debtor will fail to satisfy its obligation to the lender (that is, timely payment of principal and/or interest). That is in fact one form of risk referred to as *default risk*. Default risk is gauged by credit ratings assigned by three nationally recognized statistical rating companies: Moody's Investors Service, Standard & Poor's Corporation, and Fitch Ratings. These organizations are popularly referred to as *rating agencies*.

Bonds with default risk trade in the market at a price that is lower than comparable U.S. government securities, which are considered free of default risk. In other words, a non-U.S.-government taxable bond will trade in the market at a higher yield than a U.S.-government taxable bond that is otherwise comparable in terms of maturity and coupon rate.

Except in the case of the lowest-rated securities, known as "high-yield" or "junk bonds," an investor is normally more concerned with the changes in the perceived default risk than with the actual event of default. Even though the actual default of an issuer may be highly unlikely, an investor is concerned about the impact that a change in perceived default risk can have on a bond's price. If the perceived default risk increases, the market will require a higher yield for the security. As a result, a bond's price will decline. This risk is referred to as *credit spread risk*. A decline in the price of a bond will also occur if an issue's credit rating is lowered. By a lower credit rating, it is meant the issue is "downgraded." This risk is referred to as *downgrade risk*.

LIQUIDITY RISK   When an investor wants to sell a bond prior to the maturity date, he or she is concerned whether the price that can be obtained from dealers is close to the true value of the issue. For example, if recent trades in the market for a particular issue have been between 97.25 and 97.75 and market conditions have not changed, an investor would expect to sell the bond somewhere in the 97.25 to 97.75 area.

Liquidity risk is the risk that the investor will have to sell a bond below its true value where the true value is indicated by recent transactions. The primary measure of liquidity is the size of the spread between the bid price (the price at which a dealer is willing to buy a security) and the ask price (the price at which a dealer is willing to sell a security). The wider the bid-ask spread, the greater the liquidity risk.

A liquid market can generally be defined by "small bid-ask spreads which do not materially increase for large transactions" (Gerber, 1997, p. 278). Bid-ask spreads, and therefore liquidity risk, change over time.

For investors who plan to hold a bond until maturity and need not mark a position to market, liquidity risk is not a major concern. An institutional investor that plans to hold an issue to maturity but is periodically marked to market is concerned with liquidity risk. By marking a position to market, it is meant that the security is revalued in the portfolio based on its current market price. For example, mutual funds are required to mark to market at the end of each day the holdings in their portfolio in order to compute the net asset value (NAV). While other institutional investors may not mark to market as frequently as mutual funds, they are marked to market when reports are periodically sent to clients or the board of directors or trustees.

EXCHANGE RATE OR CURRENCY RISK   For a U.S. investor, a non-dollar-denominated bond (that is, a bond whose payments are not in U.S. dollars) has unknown U.S. dollar cash flows. The dollar cash flows are dependent on the exchange rate at the time the payments are received. For example, suppose a U.S. investor purchases a bond whose payments are in euros. If the euro depreciates relative to the U.S. dollar, then fewer dollars will be received. The risk of this occurring is referred to as *exchange rate risk* or *currency risk*. Of course, should the euro appreciate relative to the U.S. dollar, the investor will benefit by receiving more dollars.

INFLATION OR PURCHASING POWER RISK *Inflation risk* or *purchasing power risk* arises because of the variation in the value of cash flows from a security due to inflation, as measured in terms of purchasing power. For example, if an investor purchases a bond with a coupon rate of 7 percent, but the rate of inflation is 8 percent, the purchasing power of the cash flow has declined. For all but floating-rate securities, an investor is exposed to inflation risk because the interest rate the issuer promises to make is fixed for the life of the issue. To the extent that interest rates reflect the expected inflation rate, floating-rate securities have a lower level of inflation risk.

Summary

Basically, a bond is a financial obligation of an entity (the issuer) who promises to pay a specified sum of money at specified future dates. In this part we have described the basic features of bonds and their investment characteristics.

Bond prices are quoted as a percentage of par value, with par value equal to 100. The coupon rate is the interest rate that the issuer agrees to pay each year; the coupon is the annual amount of the interest payment and is found by multiplying the par value by the coupon rate. Zero-coupon bonds do not make periodic coupon payments; the bondholder realizes interest at the maturity date equal to the difference between the maturity value and the price paid for the bond. A step-up note is a security whose coupon rate increases over time.

A floating-rate security is an issue whose coupon rate resets periodically based on some formula; the typical coupon reset formula is some reference rate plus an index spread. A floating-rate security may have a cap, which sets the maximum coupon rate that will be paid at a reset date; a cap is a disadvantage to the bondholder while a floor is an advantage to the bondholder. An inverse floater is an issue whose coupon rate moves in the opposite direction from the change in the reference rate.

Accrued interest is the amount of interest accrued since the last coupon payment, and in the United States (as well as in many countries), the bond buyer must pay the bond seller the accrued interest. The full price of a security is the agreed-upon price plus accrued interest; the clean price is the agreed-upon price without accrued interest. Interest accrues on a bond from and including the date of the previous coupon up to but excluding the value date; the value date is usually, but not always, the same as the settlement date.

A bond issue may have a call provision granting the issuer an option to retire all or part of the issue prior to the stated maturity date. A call provision is an advantage to the issuer and a disadvantage to the bondholder. When a callable bond is issued, typically the issuer may not call the bond for a number of years; that is, there is a deferred call. Most new bond issues, even if currently callable, usually have some restrictions against refunding. For an amortizing security backed by a pool of loans, the borrowers typically have the right to prepay in whole or in part prior to the scheduled principal repayment date; this provision is called a prepayment option.

A puttable bond is one in which the bondholder has the right to sell the issue back to the issuer at a specified price on designated dates. A convertible bond is an issue giving the bondholder the right to exchange the bond for a specified number of shares of common stock.

The sources of return from holding a bond to maturity are the coupon interest payments, any capital gain or loss, and reinvestment income. Reinvestment income is the interest income generated by reinvesting coupon interest payments and any principal repayments from the time of receipt to the bond's maturity. The current yield relates the annual dollar coupon interest to the market price and fails to recognize any capital gain or loss and reinvestment income. The yield to maturity is the interest rate that will make the present value of the cash flows from a bond equal to the price plus accrued interest. This yield measure will only be realized if the interim cash flows can be reinvested at the yield to maturity and the bond is held to maturity. The yield to call is the interest rate that will make the present value of the expected cash flows to the assumed call date equal to the price plus accrued interest. Yield measures for callable bonds include yield to first call, yield to next call, yield to first par call, and yield to refunding. The yield to worst is the lowest yield from among all possible yield to calls, yield to puts, and the yield to maturity. For mortgage-backed and asset-backed securities, the cash flow yield based on some prepayment rate is the interest rate that equates the present value of the projected principal and interest payments to the price plus accrued interest. The cash flow yield assumes that all cash flows (principal payments and interest payments) can be reinvested at the calculated yield and that the prepayment rate will be realized over the security's life.

Bonds expose an investor to various risks. The price of a bond changes inversely with a change in market interest rates. Interest rate risk refers to the adverse price movement of a bond as a result of a change in market interest rates; for the owner of a bond it is the risk that interest rates will rise. The coupon rate and maturity of a bond affect its price sensitivity to changes in market interest rate. The duration of a bond measures the approximate percentage price change for a 100-basis-point change in interest rates.

Call risk and prepayment risk refer to the risk that a security will be paid off before the scheduled principal repayment date. From an investor's perspective, there are three disadvantages to call and prepayment provisions: (1) the cash flow pattern is uncertain, (2) reinvestment risk because proceeds received will have to be reinvested at a relatively lower interest rate, and (3) the capital appreciation potential of a bond will be reduced.

Credit risk consists of three types of risk: (1) default risk, (2) credit spread risk, and (3) downgrade risk. Default risk is gauged by the ratings assigned by the nationally recognized statistical rating organizations (rating agencies).

Liquidity risk depends on the ease with which an issue can be sold at or near its true value and is primarily gauged by the bid-ask spread quoted by a dealer. From the perspective of a U.S. investor, exchange rate risk is the risk that a currency in which a security is denominated will depreciate relative to the U.S. dollar. Inflation risk or purchasing power risk arises because of the variation in the value of cash flows from a security due to inflation.

References

Choudhry, M., and Fabozzi, F. J. (eds.) (2004). *Handbook of European Fixed Income Securities*. Hoboken, NJ: John Wiley & Sons.

Fabozzi, F. J. (1999). *Duration, Convexity, and Other Bond Risk Measures*. Hoboken, NJ: John Wiley & Sons.

Fabozzi, F. J. (ed.) (2000). *Investing in Asset-Backed Securities*. Hoboken, NJ: John Wiley & Sons.

Fabozzi, F. J. (2002). *Fixed Income Securities*. Hoboken, NJ: John Wiley & Sons.

Fabozzi, F. J. (ed.) (2005). *Handbook of Fixed Income Securities*, 7th edition. New York: McGraw-Hill.

Fabozzi, F. J. (2006). *Bond Markets, Analysis, and Strategies*, 6th edition. Upper Saddle River, NJ: Prentice Hall.

Fabozzi, F. J., Bhattacharya, A. K., and Berliner W. S. (2007). *Mortgage-Backed Securities: Products, Structuring, and Analytical Techniques*. Hoboken, NJ: John Wiley & Sons.

Fabozzi, F. J., and Mann, S. V. (2001). *Floating Rate Securities*. Hoboken, NJ: John Wiley & Sons.

Fabozzi, F. J., Mann, S. V., and Choudhry, M. (2002). *Global Money Markets*. Hoboken, NJ: John Wiley & Sons.

Gerber, R. I. (1997). A user's guide to buy-side bond trading. In F. J. Fabozzi (ed.), *Managing Fixed Income Portfolios* (pp. 277–290). Hoboken, NJ: John Wiley & Sons.

Wilson, R. W., and Fabozzi, F. J. (1996). *Corporate Bonds: Structures and Analysis*. Hoboken, NJ: John Wiley & Sons.

Part III Effective Duration and Convexity

Modified, *duration* ignores any effect on cash flows that might take place as a result of changes in interest rates. *Effective duration* does not ignore the potential for such changes in cash flows. For example, bonds with embedded options will have very different cash flow properties as interest rates (or yields) change. Modified duration ignores these effects completely. In order to apply effective duration, an available interest rate model and corresponding pricing model are needed. The example in this part shows how to compute the effective duration of securities with cash flows that are dependent on interest rates.

There is no difference between modified and effective duration for option-free or straight bonds. In fact, it can be shown that they are mathematically identical when the change in rates (or yields) becomes very small. As shown in the example, even for bonds with embedded options, the differences between the two measures are minimal over certain ranges of yields. For example, when the embedded option is far out-of-the-money, the cash flows of the bond are not affected by small changes in yields, resulting in almost no difference in cash flows between the two measures.

Convexity and effective convexity measure the curvature of the price/yield relationship. Convexity (sometimes referred to as *standard convexity*) suffers the same limitations as modified duration and is therefore not generally useful for securities with embedded options. However, similar to the duration measures, in ranges of rates (or yields) where the cash flows are not materially affected by small changes in yields, the two convexity measures are almost identical.

As with the duration measures, there is no difference between convexity and effective convexity for option-free or straight bonds. In fact, it can be shown that they are mathematically identical when the change in rates (or yields) becomes very small. As shown in the following example, even for bonds with embedded options, the differences between the two measures are minimal over certain ranges of rates. For example, when the embedded option is far out-of-the-money, the cash flows of the bond are not affected by small changes in yields.

Effective Duration and Effective Convexity—An Example

The following example illustrates how to calculate and interpret effective duration and effective convexity for straight bonds and bonds with embedded options.

Suppose we need to measure the interest rate sensitivity of the following three securities:

1. A five-year, 6.70 percent coupon straight (noncallable and nonputable) semiannual coupon bond, with a current price of 102.75 percent of par.
2. A five-year, 6.25 percent coupon bond, callable at par in years 2 through 5 on the semiannual coupon dates, with a current price of 99.80 percent of par.
3. A five-year, 5.75% coupon bond, putable at par in years 2 through 5 on the semiannual coupon dates, with a current price of 100.11% of par.

The cash flows of these securities are very different as interest rates change. Consequently, the sensitivities to changes in interest rates are also very different.

Using the Black-Derman-Toy interest rate model (Black, Derman, and Toy, 1990) that is based on the existing term structure, the term structure of interest rates is shifted up and down by 10 basis points (bps) and the resulting price changes are recorded. P_- corresponds to the price after a downward shift in interest rates, P_+ corresponds to the price after an upward shift in interest rates, P is the current price, and S is the assumed shift in the term structure. (Note that shifting the term structure in a parallel manner will result in a change in yields equal to the shift for option-free bonds.) Table 10.8 shows these prices for each bond. The formulas for calculating effective duration and effective convexity are as follows:

$$\text{Effective duration} = \frac{(P_-) - (P_+)}{2PS} \tag{10.1}$$

$$\text{Effective convexity} = \frac{(P_-) - (P_+) - 2P}{PS^2} \tag{10.2}$$

TABLE 10.8 Original Prices and Resulting Prices from a Downward and Upward 10 Basis Point Interest Rate Shift and the Corresponding Effective Duration and Effective Convexity for Three Bonds Based on the Black-Derman-Toy Model

	Price Changes Following 10 bp Shift		
Variable	Original Price P	Upward Shift of 10 bp P_+	Downward Shift of 10 bp P_-
Straight Bond Price	102.7509029	102.3191235	103.1848805
Callable Bond Price	99.80297176	99.49321718	100.1085624
Putable Bond Price	100.1089131	99.84237604	100.3819059

Effective Duration and Effective Convexity Measures Calculated from Using the Price Changes Resulting from the 10 bp Shifts in the Term Structure

	Effective Duration	Effective Convexity
Straight Bond	4.21	21.39
Callable Bond	3.08	−41.72
Putable Bond	2.70	64.49

TABLE 10.9   Effective Duration and Effective Convexity for Various Shifts in the Term Structure for Three Bonds

Term Structure Shift (bps)	Straight Bond		Callable Bond		Putable Bond	
	Effective Duration	Effective Convexity	Effective Duration	Effective Convexity	Effective Duration	Effective Convexity
−500	4.40	23.00	1.91	4.67	4.46	23.46
−250	4.30	22.19	1.88	4.55	4.37	22.66
0	4.21	21.39	3.08	−41.72	2.70	64.49
250	4.12	20.62	4.15	20.85	1.87	7.07
500	4.03	19.87	4.07	20.10	1.81	4.23
1000	3.85	18.42	3.89	18.66	1.77	4.03

It is very important to realize the importance of the pricing model in this exercise. The model must account for the change in cash flows of the securities as interest rates change. The callable and putable bonds have very different cash flow characteristics that depend on the level of interest rates. The pricing model used must account for this property. (Note that when calculating the measures, users are cautioned to not round values. Since the denominators of both the duration and convexity terms are very small, any rounding will have a significant impact on results.)

STRAIGHT BOND   The effective duration for the *straight bond* is found by recording the price changes from shifting the term structure up (P_+) and down (P_-) by 10 bps and then substituting these values into equation (10.1). The prices are shown in Table 10.9. Consequently, the computation is:

$$\text{Effective duration} = \frac{103.1848805 - 102.3191235}{2(102.7509029)(0.001)} = 4.21$$

Similarly, the calculation for effective convexity is found by substituting the corresponding prices into equation (10.2):

$$\text{Effective convexity} = \frac{103.1848805 + 102.3191235 - 2(102.7509029)}{102.7509029(0.001)^2} = 21.39$$

For the straight bond, the modified duration is 4.21 and the convexity is 21.40. These are very close to the effective measures shown in Table 10.8. This demonstrates that, for option-free bonds, the two measures are almost the same for small changes in yields.

Table 10.9 shows the effects of the term structure shifts on the effective duration and effective convexity of the straight bond. The effective duration increases as yields decrease because as yields decrease the slope of the price yield relationship for option-free bonds becomes steeper and effective duration (and modified duration) is directly proportional to the slope of this relationship. For example, the effective duration at very low yields (−500-bp shift) is 4.40 and decreases to 3.85 at very high rates (+1,000 bps), Figure 10.11 illustrates this phenomenon; as yields increase notice how the slope of the price/yield relationship decreases (becomes more horizontal or flatter).

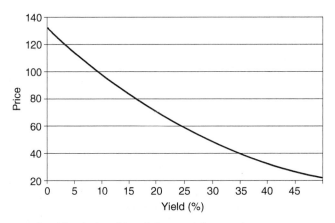

FIGURE 10.11   Price/Yield Relationship of the Straight Bond

As the term structure shifts up (that is, as rates rise), the yield to maturity on a straight bond increases by approximately the same amount. As the yield increases, its convexity decreases. Figure 10.11 illustrates this property. As yields increase, the curvature (or the rate of change of the slope) decreases. The results in Table 10.9 for the straight bond also bear this out. The effective convexity values become smaller as yields increase. For example, the effective convexity at very low yields (−500-bp shift) is 23.00 and decreases to 18.43 at very high rates (+1,000-bp shift).

These are both well-documented properties of option-free bonds. The modified duration and convexity numbers for the straight bond are almost identical to the effective measures for the straight bond shown in Table 10.9.

CALLABLE BOND   The effective duration for the *callable bond* is found by recording the price changes from shifting the term structure up (P_+) and down (P_-) by 10 bps and then substituting these values into equation (10.1). The prices are shown in Table 10.8. Note that these prices take into account the changing cash flows resulting from the embedded call option. Consequently, the computation is:

$$\text{Effective duration} = \frac{100.1085624 - 99.49321718}{2(99.800297)(0.001)} = 3.08$$

Similarly, the calculation for effective convexity is found by substituting the corresponding prices into equation (10.2):

$$\text{Effective convexity} = \frac{100.1085624 + 99.49321718 - 2(99.80297176)}{99.80297176(0.001)^2} = -41.72$$

The relationship between the shift in rates and effective duration is shown in Table 10.9 and in Figure 10.12. As rates increase, the effective duration of the callable bond becomes larger. For example, the effective duration at very low yields (−500-bp shift) is 1.91 and increases to 3.89 at very high rates (+1,000 bps). This reflects the fact that as rates increase the likelihood of the bond being called decreases and, as a result, the bond behaves more like a straight bond; hence, its effective duration increases. Conversely, as rates drop, this likelihood increases and the bond and its effective duration behave more like a bond with a two-year maturity because of the call option becoming effective in two years. As rates decrease significantly, the

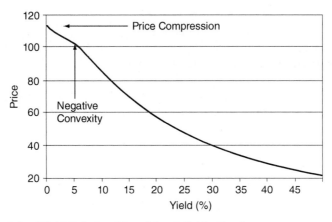

FIGURE 10.12   Price/Yield Relationship of the Callable Bond

likelihood of the issuer calling the bond in two years increases. Consequently, at very low and intermediate rates the difference between the effective duration measure and modified duration is large, and at very high rates the difference is small.

As explained above, effective convexity measures the curvature of the price/yield relationship of bonds. Low values for effective convexity simply mean that the relationship is becoming linear (an effective convexity of zero represents a linear relationship). As shown in Table 10.9 the effective convexity values of the callable bond at extremely low interest rates (that is, for the –250-bp and –500-bp shifts in the term structure) are very small positive numbers (4.55 and 4.67, respectively). This means that the relationship is almost linear but exhibits slight convexity. This is due to the call option being delayed by two years. At these extremely low interest rates, the callable bond exhibits slight positive convexity because the price compression at the call price is not complete for another two years. (Price compression for a callable bond refers to the property that a callable bond's price appreciation potential is severely limited as yields decline. As shown in Figure 10.12, as yields fall below a certain level (that is, where the yield corresponds to the call price), the price appreciation of the callable bond is being compressed). If this bond were immediately callable, the price/yield relationship would exhibit positive convexity at high yields and negative convexity at low yields. At the current level of interest rates, the effective convexity is negative as expected. At these rate levels, the embedded call option causes enough price compression to cause the curvature of the price/yield relationship to be negatively convex (that is, concave). Figure 10.12 illustrates these properties. It is at these levels that an embedded option has a significant effect on the cash flows of the callable bond.

Table 10.9 shows that for large positive yield curve shifts (that is, for the +250-bp, +500-bp, and +1,000-bp shifts in the term structure), the effective convexity of the callable bond becomes positive and very close to the effective convexity values of the straight bond. For example, the effective convexity at the +250-bp shift is 20.85 for the callable bond and 20.62 for the *straight bond*. The only reason they are not the same is because the coupon rates of the bonds are not equal. Consequently, at very low and intermediate rates the difference between effective convexity and the standard convexity is large and at very high rates the difference is small. The intuition behind these findings is straightforward. At low rates, the cash flows of the callable bond are severely affected by the likelihood of the embedded call option being exercised by the issuer. At high rates, the embedded call option is so far out-of-the-money that it has almost no effect on the cash flows of the callable bond and so the callable bond behaves like a straight bond.

PUTABLE BOND   The effective duration for the *putable bond* is found by recording the price changes from shifting the term structure up (P_+) and down (P_-) by 10 bps and then substituting these values into equation (10.1). The prices are shown in Table 10.8. Note that these prices take into account the changing cash flows resulting from the embedded put option. Consequently, the computation is:

$$\text{Effective duration} = \frac{100.3819059 + 99.84237604 - 2(99.80297176)}{2(100.1089131)(0.001)} = 2.70$$

Similarly, the calculation for effective convexity is found by substituting the corresponding prices into equation (10.2):

$$\text{Effective convexity} = \frac{100.3819059 + 99.84237604 - 2(100.1089131)}{100.1089131(0.001)^2} = 64.49$$

Because the putable bond behaves so differently from the other two bonds, the effective duration and effective convexity values are very different. As rates increase, the bond behaves more like a two-year bond because the owner will, in all likelihood, exercise his right to put the bond back at the put price as soon as possible. As a result, effective duration of the putable bond is expected to decrease as rates increase. This is due to the embedded put option severely affecting the cash flows of the putable bond. Conversely, as rates fall, the putable bond behaves more like a five-year straight bond since the embedded put option is so far out-of-the-money and has little effect on the cash flows of the putable bond. Effective duration should reflect these properties. Table 10.9 shows that this is indeed the case. For example, the effective duration at very low yields (–500-bp shift) is 4.46 and decreases to 1.77 at very high rates (+1,000 bps). Consequently, at very high rates and intermediate rates the difference between the effective duration and modified duration measures is large and at low rates the difference is small.

Table 10.9 shows that the effective convexity of the putable bond is positive for all rate shifts as would be expected, but it becomes smaller as rates increase (that is, for the +250-bp, +500-bp, and +1,000-bp shifts in the term structure). As rates increase, the putable bond price/yield relationship will become linear because of the bond's price truncation at the put price. (Price truncation for a putable bond refers to the property that the putable bond's price depreciation potential is severely limited as yields increase. As shown in Figure 10.13 as yields rise above a certain level (that is, where the yield corresponds to the put price), the price depreciation of the putable bond is truncated. This is the reason for the small effective convexity values for the putable bond for the three positive shifts in the term structure (7.07, 4.23, and 4.03, respectively). It is at these levels that the embedded put option has a significant effect on the cash flows of the putable bond. Consequently, at very high rates and intermediate rates the difference between the effective convexity and standard convexity is very large. Figure 10.13 illustrates these properties.

At very low rates (that is, for the 250-bp and 500-bp downward shifts in the term structure), the putable bond behaves like a five-year straight bond because the put option is so far out-of-the-money. Therefore, as the term structure is shifted

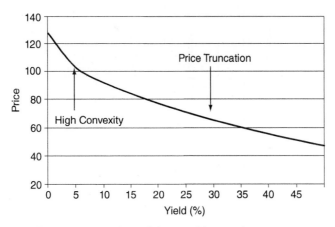

FIGURE 10.13 Price/Yield Relationship of the Putable Bond

downward, the putable bond's effective convexity values approach those of a comparable five-year straight bond. Comparing the effective convexity measures for the putable bond and the straight bond illustrates this characteristic. For example, the effective convexity at the −250-bp shift is 22.66 for the putable bond and 22.19 for the straight bond. The two convexity measures are almost identical. In fact, they would be identical if their coupon rates were equal.

Figure 10.13 illustrates these properties. Also notice how the transition from low yields to high yields forces the price/yield relationship to have a very high convexity at intermediate levels of yields. For example, the current effective convexity of the putable bond is 64.49 compared to 21.39 for the straight bond and −41.72 for the callable bond. This is because of the price truncation of the putable bond resulting from the embedded put option moving from out-of-the-money and having little influence over the cash flows to in-the-money and having a significant impact on cash flows.

Putting It All Together

Notice in Table 10.9 how effective duration changes much more across yields for the callable and putable bonds than it does for the straight bond. This is to be expected because the embedded options have such a significant influence over cash flows as yields change over a wide spectrum. Interestingly, at high (low) yields the callable (putable) bond's effective duration is very close to the straight bond. This is where the embedded call (put) option is so far out-of-the-money that the two securities behave similarly. The same intuition holds for the effective convexity measures.

A common use of effective duration and effective convexity is to estimate the percentage price changes in fixed income securities for assumed changes in yield. In fact, it is not uncommon for effective duration and effective convexity to be presented in terms of estimated percentage price change for a given change in yield (typically 100 bp), Tables 10.10 and 10.11 show this alternative presentation for a ±100 bp changes in yield. These results are computed by substituting the values from Table 10.3 into the following relationship:

$$\% \text{ Price change} = \frac{\Delta P}{P} = -(ED)\,(\Delta y)\,(100) + \frac{1}{2}\,(EC)\,(\Delta y)^2\,(100) \qquad (10.3)$$

TABLE 10.10 Percentage Price Changes Assuming an Increase in Yield of 100 bps and Effective Duration and Effective Convexity for Various Shifts in the Term Structure

Term Structure Shift (bp)	Straight Bond			Callable Bond			Putable Bond		
	% Price Change Using Effective Duration	% Price Change Using Effective Convexity	Total % Price Change	% Price Change Using Effective Duration	% Price Change Using Effective Convexity	Total % Price Change	% Price Change Using Effective Duration	% Price Change Using Effective Convexity	Total % Price Change
−500	−4.40	0.11500	−4.28500	−1.91	0.02335	−1.88665	−4.46	0.11730	−4.34270
−250	−4.30	0.11095	−4.18905	−1.88	0.02275	−1.85725	−4.37	0.11330	−4.25670
0	−4.21	0.10695	−4.10305	−3.08	−0.20860	−3.28860	−2.70	0.32245	−2.37755
250	−4.12	0.10310	−4.01690	−4.15	0.10425	−4.04575	−1.87	0.03535	−1.83465
500	−4.03	0.09935	−3.93065	−4.07	0.10050	−3.96950	−1.81	0.02115	−1.78885
1000	−3.85	0.09210	−3.75790	−3.89	0.09330	−3.79670	−1.77	0.02015	−1.74985

TABLE 10.11 Percentage Price Changes Assuming a Decrease in Yield of 100 bps and Effective Duration and Effective Convexity for Various Shifts in the Term Structure

Term Structure Shift (bp)	Straight Bond			Callable Bond			Putable Bond		
	% Price Change Using Effective Duration	% Price Change Using Effective Convexity	Total % Price Change	% Price Change Using Effective Duration	% Price Change Using Effective Convexity	Total % Price Change	% Price Change Using Effective Duration	% Price Change Using Effective Convexity	Total % Price Change
−500	4.40	0.1150	4.5150	1.91	0.0234	1.9334	4.46	0.1173	4.5773
−250	4.30	0.1110	4.4110	1.88	0.0228	1.9028	4.37	0.1133	4.4833
0	4.21	0.1070	4.3170	3.08	−0.2086	2.8714	2.70	0.3225	3.0225
250	4.12	0.1031	4.2231	4.15	0.1043	4.2543	1.87	0.0354	1.9054
500	4.03	0.0994	4.1294	4.07	0.1005	4.1705	1.81	0.0212	1.8312
1000	3.85	0.0921	3.9421	3.89	0.0933	3.9833	1.77	0.0202	1.7902

where ED is the effective duration, EC is the effective convexity, and Δy is the assumed change in yield (e.g., 100 bp). Equation (10.3) is the result of a Taylor Series expansion on the bond price function. Also, note that the effective duration (ED) and effective convexity (EC) terms can be replaced by modified duration and standard convexity, respectively, for option-free bonds.

Table 10.10 illustrates the resulting precentage price changes resulting from an increase in yield of 100 bps at various levels of the term structure. For example, the percentage price change for the callable bond at the current term structure (0-bp shift) is calculated using the values from Table 10.9 and substituting them into equation (10.3) as follows:

$$\text{\% Price change} = -(3.08)(0.01)(100) + \frac{1}{2}(-41.72)(0.01)^2(100)$$

$$= -3.08 - 0.2086 = -3.2886\%$$

This example shows that the estimated total percentage price change from effective convexity (–0,2086%) is much smaller than the percentage price change from effective duration (–3.08).

Table 10.11 illustrates the resulting percentage price changes resulting from a decrease in yield of 100 bp at the various levels of the term structure. For example, the percentage price change for the callable bond at the current term structure (0-bp shift) is calculated using the values from Table 10.9 and substituting them into equation (10.3) as follows:

$$\text{\% Price change} = -(3.08)(-0.01)(100) + \frac{1}{2}(-41.72)(-0.01)^2(100)$$

$$= 3.08 - 0.2086 = -2.8714\%$$

Summary

In this chapter we illustrated the important differences between effective duration and modified duration and effective convexity and convexity. The differences are due to changing cash flows of the security being evaluated. The effective measures account for changing cash flows and the traditional measures do not. It was shown that the differences between the two are very significant whenever the cash flows are greatly affected by the level of interest rates. However, to properly compute the effective measures, both an interest rate and a valuation model are required. Consequently, they are more computationally intensive than the traditional measures. We also showed how the effective and traditional measures are identical for option-free bonds. The geometric interpretation using the price/yield relationship was also presented, as was the translation of the measures to percentage price changes. Sometimes these measures are presented directly as percentage price change so that the analyst needs to be aware of the source of the information before interpreting them. The analyst would be best served by always using the effective measures since they properly account for the characteristics of the security.

References

Black, F., Derman, E., and Toy, W. (1990). A one-factor model of interest rates and its application to Treasury bond options. *Financial Analysts Journal* (January–February): 24–32.

Buetow, G. W., Jr., Hanke, B., and Fabozzi, F. J. (2001). The impact of different interest rate models on effective duration, effective convexity, and option-adjusted spreads. *Journal of Fixed Income* (December): 41–53.

Buetow, G., and Sochacki, J. (2001). *Term-Structure Models Using Binomial Trees.* Charlottesville, VA: The Research Foundation of the CFA Institute.

Fabozzi, F. J. (2006). *Fixed Income Mathematics.* New York: McGraw-Hill.

Fabozzi, F. J. (1999). *Duration, Convexity, and Other Bond Risk Measures.* New York: John Wiley & Sons.

Fabozzi, F. J., Buetow, G. W., Jr., and Johnson, R. B. (2005). Measuring interest-rate risk. In F. J. Fabozzi (ed.), *The Handbook of Fixed Income Securities,* 7th edition, 183–228. New York: McGraw-Hill.

Golub, B. W. (2006). Approaches for measuring duration of mortgage-related securities. In F. J. Fabozzi (ed.), *The Handbook of Mortgage-Backed Securities,* 6th edition, 823–856. New York: McGraw-Hill.

Jacob, D. P., and Lu, T. (2006). Duration and average-life drift of CMOs. In F. J. Fabozzi (ed.), *The Handbook of Mortgage-Backed Securities,* 6th edition, 857–867. New York: McGraw-Hill.

Part IV Values Tied to Bonds

Promises make debt, and debt makes promises.

—Dutch proverb

When we value an investment, we need to know its expected future cash flows and the uncertainty of receiving them. To value securities, you must understand the nature of the cash flows, their timing, and the uncertainty associated with these future cash flows. In this chapter, we focus on one type of security: bonds.

A *bond* is a legal obligation to repay an amount borrowed—the principal—along with some compensation for the time value of money and risk. Corporations, municipalities, states, and the federal government issue bonds.

Most bonds represent obligations of the borrower to pay interest at regular intervals (usually every six months) and to repay the principal amount of the loan at the end of the loan period; that is, at maturity. We also use the terms *maturity value, face value, par value,* and *redemption value* to refer to this principal.

If you buy a bond, you are entering into a contract with the issuer of that debt security, the borrower. By owning the bond, you become a creditor of the issuer. Any interest and principal that the issuer promises to pay are legal obligations, and failure to pay as promised results in dire consequences for the issuer.

For a corporate issuer, bonds are senior to equity securities: The borrower must satisfy their obligations to the creditors before making payments to owners, the stockholders. Therefore, for a given corporation, the cash flows from bonds are more certain than the cash flows of either preferred stock or common stock.

Bond Basics

A bond is a promise by the borrower to repay the principal amount. A bond may also require the borrower to pay interest periodically, typically semiannually or annually. We usually state interest as a percentage of the bond's maturity value, no matter the current price of the bond or its original offering price.

We refer to the interest payments as coupon payments or *coupons* and the percentage rate as the *coupon rate*. If these coupons are a constant amount, paid at regular intervals, we refer to the security paying them as having a *straight coupon*. A bond that does not have a promise to pay interest we refer to as a *zero-coupon* note or bond.

A bond typically has two types of cash flows:

1. Interest, which is periodic
2. Principal, which is a lump sum at maturity

The value of a bond today is the present value of the promised future cash flows; that is, the present value of the interest and the maturity value. Therefore, the present value of a debt is the sum of the present value of the interest payments and the present value of the maturity value:

$$\text{Present value of a bond} = \text{Present value of interest payments} + \text{Present value of maturity value}$$

To calculate the value of a bond, we discount the future cash flows (that is, the interest and maturity value) at some rate that reflects both the time value of money and the uncertainty of receiving these future cash flows. We refer to this discount rate as the *yield*. The more uncertain the future cash flows, the greater the yield. It follows that the greater the yield, the lower the present value of the future cash flows—hence, the lower the value of the bond.

Most U.S. bonds pay interest semiannually, though European bonds often pay interest annually.[1] In Wall Street parlance, we use the term *yield-to-maturity* (YTM) to describe an annualized yield on a security if the security is held to maturity. For example, if a bond has a return of 5 percent over a six-month period, the annualized yield-to-maturity for a year is 2×5 percent, or 10 percent.[2] The yield-to-maturity, as commonly used on Wall Street, is the *bond equivalent yield*:

$$\text{Bond equivalent yield} = \text{6-month yield} \times 2$$

When we use the term "yield" in the context of bond valuation without any qualification, the intent is that this is the bond equivalent yield.

The present value of the maturity value is the present value of a lump sum, a future amount. In the case of a straight-coupon security, the present value of the interest payments is the present value of an annuity. In the case of a zero-coupon security, the present value of the interest payments is zero, so the present value of the bond is the present value of the maturity value.

Calculation Tip

We use the coupon rates to determine the cash flows from interest.
We use the yield to maturity to determine the discount rate.

We can rewrite the formula for the present value of a bond using some new notation and some familiar notation. Because there are two different cash flows—interest and maturity value—let PMT represent the coupon payment promised each period and M represent the maturity value. Also, let N indicate the number of periods until maturity, t to indicate a specific period, and r_d to indicate the six-month yield. The present value of a bond, V, is

$$V = \left[\sum_{t=1}^{N} \frac{\text{PMT}_t}{\left(1 + r_d\right)^t} \right] + \frac{M}{\left(1 + r_d\right)^N}$$

↑   ↑

Present value   Present value
of an annuity   of a lump-sum

The discount rate, r_d, indicates the required rate of return on the bond; that is, r_d is what investors require when they invest in this particular bond. To see how the valuation of future cash flows from debt securities works, let's look at the valuation of a straight-coupon bond and then a zero-coupon bond.

Why Do They Refer to Interest Payments as Coupons?

The interest payments are referred to as *coupons* because, in the days before electronic entries for bond ownership and the payment of interest, investors would need to clip a coupon from the bond itself and present it to receive their money. Each coupon had a date printed on it so the bond owner would know when it was time to clip it.

Valuing a Straight-Coupon Bond

Suppose you are considering investing in a straight coupon bond that:

Promises interest of 10 percent each year.
Promises to pay the principal amount of $1,000 at the end of 12 years.
Has a yield of 5 percent per year.

What is this bond worth today? We have the following data:

Interest = $100 every year
Number of years to maturity = 12
Maturity value = $1,000
Yield to maturity = 5% per year

Most U.S. bonds pay interest twice a year. Therefore, we adjust the given information for the fact that interest is semiannual, producing the following:

PMT = $100 ÷ 2 = $50
N = 12 × 2 = 24
M = $1,000
r_d = 5% ÷ 2 = 2.5%

$$V = \left[\sum_{t=1}^{24} \frac{\$50}{\left(1 + 0.025\right)^t} \right] + \frac{\$1,000}{\left(1 + 0.025\right)^{24}} = \$1,447.1246$$

This value is the sum of the value of the interest payments (an ordinary annuity consisting of 24 $50 payments, discounted at 2.5 percent) and the value of the maturity value (a lump sum of $1,000, discounted 24 periods at 2.5 percent), as we depict in the time line:

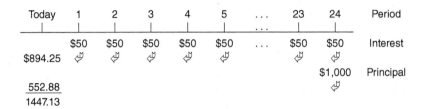

Using financial calculators or spreadsheets, we can perform this calculation in one step:

TI-83/84 Using TVM Solver	HP10B	Microsoft Excel
N = 24	1000 FV	=PV(0.025,24,50,1000)
I = 2.5	24 N	
PMT = 50	2.5 I/YR	
FV = 1000	50 PMT	
Solve for PV	PV	

Another way of representing the bond valuation is to state all the monetary inputs in terms of a percentage of the maturity value. Continuing this example, this requires the following:

$$PMT = 10 \div 2 = 5$$
$$N = 12 \times 2 = 24$$
$$M = 100$$
$$r_d = 5\% \div 2 = 2.5\%$$
$$V = \left[\sum_{t=1}^{24} \frac{5}{(1 + 0.025)^t} \right] + \frac{100}{(1 + 0.025)^{24}} = 144.71246$$

This produces a value that is in terms of a bond quote, which is a percentage of face value. For a $1,000 face value bond, this means that the present value is 144.71246% of the face value, or $1,447.1246.

Why bother with bond quotes? For two reasons: First, this is how you will see a bond's value quoted on any financial publication or website; second, this is a more general approach to communicating a bond's value and can be used regardless of the bond's face value. For example, if the bond has a face value of $500 (i.e., it's a baby bond), a bond quote of 101 translates into a bond value of $500 × 101% = $505.

TI-83/84 Using TVM Solver	HP10B	Microsoft Excel
N = 24	100 FV	=PV(0.025,24,5,100)
I = 2.5	24 n	
PMT = 5	2.5 I/YR	
FV = 100	PV	
Solve for PV		

PREMIUMS AND DISCOUNTS This bond has a present value greater than its maturity value, so we say that the bond is selling at a *premium* from its maturity value. Does this make sense? Yes: The bond pays interest of 10 percent of its face value every year. But what investors require on their investment—the capitalization rate considering the time value of money and the uncertainty of the future cash flows—is 5 percent.

So what happens? The bond paying 10 percent is attractive—so attractive that its price is bid upward to a price that gives investors the going rate, the 5 percent. In other words, an investor who buys the bond for $1,447.1246 will get a 5 percent return on it if it is held until maturity. We say that at $1,447.1246, the bond is priced to yield 5 percent per year.

Suppose that instead of priced to yield 5 percent, this bond is priced to yield 10 percent. What is the value of this bond?

$$PMT = \$100 \div 2 = \$50$$
$$N = 12 \times 2 = 24$$
$$M = \$1,000$$
$$r_d = 10\% \div 2 = 5\%$$

$$V = \left[\sum_{t=1}^{24} \frac{\$50}{(1+0.05)^t} \right] + \frac{\$1,000}{(1+0.05)^{24}} = \$1,000$$

TI-83/84 Using TVM Solver	HP10B	Microsoft Excel
N = 24	1000 FV	= PV(0.05,24,50,1000)
I = 5	24 n	
PMT = 50	5 I/YR	
FV = 1000	PV	
Solve for PV		

The bond's present value is equal to its face value and we say that the bond is selling "at par." Investors will pay face value for a bond that pays the going rate for bonds of similar risk. In other words, if you buy the 10 percent bond for $1,000.00, you will earn a 10 percent annual return on your investment if you hold it until maturity.

Suppose, instead, the interest on the bond is $20 every year—a 2 percent coupon rate. Now use the following data inputs:

$$PMT = \$20 \div 2 = \$10$$
$$N = 12 \times 2 = 24$$
$$M = \$1,000$$
$$r_d = 10\% \div 2 = 5\%$$

$$V = \left[\sum_{t=1}^{24} \frac{\$10}{(1+0.05)^t} \right] + \frac{\$1,000}{(1+0.05)^{24}} = \$448.0543$$

The bond sells at a *discount* from its face value. Why? Because investors are not going to pay face value for a bond that pays less than the going rate for bonds of similar risk. If an investor can buy other bonds that yield 5 percent, why pay the face value ($1,000 in this case) for a bond that pays only 2 percent? They wouldn't. Instead, the price of this bond would fall to a price that provides an investor earn a yield-to-maturity of 5 percent.

So when we look at the value of a bond, we see that its present value is dependent on the relation between the coupon rate and the yield. We can see this relation in our example: If the yield exceeds the bond's coupon rate, the bond sells at a discount from its maturity value and if the yield is less than the bond's coupon rate, the bond sells at a premium.

EXAMPLE 10.1 Suppose a bond has a $1,000 face value, a 10 percent coupon (paid semiannually), five years remaining to maturity, and is priced to yield 8 percent. What is its value? Answer: $1,081.14

One approach is to value the pieces separately:

The present value of the interest is $405.54 [PMT = 50; N = 10; i = 4%].
The present value of the maturity value is $675.60 [FV = 1000; N = 100; i = 4%]
Therefore, the value of the bond is $405.54 + 675.60 = $1,081.14.

Using a calculator, we can value this bond in one calculation with the following inputs:

i = 4%
N = 10
PMT = $50
FV = $1,000

We use these inputs to solve for the present value. Using Microsoft Excel's spreadsheet function, we would specify the function: = PV (.04,10,50,1000,0) and then multiply by negative 1.

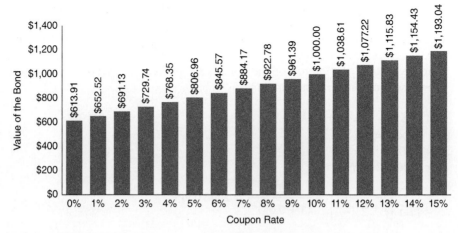

FIGURE 10.14 Value of a $1,000 Face-Value Bond That Has Five Years Remaining to Maturity and Is Priced to Yield 10 percent for Different Coupon Rates

EXAMPLE 10.2 As another example, consider a bond with five years remaining to maturity and is priced to yield 10 percent. If the coupon on this bond is 6 percent per year, the bond is priced at $845.57 (bond quote: 84.557). If the coupon on this bond is 14 percent per year, the bond is a premium bond, priced at $1,154.43 (bond quote: 115.443).

We illustrate the relation between this bond's value and its coupon in Figure 10.14.

Try It! 10.1: Bond Quotes

Complete the following table, specifying the value of the bond based on the quote and face value.

Bond	Quote	Face Value	Value of the Bond
A	103.45	$1,000	
B	98.00	$1,000	
C	89.50	$500	
D	110.00	$100,000	
E	90.00	€1000	
F	120.25	¥10,000	
G	65.45	$10,000	

DIFFERENT VALUE, DIFFERENT COUPON RATE, BUT SAME YIELD? The yield to maturity on a bond is the market's assessment of the time value and risk of the bond's cash flows. This yield will change constantly to reflect changes in interest rates in general, and it will also change as the market's perception of the debt issuer's risk changes.

At any point in time, a company may have several different bonds outstanding, each with a different coupon rate and bond quote. However, the yield on these bonds—at least those with similar other characteristics (e.g., seniority, security, indentures)—is usually the same or very close. This occurs because the bonds are issued at different times and with different coupons and maturity, but the yield on the bonds reflects the market's current perception of the risk of the bond and its time value.

Consider two bonds:

Bond A. A maturity value of $1,000, a coupon rate of 6 percent, 10 years remaining to maturity, and priced to yield 8 percent. Value = $864.0967.

Bond B. A maturity value of $1,000, a coupon rate of 12 percent, 10 years remaining to maturity, and priced to yield 8 percent. Value = $1,271.8065.

How can these bonds, one with a value of $864.0967 and another with a value of $1,271.8065, both give an investor a return of 8 percent per year if held to maturity? Bond B has a higher coupon rate than Bond A (12 percent versus 6 percent), yet it is possible for the bonds to provide the same return.

Bond B costs you more now, but also gets more interest each year ($120 versus $60). The extra $60 a year for 10 years makes up for the extra you pay now to buy the bond, considering the time value of money.

Same Bond, Different Yields, Hence Different Values

As interest rates change, the value of bonds changes in the opposite direction; that is, there is an inverse relation between bond prices and bond yields.

Let's look at another example, this time keeping the coupon rate the same, but varying the yield. Suppose we have a $1,000 face value bond with a 10 percent coupon rate that pays interest at the end of each year and matures in five years. If the yield is 5 percent, the value of the bond is

$$V = \$432.95 + \$783.53 = \$1,216.48$$

If the yield is 10 percent, the same as the coupon rate, the bond sells at face value:

$$V = \$379.08 + \$620.92 = \$1,000.00$$

If the yield is 15 percent, the bond's value is less than its face value:

$$V = \$335.21 + \$497.18 = \$832.39$$

When we hold the coupon rate constant and vary the yield, we see that there is a negative relation between a bond's yield and its value. We see a relation developing between the coupon rate, the yield, and the value of a bond:

If the coupon rate is more than the yield, the security is worth more than its face value—it sells at a premium.
If the coupon rate is less than the yield, the security is less that its face value—it sells at a discount.
If the coupon rate is equal to the yield, the security is valued at its face value.

We can see the relation between the annualized yield-to-maturity and the value of the 8 percent coupon bond in Figure 10.15. The greater the yield, the lower the present value of the bond. This makes sense since an increasing yield means that we are discounting the future cash flows at higher rates.

For a given bond, if interest rates go up, its price goes down; if interest rates go down, its price goes up.

EXAMPLE 10.3   Suppose we are interested in valuing a $1,000 face value bond that matures in five years and promises a coupon of 4 percent per year, with interest paid semiannually. This 4 percent coupon rate tells us that 2 percent, or $20, is paid every six months. What is the bond's value today if the annualized yield-to-maturity is 6 percent? 8 percent?

If the yield-to-maturity is 6 percent, the inputs to the calculation are:

Interest, PMT = $20 every six months
Number of periods, $N = 5$ times $2 = 10$ six-month periods

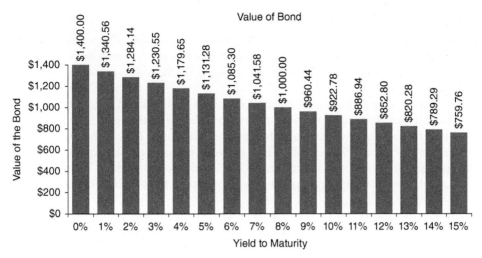

FIGURE 10.15   Value of a Five-Year, $1,000 Face Value Bond with an 8 percent Coupon for Different Yields to Maturity

Maturity value, M = $1,000

Yield, r_d = 6% ÷ 2 = 3% for six-month period and the value of the bond is $914.69797.

If the yield-to-maturity is 8 percent, the inputs to the calculation are:

Interest, PMT = $20 every six months

Number of periods, N = 5 times 2 = 10 six-month periods

Maturity value, M = $1,000

Yield, r_d = 8% ÷ 2 = 4% for six-month period and the value of the bond is $837.7821.

Try It! 10.2: Bond Values and Yields

Consider a bond that pays interest at the rate of 6 percent per year and has 10 years remaining to maturity. Calculate the value of the bond if its face value is $1,000 and the bond quote for the specific yields to maturity, completing this table:

Yield to Maturity	Value of Bond	Bond Quote
5%		
6%		
7%		
8%		

Valuing a Zero-Coupon Bond

A *zero-coupon bond* is a debt security issued without a coupon. Why would anyone ever buy a zero-coupon bond? Because they sell for deep discounts from the face value and you get your return from the increase in the value of the bond as it approaches maturity.

The value of a zero-coupon bond is easier to figure out than the value of a coupon bond. Let's see why. Suppose we are considering investing in a zero-coupon bond that matures in five years and has a face value of $1,000. If this bond does not pay interest—explicitly at least—no one will buy it at its face value. Instead, investors pay some amount less than the face value, with its return based on the difference between what they pay for it and, assuming they hold it to maturity, its maturity value.

If these bonds are priced to yield 10 percent, their present value is the present value of $1,000, discounted five years at 10 percent. We are given:[3]

$M = \$1,000$
$N = 10$
$r_d = 5\%$

Using financial calculators or a spreadsheet financial function:

TI-83/84 Using TVM Solver	HP10B	Microsoft Excel
N = 10	1000 FV	= PV(0.05,10,0,1000)
I = 5	10 N	
PMT = 0	5 I/YR	
FV = 1000	PV	
Solve for PV		

If a Zero-Coupon Bond Does Not Pay Interest, Why Use Two Compounding Periods a Year?

Perplexing, isn't it. If the zero-coupon bond does not pay interest, why do we use two compounding periods a year instead of one? That's because when we consider the available investments, we have a large number of coupon and zero-coupon bonds out there to invest in. If we want to evaluate these bonds based on what we can earn from them, we need to place their yields on a comparable basis. Convention has it—and likely because coupon bonds have been around longer and represent the vast majority of bonds—that we compare bonds on a bond equivalent yield basis. Hence, if we start with a YTM on a zero coupon bond, it's going to be a bond equivalent yield.

Does it make a difference? Yes. In our example with a 10 percent YTM on a five-year zero-coupon bond, we calculate a value of $613.91 using the correct method, but $620.92 using the incorrect method.

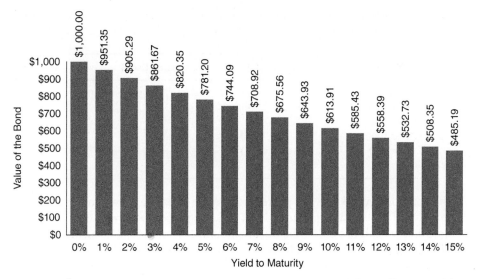

FIGURE 10.16   Value of a Five-Year Maturity Zero Coupon Bond for Different Yields to Maturity

The value of the bond is

$$V = \frac{\$1,000}{(1 + 0.05)^{10}} = \$613.91325$$

The price of the zero-coupon bond is sensitive to the yield: If the yield changes from 10 percent to 5 percent, the value of the bond increases from $613.91325 to $781.19840. We can see the sensitivity of the value of the bond's price over yields ranging from 1 percent to 15 percent in Figure 10.16.

CALCULATING THE YIELD TO MATURITY   In the previous section, we valued a bond, given a specific yield-to-maturity. But we are often concerned with the yield that is implied in a given bond's price. For example, what is the yield-to-maturity on a bond that has a current price of $900, has five years remaining to maturity, an 8 percent coupon rate, and a face value of $1,000? We have the following inputs:

$N = 10$
$PMT = \$40$
$M = \$1,000$
$V = \$900$

The six-month yield, r_d, is the discount rate that solves the following:

$$\$900 = \left[\sum_{t=1}^{10} \frac{\$40}{\left(1+r_d\right)^t} \right] + \frac{\$1,000}{\left(1+r_d\right)^{10}}$$

There is no direct solution, so we must use iteration.[4] In other words, without the help of a financial calculator or a spreadsheet, we would have to try different values of r_d until we cause the left- and right-hand sides of this equation to be equal.

Fortunately, calculators and spreadsheets make calculations much easier. Using a financial calculator or spreadsheet:

TI-83/84 Using TVM Solver	HP10B	Microsoft Excel
N = 10	1000 FV	= RATE(10,40,−900,1000)
PV = −900	900 +/−	
PMT = 40	PV	
FV = 1000	10 N	
Solve for I	40 PMT	
	I	

The six-month yield is 5.315 percent. Once we arrive at r_d, we multiply this by two to arrive at the yield-to-maturity: YTM = 5.315 percent × 2 = 10.63%.

Note that we can use either the dollar amounts (that is, $40, $1,000, and $900 for PMT, FV, PV, respectively) or in bond quote terms (that is, 4, 100, and 90 for PMT, FV, and PV, respectively) to solve for the six-month yield, that we then annualize. For example, using the bond quote terms, we calculate the YTM:

TI-83/84 Using TVM Solver	HP10B	Microsoft Excel
N = 10	100 FV	= RATE(10,4,−90,100,0)∗2
PV = −90	90 +/−	
PMT = 4	PV	
FV = 100	10 n	
Solve for i	4 PMT	
X 2	I	
	X 2	

The yield-to-maturity calculation is similar for a zero-coupon bond, with the exception that there is no interest: There is simply a present value, a future value, and a number of six-month periods. Again, we must multiply the rate from this calculation to produce the yield to maturity.

EXAMPLE 10.4   BD, Inc. has a bond outstanding with eight years remaining to maturity, a $1,000 face value, and a coupon rate of 8 percent paid semiannually. If the current market price is $880, what is the yield to maturity (YTM) on the BD bonds?

Given the following data inputs:

FV = $1,000
$N = 16$
PV = $880
PMT = $40

Solve for i:

$$i = 5.116434\%$$

$$YTM = 5.116434 \times 2 = 10.232868\%$$

EXAMPLE 10.5   Suppose a zero-coupon bond with five years remaining to maturity and a face value of $1,000 has a price of $800. What is the yield to maturity on this bond?

Given the following data inputs:

FV = $1,000
N = 10
PV = $800
PMT = $0

Solve for i:

$$i = 2.2565\%$$

$$YTM = 2.2565\% \times 2 = 4.5130\%$$

Try It! 10.3: Yields to Maturity

Consider a bond that pays interest at the rate of 6 percent per year, a face value of $1,000, and has 10 years remaining to maturity. Calculate the yield to maturity of the bond for the various bond values:

Bond Value	Yield to Maturity
$1,100	
$1,000	
$900	
$800	

Issues

CHANGES IN INTEREST RATES   We have already seen that value of a bond changes as the yield changes: If the yield increases, the bond's price decreases; if the yield decreases, the bond's price increases. Just how much a bond's value changes for a given yield change depends on the cash flows of the bond and the starting point, in terms of yield.

Consider the 8 percent coupon bond with five years to maturity that we saw earlier. If the yield changes from 5 percent to 6 percent, the price of the bond goes from $1,131.28 to $1,085.30; in percentage terms, the price declines 4.064 percent. But if the yield changes from 10 percent to 11 percent, the price changes from $922.78 to $886.94, a decline of 3.884 percent. In other words, this bond's price is more sensitive to yield changes for lower yields.

We can also compare bonds and their price sensitivities. Consider two bonds with the following characteristics:

Bond C. A 5 percent coupon bond with six years remaining to maturity and a face value of $1,000.

Bond D. Zero-coupon bond with six years remaining to maturity and a face value of $1,000.

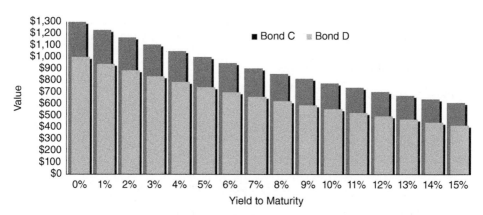

FIGURE 10.17   Value of Bonds with Six Years to Maturity: Bond C has a 5% Coupon and
Bond D is a Zero-Coupon Bond

Bond C is more valuable because it has the additional cash flows from interest,
relative to Bond D. But which bond's value is more sensitive to changes in yields? We
graph the value of each bond in Figure 10.17 for yields from 0 percent to 15 percent.
In percentage terms, the change in the price for a given yield change is greater for
the zero-coupon bond, Bond D, than the coupon bond; for example:

	Percentage Change in the Bond's Value	
Change in Yield	Bond C	Bond D
From 5% to 6%	−4.98%	−5.67%
From 8% to 9%	−4.84%	−5.59%
From 14% to 15%	−4.57%	−5.44%

This is because the entire cash flow for the zero-coupon bond is 12 periods into
the future, whereas the coupon bond has cash flows in the near periods as well,
which are not as affected by the yield change as the maturity value.

TIME PASSAGE   We have seen examples in this chapter so far of bonds that trade
at either a premium or a discount from their face values. This is usually the case:
Borrowers often issue bonds at or near their face value, but as time passes, yields
change and thus the value of the bond changes. Eventually, the value of the bond
must be equal to the maturity value.[5] If the yield holds constant throughout the life
the bond, the value of a bond approaches the maturity value as time passes. If the
yield changes during the life of the bond, the value still approaches the maturity
value as time passes, but perhaps not in a smooth path.

Consider a bond that has a 10 percent coupon, a maturity value of $1,000,
10 years (i.e., 20 periods) remaining to maturity, and is priced to yield 6 percent.
If the yield does not change until the bond matures, the price of the bond will
decline until it reaches $1,000, the maturity value, as shown in Figure 10.18. If this

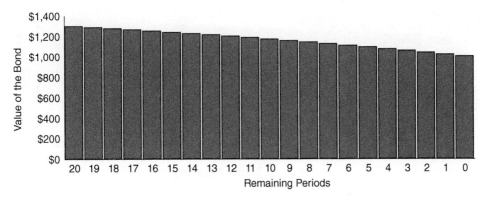

FIGURE 10.18   Value of a 10 percent Coupon, $1,000 Maturity Value Bond, with 10 Years to Maturity and Priced to Yield 6 percent

bond's yield changes, say to 4 percent with 10 periods remaining, the value adjusts appropriately (i.e., increasing) and the bond's value will decline towards $1,000 at maturity, as shown in Figure 10.19.

In a similar manner, a discount bond's value will increase over time, approaching the maturity value, as we show in Figure 10.20.

In Figure 10.21, We can see the convergence of the premium and discount bonds' values by comparing three bonds, each with a maturity of 20 years: a 4 percent coupon bond, a 6 percent coupon bond, and an 8 percent coupon bond.

REINVESTMENT RATE ISSUES   When we solve for the value of a bond for a given yield, or solve for a yield for a given bond's value, we are making an assumption about what we can do with the interest when we get it. You didn't have to do anything special to make this assumption: It is built into the mathematics.

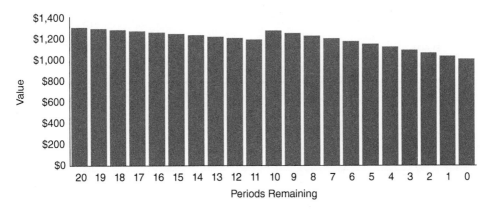

FIGURE 10.19   Value of a 10 percent Coupon, $1,000 Maturity Value Bond, with 10 Years to Maturity, and Priced to Yield 6 percent for the First Five Years and 4 percent for the Last Five Years

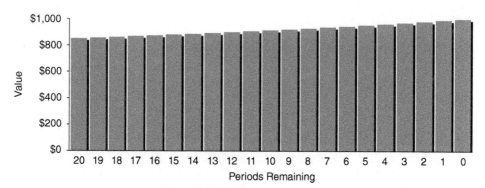

FIGURE 10.20   Value of a 4 percent Coupon, $1,000 Maturity Value Bond, with 10 Years to Maturity, and Priced to Yield 6 percent

To see this, let's use the generic valuation equation for a series of cash flows:

$$PV = \sum_{t=1}^{N} \frac{CF_t}{(1+i)^t}$$

We used the same discount rate for each period's cash flow. We allowed the cash flows to be different each period, but we specified one and only one discount rate. The mathematics that we use assumes that each CF_t we receive is reinvested at the rate i. We did the same in the bond valuation:

$$V = \left[\sum_{t=1}^{N} \frac{PMT_t}{(1+r_d)^t} \right] + \frac{M}{(1+r_d)^N}$$

We specified one and only one discount rate, r_d. Let's see why this is so—and why it may be an issue. Consider a bond that has a face value of $1,000, a coupon rate of 4 percent, is priced to yield 6 percent, and has two years remaining to maturity. The value of this bond is $962.83.

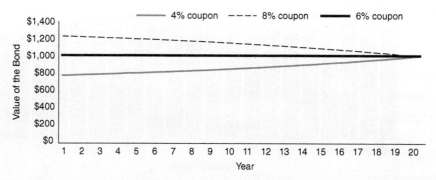

FIGURE 10.21   Comparison of Convergence of Values for Three 20-Year Bonds with Coupon Rates of 4 percent, 6 percent, and 8 percent, respectively, if the Yield to Maturity Remains at 6 percent throughout the Life of the Bonds

Now let's see how the math works on the reinvestment:

	Cash Flow	Calculation	Value at the End of Two Years
1st six-month period	$20	$(1 + 0.03)^3$	$21.85
2nd six-month period	$20	$(1 + 0.03)^2$	21.22
3rd six-month period	$20	$(1 + 0.03)^1$	20.60
4th six-month period	$1,020		1,020.00
			$1,083.67

With FV = $1,083.67; PV = $962.83; $N = 4$; the $r_d = 3$ percent and the yield to maturity is 6 percent. In other words, you will earn a return of 6 percent on your investment if you:

Buy the bond for $962.83 and hold it for two years.
Receive the coupon payments of $20 each.
Reinvest the coupons at 3 percent each six-month period, or 6 percent per year.

But what if you cannot earn 6 percent on your reinvested cash flows? What if returns on investments have changed and so have the reinvestment opportunities? In that case, your return will be something other than 6 percent.

What if the return that you can get on your reinvested cash flows is only 5 percent per year? In that case:

	Cash Flow	Calculation	Value at the End of Two Years
1st six-month period	$20	$(1 + 0.02)^3$	21.22
2nd six-month period	$20	$(1 + 0.02)^2$	20.81
3rd six-month period	$20	$(1 + 0.02)^1$	20.40
4th six-month period	$1,020		1,020.00
			$1,082.43

With FV = $1,082.43; PV = $962.83; $N = 4$; the $r_d = 2.97$ percent and the yield to maturity is 5.94 percent.

We call the risk that you will earn less than what is expected *reinvestment risk*, because reinvested coupons earn a yield different from what was expected. An investor investing in zero-coupon bonds does not have an exposure to reinvestment risk because there are no cash flows other than the initial purchase price and the maturity value.

Bottom line? The return earned by holding a security depends on not only the cash flows of the security itself, but what you can earn on any reinvested cash flows.

OTHER VALUATION ISSUES   A borrower could design a bond with any features that are necessary for the issuer's financial situation or creditors' demand. There are endless variations in debt securities' characteristics that may affect how we value the security. Consider a few of these characteristics:

Feature	Description	Valuation Considerations
Callable	At the discretion of the issuer, the bond may be bought back by the issuer at a specified price, according to a specified schedule.	The value of the security is the value of the straight bond, less the value of the option that the issuer possesses.
Convertible	At the discretion of the creditor, the bond may be exchanged for another security, such as a specified number of common shares.	The value of the security is the value of the straight bond, plus the value of the option to convert.
Deferred Interest	Interest scheduled such that it is not paid in the first few years, but begins sometime in the future.	The value of the security is the present value of the interest (a deferred annuity) and the face value.
Step-Up	The coupon rate of the bond changes from one rate to another, according to a pre-determined schedule.	The valuation requires valuing a coupon stream that is not constant, but rather changes at specific points in the security's life.

Other features include *security* (i.e., collateral), a *put option* (the investor's option to sell the security back to the issuer), a *sinking fund* (i.e., putting aside funds or periodically retiring the debt). A security issuer may combine these features, and others, in a given bond, making the valuation of the security quite challenging. Most of these features will affect the risk associated with the bond's future cash flows; for example, if the bond is secured, this reduces the risk of the bond's future cash flows because this collateral can be used to pay off the debt obligation.

Interest Rates

A casual examination of the financial news would be enough to convene the idea that nobody talks about an "interest rate." There are interest rates reported for borrowing money and for investing. These rates are not randomly determined; that is, there are factors that systematically affect how interest rates on different types of loans and debt instruments vary from each other.

The securities issued by the U.S. Department of the Treasury, popularly referred to as Treasury securities or simply Treasuries, are backed by the full faith and credit of the U.S. government.[6] Historically Treasury securities have served as the benchmark interest rates throughout the U.S. economy, as well as in international capital markets.[7]

Bonds that the U.S. Treasury do not back will have some risk of default, though for some bonds this is quite small. *Default risk* is the uncertainty that the issuer of the security is unable to make timely payments of interest and principal amount when promised. To get a better idea of what determines interest rate, let's ignore default risk for now and focus on the fundamentals.

We can think of interest rates providing compensation for the time value of money. The time value of money is compensation for not having use of the funds.

Within this interest rate are two components: the real interest rate and the expected rate of inflation:

Interest rate = Real interest rate + Expected rate of inflation

The real interest rate is what would exist in the economy in the absence of inflation. We generally look at interest rates with inflation expectations built into the rate. Consider interest rates on two securities:

Security A: 5.4 percent
Security B: 6.5 percent

The difference between the yields, or *spread*, is 1.1 percent.

Rather than refer to this spread in percentage terms, such as 1.1 percent, market participants refer to the difference in terms of basis points. A *basis point* is equal to 0.01 percent. Consequently, 1 percent is equal to 100 basis points. In our example, the spread of 1.1 percent is equal to 110 basis points.

Yield Curves

One of the influences of a bond's yield is the yield curve. The *yield curve* is the relation between the time remaining to maturity and the yield. We gauge the relation between yields and maturity by looking at the difference in yields for U.S. Treasuries. We do this so that we can look at interest rates for securities with different maturities, without having to worry about adjusting for differences in default risk. We refer to the difference in the yields at a point in time for U.S. Treasuries as the *maturity spread*.

Consider the yield curve that existed on these different dates:

Maturity	January 31, 2008	January 2, 2008	March 1, 2007	January 2, 2007
1 month	1.64%	3.09%	5.23%	4.79%
3 months	1.96%	3.26%	5.12%	5.07%
6 months	2.07%	3.32%	5.11%	5.11%
1 year	2.11%	3.17%	4.95%	5.00%
2 years	2.17%	2.88%	4.63%	4.80%
3 years	2.27%	2.89%	4.54%	4.71%
5 years	2.82%	3.28%	4.50%	4.68%
7 years	3.19%	3.54%	4.51%	4.68%
10 years	3.67%	3.91%	4.56%	4.68%
20 years	4.35%	4.39%	4.78%	4.87%
30 years	4.35%	4.35%	4.68%	4.79%

On January 2, 2007, the maturity spread for the 1-year and 30-year securities was 4.79% − 5% = −0.21% or −21 basis points, and the same spread on January 31, 2008, was 2.24 percent or 224 basic points.

We show the yield curves for two of these dates in a graph in Figure 10.22.

Yield curves may be upward sloping, downward sloping, flat, or even humped-shaped. The *normal yield curve* is upward sloping, with longer-maturity securities having higher yields than shorter-term securities. In other words, with the normal

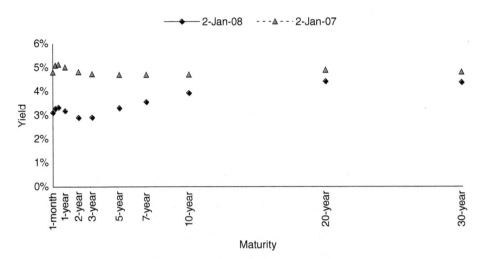

FIGURE 10.22   Yield Curves on U.S. Treasury Securities for Two Different Dates

curve, the maturity spreads are positive. The January 31, 2008, curve resembles a normal curve. However, the January 2, 2007, curve is an inverted curve, which means that, in general, the shorter-term securities had higher yields than the longer-term securities. In other words, the maturity spread is negative. Inverted curves, while unusual, are often a precursor to a recessionary economic period. It is also possible for the yield curve to be flat, which means that the yields do not differ based upon maturity.

A number of factors affect the yield curve, with the largest influence being the general economy. As we show in Figure 10.22, yield curves can shift, though more likely in the shorter-term securities. Though we depict yield curves using U.S. Treasury securities so that we can compare yields without having to worry about the effect of default risk on yields, corporate and municipal bond interest rates follow a similar pattern with respect to maturity: Longer-term securities generally have higher yields, though yields do change often.

INTEREST RATES AND CREDIT RISK   Debt instruments not issued or backed by the full faith and credit of the U.S. government are available in the market at an interest rate or yield that is different from an otherwise comparable maturity Treasury security. We refer to the difference between the interest rate offered on a non-Treasury security and a comparable maturity Treasury security as the *credit spread*. The credit spread exists because an investor is exposed to the additional risks with a security not issued by the U.S. government.

Default risk refers to the risk that the issuer of a debt obligation may be unable to make timely payment of interest and/or the principal amount when it is due.

Most market participants gauge credit risk in terms of ratings assigned by the three major commercial rating companies:

1. Moody's Investors Service
2. Standard & Poor's Corporation
3. Fitch Ratings

These companies, referred to as *rating agencies*, perform credit analyses of issuers and issues and express their conclusions by a system of ratings.

Let's see how credit risk affects spreads. For example, on August 5, 2008, the five-year Treasury yield was 3.29 percent and the same day the yield on five-year corporate bonds was as follows:[8]

Credit Rating	Yield
AAA	5.01%
AA	5.50%
A	5.78%

Therefore, the credit spreads were:

Credit Rating	Credit Spread
AAA	5.01% − 3.29% = 1.72% = 172 basis points
AA	5.50% − 3.29% = 2.21% = 221 basis points
A	5.78% − 3.29% = 2.49% = 249 basis points

Note that the lower the credit rating, the higher the credit spread.

EXAMPLE 10.6 Consider the following two bonds, as of February 2006:[9]

1. Verizon Communications: 5.55 percent coupon, with a yield of 5.492 percent and a bond rating of A.
2. Boise Cascade Corporation: 7.35 percent coupon, with a yield of 7.284 percent and a bond rating of BB.

Both bonds mature at the same time and have similar features (in this case, both are noncallable and nonconvertible, fixed-rate bonds). A similar maturity U.S. Treasury bond has a yield of 4.653 percent.

What is the credit spread of each bond?

Answer:

Verizon Communications: 5.55% − 4.653% = 0.847% or 84.7 basis points.

Boise Cascade: 7.35% − 4.653% = 2.697% or 269.7 basis points.

Bond Ratings and Yields

Bond rating agencies, such as Standard & Poor's, Moody's, and Fitch, provide a rating of the creditworthiness of bonds. The more default risk, the lower the rating. The rating systems used by the three major ratings services are similar, but the ratings don't always agree. As an example of ratings, consider Standard & Poor's system from AAA to D:[10]

	Rating	Description
	AAA	Capacity of issuer to meet obligations is extremely strong.
	AA	Capacity of issuer to meet obligations is very strong.
	A	Capacity of issuer to meet obligations is strong, but this capacity is susceptible to unfavorable economic conditions.
Investment Grade	BBB	Issuer has adequate capacity, but is vulnerable to adverse conditions.
	BB	Debt is speculative, with ongoing uncertainties that may affect the ability of the issuer to meet its obligations.
	B	Debt is speculative and vulnerable to adverse conditions that may result in nonpayment of obligations.
	CCC	Debt is speculative and currently susceptible to adverse conditions.
	CC	Issuer is likely to be unable to meet obligations.
	C	Obligations are highly vulnerable to nonpayment, payments are currently not being made, or the issuer is in bankruptcy.
Noninvestment-Grade (Junk) Bonds	D	Obligation is in default.

We can see the difference in the yields for different levels of risk by looking at a snapshot of yields on December 24, 2008:

Maturity	U.S. Treasury Bonds	Corporate AAA-Rated Bonds	Corporate A-Rated Bonds
5 years	1.54%	3.48%	4.97%
10 years	2.20%	4.82%	5.30%
20 years	2.94%	5.12%	5.73%

OTHER INFLUENCES ON INTEREST RATES AND YIELDS   We refer to the difference between a security's interest rate or yield and a Treasury security with the same maturity as the *risk premium*. The general factors that affect the risk premium between a non-Treasury security and a Treasury security with the same maturity, other than credit risk, include:

Any features provided for in the non-Treasury security that make them attractive or unattractive to investors, such as a call or conversion feature.
The tax treatment of the interest income from the non-Treasury security.
The ability of the investor to sell the security close to its true value.[11]

Therefore, it is possible that you can observe, for example, two bonds with similar ratings and maturity that have different yields because one bond is callable and the other one is not.

Summary

The valuation of bonds is an application of the time value of money mathematics. The key is to take the bond's characteristics (i.e., coupon, maturity value) and translate them into inputs for the financial mathematics.

Bond valuation can get more complicated than what we've discussed in this reading because issuers have a great deal of flexibility in designing these securities, but any feature that an issuer includes in the bond is usually just a simple extension of asset valuation principles and mathematics.

"Try It!" Solutions

10.1 Bond Quotes

Bond	Quote	Face Value	Value of Bond[12]
A	103.45	$1,000	$1,034.50
B	98.00	$1,000	$980.00
C	89.50	$500	$447.50
D	110.00	$100,000	$110,000
E	90.00	€1000	€900,000
F	120.25	¥10000	¥12,025
G	65.45	$10,000	$6,545

10.2 Bond Values and Yields

Yield to Maturity	Value of Bond	Bond Quote
5%	$1,077.95	107.795
6%	$1,000.00	100.000
7%	$928.94	92.894
8%	$864.10	86.410

10.3 Yields to Maturity

Bond Value	Yield to Maturity
$1,100	4.733%
$1,000	6.000%
$900	7.435%
$800	9.087%

Notes

1. You should assume all bonds pay interest semiannually unless specified otherwise.
2. But is this the effective yield-to-maturity? Not quite. This annualized yield does not take into consideration the compounding within the year if the bond pays interest more than once per year.
3. You will notice that we still convert the number of years into the number of six-month periods and we convert the yield to maturity to a six-month yield. This is because the convention for reporting yields on bonds, whether coupon or zero-coupon, is to assume an annualized yield that is the six-month yield multiplied by two.
4. That is, we cannot algebraically manipulate this equation to produce r_d on the left-hand side and the remainder on the right-hand side of the equation and solve.
5. Otherwise there would be a windfall gain or a large loss to someone owning the bond just prior to maturity.
6. At the time of this writing, most market participants view U.S. Treasuries as being free of default risk, although there is the possibility that unwise economic policy by the U.S. government may alter that perception.
7. Yet there are other important benchmarks used by market participants, such as the London Interbank Offered Rate (LIBOR).
8. The data is from finance.yahoo.com reported (based on information supplied by ValuBond).
9. *Source: Yahoo!Finance*, February 13, 2006.
10. For more information, check out the Standard & Poor's Ratings Definitions, available at RatingsDirect.com and StandardandPoors.com.
11. We refer to the ability to get a security's true value in the market as liquidity. The greater the chance of getting close to its true value when you sell the security, the better the liquidity.
12. Note that a comma is used in European math conventions, which is different from the U.S. convention of a decimal place.

CHAPTER **11**

Foreign Exchange Market

In a global financial marketplace where transactions take place using many different currencies, currency risk must be understood, measured, and appropriately managed by investment advisors and consultants. This chapter will review the world's largest financial market, the foreign exchange market, and discuss how risk may be managed and how opportunities may be captured.

Part I *Handbook of Finance:* An Introduction to Spot Foreign Exchange

Learning Objectives
- Describe how the foreign exchange (FX) market works and how transactions take place.
- List and describe the three types of foreign exchange exposures.
- Explain the five basic foreign exchange products including: spot transactions, forward contracts, foreign exchange futures contracts, foreign exchange swaps, and currency options.
- Describe how advisors and investors use these products to manage risk and/or enhance return.

Part II *Handbook of Finance:* Currency Overlay

Learning Objectives
- Describe and differentiate between full or unitary hedging, partial hedging, over-hedging, and cross-hedging.
- Discuss who should invest in a currency overlay.
- Describe common overlay strategies including: currency alpha, carry strategies, momentum strategies, flow strategies, valuation strategies, and quantitative currency overlay.
- Discuss the concept of strategy weighting and portfolio optimization.

Part I An Introduction to Spot Foreign Exchange

The foreign exchange market is by far the largest market in the world, and although the world's currency markets are generally thought of as the exclusive domain of the largest banks and multinational corporations, nothing could be further from the truth. Even though major currencies are traded like commodities, it is distinguished from both the commodity or equity markets by having no fixed base. In other words, the foreign exchange market exists through communications and information systems consisting of telephones, the Internet, or other means of instant communications, for example, Reuters and Bloomberg. The foreign exchange market is not located in a building, nor is it limited by fixed trading hours, but is truly a 24-hour global trading system. It knows no barriers and trading activity in general moves with the sun from one major financial center to the next—so that around the clock a foreign exchange market is active somewhere in the world. Because of this decentralization, the total size of the foreign exchange market can only be guessed at. The foreign exchange market is an over-the-counter market where buyers and sellers conduct business. Many of the traders in the markets have all started with this simplest of products: just buy low and sell high, or sell high and buy low. Thus, the foreign exchange market is a global network of buyers and sellers of currencies with a foreign exchange transaction being a contract to exchange one currency for another currency at an agreed rate on an agreed date. Today, what began as a way of facilitating trade across country borders has grown into one of the most liquid, hectic, and volatile financial markets in the world—where banks (and many hedge funds) are the major players and have the potential of generating huge profits or losses.

The foreign exchange (FX) market includes the cash market and the FX derivatives market. The focus in this chapter is on the cash market, which is more commonly referred to as the spot foreign exchange market.

A foreign exchange, or currency rate, is simply the price of one country's money in terms of another's. Although exchange rates are affected by many factors, in the end, currency prices are a result of supply-and-demand forces. The world's currency markets can be viewed as a huge melting pot: In a large and ever-changing mix of current events, supply-and-demand factors are constantly shifting, and the price of one currency in relation to another shifts accordingly. No other market encompasses as much of what is going on in the world at any given time as foreign exchange.

Approximately 80 percent of foreign exchange transactions have a dollar leg. The dollar plays such a large role in the markets because:

It is used as an investment currency throughout the world.
It is a reserve currency held by many central banks.
It is a transaction currency in many international commodity markets.
Monetary bodies use it as an intervention currency for operations in their own currencies.

The most widely traded currency pairs are:

The American dollar against the Japanese yen (USD/JPY)
The European euro against the American dollar (EUR/USD)
The British pound against the American dollar (GBP/USD)
The American dollar against the Swiss franc (USD/CHF)

In general, EUR/USD is by far the most traded currency pair and has captured approximately 30 percent of the global turnover. It is followed by USD/JPY with 20 percent and GBP/USD with 11 percent. Of course, most national currencies are represented in the foreign exchange market, in one form or another. Most currencies operate under floating exchange rate mechanisms against one another. The rates can rise or fall depending largely on economic, political, and military situations in given country.

The basic information and common definitions of foreign exchange and the foreign exchange market follow:

> *Foreign exchange market* is a global network of buyers and sellers of currencies.
> *Foreign exchange* or *FX* is the exchange of one currency for another.
> *Foreign exchange rate* is the price of one currency expressed in terms of another currency.
> *Foreign exchange transaction* is a contract to exchange one currency for another currency at an agreed rate on an agreed date.
> *Spot exchange rate* is the ratio at which one currency is exchanged for another for settlement in two business days (value date)

Foreign Exchange Exposure

By way of explanation, foreign exchange exposure is the risk of financial impact due to changes in foreign exchange rates and, in general, there are three types of foreign exchange exposures:

1. Transactions exposures principally impact a company's profit and loss and cash flow and result from transacting business in a currency or currencies different from the company's home currency.
2. Translation exposures principally impact a company's balance sheet and result from the translation of foreign assets and liabilities into the company's home currency for accounting purposes.
3. Economic exposures relate to a company's exposure to foreign markets and suppliers. More difficult to identify, economic exposure is sometimes also referred to as competitive, strategic, or operational exposure.

There are actually five basic foreign exchange products:

1. Spot transactions
2. Forward contracts
3. Foreign exchange futures contracts
4. Foreign exchange swaps
5. Currency options

The last four are referred to as foreign exchange derivative contracts.

Basic Uses

The basic uses of foreign exchange products include the following:

> For settlement and funding in order to convert cash from one currency into another for commercial transactions (e.g., import or export payables or receivables) or to convert capital flows (e.g. dividends, inter-company loans, and investments)

To hedge/manage foreign exchange exposures caused by the passage of time
and exchange rate fluctuations

For arbitrage to take advantage of short-term discrepancies between prices in
different currencies or marketplaces

For investment to take advantage of changing exchange rates and interest rates
and to optimize all components of a global investment strategy

To speculate so as to take advantage of anticipated exchange rate changes

In actual terms for spot transactions, client groups, such as corporations,
investors, funds, and institutions, will use spot transactions as part of their foreign
exchange management programs. Speculators will also use this market because it is
an extremely active and liquid market with roughly two-thirds of all foreign exchange
activity being traded. There can be plenty of movement (volatility) in any one day,
which will enable a speculator to possibly benefit from such gyrations.

Spot Foreign Exchange

Foreign exchange rates are a means of expressing the value and worth of one economy as expressed by its currency as compared to that of another. Normal market
usage is to quote the exchange rate for spot value, that is, for delivery two business
days from the trade date (except Canadian transactions against the dollar, where the
spot date is only one day). The two business days are normally required in order to
get the trade information between the counterparties involved agreed and to process
the funds through the local clearing systems. The two payments are made on the
same date, regardless of the time zone difference.

Figure 11.1 provides an example of a foreign exchange transaction.

SPOT AND RECIPROCAL RATES   The rate used in a spot deal is the spot rate and is
the price at which one currency can be bought or sold, expressed in terms of the
other currency, for delivery on the spot value date. The spot exchange rate can be
expressed in either currency; thus, this price has two parts, the base currency and
the equivalent number of units of the other currency. For example, a rate for the
U.S. dollar ($ or USD) against the Swiss franc (CHF) would be quoted as 1.2507 on
July 25, 2006. (We will use exchange rates on this date throughout the chapter.) This
means there are 1.2507 francs to $1. When one rate is known, the spot exchange

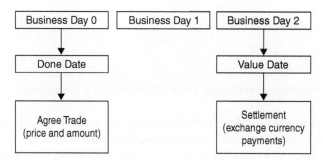

FIGURE 11.1   Example of a Foreign Exchange Transaction

rate expressed in the other currency (the reciprocal) is easily calculated. The price of $1, expressed in Swiss francs, is 1/$0.7996 or CHF 1.2507.

Although some newspapers calculate and publish both exchange rates, it has become standard market practice among traders to quote foreign exchange for most currencies as the amount of foreign currency that will be exchanged for $1. For example, if a bank trader were asked to quote a rate for Swiss francs against the dollar, the response would most likely be CHF 1.2507 rather than $0.7996. In this case, $1 is the traded commodity and the trader is quoting the price in Swiss francs. This type of quotation is known as European terms.

It should be noted that the U.S. dollar is the most popularly traded currency because it is the primary currency for international trade and official reserves (although the Euro is rapidly catching the U.S. dollar as a reserve currency). Therefore, the most frequently quoted exchange rates and the most liquid markets are those between dollars and various foreign currencies.

Risk Considerations

It must be remembered that there are risks with spot transactions. First, there is credit risk. Like the risk a bank incurs when making a loan, a foreign exchange contract poses the risk that the client will not perform according to the terms of the contract (that is, will not deliver the appropriate currency on time). In a foreign exchange transaction, the market maker and the client agree that each will deliver to the other a specified amount of a currency on a specific date, at an agreed rate. Trading the currencies of countries that are in different time zones compounds this risk.

Second, there is market/price risk. Trading in any currency has a degree of risk. Exchange rate risk is inevitable because currency values rise and fall constantly in response to market pressures. When engaging in a foreign exchange trade, the client's position is open until it is closed or covered. While that position is open, the client is exposed to the risk of changes in exchange rates. A few moments can transform a potentially profitable transaction into a loss.

Third, there is country risk. Some countries (and their currencies) are more risky than others. Country risk may be due to anything from governmental regulations and restrictions to political situations, or the amount of foreign currency reserves the country has. However, this risk is usually of less significance.

The spot exchange risk is shown graphically in Figure 11.2.

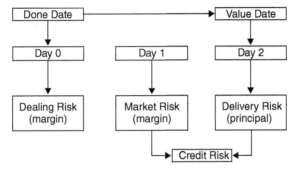

FIGURE 11.2   Spot Exchange Risk

Part II Currency Overlay

Currency risk has long been seen as the dark side of international diversification as investors realized that currency risk is always on top of asset risk. The one month return of a U.S.-based investor for buying German government bonds will be driven by movements in the German yield curve (interest rate risk) plus changes in the $/€ rate (currency risk). If left unmanaged, the diversification of interest rate risk would come at the expense of increased total risk. As a result of this the business of currency overlay management developed focusing on managing the added currency risk from international diversification.

Currency overlay management was born. It first started (in the 1980s) as a more or less passive hedging exercise. In today's language we call these risk or beta overlays. The main question at that time was: how much of the currency risk should be hedged back into the home currency? This hedge ratio was then maintained by an overlay manager such that the underlying bond and equity managers could focus on selecting bonds and stocks without having to give consideration to the currency implications. However, it did not take long until the advent of a more specialist and active approach to currency management. Paired with a trend toward outsourcing and a stronger focus on the separation between passive exposure and active management, this proved to be a catalyst for active currency overlay managers. The allocation of long short currency positions around a strategic currency benchmark became mainstream. Currencies moved from the dark side to the bright side of investing. Nowadays, a whole auxiliary business has developed around currency overlay management, ranging from consultants and investment boutiques to providers of specialized currency indices.

What is a *currency overlay*? Let us go through an example in Table 11.1. Let us assume an equally weighted physical investment into Australian, Canadian, Swiss, and European equity markets for a dollar-based investor. This resembles the asset benchmark (line 1). Suppose the investor runs a tactical equity overlay with positions implemented using long short future contracts (line 2). As a future contract is effectively long the local risk premium there is no currency risk (other than the profit-and-loss [P&L] risk) involved and while the total equity allocation changes (line 3), the currency exposure remains unchanged (line 4) relative to the physical equity investment. Note that only physical investment will create currency exposure. If the

TABLE 11.1 Currency Overlay Management

	AUD	CAD	CHF	EUR	USD	Σ
Equity Benchmark	25%	25%	25%	25%	0%	100%
Tactical Equity Overlay	−5%	5%	−10%	−10%	20%	0%
Equity Allocation	20%	30%	15%	15%	20%	100%
Currency Exposure	25%	25%	25%	25%	0%	100%
Currency Risk Overlay	−20%	−20%	−20%	−20%	80%	0%
Currency Benchmark	5%	5%	5%	5%	80%	100%
Currency Alpha Overlay	−5%	+10%	−15%	−5%	15%	0%
Total Exposure	0%	15%	−10%	0%	95%	100%

U.S. investor feels she is taking too much currency risk she could hedge 80 percent of the currency risk (assume for simplicity equally distributed around currencies) into the USD using forward contracts. This risk overlay (line 5) would create a new currency exposure of 80 percent USD and 5 percent in each other currency that is equivalent to the new benchmark for active currency management (line 6).

On top of all this the investor wants an active risk overlay to be implemented (line 7). We again assume for simplicity that all positions are implemented using forwards and no initial cash is needed. The active positions range from –15 percent to +15 percent. If we combine active and passive overlay, we arrive at a 15 percent exposure in CAD, a net 10 percent short in CHF, and the remaining currency exposure repatriated into USD (line 8). Revisiting Table 11.1 we see that all overlays are long short portfolios adding up to a zero initial cash investment (0 percent entries). To the extent that net short positions are created, overlays will create leverage. The following sections will show how to optimally derive risk (beta) overlays as well as active (alpha) overlays.

The Mathematics of Currency Overlay Management

SOME CONVENTIONS   Currency overlay management deals with the complicated interactions between currency returns and local asset returns. The overlay manager will routinely be asked questions like: "How much currency exposure should be hedged" and "Which currencies should be hedged?" We therefore need to build a theoretically sound framework to address these questions. In the terminology that follows we build on Jorion (1994) and distinguish between excess asset returns and excess currency returns. Asset excess returns (a_i) for market i (out of k markets) are given by

$$a_i = r_i + s_i - c_h \qquad (11.1)$$

where r_i, s_i, c_h denote local asset return, currency spot return, and home currency cash return (that is, the excess return is relative to domestic cash). Given that investing in foreign currencies is equivalent to investing in foreign cash we can write the currency excess (e_i) return as

$$e_i = c_i + s_i - c_h \qquad (11.2)$$

While equation (11.1) describes a 100 percent unhedged position, we can express a 100 percent hedged position (unitary hedge) as equivalent to a long exposure in (11.1) and a short exposure in (11.2). Combining (11.1) and (11.2) for $h = 1$ we arrive at

$$a_i = (r_i + s_i - c_h) - (c_i + s_i - c_h) = r_i - c_i \qquad (11.3)$$

In other words, hedged returns are equivalent to a locally funded position (e.g., by borrowing in the local repo market). A position like this is also automatically generated, if we invest into a foreign market using futures or total return swaps. We can now ask ourselves how currency hedging affects total risk. Suppose we search for the optimal, that is, risk (variance)-minimizing hedge ratio, h. Hedging a fraction h of asset excess returns, we arrive at

$$a_{i\backslash h} = (r_i + s_i - c_h) - h(c_i + s_i - c_h) \qquad (11.4)$$

Here, $a_{i\backslash h}$ denotes the asset excess returns after hedging. Imposing the variance operator on (11.4) and realizing that all cash rates have zero variance and covariance (as they are known at the beginning of the investment period), we get

$$\text{Var}(a_{i\backslash h}) = \text{Var}(r_i) + (1 - h)^2 \text{Var}(s_i) + 2(1 - h)\text{Cov}(r_i, s_i) \qquad (11.5)$$

The optimal (variance minimal) hedge ratio can now be found by minimizing (11.5). We set

$$\frac{d\text{Var}(a_{i\backslash h})}{dh} = 0 \qquad (11.6)$$

Note that all this is done under the assumption of a zero expected excess return on currencies, that is, $E(e_i) = 0$. This allows us to focus solely on risk. After some manipulations, we arrive at

$$h = 1 + \frac{\text{Cov}(r_i, s_i)}{\text{Var}(s_i)} \qquad (11.7)$$

The variance minimal hedge ratio is centered around 1 and is dependent on the covariance between currency returns and asset returns. The next section will explain (11.7) intuitively.

CURRENCY HEDGING TAXONOMY

Full or Unitary Hedging   We start with the case where $\text{Cov}(r_i, s_i) = 0$ in (11.7). In this instance currency returns are uncorrelated to asset returns and the optimal hedge ratio becomes $h = 1$ or 100 percent. Currency risk comes on top of asset risk and cannot be used to hedge out some of the underlying asset risk. Some practitioners argue with zero correlation and zero expected return currencies effectively become a "wash" and as such currency hedging becomes irrelevant. While this is true from an expected return perspective, it is painfully wrong from a risk perspective. Even if we expect the average return to be close to zero, there is substantial risk it will randomly deviate from zero.

Partial Hedging   If, however, $\text{Cov}(r_i, s_i) < 0$, that is, each positive local market return is more likely accompanied by a negative currency return, maintaining some currency exposure is desirable, that is, $h < 1$. This might be the case for a foreign bond investment, where falling interest rates create positive bond returns at the expense of an unattractive carry (and therefore falling currency) in the foreign exchange market. Alternatively, this might arise in a small export economy where a fall in the exchange rate spurs an export-led stock market rally. Hedging 100 percent currency risk is no longer optimal. If $\text{Cov}(r_i, s_i)$ is substantially negative, hedging can even increase risk.

Overhedging   In case currency returns and local returns tend to move in the same direction, that is, $\text{Cov}(r_i, s_i) > 0$, currency exposure amplifies the range of total returns (asset and currency) and the optimal hedge ratio becomes $h > 1$. The preceding taxonomy is summarized in Figure 11.3.

Cross-Hedging   What if we cannot hedge currency exposure directly due to foreign exchange controls? Let us use the idea behind (11.4) to (11.7) in order to derive

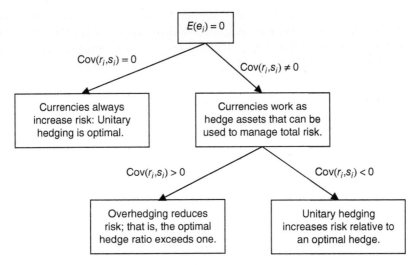

FIGURE 11.3 Currency Hedging Taxonomy

the optimal cross-hedge. Hedging asset returns in currency i with a closely related currency j (liquidity concerns, capital controls) leads to:

$$a_{i\backslash h} = (r_i + s_i - c_h) - h(c_j + s_j - c_h) \tag{11.8}$$

Imposing again the variance operator on (11.8) and taking the first derivative with respect to h, we get the optimal cross-hedge ratio.

$$h = \frac{\text{Cov}(s_i, s_j)}{\text{Var}(s_j)} + \frac{\text{Cov}(r_i, s_i)}{\text{Var}(s_j)} \tag{11.9}$$

Note first that (11.9) looks similar to (11.7). The first term will be close to one for all currencies that are closely correlated and have similar volatilities, while the second term reflects the deviation from a unitary hedge as indicated above.

BASIC OVERLAY MODEL   Following the preceding definitions, we can summarize all information about the covariance between excess asset and excess currency returns in a combined covariance matrix

$$\Omega = \begin{bmatrix} \Omega_{aa} & \Omega_{ae} \\ \Omega_{ae}^T & \Omega_{ee} \end{bmatrix} \tag{11.10}$$

where Ω_{aa} denotes the $k \times k$ covariance matrix of excess asset returns as defined in (11.10), while Ω_{ee} is the $k \times k$ covariance matrix of excess currency returns. As we implicitly assumed the number of assets equals the number of currencies, we summarize the information about asset and currency covariances in Ω_{ae}, which is also of dimension $k \times k$. Currency hedging is assumed to follow *regression hedging;* that is, the excess asset returns are regressed against all currency excess returns to capture cross correlation effects as in (11.11).

$$a_i = h_{i,1}e_1 + h_{i,2}e_2 + \dots + h_{i,k}e_k + \varepsilon_i \tag{11.11}$$

For example: an investment in U.S. commodity-related (oil) stocks is likely to be correlated with commodity currencies (Australian dollar [AUD], Canadian dollar [CAD], or New Zealand dollar [NZD]), making several coefficients in (11.11) significant. The outcome of all k hedging regressions can be summarized in the $k \times k$ matrix h of exposures

$$h = \Omega_{ae} \times \Omega_{ee}^{-1} \tag{11.12}$$

The risk after currency hedging is given by

$$\Omega_{a|e} = \Omega_{aa} - h^T \cdot \Omega_{ee} \cdot h \tag{11.13}$$

This defaults to (11.4) in the case of a single currency. Using the results for the inverse of a partitioned matrix as in Greene (2002), we can rewrite (11.10) as

$$\Omega^{-1} = \begin{bmatrix} \Omega_{a|e}^{-1} & \Omega_{a|e}^{-1} h^T \\ -h\Omega_{ae}^{-1} & \Omega_{ee}^{-1} + h\Omega_{a|e}^{-1}h^T \end{bmatrix} \tag{11.14}$$

Finally, we need to define the vector of asset and currency weights $\mathbf{w}^T = [\mathbf{w}_a \quad \mathbf{w}_e]$ as well as the vector of expected asset and currency excess returns $\mu^T = [\mu_a \quad \mu_e]$. We further assume a mean variance investor that attempts to maximize $U = \mathbf{w}^T \cdot \mu - \frac{1}{2\lambda}\mathbf{w}^T \cdot \Omega \cdot \mathbf{w}$, where λ summarizes risk preferences. The well-known solution is given by $\mathbf{w}^* = \lambda \cdot \Omega^{-1} \cdot \mu$. First, note that we do not need a full investment constraint such as $\mathbf{w}^T \mathbf{1} = 1$. The risk-free asset c_h can always be added or subtracted to generate a fully invested portfolio as cash adds neither risk nor excess return. Second, we can interpret the parameter λ as leverage. Efficient portfolios for investors with different risk aversion will not differ with respect to their relative weights but rather with respect to the scale of the positions taken.

FULLY INTERDEPENDENT SOLUTION   The optimal solution to currency overlay management is given as the simultaneous optimization of both asset as well as currency positions, taking full advantage of all information contained in the covariance matrix of asset and currency returns.

$$\mathbf{w}_{FIS}^* = \lambda\Omega^{-1} \cdot \begin{bmatrix} \mu_a \\ \mu_e \end{bmatrix} = \begin{bmatrix} \mathbf{w}_{a,FIS}^* \\ \mathbf{w}_{e,FIS}^* \end{bmatrix}$$

$$= \begin{bmatrix} \lambda\left(\Omega_{a|e}^{-1} \cdot \mu_a - \Omega_{a|e}^{-1} \cdot h^T \cdot \mu_e\right) \\ \lambda\Omega_{ee}^{-1} \cdot \mu_e - h \cdot \mathbf{w}_{a,FIS}^* \end{bmatrix} \tag{11.15}$$

In the fully interdependent solution we can decompose the optimal currency position into a speculative demand (dependent on both risk aversion as well as expected returns) as well as a hedging demand.

$$\mathbf{w}_{e,FIS}^* = \underbrace{\lambda\Omega_{ee}^{-1} \cdot \mu_e}_{\substack{\text{Speculative} \\ \text{demand}}} - \underbrace{h \cdot \mathbf{w}_{a,FIS}^*}_{\substack{\text{Hedging} \\ \text{demand}}} \tag{11.16}$$

If expected currency returns in (11.2) are substantial, so will the corresponding speculative demand. The hedging demand will in general be negative and depends on the underlying positions of the optimal asset portfolio. To shed further light on the mechanics of overlay investing, we will, as in the previous section, assume that expected currency returns are zero, that is, $\mu_e = 0$. In this case, we find

$$\mathbf{w}_{FIS}^* = \lambda \mathbf{\Omega}^{-1} \cdot \begin{bmatrix} \mu_a \\ 0 \end{bmatrix} = \begin{bmatrix} \mathbf{w}_{a,FIS}^* \\ \mathbf{w}_{e,FIS}^* \end{bmatrix} = \begin{bmatrix} \lambda \mathbf{\Omega}_{a|e}^{-1} \cdot \mu_a \\ -\mathbf{h} \cdot \mathbf{w}_{a,FIS}^* \end{bmatrix} \qquad (11.17)$$

Not surprisingly, the demand for currency exposure is entirely driven by hedging considerations. Suppose now that $\mathrm{Cov}(r_i, s_j) = 0$ for all currencies j. What does that do to $\mathbf{\Omega}_{ae}$ and $\mathbf{\Omega}_{a|e}$? We start with observing that in the previous case is $\mathrm{Cov}(a_i, e_j) = \mathrm{Cov}(r_i + s_i, s_j) = \mathrm{Cov}(s_i, s_j)$. As a consequence, $\mathbf{\Omega}_{ea} = \mathbf{\Omega}_{ee} \Rightarrow \mathbf{h} = \mathbf{\Omega}_{ea} \cdot \mathbf{\Omega}_{ee}^{-1} = 1_{k \times k}$ and the optimal currency position will be mirroring asset exposures.

$$\mathbf{w}_{FIS}^* = \lambda \mathbf{\Omega}^{-1} \cdot \begin{bmatrix} \mu_a \\ 0 \end{bmatrix} = \begin{bmatrix} \mathbf{w}_{a,FIS}^* \\ \mathbf{w}_{e,FIS}^* \end{bmatrix} = \begin{bmatrix} \lambda \mathbf{\Omega}_{a|e}^{-1} \cdot \mu_a \\ -\mathbf{w}_{a,FIS}^* \end{bmatrix} \qquad (11.18)$$

Finally, assume currency returns and local asset returns show negative enough correlation to compensate for currency volatility, respective covariance. In this case we require that covariance terms add to zero: $\mathrm{Cov}(a_i, e_j) = \mathrm{Cov}(r_i + s_i, s_j) = \mathrm{Cov}(s_i, s_j) = 0$. In terms of the involved covariance matrices we get $\mathbf{\Omega}_{ea} = 0 \Rightarrow \mathbf{h} = \mathbf{\Omega}_{ea} \cdot \mathbf{\Omega}_{ee}^{-1} = 0_{k \times k}$ and the optimal currency position become

$$\mathbf{w}_{FIS}^* = \lambda \mathbf{\Omega}^{-1} \cdot \begin{bmatrix} \mu_a \\ 0 \end{bmatrix} = \begin{bmatrix} \mathbf{w}_{a,FIS}^* \\ \mathbf{w}_{e,FIS}^* \end{bmatrix} = \begin{bmatrix} \lambda \mathbf{\Omega}_{aa}^{-1} \cdot \mu_a \\ 0 \end{bmatrix} \qquad (11.19)$$

It is best here not to hedge currency risks, as the covariances are sufficiently negative. As a consequence, $\mathbf{\Omega}_{a|e} = \mathbf{\Omega}_{aa}$. The difficulty with a fully integrated currency management lies in the requirement to arrive at positions simultaneously, which does not work well in institutional asset management, where overlay managers are often specialists that focus solely on currency management.

ACTIVE OVERLAY AND RISK OVERLAY   The majority of currency overlay managers do not consider the feedback of their currency positions on the underlying asset positions; that is, they take the asset positions as exogenously given. However, the optimal currency position still involves both a hedging as well as a speculative demand. Given current asset positions $\mathbf{w}_a$, the optimal currency position can be again decomposed into

$$\mathbf{w}_e^* = \underbrace{\lambda \mathbf{\Omega}_{ee}^{-1} \cdot \mu_e}_{\substack{Active \\ overlay}} - \underbrace{\mathbf{h} \cdot \mathbf{w}_a}_{\substack{Risk \\ overlay}} \qquad (11.20)$$

The difference to (11.16) is the exogenous treatment of asset positions (it carries no * as the position is not necessarily optimal). However, we can still separate active currency management (active overlay, that is, long/short portfolio of currency positions) from passive currency decision (risk overlay), which is the practice in institutional asset management. Usually, currency overlay management follows a two-step approach. In the first step an optimal hedge ratio h is selected given an exogenously given asset allocation. Once the currency benchmark is assigned, an active currency overlay manager is hired to manage relative to this benchmark. Note that there is a subtle relation between currency benchmark and active currency management. In case the manager faces a 100 percent hedged benchmark and is not allowed to take leverage (net short positions) he might face substantial performance limitations. In this case the manager can only open positions (unwind hedges) but is not allowed to further short currencies (no leverage); she can, on average, implement only half of their positions (only those where the foreign currency is expected to appreciate), and as such the information ratio will drop by $\sqrt{2}$.

PRACTICAL CONSIDERATIONS   While we think it is entirely intuitive that the currency hedging decision should be driven by the covariance of asset and currency returns, in practice this is often seen with strong skepticism due to several interrelated problems. First, there is parameter uncertainty in the regression hedging estimates of (11.11) due to estimation error and/or model error in the covariance matrix estimates. From a practical point of view, Larsen and Resnick (1999) have shown that the impact of estimation error on optimal hedge ratios is material and that it is unclear that sophisticated mean variance hedges will outperform naïve models (*unitary hedging* or universal hedging). Second, as model-based hedging incurs frequent updates due to model changes, this kind of rebalancing activity might prove costly. Often, these reasons are used to justify a so-called universal hedging by Black (1989), where all investors around the world get the same universal hedge ratio. But do the above arguments really build a meaningful case using a mean variance approach to hedging? Note that all previously mentioned issues are implementation problems that affect all quantitative portfolio management in general, not just currency overlay management. The correct way to address parameter instability and transaction costs is to address them directly. If the investor does not want to rely on historical covariance estimates, she should express her uneasiness within a Bayesian framework, if appropriate, with a very narrow Bayesian prior stating, for example, that the covariance between asset and currency returns is zero. When it comes to transaction costs, it again is a bad idea to manage transaction costs via a never-changing covariance matrix. Rather make rebalancing costly (using a realistic transaction cost model), and again address the problem directly, that is, via portfolio optimization.

WHO SHOULD INVEST IN A CURRENCY OVERLAY?   In order to answer this question, we need to rephrase it into two questions. Who should buy a risk overlay; that is, who needs to hedge currency risk? Who should buy active overlays; that is, who should be interested in alpha arising from the currency universe? The second question is easiest to answer. Everybody should be interested in earning alpha, whether it is in a private portfolio, a 401(k) plan, on the corporate balance sheet, or within a pension fund. Real alpha extends the investment opportunity set for private investors and provides a positive shareholder value generating net present value for institutional investors. What about the currency risk an investor should take as part of its passive (unconditional) exposure? For an asset-only investor, the question should be answered from a pure hedging perspective, as the unconditional risk premium on currencies is likely to be zero. For example, the investor in a small country might wish to hold some currencies, as it is one way to hedge against local inflation risk arising from a local policy accident. This does not affect the optimal active currency exposure, which we would regard as a separate decision. The solution changes dramatically for an asset liability investor. Pension fund management is an integral part of corporate risk management. If the corporate treasury department is not allowed to take currency risk as it does not belong to the plan sponsor's core activity, there is no argument the same currency risk should be taken in the plan sponsors pension fund. Unless the plan sponsor is in deep financial distress, we would argue that pension liabilities should be 100 percent hedged. This not only calls for a unitary hedge, but also gives little reason to move away from the local discount factor, that is, the liability mimicking portfolio.

Active Currency Overlay

COMMON STRATEGIES   Common active currency overlay strategies include currency alpha, carry strategies, momentum strategies, flow strategies, valuation strategies, and quantitative currency overlay. We describe each of these below.

Currency Alpha   Active investing is a zero-sum game. For every winner, there must by definition be a loser. Given that active management creates transaction costs, the average manager should underperform the market. This is well known as the arithmetic of active management introduced by Sharpe (1991). While the active equity manager has on average underperformed major indices, the active currency manager seems to have outperformed as studies summarized by Dales and Meese (2003) report. Who is supplying net alpha to the active currency investor; that is, who is implicitly transferring wealth? The usual folklore is that the currency market is dominated by so-called forced players that have nonprofit objectives. Central banks are said to have more macroeconomic policy objectives, corporate treasuries are more interested in corporate hedging, and tourists are treated as entirely ignorant to currency valuations. Care should be taken. The above-cited studies have neither been undertaken nor confirmed by independent sources as they are originated by players that have a strong interest in active currency management. Moreover, contrary to the conventional wisdom, it is well known that central banks make profits, corporate hedging does not lose money, and tourist flows follow currency weakness.

Carry Strategies   We start with the most well-known strategy in currency management, the so-called carry strategy, first investigated by Froot and Frankel (1989), which is also known as *forward rate bias*. For a most recent discussion, see Cochrane (2007). The basis of these strategies is that if we were running a regression for currency i (here we assume $i = \frac{AUD}{\$}$) of the form

$$i = \frac{s_{AUD}}{\$} = \gamma_0 + \gamma_1 \left(c_{AUD} - c_{\$} \right) + \epsilon \tag{11.21}$$

we would expect that the regression coefficients take values of $\gamma_0 = 0$, $\gamma_1 = 1$. Only if these conditions are met, we can possibly arrive at expected excess returns of $\frac{e_{AUD}}{\$} = \frac{s_{AUD}}{\$} + c_{AUD} - c_{\$} = 0$ in (11.2) as the uncovered interest rate parity would indicate. However, empirically countless studies confirmed that $\gamma_1 < 0$, implying that not only does the higher-yielding currency not depreciate enough to offset the interest rate differential, but it actually appreciates. Investors get both the certain interest rate differential as well as an on average positive spot return.

Most quantitative models in practice prefix $\gamma_1 = 0$. The main justification for this is that a regression like (11.21) might pick up estimation error as well as time variations in the regression coefficients, resulting in unstable forecasts. While using $(c_{AUD} - c_{\$})$ as a return forecast results most likely in a biased forecast, it will exhibit lower estimation risk. Trading off bias against estimation risk, most practitioners prefer a probably biased but less volatile forecast. Note that on any currency pair in isolation this is still a risky trade. After all, $\text{Var}(\varepsilon)$ will be around 8 percent to 15 percent, depending on currency and time period selected. In other words, the R^2 of (11.21) is low. The key to making carry strategies work is therefore to diversify across many currencies and to realize that interest rate differentials have to be adjusted by their relative risks.

Momentum Strategies   Trend models come in many forms. Their main justification in the currency arena comes from central bank activity that seems to generate trending exchange rates as described in Szakmary and Mathur (1997) and LeBaron (1999) as well as from well-known behavioral biases. Investors show under- and overreaction to economic news that are both related to momentum effects as outlined by Hong and Stein (1999).

To illustrate a simple *momentum strategy,* we show a moving average crossover signal where a currency is deemed attractive if the short-run moving average is above the long-run moving average, that is, there is current momentum in currency returns. The signal for currency i becomes

$$signal_{i,t} = \frac{1}{\#short} \sum_{j=0}^{\#short} s_{i,t-j} - \frac{1}{\#long} \sum_{j=0}^{\#long} s_{i,t-j} \qquad (11.22)$$

where *#short* and *#long* are the number of observations to calculate the long and short moving average. Often, the signals and weights are equalized such that a stronger signal also means a stronger weight. Sometimes signals are adjusted by subtracting the cross-sectional mean

$$signal^*_{i,t} = signal_{i,t} - \frac{1}{k} \sum_{i=1}^{k} signal_{i,t} \qquad (11.23)$$

which, in effect, makes the position's home currency (in this case) dollar neutral. Note that not only do we need to choose *#short* and *#long*, but we also need to define the time period we think momentum is going to last.

Suppose we think momentum continues for six months and we calculate a new signal every month. This leaves us with a dilemma. What do we do with the old signal after one month? After all, it should be good for another five months. The solution is to build overlapping portfolios. Each time a new signal arrives we throw away the portfolio and add one-sixth of the current momentum portfolio. This way, we always have a mixture of momentum portfolios, so we don't throw away information that still contains value.

Flow Strategies   The stronger role played by more increasingly open international financial markets constitutes a persuasive argument to more fully explore a possible relationship between risky assets and exchange rate dynamics. The dynamic linkage among international financial markets has become the focus of academic research as most recent in Moore, John, Dunne, and Hau (2006). Empirical research shows that net equity flows are on average positively correlated with currency returns. At the same time equity flows seem to have more explaining power for exchange rate movements than bond flows.

One possible explanation is that bond investors tend to hedge their currency exposure, while equity investors often leave the implied currency exposure unmanaged. Building on these insights, practitioners use the relative local equity market performance (relative to a currency anchor, like the U.S. dollar) as a positive signal for future currency returns.

$$signal_{i,t} = \frac{1}{n} \sum_{j=0}^{n} \left(r_{i,t-j} - r_{\$,t-j} \right) \qquad (11.24)$$

The signal for currency i is a moving average of relative currency returns. Note that this procedure tries to anticipate future flows as a function of perceived currency attractiveness rather than measuring flows directly. The latter is limited to few market participants that have access to flow data.

Valuation Strategies From a macroeconomic perspective, the fair value of currencies is a function of macroeconomic fundamentals, like money supply, current account deficit, relative gross domestic product (GDP), or inflation growth, to name a few. This is in stark contrast to the previous specifications that assumed that financial flows are triggered by interest rate differentials and relative equity market performance. Fundamental models do not have a stellar track record, as found in the classic studies by Meese and Rogoff (1983) and Frankel and Rose (1995). First, macroeconomic data are observed only at low frequency and hence offer little breadth in a strategy; they are often revised and certainly not forward looking. Second, given the importance of short-term asset-related flows, they tend to work only in the most extreme deviations from equilibrium and as such resemble a very risky contrarian strategy.

Quantitative Currency Overlay Quantitative investing is the systematic exploitation of economically motivated empirical regularities. This makes it perfectly suited for currency markets where information is vast and public rather than markets where information is largely private, and, as such, the traditional portfolio manager has little advantage from her ability to talk to individuals. While traditional managers would look at very similar information than traditional investors, they would almost erratically jump between themes given the different importance across time and would be unlikely to catch any regularity. The dark side of quantitative investing is called data mining; that is, the quantitative investor's ability to overadjust to empirical data. However, using out-of-sample and across-market validation techniques will mitigate this problem, making quantitative investing a very interesting alternative in active currency research.

ACTIVE PORTFOLIO CONSTRUCTION AND CURRENCY PERSPECTIVE Suppose we have chosen one of the preceding strategies and found a set of expected excess currency returns. The management of active overlays requires us also to estimate the covariation in excess returns Ω_{ee} in order to establish the portfolio with the highest risk-adjusted return. Assume we model s_i for $i = \{\frac{AUD}{\$}, \frac{CAD}{\$}, \frac{CHF}{\$}, \frac{EUR}{\$}\}$ by calculating the currency returns from the change in the log exchange rate. The use of log returns is convenient as we can not only draw on the well-known fact that log returns are normally distributed if exchange rates are lognormal (with the caveat, however, that log-returns are not additive), but we can also easily transform currencies from one base into another.

By definition, the log of the $\frac{AUD}{\$}$ exchange rate can be written as $\ln(\frac{AUD}{\$}) = \ln(AUD) - \ln(\$)$ spot return from

$$\ln\left(\frac{AUD}{EUR}\right) = \ln\left(\frac{AUD}{\$}\right) - \ln\left(\frac{EUR}{\$}\right) \tag{11.25}$$

This is helpful, as we can now use (11.25) to calculate volatilities on cross rate. Let us use the following definitions:

$$s_{\frac{AUD}{\$}} = \ln\left[\frac{\frac{AUD}{\$}_t}{\frac{AUD}{\$}_{t-1}}\right], s_{\frac{EUR}{\$}} = \ln\left[\frac{\frac{EUR}{\$}_t}{\frac{EUR}{\$}_{t-1}}\right] \tag{11.26}$$

It is now obvious that we can write

$$s_{\frac{AUD}{EUR}} = \ln\left[\frac{\frac{AUD}{\$}_t}{\frac{AUD}{\$}_{t-1}}\right] - \ln\left[\frac{\frac{EUR}{\$}_t}{\frac{EUR}{\$}_{t-1}}\right] = s_{\frac{AUD}{\$}} - s_{\frac{EUR}{\$}} \tag{11.27}$$

Applying the variance operator on (11.27), we get

$$\text{Var}\left(s_{\frac{AUD}{EUR}}\right) = \text{Var}\left(s_{\frac{AUD}{\$}} - s_{\frac{EUR}{\$}}\right) = \text{Var}\left(s_{\frac{AUD}{\$}}\right) + \text{Var}\left(s_{\frac{EUR}{\$}}\right) - 2\text{Cov}\left(s_{\frac{AUD}{\$}}, s_{\frac{EUR}{\$}}\right) \tag{11.28}$$

That is, we can calculate the volatility for the $\frac{AUD}{EUR}$ cross rate entirely from the existing covariance matrix. Rather than going through every entry in great detail, we take a shortcut using the early work by Sercu (1980). We define a transformation matrix, Θ, which is similar to an identity matrix (matrix of ones on the main diagonal and zero elsewhere) with the exception that the column of the new *numeraire* currency is filled with –1. The variance covariance matrix in the new numeraire currency is then given by

$$\Omega_{ee|EUR} = \Theta \cdot \Omega_{ee|\$} \cdot \Theta \tag{11.29}$$

We will illustrate the preceding calculations with an example. Using daily data from January 2001 to the end of April 2004, we arrive at the following covariance matrix from a U.S. dollar perspective, where the currencies are Australian dollar, Canadian dollar, Swiss franc, and euro all against the dollar.

$$\Omega_{ee|\$} = \begin{bmatrix} 109.42 & 37.99 & 55.65 & 55.83 \\ 37.99 & 58.18 & 30.58 & 29.37 \\ 55.65 & 30.58 & 101.87 & 87.36 \\ 55.83 & 29.37 & 87.36 & 84.17 \end{bmatrix} \tag{11.30}$$

To clarify the dimension of the entries in (11.30) the volatility of the Australian dollar relative to the USD is $10.46 = \sqrt{109.42}$, that is, about 10 percent. According to (11.29), we can transform the covariance matrix that expresses currency risk for a USD investor into a covariance matrix for a European investor. We can do this without the need to recalculate the covariance matrix by generating a new set of cross rates, simply using the information in the dollar covariance matrix. This comes in handy when the process of estimating the covariance matrix itself is complicated as, for example, it is in the case of a multivariate generalized autoregressive conditional heteroskedasticity (GARCH) model.

The covariance in euro term is simply given by

$$
\Omega_{ee|EUR} \Theta \cdot \Omega_{ee|\$} \cdot \Theta^T =
\begin{bmatrix}
1 & 0 & 0 & -1 \\
0 & 1 & 0 & -1 \\
0 & 0 & 1 & -1 \\
0 & 0 & 0 & -1
\end{bmatrix}
\begin{bmatrix}
109.42 & 37.99 & 55.65 & 55.83 \\
37.99 & 58.18 & 30.58 & 29.37 \\
55.65 & 30.58 & 101.87 & 87.36 \\
55.83 & 29.37 & 87.36 & 84.17
\end{bmatrix} \cdot
$$

$$
\cdot
\begin{bmatrix}
1 & 0 & 0 & -1 \\
0 & 1 & 0 & -1 \\
0 & 0 & 1 & -1 \\
0 & 0 & 0 & -1
\end{bmatrix}^T =
\begin{bmatrix}
81.94 & 36.96 & -3.37 & 28.34 \\
36.96 & 83.61 & -1.98 & 54.80 \\
-3.37 & -1.98 & 11.32 & -3.19 \\
28.34 & 54.80 & -3.19 & 84.17
\end{bmatrix}
$$

Note that as we transform the covariance matrix in euro, the matrix Θ is created by replacing the last column of an identity matrix with a vector containing -1. We can check this result looking at two particular entries. First we realize that $\text{Var}(s_{\$_{EUR}}) = \text{Var}(s_{EUR_\$}) = 84.17$. This directly follows from using log returns, which have the property of being symmetric. An increase from 1.3 to 1.4 in log returns exactly offset by a decrease from 1.4 to 1.3, which is the exchange rate movement from the other currency perspective: $\ln(\frac{1.4}{1.3}) = -\ln(\frac{1.3}{1.4})$. If we used simple returns, the same would not apply: $\frac{1.4}{1.3} - 1 \neq \frac{1.3}{1.4} - 1$. Second, we can also apply (11.28) to check our calculations:

$$
\text{Var}\left(s_{\frac{AUD}{EUR}}\right) = \text{Var}\left(s_{\frac{AUD}{\$}} - s_{\frac{EUR}{\$}}\right) = 109.42 + 84.17 - 2 \cdot 55.83 = 81.94 \qquad (11.31)
$$

This confirms our results. However, a new question naturally arises. Do our optimal active positions change when we transform the covariance matrix; that is, do we need to construct a different active portfolio when we construct an active overlay for U.S. investors versus European investors? We start with a set of currency forecasts. Suppose we look at the carry strategy in (11.21). For a U.S.-based investor we could have calculated (assuming $\gamma_0 = \gamma_1 = 0$ for all regressions)

$$
\mu_{e|\$} =
\begin{bmatrix}
c_{AUD} - c_\$ \\
c_{CAD} - c_\$ \\
c_{CHF} - c_\$ \\
c_{EUR} - c_\$
\end{bmatrix} =
\begin{bmatrix}
1 \\
4 \\
2 \\
1
\end{bmatrix}
$$

where $\mu_{e|\$}$ refers to currency excess returns from a USD perspective. All forecasts are relative to the USD.

We expect, for example, an AUD cash position to exhibit a 100 basis points outperformance versus a dollar cash position. For a given risk aversion parameter λ, the optimal solution to an active currency overlay is

$$w^*_{e|\$} = \lambda \cdot \Omega^{-1}_{ee|\$} \cdot \mu_{e|\$}$$

$$= \lambda \begin{bmatrix} 109.42 & 37.99 & 55.65 & 55.83 \\ 37.99 & 58.18 & 30.58 & 29.37 \\ 55.65 & 30.58 & 101.87 & 87.36 \\ 55.83 & 29.37 & 87.36 & 84.17 \end{bmatrix}^{-1} \begin{bmatrix} 1 \\ 4 \\ 2 \\ 1 \end{bmatrix}$$

$$= \lambda \begin{bmatrix} -1.35\% \\ +8.12\% \\ +8,25\% \\ -9,31\% \end{bmatrix}$$

It is worth noting that the positions do not add up to 0 percent, nor should they, as all positions are expressed against the dollar. Hence, the remaining cash position must be the dollar. So the optimal portfolio is short 1.35 percent AUD and 9.31 percent euro, while at the same time being long 8.12 percent CAD and 8.25 percent CHF. Again, as all trades are implemented versus the dollar, we have an implicit –5.71 percent short dollar position.

Let us now find the optimal positions for a European investor. We need not only to transform the covariance according to (11.29) but also expected returns using the same logic and the same transformation matrix.

$$\mu_{e|EUR} = \Theta \cdot \mu_{e|\$}$$

$$= \begin{bmatrix} 0 \\ 3 \\ 1 \\ -1 \end{bmatrix} = \begin{bmatrix} 1 & 0 & 0 & -1 \\ 0 & 1 & 0 & -1 \\ 0 & 0 & 1 & -1 \\ 0 & 0 & 0 & -1 \end{bmatrix} \begin{bmatrix} 1 \\ 4 \\ 2 \\ 1 \end{bmatrix} \qquad (11.32)$$

The calculation in (11.32) rebases return expectations. If, for example, a USD investor expects a 100 bps advantage of the AUD versus the dollar and an equal advantage of the EUR against the dollar, the implicit advantage of the AUD versus the EUR is zero.

$$\mathbf{w}^*_{e|EUR} = \lambda \cdot \Omega^{-1}_{ee|EUR} \cdot \mu_{e|EUR}$$

$$= \lambda \cdot \left(\Theta \cdot \Omega_{ee|\$} \cdot \Theta^T \right)^{-1} \cdot \Theta \cdot \mu_{e|\$} \qquad (11.33)$$

$$= (\Theta^{-1})^{-T} \mathbf{w}^*_{e|\$}$$

Again, we just have to rebase the original solution for the U.S. investor according to our transformation matrix. A closer look at

$$\left(\Theta^{-1} \right)^{-T} \mathbf{w}^*_{e|\$} = \begin{bmatrix} 1 & 0 & 0 & 0 \\ 0 & 1 & 0 & 0 \\ 0 & 0 & 1 & 0 \\ -1 & -1 & -1 & -1 \end{bmatrix} \cdot \begin{bmatrix} -1.35\% \\ +8.12\% \\ +8.25\% \\ -9.31\% \end{bmatrix}$$

$$= \begin{bmatrix} -1.35\% \\ +8.12\% \\ +8.25\% \\ -5.71\% \end{bmatrix}$$

reveals that both solutions are identical. The first three entries in $\mathbf{w}^*_{e|EUR}$ are the same as in $\mathbf{w}^*_{e|\$}$, and the fourth entry is now the dollar entry, which, as above, is the negative of the sum of the positions, that is, −5.7 percent. The euro position in turn is again the residual position amounting to a total of −9.31 percent. This is an important result. The optimal active overlay position from the perspective of a U.S. investor (all forecasts are made relative to the USD and all currency risks are also relative to the USD) remains unchanged for all investors irrespective of their reference currency. For practical purposes, this is extremely convenient as it allows us to translate a given portfolio in all reference currencies without the need for reoptimization.

STRATEGY WEIGHTING   Once an active overlay strategy is running, we need to decide how much weight should be given to a strategy (momentum, forward rate bias, flow, etc.) relative to other strategies and under which circumstances one should switch off the strategy entirely. The first question relates to strategy timing, while the second is ultimately about strategy termination.

Portfolio Optimization   The most natural approach is to weight strategies with respect to their historical performance and use some techniques to deal with the inherent estimation error that comes from using past data. Here, we can use the full range of portfolio optimization model as described in Fabozzi, Kolm, Pachamanova, and Focardi (2007). Ultimately, the foundation of these models is the idea that active returns (alpha) should, by definition, not be forecastable, and if it is, we have some factors missing in our forecasting models. If we find that a particular model works best in a rising equity market, we still have to forecast the equity market, which is not easy to forecast. Also, if past equity markets would be indicative for future signal performance, we should rather use it as a model input factor. Effectively, these optimization-based algorithms will smooth allocations over time (trying to make them not "too responsive" to past data). However, it is exactly for this reason that optimization strategies are criticized. In order to make strategies more contextual, it has been suggested to introduce on/off switches to either depend on *ex ante* expected regimes or *ex post* realized performance. We will review two of the most common approaches: an *ex ante* crisis indicator (*regime based*) that attempts to identify economic regimes that in the past have been followed with a currency crisis, and an *ex post* performance-based *stop loss* rule.

Regime-Based Weightings   Let us start with a variable X that could possibly work as a leading indicator for a currency crisis. Possible candidates are the bid-ask spread (widening might indicate a looming crisis), equity market performance, the trade-weighted exchange rate, GDP growth, or related variables. Alternatively, we might want to use principal component analysis to extract the common element in a series of indicators. The (standardized) variable x is then said to signal a crisis if it crosses a particular threshold z. How do we derive z? Take the order statistic of all realizations $x_1, \ldots, x_m$, and for any given level of the cutoff value z (percentile measure) define both signal (s) and noise (n) as

$$n(z) = \frac{\#\text{ signals with no crisis following (false alarms)}}{\#\text{ of times no crisis happened}}, s(z)$$

$$= \frac{\#\text{ signals with correct crisis specification}}{\#\text{ of times a crisis happened}} \tag{11.34}$$

Each time $x > z$, a crisis will happen (or not). We can therefore calculate (11.34) for every value of z from empirical data once we decide on the correct time frame and the definition of a currency crisis (strong negative performance in a particular currency). Our indicator is said to be at a critical level where the noise-to-signal ratio is minimized, that is, at

$$z = \arg \min \frac{n(z)}{s(z)} \tag{11.35}$$

Note that under the null hypothesis H_0:*no crisis*, equation (11.35) can also be expressed as

$$z = \arg \min \frac{\text{prob(type I error)}}{1 - \text{prob(type II error)}} \tag{11.36}$$

where we can interpret the probability of a false alarm as type I error and the probability of a missed call as type II error.

Note that our null hypothesis is H_0: *no crisis*. What are the problems with regime-based indicators? Indicators like the preceding will work more in a six- to eighteen-month time frame rather than a one- to four-week horizon. As such, it will force a given signal to be inactive for a long time, thereby reducing considerably the breadth of a strategy. For many strategies that are also sensitive to crisis risk (like the forward rate bias strategy or any short volatility strategy), this is hazardous, as these strategies live from small incremental returns that are, on average, due every day. Giving up these returns for a long time will be detrimental to performance. Given the erratic nature of currency crisis, the probability of false alarms will be high (keeping the strategy out of the market), while it is by no means guaranteed that an occurring crisis will be correctly anticipated.

Performance-Based Weightings   Alternatively, we can take the view that a currency crisis is, by definition, not forecastable. After all, it is driven by an exogenous event that probably applies all the more to currencies that are sometimes driven by geopolitical events. Practitioners often apply performance-based stop loss rules to deal with crisis risk. It is worthwhile to work out the conditions under which stop loss rules can improve performance and where they will be detrimental. Stop loss (or take profit) rules will reduce returns in a random market. Essentially, a stop loss/take profit rule is X percent of the time in the market and 1 percent to X percent in cash.

A similar question has already been solved in the literature. Kritzman (2000) explained that it is better to hold a portfolio of stocks and cash in proportions of X percent and 1 – X percent rather than a random timing strategy with these probabilities. We should expect a stop loss strategy to underperform if the underlying market is truly random. However, if the P&L of a given currency strategy has clear patterns, this result will change.

Let us take the case of a carry strategy. Its returns will be upward trending, as it offers a consistent positive return. However, in terms of a currency crisis, the strategy seems to underperform considerably, giving up the performance of the last two months in a short period. With this kind of profile, a take-profit strategy really means stop profit. On the other side, a stop loss rule seems appropriate given the short outbursts of strategy reversal. As we can neither diversify away from crisis nor

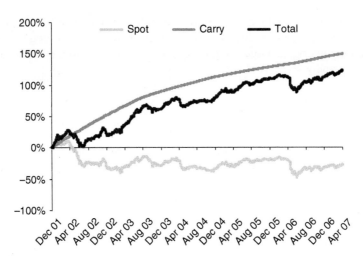

FIGURE 11.4 Carry Trade: Long Turkish Lira, Short Swiss Franc

forecast an exogenous event, we need to at least ensure that our losses in a crisis situation remain limited.

We can see the potential benefits from a stop loss strategy in Figure 11.4. While the returns from the positive interest rate differential (TLR rates exceed CHF rates) is, by definition, positive, we see that the TRL, on average, moves against the interest rate differential, but the depreciation (cumulative) is by no means large enough to erase the positive carry as indicated by the black line representing the total profit. However, we also see the temporary and sometimes very sharp breakdown (as in April 2002, November 2002, April 2004, and May 2006). Any stop loss rule filtering out extreme events that are due to local policy crisis would have helped to improve performance dramatically. Be aware that a stop loss is merely a clumsy momentum strategy. It will only add value (by avoiding losses) if downward momentum contin-ues for the stop-out period. Otherwise the opportunity cost (positive average strategy return) of not being invested will destroy its benefit. The stronger the Sharpe ratio of a strategy, the stronger its required downward momentum.

Strategy Termination   How do we react to persistently poor performance? The first reaction is to attribute it to the normal variation in active strategies or to blame it on a temporary adverse environment. However, it might also be the case that the competition has arbitraged empirical regularities away, that a structural break happened, or, worse, the anomaly never has been there. Dealing with strategy ter-mination might be the result of a subjective decision. In this case the model learns in meetings. Alternatively, the model will learn from the data (Bayesian error learning), and an optimization-based allocation algorithm will disinvest. Quantitative currency overlay management is more likely to follow the latter approach.

Summary

Currency overlays are long/short portfolios designed to create a strategic cur-rency exposure (risk overlay) or alpha-generating positions (active overlay). Both approaches can and should be embedded into a standard portfolio optimization framework. With the availability of a variety of quantitative strategies for active currency management, strategy weighting becomes an important part of currency overlay management.

References

Black, F. (1989). Equilibrium exchange rate hedging. NBER working paper #2947.

Cochrane, J. (2007). The returns to currency speculation. University of Chicago working paper.

Dales, A., and Meese, R. (2003). The case for active currency management. *AIMA Journal*, September: loads/BGI.pdf.

Fabozzi, F. J., Kolm, P. N., Pachamanova, D., and Focardi, S. (2007). *Robust Portfolio Optimization and Management*. Hoboken, NJ: John Wiley & Sons.

Frankel, J., and Rose, A. (1995). Empirical research on nominal exchange rates. In G. Grossman and K. Rogoff (eds.), *Handbook of International Economics*, 1689–1729. Amsterdam: North-Holland.

Froot, K., and Frankel, J. (1989). Forward discount bias: Is it an exchange risk premium? *Quarterly Journal of Economics* **104**, 1: 139–161.

Green, W. (2002). *Econometric Analysis*, 5th Edition. Upper Saddle River, NJ: Prentice Hall.

Hong, H., and Stein, J. (1999). A unified theory of underreaction, momentum trading and overreaction in asset markets. *Journal of Finance* **54**, 6: 2143–2184.

Jorion, P. (1994). A mean-variance analysis of currency overlays. *Financial Analysts Journal*, May/June: 48–56.

Kritzman M. (2000). *Puzzles of Finance*. New York: John Wiley & Sons.

Larsen, G., and Resnick, B. (1999). Universal currency hedging for international equity portfolios und parameter uncertainty. *International Journal of Business* **4**, 1: 1–17.

LeBaron, B. (1999). Technical trading rule profitability and foreign exchange intervention. *Journal of International Economics* **49**: 129–143.

Meese, R., and Rogoff, K. (1983). Empirical exchange rate models of the seventies: Do they fit out of sample? *Journal of International Economics* **14**: 3–24

Moore, M., John, M., Dunne, P., and Hau, H. (2006). International order flows: Explaining equity and exchange rate returns. Queen's University (Belfast), School of Management and Economics working paper.

Sercu, P. (1980). A generalization of the international asset pricing model. *Revue de l'Association Francaise de Finance* **1**, 1: 91–135.

Sharpe, W. (1991). The arithmetic of active management. *Financial Analysts Journal*, January/February: 7–9.

Szakmary, A., and Mathur, I. (1997). Central bank intervention and trading rule profits in foreign exchange markets. *Journal of International Money and Finance*, August 1997: 513–536.

CHAPTER 12

Alternative Investments

A lternative investments are one of the most popular, intriguing, debated, and misunderstood topics in investments today. Investors are lured by the prospect of higher returns that may be created through both alpha and beta. Alternative investments however come with unique and significant risks and concerns including minimal regulation; voluntary, incomplete, and inaccurate reporting; survivorship bias; illiquidity risk; high fees; high minimum investments; and lack of transparency.

Despite these risks and concerns, investors and advisors alike are drawn to these investments believing there is an undiscovered potential for growth coupled with unique diversification benefits. To be sure, there is also a "cool" factor associated with alts, as they are sometimes known.

This chapter looks at a couple of different definitions of alternative investments as not all professionals agree on what alternatives are and how to classify or characterize them. The readings review the various investment asset classes and strategies represented by alternative investments and review the various investment structures through which these investments are made available. The chapter offers a thorough discussion of how investment advisors and consultants may analyze these alternative investments and incorporate them into an investment methodology or portfolio strategy.

Part I *Handbook of Finance:* Alternative Asset Classes

Learning Objectives

- Define alternative investments and discuss whether they should be considered as an "asset class."
- Classify alternative investments based on the following categories: hedge funds, commodity and managed futures, private equity, credit derivatives, and corporate governance.
- List examples of alternative investments that are based on different trading strategies, generate risk premia based on active trading rather than systematic risk, offer opportunities to exploit market inefficiencies, employ tactical applications, or seek to capitalize on systematic risk derived from something other than stocks and bonds.

- Discuss how alternative investments fit into strategic and tactical asset allocation models.
- Discuss the concept of asset location as it relates to alternative investments.

Part II *The New Science of Asset Allocation: Risk Management in a Multi-Asset World:* Sources of Risk and Return in Alternative Investments

Learning Objectives

- Describe and discuss historical performance of alternative investments.
- Describe the historical performance of hedge funds and their correlation to stocks and bonds. Discuss the challenges that result from hedge fund performance reporting.
- Describe the structure of and strategies of hedge funds.
- Describe the historical performance of managed futures (commodity trading advisors) and their correlation to stocks and bonds.
- Describe and discuss the unique risks associated with managed futures and its sources of return.
- Describe the historical performance of private equity and its correlation to stocks and bonds.
- Describe and discuss the unique risks associated with private equity and its sources of return.
- Describe the historical performance of real estate and its correlation to stocks and bonds.
- Describe the structure of and strategies available through public and private real estate.
- Describe and discuss the unique risks associated with real estate and its sources of return.
- Describe the historical performance of commodities and their correlation to stocks and bonds.
- Describe the structure of commodities investments.
- Describe and discuss the unique risks associated with commodities and their sources of return.

Part III *Portfolio Design: A Modern Approach to Asset Allocation:* Hedge Funds

Learning Objectives

- Describe and differentiate between investment strategies offered through hedge funds including: market neutral, arbitrage, long/short equity, global macro, event driven, managed futures, and fund of funds.
- List and discuss the risks associated with investing in hedge funds.
- Discuss the historical performance of hedge fund strategies and discuss the reliability of hedge fund performance reporting (e.g., backfill bias, survivorship bias).
- Discuss the appropriateness of hedge funds in a portfolio based on client objectives, risk exposure and client risk tolerance, asset allocation, and the benefits of diversification.

Part IV *Portfolio Design: A Modern Approach to Asset Allocation:* Asset Allocation with Alternative Investments

Learning Objectives

- Discuss the structure and strategies represented in the Yale Endowment and how appropriate this allocation would or would not be for individual investors.
- Describe the availability of alternative investments to the general public and discuss different types of alternative investment structures that are now available, including so-called "liquid alternatives."
- Describe the historical performance and correlations of alternative investments in both bull and bear markets.
- Discuss the appropriateness of alternative investments in high-net-worth (HNW) and ultra-HNW client portfolios.
- List and explain lessons that can be learned from the Yale Endowment's investment portfolio.
- List and explain lessons that can be learned from holding alternative investments in the financial crises.
- Discuss whether alternative investments are attractive and appropriate for your clients.

Part I Alternative Asset Classes

Part of the difficulty of working with alternative asset classes is defining them. Are they a separate asset class or a subset of an existing asset class? Do they hedge the investment opportunity set or expand it? Are they listed on an exchange or do they trade in the over-the-counter market?

In most cases, alternative assets are a subset of an existing asset class. This may run contrary to the popular view that alternative assets are separate asset classes. However, we take the view that what many consider separate "classes" are really just different investment strategies within an existing asset class.

In most cases, they expand the investment opportunity set, rather than hedge it. Finally, alternative assets are generally purchased in the private markets, outside of any exchange. While hedge funds, private equity, and credit derivatives meet these criteria, we will see that commodity futures prove to be the exception to these general rules.

Alternative assets, then, are just alternative investments within an existing asset class. Specifically, most alternative assets derive their value from either the debt or equity market. For instance, most hedge fund strategies involve the purchase and sale of either equity or debt securities. Additionally, hedge fund managers may invest in derivative instruments whose value is derived from the equity or debt market.

One can classify five types of alternative assets: hedge funds, commodity and managed futures, private equity, credit derivatives, and corporate governance. This is the classification used in Anson (2006). Hedge funds and private equity are the best known of the alternative asset world. Typically, these investments are accomplished through the purchase of limited partner units in a private limited partnership. Commodity futures can be either passive investing tied to a commodity futures index or active investing through a commodity pool or advisory account. Private equity is the investment strategy of investing in companies before they issue their securities publicly, or taking a public company private. Credit derivatives can be purchased through limited partnership units, as a tranche of a special-purpose vehicle, or directly through the purchase of credit default swaps or credit options. Corporate governance is also a form of shareholder activism designed to improve the internal controls of a public company.

Yet, before we can discuss alternative assets we need to provide a definition for the term "asset class." We start by defining the major asset classes and then work our way to defining what is an "alternative asset."

Super Asset Classes

There are three super asset classes: capital assets, assets that are used as inputs to creating economic value, and assets that are a store of value (see Greer, 1997).

CAPITAL ASSETS   Capital assets are defined by their claim on the future cash flows of an enterprise. They provide a source of ongoing value. As a result, capital assets may be valued based on the net present value of their expected returns.

Under the classic theory of Modigliani and Miller (1958), a corporation cannot change its value (in the absence of tax benefits) by changing the method of its financing. Modigliani and Miller demonstrated that the value of the firm is dependent on its cash flows. How those cash flows are divided up between shareholders and bondholders is irrelevant to firm value.

Capital assets, then, are distinguished not by their possession of physical assets, but rather by their claim on the cash flows of an underlying enterprise. Hedge funds, private equity funds, credit derivatives, and corporate governance funds all fall within the super asset class of capital assets because the value of their funds are all determined by the present value of expected future cash flows from the securities in which they invest.

As a result, we can conclude that it is not the types of securities in which they invest that distinguishes hedge funds, private equity funds, credit derivatives, or corporate governance funds from traditional asset classes. Rather, it is the alternative investment strategies that they pursue that distinguishes them from traditional stock and bond investments.

ASSETS THAT CAN BE USED AS ECONOMIC INPUTS   Certain assets can be consumed as part of the production cycle. Consumable or transformable assets can be converted into another asset. Generally, this class of asset consists of the physical commodities: grains, metals, energy products, and livestock. These assets are used as economic inputs into the production cycle to produce other assets, such as automobiles, skyscrapers, new homes, and appliances.

These assets generally cannot be valued using a net present value analysis. For example, a pound of copper, by itself, does not yield an economic stream of revenues. Nor does it have much value for capital appreciation. However, the copper can be transformed into copper piping that is used in an office building or as part of the circuitry of an electronic appliance.

While consumable assets cannot produce a stream of cash flows, we demonstrate in our section on commodities that this asset class has excellent diversification properties for an investment portfolio. In fact, the lack of dependency on future cash flows to generate value is one of the reasons why commodities have important diversification potential vis-à-vis capital assets.

ASSETS THAT ARE A STORE OF VALUE Art is considered the classic asset that stores value. It is not a capital asset because there are no cash flows associated with owning a painting or a sculpture. Consequently, art cannot be valued in a discounted cash flow analysis. It is also not an asset that is used as an economic input because it is a finished product.

Art requires ownership and possession. Its value can be realized only through its sale and transfer of possession. In the meantime, the owner retains the artwork with the expectation that it will yield a price at least equal to that which the owner paid for it.

There is no rational way to gauge whether the price of art will increase or decrease because its value is derived purely from the subjective (and private) visual enjoyment that the right of ownership conveys. Therefore, to an owner, art is a store of value. It neither conveys economic benefits nor is it used as an economic input, but retains the value paid for it.

Gold and precious metals are another example of a store-of-value asset. In the emerging parts of the world, gold and silver are a significant means of maintaining wealth. In these countries, residents do not have access to the same range of financial products that are available to residents of more developed nations. Consequently, they accumulate their wealth through a tangible asset as opposed to a capital asset.

However, the lines between the three super classes of assets can become blurred. For example, gold can be leased to jewelry and other metal manufacturers. Jewelry makers lease gold during periods of seasonal demand, expecting to purchase the gold on the open market and return it to the lessor before the lease term ends. The gold lease provides a stream of cash flows that can be valued using net present value analysis.

Precious metals can also be used as a transformable/consumable asset because they have the highest level of thermal and electrical conductivity among the metals. Silver, for example, is used in the circuitry for most telephones and light switches. Gold is used in the circuitry for televisions, cars, airplanes, computers, and rocketships.

REAL ESTATE We provide a brief digression to consider where real estate belongs in our classification scheme. Real estate is a distinct asset class, but is it an alternative one? For purposes of this book, we do not consider real estate to be an alternative asset class. The reasons are several.

First, real estate was an asset class long before stocks and bonds became the investment of choice. In fact, in times past, land was the single most important asset class. Kings, queens, lords, and nobles measured their wealth by the amount of property that they owned. "Land barons" were aptly named. Ownership of land was reserved for only the most wealthy in a society.

However, over the past 200 years, our economic society changed from one based on the ownership of property to the ownership of legal entities. This transformation occurred as society moved from the agricultural age to the industrial age. Production of goods and services became the new source of wealth and power.

Stocks and bonds were born to support the financing needs of new enterprises that manufactured material goods and services. In fact, stocks and bonds became the "alternatives" to real estate instead of vice versa. With the advent of stock-and-bond exchanges, and the general acceptance of owning equity or debt stakes in companies, it is sometimes forgotten that real estate was the original and primary asset class of society.

In fact, it was only 25 years ago in the United States that real estate was the major asset class of most individual investors. This exposure was the result of owning a primary residence. It was not until the long bull market started in 1983 that investors began to diversify their wealth into the "alternative" assets of stocks and bonds.

Second, given the long-term presence of real estate as an asset class, several treatises have been written concerning its valuation. Finally, we do not consider real estate to be an alternative asset class as much as we consider it to be an additional asset class. Real estate is not an alternative to stocks and bonds—it is a fundamental asset class that should be included within every diversified portfolio. The alternative assets that we consider in this book are meant to diversify the stock-and-bond holdings within a portfolio context.

Asset Allocation

Asset allocation is generally defined as the allocation of an investor's portfolio across a number of asset classes (see Sharpe, 1992). Asset allocation, by its very nature shifts the emphasis from the security level to the portfolio level. It is an investment profile that provides a framework for constructing a portfolio based on measures of risk and return. In this sense, asset allocation can trace its roots to modern portfolio theory and the work of Harry Markowitz (1959).

ASSET CLASSES AND ASSET ALLOCATION   Initially, asset allocation involved four asset classes: equity, fixed income, cash, and real estate. Within each class, the assets could be further divided into subclasses. For example, stocks can be divided into large capitalized stocks, small-capitalized stocks, and foreign stocks. Similarly, fixed income can be broken down into U.S. Treasury notes and bonds, investment-grade bonds, high-yield bonds, and sovereign bonds.

The expansion of newly defined "alternative assets" may cause investors to become confused about their diversification properties and how they fit into an overall diversified portfolio. Investors need to understand the background of asset allocation as a concept for improving return while reducing risk.

For example, in the 1980s the biggest private equity game was taking public companies private. Does the fact that a corporation that once had publicly traded stock but now has privately traded stock mean that it has jumped into a new asset class? Furthermore, public offerings are the primary exit strategy for private equity; public ownership begins where private equity ends (see Horvitz, 2000). Therefore, it might be argued that private equity is just an extension of the equity markets where the dividing boundary is based on liquidity.

Similarly, credit derivatives expand the fixed income asset class, rather than hedge it. Hedge funds also invest in the stock-and-bond markets but pursue trading strategies very different from a traditional buy-and-hold strategy. Commodities fall into a different class of assets than equity, fixed income, or cash, and will be treated separately in this book.

Finally, corporate governance is a strategy for investing in public companies. It seems the least likely to be an alternative investment strategy. However, it can be demonstrated that a corporate governance program bears many of the same characteristics as other alternative investment strategies (see Anson, 2006).

STRATEGIC VERSUS TACTICAL ALLOCATIONS Alternative assets should be used in a tactical rather than strategic allocation. Strategic allocation of resources is applied to fundamental asset classes such as equity, fixed income, cash, and real estate. These are the basic asset classes that must be held within a diversified portfolio.

Strategic asset allocation is concerned with the long-term asset mix. The strategic mix of assets is designed to accomplish a long-term goal such as funding pension benefits or matching long-term liabilities. Risk aversion is considered when deciding the strategic asset allocation, but current market conditions are not. In general, policy targets are set for strategic asset classes, with allowable ranges around those targets. Allowable ranges are established to allow flexibility in the management of the investment portfolio.

Tactical asset allocation is short term in nature. This strategy is used to take advantage of current market conditions that may be more favorable to one asset class over another. The goal of funding long-term liabilities has been satisfied by the target ranges established by the strategic asset allocation. The goal of tactical asset allocation is to maximize return.

Tactical allocation of resources depends on the ability to diversify within an asset class. This is where alternative assets have the greatest ability to add value. Their purpose is not to hedge the fundamental asset classes, but rather to expand them. Consequently, alternative assets should be considered as part of a broader asset class.

An example is credit derivatives. These are investments that expand the frontier of credit risk investing. The fixed-income world can be classified simply as a choice between U.S. Treasury securities that are considered to be default free, and spread products that contain an element of default risk. Spread products include any fixed income investment that does not have a credit rating on par with the U.S. government. Consequently, spread products trade at a credit spread relative to U.S. Treasury securities that reflects their risk of default.

Credit derivatives are a way to diversify and expand the universe for investing in spread products. Traditionally, fixed income managers attempted to establish their ideal credit risk-and-return profile by buying and selling traditional bonds. However, the bond market can be inefficient and it may be difficult to pinpoint the exact credit profile to match the risk profile of the investor. Credit derivatives can help to plug the gaps in a fixed income portfolio, and expand the fixed income universe by accessing credit exposure in more efficient formats.

EFFICIENT VERSUS INEFFICIENT ASSET CLASSES Another way to distinguish alternative asset classes is based on the efficiency of the marketplace. The U.S. public stock-and-bond markets are generally considered to be the most efficient marketplaces in the world. Often, these markets are referred to as "semi-strong efficient." This means that all publicly available information regarding a publicly traded corporation, both past information and present, is fully digested in that company's traded securities.

Yet inefficiencies exist in all markets, both public and private. If there were no informational inefficiencies in the public equity market, there would be no case for active management. Nonetheless, whatever inefficiencies do exist, they are small and fleeting. The reason is that information is easy to acquire and disseminate in the publicly traded securities markets. Top-quartile active managers in the public equity market earn excess returns (over their benchmarks) of approximately 1 percent a year.

In contrast, with respect to alternative assets, information is very difficult to acquire. Most alternative assets (with the exception of commodities) are privately traded. This includes private equity, hedge funds, and credit derivatives. The difference between top-quartile and bottom-quartile performance in private equity can be as much as 25 percent.

Consider venture capital, one subset of the private equity market. Investments in start-up companies require intense research into the product niche the company intends to fulfill, the background of the management of the company, projections about future cash flows, exit strategies, potential competition, beta testing schedules, and so forth. This information is not readily available to the investing public. It is time consuming and expensive to accumulate. Furthermore, most investors do not have the time or the talent to acquire and filter through the rough data regarding a private company. One reason why alternative asset managers charge large management and incentive fees is to recoup the cost of information collection.

This leads to another distinguishing factor between alternative investments and the traditional asset classes: the investment intermediary. Continuing with our venture capital example, most investments in venture capital are made through limited partnerships, limited liability companies, or special-purpose vehicles. It is estimated that 80 percent of all private equity investments in the United States are funneled through a financial intermediary.

Investments in alternative assets are less liquid than their public market counterparts. Investments are closely held and liquidity is minimal. Furthermore, without a publicly traded security, the value of private securities cannot be determined by market trading. The value of the private securities must be estimated by book value or appraisal, or determined by a cash flow model.

CONSTRAINED VERSUS UNCONSTRAINED INVESTING   During the great bull market from 1981 to 2000 the asset management industry only had to invest in the stock market to enjoy consistent, high, double-digit returns. During this heyday, investment management shops and institutional investors divided their assets between the traditional asset classes of stocks and bonds. As the markets turned sour at the beginning of the new millennium, asset management firms and institutional investors found themselves "boxed in" by these traditional asset class distinctions. They found that their investment teams were organized along traditional asset class lines, and their investment portfolios were constrained by efficient benchmarks that reflected this "asset box" approach.

Consequently, traditional asset management shops have been slow to reorganize their investment structures. This has allowed hedge funds and other alternative investment vehicles to flourish because they are not bounded by traditional asset class lines—they can invest outside the benchmark. These alternative assets are free to exploit the investment opportunities that fall in between the traditional benchmark boxes. The lack of constraints allows alternative asset managers a degree of freedom that is not allowed the traditional asset class shops. Furthermore, traditional asset management shops remain caught up in an organizational structure that is bounded by traditional asset class lines. This provides another constraint because it inhibits the flow of information and investment ideas across the organization.

ASSET LOCATION VERSUS TRADING STRATEGY   One of the first and best papers on hedge funds by Fung and Hsieh (1997) shows a distinct difference in how mutual funds and hedge funds operate. They show that the economic exposure associated with mutual funds is defined primarily by *where* the mutual fund invests. In other words, mutual funds gain their primary economic and risk exposures by the location of the asset classes in which they invest. Thus, we get large-cap active equity funds, small-cap growth funds, Treasury bond funds, and the like.

Conversely, Fung and Hsieh show that hedge funds' economic exposures are defined more by *how* they trade. That is, a hedge fund's risk and return exposure is defined more by a trading strategy within an asset class than it is defined by the location of the asset class. As a result, hedge fund managers tend to have much greater turnover in their portfolios than mutual funds.

ALTERNATIVE BETA AND THE EFFICIENT FRONTIER   Strategic asset allocation (SAA) revolves around the most efficient combination of stocks, bonds, and other asset classes to achieve the best return and risk trade-off. This is the concept behind charting the efficient frontier—the most efficient trade-off between risk and return given a mix of asset classes. In this sense, SAA is all about capturing the systematic risk premiums that exist for investing in different asset classes. However, if additional asset classes can be added to the mix, the efficient frontier can be "pushed out" to provide a greater range of risk and return opportunities for an investor.

This is another way to consider alternative assets—as an alternative source of beta that is different from the traditional mixture of stocks and bonds. Access to alternative assets can provide new systematic risk premiums that are distinctly different than that obtained from stocks and bonds. Commodities are a good example—they provide a different risk exposure than the stocks or bonds. Consequently, the risk premium associated with commodities is less than perfectly correlated with the traditional financial markets. This is a form of "alternative beta." Investing in alternative assets does not have to focus exclusively on the quest for excess returns; it can also look at the diversification properties of alternative assets when blended with a traditional portfolio of stocks and bonds. Alternative beta can be a form of added value through diversification properties instead of a desire for excess return.

ASSET CLASS RISK PREMIUMS VERSUS TRADING STRATEGY RISK PREMIUMS   Related to the idea of trading strategy versus investment location is the notion of risk premiums. You cannot earn a return without incurring risk. Traditional investment managers earn risk premiums for investing in the large-cap value equity market, small-cap growth equity market, high-yield bond market—in other words, based on the location of the asset markets in which they invest.

Conversely, alternative asset managers also earn returns for taking risk, but the risk is defined more by a trading strategy than it is an economic exposure associated with the systematic risk contained within broad financial classes. For example, hedge fund strategies such as convertible arbitrage, statistical arbitrage, and equity market neutral can earn a "complexity" risk premium (see Jaeger, 2002).

These strategies buy and sell similar securities expecting the securities to converge in value overtime. The complexity of implementing these strategies results in inefficient pricing in the market. Additionally, many investors are constrained by the *long-only* constraint—their inability to short securities. This perpetuates inefficient pricing in the marketplace, which enables hedge funds to earn a return.

Summary

This section was meant as an introduction to the different kinds of asset classes that exist for investment portfolios. To be considered an "alternative" asset class, an investment must demonstrate one of the following: a different trading strategy, a risk premium based on active trading rather than systematic market risk, an exploitation of cracks in the financial markets, a tactical application to add excess return, or a systematic risk premium that is different from that derived from stocks and bonds. Any of these characteristics can distinguish an alternative asset from a traditional asset class. The trick is to use both to extract the greatest performance for the portfolio.

References

Anson, M. J. P. (2006). *Handbook of Alternative Assets*, 2nd edition. Hoboken, NJ: John Wiley & Sons.

Fung, W., and Hsieh, D. A. (1997). Empirical characteristics of dynamic trading strategies: The case of hedge funds. *Review of Financial Studies* 10, Summer: 275–302.

Greer, R. (1997). What is an asset class anyway? *Journal of Portfolio Management* 23, 2: 83–91.

Horvitz, J. (2000). Asset classes and asset allocation: Problems of classification. *Journal of Private Portfolio Management* 2, 4: 27–32.

Jaeger, L. (2002). Managing risk in alternative investment strategies, *Financial Times*, London: Prentice Hall.

Markowitz, H. M. (1959). *Portfolio Selection*. Cowles Foundation. New Haven, Conn.: Yale University Press.

Modigliani, F., and Miller, M. (1958). The cost of capital, corporation finance, and the theory of investment. *American Economic Review* XLVIII, June: 433–443.

Sharpe, W. F. (1992). Asset allocation: Management style and performance measurement. *Journal of Portfolio Management* 18, 2: 7–19.

Part II Sources of Risk and Return in Alternative Investments

Any investment outside of traditional fixed income, equities, or cash is often considered an alternative investment. As such this category occupies a vast space in finance. Most books on asset allocation, however, continue to emphasize the return and risk characteristics of traditional stock and bond investments. Alternative investments include hedge funds, managed futures, private equity, real estate, and commodities.[1] In this chapter a working definition for each is provided. For a range of alternative investments, the historical performance and correlation with certain performance benchmarks such as the S&P 500 are presented. The overall goal is to demonstrate how these asset classes should perform within a multiasset portfolio. Throughout the analysis the period 2001 through and including 2008 is used as a reference period. This period was chosen because 2001 corresponds to the end of the dot-com bubble and is perhaps a bit more reflective of future equity and fixed income markets. There are significant caveats, however, with this approach. First, reference periods can always be used to game pro forma return results as well as risk projections. Where a period starts and where it ends can have significant consequences as to whether the performance looks great or whether the risk looks modest. We also examine the behavior of these traditional alternative asset classes in down markets. The focus on down markets is important from the perspective of risk. So long as everyone is making money, there is very little concern about correlations. However, down markets are where the portfolio shock truly takes place and where the diversification decision is truly tested. Throughout this review the chapter focuses within each section on the sources of return and the risks inherent within each asset class.

Keep in mind that this chapter focuses on the general performance of each investment area rather than the performance of individual funds or managers. The performance of a portfolio of style pure managers (managers who consistently trade the same strategy in basically similar ways) is expected to have the same general factor sensitivities as the average manager in that strategy but with lower risk.

Asset Class Performance

In Table 12.1, results for the return and risk performance of various traditional and alternative asset classes are presented. Each equity index generally has a higher level of volatility and a higher equity beta than most fixed income investments and modern alternatives. Assets in the traditional alternative investment area (private equity, real estate, commodities) generally have the highest volatility and, depending on the asset, a high equity beta as well (as will be discussed later, real estate and private equity may not necessarily be regarded as an equity diversifier but more as a return enhancement to equity dominated portfolios). Finally, hedge funds and managed futures both report moderate volatility as well as relatively low equity market betas. In Table 12.2, the correlations across the various investment asset groupings are also presented. Results reflect those presented in Table 12.1; that is, benchmarks with equity exposure have relatively high intra-asset correlations. Lastly, asset groups that can easily take long and short positions (e.g., CTA) or which hold assets not directly linked to equity or bond markets (e.g., commodities) report low correlation with other asset classes. Figure 12.1, however, indicates that the relative benefits of these asset classes may be time-specific. For example, after ranking performance of various asset classes over the period 2001 to 2008 by the S&P 500, results indicate that in years of extreme negative stock market performance, many of the listed asset classes (with the exception of credit quality fixed income and CTAs) also reported negative returns.

TABLE 12.1 Benchmark Performance

Index Performance 2001–2008	Annualized Total Return	Annualized Standard Deviation	Information Ratio	Maximum Drawdown	Beta Russell 1000	Beta Barclays U.S. Gov	Beta Barclays U.S. HY
Equity							
Russell 1000	−2.7%	15.28%	−0.18	−41.58%	1.00	(1.25)	0.96
Russell 2000	1.7%	19.55%	0.09	−42.98%	1.13	(1.58)	1.24
MSCI EAFE	−0.1%	17.00%	0.00	−49.51%	0.98	(0.94)	1.05
MSCI Emerging Markets Index	6.8%	24.41%	0.28	−60.60%	1.31	(1.29)	1.54
Fixed Income							
BarCap U.S. Gov	6.4%	4.70%	1.36	−4.64%	(0.12)	1.00	(0.04)
BarCap U.S. Agg	5.7%	3.99%	1.44	−3.83%	(0.03)	0.79	0.08
BarCap U.S. Corporate High-Yield	3.2%	10.96%	0.29	−33.31%	0.49	(0.20)	1.00
Traditional Alternatives							
S&P GSCI	−0.5%	25.57%	−0.02	−62.16%	0.33	(0.64)	0.67
FTSE NAREIT All REITs	6.4%	20.95%	0.31	−58.79%	0.81	(0.42)	1.27
Private Equity Index	−3.7%	26.43%	−0.14	−70.33%	1.44	(1.59)	1.75
Modern Alternatives							
CISDM EW Hedge Fund	5.6%	6.62%	0.84	−21.12%	0.35	(0.37)	0.44
CISDM CTA EW	9.2%	8.75%	1.05	−8.75%	(0.14)	0.49	(0.16)

TABLE 12.2 Benchmark Correlations

Index Correlation 2001–2008	Russell 1000	Russell 2000	MSCI EAFE	MSCI Emerging Markets	BarCap U.S. Gov	BaCap U.S. Agg	BarCap U.S. Corporate High-Yield	S&P GSCI	FTSE NAREIT All REITs	Private Equity Index	CISDM EW Hedge Fund Index	CISDM CTA EW Index
Equity												
Russell 1000		0.88	0.88	0.82	−0.38	−0.13	0.69	0.20	0.59	0.83	0.81	−0.25
Russell 2000	0.88		0.81	0.78	−0.38	−0.15	0.69	0.20	0.69	0.82	0.80	−0.16
MSCI EAFE	0.88	0.81		0.88	−0.26	−0.01	0.68	0.35	0.56	0.81	0.88	−0.09
MSCI Emerging Markets	0.82	0.78	0.88		−0.25	0.00	0.69	0.36	0.52	0.80	0.93	−0.03
Fixed Income												
BaCap U.S. Gov	−0.38	−0.38	−0.26	−0.25		0.94	−0.09	−0.12	−0.10	−0.28	−0.26	0.26
BarCap U.S. Aggregate	−0.13	−0.15	−0.01	0.00	0.94		0.22	−0.02	0.13	−0.06	0.00	0.17
BarCap U.S. Corporate High-Yield	0.69	0.69	0.68	0.69	−0.09	0.22		0.29	0.66	0.72	0.73	−0.20
Traditional Alternatives												
S&P GSCI	0.20	0.20	0.35	0.36	−0.12	−0.02	0.29		0.16	0.29	0.45	0.22
FTSE NAREIT All REITs	0.59	0.69	0.56	0.52	−0.10	0.13	0.66	0.16		0.62	0.52	−0.12
Private Equity Index	0.83	0.82	0.81	0.80	−0.28	−0.06	0.72	0.29	0.62		0.80	−0.14
Modern Alternatives												
CISDM EW Hedge Fund Index	0.81	0.80	0.88	0.93	−0.26	0.00	0.73	0.45	0.52	0.80		0.02
CISDM CTA EW Index	−0.25	−0.16	−0.09	−0.03	0.26	0.17	−0.20	0.22	−0.12	−0.14	0.02	

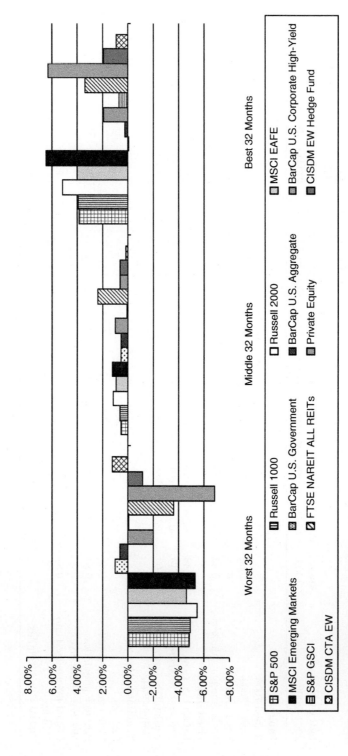

FIGURE 12.1 Benchmark Returns Ranked by S&P 500 (2001–2008)

Results at the asset class level may not reflect the potential benefits of various investment options within each class. For instance, within particular alternative asset classes, certain substrategies may have a higher correlation with other asset classes than with their own investment class (for example, within the hedge fund asset class, equity based hedge fund strategies such as equity long short may have a higher correlation with long equity strategies and distressed debt may have a higher correlation with high-yield debt than they have with a composite hedge fund index). As a result, certain subasset class groupings may be regarded as better diversifiers or return enhancers depending on the portfolio for which they are being considered as potential additions to.

As discussed in the introduction to this chapter, in the following sections we discuss (1) the various sources of return, (2) the return and risk performance, (3) the market factor sensitivity, and (4) the performance in down and up equity markets for each of five major alternative investments, that is, hedge funds, managed futures, private equity, real estate, and commodities. Results are presented both at the composite index level as well as, when available, the strategy index level.

Hedge Funds

Hedge funds have often been described as being loosely regulated private pooled investment vehicles that are often levered and generally include a performance fee. There are four principal ways in which an investor can invest in hedge funds. First, direct investments where the investor meets the standards of an "accredited investor" or "qualified purchaser." Second, an investor can invest in a fund of hedge funds. Third, there are investable hedge fund indices. Fourth, recently managers have developed hedge fund replication products. As of the end of 2009, there were more than an estimated 7,000 hedge funds managing approximately $1.5 trillion in assets. Hedge fund strategies generally fall under three primary groupings:

1. Relative value (equity market neutral, fixed income arbitrage, convertible arbitrage)
2. Event driven (merger arbitrage, distressed securities, event multi-strategy)
3. Opportunistic (equity long short, global macro)

SOURCES OF HEDGE FUND RETURN   The sources of hedge fund returns are often described as being based on the unique skill or strategy of the trader. Because hedge funds are actively managed, manager skill is important. However, academic research (Fung & Hsieh, 2002; Schneeweis, 1998; Schneeweis et al., 2002, 2003) demonstrates that hedge fund returns are also driven systematically by market factors such as changes in credit spreads or market volatility, rather than exclusively by an individual manager's alpha. Therefore, one can think of hedge fund returns as a combination of manager skill and an underlying return to the hedge fund strategy or investment style itself.

Similar to the equity and bond markets, passive security based indices have been created that are designed to capture the underlying returns to the hedge fund strategy (Schneeweis, Kazemi, and Karavas 2003; Jaeger and Wagner 2005).[2] If a manager's

TABLE 12.3   Hedge Fund and Comparison Index Performance (2001–2008)

Performance	S&P 500	BarCap U.S. Aggregate	CISDM EW Hedge Fund Index
Annualized Total Return	−2.9%	5.7%	5.6%
Annualized Standard Deviation	15.0%	4.0%	6.6%
Information Ratio	(0.19)	1.44	0.84
Maximum Drawdown	−40.7%	−3.8%	−21.1%
Correlation with Hedge Funds	0.79	0.00	1.00

Alternative Asset Performance	S&P GSCI	CISDM CTA EW Index	FTSE NAREIT All REIT	Private Equity
Annualized Total Return	−0.5%	9.2%	6.4%	−3.7%
Annualized Standard Deviation	25.6%	8.7%	20.9%	26.4%
Information Ratio	(0.02)	1.05	0.31	(0.14)
Maximum Drawdown	−62.2%	−8.7%	−58.8%	−70.3%
Correlation with Hedge Funds	0.45	0.02	0.52	0.80

performance is measured relative to the investable passive hedge fund index, for example, then the differential return may be viewed as the manager's "alpha" (return in excess of a nonmanager based strategy similar replicate portfolio). If a manager's performance is measured relative to an index of other active managers, then the relative performance simply measures the over- or underperformance to that index of manager returns.

HEDGE FUND RETURN AND RISK PERFORMANCE   Table 12.3 shows the risk and return performance of hedge funds, traditional U.S. stocks and bonds, CTAs, real estate, commodities, and private equity for the period of 2001 to 2008. Portfolio combinations that include traditional assets and alternative investments for the most recent eight-year period 2001 to 2008 are shown in Table 12.4. Over the period of

TABLE 12.4   Multiple Asset Class Portfolio Performance (2001–2008)

Portfolio	A	B	C	D
Annualized Returns	1.7%	2.1%	2.4%	2.7%
Standard Deviation	7.5%	7.3%	8.4%	8.1%
Information Ratio	0.22	0.28	0.29	0.34
Maximum Drawdown	−21.0%	−21.0%	−25.6%	−25.2%
Correlation with Hedge Funds	0.79		0.78	
Portfolio A	Equal Weights S&P 500 and BarCap U.S. Agg			
Portfolio B	90% Portfolio A and 10% Hedge Funds			
Portfolio C	75% Portfolio A and 25% CTA/Commodities/ Private Equity/Real Estate			
Portfolio D	90% Portfolio C and 10% Hedge Funds			

analysis, hedge funds reported higher annualized returns but lower volatility than the S&P 500. Compared to the returns of the Barclays Capital U.S. Bond Aggregate Index, hedge funds reported slightly lower rates of return but with higher volatility. Also, compared to CTAs and real estate, hedge funds reported a lower return but lower volatility. Next, compared to commodities and private equity, hedge funds reported higher returns and lower volatility. Table 12.4 shows that the information ratios for portfolios that include at least a 10 percent investment in hedge funds dominate those portfolios that do not contain an investment in hedge funds.

The high correlation of the CISDM EW Hedge Fund index with the S&P 500 is due in part to the dominance of hedge fund index returns by equity-biased hedge funds. As shown in Table 12.5, hedge funds (equity market neutral, convertible arbitrage, fixed income arbitrage) that have in part removed the impact of associated market factor from their returns have correlations with the S&P 500 of under .60, and global macro, which trades global markets opportunistically, has a correlation of only .30. In contrast, equity long short and emerging markets hedge funds report correlations with the S&P 500 of close to or over .70. This is as expected. As discussed previously, each unique hedge fund strategy trades in particular markets such that their performance is sensitive to the underlying movements of securities in those markets. As a result, hedge fund strategies that primarily trade equity markets (e.g., equity long short) may be viewed as return enhancers to traditional equity portfolios rather than as risk diversifiers. Other traditional hedge fund strategies such as distressed securities, fixed income arbitrage, and convertible arbitrage often trade in high-yield debt. As indicated in Table 12.5, the correlation of these three strategies

TABLE 12.5   Performance of CISDM Hedge Fund Strategy Indices (2001–2008)

	Annualized Return	Standard Deviation	Correlation S&P 500	Correlation BarCap U.S. Gov	Correlation BarCap U.S. Corporate High-Yield
CISDM Equity Market Neutral	5.6%	2.0%	0.44	−0.16	0.40
CISDM Fixed Income Arbitrage	3.6%	4.8%	0.56	−0.18	0.75
CISDM Convertible Arbitrage	3.3%	6.2%	0.46	0.05	0.69
CISDM Distressed Securities	7.6%	6.0%	0.65	−0.16	0.77
CISDM Event Driven Multi-Strategy	5.6%	6.3%	0.76	−0.27	0.78
CISDM Merger Arbitrage	4.8%	3.4%	0.66	−0.17	0.65
CISDM Emerging Markets	7.9%	10.5%	0.69	−0.17	0.71
CISDM Equity Long/Short	4.4%	6.0%	0.77	−0.32	0.62
CISDM Global Macro	6.4%	3.3%	0.30	0.05	0.28
S&P 500	−2.9%	15.0%	1.00	−0.39	0.68
BarCap U.S. Gov	6.4%	4.7%	−0.39	1.00	−0.09
BarCap U.S. Corporate High-Yield	3.2%	11.0%	0.68	−0.09	1.00

with the Barclays Capital U.S. Corporate High-Yield Index are all close to or over .70. Similarly, hedge fund strategies that primarily trade high-yield debt (e.g., distressed securities) may be viewed as return enhancers to high-yield debt portfolios rather than as risk diversifiers.

In general, hedge funds and their associated strategies cover a broad array of risk/return scenarios. In Table 12.6, the correlation of various hedge fund strategies are given. Note that strategies that trade in similar markets or are exposed to similar risks should have higher correlations (equity long short and emerging markets) than strategies that trade in fundamentally different markets (global macro and merger arbitrage).

HEDGE FUND PERFORMANCE IN DOWN AND UP EQUITY MARKETS   Figure 12.2 depicts the performance of various hedge fund strategies in months in which the S&P 500 had its worst and best performance over the period 2001 to 2008. Results show that, relative to other hedge fund strategies, hedge fund strategies with significant equity bias (e.g., event driven, equity long short, and emerging markets) had the most negative returns in the worst S&P 500 months as well as the highest positive returns in the months in which the S&P 500 had its best performance.

Managed Futures (Commodity Trading Advisors)

The term "managed futures" represents an industry composed of professional money managers known as commodity trading advisors (CTAs) or commodity pool operators (CPOs). Commodity trading advisors or commodity pool operators manage client assets on a discretionary basis, using forwards, futures, and options markets as the primary investment area. Managed futures, through their ability to take both long and short investment positions in international financial and nonfinancial asset sectors, offer risk and return patterns not easily accessible through traditional (such as long-only stock and bond portfolios) or other nontraditional investments (e.g., hedge funds, real estate, private equity, or commodities).

Investors generally invest in CTAs using individual managed accounts. Investors can also access the managed futures industry by investing through a commodity pool that resembles a mutual fund. Investments from several investors are pooled together and then invested in futures either directly by the pool operator or through one or more commodity trading advisors. CPOs may be either public or private. Currently several noninvestable as well as investable manager based CTA indices are available.

SOURCES OF MANAGED FUTURES RETURN   The sources of return to managed futures are uniquely different from traditional stocks, bonds, or even hedge funds. For instance, futures and options contracts can provide direct exposure to underlying financial and commodity markets. Therefore, while actively traded futures and options may provide similar returns to the underlying assets, but often with greater liquidity and less market impact, they may also easily take short positions or actively allocate assets between long and short positions. In addition, options traders may also directly trade market/security characteristics, such as price volatility, that underlie the contract.

TABLE 12.6 CISDM Hedge Fund Strategy Correlations (2001–2008)

	Equity Market Neutral	Fixed Income Arbitrage	Convertible Arbitrage	Distressed Securities	Event Driven Multi-Strategy	Merger Arbitrage	Emerging Markets	Equity Long/Short	Global Macro
CISDM Equity Market Neutral	1.00	0.39	0.45	0.54	0.68	0.61	0.65	0.76	0.57
CISDM Fixed Income Arbitrage	0.39	1.00	0.78	0.80	0.73	0.50	0.74	0.53	0.12
CISDM Convertible Arbitrage	0.45	0.78	1.00	0.79	0.71	0.56	0.69	0.53	0.24
CISDM Distressed Securities	0.54	0.80	0.79	1.00	0.90	0.68	0.83	0.75	0.36
CISDM Event Driven Multi-Strategy	0.68	0.73	0.71	0.90	1.00	0.82	0.86	0.89	0.47
CISDM Merger Arbitrage	0.61	0.50	0.56	0.68	0.82	1.00	0.65	0.79	0.45
CISDM Emerging Markets	0.65	0.74	0.69	0.83	0.86	0.65	1.00	0.83	0.47
CISDM Equity Long/Short	0.76	0.53	0.53	0.75	0.89	0.79	0.83	1.00	0.60
CISDM Global Macro	0.57	0.12	0.24	0.36	0.47	0.45	0.47	0.60	1.00

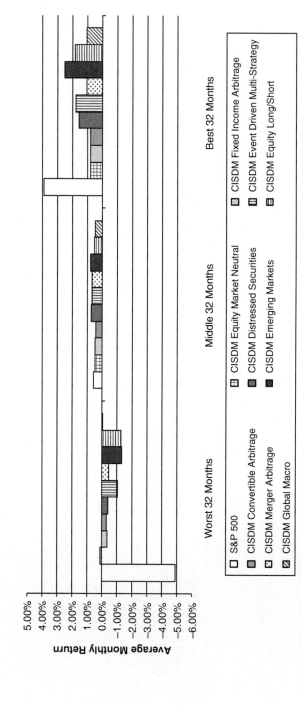

FIGURE 12.2 CISDM Hedge Fund Strategy Returns Ranked by S&P 500 (2001–2008)

As for hedge funds, the sources of managed futures returns have also been described as being based on the unique skill or strategy of the trader. Because CTAs actively trade, manager skill is important. Many managed futures strategies trade primarily in futures markets, which are zero-sum games. If CTAs were only trading against other CTAs, then it may be concluded that an individual managed futures program's returns are based solely on manager skill. However some spot market players are willing to sell or hedge positions even if they expect spot prices to rise or fall in their favor (e.g., currency and interest rate futures may trend over time due to government policy to smooth price movements). Since academic research (Schneeweis, 1998), has demonstrated that managed futures returns may be driven by systematic market factors such as changes in interest rates, exchange rates, or market volatility, rather than exclusively by an individual manager's alpha, we can also think of CTA returns as a combination of manager skill and an underlying return to the CTA strategy or investment style itself. Similar to the equity and bond markets, passive CTA security based indices have been created that are designed to capture the underlying return to the CTA strategy (Schneeweis, Kazemi, and Karavas 2003; Jaeger and Wagner 2005). If a manager's performance is measured relative to the systematic passive CTA index, for example, then the differential return may be viewed as the manager's "alpha" (return in excess of a nonmanager based strategy similar replicate portfolio). If a manager's performance is measured relative to an index of other active managers, then the relative performance simply measures the over- or underperformance to that index of manager returns.

MANAGED FUTURES RETURN AND RISK PERFORMANCE   Table 12.7 shows the risk and return performance of CTAs, traditional U.S. stocks and bonds, hedge funds, real estate, commodities, and private equity indices for the period 2001 to 2008. Portfolio combinations that include traditional and alternative investments for the most recent

TABLE 12.7   CTA and Comparison Benchmark Performance (2001–2008)

	S&P 500	BarCap U.S. Agg	CISDM CTA EW
Annualized Total Return	−2.9%	5.7%	9.2%
Annualized Standard Deviation	15.0%	4.0%	8.7%
Information Ratio	−0.19	1.44	1.05
Maximum Drawdown	−40.7%	−3.8%	−8.7%
Correlation with CTA	−0.26	0.17	1.00

	S&P GSCI	CISDM EW Hedge Funds	FTSE NAREIT All	Private Equity
Annualized Total Return	−0.5%	5.6%	6.4%	−3.7%
Annualized Standard Deviation	25.6%	6.6%	20.9%	26.4%
Information Ratio	−0.02	0.84	0.31	−0.14
Maximum Drawdown	−62.2%	−21.1%	−58.8%	−70.3%
Correlation with CTA	0.22	0.02	−0.12	−0.14

TABLE 12.8 Multiasset Portfolio Performance (2001–2008)

Portfolio	A	B	C	D
Annualized Returns	1.7%	2.5%	2.2%	2.9%
Standard Deviation	7.5%	6.6%	8.8%	7.8%
Information Ratio	0.22	0.37	0.25	0.37
Maximum Drawdown	−21.0%	−17.3%	−27.8%	−23.6%
Correlation with CTA	(0.22)		(0.14)	
Portfolio A	Equal Weights S&P 500 and BarCap U.S. Aggregate			
Portfolio B	90% Portfolio A and 10% CTA			
Portfolio C	75% Portfolio A and 25% HF/Commodities/Private Equity/ Real Estate			
Portfolio D	90% Portfolio C and 10% CTAs			

eight year period 2001 to 2008 are also reviewed in Table 12.8. Over the period of analysis, managed futures reported a higher annualized return and lower volatility than the S&P 500. Compared to the returns of the Barclays Capital U.S. Aggregate Bond Index, managed futures again reported higher rates of return albeit with higher volatility. Compared to the private equity and real estate and commodities, managed futures reported a higher return with significantly lower volatilities. Finally, compared to hedge funds, managed futures reported higher returns but higher volatilities. It can be observed from Table 12.8 that the information ratios for portfolios that include at least a 10 percent investment in CTAs dominate those portfolios that do not contain an investment in CTAs.

CTA strategies provide a broadly diverse mix of opportunities. Some CTAs trade in a more systematic fashion using an array of algorithmic based trading strategies often based on historical pricing patterns. Other CTAs trade a more discretionary style based on a wider range of economic and manager based trading systems. In addition, certain CTAs may concentrate on shorter- or longer-term models to dominate their trading focus. As a result, CTAs may be separated into a range of various strategy and market focus groupings including currency, financial, diversified CTAs, as well as systematic and discretionary CTAs. As indicated in Table 12.9, the results show that with the exception of CTAs who trade primarily in equity futures, most CTA managers (market or strategy based) have a low correlation with most traditional stock and bond markets.

In Table 12.10, the correlation of various CTA strategies are given. In general most CTAs trade using systematic trading models. As a result, results in Table 12.10 show a high correlation between the CTA systematic index and other market based CTA strategies (financial). However, results in Table 12.10 also show a low correlation between the CTA systematic index and the CTA discretionary index reflecting the differential trading styles.

MANAGED FUTURES PERFORMANCE IN DOWN AND UP EQUITY MARKETS Figure 12.3 depicts the performance over various CTA strategies in months in which the S&P 500 had its worst and best performance over the period 2001 to 2008. Results show that, relative to other CTAs, the various CTA strategies with the exception of the equity CTAs provided positive returns in the worst S&P 500 months but also provided positive returns in the best S&P 500 months.

TABLE 12.9 Performance of CISDM CTA Indices (2001–2008)

	Annualized Return	Standard Deviation	Correlation S&P 500	Correlation BarCap U.S. Gov	Correlation BarCap U.S. Corporate High-Yield
CISDM CTA EW Currency	5.9%	5.6%	0.10	0.10	-0.10
CISDM CTA EW Financials	7.8%	8.5%	-0.28	0.30	-0.22
CISDM CTA EW Diversified	10.7%	11.2%	-0.28	0.27	-0.22
CISDM CTA EW Equity	6.6%	7.9%	0.37	-0.07	0.41
CISDM CTA EW Physicals	8.3%	8.7%	-0.13	0.04	-0.10
CISDM CTA EW Systematic	9.0%	9.8%	-0.27	0.23	-0.21
CISDM CTA EW Discretionary	11.1%	6.4%	0.19	0.09	0.23
S&P 500	-2.9%	15.0%	1.00	-0.39	0.68
BarCap U.S. Government	6.4%	4.7%	-0.39	1.00	-0.09
BarCap U.S. Corporate High-Yield	3.2%	11.0%	0.68	-0.09	1.00

TABLE 12.10   CISDM CTA Indices Correlation (2001–2008)

	Currency	Financials	Diversified	Equity	Physicals	Systematic	Discretionary
CISDM CTA EW Currency	1.00	0.61	0.62	−0.02	0.30	0.65	0.20
CISDM CTA EW Financials	0.61	1.00	0.88	0.04	0.49	0.91	0.27
CISDM CTA EW Diversified	0.62	0.88	1.00	0.01	0.64	0.97	0.35
CISDM CTA EW Equity	−0.02	0.04	0.01	1.00	0.01	0.03	0.64
CISDM CTA EW Physicals	0.30	0.49	0.64	0.01	1.00	0.62	0.40
CISDM CTA EW Systematic	0.65	0.91	0.97	0.03	0.62	1.00	0.29
CISDM CTA EW Discretionary	0.20	0.27	0.35	0.64	0.40	0.29	1.00

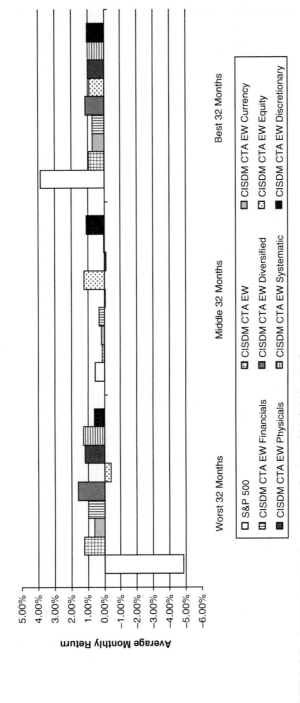

FIGURE 12.3 CISDM CTA Indices Ranked by S&P 500 (2001–2008)

593

Private Equity

Private equity is often viewed as ownership in private or nonpublicly traded business. These ownership stakes may take various forms (proprietorship, partnership, and other corporate or legal entities). It is important to note that private equity is viewed by some as including the entire range of nonpublic investments from early stage through final stage investments. For others, private equity is limited to that section of the nonpublic investment process in which capital is raised via a private placement in contrast to a public offering. Often private equity is discussed within five distinct stages or forms of investment. These include angel investors (generally seed capital), venture capital (startup/first stage), leveraged buyouts, mezzanine investing, and distressed debt investing (later-stage investing). The long-term goal of many private equity investments is to have the enterprise sold to other investors either through private sales, mergers, or initial public offerings. Investors in private equity should also be aware that the initial nonpublic nature of the private equity holdings makes valuation of the underlying shares difficult.

SOURCES OF PRIVATE EQUITY RETURN Private equity is generally regarded as an investment that offers investors the opportunity to achieve superior long-term returns compared to traditional public equity investment. The basis for returns to private equity is similar to that for traditional stock and bond investment, that is, a claim on long-term earnings, a return premium for providing capital to an illiquid and risky investment, and positive alpha generated from the value that private equity managers may create by their proactive influence on the invested companies' management and operations. However, it is difficult to determine the actual historical return to private equity investment. Private investment vehicles have a net asset value that is often determined as an internal appraisal value and not by a public market transaction. Thus actual returns are often measured as an internal rate of return or cash disbursements relative to capital investment. These cash flows may be lower at the initial stage than at later stages of the capital investment (known as the J-curve effect). However, in recent years, several forms of publicly traded private equity vehicles have come into existence. These include, among others, publicly listed investment companies, business development companies, and special purpose acquisition vehicles. These investment vehicles have provided a basis for measuring rates of return based on public market valuations.

PRIVATE EQUITY RETURN AND RISK PERFORMANCE Table 12.11 provides the risk and return characteristics of the private equity index, traditional U.S. equity and bond indices, and other alternative investment indices for the period 2001 to 2008. Portfolio combinations that include traditional assets and alternative investments for the most recent eight-year period 2001 to 2008 are also reviewed. Over the period of analysis, the private equity index reported lower annualized return and higher risk (as measured by standard deviation) than the S&P 500, the Barclays Capital Aggregate Bond, CISDM hedge fund and CTA indices, real estate, and the commodities index.

The correlations between the private equity index and other equity sensitive assets such as real estate, hedge funds, and the S&P 500 are significant. However,

TABLE 12.11   Private Equity and Comparison Benchmark Performance (2001–2008)

	S&P 500	BarCap U.S. Agg	Private Equity
Annualized Total Return	−2.9%	5.7%	−3.7%
Annualized Standard Deviation	15.0%	4.0%	26.4%
Information Ratio	(0.19)	1.44	(0.14)
Maximum Drawdown	−40.7%	−3.8%	−70.3%
Correlation with Private Equity	0.83	(0.06)	1.00

	CISDM EW Hedge Funds	CISDM CTA EW	S&P GSCI	FTSE NAREIT All REIT
Annualized Total Return	5.6%	9.2%	−0.5%	6.4%
Annualized Standard Deviation	6.6%	8.7%	25.6%	20.9%
Information Ratio	0.84	1.05	(0.02)	0.31
Maximum Drawdown	−21.1%	−8.7%	−62.2%	−58.8%
Correlation with Private Equity	0.80	(0.14)	0.29	0.62

the correlations of private equity with the other nonequity based indices are very low, suggesting that, over the most recent eight-year period, additional diversification benefits could have been achieved by adding private equity to a nonequity based portfolio, but that adding private equity to an equity biased portfolio may offer limited diversification. It can be observed from Table 12.12 that the information ratios for portfolios that include at least a 10 percent investment in private equity hedge funds failed to dominate those portfolios that do not include an investment in private equity. Investment in publicly traded private equity may therefore be based primarily on expected future returns rather than recent past performance.

PRIVATE EQUITY PERFORMANCE IN DOWN AND UP EQUITY MARKETS   Private equity often refers to a wide range of potential prepublicly traded investment opportunities. These opportunities are often grouped into angel investing (initial seed capital); venture capital (startup opportunities); mezzanine finance (bridge loans); and more mature private equity vehicles (mature or pre-IPO). These various opportunities can be broken down into specific areas of investment (e.g., biotech or computers) as well as geographical area of focus (e.g., United States, Europe, or Asia). Each subarea may

TABLE 12.12   Multiple Asset Class Portfolio Performance (2001–2008)

Portfolio	A	B	C	D
Annualized Returns	1.7%	1.34%	2.9%	2.4%
Standard Deviation	7.5%	9.0%	7.2%	8.9%
Information Ratio	0.22	0.15	0.39	0.27
Maximum Drawdown	−21.0%	−27.1%	−21.9%	−27.8%
Correlation with Real Estate	0.81		0.84	
Portfolio A	Equal Weights S&P 500 and BarCap U.S. Aggregate			
Portfolio B	90% Portfolio A and 10% Private Equity			
Portfolio C	75% Portfolio A and 25% HF/CTA/Real Estate/Commodities			
Portfolio D	90% Portfolio C and 10% Private Equity			

have its own return and risk characteristics; however, as a general class, private equity remains more of an equity return enhancer than an equity diversifier. In Figure 12.4, the high correlation between publicly traded private equity vehicles and the S&P 500 is shown, with private equity performing poorly in down S&P 500 months and performing well in positive S&P 500 months.

Real Estate

Real estate investment has generally been regarded as a primary part of individual and institutional investors' portfolios. Over the recent years, however, the sector itself has undergone a dramatic transformation. In the past, the physical real estate market has been characterized by a relative lack of liquidity, high transaction costs, high management costs, high information costs, and low transparency. However, some of the costs of investing in real estate have been reduced in recent years, since initiatives to enhance liquidity and transparency in the property markets have been put forth. Despite these changes, real estate investments are still substantially different from country to country, region to region, and property type to property type. As real estate investment opportunities differ widely, traditional real estate may be better viewed as return enhancement vehicles to equity based as well as fixed income investments. This is due, in part, to the impact of interest rates on the present value of fixed cash flows often generated by real estate and the fact that dramatic changes in global economic conditions may impact both the financing of real estate as well as the demand. Moreover, many investors access real estate investment through equity based investment vehicles (e.g., real estate investment trusts). These investment firms often have investment characteristics associated with the general equity market in addition to their more specific real estate characteristics. While traditional real estate may provide diversification and return benefits, their comovements with existing stock and bond investments as well as to certain alternative (hedge funds, private equity) portfolios must be considered carefully.

In addition, the relative performance characteristics are dependent in part on the business model of the investment firm and the characteristics of the underlying real estate (e.g., commercial, housing). Public investment involves buying shares of real estate investment companies (REITs) or other forms of indirect financial investment (e.g., futures or ETFs based on real estate). The real estate market is composed of several segments that include housing or residential real estate properties, commercial real estate properties, farmland, and timberland. Until recently, the advent of securitization has broadened investor access to include a wider range of real estate investment. The impact of recent market events on the future securitization of real estate investments depends both on future economic developments and regulatory constraints and oversight of these products.

SOURCES OF REAL ESTATE RETURN   Real estate prices are determined by a myriad of factors. Among those that have been mentioned in the literature, we can list the following (Case and Shiller 2003; Sabal 2005):

- Long-term population growth, which is in turn determined by birth rates and migration flows.

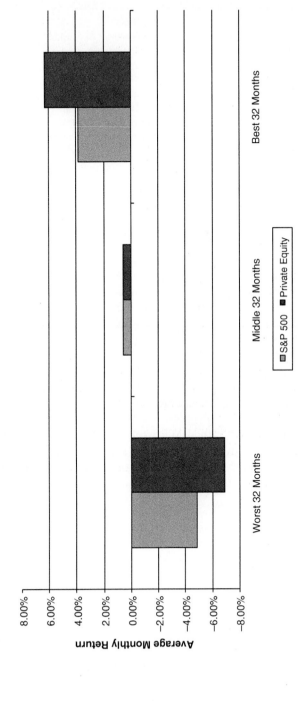

FIGURE 12.4 Private Equity Returns Ranked by S&P 500 (2001–2008)

TABLE 12.13   Real Estate and Comparison Benchmark Performance (2001–2008)

	S&P 500	BarCap U.S. Agg	FTSE NAREIT All
Annualized Total Return	−2.9%	5.7%	6.4%
Annualized Standard Deviation	15.0%	4.0%	20.9%
Information Ratio	(0.19)	1.44	0.31
Maximum Drawdown	−40.7%	−3.8%	−58.8%
Correlation with FTSE NAREIT All REIT	0.58	0.13	1.00

	CISDM EW Hedge Funds	CISDM CTA EW	S&P GSCI	Private Equity
Annualized Total Return	5.6%	9.2%	−0.5%	−3.7%
Annualized Standard Deviation	6.6%	8.7%	25.6%	26.4%
Information Ratio	84.3%	104.8%	−1.8%	−13.9%
Maximum Drawdown	−21.1%	−8.7%	−62.2%	−70.3%
Correlation with FTSE NAREIT All REIT	51.7%	−12.4%	15.9%	62.3%

- Uniqueness of the property. Since real estate is a heterogeneous asset, prices between two properties are not perfectly comparable. For example, new homes are priced differently than those in the secondary market, smaller properties are more expensive by the square foot, some homes respond better to customer needs and are thus more expensive, and so on.
- Government planning and regulations on the use of land have a crucial role in the real estate market through the influence these actions may have on real estate supply.
- Disposable income, which is closely related to unemployment and economic growth, and availability of financing are key determinants of property prices.

REAL ESTATE RETURN AND RISK PERFORMANCE   Table 12.13 shows the risk and return performance of real estate investment trusts, traditional U.S. stocks and bonds, hedge funds, CTAs, commodities, and private equity indices for the period 2001 to 2008. Table 12.14 shows portfolio combinations that include traditional assets and

TABLE 12.14   Multiasset Portfolio Performance (2001–2008)

	A	B	C	D
Annualized Returns	1.7%	2.3%	2.3%	2.8%
Standard Deviation	7.5%	8.2%	7.8%	8.5%
Information Ratio	0.22	0.28	0.29	0.33
Maximum Drawdown	−21.0%	−24.5%	−23.5%	−26.7%
Correlation with Real Estate	0.61		0.62	
Portfolio A	Equal Weights S&P 500 and BarCap U.S. Aggregate			
Portfolio B	90% Portfolio A and 10% Real Estate			
Portfolio C	75% Portfolio A and 25% HF/CTA/Private Equity/Commodities			
Portfolio D	90% Portfolio C and 10% Real Estate			

alternative investments and real estate for the most recent eight-year period 2001 to 2008. Over the period of analysis, the real estate index reported a higher annualized return and a slightly higher volatility than the S&P 500. Compared to the returns of the Barclays Capital U.S. Aggregate Bond Index, real estate investments again reported significantly higher rates of return albeit with higher volatility. In addition, when compared to the hedge funds, the real estate index reported a higher return but with higher risk. When compared to the CTAs, the real estate index reported a higher return but with higher risk. Finally, the real estate index reported higher returns than private equity and commodity investments but with lower risk levels.

We can again observe moderate correlations between the real estate index and traditional asset classes and the other alternative investments (hedge funds, private equity) with equity exposure. This again suggests that, over the most recent eight year period, the additional diversification benefits that exist by adding real estate to an already diversified equity biased portfolio may come primarily from return enhancement in contrast to risk reduction. Table 12.14 shows, however, that the information ratios for portfolios that include at least a 10 percent investment dominate those portfolios that do not contain an investment in real estate.

Similar to other alternatives, FTSE REIT securities cover a broad array of real estate concentrations. The performance characteristics and correlation of the primary FTSE REIT sectors are given in Table 12.15 and Table 12.16. The three primary sectors are:

1. **Equity REITs:** Equity REITs mostly own and operate income-producing real estate. They increasingly have become real estate operating companies engaged in a wide range of real estate activities, including leasing, maintenance, and development of real property and tenant services. One major distinction between REITs and other real estate companies is that a REIT must acquire and develop its properties primarily to operate them as part of its own portfolio rather than to resell them once they are developed.
2. **Mortgage REITs:** Mortgage REITs mostly lend money directly to real estate owners and operators or extend credit indirectly through the acquisition of loans or mortgage-backed securities. Today's mortgage REITs generally extend mortgage credit only on existing properties. Many mortgage REITs also manage their interest rate and credit risks using securitized mortgage investments, dynamic hedging techniques, and other accepted derivative strategies.
3. **Hybrid REITs:** As the name suggests, a hybrid REIT both owns properties and makes loans to real estate owners and operators. Of the various FTSE REIT sectors, those that concentrate on ownership of properties (equity REITs) have had the best performance relative to those such as mortgage and hybrid, which also include direct loans as a primary part of their portfolio.

REAL ESTATE PERFORMANCE IN DOWN AND UP EQUITY MARKETS   As with other alternative asset classes, real estate covers a wide range of potential investment opportunities. These opportunities are often grouped into retail and commercial investments. However, equity based investments in various real estate opportunities provide the most liquid and transparent of the various investment vehicles. Each subarea may have its own return and risk characteristics; however, as a general class, when returns

TABLE 12.15   Performance of Real Estate Market Segment Indices (2001–2008)

	Annualized Return	Standard Deviation	Correlation S&P 500	Correlation BarCap U.S. Government	Correlation BarCap U.S. Corporate High-Yield
FTSE NAREIT All REITs	6.4%	20.9%	–0.10	–0.10	0.66
FTSE NAREIT Equity REITs	6.8%	21.6%	0.57	–0.10	0.66
FTSE NAREIT Mortgage REITs	5.8%	24.9%	0.33	0.03	0.37
FTSE NAREIT Hybrid REITs	–4.0%	30.2%	0.48	0.00	0.64
S&P 500	–2.9%	15.0%	1.00	–0.39	0.68
BarCap U.S. Government	6.4%	4.7%	–0.39	1.00	–0.09
BarCap U.S. Corporate High-Yield	3.2%	11.0%	0.68	–0.09	1.00

TABLE 12.16 FTSE REITs Sector Correlations (2001–2008)

Correlation (2001–2008)	All REITs	Equity REITs	Mortgage REITs	Hybrid REITs
FTSE NAREIT All REITs	1.00	1.00	0.51	0.66
FTSE NAREIT Equity REITs	1.00	1.00	0.45	0.62
FTSE NAREIT Mortgage REITs	0.51	0.45	1.00	0.63
FTSE NAREIT Hybrid REITs	0.66	0.62	0.63	1.00

are ranked by the S&P 500, they provide negative returns in down S&P 500 markets and positive returns in up S&P 500 markets (see Figure 12.5). In short, public real estate vehicles also remain more of an equity return enhancer than an equity diversifier.

Commodities

Commodity indices attempt to replicate the returns available to holding long positions in agricultural, metal, energy, or livestock investments. Since returns on a fully invested futures contract reflect that of an investment in the underlying deliverable, commodity indices based on the returns of futures/forward contracts offer an efficient means to obtain commodity exposure. A number of commodities indices offer access to commodity investment. These indices may differ in a number of ways, such as the commodities included in the index, the weights of the individual commodities, as well as a number of operational trading issues (e.g., roll period or rebalancing).

SOURCES OF RETURN FOR COMMODITIES Investor benefits of commodity or commodity based products lie primarily in their ability to offer risk/return tradeoffs that cannot be easily replicated through other investment alternatives. Academic research (Williams 1986) has examined the economic determinants of returns to commodity investment. As with any futures based investment, returns are determined by both the expected returns on the deliverable and the expected cost of carry returns, as well as other storage and deliverable options. For example, as expected, Fama and French (1988) and Schneeweis, Spurgin, and Georgiev (2000) identified a strong business cycle component in industrial metals based futures contracts, a finding that is consistent with the business cycle variation of spot and futures prices of industrial metals.[3] Commodity based index returns can also benefit from multiple sources of returns, many of which tend not to be correlated. These can include spot,[4] roll,[5] beta, momentum, rebalancing, and Treasury Bill, returns. However, each index has its own unique portfolio attribution characteristics and can be impacted by additional factors like diversification, commodity component weighting, and roll schedule.

COMMODITY RETURN AND RISK PERFORMANCE Results in Table 12.17 show the risk and return performance of the S&P GSCI commodity index, traditional U.S.

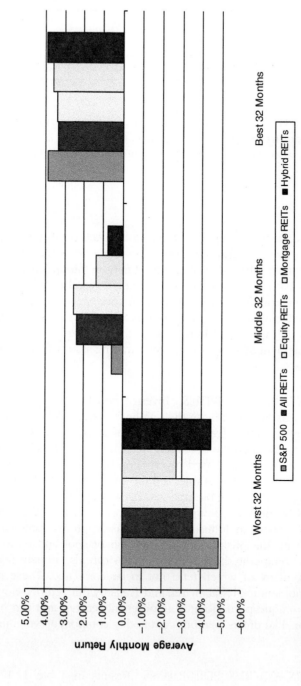

FIGURE 12.5 FTSE REIT Returns Ranked by S&P 500 (2001–2008)

TABLE 12.17   Commodity and Comparison Benchmark Performance

	S&P 500	BarCap U.S. Agg	S&P GSCI
Annualized Total Return	−2.9%	5.7%	−0.5%
Annualized Standard Deviation	15.0%	4.0%	25.6%
Information Ratio	−0.19	1.44	−0.02
Maximum Drawdown	−40.7%	−3.8%	−62.2%
Correlation with Commodities	0.18	(0.02)	1.00

	CISDM EW Hedge Funds	CISDM CTA EW	FTSE NAREIT All Reit	Private Equity
Annualized Total Return	5.6%	9.2%	6.4%	−3.7%
Annualized Standard Deviation	6.6%	8.7%	20.9%	26.4%
Information Ratio	0.84	1.05	0.31	−0.14
Maximum Drawdown	−21.1%	−8.7%	−58.8%	−70.3%
Correlation with Commodities	0.4	0.2	0.2	0.3

equity and bond indices, the hedge fund and CTA indices, and the real estate and private equity indices for the period 2001 to 2008. Portfolio combinations that include traditional assets, alternative investments (e.g., hedge funds and CTAs), and commodities for the most recent eight-year period 2001 to 2008 are also reviewed. Over the period of analysis, the S&P GSCI reported higher annualized returns as well as higher volatility than the S&P 500. Compared to the returns of the Barclays Capital U.S. Aggregate Bond index, the S&P GSCI reported a lower rate of return as well as higher volatility. Compared to the returns of the CISDM hedge fund and CTA indices, the S&P GSCI reported lower returns with higher risk. Lastly, the S&P GSCI reported higher returns and lower risk than the private equity and lower returns but with slightly higher risk than the real estate index.

In brief, the weak correlations between the S&P GSCI and hedge funds, CTAs, real estate, private equity, and traditional asset classes again suggest that over the most recent eight-year period additional diversification benefits can exist by adding commodities to an already diversified portfolio. As shown in Table 12.18, information ratios for portfolios that include at least a 10 percent investment in commodities dominate those in portfolios that do not contain an investment in commodities.

TABLE 12.18   Portfolio Performance (2001−2008)

Portfolios	A	B	C	D
Annualized Returns	1.7%	2.5%	2.6%	3.3%
Standard Deviation	7.5%	6.6%	.2%	7.3%
Information Ratio	0.22	0.37	0.32	0.46
Maximum Drawdown	−21%	−17%	−25%	−21%
Correlation with Commodity	0.21		0.27	
Portfolio A	Equal Weights S&P 500 and BarCap U.S. Aggregate			
Portfolio B	90% Portfolio A and 10% Commodities			
Portfolio C	75% Portfolio A and 25% HF/CTA/Private Equity/Real Estate			
Portfolio D	90% Portfolio C and 10% Commodities			

TABLE 12.19 Performance of S&P GSCI Market Segment Indices (2001–2008)

	Annualized Return	Standard Deviation	Correlation S&P 500	Correlation BarCap U.S. Govt	Correlation BarCap U.S. Corporate High-Yield
S&P GSCI Agriculture	−3.2%	20.8%	0.05	0.05	0.26
S&P GSCI Energy	−1.1%	33.8%	0.12	−0.12	0.23
S&P GSCI Grains	−1.6%	23.8%	0.21	0.11	0.24
S&P GSCI Industrial Metal	5.8%	23.7%	0.48	−0.26	0.40
S&P GSCI Livestock	−4.3%	15.5%	0.08	−0.13	0.08
S&P GSCI Total Petroleum	5.9%	33.3%	0.14	−0.16	0.27
S&P 500	−2.9%	15.0%	1.00	−0.39	0.68
BarCap U.S. Government	6.4%	4.7%	−0.39	1.00	−0.09
BarCap U.S. Corporate High-Yield	3.2%	11.0%	0.68	−0.09	1.00

TABLE 12.20 Commodity Sector Correlations (2001–2008)

	S&P GSCI Agriculture	S&P GSCI Energy	S&P GSCI Grains	S&P GSCI Industrial Metal	S&P GSCI Livestock	S&P GSCI Non-Livestock	S&P GSCI Petroleum
S&P GSCI Agriculture	1.00	0.17	0.96	0.37	0.05	0.31	0.17
S&P Energy	0.17	1.00	0.12	0.39	0.07	0.99	0.97
S&P GSCI Grains	0.96	0.12	1.00	0.28	0.07	0.25	0.11
S&P GSCI Industrial Metal	0.37	0.39	0.28	1.00	0.13	0.49	0.41
S&P GSCI Total Livestock	0.05	0.07	0.07	0.13	1.00	0.09	0.09
S&P GSCI Total Petroleum	0.17	0.97	0.11	0.41	0.09	0.96	1.00

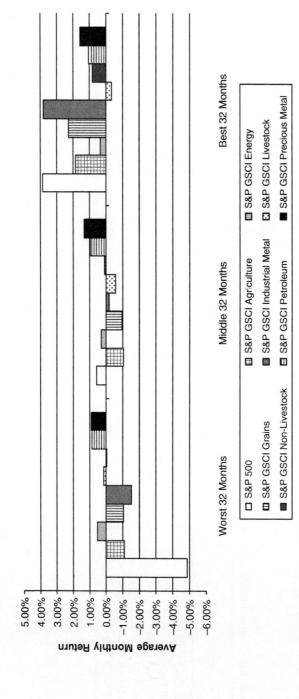

FIGURE 12.6 Commodity Benchmark Ranked by S&P 500 (2001–2008)

Commodity investments cover a wide variety of sectors. The performance characteristics and correlation of the primary S&P GSCI commodity sectors with traditional market indices are given in Table 12.19. As shown in Table 12.20, over the period 2001 to 2008, the various commodity indices reflect a low correlation to traditional market indices as well as to other comparison commodity subindices.

COMMODITY PERFORMANCE IN DOWN AND UP EQUITY MARKETS   Like other alternative investments, commodity investment is available through a number of product providers covering a wide range of alternative strategy emphasis (convenience yield, momentum patterns) as well as market emphasis (energy, livestock, precious and industrial metals, and agriculture). Each of these products has their own unique return and risk performance including their correlations with various market phenomena including inflation. While not the focus of this chapter, investors should be aware that the return and risk characteristics of any commodity product is impacted both by the commodities they trade (e.g., energy) and the form of the trading strategy (near- or far-term futures contracts). However, despite the differences between individual commodity sectors, results show in Figure 12.6 that none of the various commodity sectors showed a consistent return relationship with the S&P 500 in either down or up S&P 500 markets.

What Every Investor Should Remember

- The benefit of alternative assets in addition to stand-alone stock and bond portfolios is determined primarily by their common or differential sensitivity to common market factors.
- Analysis of individual assets at the index level often fails to provide suitable evidence of the return and risk characteristics of unique strategies at the strategy or market sector level.
- Sources of return are time sensitive and dependent upon business models. Care should be taken in understanding how and why correlations change both at the index and individual security level.

Notes

1. Modern alternatives also often incorporate unique risk and return solutions usually found in structured products. Structured products run the gamut from principal protection backed by a bank's balance sheet to quantitative driven models designed to trade at given inflection points.
2. These security-based indices are available in tradable form from various platform providers. Public research has generally indicated that, depending on the hedge fund strategy, the correlation between the passive security based index and the active trading manager based index is often greater than .75. However, public research has also indicated that the return to such passive security based trading models often underperforms active trading manager based indices by 100 to

200 basis points, depending on the strategy replicated. This lower return must, of course, be balanced with the additional benefits to passive security based indices including greater transparency, capacity, and liquidity.

3. For a full discussion of pricing and modeling commodities and commodity derivatives returns, see Geman (2005). Lastly, Schneeweis et al. (2008) have explored the degree to which commodity prices follow various momentum patterns, for which their analysis provides evidence and summarizes research results.

4. Commodity spot for a given market can be defined as the return from holding the active contract until the contract roll date and then rolling to the next active contract. From the perspective of liquidity and transparency, this is the simplest way to hold commodities, and thus is the benchmark against which other methods of holding commodity futures are measured.

5. Roll return: Positive or negative roll returns, which are the profits or losses generated from the rolling of futures contracts, also have a direct impact on index performance.

References

Case, K., and R. Shiller. "Is There a Bubble in the Housing Market?" *Brookings Papers on Economic Activity* (2003): 299–362.

Fama, E., and K. French. "Business Cycles and the Behavior of Metals Prices." *Journal of Finance* 43, Issue 5 (December 1988): 1075–1093.

Fung, W., and D. Hsieh. "Asset Based Style Factors of Hedge Funds." *Financial Analysts Journal* 58, No. 5 (September/October 2002): 16–27.

Geman, H. *Commodities and Commodity Derivatives.* Hoboken, NJ: John Wiley & Sons, 2005.

Jaeger, L., C. Wagner. "Factor Modeling and Benchmarking of Hedge Funds: Can Passive Investment in Hedge Fund Strategies Deliver?" *The Journal of Alternative Investments* 8, No. 3 (Winter 2005): 9–6.

Sabal, J. "The Determinants of Housing Prices: The Case of Spain." (2005). Available at www.sabalonline.com.

Schneeweis, T. "Dealing with Myths of Hedge Fund Investments." *The Journal of Alternative Investments* 1, No. 3 (Winter 1998): 11–15.

Schneeweis, T., H. Kazemi, and G. Martin. "Understanding Hedge Fund Performance: Research Issues Revisited—Part I." *The Journal of Alternative Investments* 5, No. 3 (Winter 2002): 6–22.

Schneeweis, T., H. Kazemi, and G. Martin. "Understanding Hedge Fund Performance: Research Issues Revisited—Part II." *The Journal of Alternative Investments* 5, No. 4 (Spring 2003): 8–30.

Schneeweis, T., H. Kazemi, and V. Karavas. "Eurex Derivative Products in Alternative Investments: The Case for Hedge Funds." Eurex, 2003.

Schneeweis, T., R. Spurgin, and G. Georgiev. "Benchmarking Commodity Trading Advisor Performance with a Passive Futures-Based Index." CISDM Working Paper, 2000.

Williams, J. *The Economic Function of Futures Markets.* Cambridge University Press, 1986.

Part III Hedge Funds

Hedge funds are difficult to define if only because they have morphed into so many different shapes. The term *hedge* used to mean that the funds attempted to hedge one set of assets with another. This was certainly true of the first hedge fund formed in 1949 by A.W. Jones, and is still true of hedge funds following market-neutral strategies (as explained later). But many hedge funds have directional strategies that are anything but hedged.

Perhaps it's better to define hedge funds by the fees they charge. The Investment Company Act of 1940 insists that a Registered Investment Company (RIC) like a mutual fund charge *symmetrical* investment fees. So their fees remain fixed in percentage terms whether the fund rises or falls. Hedge fund managers insist on *asymmetrical* fees typically consisting of a management fee paid regardless of performance and an *incentive fee* charged as a percentage of the upside. A typical fee schedule would be to charge a 1 percent or 2 percent management fee on all of the assets under management and a 20 percent incentive fee.[1] To avoid having to register as an RIC, the hedge fund must be offered to investors only through a private placement.

Hedge funds are organized as partnerships with the general partners being the managers and the limited partners being the investors. The form of the partnership is similar to that used by private equity and venture capital firms. In fact, these firms also charge asymmetrical investment fees. So how are hedge funds different from private equity and venture capital firms? The answer is that their investment horizons and their investments are very different. Hedge funds have short-term strategies and typically invest in publicly available securities such as equities and bonds. Private equity and venture capital invest for extended periods in firms and they invest in projects not generally available to the general public. Of course, the lines between the hedge funds and private equity/venture capital are not always sharply drawn, but it helps to think of them as distinct types of investments.

Under the Investment Company Act of 1940, hedge funds (and other limited partnerships) have traditionally been exempt from many regulations including SEC registration. That's because they were intended only for wealthy private investors or wealthy institutions that could presumably take care of themselves. The Act specified that only 100 limited partners could invest in a fund. More recently, a distinction has been drawn between different types of investors. Accredited investors are those who have a net worth of $1 million *or* have income of $200,000 for the last two years ($300,000 for a married couple). Qualified purchasers are investors with at least $5 million in investment assets. Hedge funds that limit investors to qualified purchasers have less onerous regulations than those open to accredited investors.[2]

The hedge fund industry has grown rapidly over the last two decades. From less than $200 billion in assets under management in 1994, the industry grew to more than $400 billion in 2000 and then to almost $2 trillion in 2007 as interest in hedge funds increased dramatically (AIMA, 2008). As the AIMA study points out, it's actually difficult to pin down the size of this industry because there is no central reporting. Hedge Fund Research estimates that there was $1.9 trillion under management in June 2008, whereas HedgeFund.net puts the number much higher at $2.8 trillion.[3] The number of hedge funds has also grown exponentially in the past two decades.

TABLE 12.21   Investors in Hedge Funds

Investor	1997	2005
Individuals	62%	44%
Fund of Funds	16%	28%
Pension Funds (Public and Private)	10%	7%
Corporations and Institutions	5%	14%
Endowments and Foundations	7%	7%

Source: Hennessee Group LLC.

In 1994 there were less than 2,000 hedge funds, but by 2007 that number had grown to 7,600 before falling off to 6,800 by the end of 2009.[4]

The investors in hedge funds (the limited partners) can be individuals, companies, or institutions. Traditionally, individual investors have provided a majority of the funding. Table 12.21 shows that in 1997, 62 percent of the investments in hedge funds came from individuals directly investing in the funds. In addition, there were also individual investors who invested through fund of funds. By 2005, the share of individual investors had fallen to 44 percent. Endowments and foundations merely maintained their shares while pension funds fell in relative importance. In contrast, corporations and institutions, the latter including educational institutions, almost tripled their share.

Investment Strategies

The investment strategies followed by hedge funds range from the absolute return strategies that aim to hedge away most market movements to directional strategies that aim to profit from directional bets in one market or another. Before getting into the terminology used to describe narrower types of strategies within the industry, let's consider strategies in terms of beta and alpha. A pure hedge or absolute return strategy would try to eliminate most of the systematic risk of the market by keeping beta close to zero. The hedge fund would then be judged by whether the manager could produce alpha. A directional strategy would earn part of its return from the market itself.[5] The manager would still try to produce additional return from the superiority of the manager's security selection, so the total return would be enhanced by alpha (much like a long-only mutual fund manager).

How would a hedge fund manage to keep its beta close to zero following an absolute return strategy? To do this, a fund might match each long position in a security with a short position in a second, highly correlated security. Suppose the fund manager is focusing on the stocks of utility companies. The manager knows that utility stocks are likely to rise and fall with the market and to be highly correlated with one another. So if the manager takes a matching long and short position in this industry, the market exposure of the position should be marginal. This matching of long and short positions results in what is called a *market-neutral* fund. The alpha of this manager depends on his or her ability to invest in utility stocks that will outperform other stocks in the industry and to choose utility stocks to short that will underperform. Security analysis is important just as it is with a long-only manager.

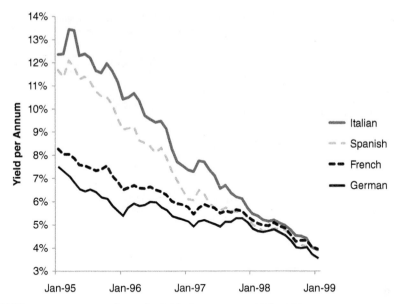

FIGURE 12.7   Convergence of Bond Yields in Europe, 1995–1998
Source: IMF, International Financial Statistics.

Market-neutral strategies can take a variety of forms. It will be helpful to consider a real-life strategy that paid off handsomely for some hedge funds in the mid-1990s. This strategy was called the convergence play in the European bond market. Under the Maastricht Treaty of 1991, the euro was to be introduced in 1999, but the countries to be admitted were to be chosen at the end of 1997. To join the new monetary union, countries had to satisfy certain conditions regarding their currencies, inflation rates, and budget deficits. Only those countries that had satisfied these conditions would be invited to join the union. Once in the union, all countries would see their interest rates converge to one level.

In 1995, the market as a whole had little faith that Italy or Spain would be able to join the union. The evidence for this is shown in Figure 12.7 where the interest rates on the government bonds of Italy, Spain, France, and Germany are displayed. The Italian government had to offer an interest rate on its bonds that was about 6 percent higher than German interest rates. The market simply did not believe that Italy could satisfy all of the conditions for the union, and therefore a huge interest rate premium was required to induce investors to buy Italian bonds.[6] In particular, there was skepticism that the Italian government could bring its fiscal deficit down from more than 9 percent of GDP in 1995 to 3 percent of GDP as required by the Treaty.

Some hedge funds, notably Long-Term Capital Management (LTCM), believed otherwise. These funds trusted that Italy would do whatever was necessary to qualify for the union by the end of 1997. So these funds bought Italian bonds. To hedge their positions and ensure market neutrality, they simultaneously borrowed and sold short German bonds (or equivalent derivatives). With offsetting positions in two European bond markets, it did not matter whether European currencies rose or fell against the dollar. A rise in the dollar, for example, would lead to losses on the

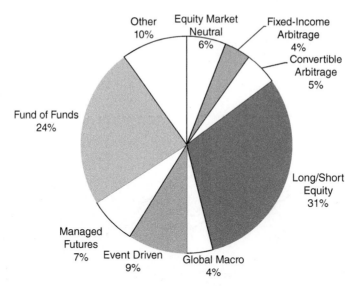

FIGURE 12.8   Hedge Funds by Strategy in TASS Database, 2004
Source: Getmansky, Lo, and Mei (2004).

long Italian bond position and gains on the short German bond position. Similarly, it did not matter whether the general level of European interest rates rose or fell. All that mattered is that Italian bonds outperformed German bonds in the run-up to the end-1997 deadline. It is evident from Figure 12.7 that this convergence strategy paid off handsomely. This was particularly true for LTCM, which made spectacular gains from the strategy.[7]

The hedge fund industry employs a variety of strategies and some of the names of the strategies vary from firm to firm. Generally, the databases accept whatever classification is used by the hedge fund itself. Figure 12.8 gives a breakdown of the strategies used by the funds in the TASS database as of August 2004.[8] The most important category of fund is the long/short equity fund representing 31 percent of the TASS database. The global fund category associated with George Soros and Julian Robertson, two famous managers from the 1990s, is only 4 percent of the total.

A brief description of some of these strategies might be useful:

Fixed income arbitrage: betting on mispricing of related interest rate securities.
Convertible arbitrage: betting on discrepancies in the prices of convertibles relative to the underlying stocks.
Equity market neutral: as its name implies, this strategy works with matching short and long positions that keep overall market risk low. The first three strategies are all normally market neutral and offer absolute returns.
Long/short equity: a variation on equity market-neutral where the manager has a larger long position than the short position that is hedging it. The manager may also make a bet on style (e.g., by favoring value over growth), size, or some other factor that makes the position more directional than a market-neutral fund. The beta of such funds could be much higher than that of market-neutral funds.

Equity hedge: this category is used by the HFRI database and encompasses both equity market-neutral and equity long-short strategies.

Relative value: also used by the HFRI database. This strategy attempts to take advantage of relative pricing discrepancies between instruments including equities, debt, options, and futures.

Global macro: big directional bets on currencies or interest rates or some other macro variable.

Event driven: bets on corporate events such as mergers and acquisitions, corporate restructurings, or share buybacks.

Managed futures: long or short bets on futures contracts for commodities or currencies.

Emerging markets: invests in the securities of companies or the sovereign debt of emerging countries

Fund of funds: a fund that invests in a number of hedge funds to diversify the manager risk.

The list of strategies will vary from one database to another. Naturally returns vary widely across strategies. But, as explained earlier, so do risks, particularly the systematic risks associated with beta. We will examine returns and risks in the next section.

Hedge Fund Returns

All mutual funds in the United States must report their returns publicly each period. Databases such as that developed by Morningstar allow investors (and researchers) to examine returns earned on the universe of mutual funds just like they can examine returns on individual stocks. Because hedge funds are offered through private placement, they cannot advertise their returns publicly. Nor is there any requirement that they report returns to official agencies. So the collection of return data is haphazard and incomplete.

Consulting firms like TASS or HFR have developed databases of returns that they sell to the investment industry. The returns are provided by the hedge funds, but only on a voluntary basis. So these consulting firms will contact all of the hedge funds of which they are aware and ask for the funds to report their returns on a regular basis. Some funds do and some don't. Some do for a while, then don't. Some don't for a while, then provide backfilled returns.[9]

To see how incomplete these data collections can be, consider the overlap of three database providers, TASS, HFR, and CISDM, as reported in Agarwal and colleagues (2009).[10] Many of the hedge funds appear in two or more of these databases, so it is important to ask to what extent is any one database capturing the universe of hedge funds? The answer is revealed in Figure 12.9 where a Venn diagram shows the overlap among the three databases.[11] Only 7 percent of the funds appear in all three databases. On the other hand, 28 percent of the funds only appear in the TASS database, 31 percent only appear in the CISDM database, and 23 percent in the HFR database. This figure shows how limited is the coverage of any single database.

The biases that develop from using these databases will be analyzed in a later section of the chapter. Before doing so, let's consider the performance of the hedge

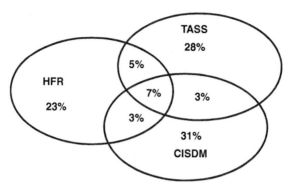

FIGURE 12.9   Overlap of Databases
Source: Agarwal, Daniel, and Naik (2009).

fund indexes developed from these databases. That is, let's ignore any biases in the data and consider the return and risk characteristics of hedge funds using the same kinds of return data that the investment industry normally analyzes. We will find the case for investing in hedge funds very compelling whether viewed on a stand-alone basis or as part of a broader portfolio strategy.

One of the most widely used set of indexes is that provided by Hedge Fund Research (HFR). Indexes have been developed for hedge funds as a whole as well as for individual strategies. As with most indexes, the series begin in the early 1990s, 1990 in the case of the HFR indexes. Table 12.22 gives a standard set of statistics examining the average return, standard deviation, and Sharpe ratio of the HFR Fund-Weighted (total) Index. This index is an equally weighted average of all of the funds in the HFR database. The statistics are based on monthly returns from 1990 through 2009. The table compares hedge fund returns with stock and bond returns. The results are quite impressive. The HFR index gives a compound return of 12.2 percent over a sample period when the Russell 3000 could barely beat the Barclays Aggregate Bond Index. And the HFR index had half of the standard deviation of the Russell series. Foreign stocks as represented by the EAFE index performed even more miserably over this same period.[12]

In most portfolios, hedge funds will represent only a portion of the asset allocation. So it makes sense to view hedge funds in a portfolio context. Table 12.23 reports correlations between the HFRI Fund-Weighted hedge fund index and other stock and bond indexes. Hedge funds are low in correlation with U.S. bonds, but

TABLE 12.22   Hedge Funds Compared with Other Assets, 1990–2009

	Geometric Average	Arithmetic Average	Standard Deviation	Sharpe Ratio
HFRI Fund-Weighted Hedge Fund Index	12.2%	11.8%	7.1%	1.13
Barclays Aggregate Bond Index	7.0%	6.9%	3.9%	0.80
Russell 3000 All-Cap Stock Index	8.4%	9.2%	15.2%	0.36
MSCI EAFE Stock Index	4.4%	5.9%	17.5%	0.12

Data Sources: HFRI, Barclays Capital, Russell®, and MSCI.

TABLE 12.23   Correlations between Hedge Funds and Other Assets, 1990–2009

	HFRI Fund-Weighted Hedge Fund Index	Barclays Aggregate Bond Index	Russell 3000 Stock Index
HFRI Fund-Weighted Hedge Fund Index	1.00		
Barclays Aggregate Bond Index	0.11	1.00	
Russell 3000 Stock Index	0.77	0.17	1.00
MSCI EAFE Stock Index	0.65	0.14	0.73

Data Sources: HFRI, Barclays Capital, Russell®, and MSCI.

have sizable correlations with domestic and foreign stocks. The correlation between the HFRI Fund-Weighted index and the Russell 3000 is 0.77, while the correlation between the hedge fund index and MSCI EAFE is 0.65. These correlations are lower than they would be between most U.S. stock indexes, but they are still relatively high.

Table 12.24 reports the betas and alphas of the HFRI Fund-Weighted (total) Index and HFRI-style hedge fund indexes. Consider first the beta of the HFRI Fund-Weighted Index. With a correlation of 0.77 with the Russell 3000 index, the beta is nonetheless only 0.36 because the standard deviation of the HFRI index is 7.1 percent compared with a standard deviation for the Russell 3000 index of 15.2 percent.[13] So it is the very low standard deviation of the hedge fund series, not its correlation with the market, which gives it a low beta. With such a low beta, the alpha is 6.1 percent.[14]

The beta is even lower for the relative value strategy reported in the table. This strategy has a relatively low correlation with respect to the Russell 3000 (0.51). The low beta is more due to its low standard deviation (4.5 percent) than to the low correlation. This strategy is not truly market neutral, but its low beta provides ample opportunity for managers to earn a high alpha (5.7 percent).

Somewhat less impressive results were obtained in Bernstein Wealth Management (2006) using the TASS database of individual hedge fund returns. To try to minimize some of the biases discussed below, the study included fund returns only after they started reporting returns to the database and kept all funds in the calculations even if they later stopped reporting returns to TASS. Bernstein created

TABLE 12.24   Betas and Alphas of HFRI Hedge Fund Indexes, 1990–2009

HFRI Hedge Fund Index	Correlation with R 3000	Standard Deviation	Beta	Alpha
Fund-Weighted (Aggregate)	0.77	7.1%	0.36	6.1%
Event Driven	0.73	7.0%	0.33	6.5%
Relative Value	0.51	4.5%	0.15	5.7%
Equity	0.75	9.2%	0.46	7.5%
Macro	0.36	7.8%	0.18	8.6%
Emerging Market	0.64	14.7%	0.62	7.2%

Note: Betas are calculated using the Russell 3000 index as the market benchmark.
Data Sources: HFRI and Russell®.

TABLE 12.25   Performance of Other Hedge Fund Indexes, 1994–2009

	HFRI	Tremont	Hennessee	MSCI
Correlation with HFRI	1.00	0.81	0.98	0.88
Average Return	9.7%	9.2%	9.1%	9.1%
Standard Deviation	7.3%	7.8%	7.1%	5.1%
Beta	0.36	0.28	0.35	0.20
Alpha	4.3%	4.3%	3.8%	4.6%

Note: The four indexes shown are those reported by Hedge Fund Research, CSFB/Tremont, Hennessee Group, and MSCI. Beta is measured with the Russell 3000 as the market benchmark.
Data Sources: HFRI, Credit Suisse/Tremont, Hennessee, MSCI, and Russell®.

equal-weighted indexes for both the directional and market-neutral funds using fund returns from 1996 to 2005. The study found that market-neutral hedge funds had an alpha of 3.1 percent, while directional hedge funds had an alpha of 3.5 percent.

It is also useful to compare the results for the HRFI Fund-Weighted Hedge Fund index with those of aggregate hedge fund indexes of three other index providers. As shown in Table 12.25, the three indexes have correlations with the HFRI index ranging from 0.81 to 0.98.[15] All of the indexes have similar returns. Average returns range from 9.1 percent to 9.7 percent, betas range from 0.20 to 0.36, and alphas range from 3.8 percent to 4.6 percent.

Beyond the standard statistics for hedge fund indexes, there should be interest in any unusual statistical properties of hedge fund returns. For example, are there reasons to believe that hedge fund returns follow a nonnormal statistical distribution? Do the measured standard deviations properly account for the potential volatility of these investments?

Malkiel and Saha (2005) provide evidence on the distribution of the hedge fund returns in the TASS index. They find that the returns are characterized by high kurtosis, so the tails of the returns distribution are fatter than what you would find in a normal distribution. And these returns have a negative skewness, so returns are asymmetrical in the downward direction (not exactly what an investor desires). They can reject normality for all strategies except managed futures and global macro. Getmansky, Lo, and Makorov (2004) show that hedge fund returns (for most strategies) have high serial correlation suggesting that hedge fund investments are relatively illiquid and/or the managers deliberately smooth their returns. The authors show that the serial correlation is higher for strategies where you would expect investments to be illiquid such as event-driven or emerging market investments.

A more difficult issue to address is whether hedge funds may perform worse in a crisis than the statistical measures indicate. Certainly the experience of hedge funds following the Russian bond default of July 1998 was not reassuring. There are two issues involved. First, in a crisis, does the systematic factor drag down hedge fund returns to the extent that they are correlated with the market? Second, does the crisis itself pose a risk to hedge funds to the extent that they become more illiquid? Both issues were at work in the crisis beginning in 2007. First, the stock market itself fell more than 50 percent at one point dragging down hedge fund returns with significant beta exposure. Second, both bond and stock markets became increasingly illiquid, particularly after the failure of Lehman Brothers in September 2008.

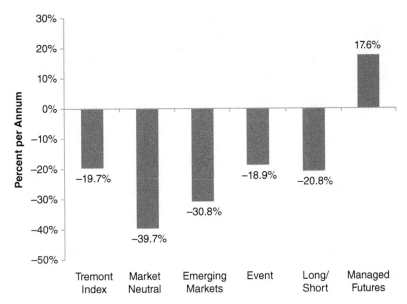

FIGURE 12.10   Hedge Fund Returns in the Crisis, October 2007 to December 2008
Source: Credit Suisse/Tremont.

In the crisis beginning in 2007, hedge funds faltered badly. Consider the returns on a range of hedge fund strategies as reported by Credit Suisse/Tremont from October 2007 (the peak of the U.S. stock market) through December 2008. Figure 12.10 reports the returns over this period. The hardest hit strategy was market neutral, down 39.7 percent. Illiquidity adversely affected this strategy, especially at the peak of the crisis after Lehman failed. The Tremont index as a whole was down almost 20 percent.[16] Only managed futures fared well with a positive 17.6 percent return. Evidently many of the managed futures managers were able to reverse their oil and other commodity bets in time for the sharp turnaround in oil prices in summer 2008.

What has this crisis taught us about hedge funds? First, hedge funds should not be referred to as absolute return investments as they so often are. Nonetheless, hedge funds did provide returns superior to virtually all equity investments. After all, the S&P 500 was down 40.1 percent over this same period, while the MSCI EAFE and MSCI Emerging Market Indexes were down by 46.2 percent and 56.3 percent, respectively. Third, investors learned that hedge fund positions were not as liquid as they expected. Many hedge funds slammed the gates on their investors and would not let them out of their investments. That's a lesson that investors are unlikely to forget.

Hedge Fund Biases

Because of the way that hedge fund returns are reported, biases inevitably develop that undermine the performance results reported by the investment industry. This section will describe the major biases and then will attempt to measure how large they are.

There are two major biases affecting hedge fund returns. One bias plagues all asset return data—survivorship bias—although usually it's relatively easy to correct for it if there is a full universe of data available. The other bias—backfill bias—is peculiar to hedge funds. We will begin by describing backfill bias because it affects data sets from the very beginning.

1. **Backfill bias.** This is the bias that arises when hedge funds first begin reporting to a database. If a hedge fund has been operating for a few years prior to its first reporting, it's natural for the managers to offer all of their return data including returns that occurred before database reporting began. Thus the database backfills the return data for that fund. The bias is important in the hedge fund industry because many hedge funds are incubated in their early stages. Families and friends of the manager may be the only investors in the fund at start-up. Or the manager may choose not to report returns at first because the fund is too small. Or the manager may want to see how the fund performs before providing data to an outside consultant. In some cases, hedge fund managers may start multiple funds at the same time and then see which funds perform well. In any case, the result is that there is a bias toward reporting the results of funds that do well. Those that close or get merged into other funds never get reported. Sometimes this bias is called *instant history bias* because the backfilled returns provide an instant history. Another term used is *incubation bias*. Mutual fund data sets should not be plagued by this type of bias because they have reporting obligations right from their beginning.

2. **Survivorship bias.** This bias arises when a database keeps track of only the live funds. The reason why you would like to keep track of all funds is that the investor, *ex ante*, does not know which funds will disappear. Dead funds often have ugly returns during their death spiral, so it's important to keep track of these funds. But other funds may disappear from the database because they have been *too successful* and have closed to new investors. A third class of fund may be closed because the managers have moved on to other opportunities. Or the managers may just choose not to report for some other reason. Because funds that disappear from the database may not be dead, we will follow other authors in calling disappearing funds defunct. It's important to determine (a) what percentage of funds in a database are defunct, and (b) how their returns compare with those that remain in the database.

One other bias is worth noting although it's difficult to treat it empirically. This is *liquidation bias*. This bias refers to the fact that managers of hedge funds that are failing are likely to stop reporting returns to a database before the final liquidation value of the fund is realized. For example, the funds that lost their capital in the Russian debt crisis of August 1998 did not report returns of −100 percent in that month. Instead, the returns ended in July 1998.[17] Any attempts to adjust for survivorship bias will miss the liquidation bias when the fund closes down.

Quantitative estimates of backfill bias range widely from one study to another. That's because the methodology for determining the bias varies as well. Malkiel and Saha (2005) estimate backfill and survivorship bias using the TASS database from 1994 to 2003. The TASS database distinguishes between returns that have been backfilled into the TASS database from returns subsequently recorded by the same fund. And it keeps track of defunct funds as well as the funds still alive in each year.

TABLE 12.26   Biases in Hedge Fund Returns in TASS Database

Malkeil and Saha Estimates		Fung and Hsieh Estimates	
1994–2003		1994–2004	
Backfill Bias			
Backfilled Returns	14.6%	Backfill Bias	
Nonbackfilled	7.3%	All Funds	12.0%
Bias	7.3%	Exclude 1st 14 Months	10.5%
Survivorship Bias		Bias	1.5%
Live Funds*	13.7%	Survivorship Bias	
Live and Defunct*	9.3%	Live Funds	14.4%
Bias	4.4%	Live and Defunct	12.0%
		Bias	2.4%

*The returns for the live and defunct funds exclude backfilled returns. The estimates of survivorship bias are for 1996 to 2003.

Malkiel and Saha define the backfill bias as being the gap between the backfilled and nonbackfilled returns. As shown in Table 12.26, the bias is estimated to be 7.3 percent per year. This is a huge gap. The authors do not calculate what might be a more interesting statistic, the gap between the nonbackfilled returns and all of the returns together.

Fung and Hsieh (2006) criticize this methodology for determining backfill bias. They point out that hedge funds typically report to several databases, and the returns that appear to be backfilled in one database may have already been reported to another database. Fung and Hsieh are particularly concerned about the TASS database because Tremont bought TASS in 2001 and then added the funds in the Tremont database to the TASS database at that time. Fung and Hsieh propose to estimate backfill bias by trying to determine the average incubation period of a fund. They do this by examining the dropout rates for hedge funds in three databases, TASS, HFR, and CISDM. Using a data set of hedge funds over the period 1994-2004, they find that the highest dropout rate occurs at about 14 months. They then eliminate the first 14 months of returns for the hedge funds in the three databases. The resulting bias estimate of 1.5 percent for the TASS database is shown in Table 12.26. The biases for the other two databases are almost identical.

The backfill bias estimates of the two studies are so far apart that it is difficult to reconcile them. But it's natural to ask the question: If the Malkiel-Saha estimates are measuring returns that are not truly backfilled, but merely previously missing from that database, why are those returns so much lower than the non back-filled returns?

Survivorship bias is potentially quite large given the high rates of exit from the industry. Consider first how many funds survive over time. Malkiel and Saha (2005) use the TASS database to follow firms through time from the first date that they entered the database. (So no backfilled returns are used.) They divide firms into the live firms that continued to exist at the end of the data set, December 2003, from the defunct firms that dropped out of the data set prior to that date. To determine the resulting survivorship bias, it's necessary to compare the returns of the live firms with the live and defunct firms together. In Table 12.26, Malkiel and Saha estimate survivorship bias to be 4.4 percent. Fung and Hsieh (2006) measure survivorship bias using their three databases from 1994 to 2004. Unlike Malkiel and Saha, Fung and

Hsieh include all returns in their estimate of this bias, including backfilled returns. Table 12.26 reports a survivorship bias of 2.4 percent using the TASS database. Their estimates for the other two databases are similar, 1.8 percent for the HFR database and 2.4 percent for the CISDM database.

Even if the lower set of estimates from Fung and Hsieh (2006) are used, 1.5 percent for backfill bias and 1.8 to 2.4 percent for survivorship bias, the effects on hedge fund returns are enormous. If you reduce the returns in Table 12.24 by about 3.5 percent to 4 percent, the alphas then become much more modest in size. So taking into account biases is really important in assessing hedge fund returns. The previous discussion shows that it's difficult to assess this bias, and leading researchers can come to different quantitative conclusions. But the importance of bias is undisputed.

Performance across Managers

Managers are not created equal. That's true of any asset class where active management is pursued since managers differ in their abilities to select assets. But it's especially true of hedge funds. The performance of managers varies widely because different strategies are pursued. But the dispersion in performance across managers is much too large to be explained by whether one strategy, such as market-neutral equity, is chosen rather than another, like fixed-income arbitrage. Generating alpha is not easy, especially not the large alphas that are found for some hedge funds.

To investigate the dispersion in manager performance, it's helpful to compare hedge funds with other types of investments. That's exactly what Malkiel and Saha (2004) did in the working paper version of the study cited earlier. Using TASS data for hedge fund managers and Lipper data for mutual fund managers, they calculated the returns of the top quartile and third quartile managers for each of five asset classes. These were hedge funds and four types of mutual funds for real estate, international equity, U.S. equity, and U.S. fixed income. Figure 12.11 reports the *excess returns* of the first quartile and third quartile managers over the median manager for that asset class. Thus in the case of U.S. equity mutual funds, the top quartile manager delivered 0.9 percent more than the median manager while the third quartile manager delivered 0.5 percent less than the median manager. For hedge funds, the gap between quartile returns was much larger. The top quartile manager delivered 8.6 percent more than the median manager. And the third quartile manager delivered 8.1 percent less. Manager *selection* is everything when it comes to hedge funds. Or, perhaps since so many managers are closed to new investors, manager *access* is everything.

A second source of information about manager dispersion is provided by Bernstein Wealth Management Research (2006). Using the same set of data described earlier for hedge funds and long-only equity and bond managers, Bernstein sorted managers by performance using the *alphas* of each manager net of fees. Figure 12.12 shows alphas for the top-decile manager and bottom-decile manager for each asset class. All alphas are shown relative to the median alpha for that asset class. The top decile long-only equity manager delivers an alpha that is 2.5 percent above that of the bottom-decile manager, a reasonably small range. In contrast, the gap in alphas between the top and bottom decile managers for hedge funds is more than 25 percent for directional hedge funds and more than 15 percent for market-neutral hedge funds. As with the Malkiel-Saha data set, it really matters which manager you choose (or get access to).

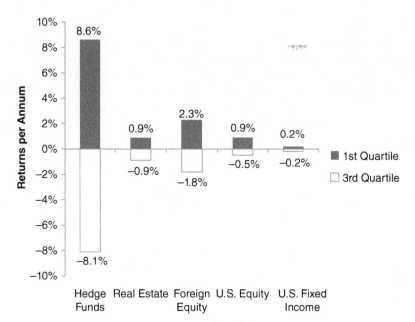

FIGURE 12.11   Excess Returns of First and Third Quartile Managers (Relative to Median Manager), 1994–2004

Source: Malkiel and Saha (2004).

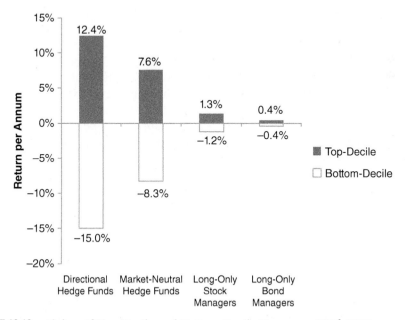

FIGURE 12.12   Alphas of Top Decile and Bottom Decile Managers, 1996–2005

Source: Bernstein (2006).

Fund of Funds

Manager risk represents a significant problem for hedge fund investors. Not only is there great variation in performance across managers, but there is also the risk that managers might blow up. So many investors have chosen to diversify the manager risk by investing through a *fund of hedge funds*. Figure 12.8 shows that 24 percent of the hedge funds in the TASS database are funds of hedge funds.

What advantages do fund of funds offer to the investor? There are two major advantages. First, the funds of funds offer due diligence and expertise in choosing hedge funds. With about 10,000 hedge funds to choose from, many of which have short track records, it's difficult for an investment advisor to make decisions about which funds to invest in. A fund of funds offers a group of recommended hedge funds that the fund of funds manager has investigated. And a fund of funds manager should be able to constantly monitor the hedge funds that are chosen in case there are changes in personnel or other material changes in operations. Due diligence by the managers of the funds of funds will not ensure against blow ups, but probably reduces their number.

The second advantage of the fund of funds lies in the diversification of manager risk. As with all assets, investing in 15 managers rather than two managers undoubtedly reduces risk. Just as importantly, a fund of funds can give the investor diversification across hedge fund styles. So if convertible arbitrage falls out of favor, perhaps long-short will begin outperforming. Funds of funds may have an additional advantage over direct investment in hedge funds. Investors may obtain *access* to better hedge fund managers. As shown above, there is very large dispersion in the performance of managers. If funds of funds can get an investor into superior funds, the extra cost of hiring a fund of funds manager may be worth it. But there is no evidence whether funds of funds provide superior access.

There must be some disadvantages to investing through fund of funds since only 24 percent of hedge fund investments follow this strategy. One obvious disadvantage is diversification. (Diversification is always a disadvantage if you are trying to strike it rich.) With 15 hedge funds, there is virtually no chance to end up in the top quartile of hedge funds. It's true that some of the 15 hedge funds may be in the top quartile, but lightning only strikes so many times in one place—even if the fund of funds manager has strung lightning rods all over.

There is another disadvantage that should be important to all investors. Fund of fund managers charge an extra layer of fees, and these fees are often quite high. Consider the evidence about hedge fund fees reported in Brown et al. (2004). In that study, management and incentive fee for hedge funds averaged 1.4 percent and 18.5 percent, respectively. On top of those fees, funds of funds charged a 1.5 percent management fee and a 9.1 percent incentive fee. To overcome two layers of fees, the hedge fund managers had better deliver some very high returns.

Consider the effects of fees on performance. Let's assume that hedge funds charge 1 percent management fees and 20 percent incentive fees. In order for the investor to earn an 8 percent net return, a hedge fund must earn 11 percent gross return:

$$(0.11 - 0.01) * (1 - 0.20) = 0.08$$

An investor in a fund of funds, however, must find hedge funds earning much higher gross returns in order to earn the same 8 percent net return. Let's assume that the funds of funds charge an extra 1 percent management fee and an extra 10 percent incentive fee. Then the hedge funds must earn a gross return of 13.4 percent to net the investor 8 percent:

$$[(0.134 - 0.01) * (1 - 0.20) - 0.01] * (1 - 0.10) = 0.08$$

It's probably unlikely that the expertise of the fund of funds in selecting managers is going to deliver, on average, the extra 2.4 percent required to keep net returns at 8 percent. So investing through a fund of funds is costly. Whether the extra layer of fees is worthwhile depends on how much the investor values the due diligence and diversification provided by the fund of funds.

How costly is the fund of funds approach to investing in hedge funds? One way to approach this question is to compare fund of funds returns with those on the hedge funds themselves. HFRI provides two aggregate indexes of hedge fund returns: the Fund-Weighted index previously introduced and a Fund of Funds index. Over the period from January 1990 through December 2009, the former has a compound average return of 12.2 percent compared with an 8.2 percent compound return for the latter. Of course, the mix of hedge funds in the two indexes is undoubtedly different since one consists of an equal weighted average of hedge funds while the other is a mix of whatever hedge funds the managers of the funds of funds select. But nonetheless this gap in returns of 4 percent is quite sizable. Apparently the average manager of the funds of funds in the HFRI index is not able to overcome the extra layer of fees with superior access to managers. Figure 12.13 compares the HFRI fund of funds index with two hedge funds indexes, the HFRI Fund-Weighted

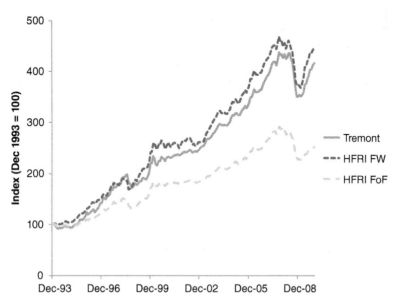

FIGURE 12.13   Hedge Fund and Fund of Fund Returns, 1994–2009

Sources: HFRI and Credit Suisse/Tremont.

Index and the Credit Suisse/Tremont (total) Hedge Fund Index. The latter begins in 1994, so the figure traces out the three returns from 1994 to 2008. It is apparent from the figure that the funds of funds index lags consistently behind the two hedge fund indexes. The extra layer of fees does create quite a drag of cumulative returns.

Yet perhaps this comparison is misleading. An investor with $5 million or $10 million cannot earn the HFRI Fund-Weighted hedge fund return because there is no way for such an investor to invest in a diversified array of hedge funds. Minimum investments in hedge funds are typically in the $1 million range or more. It's true that an endowment with $500 million can choose a diversified array of funds as can an ultra-high net worth family with that much wealth. But there are few investors with sufficient wealth to get diversification on their own. Suppose an investor is forced to approach hedge funds through a fund of fund investment. Would it still pay to invest in hedge funds?

Hedge Funds in a Portfolio

Table 12.27 reports on a diversification experiment where an investor shifts from an all-traditional portfolio to a portfolio that includes 10 percent investment in hedge funds. The traditional portfolio (A) consists of 25 percent in the Barclays Aggregate U.S. bond index, 50 percent in the Russell 3000, and 25 percent in the MSCI EAFE index. Portfolio B shifts 10 percent of the U.S. stock investment into the HFRI Fund-Weighted Index. Portfolio C shifts 10 percent of the U.S. stock investment into the HFRI Fund of Funds index.

The most impressive results are obtained when the HFRI Fund-Weighted index is chosen as the hedge fund vehicle. The compound return on the portfolio is lifted by 0.4 percent and the Sharpe ratio is increased from 0.35 to 0.41. That translates into an Alpha* of 0.6 percent. But investment in the fund of funds index also improves performance of the portfolio. The return on the portfolio is not increased, but the Sharpe ratio is increased from 0.35 to 0.38. That translates into an Alpha* of about 0.3 percent. This is admittedly a very small improvement. In fact, Table 12.27 shows that hedge funds are not the wonder drug that some observers claim. But, according to these results, they do add to risk-adjusted performance.

TABLE 12.27   Effects of Hedge Funds on Portfolio Performance, 1990–2009

	Geometric Average	Arithmetic Average	Standard Deviation	Sharpe Ratio
Portfolio A (No hedge fund)	7.4%	7.8%	11.4%	0.35
Portfolio B (Fund Weighted)	7.8%	8.1%	10.5%	0.41
Portfolio C (Fund of Funds)	7.4%	7.7%	10.3%	0.38

Portfolio A consists of 25 percent in the Barclays Aggregate Bond Index, 50 percent in the Russell 3000 all-stock index, and 25 percent in MSCI EAFE index. Portfolio B replaces 10 percent of the Russell 3000 with the HFRI Fund-Weighted hedge fund index, while Portfolio C replaces the Russell 3000 with the HFRI Fund of Funds index.
Data Sources: HFRI, Barclays Capital, Russell®, and MSCI.

Summary—Key Features of Hedge Funds

With stock and bond markets unlikely to deliver the stellar returns of the last 25 years, hedge funds have become increasingly popular among investors. The growth in this asset class in the last 15 years is nothing short of phenomenal. The hedge fund industry has developed a multitude of strategies aimed at generating much more alpha than long-only managers have been able to produce. Some of these strategies are actually hedged against market risk, while others are directional with significant market risk.

The record for returns is impressive. These returns are large whether they are measured in absolute terms or relative to market benchmarks. Alphas higher than 5 percent are found for some hedge fund strategies. Hedge fund returns do not extend back very far since most databases were only developed in the 1990s. But the biggest problem is that these returns are plagued with backfill and survivor bias. Once you adjust for these biases, the returns look much less impressive.

When investing in hedge funds, manager skill is everything. And that skill is very unevenly distributed. The gap between the top-performing and lower-performing manager is far larger than for traditional asset classes. Manager selection and manager access are absolutely crucial to successful hedge fund investing. Does that mean that an investor should choose a fund of funds? The answer must weigh the advantages of a fund of funds manager, due diligence and expertise in choosing managers, as well as diversification against the biggest disadvantage, an extra layer of fees.

Hedge funds are not just the latest passing fad for investors. In a world with moderate long-only returns, it's inevitable that investors will hunt for returns with managers who pursue more complex strategies. And investment managers will continue to be attracted to the huge fees offered by this industry.

Notes

1. Fung and Hsieh (2006) report that between 78 percent and 86 percent of managers in three major databases charge 20 percent incentive fees. More than 70 percent of the management fees in these three databases lie between 1 percent and 1.99 percent.
2. For further details, see Hodge (2003).
3. AIMA (2008), p. 16.
4. CNNMoney.com, Hedge Funds: They're Back, March 12, 2010 using figures from Hedge Fund Research.
5. Not all directional strategies are correlated with the stock market, of course, since the hedge fund manager may be making a bet on interest rates or currencies or the direction of some other market.
6. The 6 percent premium was primarily a currency premium designed to compensate the investor if Italy failed to qualify and subsequently allowed the Lira to depreciate against the Deutschmark. Once a country has joined a currency union, differentials between interest rates such as those between Greece and Germany seen in 2010 reflect default risks rather than currency premiums.
7. Lowenstein (2000) provides a lively account of LTCM's brief history. The convergence strategy was one of LTCM's most profitable strategies, helping LTCM

earn 60 percent returns in both 1996 and 1997. At the beginning of 1998, after this strategy had played out, LTCM returned half of the capital to its investors citing the lack of comparable investment opportunities. Nine months later it had to be rescued.

8. This is the breakdown of 2,771 live funds in the TASS database as reported in Getmansky, Lo, and Mei (2004). The authors eliminate funds that give only gross returns or quarterly, not monthly, returns.

9. As discussed below, those that do, then don't cause survivorship bias. Those that don't, then backfill cause backfill bias.

10. These databases are provided by Lipper TASS, Hedge Fund Research (HFR), and the Center for International Securities and Derivative Markets (CISDM) at the University of Massachusetts. All three have more than 10 years of data collection experience.

11. This figure is based on a Venn diagram in Agarwal et al. (2009) showing overlap among four databases including a newer one developed by MSCI. The four databases together have 3,924 live funds at the end of December 2002. The overlap among the three largest databases was analyzed after eliminating the funds that only appeared in MSCI. The percentages were rounded to the nearest decimal.

12. The underperformance of EAFE relative to U.S. stocks is almost entirely due to Japan.

13. Recall that beta is equal to the correlation coefficient times the ratio of the standard deviation of the asset relative to the standard deviation of the benchmark. The beta is $0.36 = 0.77 * (0.071/0.152)$.

14. Since the average return on the risk-free Treasury bill is 3.8 percent and the average return on the Russell 3000 is 9.2 percent, the alpha = 11.8 percent − [3.8% + 0.36 * (9.2% − 3.8%)] = 6.1%.

15. Over the same period, the correlation between the S&P 500 index and the Russell 1000 large-cap index is 1.00 and the correlation between the S&P 500 and the Russell 3000 all-cap index is 0.99. This is further evidence that each hedge fund index is measuring the performance of a somewhat different set of hedge funds than another index.

16. Similar results are found for the other indexes in Table 12.25. HFRI was down 20.4 percent, Hennessee was down 21.0 percent, while MSCI was down 14.0 percent over this same 15 month period.

17. This example is due to Fung and Hsieh (2006).

References

Agarwal, Vikas, Naveen D. Daniel, and Narayan Y. Naik, 2009, "Role of Managerial Incentives and Discretion in Hedge Fund Performance," *Journal of Finance* (October), 2221–2256.

Alternative Investment Management Association, 2008, "AIMA's Roadmap to Hedge Funds," November.

Bernstein Wealth Management Research, 2006, "Hedge Funds: Too Much of a Good Thing?," Bernstein Global Wealth Management (June).

Brown, Stephen J., William N. Goetzmann, and Bing Liang, 2004, "Fees on Fees in Funds of Funds," *Journal of Investment Management* (4th Quarter), 39–56.

Fung, K.H., and David A. Hsieh, 2006, "Hedge Funds: An Industry in Its Adolescence," *Federal Reserve Bank of Atlanta Economic Review* (Fourth Quarter), 1–33.

Getmansky, Mila, Andrew W. Lo, and Igor Makorov, 2004, "An Econometric Model of Serial Correlation and Liquidity in Hedge Fund Returns," *Journal of Financial Economics* (December), 529–609.

Getmansky, Mila, Andrew W. Lo, and Shauna X. Mei, 2004, "Sifting through the Wreckage: Lessons from Recent Hedge-Fund Liquidations," *Journal of Investment Management* (4th Quarter), 6–38.

Hodge, Nicholas, 2003, "Marketing Alternative Investments: Law and Regulation in the United States," Chapter 41 in *Evaluating and Implementing Hedge Fund Strategies: The Experience of Managers and Investors*, 3rd ed., edited by Ronald A. Lake, Euromoney Institutional Investor.

Lowenstein, Roger, 2000, *When Genius Failed: the Rise and Fall of Long-term Capital Management*, Random House.

Malkiel, Burton G., and Atanu Saha, 2004, "Hedge Funds: Risk and Return," working paper.

Malkiel, Burton G., and Atanu Saha, 2005, "Hedge Funds: Risk and Return," *Financial Analyst Journal* (November/December), 80–88.

Hennessee Group LLC, 2007, "Sources of Hedge Fund Capital," The 2007 Manager Survey.

Part IV   Asset Allocation with Alternative Investments

Alternative investments have captured the fancy of investors, both individuals and institutions. Many of these investors have become convinced that the bull market in equities experienced in the 1980s and 1990s is over, and that the secular downturn in inflation that led to unusually high bond returns is also drawing to a close. Many of those same investors have heard of the incredible returns earned by institutional investors like Yale University who have shifted from conventional stock and bond investments to alternative investments like real estate, hedge funds, and private equity. Previously, we have examined the chief alternative investments one by one. These investments have many attractive features as well as some important drawbacks. Now it is time to consider how well they perform in a portfolio. The first section of Part IV considers what we might term alternative investments for the ordinary investor as recommended by a leading institutional investor. The second section then introduces what we might term more exotic alternative investments, namely hedge funds, commodity futures, and private equity. The investments are evaluated in portfolios designed for high net worth and ultra-high net worth investors, respectively. The third section then examines the extraordinary record of one institutional investor, the Yale University Endowment, over the period since 1985 when David Swensen took over its direction. The analysis of the Yale endowment will be designed to disentangle the effects of asset allocation from the superior access to managers provided by the Yale Endowment. The final section examines how alternative investments performed in the financial crisis.

Diversifying into Real Estate—Alternatives for Ordinary Investors

In 2005 David Swensen, the director of the Yale Endowment since 1985, published a book on investment designed for the ordinary investor. The book, entitled *Unconventional Success: A Fundamental Approach to Personal Investment* presented a model portfolio for investors not wealthy enough (or perhaps too risk averse) to invest in exotic alternative investments. Swensen recommended that such investors consider two somewhat unconventional investments, real estate and Treasury inflation-protected bonds.

Let's consider the diversifying power of real estate first. There are many ways to invest in real estate. Most investors own a residence, but here we are discussing investable real estate including apartment buildings, office buildings, retail office space, and factory buildings. Many wealthy investors own such real estate directly rather than through funds. For these investors, the common feature of their real estate holdings is their lack of diversification. The real estate is typically in a single area of the country and often in the same type of real estate. For example, an investor may own apartment buildings or office buildings in the Los Angeles area, but not elsewhere in the country. Or an investor may own rental real estate in a vacation area, but little else.

REITs offer diversification to an investor, both geographic diversification and diversification in the types of real estate. For that reason, we will study real estate by focusing on the REIT market. The series we will use is the same one discussed in Part II of this chapter, the FTSE NAREIT index of REIT equity returns provided by the National Association of Real Estate Investment Trusts. Returns from the REIT index begin in 1972. Over the period since then, REITs have earned a premium over the S&P 500 of 1.6 percent. The correlation between REITs and the S&P 500 is only 0.56. No wonder Swensen believes that real estate could help to improve the performance of a portfolio.

To see the potential for diversification into real estate, consider Figure 12.14 where two portfolios are compared. There is a stock and bond portfolio consisting of the Russell 3000 all-cap U.S. stock index, the MSCI EAFE index, and the Barclays Capital Aggregate bond index. This three-asset portfolio provides diversification across the entire U.S. stock market, international diversification, and diversification across different types of U.S. investment grade bonds. The three asset stock and bond portfolio is compared with a portfolio that also includes REITs. The sample period used to measure standard errors and correlations is 1979 to 2009 (truncated because the Russell series begins in 1979). The returns are measured through 2009 using the premium method described in Table 12.28 following. The addition of REITs to the portfolio shifts the frontier in a northwesterly direction. The shift is not dramatic, but it's at no cost to the investor.

It should be noted that the optimization is done without imposing constraints on the portfolio allocation. The optimizer often chooses portfolios that might appear strange to the investor. For example, the portfolio with bonds at 30 percent of the allocation has 36.7 percent in REITs, 21.5 percent in EAFE, and only 11.8 percent in U.S. stocks. This allocation shows the diversifying power of real estate, but it is not one that most investors would choose.

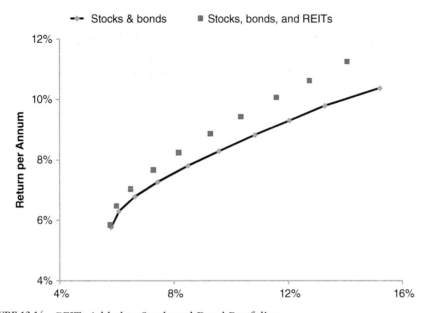

FIGURE 12.14   REITs Added to Stock and Bond Portfolios

Source: Swensen, *Unconventional Success* (2005). Expected returns are from Tables 8.3 and 13.2.

TABLE 12.28   Comparison between Swensen's *Unconventional Success* Portfolio and Conventional Portfolio

Portfolio Shares	*Unconventional Success* Portfolios		Conventional Portfolio
	With Real Estate and TIPS	With No TIPS	
U.S. Treasury Bonds (SBBI MT)	15%	30%	30%
U.S. TIPS (Barclays TIPS)	15%		
Domestic Equity (Russell 3000)	30%	30%	42%
Foreign Developed Equity (EAFE)	15%	15%	21%
Emerging Market Equity (MSCI EM)	5%	5%	7%
Real Estate (FTSE NAREIT)	20%	20%	
Average Return	9.3%	9.3%	9.0%
Standard Deviation	10.5%	10.3%	10.5%
Sharpe Ratio	0.56	0.57	0.53
Alpha*	0.3%	0.4%	

*The *Unconventional Success* portfolio refers to the portfolio recommended for ordinary investors by David Swensen. Standard deviations are calculated using Zephyr AllocationADVISOR for sample period from 1990 to 2009 except for the TIPS series, which begins in March 1997.
Data Sources: ©Morningstar, Barclays Capital, Russell®, MSCI, and ©FTSE.

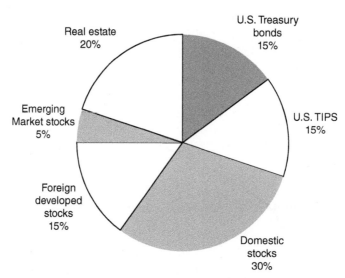

FIGURE 12.15 David Swensen's Portfolio for Individual Investors
Source: Swensen, *Unconventional Success* (2005).

For that reason, we will consider constrained portfolios. For guidance in how to constrain the portfolio, let's consult David Swensen's book, *Unconventional Success* (2005). The portfolio he recommends to ordinary investors is displayed in Figure 12.15. He recommends that investors diversify a conventional stock and bond portfolio by adding two assets: (a) real estate and (b) Treasury inflation-protected securities (TIPS). The latter were introduced in 1997 by the Clinton Administration, so the historical series of returns is rather short. Swensen recommends TIPS as a hedge against unexpected inflation much like an endowment might look to commodities or timberland for such protection. Swensen allocates half of the 30 percent bond portion of the portfolio to TIPS. The other half is allocated to conventional Treasury bonds since Swensen is skeptical about the advantages of incurring credit risk by investing in non-Treasury bonds. Swensen also allocates 20 percent of the portfolio to real estate. This is truly an unconventional portfolio. But given Swensen's extraordinary success in investing Yale's endowment, his views ought to be considered seriously.

To evaluate the Swensen portfolio, we again employ the premium method for estimating returns. The premium method builds on the fundamental capital market assets, U.S. Treasury bonds and the S&P 500. Those returns were estimated to be 4.9 percent and 9.4 percent, respectively.[1] Since REITs earned a premium over the S&P 500 of 1.6 percent from 1972 to 2009, the REIT return is estimated to be 11.2 percent.[2] TIPS were introduced in 1997, so the data set extends only from March 1997 through December 2009. Over this period, TIPS earned a 0.5 percent premium over the medium-term Treasury bond, so the TIPS return is estimated to be 5.4 percent. As an alternative to the portfolio recommended by Swensen, a conventional portfolio is chosen with ordinary Treasury bonds replacing the TIPS allocation and stocks replacing the REIT allocation (with the foreign/domestic proportions for equities remaining the same). The two portfolios were evaluated using

Zephyr AllocationADVISOR. The standard deviations and correlation coefficients for both portfolios were based on the same sample period beginning in 1990 (when the MSCI Emerging Markets Index begins) except that the TIPS returns begin only in March 1997.[3]

The results of this comparison are reported in Table 12.28. Swensen's recommended portfolio with REITs and TIPS earned 0.3 percent more than the conventional portfolio (9.3 percent versus 9.0 percent). Since the standard deviations of the two portfolios are identical, the Sharpe ratio of Swensen's recommended portfolio is higher than that of the conventional portfolio, 0.56 versus 0.53. That translates into an excess return, or alpha*, of 0.3 percent for Swensen's portfolio.[4] That's certainly not much of an improvement in performance, but it's achieved while staying with quite conventional alternative investments. Swensen designed the portfolio for the ordinary investor, and there is nothing about this portfolio that should alarm such an investor.

How much of that outperformance is due to the addition of real estate and how much to the addition of TIPS? The answer is provided in Table 12.28 in the middle column of the table where the allocation to TIPS is replaced by conventional Treasury securities. The portfolio without TIPS actually performs a little better than Swensen's recommended portfolio. The modified Swensen portfolio outperforms the conventional portfolio by 0.4 percent in risk-adjusted terms. So it's the real estate investment that delivers the improvement in performance in Swensen's portfolio. A 20 percent allocation to real estate gives the investor an extra boost in terms of risk-adjusted returns.

The statistics in Table 12.28 may not do true justice to Swensen's argument for diversification into TIPS. The main reason that Swensen adds TIPS to a conventional portfolio is to guard against unexpected inflation. In an endowment portfolio like Yale's there are several types of investments, like timberland and oil and gas properties, that will help protect the portfolio against inflation. The value of these assets is never fully appreciated unless inflation rises unexpectedly. Since 1997 when TIPS were introduced, it's been deflation rather than inflation that has preoccupied many minds.

Swensen's portfolio suggests that there are advantages to diversifying the portfolio beyond conventional stocks and bonds. Institutional investors as well as high net worth investors, however, often consider alternative investments more exotic than those in this portfolio designed by Swensen for ordinary investors. The next section of this chapter will consider how investments like hedge funds, commodities, and private equity can help to diversify the portfolio. Then in the following section, the Yale endowment portfolio will be analyzed. Yale's portfolio combines many of these alternative investments in a very unconventional way.

Expanding the Menu of Alternative Assets

In earlier chapters, several different types of alternative investments were discussed in detail, among them hedge funds, commodities, and private equity, along with real estate. This section will analyze how these alternative assets help to diversify the portfolio. Several portfolios containing conventional and alternative assets will be examined.

In addition to the FTSE NAREIT index discussed in Part II, the indexes chosen are as follows:

Hedge funds: the HFRI Fund of Funds Index and Credit Suisse/Tremont Hedge Fund Index. The HFRI index begins in 1990 while the Credit Suisse/Tremont index begins in 1994.[5]

Commodity futures: the Dow Jones UBS Commodity Index. This index limits the weight of any individual commodity to 33 percent of the index, so it is a more representative index than the Goldman Sachs Commodity Index (which is dominated by energy). The DJ UBS index begins in February 1991.

Venture capital: the Cambridge Associates LLC U.S. Venture Capital Index®. This index begins in the second quarter of 1981.

Private equity: the Cambridge Associates LLC U.S. Private Equity Index®. This index, which begins in the second quarter of 1986, consists primarily of buyout funds.

It should be noted that some of these indexes for alternative investments are quite different from the stock and bond indexes used in a conventional indexed portfolio. First, unlike the DJ AIG commodity futures index, which measures the returns on a passive investment in commodity futures contracts, the indexes for REITs, hedge funds, and private equity all measure the performance of *active managers*. For example, the FTSE NAREIT real estate index measures the returns of REIT managers who actively manage portfolios of real estate assets. Similarly, hedge fund and private equity managers actively manage their portfolios of assets, so indexes for hedge funds and private equity measure some average of the managers' performance. Second, some of these indexes, notably the hedge fund indexes, have *significant biases* in measuring the set of active managers. So they should be regarded as asset benchmarks rather than genuine indexes.

To obtain measures of the expected returns on these alternative investments, we use the premium method. Table 12.29 reports the premiums for these alternative assets. The table reports the index used for each alternative asset, the premium over the S&P 500, the period of measurement, and the resulting estimated return. For example, as discussed in the first section of this chapter, the FTSE NAREIT Index of REITs has a premium of 1.6 percent above the S&P 500 over the period starting in 1972 (when the FTSE NAREIT series begins). If the expected return on the S&P 500 in the long run is 9.4 percent, this results in an expected return on the REIT index of 11.2 percent. In contrast, the Dow Jones AIG Index of commodity futures returns has a negative premium of −2.5 percent over the period from February 1991 to December 2009. So the estimated return is 6.7 percent.[6]

Portfolios containing alternative investments will be compared with a conventional portfolio of stocks and bonds. The conventional portfolio to be used as a benchmark in all of the comparisons consists of the same four indexes used in earlier experiments: the Barclays Capital Aggregate index of investable U.S. bonds, the Russell 3000 all-cap U.S. stock index, the MSCI EAFE Index of foreign developed country stocks, and the MSCI Emerging Market Index. The benchmark portfolio consists of 25 percent in bonds and 75 percent in stocks. Forty percent of the stocks (or 30 percent of the portfolio) is invested overseas with one-third of the foreign stocks

TABLE 12.29   Premiums of Alternative Investment Returns over S&P 500

Alternative Asset Index	Premium over S&P 500	Estimated Return	Period of Measurement
FTSE NAREIT	+1.6%	11.2%	1972–2009
HRFI Fund of Funds	+0.0%	9.4%	1990–2009
Credit Suisse/Tremont Hedge Fund	+1.6%	11.2%	1994–2009
DJ UBS Commodity	−2.5%	6.7%	Feb 1991–Dec 2009
Venture Capital	+2.1%	11.7%	1981 Q2–2009 Q3
Private Equity	+3.4%	13.1%	1986 Q2–2009 Q3

The alternative indexes are the FTSE NAREIT Index for REITs, the HFRI Fund of Funds and Credit Suisse/Tremont Hedge Fund indexes, the Dow Jones UBS commodity futures index, and the Cambridge Associates LLC U.S. indexes for venture capital and private equity. The premiums are measured relative to the S&P 500 over the periods indicated and applied to the long-run S&P 500 (geometric average) estimated return of 9.4 percent.
Data Sources: S&P, ©FTSE, HFRI, Credit Suisse/Tremont, Dow-Jones-UBS Commodity Indexes©, Cambridge Associates LLC U.S. Venture Capital Index®, and U.S. Private Equity Index®.

invested in emerging markets. This portfolio is illustrated on the left side of Figure 12.16. When alternative assets are added to the portfolio, domestic and foreign stocks remain in the same proportion as in the benchmark portfolio.

High Net Worth (HNW) Portfolios

Several portfolios with alternative investments are examined. The first two portfolios are designed for high net worth investors who are willing to invest in hedge funds and commodity futures as well as in real estate, stocks, and bonds. Both HNW portfolios have 25 percent invested in bonds, 50 percent in stocks, and 25 percent in

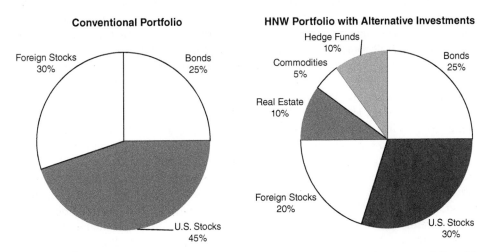

FIGURE 12.16   Conventional Portfolio with Traditional Investments and HNW Portfolio with Alternative Investments

TABLE 12.30   Comparison between HNW Portfolios (with Alternative Investments) and Conventional Portfolio (No Alternatives)

| Portfolio Shares | HNW Portfolios | | Conventional Portfolio |
	With Commodities	Without Commodities	
Barclays Aggregate	25%	25%	25%
Russell 3000	30%	30%	45%
MSCI EAFE	13.3%	13.3%	20%
MSCI Emerging Markets	6.7%	6.7%	10%
FTSE NAREIT	10%	15%	
HFRI Fund of Funds	10%	10%	
DJ UBS Commodity Index	5%		
Average Return	9.2%	9.5%	9.4%
Standard Deviation	9.7%	10.1%	11.5%
Sharpe Ratio	0.59	0.59	0.52
Alpha*	0.7%	0.7%	

The returns for individual assets are based on the premium method as reported in Tables and Standard deviations are measured starting in February 1991.
Data Sources: Barclays Capital, Russell®, MSCI, ©FTSE, HFRI, Dow-Jones-UBS Commodity Indexes©.

alternative investments (including real estate). The first of these portfolios has 10 percent in hedge funds, 5 percent in commodity futures, and 10 percent in REITs. This portfolio is illustrated on the right side of Figure 12.16. The second HNW portfolio excludes commodity futures with the REIT allocation increased to 15 percent from 10 percent. The other portfolios are designed for ultra-high net worth investors who can cope with the illiquidity of venture capital and private equity investments. These portfolios will be discussed later.

The two HNW portfolios are examined in Table 12.30. The hedge fund index used for these portfolios is the HFRI Fund of Funds index since high net worth investors usually cannot diversify manager risk adequately by investing directly in hedge funds.[7] The expected returns of each portfolio are calculated using Zephyr AllocationADVISOR, but only after the individual asset returns are replaced by the estimated returns obtained using the premium method (as in Table 12.29).[8] The standard deviations and correlations for each portfolio are measured by Zephyr from February 1991 (when the DJ UBS index begins) until December 2009.

Consider the first HNW portfolio that includes 10 percent in hedge funds, 5 percent in commodities, and 10 percent in REITs. This portfolio is shown in the second column of Table 12.30. The addition of three alternative investments—real estate, hedge funds, and commodities—lowers risk by 1.8 percent while lowering the average return by 0.2 percent. The Sharpe ratio for this HNW portfolio is 0.59 compared with the Sharpe ratio of 0.52 for the conventional portfolio measured over the same period. In Figure 12.17, this portfolio is compared with the conventional portfolio. After adjusting the risk of the conventional portfolio down to that of the HNW portfolio, the return on the latter exceeds that of the conventional portfolio by 0.7 percent. So the shift of 25 percent of the portfolio from stocks to the three alternative assets raises the risk-adjusted return 70 basis points.

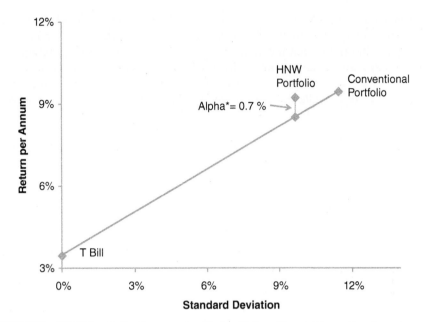

FIGURE 12.17 HNW Portfolio Compared with Portfolio without Alternative Investments
Sources: Barclays Capital, Russell®, MSCI, ©FTSE, HFRI, Dow-Jones-UBS Commodity Indexes©.

Table 12.30 also shows the performance of a second HNW portfolio that replaces the 5 percent allocation to commodity futures with an additional 5 percent in REITs. So this portfolio has 10 percent in hedge funds and 15 percent in REITs. The results are very similar to those for the first HNW portfolio. This portfolio has a higher return than the first HNW portfolio because REITs have earned a higher return than commodities, but the Sharpe ratios of the two HNW portfolios are identical.

So does a HNW investor with access to alternative investments do much better than an ordinary investor confined to conventional assets? The answer is provided by the alpha* calculations. Yes, the HNW investor does earn an extra 0.7 percent adjusted for risk. It should be noted, though, that an excess return of that size could easily be swamped by excessive investment expenses or taxes, or other sources of investment expense. And remember that the hedge fund returns are upwardly biased. So the alpha* calculation may overstate the actual advantage of the alternative strategy.

Ultra HNW Portfolios

Ultra HNW investors are in a somewhat different investment world than the rest of us. Those investors are able to tie up capital for extended periods of time, so the world of venture capital and private equity is open to them. At what wealth level do such investments become possible? Some brokerage firms define ultra HNW investors as having as little as $20 million or $30 million in wealth.[9] But it's not clear that an investor with \$20 or \$30 million could afford to tie up 10 percent of the portfolio in an investment that would be illiquid for 10 years or more. Certainly such an investor could not obtain much diversification within the private equity portion of the portfolio, since the minimums for investment in venture capital or buyouts would preclude more than one or two investments (if the total amount to be invested was \$2 or \$3 million). In any case, our definition of the ultra HNW investor will be made in terms of eligible investments rather than in terms of wealth. *An ultra HNW investor is any investor who can devote 10 percent or more of the portfolio to private equity or other illiquid investments.* This definition is useful because we are primarily interested in portfolio performance rather than levels of wealth per se.

Since many ultra-HNW investors can obtain sufficient diversification of hedge fund investments by directly investing in hedge funds, the Credit Suisse/Tremont Hedge Fund index will be used to measure hedge fund performance rather than the HFRI Fund of Funds index. The Tremont index begins in 1994, so standard deviations and correlations will be measured over the period from 1994 through the third quarter of 2009. To measure private equity returns, two Cambridge Associates series are used. These series are for venture capital and private equity.[10] The portfolios described below will allocate equal proportions to each type of investment. The CA series are available only quarterly, so the correlations and standard deviations had to be loaded manually into the Zephyr program (since all other series are available monthly). The volatility of these investments is probably seriously underestimated because the returns are smoothed by infrequent valuations. So the standard deviations of the resulting portfolios are downwardly biased. The measured correlations are also probably lower than in reality.

Table 12.31 compares portfolios for the ultra HNW investor with the conventional portfolio previously described. The table examines two ultra HNW portfolios. In the second column, Portfolio A assigns 25 percent to alternative investments overall with 5 percent allocated to venture capital and another 5 percent to private equity. In the third column, Portfolio B doubles the allocation to alternatives to 50 percent of the portfolio.

Consider first Portfolio A with 25 percent invested in alternatives. The return on this portfolio is 0.3 percent higher than that of the conventional portfolio and the standard deviation is 1.4 percent lower. So the Sharpe ratio of the ultra HNW portfolio is higher. Translated into an excess return, this higher Sharpe ratio results in an alpha* of 1.0 percent. That's a little higher than achieved by the HNW investor who is confined to real estate and hedge funds. But the addition of venture capital and private equity to the portfolio does not matter that much.

Portfolio B doubles the allocation to alternative investments to 50 percent of the portfolio. That has the predictable effect of increasing the relative performance of the ultra HNW portfolio. The return of Portfolio B is 0.6 percent above that of the conventional portfolio while the risk is 2.4 percent lower. The Sharpe ratio is high enough to result in an alpha* of 1.9 percent relative to that of the conventional portfolio. These results in Table 12.31 are notable, but they are not as impressive as we might expect. Remember that these returns are obtained only after tying up part of the portfolio in very illiquid investments. Surely an extra 0.3 percent return (comparing the alpha* of 1.0 percent for Portfolio A with the alpha* of 0.7 percent for

TABLE 12.31 Comparison between Portfolios for Ultra-HNW Investors and Conventional Portfolio

Portfolio Shares	Ultra-HNW Portfolios		Conventional Portfolio
	Portfolio A	Portfolio B	
Barclays Aggregate	25%	25%	25%
Russell 3000	30%	15%	45%
MSCI EAFE	13.3%	6.7%	20%
MSCI Emerging Markets	6.7%	3.3%	10%
FTSE NAREIT	5%	10%	
Credit Suisse/Tremont Hedge Fund	10%	20%	
Venture Capital	5%	10%	
Private Equity	5%	10%	
Average Return	9.7%	10.0%	9.4%
Standard Deviation	10.4%	9.4%	11.8%
Sharpe Ratio	0.60	0.70	0.50
Alpha*	1.0%	1.9%	

*The returns for individual assets are based on the premium method as reported in Tables and Standard deviations are measured from 1994 to 2009 Q3.
Data Sources: Barclays Capital, Russell®, MSCI, ©FTSE, Credit Suisse/Tremont, Cambridge Associates LLC U.S. Venture Capital Index®, and Private Equity Index®.

the HNW portfolio in Table 12.30) is not much compensation for investing 10 percent of the portfolio in illiquid VC and PE investments.

The results developed in this section must puzzle some readers. It's well known that some wealthy institutions have made huge returns by investing in alternative investments. The Yale Endowment is perhaps the best example, but other institutions such as Harvard University and the Rockefeller Foundation have also achieved superior returns by investing in alternatives. How we reconcile their results with those analyzed above is the subject of the next section of this chapter.

Lessons about Alternatives from the Yale Endowment

Interest in alternative investments has been enhanced dramatically by the remarkable performance of the Yale Endowment under its long-term director, David Swensen. Since he took over direction of the Endowment in 1985, the Endowment has compiled one of the most impressive records of any investment organization. As will be shown in this section, Yale beats all normal benchmarks including those of peer institutions. What is more impressive perhaps is that it has led the way in revolutionizing the investment practices of educational institutions nationwide. Under David Swensen, Yale has embraced alternative investments and they have been the key to its success. Whether other investors should emulate Yale is a question that will be addressed in this section.

Consider the strategic asset allocation reported in the 2009 Yale Endowment report as illustrated in Figure 12.18. Only 22 percent of the portfolio is in traditional

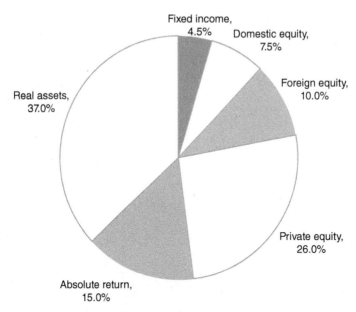

FIGURE 12.18   Target Portfolio of Yale Endowment, (2009)
Sources: The Yale Endowment, 2009.

stock and bond investments. It's interesting that Yale has more invested in foreign equity (10 percent) than in U.S. equity (7.5 percent). All of the rest of the portfolio is in three alternative asset classes:

Private equity (26 percent of portfolio), primarily in *venture capital* and *buyouts*
Absolute return (15 percent), split between *event-driven strategies* (tied to merg-
     ers, bankruptcy restructurings, or other corporate events) and *value-driven*
     strategies
Real assets (37 percent), primarily *real estate, oil and gas properties*, and *timber-*
     land

A small investment staff led by Swensen and Dean Takahashi, Swensen's deputy, chooses the management firms that in turn invest in all of these alternative asset classes.

With such a large allocation to alternative investments, the Yale endowment has lowered risk to much lower levels than would normally be associated with a portfolio allocation with so little in fixed income.[11] In fact, over the period from 1986 to 2009, a period that covers Swensen's tenure to date at Yale, the standard deviation of the portfolio has been only 13.3 percent compared with a standard deviation for the Russell 3000 of 16.3 percent. The fact that Yale has averaged a return of 14.2 percent is quite impressive given that the Russell 3000 return was only 9.2 percent over the same period and the S&P 500 return only 9.3 percent.[12] Lower risk and much higher returns—that's an impressive record. Adjusting the Russell 3000 (all-equity) return down to the risk level of the Yale endowment, the excess return of that endowment is an impressive 5.7 percent per annum. In other words, Yale has outperformed the U.S. stock market *adjusted for risk* by almost 6 percent per year on average since 1986.

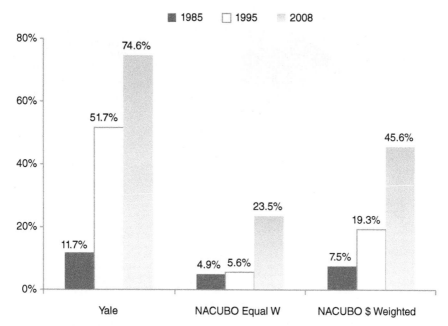

FIGURE 12.19 Allocation to Alternative Investments: Yale Endowment and University Endowments (NACUBO Survey)

Sources: Yale Endowment (various reports) and NACUBO.

In 1986 when Swensen took over the portfolio, Yale invested only 3.2 percent in private equity, 8.5 percent in real assets (mostly real estate) and nothing in absolute return assets.[13] Between 1985 and 2009, the Yale Endowment increased its commitment to alternative investments from 11.7 percent of the portfolio to 78 percent. Figure 12.19 compares Yale's allocation to alternatives with those of other university endowments as reported by NACUBO, the National Association of College and University Business Officers. Each year NACUBO conducts a survey of its members to determine the asset allocations that their endowments are following. NACUBO reports two sets of figures, those that equally weight all colleges and universities and a dollar-weighted average. The massive size of the endowments of the richest institutions ensures that the dollar-weighted average is heavily influenced by the asset allocation decisions of the biggest endowments. In 2008, the top 10 institutions had 36 percent of the endowment monies of the 791 institutions in the survey. The dollar-weighted average, therefore, better reflects the asset allocations of Yale's peers.

Figure 12.19 shows the asset allocations over more than three decades. In 1985 when Swensen took over the Yale Endowment, Yale's allocation to alternatives was still only 11.7 percent compared with NACUBO's equal-weighted average of 4.9 percent.[14] By 2008, NACUBO's average allocation to alternatives had increased to 23.5 percent while Yale's had risen to 74.6 percent. Interestingly enough, the NACUBO dollar-weighted average allocation had increased from 7.5 percent in 1985 to 45.6 percent in 2008. So Yale's shift toward alternatives is part of a larger trend in the endowments of many universities.[15]

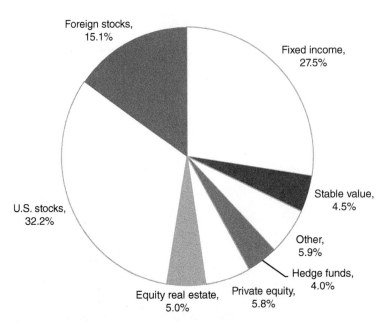

FIGURE 12.20   Investments of Pension Plans, Endowments, and Foundations
Source: Greenwich Investment Report, 2009.

To what extent is the shift toward alternatives by Yale part of a larger shift by all institutional investors? Some evidence about this issue is provided by the 2009 Greenwich Associate survey of pension plans, endowments, and foundations. The average asset allocation of the institutions in this survey is given in Figure 12.20.[16] These institutions devoted only 14.8 percent of their portfolios to alternative investments (defined to include real estate, private equity, and hedge funds). So there is a large gap between the allocations to alternatives by Yale and its peers on the one hand, and noneducational institutions on the other hand.

Investments in hedge funds provide the biggest contrast between university endowments and the other institutional investors studied in the Greenwich surveys. In 1999, the Greenwich survey did not even have a category for hedge funds. Between 2001 (when hedge funds were first reported) and 2009, average allocations to hedge funds increased from 0.6 percent to 4.0 percent. That's a large percentage increase in hedge funds, but the 4 percent allocation in 2009 is very small relative to the 15 percent strategic allocation of the Yale Endowment or the 12.9 percent allocation of the average university endowment.[17] So the institutional investor world has started to embrace hedge funds, but the university endowments have gone on to full courtship.

Yale's push into alternative investments has evidently been a key reason for its investment success. One way to see how well the Yale endowment has performed is to compare it with the conventional portfolio discussed earlier that is made up of traditional stock and bond investments. This is the portfolio shown on the left side of Figure 12.16. Figure 12.21 compares the Yale and conventional portfolios for the period since Swensen's tenure began. Since the conventional portfolio has

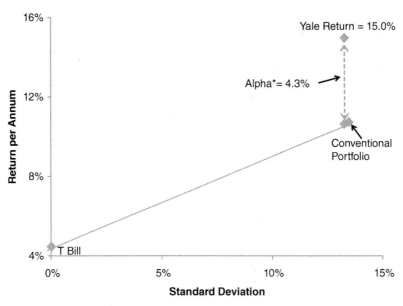

FIGURE 12.21 Alpha* of Yale Endowment Returns Relative to Conventional Portfolio, 1985–2009

Sources: Yale Endowment (various reports), ©Morningstar, Russell®, and MSCI.

a slightly higher risk standard deviation than the Yale portfolio (13.5 percent versus 13.3 percent), its risk is reduced to that of the Yale portfolio in order to make a proper comparison. The alpha* of the Yale portfolio relative to this benchmark portfolio is an impressive 4.3 percent.

It's important to try to disentangle the sources of Yale's success. Is the extraordinary return due to Yale's devotion to alternative investments? Or is it due to Yale's selection of (and access to) superior managers? We can try to extract an answer to these questions by constructing an experiment. Let's set up a portfolio with the same asset allocation that Yale followed each year over the period from 1986 to 2009, but with each asset invested in an index rather than in the managers that Yale selected. As previously noted, the indexed portfolio will reflect active management in some of the alternative asset classes such as hedge funds, venture capital, and private equity. So the returns on what we call the indexed portfolio will reflect the asset allocation chosen by Yale together with the performance of the average fund managers in the alternative investment indexes. And recall that some of these alternative investment indexes, particularly those for hedge funds, are upwardly biased. Comparing the return on this indexed portfolio with Yale's actual return gives us a measure of how much value added has come from Yale's manager selection and access to superior managers. This is an important issue because ordinary investors may not have the same access to managers that Yale does and because ordinary investors may not have the resources to find the best managers in the first place. But because of the biases in the indexes used, we will *underestimate the value added provided by Yale's superior manager selection and manager access.*

To apply this methodology, we must identify an index or indexes for each asset class. For some alternative asset classes, this is a difficult task since the range of alternatives chosen by Yale is difficult to capture in indexes. The following is a list of indexes chosen to represent each asset class:[18]

Cash: One-month Treasury bill return from SBBI
Bonds: Medium-term Treasury bond from SBBI (since Yale's bond portfolio is made up primarily of Treasuries)
Domestic equity: Russell 3000 all-cap stock index
Foreign equity: MSCI EAFE and MSCI Emerging Market indexes (with two-thirds weight on MSCI EAFE)
Private equity: Cambridge Associates indexes for private equity and venture capital (one-half weight for each)[19]
Absolute return: HFRI fund-weighted composite hedge fund index through 1993 and Credit Suisse/Tremont thereafter[20]
Real assets: NCREIF institutional real estate index and Goldman Sachs Commodity Futures Index (one-half weight to each)

The real asset category in Yale's portfolio consists mainly of real estate, timberland, and oil and gas properties. For real estate, the NCREIF institutional real estate index is used instead of the FTSE NAREIT index because Yale uses it as its real estate benchmark. Since there are no good indexes for timberland and oil and gas properties, the GS commodity futures index, with its heavy weight on energy, is used instead.[21]

If Yale had invested in all of these indexes during Swensen's tenure, the endowment would have earned a return of 13.0 percent with a standard deviation of 13.4 percent (compared with Yale's 13.3 percent). An alpha* calculation can compare the relative returns on a risk-adjusted basis. Figure 12.22 shows the calculation. If an investor chose the Yale allocation each year, but invested in indexes, that investor would have earned *on a risk-adjusted basis* 2.3 percent more than an investment in the benchmark (traditional) portfolio. Yale's choice of managers then added *an extra 2.0 percent* to its performance. So *Yale's performance was based on its manager selection and access as well as on its reliance on alternative investments.* That's exactly what David Swensen told investors in his book *Unconventional Success* (2005). It's important to reiterate that the return calculated using indexes is probably upwardly biased because some of the indexes for alternative investments, particularly the hedge fund indexes, are upwardly biased. So the estimate of what Yale earned due to manager selection and access is probably larger than indicated above. It's impressive enough as it is.

If Yale has led the charge into alternative investments, how well has it done relative to other universities? In Table 12.32, the returns of the Yale Endowment are compared with the average returns reported in the NACUBO studies. Over the period from 1986 to 2009, Yale has achieved a compound return of 14.2 percent compared with a return of 8.8 percent for the NACUBO equal-weighted return.[22] The NACUBO returns have less risk than Yale's, so it's important to compare the returns adjusted for risk. The Sharpe ratio for the Yale endowment is 0.79 compared with a Sharpe ratio for the NACUBO index of 0.48. The risk-adjusted excess return, or alpha*, for the Yale endowment is an impressive 4.2 percent per annum. This excess return

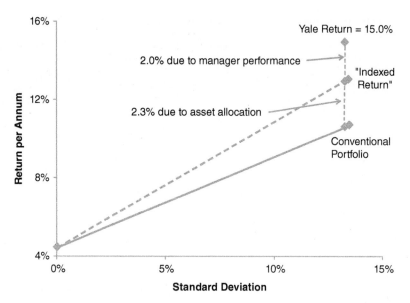

FIGURE 12.22 Alpha* of Yale Endowment Returns Relative to Indexed Portfolio and Conventional Portfolio

Sources: Yale Endowment (various reports) ©Morningstar, Russell®, MSCI, NCREIF, S&P, Cambridge Associates LLC U.S. Venture Capital Index® and Private Equity Index®, HFRI, and Credit Suisse/Tremont.

implies that Yale's endowment has delivered a cumulative excess return over the 24-year period of more than 160 percent. Not bad for a handful of staff in a New Haven office far from Wall Street!

Lessons about Alternative Investments Learned in the Financial Crisis

Yale and other institutional investors suffered along with the rest of us when the financial crisis hit in 2007 to 2009. Yale's portfolio suffered a loss of 24.6 percent in the fiscal year 2009 (from July 2008 to June 2009). Harvard's portfolio was down 27.3 percent. The average return of NACUBO members was −18.7 percent. How do we explain these results? This section will examine how different types of alternatives fared during the crisis. Then it will examine Yale's performance.

TABLE 12.32 Performance of Yale Endowment Compared with University Endowments, 1986–2009

	Geometric Average	Arithmetic Average	Standard Deviation	Sharpe Ratio	Alpha*
Yale Endowment	14.2%	15.0%	13.3%	0.79	4.2%
NACUBO	8.8%	9.2%	10.0%	0.48	

Sources: Yale Endowment (various reports) and NACUBO.

TABLE 12.33   Returns on Stocks and Alternative Investments during Financial Crisis

Index	October 2007–March 2009*	Fiscal 2009**
S&P 500	−46.7%	−26.2%
Venture Capital	−15.6%	−17.3%
Private Equity	−22.6%	−22.0%
FTSE NAREIT	−63.4%	−43.3%
NCREIF	−10.5%	−19.6%
GSCI	−51.3%	−59.7%
Credit Suisse/Tremont Hedge Fund	−19.0%	−13.7%

*S&P 500 peaked in October 2007 and fell until March 2009. Venture capital, private equity, and NCREIF returns are quarterly from 2007 Q4 through 2009 Q1.
**Fiscal year is the 12 months ending in June 2009.
Data Sources: S&P, Cambridge Associates LLC U.S. Venture Capital Index® and Private Equity Index®, ©FTSE, NCREIF, and Credit Suisse/Tremont.

One important feature of investments during the crisis was that they varied widely in how accurately they reflected true economic values. Stocks are priced on organized exchanges—marked to market at every point in time. The same is true of REITs and the commodity futures contracts measured by the GSCI or DJ UBS commodity indexes. The same cannot be said of private equity or the NCREIF valuation-based index of real estate returns.

Consider first the damage inflicted on publicly traded equities during the crisis. The S&P 500 index reached a peak for this cycle on October 9, 2007. For the next 17 months it fell 56.8 percent until reaching a trough on March 9, 2009. Using monthly data for total returns on the S&P 500 (including dividends), the cumulative return on the S&P 500 was −46.7 percent from October 2007 through March 2009. Over the same 17 months, the return on the EAFE index was −53.6 percent and the return on the MSCI Emerging Markets index was −55.9 percent.

Over the same period, private equity suffered, but their returns were far better than those of public equity. Table 12.33 compares returns on the S&P 500 with those on venture capital and private equity from Cambridge Associates. In contrast to the −46.7 percent return on the S&P 500, venture capital returned −15.6 percent and private equity −22.6 percent. The returns on VC and PE are based on valuations, which often reflect stale prices for the projects being evaluated. During the crisis, these valuations must have lagged far behind the public equity's pricing of similar companies. After all, private equity firms are trying to prepare their investments for eventual sale to the public equity markets. When the latter are down more than 40 percent, how can the private equity valuations be down less than half as much?[23]

A similar pattern is seen in real estate returns. Over this same period, the FTSE NAREIT return on publicly traded REITs was down 63.4 percent. But the NCREIF index reflecting the real estate holdings of institutional investors was down only 10.5 percent. Surely there cannot be that large a difference in the commercial real estate properties held in REITs on the one hand, and those held in institutional portfolios on the other hand. The NCREIF index is based on appraisals, not market prices.

Illiquid investments have stale valuations, which are slow to reflect falling market values. Those stale valuations seem to shield investors from market downturns. But surely this is misleading.

Not all alternative investments are illiquid. Nor do all of them fail to reflect current pricing. The Dow Jones UBS Commodity Index and the Goldman Sachs Commodity Index are made up of commodity futures contracts which are constantly marked to market. So these indexes reflect current values. Nonetheless, commodities failed to protect investors from the crisis. The world recession that crushed equity valuations also leveled commodity markets. The GSCI fell 51.3 percent from October 2007 through March 2009, while the Dow Jones UBS Commodity Index fell 38.9 percent. Hedge funds, in contrast to commodities, did help to cushion investors from market turmoil during this period even though they are also marked to market.[24] The Credit Suisse/Tremont Hedge Fund Index was down only 19.0 percent over the 17-month period beginning in October 2007. It's true that some individual hedge fund strategies were down much more. Indeed, the Tremont market-neutral hedge fund index had a return of −41.8 percent over this same period. And it's also true that many hedge funds shut their gates, preventing investors from cashing out. In such cases, it was not very reassuring that your hedge fund investments were only down 19.0 percent if you had no access to them in the crisis period.

This crisis provided almost no place to hide from losses even if losses on some asset classes were smaller than on others. Almost every investment yielded negative returns. The most important exception was Treasury bonds. As the financial world came close to crumbling, investors fled to the safety of U.S. Treasury bonds and the dollar. The return on Barclays Capital Long-Term Treasury Index was a positive 22.5 percent over this same 17-month period! In contrast, bonds with credit risk fell in the crisis. The Barclays (investment-grade) Corporate Bond Index returned −6.1 percent and the Barclays High Yield Index returned −23.2 percent.

So for investors who only invested in stocks and bonds, Treasury bonds alone shielded the investor from losses. For investors who also had alternative investments, some but not all alternative investments helped to limit losses in the portfolio. First, there were hedge funds, which fell much less than stocks. The cushion to portfolios was provided not by nonmarket pricing but because hedge fund betas are relatively low. Then there were the illiquid assets where the *reported* returns, at least, were less negative than those of publicly traded equities or publicly traded REITs. So a portfolio with alternatives declined less than a comparable portfolio with only publicly traded assets (both equity and real estate).

Consider the ultra HNW Portfolio A described in Table 12.31. Recall that this portfolio had 25 percent in bonds, 50 percent in stocks, and 25 percent in alternatives. This portfolio fell 30.0 percent from October 2007 through March 2009.[25] The conventional portfolio in Table 12.31 with 75 percent in stocks and no alternatives had a −35.5 percent return. So holding private equity and hedge funds did help to cushion the returns reported during the crisis. But as discussed above, some of that cushioning was more apparent than real.

With this discussion of asset returns during the crisis as background, we can now consider Yale's performance during the crisis. As stated earlier, for the fiscal year ended June 2009 Yale had a return of −24.6 percent. How much of that is due to Yale's asset allocation and how much is due to manager performance? Table 12.34

TABLE 12.34   Performance of Yale Endowment Compared with Indexes in Fiscal Year 2009
(July 2008 to June 2009)

Asset	Index	Weight	2009 Return
Bonds	MT Treasury	4.0%	5.5%
Cash	Treasury Bill	−3.9%	0.6%
Domestic Equity	Russell 3000	10.1%	−26.6%
Foreign Equity	2/3 EAFE, 1/3 EM	15.2%	−29.9%
Real Assets	1/2 NCREIF, 1/2 GSCI	29.3%	−39.6%
Private Equity	1/2 VC, 1/2 PE	20.2%	−19.6%
Absolute Return	Credit Suisse/Tremont Hedge Fund	25.1%	−13.7%
Weighted Average			−26.0%
Yale Return			−24.6%

Notes: Weights represent Yale's actual asset allocation in June 2008 (before the 2009 fiscal year began). The
foreign equity return is based on the EAFE return of −31.0 percent and MSCI EM return of −27.8 percent.
Other returns are in Table 12.33.
Data Sources: Yale (2009), ©Morningstar, Russell®, MSCI, NCREIF, S&P, Cambridge Associates LLC U.S.
Venture Capital Index®, and Private Equity Index®, and Credit Suisse/Tremont.

attempts to estimate the return Yale would have earned just based on index performance. The table uses Yale's *actual* asset allocation in *June 2008*, just before the
beginning of the 2009 fiscal year. The indexes used for each asset class are the same
ones used for the indexed portfolio in Figure 12.22. As Table 12.34 reports, Yale's
portfolio should have earned −26.0 percent in the 2009 fiscal year if it had just
invested in the indexes themselves. Instead Yale actually earned −24.6 percent.[26]
That's a relatively small difference given the large losses suffered in almost every
asset class. So at least according to this (admittedly imperfect) measure of the indexed
return, Yale's losses are due to its asset allocation and not due to the failure of its
managers to perform relative to their benchmarks. Indeed, the managers on balance
seem to have added marginally to Yale's performance even in the crisis.

So does Yale's loss in 2009 undermine its earlier performance? As David Swensen
said in February 2009, *Propublica* (February 18, 2009).

- For the period during which we're in crisis, the hoped-for benefits of diversification disappear. But once the crisis passes, then the fact that these different
  asset classes are driven by fundamentally different factors will reassert itself, and
  you'll get the benefits of diversification. It would be nice if we could always have
  the benefit of diversification, but life doesn't work that way.

Verdict on Alternative Investments

No doubt asset allocation is improved with the addition of alternative investments.
The adoption of alternatives will not guarantee Yale-size returns because other
investors do not have the advantages of the Yale Endowment. But alternatives
do shift the efficient frontier in a northwesterly direction. This chapter has documented this shift by examining the alpha* of portfolios with and without alternatives. Investors can improve their risk-adjusted performance with alternatives. They

can reduce risk for a given return or increase return for a given risk. So alternatives are clearly desirable.

David Swensen expressed the view that ordinary investors could achieve a lot of this gain from diversification by sticking with conventional alternatives, real estate, and TIPS. In Swensen's portfolio for the ordinary investor, 20 percent of the allocation is given to real estate. The analysis above showed real estate investments do raise risk-adjusted returns, but the gain is small.

Diversifying beyond real estate to hedge funds and other alternatives is desirable, at least for those investors who are wealthy enough. But alternatives are no panacea for high-net-worth investors. Unless investors have access to the best managers, hedge funds or other alternatives are going to provide only modest improvement to the portfolio. The shift to the northwest is limited, or if excess returns are measured at a given level of risk, the alpha* is positive but relatively small. For HNW investors, that should still be enough of a recommendation.

Notes

1. Estimated returns for these two assets are based on the real geometric average returns earned since 1951 of 2.4 percent and 6.7 percent, respectively. If long-term expected inflation is 2.5 percent a year, then the nominal compound returns are 4.9 percent and 9.4 percent per annum. These compound averages translate into the arithmetic averages needed for optimization of 5.0 percent and 10.0 percent, respectively.
2. Since the premium is measured using geometric returns, the estimated return on REITs is calculated as $(1.094) * (1.016) - 1 = 11.2\%$.
3. The standard deviations and correlations for the Barclays Capital TIPS Index were calculated beginning in March 1997 and entered manually in the Zephyr software.
4. Since the two portfolios have identical standard deviations, alpha* is just the difference between the two returns.
5. The Credit Suisse/Tremont index is a value-weighted index. The HFRI Fund Weighted index starts earlier in 1990, but it is an equally weighted index so it seems preferable to use the Tremont index whenever possible.
6. So the estimated return is 2.7 percent below the S&P 500 return because the return is calculated using the compound formula $1.094 * (1 - 0.025) - 1 = 6.7\%$.
7. This would certainly be true of an investor with $5 million in wealth since many hedge funds have a minimum investment of at least $1 million. In the analysis of ultra HNW portfolios that follows, we will consider the returns from direct investment in hedge funds using the Credit Suisse/Tremont index because diversification of manager risk should be possible for those investors.
8. The returns required by the Zephyr optimizer are arithmetic averages, so the geometric averages must be converted to arithmetic averages.
9. In the Merrill Lynch-Cap Gemini World Wealth Report (2008), for example, ultra HNW investors are those who have at least $30 million in financial assets excluding collectibles, consumer durables, and primary residences.

10. Recall that the private equity return measures buyout investments primarily.

11. Yale's allocation to fixed income was as much as 22 percent in the early 1990s, but that is still below the allocation to fixed income in most institutional portfolios.

12. The figures quoted are compound (geometric) averages. The arithmetic average returns were 15.0 percent for the Yale Endowment, 10.4 percent for the Russell 3000, and 10.7 percent for the S&P 500, the latter two indexes measured like the Endowment for the 12 months ending in June of each year.

13. The Yale Endowment (various years).

14. The chief real estate holding in 1985 was a single Manhattan office building at 717 Fifth Avenue. By the time Yale sold it in 2002, it had earned a 19.5 percent per annum return on its investment over a 24-year period! (Lerner, 2007).

15. Perhaps Yale has had influence on the allocations of other university endowments, particularly the larger endowments. Some of Swensen's colleagues have moved on to lead the endowments of other institutions, so Yale's influence may be both direct and indirect.

16. Percentages are U.S. dollar-weighted. Excludes U.S. assets held by public funds in defined contribution accounts. U.S. assets are projected to the 2009 Greenwich Associates universe of 2,040 institutional investors with $250 million or more in total assets based on responses from 1,009 institutions.

17. The NACUBO figure is for 2008. In 2008, Yale's actual allocation to absolute return investments was 25.1 percent. In 2009, that allocation had fallen to 24.3 percent, but it's notable that the target portfolio allocation illustrated in Figure 12.12 includes only 15 percent in absolute return. So Yale evidently intends to cut back sharply on its absolute return investments in the future.

18. These benchmarks are not identical to those used by Yale itself. For example, Yale uses the Wilshire 5000 as its benchmark for U.S. equity investments. The correlation between this index and the Russell 3000 is 0.998, so this study will continue to use the Russell 3000 as the equity benchmark. For real assets, Yale uses the NCREIF real estate index as well as a Cambridge Associates composite. This study instead uses NCREIF plus a commodity index.

19. The private equity index begins in the second quarter of 1986, so only the venture capital index is used for 1985 and 1986.

20. The HFRI index begins only in 1990, but Yale added absolute return assets to its portfolio only in 1991. The Credit Suisse/Tremont value-weighted index is used as soon as it becomes available in 1994.

21. The Goldman Sachs index is preferable to the Dow Jones AIG index because the latter puts a limit on energy at 33 percent of the index.

22. NACUBO did not provide a dollar-weighted return for 2009. Through 2008, the dollar-weighted return was 3.8 percent below that of the Yale Endowment.

23. Harvard's experience with private equity supports this view. In late 2008, Harvard was reported to have tried selling some of its private equity stake only to have to withdraw the sale because of low bids. In its 2009 endowment report, Harvard estimates that its private equity investments returned −31.6 percent in fiscal 2009 (Harvard, 2009). That return includes realized capital losses of $439 million reported by *Forbes* (2009).

24. It should be noted that many hedge funds invest in illiquid securities, and marking to market involves estimation of the value of these securities, but on the

whole hedge funds' returns rely much more on market pricing than private equity or direct real estate investments.

25. The crisis return of 30.0 percent is based on a 5 percent allocation to REITs (as in Table 12.31). If instead, the NCREIF valuation-based return is used for the real estate investment, then the portfolio return is −27.4 percent.

26. If the FTSE NAREIT index (instead of the NCREIF index) is used in the calculation of the real asset return, the benchmark return is −29.5 percent, so the difference between Yale's performance and the benchmark widens considerably.

References

Forbes, 2009, "Did Harvard Sell at the Bottom?," October 26, 2009.

Lerner, Josh, 2007, "Yale University Investments Office: August 2006," HBS Case Study 9-807-073, revised May 8, 2007.

Merrill Lynch-Capgemini, 2008, World Wealth Report.

Swensen, David F., 2005, *Unconventional Success: A Fundamental Approach to Personal Investment*, New York: Free Press.

Yale Endowment, 2009, "2009 The Yale Endowment."

CHAPTER 13

Options, Futures, and Other Derivatives

I nvestment advisors and consultants must have foundational knowledge of options, futures, and other derivatives. This chapter describes and analyzes various options and futures products and strategies. The author reviews the structures, risk-reward tradeoffs, and potential purposes of numerous trades and positions. The second reading discusses how investors and advisors may integrate these tools to enhance or supplement their strategic or tactical asset allocation strategies.

Part I *The Theory and Practice of Investment Management: Asset Allocation, Valuation, Portfolio Construction, and Strategies:* Fundamentals of Equity Derivatives

Learning Objectives

- Discuss the four primary roles of derivatives in investment portfolios including: risk management, returns management, cost management, and regulatory management.
- Differentiate between futures and forwards contracts, options, and swaps.
- Describe the differences between listed and over-the-counter (OTC) options.
- Explain the risk and return characteristics of options including: buying and writing call options, buying and writing put options.
- Explain the basic components of an option price including: intrinsic value and time value.
- List and explain the six factors that influence an option price including: spot price of the underlying, strike price, time to expiration of the option, expected price volatility of the underlying over the life of the option, short-term risk-free rate over the life of the option, and the anticipated cash dividends on the underlying stock or index over the life of the option.
- Describe the Black-Scholes options pricing model and the Greeks (e.g., delta, gamma, theta, and vega) that measure the sensitivity of the option price to changes in factors.
- Describe a futures contract and differentiate between futures and options.
- Describe OTC equity derivatives including: equity forwards, OTC options, and equity swaps.
- Describe structured products including "special purpose vehicles" (SPVs).

Part II *The Theory and Practice of Investment Management: Asset Allocation, Valuation, Portfolio Construction, and Strategies:* Using Equity Derivatives in Portfolio Management

Learning Objectives

- List and describe risk management strategies using derivatives.
- Describe cost management strategies including a cash-secured put and naked calls.
- List and describe return enhancement strategies using derivatives.
- Describe market risk hedges using stock index futures.
- List and describe various uses of over-the-counter (OTC) derivatives for equity strategies.
- Explain the role and application of OTC options and exotics, equity-linked debt, and equity swaps strategies.
- List several hedging strategies using derivatives.
- Discuss the risk and expected return of options strategies.

Part I Fundamentals of Equity Derivatives

Derivative securities, or simply derivatives, are financial agreements or contracts between two parties that "derive" their value from an underlying asset. The contract specifies the terms of a payout from one party to another. The underlying asset is typically a cash market instrument such as a stock, a bond or a commodity. When the underlying instrument is an equity security, the contract is called an *equity derivative*. The equity security can be a stock, a basket of stocks, an index or a group of indexes.

The purpose of this chapter is to explain these instruments, their investment characteristics, and to provide an overview as to how they are priced. In the next section, we look at how equity derivatives can be used in the management of equity portfolios.

The Role of Derivatives

Equity derivatives have several properties that provide economic benefits that make them excellent candidates for use in equity portfolio management. These properties are linked to the four roles that derivatives serve in portfolio management:

1. *Risk management.* Modifying the risk characteristics of a portfolio.
2. *Returns management.* Enhancing the expected return of a portfolio.
3. *Cost management.* Reducing transaction costs associated with managing a portfolio.
4. *Regulatory management.* Achieving efficiency in the presence of legal, tax, or regulatory obstacles.

We can further reduce the role of derivatives to the single purpose of risk management and incorporate the other three roles into this one role. Thus, it can be argued that equity derivatives are used primarily to manage risk or to buy and sell risk at a favorable price.

Risk management is a dynamic process that allows portfolio managers to identify, measure, and assess the current risk attributes of a portfolio and to measure the potential benefits from taking the risk. Moreover, risk management involves understanding and managing the factors that can have an adverse impact on the targeted rate of return. The objective is to attain a desired return for a given level of corresponding risk on an after-cost basis. This is consistent with the Markowitz efficient frontier and modern portfolio theory.

The role of equity derivatives in this process is to shift the frontier in favor of the investor by implementing a strategy at a lower cost, lower risk, and higher return or to gain access to an investment that was not available due to some regulatory or other restriction. We can therefore regard the management of equity portfolios as a sophisticated exercise in risk management.

Equity derivatives give investors more degrees of freedom. In the past, the implementation and management of an investment strategy for pension funds, for example, was a function of management style and was carried out in the cash market. Pension funds managed risk by diversifying among management styles. Prior to the advent of the over-the-counter (OTC) derivatives market in the late 1980s and the structured products market in the 1990s, the first risk management tools available to investors were limited to the listed futures and options markets. Although providing a valuable addition to an investor's risk management toolkit, listed derivatives were limited in application due to their standardized features, limited size, and liquidity constraints. The OTC derivatives market gives investors access to longer-term products that better match their investment horizon and flexible structures to meet their exact risk–reward requirements. The structured products market allows investors to gain synthetic exposure to risk and return relating to an equity security. The number of unique equity derivative structures is essentially unlimited.

EQUITY DERIVATIVES MARKET   There are generally three segments of what we define as the equity derivatives markets. These include the exchange-listed market, the OTC market, and the market for structured products. Often the structured product market is considered an extension of the OTC market.

There are also three general categories of derivatives that are created and traded across three markets: (1) futures and forwards, (2) options, and (3) swaps. The most fundamental derivative securities are futures or forward contracts and options. Swaps and other derivative structures with more complicated payoffs are regarded as hybrid securities, which can be shown to be portfolios of forwards, options, and cash instruments in varying combinations.

The listed market consists of options, warrants, and futures contracts. The principal listed options market consists of exchange-traded options with standardized strike prices, expirations, and payout terms traded on individual stocks, equity indexes, and futures contracts on equity indexes. A Flexible Exchange (FLEX) Option traded on the Chicago Board Options Exchange (CBOE) provides the customization feature of the OTC market, but with the guarantee of the exchange. More recently, the NYSE LIFFE (New York Stock Exchange/London International Financial Futures and Options Exchange) launched a hybrid trading platform that combines the flexibility of the OTC market with the security and benefits associated with exchange-traded derivatives. The listed futures market consists of exchange-traded equity index futures and single stock futures with standardized settlement dates and settlement returns. Other innovations offered by the CBOE include *weeklys, quarterlys,* and *binaries.* Weeklys are options that are listed for approximately one week to expiration, which provides a cost advantage for investors with derivative needs and short-term horizons. Similarly, quarterlys are options that expire on the last trading day of the calendar quarter. Binaries are options contracts that pay out a predetermined, fixed amount of money or nothing at all (all or nothing options). This brings the so-called second generation OTC "exotic" options to the listed exchange-traded space.

OTC equity derivatives are not traded on an exchange and have an advantage over listed derivatives because they provide complete flexibility and can be tailored to fit an investment strategy. The OTC equity derivatives market can be divided into four components: OTC forwards, options and warrants, equity-linked debt investments, and equity swaps. Equity forward contracts are not unlike listed futures contracts where the long party agrees to take delivery of a specified number of shares of stock from the counterparty for delivery at some future date for a price agreed upon in the contract. The difference is that forwards are settled at the settlement date while futures are marked-to-the-market. OTC equity options are customized option contracts that can be applied to any equity index, basket of stocks or an individual stock. OTC options are privately negotiated agreements between an investor and an issuing dealer. The structure of the option is completely flexible in terms of strike price, expiration, and payout features. A fundamental difference between listed and OTC derivatives, however, is that listed options and futures contracts are guaranteed by the exchange, while in the OTC market the derivative is the obligation of a nonexchange entity that is the counterparty. Thus, the investor is subject to credit risk or counterparty risk.

Structured products are packaged investment strategies that typically embed equity derivatives technology with other financial instruments.[1] The financial instruments might include a single security, a basket of securities, an index, an interest rate product or a commodity. One common feature of structured products is a principal guarantee. Other features might include tax considerations, returns enhancement or reduced volatility. They are an alternative to direct investment and are often useful for asset allocation purposes.

Other equity derivatives might include exchange-traded funds (ETFs), which are index investment products listed and traded on an exchange.

Listed Equity Options

Equity derivative products are either exchange-traded listed derivatives or OTC derivatives. In this section we will look at listed equity options.[2]

An *option* is a contract in which the option seller grants the option buyer the right to enter into a transaction with the seller to either buy or sell an underlying

---

[1] For a more detailed discussion of structured products, see Peter Green and Jeremy Jennings-Mares, "Types of Structured Products," *Equity Derivatives: Documenting and Understanding Equity Derivative Products*, ed. Edmund Parker (London: Global Business Publishing Ltd., 2009), 85–106.

[2] The CBOE is the largest listed options exchange in the U.S. trading equity, index, ETF, and hybrid options contracts. Eurex is one of the world's leading derivatives exchanges including listed options. It owns the International Securities Exchange (ISE), which is an electronic trading platform for listed options in the United States.

asset at a specified price on or before a specified date. The specified price is called the *strike price* or *exercise price* and the specified date is called the *expiration date*. The option seller grants this right in exchange for a certain amount of money called the *option premium* or *option price*.

The option seller is also known as the option writer, while the option buyer is the option holder. The asset that is the subject of the option is called the underlying. The underlying can be an individual stock, a basket of stocks, a stock index or group of indexes, or another derivative instrument such as a futures contract or an ETF. The option writer can grant the option holder one of two rights. If the right is to purchase the underlying, the option is a call option. If the right is to sell the underlying, the option is a put option.

An option can also be categorized according to when it may be exercised by the buyer. This is referred to as the exercise style. A European option can only be exercised at the expiration date of the contract. An American option can be exercised any time on or before the expiration date. A Bermudan option is in between an American and a European and can be exercised only on certain dates over the life of the option.

The terms of exchange are represented by the contract unit, which is typically 100 shares for an individual stock and a multiple times an index value for a stock index. The terms of exchange are standard for most contracts. The contract terms for a FLEX option can be customized along four dimensions: underlying, strike price, expiration date, and settlement style. These options are discussed further below.

The option holder enters into the contract with an opening transaction. Subsequently, the option holder then has the choice to exercise or to sell the option. The sale of an existing option by the holder is a closing sale.

LISTED VERSUS OTC EQUITY OPTIONS   There are three advantages of listed options relative to OTC options. First, the strike price and expiration dates of the contract are standardized. Second, the direct link between buyer and seller is severed after the order is executed because of the fungible nature of listed options. The Options Clearing Corporation (OCC) serves as the intermediary between buyer and seller. Finally, transaction costs are lower for listed options than their OTC counterparts.

There are many situations in which an institutional investor needs a customized option. Such situations will be identified when we discuss the applications of OTC options in the next section. The higher cost of OTC options reflects this customization. However, some OTC exotic option structures may prove to cost less than the closest standardized option because a more specific payout is being bought.

A significant distinction between a listed option and an OTC option is the presence of credit risk or counterparty risk. Only the option buyer is exposed to counterparty risk. Options traded on exchanges and OTC options traded over a network of market makers have different ways of dealing with the problem of credit risk. Organized exchanges reduce counterparty risk by requiring margin, marking to the market daily, imposing size and price limits, and providing an intermediary that takes both sides of a trade. The clearing process provides three levels of protection: (1) the customer's margin, (2) the member firm's guarantee, and (3) the clearinghouse. The OTC market has incorporated a variety of terms into the contractual agreement between counterparties to address the issue of credit risk and these are described when we discuss OTC derivatives.

For listed options, there are no margin requirements for the buyer of an option once the option price has been paid in full. Because the option price is the maximum amount that the option buyer can lose, no matter how adverse the price movement of the underlying, margin is not necessary. The option writer has agreed to transfer the risk inherent in a position in the underlying from the option buyer to itself. The writer, on the other, has certain margin requirements.

BASIC FEATURES OF LISTED OPTIONS   The basic features of listed options are summarized in Table 13.1. The table is grouped into four categories with each option category presented in terms of its basic features. These include the type of option, underlying, strike price, settlement information, expiration cycle, exercise style, and some trading rules.

Stock options refer to listed options on individual stocks or American Depository Receipts (ADRs). The underlying is 100 shares of the designated stock. All listed stock options in the United States may be exercised any time before the expiration date; that is, they are American-style options.

Index options are options where the underlying is a stock index rather than an individual stock. An index call option gives the option buyer the right to buy the underlying stock index, while a put option gives the option buyer the right to sell the underlying stock index. Unlike stock options where a stock can be delivered if the option is exercised by the option holder, it would be extremely complicated to settle an index option by delivering all the stocks that constitute the index. Instead, index options are cash settlement contracts. This means that if the option is exercised by the option holder, the option writer pays cash to the option buyer. There is no delivery of any stocks.

Among the most liquid index options are those on the S&P 100 index (OEX) and the S&P 500 index (SPX). Other indexes that have gained in popularity include options on the Nasdaq 100 Index (NDX) and the Dow Jones Industrial Average Index (DJX). All trade on the CBOE. Index options can be listed as American or European. The S&P 500 index option contract is European, while the OEX is American. Both index option contracts have specific standardized features and contract terms. Moreover, both have short expiration cycles.

Currently, the CBOE trades approximately 40 index options. Two of the latest products that are being prepared for listing as of this writing include the CBOE China Index Options (CYX) and the Morgan Stanley Multinational Company Index (NFT).[3]

Among a wide group of international contracts are options traded on the Dow Jones STOXX 50 and the Dow Jones EURO 50 stock indexes.[4] Other international index options include options traded on the FTSE 100, the CaC-40 and a host of Euro Stoxx indexes.[5] There are over 100 stock index option contracts listed across 26 separate exchanges and 20 countries.

---

[3] You can find a complete description of these products at www.cboe.com under products.

[4] The indexes are comprised of 50 industrial, commercial, and financial European blue chip companies.

[5] The EURO STOXX Index is a group of sector indexes and is a broad subset of the STOXX Europe 600 Index. The number of components is variable, and the index encompasses large-, mid-, and small-capitalization companies of 12 Euro zone countries: Austria, Belgium, Finland, France, Germany, Greece, Ireland, Italy, Luxembourg, the Netherlands, Portugal, and Spain. There are options and futures contracts available on the indexes.

TABLE 13.1   Basic Features of Listed Equity Options

Stock Options

Option type	Call or put
Option category	Equity
Underlying security	Individual stock or ADR
Contract value	Equity: 100 shares of common stock or ADRs
Strike price	$2\frac{1}{2}$ points when the strike price is between $5 and $25, 10 points when the strike price is over $200. Strikes are adjusted for splits, recapitalizations, etc.
Settlement and delivery	100 shares of stock
Exercise style	American
Expiration cycle	Two near-term months plus two additional months from the January, February, or March quarterly cycles
Transaction costs	$1–$3 commissions and $\frac{1}{8}$ market impact
Position and size limits	Large capitalization stocks have an option position limit of 25,000 contracts (with adjustments for splits, recapitalizations, etc.) on the same side of the market; smaller capitalization stocks have an option position limit of 20,000, 10,500, 7,500, or 4,500 contracts (with adjustments for splits, recapitalizations, etc.) on the same side of the market.

Index Options

Option type	Call or put
Option category	Indexes
Underlying security	Stock index
Contract value	Multiplier × Index price
Strike price	Five points. 10-point intervals in the far-term month.
Settlement and delivery	Cash
Exercise style	American
Expiration cycle	Four near-term months
Transaction costs	$1–$3 commissions and $\frac{1}{8}$ market impact
Position and size limits	150,000 contracts on the same side of the market with no more than 100,000 of such contracts in the near-term series

LEAP Options

Option type	Call or put
Option category	LEAP
Underlying security	Individual stock or stock index
Contract value	Equity: 100 shares of common stock or ADRs Index: full or partial value of stock index
Strike price	Equity: Same as equity option Index: Based on full or partial value of index. $\frac{1}{5}$ value translates into $\frac{1}{5}$ strike price
Settlement and delivery	Equity: 100 shares of stock or ADR Index: Cash
Exercise style	American or European
Expiration cycle	May be up to 39 months from the date of initial listing, January expiration only
Transaction costs	$1–$3 commissions and $\frac{1}{8}$ market impact
Position and size limits	Same as equity options and index options

(continued)

TABLE 13.1 (*Continued*)

FLEX Options	
Option type	Call, put, or cap
Option category	Equity: E-FLEX option
	Index: FLEX option
Underlying security	Individual stock or index
Contract value	Equity: 100 shares of common stock or ADRs
	Index: multiplier × index value
Strike price	Equity: Calls, same as standard calls
	Puts, any dollar value or percentage
	Index: Any index value, percentage, or deviation from index value
Settlement and delivery	Equity: 100 shares of stock
	Index: Cash
Exercise style	Equity: American or European
	Index: American, European, or cap
Expiration cycle	Equity: 1 day to 3 years
	Index: Up to 5 years
Transaction costs	$1–$3 commissions and $1/_8$ market impact
Position and size limits	Equity: Minimum of 250 contracts to create FLEX
	Index: $10 million minimum to create FLEX No size or position limits

The following mechanics should be noted for index options. The dollar value of the stock index underlying an index option is equal to the current cash index value multiplied by the contract's multiple.[6] That is,

Dollar value of the underlying index = Cash index value × Contract multiple

For example, if the cash index value for the S&P 500 is 1150, then the dollar value of the S&P 500 contract is 1150 × $100 = $115,000.

For a stock option, the price at which the buyer of the option can buy or sell the stock is the strike price. For an index option, the strike index is the index value at which the buyer of the option can buy or sell the underlying stock index. The strike index is converted into a dollar value by multiplying the strike index by the multiple for the contract. For example, if the strike index is 1150, the dollar value is $115,000 (1150 × $100). If an investor purchases a call option on the S&P 500 with a strike index of 1150, and exercises the option when the index value is 1175, then the investor has the right to purchase the index for $115,000 when the market value of the index is $117,500. The buyer of the call option would then receive $2,500 from the option writer.

The next two categories listed in Table 13.1, LEAPS and FLEX options, essentially modify an existing feature of either a stock option, an index option, or both. For example, stock option and index option contracts have short expiration cycles. Long-Term Equity Anticipation Securities (LEAPS) are designed to offer options with longer

---

[6] Non-U.S. index options follow the same valuation specification: Multiplier × Index value. For example, EURO STOXX products are €50 multiplied by the value of the index.

maturities. These contracts are available on individual stocks and some indexes. Stock option LEAPS are comparable to standard stock options except the maturities can range up to 39 months from the origination date. Index options LEAPS differ in size compared with standard index options having a multiplier of 10 rather than 100.

FLEX options allow users to specify the terms of the option contract for either a stock option or an index option. The value of FLEX options is the ability to customize the terms of the contract along four dimensions: underlying, strike price, expiration date, and settlement style. Moreover, the exchange provides a secondary market to offset or alter positions and an independent daily marking of prices. The development of the FLEX option is a response to the growing OTC market. The exchanges seek to make the FLEX option attractive by providing price discovery through a competitive auction market, an active secondary market, daily price valuations, and the virtual elimination of counterparty risk. The FLEX option represents a link between listed options and OTC products.

There are two other categories, ETF options and binary options, which are recent developments in the listed market. The CBOE trades nearly 240 option contracts on ETFs. ETFs are shares of trusts that hold a basket of stocks designed to replicate the performance of a benchmark index. The equity index might be a broad-based index or a narrowly defined sector index. ETFs effectively trade like stocks and options on these products are operationally similar to traditional stock options. Options on ETFs are America style options but are not cash-settled like index options. They are instead physically settled like individual stock options. LEAPS are also offered on some ETF products.

CBOE Binary Options are all or nothing options that allow investors to trade based on market direction.[7] These options are also a link between listed options and OTC products. The contracts pay out a pre-determined fixed amount of $100 or nothing at all. The CBOE lists both calls and puts on the S&P 500 index with a variety of strike prices and expirations. If, at expiration, the price of the underlying index is above the strike, there is a payout of $100 for the buyer in the case of a call option and nothing in the case of a put option. These options trade like ordinary options prior to expiration with the price reflect the market's assessment of the probability that the S&P 500 will exceed or fail to reach a selected strike price. For example, if the strike price for a binary option on the S&P 500 is 1200 then the payout is $100 if the S&P 500 is above 1200 at expiration and 0 otherwise.

RISK AND RETURN CHARACTERISTICS OF OPTIONS   Now let's illustrate the risk and return characteristics of the four basic option positions—buying a call option (long a call option), selling a call option (short a call option), buying a put option (long a put option), and selling a put option (short a put option). We will use stock options in our example. The illustrations assume that each option position is held to the expiration date. Also, to simplify the illustrations, we assume that the underlying for each option is for one share of stock rather than 100 shares and we ignore transaction costs.

---

[7] Binary options, also known as digitals, can be structured as "cash or nothing" or "asset of nothing" products. The CBOE S&P 500 binary is a "cash or nothing" structure.

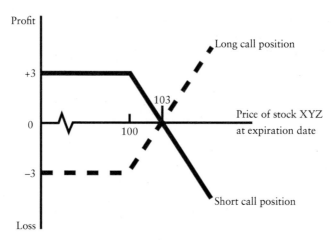

FIGURE 13.1   Profit/Loss Profile at Expiration Call

Buying Call Options   Assume that there is a call option on stock XYZ that expires in one month and has a strike price of $100. The option price is $3. Suppose that the current or spot price of stock XYZ is $100. (The *spot price* is the cash market price.) The profit and loss will depend on the price of stock XYZ at the expiration date. The buyer of a call option benefits if the price rises above the strike price. If the price of stock XYZ is equal to $103, the buyer of a call option breaks even. The maximum loss is the option price, and there is substantial upside potential if the stock price rises above $103. Figure 13.1 shows using a graph the profit/loss profile for the buyer of this call option at the expiration date.

It is worthwhile to compare the profit and loss profile of the call option buyer with that of an investor taking a long position in one share of stock XYZ. The payoff from the position depends on stock XYZ's price at the expiration date. An investor who takes a long position in stock XYZ realizes a profit of $1 for every $1 increase in stock XYZ's price. As stock XYZ's price falls, however, the investor loses, dollar for dollar. If the price drops by more than $3, the long position in stock XYZ results in a loss of more than $3. The long call position, in contrast, limits the loss to only the option price of $3 but retains the upside potential, which will be $3 less than for the long position in stock XYZ. Which alternative is better, buying the call option or buying the stock? The answer depends on what the investor is attempting to achieve.

Writing Call Options   To illustrate the option seller's, or writer's, position, we use the same call option we used to illustrate buying a call option. The profit/loss profile at expiration of the short call position (that is, the position of the call option writer) is the mirror image of the profit and loss profile of the long call position (the position of the call option buyer). That is, the profit of the short call position for any given price for stock XYZ at the expiration date is the same as the loss of the long call position. Consequently, the maximum profit the short call position can produce is the option price. The maximum loss is not limited because it is the highest price reached by stock XYZ on or before the expiration date, less the option price; this

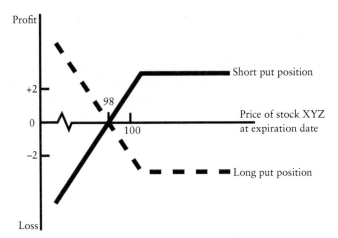

FIGURE 13.2   Profit/Loss Profile at Expiration Put

price can be indefinitely high. Figure 13.1 shows a graph of the profit/loss profile for the seller of this call option at the expiration date.

Buying Put Options   To illustrate a long put option position, we assume a hypothetical put option on one share of stock XYZ with one month to maturity and a strike price of $100. Assume that the put option is selling for $2 and the spot price of stock XYZ is $100. The profit or loss for this position at the expiration date depends on the market price of stock XYZ. The buyer of a put option benefits if the price falls. Figure 13.2 shows a graph of the profit/loss profile for the buyer of this put option at the expiration date. As with all long option positions, the loss is limited to the option price. The profit potential, however, is substantial: The theoretical maximum profit is generated if stock XYZ's price falls to zero. Contrast this profit potential with that of the buyer of a call option. The theoretical maximum profit for a call buyer cannot be determined beforehand because it depends on the highest price that can be reached by stock XYZ before or at the option expiration date.

To see how an option alters the risk–return profile for an investor, we again compare it with a position in stock XYZ. The long put position is compared with a short position in stock XYZ because such a position would also benefit if the price of the stock falls. While the investor taking a short stock position faces all the downside risk as well as the upside potential, an investor taking the long put position faces limited downside risk (equal to the option price) while still maintaining upside potential reduced by an amount equal to the option price.

Writing Put Options   The profit and loss profile for a short put option is the mirror image of the long put option. The maximum profit to be realized from this position is the option price. The theoretical maximum loss can be substantial should the price of the underlying fall; and if the price were to fall all the way to zero, the loss would be as large as the strike price less the option price the seller received. Figure 13.1 shows a graph of the profit/loss profile for the seller of this put option at the expiration date.

THE VALUE OF AN OPTION   Now we will look at the basic factors that affect the value of an option and discuss a well-known option pricing model.

Basic Components of the Option Price   The price of an option is a reflection of the option's *intrinsic value* and any additional amount above its intrinsic value. The premium over intrinsic value is often referred to as the *time value*.

Intrinsic Value. The intrinsic value of an option is its economic value if it is exercised immediately. For a call option, the intrinsic value is positive if the spot price (i.e., cash market price) of the underlying is greater than the strike price. For example, if the strike price for a call option is $100 and the spot price of the underlying is $105, the intrinsic value is $5. That is, an option buyer exercising the option and simultaneously selling the underlying would realize $105 from the sale of the underlying, which would be covered by acquiring the underlying from the option writer for $100, thereby netting a $5 gain.

When an option has intrinsic value, it is said to be *in the money* (ITM). When the strike price of a call option exceeds the spot price of the underlying, the call option is said to be *out of the money* (OTM); it has no intrinsic value. An option for which the strike price is equal to the spot price of the underlying is said to be at the money. Both at-the-money and out-of-the-money options have an intrinsic value of zero because they are not profitable to exercise.

For a put option, the intrinsic value is equal to the amount by which the spot price of the underlying is below the strike price. For example, if the strike price of a put option is $100 and the spot price of the underlying is $92, the intrinsic value is $8. The buyer of the put option who exercises the put option and simultaneously sells the underlying will net $8 by exercising since the underlying will be sold to the writer for $100 and purchased in the market for $92. The intrinsic value is zero if the strike price is less than or equal to the underlying's spot price.

Time Value. The *time value of an option* is the amount by which the option price exceeds its intrinsic value. The option buyer hopes that at some time prior to expiration, changes in the market price of the underlying will increase the value of the rights conveyed by the option. For this prospect, the option buyer is willing to pay a premium above the intrinsic value. For example, if the price of a call option with a strike price of $100 is $9 when the spot price of the underlying is $105, the time value of this option is $4 ($9 minus its intrinsic value of $5). Had the current price of the underlying been $90 instead of $105, then the time value of this option would be the entire $9 because the option has no intrinsic value. Other factors being equal, the time value of an option will increase with the amount of time remaining to expiration since the opportunity for a favorable change in the price of the underlying is greater.

There are two ways in which an option buyer may realize the value of a position taken in an option: the first is to exercise the option, and the second is to sell the option. In the first example above, since the exercise of an option will realize a gain of only $5 and will cause the immediate loss of any time value ($4 in our first example), it is preferable to sell the call. In general, if an option buyer wishes to realize the value of a position, selling will be more economically beneficial than exercising. However, there are circumstances under which it is preferable to exercise prior to the expiration date, depending on whether the total proceeds at the expiration date would be greater by holding the option or by exercising it and reinvesting any cash proceeds received until the expiration date.

TABLE 13.2   Summary of Factors That Affect the Price of an American Option

	Effect of an Increase of Factor on	
Factor	Call Price	Put Price
Spot price of underlying	Increase	Decrease
Strike price	Decrease	Increase
Time to expiration of option	Increase	Increase
Expected price volatility	Increase	Increase
Short-term rate	Increase	Decrease
Anticipated cash dividends	Decrease	Increase

Factors That Influence the Option Price   The following six factors influence the option price:

1. Spot price of the underlying.
2. Strike price.
3. Time to expiration of the option.
4. Expected price volatility of the underlying over the life of the option.
5. Short-term risk-free rate over the life of the option.
6. Anticipated cash dividends on the underlying stock or index over the life of the option.

The impact of each of these factors depends on whether (1) the option is a call or a put and (2) the option is an American option or a European option. A summary of the effects of each factor on American put and call option prices is presented in Table 13.2.

Notice how the expected price volatility of the underlying over the life of the option affects the price of both a put and a call option. All other factors being equal, the greater the expected volatility (as measured by the standard deviation or variance) of the price of the underlying, the more an investor would be willing to pay for the option, and the more an option writer would demand for it. This is because the greater the volatility, the greater the probability that the price of the underlying will move in favor of the option buyer at some time before expiration.

Option Pricing Models   Several models have been developed to determine the theoretical value of an option.[8] The most popular one was developed by Fischer Black and Myron Scholes in 1973 for valuing European call options.[9] Several modifications

---

[8] The most common are the Black-Scholes-Merton model and the Binomial Pricing models. Other models have been developed to deal with the shortcomings of these two basic models.
[9] Fischer Black and Myron Scholes, "The Pricing of Corporate Liabilities," *Journal of Political Economy* 81 (May–June 1973): 637–659. Today, many practitioners refer to the basic model as the Black-Scholes-Merton model. Robert Merton was awarded the Nobel Prize for economics along with Myron Scholes for their work on options pricing. See R. C. Merton, "Theory of Rational Option Pricing," *Bell Journal of Economics and Management Science* 4, no. 1 (1973): 141–183.

to their model have followed since then. We discuss this model here to explain how to price an option.

By imposing certain assumptions and using arbitrage arguments, the Black-Scholes option pricing model provides the fair (or theoretical) price of a European call option on a non-dividend-paying stock. Basically, the idea behind the arbitrage argument in deriving this and other option pricing models is that if the payoff from owning a call option can be replicated by (1) purchasing the stock underlying the call option and (2) borrowing funds, then the price of the option will be (at most) the cost of creating the replicating strategy.

The formula for the Black-Scholes model is

$$C = SN(d_1) - Xe^{-rt}N(d_2)$$

where

$$d_1 = \frac{\ln(S/K) + (r + 0.5s^2)t}{s\sqrt{t}}$$

$$d_2 = d_1 - s\sqrt{t}$$

ln   = natural logarithm
C = call option price
S = price of the underlying
K = strike price
r = short-term risk-free rate
e = 2.718 (natural antilog of 1)
t = time remaining to the expiration date (measured as a fraction of a year)
s = standard deviation of the change in stock p
$N(.)$ = the cumulative probability density[10]

Notice that five of the factors that we said earlier in this chapter influence the price of an option are included in the formula. However, the sixth factor, anticipated cash dividends, is not included because the model is for a non-dividend-paying stock. In the Black-Scholes model, the direction of the influence of each of these factors is the same as stated earlier. Four of the factors—strike price, price of underlying, time to expiration, and risk-free rate—are easily observed. The standard deviation of the price of the underlying must be estimated. The option price derived from the Black-Scholes model is "fair" in the sense that if any other price existed, it would be possible to earn riskless arbitrage profits by taking an offsetting position in the underlying. That is, if the price of the call option in the market is higher than that derived from the Black-Scholes model, an investor could sell the call option and buy a certain quantity of the underlying. If the reverse is true, that is, the market price of the call option is less than the "fair" price derived from the model, the investor could buy the call option and sell short a certain amount of the underlying. This process of hedging by taking a position in the underlying allows the investor to lock in the riskless arbitrage profit. The number of shares necessary to hedge the position

---

[10]The value for $N(.)$ is obtained from a normal distribution function that is tabulated in most statistics textbooks or from spreadsheets that have this built-in function.

changes as the factors that affect the option price change, so the hedged position must be changed constantly.

To illustrate the Black-Scholes model, assume the following values:

Strike price	= $45
Time remaining to expiration	= 183 days
Spot stock price	= $47
Expected price volatility	= standard deviation = 25%
Risk-free rate	= 10%

In terms of the values in the formula:

$S = 47$
$K = 45$
$t = 0.5$ (183 days/365, rounded)
$s = 0.25$
$r = 0.10$

Substituting these values into the equations above, we get

$$d_1 = \frac{\ln(47/45) + [0.10 + 0.5(0.25)^2]0.5}{0.25\sqrt{0.5}} = 0.6172$$

$$d_2 = 0.6172 - 0.25\sqrt{0.5} = 0.4404$$

From a normal distribution table,

$$N(0.6172) = 0.7315 \text{ and } N(0.4404) = 0.6702$$

Then

$$C = 47(0.7315) - 45(e^{-(0.10)(0.5)})(0.6702) = \$5.69$$

How do we determine the value of put options? There is relationship that shows the relationship among the spot price of the underlying, the call option price, and the put option price. This is called the *put-call parity relationship*. If we can calculate the fair value of a call option, the fair value of a put with the same strike price and expiration on the same stock can be calculated from the put-call parity relationship.

Sensitivity of the Option Price to a Change in Factors   In employing options in investment strategies, a manager would like to know how sensitive the price of an option is to a change in any one of the factors that affect its price. Let's discuss the sensitivity of a call option's price to changes in the price of the underlying, the time to expiration, and expected price volatility. These measures are commonly referred to as the "Greeks" since Greek letters are used to describe them.

The Call Option Price and the Price of the Underlying. A manager employing options for risk management wants to know how the option position will change as the price of the underlying changes. Figure 13.3 shows the theoretical price of a call option based on the price of the underlying. The horizontal axis is the price of the underlying at any point in time. The vertical axis is the theoretical call option price. The shape of the curve representing the theoretical price of a call option, given the

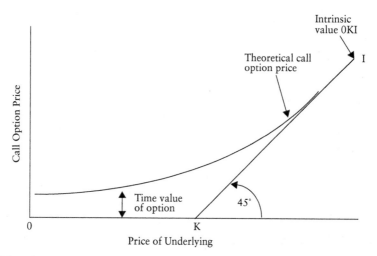

FIGURE 13.3   Theoretical Call Price and Price of Underlying

price of the underlying, would be the same regardless of the actual option pricing model used. In particular, the relationship between the price of the underlying and the theoretical call option price is convex.

The line from the origin to the strike price on the horizontal axis in Figure 13.3 is the intrinsic value of the call option when the price of the underlying is less than the strike price since the intrinsic value is zero. The 45-degree line extending from the horizontal axis is the intrinsic value of the call option once the price of the underlying exceeds the strike price. The reason is that the intrinsic value of the call option will increase by the same dollar amount as the increase in the price of the underlying. For example, if the strike price is $100 and the price of the underlying increases from $100 to $101, the intrinsic value will increase by $1. If the price of the underlying increases from $101 to $110, the intrinsic value of the option will increase from $1 to $10. Thus, the slope of the line representing the intrinsic value after the strike price is reached is 1.

Since the theoretical call option price is shown by the convex curve, the difference between the theoretical call option price and the intrinsic value at any given price for the underlying is the time value of the option. Figure 13.4 shows the theoretical call option price, but with a tangent line drawn at the price p∗. The tangent line in the figure can be used to estimate what the new option price will be (and therefore what the change in the option price will be) if the price of the underlying changes. Because of the convexity of the relationship between the option price and the price of the underlying, the tangent line closely approximates the new option price for a small change in the price of the underlying. For large changes, however, the tangent line does not provide as good an approximation of the new option price. The slope of the tangent line shows how the theoretical call option price will change for small changes in the price of the underlying. The slope of the tangent line is popularly referred to as the *delta* of the option. Specifically,

$$\text{Delta} = \frac{\text{Change in price of call option}}{\text{Change in price of underlying}}$$

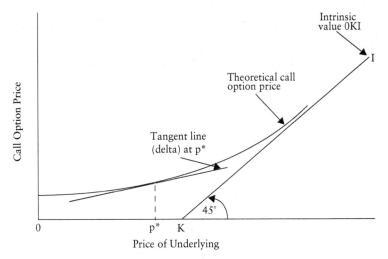

FIGURE 13.4   Estimating the Theoretical Option Price

For example, a delta of 0.4 means that a $1 change in the price of the underlying will change the price of the call option by approximately $0.40.

Thus, the delta for a call option varies from zero (for call options deep out of the money) to 1 (for call options deep in the money). The delta for a call option at the money is approximately 0.5. The curvature of the convex relationship can also be approximated. This is the rate of change of delta as the price of the under-lying changes. The measure is commonly referred to as *gamma* and is defined as follows:

$$\text{Gamma} = \frac{\text{Change in delta}}{\text{Change in price of underlying}}$$

The Call Option Price and Time to Expiration. All other factors constant, the longer the time to expiration, the greater is the option price. Since each day the option moves closer to the expiration date, the time to expiration decreases. The *theta* of an option measures the change in the option price as the time to expira-tion decreases, or equivalently, it is a measure of time decay. Theta is measured as follows:

$$\text{Theta} = \frac{\text{Change in price of option}}{\text{Decrease in time to expiration}}$$

Assuming that the price of the underlying does not change (which means that the intrinsic value of the option does not change), theta measures how quickly the time value of the option changes as the option moves toward expiration. Buyers of options prefer a low theta so that the option price does not decline quickly as it moves toward the expiration date. An option writer benefits from an option that has a high theta.

The Call Option Price and Expected Price Volatility. All other factors constant, a change in the expected price volatility will change the option price. The *vega* (also called *kappa*) of an option measures the dollar price change in the price of the option for a 1 percent change in the expected price volatility. That is,

$$\text{Vega} = \frac{\text{Change in option price}}{1\% \text{ change in expected price volatility}}$$

Critique of Black-Scholes Pricing Model   The Black-Scholes pricing model while groundbreaking and innovative is based on a set of assumptions some of which do not hold up in the real world. First of all, the model cannot be used to price American-style options that pay dividends. Second, the underlying assumption that stock returns are normally distributed is inconsistent with the empirical finding of "fat tails" in equity returns. The implication of fat tails is that the Black-Scholes pricing model misprices OTM options. Finally, the model assumes that volatility is constant across the entire price distribution.

Because of these shortcomings, there have been many developments in option pricing models. The most famous perhaps is the binomial option pricing model. The major advantage this model has over the Black-Scholes model is that it can be used to price American-style options. Other modifications have included incorporating stochastic volatility into the model and to consider alternative price distribution that takes into account fat tails.[11]

Futures Contracts

A *futures contract* is an agreement between two parties, a buyer and a seller, where the parties agree to transact with respect to the underlying at a predetermined price at a specified date. Both parties are obligated to perform over the life of the contract, and neither party charges a fee. Once the two parties have consummated the trade, the exchange where the futures contract is traded becomes the counterparty to the trade, thereby severing the relationship between the initial parties.

Each futures contract is accompanied by an exact description of the terms of the contract, including a description of the underlying, the contract size, settlement cycles, trading specifications, and position limits. The fact is that in the case of futures contracts, delivery is not the objective of either party because the contracts are used primarily to manage risk or costs.

The nature of the futures contract specifies a buyer and a seller who agree to buy or sell a standard quantity of the underlying at a designated future date. However, when we speak of buyers and sellers, we are simply adopting the language of the futures market, which refers to parties of the contract in terms of the future obligation they are committing themselves to. The buyer of a futures contract agrees to take delivery of the underlying and is said to be *long futures*. Long futures positions benefit when the price of the underlying rises. Since futures can be considered a substitute for a subsequent transaction in the cash market, a long futures

---

[11] Most models used to price options rely on the assumption that asset price behavior can be represented by a geometric Brownian motion. A discussion of the weaknesses of this assumption and presentation of alternative models is found in Chapters 19 and 26 of John C. Hull, *Options, Futures, and Other Derivatives*, 7th ed. (Upper Saddle River, NJ: Pearson Prentice Hall, 2009).

position is comparable to holding the underlying without the financial cost of purchasing the underlying or the income that comes from holding the underlying. The seller, on the other hand, is said to be *short futures* and benefits when the price of the underlying declines.

The designated price at which the parties agree to transact is called the *futures price*. The designated date at which the parties must transact is the *settlement date* or *delivery date*. Unlike options, no money changes hands between buyer and seller at the contract's inception. However, the futures broker and the futures exchange require initial margin as a "good faith" deposit. In addition, a minimum amount of funds referred to as *maintenance margin* is required to be maintained in the corresponding futures account. The initial margin and the maintenance margin can be held in the form of short-term credit instruments.

Futures are marked-to-the-market on a daily basis. This means that daily gains or losses in the investor's position are accounted for immediately and reflected in his or her account. The daily cash flow from a futures position is called *variation margin* and essentially means that the futures contract is settled daily. Thus, the buyer of the futures contract pays when the price of the underlying falls and the seller pays when the price of the underlying rises. Variation margin differs from other forms of margin because outflows must be met with cash.

Futures contracts have a settlement cycle and there may be several contracts trading simultaneously. The contract with the closest settlement is call the *nearby futures contract* and is usually the most liquid. The next futures contract is the one that settles just after the near contract. The contract with the furthest away settlement is called the *most distant futures contract.*

DIFFERENCES BETWEEN OPTIONS AND FUTURES   The fundamental difference between futures and options is that buyer of an option (the long position) has the right but not the obligation to enter into a transaction. The option writer is obligated to transact if the buyer so desires. In contrast, both parties are obligated to perform in the case of a futures contract. In addition, to establish a position, the party who is long futures does not pay the party who is short futures. In contrast, the party long an option must make a payment to the party who is short the option in order to establish the position. The price paid is the option price.

The payout structure also differs between a futures contract and an options contract. The price of an option contract represents the cost of eliminating or modifying the risk–reward relationship of the underlying. In contrast, the payout for a futures contract is a dollar-for-dollar gain or loss for the buyer and seller. The buyer gains at the expense of the seller when the futures price rises, while the buyer suffers a dollar-for dollar loss when the futures price drops.

Thus, futures payout is symmetrical, while the payout for options is skewed. The maximum loss for the option buyer is the option price. The loss to the futures buyer is the full value of the contract. The option buyer has limited downside losses but retains the benefits of an increase in the value in the position of the underlying. The maximum profit that can be realized by the option writer is the option price, which is offset by significant downside exposure. The losses or gains to the buyer and seller of a futures contract are completely symmetrical. Consequently, futures can be used as a hedge against symmetric risk, while options can be used to hedge asymmetric risk.

FEATURES OF FUTURES   The key elements of a futures contract include the futures price, the amount or quantity of the underlying, and the settlement or delivery date.

Stock Index Futures   The underlying for a stock index futures contract is the portfolio of stocks represented by the index.

The value of the underlying portfolio is the value of the index in a specified currency times a number called a *multiplier*. For example, if the current value of the S&P 500 index is 1100, then the seller of a December S&P 500 futures contract is theoretically obligated to deliver in December a portfolio of the 500 stocks that comprise the index. The multiplier for this contract is 250. The portfolio would have to exactly replicate the index with the weights of the stocks equal to their index weights. The current value of one futures contract is $275,000 (= 1100 × 250).

However, because of the problems associated with delivering a portfolio of 500 stocks that exactly replicate the underlying index, stock index futures substitute cash delivery for physical delivery. At final settlement, the futures price equals the spot price and the value of a futures contract is the actual market value of the underlying replicating portfolio that represents the stock index. The contract is marked-to-market based on the settlement price, which is the spot price, and the contract settles. Table 13.3 provides a list of selected stock index futures traded in the United States and Europe.

TABLE 13.3   Selected Equity Futures Contracts Traded in the United States and Europe

Index Futures Contract	Index Description	Exchange	Contract Size
U.S. Contracts			
S&P 500	500 cap-weighted stocks	CME	Index × 250 Index × 50 E-mini
S&P MidCap 400	400 cap-weighted stocks	CME	Index × 500 Index × 100 E-mini
Russell 200 Index	2,000 cap-weighted stocks	ICE	Index × 500 Index × 100 mini
S&P Growth Index	165 cap-weighted stocks	CME	Index × 250
S&P Value Index	165 cap-weighted stocks	CME	Index × 250
European Contracts			
EURO STOXX 50	50 cap-weighted European stocks	Eurex	Several multiples[a] 5, 10, 25, 50, 100, 200
DAX	30 cap-weighted German stocks	Eurex	Several multiples[a] 5, 10, 25, 50, 100, 200
FTSE 100 Index	100 cap-weighted UK stocks	NYSE Euronext	Index × 10[b]
CAC 40 Index	40-cap-weighted stocks on Euronext Paris	NYSE Euronext	Index × 10[c]

[a]Multiples in euros. Some available in Swiss francs or U.S. dollars.
[b]Multiple in British pounds.
[c]Multiple in euros.

Single Stock Futures A *single stock futures* (SSF) contract is an agreement between two parties to buy or sell shares of individual companies (as opposed to a stock index in the case of a stock index futures contract) at some time in the future with the terms agreed upon today. The value of traditional futures contracts is captured by SSFs as well because the agreement requires a low capital commitment upfront in the form of initial margin. Originally there were two key benefits to investors. These included that shorting was not constrained by the uptick rule or complicated by stock loans and a simple long or short strategy in the underlying stock can be created.[12]

SSFs currently trade on numerous exchanges around the world including those in Australia, Denmark, Finland, Hong Kong, Hungary, Portugal, South Africa, Sweden, and, most recently, Canada, the UK, the United States, and Iran. As of this writing, there has been modest success for these products. In January 2001, the London International Financial Futures Exchange (LIFFE) introduced SSFs on 30 stocks including seven U.S. companies and the Bourse de Montreal began trading a SSF contract on Nortel Networks. In May of that year, LIFFE expanded the number by 25 contracts to a total of 65 listed SSF contracts on global stocks.

The importance of the LIFFE development is that it is the first time SSFs have been listed on a major global exchange. The contracts are referred to as Universal Stock Futures (USF) and are standardized futures contracts based on shares of European and U.S. companies. Since the Euronext takeover of LIFFE, it is now part of NYSE Euronext and current trades 143 single stock futures contracts.

Recently, the CBOE, the CME (Chicago Mercantile Exchange) and the CBOT (Chicago Board of Trade) formed a joint venture to establish an electronic trading platform for SSFs called OneChicago, LLC. Trading in SSFs on OneChicago began in November 2002. OneChicago lists futures on 1,548 stocks including some bellwether stocks as IBM, Apple, Google and others.

The standardized features of the contracts for the NYSE Euronext market and the emerging U.S. market at OneChicago include a contract size of 100 shares with quotes in dollars or euros.[13] The minimum tick increment is $0.01 per share or $1 dollar per contract. Settlement calls for the physical delivery of 100 shares (adjusted for corporate events) of stock. The NYSE Euronext contract is also available as cash delivery. There is no daily price limits imposed on the contracts, but OneChicago has position limits of 13,500 net contracts on the 100 shares contracts and 1,350 net contracts on the 1,000 share contracts, which apply only during the last five trading days prior to expiration and are required by CFTC regulation.

Pricing Stock Index Futures

Futures contracts are priced based on the spot price and cost of carry considerations. For equity contracts these include the cost of financing a position in the underlying

---

[12] SEC Rule 10a-1(a)(1) (the uptick rule) was removed when Rule 201 Regulation SHO became effective in 2007. In February 2010, the SEC created an alternative rule that triggers a circuit breaker after a stock has fallen 10 percent. After the breaker is triggered an uptick rule is in effect.

[13] OneChicago also offers a 1,000 share contract size and as of this writing the NYSE Euronext Universal stock futures contract for Italy offers a 1,000-share size.

asset, the dividend yield on the underlying stocks, and the time to settlement of the futures contract. The theoretical futures price is derived from the spot price adjusted for the cost of carry. This can be confirmed using risk-free arbitrage arguments.

The logic of the pricing model is that the purchase of a futures contract can be looked at as a temporary substitute for a transaction in the cash market at a later date. Moreover, futures contracts are not assets to be purchased and no money changes hands when the agreement is made. Futures contracts are agreements between two parties that establish the terms of a later transaction. It is these facts that lead us to a pricing relationship between futures contracts and the underlying. The seller of a futures contract is ultimately responsible for delivering the underlying and will demand compensation for incurring the cost of holding it. Thus, the futures price will reflect the cost of financing the underlying. However, the buyer of the futures contract does not hold the underlying and therefore does not receive the dividend. The futures price must be adjusted downward to take this into consideration. The adjustment of the yield for the cost of financing is what is called the *net cost of carry*. The futures price is then based on the net cost of carry, which is the cost of financing adjusted for the yield on the underlying. That is,

$$\text{Futures price} = \text{Spot price} + \text{Cost of financing} - \text{Dividend yield}$$

The borrowing or financing rate is an interest rate on a money market instrument and the yield in the case of equity futures is the dividend yield on an individual stock or a portfolio of stocks that represent the stock index.

The theoretical futures price derived from this process is a model of the fair value of the futures contract. It is the price that defines a no-arbitrage condition. The no-arbitrage condition is the futures price at which sellers are prepared to sell and buyers are prepared to buy, but no risk-free profit is possible. The theoretical futures price expressed mathematically depends on the treatment of dividends. For individual equities with quarterly dividend payout, the theoretical futures price can be expressed as the spot price adjusted for the present value of expected dividends over the life of the contract and the cost of financing. The expression is given below as

$$F(t, T) = [S(t) - D] \times [1 + R(t, T)]$$

where

$F(t,T)$ = futures price at time t for a contract that settles in the future at time T
$S(t)$ = current spot price
D = present value of dividends expected to be received over the life of the contract
$R(t,T)$ = borrowing rate for a loan with the same time to maturity as the futures settlement date

For example, if the current price of the S&P 500 stock index is 1150, the borrowing rate is 0.4 percent, the time to settlement is 60 days, and the index is expected to yield 2.14 percent.[14] An annualized dividend yield of 2.14 percent corresponds

---

[14] The dividend yield and borrowing rate are derived from actual data as of July 2010.

to 4.045 index points when the S&P 500 stock index is 1150 and the contract has 60 days to expiration.

$$1150 \times [0.0214 \times 60/365] = 4.045 \text{ index points}$$

The theoretical futures price can be calculated as follows:

$$D = 4.05/(1 + 0.004)^{60/365} = 4.043$$

$$R = (1 + 0.004)^{(60/365)} - 1 = 0.000656 \text{ or } 0.0656\%$$

$$F(t, 60) = [1150 - 4.043] \times 1.000656 = 1146.71$$

If the actual futures price is above or below 1146.71, then risk-free arbitrage is possible. For actual futures prices greater than fair value, the futures contract is overvalued. Arbitrageurs will sell the futures contract, borrow enough funds to purchase the underlying stock index, and hold the position until fair value is restored or until the settlement date of the futures contract.

If, for example, we assume the actual futures price is 1151, then the following positions would lead to risk-free arbitrage:

Sell the overvalued futures at 1151.
Borrow an amount equivalent to 1150.
Purchase a stock portfolio that replicates the index for the equivalent of 1150.

The position can be unwound at the settlement date in 60 days at no risk to the arbitrageur. At the settlement date, the futures settlement price equals the spot price. Assume the spot price is unchanged at 1150. Then,

Collect 4.045 in dividends.
Settle the short futures position by delivering the index to the buyer for 1151.
Repay 1150.755 (1150 × 1.000656) to satisfy the loan (remember the interest rate for the 60 days is 0.0656%).

The net gain is $[1151 + 4.045] - 1150.755 = 4.29$. That is, the arbitrageur "earned" 4.29 index points or 37 basis points (4.29/1150) without risk or without making any investment. This activity would continue until the price of the futures converged on fair value.

It does not matter what the settlement price for the index is at the settlement date. This can be clearly shown by treating the futures position and stock position separately. The futures position delivers the difference between the original futures price and the settlement price or $1151 - 1150$, which equals 1 index point. The long stock position earned only the dividends and no capital gain. The cost of financing the position in the stock is 0.755 and the net return to the combined short futures and long stock position is 1(futures) + 4.045(stock) less the 0.755 cost of financing, which is a net return of 4.29. Now consider what happens if the spot price is at any other level at the settlement date. Table 13.4 shows the cash flows associated with the arbitrage. We can see from the results that regardless of the movement of the spot price, the arbitrage profit is preserved.

For actual futures prices less than fair value, the futures contract is undervalued. Arbitrageurs will buy the futures contract, short or sell the underlying, lend the proceeds, and hold the position until fair value is restored or until settlement date of the futures contract.

TABLE 13.4   Arbitrage Cash Flows: Short Futures at 1151

Futures Stock Index Settlement Price	Futures Cash Flows	Stock Cash Flows	Interest	Profits
1175	1151 − 1175 = −24	25 + 4.045 = 29.045	0.755	4.29
1165	1151 − 1165 = −14	15 + 4.045 = 19.045	0.755	4.29
1150	1151 − 1150 = 1	0 + 4.045 = 4.045	0.755	4.29
1140	1151 − 1140 = 11	−10 + 4.045 = −5.955	0.755	4.29
1135	1151 − 1135 = 16	−15 + 4.045 = −10.955	0.755	4.29
1125	1151 − 1125 = 26	−25 + 4.045 = −20.955	0.755	4.29

The theoretical futures price can also be expressed mathematically based on a security with a known dividend yield. For equities that pay out a constant dividend over the life of a futures contract, this rendition of the model is appropriate. This may apply to stock index futures contracts where the underlying is an equity index of a large number of stocks. Rather than calculating every dividend, the cumulative dividend payout or the weighted-average dividend produces a constant and known dividend yield. The cost of carry valuation model is modified to reflect the behavior of dividends. This is expressed in the following equation:

$$F(t, T) = S(t) \times [1 + R(t, T) - Y(t, T)]$$

where $Y(t,T)$ is the dividend yield on the underlying over the life of the futures contract and $F(t,T)$, $S(t)$, and $R(t,T)$ are as defined earlier.

For example, if the current price of a stock is 1150, the borrowing rate is 0.4 percent, the time to settlement is 60 days, and the annualized dividend yield is 2.14 percent, the theoretical futures price can be calculated as follows:

$$Y = (1 + 0.0214)^{60/365} - 1 = 0.003487 \text{ or } 0.3487\%$$

$$R = (1 + 0.004)^{(60/365)} - 1 = 0.000656 \text{ or } 0.0656\%$$

$$F(t, 60) = 1150 \times [1 + 0.000656 - 0.003487] = 1146.75$$

In practice, it is important to remember to use the borrowing rate and dividend yield for the term of the contract and not the annual rates. The arbitrage conditions outlined above still hold in this case. The model is specified differently, but the same outcome is possible. When the actual futures price deviates from the theoretical price suggested by the futures pricing model, arbitrage would be possible and likely. The existence of risk-free arbitrage profits will attract arbitrageurs.

Also in practice, there are several factors that may violate the assumptions of the futures valuation model. Because of these factors, arbitrage must be carried out with some degree of uncertainty and the fair value futures price is not a single price, but actually a range of prices where the upper and lower prices act as boundaries around an arbitrage-free zone. Furthermore, the violation of various assumptions can produce mispricing and risk that reduce arbitrage opportunities.

The futures price ought to gravitate toward fair value when there is a viable and active arbitrage mechanism. Arbitrage activity will only take place beyond the upper and lower limits established by transaction and other costs, uncertain cash flows, and divergent borrowing and lending rates among participants. The variability of the spread between the spot price and futures price, known as the *basis*, is a consequence of mispricing due to changes in the variables that influence the fair value.

The practical aspects of pricing produce a range of prices. This means that the basis can move around without offering a profit motive for arbitrageurs. The perspective of arbitrageurs in the equity futures markets is based on dollar profit but can be viewed in terms of an interest rate. The borrowing or financing rate found in the cost of carry valuation formula assumes borrowing and lending rates are the same. In practice, however, borrowing rates are almost always higher than lending rates. Thus, the model will yield different values depending on the respective borrowing and lending rates facing the user. Every futures price corresponds to an interest rate. We can manipulate the formula and solve for the rate implied by the futures price, which is called the *implied futures rate*. For each market participant there is a theoretical fair value range defined by its respective borrowing and lending rates and transaction costs.

OTC Equity Derivatives

An OTC equity derivative can be delivered on a stand-alone basis or as part of a structured product. Structured products involve packaging standard or exotic options, equity swaps, or equity-linked debt into a single product in any combination to meet the risk–return objectives of the investor and may represent an alternative to the cash market even when cash instruments are available.

The four basic components of OTC equity derivatives are equity forwards, OTC options, equity swaps, and equity-linked debt. These components offer an array of product structures that can assist investors in developing and implementing investment strategies that respond to a changing financial world. OTC derivatives can assist the investor with cost minimization, diversification, hedging, asset allocation, and risk management.

Before we provide a product overview, let's look at counterparty risk. For exchange-listed derivative products counterparty or credit risk is minimal because of the clearinghouse associated with the exchange. However, for OTC products there is counterparty risk. For parties taking a position where performance of both parties is required, both parties are exposed to counterparty risk. The OTC market has incorporated a variety of terms into the contractual agreement between counterparties to address the issue of credit risk. These include netting arrangements, position limits, the use of collateral, recouponing, credit triggers, and the establishment of Derivatives Product Companies (DPCs).

Netting arrangements between counterparties are used in master agreements specifying that in the event of default, the bottom line is the net payment owed across all contractual agreements between the two counterparties. *Position limits* may be imposed on a particular counterparty according to the cumulative nature of their positions and creditworthiness. As the OTC market has grown, the creditworthiness of customers has become more diverse. Consequently, dealers are requiring some counterparties to furnish collateral in the form of a liquid short-term credit instrument. *Recouponing* involves periodically changing the coupon such that the marked-to-market value of the position is zero. For long-term OTC agreements, a *credit trigger provision* allows the dealer to have the position cash settled if the counterparty's credit rating falls below investment grade. Finally, dealers are establishing

DPCs as separate business entities to maintain high credit ratings that are crucial in competitively pricing OTC products.

EQUITY FORWARDS   Equity forward contracts are OTC products where the underlying equity security can be a single stock, a basket of stocks or based on a stock index.[15] The buyer of the forward is in a long position to take delivery of the underlying at settlement. The seller is responsible for delivery and is short the underlying. The forward price is determined by cost of carry considerations versus the current spot price. The buyer gains if, at settlement, the spot price exceeds the forward price. Equity forwards are a useful mechanism for hedging price risk on either the long or the short side. A long position is stock can be hedged by a short forward contract, while a short position such as anticipatory purchase can be hedged with a long forward contract.

OTC OPTIONS   OTC options can be classified as first generation and second generation options. The latter are called *exotic options*. We describe each type of OTC option below.

FIRST GENERATION OF OTC OPTIONS   The basic type of first generation OTC options either extends the standardized structure of an existing listed option or created an option on stocks, stock baskets, or stock indexes without listed options or futures. Thus, OTC options were first used to modify one or more of the features of listed options: the strike price, maturity, size, exercise type (American or European), and delivery mechanism. The terms were tailored to the specific needs of the investor. For example, the strike price can be any level, the maturity date at any time, the contract of any size, the exercise type American or European, the underlying can be a stock, a stock portfolio, or an equity index or a foreign equity index, and the settlement can be physical, in cash or a combination.

An example of how OTC options can differ from listed options is exemplified by an Asian option. Listed options are either European or American in structure relating to the timing of exercise. Asian options are options with a payout that is dependent on the average price of the spot price over the life of the option. Due to the averaging process involved, the volatility of the spot price is reduced. Thus, Asian options are cheaper than similar European or American options.

The first generation of OTC options offered flexible solutions to investment situations that listed options did not. For example, hedging strategies using the OTC market allow the investor to achieve customized total risk protection for a specific time horizon. The first generation of OTC options allow investors to fine tune their traditional equity investment strategies through customizing strike prices, and maturities, and choosing any underlying equity security or portfolio of securities. Investors could now improve the management of risk through customized hedging strategies or enhance returns through customized buy writes. In addition, investors could invest

---

[15] For a treatment of equity forward contracts see Julian Barrow and Richard Hart, "Types of OTC Equity Products," in *Equity Derivatives, Documenting and Understanding Equity Derivative Products*, ed. Edmund Parker (London: Global Business Publishing Ltd., 2009), 63–84.

in foreign stocks without the need to own them, profit from an industry downturn without the need to short stocks.

Exotics: Second Generation OTC Options The second generation of OTC equity options includes a set of products that have more complex payoff characteristics than standard American or European call and put options. These second-generation options are sometimes referred to as "exotic" options and are essentially options with specific rules that govern the payoff.[16] Exotic option structures can be created on a stand-alone basis or as part of a broader financing package such as an attachment to a bond issue, which are considered structured products.

Some OTC option structures are path dependent, which means that the value of the option to some extent depends on the price pattern of the underlying asset over the life of the option. In fact, the survival of some options, such as barrier options, depends on this price pattern. Other examples of path dependent options include Asian options, look-back options, and reset options. Another group of OTC option structures has properties similar to step functions. They have fixed singular payoffs when a particular condition is met. Examples of this include digital or binary options and contingent options. A third group of options is classified as multivariate because the payoff is related to more than one underlying asset. Examples of this group include a general category of rainbow options such as spread options and basket options.

Competitive market makers are now prepared to offer investors a broad range of derivative products that satisfy the specific requirements of investors. The fastest growing portion of this market pertaining to equities involves products with option-like characteristics on major stock indexes or stock portfolios.

Equity Swaps Equity swaps have the same structure as interest rate swaps in that they are agreements between two counterparties that provide for the periodic exchange of a schedule of cash flows over a specified time period based on some notional amount. For equity swaps at least one of the two payments is linked to the performance of an equity index, a basket of stocks, or a single stock. The unique feature of an equity swap is that the net cash flows are often based on two different markets typically equity, bonds or money markets. In a standard or plain vanilla equity swap, one counterparty agrees to pay the other the total return to an equity index in exchange for receiving either the total return of another asset or a fixed or floating interest rate. All payments are based on a fixed notional amount and payments are made over a fixed time period.

Equity swap structures are very flexible with maturities ranging from a few months to 10 years. The returns of virtually any asset can be swapped for another without incurring the costs associated with a transaction in the cash market. Payment schedules can be denominated in any currency irrespective of the equity asset and payments can be exchanged monthly, quarterly, annually, or at maturity. The equity asset can be any equity index or portfolio of stocks, hedged or unhedged.

---

[16] For a description of exotic options, see Chapter 10 in Bruce M. Collins and Frank J. Fabozzi, *Derivatives and Equity Portfolio Management* (Hoboken, NJ: John Wiley & Sons, 1999).

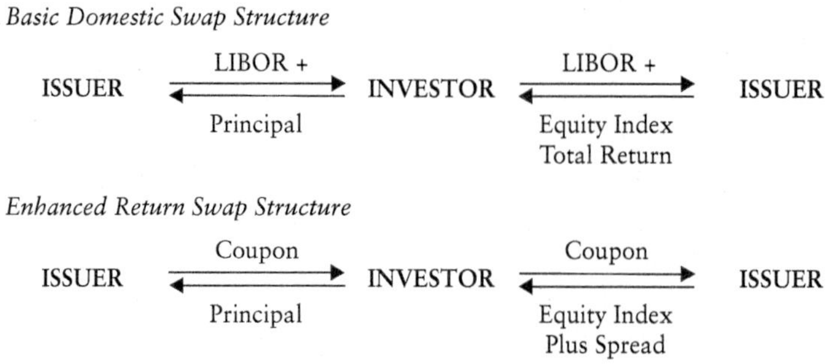

Basic Domestic Swap Structure

$$\text{ISSUER} \xrightarrow[\text{Principal}]{\text{LIBOR +}} \text{INVESTOR} \xleftarrow[\substack{\text{Equity Index} \\ \text{Total Return}}]{\text{LIBOR +}} \text{ISSUER}$$

Enhanced Return Swap Structure

$$\text{ISSUER} \xrightarrow[\text{Principal}]{\text{Coupon}} \text{INVESTOR} \xleftarrow[\substack{\text{Equity Index} \\ \text{Plus Spread}}]{\text{Coupon}} \text{ISSUER}$$

FIGURE 13.5   Equity Swaps

Variations of the plain vanilla equity swap include: international equity swaps where the equity return is linked to an international equity index; currency-hedged swaps where the swap is structured to eliminate currency risk; and call swaps where the equity payment is paid only if the equity index appreciates (depreciation will not result in a payment from the counterparty receiving the equity return to the other counterparty because of call protection).

A basic swap structure is illustrated in Figure 13.5. In this case, the investor owns a short-term credit instrument that yields LIBOR (London Interbank Offered Rate) plus a spread. The investor then enters into a swap to exchange LIBOR plus the spread for the total return to an equity index. The counterparty pays the total return to the index in exchange for LIBOR plus a spread. Assuming the equity index is the Nikkei 225, a U.S. investor could swap dollar-denominated LIBOR plus a spread for cash flows from the total return to the Nikkei denominated in yen or U.S. dollars. The index could be any foreign or domestic equity index. A swap could also be structured to generate superior returns if the financing instrument in the swap yields a higher return than LIBOR.

There are a number of reasons for using equity swaps versus a direct investment in a portfolio of physical shares of equity. These benefits are consistent with the role of derivatives outlined previously. Swaps can serve as an effective means of cost management by offering lower administrative and execution costs. Swap structures are particularly suitable for returns management because they serve as a substitute for passive index funds or core portfolios with performance benchmarks. There might be regulatory constraints associated with international investments that can be managed with swaps. In addition, swap structures can be devised to effectively manage currency risk.

Equity swaps can be used by fund and portfolio managers for a variety of applications including asset allocation, accessing international markets, enhancing equity returns, hedging equity exposure, and synthetically shorting stocks. A swap structure can create the same economics of a direct investment in an asset. Unlike interest rate swaps where both legs produce positive cash flows, the equity leg can produce a negative cash flow leading to cash outflows on both legs of the swap. An investor who wants to invest $100 million in equities can instead put the money into a short-term credit instrument and enter into an equity swap. Every payment date, the investor uses the proceeds from the investment to pay the floating leg and will either invest or divest the equity leg. Thus, this is the equivalent of an equity investment financed with LIBOR.

Another example of an equity swap is a one-year agreement where the counterparty agrees to pay the investor the total return to the S&P 500 Index in exchange for dollar-denominated LIBOR on a quarterly basis. The investor would pay LIBOR plus a spread × 91/360 × notional amount. This type of equity swap is the economic equivalent of financing a long position in the S&P 500 Index at a spread to LIBOR. The advantages of using the swap are: no transaction costs, no sales or dividend-withholding tax, and no tracking error or basis risk versus the index.

The basic mechanics of equity swaps are the same regardless of the structure. However, the rules governing the exchange of payments may differ. For example, a U.S. investor wanting to diversify internationally can enter into a swap and, depending on the investment objective, exchange payments on a currency-hedged basis. If the investment objective is to reduce U.S. equity exposure and increase Japanese equity exposure, for example, a swap could be structured to exchange the total returns to the S&P 500 Index for the total returns to the Nikkei 225 Index. If, however, the investment objective is to gain access to the Japanese equity market, a swap can be structured to exchange LIBOR plus a spread for the total returns to the Nikkei 225 Index. This is an example of diversifying internationally and the cash flows can be denominated in either yen or dollars. The advantages of entering into an equity swap to obtain international diversification are that the investor exposure is devoid of tracking error, and the investor incurs no sales tax, custodial fees, withholding fees, or market impact associated with entering and exiting a market. This swap is the economic equivalent of being long the Nikkei 225 financed at a spread to LIBOR at a fixed exchange rate.

Structured Products

It is difficult to precisely define a structured product or separate it from an OTC product. The market is part of the OTC market, but goes beyond the traditional set of OTC products. It includes equity-linked debt investments, but is mostly identified with a "wrapper," which is a legal structure that houses the product by which it is sold to the public. The most common of structures are transferable securities such as a note or a unit in a fund such as an equity certificate. These products are often issued by a *Special Purpose Vehicle* (SPV) that is created specifically to sell the product to the public. The SPV will hold assets that are part of the product and obtain the necessary credit rating to meet the needs of its investors. Structured products are commonly issued to investors by financial institutions. Another differentiating factor for structured products versus OTC products is that some products embed an actively managed portfolio while others have principal protection guarantees. Thus, structured products can be created to enhance returns or manage specific risks. The first structures emerging from the OTC market were equity linked debt products. The wrapper is a note or a bond and the product embeds a derivative structure that can limit downside exposure, cap the upside, offer coupon payments, or include an exotic option like a barrier or Asian option.

Key Points

- The equity security underlying an equity derivative can be a stock, a basket of stocks, an index, or a group of indexes.

- Equity derivatives have four basic roles: risk management, returns management, cost management, and regulatory management.
- There are three segments of the equity derivatives market: exchange-listed market, OTC market, and the market for structured products.
- There are three general categories of derivatives: futures and forwards, options, and swaps.
- OTC derivatives provide more flexible terms than listed derivatives and can be customized to meet the specific needs of investors.
- The listed market has sought to incorporate products with OTC characteristics such as FLEX options and binary options.
- The fundamental difference between futures and options is that the buyer of an option has the right but not the obligation to perform whereas the seller of an option is obligated to perform; in contrast, in the case of a futures contract both parties are required to perform.
- The payout structure of a futures contract and an options contract differ. The price of an option contract represents the cost of eliminating or modifying the risk–reward relationship of the underlying. The payout for a futures contract is a dollar-for-dollar gain or loss for the buyer and seller. Consequently, a futures payout is symmetrical, while the payout for options is skewed.
- The Black-Scholes model is the basic options pricing model. There are many extensions of this model, but it remains the basic model in practice.
- The six factors that affect an option's price are (1) spot price of the underlying, (2) strike price, (3) time to expiration of the option, (4) expected price volatility of the underlying over the life of the option, (5) short-term risk-free rate over the life of the option, and (6) anticipated cash dividends on the underlying stock or index over the life of the option.
- In employing options in investment strategies, a portfolio manager can calculate the sensitivity of the price of an option to a change in any one of the factors that affect its price.
- There are numerous stock index futures contracts that have been developed around the world that can be used to implement an equity investment strategy.
- Single stock futures contracts trade around the world including on the OneChicago exchange in the United States.
- Futures can be priced using a cost of carry valuation model.
- The OTC derivatives market includes equity forwards, options and warrants, equity linked debt and equity swaps.
- Structured products are an extension of the OTC market and can include a "wrapper" to house the product and sell in to the public.

Part II Using Equity Derivatives in Portfolio Management

Previously, we described the basic characteristics of the different types of equity derivatives. We identified four primary roles for derivatives: (1) to modify the risk characteristics of an investment portfolio, (2) to enhance the expected return of a portfolio, (3) to reduce transaction costs associated with managing a portfolio, and (4) to circumvent regulatory obstacles. In this chapter, we discuss several basic applications of these instruments to equity portfolio management that reflect a cross section of these four primary roles across passive, active, and semi-active approaches to equity investment management.[1] In addition, because options will change the risk reward characteristics of an investment portfolio, we also provide an overview of the relationship between expected returns and risk for strategies employing options.

While forward and futures contracts are time dependent linear derivatives with similar payouts and risk characteristics as the underlying, options are nonlinear derivatives that have fundamentally different risk characteristics than the underlying asset. The real value of options in portfolio management regardless of the motivation for their use is that they allow the investor a means of modifying the risk and return characteristics of their investment portfolio. This makes options valuable vehicles for implementing active or semi-active strategies. The impact of adding options to an existing portfolio or using options as an investment vehicle is to create skewed distributions that reflect different risks than an investment in the underlying asset.[2] For example, the purchase of a call option rather than a stock changes the payout profile of the investment by capping the losses and thus truncates the probability distribution associated with possible outcomes and necessarily changes the expected return and risk of the investment.[3]

Equity Investment Management

Equities represent a significant asset class comprising a major proportion of investors' investment portfolios. The asset allocation for investor spans across equity markets in terms of domestic and international, based on capitalization, style, and investment approach.

There are two basic approaches to equity investment management: passive and active.[4] Passive management involves gaining broad exposure to equities as defined

---

[1] Semi-active might also fall under active strategies. It is semi-active because it involves a core exposure to equities and adding some value without actively pursuing alpha as the case with stock selection.

[2] The use of options can create so-called "fat tails" in the returns distribution because volatility changes. Options also create an asymmetric or skewed distribution to reflect their contingent payout pattern. The extent of the skewness depends on the option. In addition, the degree of the volatility affects the peakedness or kurtosis of the distribution as well. High volatility conditions, for example, correspond to distributions with thicker tails and low volatility conditions correspond to distributions with higher peaks. For a discussion of these issues see Nassim Taleb, *Dynamic Hedging* (New York: John Wiley & Sons, 1997).

[3] The probability distribution for an option is not normally distributed as the underlying is assumed to be in Black-Scholes-Merton option pricing model. However, even in the case when returns are not normally distributed, it is still true that the expected returns and variance of the portfolio can be calculated. The normal distribution assumption of Black-Scholes-Merton models allows the mapping to a skewed distribution. The expected returns can be estimated directly from a Taylor expansion, through the use of a factor model or through the use of Monte Carlo simulation to generate the probability distribution for the option price.

[4] For an additional discussion of equity portfolio management see Gary Gastineau, Andrew Olma, and Robert Zielinski, "Equity Portfolio Management," Chapter 7 in John Maginn, Donald Tuttle, Dennis McLeavey, and Jerald Pinto (eds.), *Managing Investment Portfolios* (Hoboken, NJ: John Wiley & Sons, 2007). Some have established a third approach called semi-active investing, which traditionally has been considered an active strategy.

by a tracking index such as the S&P 500 stock index. Equity indexing is an approach to equity investing that seeks to replicate the performance of a benchmark. Equity derivatives can be used as important investment vehicles for implementing passive strategies. As an alternative to an investment in a replicating portfolio of stocks designed to track the index, investors can use a combination of a long cash investment and stock index futures or an equity swap.[5]

Active equity investment strategies are designed to outperform a passive equity benchmark. These strategies might use superior stock selection techniques or quantitative techniques to produce superior returns to the benchmark. The specific approach to active management is often categorized according to some concept of style. The most common two styles include growth and value investing. It might also involve a capitalization filter or the use of technical analysis. Once a style has been identified, a style benchmark is established for measuring performance. Equity derivatives can be used as investment vehicles through a long cash position and a long position in stock index futures based on a style index.[6]

An approach to investment management that falls into an alternative category is long-short investing.[7] The investor can use stock selection to buy undervalued stocks and sell overvalued stocks. Equity derivatives can be used to isolate alpha on the long or short side. For example, a long stock portfolio with positive alpha can be traded against a short stock index futures position that neutralizes systematic risk. Equity swaps can also be used to implement an active or passive strategy.

We know that investors developed a strategy known as *enhanced indexing* based on the concept of matching the risk characteristics of a benchmark portfolio with the chance of higher returns. This approach seeks superior risk-adjusted returns versus a benchmark. The other side of this approach is to match expected returns to a benchmark with lower risk. These two approaches are considered *semi-active equity investment strategies*. Once again as with passive and active approaches, the vehicles to implement these strategies can be based on building a stock portfolio or derivatives-based. The derivatives approach can use stock index futures or equity swaps to equitize[8] cash and add value through a nonequity asset. For example, an equity swap can be structured such that the investor receives the total returns to the benchmark and pays LIBOR plus a spread. The investor can achieved added value by investing in a higher return bond.

---

[5] Other passive investment vehicles might include index mutual funds or exchange-traded funds (ETFs).

[6] An example is the S&P 500 Growth and Value contracts that trade on the Chicago Mercantile Exchange (CME). There are also numerous stock index futures contracts based on capitalization.

[7] Alternative investments are usually regarded as those outside the three major asset classes: stocks, bonds, and cash. However, active management strategies that are not long-only and typically implemented by hedge funds also fall into this category. The implementation of an alternative strategy in this context can utilize passive or active investment vehicles or both.

[8] Equitizing cash involves using derivatives to maintain exposure to equities.

Portfolio Applications of Listed Options

Investors can use the listed options market to address a range of investment problems particularly for active and semiactive managers. We discuss the use of OTC options later. Advantages of listed options relative to OTC options are that they provide accurate and consistent information about pricing and virtually eliminate credit risk. Moreover, because of these characteristics and the standardization of products, listed options often have low transaction costs and moderate to high liquidity. The issue of transaction costs and liquidity can play an important role in the decision to use derivatives as part of the investment process.

RISK MANAGEMENT STRATEGIES   Risk management in the context of equity portfolio management focuses on price risk. Consequently, the strategies discussed here in some way address the risk of a price decline or a loss due to adverse price movement. Options can be used to create asymmetric risk exposures across all or part of the core equity portfolio. This allows the investor to hedge downside risk at a fixed cost with a specific limit to losses should the market turn down. This tactical investment approach can improve risk-adjusted performance versus a benchmark.

The most common strategy for risk management is a *protective put buying strategy*. This strategy is used by investors who currently hold a long position in the underlying security or investors who desire upside exposure and downside protection. The motivation is either to hedge some or all of the total risk. Index put options hedge mostly market risk, while put options on an individual stock hedge the total risk associated with a specific stock. This allows portfolio managers to use protective put strategies for separating tactical and strategic strategies. Consider, for example, a manager who is concerned about nonfinancial events increasing the level of risk in the marketplace. Furthermore, assume the manager is satisfied with the core portfolio holdings and the strategic mix. Put options could be employed as a tactical risk reduction strategy designed to preserve capital and still maintain strategic targets for portfolio returns. In recent years, the U.S. equity market has experienced significant volatility. A *protective put buying strategy* implemented in a timely fashion could have produced superior risk-adjusted returns.[9]

Thus, any investor concerned about downside risk is a candidate for a protective put strategy. Nonetheless, protective put strategies may not be suitable for all investors. The value of protective put strategies, however, is that they provide the investor with the ability to invest in volatile stocks with a degree of desired insurance and unlimited profit potential over the life of the strategy.

The protective put involves the purchase of a put option combined with a long stock position. The put option is comparable to an insurance policy written against the long stock position. The option price is the cost of the insurance premium and the amount the option is out-of-the money is the deductible. Just as in the case of insurance, the deductible is inversely related to the insurance premium. The deductible is reduced as the strike price increases, which makes the put option more in-the money or less out-of-the-money. The higher strike price causes the put price to

---

[9] Since 2000, the equity market has experienced two market corrections in excess of 35 percent. Protective put strategies or collar strategies could have produced higher risk-adjusted returns.

increase and makes the insurance policy more expensive. The put can be paid for through the sale of an out-of-the-money call option creating a *collar strategy*. The upside is limited to the strike price.

COST MANAGEMENT STRATEGIES Equity managers are evaluated in terms of performance versus a benchmark. Often costs cause a drag on portfolio performance. Options can be used to manage the cost of maintaining an equity portfolio in a number of ways. Among the strategies is the use of short put and short call positions to serve as a substitute for a limit order in the cash market. Cash-secured put strategies can be used to purchase stocks at the target price, while covered calls or overwrites can be used to sell stocks at the target price. The target price is the one consistent with the portfolio manager's valuation or technical models and the price intended to produce the desired rate of return.

In addition, synthetic strategies may allow the investor to implement a position at a lower cost than a direct investment in the cash market. For example, foreign investors subject to dividend withholding taxes may find a synthetic long stock position using options an attractive alternative to the cash investment. Moreover, there is always an alternative method of creating a position. Synthetic calls, for example, can be created by borrowing, investing in stock, and buying put options. Likewise, a synthetic protective put strategy can be established by buying call options and discount bonds.

Cash-Secured Put The motivation behind a *cash-secured put strategy* is to reduce market impact costs associated with the purchase of a stock. The strategy can be used by managers to transact in the cash market without bearing the total cost of the perceived risk to the seller. The demand for the stock may bid up the price of the security regardless of the motivation behind the trade. If, for example, the manager believes that the stock is attractive at or below a particular price, a cash-secured put can be established using a strike price consistent with the target price. If the purchase is not motivated by firm-specific information, but is strategic in nature, part of a passive rebalancing, or based on relative valuation models, then using an option mechanism to purchase the stock may make sense.

The strategy is similar to a limit order in the cash market with two notable differences. First, the option approach pays the buyer a premium, while no such premium exists for a limit order. Second, the limit order can be ended at any time, while the option is only extant over the life of the contract.

A cash market transaction may bid up the price of the stock because sellers believe the trade is motivated by new information. The use of short put options is a means to convey the intent of the buyer. The put seller indicates to the market a willingness to accept the downside risk of a further stock price decline. Consequently, this makes it clear to the market that the interested party does not expect an immediate increase in the stock price. This may reduce the immediacy cost of market impact.

Thus, the short put mechanism of purchasing stock may be appropriate for managers with strategic interest in the stock, but no compelling need for immediate execution. The short put premium provides some downside cushion, which further reduces the effective cost of the stock. If the stock rises over the life of the option and the put expires worthless, then an overvalued stock has become more overvalued.

If, on the other hand, the manager wants to own the stock immediately, then a put option strategy is not appropriate.

Naked Calls Similarly, short calls can be used as a mechanism for selling current holdings at a price consistent with the rate of return objective of the manager. The intention is twofold: (1) to reduce market impact costs and (2) to receive a favorable price for selling the stock shares.

Consider a manager who currently holds a number of stocks based on a quantitative valuation model. The model has created a sell price for each holding based on the investment horizon under consideration. The alternative methods for selling a substantial holding are to work it upstairs through a broker/dealer or establish a short call position with a strike price consistent with investment objectives. The disadvantage of a sizable cash market transaction is that the buyer will interpret the sale as information motivated and adjust the price accordingly. This could result in a meaningful decline in price and lower the return contribution of the stock to the overall portfolio.

A naked call can be written with a strike price as a substitute for a limit order. The investor selling the stock is conveying a clearer message to the market regarding intent. The stock is being sold for reasons other than the possession of adverse information regarding the company's future. The seller's intent is clearer for more aggressive OTM strike prices because it requires a rise in price for exercise. The effect of the overwrite position on portfolio performance is positive for neutral to slightly rising markets and negative for declining markets. The trade will undoubtedly incur transaction costs of some kind in either market. However, the prudent use of options is a useful way to be more specific about the motivation behind the trade.

RETURN ENHANCEMENT STRATEGIES Recall that semi-active management seeks to improve risk-adjusted performance through enhanced returns or less risk. The most popular return enhancement strategies employing listed options are *covered call strategies.* If the investor currently owns the stock and writes a call on that stock, the strategy has been referred to as an "overwrite." If the strategy is implemented all at once (simultaneously buying the stock and selling the call), it is referred to as a "buy write." The essence of the covered call is to trade price appreciation for income. The strategy is appropriate for slightly bullish investors who don't expect much out of the stock and want to produce additional income. These are investors who are willing either to limit upside appreciation for limited downside protection or to manage the costs of selling the underlying stock. The primary motive is to generate additional income from owning the stock.

Although the call premium provides some limited downside protection, this is not an insurance strategy because it has significant downside risk. Consequently, investors should proceed with caution when considering a covered call strategy.

A covered call is less risky than buying the stock because the call premium lowers the break-even recovery price. The strategy behaves like a long stock position when the stock price is below the strike price. On the other hand, the strategy is insensitive to stock prices above the strike price and is therefore capped on the upside. The maximum profit is given by the call premium and the OTM amount of the call option.

REGULATORY ISSUES   The regulation of derivatives markets and equity markets is quite extensive in the United States. The Securities and Exchange Commission (SEC) is the primary regulator of equity markets and option markets. One focus of the SEC is to protect the investor by making certain that brokers identify the suitability of the investor for trading in options. This has mostly been a problem for smaller investors and not for institutional investors. However, numerous institutional investors are still subject to a variety of antiquated restrictions that prohibit such investment management choices as short selling. Options can be used to establish a synthetic short position held in lieu of a short position in the cash market. In addition, options can be useful to foreign investors subject to local tax consequences by avoiding a cash market transaction.

Portfolio Applications of Stock Index Futures

Now let's look at how stock index futures can work with passive or active equity investment strategies. Our focus is on how stock index futures can be used to manage all types of equity strategies more efficiently. We begin by examining how futures can help change equity exposure in order to achieve the desired level of exposure at the lowest possible cost. The two strategies examined are hedging strategies (a special case of risk management) and asset allocation strategies.

Stock index futures contracts are often ideal instruments for managing equity exposure in passive or active strategies due to their liquidity, flexibility, and low transaction costs. An equity position of comparable dollar value can be managed in the stock index futures market at a fraction of the cost in the cash market. The futures market is also an alternative means of implementing an investment strategy to the cash market.

The choice of whether to use the cash market or the futures market to alter equity exposure depends on the objectives of the manager and the size of the equity exposure. Despite apparent cost advantages, there are limits to the amount of stock index futures available to large institutional investors such as pension funds due to regulatory, size, and liquidity constraints. Nonetheless, stock index futures can still be an effective and valuable tool for portfolio management.

The motivation behind the choice to change equity exposure is important in deciding between the cash market or the stock index futures market. If the decision is a strategic asset allocation decision then it can be viewed as long term. If, on the other hand, the decision is tactical, it is a short-term situation. Stock index futures allow managers to quickly adjust imbalances in their asset allocation positions effectively without the need to purchase individual stocks. This effectively allows portfolio managers to increase or decrease equity exposure without altering the status of their core portfolio or disturbing their long-term investment objectives.

The appropriate way to analyze the cash and futures alternatives is to compare the costs of the two transactions.

HEDGING MARKET RISK   Since stock index futures were first introduced, the most common application is to hedge market risk. The motivation for hedging market risk might be tactical based on market conditions or strategic as part of an active long-short management strategy or as part of an arbitrage strategy. Active managers with positive alpha derived from long portfolios can neutralize market risk by shorting stock index futures. Arbitragers will buy or sell stock index futures to take advantage of mispricing. Using arbitrage to enhance returns is considered a semi-active approach to equity management. Regardless of the motivation, hedging involves the transfer of risk from one party to another. Stock index futures serve as a valuable hedging instrument for both domestic and global equity portfolio managers. The global proliferation of viable futures contracts has brought the capability from the traditional S&P 500–type funds to a broad range of hedging possibilities. The methodology is identical except that hedging foreign equity positions requires currency hedges as well.

Hedging strategies involve cross-hedging when the hedging instrument is not perfectly correlated with the investor's equity portfolio. This is the case with active portfolios. A perfectly hedged position is one without risk. If the underlying index is the same as the portfolio being hedged, then the hedge is an arbitrage and will generate a certain profit. If the futures contract is fairly priced at the risk-free rate, then the hedge is comparable to a risk-free investment and it will produce the risk-free rate of return. If the portfolio being hedged has some tracking error versus the underlying index, then the rate of return is comparable to a money market instrument with small levels of tracking error.

As a hedging instrument, stock index futures provide investors with a means to manage risk whether holding long or short positions in the equity market. By taking the opposite side of their position, equity managers can insulate the performance of their equity position from market movements. The residual performance is directly related to the level of nonmarket risk in the portfolio. The most sophisticated hedging techniques do not completely eliminate risk because the gains or losses on the futures side do not precisely offset the gains or losses on the cash equity portfolio. Nonetheless, the hedged position is clearly a low-risk strategy particularly when the equity portfolio is highly correlated with the index underlying the stock index futures contract.

For equity portfolios designed to track known indexes with corresponding futures contracts, tracking error is not a huge problem. However, alternative equity portfolios with low correlations might have significant tracking error versus any particular hedging instrument that will subject the hedge to significant risk. This means that stock index futures can only insulate an equity portfolio from some portion of total risk. If the equity portfolio happens to be a broad market index fund, then S&P 500 index futures can pretty much take care of total risk because nonmarket risk was eliminated through diversification. However, when this is not the case and the equity portfolio is subject to significant nonmarket risk, then it exposes the hedging strategy to those same risks.

On the other hand, when the stock index futures contract is based on a broad-market index, it gives managers the ability to hedge systematic risk and take advantage of superior stock selection ability that will produce a positive return even in declining markets. These contracts can be used to isolate the nonmarket component of total risk. This feature benefits active managers who have the ability to pick high-performance stocks, but who do not necessarily like the market. There is no need to stay out of equities. The manager can use stock index futures to remove the market component from the strategy. Over the investment horizon, the returns to the hedged portfolio will include an incremental return to the selected stocks versus the market and any dividends from the stocks.

HEDGE RATIOS   In order to hedge a position, the amount of the position to be taken in the stock index futures contract must be determined. That is, a risk equivalent position of the cash market portfolio is needed for the stock index futures position in order to hedge the portfolio. The *hedge ratio* indicates the amount of the futures position that must be taken to hedge the cash market portfolio. For example, using the S&P 500 futures contract, a hedge ratio of 1 means that if a manager wants to hedge a $10 million stock portfolio, a $10 million S&P 500 futures position must be sold. If the hedge ratio is 0.9, this means that $9 million of S&P 500 futures contracts must be sold to hedge a $10 million stock portfolio.

It is tempting to use the portfolio's beta as a hedge ratio because it is an indicator of the sensitivity of the portfolio returns to the stock index returns. It appears, then, to be an ideal sensitivity adjustment. However, applying beta relative to a stock index as a sensitivity adjustment to a stock index futures contract assumes that the index and the futures contract have the same volatility. If futures always sold at their fair value, this would be a reasonable assumption. However, mispricing is an extra element of volatility in a stock index futures contract. Since the stock index futures contract is more volatile than the underlying stock index, using a portfolio beta as a sensitivity measure would result in a portfolio being overhedged.

The most accurate sensitivity adjustment would be the beta of a portfolio relative to the futures contract. It can be shown that the beta of a portfolio relative to a stock index futures contract is equivalent to the product of the portfolio relative to the underlying index and the beta of the index relative to the futures contract.[10] The beta in each case is estimated using regression analysis in which the data are historical returns for the portfolio to be hedged, the stock index, and the stock index futures contract. The regressions estimated are

$$r_P = a_P + B_{PI} r_I + e_P$$

where

r_P = the return on the portfolio to be hedged
r_I = the return on the stock index
B_{PI} = the beta of the portfolio relative to the stock index
a_P = the intercept of the relationship
e_P = the error term

and

$$r_I = a_I + B_{IF} r_F + e_I$$

---

[10] Edgar Peters, "Hedged Equity Portfolios: Components of Risk and Return," in *Advances in Futures and Options Research*, vol. 1B, ed. F. J. Fabozzi (Stamford, CT: JAI Press, 1987), 75–91.

where

r_F = the return on the stock index futures contract
r_I = the return on the stock index
B_{IF} = the beta of the stock index relative to the stock index futures contract
a_I = the intercept of the relationship
e_I = the error term

Given B_{PI} and B_{IF}, the minimum risk hedge ratio can then be found by:

$$\text{Hedge ratio} = h = B_{PI} \times B_{IF}$$

The hedge ratio h in the above expression is referred to as a *minimum risk hedge ratio* (also called an *optimal hedge ratio*) because the ratio minimizes the variance of returns to the hedged position.

There is a special case where the portfolio beta can be used as the hedge ratio. This is the case if the manager can hedge the portfolio until the settlement date. This is because the return to mispricing is no longer an unknown factor when the portfolio can be held to the futures settlement date.

Given the hedge ratio, the manager must determine the number of stock index futures contracts to sell. The number needed can be calculated using the following three steps after B_{PI} and B_{IF} are estimated:

Step 1. Determine the "equivalent market index units" of the market by dividing the market value of the portfolio to be hedged by the current value of the futures contract:

$$\text{Equivalent market index units} = \frac{\text{Market value of the portfolio to be hedged}}{\text{Current value of the futures contract}}$$

Step 2. Multiply the equivalent market index units by the hedge ratio to obtain the "beta-adjusted equivalent market index units":

$$\text{Beta-adjusted equivalent market index units} = \text{Hedge ratio} \times \text{Equivalent market index units}$$

or

$$B_{PI} \times B_{IF} \times \text{Equivalent market index units}$$

Step 3. Divide the beta-adjusted equivalent index units by the multiple specified by the stock index futures contract:

$$\text{Number of contracts} = \frac{\text{Beta-adjusted equivalent market index units}}{\text{Multiple of the contract}}$$

ASSET ALLOCATION   All investment decisions ultimately are asset allocation decisions. The choice to invest new cash in a domestic index fund instead of a global portfolio or the choice to reduce bond exposure is a clear example. If the decision is a long-term one, then it is a strategic asset allocation decision. Strategic decisions are made with the careful analysis of a client's long-term needs. If, instead, the decision is short-term, it is a tactical asset allocation decision. Tactical asset allocation (TAA) is actually a short-term to intermediate-term timing strategy designed to benefit from identifiable misevaluation in an asset class and seeks to add value to the overall fund performance. TAA could also include a defensive strategy to avoid adverse market movements. The classic example is a shift from equities to bonds or equity to cash in anticipation of a market correction. Asset allocation is not limited to domestic financial assets, but reaches into foreign markets as well. Once the asset allocation decision is made, for the equity investor the implementation of that decision takes place on two levels. First, the asset allocation decision determines the overall exposure to equity as an asset class. Second, the intra-asset allocation determines how the equity exposure is realized—passively or actively. Equity derivatives can play an important role at both levels of the asset allocation process.

The mechanics of implementing asset allocation decisions depend upon the investor's choice of an instrument. Whether managers choose to diversify internationally or not, superior security selection may be blown over by the adverse winds of a bear market. There are several ways that managers can respond to tactical asset allocation models that signal a danger of a market reversal. Tactical asset allocation is comparable to dynamic hedging. The choice to reduce or increase exposure to an asset class effectively hedges one risk in favor of another or none. The instruments to hedge market risk are also available for asset allocation decisions.

Managers have a choice of vehicles and methods to implement an asset allocation strategy. The stock index futures solution is available across a number of countries and asset classes, enabling managers to manage the systematic risk of equity portfolios regardless of the country of origin. The derivatives solution to the asset allocation decision allows managers to separate the security selection decision from the market timing or the asset allocation decision. (See Table 13.6.) Later in this chapter we discuss the OTC derivatives alternative to stock index futures.

The choice of whether to use cash or futures to accomplish an allocation-related strategy was discussed earlier. Once again the choice comes down to whether the decision is long term or short term.

Applications of OTC Equity Derivatives

The array of OTC derivative-based equity portfolio management strategies cuts across the two primary categories of investment philosophy—active and passive management. We consider several strategies in this section, which are listed in Table 13.5, together with the purpose of using an OTC derivatives and a product candidate.

Table 13.6 summarizes various OTC equity derivative structures in terms of the role of derivatives for long-term investors and hedgers.[11] A broad spectrum of equity investment activities emanating from the role of derivatives can benefit from

---

[11] The investors referred to in Table 13.6—pension funds, insurance companies, high net work individuals, and hedge funds—might create an index fund or use active managers to meet their respective investment objectives. All are candidates for using equity derivatives.

TABLE 13.5 The Use of OTC Derivatives for Equity Strategies

Equity Strategy	Purpose	Product Candidate
Return-enhancement strategies	Outperform benchmark	Equity swap
Hedging strategies	Risk management	Exotics, swaps, debt[a]
Spread strategies	Risk management	Equity swaps, exotics
Market access strategies	Reduce costs	Swaps, debt, warrants,
Changing equity exposure	Reduce costs	exotics
Index funds	Outperform benchmark	Swaps, debt, exotics
Standard		Swaps, debt
Enhanced		
Style		
Asset allocation	Risk management	Swaps
Active manager transition	Cost management	Swaps, exotics

[a]Debt refers to equity-linked debt products.

these three basic categories of OTC equity derivative structures: options and exotics, equity-linked notes, and equity swaps.

Creation of Structured Product Solutions

One of the most important applications of derivative securities is in the creation of structured product solutions to the financial needs or objectives of an institutional investor.[12] Structured products are, like derivative securities, financial products representing contractual agreements between two parties—an issuer (the designer or creator of the structure) and a purchaser (the user or holder of the structure). The structure is designed with a linkage to the performance of an existing security or securities. The linkage could be to an equity index or portfolio, an interest rate, an exchange rate, or a commodity price and based on spreads, correlations, convergences, or divergences. The objective could be to protect principal, enhance returns, defer taxes, gain access to difficult markets, manage costs or manage regulatory risks. The process of creating or establishing a structured product is known as "financial engineering" and involves the creation of a structure that meets the specific needs of the client in terms of the objectives listed above. The value of structured products is that they provide great flexibility in design and application.

Typically, structured products are used to provide some form of principal protection while having the potential for upside returns. Thus, a basic structure consists of a fixed income component and a returns generating component. An alternative basic structure offers a leverage factor that can generate a higher magnitude of returns than a traditional investment or a principal protected structure. Examples of structured products include but are not restricted to warrants, principal protection notes, asset-linked notes, various types of swaps, credit linked products, monetization

---

[12] For an discussion of structured products see, John C. Braddock, *Derivatives Demystified: Using Structured Financial Products* (New York: John Wiley and Sons, 1997).

TABLE 13.6   OTC Derivative Structures and Investment Management

Derivative Structure	Investor	Role	Application
OTC options and exotics	Long-term Index funds Style funds Active managers Strategic asset allocators	Risk management	Customized protective puts Collar structures Portfolio insurance Currency hedging Asset exposure Probability exposure
		Return management	Index arbitrage Option writing Volatility forecasting Intra-asset allocation Leverage strategies
		Cost management	Option writing Market access Valuation estimation Structured products
		Regulatory management	Foreign market exposure Tax deferral Asset exposure
Equity-linked debt	Long-term Index funds Style funds Active managers Strategic asset allocators	Risk management	Customized structures Collar structures Portfolio insurance Currency hedging Asset exposure
		Return management	Spread premiums
		Cost management	Foreign market cost avoidance Asset allocation
		Regulatory management	Asset exposure Foreign market exposure Capital requirement
Equity swaps	Long-term Index funds Style funds Active managers Strategic asset allocators	Risk management	Diversification Asset allocation Minimize tracking error Currency hedging
		Return management	Tracking portfolio Spread premium
		Cost management	Foreign market cost avoidance Asset allocation
		Regulatory management	Foreign market exposure Tax deferral Asset exposure

strategies for restricted or concentrated situations, caps and floor products, and securitized cash flows.

Risk Management Strategies

As we have noted, a common use of derivatives is to hedge financial risk. Stock index futures can insulate an equity portfolio from only some portion of total risk. If the equity portfolio happens to be a broad market index fund, then S&P 500 index futures can pretty much take care of total risk because nonmarket risk was eliminated through diversification. However, when this is not the case and the equity portfolio is subject to significant nonmarket risk, then it exposes the hedging strategy to those same risks.

Stock index futures contracts in which the underlying is a broad market index allow portfolio managers the ability to hedge systematic risk and to take advantage of superior stock selection ability that will produce a positive return even in declining markets. Stock index futures can be used to isolate the nonmarket component of total risk. This feature benefits active managers who have the ability to pick high performance stocks, but who have little market timing skills. There is no need to stay out of equities during volatile markets. The manager can use stock index futures to hedge market risk.

Consequently, over the investment horizon, the returns to the hedged portfolio will include an incremental return to the selected stocks versus the market and any dividends from the stocks. However, the resulting strategy may go beyond the desired risk-return trade-off. OTC derivative structures can be designed to address all these issues and achieve the exact hedged position desired. All costs can be known up front with no additional risk to investors, with the exception of some credit risk and market failure risk that accompanies all financial transactions.

Despite the benefits of using stock index futures, listed index futures products do not provide a full range of hedging choices for equity investors. OTC equity derivatives go a long way to fill this gap. Investors can choose among equity swaps, equity-linked debt, and a structured option-like product to hedge with greater precision the specific risk they want to shed and to acquire the risk they want to bear. Table 13.7 provides a list of derivative alternatives for hedging equity portfolios.

TABLE 13.7   Hedging with Derivatives

	Hedging Instrument	
Hedging Strategy	Listed	OTC
Reduce Market Risk	Stock index futures	Option, swap, debt
Reduce Total Risk	Multiple SIFs contracts	Option, swap, debt
Change Risk Components	Stock index futures	Option, swap, debt
Reduce Currency Risk	Quanto futures	Option, swap, debt
Reduce Interest Rate Risk	Interest rate derivatives	Option, swap, debt
Reduce Inflation Risk	Interest rate derivatives Commodity index derivatives	Option, swap, debt

With the advent of second-generation "exotic" options, investors can now implement a hedging strategy with the degree of precision they desire. Market risk can be hedged in any country using any derivative structure. Equity swaps can exchange the total return of a portfolio for another less risky asset class. The structure can be designed to hedge currency risk if necessary and desired.

A structured product using exotics can design a payout that is contingent on certain market activity. For example, a barrier put option can be used to obtain a specific degree of protection without paying extra for outcomes that are not relevant. Ladder options can lock in a market decline, while flexible strike options can ratchet up when the market moves opposite to expectations.

Once again, the bottom line is that structured OTC equity derivative products can overcome the risk inherent in cash or futures market hedging strategies. Investors have the means to hedge all or a specific part of total risk.

ASSET ALLOCATION The mechanics of implementing asset allocation decisions depend upon the investor's choice of an investment vehicle. Table 13.8 presents a list of candidates for a global asset shift, which changes foreign equity exposure in the overall asset allocation strategy using listed derivatives and OTC derivatives.

The problem is the same one presented in an earlier discussion of equity investment strategies. The choices unfold similarly. The option-based solution may suffer from high costs due to a highly volatile portfolio or due to significant liquidity risk. However, exotic option structures provide a means to fine-tune the strategy to reflect very precisely forecasted returns. Basket options, such as index options, are cheaper than a portfolio of options. They also provide a portfolio manager with a means of eliminating tracking error between the underlying for the hedging vehicle and the equity portfolio.

Listed options have the additional problem of size limits for standardized contracts. FLEX options resolve some but not all of those limitations. The stock index futures alternative comes with some administrative issues and risks. The equity swap solution incorporates the asset allocation decision into a single transaction, but necessitates a counterparty and has credit risk. In Figure 13.6, we present a case where an active manager with $100 million portfolio that is currently allocated 50 percent

TABLE 13.8 Alternative Investment Vehicles Global Asset Allocation Strategy

Investment Category	Vehicle	Advantages	Disadvantages
Cash market	Stock portfolio	Ownership	Costs and management
Listed derivatives	Stock index futures	Cost	Managing futures
	Stock index options	Listed	Size, standardization
Flex options		Flexibility, listed	Size, tracking error
OTC options	Baskets	No tracking error	Cost
Spread		Any market	Cost
Barriers		Low cost	Volatile markets
Compound		Low cost	Multiple transactions
Swaps	Equity swap	Quick, efficient	Negative payments
International swap			Credit risk

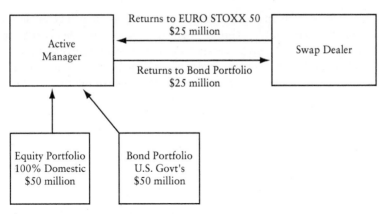

FIGURE 13.6   Asset Allocation Using an Equity Swap Structure

equities and 50 percent bonds and seeks to increase equity exposure to 75 percent. The equity exposure is currently 100 percent domestic and the manager wants to diversity into Europe. The swap dealer can structure an equity swap to accomplish this asset allocation objective. The new allocation is $50 million domestic equity, $25 million foreign equity, and $25 million bonds.

The derivatives solution to the asset allocation decision allows fund managers or portfolio managers to separate the security selection decision from the market timing or the asset allocation decision. The choice of what mechanism to use to accomplish the investment objective depends on whether the decision is long term or short term and the relative costs.

RETURN MANAGEMENT STRATEGIES   Return management strategies focus on structuring an investment strategy to increase returns but not risk. Here we include passive index funds and enhanced index funds because they are investment strategies designed to meet the performance criterion of matching or exceeding a benchmark. We could just as easily think of index funds as a means to match the risk characteristics of a benchmark, which is one of the features of this strategy. However, once the risk profile is established, the focus of index funds is performance relative to a benchmark.

The modified index fund strategies might also be called return enhancement strategies. The purpose behind return-enhancement strategies is to increase return without an accompanying increase in risk. This means that an "enhanced" index fund ought to do better than the benchmark index without incurring additional risk. However, it may not be an easy task to outperform a benchmark without incurring tracking error risk. This risk will usually emerge whenever the replicating portfolio does not exactly mimic the composition of the benchmark. Nonetheless, the incremental returns are expected to more than compensate for the small increase in risk and, over time, the enhanced index fund is expected to outperform the benchmark on a risk-adjusted basis.

The goal of indexing is to construct a portfolio to exactly match the performance of the benchmark. When this is accomplished, tracking error is zero. In addition to performance reasons, plan sponsors are attracted to index funds because they provide investment diversification and are a means to control costs. Many plan sponsors have combined active and passive management using index funds as a risk management tool. Index funds can also provide a means for market timing. Thus we see that index funds can fall into return management, risk management, or cost management categories. This also can fall into a passive or active investment category as well. Part of the reason is that the use of index funds makes performance attribution and cost control more manageable because of the use of an established index as a benchmark. For the plan sponsor, an index fund can represent an entire asset class within the framework of its strategic asset allocation strategy or as part of an intra-asset allocation strategy that mixes active and passive management.

Indexing has taken on many different forms that have broad applications. If we generalize our definition of index funds as a portfolio of stocks designed to match or exceed the returns of a benchmark while maintaining the same risk exposure, then there are many extensions of the original index fund. The many applications of index funds provide a rich landscape for using derivatives to further reduce costs. In fact, the prudent use of equity derivatives can reduce transaction costs to near zero. We regard the reduction of costs as any increase in after-cost return without changing the fundamental composition of the portfolio. This means that the returns are derived from the same sources in the cash market. Thus, it is comparable to getting a better execution in the cash market. Superior execution leads to lower costs, which increases return. The following is a list of index fund applications:

Extended funds. An *extended funds strategy* involves constructing a portfolio linked to an index that "extends" beyond the traditional S&P 500 index and may include a significantly larger group of stocks. The purpose of this strategy is to gain U.S. equity diversification. The universe of over 5,000 stocks across many sectors is more representative of the U.S. equity market and the U.S. economy. In addition, it provides a means of reducing risk versus a more narrow view represented by the S&P 500 index. No real liquid listed derivatives are available to create a synthetic fund. OTC derivative structures such as equity swaps and equity-linked debt instruments can provide an alternative investment vehicle to an exclusive cash approach.

Non-S&P 500 index funds. A non-S&P 500 index fund's strategy involves constructing a portfolio linked to a broad-based non-S&P 500 stock index. The strategy underlying these funds is to expand U.S. equity market exposure. Investors who currently have an S&P 500 index fund can combine it with a separate index fund that captures a neglected portion of the market. The end result can effectively be an extended fund with the added advantage of making intra-asset allocation rebalancings when desired. Once we travel outside the plain vanilla index fund, using listed derivatives becomes more difficult. OTC equity derivatives are available for implementing and managing non-S&P 500 index funds.

Foreign or international index funds. A foreign or international index funds strategy seeks to design a portfolio that is linked to a foreign or international stock index. Thus, investors who do not invest beyond the borders of the United States are ignoring about half of world equities. The strategy objective of foreign investments is to gain international diversification. Furthermore, as global financial markets continue to deregulate and integrate, emerging markets in other parts of the world will provide additional opportunities. There are, however, direct investment expenses associated with owning foreign securities that exceed similar domestic investments. These may include larger commissions and spreads, stamp taxes, dividend withholding taxes, custody fees, and research fees. Many of these costs can be better managed through the use of OTC index derivatives.

Special-purpose index funds. A portfolio can be constructed to be linked to the performance of a subindex, such as a market sector, or a portfolio with the same risk profile as a benchmark but with a tilt toward a specific parameter such as yield or price-earnings ratio. This strategy is called a *special-purpose index funds strategy*. Tilted portfolios are designed to enhance the returns to an index fund without assuming additional risk. Sometimes referred to as "enhanced" index funds, this strategy may also involve the use of futures or options to provide incremental return. An enhanced index fund begins with a traditional index fund and then utilizes financing techniques and derivative strategies to enhance return.

Having decided on a passive investment strategy and an appropriate benchmark, the investor's next consideration is how to implement the strategy. A cash market solution needs to address the design and construction of a replicating or tracking portfolio. In the presence of transaction costs, the optimal portfolio may still underperform the benchmark. Thus, in order to overcome the risk of underperformance the investor may have to assume more tracking error risk. The final choice of a replicating portfolio must be made within a cost management framework. The trade-off can be represented by expected tracking error versus expected trading costs. Costs are related to portfolio size and liquidity. Part of the skill of portfolio construction is to find the optimal balance between costs and risk. The marginal trade-off between risk and cost is greater for small sized portfolios.

Earlier we discussed the benefits of using stock index futures to manage an index fund. Synthetic index funds can be created using stock index futures that exactly replicate the returns to the underlying index. Recently, OTC index derivatives have been developed for investors with restrictions on using derivatives. These include equity-linked debt instruments and equity swaps. Equity swaps are important because they are the economic equivalent of financing an equity investment with a fixed-income security, typically a LIBOR-based security. Because there are many stock indexes that are not covered by stock index futures or ETFs, equity index swaps offer a means to invest in these indexes that make them attractive to investors. Equity index swaps provide a low-cost structure that can eliminate tracking risk and provide longer term maturities than stock index futures.

There are some index funds that use futures almost exclusively. It is not practical for large pension funds to rely exclusively on synthetic index funds due to market constraints. Thus, some combination of the cash market and futures market is appropriate. Index funds can be developed as a more dynamic strategy, and can be used as a risk management tool and a platform for better performance. However, stock index futures have their own administrative considerations and are limited in application because they have a linear pay off.

In order to provide a richer body of choices for implementing and managing index funds over the long haul, the use of OTC derivative structures provides the missing link to more complete and effective global risk management solutions to the investment problem. Equity swaps can be used to create the exact desired equity exposure in a single transaction, which makes them convenient, cost effective, and economically sound.

Return Enhancement Strategies

There are three basic approaches to enhanced indexing that apply to other investment strategies as well. These strategies cut across passive and active management, which is why they are often referred to as semi-active strategies. The objective is to increase risk-adjusted returns and this can be accomplished through returns management or risk management. The first approach involves changing the composition of the equity portfolio in order to position the portfolio to take advantage of stocks, stock sectors, some different weighting allotments, or other criteria that the manager believes will cause the portfolio to perform better than a passive benchmark. In the case of index funds, the equity portfolio is the replicating portfolio. Changing the portfolio involves modifying the content of the portfolio and yet maintaining the current level of risk. The resulting portfolio is typically designed to minimize tracking error. For return management strategies, the equity portfolio is designed to match the risk characteristics of a benchmark and not its expected return.

In the second approach, index fund managers can use a stock index futures arbitrage to increase or enhance returns. The strategy is formalized as a stock replacement program, which invests in the less expensive of the cash portfolio or futures. The incremental return is the result of futures pricing inefficiencies rather than estimated mispricing of equities.

OTC equity derivatives can be a useful tool to modify the composition of the portfolio at low cost or to enhance returns. The use of derivatives would enter the picture as part of the implementation process. The investor would first establish the necessary rebalancing to achieve the desired exposure to a new set of stocks on either an individual basis, an industry sector basis, or with the intent to modify a portfolio parameter such as price-earnings ratio. In any case, the result in the cash market is a set of sell orders and a set of buy orders. The investor is shedding some risks in favor of others. The rebalanced portfolio represents the right equity exposure to add incremental return necessary to improve performance with no added risk.

As explained earlier, a structured product can be used to enhance returns by providing a means of accessing other sources of additional returns. Various structures are capable of accomplishing these objectives. For example, investors can invest in a triple-B-rated bond at a spread above Treasuries and enter into an equity swap to receive the total returns to the benchmark index and pay the yield on Treasuries. The spread then enhances the total return to the strategy above the benchmark index. Because of recent market volatility, other types of structures have been developed to improve returns through effective risk management.[13]

---

[13] Equity linked note structures that vary the level of principal guarantee and upside participation are available. Also, structures such as those provided by "Himalaya products" are linked to the performance of a group of indexes or baskets over an observation period. The best performing index is locked in at that time until the maturity of the product when the investor

Risk and Expected Return of Option Strategies

Options are like any other risky asset because they compensate investors for assuming systematic risk. Therefore, if options have higher exposure to systematic risk, investors will require and expect higher returns from holding options. Naturally, call options, which pay off in states of the world where the underlying asset's price rises, will have higher expected returns than the underlying asset. In contrast, put options, which pay off in states of the world where the asset's price declines, will have lower expected returns than the risk-free asset that are often negative.[14] Furthermore, adding options to a stock portfolio or writing options against an existing long position will change the risk-return characteristics of the investment and therefore its expected return.

According to the asset pricing framework of Merton and the Black-Scholes model, the instantaneous expected return to an option ought to be the same as the return implied by the CAPM.[15] Hence, it can be shown that an option's instantaneous beta is related to the beta of the underlying stock and the elasticity of the option.[16] Rendleman demonstrates that the expected returns and risks for options should be consistent with the principles of risk and return from the CAPM.[17] He shows the impact on expected returns for various investment strategies that use options. One observation is that call options with high positive betas should have high expected returns and put options with negative betas should have low expected returns. The discussion below follows the presentations by Rendleman and Coval and Shumway.[18]

EXPECTED RETURNS FROM LONG CALLS AND COVERED CALLS   From the CAPM derived by Merton, the expected value of a call can be derived:

$$E[R_{call}] = R_f + \beta_{call}[E[R_M] - R_f]$$

The expected return from buying call options is higher than the underlying stock. However, the difference in returns is less the further the option is in-the-money and

---

receives the weighted average performance of the locked-in indexes. In seeking protection from market volatility investors hope to improve performance.

[14] Coval and Shumway find empirical evidence that the returns to option strategies are lower than predicted by the CAPM. They argue that this suggests that other factors besides the market are important for pricing the risk associated with options. See Joshua D. Coval and Tyler Shumway, "Expected Option Returns," *Journal of Finance* 56, no. 3 (2001): 983–1009.

[15] See Robert C. Merton, "An Intertemporal Capital Asset Pricing Model," *Econometrica* 41, no. 5 (1973): 867–887; and Fischer Black and Myron Scholes, "The Pricing of Options and Corporate Liabilities," *Journal of Political Economy* 81, no. 3 (1973): 637–654.

[16] That is, $\beta_{option} = \beta_{stock}(\delta P/\delta S)(S/P)$ where P = price of the option and S = price of the underlying stock.

[17] Richard J. Rendleman, "Option Investing from a Risk-Return Perspective," *Journal of Portfolio Management* 25, special issue (May 1999): 109–121.

[18] Rendleman, "Option Investing from a Risk-Return Perspective"; and Coval and Shumway, "Expected Option Returns." For a graphical treatment of the expected return and risk for option strategies, see Hans E. Stoll and Robert E. Whaley, *Futures and Options: Theory and Applications* (Cincinnati, Ohio: South-Western Publishing, 1993).

converges on the stock's expected return for very high stock prices. The reason for this relationship is that the option's beta exceeds that of the underlying stock and in fact can be much higher. For stocks with positive betas, the beta of the option will be higher because of its exposure to greater systematic risk. The fact that an option is a leveraged position in the underlying would also lead to the higher risk and expected returns conclusion. In a portfolio context, adding an option to a diversified portfolio will heighten the systematic risk in the portfolio. Consequently, investors should require a higher rate of return.

For covered calls, which reduce the risk of holding the stock, the expected return ought to be lower than a long stock position. The important behavioral aspect of covered call writing from an expected return perspective is that writing calls on a long stock position reduces risk and consequently will lower expected returns. The fact that covered call strategies are viewed as a means to generate income during flat markets does not change the fact that across the spectrum of possible outcomes, risk is lower, as is expected returns.

EXPECTED RETURNS FROM PROTECTIVE PUT STRATEGIES   From the CAPM, if a stock has a positive beta, then a put ought to have a negative beta. This can be demonstrated by viewing the put option as a portfolio of a short position and a discount loan. The expected return must necessarily be below the risk-free rate because the equity risk premium is positive. This can be seen in the following expression:

$$E[R_{\text{put}}] = R_f + \beta_{\text{put}}[E[R_M] - R_f]$$

Investors are willing to hold puts because they view it as purchasing insurance. Hence, a put is bought for the same reasons that motivate consumers to buy automobiles or homeowners insurance—to hedge against adverse events. In neither case does the consumer expect to generate earnings because the purchase of an insurance policy is basically the purchase of utility in exchange for the expected loss. Consequently, protective put strategies will lower expected returns compared with a long-only strategy.

For more complicated option-based strategies, the outcomes will also result in a different risk-return profile depending on the payout of the strategy. Straddles, for example, with zero betas ought to return the risk-free rate.

The relationship between expected return and beta for the basic option strategies is illustrated in Figure 13.7. From the exhibit, we see that the relationship between strike price and expected return shows that the more in-the-money the option, the closer to the risk-return position of the underlying stock. We also observe that the covered call and the protective put strategy both result in lower risk and expected returns versus the long stock position. The riskless asset and the zero beta straddle ought to be similarly positioned in terms of expected return and beta. On the lower end of the exhibit, we find a similar relationship among put options as call options except with negative betas.[19]

---

[19] See Thomas Schneeweis and Richard Spurgin, "The Benefits of Index Option-Based Strategies for Institutional Portfolios," *Journal of Alternative Investments* 3, no. 4 (2001): 44–52.

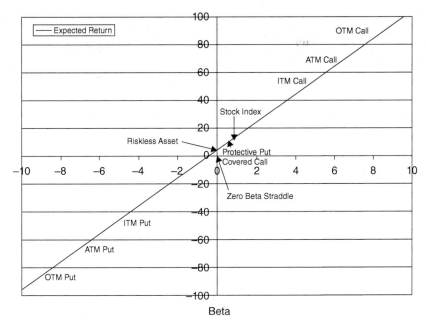

FIGURE 13.7   Expected Return and Beta for Option Strategies

Key Points

- Equity portfolio management applications fall across the four roles of derivatives (returns management, risk management, cost management, and regulatory management) and the two basic categories of equity investing: passive and active.
- Equity derivatives can be used as investment vehicles by active or passive managers in the context of the four roles of derivatives.
- Portfolio applications exist for listed derivatives and OTC derivatives.
- Protective put buying is the most common risk management strategy using listed options.
- Cash secured puts and naked calls can be used to reduce market impact costs of implementing a strategy.
- Buy writes are the most popular way to use listed options to enhance returns.
- Stock index futures contracts are often ideal instruments for managing equity exposure in passive or active strategies due to their liquidity, flexibility, and low transaction costs.
- Stock index futures can be used to hedge systematic risk, create synthetic index funds or in an enhanced index fund program.
- A hedge ratio is needed to determine the appropriate number of stock index futures in a hedging strategy.

Schneeweis and Spurgin report that over the period of analysis (1987–1999) passive option-based strategies such as covered calls, protective puts, and collars produced higher risk-adjusted returns than the underlying equity benchmarks.

- Equity listed or OTC derivatives can be used to implement an asset allocation program.
- A broad spectrum of equity investment activities emanating from the role of derivatives can benefit from three basic categories of OTC equity derivative structures: options and exotics, equity-linked notes, and equity swaps.
- The instantaneous expected return to an option should be the same as the return implied by the CAPM.

CHAPTER 14

Tools and Strategies Based on Technical Analysis

Technical analysis has long been questioned and even ridiculed by many, particularly those in academia. Recent research in areas including behavioral economics, however, may better be able to explain why asset prices move the way they do and why certain trends and patterns develop. Technical analysis shows "what" has happened while behavioral research attempts to explain "why" it has happened. Consequently a newfound interest in technical analysis appears to be rising among investors, financial professionals, and even some academicians.

This chapter takes a quick look back at the history of technical analysis and discusses the underlying logic and primary tools used to analyze assets and markets. The reading that follows explores many types of charts including the line chart, bar chart, candlestick chart, and point and figure chart. The author looks at a number of chart patterns including reversal and continuation patterns and what each could be indicating.

Numerous technical indicators including price-based indicators (e.g., moving averages), momentum oscillators (e.g., relative strength index), sentiment indicators (e.g., put/call ratio), and flow-of-funds indictors (e.g., Arms Index) will be studied. Volume, relative strength analysis, time intervals, and trend analysis will also be reviewed.

The reading looks at market cycles more closely and explores several theories including the Kondratieff Wave, Elliott Wave Theory, and Dow Theory. Lastly, inter-market analysis, which incorporates economic analysis and seeks to draw connections between economic activity, asset prices, and the financial markets, is explained.

Investments: Principles of Portfolio and Equity Analysis: Technical Analysis

Learning Objectives

- Explain the principles of technical analysis, its applications, and its underlying assumptions.
- Discuss the construction and interpretation of different types of technical analysis charts.
- Demonstrate the uses of trend, support, and resistance lines, and change in polarity.

- Identify and interpret common chart patterns.
- Discuss common technical analysis indicators: price-based indicators, momentum oscillators, sentiment, and flow of funds.
- Explain the use of cycles by technical analysts.
- Discuss the key tenets of Elliott Wave Theory and the importance of Fibonacci numbers.
- Describe intermarket analysis as it relates to technical analysis and asset allocation.

Technical Analysis

Technical analysis has been used by traders and analysts for centuries, but it has only recently achieved broad acceptance among regulators and the academic community. This chapter gives a brief overview of the field, compares technical analysis with other schools of analysis, and describes some of the main tools in technical analysis. Some applications of technical analysis are subjective. That is, although certain aspects, such as the calculation of indicators, have specific rules, the interpretation of findings is often subjective and based on the long-term context of the security being analyzed. This aspect is similar to fundamental analysis, which has specific rules for calculating ratios, for example, but introduces subjectivity in the evaluation phase.

Technical Analysis: Definition and Scope

Technical analysis is a form of security analysis that uses price and volume data, which is often graphically displayed, in decision making. Technical analysis can be used for securities in any freely traded market around the globe. A freely traded market is one where willing buyers trade with willing sellers without external intervention or impediment. Prices are the result of the interaction of supply and demand in real time. Technical analysis is used on a wide range of financial instruments, including equities, bonds, commodity futures, and currency futures.

The underlying logic of technical analysis is simple:

Supply and demand determine prices.
Changes in supply and demand cause changes in prices.
Prices can be projected with charts and other technical tools.

Technical analysis of any financial instrument does not require detailed knowledge of that instrument. As long as the chart represents the action in a freely traded market, a technician does not even need to know the name or type of the security to conduct the analysis. Technical analysis can also be applied over any time frame—from short-term price movements to long-term movements of annual closing prices. Trends that are apparent in short-term charts may also appear over longer time frames. Because fundamental analysis is more time consuming than technical analysis, investors with short-term time horizons, such as traders, tend to prefer technical analysis—but not always. For example, fundamental analysts with long time frames often perform technical analysis to time the purchase and sale of the securities they have analyzed.

PRINCIPLES AND ASSUMPTIONS   Technical analysis can be thought of as the study of collective investor psychology, or sentiment. Prices in any freely traded market are set by human beings or their automated proxies (such as computerized trading programs), and price is set at the equilibrium between supply and demand at any instant in time. Various fundamental theorists have proposed that markets are efficient and rational, but technicians believe that humans are often irrational and emotional and that they tend to behave similarly in similar circumstances.

Although fundamental data are key inputs into the determination of value, these data are analyzed by humans, who may be driven, at least partially, by factors other than rational factors.[1] Human behavior is often erratic and driven by emotion in many aspects of one's life, so technicians conclude that it is unreasonable to believe that investing is the one exception where humans always behave rationally. Technicians believe that market trends and patterns reflect this irrational human behavior. Thus, technical analysis is the study of market trends or patterns. And technicians believe the trends and patterns tend to repeat themselves and are, therefore, somewhat predictable. So, technicians rely on recognition of patterns that have occurred in the past in an attempt to project future patterns of security prices.

Another tenet of technical analysis is that the market reflects the collective knowledge and sentiment of many varied participants and the amount of buying and selling activity in a particular security. In a freely traded market, only those market participants who actually buy or sell a security have an impact on price. And the greater the volume of a participant's trades, the more impact that market participant will have on price. Those with the best information and most conviction have more say in setting prices than others because the informed traders trade higher volumes. To make use of their information, however, they must trade. Technical analysis relies on knowledgeable market participants putting this knowledge to work by trading in the market, thereby influencing prices and volume. Without trading, the information is not captured in the charts. Arguably, although insider trading is illegal for a variety of reasons, it improves the efficiency of technical analysis.

Trades determine volume and price. The impact occurs instantaneously and frequently anticipates fundamental developments correctly. So, by studying market technical data—price and volume trends—the technician is seeking to understand investor sentiment. The technician is benefiting from the wide range of knowledge of market participants and the collective conclusion of market participants about a security. In contrast, the fundamental analyst must wait for the release of financial statements to conduct financial statement analysis, so a time lag occurs between the market's activities and the analyst's conclusions.

Charles Dow, creator in 1896 of what is now known as the Dow Jones Industrial Average, described the collective action of participants in the markets as follows:

The market reflects all the jobber knows about the condition of the textile trade; all the banker knows about the money market; all that the best-informed president knows of his own business, together with his knowledge of all other businesses;

---

[1] Fundamental analysts use a wide variety of inputs, including financial statements, legal documents, economic data, first-hand observations from visiting the facilities of subject companies, and interviews with corporate managers, customers, suppliers, and competitors.

it sees the general condition of transportation in a way that the president of no single railroad can ever see; it is better informed on crops than the farmer or even the Department of Agriculture. In fact, the market reduces to a bloodless verdict all knowledge bearing on finance, both domestic and foreign.

A similar notion was expressed by George A. Akerlof and Robert J. Shiller:

To understand how economies work and how we can manage them and prosper, we must pay attention to the thought patterns that animate people's ideas and feelings, their animal spirits. We will never really understand important economic events unless we confront the fact that their causes are largely mental in nature.[2]

Market participants use many inputs and analytical tools before trading. Fundamental analysis is a key input in determining security prices, but it is not the only one. Technical analysts believe that emotions play a role. Investors with a favorable fundamental view may nonetheless sell a financial instrument for other reasons, including pessimistic investor sentiment, margin calls, and requirements for their capital—for example, to pay for a child's college tuition. Technicians do not care why market participants are buying or selling, just that they are doing so.

Some financial instruments have an associated income stream that contributes to the security's intrinsic value. Bonds have regular coupon payments, and equity shares may have underlying cash flows or dividend streams. A fundamental analyst can adjust these cash flows for risk and use standard time value of money techniques to determine a present value. Other assets, such as a bushel of wheat, gallon of crude oil, or ounce of silver, do not have underlying financial statements or an income stream, so valuation models cannot be used to derive their fundamental intrinsic values. For these assets, technical analysis is the only form of analysis possible. So, whereas fundamental analysis is widely used in the analysis of fixed-income and equity securities, technical analysis is widely used in the analysis of commodities, currencies, and futures.

Market participants attempt to anticipate economic developments and enter into trades to profit from them. Technicians believe that security price movements occur before fundamental developments unfold—certainly before they are reported. This belief is reflected in the fact that stock prices are one of the 12 components of the National Bureau of Economic Research's Index of Leading Economic Indicators. A key tenet of technical analysis is that the equity market moves roughly six months ahead of inflection points in the broad economy.

TECHNICAL AND FUNDAMENTAL ANALYSIS   Technical analysis and fundamental analysis are both useful and valid, but they approach the market in different ways. Technicians focus solely on analyzing markets and the trading of financial instruments. Fundamental analysis is a much wider field, encompassing financial and economic analysis as well as analysis of societal and political trends. Technicians analyze the result of this extensive fundamental analysis in terms of how it affects market prices.

---

[2] Akerlof and Shiller (2009).

A technician's analysis is derived solely from price and volume data, whereas a fundamental equity analyst analyzes a company and incorporates data that are external to the market and then uses this analysis to predict security price movements. As the quotation from Dow shown earlier illustrates, technical analysis assumes that all of the factors considered by a fundamental analyst are reflected in the price of a financial instrument through buying and selling activity.

A key distinction between technical analysis and fundamental analysis is that the technician has more concrete data, primarily price and volume data, to work with. The financial statements analyzed by fundamental analysts are not objective data but are the result of numerous estimates and assumptions that have been added together to arrive at the line items in the financial statements. Even the cash line on a balance sheet is subject to corporate management's opinion about which securities are liquid enough to be considered "cash." This opinion must be agreed to by auditors and, in many countries, regulators (who sometimes differ with the auditors). Financial statements are subject to restatements because of such issues as changes in accounting assumptions and even fraud. But the price and volume data used in technical analysis are objective. When the data become subject to analysis, however, both types of analysis become subjective because judgment is exercised when a technician analyzes a price chart and when a fundamental analyst analyzes an income statement.

Fundamental analysis can be considered to be the more theoretical approach because it seeks to determine the underlying long-term (or intrinsic) value of a security. Technical analysis can be considered to be the more practical because a technician studies the markets and financial instruments as they exist, even if trading activity appears, at times, to be irrational. Technicians seek to project the level at which a financial instrument *will* trade, whereas fundamental analysts seek to predict where it *should* trade.

Being a fundamental analyst can be lonely if the analyst is the first to arrive at a fundamental conclusion, even though it is correct, because deviations from intrinsic value can persist for long periods. The reason these deviations may persist is that it takes buying activity to raise (or lower) the price of a security in a freely traded market.

A drawback of technical analysis is that technicians are limited to studying market movements and do not use other predictive analytical methods, such as interviewing the customers of a subject company, to determine future demand for a company's products. Technicians study market trends and are mainly concerned with a security's price trend: Is the security trading up, down, or sideways? Trends are driven by collective investor psychology, however, and can change without warning. Additionally, it can take some time for a trend to become evident. Thus, technicians may make wrong calls and have to change their opinions. Technicians are better at identifying market moves after the moves are already under way.

Moreover, trends and patterns must be in place for some time before they are recognizable, so a key shortcoming of technical analysis is that it can be late in identifying changes in trends or patterns. This shortcoming mirrors a key shortcoming of fundamental analysis in that securities often overshoot fundamental fair values in an uptrend and undershoot fundamental fair values in a downtrend. Strictly relying on price targets obtained by fundamental analysis can lead to closing profitable investment positions too early because investors may irrationally bid securities prices well above or well below intrinsic value.

Fundamental analysis is a younger field than technical analysis because reliable fundamental data are a relatively new phenomenon. In contrast, the first recorded use of technical analysis was in Japan in the 1700s, where it was used to analyze trading in the rice market. The Japanese developed a detailed field of technical analysis with their own chart design and patterns. These tools were translated and widely understood outside Japan only in the 1980s.

Western use of technical analysis was pioneered by Dow, who was also the first editor of the *Wall Street Journal*, in the 1890s. At the time, publicly traded companies were under no requirement to release their financial information even to shareholders, and insider trading was common and legal. Dow created the Dow Jones Industrial Average and the Dow Jones Railroad Average (now the Transportation Average) as a proxy to gauge the health of the economy, because fundamental data were not available. By his logic, if industrial stocks were doing well, industrial companies themselves must be doing well and if railroad stocks were doing well, railroad companies must be doing well. And if both manufacturers and the companies that transported goods to market were prospering, the economy as a whole must be prospering.

Not until the Securities Exchange Act of 1934 were public companies in the United States required to regularly file financial statements that were available to the public. In that year, Benjamin Graham published his seminal work, *Security Analysis*, and three years later, he and several others founded one of the first societies devoted to fundamental analysis, the New York Society of Security Analysts.[3] Fundamental analysis quickly overtook technical analysis in terms of acceptance by practitioners, regulators, and academics.

Acceptance of technical analysis by practitioners was revived in the 1970s with the creation of the Market Technicians Association in New York and the International Federation of Technical Analysts a few years later. Only in the last decade, however, has the field started to achieve widespread acceptance by regulators and academics. An important impediment to acceptance by academics is the difficulty of capturing the subjectivity involved in technical analysis. The human brain can recognize, analyze, and interpret technical information that is difficult for statistical computer models to recognize and test.

Although technical analysis can be applied to any freely traded security, it does have its limits. In markets that are subject to large outside manipulation, the application of technical analysis is limited. For example, the central banks of many countries intervene in their currency markets from time to time to maintain exchange rate stability. Interestingly, traders claim to have been able to successfully predict interventions in some countries, especially those where the central bank is itself using technical analysis. Technical analysis is also limited in illiquid markets, where even modestly sized trades can have an inordinate impact on prices. For example, in considering a thinly traded American Depositary Receipt (ADR), analyzing the more

---

[3] The New York Society of Security Analysts was a successor to the New York Society of Financial Statisticians, which was founded in 1916.

heavily traded local security frequently yields a better analysis.[4] Another example of when technical analysis may give an incorrect reading is in the case of a company that has declared bankruptcy and announced that its shares will have zero value in a restructuring. A positive technical trend may appear in such cases as investors who hold short positions buy shares to close out their positions.

A good example of when technical analysis is a superior tool to fundamental analysis is in the case of securities fraud, such as occurred at Enron Corporation and WorldCom. These companies were issuing fraudulent financial statements, but many fundamental analysts continued to hold favorable views of the companies' equity securities even as the share prices declined. Simultaneously, a small group of investors came to the opposite view and expressed this view through high-volume sales of the securities. The result was clearly negative chart patterns that could then be discerned by technical analysis.

Technical Analysis Tools

The primary tools used in technical analysis are charts and indicators. Charts are the graphical display of price and volume data, and the display may be done in a number of ways. Charts are then subjected to various analyses, including the identification of trends, patterns, and cycles. Technical indicators include a variety of measures of relative price level—for example, price momentum, market sentiment, and funds flow. We will discuss charts first.

CHARTS Charts are an essential component of the technical analyst's toolkit. Charts provide information about past price behavior and provide a basis for inferring likely future price behavior. A variety of charts can be useful in studying the markets. The selection of the chart to use in technical analysis is determined by the intended purpose of the analysis.

Line Chart **Line charts** are familiar to all types of analysts and are a simple graphic display of price trends over time. Usually, the chart is a plot of data points, such as share price, with a line connecting these points. Line charts are typically drawn with closing prices as the data points. The vertical axis (y-axis) reflects price level, and the horizontal axis (x-axis) is time. Even though the line chart is the simplest chart, an analyst can quickly glean information from this chart.

The chart in Figure 14.1 is a quarterly chart of the FTSE 100 Index from 1984 through mid-2009. Up years and down years are clearly evident. The strong rally from 1984 through 1999 and the market decline from late 1999 to late 2002 are also clearly visible. The 2003–2007 rally did not exceed the high reached in 1999, which suggests that investors were not willing to pay as high a price for stocks on the London Stock Exchange during that rally as they were in the prior rally. This information provides a broad overview of investor sentiment and can lead to further analysis. Importantly, the analyst can access and analyze this information quickly.

---

[4] An American Depositary Receipt is a negotiable certificate issued by a depositary bank that represents ownership in a non-U.S. company's deposited equity (i.e., equity held in custody by the depositary bank in the company's home market).

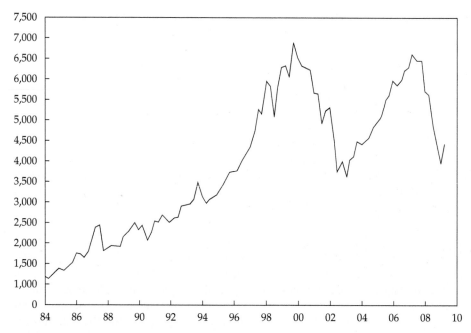

FIGURE 14.1   Line Chart: FTSE 100 Quarterly Price Data, 1984–2009 (price measured in British pounds sterling)

Collecting and analyzing the full array of data normally incorporated in fundamental analysis would take much longer.

Bar Chart   A line chart has one data point per time interval. A **bar chart**, in contrast, has four bits of data in each entry—the high and low price encountered during the time interval plus the opening and closing prices. Such charts can be constructed for any time period, but they are customarily constructed from daily data.

As Figure 14.2 shows, a vertical line connects the high and low price of the day; a crosshatch to the right indicates the closing price, and a crosshatch to the left indicates the opening price. The appeal of this chart is that the analyst immediately gets a sense of the nature of that day's trading. A short bar indicates little price

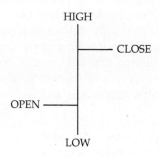

FIGURE 14.2   Bar Chart Notation

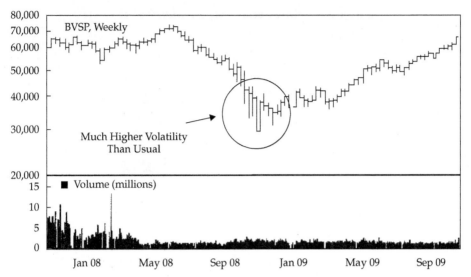

FIGURE 14.3   Bar Chart: Bovespa Index, November 2007–November 2009 (price in Brazilian reais)

movement during the day; that is, the high, low, and close were near the open-ing price. A long bar indicates a wide divergence between the high and the low for the day.

Figure 14.3 shows daily performance of the Brazilian Bovespa Index (BVSP) from late 2007 through late 2009. The top part provides the price open, close, high, and low; the bottom part shows volume. The downturn in the second half of 2008 is obvious, but also notable are the extreme price movements in the fourth quarter of 2008. There were 40 trading days from 29 September to 24 November. On 20 of those days, the closing value of the index changed from the previous close by at least 4 percent, a huge move by historical standards. During the same period, the average daily price range (high to low) was 7 percent, compared with 3.7 percent in the previous two months. This potentially important information would not be captured in a line chart.

Candlestick Chart   Candlestick charts trace their roots to Japan, where technical anal-ysis has been in use for centuries. Like a bar chart, a *candlestick chart* also provides four prices per data point entry: the opening and closing prices and the high and low prices during the period. As shown in Figure 14.4, a vertical line represents the range through which the security price traveled during the time period. The line is known as the wick or shadow. The body of the candle is shaded if the opening price was higher than the closing price, and the body is clear if the opening price was lower than the closing price.

The advantage of the candlestick chart over the bar chart is that price moves are much more visible in the candlestick chart, which allows faster analysis. The bar chart indicates market volatility only by the height of each bar, but in candlestick charts, the difference between opening and closing prices and their relationship to the highs and lows of the day are clearly apparent. Compare the sixth candle with

Each candle has two elements: body and wick/shadow

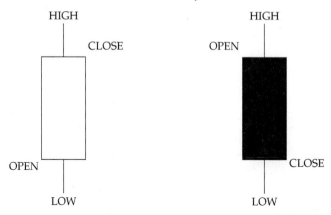

White body means market closed UP   Dark body means market closed DOWN
          Close > Open   Close < Open

FIGURE 14.4   Construction of a Candlestick Chart

the twelfth in Figure 14.5. In the sixth candle, the analyst can see significant volatility because the high of the day and low of the day are so far apart. The stock opened near the low of the day and closed near the high, suggesting a steady rally during the day. In contrast, the twelfth candle shows no difference between the high and low, and the shares opened and closed at the same price, creating a cross pattern. In Japanese terminology used in candlestick charting, this pattern is called a doji. The doji signifies that after a full day of trading, the positive price influence of buyers and the negative price influence of sellers exactly counteracted each other, which tells the analyst that this market is in balance. If a doji occurs at the end of a long uptrend or downtrend, it signals that the trend will probably reverse.

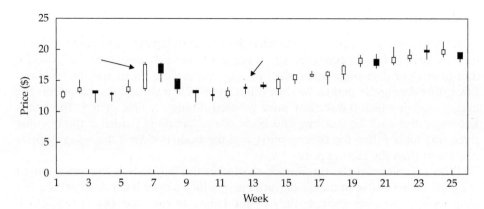

FIGURE 14.5   Candlestick Chart: Companhia Vale do Rio Doce, January 1–June 15, 2009 (prices in U.S. dollars)

Point and Figure Chart Point and figure charts were widely used in the United States in the early 1900s and were favored because they were easy to create and update manually in the era before computers. As with any technical analysis tool, these charts can be used with equities, fixed-income securities, commodities, or foreign exchange.

Where the point and figure chart originated is unclear; the chart is referred to in a number of books in the United States dating back to 1898. The methodology evolved until 1934 when the first book was published on the topic: *The Point and Figure Method of Anticipating Stock Price Movements* by Victor de Villiers and Owen Taylor. With the advent of powerful charting software and Internet websites, complex chart types, such as the candlestick chart, have become more popular. But point and figure charts still offer tremendous value if one knows their limitations and their advantages. The key reason this knowledge is necessary, as explained next, is that point and figure charts are constructed differently from other charts; they have a clear focus on entry and exit levels but no focus on holding periods.

As illustrated in Figure 14.6, a point and figure chart is drawn on a grid and consists of columns of X's alternating with columns of O's. Neither time nor volume is represented on this type of chart, and *the horizontal axis represents the number of changes in price, not time.* Movement along the horizontal axis does reflect the passage of time, but not in any uniform fashion. The analyst makes entries on a point and figure chart only when the price changes by the "box size," which is explained below. This lack of a normal time dimension is perhaps the most unusual characteristic of a point and figure chart.

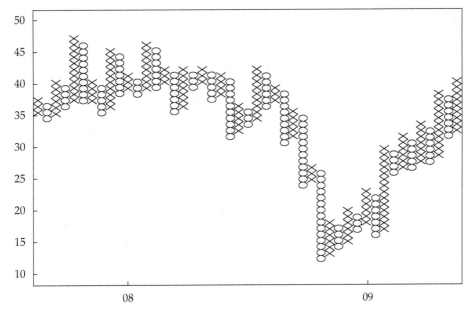

FIGURE 14.6 Point and Figure Chart: Wharf Holdings Daily Price Chart, 2007–2009 (in Hong Kong dollars)

Note: The box size is HK$1, and the reversal size is three.

To construct a point and figure chart, the analyst must determine both the box size and the reversal size. Box size refers to the change in price represented by the height of each box (boxes are generally square, but the width has no meaning). In Figure 14.6, the box size is HK$1. The reversal size is used to determine when to create a new column. In Figure 14.6, the reversal size is three, meaning a reversal in price of three or more boxes.

Although a point and figure chart can be constructed in several ways, these charts are always drawn on graph paper to facilitate seeing the "columns and rows" nature of the data. The vertical axis measures *discrete increments of price*. For example, an analyst in Europe might draw an h1 chart, an h2 chart, or any other increment. In an h1 chart, boxes would be h1 apart (e.g., h40, h41, h42), whereas in an h2 chart they would be h2 apart (h40, h42, h44). The most commonly used box size is 1 unit of currency, which is used when prices range from 20 to 100 per share of the currency.

The next decision the technician needs to make is the reversal size. The most common size is three, meaning a reversal in price of three or more boxes (h3 in the case of a box size of h1). This use of a multibox reversal helps eliminate "noise" in the price data. (*Noise* refers to short-term trading volatility that does not alter the long-term trend of the security.)

In a point and figure chart, X represents an increase in price and O represents a decline in price. In constructing a chart, the technician draws an X in a column of boxes every time the security price closes up by the amount of the box size. (Ideally, all security prices are considered on an intraday basis, but this practice has given way to using closing prices only.) If the price increases by twice the box size, the technician draws two X's to fill in two boxes, one on top of the other. The technician fills in more boxes for larger price moves. The resulting column starts at the opening price level and extends to the closing price level. As long as the security keeps closing at higher prices, the technician keeps filling in boxes with X's, which makes the column higher and higher. If the price does not increase by at least the box size, no indication is made on the chart. Thus, in some cases, the chart is not updated for long periods, but no indication of this passage of time is made on the chart.

The reversal size determines when to create a new column. In the case of an h1 box size, and three-box reversal size, a decline of h3 or more would result in the technician shifting to the next column over and beginning a column of O's. The first box to be filled in is to the right and below the highest X in the prior column. The technician then fills in an O to bring the column down to the price level at the close. Again, each filled-in box (if the box size is h1) represents an h1 decline in the security price. As long as the downtrend continues, without an h3 increase in price, the technician continues adding O's to the column below the prior O's. A reversal in the downtrend by at least the amount of the reversal size prompts the technician to move to the next column and begin drawing a series of X's again. Computer technology makes the process easy, but many technicians prefer to keep point and figure charts on their wall and update them manually because doing so provides a vivid reminder of the market trend.

Point and figure charts are particularly useful for making trading decisions because they clearly illustrate price levels that may signal the end of a decline or advance. They also clearly show price levels at which a security may frequently trade. In using the point size and reversal size to make trading decisions, for uptrends, or columns of X's, the practitioner would maintain long positions. The reversal size could be considered the amount of loss that would prompt the closing of a long position and the establishment of a new short position. The larger the reversal size, the fewer columns in the chart and the longer uptrends and downtrends will run.

The box size can be varied in relation to the security price. For a security with a very low price—say, below h5—an h1 box size might mean few or no updates on the chart because the price would only rarely change by this amount. Thus, the technician could reduce the box size to cents. For highly priced securities, much larger box sizes could be used. The reversal size is a multiple of the box size, so if the box size is changed, the reversal size changes. Practitioners who want fewer columns or trade signals can use a large reversal size.

Analysis of a point and figure chart is relatively straightforward as long as the technician understands its construction and limitations. The chart is relatively simple, and repeated high and low prices are evident. Congestion areas, where a security trades up and down in a narrow range, are evidenced by a series of short columns of X's and O's spanning roughly the same price range. Major, sustained price moves are represented by long columns of X's (when prices are moving up) or O's (when prices are moving down).

Scale For any chart—line, bar, or candlestick—the vertical axis can be constructed with either a **linear scale** (also known as an arithmetic scale) or a **logarithmic scale**, depending on how you want to view the data. With a logarithmic scale, equal vertical distances on the chart correspond to an equal percentage change. A logarithmic scale is appropriate when the data move through a range of values representing several orders of magnitude (e.g., from 10 to 10,000); a linear scale is better suited for narrower ranges (e.g., prices from $35 to $50). The share price history of a particular company, for instance, is usually best suited to a linear scale because the data range is usually narrow.

The horizontal axis shows the passage of time. The appropriate time interval depends on the nature of the underlying data and the specific use of the chart. An active trader, for instance, may find 10-minute, 5-minute, or even tick-by-tick data useful, but other technical analysts may prefer daily or weekly data. In general, the greater the volatility of the data, the greater the likelihood that an analyst can find useful information in more-frequent data sampling.

Consider Figures 14.7 and 14.8, which both show the yearly history of the Dow Jones Industrial Average (DJIA) from 1928 to 2010. Plotting the index on a linear scale, as in Figure 14.7, makes it difficult to gather much information from the first 50 years of the data series. Analysts can see a slight uptrend but not much else. The eye is drawn to the bull market of the 1980s, the subsequent dot-com bubble, and the recent era of the subprime crisis. When plotted on a logarithmic scale, as in Figure 14.8, however, many people would find that the data tell a more comprehensive story. The Great Depression of the 1930s stands out, but over the following 75 years, the data follow a relatively stable upward trend.

Volume Volume is an important characteristic that is included at the bottom of many charts; see, for example, Figure 14.3. Volume is used to assess the strength or conviction of buyers and sellers in determining a security's price. For example, on a daily

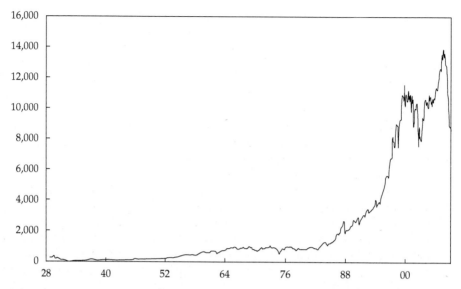

FIGURE 14.7   Dow Jones Industrial Average on Linear Scale, 1928–2010 (in U.S. dollars)

price chart, below the price section would be a column chart showing the volume traded for that day.

Some technicians consider volume information to be crucial. If volume increases during a time frame in which price is also increasing, that combination is considered positive and the two indicators are said to "confirm" each other. The signal would be interpreted to mean that over time, more and more investors are buying the

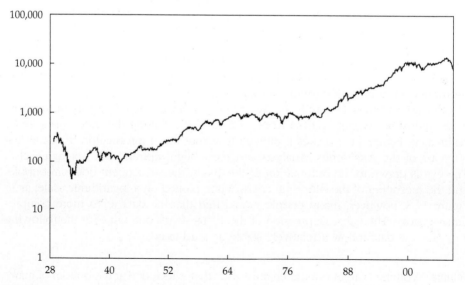

FIGURE 14.8   Dow Jones Industrial Average on Logarithmic Scale, 1928–2010 (in U.S. dollars)

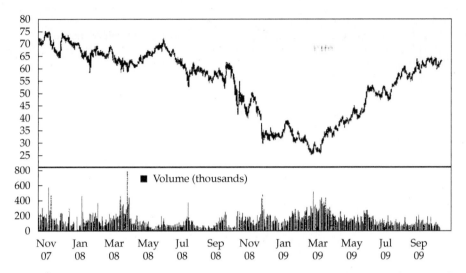

FIGURE 14.9   Daily Candlestick Price Chart and Volume Bar Chart: TD Bank, November 2007–November 2009 (price in Canadian dollars)

financial instrument and they are doing so at higher and higher prices. This pattern is considered a positive technical development.

Conversely, if volume and price diverge—for example, if a stock's price rises while its volume declines—the implication is that fewer and fewer market participants are willing to buy that stock at the new price. If this trend in volume continues, the price rally will soon end because demand for the security at higher prices will cease. Figure 14.9 shows a chart for Toronto-Dominion Bank (TD Bank) with volume displayed separately.

Time Intervals   Most of the chart examples in this chapter are daily price charts in that they show the price and volume on a daily basis. Daily frequency is not required, however, because charts can be constructed by using any time interval. For short-term trading, the analyst can create charts with one-minute or shorter intervals. For long-term investing, the analyst can use weekly, monthly, or even annual intervals. The same analytical approach applies irrespective of the time interval. Using long intervals allows the analyst to chart longer time periods than does using short time intervals for the simple reason that long intervals contain fewer data points, so a longer time frame can be presented on the chart. Using short intervals allows the analyst to see more detail. A useful step for many analysts is to begin the analysis of a security with the chart for a long time frame, such as a weekly or monthly chart, and then construct charts with shorter and shorter time intervals, such as daily or hourly charts.

Relative Strength Analysis   **Relative strength analysis** is widely used to compare the performance of a particular asset, such as a common stock, with that of some benchmark—such as, in the case of common stocks, the FTSE 100, the Nikkei 225, or the S&P 500 Index—or the performance of another security. The intent is to show

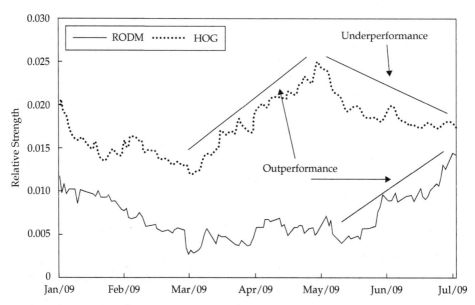

FIGURE 14.10   Relative Strength Analysis: HOG versus the S&P 500 and RODM versus the
S&P 500, January–June 2009

out- or underperformance of the individual issue relative to some other index or
asset. Typically, the analyst prepares a line chart of the ratio of two prices, with
the asset under analysis as the numerator and with the benchmark or other security as the denominator. A rising line shows the asset is performing better than the
index or other stock; a declining line shows the opposite. A flat line shows neutral
performance.

Suppose a private investor is researching two investment ideas she read about.
Harley-Davidson Motor Company (HOG) is a well-known motorcycle company; Rodman and Renshaw (RODM) is a small investment bank. The investor wants to determine which of these two has been the stronger performer (relative to the S&P 500)
over the past few months. Figure 14.10 shows relative strength lines for the two
stocks for the first six months of 2009. Each point on the relative strength plot is
simply the ratio of a share price to the S&P 500. For example, on March 9, 2009,
HOG closed at US$8.42 and the S&P 500 closed at $676.53. The relative strength data
point is, therefore, 8.42/676.53, or 0.0124. On 27 April, HOG closed at US$19.45, with
the S&P 500 at $857.51. The relative strength value is 19.45/857.51, or 0.0227, nearly
double the March 9, value.

The units on the vertical axis are not significant; the ratio is a function of the
relative prices of the assets under consideration. The important information is how
the ratio has changed. This type of chart allows an analyst to make a visual determination of that change. As Figure 14.10 illustrates, Harley-Davidson was a strong
performer in March and April but lagged the index beginning in May. In contrast, the
stock of Rodman and Renshaw began a significant rise in mid-May that outperformed
the market average.

TREND   The concept of a **trend** is perhaps the most important aspect of technical analysis. Trend analysis is based on the observation that market participants tend to act in herds and that trends tend to stay in place for some time. A security can be considered to be in an upward trend, a downward trend, a sideways trend, or no apparent trend. Not all securities are in a trend, and little useful forecasting information can be gleaned from technical analysis when a security is not in a trend. Not every chart will have obvious or clear implications, so the analyst must avoid the temptation to force a conclusion from every chart and thus reach a wrong interpretation.

An uptrend for a security is when the price goes to higher highs and higher lows. As the security moves up in price, each subsequent new high is higher than the prior high and each time there is a **retracement**, which is a reversal in the movement of the security's price, it must stop at a higher low than the prior lows in the trend period. To draw an uptrend line, a technician draws a line connecting the lows of the price chart. Major breakdowns in price, however, when the price drops through and below the trendline by a significant amount (many technicians use 5–10 percent below the trendline) indicate that the uptrend is over and may signal a further decline in the price. Minor breakthroughs below previous lows simply call for the line to be moderately adjusted over time. Time is also a consideration in trends: The longer the security price stays below the trendline, the more meaningful the breakdown is considered to be.

In an uptrend, the forces of demand are greater than the forces of supply. So, traders are willing to pay higher and higher prices for the same asset over time. Presumably, the strong demand indicates that investors believe the intrinsic value of the security is increasing.

A downtrend is when a security makes lower lows and lower highs. As the security moves down in price, each subsequent new high must be lower than the prior high and each time there is a retracement, it must stop at a lower low than the prior lows in the trend period. To draw a downtrend line, a technician draws a line connecting the highs of the price chart. Major breakouts above the downtrend line (e.g., 5–10 percent) indicate that the downtrend is over and a rise in the security's price may occur. And as with an uptrend, the longer the security price stays above the trendline, the more meaningful the breakout is considered to be.

In a downtrend, supply is overwhelming demand. Over time, sellers are willing to accept lower and lower prices to exit long positions or enter new short positions. Both motives of the sellers generally indicate deteriorating investor sentiment about the asset. However, selling may be prompted by factors not related to the fundamental or intrinsic value of the stock. For example, investors may be forced to sell to meet margin calls in their portfolios. From a purely technical standpoint, the reason is irrelevant. The downtrend is assumed to continue until contrary technical evidence appears. Combining fundamental analysis with technical analysis in such a case, however, might reveal a security that has attractive fundamentals but a currently negative technical position. In uptrends, however, a security with an attractive technical position but unattractive fundamentals is rare because most buying activity is driven by traders who expect the security price to increase in the future. The rare exception is covering short positions after a sizable decline in the share price.

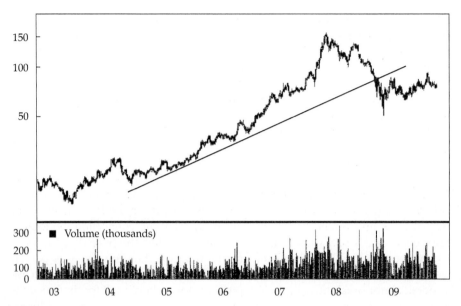

FIGURE 14.11   Trend Analysis: China Mobile Weekly Price Chart, 2002–2010 (prices in Hong Kong dollars)

A security may trade in a fairly narrow range, moving sideways on the price chart without much upward or downward movement. This pattern indicates a relative balance between supply and demand. A technical analyst may not expect to profit from long or short trades in such securities but might devise profitable option strategies for short-term investors with the ability to accept the risks.

Figure 14.11 shows the application of trend analysis. Depicted is an uptrend line for the shares of China Mobile Limited. Note that through late 2007, every rally took the shares to a new high whereas sell-offs stopped at increasingly higher levels. The first sign of trouble came in the spring of 2008 when the rally terminated at a lower price point than the prior rally of late 2007. This movement was followed by the shares breaking through the trendline.

The chart in Figure 14.11 covers roughly seven years and would most likely be used by investors with a long time horizon. Investors with a shorter horizon might use a chart with a shorter time frame and would thus obtain a different trendline as well as a different trendline breakdown.

Two concepts related to trend are support and resistance. **Support** is defined as a low price range in which buying activity is sufficient to stop the decline in price. It is the opposite of **resistance**, which is a price range in which selling is sufficient to stop the rise in price. The psychology behind the concepts of support and resistance is that investors have come to a collective consensus about the price of a security. Support and resistance levels can be sloped lines, as in trendlines, or horizontal lines.

A key tenet of support and resistance as a part of technical analysis is the **change in polarity principle**, which states that once a support level is breached, it becomes a resistance level. The same holds true for resistance levels; once breached, they become support levels. For example, if the price of a security never rises above SFr10 over a long period of time and begins to decline each time it reaches this level

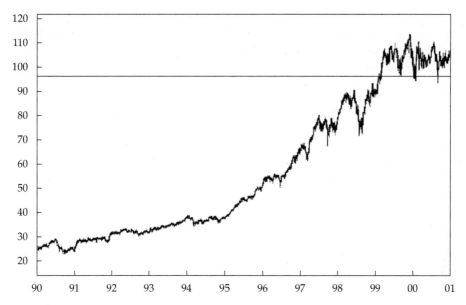

FIGURE 14.12   Support Level: DJIA Weekly Price Chart, 1990–2001 (price in U.S. dollars ÷ 100)

but then finally breaks through this level by a significant amount, the point to which the price rises becomes a support level.

Support and resistance levels are commonly round numbers. Support indicates that at some price level, investors consider a security to be an attractive investment and are willing to buy, even in the wake of a sharp decline (and for resistance, at some level, investors are not willing to buy, even in an uptrend). The fact that these price points tend to be round numbers strongly suggests that human sentiment is at work.

One of the most widely publicized examples of support and resistance is when the DJIA broke through the 10,000 mark in 1999, shown in Figure 14.12. Previously, 10,000 had been viewed as a resistance line, but from 1999 through the end of the chart in 2001, 10,000 served as a support level.

CHART PATTERNS   Chart patterns are formations that appear in price charts that create some type of recognizable shape. Common patterns appear repeatedly and often lead to similar subsequent price movements. Thus, the identification and analysis of chart patterns is a common aspect of technical analysis used to predict security prices. An important connection to understand is that patterns form as a result of the behavior of market participants and that these patterns represent graphical depictions of the collective psychology of the market at a given time.

The recurring patterns that appear in charts can be used as a basis for market forecasting. The reason chart patterns have predictive value is that they are graphic representations of human trading activity and human behavior is frequently repeated, especially trading activity that is driven by fear (in market sell-offs) or hope and greed (as evidenced in bubbles—that is, rallies that extend well beyond valuation levels that would be derived by fundamental values). An example of a rally driven by greed is the recent real estate bubble, which took home prices to unsustainably high levels. This bubble started a few years after the Internet stock bubble of the 1990s, which also took prices to unsustainably high levels. In bubbles, investors, driven by hope and greed, drive the price of an asset to irrationally high levels, in the expectation that another buyer will be willing to pay an even higher price for the asset. The housing bubble was notable because it so closely followed the Internet stock bubble, despite all that had been written about the "irrational exuberance" of the Internet bubble of the 1990s.

Chart patterns can be divided into two categories: **reversal patterns** and **continuation patterns**. These terms refer to the trend for the security in question prior to the formation of the pattern. The most important concept to understand in using chart patterns is that without a clear trend in place prior to the pattern, the pattern has no predictive value. This aspect is frequently forgotten by investors who are so eager to identify and use patterns that they forget the proper application of charts.

Reversal Patterns   As the name implies, a reversal pattern signals the end of a trend, a change in direction of the financial instrument's price. Evidence that the trend is about to change direction is obviously important, so reversal patterns are noteworthy.

Head and Shoulders   Perhaps the most widely recognized reversal pattern is the **head-and-shoulders pattern**. The pattern consists of three segments. Volume is an important characteristic in interpreting this pattern. Because a head-and-shoulders pattern indicates a trend reversal, a clear trend must exist prior to the formation of the pattern in order for the pattern to have predictive validity. For a head-and-shoulders pattern, the prior trend must be an uptrend. Later, we will discuss the *inverse* head-and-shoulders pattern (preceded by a downtrend).

Figure 14.13 depicts a head-and-shoulders pattern for Marvell Technology Group during 2006. The three parts of the pattern are as follows:

Left shoulder: This part appears to show a strong rally, with the slope of the rally being greater than the prior uptrend, on strong volume. The rally then reverses back to the price level where it started, forming an inverted V pattern, but on lower volume.

Head: The head is a more pronounced version of the left shoulder. A rally following the first shoulder takes the security to a higher high than the left shoulder by a significant enough margin to be clearly evident on the price chart. Volume is typically lower in this rally, however, than in the one that formed the first, upward side of the left shoulder. This second rally also fails, with price falling back to the same level at which the left shoulder began and ended. This price level is called the neckline. This price level also will be below the uptrend line formed by connecting the low prices in the uptrend preceding the beginning of the head-and-shoulders pattern. This head pattern is the first signal that the rally may be coming to an end and that a reversal may be starting.

Right shoulder: The right shoulder is a mirror image (or close to a mirror image) of the left shoulder but on lower volume, signifying less buying enthusiasm. The price rallies up to roughly the same level as the first shoulder, but the rally reverses at a lower high price than the rally that formed the head.

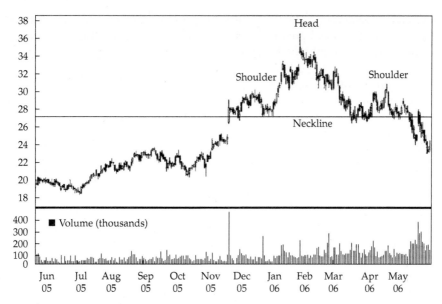

FIGURE 14.13 Head-and-Shoulders Pattern: Marvell Technology Daily Price Chart, June 2005–June 2006 (price in U.S. dollars ÷ 100)

Rarely will an analyst see a perfectly formed head-and-shoulders pattern; variations include two tops on the shoulders or on the head. The head, however, should rise to a higher price level than either shoulder, whereas the shoulders should be roughly symmetrical. In terms of the neckline price level, the first rally should begin at this level and the left shoulder and head should also decline to roughly this level. But necklines may not always form exactly horizontal lines. These imperfect variations make this (and other) technical patterns difficult for quantitative analysts or academicians to model, but the human brain can detect the pattern even if it is imperfectly formed.

Volume is important in analyzing head-and-shoulders patterns. A new high in price at the top of the head without a new high in volume signals fewer bullish market participants. When one indicator is making a new high (or low) but another is not, this situation is called divergence. In divergence, the right shoulder will have even lower volume, signaling that buying interest or demand is tapering off and will soon be overwhelmed by supply. The result will be a price decline.

Once the head-and-shoulders pattern has formed, the expectation is that the share price will decline down through the neckline price. Technicians tend to use filtering rules to make sure that a clear breakdown of the neckline has occurred. These rules may take the form of waiting to trade until the price falls to a meaningful level below the neckline (3 percent or 5 percent are commonly used) and/or a time limit for the price to remain below the neckline before trading; when a daily price chart is used, the rule may be several days to a week. Prices commonly rebound to the neckline levels, even after a decline has exceeded the filter levels. Prices generally stop, however, at or around the neckline. The neckline was a support level, and under the change in polarity principle, once a support level is breached, it becomes a resistance level.

Inverse Head-and-Shoulders   The head-and-shoulders pattern can also form upside down and act as a reversal pattern for a preceding downtrend. The three parts of the inverse head-and-shoulders are as follows:

Left shoulder: This shoulder appears to show a strong decline, with the slope of the decline greater than the prior downtrend, on strong volume. The rally then reverses back to the price level where it started, forming a V pattern, but on lower volume.

Head: The head is a more pronounced version of the left shoulder. Another decline follows but on diminishing volume, which takes the price to a lower low than the prior shoulder by a significant enough margin that it is clearly evident on the price chart. This second decline also reverses, with price rising to the same level at which the left shoulder began and ended. This price level, the neckline, will also be above the uptrend line formed by connecting the high prices in the downtrend preceding the beginning of the inverse head-and-shoulders pattern. This pattern is the first signal that the decline may be coming to an end and that a reversal may be near.

Right shoulder: The right shoulder is roughly a mirror image of the left shoulder but on lower volume, signifying less selling enthusiasm. The price declines down to roughly the same level as the first shoulder, but the rally reverses at a higher low price than the rally that formed the head.

Setting Price Targets with Head-and-Shoulders Pattern   As with all technical patterns, the head-and-shoulders pattern must be analyzed from the perspective of the security's long-term price trend. The rally that happened before the formation of the pattern must be large enough for there to be something to reverse. The stronger and more pronounced the rally was, the stronger and more pronounced the reversal is likely to be. Similarly, once the neckline is breached, the security is expected to decline by the same amount as the change in price from the neckline to the top of the head. If the preceding rally started at a price higher than the neckline, however, the correction is unlikely to bring the price lower than the price level at the start of the rally. Because a head-and-shoulders formation is a bearish indicator (i.e., a technician would expect the previously established uptrend to end and a downtrend to commence), a technician would seek to profit by shorting the security under analysis. When attempting to profit from the head-and-shoulders pattern, a technician will often use the price differences between the head and the neckline to set a price target, which is the price at which the technician anticipates closing the investment position. The price target for the head-and-shoulders pattern is calculated as follows:

$$\text{Price target} = \text{Neckline} - (\text{Head} - \text{Neckline})$$

For example, in Figure 14.14, the high price reached at the top of the head is roughly \$37 and the neckline formed at roughly \$27 for a difference of \$10. So a technician would expect the price to decline to a level \$10 below the neckline, or to \$17; that is,

$$\text{Price target} = \$27 - (\$37 - \$27) = \$17$$

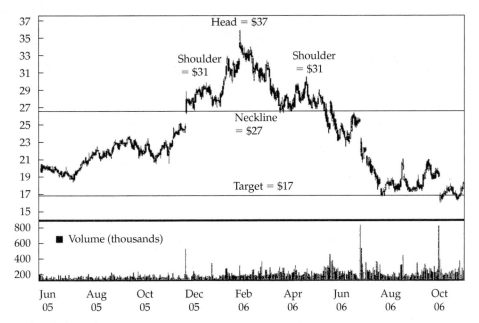

FIGURE 14.14   Calculating Price Target: Marvell Technology Daily Price Chart, June 2005–November 2006 (price in U.S. dollars)

EXAMPLE 14.1   Determining a Price Target from a Head-and-Shoulders Pattern

Danielle Waterhouse is the technical analyst at Kanektok Securities. One of the companies her firm follows is LPA Petroleum. Waterhouse believes that a graph of LPA's share prices over the past six months reveals a classic head-and-shoulders pattern. The share price peaked at US$108, and she estimates the neckline at US$79. At today's close, the shares traded at US$78. Based on the head-and-shoulders pattern, what price target should Waterhouse estimate?

Solution: Waterhouse estimates the neckline at US$79, which is US$108 minus US$79, or US$29 lower than the head. Her price target is thus US$79 minus US$29, which is US$50. Waterhouse would attempt to sell LPA short at today's price of US$78 and anticipate closing the position at US$50 for a profit of US$28 per share (not accounting for transaction costs).

Setting Price Targets with Inverse Head-and-Shoulders Pattern   Calculating price targets for inverse head-and-shoulders patterns is similar to the process for head-and-shoulders patterns, but in this case, because the pattern predicts the end of a downtrend, the technician calculates how high the price is expected to rise once it breaches the neckline. Figure 14.15 illustrates an inverse head-and-shoulders pattern.

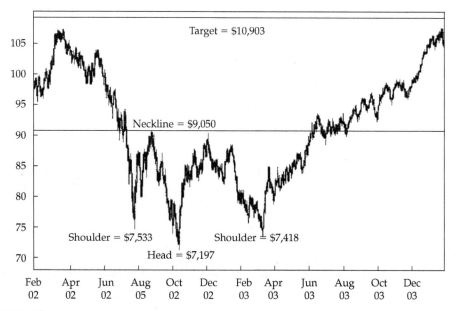

FIGURE 14.15   Calculating Price Target for Inverse Head-and-Shoulders Pattern: DJIA Daily Price Chart, February 2002–January 2004 (price in U.S. dollars ÷ 100)

EXAMPLE 14.2   Determining a Price Target from a Double-Top Pattern

Richard Dupuis is a technician who trades Eurodollar futures for his own account. He analyzes charts based on one-minute time intervals looking for short-term trading opportunities. Eurodollar futures contracts have been trending upward most of the morning, but Dupuis now observes what he believes is a double-top pattern: After peaking at US\$97.03, the futures contract price fell to US\$96.42, climbed again to US\$97.02, and then started a decline. Because of the double top, Dupuis anticipates a reversal from the uptrend to a downtrend. Dupuis decides to open a short position to capitalize on the anticipated trend reversal. What price target should Dupuis estimate for closing the position?

Solution: Dupuis estimates the price target as \$96.42 – (\$97.02 – \$96.42) = \$95.82.

For an inverse head-and-shoulders pattern, the formula is similar to a head-and-shoulders pattern:

$$\text{Price target} = \text{Neckline} + (\text{Neckline} - \text{Head})$$

For example, in the price chart in Figure 14.15, the low price reached at the bottom of the head is roughly US\$7,197 and the neckline formed at roughly US\$9,050. The target can thus be found as \$9,0501(9,050 – \$7,197) = \$10,903. In this case, a technician might have taken a long position in the summer of 2003 with the hope of eventually exiting the position at about US\$10,903 for a profit.

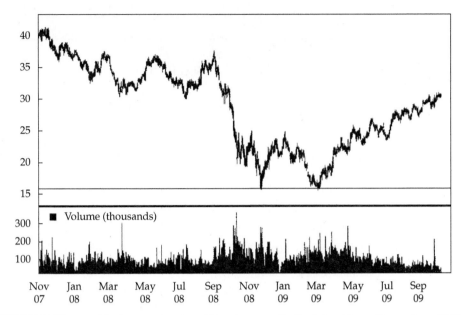

FIGURE 14.16 Double-Bottom Pattern: Time Warner Daily Price Chart, November 2007–October 2009 (price in U.S. dollars)

Double Tops and Bottoms   A **double top** is when an uptrend reverses twice at roughly the same high price level. Typically, volume is lower on the second high than on the first high, signaling a diminishing of demand. The longer the time is between the two tops and the deeper the sell-off is after the first top, the more significant the pattern is considered to be. Price targets can be calculated from this pattern in a manner similar to the calculation for the head-and-shoulders pattern. For a double top, price is expected to decline below the low of the valley between the two tops by at least the distance from the valley low to the high of the double tops.

Double bottoms are formed when the price reaches a low, rebounds, and then sells off back to the first low level. Figure 14.16 depicts a double bottom pattern for Time Warner. Technicians use the double bottom to predict a change from a downtrend to an uptrend in security prices. For double bottoms, the price is expected to appreciate above the peak between the two bottoms by at least the distance from the valley lows to the peak.

The reason these patterns are significant is that they show that at some price point, investors step in to reverse trends that are under way. For an uptrend, a double top implies that at some price point, enough traders are willing to either sell positions (or enter new short positions) that their activities overwhelm and reverse the uptrend created by demand for the shares. A reasonable conclusion is that this price level has been fundamentally derived and that it represents the intrinsic value of the security that is the consensus of investors. With double bottoms, if a security ceases to decline at the same price point on two separate occasions, the analyst can conclude that the market consensus is that at that price point, the security is now cheap enough that it is an attractive investment.

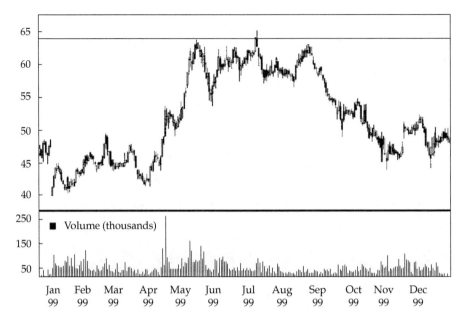

FIGURE 14.17   Triple-Top Pattern: Rockwell Automation Daily Price Chart, 1999 (price in U.S. dollars)

Triple Tops and Bottoms   **Triple tops** consist of three peaks at roughly the same price level, and **triple bottoms** consist of three troughs at roughly the same price level. A triple top for Rockwell Automation during 1999 is shown in Figure 14.17.

One of the challenges in double-top and triple-top patterns, and one of the valid criticisms of technical analysis in general, is that an analyst cannot know which pattern will result until after the fact. For example, after the broad equity market sell-off in the first quarter of 2009, a number of investment professionals were quoted as calling for a "retest of the lows"—in technical terms, a double bottom.

There is no evidence that market corrections (or rallies) must end with a double bottom (or double top in the case of an uptrend), and there is no generally accepted technical theory that predicts whether a low will be repeated once or even twice before a reversal occurs. A double bottom is considered to be a more significant pattern than a single bottom because traders have stepped in on two occasions to halt declines. However, traders have no way to determine whether a double top or bottom will be followed by a third top or bottom. Triple tops and triple bottoms are rare, but when they occur, they are more significant reversal patterns than double tops or double bottoms. On three separate occasions, traders stepped in to sell or buy shares with enough volume to end a rally or decline under way at the time. Nevertheless, the greater the number of times the price reverses at the same level, and the greater the time interval over which this pattern occurs, the greater the significance of the pattern.

Continuation Patterns   A continuation pattern is used to predict the resumption of a market trend that was in place prior to the formation of a pattern. From a supply-and-demand standpoint, a continuation pattern indicates a change in ownership from one group of investors to another. For example, if a positive trend was in place prior to a pattern and then one group of investors begins selling, the negative impact on price is quickly offset by other investors buying, so the forces of supply and demand go back and forth in terms of their impact on price. But neither has an overwhelming advantage. This type of pattern is often called "a healthy correction" because the long-term market trend does not change and because while one set of investors is seeking to exit, they are replaced by another set of investors willing to take their positions at roughly the same share price.

Triangles   **Triangle patterns** are a type of continuation pattern. They come in three forms, symmetrical triangles, ascending triangles, and descending triangles. A triangle pattern forms as the range between high and low prices narrows, visually forming a triangle. In old terminology, triangles were referred to as "coils" (which was also synonymous with "springs") because a triangle was considered analogous to a spring being wound up tighter and tighter and storing energy that would at some point be released. In a triangle, a trendline connects the highs and a trendline connects the lows. As the distance between the highs and lows narrows, the trendlines meet, forming a triangle. In a daily price chart, a triangle pattern usually forms over a period of several weeks.

In an ascending triangle, as shown in Figure 14.18, the trendline connecting the high prices is horizontal and the trendline connecting the low prices forms an uptrend. What this pattern means is that market participants are selling the stock at the same price level over a period of time, putting a halt to rallies at the same price point, but that buyers are getting more and more bullish and stepping in at increasingly higher prices to halt sell-offs instead of waiting for further price declines. An ascending triangle typically forms in an uptrend. The horizontal line represents sellers taking profits at around the same price point, presumably because they believe that this price represents the fundamental, intrinsic value of the security. The fact that the rally continues beyond the triangle may be a bullish signal; it means that another set of investors is presumably willing to buy at an even higher price because their analysis suggests the intrinsic value of the security is higher. Alternatively, the

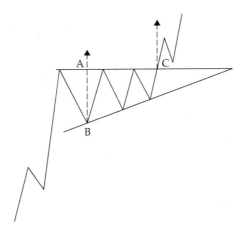

FIGURE 14.18   Ascending Triangle Pattern

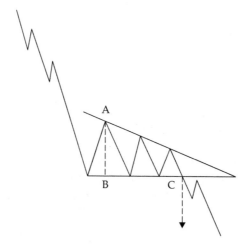

FIGURE 14.19   Descending Triangle

fundamental facts themselves may have changed; that is, the security's fundamental value may be increasing over time. The technician does not care which explanation is true; the technician is relying solely on the information conveyed by the security price itself, not the underlying reason.

In the descending triangle, shown in Figure 14.19, the low prices form a horizontal trendline and the high prices form a series of lower and lower highs. Typically, a descending triangle will form in a downtrend. At some point in the sell-offs, buyers appear with enough demand to halt sell-offs each time they occur, at around the same price. Again, this phenomenon may be the result of fundamental analysts believing that the security has reached a price where it represents a significant discount to its intrinsic value and these analysts step in and buy. As the triangle forms, each rally ceases at a lower and lower high price point, suggesting that the selling demand is exerting greater price influence than the buying demand.

In a symmetrical triangle, the trendline formed by the highs angles down and the trendline formed by the lows angles up, both at roughly the same angle, forming a symmetrical pattern. Figure 14.20 contains a symmetrical triangle formed by the price for Transocean in early 2000. What this triangle indicates is that buyers are becoming more bullish while, simultaneously, sellers are becoming more bearish, so they are moving toward a point of consensus. Because the sellers are often dominated by long investors exiting positions (as opposed to short sellers creating new short positions), the pressure to sell diminishes once the sellers have sold the security. Thus, the pattern ends in the same direction as the trend that preceded it, either uptrend or downtrend.

The term "measuring implication" refers to the height of a triangle, as illustrated with a dark vertical bar in Figure 14.20. The measuring implication is derived by calculating the difference in price from the two trendlines at the start of the triangle. Once the pattern is broken and the price breaks through one of the trendlines that form the triangle, the analyst expects the price to move by at least the amount of the breakthrough above or below the trendline. Typically, price breaks out of a triangle pattern between halfway and three-quarters of the way through the pattern. The

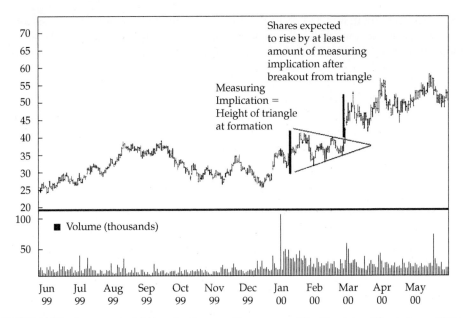

FIGURE 14.20 Symmetrical Triangle Pattern: Transocean Weekly Price Chart, June 1999–June 2000 (price in U.S. dollars)

longer the triangle pattern persists, the more volatile and sustained the subsequent price movement is likely to be.

Rectangle Pattern A rectangle pattern is a continuation pattern formed by two parallel trendlines, one formed by connecting the high prices during the pattern, and the other formed by the lows. Figure 14.21 shows two rectangle patterns. As is the case with other patterns, the rectangle pattern is a graphical representation of what

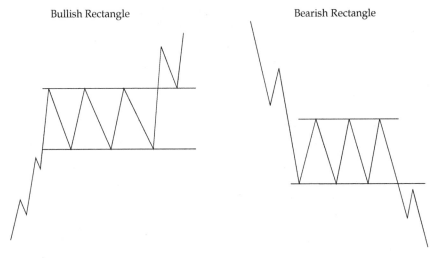

FIGURE 14.21 Rectangle Patterns

has been occurring in terms of collective market sentiment. The horizontal resistance line that forms the top of the rectangle shows that investors are repeatedly selling shares at a specific price level, bringing rallies to an end. The horizontal support line forming the bottom of the rectangle indicates that traders are repeatedly making large enough purchases at the same price level to reverse declines. The support level in a bullish rectangle is natural because the long-term trend in the market is bullish. The resistance line may simply represent investors taking profits. Conversely, in a bearish rectangle, the support level may represent investors buying the security. Again, the technician is not concerned with why a pattern has formed, only with the likely next price movement once the price breaks out of the pattern.

Flags and Pennants   Flags and pennants are considered minor continuation patterns because they form over short periods of time—on a daily price chart, typically over a week. They are similar to each other and have the same uses. A flag is formed by parallel trendlines, in the same way that most countries' flags are rectangular and create a parallelogram. Typically, the trendlines slope in a direction opposite to the trend up to that time; for example, in an uptrend, they slope down. A pennant formation is similar except that the trendlines converge to form a triangle, similar to the pennants of many sports teams or pennants flown on ships. The key difference between a triangle and pennant is that a pennant is a short-term formation whereas a triangle is a long-term formation.

The expectation for both flags and pennants is that the trend will continue after the pattern in the same direction it was going prior to the pattern. The price is expected to change by at least the same amount as the price change from the start of the trend to the formation of the flag or pennant. In Figure 14.22, a downtrend

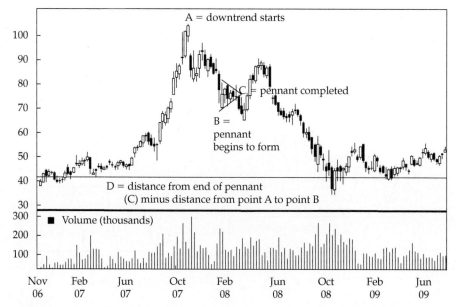

FIGURE 14.22   Pennant Formation: China Mobile ADR, November 2006–July 2009 (price in U.S. dollars)

begins at point A, which is $104. At point B, which is $70, a pennant begins to form. The distance from point A to point B is $34. The pennant ends at point C, which is $76. The price target is $76 minus $34, which is $42, the line labeled D.

TECHNICAL INDICATORS The technical analyst uses a variety of **technical indicators** to supplement the information gleaned from charts. A technical indicator is any measure based on price, market sentiment, or funds flow that can be used to predict changes in price. These indicators often have a supply-and-demand underpinning; that is, they measure how potential changes in supply and demand might affect a security's price.

Price-Based Indicators Price-based indicators somehow incorporate information contained in the current and past history of market prices. Indicators of this type range from simple (e.g., a moving average) to complex (e.g., a stochastic oscillator).

Moving Average A **moving average** is the average of the closing price of a security over a specified number of periods. Moving averages smooth out short-term price fluctuations, giving the technician a clearer image of market trend. Technicians commonly use a simple moving average, which weights each price equally in the calculation of the average price. Some technicians prefer to use an exponential moving average (also called an exponentially smoothed moving average), which gives the greatest weight to recent prices while giving exponentially less weight to older prices.

The number of data points included in the moving average depends on the intended use of the moving average. A 20-day moving average is commonly used because a month contains roughly 20 trading days. Also, 60 days is commonly used because it represents a quarter year (three months) of trading activity.

Moving averages can be used in conjunction with a price trend or in conjunction with one another. Moving averages are also used to determine support and resistance.

Because a moving average is less volatile than price, this tool can be used in several ways. First, whether price is above or below its moving average is important. A security that has been trending down in price will trade below its moving average, and a security that has been trending up will trade above its moving average. Second, the distance between the moving- average line and price is also significant. Once price begins to move back up toward its moving-average line, this line can serve as a resistance level. The 65-day moving-average line is commonly cited in the press, and when the price approaches the moving-average line, many investors become concerned that a rally will stall, so they sell the security.

Two or more moving averages can be used in conjunction. Figure 14.23 shows the price chart of Gazprom SP European Depositary Receipts (EDRs) on the Frankfurt Stock Exchange overlaid with 20-day and 60-day EDR moving averages for late 2007 to mid-2009.[5] Note that the longer the time frame used in the creation of a moving average, the smoother and less volatile the line. Investors often use moving-average

---

[5] A European Depositary Receipt is a negotiable certificate issued by a depositary bank in one country against equity that is traded on the stock exchange of another country.

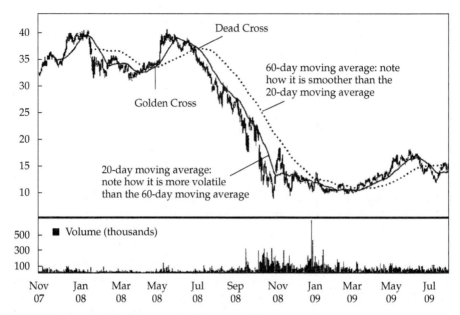

FIGURE 14.23   Daily Price Chart with 20-Day and 60-Day Moving Averages: Gazprom EDR, November 2007–August 2009 (price in euros)

crossovers as a buy or sell signal. When a short-term moving average crosses from underneath a longer-term average, this movement is considered bullish and is termed a **golden cross**. Conversely, when a short-term moving average crosses from above a longer-term moving average, this movement is considered bearish and is called a **dead cross**. In the case shown in Figure 14.23, a trading strategy of buying on golden crosses and selling on dead crosses would have been profitable.

Moving averages are easy to construct, and simple trading rules can be derived for using them. Computers can optimize what time lengths to set when using two moving averages. This optimization may take the form of changing the number of days included in each moving average or adding filter rules, such as waiting several days after a trade signal is given to make a trade. Reasons for optimization include the desire to manage capital drawdowns, to maximize gains, or to minimize losses. Once the moving average is optimized, even if a profitable trading system is devised for that security, the strategy is unlikely to work for other securities, especially if they are dissimilar. Also, as market conditions change, a previously optimized trading system may no longer work.

Bollinger Bands   Market veteran John Bollinger combined his knowledge of technical analysis with his knowledge of statistics to create an indicator called **Bollinger Bands**. Bollinger Bands consist of a moving average plus a higher line representing the moving average plus a set number of standard deviations from average price (for the same number of periods as used to calculate the moving average) and a lower line that is a moving average minus the same number of standard deviations. Figure 14.24 depicts Bollinger Bands for the Gazprom EDR.

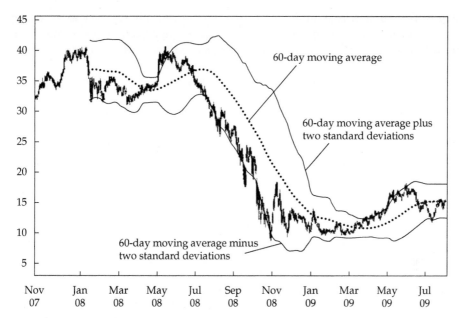

FIGURE 14.24 Bollinger Band Using 60-Day Moving Average and Two Standard Deviations: Gazprom EDR Daily Price Chart, November 2007–August 2009 (price in euros)

The more volatile the security being analyzed becomes, the wider the range becomes between the two outer lines or bands. Similar to moving averages, Bollinger Bands can be used to create trading strategies that can be easily computerized and tested. A common use is as a contrarian strategy, in which the investor sells when a security price reaches the upper band and buys when it reaches the lower band. This strategy assumes that the security price will stay within the bands.

This type of strategy is likely to lead to a large number of trades, but it also limits risk because the trader can quickly exit unprofitable trades. In the event of a sharp price move and a change in trend, however, a contrarian strategy based on Bollinger Bands would be unprofitable. So, long-term investors might actually buy on a significant breakout above the upper boundary band because a major breakout would imply a change in trend likely to persist for some time. The long-term investor would sell on a significant breakout below the lower band. In this strategy, significance would be defined as breaking above or below the band by a certain percentage (say, 5 percent or 10 percent) and/or for a certain period of time (say, a week for a daily price chart). Again, such rules can easily be computerized and tested.

Momentum Oscillators One of the key challenges in using indicators overlaid on a price chart is the difficulty of discerning changes in market sentiment that are out of the ordinary. **Momentum oscillators** are intended to alleviate this problem. They are constructed from price data, but they are calculated so that they either oscillate between a high and low (typically 0 and 100) or oscillate around a number (such as 0 or 100). Because of this construction, extreme highs or lows are easily discernible. These extremes can be viewed as graphic representations of market sentiment when selling or buying activity is more aggressive than historically typical. Because they are price based, momentum oscillators also can be analyzed by using the same tools technicians use to analyze price, such as the concepts of trend, support, and resistance.

Technicians also look for **convergence** or **divergence** between oscillators and price. Convergence is when the oscillator moves in the same manner as the security being analyzed, and divergence is when the oscillator moves differently from the security. For example, when price reaches a new high, this sign is considered bullish, but if the momentum oscillator being used does not also reach a new high at the same time, this pattern is divergence. It is considered to be an early warning of weakness, an indication that the uptrend may soon end.

Momentum oscillators should be used in conjunction with an understanding of the existing market (price) trend. Oscillators alert a trader to **overbought** or **oversold** conditions. In an overbought condition, market sentiment is unsustainably bullish. In an oversold condition, market sentiment is unsustainably bearish. In other words, the oscillator *range* must be considered separately for every security. Some securities may experience wide variations, and others may experience only minor variations.

Oscillators have three main uses. First, oscillators can be used to determine the strength of a trend. Extreme overbought levels are warning signals for uptrends, and extreme oversold levels are warning signals for downtrends. Second, when oscillators reach historically high or low levels, they may be signaling a pending trend reversal. For oscillators that move above and below 0, crossing the 0 level signals a change in the direction of the trend. For oscillators that move above and below 100, crossing the 100 level signals a change in the direction of the trend. Third, in a non-trending market, oscillators can be used for short-term trading decisions—that is, to sell at overbought levels and to buy at oversold levels.

Momentum or Rate of Change Oscillator   The terms *momentum oscillator* and *rate of change oscillator* are synonymous. "Rate of change" is often abbreviated ROC. The ROC oscillator is calculated by taking the most recent closing price, subtracting the closing price from a prior date that is a set number of days in the past, and multiplying the result by 100:

$$M = (V - Vx) \times 100$$

where

> M = momentum oscillator value
> V = last closing price
> Vx = closing price x days ago, typically 10 days

When the ROC oscillator crosses zero in the same direction as the direction of the trend, this movement is considered a buy or sell signal. For example, if the ROC oscillator crosses into positive territory during an uptrend, it is a buy signal. If it enters into negative territory during a downtrend, it is considered a sell signal. The technician will ignore crossovers in opposition to the trend because the technician must *always* first take into account the general trend when using oscillators.

An alternative method of constructing this oscillator it to set it so that it oscillates above and below 100, instead of 0, as follows:

$$M = \frac{V}{Vx} \times 100$$

This approach is shown in Figure 14.25 for Toyota Motor Corporation.

In Figure 14.25, the calculation method for the ROC oscillator for Toyota stock, traded on the Tokyo Stock Exchange, is for the oscillator to move around 100 and *x* is 12 days. Note that for this stock, the ROC oscillator tends to maintain a range between f85 and f115. So episodes when the oscillator moves outside this range are of particular interest to the technician. An extreme high means that the stock has posted its highest gain in any 12-day period at this point, and an extreme low reading means it has posted its greatest loss over any 12-day period. When investors bid up the price of a security too rapidly, the indication is that sentiment may be unduly bullish and the market may be overbought. Figure 14.25 shows that overbought levels of the ROC oscillator coincide with temporary highs in the stock price. So, those levels would have been signals to sell the stock. The other notable aspect of Figure 14.25 is the divergence when the share price hit a new low in December 2008

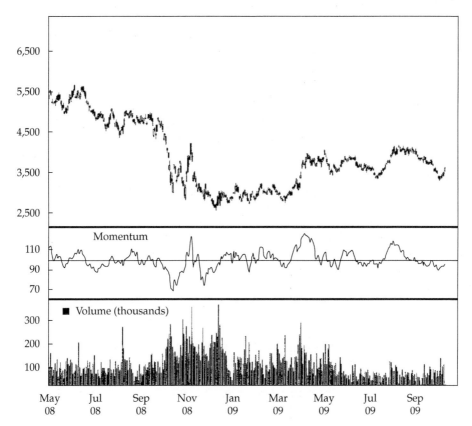

FIGURE 14.25 Momentum Oscillator with 100 as Midpoint: Toyota Motor, May 2008–October 2009 (price in Japanese yen)

but the ROC oscillator did not. This divergence would have been a bullish signal and would have been interpreted to mean that, although the share price hit a new low, investor sentiment was actually higher than it had been previously. In itself, this information would not have been enough to warrant buying the shares because a downtrend in price was still in place, but it alerted the technician to the fact that the trend might end soon. The technician could then look for further indication of the trend's end and, with confirmation, might buy the stock.

Relative Strength Index   A **relative strength index** (RSI) is computed over a rolling time period.[6] It graphically compares a security's gains with its losses over the set period. The creator of the RSI, Welles Wilder, suggested a 14-day time period, and this period is generally the period used in most technical analysis software. The technician should understand that this variable can be changed and that the optimal time range should be determined by how the technician intends to use the RSI information. Factors that influence selection of the time period are similar to those that influence the selection of a time period for moving averages. Short time periods (such as 14 days) provide information about short-term price behavior. If 200 days is used, this short-term information will be smoothed out and, perhaps, will not be apparent at all.

RSI is a momentum oscillator and is not to be confused with the charting method called "relative strength analysis," in which the ratio of two security prices is plotted over time. The RSI provides information on whether an asset is overbought. The formula for the RSI is not intuitive and is best understood with an example. The formula is:

$$RSI = 100 - \frac{100}{1 + RS}$$

$$\text{where RS} = \frac{\sum (\text{Up changes for the period under consideration})}{\sum (\text{Down changes for the period under consideration})}$$

Table 14.1 shows closing prices for Ford Motor Company during the month of June 2009.

During this time, markets were still rebounding from the subprime crisis; automobile company stocks were unusually volatile and, to some speculators, presented interesting short-term trading opportunities. Suppose a trader decided to compute an RSI for the month of June. It would be a 22-day RSI with 21 price changes— 11 up, 9 down, and 1 unchanged. To calculate the RSI, the trader would sum the 11 up changes, which sum to US$1.45. The down changes total –US$1.51; the absolute value drops the minus sign. The ratio of these two numbers is 0.96, so the RSI is

$$RSI = 100 - \frac{100}{1 + 0.96} = 100 - 51.02 = 48.98$$

The index construction forces the RSI to lie within 0 and 100. A value above 70 represents an overbought situation. Values below 30 suggest the asset is oversold. Again, as is the case with most technical tools, an analyst cannot simply learn the default settings and use them in every case. The 30–70 range is a good rule of

---

[6] This indicator is sometimes called the Wilder RSI.

TABLE 14.1   Computation of RSI: Ford, June 2009

Date	Close	Up Changes	Down Changes
6/1/2009	6.13		
6/2/2009	6.41	0.28	
6/3/2009	6.18		−0.23
6/4/2009	6.36	0.18	
6/5/2009	6.36		
6/8/2009	6.38	0.02	
6/9/2009	6.26		−0.12
6/10/2009	6.19		−0.07
6/11/2009	5.98		−0.21
6/12/2009	6.11	0.13	
6/15/2009	5.93		−0.18
6/16/2009	5.67		−0.26
6/17/2009	5.71	0.04	
6/18/2009	5.68		−0.03
6/19/2009	5.72	0.04	
6/22/2009	5.38		−0.34
6/23/2009	5.53	0.15	
6/24/2009	5.63	0.10	
6/25/2009	5.68	0.05	
6/26/2009	5.61		−0.07
6/29/2009	5.78	0.17	
6/30/2009	6.07	0.29	
		1.45	−1.51

thumb, but because the oscillator is a measure of volatility, less volatile stocks (such as utilities) may normally trade in a much narrower range. More volatile stocks (such as small-capitalization technology stocks) may trade in a wider range. The range also does not have to be symmetrical around 50. For example, in an uptrend, one might see a range of 40–80 but in downtrends, a range of 20–60.

The RSI measure often appears at the bottom or top of a price chart. Figure 14.26 shows a candlestick chart of Ford stock in 2009 with the corresponding RSI.

The candlestick chart of Ford stock prices in Figure 14.26 illustrates several aspects of the use of an RSI. For example, because the RSI oscillator was higher than 70 on March 23 so the stock was overbought at that time, a simple reading of the chart might have led to the conclusion that the trader should sell the stock. Doing so, however, would have caused the trader to miss a significant advance in the shares. A more careful technical analysis that took into account the trend would have indicated that the stock was in an uptrend, so RSI readings above 70 could be expected.

Because RSI is a price-based oscillator, the trader can also apply trend lines to analyze it. Note in Figure 14.26 that both the share price and the RSI oscillator were in uptrends from February until April but that the RSI uptrend was broken on 15 April, a potential warning that the uptrend in price might also break downward. In June, the share price broke its uptrend support line.

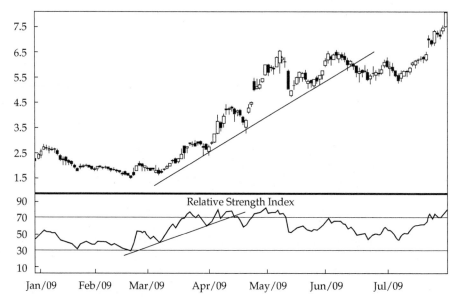

FIGURE 14.26   Candlestick Chart with RSI: Ford, January–August 2009 (price in U.S. dollars)

Stochastic Oscillator   The stochastic oscillator is based on the observation that in uptrends, prices tend to close at or near the high end of their recent range and in downtrends, they tend to close near the low end. The logic behind these patterns is that if the shares of a stock are constantly being bid up during the day but then lose value by the close, continuation of the rally is doubtful. If sellers have enough supply to overwhelm buyers, the rally is suspect. If a stock rallies during the day and is able to hold on to some or most of those gains by the close, that sign is bullish.

The stochastic oscillator oscillates between 0 and 100 and has a default setting of a 14-day period, which, again, might be adjusted for the situation as we discussed for the RSI. The oscillator is composed of two lines, called %*K* and %*D*, that are calculated as follows:

$$\%K = 100 \left(\frac{C - L14}{H14 - L14} \right)$$

where

C = latest closing price
$L14$ = lowest price in past 14 days
$H14$ = highest price in past 14 days

and

%*D* = average of the last three %*K* values calculated daily

Analysts should think about the %*D* in the same way they would a long-term moving-average line in conjunction with a short-term line. That is, %*D*, because it is the average of three %*K* values, is the slower moving, smoother line and is called the signal line. And %*K* is the faster moving line. The %*K* value means that the latest closing price (*C*) was in the %*K* percentile of the high–low range (*L*14 to *H*14).

The default oversold–overbought range for the stochastic oscillator is based on reading the signal line relative to readings of 20 and 80, but warnings about always using the default range for the RSI oscillator also apply in the case of the stochastic oscillator. In fact, noted technician Constance Brown has coined a term called the "stochastics default club" to refer to neophyte technicians who trade based solely on these defaults.[7] She has reported being able to develop successful trading strategies by using a time frame shorter than the 14-day default to calculate the stochastic oscillator. Apparently, enough traders are basing trades on the defaults to move the market for certain stocks. So, using shorter time frames than the default, she could trade ahead of the traders in the default stochastic club and generate a profit. Of course, other traders might be tempted to use an even shorter time frame, but there is a drawback to using a short time frame; namely, the shorter the time frame is, the more volatile the oscillator becomes and the more false signals it generates.

The stochastic oscillator should be used with other technical tools, such as trend analysis or pattern analysis. If both methods suggest the same conclusion, the trader has convergence (or confirmation), but if they give conflicting signals, the trader has divergence, which is a warning signal suggesting that further analysis is necessary.

The absolute level of the two lines should be considered in light of their normal range. Movements above this range indicate to a technician an overbought security and are considered bearish; movements below this range indicate an oversold security and are considered bullish. Crossovers of the two lines can also give trading signals the same way crossovers of two moving averages give signals. When the %*K* moves from below the %*D* line to above it, this move is considered a bullish short-term trading signal; conversely, when %*K* moves from above the %*D* line to below it, this pattern is considered bearish. In practice, a trader can use technical analysis software to adjust trading rules and optimize the calculation of the stochastic oscillator for a particular security and investment purpose (e.g., short-term trading or long-term investing).

The reason technicians use historical data to test their trading rules and find the optimal parameters for each security is that each security is different. The group of market participants actively trading differs from security to security. Just as each person has a different personality, so do groups of people. In effect, the groups of active market participants trading each security are imparting their personality on the trading activity for that security. As this group changes over time, the ideal parameters for a particular security may change.

Figure 14.27 provides a good example of how the stochastic oscillator can be used together with trend analysis. The figure provides the weekly price chart and stochastic oscillator for Petroleo Brasileiro ADRs, which are traded on the New York Stock Exchange, for June 2008 through June 2009. Note that during the downtrend on the left side of the chart the stochastic oscillator often moved below 20. Each time it reached 80, however, it provided a valid sell signal. When the downtrend ended in November 2008 and an uptrend began, the stochastic oscillator was regularly moving above 80 but each time the %*D* line moved above %*K*, a valid buy signal was given.

---

[7] Brown (1999).

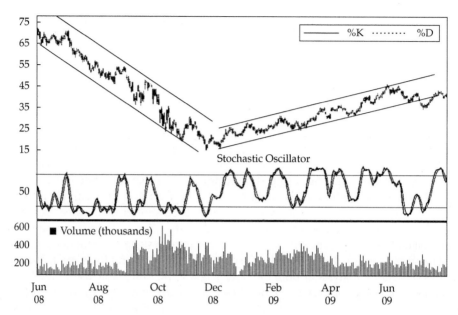

FIGURE 14.27   Weekly Price Chart and Stochastic Oscillator: Petroleo Brasileiro ADR, June 2008–July 2009 (price in U.S. dollars)

Moving-Average Convergence/Divergence Oscillator   The **moving-average convergence/ divergence oscillator** is commonly referred to as MACD, which is pronounced Mack Dee. The MACD is the difference between a short-term and a long-term moving average of the security's price. The MACD is constructed by calculating two lines, the MACD line and the signal line:

MACD line: difference between two exponentially smoothed moving averages, generally 12 and 26 days

Signal line: exponentially smoothed average of MACD line, generally 9 days

The indicator oscillates around zero and has no upper or lower limit. Rather than using a set overbought–oversold range for MACD, the analyst compares the current level with the historical performance of the oscillator for a particular security to determine when a security is out of its normal sentiment range.

MACD is used in technical analysis in three ways. The first is to note crossovers of the MACD line and the signal line, as discussed for moving averages and the stochastic oscillator. Crossovers of the two lines may indicate a change in trend. The second is to look for times when the MACD is outside its normal range for a given security. The third is to use trend lines on the MACD itself. When the MACD is trending in the same direction as price, this pattern is convergence, and when the two are trending in opposite directions, the pattern is divergence.

Figure 14.28 shows a daily price chart of Exxon Mobil (at the top) with the MACD oscillator for March through October of 2005. Note the convergence in the bottoming of both the oscillator and price in May, which provided confirmation of a change in trend. This change was further confirmed by the MACD line crossing

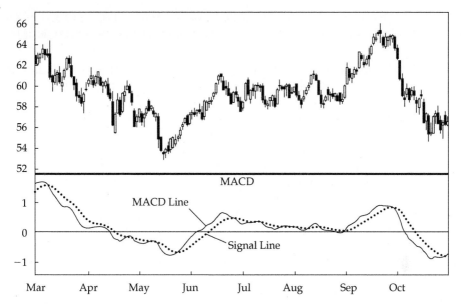

FIGURE 14.28 MACD and Daily Price Chart: Exxon Mobil, March–November 2005 (price in U.S. dollars)

above the signal line. A bearish signal was given in September with the change in trend of both price and the oscillator and the crossover of the signal line by the MACD line. The fact that the MACD oscillator was moving up to a level that was unusually high for this stock would have been an early warning signal in September.

Sentiment Indicators Sentiment indicators attempt to gauge investor activity for signs of increasing bullishness or bearishness. Sentiment indicators come in two forms—investor polls and calculated statistical indices.

Opinion Polls A wide range of services conduct periodic polls of either individual investors or investment professionals to gauge their sentiment about the equity market. The most common of the polls are the Investors Intelligence Advisors Sentiment reports, Market Vane Bullish Consensus, Consensus Bullish Sentiment Index, and Daily Sentiment Index, all of which poll investment professionals, and reports of the American Association of Individual Investors (AAII), which polls individual investors. All but the AAII survey are subscription-based services. *Barron's* magazine publishes data from four of these surveys on a weekly basis.

By regularly polling, compiling these data over time, and presenting it graphically, these services provide technicians with an analyzable snapshot of investor sentiment over time. Technicians look at prior market activity and compare it with highs or lows in sentiment, as well as inflection points in sentiment, as a gauge when they are forecasting the future direction of the market.

The most widely used investor polls are all U.S.-based. One reason is that interpretation of the surveys is determined by comparing the survey results with market performance over time. To gauge a survey's usefulness in predicting major market turns, the survey must have been published over several cycles, and each of the surveys mentioned here, based on U.S. data, has been available for several decades.

Calculated Statistical Indices   The other category of sentiment indicators are indicators that are calculated from market data, such as security prices. The two most commonly used are derived from the options market; they are the put/call ratio and the volatility index. Additionally, many analysts look at margin debt and short interest.

The **put/call ratio** is the volume of put options traded divided by the volume of call options traded for a particular financial instrument. Investors who buy put options on a security are presumably bearish, and investors who buy call options are presumably bullish. The volume in call options is greater than the volume traded in put options over time, so the put/call ratio is normally below 1.0. The ratio is considered to be a contrarian indicator, meaning that higher values are considered bearish and lower values are considered bullish. But, its usefulness as a contrarian indicator is limited except at extreme low or high levels in relation to the historical trading level of the put/call ratio for a particular financial instrument. The actual value of the put/call ratio, and its normal range, differs for each security or market, so no standard definitions of overbought or oversold levels exist. At extreme lows where call option volume is significantly greater than put option volume, market sentiment is said to be so overly positive that a correction is likely. At extreme highs in the put/call ratio, market sentiment is said to be so extremely negative that an increase in price is likely.

The **CBOE Volatility Index** (VIX) is a measure of near-term market volatility calculated by the Chicago Board Options Exchange. Since 2003, it has been calculated from option prices on the stocks in the S&P 500. The VIX rises when market participants become fearful of an impending market decline. These participants then bid up the price of puts, and the result is an increase in the VIX level. Technicians use the VIX in conjunction with trend, pattern, or oscillator tools, and it is interpreted from a contrarian perspective. When other indicators suggest that the market is oversold and the VIX is at an extreme high, this combination is considered bullish. Figure 14.29 shows the VIX form March 2005 to December 2009.

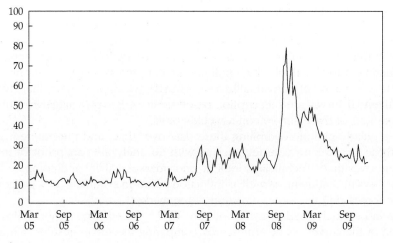

FIGURE 14.29   VIX, March 2005–December 2009

Margin debt is also often used as an indication of sentiment. As a group, investors have a history of buying near market tops and selling at the bottom. When the market is rising and indices reach new highs, investors are motivated to buy more equities in the hope of participating in the market rally. A margin account permits an investor to borrow part of the investment cost from the brokerage firm. This debt magnifies the gains or losses resulting from the investment.

Investor psychology plays an important role in the intuition behind margin debt as an indicator. When stock margin debt is increasing, investors are aggressively buying and stock prices will move higher because of increased demand. Eventually, the margin traders use all of their available credit, so their buying power (and, therefore, demand) decreases, which fuels a price decline. Falling prices may trigger margin calls and forced selling, thereby driving prices even lower.

Brokerage firms must report activity in their customers' margin accounts, so keeping track of borrowing behavior is relatively easy. Figure 14.30 provides a 10-year comparison of margin debt with the S&P 500. The correlation is striking: Rising margin debt is generally associated with a rising index level, and falling margin debt is associated with a falling index level. In fact, for the 113 months shown in Figure 14.30, the correlation coefficient between the levels of margin debt and the S&P 500 is 80.2 percent. When margin debt peaked in the summer of 2007, the market also topped out. Margin debt dropped sharply during the latter part of 2008 as the subprime crisis took the market down. Investors began to use borrowed funds again in the first half of 2009 when heavily discounted shares became increasingly attractive. Margin debt was still well below the average of the last decade, but the upturn would be viewed as a bullish sign by advocates of this indicator.

Short interest is another commonly used sentiment indicator. Investors sell shares short when they believe the share prices will decline. Brokerage firms must report

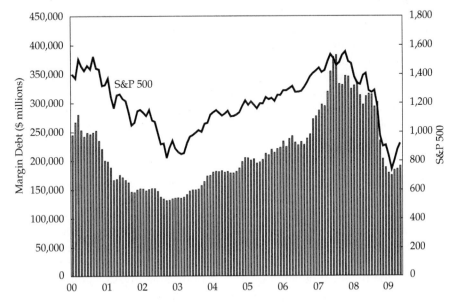

FIGURE 14.30   Margin Debt in U.S. Markets versus S&P 500, 2000–09
Source: New York Stock Exchange Fact Book.

short-sale activity, and these statistics are aggregated and reported by the exchanges and the financial press on a monthly basis. The number of shares of a particular security that are currently sold short is called "short interest." The short interest ratio represents the number of days trading activity represented by short interest. To facilitate comparisons of large and small companies, common practice is to "normalize" this value by dividing short interest by average daily trading volume to get the short interest ratio:

$$\text{Short interest ratio} = \text{Short interest} / \text{Average daily trading volume}$$

EXAMPLE 14.3   Short Interest Ratio

At the end of September 2009, *Barron's* reported short interest of 10,936,467 shares in Goldman Sachs, with average daily trading volume of 9,086,174. At the same time, the short interest in TD Banknorth was 20,420,166 on average trading volume of 1,183,558 shares. Calculate the short interest ratio for both firms.

Solution: The short interest ratio for Goldman Sachs was 10,936,467 divided by 9,086,174, or 1.2 days. For TD Banknorth, the short interest ratio was 20,420,166 divided by 1,183,558, or 17.25 days.

There are differences of opinion about how to interpret short interest as an indicator. It is considered to show market sentiment and to be a contrarian indicator. Some people believe that if a large number of shares are sold short and the short interest ratio is high, the market should expect a falling price for the shares because of so much negative sentiment about them. A counterargument is that, although the short sellers are bearish on the security, the effect of their short sales has already been felt in the security price. The short sellers' next action will be to buy shares back to cover their short positions. When the short sellers cover their positions, those actions will provide a boost to the share price. Therefore, the short interest ratio constitutes future (and known) demand for the shares.

Regardless of the analyst's perspective, in Example 14.3, the TD Banknorth short interest ratio of approximately 17 is more noteworthy than the much lower figure for Goldman Sachs.

Flow-of-Funds Indicators   Technicians look at fund flows as a way to gauge the potential supply and demand for equities. Demand can come in the form of margin borrowing against current holdings or cash holdings by mutual funds and other groups that are normally large holders of equities, such as insurance companies and pension funds. The more cash these groups hold, the more bullish is the indication for equities. One caveat in looking at potential sources of demand is that, although these data indicate the potential buying power of various large investor groups, the data say nothing about the likelihood that the groups will buy.

On the supply side, technicians look at new or secondary issuance of stock because these activities put more securities into the market and increase supply.

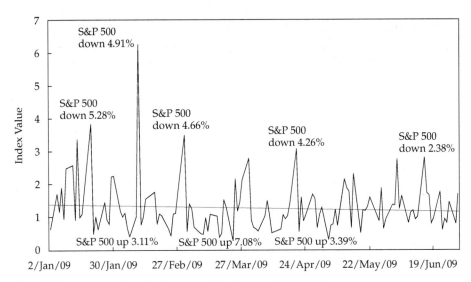

FIGURE 14.31   Arms Index for the S&P 500, January–July 2009

Arms Index A common flow of funds indicator is the **Arms Index**, also called the **TRIN** (for "short-term trading index").[8] This indicator is applied to a broad market (such as the S&P 500) to measure the relative extent to which money is moving into or out of rising and declining stocks. The index is a ratio of two ratios:

$$\text{Arms Index} = \frac{\text{Number of advancing issues/Number of declining issues}}{\text{Volume of advancing issues/Volume of declining issues}}$$

When this index is near 1.0, the market is in balance; that is, as much money is moving into rising stocks as into declining stocks. A value above 1.0 means that there is more volume in declining stocks; a value below 1.0 means that most trading activity is in rising stocks. Figure 14.31 shows the Arms Index for the S&P 500 on a daily basis for the first six months of 2009. The majority of the points lie above the 1.0 level, suggesting that the market continued to be in a selling mood. Note that the up spikes are associated with large price decreases in the index level and the down spikes reflect the opposite. The trendline shows a slightly negative slope, providing some slight encouragement for the bulls.

EXAMPLE 14.4   TRIN Indicator

Sarah Johannson, CFA, recently installed some investment software and is verifying the calculation of some of the statistics it produces. Her screen indicates a TRIN value of 1.02 for the NYSE and 1.80 for the Nasdaq market. These values seem to be unusually far apart to her, and she wonders whether they are both real-time statistics like the other market price data. To check whether they are

---

[8] This tool was first proposed by Richard W. Arms, Jr., a well-known technical analyst.

real-time statistics, a few minutes later, she simultaneously captures the TRIN from her software display (slightly changed to 1.01 for the NYSE and 1.81 for Nasdaq) and on a separate monitor, she does a screen capture of NYSE and Nasdaq data, as follows:

		NYSE	Nasdaq
Number of issues	Advancing	850	937
	Declining	1,982	1,472
Volume	Advancing	76,921,200	156,178,475
	Declining	185,461,042	441,970,884

How does Johannson recalculate and interpret the TRIN value for the NYSE and Nasdaq?

Solution:
Johannson calculates the TRIN values for the NYSE and Nasdaq as follows:

$$\text{TRIN (NYSE)} = \frac{(850 \div 1,982)}{(76,921,200 \div 185,461,042)} = 1.03$$

$$\text{TRIN (Nasdaq)} = \frac{(937 \div 1,472)}{(156,178,475 \div 441,970,884)} = 1.80$$

Johannson concludes that her software is giving her current values and that the Nasdaq is having a much worse day than the NYSE.

Margin Debt The previous section discussed the use of margin debt as an indicator of market sentiment. Margin debt is also widely used as a flow-of-funds indicator because margin loans may increase the purchases of stocks and declining margin balances may force the selling of stocks.

Mutual Fund Cash Position Mutual funds hold a substantial proportion of all investable assets. Some analysts use the *percentage of mutual fund assets held in cash* as a predictor of market direction. It is called the "mutual fund cash position indicator." Mutual funds must hold some of their assets in cash in order to pay bills and send redemption checks to account holders. Cash arrives on a daily basis from customer deposits, interest earned, and dividends received. Cash also increases after a fund manager sells a position and holds the funds before reinvesting them. During a bull market, the manager wants to buy shares as quickly as possible to avoid having a cash "drag" hurt the fund's performance. If prices are trending lower, however, the manager may hold funds in cash to improve the fund's performance.

Figure 14.32 shows year-end mutual fund cash in the United States as a percentage of assets from 1984 through 2008. Over this period, the average cash percentage was 6.8 percent. An analyst's initial intuition might be that when cash is relatively low, fund managers are bullish and anticipate rising prices but when fund managers are bearish, they conserve cash to wait for lower prices. Advocates of this technical

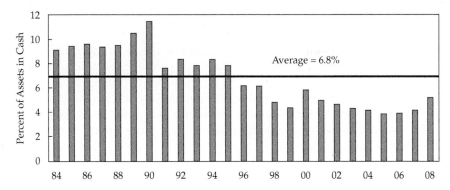

FIGURE 14.32   Mutual Fund Cash Position, 1984–2008

indicator argue exactly the opposite: When the mutual fund cash position is low, fund managers have already bought, and the effects of their purchases are already reflected in security prices. When the cash position is high, however, that money represents buying power that will move prices higher when the money is used to add positions to the portfolio. The mutual fund cash position is another example of a contrarian indicator.

Some analysts modify the value of the cash percentage to account for differences in the level of interest rates. Cash is not sitting in a desk drawer; it is on deposit somewhere earning interest. When interest rates are low, holding cash can be a substantial drag on the fund's performance if the broad market advances. When interest rates are high, holding cash is less costly.

EXAMPLE 14.5   Market Indicators

At the request of a wealthy client, Erik Nielson is preparing a proprietary research report on the shares of a U.S. company. He has completed the part of the report dealing with fundamental analysis and wants to include a section on technical analysis. Nielson has gathered the following information:

Company Information:

> The 20-day moving average of the share price just rose through the 200-day moving average.
> RSI = 40.6.

Market Information:

> TRIN = 1.9.
> Mutual fund cash position = 7.0%

1. How should Nielson interpret each item of information?
2. Do these indicators, in the aggregate, lead Nielson to a buy, hold, or sell recommendation for the company's shares?

Solution to 1:

> Moving average: When a short-term moving average moves above a longer-term moving average, the movement is a golden cross and is a bullish signal.
>
> RSI: An RSI of 40.6 would be considered neutral. The RSI ranges between 0 and 100. Values greater than 70 are bearish; values below 30 are bullish.
>
> TRIN: A TRIN value above 1.0 means that there is more volume in declining stocks than in advancing stocks; therefore, a value of 1.9 is bearish.
>
> Mutual fund cash position: The 7.0 percent figure is near the long-term average, so it is a neutral signal.

Solution to 2: Of the four indicators, one is bullish, one is bearish, and two are neutral. Most analysts would view this result as "net neutral" and would recommend continuing to hold the stock. An alternative point of view might be that seeing a bullish indicator for the stock while the indicator for the overall market is bearish could be an argument for overweighting the stock.

New Equity Issuance When a company's owners decide to take a company public and offer shares for sale, the owners want to put those shares on the market at a time when investors are eager to buy. That is, the owners want to offer the shares when they can sell them at a premium price. Premium prices occur near market tops. The new equity issuance indicator suggests that as the number of initial public offerings (IPOs) increases, the upward price trend may be about to turn down.

A supply-and-demand effect is also at work. Putting more shares on the market increases the aggregate supply of shares available for investors to purchase. The investment community has a finite quantity of cash to spend, so an increase in IPOs may be viewed as a bearish factor.

Secondary Offerings Technicians also monitor secondary offerings to gauge potential changes in the supply of equities. Although secondary offerings do not increase the supply of shares, because existing shares are sold by insiders to the general public, they do increase the supply available for trading or the float. So, from a market perspective, secondary offerings of shares have the potential to change the supply-and-demand equation as much as IPOs do.

CYCLES Over the centuries, technicians have noted recurring cycles of various frequencies in the capital markets. The study of cycles in the markets is part of broader cycle studies that exist in numerous fields of study. Many observed cycles, such as one in U.S. equities tied to the cycle of U.S. presidential elections, have an obvious and rational justification. Other cycles do not. However, why cycles in fields seemingly unrelated to finance, such as astronomy or weather patterns, may influence the economy (and thus the capital markets) may have a logical explanation. For example, sunspots affect weather patterns on earth, which in turn affect agriculture and, therefore, capital markets because they are related to agriculture.

Kondratieff Wave The longest of the widely recognized cycles was identified by Nikolai Kondratieff in the 1920s. Kondratieff was an economist in the Soviet Union who suggested that Western economies had a 54-year cycle. He traced cycles from the 1780s to the time he published this theory in the 1920s, and the economic depression of the 1930s was consistent with the cycle he identified. His theory was mainly tied to economic cycles and commodity prices, but cycles can also be seen in the prices of equities during the time of his work.

Kondratieff was executed in a Soviet purge in 1938, but his ideas have come into widespread acceptance, particularly since his works were translated into English in the 1980s. Two economists at the London School of Economics, E. H. Phelps Brown and Sheila Hopkins, identified a 50–52 year economic cycle in the United Kingdom. Together with Kondratieff, credit should be given to two Dutch economists, Jacob van Gelderen and Samuel de Wolff, who wrote about a 50–60 year economic cycle but published their work earlier, in 1913. Their work came to light only recently, however, so the long 54-year economic cycle is known as the **Kondratieff Wave** or K Wave.

The 18-Year Cycle   The 18-year cycle is interesting because three 18-year cycles make up the longer 54-year Kondratieff Wave. The 18-year cycle is most often mentioned in connection with real estate prices, but it can also be found in equities and other markets.

Decennial Pattern   The decennial pattern is the pattern of average stock market returns (based on the DJIA) broken down on the basis of the last digit in the year. Years ending with a 0 have had the worst performance, and years ending with a 5 have been by far the best. The DJIA was up every year ending in a 5 from 1885 until 1995, but it declined 0.6 percent in 2005.

Presidential Cycle   This cycle in the United States connects the performance of the DJIA with presidential elections. In this theory, years are grouped into categories on the basis of whether they were election years or the first, second, or third year following an election. The third year is the year prior to the next election. The third year shows the best performance; in fact, the DJIA experienced a positive return in every pre-election year from 1943 through 2007. One explanation for this outcome is that with so many politicians up for re-election, they inject stimulus into the economy in an attempt to improve their chances to be re-elected.[9] Election years are also usually positive years for the stock market, but with less consistency. Postelection years and the so-called midterm year have the worst performance.

These long cycles are important to keep in mind when using other technical analysis tools. However, the long cycles described here and other theories about long cycles present a number of problems. The primary problem is the small sample size. Only 56 presidential elections have been held in the United States, and only four completed Kondratieff cycles have occurred in U.S. history. Another problem is that even with the small number of cycles, the data do not always fit the cycle theory, and when they do, that fit may not be obvious.

---

[9] In U.S. presidential election years, the vice presidency, all 435 House of Representatives seats, and 33 of the 100 Senate seats are also up for election.

Elliott Wave Theory

In a theory proposed by R. N. Elliott in 1938, the market moves in regular, repeated waves or cycles. He identified and categorized these waves and wrote in detail about aspects of market cycles. Elliott was an accountant by training, but in 1929, after he contracted a progressive intestinal illness at age 58 while working in Latin America, he was forced to retire. Then, he turned his attention to a detailed study of equity prices in the United States.

A decade later, in 1938, he published his findings in a book titled *The Wave Principle*. In developing the concept that the market moves in waves, Elliott relied heavily on Charles Dow's early work. Elliott described how the market moved in a pattern of five waves moving up in a bull market in the following pattern: 1 = up, 2 = down, 3 = up, 4 = down, and 5 = up. He called this wave the "impulse wave." The impulse wave was followed by a corrective wave with three components: a = down, b = up, and c = down.

When the market is a bear market, as defined in Dow Theory—that is, with both of Dow's major indices in bear markets—the downward movements are impulse waves and are broken into five waves with upward corrections broken into three subwaves.

Elliott also noted that each wave could be broken down into smaller and smaller subwaves.

The longest of the waves is called the "grand supercycle" and takes place over centuries. Elliott traced grand supercycles back to the founding of the United States, and his successors have continued his work. Each grand supercycle can be broken down into subcycles until ending with the "subminuette," which unfolds over several minutes. The major cycles are:

Grand supercycle
Supercycle
Cycle
Primary
Intermediate
Minor
Minute
Minuette
Subminuette

An important aspect of Elliott's work is that he discovered that market waves follow patterns that are ratios of the numbers in the **Fibonacci sequence**. Leonardo Fibonacci was an eleventh-century Italian mathematician who explained this sequence in his book *Liber Abaci*, but the sequence was known to mathematicians as far back as 200 B.C.E. in India. The Fibonacci sequence starts with the numbers 0, 1, 1, and then each subsequent number in the sequence is the sum of the two preceding numbers:

0, 1, 1, 2, 3, 5, 8, 13, 21, 34 . . .

Elliott was more interested in the ratios of the numbers in the sequence because he found that the ratio of the size of subsequent waves was generally a Fibonacci

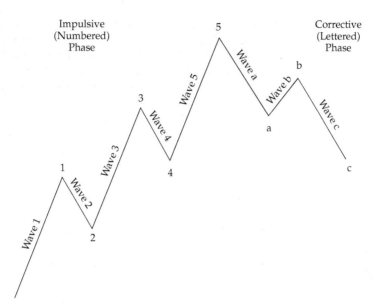

FIGURE 14.33   Impulse Waves and Corrective Waves

ratio. The ratios of one Fibonacci number to the next that Elliott considered most important are the following:

1/2 = 0.50, 2/3 = 0.6667, 3/5 = 0.6, 5/8 = 0.625, 8/13 = 0.6154

He also noticed that the ratio of a Fibonacci sequence number to its preceding number is important:

2/1 = 2, 3/2 = 1.5, 5/3 = 1.6667, 8/5 = 1.600, 8/13 = 1.6250

These ratios converge around 1.618. In mathematics, 1.618 is called the "golden ratio," and it can be found throughout nature—in astronomy, biology, botany, and many other fields. It is also widely used in art and architecture. The ancient Egyptians built the pyramids on the basis of this ratio, and the ancient Greeks used it widely.

As noted, Elliott numbered the impulse waves 1–5 and the corrective waves, a, b, and c. Figure 14.33 depicts the impulse and corrective waves in a bull market.

Elliott described the characteristics of each wave. Note the following, as shown in Figure 14.33:

Wave 1 starts as a basing pattern and displays an increase in price, volume, and breadth.[10] Wave 1 consists of five smaller waves.

Wave 2 moves down, retracing much of the gain in Wave 1 but not all of it. Common percentage retracements are Fibonacci ratios, such as 50 percent or 62 percent. Wave 2 never erases all of the gains from Wave 1. Wave 2 consists of three smaller waves.

---

[10] Breadth is defined as the ratio of the number of advancing securities in an index or traded on a given stock market to the number of declining issues.

Wave 3 moves above the high of the first wave and has strong breadth, volume, and price movement. Most of the price movement in an uptrend typically occurs in Wave 3. Wave 3 consists of five smaller waves. Wave 3 often moves prices 1.68 times higher than the length of Wave 1, which is a Fibonacci ratio.

Wave 4 is, again, a correction, and the ratio of the change in price during this wave to the price change during the third wave is also generally a Fibonacci ratio. Wave 4 commonly reverses 38 percent of the gain in Wave 3. Wave 5 is also an up wave. Generally, the price movement in Wave 5 is not as great as that in Wave 3. The exception to the rule is that Wave 5 may become extended, as when euphoria overtakes the market. Wave 5 consists of five smaller waves.

After Wave 5 is completed, the market traces out a series of three corrective waves, labeled a, b, and c in Figure 14.33.

Wave a is a down-wave in a bull market; Wave a itself breaks down into three waves.

Wave b is an upward movement and breaks down into five waves. Wave b is a false rally and is often called a "bull trap."

Wave c is the final corrective wave. In a bull market, it does not move below the start of the prior Wave 1 pattern. Wave c breaks down into three subwaves.

This description of the waves applies to bull markets; in bear markets, the impulse waves are labeled A through E and the corrective waves are labeled 1, 2, and 3. Waves in the direction of the trend consist of five subwaves, and counter-waves consist of three subwaves.

In practice, a good deal of time is required to become proficient with **Elliott Wave Theory**. Wave counts may not become evident at first, and Elliotticians often have to renumber their wave counts on the basis of changes in market trends. This theory is widely used, however, and the patterns Elliott described can still be observed today.

As a technician begins to make initial judgments on wave counts, the next step is to draw lines representing Fibonacci ratios on the charts. These lines alert the technician to the levels at which trends may change in the future and can be used in conjunction with other technical tools for forecasting. Positive price movements generally take prices up by some Fibonacci ratio of prior highs (e.g., 1.5 or 1.62), and price declines generally reverse prices by a Fibonacci ratio (e.g., 0.50 or 0.667). Elliott Wave Theory is used in practice with Dow Theory, trend analysis, pattern analysis, and oscillator analysis to provide a sense of the general trend in the market. As Elliott's nine cycles imply, Elliott Wave Theory can be applied in both very short term trading as well as in very long term economic analysis, as is the case with most tools used in technical analysis.

Intermarket Analysis

Intermarket analysis is a field within technical analysis that combines analysis of major categories of securities—namely, equities, bonds, currencies, and commodities—to identify market trends and possible inflections in a trend. Intermarket analysis also looks at industry subsectors, such as the nine sectors the S&P 500 is divided into, and the relationships among the major stock markets of countries with the largest economies, such as the New York, London, and Tokyo stock exchanges.

Intermarket analysis relies heavily on the field of economic analysis for its theoretical underpinning. The field was pioneered by John Murphy with his 1991 book *Intermarket Technical Analysis*. Murphy noted that all markets are interrelated and that these relationships are strengthening with the globalization of the world economy.[11]

- Stock prices are affected by bond prices. High bond prices are a positive for stock prices since this means low interest rates. Lower interest rates benefit companies with lower borrowing costs and lead to higher equity valuations in the calculation of intrinsic value using discounted cash flow analysis in fundamental analysis. Thus rising bond prices are a positive for stock prices, and declining bond prices are a bearish indicator.
- Bond prices impact commodity prices. Bond prices move inversely to interest rates. Interest rates move in proportion to expectations to future prices of commodities or inflation. So declining bond prices are a signal of possible rising commodity prices.
- Currencies impact commodity prices. Most commodity trading is denominated in U.S. dollars and so prices are commonly quoted in U.S. dollars. As a result, a strong dollar results in lower commodity prices and vice versa.

In intermarket analysis, technicians often look for inflection points in one market as a warning sign to start looking for a change in trend in a related market. To identify these intermarket relationships, a commonly used tool is relative strength analysis, which charts the price of one security divided by the price of another.

Figure 14.34 shows the relative price of 10-year U.S. Treasury bonds compared with the S&P 500. The rise in T-bond price relative to the S&P 500 can be clearly seen. The inflection point in this chart occurs in March 2009. This point would signal that the time had come to move investments from bonds to stocks.

Figure 14.35 is a relative strength chart depicting the ratio between the S&P 500 and commodity prices. It shows a clear top and reversal of trend in December 2008. This inflection point shows U.S. stocks weakening relative to commodities and would indicate that allocating funds away from the U.S. stocks and into commodities might be appropriate.

In addition to the preceding comparisons, once an asset category has been identified, relative strength analysis can be used to identify the strongest performing securities in a sector. For example, if commodities look promising, an investor can analyze each of the major commodities relative to a broad commodity index in order to find the strongest commodity.

Intermarket analysis can also be used to identify sectors of the equity market to invest in—often in connection with technical observations of the business cycle at any time. The equities of certain industry sectors tend to perform best at the beginning of an economic cycle. These sectors include utilities, financials, consumer nondurables, and transportation stocks. As an economic recovery gets under way,

---

[11] Murphy (1991).

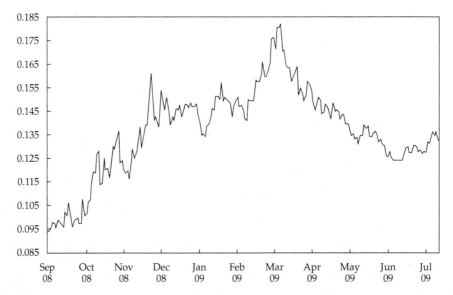

FIGURE 14.34   Relative Strength of 10-Year T-Bonds versus S&P 500, September 2008–July 2009

retailers, manufacturers, health care, and consumer durables tend to outperform. Lagging sectors include those tied to commodity prices, such as energy and basic industrial commodities, and also technology stocks.

Observations based on intermarket analysis can also help in allocating funds across national markets. Certain countries' economies are closely tied to commodities—for example, Australia, Canada, and South Africa. As economies evolve, these relationships change. So, the relationships must be monitored closely. For example, the Chinese equity markets have become much more advanced since

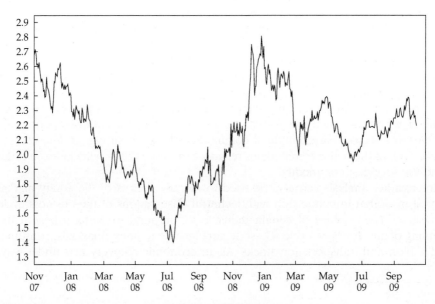

FIGURE 14.35   S&P 500 Index versus Commodity Prices, November 2007–November 2009

2000, the Chinese economy is much more industrialized than in the past, and its dependence on exports is currently strong.

Summary

- Technical analysis is a form of security analysis that uses price and volume market data, often graphically displayed.
- Technical analysis can be used for any freely traded security in the global market and is used on a wide range of financial instruments, such as equities, bonds, commodity futures, and currency futures.
- Technical analysis is the study of market trends or patterns and relies on recognition of patterns that have worked in the past in an attempt to predict future security prices. Technicians believe that market trends and patterns repeat themselves and are somewhat predictable because human behavior tends to repeat itself and is somewhat predictable.
- Another tenet of technical analysis is that the market brings together the collective wisdom of multiple participants, weights it according to the size of the trades they make, and allows analysts to understand this collective sentiment. Technical analysis relies on knowledgeable market participants putting this knowledge to work in the market and thereby influencing prices and volume.
- Technical analysis and fundamental analysis are equally useful and valid, but they approach the market in different ways. Technical analysis focuses solely on analyzing markets and the trading of financial instruments, whereas fundamental analysis is a much wider ranging field encompassing financial and economic analysis as well as analysis of societal and political trends.
- Technical analysis relies primarily on information gathered from market participants that is expressed through the interaction of price and volume. Fundamental analysis relies on information that is external to the market (e.g., economic data, company financial information) in an attempt to evaluate a security's value relative to its current price.
- The usefulness of technical analysis is diminished by any constraints on the security being freely traded, by large outside manipulation of the market, and in illiquid markets.
- Charts provide information about past price behavior and provide a basis for inferences about likely future price behavior. Various types of charts can be useful in studying the markets: line charts, bar charts, candlestick charts, and point and figure charts.
- Relative strength analysis is based on the ratio of the prices of a security to a benchmark and is used to compare the performance of one asset with the performance of another asset.
- Many technicians consider volume information to be very important and watch for the confirmation in volume of a price trend or the divergence of volume from a price trend.
- The concept of trend is perhaps the most important aspect of technical analysis. An uptrend is defined as a security making higher highs and higher lows. To draw an uptrend line, a technician draws a line connecting the lows of the price chart. A downtrend is defined as a security making lower highs and lower lows. To draw a downtrend line, a technician draws a line connecting the highs of the price chart.

- Support is defined as a low price range in which the price stops declining because of buying activity. It is the opposite of resistance, which is a price range in which price stops rising because of selling activity.
- Chart patterns are formations appearing in price charts that create some type of recognizable shape.
- Reversal patterns signal the end of a trend. Common reversal patterns are the head-and-shoulders, the inverse head-and-shoulders, double tops and bottoms, and triple tops and bottoms.
- Continuation patterns indicate that a market trend in place prior to the pattern formation will continue once the pattern is completed. Common continuation patterns are triangles, rectangles, flags, and pennants.
- Price-based indicators incorporate information contained in market prices. Common price-based indicators are the moving average and Bollinger Bands.
- Momentum oscillator indicators are constructed from price data, but they are calculated so that they fluctuate either between a high and low, typically 0 and 100, or around 0 or 100. Some examples are momentum (or rate of change) oscillators, the RSI, stochastic measures, and MACD.
- Sentiment indicators attempt to gauge investor activity for signs of increasing bullishness or bearishness. Sentiment indicators come in two forms—investor polls and calculated statistical indices. Opinion polls to gauge investors' sentiment toward the equity market are conducted by a variety of services. Commonly used calculated statistical indices are the put/call ratio, the VIX, margin debt, and the short interest ratio.
- Flow-of-funds indicators help technicians gauge potential changes in supply and demand for securities. Some commonly used indicators are the ARMS Index (also called the TRIN), margin debt (also a sentiment indicator), mutual fund cash positions, new equity issuance, and secondary equity offerings.
- Many technicians use various observed cycles to predict future movements in security prices; these cycles include Kondratieff waves, decennial patterns, and the U.S. presidential cycle.
- Elliott Wave Theory is an approach to market forecasting that assumes that markets form repetitive wave patterns, which are themselves composed of smaller and smaller subwaves. The relationships among wave heights are frequently Fibonacci ratios.
- Intermarket analysis is based on the principle that all markets are interrelated and influence each other. This approach involves the use of relative strength analysis for different groups of securities (e.g., stocks versus bonds, sectors in an economy, and securities from different countries) to make allocation decisions.

References

Akerlof, George A., and Robert J. Shiller. 2009. *Animal Spirits: How Human Psychology Drives the Economy, and Why It Matters for Global Capitalism.* Princeton, NJ: Princeton University Press.

Brown, Constance. 1999. *Technical Analysis for the Trading Professional.* New York McGraw-Hill.

Murphy, John J. 1991. *Intermarket Technical Analysis: Trading Strategies for the Global Stock, Bond, Commodity, and Currency Markets.* New York: John Wiley & Sons.

CHAPTER 15

Portfolio Theories and Models

W hile there is no consensus among investment advisors and consultants on a single blueprint for building and managing optimal portfolios, there is value in understanding the core theories and models from which so many different investment strategies are built.

This chapter will explore several foundational portfolio theories and models that have been developed over time. It is important to remember that these investment theories are just that, "theories." Consequently, they should not be considered "law" in a scientific sense. The results of these models are not always consistent or predictable, and past performance is no guarantee of future results. They do however play an important role in creating a framework from which investors may think about the relationship between risk and return and how to build more efficient portfolios.

Modern Portfolio Theory (MPT), the Capital Allocation Line (CAL), the Efficient Market Hypothesis (EMH), the Capital Asset Pricing Model (CAPM), the Security Market Line (SML), the Arbitrage Pricing Theory (APT), and various studies and models that are now considered Post-MPT (post Modern Portfolio Theory) are all reviewed in depth.

Part I *The New Science of Asset Allocation:* A Brief History of Asset Allocation

Learning Objectives
- Explain the concept of asset allocation and briefly describe its history.
- Describe and differentiate between strategic, tactical, and dynamic asset allocation strategies.
- Describe the Capital Asset Pricing Model (CAPM), the Security Market Line (SML), the Capital Market Line (CML).
- Discuss the importance of correlation and covariance between assets.
- Describe the conclusions of and importance of the Efficient Markets Hypothesis (EMH).
- Describe the key assumptions of and the challenges made to the Capital Asset Pricing Model (CAPM) and Modern Portfolio Theory (MPT).

Part II *Investments: Principles of Portfolio and Equity Analysis:* Market Efficiency

Learning Objectives
- Discuss market efficiency and related concepts including their importance to practitioners.
- Explain the factors affecting a market's efficiency.
- Distinguish between market value and intrinsic value.
- Compare and contrast weak-form, semistrong-form, and strong-form market efficiency.

Part III *Investments: Principles of Portfolio and Equity Analysis:* Portfolio Risk and Return

Learning Objectives
- Describe the "investment opportunity set."
- Explain the importance of diversification.
- Describe the effect on a portfolio's risk of investing in assets that are less than perfectly correlated.
- Describe and interpret the minimum-variance and efficient frontiers of risky assets and the global minimum-variance portfolio.
- Explain Markowitz's efficient frontier and how it is commonly used to build investment portfolios.
- Describe the Capital Allocation Line (CAL) and plot investments along and around the CAL.
- Discuss the selection of the optimal portfolio, given an investor's utility or (risk aversion) and the capital allocation line.

Part IV *The Handbook of Finance:* Asset Pricing Models

Learning Objectives
- Describe the characteristics and applications of the Capital Asset Pricing Model (CAPM).
- List the assumptions of the CAPM.
- Draw and explain the Capital Market Line (CML).
- Differentiate between systematic and unsystematic risk.
- Draw and explain the Security Market Line (SML).
- Discuss tests of and challenges to the CAPM.
- Describe the Arbitrage Pricing Theory (APT).
- List and explain various multifactor risk models including statistical factor models, macroeconomic factor models, and fundamental factor models.

Part I A Brief History of Asset Allocation

For most investors, asset allocation and its meaning seems relatively straightforward, that is, the process of allocating assets. It is the how and the why of asset allocation that has led to an entire asset management industry dedicated to its operation. Given the amount of resources and effort dedicated to understanding asset allocation, it would be reasonable to expect that after almost 5,000 years of human history there would be a suitable solution. The fact that the investment management industry is still groping for an answer is illustrated in the millions of references to "asset allocation" from any Internet search and the fact that there are enough practitioner books and academic articles on "how to allocate assets" to fill any investor's library. This part provides a brief history of how major advances in financial theory and investment practice affected investors' approaches to asset allocation and how asset allocation has had to evolve to meet changes in economic, regulatory, and technological environments. However, given the range of current and past efforts to diagnose, describe, and prescribe the process of asset allocation, it seems relatively futile to provide any reasonable summary of how we got here, much less what "here" is.

Before reviewing how we have arrived at current approaches to asset allocation, a brief review of what asset allocation is seems appropriate. Simply put, the ability to estimate what the future returns and risks of a range of investors' acceptable investments are and to choose a course of action based upon those alternatives is at the heart of asset allocation. As a result, much of asset allocation is centered on the quantitative tools or approaches used to estimate the probabilities of what may happen (risk) and the alternative approaches to managing that risk (risk management). While the concept of risk is multidimensional—including various types of market risks as well as liquidity risk, operational risk, legal risk, counterparty risk, and so on—for many it is simply the probability of a bad outcome. There is simply no single approach to asset allocation that covers each individual's sense of risk tolerance or even what risk is. In the world of asset allocation, we generally concentrate on the concept of statistically driven risk management, since those risk measurements are often centered on statistical estimates of probability (which is measurable) rather than on the concept of uncertainty (or possibility management), on which our empirically driven asset allocation models have little to say.

As a consequence, there is risk or uncertainty even in the most basic concept of asset allocation. Much of what we do in asset allocation is based on the trade-offs between the risks and returns of various investable assets as well as the risks and returns of various aspects of asset allocation, including alternative approaches to return and risk estimation. Choosing among the various courses of action lies at the heart of a wide range of asset allocation approaches, including:

Strategic asset management (allocation across various investment classes with the goal of achieving a desired long-term risk exposure)

Tactical asset management (allocation within or across investment classes with the goal of maximizing the portfolio's short-term return-risk profile)

Dynamic asset management (systematic changes in allocation across assets with the goal of fundamentally changing the portfolio's risk exposure in a predetermined way)

Asset allocation is not about solely maximizing expected return. It is a central thesis of this book as well as years of academic theory and investment practice that expected return is a function of the risks taken and that those risks may not be able to be measured or managed solely through systematic algorithmic-based risk management. Thus, asset allocation must focus on risk management in a broader context, including the benefit of an individual asset allocators's discretionary oversight in order to provide a suitable return to risk trade-off consistent with an investor's risk tolerance or investment goals. The story of the evolution of our understanding of that return to risk trade-off is the subject of this part. It is important to emphasize the "evolution" part as our understanding of the expected return to risk relationship keeps changing. First, because through time we learn more about how individuals react to risk and second, because the world itself changes (the financial world included).[1]

An individual's or institution's approach to asset allocation depends of course in part on the relative understanding of the alternative approaches and the underlying risks and returns of each. For the most part, this book does not attempt to depict the results of the most current research on various approaches to asset allocation. In many cases, that research has not undergone a full review or critical analysis and is often based solely on algorithmic-based model building. Also, many individuals are simply not aware of or at ease with this current research since their investment background is often rooted in traditional investment books in which much of this "current research" is not included.[2]

In the Beginning

It should be no surprise to investors that the two fundamental directives of asset allocation—(1) estimate what may happen and (2) choose a course of action based on those estimates—have been at the core of practitioner and academic debate. For our purposes, the timeline of that debate is illustrated in Figure 15.1. The advent of Modern Portfolio Theory and practice is often linked to the publication of Harry Markowitz's 1952 article "Portfolio Selection." For many the very words "Modern Portfolio Theory" are synonymous with Markowitz. It is important to point out that Modern Portfolio Theory is now almost 60 years old. As such, and not merely as a result of age, MPT (Modern Portfolio Theory) is really IPT (Initial Portfolio Theory) or OPT (Old Portfolio Theory). Moreover, the fundamental concept expressed in Markowitz's article (the ability to manage risk based on the expected correlation relationships between assets) was well known by practitioners at the time of its publication.

Markowitz formalized the return and risk relationship between securities in what is known today as the mathematics of diversification. If expected single-period returns and standard deviations of available securities as well as the correlations among them are estimated, then the standard deviation and the expected return of any portfolio consisting of those securities can be calculated. This means that

---

[1] One of the least emphasized parts of asset allocation is that an asset's marginal risks to a market portfolio may change when assets that were once noninvestable are added to the investable pool, since the marginal risks change when the composition of the investable portfolio changes.

[2] Most current investment textbooks (Bodie, Kane, and Marcus 2008; Reilly and Brown 2008) provide an excellent review of basic investment concepts, but for the most part they do not deal in great depth with the wide range of asset alternatives available to investors or with the range of alternative approaches to return and risk estimation. As discussed earlier, a book (including this one) published in 2010 was often written two years earlier (2008) using research material published in 2006, which was written in 2004 based on data from an even earlier period. In short, basic textbooks often rely on material that is 6 to 10 years old.

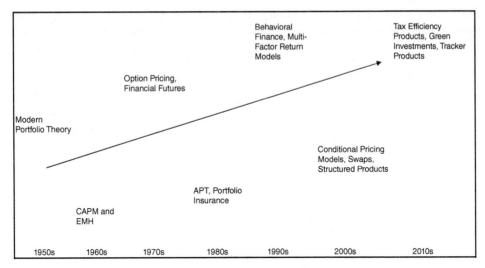

FIGURE 15.1   Timeline of Financial Advances in Asset Allocation

portfolios can be constructed with desirable standard deviation and expected return profiles. One particular set of such portfolios is the so-called mean-variance efficient portfolios, which have the highest expected rate of return for a given level of risk (variance). The collection of such portfolios for various levels of variance leads to the mean-variance efficient frontier.[3] In the mid-1950s, James Tobin (1958) expanded on Markowitz's work by adding a risk-free asset to the analysis.[4] This brought into focus an individual's ability to hold only two types of assets (risky and riskless) and to lend or borrow such that those two assets provided the tools necessary to match a wide range of investor return and risk preferences.[5]

The next major advancement in asset allocation expanded the work of Markowitz and Tobin into a general equilibrium model of risk and return. In this work, academics treated volatility and expected return as proxies for risk and reward. In the early 1960s, academics (Sharpe, 1964) proposed a theoretical relationship between expected return and risk based on a set of assumptions of individual behavior

---

[3] By the 1950s, other economic concepts such as the existence of pure securities were also commonplace (Arrow & Debreu, 1954).

[4] An example of the continued debate as to the development of asset pricing is the debate as to whether the MPT and the CAPM are positive or normative in construction. The author(s) will leave it up to the readers to decide. As to the basis for positive and normative models, see Milton Friedman (1953), *Essays in Positive Economics*, University of Chicago Press. Note that Friedman gave proper credit to John Maynard Keynes. Friedman starts his introduction by pointing out that "In his admirable book on *The Scope and Method of Political Economy* John Neville Keynes distinguishes among '*a positive science* ... a body of systematized knowledge concerning what is; a *normative* or *regulative science* ..., a body of systematized knowledge discussing criteria of what ought to be.'"

[5] This concept was later expanded with the growth of the capital asset pricing theory and the development of the capital market line in which the investment choice was really between two assets (the risk-free asset and the tangent risky portfolio).

and market conditions. These author(s) proposed that if investors invested in the mean-variance efficient market portfolio, then the required rate of return of an individual security would be directly related to its marginal contribution to the volatility of that mean-variance efficient market portfolio; that is, the risk of a security (and therefore its expected return) could not be determined while ignoring its role in a diversified portfolio.

A Review of the Capital Asset Pricing Model

The model developed by Sharpe and others is known as the Capital Asset Pricing Model (CAPM). While the results of this model are based on several unrealistic assumptions, it has dominated the world of finance and asset allocation for the past 40 years. The main foundation of the CAPM is that regardless of their risk-return preference, all investors can create desirable mean-variance efficient portfolios by combining two portfolios/assets: One is a unique, highly diversified, mean-variance efficient portfolio (market portfolio) and the other is the riskless asset. By combining these two investments, investors should be able to create mean-variance efficient portfolios that match their risk preferences. The combination of the riskless asset and the market portfolio (the Capital Market Line [CML] as shown in Figure 15.2) provides a solution to the asset allocation problem in a very simple and intuitive manner: Just combine the market portfolio with riskless asset and you will create a portfolio that has optimal risk-return properties.

In such a world, the risk of an individual security is then measured by its marginal contribution to the volatility (risk) of the market portfolio. This leads to the so-called CAPM:

$$E(R_i) - R_f = [E(R_m) - R_f]\beta_i$$

$$\beta_i = Corr(R_i, R_m) \times \frac{\sigma_i}{\sigma_m}$$

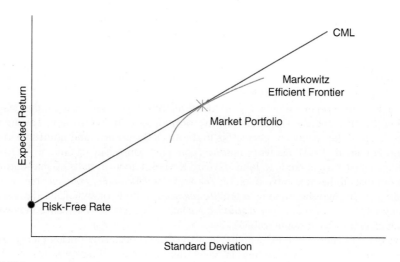

FIGURE 15.2   Capital Market Line

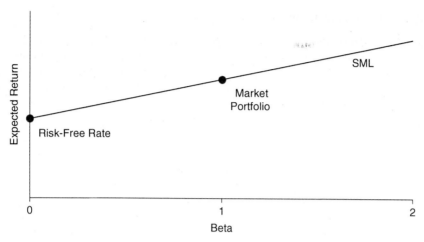

FIGURE 15.3   Security Market Line

where

R_f = Return on the riskless asset
$E(R_m)$ and $E(R_i)$ = Expected returns on the market portfolio and a security
σ_m and σ_i = Standard deviations of the market portfolio and the security
$Corr(R_i,R_m)$ = Correlation between the market portfolio and the security

Thus, in the world of the CAPM all the assets are theoretically located on the same straight line that passes through the point representing the market portfolio with beta equal to 1. That line is called the Security Market Line (SML), as shown in Figure 15.3. The basic difference between the CML and the SML is one of reference system. In the CML the risk measured is total risk (standard deviation), while the risk measured in the SML is a security's marginal risk to the market portfolio (beta).

While the most basic messages of MPT and CAPM (that diversification is important and that risk has to be measured in the context of an asset's marginal contribution to the risk of reference market portfolio) are valid and accepted widely by both academics and practitioners, many of their specific recommendations and predictions are not yet fully accepted and in some cases have been rejected by empirical evidence.[6] For instance, observed security returns are very weakly, if at all, related to a security's beta, and most investors find a simple combination of the market portfolio and the riskless asset totally inadequate in meeting their risk-return requirements.

---

[6] The initial tests indicated that while the empirical return to risk relationships derived from the CAPM were superior to similar single-factor volatility-based models, the residual error (unexplained return volatility) was so large as to question whether the underlying CAPM fit practice. The decade following the CAPM's introduction saw numerous articles (Roll, 1978) that detailed the problems with empirically testing the CAPM, which—while not denying the significant contributions of the CAPM—did imply that a more complete and dynamic process of risk estimation and return determination would more adequately describe the expected return and risk trade-off.

Asset Pricing in Cash and Derivative Markets

CAPM AND EMH   The CAPM profoundly shaped how asset allocation within and across asset classes was first conducted. Individual assets could be priced using a limited set of parameters. Securities could be grouped by their common market sensitivity into different risk classes and evaluated accordingly and, to the degree that an expected market risk premia could be modeled, it would also be possible (if desired) to adjust the underlying risk or beta of a portfolio to take advantage of changes in expected market risk premia (i.e., increase the beta of the portfolio if expected market risk premia is high and reduce the beta of the portfolio if the expected market risk premia is low). Here, market risk premia is defined as the difference between the expected rate of return of the market portfolio and the "riskless rate of interest."

While the CAPM is at its heart a model of expected return determination, it quickly became the basis for a number of asset allocation based decision models. The rudimentary nature of computers in the early 1960s is often forgotten and, while the mathematics of the Markowitz portfolio optimization model were well known, the practical application was limited due primarily to the number of numerical calculations. Specifically, the amount of data needed to obtain reasonable estimates of the covariance matrix is significant. For instance, if we have 100 securities, then to estimate the covariance matrix, we would need to estimate 100 variances and $(100^2 - 100)/2$ covariances, which add up to 5,050 parameters, have to be estimated. This would be computationally difficult and would have required many hours of work. As an alternative, the number of calculations can be significantly reduced if it is assumed that returns are driven by only one factor (e.g., the market portfolio). Note that this does not assume that CAPM holds. In other words, suppose we use a simple linear regression to estimate the beta of an asset with respect to a well-diversified portfolio.

$$R_{it} = \alpha_i + \beta_i R_{mt} + e_{it}$$

The rate of return on the asset at time t is given by R_{it}, the rate of return on the diversified portfolio is given by R_{mt}, the intercept and the slope (beta) are given by α_i and β_i respectively. Finally, the error term for asset i is given by e_{it}. Suppose we run the same regression for another asset, denoted asset j. If the error term for asset j is uncorrelated with the error term for asset i, then the covariance between the two assets is given by

$$\text{Cov}(R_i, R_j) = \beta_i \beta_j \text{Var}(R_m)$$

Notice that to estimate covariance between the two assets, we need an estimate of the variance of the market portfolio as well ($\text{Var}(R_m)$). However, this term will be common to all estimates of covariance. The result is that the number calculations required to estimate covariance matrix is now reduced to $(2 \times 100 + 1)$.

It is important to note that the above regression model, known as the market model, has nothing to do with the CAPM. The above regression makes no prediction about the size or the sign of intercept. It is simply a statistical relationship used to estimate the beta. On the other hand, the CAPM predicts that the market model intercept will be $(1 - \beta_i)R_f$.

It is fair to say, however, that almost 40 years ago most academics and professionals knew that the CAPM was an "incomplete" model of expected return. We now know that Sharpe and his fellow academics had unwittingly created a sort of "Asset Pricing Vampire," which rose from their model and, despite 30 years of stakes driven into its heart lives to this day for many practitioners as the primary approach to return estimation.[7] In the early years of the CAPM, financial economists were like kids with a new hammer and to them everything in the financial world looked like a nail. For example, if an asset's expected return can be estimated, then that estimate could be used as a basis for determining if an individual could consistently choose assets that were fundamentally underpriced and offered an ex post return greater than that consistent with its underlying risk. In sum, it provided the basis for determining if managers could obtain an alpha (excess return above that consistent with the expected return of a similar risk-passive investable asset).

The combination of the full information assumptions in the CAPM, along with the "presumed" ability to measure expected returns consistent with risk, offered academics the chance to measure the true informational efficiency of the marketplace. Initial studies by academics indicated that active managers underperformed similar risk-passive indices. This empirical result helped give rise later to the creation of a series of passive noninvestable and investable indices that would form the basis for the asset allocation consulting industry. As important, the combination of presumed informational efficiency with the ability to measure expected return led to the development of the Efficient Market Hypothesis (Fama, 1970) in which assets' prices were described relative to the degree to which their current prices reflected various types of information; that is, an asset's current price may be consistent with (a) past price information (weak form efficiency), (b) public information (semi-strong efficiency), and (c) private information (strong form efficiency). If market inefficiencies existed, this implied that investors could earn returns that would exceed what is predicted by the asset's underlying risk, as if there were some violation of information efficiency (similar to a monopoly or oligopolies). However, if the Efficient Market Hypothesis (EMH) is true, most investors should not waste their time trying to pick individual stocks using well-known public information but concentrate instead on risk determination and the proper set of assets to capture the expected risk that matches their risk preferences.

Today it is realized that the Efficient Market Hypothesis would be more correctly named the "Excess Return If We Only Knew How to Measure Expected Return Hypothesis"; it did provide the impetus for moving from a "Managers Only Matter" state of mind to an asset allocation process based on "Managers May Matter But Let Us Measure It First" plus a "Passive Approach to Asset Class/Security Selection." Again, it is important to come to terms with what the EMH says and does not say. EMH does not say that prices fluctuate randomly. EMH states that prices randomly fluctuate with a drift; that is, tomorrow's expected price is equal to today's price times the asset's expected return where expected return is based on current information

---

[7] For example, the Sharpe Ratio, defined as:

$$S_i = \frac{(\bar{R}_i - R_f)}{\sigma_i}$$

as meant to provide evidence of the relative benefit of two efficient risky portfolios on the capital market line and became the performance measurement vehicle of choice. Note that the Sharpe Ratio for an individual asset or portfolio merely provides evidence of the number of standard deviations the mean return of a portfolio/asset is from the risk-free rate.

(risk assessment). EMH says that there are no free lunches. Such profit opportunities are quickly eliminated, and the only way one can earn a high rate of return is through assuming a higher level of risk.

The quintessential problem is that there is no firm understanding of how people determine expected risk-adjusted return since there are no conclusive models that demonstrate how people price risk. All we can say is whether a manager has been able to create excess return (return above some arbitrarily chosen expected return model). The EMH does not say that an investment manager cannot make a gross return in excess of a passive approach. The EMH only says that if a manager makes such an excess return (e.g., because of access to technology or information), the investor may be charged a fee equal to the excess return such that the net return will be similar to that of investment in the passive index (e.g., manager returns – manager fee ≥ return on passive index). The manager's fee is supposed to cover the cost of acquiring the technology and/or information plus the investment made in time and effort to use that technology and information.

The combination of the CAPM and the EMH gave the marketplace the twin academic pillars required for the development of the asset allocation industry. All that was needed was a third pillar, a business model capable of developing the infrastructure required to market this new industry. Fortunately, computers and information technology had advanced such that in the late 1960s the investment industry witnessed the expansion of the index business. Both within the United States and overseas, monthly and even daily data series of domestic and global stock indices were being created. These indices could be used to provide estimates of the benefits of various approaches to asset allocation. For instance, newly developed global stock indices were used in a number of studies to illustrate the potential benefits of combining domestic stock indices (asset classes) with foreign and international stock indices (Grubel, 1968; Levy and Sarnet, 1970).[8]

Lost, of course, in this academic and practitioner euphoria were some of the practical realities relating to the underlying assumptions of the CAPM and EMH. First, the available empirical evidence had not strictly supported the CAPM's expected return and risk relationship. There was no means to estimate the "True Market Portfolio," so any empirically estimated betas were only estimates subject to unknown measurement errors. More complex multifactor models were required to capture expected return processes. While the market for financial products aimed at providing such multifactor models came into existence (e.g., Barr Rosenberg and Barr's better betas), most academics remained wedded to single-factor models. As academics came to appreciate the statistical problems associated with using underspecified single factor (beta) models of return determination or the data problems associated with the use of international data (e.g., timing of data or liquidity), attempts were made to "tweak"

---

[8] It is hard to remember the importance of the initial studies that demonstrated the return to risk benefits of international investment. However, the studies failed to emphasize the point that if the two international financial markets were separated to any great detail, the historical risk relationships may not tell us much about the expected return to risk relationships after the two countries became integrated (e.g., new market portfolio). The implications of that simple point—that as markets evolve, historical return to risk relationships may also evolve—has remained a problem for most asset allocation practitioners.

the CAPM. Throughout the 1970s, various forms of zero beta and multibeta APT models came into existence—better to explain the previously unexplained residual error of the single factor models of return estimation. These models provided additional statistical tools for measuring the efficacy of the EMH.

As with most people, when given the choice between the familiar and the unfamiliar, academics and practitioners kept using the hammers they had (CAPM and EMH) to nail down the problem of expected return estimation and the degree to which individual managers provided returns in excess of similar risk passively produced portfolio returns. In truth, the CAPM and EMH models did an excellent job of describing most market conditions. For the most part, markets do work. It should be expected that for financial markets with low-cost information (e.g., Treasury Bill market), asset prices would reflect current information and a common risk-based return model. Other markets and/or assets may require enlarged risk-based factor models that capture an enlarged set of underlying risks and therefore expected returns. Small firms with few analysts following them, with less ability to raise capital, with a less diversified client base, limited legal support, and so on may be priced to reflect those risks. Many assets are simply not tradable or have high transaction costs (e.g., housing, commodities, employment contracts, or distressed debt). How they could or should be priced in a single-factor or even a multifactor model framework was explored, but a solution was rarely found.[9]

OPTION PRICING MODELS AND GROWTH OF FUTURES MARKETS We have spent a great deal of time focusing on the equity markets. During this period of market innovation, considerable research also centered on direct arbitrage relationships. Arbitrage relationships in capital and corporate markets were explored during the 1930s (forward interest rates implied in yield curve models)[10] and in the 1950s (corporate dividend policy and debt policy). Similarly, cost of carry arbitrage models had long been the focal point of pricing in most futures-based research. In the early 1970s Fischer Black and Myron Scholes (1973) and Merton (1973) developed a simple-to-use option-pricing model based in part on arbitrage relationships between investment vehicles. Soon after, fundamental arbitrage between the relative prices of a put option (the right to sell) and a call option (the right to buy) formed a process to become known as the Put-Call Parity Model, which provided a means to explain easily the various ways options can be used to modify the underlying risk characteristics of existing portfolios. Exchange-based trading floors soon came into existence, which helped eventually to develop a market for a wide range of option based financial derivatives. While a range of dynamic futures based approaches should provide similar risk management opportunities, options provided a direct and easily measured approach to fundamentally change the risk composition of an asset or a portfolio.

---

[9] While lost to history, in the early 1970s the University of California at Berkeley held a series of seminars discussing the problem of tradable and nontradable assets in a market portfolio context.

[10] Research in the 1930s also addressed the ability to manage investment horizon risk in fixed income through the use of duration-based modeling. In addition, at the same time that Markowitz was publishing his views on MPT, Frank Redington (1952) was conducting research on how to best manage the risk of bond funds (duration).

As important, the model allowed one to estimate the cost for modifying the risk of a portfolio.

The growth of options as a means to provide risk management was centered primarily on equity markets. The 1970s also witnessed the creation and growth of new forms of financial futures, including currency futures in the early part of that decade and various forms of fixed income futures in the latter half (Treasury Bond futures). The creation of the Commodity Futures Trading Commission (CFTC) in the mid-1970s provided the additional government oversight necessary for the growth and development of new forms of financial futures as well as options products based on them. It is well known that futures provide a means to directly track underlying investment markets as well as to provide risk reduction opportunities. Futures contracts offer the ability to reduce or increase the underlying variability of an asset but futures alone do not permit one to fundamentally change the risk structure of the asset. The ability to directly change the distributional form of an asset is left for options. It can simply be said that the creation and development of options and futures trading in the 1970s led the way for the creation of an entire new industry dedicated to new means of managing risk.

Models of Return and Risk Post-1980

Models of investors' behavior as well as models of return and risk relationships, like so much of modern finance as well as life, are evolutionary. Given the tools and information at hand, various theories of expected return and risk relationships were put forth and were tested against the available data and technology of the period. Whether realized or not, none of the theories presented offered stopping points. They were in fact evolutionary steps with each reaching a conclusion within the confines of their stated parameters. As noted above, the EMH only states that expected return is a function of expected risk, which is a function of expected information. Nothing says that individuals do not get it wrong ex post or even that they had it right ex ante. In any market there is a process of information discovery and market reaction. The fact that, on average, individuals do not correctly value factors such as ratings or real estate payment cycles is less a critique of market efficiency than the process by which individuals assess information. Whatever the criticisms of the EMH, it became a staple of the investment jargon along with the CAPM as the benchmarks by which products were designed or marketed. Even other markets and products were discussed in terms of their performance or risk attributes relative to EMH or CAPM. For example, in the early 1970s the benefits of commodity futures were even discussed in terms of their equity market betas (Dusak, 1973). Fixed income securities (while developing their own multifactor jargon such as duration and convexity) were also discussed with regard to offering expected returns in terms of their betas with some weighted stock and bond market portfolio.

By the early 1980s a range of financial products and databases had come into existence that provided the ability to empirically test asset allocation decision rules (Ibbotson and Sinquefield, 1979). Options trading had grown and financial futures markets had evolved (S&P 500 futures contracts came into existence in the mid-1980s). Other changes had taken place in terms of technology, regulation, and market structure to provide an enhanced set of conditions that supported further development of asset allocation within a risk-controlled environment. During this period, systemized approaches to tactical asset allocation were being developed and marketed. By the mid-1980s concepts such as alpha transfer (Schwarz et al., 1986) and dynamic portfolio insurance (Leland, 1988) were well understood. In addition, during the 1980s advances in computer technology and software (e.g., Lindo) made available for the first time a series of self-serve portfolio management tools that enabled investors the ability to directly manage and adjust portfolio risk exposure.

It is fair to say that throughout the 1980s and 1990s markets continued to expand, which provided additional investable products that further expanded the available investable set. As technology advanced and markets expanded, the ability to dissect and reset asset flows led to the development of a wide range of new structured products and investment vehicles designed to meet the unique return and risk profile of individual investors. Financial regulation made it profitable for banks to offload certain trading processes, and new forms of external product-based hedge funds and managed futures programs were developed. By the mid-1990s, globalization had led to the development of new forms of emerging market securities, new commodity products, as well as new forms of non-exchange-traded financial products such as swaps to manage unique investor risks not fulfilled by more general exchange-based products. The development of these non-exchange-traded products culminated in the growth of various fixed income products (e.g., credit default swaps), which helped manage not only the exposure to interest rates but also the credit risk as well.

The evolution, if not revolution, in the market structure and trading also impacted the way practitioners and academics viewed the asset-pricing process. Concerns over the deviations from the strict CAPM process led to new research focused on issues that have been expanded under the topic "behavioral economics," which offers for some a more plausible picture of investor behavior. As these alternative models became popular, alternative views as to the underlying process by which excess return was determined evolved. Fama and French (1992, 1995) and others developed a series of empirical models that indicated that sources of returns could be related to firm size as well as style (growth and value).

Although behavioral economics and other expanded models of return to risk models dominated the market, the challenge remained as to how to hang on to the baby as the bathwater was thrown out. The development of more behavioral approaches to risk and return determination did focus on a more activist approach to asset price determination and the fact that the process of price determination is not instantaneous.[11] Arguments about the benefit of such behavioral approaches to asset pricing in some cases missed the point. EMH does not say that there are no risk-free $100 bills lying on the street; rather, it states that there are unforeseen risks

---

[11] While a summary of empirical tests of various equity-based pricing models is not the focus of this book, the changing market structure and risk and return opportunities are. Just as the CAPM and its empirical variant (e.g., the market model) became a primary expected factor model for decades, the Fama and French three-factor model plus one (momentum) has somewhat dominated the academic world for the past 20 years, despite evidence that the underlying factors may have become less important in terms of explaining return. Thomas Kuhn (*The Structure of Scientific Revolutions*, 2nd ed. 1970) offers one explanation as to why the movement from one mode of explaining market returns to another is so difficult. The point is simple: there is risk in the use of any risk or return model.

in attempting to pick them up. Moreover, the fact that there are some "irrational investors" may have little impact on market prices. The current price is always only a clearing price. There are other individuals who will pay more but do not have to and others who would sell it for less but do not have to. The market price mostly reflects those with the most money and does not generally reflect small rational or irrational investors who for the most part are price-takers. Also, people may behave predictably when faced with simple choices in a psychology lab, but when faced with extreme amounts of money, especially in arbitrage markets, it is rare that ex ante market prices do not reflect the best of the brightest; there is just too much money to make or lose.[12]

Asset Allocation in the Modern World

Looking back over the past decade, the issues in asset allocation had less to do with the theoretical models underlying return determination than the changes in market and trading structures that have led to a rapid increase in the number of available investable alternatives. Today, the number of investment choices has expanded beyond that available in traditional stock and bond investment to a wider range of alternative investments, including traditional alternatives such as private equity, real estate, and commodities, as well as more modern alternatives such as hedge funds and managed futures. In the past 10 years, academics and practitioners have also come to appreciate that both traditional stocks and bonds as well as alternatives (real estate, commodities, private equity, hedge funds, and managed futures) have common risk factors that drive returns and that those risk factors are conditional on changing market conditions. Moreover, global and domestic regulatory forces as well as market forces have created a new list of investable products (exchange traded and over the counter). These products include more liquid and readily available forms of traditional stock and bond investment (e.g., ETFs, OTC forward and options contracts) as well as more liquid and readily investable alternative investment forms (e.g., passive investable benchmark products).

The addition of new investment forms has permitted individuals to more readily access previously illiquid or less transparent asset classes (e.g., private equity or real estate) and has increased the number of assets that provide the potential for risk diversification in various states of the world. In fact, risk itself has become a more tradable asset. While options had always provided a means for individuals to directly manage risk, previous attempts to directly trade risk had not met with success. In the mid-2000s, various forms of VIX (VIX is the ticker symbol for the CBOE Volatility Index) began to be traded directly on central exchanges. In addition, advances in various forms of structuring along with algorithmic-based trading products have offered investors a broader set of domestic and international vehicles

---

[12] One can always take this to various extremes. The fact that over time return to risk is correctly priced does not mean that at some point assets may offer known excess to risk opportunities for which others take the anticipated loss (e.g., government policy may force losses on some for the benefit of others); however, this is simply another risk that must be considered when investing. Some markets are more prone to mispricing than others. Fortunately, the markets that are most prone to mispricing are so small in valuation that they have little impact on global valuation, although they make interesting television.

by which to manage asset portfolios. Lastly, the development of the Internet, along with the expansion of data and product availability as well as computer technology have permitted the development of a wide set of new approaches to asset allocation and risk management.

The problem still exists that we do not know what we can reasonably expect from these new products as well as the various asset allocation systems. Investor asset choices exist under a wide range of investment constraints. Regulation prevents some individuals from investing in certain forms of asset classes except in the most rudimentary form. Investment size restricts certain investors from taking advantage of more cost-efficient asset classes (e.g., swaps may be the preferred form of accessing a particular asset class but many investors are limited to investing in exchange-traded variants, which do not have the same statistical properties). As pointed out, the market is never efficient for everyone; that is, transaction costs differ, borrowing costs differ, taxation differs such that the actual after-tax return for individuals and institutions varies greatly. Finally, the ability to process and understand information and its consequences differs.

The very unpredictable nature of risky asset pricing raises the issue of how best to manage that risk. Certainly, the Markowitz model based on estimates obtained from historical figures continues as a primary means by which individuals attempt to estimate portfolio risk; however, the 2007 and 2008 market collapse illustrated the fundamental flaw of the Markowitz diversification approach; that is, Murphy's Law of Diversification—assets and markets only offer diversification benefits when you do not need them.

Until recently, investors felt secure that they had available to themselves not only a wide range of potential assets to invest in but also a wide range of risk management tools to manage that risk. It is not that investors are unaware of the potential issues in risk management. While many practitioners continued to concentrate on return maximization, many academics focused on the conditional risk, and, therefore, changing return to risk properties of various investments. Portfolio rebalancing based on the conditional nature of risk appeared to offer a more consistent approach to managing a portfolio's risk. However, even these models were incapable of anticipating the risk exposures of typical portfolios under extreme economic conditions witnessed in 2008. The market collapse of 2007 and 2008 provided conclusive evidence that while risk could be understood and in certain cases even managed, it could not be eliminated. The real problem remained now among market participants—what is risk and how to manage it?

Product Development: Yesterday, Today, and Tomorrow

The touchstone of evolution is that an entity has to develop to survive within its environment. Understand that the operative word is survive, and survival does not carry an optimization requirement. So we will not find the perfect theory or grouping of products as change comes to the corporate or investment world or, for that matter, to academic research. Rather, we will find that we have a better understanding of risk and return relationships. Today's growth in off-exchange and screen-traded markets, in contrast to floor-traded markets, is only one example of such understanding and change. There can be, however, a gulf between reality and perception. A delay in an investor's (and here the term is used broadly to incorporate regulators and corporate boards) understanding or market awareness of new research or market relationships often results in a delay in an appreciation of these changes and leads to a significant disadvantage in the marketplace.

Change comes from many sources. Modern investment products grew out of economic necessity, regulation, and technological innovations. Currency derivatives came into existence out of the failure of the United States to manage its own currency; thus the market had to devise an approach to facilitate international trade in a world of uncertain currency values. Individual options grew in the early 1970s as risk management tools, partly in response to the collapse of the stock markets of the late 1960s and the demand for new means of equity risk management. In the 1980s the expansion of interest rate futures and the development of equity futures followed, in part, from earlier ERISA laws, which created the pension fund asset base that required investment managers to hedge their asset risks. During the 1990s and into the current era, new product creations (e.g., swaps) were part of the changing world of technology and the resulting increasing ability to manage and monitor an ever more complex series of financial and nonfinancial products.

Thus, while we know very few fundamental truths, one, however, that we can collectively agree upon is that the evolution of asset allocation draws upon the aforementioned changes flowing from a dynamic world in which new forms of assets and risk management tools are constantly being created. Relative risks and returns and the ability to monitor and manage the process by which these evolving assets fit into portfolios will change and will be based on currently unknown relationships and information. Certainly today the challenge is greater, not only because we are working in a more dynamic market but the number of investment vehicles available to investors has increased as well.

What Every Investor Should Remember

- Much of what we do in asset allocation is based on the trade-offs between the costs and returns of various approaches to return and risk estimation. Choosing among the various courses of action based on those risky alternatives lies at the heart of a wide range of various approaches to asset allocation, including strategic asset management, tactical asset management, and dynamic asset management.
- MPT (Modern Portfolio Theory) is really IPT (Initial Portfolio Theory) or OPT (Old Portfolio Theory). The CAPM and Efficient Market Hypothesis, as well as more modern multifactor risk approaches to asset pricing, while providing a basic framework for addressing return and risk dynamics in the marketplace, are in most cases 60, 40, 30, or 20 years old. In short, the sources of asset returns and risks are known to be more dynamic than currently considered in the most basic asset allocation models such that a more nuanced and in some cases discretionary approach of the return and risk process must be considered when viewing the asset allocation process.

- The continued evolution of market structure, regulatory oversight, and trading technology has produced an increasing number of investable products as well as the means to monitor those products' interactions. Asset allocation is more than a simple breakdown of investment alternatives into stocks and bonds and now includes a broader range of traditional alternatives (private equity, real estate, and commodities) along with new alternatives such as hedge funds and managed futures. In addition, the ability to provide a greater number of unique targeted products designed to meet investors' needs has increased the asset allocation choices to investors.

References

Arrow, K., and G. Debreu. "The Existence of an Equilibrium for a Competitive Economy." *Econometrics* 22, No. 3 (1954): 265–290.

Black, F., and M. Scholes. "The Pricing of Options and Corporate Liabilities." *The Journal of Political Economy* 81, No. 3 (May/June 1973): 637–654.

Bodie, Z., A. Kane, and A. Marcus. *Investments.* New York: McGraw-Hill, 2008.

Dusak, Katherine. "Futures Trading and Investor Returns: An Investigation of Commodity Market Risk Premiums." *Journal of Political Economy* 81, Issue 6 (November/December 1973): 1387–1406.

Fama, E. "Efficient Capital Markets: A Review of Theory and Empirical Work." *Journal of Finance* 25, No. 2 (May 1970): 383–417.

Fama, E., and K. French. "The Cross Section of Expected Stock Returns." *Journal of Finance* 47, No. 2 (June 1992): 427–465.

Fama, E., and K. French. "Size and Book-to-Market Factors in Earnings and Returns." *Journal of Finance* 50, No. 1 (March 1995): 131–155.

Friedman, Milton. *Essays in Positive Economics.* Chicago: University of Chicago Press, 1953.

Grubel, Herbert. "Internationally Diversified Portfolio: Welfare Gains and Capital Flows." *The American Economic Review* 58, No. 5 (December 1968): 1299–1314.

Ibbotson, R.G., and R.A. Sinquefield. "Stocks, Bonds, Bills and Inflation: Update." *Financial Analysts Journal* 35, No. 4 (1979): 40–44.

Kuhn, T.S. *The Structure of Scientific Revolutions.* 2nd ed. University of Chicago Press, 1970.

Leland, H. "Portfolio Insurance and October 19th." *California Management Review* (Summer 1988).

Levy, H., and M. Sarnat. "International Diversification of Investment Portfolios." *American Economic Review* 60, Issue 4 (September 1970): 668–675.

Merton, R. "Theory of Rational Option Pricing." *Bell Journal of Economics* 4, Issue 1 (Spring 1973): 141–183.

Redington, F. "Review of the Principles of Life-Office Valuations." *Journal of the Institute of Actuaries* 78 (1952): 286–340.

Reilly, F.K., and K. Brown. *Investment Analysis and Portfolio Management*. 6th ed. South-Western College Publishing, 2008.

Roll, R. "Ambiguity When Performance Is Measured by the Securities Market Line." *Journal of Finance* 33, Issue 4 (September 1978): 1051–1069.

Schwarz, E., J. Hill, and T. Schneeweis. *Financial Futures: Fundamentals, Strategies, and Applications*. Homewood, IL: Irwin, 1986.

Sharpe, W.F. "Capital Asset Prices: A Theory of Market Equilibrium Under Conditions of Risk." *Journal of Finance* 19, Issue 3 (September 1964): 425–442.

Tobin, James. "Liquidity Preference as Behavior Toward Risk." *Review of Economic Studies* 25, Issue 2 (February 1958): 65–86.

Part II Market Efficiency

Market efficiency concerns the extent to which market prices incorporate available information. If market prices do not fully incorporate information, then opportunities may exist to make a profit from the gathering and processing of information. The subject of market efficiency is, therefore, of great interest to investment managers, as illustrated in Example 15.1.

EXAMPLE 15.1   Market Efficiency and Active Manager Selection

The chief investment officer (CIO) of a major university endowment fund has listed eight steps in the active manager selection process that can be applied both to traditional investments (e.g., common equity and fixed-income securities) and to alternative investments (e.g., private equity, hedge funds, and real assets). The first step specified is the evaluation of market opportunity:

> What is the opportunity and why is it there? To answer this question we start by studying capital markets and the types of managers operating within those markets. We identify market inefficiencies and try to understand their causes, such as regulatory structures or behavioral biases. We can rule out many broad groups of managers and strategies by simply determining that the degree of market inefficiency necessary to support a strategy is implausible. Importantly, we consider the past history of active returns meaningless unless we understand why markets will allow those active returns to continue into the future.[1]

> The CIO's description underscores the importance of not assuming that past active returns that might be found in a historical dataset will repeat themselves in the future. The term *active returns* refers to returns earned by strategies that do *not* assume that all information is fully reflected in market prices.

---

[1] The CIO is Christopher J. Brightman, CFA, of the University of Virginia Investment Management Company, as reported in Yau, Schneeweis, Robinson, and Weiss (2007, pp. 481–482).

Governments and market regulators also care about the extent to which market prices incorporate information. Efficient markets imply informative prices—prices that accurately reflect available information about fundamental values. In market-based economies, market prices help determine which companies (and which projects) obtain capital. If these prices do not efficiently incorporate information about a company's prospects, then it is possible that funds will be misdirected. By contrast, prices that are informative help direct scarce resources and funds available for investment to their highest-valued uses.[2] Informative prices thus promote economic growth. The efficiency of a country's capital markets (in which businesses raise financing) is an important characteristic of a well-functioning financial system.

The Concept of Market Efficiency

THE DESCRIPTION OF EFFICIENT MARKETS An informationally efficient market (an efficient market) is a market in which asset prices reflect new information quickly and rationally. An efficient market is thus a market in which asset prices reflect all past and present information.[3]

In this section we expand on this definition by clarifying the time frame required for an asset's price to incorporate information as well as describing the elements of information releases assumed under market efficiency. We discuss the difference between market value and intrinsic value and illustrate how inefficiencies or discrepancies between these values can provide profitable opportunities for active investment. As financial markets are generally not considered being either completely efficient or inefficient, but rather falling within a range between the two extremes, we describe a number of factors that contribute to and impede the degree of efficiency of a financial market. Finally, we conclude our overview of market efficiency by illustrating how the costs incurred by traders in identifying and exploiting possible market inefficiencies affect how we interpret market efficiency.

Investment managers and analysts, as noted, are interested in market efficiency because the extent to which a market is efficient affects how many profitable trading opportunities (market inefficiencies) exist. Consistent, superior, risk-adjusted returns (net of all expenses) are not achievable in an efficient market.[4] In a highly efficient market, a passive investment strategy (i.e., buying and holding a broad market portfolio) that does not seek superior risk-adjusted returns is preferred to an active investment strategy because of lower costs (for example, transaction and information-seeking costs). By contrast, in a very inefficient market, opportunities may exist for

---

[2] This concept is known as *allocative efficiency.*

[3] This definition is convenient for making several instructional points. The definition that most simply explains the sense of the word *efficient* in this context can be found in Fama (1976): "An efficient capital market is a market that is efficient in processing information" (p. 134).

[4] The technical term for *superior* in this context is *positive abnormal* in the sense of higher than expected given the asset's risk (as measured, according to capital market theory, by the asset's contribution to the risk of a well-diversified portfolio).

an active investment strategy to achieve superior risk-adjusted returns (net of all expenses in executing the strategy) as compared with a passive investment strategy. In inefficient markets, an active investment strategy may outperform a passive investment strategy on a risk-adjusted basis. Understanding the characteristics of an efficient market and being able to evaluate the efficiency of a particular market are important topics for investment analysts and portfolio managers.

An efficient market is a market in which asset prices reflect information quickly. But what is the time frame of "quickly"? Trades are the mechanism by which information can be incorporated into asset transaction prices. The time needed to execute trades to exploit an inefficiency may provide a baseline for judging speed of adjustment.[5] The time frame for an asset's price to incorporate information must be at least as long as the shortest time a trader needs to execute a transaction in the asset. In certain markets, such as foreign exchange and developed equity markets, market efficiency relative to certain types of information has been studied using time frames as short as one minute or less. If the time frame of price adjustment allows many traders to earn profits with little risk, then the market is relatively inefficient. These considerations lead to the observation that market efficiency can be viewed as falling on a continuum.

Finally, an important point is that in an efficient market, prices should be expected to react only to the elements of information releases that are not anticipated fully by investors—that is, to the "unexpected" or "surprise" element of such releases. Investors process the unexpected information and revise expectations (for example, about an asset's future cash flows, risk, or required rate of return) accordingly. The revised expectations enter or get incorporated in the asset price through trades in the asset. Market participants who process the news and believe that at the current market price an asset does not offer sufficient compensation for its perceived risk will tend to sell it or even sell it short. Market participants with opposite views should be buyers. In this way the market establishes the price that balances the various opinions after expectations are revised.

MARKET VALUE VERSUS INTRINSIC VALUE   **Market value** is the price at which an asset can currently be bought or sold. **Intrinsic value** (sometimes called **fundamental value**) is, broadly speaking, the value that would be placed on it by investors if they had a complete understanding of the asset's investment characteristics.[6] For a bond, for example, such information would include its interest (coupon) rate, principal value, the timing of its interest and principal payments, the other terms of the bond contract (indenture), a precise understanding of its default risk, the liquidity of its market, and other issue-specific items. In addition, market variables such as the term structure of interest rates and the size of various market premiums applying to the issue (for default risk, etc.) would enter into a discounted cash flow estimate of the bond's intrinsic value (discounted cash flow models are often used for such

---

[5] Although the original theory of market efficiency does not quantify this speed, the basic idea is that it is sufficiently swift to make it impossible to consistently earn abnormal profits. Chordia, Roll, and Subrahmanyam (2005) suggest that the adjustment to information on the New York Stock Exchange (NYSE) is between 5 and 60 minutes.

[6] Intrinsic value is often defined as the present value of all expected future cash flows of the asset.

estimates). The word *estimate* is used because, in practice, intrinsic value can be estimated but is not known for certain.

If investors believe a market is highly *efficient*, they will usually accept market prices as accurately reflecting intrinsic values. Discrepancies between market price and intrinsic value are the basis for profitable active investment. Active investors seek to own assets selling below perceived intrinsic value in the marketplace and to sell, or sell short, assets selling above perceived intrinsic value.

If investors believe an asset market is relatively *inefficient*, they may try to develop an independent estimate of intrinsic value. The challenge for investors and analysts is estimating an asset's intrinsic value. Numerous theories and models, including the dividend discount model, can be used to estimate an asset's intrinsic value, but they all require some form of judgment regarding the size, timing, and riskiness of the future cash flows associated with the asset. The more complex an asset's future cash flows, the more difficult it is to estimate its intrinsic value. These complexities and the estimates of an asset's market value are reflected in the market through the buying and selling of assets. The market value of an asset represents the intersection of supply and demand—the point that is low enough to induce at least one investor to buy while being high enough to induce at least one investor to sell. Because information relevant to valuation flows continually to investors, estimates of intrinsic value change, and hence, market values change.

FACTORS CONTRIBUTING TO AND IMPEDING A MARKET'S EFFICIENCY   For markets to be efficient, prices should adjust quickly and rationally to the release of new information. In other words, prices of assets in an efficient market should "fully reflect" all information. Financial markets, however, are generally not classified at the two extremes as either completely inefficient or completely efficient but, rather, as exhibiting various degrees of efficiency. In other words, market efficiency should be viewed as falling on a continuum between extremes of completely efficient, at one end, and completely inefficient, at the other. Asset prices in a highly efficient market, by definition, reflect information more quickly and more accurately than in a less-efficient market. These degrees of efficiency also vary through time, across geographical markets, and by type of market. A number of factors contribute to and impede the degree of efficiency in a financial market.

Market Participants   One of the most critical factors contributing to the degree of efficiency in a market is the number of market participants.

A large number of investors (individual and institutional) follow the major financial markets closely on a daily basis, and if mispricings exist in these markets, investors will act so that these mispricings disappear quickly. Besides the number of investors, the number of financial analysts who follow or analyze a security or asset should be positively related to market efficiency. The number of market participants and resulting trading activity can vary significantly through time. A lack of trading activity can cause or accentuate other market imperfections that impede market efficiency. In fact, in many of these markets, such as China, trading in many of the listed stocks is restricted for foreigners. By nature, this limitation reduces the number of market participants, restricts the potential for trading activity, and hence reduces market efficiency.

Information Availability and Financial Disclosure   Information availability (e.g., an active financial news media) and financial disclosure should promote market efficiency. Information regarding trading activity and traded companies in such markets as the New York Stock Exchange, the London Stock Exchange, and the Tokyo Stock Exchange is readily available. Many investors and analysts participate in these markets, and analyst coverage of listed companies is typically substantial. As a result, these markets are quite efficient. In contrast, trading activity and material information availability may be lacking in smaller securities markets, such as those operating in some emerging markets.

Similarly, significant differences may exist in the efficiency of different types of markets. For example, many securities trade primarily or exclusively in dealer or over-the-counter (OTC) markets, including bonds, money market instruments, currencies, mortgage-backed securities, swaps, and forward contracts. The information provided by the dealers who serve as market makers for these markets can vary significantly in quality and quantity, both through time and across different product markets.

Treating all market participants fairly is critical for the integrity of the market and explains why regulators place such an emphasis on "fair, orderly, and efficient markets."[7] A key element of this fairness is that all investors have access to the information necessary to value securities that trade in the market. Rules and regulations that promote fairness and efficiency in a market include those pertaining to the disclosure of information and illegal insider trading.

For example, U.S. Securities and Exchange Commission's (SEC's) Regulation FD (Fair Disclosure) requires that if security issuers provide nonpublic information to some market professionals or investors, they must also disclose this information to the public.[8] This requirement helps provide equal and fair opportunities, which is important in encouraging participation in the market. A related issue deals with illegal insider trading. The SEC's rules, along with court cases, define illegal insider trading as trading in securities by market participants who are considered insiders "while in possession of material, nonpublic information about the security."[9,10] Although these rules cannot guarantee that some participants will not have an advantage over others and that insiders will not trade on the basis of inside information, the civil and

---

[7] "The Investor's Advocate: How the SEC Protects Investors, Maintains Market Integrity, and Facilitates Capital Formation," U.S. Securities and Exchange Commission (www.sec.gov/about/whatwedo.shtml).

[8] Regulation FD, "Selective Disclosure and Insider Trading," 17 CFR Parts 240, 243, and 249, effective 23 October 2000.

[9] Although not the focus of this particular part, it is important to note that a party is considered an insider not only when the individual is a corporate insider, such as an officer or director, but also when the individual is aware that the information is nonpublic information [Securities and Exchange Commission, Rules 10b5-1 ("Trading on the Basis of Material Nonpublic Information in Insider Trading Cases") and Rule 10b5-2 ("Duties of Trust or Confidence in Misappropriation Insider Trading Cases")].

[10] In contrast to the situation in the United States, in other developed markets, the insider trading laws are generally promulgated by the courts, although the definition of "insider trading" is generally through statutes. See, for example, the European Community's (EC's) Insider Trading Directive, *Council Directive Coordinating Regulations on Insider Dealing*, Directive 89/592, article 32, 1989 OJ (L 334) 30, 1.

criminal penalties associated with breaking these rules are intended to discourage illegal insider trading and promote fairness.

Limits to Trading **Arbitrage** is a set of transactions that produces riskless profits. Arbitrageurs are traders who engage in such trades to benefit from pricing discrepancies (inefficiencies) in markets. Such trading activity contributes to market efficiency. For example, if an asset is traded in two markets but at different prices, the actions of buying the asset in the market in which it is underpriced and selling the asset in the market in which it is overpriced will eventually bring these two prices together. The presence of these arbitrageurs helps pricing discrepancies disappear quickly. Obviously, market efficiency is impeded by any limitation on arbitrage resulting from operating inefficiencies, such as difficulties in executing trades in a timely manner, prohibitively high trading costs, and a lack of transparency in market prices.

Some market experts argue that restrictions on short selling limit arbitrage trading, which impedes market efficiency. **Short selling** is the transaction whereby an investor sells shares that he or she does not own by borrowing them from a broker and agreeing to replace them at a future date. Short selling allows investors to sell securities they believe to be overvalued, much in the same way they can buy those they believe to be undervalued. In theory, such activities promote more efficient pricing. Regulators and others, however, have argued that short selling may exaggerate downward market movements, leading to crashes in affected securities. In contrast, some researchers report evidence indicating that when investors are unable to borrow securities (that is, to short the security), or when costs to borrow shares are high, market prices may deviate from intrinsic values.[11] Furthermore, research suggests that short selling is helpful in price discovery (that is, it facilitates supply and demand in determining prices).[12]

TRANSACTION COSTS AND INFORMATION-ACQUISITION COSTS The costs incurred by traders in identifying and exploiting possible market inefficiencies affect the interpretation of market efficiency. The two types of costs to consider are transaction costs and information-acquisition costs.

> *Transaction costs:* Practically, transaction costs are incurred in trading to exploit any perceived market inefficiency. Thus, "efficient" should be viewed as efficient within the bounds of transaction costs. For example, consider a violation of the principle that two identical assets should sell for the same price in different markets. Such a violation can be considered to be a rather simple possible exception to market efficiency because prices appear to be inconsistently processing information. To exploit the violation, a trader could arbitrage by simultaneously shorting the asset in the higher-price market and buying the asset in the lower-price market. If the price discrepancy between the two markets is smaller than the transaction costs involved in the arbitrage for the lowest cost traders, the arbitrage will not occur, and both prices are in effect efficient within the bounds of arbitrage. These bounds of arbitrage

---

[11] A significant amount of research supports this view, including Jones and Lamont (2002) and Duffie, Garleanu, and Pederson (2002).

[12] See Bris, Goetzmann, and Zhu (2009).

are relatively narrow in highly liquid markets, such as the market for U.S. Treasury bills, but could be wide in illiquid markets.

Information-acquisition costs: Practically, expenses are always associated with gathering and analyzing information. New information is incorporated in transaction prices by traders placing trades based on their analysis of information. Active investors who place trades based on information they have gathered and analyzed play a key role in market prices adjusting to reflect new information. The classic view of market efficiency is that active investors incur information acquisition costs but that money is wasted because prices already reflect all relevant information. This view of efficiency is very strict in the sense of viewing a market as inefficient if active investing can recapture any part of the costs, such as research costs and active asset selection. Grossman and Stiglitz (1980) argue that prices must offer a return to information acquisition; in equilibrium, if markets are efficient, returns net of such expenses are just fair returns for the risk incurred. The modern perspective views a market as inefficient if, after deducting such costs, active investing can earn superior returns. Gross of expenses, a return should accrue to information acquisition in an efficient market.

In summary, a modern perspective calls for the investor to consider transaction costs and information-acquisition costs when evaluating the efficiency of a market. A price discrepancy must be sufficiently large to leave the investor with a profit (adjusted for risk) after taking account of the transaction costs and information-acquisition costs to reach the conclusion that the discrepancy may represent a market inefficiency. Prices may not fully reflect available information but still not provide a true market opportunity for active investors.

Forms of Market Efficiency

Eugene Fama developed a framework for describing the degree to which markets are efficient.[13] In his efficient market hypothesis, markets are efficient when prices reflect *all* relevant information at any point in time. This means that the market prices observed for securities, for example, reflect the information available at the time.

In his framework, Fama defines three forms of efficiency: weak, semistrong, and strong. Each form is defined with respect to the available information that is reflected in prices.

	Market Prices Reflect:		
Forms of Market Efficiency	Past Market Data	Public Information	Private Information
Weak form of market efficiency	√		
Semistrong form of market efficiency	√	√	
Strong form of market efficiency	√	√	√

---

[13] Fama (1970).

A finding that investors can consistently earn **abnormal returns** by trading on the basis of information is evidence contrary to market efficiency. In general, abnormal returns are returns in excess of those expected given a security's risk and the market's return. In other words, abnormal return equals actual return less expected return.

WEAK FORM   In the **weak form** of the efficient market hypothesis, security prices fully reflect *all past market data*, which refers to all historical price and trading volume information. If markets are weak-form efficient, past trading data are already reflected in current prices and investors cannot predict future price changes by extrapolating prices or patterns of prices from the past.[14]

Tests of whether securities markets are weak-form efficient require looking at patterns of prices. One approach is to see whether there is any serial correlation in security returns, which would imply a predictable pattern.[15] Although there is some weak correlation in daily security returns, there is not enough correlation to make this a profitable trading rule after considering transaction costs.

An alternative approach to test weak-form efficiency is to examine specific trading rules that attempt to exploit historical trading data. If any such trading rule consistently generates abnormal risk-adjusted returns after trading costs, this evidence will contradict weak-form efficiency. This approach is commonly associated with **technical analysis**, which involves the analysis of historical trading information (primarily pricing and volume data) in an attempt to identify recurring patterns in the trading data that can be used to guide investment decisions. Many technical analysts, also referred to as "technicians," argue that many movements in stock prices are based, in large part, on psychology. Many technicians attempt to predict how market participants will behave, based on analyses of past behavior, and then trade on those predictions. Technicians often argue that simple statistical tests of trading rules are not conclusive because they are not applied to the more sophisticated trading strategies that can be used and that the research excludes the technician's subjective judgment. Thus, it is difficult to definitively refute this assertion because there are an unlimited number of possible technical trading rules.

Can technical analysts profit from trading on past trends? Overall, the evidence indicates that investors cannot consistently earn abnormal profits using past prices or other technical analysis strategies in developed markets.[16] Some evidence suggests, however, that there are opportunities to profit on technical analysis in countries with developing markets, including China, Hungary, Bangladesh, and Turkey.[17]

SEMISTRONG FORM   In a **semistrong-form efficient market**, prices reflect all publicly known and available information. Publicly available information includes financial statement data (such as earnings, dividends, corporate investments, changes

---

[14] Market efficiency should not be confused with the *random walk hypothesis* in which price changes over time are independent of one another. A random walk model is one of many alternative expected-return-generating models. Market efficiency does not require that returns follow a random walk.

[15] Serial correlation is a statistical measure of the degree to which the returns in one period are related to the returns in another period.

[16] Bessembinder and Chan (1998) and Fifield, Power, and Sinclair (2005).

[17] Fifield, Power, and Sinclair (2005), Chen and Li (2006), and Mobarek, Mollah, and Bhuyan (2008).

in management, etc.) and financial market data (such as closing prices, shares traded, etc.). Therefore, the semistrong form of market efficiency encompasses the weak form. In other words, if a market is semistrong efficient, then it must also be weak-form efficient. A market that quickly incorporates all publicly available information into its prices is semistrong efficient.

EXAMPLE 15.2   Information Arrival and Market Reaction

Consider an example of a news item and its effect on a share's price. In June 2008, the U.S. Federal Trade Commission (FTC) began an investigation of Intel Corporation regarding noncompetitiveness, and on December 16, 2009, the FTC announced that it was suing Intel over noncompetitive issues. This announcement was made before the market opened for trading on December 16.

Intel stock closed at $19.78 on December 15, 2009, but opened at $19.50 on December 16. The stock then traded in the range from $19.45 to $19.68 within the first half hour as the news of the suit and Intel's initial response were spreading among investors. Figure 15.4 illustrates the price of Intel for the first 90 minutes of trading on December 16.

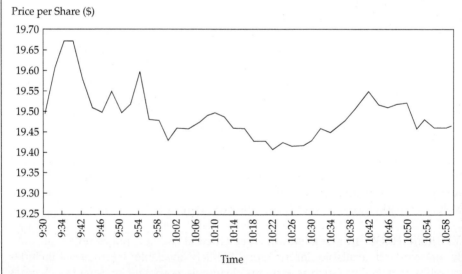

Price per Share ($)

FIGURE 15.4   Price of Intel: December 16, 2009
Source: Price data from Yahoo! Finance.

Is the fact that the price of Intel moves up immediately and then comes down indicative of an inefficiency regarding information? Not necessarily. Does it mean that investors overreacted? Not necessarily. During the morning, both before and after the market opened, news flowed about the lawsuit and the company's reaction to the lawsuit. The price of the shares reflects investors' reactions to this news. Why didn't Intel's shares simply move to a new level and stay there? Because (a) information continued to flow during the day on Intel and investors' estimate of the importance of this news on Intel's stock value continued to change, and (b) other news, related to other events and issues (such as the economy), affected stock prices.

In a semistrong market, efforts to analyze publicly available information are futile. That is, analyzing earnings announcements of companies to identify under-priced or overpriced securities is pointless because the prices of these securities already reflect all publicly available information. If markets are semistrong efficient, no single investor has access to information that is not already available to other market participants, and as a consequence, no single investor can gain an advantage in predicting future security prices. In a semistrong efficient market, prices adjust quickly and accurately to new information. Suppose a company announces earnings that are higher than expected. In a semistrong efficient market, investors would not be able to act on this announcement and earn abnormal returns.

STRONG FORM In the strong form of efficient markets, security prices fully reflect both public and private information. A market that is strong-form efficient is, by definition, also semistrong- and weak-form efficient. In the case of a strong-form efficient market, insiders would not be able to earn abnormal returns from trading on the basis of private information. A strong-form efficient market also means that prices reflect all private information, which means that prices reflect everything that the management of a company knows about the financial condition of the company that has not been publicly released. However, this is not likely because of the strong prohibitions against insider trading that are found in most countries. If a market is strong-form efficient, those with insider information cannot earn abnormal returns.

Researchers test whether a market is strong-form efficient by testing whether investors can earn abnormal profits by trading on nonpublic information. The results of these tests are consistent with the view that securities markets are not strong-form efficient; many studies have found that abnormal profits can be earned when nonpublic information is used.[18]

IMPLICATIONS OF THE EFFICIENT MARKET HYPOTHESIS The implications of efficient markets to investment managers and analysts are important because they affect the value of securities and how these securities are managed. Several implications can be drawn from the evidence on efficient markets for developed markets:

- Securities markets are weak-form efficient, and therefore, investors cannot earn abnormal returns by trading on the basis of past trends in price.

---

[18] Evidence that finds that markets are not strong-form efficient include Jaffe (1974) and Rozeff and Zaman (1988).

- Securities markets are semistrong efficient, and therefore, analysts who collect and analyze information must consider whether that information is already reflected in security prices and how any new information affects a security's value.[19]
- Securities markets are not strong-form efficient because securities laws are intended to prevent exploitation of private information.

Summary

This part has provided an overview of the theory and evidence regarding market efficiency and has discussed the different forms of market efficiency as well as the implications for fundamental analysis, technical analysis, and portfolio management. The general conclusion drawn from the efficient market hypothesis is that it is not possible to beat the market on a consistent basis by generating returns in excess of those expected for the level of risk of the investment.

Additional key points include the following:

- The efficiency of a market is affected by the number of market participants and depth of analyst coverage, information availability, and limits to trading.
- There are three forms of efficient markets, each based on what is considered to be the information used in determining asset prices. In the weak form, asset prices fully reflect all market data, which refers to all past price and trading volume information. In the semistrong form, asset prices reflect all publicly known and available information. In the strong form, asset prices fully reflect all information, which includes both public and private information.
- Intrinsic value refers to the true value of an asset, whereas market value refers to the price at which an asset can be bought or sold. When markets are efficient, the two should be the same or very close. But when markets are not efficient, the two can diverge significantly.
- Most empirical evidence supports the idea that securities markets in developed countries are semistrong-form efficient; however, empirical evidence does not support the strong form of the efficient market hypothesis.
- A number of anomalies have been documented that contradict the notion of market efficiency, including the size anomaly, the January anomaly, and the winners–losers anomalies. In most cases, however, contradictory evidence both supports and refutes the anomaly.
- Behavioral finance uses human psychology, such as cognitive biases, in an attempt to explain investment decisions. Whereas behavioral finance is helpful in understanding observed decisions, a market can still be considered efficient even if market participants exhibit seemingly irrational behaviors, such as herding.

---

[19] In the case of the Intel example, this implication would mean estimating how the actual filing of the lawsuit and the company's reaction to the lawsuit affect the value of Intel, while keeping in mind that the expectation of a lawsuit was already impounded in Intel's stock price.

References

Bessembinder, Hendrik, and Kalok Chan. 1998. "Market Efficiency and the Returns to Technical Analysis." *Financial Management*, Vol. 27, No. 2: 5–17.

Bris, Arturo, William N. Goetzmann, and Ning Zhu. 2009. "Efficiency and the Bear: Short Sales and Markets around the World." *Journal of Finance*, Vol. 62, No. 3: 1029–1079.

Chen, Kong-Jun, and Xiao-Ming Li. 2006. "Is Technical Analysis Useful for Stock Traders in China? Evidence from the SZSE Component A-Share Index." *Pacific Economic Review*, Vol. 11, No. 4: 477–488.

Chordia, Tarun, Richard Roll, and Avanidhar Subrahmanyam. 2005. "Evidence on the Speed of Convergence to Market Efficiency." *Journal of Financial Economics*, Vol. 76, No. 2: 271–292.

Duffie, Darrell, Nicholae Garleanu, and Lasse Heje Pederson. 2002. "Securities Lending, Shorting and Pricing." *Journal of Financial Economics*, Vol. 66, Issue 2–3: 307–339.

Fama, Eugene. "Efficient Capital Markets: A Review of Theory and Empirical Work." *Journal of Finance* 25, No. 2 (May 1970): 383–417.

Fama, Eugene. 1976. *Foundations of Finance*. New York: Basic Books.

Fifield, Suzanne, David Power, and C. Donald Sinclair. 2005. "An Analysis of Trading Strategies in Eleven European Stock Markets." *European Journal of Finance*, Vol. 11, No. 6: 531–548.

Grossman, Sanford J., and Joseph E. Stiglitz. 1980. "On the Impossibility of Informationally Efficient Markets." *American Economic Review*, Vol. 70, No. 3: 393–408.

Jaffe, Jeffrey. 1974. "Special Information and Insider Trading." *Journal of Business*, Vol. 47, No. 3: 410–428.

Jones, Charles M., and Owen A. Lamont. 2002. "Short-Sale Constraints and Stock Returns." *Journal of Financial Economics*, Vol. 66, Nos. 2–3: 207–239.

Mobarek, Asma, A. Sabur Mollah, and Rafiqul Bhuyan. 2008. "Market Efficiency in Emerging Stock Market." *Journal of Emerging Market Finance*, Vol. 7, No. 1: 17–41.

Rozeff, Michael S., and Mir A. Zaman. 1988. "Market Efficiency and Insider Trading: New Evidence." *Journal of Business*, Vol. 61: 25–44.

Yau, Jot, Thomas Schneeweis, Thomas Robinson, and Lisa Weiss. 2007. "Alternative Investments Portfolio Management." *Managing Investment Portfolios: A Dynamic Process*. Hoboken, NJ: John Wiley & Sons.

Part III Portfolio Risk and Return

Efficient Frontier and Investor's Optimal Portfolio

In this section, we formalize the effect of diversification and expand the set of investments to include all available risky assets in a mean–variance framework. The addition of a risk-free asset generates an optimal risky portfolio and the capital allocation line. We can then derive an investor's optimal portfolio by overlaying the capital allocation line with the indifference curves of investors.

INVESTMENT OPPORTUNITY SET   If two assets are perfectly correlated, the risk–return opportunity set is represented by a straight line connecting those two assets. The

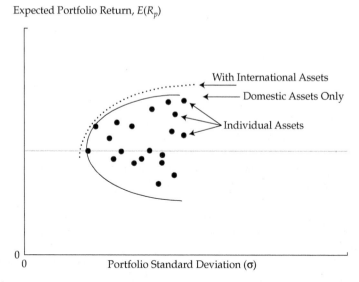

Expected Portfolio Return, $E(R_p)$

With International Assets

Domestic Assets Only

Individual Assets

0

0   Portfolio Standard Deviation (σ)

FIGURE 15.5   Investment Opportunity Set

line contains portfolios formed by changing the weight of each asset invested in the portfolio. This correlation is depicted by the straight line (with $\rho = 1$) in Figure 15.5. If the two assets are not perfectly correlated, the portfolio's risk is less than the weighted average risk of the components and the portfolio formed from the two assets bulges on the left as shown by curves with the correlation coefficient (ρ) less than 1.0 in Figure 15.5. All of the points connecting the two assets are achievable (or feasible). The addition of new assets to this portfolio creates more and more portfolios that are either a linear combination of the existing portfolio and the new asset or a curvilinear combination depending on the correlation between the existing portfolio and the new asset.

As the number of available assets increases, the number of possible combinations increases rapidly. When all investable assets are considered, and there are hundreds and thousands of them, we can construct an opportunity set of investments. The opportunity set will ordinarily span all points within a frontier because it is also possible to reach every possible point within that curve by judiciously creating a portfolio from the investable assets.

We begin with individual investable assets and gradually form portfolios that can be plotted to form a curve as shown in Figure 15.5. All points on the curve and points to the right of the curve are attainable by a combination of one or more of the investable assets. This set of points is called the *investment opportunity set*. Initially, the opportunity set consists of domestic assets only and is labeled as such in Figure 15.5.

ADDITION OF ASSET CLASSES   Figure 15.5 shows the effect of adding a new asset class, such as international assets. As long as the new asset class is not perfectly correlated with the existing asset class, the investment opportunity set will expand out further to the northwest providing a superior risk–return trade-off.

The investment opportunity set with international assets dominates the opportunity set that includes only domestic assets. Adding other asset classes will have the same impact on the opportunity set. Thus, we should continue to add asset classes until they do not further improve the risk–return trade-off. The benefits of diversification can be fully captured in this way in the construction of the investment opportunity set, and eventually in the selection of the optimal portfolio.

In the discussion that follows in this section, we will assume that *all* investable assets available to an investor are included in the investment opportunity set and no special attention needs to be paid to new asset classes or new investment opportunities.

MINIMUM-VARIANCE PORTFOLIOS The investment opportunity set consisting of all available investable sets is shown in Figure 15.6. There are a large number of portfolios available for investment, but we must choose a single optimal portfolio. In this subsection, we begin the selection process by narrowing the choice to fewer portfolios.

MINIMUM-VARIANCE FRONTIER Risk-averse investors seek to minimize risk for a given return. Consider points A, B, and X in Figure 15.6 and assume that they are on the same horizontal line by construction. Thus, the three points have the same expected return, $E(R_1)$, as do all other points on the imaginary line connecting A, B, and X. Given a choice, an investor will choose the point with the minimum risk, which is point X. Point X, however, is unattainable because it does not lie within the investment opportunity set. Thus, the minimum risk that we can attain for $E(R_1)$ is at point A. Point B and all points to the right of point A are feasible but they have higher risk. Therefore, a risk-averse investor will choose only point A in preference to any other portfolio with the same return.

Similarly, point C is the minimum variance point for the return earned at C. Points to the right of C have higher risk. We can extend the above analysis to all possible returns. In all cases, we find that the **minimum variance portfolio** is the one that lies on the solid curve drawn in Figure 15.6. The entire collection of these

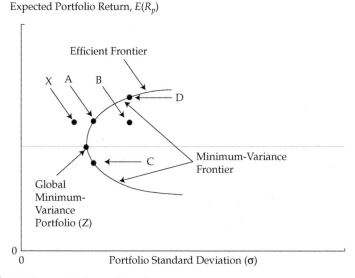

FIGURE 15.6   Minimum-Variance Frontier

minimum-variance portfolios is referred to as the minimum-variance frontier. The minimum-variance frontier defines the smaller set of portfolios in which investors would want to invest. Note that no risk-averse investor will choose to invest in a portfolio to the right of the minimum-variance frontier because a portfolio on the minimum-variance frontier can give the same return but at a lower risk.

Global Minimum-Variance Portfolio   The left-most point on the minimum-variance frontier is the portfolio with the minimum variance among all portfolios of risky assets, and is referred to as the **global minimum-variance portfolio**. An investor cannot hold a portfolio consisting of *risky* assets that has less risk than that of the global minimum-variance portfolio. Note the emphasis on "risky" assets. Later, the introduction of a risk-free asset will allow us to relax this constraint.

Efficient Frontier of Risky Assets   The minimum-variance frontier gives us portfolios with the minimum variance for a given return. However, investors also want to maximize return for a given risk. Observe points A and C on the minimum-variance frontier shown in Figure 15.6. Both of them have the same risk. Given a choice, an investor will choose portfolio *A* because it has a higher return. No one will choose portfolio *C*. The same analysis applies to all points on the minimum-variance frontier that lie below the global minimum-variance portfolio. Thus, portfolios on the curve below the global minimum-variance portfolio and to the right of the global minimum-variance portfolio are not beneficial and are inefficient portfolios for an investor.

The curve that lies above and to the right of the global minimum-variance portfolio is referred to as the **Markowitz efficient frontier** because it contains all portfolios of risky assets that rational, risk-averse investors will choose.

An important observation that is often ignored is the slope at various points on the efficient frontier. As we move right from the global minimum-variance portfolio (point Z) in Figure 15.6, there is an increase in risk with a concurrent increase in return. The increase in return with every unit increase in risk, however, keeps decreasing as we move from left to right because the slope continues to decrease. The slope at point D is less than the slope at point A, which is less than the slope at point Z. The increase in return by moving from point Z to point A is the same as the increase in return by moving from point A to point D. It can be seen that the additional risk in moving from point A to point D is three to four times more than the additional risk in moving from point Z to point A. Thus, investors obtain decreasing increases in returns as they assume more risk.

A RISK-FREE ASSET AND MANY RISKY ASSETS   Until now, we have only considered risky assets in which the return is risky or uncertain. Most investors, however, have access to a risk-free asset, most notably from securities issued by the government. The addition of a risk-free asset makes the investment opportunity set much richer than the investment opportunity set consisting only of risky assets.

Capital Allocation Line and Optimal Risky Portfolio   By definition, a risk-free asset has zero risk so it must lie on the y-axis in a mean-variance graph. A risk-free asset with a return of R_f is plotted in Figure 15.7. This asset can now be combined with a portfolio of risky assets. The combination of a risk-free asset with a portfolio of risky assets is a straight line (see Figure 15.7). Here, we have many risky portfolios to choose from instead of a single risky portfolio.

Expected Portfolio Return, $E(R_p)$

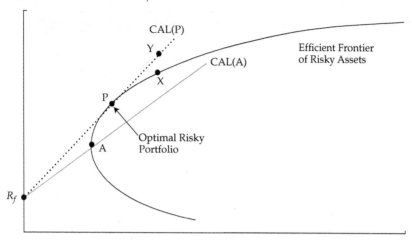

FIGURE 15.7   Optimal Risky Portfolio

All portfolios on the efficient frontier are candidates for being combined with the risk-free asset. Two combinations are shown in Figure 15.7: one between the risk-free asset and efficient portfolio A and the other between the risk-free asset and efficient portfolio P. Comparing capital allocation line A and capital allocation line P reveals that there is a point on CAL(P) with a higher return and same risk for each point on CAL(A). In other words, the portfolios on CAL(P) dominate the portfolios on CAL(A). Therefore, an investor will choose CAL(P) over CAL(A). We would like to move further northwest to achieve even better portfolios. None of those portfolios, however, is attainable because they are above the efficient frontier.

What about other points on the efficient frontier? For example, point X is on the efficient frontier and has the highest return of all risky portfolios for its risk. However, point Y on CAL(P), achievable by leveraging portfolio P, lies above point X and has the same risk but higher return. In the same way, we can observe that not only does CAL(P) dominate CAL(A) but it also dominates the Markowitz efficient frontier of risky assets.

CAL(P) is the optimal capital allocation line and portfolio P is the optimal risky portfolio. Thus, with the addition of the risk-free asset, we are able to narrow our selection of risky portfolios to a single optimal risky portfolio, P, which is at the tangent of CAL(P) and the efficient frontier of risky assets.

The Two-Fund Separation Theorem   The **two-fund separation theorem** states that all investors, regardless of taste, risk preferences, and initial wealth, will hold a combination of two portfolios or funds: a risk-free asset and an optimal portfolio of risky assets.

The separation theorem allows us to divide an investor's investment problem into two distinct steps: the investment decision and the financing decision. In the first step, as in the previous analysis, the investor identifies the optimal risky portfolio. The optimal risky portfolio is selected from numerous risky portfolios without considering the investor's preferences. The investment decision at this step is based on the optimal risky portfolio's (a single portfolio) return, risk, and correlations.

The capital allocation line connects the optimal risky portfolio and the risk-free asset. All optimal investor portfolios must be on this line. Each investor's optimal portfolio on the CAL(P) is determined in the second step. Considering each individual investor's risk preference, using indifference curves, determines the investor's allocation to the risk-free asset (lending) and to the optimal risky portfolio. Portfolios beyond the optimal risky portfolio are obtained by borrowing at the risk-free rate (i.e., buying on margin). Therefore, the individual investor's risk preference determines the amount of financing (i.e., lending to the government instead of investing in the optimal risky portfolio or borrowing to purchase additional amounts of the optimal risky portfolio).

EXAMPLE 15.3   Choosing the Right Portfolio

In Figure 15.8, the risk and return of the points marked are as follows:

Point	Return	Risk	Point	Return	Risk
A	15%	10%	B	11%	10%
C	15%	30%	D	25%	30%
F	4%	0%	G (gold)	10%	30%
P	16%	17%			

Answer the following questions with reference to the points plotted on Figure 15.8 and explain your answers. The investor is choosing one portfolio based on the graph.

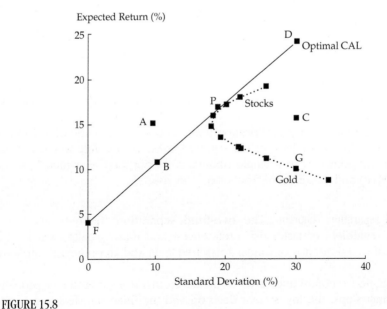

FIGURE 15.8

1. Which of the above points is not achievable?
2. Which of these portfolios will not be chosen by a rational, risk-averse investor?
3. Which of these portfolios is most suitable for a risk-neutral investor?
4. Gold is on the inefficient part of the feasible set. Nonetheless, gold is owned by many rational investors as part of a larger portfolio. Why?
5. What is the utility of an investor at point P with a risk aversion coefficient of 3?

Solution to 1: Portfolio A is not attainable because it lies outside the feasible set and not on the capital allocation line.

Solution to 2: Portfolios G and C will not be chosen because D provides higher return for the same risk. G and C are the only investable points that do not lie on the capital allocation line.

Solution to 3: Portfolio D is most suitable because a risk-neutral investor cares only about return and portfolio D provides the highest return. A = 0 in the utility formula.

Solution to 4: Gold may be owned as part of a portfolio (not as *the* portfolio) because gold has low or negative correlation with many risky assets, such as stocks. Being part of a portfolio can thus reduce overall risk even though its standalone risk is high and return is low. Note that gold's price is not stable—its return is very risky (30 percent). Even risk-seekers will choose D over G, which has the same risk but higher return.

Solution to 5: $U = [E(r) - (0.5 \times A \times \sigma^2)] = [0.16 - (0.5 \times 3 \times 0.0289)] = (0.16 - 0.4335) = 0.1167 = 11.67\%$.

OPTIMAL INVESTOR PORTFOLIO The CAL(P) contains the best possible portfolios available to investors. Each of those portfolios is a linear combination of the risk-free asset and the optimal risky portfolio. Among the available portfolios, the selection of each investor's optimal portfolio depends on the risk preferences of an investor. In a previous section we discussed how an individual investor's risk preferences are incorporated into his or her indifference curves. These can be used to select the optimal portfolio.

Figure 15.9 shows an indifference curve that is tangent to the capital allocation line, CAL(P). Indifference curves with higher utility than this one lie above the capital allocation line, so their portfolios are not achievable. Indifference curves that lie below this one are not preferred because they have lower utility. Thus, the optimal portfolio for the investor with this indifference curve is portfolio C on CAL(P), which is tangent to the indifference curve.

Investor Preferences and Optimal Portfolios The location of an optimal investor portfolio depends on the investor's risk preferences. A highly risk-averse investor may invest a large proportion, even 100 percent, of his/her assets in the risk-free

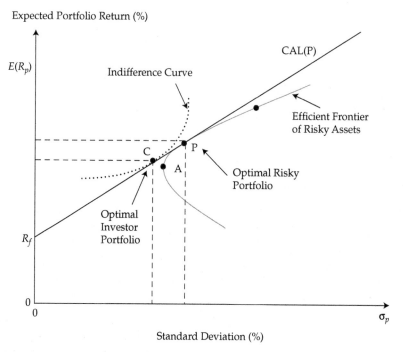

FIGURE 15.9   Optimal Investor Portfolio

EXAMPLE 15.4   Comprehensive Example of Portfolio Selection

This comprehensive example reviews many concepts learned in this chapter. The example begins with simple information about available assets and builds an optimal investor portfolio for the Lohrmanns.

Suppose the Lohrmanns can invest in only two risky assets, A and B. The expected return and standard deviation for asset A are 20 percent and 50 percent, and the expected return and standard deviation for asset B are 15 percent and 33 percent. The two assets have zero correlation with one another.

1. Calculate portfolio expected return and portfolio risk (standard deviation) if an investor invests 10 percent in A and the remaining 90 percent in B.

Solution to 1: The subscript "rp" means risky portfolio.

$$R_{rp} = [0.10 \times 20\%] + [(1 - 0.10) \times 15\%] = 0.155 = 15.50\%$$

$$\sigma_{rp} = \sqrt{w_A^2 \sigma_A^2 + w_B^2 \sigma_B^2 + 2w_A w_B \rho_{AB} \sigma_A \sigma_B}$$

$$= \sqrt{(0.10^2 \times 0.50^2) + (0.90^2 \times 0.33^2) + (2 \times 0.10 \times 0.90 \times 0.0 \times 0.50 \times 0.33)}$$

$$= 0.3012 = 30.12\%$$

Note that the correlation coefficient is 0, so the last term for standard deviation is zero.

2. Generalize the above calculations for portfolio return and risk by assuming an investment of w_A in asset A and an investment of $(1 - w_A)$ in asset B.

Solution to 2:

$$R_{rp} = w_A \times 20\% + (1 - w_A) \times 15\% = 0.05w_A + 0.15$$

$$\sigma_{rp} = \sqrt{w_A^2 \times 0.5^2 + (1 - w_A)^2 \times 0.33^2} = \sqrt{0.25w_A^2 + 0.1089\left(1 - 2w_A + w_A^2\right)}$$

$$= \sqrt{0.3589w_A^2 - 0.2178w_A + 0.1089}$$

The investment opportunity set can be constructed by using different weights in the expressions for $E(R_{rp})$ and σ_{rp} in Part 1 of this example. Figure 15.10 shows the combination of assets A and B.

Expected Portfolio Return, $E(R_p)$, %

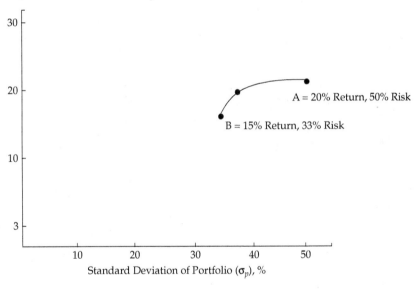

FIGURE 15.10

3. Now introduce a risk-free asset with a return of 3 percent. Write an equation for the capital allocation line in terms of w_A that will connect the risk-free asset to the portfolio of risky assets. (Hint: Use the following equation and substitute the expressions for a risky portfolio's risk and return from number 2.)

$$E(R_p) = w_1 R_f + (1 - w_1)E(R_i)$$

$$\sigma_p^2 = w_1^2 \sigma_f^2 + (1 - w_1)^2 \sigma_i^2 + 2w_1(1 - w_1)\rho_{12}\sigma_f\sigma_i = (1 - w_1)^2 \sigma_i^2$$

$$\sigma_p = (1 - w_1)\sigma_i$$

Solution to 3: The equation of the line connecting the risk-free asset to the portfolio of risky assets is given below, where the subscript "*rp*" refers to the risky portfolio instead of "*I*," and the subscript "*p*" refers to the new portfolio of two risky assets and one risk-free asset.

$$E(R_p) = R_f + \frac{E(R_i) - R_f}{\sigma_i}\sigma_p, \text{rewritten as}$$

$$E(R_p) = R_f + \frac{E(R_{rp}) - R_f}{\sigma_{rp}}\sigma_p$$

$$= 0.03 + \frac{0.05w_A + 0.15 - 0.03}{\sqrt{0.3589w_A^2 - 0.2178w_A + 0.1089}}\sigma_p$$

$$= 0.03 + \frac{0.05w_A + 0.12}{\sqrt{0.3589w_A^2 - 0.2178w_A + 0.1089}}\sigma_p$$

The capital allocation line is the line that has the maximum slope because it is tangent to the curve formed by portfolios of the two risky assets. Figure 15.11 shows the capital allocation line based on a risk-free asset added to the group of assets.

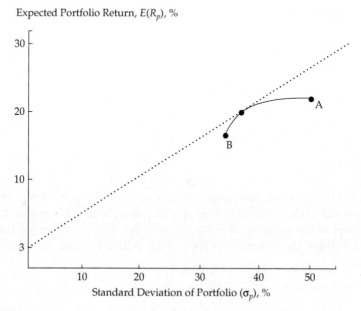

FIGURE 15.11

4. The slope of the capital allocation line is maximized when the weight in asset A is 38.20 percent.[1] What is the equation for the capital allocation line using w_A of 38.20 percent?

Solution to 4: By substituting 38.20 percent for w_A in the equation in 3 above we get $E(R_p) = 0.03 + 0.4978\ \sigma_p$ as the capital allocation line.

5. Having created the capital allocation line, we turn to the Lohrmanns. What is the standard deviation of a portfolio that gives a 20 percent return and is on the capital allocation line? How does this portfolio compare with asset A?

Solution to 5: Solve the equation for the capital allocation line to get the standard deviation: $0.20 = 0.03 + 0.4978\ \sigma_p.$ $\sigma_p = 34.2\%$. The portfolio with a 20 percent return has the same return as asset A but a lower standard deviation, 34.2 percent instead of 50.0 percent.

6. What is the risk of portfolios with returns of 3 percent, 9 percent, 15 percent, and 20 percent?

Solution to 6: You can find the risk of the portfolio using the equation for the capital allocation line: $E(R_p) = 0.03 + 0.4978\ \sigma_p$.

For a portfolio with a return of 15 percent, write $0.15 = 0.03 + 0.4978\ \sigma_p$. Solving for σ_p gives 24.1 percent. You can similarly calculate risks of other portfolios with the given returns.

The risk of the portfolio for a return of 3 percent is 0.0 percent, for a return of 9 percent is 12.1 percent, for a return of 15 percent is 24.1 percent, and for a return of 20 percent is 34.2 percent. The points are plotted in Figure 15.12.

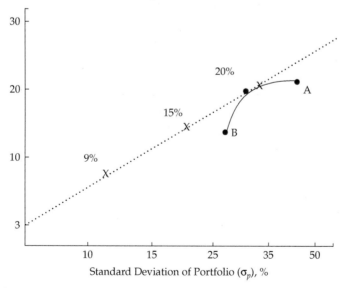

FIGURE 15.12

7. What is the utility that the Lohrmanns derive from a portfolio with a return of 3 percent, 9 percent, 15 percent, and 20 percent? The risk aversion coefficient for the Lohrmanns is 2.5.

Solution to 7: To find the utility, use the utility formula with a risk aversion coefficient of 2.5:

Utility $= E(R_p) - 0.5 \times 2.5 \ \sigma_p^{\ 2}$
Utility (3%) $= 0.0300$.
Utility (9%) $= 0.09 - 0.5 \times 2.5 \times 0.121^2 = +0.0717$
Utility (15%) $= 0.15 - 0.5 \times 2.5 \times 0.241^2 = +0.0774$
Utility (20%) $= 0.20 - 0.5 \times 2.5 \times 0.341^2 = +0.0546$

Based on the above information, the Lohrmanns choose a portfolio with a return of 15 percent and a standard deviation of 24.1 percent because it has the highest utility: 0.0774. Finally, Figure 15.13 shows the indifference curve that is tangent to the capital allocation line to generate the Lohrmanns' optimal investor portfolio.

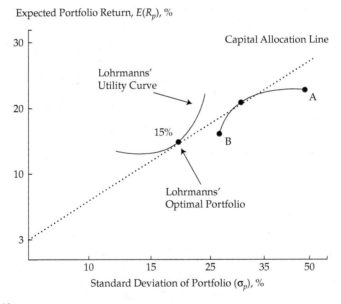

FIGURE 15.13

---

[1] You can maximize $\dfrac{0.05w_A + 0.12}{\sqrt{0.3589w_A^2 - 0.2178w_A + 0.1089}}$ by taking the first derivative of the slope with respect to w_A and setting it to 0.

asset. The optimal portfolio in this investor's case will be located close to the *y*-axis. A less risk-averse investor, however, may invest a large portion of his/her wealth in the optimal risky asset. The optimal portfolio in this investor's case will lie closer to point P in Figure 15.9.

Some less risk-averse investors (i.e., with a high risk tolerance) may wish to accept even more risk because of the chance of higher return. Such an investor may borrow money to invest more in the risky portfolio. If the investor borrows 25 percent of his wealth, he/she can invest 125 percent in the optimal risky portfolio. The optimal investor portfolio for such an investor will lie to the right of point P on the capital allocation line.

Thus, moving from the risk-free asset along the capital allocation line, we encounter investors who are willing to accept more risk. At point P, the investor is 100 percent invested in the optimal risky portfolio. Beyond point P, the investor accepts even more risk by borrowing money and investing in the optimal risky portfolio.

Note that we are able to accommodate all types of investors with just two portfolios: the risk-free asset and the optimal risky portfolio. Figure 15.9 is also an illustration of the two-fund separation theorem. Portfolio P is the optimal risky portfolio that is selected without regard to investor preferences. The optimal investor portfolio is selected on the capital allocation line by overlaying the indifference curves that incorporate investor preferences.

Part IV Asset Pricing Models

The theory of portfolio selection as formulated in 1952 by Markowitz together with asset-pricing theory provide the foundation for the management of portfolios. The goal of portfolio selection is the construction of portfolios that maximize expected returns consistent with individually acceptable levels of risk. The theory of portfolio selection, popularly referred to as mean-variance portfolio analysis, is a normative theory. That is, it is a theory that describes a standard or norm of behavior that investors should pursue in constructing a portfolio, in contrast to a theory that is actually followed. Asset pricing theory goes on to formalize the relationship that should exist between asset returns and risk if investors behave in a hypothesized manner. In contrast to a normative theory, asset-pricing theory is a positive theory— a theory that hypothesizes how investors behave rather than how investors should behave. Based on that hypothesized behavior of investors, a model that provides the expected return (a key input into constructing portfolios based on mean-variance portfolio analysis) is derived and is called an asset-pricing model. In this part, major theories about a security's expected return based on asset-pricing models are described.

Together, portfolio selection theory and asset-pricing theory provide a framework to specify and measure investment risk and to develop relationships between expected asset return and risk (and hence between risk and required return on an investment). However, it is critically important to understand that portfolio selection theory is a theory that is independent of any theories about asset pricing. The validity of portfolio selection theory does not rest on the validity of asset-pricing theory.

Characteristics of an Asset-Pricing Model

In well-functioning capital markets, an investor should be rewarded for accepting the various risks associated with investing in an asset. Risks are also referred to as "risk factors" or "factors." We can express an *asset-pricing model* in general terms based on risk factors as follows:

$$E(R_i) = f(F_1, F_2, F, \ldots, F_N) \tag{15.1}$$

where

$E(R_i)$ = expected return for asset i
F_k = risk factor k
N = number of risk factors

Equation (15.1) says that the expected return is a function of N risk factors. The trick is to figure out what the risk factors are and to specify the precise relationship between expected return and the risk factors.

We can fine-tune the asset-pricing model given by equation (15.1) by thinking about the minimum expected return we would want from investing in an asset. There are securities issued by the U.S. Department of the Treasury that offer a known return if held over some period of time. The expected return offered on such securities is called the risk-free return or the risk-free rate. By investing in an asset other than such securities, investors will demand a premium over the risk-free rate. That is, the expected return that an investor will demand is

$$E(R_i) = R_f + \text{Risk premium}$$

where R_f is the risk-free rate.

The "risk premium" or additional return expected over the risk-free rate depends on the risk factors associated with investing in the asset. Thus, we can rewrite the general form of the asset-pricing model given by equation (15.1) as follows:

$$E(R_i) = R_f + f(F_1, F_2, F, \ldots, F_N) \tag{15.2}$$

Risk factors can be divided into two general categories. The first category is risk factors that cannot be diversified away. That is, no matter what the investor does, the investor cannot eliminate these risk factors. These risk factors are referred to as *systematic risk factors* or *nondiversifiable risk factors*. The second category is risk factors that can be eliminated via diversification. These risk factors are unique to the asset and are referred to as *unsystematic risk factors* or *diversifiable risk factors*.

Capital Asset Pricing Model

The first asset-pricing model derived from economic theory was formulated by Sharpe (1964), Lintner (1965), Treynor (1961), and Mossin (1966) and is called the *capital asset-pricing model (CAPM)*. The CAPM has only one systematic risk factor—the risk of the overall movement of the market. This risk factor is referred to as "market risk." So, in the CAPM, the terms "market risk" and "systematic risk" are used interchangeably. By "market risk" it is meant the risk associated with holding a portfolio consisting of all assets, called the "market portfolio." As will be explained later, in the market portfolio an asset is held in proportion to its market value. So, for example, if the total market value of all assets is X and the market value of asset j is Y, then asset j will comprise $Y/$X$ of the market portfolio.

The CAPM is given by the following formula:

$$E(R_i) = R_f + \beta_i[E(R_M) - R_f] \tag{15.3}$$

where

$E(R_M)$ = expected return on the "market portfolio"

β_i = measure of systematic risk of asset i relative to the "market portfolio"

We will derive the CAPM later. For now, let's look at what this asset-pricing model says.

The expected return for an asset i according to the CAPM is equal to the risk-free rate plus a risk premium. The risk premium is

$$\text{Risk premium in the CAPM} = \beta_i[E(R_M) - R_f]$$

First look at *beta* (β_i) in the risk premium component of the CAPM. Beta is a measure of the sensitivity of the return of asset i to the return of the market portfolio. A beta of 1 means that the asset or a portfolio has the same quantity of risk as the market portfolio. A beta greater than 1 means that the asset or portfolio has more market risk than the market portfolio and a beta less than 1 means that the asset or portfolio has less market risk than the market portfolio. The second component of the risk premium in the CAPM is the difference between the expected return on the market portfolio, $E(R_M)$, and the risk-free rate. It measures the potential reward for taking on the risk of the market above what can earned by investing in an asset that offers a risk-free rate.

Taken together, the risk premium is a product of the quantity of market risk (as measured by beta) and the potential compensation of taking on market risk (as measured by $[E(R_M) - R_f]$).

Let's use some values for beta to see if all of this makes sense. Suppose that a portfolio has a beta of zero. That is, the return for this portfolio has no market risk. Substituting zero for β in the CAPM given by equation (15.3), we would find that the expected return is just the risk-free rate. This makes sense since a portfolio that has no market risk should have an expected return equal to the risk-free rate.

Consider a portfolio that has a beta of 1. This portfolio has the same market risk as the market portfolio. Substituting 1 for β in the CAPM given by equation (15.3) results in an expected return equal to that of the market portfolio. Again, this is what one should expect for the return of this portfolio since it has the same market risk exposure as the market portfolio.

If a portfolio has greater market risk than the market portfolio, beta will be greater than 1 and the expected return will be greater than that of the market portfolio. If a portfolio has less market risk than the market portfolio, beta will be less than 1 and the expected return will be less than that of the market portfolio.

DERIVATION OF THE CAPM The CAPM is an equilibrium asset-pricing model derived from a set of assumptions. Here, we demonstrate how the CAPM is derived.

Assumptions The CAPM is an abstraction of the real world capital markets and, as such, is based on some assumptions. These assumptions simplify matters a great deal, and some of them may even seem unrealistic. However, these assumptions make the CAPM more tractable from a mathematical standpoint. The seven CAPM assumptions are as follows:

Assumption 1:	Investors make investment decisions based on the expected return and variance of returns.
Assumption 2:	Investors are rational and risk averse.
Assumption 3:	Investors subscribe to the Markowitz method of portfolio diversification.
Assumption 4:	Investors all invest for the same period of time.
Assumption 5:	Investors have the same expectations about the expected return and variance of all assets.
Assumption 6:	There is a risk-free asset and investors can borrow and lend any amount at the risk-free rate.
Assumption 7:	Capital markets are completely competitive and frictionless.

The first five assumptions deal with the way investors make decisions. The last two assumptions relate to characteristics of the capital market.

Capital Market Line To derive the CAPM, we begin with the efficient frontier. In creating an efficient frontier, there is no consideration of a risk-free asset. In the absence of a risk-free rate, efficient portfolios can be constructed based on expected return and variance, with the optimal portfolio being the one portfolio that is tangent to the investor's indifference curve. The efficient frontier changes, however, once a risk-free asset is introduced and assuming that investors can borrow and lend at the risk-free rate (Assumption 6). This is illustrated in Figure 15.14.

Every combination of the risk-free asset and the efficient portfolio denoted by point M is shown on the line drawn from the vertical axis at the risk-free rate tangent to the efficient frontier. The point of tangency is denoted by M, which represents portfolio M. All the portfolios on the line are feasible for the investor to construct.

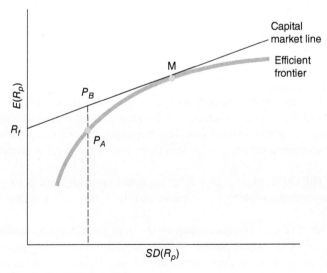

FIGURE 15.14   The Capital Market Line

Portfolios to the left of portfolio *M* represent combinations of risky assets and the risk-free asset. Portfolios to the right of *M* include purchases of risky assets made with funds borrowed at the risk-free rate. Such a portfolio is called a *leveraged portfolio* since it involves the use of borrowed funds. The line from the risk-free rate that is tangent to portfolio *M* is called the *capital market line (CML)*.

Let's compare a portfolio on the CML to a portfolio on the efficient frontier with the same risk. For example, compare portfolio P_A, which is on the efficient frontier, with portfolio P_B, which is on the CML and therefore is comprised of some combination of the risk-free asset and the efficient portfolio *M*. Notice that for the same risk the expected return is greater for P_B than for P_A. By Assumption 2, a risk-averse investor will prefer P_B to P_A. That is, P_B will dominate P_A. In fact, this is true for all but one portfolio on the CML: portfolio *M*, which is on the efficient frontier.

With the introduction of the risk-free asset, we can now say that an investor will select a portfolio on the CML, which represents a combination of borrowing or lending at the risk-free rate and the efficient portfolio *M*. The particular efficient portfolio on the CML that the investor will select will depend on the investor's risk preference. This can be seen in Figure 15.15, which is the same as Figure 15.14 but has the investor's indifference curves included. The investor will select the portfolio on the CML that is tangent to the highest indifference curve, u_3 in the exhibit. Notice that without the risk-free asset, an investor could only get to u_2, which is the indifference curve that is tangent to the efficient frontier. Thus, the opportunity to borrow

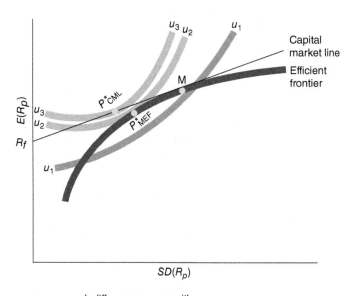

u_1, u_2, u_3 = Indifference curves with $u_1 < u_2 < u_3$

M = Market portfolio

R_f = Risk-free rate

P^*_{CML} = Optimal portfolio on capital market line

P^*_{MEF} = Optimal portfolio on efficient frontier

FIGURE 15.15   Optimal Portfolio and the Capital Market Line

or lend at the risk-free rate results in a capital market where risk-averse investors will prefer to hold portfolios consisting of combinations of the risk-free asset and some portfolio M on the efficient frontier.

We can derive a formula for the CML algebraically. Based on the assumption of homogeneous expectations (Assumption 5), all investors can create an efficient portfolio consisting of w_f placed in the risk-free asset and w_M in the market portfolio, where w represents the corresponding percentage (weight) of the portfolio allocated to each asset. Thus,

$$w_f + w_M = 1 \text{ or } w_f = 1 - w_M$$

The expected return is equal to the weighted average of the expected return of the two assets. Therefore, the expected portfolio return, $E(R_p)$, is equal to

$$E(R_p) = w_f R_f + w_M E(R_M)$$

Since we know that $w_f = 1 - w_M$, we can rewrite $E(R_p)$ as follows:

$$E(R_p) = (1 - w_M)R_f + w_M E(R_M)$$

This can be simplified as follows:

$$E(R_p) = R_f + w_M[E(R_M) - R_f] \tag{15.4}$$

The variance of the portfolio consisting of the risk-free asset and portfolio M can be found using the formula for the variance of a two-asset portfolio. It is

$$\text{Var}(R_p) = w_f^2 \, \text{Var}(R_f) + w_M^2 \, \text{Var}(R_M) + 2w_f w_M \, \text{Cov}(R_f, R_M)$$

The variance of the risk-free asset, $\text{Var}(R_f)$, is equal to zero. This is because there is no possible variation in the return since the future return is known. The covariance between the risk-free asset and portfolio M, $\text{Cov}(R_f, R_M)$, is zero. This is because the risk-free asset has no variability and therefore does not move at all with the return on portfolio M, which is a risky portfolio. Substituting these two values into the formula for the portfolio's variance, we get

$$\text{Var}(R_p) = w_M^2 \, \text{Var}(R_M)$$

In other words, the variance of the portfolio is represented by the weighted variance of portfolio M.

We can solve for the weight of portfolio M by substituting standard deviations for variances. Since the standard deviation (SD) is the square root of the variance, we can write

$$\text{SD}(R_p) = w_M \text{SD}(R_M)$$

and therefore

$$w_M = \frac{\text{SD}(R_p)}{\text{SD}(R_M)}$$

If we substitute the above result for w_M in equation (15.4) and rearrange terms we get the CML:

$$E(R_p) = R_f + \left[\frac{E(R_M) - R_f}{\text{SD}(R_M)} \right] \text{SD}(R_p) \tag{15.5}$$

WHAT IS PORTFOLIO *M*?   Now that we know that portfolio *M* is pivotal to the CML, we need to know what portfolio *M* is. That is, how does an investor construct portfolio *M*? Fama (1970) demonstrated that portfolio *M* must consist of all assets available to investors, and each asset must be held in proportion to its market value relative to the total market value of all assets. That is, portfolio *M* is the "market portfolio" described earlier. So, rather than referring to the market portfolio, we can simply refer to the "market."

Risk Premium in the CML   With homogeneous expectations, $SD(R_M)$ and $SD(R_p)$ are the market's consensus for the expected return distributions for portfolio *M* and portfolio *p*. The risk premium for the CML is

$$\left[\frac{E(R_M) - R_f}{SD(R_M)} \right] SD(R_p)$$

Let's examine the economic meaning of the risk premium.

The numerator of the first term is the expected return from investing in the market beyond the risk-free return. It is a measure of the reward for holding the risky market portfolio rather than the risk-free asset. The denominator is the market risk of the market portfolio. Thus, the first term measures the reward per unit of market risk. Since the CML represents the return offered to compensate for a perceived level of risk, each point on the CML is a balanced market condition, or equilibrium. The slope of the CML (that is, the first term) determines the additional return needed to compensate for a unit change in risk. That is why the slope of the CML is also referred to as the equilibrium market price of risk.

The CML says that the expected return on a portfolio is equal to the risk-free rate plus a risk premium equal to the market price of risk (as measured by the reward per unit of market risk) times the quantity of risk for the portfolio (as measured by the standard deviation of the portfolio). That is,

$$E(R)_p = R_f + \text{Market price of risk} \times \text{Quantity of risk}$$

Systematic and Unsystematic Risk   Now we know that a risk-averse investor who makes decisions based on expected return and variance should construct an efficient portfolio using a combination of the market portfolio and the risk-free rate. The combinations are identified by the CML. Based on this result, Sharpe (1964) derived an asset-pricing model that shows how a risky asset should be priced. In the process of doing so, we can fine-tune our thinking about the risk associated with an asset. Specifically, we can show that the appropriate risk that investors should be compensated for accepting is not the variance of an asset's return but some other quantity. In order to do this, let's take a closer look at risk.

We can do this by looking at the variance of the portfolio. It can be demonstrated that the variance of the market portfolio containing *N* assets can be shown to be equal to:

$$\text{Var}(R_M) = w_{1M} \, \text{Cov}(R_1, R_M) + w_{2M} \, \text{Cov}(R_2, R_M) + \dots + w_{NM} \, \text{Cov}(R_N, R_M) \quad (15.6)$$

where w_{iM} is equal to the proportion invested in asset *i* in the market portfolio.

Notice that the portfolio variance does not depend on the variance of the assets comprising the market portfolio but their covariance with the market portfolio.

Sharpe defined the degree to which an asset covaries with the market portfolio as the asset's systematic risk. More specifically, he defined systematic risk as the portion of an asset's variability that can be attributed to a common factor. Systematic risk is the minimum level of risk that can be obtained for a portfolio by means of diversification across a large number of randomly chosen assets. As such, systematic risk is that which results from general market and economic conditions that cannot be diversified away.

Sharpe defined the portion of an asset's variability that can be diversified away as nonsystematic risk. It is also sometimes called unsystematic risk, diversifiable risk, unique risk, residual risk, and company-specific risk. This is the risk that is unique to an asset.

Consequently, total risk (as measured by the variance) can be partitioned into systematic risk as measured by the covariance of asset i's return with the market portfolio's return and nonsystematic risk. The relevant risk is the systematic risk. We will see how to measure the systematic risk later.

How diversification reduces nonsystematic risk for portfolios is illustrated in Figure 15.16. The vertical axis shows the variance of the portfolio return. The variance of the portfolio return represents the total risk for the portfolio (systematic plus nonsystematic). The horizontal axis shows the number of holdings of different assets (e.g., the number of common stock held of different issuers). As can be seen, as the number of asset holdings increases, the level of nonsystematic risk is almost completely eliminated (that is, diversified away). Studies of different asset classes support this. For example, for common stock, several studies suggest that a portfolio size of about 20 randomly selected companies will completely eliminate nonsystematic risk leaving only systematic risk (see Wagner and Lau, 1971).

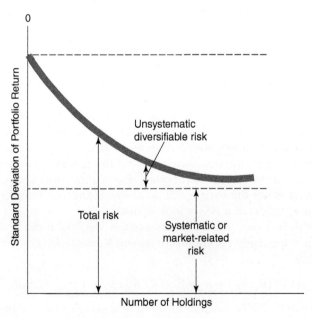

FIGURE 15.16   Systematic and Unsystematic Portfolio Risk

Security Market Line The CML represents an equilibrium condition in which the expected return on a portfolio of assets is a linear function of the expected return of the market portfolio. Individual assets do not fall on the CML. Instead, Sharpe (1970) demonstrated that the following relationship holds for individual assets:

$$E(R_i) = R_f + \left[\frac{E(R_i) - R_f}{\mathrm{Var}(R_M)}\right] \mathrm{Cov}(R_i, R_M) \tag{15.7}$$

Equation (15.7) is called the *security market line (SML)*.

In equilibrium, the expected return of individual securities will lie on the SML and not on the CML. This is true because of the high degree of nonsystematic risk that remains in individual assets that can be diversified out of portfolios. In equilibrium, only efficient portfolios will lie on both the CML and the SML.

The SML also can be expressed as

$$E(R_i) = R_f + [E(R_i) - R_f]\left[\frac{\mathrm{Cov}(R_i, R_M)}{\mathrm{Var}(R_M)}\right] \tag{15.8}$$

How can the ratio in equation (15.8) be estimated for each asset? It can be estimated empirically using return data for the market portfolio and the return on the asset. The empirical analogue for equation (15.8) is:

$$r_{it} - r_{ft} = \alpha_i + \beta_i[r_{Mt} - r_{ft}] + e_{it} \tag{15.9}$$

where e_{it} is the error term. Equation (15.9) is called the *characteristic line*.

β_i, beta, in equation (15.9) is the estimate of the ratio in equation (15.8); that is,

$$\beta_i = \frac{\mathrm{Cov}(R_i, R_M)}{\mathrm{Var}(R_M)} \tag{15.10}$$

Substituting β_i into the SML given by equation (15.8) gives the beta version of the SML:

$$E(R_i) = R_f + b_i[E(R_M) - R_f] \tag{15.11}$$

This is the CAPM form given by equation (15.3). This equation states that, given the assumptions of the CAPM, the expected return on an individual asset is a positive linear function of its index of systematic risk as measured by beta. The higher the beta, the higher the expected return.

An investor pursuing an active strategy will search for underpriced securities to purchase or retain and overpriced securities to sell or avoid (if held in the current portfolio, or sold short if permitted). If an investor believes that the CAPM is the correct asset-pricing model, then the SML can be used to identify mispriced securities. A security is perceived to be underpriced (that is, undervalued) if the "expected" return projected by the investor is greater than the "required" return stipulated by the SML. A security is perceived to be overpriced (that is, overvalued), if the "expected" return projected by the investor is less than the "required" return stipulated by the SML. Said another way, if the expected return plots above (over) the SML, the security is "underpriced"; if it plots below the SML, it is "overpriced."

TESTS OF THE CAPM   Now that's the theory. The question is whether the theory is supported by empirical evidence. There has been probably more than 1,000 academic papers written on the subject. (Almost all studies use common stock to test the theory.) These papers cover not only the empirical evidence but the difficulties of testing the theory.

Let's start with the empirical evidence. There are two important results of the empirical tests of the CAPM that question its validity. First, it has been found that stocks with low betas have exhibited higher returns than the CAPM predicts and stocks with high betas have been found to have lower returns than the CAPM predicts. Second, market risk is not the only risk factor priced by the market. Several studies have discovered other factors that explain stock returns.

While on the empirical level there are serious questions raised about the CAPM, there is an important paper challenging the validity of these empirical studies. Roll (1977) demonstrates that the CAPM is not testable until the exact composition of the "true" market portfolio is known, and the only valid test of the CAPM is to observe whether the *ex ante* true market portfolio is mean-variance efficient. As a result of his findings, Roll states that he does not believe there ever will be an unambiguous test of the CAPM. He does not say that the CAPM is invalid. Rather, Roll says that there is likely to be no unambiguous way to test the CAPM and its implications due to the nonobservability of the true market portfolio and its characteristics.

MODIFICATIONS OF THE CAPM   Several researchers have modified the CAPM. Here we will briefly describe two modifications.

Suppose that there is no risk-free rate and that investors cannot borrow and lend at the risk-free rate (Assumption 6). How does that affect the CAPM? Black (1972) examined how the original CAPM would change if there is no risk-free asset in which the investor can borrow and lend. He demonstrated that neither the existence of a risk-free asset nor the requirement that investors can borrow and lend at the risk-free rate is necessary for the theory to hold. Black's argument was as follows. The beta of a risk-free asset is zero. Suppose that a portfolio can be created such that it is uncorrelated with the market. That portfolio would then have a beta of zero, and Black labeled that portfolio a *zero-beta portfolio*. He set forth the conditions for constructing a zero-beta portfolio and then showed how the CAPM can be modified accordingly. Specifically, in equation (15.3), the return on the zero-beta portfolio is substituted for the risk-free rate.

Now let's look at the assumption that the only relevant risk is the variance of asset returns (Assumption 1). That is, it is assumed that the only risk factor that an investor is concerned with is the uncertainty about the future price of a security. Investors, however, usually are concerned with other risks that will affect their ability to consume goods and services in the future. Three examples would be the risks associated with future labor income, the future relative prices of consumer goods, and future investment opportunities. Consequently, using the variance of expected returns as the sole measure of risk would be inappropriate in the presence of these other risk factors. Recognizing these other risks that investors face, Merton (1973) modified the CAPM based on consumers deriving their optimal lifetime consumption when they face such nonmarket risk factors.

Arbitrage Pricing Theory Model

An alternative to the equilibrium asset-pricing model just discussed, an asset-pricing model based purely on arbitrage arguments was derived by Ross (1976). The model, called the *arbitrage pricing theory (APT) model*, postulates that an asset's expected return is influenced by a variety of risk factors, as opposed to just market risk as suggested by the CAPM. The APT model states that the return on a security is linearly related to H risk factors. However, the APT model does not specify what these risk factors are, but it is assumed that the relationship between asset returns and the risk factors is linear. Moreover, unsystematic risk can be eliminated so that an investor is only compensated for accepting the systematic risk factors.

ARBITRAGE PRINCIPLE   Since the model relies on arbitrage arguments, we will digress at this point to define what is meant by arbitrage. In its simple form, arbitrage is the simultaneous buying and selling of an asset at two different prices in two different markets. The arbitrageur profits without risk by buying cheap in one market and simultaneously selling at the higher price in the other market. Investors don't hold their breath waiting for such situations to occur because they are rare. In fact, a single arbitrageur with unlimited ability to sell short could correct a mispricing condition by financing purchases in the underpriced market with proceeds of short sales in the overpriced market. (Short-selling means selling an asset that is not owned, in anticipation of a price decline.) This means that riskless arbitrage opportunities are short-lived.

Less obvious arbitrage opportunities exist in situations where a package of assets can produce a payoff (expected return) identical to an asset that is priced differently. This arbitrage relies on a fundamental principle of finance called the law of one price, which states that a given asset must have the same price regardless of the means by which one goes about creating that asset. The law of one price implies that if the payoff of an asset can be synthetically created by a package of assets, the price of the package and the price of the asset whose payoff it replicates must be equal.

When a situation is discovered whereby the price of the package of assets differs from that of an asset with the same payoff, rational investors will trade these assets in such a way so as to restore price equilibrium. This market mechanism is assumed by the APT model, and is founded on the fact that an arbitrage transaction does not expose the investor to any adverse movement in the market price of the assets in the transaction.

For example, let us consider how we can produce an arbitrage opportunity involving the three assets A, B, and C. These assets can be purchased today at the prices shown below, and can each produce only one of two payoffs (referred to as State 1 and State 2) a year from now:

Asset	Price	Payoff in State 1	Payoff in State 2
A	$70	$50	$100
B	60	30	120
C	80	38	112

While it is not obvious from the data presented above, an investor can construct a portfolio of assets A and B that will have the identical return as asset C in both State 1 and State 2. Let w_A and w_B be the proportion of assets A and B, respectively, in the portfolio. Then the payoff (that is, the terminal value of the portfolio) under the two states can be expressed mathematically as follows:

If State 1 occurs: $50 w_A + \$30 w_B$
If State 2 occurs: $100 w_A + \$120 w_B$

We create a portfolio consisting of A and B that will reproduce the payoff of C regardless of the state that occurs one year from now. Here is how: For either condition (State 1 and State 2) we set the expected payoff of the portfolio equal to the expected payoff for C as follows:

State 1: $50 w_A + \$30 w_B = \$38$
State 2: $100 w_A + \$120 w_B = \$112$

We also know that $w_A + w_B = 1$.

If we solved for the weights for w_A and w_B that would simultaneously satisfy the above equations, we would find that the portfolio should have 40% in asset A (that is, $w_A = 0.4$) and 60% in asset B (that is, $w_B = 0.6$). The cost of that portfolio will be equal to

$$(0.4)(\$70) + (0.6)(\$60) = \$64$$

Our portfolio (that is, package of assets) comprised of assets A and B has the same payoff in State 1 and State 2 as the payoff of asset C. The cost of asset C is $80 while the cost of the portfolio is only $64. This is an arbitrage opportunity that can be exploited by buying assets A and B in the proportions given above and shorting (selling) asset C.

For example, suppose that $1 million is invested to create the portfolio with assets A and B. The $1 million is obtained by selling short asset C. The proceeds from the short sale of asset C provide the funds to purchase assets A and B. Thus, there would be no cash outlay by the investor. The payoffs for States 1 and 2 are shown below:

Asset	Investment	Payoff in State 1	Payoff in State 2
A	$400,000	$285,715	$571,429
B	600,000	300,000	1,200,000
C	−1,000,000	−475,000	−1,400,000
Total	0	110,715	371,429

In either State 1 or 2, the investor profits without risk. The APT model assumes that such an opportunity would be quickly eliminated by the marketplace.

APT MODEL FORMULATION The APT model postulates that an asset's expected return is influenced by a variety of risk factors, as opposed to just market risk of the CAPM. That is, the APT model asserts that the return on an asset is linearly related to H "factors." The APT does not specify what these factors are, but it is assumed that the relationship between asset returns and the factors is linear. Specifically, the APT model asserts that the rate of return on asset i is given by the following relationship:

$$R_i = E(R_i) + \beta_{i,1}F_1 + \beta_{i,2}F_2 + \cdots + \beta_{i,H}F_H + e_i$$

where

R_i = the rate of return on asset i
$E(R_i)$ = the expected return on asset i
F_b = the b-th factor that is common to the returns of all assets ($b = 1, ..., H$)
$\beta_{i,b}$ = the sensitivity of the i-th asset to the b-th factor
e_i = the unsystematic return for asset i

For equilibrium to exist, the following conditions must be satisfied: Using no additional funds (wealth) and without increasing risk, it should not be possible, on average, to create a portfolio to increase return. In essence, this condition states that there is no "money machine" available in the market.

Ross (1976) derived the following relationship, which is what is referred to as the APT model:

$$E(R_i) = R_f + \beta_{i,F1}[E(R_{F1}) - R_F] + \beta_{i,F2}[E(R_{F2}) - R_F] + \cdots + \beta_{i,FH}[E(R_{FH}) - R_F] \quad (15.12)$$

where $[E(R_{Fj}) - R_f]$ is the excess return of the jth systematic risk factor over the risk-free rate, and can be thought of as the price (or risk premium) for the jth systematic risk factor.

The APT model as given by equation (15.12) asserts that investors want to be compensated for all the risk factors that systematically affect the return of a security. The compensation is the sum of the products of each risk factor's systematic risk ($\beta_{i,FH}$), and the risk premium assigned to it by the financial market $[E(R_{Fb}) - R_f)]$. As in the case of the CAPM, an investor is not compensated for accepting unsystematic risk.

It turns out that the CAPM is actually a special case of the APT model. If the only risk factor in the APT model as given by equation (15.12) is market risk, the APT model reduces to the CAPM. Now contrast the APT model given by equation (15.3). They look similar. Both say that investors are compensated for accepting all systematic risk and no nonsystematic risk. The CAPM states that systematic risk is market risk, while the APT model does not specify the systematic risk.

Supporters of the APT model argue that it has several major advantages over the CAPM or multifactor CAPM. First, it makes less restrictive assumptions about investor preferences toward risk and return. As explained earlier, the CAPM theory assumes investors trade off between risk and return solely on the basis of the expected returns and standard deviations of prospective investments. The APT model, in contrast, simply requires some rather unobtrusive bounds be placed on potential investor utility functions. Second, no assumptions are made about the distribution of asset returns. Finally, since the APT model does not rely on the identification of the true market portfolio, the theory is potentially testable.

Multifactor Risk Models in Practice

The APT model provides theoretical support for an asset-pricing model where there is more than one risk factor. Consequently, models of this type are referred to as *multifactor risk models*. These models provide the tools for quantifying the risk profile of a portfolio relative to a benchmark, for constructing a portfolio relative to a benchmark, and controlling risk. Below we provide a brief review of the multifactor risk models used in portfolio management. The three types are statistical factor models, macroeconomic factor models, and fundamental factor models (see Connor, 1995).

STATISTICAL FACTOR MODELS In a *statistical factor model*, historical and cross-sectional data on stock returns are tossed into a statistical model. The goal of the statistical model is to best explain the observed stock returns with "factors" that are linear return combinations and uncorrelated with each other.

For example, suppose that monthly returns for 5,000 companies for ten years are computed. The goal of the statistical analysis is to produce "factors" that best explain the variance of the observed stock returns. For example, suppose that there are six "factors" that do this. These "factors" are statistical artifacts. The objective in a statistical factor model then becomes to determine the economic meaning of each of these statistically derived factors.

Because of the problem of interpretation, it is difficult to use the factors from a statistical factor model for valuation, portfolio construction, and risk control. Instead, practitioners prefer the two other models described next, which allow them to pre-specify meaningful factors, and thus produce a more intuitive model.

MACROECONOMIC FACTOR MODELS In a *macroeconomic factor model*, the inputs to the model are historical stock returns and observable macroeconomic variables. These variables are called raw descriptors. The goal is to determine which macroeconomic variables are pervasive in explaining historical stock returns. Those variables that are pervasive in explaining the returns then become the factors and are included in the model. The responsiveness of a stock to these factors is estimated using historical time series data.

An example of a proprietary macroeconomic factor model is the one developed by Burmeister, Roll, and Ross (2003). In this model, there are five macroeconomic factors that reflect unanticipated changes in the following macroeconomic variables: investor confidence (confidence risk); interest rates (time horizon risk); inflation (inflation risk); real business activity (business cycle risk); and a market index (market timing risk). For each stock, the sensitivity of the stock to a risk factor is statistically estimated. In addition, for each risk factor a market price for that risk is statistically estimated. Given these two estimates, the expected return can be projected.

FUNDAMENTAL FACTOR MODELS *Fundamental factor models* use company and industry attributes and market data as raw descriptors. Examples are price/earnings ratios, book/price ratios, estimated economic growth, and trading activity. The inputs into a fundamental factor model are stock returns and the raw descriptors about a company. Those fundamental variables about a company that are pervasive in explaining stock returns are then the raw descriptors retained in the model. Using cross-sectional analysis, the sensitivity of a stock's return to a raw descriptor is estimated. There are several fundamental factor models available from vendors.

Summary

This part explains the implications of modern portfolio theory as formulated by Markowitz (1952), a theory that deals with the construction of Markowitz efficient portfolios by rational risk-averse investors. Once a risk-free asset is introduced, the new efficient frontier is the capital market line, which represents a combination of a risk-free asset and the market portfolio. The capital asset-pricing model is an economic theory that describes the relationship between risk and expected return, or, equivalently, it is a model for the pricing of risky securities. The CAPM asserts that the only risk that is priced by rational investors is systematic risk, because that risk cannot be eliminated by diversification. Essentially, the CAPM says that the expected return of a security or a portfolio is equal to the rate on a risk-free security plus a risk premium. The risk premium in the CAPM is the product of the quantity of risk times the market price of risk.

The beta of a security or portfolio is an index of the systematic risk of the asset and is estimated statistically. Historical beta is calculated from a time series of observations on both the asset's return and the market portfolio's return. This assumed relationship is called the characteristic line and is not an equilibrium model for predicting expected return, but rather a description of historical data.

There have been numerous empirical tests of the CAPM, and, in general, these have failed to fully support the theory. Roll (1977) criticized these studies because of the difficulty of identifying the true market portfolio. Furthermore, Roll asserts that such tests are not likely to appear soon, if at all.

The arbitrage pricing theory is developed purely from arbitrage arguments. It postulates that the expected return on a security or a portfolio is influenced by several factors. Proponents of the APT model cite its less restrictive assumptions as a feature that makes it more appealing than the CAPM. Moreover, testing the APT model does not require identification of the "true" market portfolio. It does, however, require empirical determination of the factors because they are not specified by the theory. Consequently, the APT model replaces the problem of identifying the market portfolio in the CAPM with the problem of choosing and measuring the underlying factors.

Despite the fact that the theories presented are controversial or may be difficult to implement in practice, there are several principles of investing that are not controversial and can be used in developing investment strategies. First, investing has two dimensions, risk and return. Therefore, focusing only on the actual return of an asset or portfolio without looking at the risk that had to be accepted to achieve that return is inappropriate. Second, it is also inappropriate to look at the risk of an individual asset when deciding whether it should be included in a portfolio. What is important is how the inclusion of an asset into a portfolio will affect the risk of the portfolio. Third, whether investors consider one risk or a thousand risks, risk can be divided into two general categories: systematic risks that cannot be eliminated by diversification, and unsystematic risk that can be diversified away. Finally, investors should be compensated only for accepting systematic risks. Thus, it is critical in formulating an investment strategy to identify the systematic risks.

References

Black, F. 1972. Capital market equilibrium with restricted borrowing. *Journal of Business* 45, 3: 444–455.

Burmeister, B., R. Roll, and S. A. Ross. 2003. Using macroeconomic factors to control portfolio risk. Unpublished paper.

Connor, G. 1995. The three types of factor models: A comparison of their explanatory power. *Financial Analysts Journal* (May/June): 42–36.

Fama, E. F. 1970. Efficient capital markets: A review of theory and empirical work. *Journal of Finance* 25, 2: 383–417.

Lintner, J. 1965. The valuation of risk assets and the selection of risky investments in stock portfolio and capital budgets. *Review of Economics and Statistics* 1: 13–37.

Markowitz, H. M. 1952. Portfolio selection. *Journal of Finance* 7, 1: 77–91.

Merton, R. C. 1973. An intertemporal capital asset pricing model. *Econometrica* 41, September: 867–888.

Mossin, J. (1966). Equilibrium in a capital asset market. *Econometrica* 34, October: 768–783.

Roll, R. (1977). A critique of the asset pricing theory's tests. *Journal of Financial Economics* 4, March: 129–176.

Ross, R. A. (1976). The arbitrage theory of capital asset-pricing. *Journal of Economic Theory* 13, December: 343–362.

Sharpe, W. F. (1964). Capital asset prices. *Journal of Finance* 19, 3: 425–442.

Sharpe, W. F. 1970. *Portfolio theory and capital markets*. New York: McGraw-Hill.

Treynor, J. L. 1961. Toward a theory of market value of risky assets. Unpublished paper, Arthur D. Little, Cambridge, MA.

Wagner, W. H., and S. Lau, S. 1971. The effect of diversification on risks. *Financial Analysts Journal* 27, 3: 48–53.

CHAPTER 16

Behavioral Finance Theory

M any traditional investment theories and models make assumptions that investors act rationally and in a consistent manner. Behavioral finance argues that investors are subject to numerous conditions that in effect cause them to act irrationally much of the time. Research in this field can help investment professionals identify the more common biases and mental heuristics and when investors are more likely to make mistakes.

This chapter will take a quick look at the origins of the field and some of the more important concepts originally established in the field of behavioral finance. The focus then turns to the application of behavioral finance as it applies to investor behavior.

The reading reviews the basic descriptions of these mental and emotional traps and reviews practical applications and recommendations for how to deal more effectively with each. The author discusses numerous examples of common situations facing investors and the unhealthy choices that typically follow. Investment advisors and consultants should recognize most of these biases, having observed them in the behaviors of their clients and themselves as well.

Behavioral Finance and Wealth Management: Behavioral Finance

Learning Objectives

- Describe the concept of behavioral finance and how it supplements traditional financial and investment theory.
- Describe "prospect theory" and explain its importance as a pillar in behavioral finance.
- Describe and differentiate among the mental and emotional heuristics listed here.
- Identify the behaviors following in practice and prescribe ways to better manage each.

Related to existing beliefs
- cognitive dissonance
- conservatism
- confirmation
- representativeness
- illusion of control
- hindsight bias

Related to information processing
- mental accounting

- anchoring and adjustment
- framing
- availability bias
- self-attribution
- outcome bias
- recency bias

Related to emotions
- loss aversion
- overconfidence
- self-control bias
- status quo
- endowment
- regret aversion
- affinity

- Identify the following investor types and their characteristics.

Investor types
- preservers, followers, independents, accumulators

- Describe how findings in the field of behavioral finance may help investment advisors and consultants better manage the thoughts, feelings, and actions of themselves and their clients.

Behavioral Finance

At its core, behavioral finance attempts to understand and explain actual investor and market behaviors versus theories of investor behavior. This idea differs from traditional (or standard) finance, which is based on assumptions of how investors and markets should behave. Wealth managers from around the world who want to better serve their clients have begun to realize that they cannot rely solely on theories or mathematical models to explain individual investor and market behavior. As Meir Statman's quote puts it, standard finance people are modeled as "rational," whereas behavioral finance people are modeled as "normal." This can be interpreted to mean that "normal" people may behave irrationally—but the reality is that almost no one (actually, I will go so far as to say absolutely no one) behaves perfectly rationally. We will delve into the topic of the irrational behaviors of markets at times; however, the focus of the chapter is on individual investor behavior.

Fundamentally, behavioral finance is about understanding how people make financial decisions, both individually and collectively. By understanding how investors and markets behave, it may be possible to modify or adapt to these behaviors in order to improve financial outcomes. In many instances, knowledge of and integration of behavioral finance may lead to better than expected results for both advisors and their clients. But advisors cannot view behavioral finance as a panacea or "the answer" to problems with clients. Working with clients is as much an art as it is a science. Behavioral finance can add many arrows to the art quiver.

The Role of Behavioral Finance with Private Clients

Private clients can greatly benefit from the application of behavioral finance to their unique situations. Because behavioral finance is a relatively new concept in application to individual investors, investment advisors may feel reluctant to accept its validity. Moreover, advisors may not feel comfortable asking their clients psychological or behavioral questions to ascertain biases, especially at the beginning of the advisory relationship.

One of the objectives of this chapter is to position behavioral finance as a more mainstream aspect of the wealth management relationship, for both advisors and clients.

As behavioral finance is increasingly adopted by practitioners, clients will begin to see the benefits. There is no doubt that an understanding of how investor psychology impacts investment outcomes will generate insights that benefit the advisory relationship. The key result of a behavioral finance–enhanced relationship will be a portfolio to which the advisor can comfortably adhere while fulfilling the client's long-term goals. This result has obvious advantages—advantages that suggest that behavioral finance will continue to play an increasing role in portfolio structure.

How Practical Application of Behavioral Finance Can Create a Successful Advisory Relationship

Wealth management practitioners have different ways of measuring the success of an advisory relationship. Few could argue that every successful relationship shares some fundamental characteristics:

The advisor understands the client's financial goals.
The advisor maintains a systematic (consistent) approach to advising the client.
The advisor delivers what the client expects.
The relationship benefits both client and advisor.

So, how can behavioral finance help?

FORMULATING FINANCIAL GOALS Experienced financial advisors know that defining financial goals is critical to creating an investment program appropriate for the client. To best define financial goals, it is helpful to understand the psychology and the emotions underlying the decisions behind creating the goals. Such insights equip the advisor in deepening the bond with the client, producing a better investment outcome and achieving a better advisory relationship.

MAINTAINING A CONSISTENT APPROACH Most successful advisors exercise a consistent approach to delivering wealth management services. Incorporating the benefits of behavioral finance can become part of that discipline and would not mandate large-scale changes in the advisor's methods. Behavioral finance can also add more professionalism and structure to the relationship because advisors can use it in the process for getting to know the client, which precedes the delivery of any actual investment advice. This step will be appreciated by clients, and it will make the relationship more successful.

DELIVERING WHAT THE CLIENT EXPECTS Perhaps there is no other aspect of the advisory relationship that could benefit more from behavioral finance. Addressing client expectations is essential to a successful relationship; in many unfortunate instances, the advisor doesn't deliver the client's expectations because the advisor doesn't understand the needs of the client. Behavioral finance provides a context in which the advisor can take a step back and attempt to really understand the motivations of the client. Having gotten to the root of the client's expectations, the advisor is then more equipped to help realize them.

ENSURING MUTUAL BENEFITS There is no question that measures taken that result in happier, more satisfied clients will also improve the advisor's practice and work life. Incorporating insights from behavioral finance into the advisory relationship will enhance that relationship, and it will lead to more fruitful results.

It is well known by those in the individual investor advisory business that investment results are not the primary reason that a client seeks a new advisor. The number-one reason that practitioners lose clients is that clients do not feel as though their advisors understand, or attempt to understand, the clients' financial objectives—resulting in poor relationships. The primary benefit that behavioral finance offers is the ability to develop a strong bond between client and advisor. By getting inside the head of the client and developing a comprehensive grasp of his or her motives and fears, the advisor can help the client to better understand why a portfolio is designed the way it is and why it is the "right" portfolio for him or her—regardless of what happens from day to day in the markets.

Seminal Research in Behavioral Finance

KAHNEMAN AND TVERSKY At approximately the same time that Howard Raiffa published his work on decision theory, two relatively unknown cognitive psychologists, Amos Tversky and Daniel Kahneman, began research on decision making under uncertainty. This work ultimately produced a very important book published in 1982 entitled *Judgment under Uncertainty: Heuristics and Biases.*

In an interview conducted by a publication called Current Contents of ISI in April 1983, Tversky and Kahneman discussed their findings with respect to mainstream investors' thinking:

> *The research was sparked by the realization that intuitive predictions and judgments under uncertainty do not follow the laws of probability or the principles of statistics. These hypotheses were formulated very early in conversations between us, but it took many years of research and thousands of subject hours to study the role of representativeness, availability, and anchoring, and to explore the biases to which they are prone. The approach to the study of judgment that is reflected in the paper is characterized by (1) a comparison of intuitive judgment to normative principles of probability and statistics, (2) a search for heuristics of judgment and the biases to which they are prone, and (3) an attempt to explore the theoretical and practical implications of the discrepancy between the psychology of judgment and the theory of rational belief.*

Essentially, Tversky and Kahneman brought to light the incidence, causes, and effects of human error in economic reasoning. Building on the success of their 1974 paper, the two researchers published in 1979 what is now considered the seminal work in behavioral finance: "Prospect Theory: An Analysis of Decision under Risk." The following is the abstract of the paper.

This paper presents a critique of expected utility theory as a descriptive model of decision making under risk, and develops an alternative model, called prospect theory. Choices among risky prospects exhibit several pervasive effects that are inconsistent with the basic tenets of utility theory. In particular, people under-weight outcomes that are merely probable in comparison with outcomes that are obtained with certainty. This tendency, called the certainty effect, contributes to risk aversion in choices involving sure gains and to risk seeking in choices involving sure losses. In addition, people generally discard components that are shared by all prospects under consideration. This tendency, called the isolation effect, leads to inconsistent preferences when the same choice is presented in different forms. An alternative theory of choice is developed, in which value is assigned to gains and losses rather than to final assets and in which probabilities are replaced by decision weights. The value function is normally concave for gains, commonly convex for losses, and is generally steeper for losses than for gains. Decision weights are generally lower than the corresponding probabilities, except in the range of low probabilities. Overweighting of low probabilities may contribute to the attractiveness of both insurance and gambling.

Prospect theory, in essence, describes how individuals evaluate gains and losses. The theory names two specific thought processes: editing and evaluation. During the editing state, alternatives are ranked according to a basic "rule of thumb" (heuristic), which contrasts with the elaborate algorithm in the previous section. Then, during the evaluation phase, some reference point that provides a relative basis for apprais-ing gains and losses is designated. A value function, passing through this reference point and assigning a "value" to each positive or negative outcome, is S-shaped and asymmetrical in order to reflect loss aversion (i.e., the tendency to feel the impact of losses more than gains). This can also be thought of as risk seeking in domain losses (the reflection effect). Figure 16.1 depicts a value function, as typically diagrammed in prospect theory.

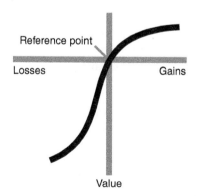

FIGURE 16.1   The Value Function—a Key Tenet of Prospect Theory
Source: The Econometric Society.

It is important to note that prospect theory also observes how people mentally "frame" predicted outcomes, often in very subjective terms; this accordingly affects expected utility. An exemplary instance of framing is given by the experimental data cited in the 1979 article by Kahneman and Tversky, where they reported that they presented groups of subjects with a number of problems. One group was presented with this problem:

1. In addition to whatever you own, you have been given $1,000. You are now asked to choose between:
   A. A sure gain of $500.
   B. A 50 percent chance to gain $1,000 and a 50 percent chance to gain nothing.

Another group of subjects was presented with a different problem:

2. In addition to whatever you own, you have been given $2,000. You are now asked to choose between:
   C. A sure loss of $500.
   D. A 50 percent chance to lose $1,000 and a 50 percent chance to lose nothing.

In the first group, 84 percent of participants chose A. In the second group, the majority, 69 percent, opted for B. The net expected value of the two prospective prizes was, in each instance, identical. However, the phrasing of the question caused the problems to be interpreted differently.

KAHNEMAN AND RIEPE   One of the next significant steps in the evolution of BFMI also involves Daniel Kahneman. Along with Mark Riepe, Kahneman wrote a paper entitled "Aspects of Investor Psychology: Beliefs, Preferences, and Biases Investment Advisors Should Know About." This work leveraged the decision theory work of Howard Raiffa, categorizing behavioral biases on three grounds: (1) *biases of judgment,* (2) *errors of preference,* and (3) *biases associated with living with the consequences of decisions.* Kahneman and Riepe also provide examples of each type of bias in practice.

Biases of judgment include overconfidence, optimism, hindsight, and overreaction to chance events. Errors of preference include nonlinear weighting of probabilities; the tendency of people to value changes, not states; the value of gains and losses as a function; the shape and attractiveness of gambles; the use of purchase price as a reference point; narrow framing; tendencies related to repeated gambles and risk policies; and the adoption of short versus long views. Living with the consequences of decisions gives rise to regrets of omission and commission, and also has implications regarding the relationship between regret and risk taking.

One of the reasons that this paper is so important from the practical application perspective is that it was the first scholarly work to really challenge financial advisors to examine their practice from a behavioral standpoint. Moreover, the authors encapsulate their challenge in the form of a detailed "Checklist for Financial Advisors."

Introduction to Behavioral Biases

Numerous research studies have shown that when people are faced with complex decision-making problems that demand substantial time and cognitive decision-making requirements, they have difficulty devising a rational approach to developing and analyzing a proper course of action. This problem is exacerbated by the fact that many consumers need to contend with a potential overload of information to process. Have you walked down the toothpaste aisle lately? Way too many choices—how do you pick? And this is one of the easier decisions we face! For more meaningful decisions, people don't systematically describe problems, record necessary data, and/or synthesize information to create rules for making decisions, which is really the best way make complex decisions. Instead, people usually follow a more subjective path of reasoning to determine a course of action consistent with their desired outcome or general preferences.

Individuals make decisions, although typically suboptimal ones, by simplifying the choices presented to them, typically using a subset of the information available, and discarding some (usually complicated but potentially good) alternatives to get down to a more manageable number. They are content to find a solution that is "good enough" rather than arriving at the optimal decision. In doing so, they may (unintentionally) bias the decision-making process. These biases may lead to irrational behaviors and flawed decisions. In the investment realm, this happens a lot; many researchers have documented numerous biases that investors have. This chapter will introduce these biases, while highlighting the importance of understanding and dealing with them before they have a chance to negatively impact the investment decision-making process.

Behavioral Biases Defined

The dictionary defines a "bias" in several different ways, including: (a) a statistical sampling or testing error caused by systematically favoring some outcomes over others; (b) a preference or an inclination, especially one that inhibits impartial judgment; (c) an inclination or prejudice in favor of a particular viewpoint; and (d) an inclination of temperament or outlook, especially, a personal and sometimes unreasoned judgment. We are naturally concerned with biases that cause irrational financial decisions due to either (a) faulty cognitive reasoning or (b) reasoning influenced by emotions, which can also be considered feelings, or, unfortunately, due to both. The first dictionary definition (a) of bias is consistent with faulty *cognitive* reasoning or thinking while (b), (c), and (d) are more consistent with impaired reasoning influenced by feelings or *emotion*.

Behavioral biases are defined, essentially, the same way as systematic errors in judgment. Researchers distinguish a long list of specific biases, and have applied over 50 of these to individual investor behaviors in recent studies. When one considers the derivative and the undiscovered biases awaiting application in personal finance, the list of systematic investor errors seems very long indeed. More brilliant research seeks to categorize these biases according to a meaningful framework. Some authors refer to biases as heuristics (rules of thumb), while others call them beliefs, judgments, or preferences. Psychologists' factors include cognitive information processing shortcuts or heuristics, memory errors, emotional and/or motivational factors, and social influences such as family upbringing or societal culture. Some biases identified by psychologists are understood in relation to human needs such as those identified by Maslow—physiological, safety, social, esteem, and self-actualizing. In satisfying these needs, people will generally attempt to avoid pain and seek pleasure. The avoidance of pain can be as subtle as refusing to acknowledge mistakes in order to maintain a positive self-image. The biases that help to avoid pain and instead produce pleasure may be classified as emotional. Other biases are attributed by psychologists to the particular way the brain perceives, forms memories, and makes judgments; the inability to do complex mathematical calculations, such as updating probabilities; and the processing and filtering of information.

This sort of bias taxonomy is helpful as an underlying theory about why and how people operate under bias, but no universal theory has been developed. Instead of a universal theory of investment behavior, behavioral finance research relies on a broad collection of evidence pointing to the ineffectiveness of human decision making in various economic decision-making circumstances.

Differences between Cognitive and Emotional Biases

In this book, behavioral biases are classified as either cognitive or emotional biases, not only because the distinction is straightforward but also because the cognitive-emotional breakdown provides a useful framework for understanding how to effectively deal with them in practice. I recommend thinking about investment decision making as occurring along a (somewhat unrealistic) spectrum, from the completely rational decision making of traditional finance to purely emotional decision making. In that context, cognitive biases are basic statistical, information processing, or memory errors that cause the decision to deviate from rationality. Emotional biases are those that arise spontaneously as a result of attitudes and feelings and that cause the decision to deviate from the rational decisions of traditional finance.

Cognitive errors, which stem from basic statistical, information processing, or memory errors, are more easily corrected for than are emotional biases. Why? Investors are better able to adapt their behaviors or modify their processes if the source of the bias is illogical reasoning, even if the investor does not fully understand the investment issues under consideration. For example, an individual may not understand the complex mathematical process used to create a correlation table of asset classes, but he can understand that the process he is using to create a portfolio of uncorrelated investments is best. In other situations, cognitive biases can be thought of as "blind spots" or distortions in the human mind. Cognitive biases do not result from emotional or intellectual predispositions toward certain judgments, but rather from subconscious mental procedures for processing information. In general, because cognitive errors stem from faulty reasoning, better information, education, and advice can often correct for them.

A Final Word on Biases

The cognitive-emotional distinction will help us determine when and how to adjust for behavioral biases in financial decision making. However, it should be noted that specific biases may have some common aspects and that a specific bias may seem to have both cognitive and emotional aspects. Researchers in financial decision making have identified numerous and specific behavioral biases. This chapter will not attempt to discuss all identified biases but rather will discuss what I consider to be the most important biases within the cognitive-emotional framework for considering potential biases. This framework will be useful in developing an awareness of biases, their implications, and ways of moderating their impact or adapting to them. The intent is to help investors and their advisors to have a heightened awareness of biases so that financial decisions and resulting economic outcomes are potentially improved.

Belief Perserverance Biases Defined and Illustrated

COGNITIVE DISSONANCE BIAS

> **Bias Name:** Cognitive dissonance
> **Bias Type:** Cognitive
> **Subtype:** Belief perseverance

General Description   When newly acquired information conflicts with preexisting understandings, people often experience mental discomfort—a psychological phenomenon known as cognitive dissonance. *Cognitions,* in psychology, represent attitudes, emotions, beliefs, or values; *cognitive dissonance* is a state of imbalance that occurs when contradictory cognitions intersect.

The term *cognitive dissonance* encompasses the response that arises as people struggle to harmonize cognitions and thereby relieve their mental discomfort. For example, a consumer might purchase a certain brand of mobile phone, initially believing that it is the best mobile phone available. However, when a new cognition that favors a substitute mobile phone is introduced, representing an imbalance, cognitive dissonance occurs in an attempt to relieve the discomfort that comes with the notion that perhaps the buyer did not purchase the right mobile phone. People will go to great lengths to convince themselves that the mobile phone they actually bought is better than the one they just learned about, to avoid mental discomfort associated with their initial purchase. In essence, they persist in their belief that they are correct. In that sense, cognitive dissonance bias is the basis for all of the belief perseverance biases in this section, with different variations on the same theme.

Technical Description   Psychologists conclude that people often perform far-reaching rationalizations in order to synchronize their cognitions and maintain psychological stability. When people modify their behaviors or cognitions to achieve cognitive harmony, however, the modifications that they make are not always rational or in their self-interest. Figure 16.2 illustrates this point.

Any time someone feels compelled to choose between alternatives, some sense of conflict is sure to follow the decision. This is because the selected alternative often poses downsides, while the rejected alternative has redeeming characteristics. These factors challenge the decision maker's confidence in the trade-off he or she has just negotiated. Commitment, which indicates an emotional attachment by an individual to the final decision, always precedes the surfacing of cognitive dissonance. If facts challenge the course to which a subject is emotionally attached, then those facts pose emotional threats. Most people try to avoid dissonant situations and will

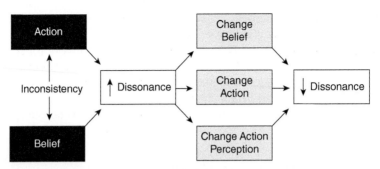

FIGURE 16.2   Cognitive Dissonance Theory

Reprinted from R. H. Rolla, "Cognitive Dissonance Theory," with permission by *Psychology World*. Department of Psychology, Univeristy of Missouri—www.umr.edu/~psyworld.

even ignore potentially relevant information to avoid psychological conflict. Theorists have identified two different aspects of cognitive dissonance that pertain to decision making.

1. *Selective perception.* Subjects suffering from selective perception register only information that appears to affirm a chosen course, thus producing a view of reality that is incomplete and, hence, inaccurate. Unable to objectively understand available evidence, people become increasingly prone to subsequent miscalculations.
2. *Selective decision making.* Selective decision making usually occurs when commitment to an original decision course is high. Selective decision making rationalizes actions that enable a person to adhere to that course, even if at an exorbitant economic cost. Selective decision makers might, for example, continue to invest in a project whose prospects have soured in order to avoid "wasting" the balance of previously sunk funds. Many studies show that people will subjectively reinforce decisions or commitments they have already made.

Practical Application   Smoking is a classic example of cognitive dissonance. Although it is widely accepted by the general public that cigarettes cause lung cancer and heart disease, virtually everyone who smokes wants to live a long and healthy life. In terms of cognitive dissonance theory, the desire to live a long life is dissonant with the activity of doing something that will most likely shorten one's life. The tension produced by these contradictory ideas can be reduced by denying the evidence of lung cancer and heart disease or justifying one's smoking because it reduces stress or provides a similar benefit. A smoker might rationalize his or her behavior by believing that only a few smokers become ill (it won't be me), that it only happens to two-pack-a-day smokers, or that if smoking does not kill them, something else will. While chemical addiction may operate in addition to cognitive dissonance for existing smokers, new smokers may exhibit a simpler case of the latter.

This case of dissonance could also be interpreted in terms of a threat to the self-concept.[1] The thought, "I am increasing my risk of lung cancer," is dissonant with the self-related belief, "I am a smart, reasonable person who makes good decisions." Because it is often easier to make excuses than it is to change behavior, dissonance

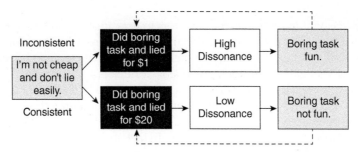

FIGURE 16.3 Modeling Cognitive Dissonance in Festinger's Peg Experiment

Reprinted from R. H. Rolla, "Cognitive Dissonance Theory," with permission by *Psychology World*. Department of Psychology, Univeristy of Missouri—www.umr.edu/~psyworld.

theory leads to the conclusion that humans are sometimes rationalizing, and not always rational beings.

Investors, like everyone else, sometimes have trouble living with their decisions. Many wealth management practitioners note that clients often go to great lengths to rationalize decisions on prior investments, especially failed investments. Moreover, people displaying this tendency might also irrationally delay unloading assets that are not generating adequate returns. In both cases, the effects of cognitive dissonance are preventing investors from acting rationally and, in certain cases, preventing them from realizing losses for tax purposes and reallocating at the earliest opportunity. Furthermore, and perhaps even more important, the need to maintain self-esteem may prevent investors from learning from their mistakes. To ameliorate dissonance arising from the pursuit of what they perceive to be two incompatible goals—self-validation and acknowledgment of past mistakes—investors will often attribute their failures to chance rather than to poor decision making. Of course, people who miss opportunities to learn from past miscalculations are likely to miscalculate again, renewing a cycle of anxiety, discomfort, dissonance, and denial (see Figure 16.3).

Both selective perception (information distortion to meet a need, which gives rise to subsequent decision-making errors) and selective decision making (an irrational drive to achieve some specified result for the purpose of vindicating a previous decision) can have significant effects on investors. The following inset illustrates four behaviors that result from cognitive dissonance and that cause investment losses.

Cognitive Dissonance Bias: Behaviors That Can Cause Investment Mistakes

1. Cognitive dissonance can cause investors to hold losing securities positions that they otherwise would sell because they want to avoid the mental pain associated with admitting that they made a bad decision.
2. Cognitive dissonance can cause investors to continue to invest in a security that they already own after it has gone down (average down) to confirm an earlier decision to invest in that security without judging the new investment with objectivity and rationality. A common phrase for this concept is "throwing good money after bad."

3. Cognitive dissonance can cause investors to get caught up in herds of behavior; that is, people avoid information that counters an earlier decision (cognitive dissonance) until so much counter information is released that investors herd together and cause a deluge of behavior that is counter to that decision.
4. Cognitive dissonance can cause investors to believe "it's different this time." People who purchased high-flying, hugely overvalued growth stocks in the late 1990s ignored evidence that there were no excess returns from purchasing the most expensive stocks available. In fact, many of the most high-flying companies are now far below their peaks in price.

CONSERVATISM BIAS

Bias Name: Conservatism
Bias Type: Cognitive
Subtype: Belief perseverance

General Description   *Conservatism bias* is a mental process in which people cling to their prior views or forecasts at the expense of acknowledging new information. For example, suppose that an investor receives some bad news regarding a company's earnings and that this news negatively contradicts another earnings estimate issued the previous month. Conservatism bias may cause the investor to *underreact* to the new information, maintaining impressions derived from the previous estimate rather than acting on the updated information. Investors persevere in a previously held belief rather than acknowledging new information.

Technical Description   Conservatism causes individuals to overweight base rates and to underreact to sample evidence. As a result, they fail to react as a rational person would in the face of new evidence. A classic experiment by Ward Edwards in 1968 eloquently illustrated the technical side of conservatism bias. Edwards presented subjects with two urns—one containing three blue balls and seven red balls, the other containing seven blue balls and three red ones. Subjects were given this information and then told that someone had drawn randomly 12 times from one of the urns, with the ball after each draw restored to the urn in order to maintain the same probability ratio. Subjects were told that this draw yielded eight reds and four blues. They were then asked, "What is the probability that the draw was made from the first urn?" While the correct answer is 0.97, most people estimate a number around 0.7. They apparently overweight the base rate of 0.5—the random likelihood of drawing from one of two urns as opposed to the other—relative to the "new" information regarding the produced ratio of reds to blues.

Professor David Hirshleifer of Ohio State University noted that one explanation for conservatism is that processing new information and updating beliefs is cognitively costly. He noted that information that is presented in a cognitively costly form, such as information that is abstract and statistical, is weighted less. Furthermore, people may overreact to information that is easily processed, such as scenarios and concrete examples. The argument for costly processing can be extended to explain base rate underweighting. If an individual underweights new information received about population frequencies (base rates), then base rate underweighting is really a form of conservatism. Indeed, base rates are underweighted less when they are presented in more salient form or in a fashion that emphasizes their causal relation to the decision problem. This argument for costly processing of new information does not suggest that an individual will underweight his or her preexisting internalized prior belief. If base rate underweighting is a consequence of the use of the representativeness heuristic, there should be underweighting of priors.

Portions of this analysis resonate interestingly with Edwards's experiment. For example, perhaps people overweight the base rate probability of drawing randomly from one of two urns, relative to the sample data probability of drawing a specific combination of items, because the former quantity is simply easier to compute.

Practical Application James Montier is author of the 2002 book *Behavioural Finance: Insights into Irrational Minds and Markets* and analyst for DKW in London. Montier has done some exceptional work in the behavioral finance field. Although Montier primarily studied the stock market in general, concentrating on the behavior of securities analysts in particular, the concepts presented here can and will be applied to individual investors later on.

Commenting on conservatism as it relates to the securities markets in general, Montier noted: "The stock market has a tendency to underreact to fundamental information—be it dividend omissions, initiations, or an earnings report. For instance, in the United States, in the 60 days following an earnings announcement, stocks with the biggest positive earnings surprise tend to outperform the market by 2 percent, even after a 4 to 5 percent outperformance in the 60 days prior to the announcement."

In relating conservatism to securities analysts, Montier wrote:

■ People tend to cling tenaciously to a view or a forecast. Once a position has been stated, most people find it very hard to move away from that view. When movement does occur, it does so only very slowly. Psychologists call this conservatism bias. The chart shown in Figure 16.4 shows conservatism in analysts' forecasts. We have taken a linear time trend out of both the operating earnings

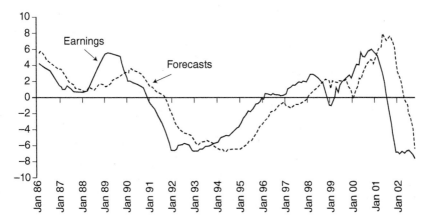

FIGURE 16.4   Montier Observes That Analysts Cling to Their Forecasts
Source: Dresdner Kleinwort Wasserstein, 2002.

numbers and the analysts' forecasts. A cursory glance at the chart reveals that analysts are exceptionally good at telling you what has just happened. They have invested too heavily in their view and hence will only change it when presented with indisputable evidence of its falsehood.

This is clear evidence of conservatism bias in action. Montier's research documents the behavior of securities analysts, but the trends observed can easily be applied to individual investors, who also forecast securities prices, and will cling to these forecasts even when presented with new information.

Implications for Investors

Investors too often give more attention to forecast outcomes than to new data that actually describes emerging outcomes. Many wealth management practitioners have observed clients who are unable to rationally act on updated information regarding their investments because the clients are "stuck" on prior beliefs. The inset following lists three behaviors stemming from conservatism bias that can cause investment mistakes.

Conservatism Bias: Behaviors That Can Cause Investment Mistakes

1. Conservatism bias can cause investors to cling to a view or a forecast, behaving too inflexibly when presented with new information. For example, assume an investor purchases a security based on the knowledge that the company is planning a forthcoming announcement regarding a new product. The company then announces that it has experienced problems bringing the product to market. The investor may cling to the initial, optimistic impression of some imminent, positive development by the company and may fail to take action on the negative announcement.
2. When conservatism-biased investors do react to new information, they often do so too slowly. For example, if an earnings announcement depresses a stock that an investor holds, the conservative investor may be too slow to sell. The preexisting view that, for example, the company has good prospects, may linger too long and exert too much influence, causing an investor exhibiting conservatism to unload the stock only after losing more money than necessary.
3. Conservatism can relate to an underlying difficulty in processing new information. Because people experience mental stress when presented with complex data, an easy option is to simply stick to a prior belief. For example, if an investor purchases a security on the belief that the company is poised to grow and then the company announces that a series of difficult-to-interpret accounting changes may affect its growth, the investor might discount the announcement rather than attempt to decipher it. More clear-cut and, therefore, easier to maintain is the prior belief that the company is poised to grow.

CONFIRMATION BIAS

Bias Name: Confirmation bias
Bias Type: Cognitive
Subtype: Belief perseverance

General Description *Confirmation bias* refers to a type of selective perception that emphasizes ideas that confirm our beliefs, while devaluing whatever contradicts our beliefs. For example, it is quite typical for someone to decide, after having bought a much desired item such as a television, to look for the same television at a store that is known to have higher prices in order to confirm that he or she made a good purchase decision. This behavior, going back to cognitive dissonance in the last chapter, is caused by our attempt to resolve the post-decisional dissonance between the decision made and the possibility of being wrong.

To describe this phenomenon another way, we might say that confirmation bias refers to our all-too-natural ability to convince ourselves of whatever it is that we want to believe. We attach undue emphasis to events that corroborate the outcomes we desire and downplay whatever contrary evidence arises.

Technical Description Confirmation bias can be thought of as a form of selection bias in collecting evidence for supporting certain beliefs, whereby decision makers observe, overvalue, or actively seek out information that confirms their claims, while simultaneously ignoring or devaluing evidence that might discount their claims. A classic demonstration of confirmation bias, of which there are many versions, is one in which subjects are shown four cards, each with a number on one side and a letter on the other. They are then told the following rule: "If the card has a vowel on one side, then it *must* have an even number on the other side." The cards are then laid out as depicted in Figure 16.5. Subjects are then asked, "Which two cards would you turn over to test the rule?"

When this experiment is run, most participants do not choose the correct cards (the card reading "A" and the card reading "9"). Instead, the most frequent responses are "A" and "2." This pairing demonstrates a common logical fallacy: People choose "2" because the discovery of an accompanying vowel could indeed uphold the hypothesis. However, exposing the opposite side of the "2" card can't possibly invalidate the hypothesized condition, so this can't be the correct response. People more readily identify "2" rather than "9" because confirmation bias makes them *want* to validate the hypothesis—not refute it as directed.

Another lesson here is that beliefs don't need to be logically entrenched in order to kindle confirmation bias. The hypothesis as stated becomes an immediate if subtle aspect of the participant's choice of cards. Even though subjects have no reason to accept the hypothesis, they become loyal enough to its validity that they are unable

A	2
9	x

FIGURE 16.5   Classic Confirmation Bias Experiment

to recognize the correct answer choice. In fact, when beliefs *are* firmly established in evidence, the effects of confirmation bias become less overt. This is due to a tendency to give more attention and weight to data that fit with beliefs with stronger foundations.

Numerous studies have demonstrated that people excessively value confirmatory information, that is, positive or supportive data. The "most likely reason for the excessive influence of confirmatory information is that it is easier to deal with cognitively"[2] than contradictory information is; that is, most people find it easier to discern how a piece of data might support rather than challenge a given position. Researchers are sometimes guilty of confirmation bias, as they occasionally design experiments or frame data in ways likely to confirm their hypotheses. To compound the problem, some scholars also avoid dealing with data that would contradict their hypotheses.

Practical Application   To demonstrate confirmation bias, we discuss employees' penchant for overconcentrating in company stock. Most practitioners have encountered clients who rationalize their disproportionate holdings by citing the promising "big things" that are developing at their companies. Numerous shareholders in Enron and WorldCom (during the technology bubble of the 1990s), and Lehman Brothers and Bear Stearns (during the most recent crisis) probably speculated that great growth was going to be sustained forever—if only these investors had had some clue as to the nature of the "big things" that would soon befall their employers! When employees load up on company stock en masse and bullish commentary on employer stock prices dominates water cooler conversation, inauspicious details can be easily overlooked. For a more elaborate example, we are going "retro" back to the early 1990s. A strong cautionary tale emerged during that time at a well-established tech firm: IBM.

In the early 1990s, many IBM employees were convinced that their company's OS/2 operating system would achieve industry standard status. They frequently ignored unfavorable signs, including evidence of compettion from Microsoft Windows. These employees loaded up on IBM stock, anticipating that OS/2's performance would drive the company forward. In 1991, IBM stock reached a split-adjusted peak of $35 per share. Over the course of the next two years, however, IBM slid to a low of $10. It would not reach $35 again until the end of 1996. During this five-year slump, IBM employees rallied around seemingly positive developments that "confirmed" that IBM was making a comeback. Some even delayed retirement. Unfortunately, in an effort to engineer a turnaround, IBM laid off a number of its employees. In the end, OS/2 caused many people to become less wealthy. For some, the failed operating system even led to unemployment. This is a classic case of confirmation bias in action.

Experienced practitioners have seen similar scenarios play out repeatedly. Clients ignore downside risks of, for example, employer stock and focus only on the upside potential. Why? In this case, confirmation bias played a significant role in the behavior of the IBM employees. It led them to accept information that supported their rosy predictions regarding IBM while discounting evidence of increased competition from Microsoft. Consequently, these employees lost money as IBM's stock price fell. Only those few who were able to hang on, over the course of five years of uncertainty—history, remember, shows us that most investors "panic" in such a situation—had the opportunity to profit in the end.

Implications for Investors   Anyone who has played a hand or two of poker knows well the downside of confirmation bias. Suppose you are entrenched in a game, and you get three kings on the flop. Your opponent raises the pot, and you are only happy to raise him back. You aren't really paying attention as the turn card comes out. Your cards are telling you "I can't lose." You are oblivious to the fact that a series of hearts are showing up. A two comes up on the river and you are pretty much guaranteed to win. You bet big. You get called. Oops, someone had a flush, and you lose.

In the context of the poker analogy, what's important to note is that, by "listening" only to information that confirms your belief that you have the best hand, you ignore the other players' cards. Focusing on the payoff of the present hand might eventually earn a profit; however, you don't analyze the implications of a loss— even if some indication has cropped up during the game that another player might be collecting hearts. While the poker metaphor isn't flawless, it gets the point across: people believe what they want to believe and ignore evidence to the contrary. This is the essence of confirmation bias.

In finance, the effects of confirmation bias can be observed almost daily. Investors often fail to acknowledge anything negative about investments they've just made, even when substantial evidence begins to argue against these investments. A classic example took place on the Internet message boards during the technology stock boom of the late 1990s. Many of these chat roomers would harass anyone who voiced a negative opinion of the company they invested in. Rather than try to glean some useful insight into their company through other investors, they sought only confirmations of their own beliefs.

The following is a summary investment mistakes that can be caused by confirmation bias.

Confirmation Bias: Behaviors That Can Cause Investment Mistakes

1. Confirmation bias can cause investors to seek out only information that confirms their beliefs about an investment that they have made and to not seek out information that may contradict their beliefs. This behavior can leave investors in the dark regarding, for example, the imminent decline of a stock.
2. When investors believe strongly in predetermined "screens," such as stocks breaking through a 52-week price high, confirmation bias is usually at work. These investors use only the information that confirms their beliefs. They may blind themselves to information that demonstrates that a stock breaking through its 52-week high may not make a good investment.
3. Confirmation bias can cause employees to overconcentrate in company stock. As IBM and other examples demonstrate, intraoffice buzz about a company's prospects does not justify indiscriminate reliance by employees on company stock. People naturally tend to unduly emphasize evidence suggesting that the companies they work for will do well.
4. Confirmation bias can cause investors to continue to hold underdiversified portfolios. Many practitioners have seen clients become infatuated with certain stocks—not always the stocks of employer corporations. Over the course of years, such a client might accrue a large position that ultimately produces

a lopsided portfolio. These clients do not want to hear anything negative about favored investments but rather seek, single-mindedly, confirmation that the position will pay off.

REPRESENTATIVENESS BIAS

Bias Name: Representativeness
Bias Type: Cognitive
Subtype: Belief perseverance

General Description   In order to derive meaning from life experiences, people have developed an innate propensity for classifying objects and thoughts. When they confront a new phenomenon that is inconsistent with any of their preconstructed classifications, they subject it to those classifications anyway, relying on a rough best-fit approximation to determine which category should house and, thereafter, form the basis for their understanding of the new element. This perceptual framework provides an expedient tool for processing new information by simultaneously incorporating insights gained from (usually) relevant/analogous past experiences. It endows people with a quick response reflex that helps them to survive. Sometimes, however, new stimuli resemble—are *representative* of—familiar elements that have already been classified. In reality, these are drastically different analogues. In such an instance, the classification reflex leads to deception, producing an incorrect understanding of the new element that often persists and biases all our future interactions with that element.

Similarly, people tend to perceive probabilities and odds that resonate with their own preexisting ideas—even when the resulting conclusions drawn are statistically invalid. For example, the "Gambler's Fallacy" refers to the commonly held impression that gambling luck runs in streaks. However, subjective psychological dynamics, not mathematical realities, inspire this perception. Statistically, the streak concept is nonsense. Humans also tend to subscribe to something researchers call "the law of small numbers," which is the assumption that small samples faithfully represent entire populations. No scientific principle, however, underlies or enforces this "law."

Technical Description   Two primary interpretations of *representativeness bias* apply to individual investors.

1. *Base-Rate Neglect.* In base-rate neglect, investors attempt to determine the potential success of, say, an investment in Company A by contextualizing the venture in a familiar, easy-to-understand classification scheme. Such an investor might categorize Company A as a "value stock" and draw conclusions about the risks and rewards that follow from that categorization. This reasoning, however, ignores other unrelated variables that could substantially impact the success of the investment. Investors often embark on this erroneous path because it looks like an alternative to the diligent research actually required when evaluating an

investment. To summarize this characterization, some investors tend to rely on *stereotypes* when making investment decisions.

2. *Sample-Size Neglect.* In sample-size neglect, investors, when judging the likelihood of a particular investment outcome, often fail to accurately consider the sample size of the data on which they base their judgments. They incorrectly assume that small sample sizes are *representative* of populations (or "real" data). Some researchers call this phenomenon the "law of small numbers." When people do not initially comprehend a phenomenon reflected in a series of data, they will quickly concoct assumptions about that phenomenon, relying on only a few of the available data points. Individuals prone to sample-size neglect are quick to treat properties reflected in such small samples as properties that accurately describe universal pools of data. The small sample that the individual has examined, however, may not be representative whatsoever of the data at large.

Practical Application This section presents and analyzes two miniature case studies that demonstrate potential investor susceptibility to each variety of representativeness bias and then conducts a practical application research review.

Miniature Case Study Number 1: Base-Rate Neglect: Case Presentation. Suppose George, an investor, is looking to add to his portfolio and hears about a potential investment through a friend, Harry, at a local coffee shop. The conversation goes something like this:

George: Hi, Harry. My portfolio is really suffering right now. I could use a good long-term investment. Any ideas?

Harry: Well, George, did you hear about the new IPO [initial public offering] pharmaceutical company called PharmaGrowth (PG) that came out last week? PG is a hot new company that should be a great investment. Its president and CEO was a mover and shaker at an Internet company that did great during the tech boom, and she has PharmaGrowth growing by leaps and bounds.

George: No, I didn't hear about it. Tell me more.

Harry: Well, the company markets a generic drug sold over the Internet for people with a stomach condition that millions of people have. PG offers online advice on digestion and stomach health, and several Wall Street firms have issued "buy" ratings on the stock.

George: Wow, sounds like a great investment!

Harry: Well, I bought some. I think it could do great.

George: I'll buy some, too.

George proceeds to pull out his cell phone, call his broker, and place an order for 100 shares of PG.

Analysis. In this example, George displays base-rate neglect representativeness bias by considering this hot IPO is, necessarily, representative of a good long-term investment. Many investors like George believe that IPOs make good long-term investments due to all the up-front hype that surrounds them. In fact, numerous studies have shown that a very low percentage of IPOs actually turn out to be good long-term investments. This common investor misperception is likely due to the fact that investors in hot IPOs usually make money in the first few days after the offering. Over time, however, these stocks tend to trail their IPO prices, often never returning to their original levels.

George ignores the statistics and probabilities by not considering that, in the long run, the PG stock will most likely incur losses rather than gains. This concept can be applied to many investment situations. There is a relatively easy way to analyze how an investor might fall prey to base-rate neglect. For example, what is the probability that person A (Simon, a shy, introverted man) belongs to Group B (stamp collectors) rather than Group C (BMW drivers)? In answering this question, most people typically evaluate the degree to which A (Simon) "represents" B or C; they might conclude that Simon's shyness seems to be more representative of stamp collectors than BMW drivers. This approach neglects base rates, however: Statistically, far more people drive BMWs than collect stamps.

Similarly, George, our hypothetical investor, has effectively been asked: What is the probability that Company A (PharmaGrowth, the hot IPO) belongs to Group B (stocks constituting successful long-term investments) rather than Group C (stocks that will fail as long-term investments)? Again, most individuals approach this problem by attempting to ascertain the extent to which A appears characteristically representative of B or C. In George's judgment, PG possesses the properties of a successful long-term investment rather than a failed one. Investors arriving at this conclusion, however, ignore the base-rate fact that IPOs are more likely to fail than to succeed.

Miniature Case Study Number 2: Sample-Size Neglect   *Case Presentation.* Suppose George revisits his favorite coffee shop the following week and this time encounters bowling buddy Jim. Jim raves about his stockbroker, whose firm employs an analyst who appears to have recently made many successful stock picks. The conversation goes something like this:

George: Hi, Jim, how are you?

Jim: Hi, George. I'm doing great! I've been doing superbly in the market recently.

George: Really? What's your secret?

Jim: Well, my broker has passed along some great picks made by an analyst at her firm.

George: Wow, how many of these tips have you gotten?

Jim: My broker gave me three great stock picks over the past month or so. Each stock is up now, by over 10 percent.

George: That's a great record. My broker seems to give me one bad pick for every good one. It sounds like I need to talk to your broker; she has a much better record!

Analysis. (As in Case Study 1.) As we'll see in a moment, this conversation exemplifies sample-size neglect representativeness bias. Jim's description has prompted George to arrive at a faulty judgment regarding the success rate of Jim's broker/analyst. George is impressed, but his assessment is based on a very small sample size; the recent, successful picks Jim cites are inevitably only part of the story. George concluded that Jim's broker is successful because Jim's account of the broker's and analyst's performances seems *representative* of the record of a successful team. However, George disproportionately weighs Jim's testimony, and if he were to ask more questions, he might discover that his conclusion draws on too small a sample size. In reality, the analyst that Jim is relying on happens to be one who covers an industry that is popular at the moment, and *every* stock that this analyst covers has enjoyed recent success. Additionally, Jim neglected to mention that last year, this same broker/analyst team made a string of three *losing* recommendations. Therefore, both Jim's and George's brokers are batting 50 percent. George's reasoning demonstrates the pitfalls of sample-size neglect representativeness bias.

Implications for Investors. Both types of representativeness bias can lead to substantial investment mistakes. In the following section, we list examples of behaviors, attributable to base-rate neglect and sample-size neglect, respectively, that can cause harm to an investor's portfolio. Advice on these four areas will come later.

Harmful Effects of Representativeness Bias

Examples of the Harmful Effects of Sample-Size Neglect for Investors

1. Investors can make significant financial errors when they examine a money manager's track record. They peruse the past few quarters or even years and conclude, based on inadequate statistical data, that the fund's performance is the result of skilled allocation and/or security selection.
2. Investors also make similar mistakes when investigating track records of stock analysts. For example, they look at the success of an analyst's past few recommendations, erroneously assessing the analyst's aptitude based on this limited data sample.

Examples of the Harmful Effects of Base-Rate Neglect for Investors

1. What is the probability that Company A (ABC, a 75-year-old steel manufacturer that is having some business difficulties) belongs to group B (value stocks that will likely recover) rather than to Group C (companies that will go out of business)? In answering this question, most investors will try to judge the degree to which A is representative of B or C. In this case, some headlines featuring recent bankruptcies by steel companies make ABC Steel appear more representative of the latter categorization, and some investors conclude that they had best unload the stock. They are ignoring, however, the base-rate reality that far more steel companies survive or get acquired than go out of business.
2. What is the probability that AAA-rated Municipal Bond A (issued by an "inner city" and racially divided county) belongs to Group B (risky municipal bonds) rather than to Group C (safe municipal bonds)? In answering this question, most investors will again try to evaluate the extent to which A seems representative of B or C. In this case, Bond A's characteristics may seem representative of Group A (risky bonds) because of the county's "unsafe" reputation; however, this conclusion ignores the base-rate fact that, historically, the default rate of AAA bonds is virtually zero.

ILLUSION OF CONTROL BIAS

Bias Name: Illusion of control
Bias Type: Cognitive
Subtype: Belief perseverance

General Description   The *illusion of control bias,* another form of dissonant behavior, describes the tendency of human beings to believe that they can control or at least influence outcomes when, in fact, they cannot. This bias can be observed in Las Vegas, where casinos play host to many forms of this psychological fallacy. Some casino patrons swear that they are able to impact random outcomes such as the product of a pair of tossed dice. In the casino game "craps," for example, various research has demonstrated that people actually cast the dice more vigorously when they are trying to attain a higher number or when an "important" roll is happening. Some people, when successful at trying to predict the outcome of a series of coin tosses, actually believe that they are "better guessers," and some claim that distractions might diminish their performance at this statistically arbitrary task.

Technical Description   Ellen Langer, PhD, of Harvard University's psychology department, defines the illusion of control bias as the "expectancy of a personal success probability inappropriately higher than the objective probability would warrant." Langer found that choice, task familiarity, competition, and active involvement can all inflate confidence and generate such illusions. For example, Langer observed that people who were permitted to select their own numbers in a hypothetical lottery game were also willing to pay a higher price per ticket than subjects gambling on randomly assigned numbers. Since this initial study, many other researchers have uncovered similar situations where people perceived themselves to possess more control than they did, inferred causal connections where none existed, or displayed surprisingly great certainty in their predictions for the outcomes of chance events.

A relevant analogy can be found in a humorous, hypothetical anecdote: In a small town called Smallville, a man marches to the town square every day at 6 p.m. carrying a checkered flag and a trumpet. When the man reaches an appointed spot, he brandishes the flag and blows a few notes on the trumpet. Then, he returns home to the delight of his family.

A police officer notices the man's daily display and eventually asks him, "What are you doing?"

The man replies, "Keeping the elephants away."

"But there aren't any elephants in Smallville," the officer replies.

"Well, then, I'm doing a fine job, aren't I?" At this, the officer rolls his eyes and laughs.

This rather absurd tale illustrates the fallacy inherent in the illusion of control bias.

Practical Application   When subject to illusion of control bias, people feel as if they can exert more control over their environment than they actually can. An excellent application of this concept was devised by Andrea Breinholt and Lynnette Dalrymple, two researchers at Westminster College in Salt Lake City, Utah. Their study entitled "The Illusion of Control: What's Luck Got to Do with It?" illustrates that people often harbor unfounded illusions of control.

Breinholt and Dalrymple sought to examine subjects' susceptibility to illusions of control as determined by the intersection of two common impulses: the desire for control and the belief in good luck as a controllable attribute. Two hundred eighty-one undergraduate students participated in the study, and all rated themselves based on a "Desirability of Control Scale" and a "Belief in Luck Scale" immediately prior to the experiment. The subjects then participated in an online, simulated gambling task. Participants were randomly assigned either a high-involvement or a low-involvement condition and, also randomly, were rewarded with either a descending or a random sequence of outcomes.

All participants played 14 hands of "Red & Black," using four cards from a standard poker deck. Each card was presented facedown on the screen, and subjects were asked to wager as to whether a chosen card matched a selected, target color. Each player began with 50 chips. In each hand, participants could wager between zero and five chips; winning increased the participant's total stock of chips by the wagered amount. Likewise, following a lost hand, a player's supply of chips automatically decreased by the wagered amount. The odds of winning each hand were calibrated at 50:50.

Participants randomly assigned to the high-involvement condition were allowed to "shuffle" and "deal" the cards themselves. They could also choose, in each hand, the target color and the amount wagered. After the high-involvement participants chose their cards, the computer revealed each result accordingly. This sequence repeated over the course of 14 trials. The high-involvement condition was designed to maximize the participants' perception that they were controlling the game.

In the low-involvement condition, the computer shuffled and dealt the cards. The participants chose the amounts wagered, but the computer randomly selected the card on which the outcome of each hand would rest.

The descending outcome sequence was designed to maximize the illusion of control, letting the majority of successful outcomes occur during the first seven trials. The descending sequence, for example, consisted of the outcomes depicted in Figure 16.6.

The random outcome sequence was designed to minimize the illusion of control by spacing the successful outcomes more evenly over the course of the 14 trials. Figure 16.7 demonstrates a sample distribution.

Ultimately, participants in the high-involvement condition tended to wager more chips on each hand than did participants in the low-involvement condition.

Win	Win	Lose	Win	Win	Win	Lose	Lose	Win	Lose	Lose	Lose	Win	Lose

FIGURE 16.6   A Sample Distribution of the Descending Outcome Sequence in "The Illusion of Control: What's Luck Got to Do with It?"

Source: Andrea Breinholt and Lynnette A. Dalrymple, "The Illusion of Control: What's Luck Got to Do with It?" *The Myriad: Westminster College Undergraduate Academic Journal* (Summer 2004).

Win	Lose	Lose	Win	Win	Lose	Lose	Lose	Win	Lose	Win	Lose	Win	Win

FIGURE 16.7   Sample Distribution of the Random Outcome Sequence in "The Illusion of Control: What's Luck Got to Do with It?"

Source: Andrea Breinholt and Lynnette A. Dalrymple, "The Illusion of Control: What's Luck Got to Do with It?" *The Myriad: Westminster College Undergraduate Academic Journal* (Summer 2004).

Moreover, in the low-involvement condition, wagers did not differ reliably as a function of distributed feature composition (DFC)—in other words, participants receiving the descending sequence of outcomes did not wager more or less, on average, than did participants allotted the random outcome sequence. In contrast, in the high-involvement condition, high-DFC participants wagered more than did low-DFC participants. These findings support the presence of an illusion of control phenomenon in the traditional sense.

This study clearly demonstrates the illusion-of-control bias in practice. Investors are very much susceptible to this bias.

Implications for Investors   Following we list four primary behaviors that can lead to investment mistakes by investors who are susceptible to illusion of control bias.

Illusion of Control Bias: Behaviors That Can Cause Investment Mistakes

1. Illusion of control bias can lead investors to trade more than is prudent. Researchers have found that traders, especially online traders, believe themselves to possess more control over the outcomes of their investments than they actually do. An excess of trading results, in the end, in decreased returns.

2. Illusions of control can lead investors to maintain underdiversified portfolios. Researchers have found that investors hold concentrated positions because they gravitate toward companies over whose fate they feel some amount of control. That control proves illusory, however, and the lack of diversification hurts the investors' portfolios.

3. Illusion of control bias can cause investors to use limit orders and other such techniques in order to experience a false sense of control over their investments. In fact, the use of these mechanisms can often lead to an overlooked opportunity or, worse, a detrimental, unnecessary purchase based on the occurrence of an arbitrary price.

4. Illusion of control bias contributes, in general, to investor overconfidence. In particular, investors who have been successful in business or other professional pursuits believe that they should also be successful in the investment realm. What they find is that they may have had the ability to shape outcomes in their vocation, but investments are a different matter altogether.

HINDSIGHT BIAS

Bias Name: Hindsight bias
Bias Type: Cognitive
Subtype: Belief perseverance

General Description   Described in simple terms, *hindsight bias* is the impulse that insists: "I knew it all along!" This is perhaps the most pronounced version of belief perseverance biases. Once an event has elapsed, people afflicted with hindsight bias tend to perceive that the event was predictable—even if it wasn't. This behavior is precipitated by the fact that *actual* outcomes are more readily grasped by people's minds than the infinite array of outcomes that could have but didn't materialize. Therefore, people tend to overestimate the accuracy of their own predictions. This is not to say, obviously, that people cannot make accurate predictions, but merely that people may believe that they made an accurate prediction in hindsight. Hindsight bias has been demonstrated in experiments involving investing—a few of which will be examined shortly—as well as in other diverse settings, ranging from politics to medicine. Unpredictable developments bother people, since it's always embarrassing to be caught off guard. Also, people tend to remember their own predictions of the future as more accurate than they actually were because they are biased by having knowledge of what actually happened. To alleviate the discomfort associated with the unexpected, people tend to view things that have already happened as being relatively inevitable and predictable. This view is often caused by the reconstructive nature of memory. When people look back, they do not have perfect memory; they tend to "fill in the gaps" with what they prefer to believe. In doing so, people may prevent themselves from learning from the past.

Technical Description   Hindsight bias is the tendency of people, with the benefit of hindsight following an event, to falsely believe that they predicted the outcome of that event in the beginning. Hindsight bias affects future forecasting. A person subject to hindsight bias assumes that the outcome he or she ultimately observes is, in fact, the only outcome that was ever possible. Thus, he or she underestimates the uncertainty preceding the event in question and underrates the outcomes that could have materialized but did not.

Baruch Fischhoff described an experiment in which he asked subjects to answer general knowledge questions from almanacs and encyclopedias. Later, after revealing the correct answers, Fischhoff asked his subjects to recall their original responses from memory. The results are revealing: in general, people overestimated the quality of their initial knowledge and forgot their initial errors. Hindsight bias is a serious problem for market followers. Once an event is part of market history, there is a tendency to see the sequence that led up to it, making the event appear inevitable. As Richard Posner noted, outcomes exert irresistible pressure on their own interpretations. In hindsight, blunders with happy results are described as brilliant tactical moves, and unfortunate results of choices that were well grounded in available information are described as avoidable blunders.

One detriment of hindsight bias is that it can prevent learning from mistakes. People with hindsight bias connected to another psychological bias, anchoring, find it difficult to reconstruct an unbiased state of mind—it is easier to argue for the inevitability of a reported outcome and convince oneself that it would not have turned out otherwise. In sum, hindsight bias leads people to exaggerate the quality of their foresight.

Practical Application   Many people have observed hindsight bias in the investment realm. They watch people fool themselves into thinking that they could have predicted the outcome of some financial gamble, but they achieve such crystal-clear insight only after the fact. Perhaps the most obvious example recalls the prevailing response by investors to the behavior of the U.S. stock market between 1998 and 2003. In 1998 and 1999, virtually nobody viewed the soaring market indexes as symptomatic of a short-lived "bubble" (or if they did harbor such misgivings, investors did not act on them). Above-average returns were the norm, though even a casual glance at historical business-cycle trends should have foretold that, eventually, the 1990s bull market had to recede. Still, sadly, even some of the most sophisticated investors succumbed to the fantasy: "It's different this time!" Similarly, in 2006, it was inconceivable to most people that housing could be an unsafe "investment" and that a financial crisis of epic proportions was in the making. Now, in 2011, most people concede the reality of the housing and credit bubbles, the Internet stock bubble, and the subsequent meltdown in a distant memory or have forgotten altogether. In fact, chatting with most investors today, you'll get the impression that they expected the collapse of housing prices. The collapse of late 2000's prosperity was "clearly in the cards," or they comment: "Wasn't it obvious that we were in a bubble?" Giving in to hindsight bias can be very destructive because it leads investors to believe that they have better predictive powers than they actually do. Relying on these "powers" can invite poor decision making in the future.

Implications for Investors   Perhaps the hindsight bias's biggest implication for investors is that it gives investors a false sense of security when making investment decisions. This can manifest itself in excessive risk-taking behavior and place people's portfolios at risk. In the following, we review some common behaviors, rooted in hindsight bias that can cause investment mistakes.

Hindsight Bias: Behaviors That Can Cause Investment Mistakes

1. When an investment appreciates, hindsight-biased investors tend to rewrite their own memories to portray the positive developments as if they were predictable. Over time, this rationale can inspire excessive risk taking because hindsight-biased investors begin to believe that they have superior predictive powers, when, in fact, they do not. The bursting of the technology bubble is an example of this bias in action.

2. Hindsight-biased investors also "rewrite history" when they fare poorly and block out recollections of prior, incorrect forecasts in order to alleviate embarrassment. This form of self-deception, in some ways similar

to cognitive dissonance, prevents investors from learning from their mistakes. A clear example of this bias took place in the early 1980s, when energy stocks generated over 20 percent of S&P 500 returns, and lots of investors were caught up in the boom. By the 1990s, though, the energy bubble subsided, and many stockholders lost money. Most now prefer, in hindsight, to not recognize that the speculative frenzy clouded their judgments.

3. Hindsight-biased investors can unduly fault their money managers when funds perform poorly. Looking back at what has occurred in securities markets, these investors perceive every development as inevitable. How, then, could a worthwhile manager be caught by surprise? In fact, even top-quartile managers who implement their strategies correctly may not succeed in every market cycle. Managers of small-cap value funds in the late 1990s, for example, drew a lot of criticism. However, these people weren't poor managers; their style was simply out of favor at the time.

4. Conversely, hindsight bias can cause investors to unduly praise their money managers when funds perform well. The clarity of hindsight obscures the possibility that a manager's strategy might simply have benefited from good timing or good fortune. Consider the wisdom attributed to managers of aggressive-growth tech funds in the late 1990s.

Information Processing Biases Defined and Illustrated

MENTAL ACCOUNTING BIAS

> **Bias Name:** Mental accounting
> **Bias Type:** Cognitive
> **Subtype:** Information processing

General Description   First coined by University of Chicago professor Richard Thaler, *mental accounting* describes people's tendency to code, categorize, and evaluate economic outcomes by grouping their assets into any number of nonfungible (noninterchangeable) mental accounts. A completely rational person would never succumb to this sort of psychological process because mental accounting causes subjects to take the irrational step of treating various sums of money differently based on where these sums are mentally categorized, for example, the way that a certain sum has been obtained (work, inheritance, gambling, bonus, etc.) or the nature of the money's intended use (leisure, necessities, etc.). Money is money, regardless of the source or intended use.

The concept of framing is important in mental accounting analysis. In framing, people alter their perspectives on money and investments according to the surrounding circumstances that they face. Thaler performed an experiment in which he offered one group of people $30 and an accompanying choice: either pocket the money, no strings attached, or gamble on a coin toss, wherein a win would add $9 and a loss would subtract $9 from the initial $30 endowment. Seventy percent of the people offered this choice elected to gamble, because they considered the $30 to be "found" money—a little fortuitous windfall, not the sum of pennies meticulously saved and not the wages of hours spent slaving at some arduous task. So, why not have a little fun with this money? After all, what did these subjects really stand to lose?

A second group of people confronted a slightly different choice. Outright, they were asked: Would you rather gamble on a coin toss, in which you will receive $39 for a win and $21 for a loss? Or, would you rather simply pocket $30 and forgo the coin toss? The key distinction is that these people were not awarded $30, seemingly out of the blue, in the initial phase, as was the first group. Rather, at the outset of the exercise, the options were presented in terms of their ultimate payoffs. As you might expect, the second group reacted differently from the first. Only 34 percent of them chose to gamble, even though the economic prospects they faced were identical to those offered to group one. Sometimes people create mental accounts in order to justify actions that seem enticing but that are, in fact, unwise. Other times, people derive benefits from mental accounting; for example, earmarking money for retirement may prevent some households from spending that money prematurely.

Technical Description　Mental accounting refers to the coding, categorization, and evaluation of financial decisions. There are numerous interpretations of mental accounting, two of which will be reviewed here.

The first interpretation stems from Shefrin and Thaler's behavioral life-cycle theory and submits that people mentally allocate wealth over three classifications: (1) current income, (2) current assets, and (3) future income. The propensity to consume is greatest from the current income account, while sums designated as future income are treated more conservatively.

Another interpretation of mental accounting describes how distinct financial decisions may be evaluated jointly (i.e., as though they pertain to the same mental account) or separately. For example, Kahneman and Tversky conducted a study in which a majority of subjects declined to pay for a new theater ticket, which they were told would replace an identically priced ticket previously bought and lost. However, when the premise was altered and the subjects were told to imagine that they had not mislaid a previous ticket but, rather, an equivalent sum of cash—and so were contemplating the ticket purchase itself for the first time—a majority did decide to pay. Kahneman and Tversky concluded that subjects tended to evaluate the loss of a ticket and the purchase price of a new ticket in the same mental account; losing a ticket and shelling out for a new one would represent two losses incurred successively, debited from the same cluster of assets. The loss of actual cash, however, and the purchase of a ticket were debits evaluated separately. Therefore, the same aggregate loss felt less drastic when disbursed over two different accounts.

Practical Application　Marketing professors Drazen Prelec and Duncan Simester of Massachusetts Institute of Technology (MIT) brought mental accounting to life through an ingenious experiment. Prelec and Simester organized a sealed-bid auction for tickets to a Boston Celtics game during the team's victorious Larry Bird era in the 1980s. Half the participants in the auction were told that whoever won the bidding would need to pay for the tickets in cash within 24 hours. The other half was informed that the winning bidder would pay by credit card. Prelec and Simester then compared the average bids put forth within each group. As predicted, bidders who thought that they were relying on their credit cards wagered, on average, nearly twice the average cash bid.

This experiment illustrated that people put money in separate "accounts" when presented with a financial decision. In this case, the auction participants value cash more highly than credit card remittances, even though both forms of payment draw, ultimately, from the participant's own money. People may allocate money to a "cash" (expenditures paid only in cash) account, while simultaneously placing additional funds in a "credit card" (expenditures paid only by credit card) account. Viewed in light of the life-cycle theory mentioned in the previous section, the cash might be more likely to represent a "current asset," and the credit card might represent "future income," which are two separate accounts. It probably goes without saying that this behavior touches on another bias previously reviewed: self-control.

Implications for Investors Mental accounting is a deep-seated bias with many manifestations, and it can cause a variety of problems for investors. The most basic of these problems is the placement of investment assets into discrete "buckets" according to asset type, without regard for potential correlations connecting investments across categories. Tversky and Kahneman contended that the difficulty individuals have in addressing interactions between investments leads investors to construct portfolios in a layered, pyramid format. Each tier addresses a particular investment goal independently of any additional investment goals. For example, when the objective is to preserve wealth, investors tend to target low-risk investments, like cash and money market funds. For income, they rely mostly on bonds and dividend-paying stocks. For a chance at a more drastic reward, investors turn to riskier instruments, like emerging market stocks and initial public offerings (IPOs). Combining different assets whose performances do *not* correlate with one another is an important consideration for risk reduction, but it is often neglected in this "pyramid" approach. As a result, investment positions held without regard to correlations might offset one another in a portfolio context, creating suboptimal inefficiencies. People quite often fail to evaluate a potential investment based on its contribution to overall portfolio return and aggregate portfolio risk; rather, they look at only the recent performance of the relevant asset layer. This common, detrimental oversight stems from mental accounting.

Following we review five investment mistakes that mental accounting can cause. Please note that this list is not exhaustive, as mental accounting bias is a vast, varied topic in application to private clients. Advice on each of the five potential pitfalls will follow in subsequent portions of this chapter.

Mental Accounting Bias: Behaviors That Can Cause Investment Mistakes

1. Mental accounting bias can cause people to imagine that their investments occupy separate "buckets," or accounts. These categories might include, for example, college fund or money for retirement. Envisioning distinct accounts to correspond with financial goals, however, can cause investors to neglect positions that offset or correlate across accounts. This can lead to suboptimal aggregate portfolio performance.

2. Mental accounting bias can cause investors to irrationally distinguish between returns derived from income and those derived from capital appreciation. Many people feel the need to preserve capital (i.e., principal) sums and prefer to spend interest. As a result, some investors chase income streams and can unwittingly erode principal in the process. Consider, for example, a high-income bond fund or a preferred stock that pays a high dividend yet, at times, can suffer a loss of principal due to interest rate fluctuations. Mental accounting can make instruments like these appealing, but they may not benefit the investor in the long run.

3. Mental accounting bias can cause investors to allocate assets differently when employer stock is involved. Studies have shown that participants in company retirement plans that offer no company stock as an option tend to invest in a balanced way between equities and fixed-income instruments. However, when employer stock is an option, employees usually allocate a portion of contributions to company stock, with the remainder disbursed evenly over equity and fixed-income investments. Total equity allocation, then, could be too high when company stock was offered, causing these investors' portfolios to potentially be underdiversified. This can be a suboptimal condition because these investors do not fully comprehend the risk that exists in their portfolio.

4. In the same vein as anchoring bias, mental accounting bias can cause investors to succumb to the "house money" effect, wherein risk-taking behavior escalates as wealth grows. Investors exhibiting this rationale behave irrationally because they fail to treat all money as fungible. Biased financial decision making can, of course, endanger a portfolio.

5. Mental accounting bias can cause investors to hesitate to sell investments that once generated significant gains but, over time, have fallen in price. During the bull market of the 2000s, investors became accustomed to healthy, unrealized gains. When most investors had their net worth deflated by the market correction, they hesitated to sell their positions at the then-smaller profit margin. Many today still regret not reaping gains when they could; a number of investments to which people clung following the 1990s boom have become nearly worthless.

ANCHORING AND ADJUSTMENT BIAS

Bias Name: Anchoring and adjustment
Bias Type: Cognitive
Subtype: Information processing

General Description   When required to estimate a value with unknown magnitude, people generally begin by envisioning some initial, default number—an "anchor"—which they then adjust up or down to reflect subsequent information and analysis. The anchor, once fine-tuned and reassessed, matures into a final estimate. Numerous studies demonstrate that regardless of how the initial anchors were chosen, people tend to adjust their anchors insufficiently and produce end approximations that are, consequently, biased. People are generally better at estimating relative comparisons rather than absolute figures, which the following example illustrates.

Suppose you are asked whether the population of Canada is greater than or less than 20 million. Obviously, you will answer either above 20 million or below 20 million. If you were then asked to guess an absolute population value, your estimate would probably fall somewhere near 20 million, because you are likely subject to anchoring by your previous response.

Technical Description *Anchoring and adjustment* is a psychological heuristic that influences the way people intuit probabilities. Investors exhibiting this bias are often influenced by purchase "points"—or arbitrary price levels or price indexes—and tend to cling to these numbers when facing questions like "Should I buy or sell this security?" or "Is the market overvalued or undervalued right now?" This is especially true when the introduction of new information regarding the security further complicates the situation. Rational investors treat these new pieces of information objectively and do not reflect on purchase prices or target prices in deciding how to act. Anchoring and adjustment bias, however, implies that investors perceive new information through an essentially warped lens. They place undue emphasis on statistically arbitrary, psychologically determined anchor points. Decision making therefore deviates from neoclassically prescribed "rational" norms.

Practical Application This section reviews one miniature case study and provides an accompanying analysis and interpretation that will demonstrate investor potential for anchoring and adjustment bias.

Miniature Case Study: Anchoring and Adjustment Bias

Case Presentation Suppose Alice owns stock in Corporation ABC. She is a fairly astute investor and has recently discovered some new information about ABC. Her task is to evaluate this information for the purpose of deciding whether she should increase, decrease, or simply maintain her holdings in ABC. Alice bought ABC two years ago at $12, and the stock is now at $15. Several months ago, ABC reached $20 after a surprise announcement of higher-than-expected earnings, at which time Alice contemplated selling the stock but did not. Unfortunately, ABC then dropped to $15 after executives were accused of faulty accounting practices. Today, Alice feels as though she has "lost" 25 percent of the stock's value, and she would prefer to wait and sell her shares in ABC once it returns to its recent $20 high.

Alice has a background in accounting, and she does some research that leads her to conclude that ABC's methods are indeed faulty, but not extremely so. However, Alice cannot entirely gauge the depth of the problem and realizes that holding ABC contains risk, but ABC is also a viable corporate entity with good prospects. Alice must make a decision. On one hand, she has confirmed that ABC does have an accounting problem, and she is unsure how severe the problem might become. On the other hand, the company has a solid business, and Alice wants to recoup the 25 percent that she feels she lost. What should Alice do?

Analysis Most investors have been confronted with situations similar to this one. They decide to invest in a stock; the stock goes up and then declines. Investors become conflicted and must evaluate the situation to determine whether to hold on to the stock. A rational investor would examine the company's financial situation; make an objective assessment of its business fundamentals; and then decide to buy, hold, or sell the shares. Conversely, some irrational investors—even after going through the trouble of performing the aforementioned rational analysis—permit cognitive errors

TABLE 16.1   Estimates by Real Estate Agents in Northcraft and Neale's 1987 Study

Real Estate Agent Group 1	Real Estate Agent Group 2
Given asking price = $119,900	Given asking price = $149,900
Predicted appraisal value = $144,202	Predicted appraisal value = $128,752
Listing price = $117,745	Listing price = $130,981
Purchase price = $111,454	Purchase price = $127,316
Lowest acceptable offer = $111,136	Lowest acceptable offer = $111,136

Reprinted from Gregory Northcroft and Margaret Neale, "Experts, Amateurs, and Real Estate: An Anchoring-and-Adjustment Perspective on Property Pricing Decisions," *Organizational Behavior and Human Decision Processes* 39, no. 1 (1987): 84–97. Copyright © 1987, with permission from Elsevier.

to cloud their judgment. Alice, for example, may irrationally disregard the results of her research and "anchor" herself to the $20 figure, refusing to sell unless ABC once again achieves that price. This type of response reflects an irrational behavioral bias and should be avoided.

Implications for Investors   A wide variety of investor behaviors can indicate susceptibility to anchoring and adjustment bias. Below we highlight some important examples of which investors and advisors should be aware.

Some excellent research into the effects of anchoring and adjustment was performed in 1987 by University of Arizona researchers Gregory Northcraft and Margaret Neale. Their study asked a group of real estate professionals to value a property after being given a proposed selling price quoted by the researchers at the outset of the experiment. The agents were also given 20 minutes to examine the premises before being asked to estimate its worth. Specifically, the study asked each researcher to provide the appraised value of the property, the value of the property should it be put up for sale, the price that a potential buyer should be advised to regard as reasonable, and the minimum offer that the seller should be advised to accept. Table 16.1 summarizes the results with respect to the first two categories—appraised value and salable value (the remaining estimates followed patterns similar to those evidenced here).

During the experiment, the real estate agents were divided into two groups. Each group received a guided tour of the home, a 10-page packet of information describing the home, and a list price for the property. The two trials proceeded identically but with one twist: The first group of agents was quoted a list price higher than that quoted to the second group. When both groups subsequently appraised the property, anchoring and adjustment theory held: other things held constant, the higher proposed list price was determined to have led to higher appraisal estimates. The appraisals, then, did not necessarily reflect the objective characteristics of the property. Rather, they were influenced by the initial values on which the agents "anchored" their estimates.

Anchoring and Adjustment Bias: Behaviors That Can Cause Investor Mistakes

1. Investors tend to make general market forecasts that are too close to current levels. For example, if the Dow Jones Industrial Average (DJIA) is at 10,500, investors are likely to forecast the index in a way narrower than what might be suggested by historical fluctuation. For example, an investor

subject to anchoring might forecast the DJIA to fall between 10,000 and 11,000 at year-end, versus making an absolute estimate based on historical standard deviation (rational) analysis.

2. Investors (and securities analysts) tend to stick too closely to their original estimates when new information is learned about a company. For example, if an investor determines that next year's earnings estimate is $2 per share and the company subsequently falters, the investor may not readjust the $2 figure enough to reflect the change because he or she is "anchored" to the $2 figure. This is not limited to downside adjustments—the same phenomenon occurs when companies have upside surprises. (At the end of the part, we will review a behaviorally based investment strategy leveraging this concept that has proven to be effective at selecting investments.)

3. Investors tend to make a forecast of the percentage that a particular asset class might rise or fall based on the current level of returns. For example, if the DJIA returned 10 percent last year, investors will be anchored on this number when making a forecast about next year.

4. Investors can become anchored on the economic states of certain countries or companies. For example, in the 1980s, Japan was an economic powerhouse, and many investors believed that they would remain so for decades. Unfortunately for some, Japan stagnated for years after the late 1980s. Similarly, IBM was a bellwether stock for decades. Some investors became anchored to the idea that IBM would always be a bellwether. Unfortunately for some, IBM did not last as a bellwether stock.

FRAMING BIAS

Bias Name: Framing bias
Bias Type: Cognitive
Subtype: Information processing

General Description   *Framing bias* notes the tendency of decision makers to respond to various situations differently, based on the context in which a choice is presented (framed). This can happen in a number of contexts, including how word problems are described, how data is presented in tables and charts, and how figures are illustrated. For example, take a look at Figure 16.8. Which line is longer?

People subject to visual framing bias experience an optical illusion, which leads them to insist that the line on the bottom is longer. The graphic is reproduced, however, in Figure 16.9, this time with vertical marks added in as a guide. Which line is longer?

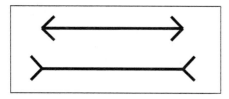

FIGURE 16.8   Which Line Is Longer?

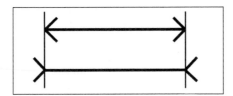

FIGURE 16.9   Which Line Is Longer?

With the framing effect of the "arrow" detail neutralized, it becomes clear that the line on the top and the line on the bottom are equal in length.

In the context of everyday evidence of framing bias, we can look at how retailers price their products. Many grocers, for example, will price items in multiples: "2 for $2" or "3 for $7."

This doesn't necessarily imply, however, that any kind of bulk discount is being offered. Have you ever found an item priced at "3 for $7" also available at a unit price of $2.33? This isn't unusual. Shopping represents a rudimentary rational choice problem ("How many oranges should I buy?"), and good salespeople try to frame a solution for a buyer that benefits the store. "Don't buy oranges in units of one," suggests the price policy. "Buy them in multiples of three." This takes advantage of people's susceptibility to framing.

Technical Description   A decision frame is the decision maker's subjective conception of the acts, outcomes, and contingencies associated with a particular choice. The frame that a decision maker adopts is controlled partly by the formulation of the problem and partly by the norms, habits, and personal characteristics of the decision maker.

It is often possible to frame a given decision problem in more than one way. Framing effects occur when preferences change as a function of some variation in framing. For example, one prospect can be formulated in two ways: as a gain ("25 percent of crops will be saved if they are provided with fertilizer XYZ") or as a loss ("75 percent of crops will die without fertilizer XYZ"). Most people in the first case will adopt a gain frame, which generally leads to risk-averse behavior. In the second case—75 percent of crops will die—most people will adopt a loss frame and thereby become more likely to engage in risk-seeking behavior.

Framing bias also encompasses a sub-categorical phenomenon known as *narrow framing,* which occurs when people focus too restrictively on one or two aspects of a situation, excluding other crucial aspects and thus compromising their decision making. For example, take the case of a lawnmower purchase. A consumer working within too narrow a frame of reference might shop for a mower that is fast, while overlooking blade width, fuel economy, and other factors that affect the length of time required to mow a lawn.

Practical Application   Decision frames are quite prevalent in the context of investor behavior. Building on the definitions outlined in the preceding section, we can now use our newly acquired insights into framing bias as we consider a typical investor risk tolerance questionnaire. This will demonstrate how framing bias is applied in practice and how advisors should be aware of its effects.

Suppose that an investor completes a risk tolerance questionnaire for the purpose of determining the "risk category" into which he or she falls. The responses the investor selects are highly relevant because the risk category outcome will determine the types of investments that are selected for this individual's portfolio. Ideally, question phrasing and framing—elements uncorrelated with the investor's actual level of risk tolerance—should not be factors that affect the questionnaire's results. Let's examine some of the material that might appear on a typical risk tolerance questionnaire.

First, suppose that the items on the questionnaire refer to a hypothetical securities portfolio, Portfolio ABC. Over a 10-year period, ABC has historically returned an annual average of 10 percent, with a standard deviation of 15 percent. (Recall that standard deviation quantifies the amount of expected variation in an investment's performance from year to year.) Basic statistics dictate that 67 percent of ABCs returns will fall within one standard deviation of the mean, or annual average, return that ABC generates. Similarly, 95 percent of returns will fall within two standard deviations, and 99.7 percent within three standard deviations of the mean. So, if ABC's mean return was 10 percent and its standard deviation was 15 percent, then two-thirds of all returns produced by ABC would equal 10 percent plus-or-minus no more than 15 percent; that is, 67 percent of the time, ABC's return will likely be somewhere between –5 percent and 25 percent. It follows that 95 percent of ABC's returns will fall between –20 percent and 40 percent and that 99.7 percent will fall somewhere between –35 percent and 55 percent.

Now, imagine that one, but not both, of the following questions is to appear on an investor's risk tolerance questionnaire. Both concern Portfolio ABC, and both try to measure an investor's comfort level with ABC, given its average returns, volatility, and so on. However, the two questions frame the situation very differently. As you compare questions 1 and 2, try to imagine how an average investor, probably subject to a few common behavioral biases, might respond to each respective frame. Do you think most investors' answers would be identical in each instance?

1. Based on Table 16.2, which investment portfolio seems like the best fit, bearing in mind your own risk tolerance as well as your desire for long-term return?
   a. Portfolio XYZ
   b. Portfolio DEF
   c. Portfolio ABC
2. Assume that you own Portfolio ABC and that it lost 15 percent of its value over the past year, despite previous years of good performance. This loss is consistent with the performance of similar funds during the past year. What is your reaction to this situation?
   a. Sell all Portfolio ABC shares.
   b. Sell some, but not all, Portfolio ABC shares.
   c. Continue to hold Portfolio ABC shares.
   d. Increase investment in Portfolio ABC.

There is a chance that a person will select similar answers for both questions. However, there is also a significant probability that inconsistent framing will generate inconsistent responses from many investors. Specifically, respondents might reject Portfolio ABC in Question 1, yet decide to proceed with ABC in Question 2.

TABLE 16.2   Portfolio Selection: Which Portfolio Seems Best?

Portfolio Number	95% Probability Gain/Loss Range	Long-Term Return
XYZ	2% to 4%	3%
DEF	−6% to 18%	6%
ABC	−20% to 40%	10%

In Question 1, "95 Percent Probability Gain/Loss Range" refers (in Table 16.2) to an interval of two standard deviations above and below the mean. In 95 percent of all cases, ABC returned 10 percent plus-or-minus 30 percent; its standard deviation is 15 percent.

In Question 2, ABC produced a return that, in two-thirds of all cases, would have been the worst return imaginable: It returned one standard deviation below the mean. However, because Question 2 employs one standard deviation rather than two, readers are less likely to consider the one-third of all cases in which ABC could lose more than 5 percent of its value (entering into the 95 percent, rather than the 67 percent, probable gain/loss range).

Like the method employed by grocers (pricing produce in multiples), which subtly suggests some arbitrary, benchmark quantity of oranges for purchase, Question 1 similarly invites people to more intuitively consider the rarer, heavier losses Portfolio ABC could incur if returns breached the 67 percent confidence interval. Here, the implications of framing are important: Inconsistent responses to Questions 1 and 2 could make the questionnaire inconsistent and an inaccurate measure of investor risk tolerance (the questionnaire's outcome would be, accordingly, a flawed basis for structuring an allocation). Practitioners need to be acutely aware of how framing can affect the outcome of various investment choices.

Implications for Investors

An individual's willingness to accept risk can be influenced by how questions/scenarios are framed—positively or negatively. Recall, for example, the subjective difference between "25 percent of crops will be saved" and "75 percent of crops will die." The same optimism or pessimism in framing can affect investment decision making. For example, suppose that Mrs. Smith chooses to invest in either Portfolio A or Portfolio B. Further suppose that Portfolios A and B are identical in every respect. Mrs. Smith learns that Portfolio A will offer her a 70 percent chance of attaining her financial goals, whereas Portfolio B offers Mrs. Smith a 30 percent chance of not attaining her financial goals. If Mrs. Smith is like most people, she will choose Portfolio A, because its performance prospects were more attractively framed.

Another key point to keep in mind is that framing bias and loss aversion bias can and do work together. When people have suffered losses, they may view losses as the right time to embark on risk-taking behavior; when people have gained, they may feel threatened by options that entail additional risk. For example, an investor who has just suffered a net loss is likely to seek risk with his or her investments. Someone who has gained, however, is more likely to opt for a sure thing.

In the following we review four investor mistakes caused by framing bias.

Framing Bias: Behaviors That Can Cause Investment Mistakes

1. Depending on how questions are asked, framing bias can cause investors to communicate responses to questions about risk tolerance that are either unduly conservative or unduly aggressive. For example, when questions are worded in the "gain" frame, a risk-averse response is more likely. When questions are worded in the "loss" frame, risk-seeking behavior is the likely response.
2. The optimistic or pessimistic manner in which an investment or asset allocation recommendation is framed can affect people's willingness or lack of willingness to invest. Optimistically worded questions are more likely to garner affirmative responses, and optimistically worded answer choices are more likely to be selected than pessimistically phrased alternatives. Framing contexts are often arbitrary and uncorrelated and therefore shouldn't impact investors' judgments . . . but, they do.
3. *Narrow framing,* a subset of framing bias, can cause even long-term investors to obsess over short-term price fluctuations in a single industry or stock. This behavior works in concert with myopic loss aversion: The risk here is that by focusing only on short-term market fluctuations, excessive trading may be the result. This trading behavior has proven to be less than optimal for investors.
4. Framing and loss aversion can work together to explain excessive risk aversion. An investor who has incurred a net loss becomes likelier to select a riskier investment, whereas a net gainer feels predisposed toward less risky alternatives.

AVAILABILITY BIAS

Bias Name: Availability bias
Bias Type: Cognitive
Subtype: Information processing

General Description The *availability bias* is a rule of thumb, or mental shortcut, that causes people to estimate the probability of an outcome based on how prevalent or familiar that outcome appears in their lives. People exhibiting this bias perceive easily recalled possibilities as being more likely than those prospects that are harder to imagine or difficult to comprehend.

One classic example cites the tendency of most people to guess that shark attacks more frequently cause fatalities than airplane parts falling from the sky do. However, as difficult as it may be to comprehend, the latter is actually 30 times more likely to occur. Shark attacks are probably assumed to be more prevalent because sharks invoke greater fear or because shark attacks receive a disproportionate degree of media attention. Consequently, dying from a shark attack is, for most respondents, easier to imagine than death by falling airplane parts. In sum, the availability rule of thumb underlies judgments about the likelihood or frequency of an occurrence based on readily available information, not necessarily based on complete, objective, or factual information.

Technical Description People often inadvertently assume that readily available thoughts, ideas, or images represent unbiased indicators of statistical probabilities. People estimate the likelihoods of certain events according to the degree of ease with which recollections or examples of analogous events can be accessed from memory. Impressions drawn from imagination and past experience combine to construct an array of conceivable outcomes, whose real statistical probabilities are, in essence, arbitrary. There are several categories of availability bias, of which the four that apply most to investors are: (1) *retrievability,* (2) *categorization,* (3) *narrow range of experience,* and (4) *resonance.* Each category will be described and corresponding examples given.

1. *Retrievability.* Ideas that are *retrieved* most easily also seem to be the most credible, though this is not necessarily the case. For example, Daniel Kahneman, Paul Slovic, and Amos Tversky performed an experiment in which subjects were read a list of names and then were asked whether more male or female names had been read. In reality, the majority of names recited were unambiguously female; however, the subset of male names contained a much higher frequency of references to celebrities (e.g., "Richard Nixon"). In accordance with availability theory, most subjects produced biased estimates indicating, mistakenly, that more male than female names populated the list.

2. *Categorization.* "Representativeness bias" describes how people's minds comprehend and archive perceptions according to certain classification schemes. Here, we will discuss how people attempt to categorize or summon information that matches a certain reference. The first thing that their brains do is generate a set of search terms, specific to the task at hand, that will allow them to efficiently navigate their brain's classification structure and locate the data they need. Different tasks require different search sets, however; and when it is difficult to put together a framework for a search, people often mistakenly conclude that the search simply references a more meager array of results. For example, if a French person simultaneously tries to come up with a list of high-quality U.S. vineyards and a corresponding list of French vineyards, the list of U.S. vineyards is likely to prove more difficult to create. The French person, as a result, might predict that high-quality U.S. vineyards exist with a lower probability than famous French vineyards, even if this is not necessarily the case.

3. *Narrow range of experience.* When a person possesses an overly restrictive frame of reference from which to formulate an objective estimate, then *narrow range of experience bias* often results. For example, assume that a very successful college basketball player is drafted by a National Basketball Association (NBA) team, where he proceeds to enjoy several successful seasons. Because this person encounters numerous other successful former college basketball players on a daily basis in the NBA, he is likely to overestimate the relative proportion of successful college basketball players that go on to play professionally. He will, likewise, probably underestimate the relative frequency of failed college basketball players, because most of the players he knows are those who have gone

on to reap great rewards from their undergraduate basketball careers. In reality, only an extremely small percentage of college basketball players will ever graduate to the NBA.

4. *Resonance.* The extent to which certain, given situations *resonate* vis-à-vis individuals' own, personal situations can also influence judgment. For example, fans of classical music might be likely to overestimate the portion of the total population that also listens to classical music. Those who dislike classical music would probably underestimate the number of people who listen to classical music.

Practical Application   Each variation of the availability bias just outlined has unique implications in personal finance, both for advisory practitioners and for clients. Let's explore these now.

1. *Retrievability.* Most investors, if asked to identify the "best" mutual fund company, are likely to select a firm that engages in heavy advertising, such as Fidelity or Schwab. In addition to maintaining a high public relations profile, these firms also "cherry pick" the funds with the best results in their advertising, which makes this belief more "available" to be recalled. In reality, the companies that manage some of today's highest-performing mutual funds undertake little to no advertising. Consumers who overlook these funds in favor of more widely publicized alternatives may exemplify retrievability/availability bias.

2. *Categorization.* Although this is changing, most Americans, if asked to pinpoint one country, worldwide, that offers the best investment prospects, would designate their own: the United States. Why? When conducting an inventory of memories and stored knowledge regarding "good investment opportunities" in general, the country category that most Americans most easily recall is the United States. However, to dismiss the wealth of investment prospects abroad as a result of this phenomenon is irrational. In reality, over 50 percent of equity market capitalization exists outside the United States. People who are unduly "patriotic" when looking for somewhere to invest often suffer from availability bias.

3. *Narrow range of experience.* Assume that an employee of a fast-growing, high-tech company is asked: "Which industry generates the most successful investments?" Such an individual, who probably comes into contact with other triumphant tech profiteers each and every day, will likely overestimate the relative proportion of corporate successes stemming from technologically intensive industries. Like the NBA star who got his start in college and, therefore, too optimistically estimates the professional athletic prospects of college basketball players, this hypothetical high-tech employee demonstrates narrow range of experience availability bias.

4. *Resonance.* People often favor investments that they feel match their personalities. A thrifty individual who discount shops, clips coupons, and otherwise seeks out bargains may demonstrate a natural inclination toward value investing. At the same time, such an investor might not heed the wisdom of balancing value assets with more growth-oriented ventures, owing to a reluctance to front the money and acquire a quality growth stock. The concept of value is easily available in such an investor's mind, but the notion of growth is less so. This person's portfolio could perform suboptimally as a result of resonance availability bias.

A Classic Example of Availability Bias   In the period 1927 to 1999, which political party's leadership has correlated with higher stock market returns? Many Wall Street professionals are known to lean Republican, so a lot of people, given this readily available information, might speculate that the markets benefit from Republican political hegemony. After all, why would so many well-informed individuals, whose livelihoods depend on the success of the stock market, vote for Republicans if Democrats produced higher returns? According to a study done by University of California at Los Angeles professors Pedro Santa-Clara and Rossen Valkanov, the 72-year period between 1927 and 1999 showed that a broad stock index, similar to the Standard & Poor's (S&P) 500, returned approximately 11 percent more a year on average under a Democratic president than safer, three-month Treasury bonds (T-bonds). By comparison, the index returned 2 percent a year more than the T-bonds when Republicans were in office. If your natural reaction was to answer "Republican" to this question, you may suffer from availability bias.

Implications for Investors   In the following we summarize the primary implications for investors of susceptibility to availability bias in each of the four forms we've reviewed. In all such instances, investors ignore potentially beneficial investments because information on those investments is not readily available, or they make investment decisions based on readily available information, avoiding diligent research.

Availability Bias: Behaviors That Can Cause Investment Mistakes

1. *Retrievability.* Investors will choose investments based on information that is available to them (advertising, suggestions from advisors, friends, etc.) and will not engage in disciplined research or due diligence to verify that the investment selected is a good one.
2. *Categorization.* Investors will choose investments based on categorical lists that they have available in their memory. In their minds, other categories will not be easily recalled and, thus, will be ignored. For example, U.S. investors may ignore countries where potentially rewarding investment opportunities may exist because these countries may not be an easily recalled category in their memory.
3. *Narrow range of experience.* Investors will choose investments that fit their narrow range of life experiences, such as the industry they work in, the region they live in, and the people they associate with. For example, investors who work in the technology industry may believe that only technology investments will be profitable.
4. *Resonance.* Investors will choose investments that resonate with their own personality or that have characteristics that investors can relate to their own behavior. Taking the opposite view, investors ignore potentially good investments because they can't relate to or do not come in contact with characteristics of those investments. For example, thrifty people may not relate to expensive stocks (high price/earnings multiples) and potentially miss out on the benefits of owning these stocks.

SELF-ATTRIBUTION BIAS

Bias Name: Self-attribution bias
Bias Type: Cognitive
Subtype: Information processing

General Description   *Self-attribution bias* (or self-serving attribution bias) refers to the tendency of individuals to ascribe their successes to innate aspects, such as talent or foresight, while more often blaming failures on outside influences, such as bad luck. Students faring well on an exam, for example, might credit their own intelligence or work ethic, while those failing might cite unfair grading. Similarly, athletes often reason that they have simply performed to reflect their own superior athletic skills if they win a game, but they might allege unfair calls by a referee when they lose a game.

Technical Description   Self-attribution is a cognitive phenomenon by which people attribute failures to situational factors and successes to dispositional factors. Self-serving bias can actually be broken down into two constituent tendencies or subsidiary biases.

1. *Self-enhancing bias* represents people's propensity to claim an irrational degree of credit for their successes.
2. *Self-protecting bias* represents the corollary effect—the irrational denial of responsibility for failure.

Self-enhancing bias can be explained from a cognitive perspective. Research has shown that if people intend to succeed, then outcomes in accordance with that intention—successes—will be perceived as the result of people acting to achieve what they've originally intended. Individuals, then, will naturally accept more credit for successes than failures, since they intend to succeed rather than to fail. Self-protecting bias can also be partially explained from an emotional perspective. Some argue that the need to maintain self-esteem directly affects the attribution of task outcomes because people will protect themselves psychologically as they attempt to comprehend their failures. Because these cognitive and emotional explanations are linked, it can be difficult to ascertain which form of the bias is at work in a given situation.

Practical Application   Dr. Dana Dunn, a professor of psychology at Moravian College in Bethlehem, Pennsylvania, has done some excellent work regarding self-serving bias. She observed that her students often have trouble recognizing self-serving attributional bias in their own behaviors. To illustrate this phenomenon, she performs an experiment in which she asks students to take out a sheet of paper and draw a line down the middle of the page. She then tells them to label one column "strengths" and the other "weaknesses" and to list their personal strengths and weaknesses in the two columns. She finds that students consistently list more strengths than weaknesses.

Dunn's result suggests that her students tend to suffer from self-serving attributional bias. Investors are not immune from this behavior. The old Wall Street adage "Don't confuse brains with a bull market" is relevant here. When an investor who is susceptible to self-attribution bias purchases an investment and it goes up, then it was due, naturally, to their business and investment savvy. In contrast, when an investor who is susceptible to self-attribution bias purchases an investment and it goes down, then it was due, naturally, to bad luck or some other factor that was not the fault of the investor. People's strengths, generally, consist of personal qualities that they believe empower them to succeed, whereas weaknesses are traits they possess that predispose them to fail. Investors subject to self-attribution bias perceive that investment successes are more often attributable to innate characteristics and that investment failures are due to exogenous factors.

Implications for Investors Irrationally attributing successes and failures can impair investors in two primary ways. First, people who aren't able to perceive mistakes they've made are, consequently, unable to learn from those mistakes. Second, investors who disproportionately credit themselves when desirable outcomes do arise can become detrimentally overconfident in their own market savvy. Below we describe the pitfalls of self-serving behavior that often lead to financial mistakes.

Self-Attribution Bias: Behaviors That Can Cause Investment Mistakes

1. Self-attribution investors can, after a period of successful investing (such as one quarter or one year) believe that their success is due to their acumen as investors rather than to factors out of their control. This behavior can lead to taking on too much risk, as the investors become too confident in their behavior.
2. Self-attribution bias often leads investors to trade more than is prudent. As investors believe that successful investing (trading) is attributed to skill versus luck, they begin to trade too much, which has been shown to be "hazardous to your wealth."
3. Self-attribution bias leads investors to "hear what they want to hear." That is, when investors are presented with information that confirms a decision that they made to make an investment, they will ascribe "brilliance" to themselves. This may lead to investors making a purchase or holding an investment that they should not.
4. Self-attribution bias can cause investors to hold underdiversified portfolios, especially among investors that attribute the success of an company's performance to their own contribution, such as corporate executives, board members, and so on. Often, the performance of a stock is not attributed to the skill of an individual person, but rather many factors, including chance; thus, holding a concentrated stock position can be associated with self-attribution and should be avoided.

OUTCOME BIAS

Bias Name: Outcome bias
Bias Type: Cognitive
Subtype: Information processing

General Description   *Outcome bias* refers to the tendency of individuals to decide to do something—such as make an investment in a mutual fund—based on the outcome of past events (such as returns of the past five years) rather than by observing the process by which the outcome came about (the investment process used by the mutual fund manager over the past five years). An investor might think, "This manager had a fantastic five years, I am going to invest with her," rather than understanding how such great returns were generated or why the returns generated by other managers might not have had good results over the past five years.

Technical Description   In the name of attempting to make better decisions themselves, people are prone to evaluating the decisions others make (and subsequent results of those decisions). We do this because it helps people, for example, to determine who they want to lead their country, who they want to be their local judges and officials, who they wish to associate with personally, and who they want to manage their money. However, in evaluating someone else's decisions after they have made them, observers possess information that the decision makers may not have had while they made their decisions (such as what kind of impact their decision had on us and other outside or big picture information), and it is possible that we judge others too kindly or too harshly. As Baron states in his work, ". . . Reasonable decisions are criticized by Monday morning quarterbacks who think they might have decided otherwise, and decision makers end up being punished for their bad luck." Similarly, people who make flawed decisions that turn out okay should not necessarily be judged on the outcome, however good it was, but rather on the process they used during the decision making process.

Information that becomes available only after a decision is made should not be considered in judging the quality of someone's decision, since having knowledge of the information after the fact does not help to teach the decision maker any valuable lessons. That is, because decision makers do not know what the outcome of their decision may be, but outcome information is available to those who evaluate the decisions afterwards, decisions are often unfairly judged since outcome information is never available while making decisions. In the context of investing, it is therefore important when evaluating the results of a money manager to not only consider their results, however good or bad, but rather the decision-making process by which they achieved their results.

Practical Application   Jonathan Baron and John C. Hershey of the University of Pennsylvania administered several experiments on outcome bias. Subjects were given descriptions of decisions made by others under conditions of uncertainty, together with outcomes of those decisions. Some decisions were medical decisions made by a physician or a patient, and others were decisions about monetary gambles. Subjects rated the quality of thinking that went into the decisions, the competence of the decision maker, or their willingness to let the decision maker act on their behalf. Subjects understood that all relevant information was available to the decision maker. Subjects rated the thinking as better (i.e., rated the decision maker as more competent, or indicated greater willingness to yield the decision) when the outcome was favorable than when it was unfavorable. In monetary gambles, subjects rated the thinking as better when the outcome of the option *not* chosen turned out poorly than when it turned out positively. When asked, subjects felt that they should not take outcomes into account in making these evaluations. However, they did exactly that. In part, the effect of outcome knowledge on evaluation may be explained in terms of its effect on the salience of arguments for each side of the choice.

Baron and Hershey's results suggest that subjects suffer from outcome bias. Investors are not immune to this behavior. For example, when investors who are susceptible to outcome bias make mutual fund investments, they may be doing so because they are focused on the outcome of a past investment experience related to this decision—such as their manager's track record or the asset class performance of that particular investment—and are not focused on *how* the returns were generated or why they should be investing in that asset class. On the contrary, when investors who are not susceptible to outcome bias make investments, they may not make an investment with that manager or asset class (well, they might, but for different reasons) because they may see that the manager took too much risk to obtain a given set of returns or the asset class is overvalued and should be avoided. Investors subject to outcome bias are not focusing on the process, but rather the result—and this can be dangerous.

Implications for Investors Irrationally attributing successes and failures can impair investors in two primary ways. First, people who aren't able to perceive the mistakes that they have made are, consequently, unable to learn from those mistakes. Secondly, investors who disproportionately credit themselves when desirable outcomes do arise can become detrimentally overconfident in their own market savvy. The following three points describe the pitfalls of self-serving behavior that can often lead to financial losses:

1. Investors may invest in funds that they should not because they are focused on the outcome of a prior action, such as the performance record of the manager, rather than on the process by which the manager achieved the results. This may cause investors to subject themselves to excessive risk if the source of the performance was a risky strategy.
2. Investors may avoid investing in funds that they should not because they are focused on the outcome of a prior action, such as the performance record of the manager, rather than on the process by which the manager achieved the results. Investors may avoid a manager based on a bad outcome while ignoring the potentially sound process by which the manager made the decision.
3. Investors may invest in overvalued asset classes based on recent outcomes, such as strong performance in gold or housing prices, and not pay heed to valuations or past price history of the asset class in question, thereby exposing them to the risk that the asset class may be peaking, which can be "hazardous to one's wealth."

RECENCY BIAS

Bias Name: Recency bias
Bias Type: Cognitive
Subtype: Information processing

General Description *Recency bias* is a cognitive predisposition that causes people to more prominently recall and emphasize recent events and observations than those that occurred in the near or distant past. Suppose, for example, that a cruise passenger peering off the observation deck of a ship spots precisely equal numbers of green boats and blue boats over the duration of the trip. However, if the green boats pass by more frequently toward the end of the cruise, with the passing of blue boats dispersed evenly or concentrated toward the beginning, then recency bias would influence the passenger to recall, following the cruise, that more green than blue boats sailed by.

Technical Description In order to best understand the technical description of recency bias, it is helpful to examine human memory recall testing, the two main components of which are primacy effect and the recency effect.

When studying human memory, psychologists use a paradigm called free recall. In a free recall task, a subject is presented a list of to-be-recalled items, one after another. For example, an experimenter might read off a list of 15 words, presenting a new word to the test taker every 5 seconds. When the experimenter has read the entire list, the subject is asked to recall as many of the listed items as possible (e.g., by writing them down). This is known as a *free recall task* because the subject is free to recall the items in any order that he or she desires.

The results of a free recall task are plotted on something called a *serial position curve,* which is normally U-shaped. The serial position curve is graphed on a basic, coordinate plane, in which the x-axis plots the serial position of to-be-remembered items in the list (e.g., the first item, the second item, the third item, and so on). The y-axis, meanwhile, indicates the probability of recalling the item, which is based on the average frequency of recall across a number of subjects in a given trial. The serial position curve, once constructed, tends to exhibit both a recency and a primacy effect.

The primacy effect describes the left portion of the U shape, that is, the elevated portion at the beginning of the curve, which precedes the concavity at the middle. The primacy effect dictates that, in a free recall experiment like the one just described, articles presented at the beginning of a list of to-be-remembered items are remembered better than ones presented in the middle of the list. The primacy effect appears to result from subjects recalling items directly from semantic memory—a type of memory that might be thought of as the "hard drive" of a computer brain. The first items inscribed in a given session onto this hard drive are more precisely retained and are easier to access than items inscribed later on.

The recency effect describes the right portion of the serial position curve. When the recency effect appears in a free recall experiment, it means that subjects recall items appearing toward the end of the to-be-remembered list better than they remember items appearing in the middle. The effect is named in such a way because the observations comprising the right-hand tail of the serial position curve correspond to the items the subjects heard most recently prior to the recall challenge. Recency bias is the result of subjects recalling items directly from short-term memory. In continuing the computer analogy, if semantic memory represents a portion of your brain's long-term memory, or "hard drive," then short-term memory is like random access memory (RAM), which contains data that your computer can access dynamically during a session, but which it may also lose after rebooting. Short-term memory stores only limited quantities of information over limited periods of time. Therefore, while the primacy effect results from the extra-long-term memory rehearsal accorded to primary items on a list, the recency effect occurs because the items the subject heard most recently are more likely to persist in short-term memory than previous, "older" items that have been discarded.

The technical description of recency bias refers to the errors people make when the recency effect prejudices their recollections. Recency bias privileges information recently retained and neglects events and observations not as fresh in the mind.

Practical Application   One of the most obvious and most pernicious manifestations of recency bias among investors pertains to their misuse of investment performance records for mutual funds and other types of funds. Investors track managers who produce temporary outsized returns during a one-, two-, or three-year period and then make investment decisions based only on such recent experiences. These investors do not pay heed to the cyclical nature of asset class returns, and so, for them, funds that have performed spectacularly in the very recent past appear unduly attractive. To counteract the effects of this bias, many practitioners wisely use what has become known as the "periodic table of investment returns," an adaptation of scientists' periodic table of chemical elements (see Table 16.3).

As the periodic table of investment returns in Table 16.3 demonstrates, asset class returns are highly variable. Many investors fail to heed the advice offered by the chart—namely, that it is nearly impossible to accurately predict which asset class will be the best performer from one year to the next. Thus, diversification is prudent (note how the diversified portfolio consistently appears near the center of each column). Practitioners would be wise to present this chart when establishing asset allocations with new clients to emphasize the advantages of diversification over return chasing.

Implications for Investors   As many wealth managers know, recency bias ran rampant during the bull market period between 2004 and 2007. Many investors implicitly presumed, as they have during other cyclical peaks, that the market would continue its enormous gains forever. They all but forgot the fact that bear markets can and do occur. Investors, who based decisions on their own subjective short-term memories, hoped that near-term history would continue to repeat itself. Intuitively, they insisted that evidence gathered from recent experience narrowed the range of potential outcomes and thus enabled them to project future returns. All too often, this behavior creates misguided confidence and becomes a catalyst for error.

When studying the market, good investors analyze large data samples to determine probabilities. By doing so, solid conclusions can be scientifically obtained. Recency bias causes investors to place too much emphasis on data recently gathered, rather than examining entire, relevant bodies of information, which often span much more extensive intervals of time. Investors need to be advised to look at underlying value and not just recent performance. If prices have just risen strongly, for example, then assets may be approaching or may have exceeded their fair value. This should imply that there are, perhaps, better investment opportunities elsewhere. In what follows we summarize investment mistakes that can stem from recency bias.

TABLE 16.3   Sample of a Periodic Table of Investment Returns

1995	1996	1997	1998	1999	2000	2001	2002	2003
Large-Cap Value 38.35%	Real Estate 37.04%	Large-Cap Value 35.19%	Large-Cap Growth 38.70%	Small-Cap Growth 43.10%	Commodities 31.84%	Small-Cap Value 14.02%	Commodities 25.91%	Small-Cap Growth 48.54%
Large-Cap Growth 37.19%	Commodities 23.16%	Small-Cap Value 31.80%	International Stocks 20.34%	Large-Cap Growth 33.16%	Real Estate 31.04%	Real Estate 12.36%	Long-Term Bonds 16.79%	Small-Cap Value 46.035
Small-Cap Growth 31.04%	Large-Cap Growth 23.11%	Large-Cap Growth 30.48%	Large-Cap Value 15.65%	International Stocks 27.31%	Small-Cap Value 22.80%	Interm-Term Bonds 8.44%	Interm-Term Bonds 10.26%	International Stocks 39.17%
Long-Term Bonds 30.69%	Large-Cap Value 21.64%	Real Estate 19.66%	Long-Term Bonds 13.52%	Commodities 24.35%	Long-Term Bonds 20.27%	Short-Term Bonds 8.30%	Foreign Bonds 7.01%	Large-Cap Value 30.03%
Small-Cap Value 25.74%	Small-Cap Value 21.37%	Long-Term Bonds 15.08%	Foreign Bonds 12.09%	Large-Cap Value 7.34%	Interm-Term Bonds 11.63%	Foreign Bonds 6.05%	Short-Term Bonds 5.76%	Large-Cap Growth 29.75%
High-Yield Bonds 20.46%	Foreign Bonds 12.16%	High-Yield Bonds 13.27%	Interm-Term Bonds 8.69%	Cash 4.74%	Foreign Bonds 9.71%	High-Yield Bonds 4.48%	Real Estate 3.60%	High-Yield Bonds 28.15%
Interm-Term Bonds 18.47%	High-Yield Bonds 11.27%	Small-Cap Growth 12.95%	Short-Term Bonds 7.00%	Short-Term Bonds 3.06%	Short-Term Bonds 8.00%	Long-Term Bonds 4.21%	Cash 1.70%	Real Estate 27.75%
Foreign Bonds 18.24%	Small-Cap Growth 11.26%	Foreign Bonds 11.32%	Cash 5.06%	High-Yield Bonds 2.51%	Large-Cap Value 7.02%	Cash 4.09%	High-Yield Bonds −1.89%	Commodities 23.93%
Commodities 15.21%	International Stocks 6.36%	Interm-Term Bonds 9.65%	High-Yield Bonds 2.95%	Foreign Bonds 2.48%	Cash 5.95%	Large-Cap Value −5.59%	Small-Cap Value −11.42%	Interm-Term Bonds 4.10%

(continued)

TABLE 16.3 (*Continued*)

1995	1996	1997	1998	1999	2000	2001	2002	2003
Real Estate 12.24%	Cash 5.25%	Short-Term Bonds 6.66%	Small-Cap Growth 1.24%	Interm-Term Bonds -0.82%	High-Yield Bonds -5.12%	Small-Cap Growth -9.23%	Large-Cap Value -15.52%	Long-Term Bonds 2.48%
International Stocks 11.55%	Short-Term Bonds 4.98%	Cash 5.25%	Small-Cap Value -6.43%	Small-Cap Value -1.49%	International Stocks -13.95%	Commodities -19.51%	International Stocks -15.64%	Foreign Bonds 1.98%
Short-Term Bonds 11.00%	Interm-Term Bonds 3.63%	International Stocks 2.06%	Real Estate -17.00%	Real Estate -2.57%	Large-Cap Growth -22.43%	Large-Gap Growth -20.42%	Large-Cap Growth -27.89%	Short-Term Bonds 1.90%
Cash 5.76%	Long-Term Bonds -0.87%	Commodities -3.39%	Commodities -27.03%	Long-Term Bonds -8.74%	Small-Cap Growth -22.44%	International Stocks -21.21%	Small-Cap Growth -30.27%	Cash 1.07%

Recency Bias: Behaviors That Can Cause Investment Mistakes

1. Recency bias can cause investors to extrapolate patterns and make projections based on historical data samples that are too small to ensure accuracy. Investors who forecast future returns based too extensively on only a recent sample of prior returns are vulnerable to purchasing at price peaks. These investors tend to enter asset classes at the wrong times and end up experiencing losses.
2. Recency bias can cause investors to ignore fundamental *value* and to focus only on recent upward price performance. When a return cycle peaks and recent performance figures are most attractive, human nature is to chase promise of a profit. Asset classes can and do become overvalued. By focusing only on price performance and not on valuation, investors risk principal loss when these investments revert to their mean or long-term averages.
3. Recency bias can cause investors to utter the words that many market veterans consider the most deceptive and damning of all: "It's different this time." In 1998 and 1999, for example, the short-term memory of recent gains influenced some investors so strongly as to overrule, in their minds, historical facts regarding rational valuations and the bubbles, peaks, and valleys that naturally occur. If your client ever seems to be yielding to this rationale, then it is time for a reality check.
4. Recency bias can cause investors to ignore proper asset allocation. Professional investors know the value of proper asset allocation, and they rebalance when necessary in order to maintain proper allocations. Recency bias can cause investors to become infatuated with a given asset class that, for example, appears in vogue. They often concentrate their holdings accordingly. Proper asset allocation is crucial to long-term investment success.

Emotional Biases Defined and Illustrated

LOSS AVERSION BIAS

> **Bias Name:** Loss aversion bias
> **Bias type:** Emotional

General Description   *Loss aversion bias* was developed by Daniel Kahneman and Amos Tversky in 1979 as part of the original prospect theory; specifically, in response to prospect theory's observation that people generally feel a stronger impulse to avoid losses than to acquire gains. A number of studies on loss aversion have given birth to a common rule of thumb: psychologically, the possibility of a loss is, on average, twice as powerful a motivator as the possibility of making a gain of equal magnitude; that is, a loss-averse person might demand, at minimum, a \$2 gain for every \$1 placed at risk. In this scenario, risks that don't "pay double" are unacceptable.

Loss aversion can prevent people from unloading unprofitable investments, even when they see little to no prospect of a turnaround. Some industry veterans have coined a diagnosis of "get-even-itis" to describe this widespread affliction, whereby

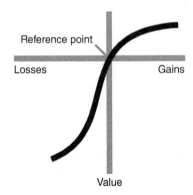

FIGURE 16.10   The Value Function—a Key Tenet of Prospect Theory
Source: The Econometric Society. Reprinted by permission.

a person waits too long for an investment to rebound following a loss. Get-even-itis can be dangerous because, often, the best response to a loss is to sell the offending security and to redeploy those assets. Similarly, loss aversion bias can make investors dwell excessively on risk avoidance when evaluating possible gains, since dodging a loss is a more urgent concern than seeking a profit. When their investments do begin to succeed, loss-averse individuals hasten to lock in profits, fearing that, otherwise, the market might reverse itself and rescind their returns. The problem here is that divesting prematurely to protect gains limits upside potential. In sum, loss aversion causes investors to hold their losing investments and to sell their winning ones, leading to suboptimal portfolio returns.

Technical Description   The technical definition of loss aversion comes from prospect theory, wherein Kahneman and Tversky don't explicitly mention concrete, relative preferences (e.g., "I prefer avoiding a loss to realizing a gain"). Rather, they discuss loss aversion in the context of the S-shaped, utility representative value function that models the entire evaluation stage in prospect theory. According to Kahneman and Tversky, people weigh all potential gains and losses in relation to some benchmark reference point (the point of origin on the graph in Figure 16.10).

   The value function that passes through this point is asymmetric; and its profile implies, given the same variation in absolute value, a bigger impact of losses than of gains. The result is that risk-seeking behavior prevails in the domain of losses (below the x-axis), while risk-averse behavior prevails in the domain of gains (above the x-axis). An important concept embedded in this utility representation is Hersh Shefrin and Meir Statman's disposition effect. The disposition effect is the desire to hold losing investments too long (risk-seeking behavior) and to sell winning investments too quickly (risk-avoidance behavior).

Practical Application   Loss aversion bias, observed in practice as the *disposition effect,* is seen often by wealth management practitioners. Investors open up the monthly statements prepared by their advisors, skim columns of numbers, and usually notice both winners and losers. In classic cases of loss aversion, clients dread selling the securities that haven't performed well. Get-even-itis takes hold, and the instinct is to hold onto a losing investment until, at the very least, it rebounds enough for the client to break even. Often, however, research into a losing investment would reveal a company whose prospects don't forecast a rebound. Continuing to hold stock in that company actually adds risk to an investor's portfolio (hence, the client's behavior is risk seeking, which accords with the path of the value function in Figure 16.10).

Conversely, when the monthly statement indicates that profits are being made, the loss-averse client is gripped by a powerful urge to "take the money and run," rather than to assume continued risk. Of course, frequently, holding on to a winning stock isn't a risky proposition, if the company is performing well; that is, profitable investments that the loss-averse investor wants to sell might actually be improving the portfolio's risk/return profile. Therefore, selling deteriorates that risk/return profile and eliminates the potential for further gains. When the increased risks associated with holding on to losing investments are considered in combination with the prospect of losing future gains that occur when selling winners, the degree of overall harm that a loss-averse investor can suffer begins to become clear.

A final thought on taking losses: Some investors, remarking on losing investments that haven't yet been sold, rationalize that "it's only a paper loss." In one sense, yes, this is true. Inasmuch as the investment is still held, a loss has technically not been triggered for tax purposes.

In reality, though, this kind of rationale covers up the fact that a loss has taken place. If you went to the market to sell, having just incurred a "paper loss," the price you would obtain for your investment would be lower than the price you paid— effecting a very "real" loss indeed. Thus, if holding on to a losing investment does not objectively enhance the likelihood of recouping a loss, then it is better to simply realize the loss, which won't remain on paper forever.

Implications for Investors   Loss aversion is a bias that simply cannot be tolerated in financial decision making. It instigates the exact opposite of what investors want: increased risk, with lower returns. Investors should take risk to increase gains, not to mitigate losses. Holding losers and selling winners will wreak havoc on a portfolio. The following inset summarizes some common investment mistakes linked to loss aversion bias.

Loss Aversion Bias: Behaviors That Can Cause Investment Mistakes

1. Loss aversion causes investors to hold losing investments too long. This behavior is sometimes described in the context of a debilitating disease: *get-even-itis*. This is the affliction in which investors hold losing investments in the hope that they get back what they lost. This behavior has seriously negative consequences by depressing portfolio returns.
2. Loss aversion can cause investors to sell winners too early, in the fear that their profit will evaporate unless they sell. This behavior limits upside potential of a portfolio, and can lead to too much trading, which has been shown to lower investment returns.

3. Loss aversion can cause investors to unknowingly take on more risk in their portfolio than they would if they simply eliminated the investment and moved into a better one (or stayed in cash).
4. Loss aversion can cause investors to hold unbalanced portfolios. If, for example, several positions fall in value and the investor is unwilling to sell due to loss aversion, an imbalance can occur. Without proper rebalancing, the allocation is not suited to the long-term goals of the client, leading to suboptimal returns.

OVERCONFIDENCE BIAS

Bias Name: Overconfidence
Bias Type: Emotional

General Description In its most basic form, *overconfidence* can be summarized as unwarranted faith in one's intuitive reasoning, judgments, and cognitive abilities. Although the concept of overconfidence derives from psychological experiments and surveys in which subjects overestimate both their own predictive abilities and the precision of the information they've been given (essentially cognitive weaknesses), these faulty cognitions lead to emotionally charged behavior, such as excessive risk taking, and therefore overconfidence is classified as an emotional rather than cognitive bias. In short, people think they are smarter and have better information than they actually do. For example, they may get a tip from a financial advisor or read something on the Internet, and then they're ready to take action, such as making an investment decision, based on their perceived knowledge advantage.

Technical Description Numerous studies have shown that investors are overconfident in their investing abilities. Specifically, the confidence intervals that investors assign to their investment predictions are too narrow. This type of overconfidence can be called *prediction overconfidence*. For example, when estimating the future value of a stock, overconfident investors will incorporate far too little leeway into the range of expected payoffs, predicting something between a 10 percent gain and decline, while history demonstrates much more drastic standard deviations. The implication of this behavior is that investors may underestimate the downside risks to their portfolios (being, naturally, unconcerned with "upside risks"!).

Investors are often also too certain of their judgments. We will refer to this type of overconfidence as certainty overconfidence. For example, having resolved that a company is a good investment, people often become blind to the prospect of a loss and then feel surprised or disappointed if the investment performs poorly. This behavior results in the tendency of investors to fall prey to a misguided quest to identify the "next hot stock." Thus, people susceptible to certainty overconfidence often trade too much in their accounts and may hold portfolios that are not diversified enough.

Practical Application

Prediction Overconfidence Roger Clarke and Meir Statman demonstrated a classic example of prediction overconfidence in 2000 when they surveyed investors on the following question: "In 1896, the Dow Jones Average, which is a price index that does not include dividend reinvestment, was at 40. In 1998, it crossed 9,000. If dividends had been reinvested, what do you think the value of the DJIA would be in 1998? In addition to that guess, also predict a high and low range so that you feel 90 percent confident that your answer is between your high and low guesses." In the survey, few responses reasonably approximated the potential 1998 value of the Dow, and no one estimated a correct confidence interval. (If you are curious, the 1998 value of the Dow Jones Industrial Average [DJIA], under the conditions postulated in the survey, would have been 652,230!)

A classic example of investor prediction overconfidence is the case of the former executive or family legacy stockholder of a publicly traded company such as Johnson & Johnson, ExxonMobil, or DuPont. These investors often refuse to diversify their holdings because they claim "insider knowledge" of, or emotional attachment to, the company. They cannot contextualize these stalwart stocks as risky investments. However, dozens of once-iconic names in U.S. business—AT&T, for example—have declined or vanished.

Certainty Overconfidence People display certainty overconfidence in everyday life situations, and that overconfidence carries over into the investment arena. People tend to have too much confidence in the accuracy of their own judgments. As people find out more about a situation, the accuracy of their judgments is not likely to increase, but their confidence does increase, as they fallaciously equate the quantity of information with its quality. In a pertinent study, Baruch Fischhoff, Paul Slovic, and Sarah Lichtenstein gave subjects a general knowledge test and then asked them how sure they were of their answer. Subjects reported being 100 percent sure when they were actually only 70 percent to 80 percent correct. A classic example of certainty overconfidence occurred during the technology boom of the late 1990s. Many investors simply loaded up on technology stocks, holding highly concentrated positions, only to see these gains vanish during the meltdown.

Implications for Investors Both prediction and certainty overconfidence can lead to making investment mistakes. Below we list four behaviors, resulting from overconfidence bias, that can cause harm to an investor's portfolio.

Overconfidence Bias: Behaviors That Can Cause Investment Mistakes

1. Overconfident investors overestimate their ability to evaluate a company as a potential investment. As a result, they can become blind to any negative information that might normally indicate a warning sign that either a stock purchase should not take place or a stock that was already purchased should be sold.

2. Overconfident investors can trade excessively as a result of believing that they possess special knowledge that others don't have. Excessive trading behavior has proven to lead to poor returns over time.

3. Because they either don't know, don't understand, or don't heed historical investment performance statistics, overconfident investors can underestimate their downside risks. As a result, they can unexpectedly suffer poor portfolio performance.

4. Overconfident investors hold underdiversified portfolios, thereby taking on more risk without a commensurate change in risk tolerance. Often, overconfident investors don't even know that they are accepting more risk than they would normally tolerate.

SELF-CONTROL BIAS

Bias Name: Self-control bias
Bias Type: Emotional

General Description   Simply put, *self-control bias* is a human behavioral tendency that causes people to fail to act in pursuit of their long-term, overarching goals because of a lack of self-discipline. Money is an area in which people are notorious for displaying a lack of self-control. Attitudes toward paying taxes provide a common example. Imagine that you, a taxpayer, estimate that your income this year will cause your income tax to increase by $3,600, which will be due one year from now. In the interest of conservatism, you decide to set money aside. You contemplate two choices: Would you rather contribute $300 per month over the course of the next 12 months to some savings account earmarked for tax season? Or would you rather increase your federal income tax withholding by $300 each month, sparing you the responsibility of writing out one large check at the end of the year? Rational economic thinking suggests that you would prefer the savings account approach because your money would accrue interest and you would actually net more than $3,600. However, many taxpayers choose the withholding option because they realize that the savings account plan might be complicated in practice by a lack of self-control (i.e., one might overspend and then the tax money might not be there when one needs it.)

Self-control bias can also be described as a conflict between people's overarching desires and their inability, stemming from a lack of self-discipline, to act concretely in pursuit of those desires. For example, a college student desiring an "A" in history class might theoretically forgo a lively party to study at the library. An overweight person desperate to shed unwanted pounds might decline a tempting triple fudge sundae. Reality demonstrates, however, that plenty of people do sabotage their own long-term objectives for temporary satisfaction in situations like the ones described.

Investing is no different. The primary challenge in investing is saving enough money for retirement. Perhaps the best framework for understanding how to advise clients on self-control bias is done in the context of life-cycle hypothesis, a rational theory of savings behavior.

Technical Description   The technical description of self-control bias is best under-stood in the context of the *life-cycle hypothesis,* which describes a well-defined link between the savings and consumption tendencies of individuals and those individ-uals' stages of progress from childhood, through years of work participation, and finally into retirement. The foundation of the model is the *saving decision,* which directs the division of income between consumption and saving. The saving decision reflects an individual's relative preferences over present versus future consumption. Because the life-cycle hypothesis is firmly grounded in expected utility theory and assumes rational behavior, an entire lifetime's succession of optimal saving decisions can be computed given only an individual's projected household income stream vis-à-vis the utility function.

The income profile over the life cycle starts with low income during the early working years, followed by increasing income that reaches a peak prior to retire-ment. Income during retirement, based on assumptions regarding pensions, is then substantially lower. To make up for the lower income during retirement and to avoid a sharp drop in utility at the point of retirement, individuals will save some fraction of their income when they're still working, spending it later during retirement. The main prediction, then, of the life-cycle hypothesis is a lifetime savings profile char-acterized by a "hump"-shaped curve, with savings building gradually, maxing out, and finally declining again as a function of time.

Two common tendencies of individuals underlie spending patterns, according to the life-cycle hypothesis:

1. Most people prefer a higher standard of living to a lower standard of living; that is, people want to maximize consumption spending in the present.
2. Most people prefer to maintain a relatively constant standard of living through-out their lives. They dislike volatility and don't desire abrupt intervals of feast interspersed with famine.

Basically, the life-cycle hypothesis envisions that people will try to maintain the highest, smoothest consumption paths possible.

Now that we have an understanding of the life-cycle hypothesis, we can integrate behavioral concepts that account for real-world savings behavior. In 1998, Hersh Shefrin and Richard Thaler introduced a behaviorally explained life-cycle hypothesis, which is a descriptive model of household savings in which self-control plays a key role. The key assumption of the behavioral life-cycle theory is that households treat components of their wealth as "nonfungible" or noninterchangeable even in the absence of credit rationing. Specifically, wealth is assumed to be divided into three "mental" accounts: (1) current income, (2) current assets, and (3) future income. The temptation to spend is assumed to be greatest for current income and least for future income.

Considerable empirical evidence supporting the behavioral life-cycle theory exists. In a survey of students' expectations of future consumption, Shefrin and Thaler obtained direct support for the tenets of behavioral life-cycle theory. Specifically, they found that subjects envisioning themselves to be the beneficiaries of some financial windfall predicted that they would consume, immediately, a greater portion of that windfall during the same year if the money was coded as current income rather than current assets. Subjects said that they would consume the smallest portions of income coded as future income. For most people, consumption and income (i.e., saving) are mediated by institutions, not individual decisions. Examples include home mortgage repayment schedules, 401(k) plans, and individual retirement accounts (IRAs); often, these instruments represent an individual's only real savings, with no additional funds being set aside.

Self-control has a cost, and people are willing to pay a price to avoid reigning in their natural impulses. Consumers act as if they are maintaining separate funds within their individual accounting systems, separating income into current income and wealth. The marginal propensity to consume varies according to the source of income (e.g., salary versus bonus), even if the measure taken to activate or to sustain the source of income (e.g., work) is the same. People are more likely to build assets or savings with money they view, or "frame," as wealth, whereas they are less likely to build savings using what they consider to be current income. Many researchers have continued to elaborate on the behavioral life-cycle model, particularly as it relates to retirement savings.

Practical Application   Encouraging people to save more is a task that constantly challenges financial advisors. The "Save More Tomorrow Program," developed by Professors Richard H. Thaler of the University of Chicago and Shlomo Benartzi of the Anderson School of Business at UCLA, aims to help corporate employees who would like to save more but lack the willpower to act on this desire. The program offers many useful insights into saving behavior, and
The "Save More Tomorrow Program" has four primary aspects:

1. Employees are approached about increasing their contribution rates a considerable time before their scheduled pay increases occur.
2. The contributions of employees who join the plan are automatically increased, beginning with the first paycheck following a raise.
3. Participating employees' contribution rates continue to increase automatically with each scheduled raise, until rates reach a preset maximum.
4. Employees can opt out of the plan at any time.

Let's examine the results of a trial of the Save More Tomorrow Program (SMTP) by a midsize manufacturing company in 1988. Prior to the adoption of the SMTP, the company suffered from a low participation rate as well as low saving rates. In an effort to increase the saving rates of the employees, the company hired an investment consultant and offered this service to every employee eligible for its retirement savings plan. Of the 315 eligible participants, all but 29 agreed to meet with the consultant and get his advice. Based on information that the employee provided, the consultant used commercial software to compute a desired saving rate. The consultant also discussed with each employee how much of an increase in saving would be considered economically feasible. If the employee seemed very reluctant to increase his or her saving rate substantially, the consultant would constrain the program to increase the saving contribution by no more than 5 percent.

Of the 286 employees who talked to the investment consultant, only 79 (28 percent) were willing to accept the consultant's advice, even with the adjustment to constrain some of the saving rate increases to 5 percent. For the rest of the participants, the planner offered a version of the SMTP, proposing that they increase their saving rates by 3 percentage points a year, starting with the next pay increase. Even with the aggressive strategy of increasing saving rates, the SMTP proved to be extremely popular with the participants. Of the 207 participants who were unwilling to accept the saving rate proposed by the investment consultant, 162 (78 percent) agreed to join the SMTP.

The majority of these participants did not change their minds once the saving increases took place. Only four participants (2 percent) dropped out of the plan prior to the second pay raise, with 29 more (18 percent) dropping out between the second and third pay raises. Hence, the vast majority of the participants (80 percent) remained in the plan through three pay raises. Furthermore, even those who withdrew from the plan did not reduce their contribution rates to the original levels; they merely stopped the future increases from taking place. So, even these workers are saving significantly more than they were before joining the plan.

The key lesson here is that people are generally poor at planning and saving for retirement. They need to have self-discipline imposed on them consistently in order to achieve savings.

Implications for Investors   As previously noted, the primary issue with regard to self-control is the lack of ability to save for retirement. In addition, there are several other self-control behaviors that can cause investment mistakes. We summarize some of these in the feature box.

Self-Control Bias: Behaviors That Can Cause Investment Mistakes

1. Self-control bias can cause investors to spend more today at the expense of saving for tomorrow. This behavior can be hazardous to one's wealth, because retirement can arrive too quickly for investors to have saved enough.

   Frequently, then, people incur inappropriate degrees of risk in their portfolios in effort to make up for lost time. This can, of course, aggravate the problem.
2. Self-control bias may cause investors to fail to plan for retirement. Studies have shown that people who do not plan for retirement are far less likely to retire securely than those who do plan. Studies have shown that people who do not plan for retirement are also less likely to invest in equity securities.
3. Self-control bias can cause asset-allocation imbalance problems. For example, some investors may prefer income-producing assets, due to a "spend today" mentality. This behavior can be hazardous to long-term wealth because too many income-producing assets can inhibit a portfolio to keep up with inflation. Other investors might favor different asset classes, such as equities over bonds, simply because they like to take risks and can't control their behavior.
4. Self-control bias can cause investors to lose sight of basic financial principles, such as compounding of interest, dollar cost averaging, and similar discipline behaviors that, if adhered to, can help create significant long-term wealth.

STATUS QUO BIAS

Bias Name: Status quo bias
Bias Type: Emotional

General Description   *Status quo bias,* a term coined by William Samuelson and Richard Zeckhauser in 1988, is an emotional bias that predisposes people facing an array of choice options to elect whatever option ratifies or extends the existing condition (i.e., the "status quo") in lieu of alternative options that might bring about change. In other words, status quo bias operates in people who prefer that things stay relatively the same. The scientific principle of inertia bears a lot of intuitive similarity to status quo bias; it states that a body at rest shall remain at rest unless acted on by an outside force. A simple real-world example illustrates. In the early 1990s, the states of New Jersey and Pennsylvania reformed their insurance laws and offered new programs. Residents had the opportunity to select one of two automotive insurance packages: (1) a slightly more expensive option that granted policyholders extensive rights to sue one another following an accident, and (2) a less expensive option with more restricted litigation rights. Each insurance plan had a roughly equivalent expected monetary value. In New Jersey, however, the more expensive plan was instituted as the default, and 70 percent of citizens "selected" it. In Pennsylvania, the opposite was true—residents would have to opt out of the default, less-expensive option in order to opt into the more expensive option. In the end, 80 percent of the residents "chose" to pay less.

Technical Description   Status quo bias refers to the finding that an option is more desirable if it is designated as the "status quo" than when it is not. Status quo bias can contribute to the aforementioned inertia principle, but inertia is not as strong as status quo bias. Inertia means that an individual is relatively more reluctant to move away from some state identified as the status quo than from any alternative state not identified as the status quo. People less readily abandon a condition when they're told, "Things have always been this way." Status quo bias implies a more intense "anchoring effect."

Status quo bias is often discussed in tandem with other biases, namely endowment bias and loss aversion bias. Status quo bias differs from these two in that it does not depend on framing changes in terms of losses and potential gains. When loss aversion bias and status quo bias cross paths, it is probable that an investor, choosing between two investment alternatives, will stick to the status quo if it seems less likely to trigger a loss—even if the status quo also guarantees a lower return in the long run. Endowment bias implies that ownership of a piece of property imbues that property with some perceived, intangible added value—even if the property doesn't really increase the utility or wealth of the owner. By definition, endowment bias favors the status quo—people don't want to give up their endowments. Loss aversion bias, endowment bias, and status quo bias often combine; and the result is an overall tendency to prefer things to stay as they are, even if the calm comes at a cost.

Practical Application   Investors with inherited, concentrated stock positions often exhibit classic status quo bias. Take the case of a hypothetical grandson who hesitates to sell the bank stock he's inherited from his grandfather. Even though his portfolio is underdiversified and could benefit from such an adjustment, the grandson favors the status quo. A number of motives could be at work here. First, the investor may be unaware of the risk associated with holding an excessively concentrated equity position. He may not foresee that if the stock tumbles, he will suffer a significant decrease in wealth. Second, the grandson may experience a personal attachment to the stock, which carries an emotional connection to a previous generation. Third, he may hesitate to sell because of his aversion to the tax consequences, fees/commissions, or other transaction costs associated with unloading the stock.

Implications for Investors In the following, we review four investment mistakes that can stem from status quo bias.

Status Quo Bias: Behaviors That Can Cause Investment Mistakes

1. Status quo bias can cause investors, by taking no action, to hold investments inappropriate to their own risk/return profiles. This can mean that investors take excessive risks or invest too conservatively.
2. Status quo bias can combine with loss aversion bias. In this scenario, an investor facing an opportunity to reallocate or alter an investment position may choose, instead, to maintain the status quo because the status quo offers the investor a lower probability of realizing a loss. This will be true even if, in the long run, the investor could achieve a higher return by electing an alternative path.
3. Status quo bias causes investors to hold securities with which they feel familiar or of which they are emotionally fond. This behavior can compromise financial goals, however, because a subjective comfort level with a security may not justify holding onto it despite poor performance.
4. Status quo bias can cause investors to hold securities, either inherited or purchased, because of an aversion to transaction costs associated with selling. This behavior can be hazardous to one's wealth because a commission or a tax is frequently a small price to pay for exiting a poorly performing investment or for properly allocating a portfolio.

ENDOWMENT BIAS

> **Bias Name:** Endowment bias
> **Bias Type:** Emotional

General Description People who exhibit *endowment bias* value an asset more when they hold property rights to it than when they don't. Endowment bias is inconsistent with standard economic theory, which asserts that a person's *willingness to pay* for a good or an object should always equal the person's *willingness to accept dispossession* of the good or the object, when the dispossession is quantified in the form of compensation. Psychologists have found, however, that the minimum selling prices that people state tend to exceed the maximum purchase prices that they are willing to pay for the same good. Effectively, then, ownership of an asset instantaneously "endows" the asset with some added value. Endowment bias can affect attitudes toward items owned over long periods of time or can crop up immediately as the item is acquired.

Technical Description   Endowment bias is described as a mental process in which a differential weight is placed on the value of an object. That value depends on whether one possesses the object and is faced with its loss or whether one does not possess the object and has the potential to gain it. If one loses an object that is part of one's endowment, then the magnitude of this loss is perceived to be greater than the magnitude of the corresponding gain if the object is newly added to one's endowment. Professor Richard Thaler of the University of Chicago defines the endowment bias:

> *If out-of-pocket costs are viewed as losses and opportunity costs are viewed as foregone gains, the former will be more heavily weighted. Furthermore, a certain degree of inertia is introduced into the consumer choice process since goods that are included in the individual's endowment will be more highly valued than those not held in the endowment, ceteris paribus. This follows because removing a good from the endowment creates a loss while adding the same good (to an endowment without it) generates a gain. Henceforth, I will refer to the underweighting of opportunity costs as the endowment effect.*

In 1989, a researcher named J. L. Knetsch reported results from experiments designed to examine the endowment bias. Knetsch's results provided an excellent practical application of endowment bias and concerned an experiment involving two groups of subjects. The 76 subjects in the first group were each given a coffee mug. They were then asked to complete a questionnaire, after which they were shown some candy bars. It had been determined earlier that the 76 subjects were about evenly divided over whether they generally preferred candy bars or coffee mugs if given a choice. But when told that they could substitute a candy bar for the coffee mug they had been given, 89 percent chose to keep the coffee mug. The second group consisted of 87 subjects. Again, about 50 percent preferred candy bars, and 50 percent preferred coffee mugs. The second group participated in the same exercise as the first group, except this time the candy bars were the endowment good and the coffee mugs were offered subsequently as substitutes. In the second group, 90 percent declined to trade their endowed candy bars. Knetsch concluded that this dramatic asymmetry resulted because "subjects weigh the loss of giving up their initial reference entitlement far more heavily than the foregone gains of not obtaining the alternative entitlement." Neither coffee mugs nor candy bars seemed, in this experiment, innately more desirable by any significant margin; rather, subjects' preferences depended on their respective endowments.

Practical Application   Investors prove resistant to change once they become endowed with (take ownership of) securities. We will examine endowment bias as it relates to both inherited securities and purchased securities. Then, we'll look at two common causes of endowment bias.

Inherited Securities William Samuelson and Richard Zeckhauser performed an enlightening study on endowment bias that aptly illustrates investor susceptibility to this bias. Samuelson and Zeckhauser conducted an experiment in which investors were told to imagine that they had to newly acquire one of four investment options:

1. A moderately risky stock
2. A riskier stock
3. A Treasury security
4. A municipal security

Another group of investors was given the same list of options. However, they were instructed to imagine that they had already inherited one specified item on the list. If desired, the investors were told, they could cede their hypothetical inheritance in favor of a different option and could do so without penalty. In every case, however, the investors in the second group showed a tendency to retain whatever was "inherited." This is a classic case of endowment bias. Most wealth management practitioners have encountered clients who are reluctant to sell securities bequeathed by previous generations. Often, in these situations, investors cite feelings of disloyalty associated with the prospect of selling inherited securities, general uncertainty in determining "the right thing to do," and tax issues.

Purchased Securities Endowment bias also often influences the value that an investor assigns to a recently purchased security. Here is an example to illustrate this point: Assume that you have a great need for income. How much would you pay for a municipal bond that pays you triple your pretax income? Further assume that you have purchased this bond and that it is performing as expected. Interest rates have not changed, the market for securities is highly liquid, and you have the type of account that offers unlimited transactions for one fee. How much would you demand in exchange for the bond if someone wanted to buy it from you?

Rational economic theories predict that your willingness to pay (WTP) for the bond would equal your willingness to accept (WTA) compensation for it. However, this is unlikely to be the case. Once you are endowed with the bond, you are probably inclined to demand a selling price that exceeds your original purchase price. Many wealth managers have observed that investor decision making regarding both inherited and purchased securities can exhibit endowment bias and that "decision paralysis" often results: Many clients have trouble making decisions regarding the sale of securities that they either inherited or purchased themselves, and their predicament is attributable to endowment bias.

Implications for Investors There are some practical explanations as to why investors are susceptible to endowment bias. Understanding the origins of endowment bias can help to provide intuition that guards against the mistakes that the bias can cause. First, investors may hold onto securities that they already own in order to *avoid the transaction costs* associated with unloading those securities. This is particularly true regarding bonds. Such a rationale can be hazardous to one's wealth, because failure to take action and sell off certain assets can sometimes invite otherwise avoidable losses, while forcing investors to forgo the purchase of potentially more profitable, alternative assets. Second, investors hold onto securities because of familiarity. If investors know from experience the characteristics of the instruments that they already own (the behavior of particular government bonds, for example), then they may feel reluctant to transition into instruments that seem relatively unknown. Familiarity, effectively, has value. This value adds to the actual market value of a security that an investor possesses, causing WTA to exceed WTP.

The list following contains a summary of investment mistakes that arise from endowment bias.

Endowment Bias: Behaviors That Can Cause Investment Mistakes

1. Endowment bias influences investors to hold onto securities that they have inherited, regardless of whether retaining those securities is financially wise. This behavior is often the result of the heirs' fear that selling will demonstrate disloyalty to prior generations or will trigger tax consequences.
2. Endowment bias causes investors to hold securities they have purchased (already own). This behavior is often the result of decision paralysis, which places an irrational premium on the compensation price demanded in exchange for the disposal of an endowed asset.
3. Endowment bias causes investors to hold securities that they have either inherited or purchased because they do not want to incur the transaction costs associated with selling the securities. These costs, however, can be a very small price to pay when evacuating an unwise investment.
4. Endowment bias causes investors to hold securities that they have either inherited or purchased because they are familiar with the behavioral characteristics of these endowed investments. Familiarity, though, does not rationally justify retaining a poorly performing stock or bond.

REGRET AVERSION BIAS

> **Bias Name:** Regret aversion bias
> **Bias Type:** Emotional

GENERAL DESCRIPTION People exhibiting *regret aversion* avoid taking decisive actions because they fear that, in hindsight, whatever course they select will prove less than optimal. Basically, this bias seeks to avoid the emotional pain of regret associated with poor decision making. Regret aversion makes investors, for example, unduly apprehensive about breaking into financial markets that have recently generated losses. When they experience negative investment outcomes, they feel instinctually driven to conserve, to retreat, and to lick their wounds—not to press on and snap up potentially undervalued stocks. However, periods of depressed prices often present the greatest buying opportunities. People suffering from regret aversion bias hesitate most at moments that actually merit aggressive behavior.

Regret aversion does not come into play only following a loss; it can also affect a person's response to investment gains. People exhibiting regret aversion can be reluctant, for example, to sell a stock whose value has climbed recently—even if objective indicators attest that it's time to pull out. Instead, regret-averse investors may cling to positions that they ought to sell, pained by the prospect that a stock, once unloaded, might soar even higher.

TECHNICAL DESCRIPTION   An extensive body of literature in experimental psychology suggests that regret does influence decision making under conditions of uncertainty. Regret causes people to challenge past decisions and to question their beliefs. People who are regret averse try to avoid distress arising from two types of mistakes: (1) errors of commission and (2) errors of omission. Errors of *commission* occur when we take misguided *actions*. Errors of *omission* arise from misguided *inaction*, that is, opportunities overlooked or foregone.

Regret is different from disappointment, because the former implies that the sufferer had some sense of agency in achieving the negative outcome. Also, feelings of regret are more intense when unfavorable outcomes emerge from errors of commission rather than errors of omission. The Implications for Investors section uses an example to examine more concretely the distinction between errors of commission and errors of omission in the context of regret aversion bias.

Regret is most palpable and takes the greatest toll on decision making when the outcomes of forgone alternatives are highly "visible" or "accessible." By the same token, regret becomes a less influential factor when consequences of mistakes are less discernible. Some researchers have proposed theories of choice under uncertainty that incorporate regret bias as a partial explanation for observed violations of traditional expected utility theory. Regret theory assumes that agents are rational but base their decisions not only on expected payoffs but also on expected regret. Regret theory bears some similarities to prospect theory (discussed earlier), and many of its predictions are consistent with the empirical observations of human behavior that constitute the building blocks of prospect theory.

Practical Application   The following case study illustrates both aspects of regret bias: *error of commission* and *error of omission*. The case shows a regret-averse investor under two sets of circumstances: (1) an investor experienced a loss and regrets his decision to invest; and (2) an investor missed an opportunity to invest in something that later appreciated in value and regrets his failure to reap profits.

Suppose that Jim has a chance to invest in Schmoogle, Inc., an initial public offering (IPO) that has generated a great buzz following its recent market debut. Jim thinks that Schmoogle has high potential and contemplates buying in because Schmoogle's price has recently declined by 10 percent due to some recent market weakness. If Jim invests in Schmoogle, one of two things will happen: (1) Schmoogle will drop further (Jim made the wrong decision), or (2) Schmoogle will rebound (Jim made the right decision). If Jim doesn't invest, one of two things will happen: (1) Schmoogle will rebound (Jim made the right decision), or (2) Schmoogle will drop further (Jim made the wrong decision).

Suppose that Jim does invest and Schmoogle goes down. Jim will have committed an error of commission because he actually committed the act of investing and will likely feel regret strongly because he actually lost money.

Now suppose that Jim does not invest and Schmoogle goes up. Jim will have committed an error of omission because he omitted the purchase of Schmoogle and lost out. This regret may not be as strong as the regret associated with the error of commission. Why? First, investors dislike losing money more than they like gaining money. Second, in the first possibility, the investor actually committed the act of investing and lost money; in the second possibility, the investor merely did not act and only lost out on the opportunity to gain.

Implications for Investors   Regret aversion causes investors to anticipate and fear the pain of regret that comes with incurring a loss or forfeiting a profit. The potential for financial injury isn't the only disincentive that these investors face; they also dread feeling responsible for their own misfortunes (because regret implies culpability, whereas simple disappointment does not). The anxiety surrounding the prospect of an error of commission, or a "wrong move," can make investors timid and can cause them to subjectively and perhaps irrationally favor investments that seem trust-worthy (e.g., "good companies"). Suppose that regret-averse Jim is now considering two investments, both with equal projected risk and return. One stock belongs to Large Company, Inc., while the other confers a share in Medium-Size Company, Inc. Even though, mathematically, the expected payoffs of investing in these two com-panies are identical, Jim will probably feel more comfortable with Large Company. If an investment in Large Company, Inc., fails to pay off, Jim can rationalize that his decision making could not have been too egregiously flawed, because Large Com-pany, Inc., must have had lots of savvy investors. Jim doesn't feel uniquely foolish, and so the culpability component of Jim's regret is reduced. Jim can't rely on the same excuse, however, if an investment in Medium-Size Company fails. Instead of exonerating himself ("Lots of high-profile people made the same mistake that I did—perhaps some market anomaly is at fault?"), Jim may condemn himself ("Why did I do that? I shouldn't have invested in Medium-Size. Only small-time players invested in Medium-Size, Inc. I feel stupid!"), adding to his feelings of regret. It's important to recall here that Large Company and Medium-Size Company stocks were, objec-tively, equally risky. This underscores the fact that aversion to regret is different from aversion to risk. We review in the following six investor mistakes that can stem from regret aversion bias. Remedies for these biases will be reviewed in the Advice section.

Regret Aversion Bias: Behaviors That Can Cause Investment Mistakes

1. Regret aversion can cause investors to be too conservative in their invest-ment choices. Having suffered losses in the past (i.e., having felt pain of a poor decision regarding a risky investment), many people shy away from making new bold investment decisions and accept only low-risk positions. This behavior can lead to long-term underperformance, and can jeopardize investment goals.
2. Regret aversion can cause investors to shy away, unduly, from markets that have recently gone down. Regret-averse individuals fear that if they invest, such a market might subsequently continue its downward trend, prompting

them to regret the decision to buy in. Often, however, depressed markets offer bargains, and people can benefit from seizing, decisively, these under-valued investments.

3. Regret aversion can cause investors to hold on to losing positions too long. People don't like to admit when they're wrong, and they will go to great lengths to avoid selling (i.e., confronting the reality of) a losing investment. This behavior, similar to loss aversion, is hazardous to one's wealth.

4. Regret aversion can cause "herding behavior" because, for some investors, buying into an apparent mass consensus can limit the potential for future regret. The demise of the technology stock bubble of the late 1990s demon-strated that even the most massive herd can stampede in the wrong direction.

5. Regret aversion leads investors to prefer stocks of subjectively designated *good companies,* even when an alternative stock has an equal or a higher expected return. Regret-averse investors may feel that "riskier" companies require bolder decision making; hence, if the investment fails, the conse-quences reflect more dramatically on an individual's judgment than do the consequences of investing in a "routine," "safe," or "reliable" stock. With increased perception of personal responsibility, of course, comes increased potential for regret. Investing in *good companies* may not permit investors any more return or less return than those companies perceived to be risky.

6. Regret aversion can cause investors to hold on to winning stocks for too long. People fear that by selling a stock that has been doing well, they might miss out on further imminent gains. The danger here is that in finance, as in physics, whatever goes up must come down.

AFFINITY BIAS

Bias Name: Affinity bias
Bias Type: Emotional
Subtype: Information processing

General Description   Affinity bias refers to an individual's tendency to make irrationally uneconomical consumer choices or investment decisions based on how they believe a certain product or service will reflect their values. This idea focuses on the *expressive benefits* of a product rather than on what the product or service actually does for someone (the utilitarian benefits). A common example of this behavior in the consumer product realm is when one purchases wine. A consumer may purchase a fine bottle of well-known wine in a restaurant or wine shop for hundreds of dollars to impress their dinner guests, while a bottle that costs much less could be equally delicious but would not convey the same status. Automobiles are another example. A person may purchase a Range Rover or a similar sport utility vehicle because they want to be viewed by others as someone who is "outdoorsy" (sometimes regardless of the extent to which the person actually engages in outdoor activities) when a much more affordable vehicle would easily transport them from point A to point B. Similarly, in the investment realm, individuals may invest in certain companies, such as those that produce Range Rovers, because they feel that this company reflects their values or self-image. This behavior may lead to suboptimal investment results if the company producing the product or service is poorly managed or has financial or business-related problems.

Technical Description A technical way of describing the phenomenon listed above is to describe the products as having either expressive or image-related value as opposed to utilitarian or functional value. As a practical example, advertisers target their consumers with different types of advertising by using two common approaches to influence consumer behavior: value-expressive (image) and utilitarian (functional) appeal (see Park, Jaworski, and MacInnis 1986; Snyder and DeBono 1985). The value-expressive strategy involves building a "personality" for a product or creating an image of the product user with which the consumer can identify. This value-expressive advertising appeal has the innovative objective of creating an image of the generalized user of the advertised product (or brand). However, the utilitarian strategy involves informing the target consumers about one or more key benefits that they may perceive as highly functional or important. The utilitarian advertising strategy is simply a creative strategy that highlights the functional features of the product (or brand). Those who are subject to affinity bias will focus on value-expressive characteristics rather than utilitarian benefits.

Practical Application

Affinity Bias A useful application of affinity bias in the investment realm is *patriotism*. Investors who concentrate their holdings in their home country or state gain the expressive benefit of patriotism but may potentially lose the utilitarian benefits of high returns and low risk that come to those who invest elsewhere. Adair Morse and Sophie Shive (2003) of the University of Chicago Booth School of Business and the University of Notre Dame, respectively, found that patriotism continuously affects investment behavior in their study, "Patriotism in Your Portfolio." They explored the role of devotion and loyalty to one's country in explaining an "equity home bias" and found that investors in more patriotic countries and regions within the United States discriminate more in favor of domestic stocks. Much like betting on the home team despite unfavorable odds or allocating retirement savings only to one's own company stock, patriotic investors choose to invest more of their stocks in firms based in their homeland. For example, the study found that U.S. investors hold 92 percent of their equity portfolio in domestic stock, although portfolio theory suggests that the optimally diversified portfolio should consist of only one third invested in domestic stocks.

Using data on 33 countries from the U-M World Values Survey, the researchers found that more patriotic countries and regions within the United States hold smaller foreign equity positions—in other words, investors discriminate in favor of domestic stocks. For example, Americans and South Africans invest less in foreign stocks than do several European investors, while investors in the very patriotic regions of Texas, Oklahoma, Louisiana, and Arkansas invest less in international equities than do investors in the less patriotic New England states.

Morse and Shive found that patriotism accounts for an additional 7 percent of the cross-country variation in foreign equity holdings. Further, a 10 percent decrease in patriotism is associated with a 29 to 48 percent increase in foreign equity in the home country portfolio. The study also presented evidence that U.S. demand for French stocks traded in the United States declined in reaction to French opposition to the recent war in Iraq. The proportion of American Depositary Receipts (ADRs) sold increased by 15 to 18 percent during the prewar period of anti-French sentiment and the average U.S. price of the ADR decreased relative to the French price (ADRs are certificates issued by a U.S. depository bank, representing foreign shares held by the bank).

Overall, Morse and Shive say their research has two implications: patriotic behavior explains a part of the mysterious equity home bias and policies aimed at increasing investors' portfolio diversification may need to account for "irrational" investor behavior. Shive said of her research:

> *Patriotism results in a winner's curse in the sense that the person valuing a stock most highly will ultimately be the highest bidder. . . . The citizens of a country will likely be the highest bidders for their own country's assets, thus possibly driving up prices in their own market.*

Implications for Investors   One of the previously referenced implications for affinity bias is that investors decide to invest in weak or otherwise unsound companies that reflect expressive characteristics rather than utilitarian characteristics in a misguided attempt to achieve investment success. A classic example of this can be found in individuals who invest in retail chain stores that produce popular products such as blue jeans, watches, or other products that reflect expressive benefits, only to discover that the company is a disaster from an investment standpoint. Other investors may also wish to invest in companies that they feel reflect their environmental, social, or governance values (ESG), which may or may not prove to be a successful strategy. Some studies have shown that ESG-type (socially responsible) investing is a successful strategy, while others have shown that ESG is not a winning investment strategy. Regardless, investors and their advisors need to be aware that some clients may wish to invest in companies that reflect their social values and that this behavior has investment implications. Another implication of affinity bias is that some investors may wish to invest in things that convey status but that they know little about or that may involve risks, such as investing in hedge funds or other alternative investments that their social acquaintances are investing in, in order to demonstrate status or be part of an investment club—only to find that they made a bad decision by doing so. Finally, patriotic behavior may cause investors to have home country bias, which can limit the success of any portfolio, especially in the globally diverse world we now live in.

The next box summarizes affinity bias behaviors that can cause poor investment outcomes.

Affinity Bias Behaviors That Can Lead to Poor Investment Outcomes

1. Investors subject to affinity bias can make investments in companies that make products or deliver services that they like but don't examine carefully enough the soundness of the investment characteristics of those companies.

2. Investors subject to affinity bias can invest in companies that reflect their ESG values but don't carefully examine the soundness of the investment characteristics of those companies.
3. Investors subject to affinity bias can invest in their home countries at the expense of investing in foreign countries due to home country bias.
4. Investors subject to affinity bias can sometimes invest in "sophisticated" investment products that convey status only to find they have invested in something they don't understand, which can be "hazardous to your wealth."

Introduction to Behavioral Investor Types

Behavioral investor types (BITs) were designed to help financial market participants (FMPs) make a speedy yet insightful assessment of what type of biases dominate investment decision making. Based on my experience as a financial advisor, combined with the research I have done in behavioral finance, I have identified four BITs: the Preserver, the Follower, the Independent, and the Accumulator. Each BIT has biases that are associated with it, which will be discussed extensively in the next section. BITs are not intended to be "absolutes" but rather "guideposts." For example, you may find that you have classified yourself or a client as a Preserver, but find that they have traits (biases) of a Follower or even an Individualist. The grouping or clustering of biases to define a BIT is done to show that certain investors have a strong *tendency* to certain biases that can dominate investment decision-making behavior. The goal of the use of BITs is to discover irrational behaviors and then, ultimately, to create a behaviorally modified (best practical) asset allocation that FMPs can comfortably adhere to, to meet long-term financial goals.

One of the most important concepts readers should keep in mind as they go through this part of the chapter is that the least risk-tolerant BIT and the most risk-tolerant BIT clients are emotionally biased in their behavior. In the middle of the risk scale are BITs that are affected mainly by cognitive biases. This should make intuitive sense. Investors who have a high need for security (i.e., a low risk tolerance) do so because emotion is driving this behavior; they get emotional about losing money and get uneasy during times of stress or change. Similarly, highly aggressive investors are also emotionally charged people who adamantly want to accumulate assets. They typically suffer from a high level of overconfidence and mistakenly believe they can control the outcomes of their investments. In between these two extremes are the investors who suffer mainly from cognitive biases and can benefit from education and information about their biases so they can make better investment decisions.

A brief diagnostic is provided for each of the biases associated with each BIT. Advice, which is geared toward the advisor, is also provided. An overarching point that readers should keep in mind as they proceed is that investors who are emotional about their investing need to be advised differently from those who make mainly cognitive errors. When advising emotionally charged investors, advisors need to focus on how the investment program being created impacts important emotional issues like financial security, retirement, or the goals for future generations rather than focusing on portfolio details like standard deviation and Sharpe ratios. A quantitative approach is more effective with clients who are less emotional and tend to make cognitive errors. Emotional clients tend to be more difficult clients to work with, and advisors who can recognize the type of client they are dealing with prior to making investment recommendations will be much better prepared to deal with irrational behavior when it arises. At the end of the day, the goal is to build better long-term relationships with clients; BITs are designed to help in this effort. In the next section, we begin with a passive, conservative investor, the Preserver.

PRESERVER

Basic type: Passive
Risk tolerance level: Low
Primary bias: Emotional

Preservers are, as the name implies, passive investors who place a great deal of emphasis on financial security and preserving wealth rather than taking risks to grow wealth. Because they have gained wealth by not risking their own capital, Preservers may not be highly financially sophisticated. A common situation is a Preserver who has gained wealth through inheritance or conservatively by working in a large company. Some Preservers are "worriers" in that they obsess over short-term performance (losses) and are slow to make investment decisions because they aren't entirely comfortable with change—which is consistent with the way they have approached their professional lives—being careful not to take excessive risks.

Many Preservers are focused on taking care of their family members and future generations, especially funding life-enhancing experiences such as education and home buying. Because the focus is on family and security, Preserver biases tend to be emotional rather than cognitive. As age and wealth level increase, this BIT becomes more common. Although not always the case, many Preservers enjoy the wealth management process—they like the idea of being catered to because of their financial status—and thus are generally good clients. Behavioral biases of Preservers tend to be emotional, security-oriented biases such as endowment bias, loss aversion, and status quo. Preservers also exhibit cognitive biases such as anchoring and mental accounting. The following is a description of the biases just discussed (this should be a review for you) and a simple diagnostic for each bias.

Loss Aversion Bias

Bias type: Emotional

Preservers tend to feel the pain of losses more than the pleasure of gains as compared to other client types. As such, these Preservers may hold on to losing investments too long—even when they see no prospect of a turnaround. Loss aversion is a very common bias and is seen by large numbers of financial advisors with this type of client.

Simple diagnostic for loss aversion bias: On a scale of 1 to 5, with 5 being full agreement, how much do you agree with the following:

The pain of financial loss is at least two times stronger than the pleasure of financial gain.

Answering 3 to 5 shows a tendency toward loss aversion bias.

Status Quo Bias

Bias type: Emotional

Preservers often prefer to keep their investments (and other parts of their life for that matter) the same or keep the "status quo." These investors tell themselves "things have always been this way" and thus feel safe keeping things the same.

Simple diagnostic for status quo bias: On a scale of 1 to 5, with 5 being full agreement, how much do you agree with the following:

When considering changing my portfolio, I spend time thinking about options but often end up changing little or sometimes nothing.

Answering 3 to 5 shows a tendency toward status quo bias.

Endowment Bias

Bias type: Emotional

Preservers, especially those who inherit wealth, tend to assign a greater value to an investment they already own (such as a piece of real estate or an inherited stock position) than they would if they didn't possess that investment and had the potential to acquire it.

Simple diagnostic for endowment bias: On a scale of 1 to 5, with 5 being full agreement, how much do you agree with the following:

I sometimes get attached to certain of my investments, which may cause me not to take action on them.

Answering 3 to 5 shows a tendency toward endowment bias.

Anchoring Bias

Bias type: Cognitive

Investors in general, and Preservers in particular, are often influenced by purchase points or arbitrary price levels, and tend to cling to these numbers when facing questions like "should I buy or sell this investment?" Suppose that the stock is down 25 percent from the high that it reached five months ago ($75/share vs. $100/share). Frequently, a Preserver client will resist selling until its price rebounds to the $100/share it achieved five months ago.

Simple diagnostic for anchoring bias: On a scale of 1 to 5, with 5 being full agreement, how much do you agree with the following:

> When thinking about selling an investment, the price I paid is a big factor I consider before taking any action.

Answering 3 to 5 shows a tendency toward anchoring bias.

Mental Accounting Bias

Bias type: Cognitive

Many Preservers treat various sums of money differently based on where these sums are mentally categorized. For example, Preservers often segregate their assets into safe "buckets." If all of these assets are viewed as safe money, suboptimal overall portfolio returns are usually the result.

> **Simple diagnostic for mental accounting bias:** On a scale of 1 to 5, with 5 being full agreement, how much do you agree with the following:
> I tend to categorize my investments in various accounts, for example, leisure, bill pay, college funding, and so forth.

Answering 3 to 5 shows a tendency toward mental accounting bias.

ADVICE FOR PRESERVERS   After reviewing this section, readers might correctly conclude that Preservers are difficult to advise because they are driven mainly by emotion. This is true; however, they are also greatly in need of good financial advice. Advisors should take the time to interpret behavioral signs provided to them by Preserver clients. Preservers need "big picture" advice, and advisors shouldn't dwell on details like standard deviations and Sharpe ratios or else they will lose the client's attention. Preservers need to understand how the portfolio they choose to create will deliver desired results to emotional issues such as family members or future generations. Once they feel comfortable discussing these important emotional issues with their advisor, and a bond of trust is established, they will take action. After a period of time, Preservers are likely to become an advisor's best clients because they value greatly the advisor's professionalism, expertise, and objectivity in helping make the right investment decisions.

FOLLOWER

Basic type: Passive
Risk tolerance level: Low to medium
Primary bias: Cognitive

Followers are typically passive investors who do not have their own ideas about investing. They often follow the lead of their friends and colleagues in investment decisions, and want to be in the latest, most popular investments without regard to a long-term plan. One of the key challenges of working with Followers is that they often overestimate their risk tolerance. Advisors need to be careful not to suggest too many "hot" investment ideas—Followers will likely want to do all of them. Some don't like, or even fear, the task of investing, and many put off making investment decisions without professional advice; the result is that they maintain, often by default, high cash balances. Followers generally comply with professional advice

when they get it, and they educate themselves financially, but can at times be difficult because they don't enjoy or have an aptitude for the investment process. Biases
of Followers are cognitive: recency, hindsight, framing, regret, cognitive dissonance,
and outcome.

Recency Bias

Bias type: Cognitive

Recency bias is a predisposition for investors to recall and emphasize recent
events and/or observations. Followers may extrapolate patterns where none really
exist. Recency bias ran rampant during the bull market period between 2003 and
2007 when many investors wrongly presumed that the stock market, particularly
energy, housing, and international stocks, would continue gains. Moderate investors
are known to enter or hold on to investments when prices are peaking, which can
end badly, with sharp price declines.

> **Simple diagnostic for recency bias:** On a scale of 1 to 5, with 5 being full
> agreement, how much do you agree with the following:
>> **When considering the track record of an investment, I put more weight on
>> how it has performed recently versus how it has performed historically.**
> Answering 3 to 5 shows a tendency toward recency bias.

Hindsight Bias

Bias type: Cognitive

Followers often lack independent thoughts about their investments and are susceptible to hindsight bias, which occurs when an investor perceives investment outcomes as if they were predictable. The result of hindsight bias is that it gives investors
a false sense of security when making investment decisions, emboldening them to
take excessive risk without recognizing it.

> **Simple diagnostic for hindsight bias:** On a scale of 1 to 5, with 5 being full
> agreement, how much do you agree with the following:
>> **When reflecting on past investment mistakes, I see that many could have
>> been easily avoided.**
> Answering 3 to 5 shows a tendency toward hindsight bias.

Framing Bias

Bias type: Cognitive

Framing bias is the tendency of Followers to respond to situations differently
based on the context in which a choice is presented (framed). Often, Followers focus
too restrictively on one or two aspects of a situation, excluding other considerations.
The use of risk tolerance questionnaires provides a good example. Depending on

how questions are asked, framing bias can cause investors to respond to risk tolerance questions in an either unduly risk-averse or risk-taking manner. For example, when questions are worded in the gain frame (e.g., an investment goes up), then a risk-taking response is more likely. When questions are worded in the "loss" frame (e.g., an investment goes down), then risk-averse behavior is the likely response.

> **Simple diagnostic for framing bias:** On a scale of 1 to 5, with 5 being full agreement, how much do you agree with the following:
> **I trust more the advice of national investment firms than smaller, local firms.**
> Answering 3 to 5 shows a tendency toward framing bias.

Cognitive Dissonance Bias

> **Bias type:** Cognitive

In psychology, cognitions represent attitudes, emotions, beliefs, or values. When multiple cognitions intersect–for example when a person believes in something only to find out it is not true—Followers try to alleviate their discomfort by ignoring the truth and/or rationalizing their decisions. Investors who suffer from this bias may continue to invest in a security or fund they already own after it has gone down (average down) even when they know they should be judging the new investment with objectivity. A common phrase for this concept is "throwing good money after bad."

> **Simple diagnostic for cognitive dissonance bias:** On a scale of 1 to 5, with 5 being full agreement, how much do you agree with the following:
> **When making investment decisions, I tend to focus on the positive aspect of an investment rather than on what might go wrong with the investment.**
> Answering 3 to 5 shows a tendency toward cognitive dissonance bias.

Regret Aversion Bias

> **Bias type:** Emotional

Followers often avoid taking decisive actions because they fear that, in hindsight, whatever course they select will prove less than optimal. Regret aversion can cause some investors to be too timid in their investment choices because of losses they have suffered in the past.

> **Simple diagnostic for regret aversion bias:** On a scale of 1 to 5, with 5 being full agreement, how much do you agree with the following:
> **Poor past financial decisions have caused me to change my current investing behavior.**
> Answering 3 to 5 shows a tendency toward regret aversion bias.

ADVICE FOR FOLLOWERS　Advisors to Followers first and foremost need to recognize that Followers often overestimate their risk tolerance. Risky trend-following behavior occurs in part because Followers don't like situations of ambiguity that may accompany the decision to enter an asset class when it is out of favor. They also may convince themselves that they "knew it all along" when an investment idea goes their way, which also increases future risk-taking behavior. Advisors need to handle Followers with care because they are likely to "say yes" to investment ideas that make sense to them, regardless of whether the advice is in their best long-term interest. Advisors need to encourage Followers to take a hard look at behavioral tendencies that may cause them to overestimate their risk tolerance. Because Follower biases are mainly cognitive, education on the benefits of portfolio diversification and sticking to a long-term plan is usually the best course of action. Advisors should challenge Follower clients to be introspective and provide data-backed substantiation for recommendations. Offering education in clear, unambiguous ways so they have the chance to "get it" is a good idea. If advisors take the time, this steady, educational approach will generate client loyalty and adherence to long-term investment plans.

INDEPENDENT

> **Basic type**: Active
> **Risk tolerance**: Medium to high
> **Primary bias**: Cognitive

With Independents, we are entering the realm of the active investor. As we reviewed in earlier articles, these investors have been actively involved in their wealth creation, typically risking their own capital in achieving their wealth objectives. Active investors have a higher tolerance for risk than they have need for security. Their tolerance for risk is high because they believe in themselves. Related to their high risk tolerance is the fact that active investors prefer to maintain at least some amount of control of their own investments. They want to get very involved in investment decision making and aren't afraid to roll up their sleeves and do due diligence on contemplated investments. Let's turn our attention to the first of two active behavioral investor types, the Independent Individualist (II).

An Independent is an active investor with medium- to high-risk tolerance who is strong-willed and an independently minded thinker. Independents are self-assured and "trust their instincts" when making investment decisions; however, when they do research on their own, they may be susceptible to acting on information that is available to them rather than getting corroboration from other sources. Sometimes advisors find that an Independent client made an investment without consulting anyone. This approach can be problematic because, due to their independent mindset, these clients often irrationally cling to the views they had when they made an investment, even when market conditions change, making advising Independents challenging. They often enjoy investing, however, and are comfortable taking risks, but often resist following a rigid financial plan.

Some Independents are obsessed with trying to beat the market and may hold concentrated portfolios. Of all behavioral investor types, Independents are the most likely to be contrarian, which can benefit them—and lead them to continue their contrarian practices. Independent Individualist biases are cognitive: conservatism, availability, confirmation, representativeness, and self-attribution.

Conservatism Bias

Bias type: Cognitive

Conservatism bias occurs when people cling to a prior view or forecast at the expense of acknowledging new information. Independents often cling to a view or forecast, behaving too inflexibly when presented with new information. For example, assume an investor purchases a security based on the knowledge about a forthcoming new product announcement. The company then announces that it is experiencing problems bringing the product to market. Independents may cling to the initial, optimistic impression of the new product announcement and may fail to take action on the negative announcement.

> **Simple diagnostic for conservatism bias:** On a scale of 1 to 5, with 5 being full agreement, how much do you agree with the following:
> **I don't easily change my views about investments once they are made.**
> Answering 3 to 5 shows a tendency toward conservatism bias.

Availability Bias

Bias type: Cognitive

Availability bias occurs when people estimate the probability of an outcome based on how prevalent that outcome appears in their lives. People exhibiting this bias perceive easily recalled possibilities as being more likely than those prospects that are harder to imagine or difficult to comprehend. As an example, suppose an Independent is asked to identify the "best" mutual funds. Many of these investors would perform a Google search and, most likely, find funds from firms that engage in heavy advertising—such as Fidelity or Schwab. Investors subject to availability bias are influenced to pick funds from such companies, despite the fact that some of the best-performing funds advertise very little if at all.

> **Simple diagnostic for availability bias:** On a scale of 1 to 5, with 5 being full agreement, how much do you agree with the following:
> **I often take action on a new investment right away, if it makes sense to me.**
> Answering 3 to 5 shows a tendency toward availability bias.

Representativeness Bias

Bias type: Cognitive

Representativeness bias occurs as a result of a flawed a perceptual framework when processing new information. To make new information easier to process, some investors project outcomes that resonate with their own preexisting ideas. An Independent might view a particular stock, for example, as a value stock because it resembles an earlier value stock that was a successful investment—but the new investment is actually not a value stock. For instance, a high-flying biotech stock with scant earnings or assets drops 25 percent after a negative product announcement. Some Independents may take this situation to be representative of a "value" stock because it is cheap; but biotech stocks don't typically have earnings, while traditional value stocks have had earnings in the past but are temporarily underperforming.

> **Simple diagnostic for representativeness bias:** On a scale of 1 to 5, with 5 being full agreement, how much do you agree with the following:
>> **Many investment choices I make are based upon my knowledge of how similar past investments have performed.**
> Answering 3 to 5 shows a tendency toward representativeness bias.

Self-Attribution (Self-Enhancing) Bias

Bias type: Cognitive

Self-attribution bias refers to the tendency of Independents to ascribe their successes to innate talents while blaming failures on outside influences. For example, suppose an Independent makes an investment in a particular stock that goes up in value. The reason it went up is not due to random factors such as economic conditions or competitor failures (the most likely reason for the investment success), but rather to the investor's investment savvy (likely not the reason for the investment success.) This is classic self-enhancing bias.

> **Simple diagnostic for self-attribution bias:** On a scale of 1 to 5, with 5 being full agreement, how much do you agree with the following:
>> **I often find that many of my successful investments can be attributed to my decisions, while those that did not work out were based on the guidance of others.**
> Answering 3 to 5 shows a tendency toward self-attribution bias.

Confirmation Bias

Bias type: Cognitive

Confirmation bias occurs when people observe, overvalue, or actively seek out information that confirms their claims, while ignoring or devaluing evidence that might discount their claims. Confirmation bias can cause investors to seek out only information that confirms their beliefs about an investment, and not seek out information that may contradict their beliefs. This behavior can leave investors in the dark regarding, for example, the imminent decline of a stock. Independents often find themselves subject to this bias.

Simple diagnostic for confirmation bias: On a scale of 1 to 5, with 5 being full agreement, how much do you agree with the following:

When an investment is not going well, I usually seek information that confirms I made the right decision about it.

Answering 3 to 5 shows a tendency toward confirmation bias.

ADVICE FOR INDEPENDENTS Independents can be difficult clients to advise due to their independent mindset, but they are usually grounded enough to listen to sound advice when it is presented in a way that respects their independent views. As we have learned, Independent Individualists are firm in their belief in themselves and their decisions, but can be blinded to contrary thinking. As with Followers, education is essential to changing behavior of Independents; their biases are predominantly cognitive. A good approach is to have regular educational discussions during client meetings. This way, the advisor doesn't point out unique or recent failures, but rather educates regularly and can incorporate concepts that he or she feels are appropriate for the client. Because Independents' biases are mainly cognitive, education on the benefits of portfolio diversification and sticking to a long-term plan is usually the best course of action. Advisors should challenge Independents to reflect on how they make investment decisions and provide data-backed substantiation for recommendations. Offering education in clear, unambiguous ways is an effective approach. If advisors take the time, this steady, educational approach should yield positive results.

ACCUMULATOR

Basic type: Active
Risk tolerance: High
Primary bias: Emotional

With Accumulators, we continue within the realm of the active investor. As we reviewed in earlier articles, active investors have been actively involved in their wealth creation, typically risking their own capital in achieving their wealth objectives. Active investors have a higher tolerance for risk than they have need for security. Their tolerance for risk is high because they believe in themselves. Related to their high risk tolerance is the fact that active investors prefer to get very involved in investment decision making and aren't afraid to roll up their sleeves and do due diligence on contemplated investments. Let's turn our attention now to the last of the two active behavioral investor types, the Accumulator.

The Accumulator is the most aggressive behavioral investor type. These clients are entrepreneurial and often the first generation to create wealth, and they are even more strong-willed and confident than Independents. At high wealth levels, they often have controlled the outcomes of noninvestment activities and believe they can do the same with investing. This behavior can lead to overconfidence in investing activities. Left unadvised, they often trade too much, which can be a drag on investment performance. Accumulators are quick decision makers but may chase higher-risk investments than their friends. If successful, they enjoy the thrill of making a good investment. Some Accumulators can be difficult to advise because they don't believe in basic investment principles such as diversification and asset allocation. They are often "hands-on," wanting to be heavily involved in the investment decision-making process. Biases of Accumulators are overconfidence, self-control, affinity, and illusion of control.

Overconfidence Bias

Bias type: Emotional

Overconfidence is best described as unwarranted faith in one's own thoughts and abilities, which contains both cognitive and emotional elements. Overconfidence manifests itself in investors' overestimation of the quality of their judgment. Many Accumulators claim an above-average aptitude for selecting stocks; however, numerous studies have shown this to be a fallacy. For example, a study done by researchers Odean and Barber showed that after trading costs (but before taxes), the average investor underperformed the market by approximately 2 percent per year due to unwarranted belief in their ability to assess the correct value of investment securities.

> **Simple diagnostic for overconfidence bias:** On a scale of 1 to 5, with 5 being full agreement, how much do you agree with the following:
> **I am confident that my investment knowledge is above average and I can accurately predict how my investments will do.**
> Answering 3 to 5 shows a tendency toward overconfidence bias.

Self-Control Bias

Bias type: Emotional

Self-control bias is the tendency to consume today at the expense of saving for tomorrow. The primary concern for advisors with this bias is a client with high risk tolerance coupled with high spending. For example, suppose you have an Accumulator client who prefers high volatility investments and has high current spending needs and suddenly the financial markets hit some severe turbulence. This client may be forced to sell solid long-term investments that have had been priced down due to current market conditions just to meet current expenses.

> **Simple diagnostic for self-control bias:** On a scale of 1 to 5, with 5 being full agreement, how much do you agree with the following:
> **I will buy things I want even if they are not the best financial choices.**
> Answering 3 to 5 shows a tendency toward self-control bias.

Affinity Bias

Bias type: Emotional

Affinity bias refers to an individual's tendency to make irrationally uneconomical consumer choices or investment decisions based on how they believe a certain product or service will reflect their values. Accumulators sometimes succumb to this bias.

Simple diagnostic for affinity bias: On a scale of 1 to 5, with 5 being full agreement, how much do you agree with the following:

I invest in companies that make products I like or companies that reflect my personal values.

Answering 3 to 5 shows a tendency towards affinity bias.

Illusion of Control Bias

Bias type: Cognitive

The illusion of control bias occurs when investors believe that they can control or, at least, influence investment outcomes when, in fact, they cannot. Accumulators who are subject to illusion of control bias believe that the best way to manage an investment portfolio is to constantly adjust it. For example, trading-oriented Accumulators who accept high levels of risk, believe themselves to possess more "control" over the outcome of their investments than they actually do because they are "pulling the trigger" on each decision.

Simple diagnostic for outcome bias: On a scale of 1 to 5, with 5 being full agreement, how much do you agree with the following:

I am more likely to have a better outcome if I make my own investment choices rather than relying on others.

Answering 3 to 5 shows a tendency toward outcome bias.

Outcome Bias

Bias type: Cognitive

Outcome bias refers to the tendency of individuals to decide to do something—such as make an investment in a mutual fund—based on the outcome of past events (such as returns of the past five years) rather than by observing the process by which the outcome came about (the investment process used by the mutual fund manager over the past five years). Accumulators often are prone to outcome bias.

Simple diagnostic for outcome bias: On a scale of 1 to 5, with 5 being full agreement, how much do you agree with the following:

What's most important is that my investments make money—I'm not that concerned with following a structured plan.

Answering 3 to 5 shows a tendency toward outcome bias.

ADVICE FOR ACCUMULATORS   Aggressive clients are generally the most difficult clients to advise, particularly those who have experienced losses. Because they like to control or at least get deeply involved in the details of investment decision making, they tend to eschew advice that might keep their risk tolerance in check. And they are emotionally charged and optimistic that their investments will do well, even if that optimism is irrational. Some Accumulators need to be monitored for excess spending, which, when out of control, can inhibit performance of a long-term portfolio. The best approach to dealing with these clients is to take control of the situation. If the advisor lets the Accumulator client dictate the terms of the advisory engagement, they will always be at the mercy of the client's emotionally driven decision making and the result will likely be an unhappy client and an unhappy advisor. Advisors to Accumulators need to demonstrate the impact financial decisions have on family members, lifestyle, or the family legacy. If these advisors can prove to the client that they have the ability to help the client to make sound long-term decisions, they will likely see their Accumulator clients fall into step and be better clients that are easier to advise.

Notes

1. E. Aronson, "The Theory of Cognitive Dissonance: A Current Perspective," in L. Berkowitz, ed., *Advances in Experimental Social Psychology*, Vol. 4 (New York: Academic Press, 1969), 1–34.
2. T. Gilovich, *How We Know What Isn't So: The Fallibility of Human Reason in Everyday Life* (New York: Free Press, 1993).

References

Ackert, Lucy F., Narat Charupat, Bryan K. Church, and Richard Deaves. 2003. "An experimental examination of the house money effect in a multiperiod setting." Working paper, Federal Reserve of Atlanta, September.

Aronson, E. 1969. "The theory of cognitive dissonance: A current perspective," in *Advances in Experimental Social Psychology*, Vol. 4, ed. L. Berkowitz (New York: Academic Press), 1–34.

Barber, Brad M., and Terrance Odean. 2001. "Boys will be boys: Gender, overconfidence, and common stock investment," *Quarterly Journal of Economics* 116(1) (February): 261–292.

Barber, Brad M., and Terrance Odean. 2002. "All that glitters: The effect of attention and news on the buying behavior of individual and institutional investors." Working paper, University of California-Berkeley.

Barberis, Nicholas, Robert W. Vishny, and Andrei Shleifer. 1998. "A model of investor sentiment," *Capital Ideas* [University of Chicago] 1(2) (Winter).

Baron, Jonathan, and John C. Hershey. 2008. "Outcome bias in decision evaluation," *Journal of Personality and Social Psychology* 54: 569–579.

Benartzi, Shlomo, and Richard H. Thaler. 1995. "Myopic loss aversion and the equity premium puzzle," *Quarterly Journal of Economics* (February): 73–92. See http://gsbwww.uchicago.edu/fac/richard.thaler/research/myopic.pdf.

Benos, Evangelos, and Marek Jochec. 2009. "Liberalism and home equity bias." *University of Illinois Urbana-Champaign*, 1–26.

Breinholt, Andrea, and Lynnette A. Dalrymple. 2004. "The illusion of control: What's luck got to do with It?" *The Myriad: Westminster College Undergraduate Academic Journal* (Summer).

Brunel, Jean L. P. 2003. "Revisiting the asset allocation challenge through a behavioral finance lens," *Journal of Wealth Management* (Fall): 10–20.

Clarke, Roger G., and Meir Statman. 2000. "The DJIA crossed 652,230," *Journal of Portfolio Management* 26 (Winter): 89–93.

Cooper, Ian, and Evi Kaplanis. 1994. "Home bias in equity portfolios, inflation hedging and international capital market equilibrium." *The Review of Financial Studies* 7 (1): 45–60.

Cooper, Michael, Roberto Gutierrez, and William Marcum. 2005 "On the predictability of stock returns in real time." *Journal of Business* 78 (2) (April): 469–499.

De Bondt, Werner F. M., and Richard Thaler. 1985. "Does the stock market overreact?" *Journal of Finance* 40 (3) (July): 793–805.

Dunn, Dana S. 1989. "Demonstrating a self-serving bias." *Teaching of Psychology* 16: 21–22.

Edwards, Ward. 1968. "Conservatism in human information processing," in B. Kleinmutz, ed., *Formal Representation of Human Judgment*, ed. B. Kleinmutz. New York: John Wiley & Sons.

Fellner, Gerlinde. 2004. "Illusion of control as a source of poor diversification: An experimental approach," published by Max Planck Institute for Research into Economic Systems in Jena, Germany, May.

Festinger, L. 1957. *A theory of cognitive dissonance*. Stanford, CA: Stanford University Press. See www.money.cnn.com/1998/06/12/mutualfunds/q_worstfunds.

Fischhoff, Baruch. "Hindsight/foresight: The effect of outcome knowledge on judgment under uncertainty." *Journal of Experimental Psychology: Human Perception and Performance* 1 (3): 288–299.

Fisher, Kenneth L., and Meir Statman. 1999. "A Behavioral Framework for Time Diversification," *Financial Analysts Journal* (May/June 1999).

French, Kenneth, and James Poterba. 1991. "Investor diversification and international equity markets." *American Economic Review* 81: 221–226.

Gadarowski, Christopher. 2001. "Financial press coverage and expected stock returns" Working paper, Cornell University.

Gervais, Simon, and Terrance Odean. "Learning to be overconfident." *Review of Financial Studies* 14 (1): 1–27.

Gilovich, T. 1993. *How we know what isn't so: The fallibility of human reason in everyday life* (New York: Free Press, 1993).

Goetzmann, W. N., and N. Peles. 1997. "Cognitive dissonance and mutual fund investors." *Journal of Financial Research* 10 (Summer): 145–158.

Hang, Ming, Nicholas Barberis, and Tano Santos. 2001. "Prospect theory and asset prices," *Quarterly Journal of Economics* (February).

Hirshleifer, David. 2001. "Investor psychology and asset pricing." Working paper, Fisher College of Business, Ohio State University.

Kahneman, Daniel, J. L. Knetsch, and Richard H. Thaler. 1991. "The endowment effect, loss aversion, and status quo bias: Anomalies." *Journal of Economic Perspectives* 5(1): 193–206.

Kahneman, Daniel, and Mark Riepe. 1998. "Aspects of investory psychology: Beliefs, preferences, and biases investment advisors should know about." *Journal of Portfolio Management* 24: 52–65.

Kahneman, Daniel, Paul Slovic, and Amos Tversky (eds.), 1982. *Judgment under uncertainty: Heuristics and biases*. New York: Cambridge University Press.

Kahneman, Daniel, and Amos Tversky. 1979. "Prospect theory: An analysis of decision under risk." *Econometrica* 47: 263–291.

Kahneman, Daniel, and Amos Tversky. 1984. "Choices, values, and frames." *American Psychologist* 39: 341–50. Reprinted as Chapter 1 in *Choices, values, and frames,* eds. Daniel Kahneman and Amos Tversky (New York: Cambridge University Press and the Russell Sage Foundation, 2000).

Knetsch, J. L. "The endowment effect and evidence of nonreversible indifference curves." *American Economic Review* 79(5): 1277–1284.

Langer, Ellen. 1975. "The illusion of control." *Journal of Personality and Social Psychology* 32: 311–328.

Lewis, Karen. 1999. "Trying to explain home bias in equities and consumption." *Journal of Economic Literature* 37: 571–608.

List, John A. 2003. "Does market experience eliminate market anomalies?" *Quarterly Journal of Economics* 118 (February): 41–71.

Lusardi, Annamaria. 1999. "Information, expectations, and savings for retirement." In *Behavioral dimensions of retirement economics,* ed. Henry J. Aaron. Washington, DC: Brookings Institution and Russell Sage Foundation, 81–155.

Lusardi, Annamaria. 2000. "Explaining why so many households do not save." Working paper, Irving Harris Graduate School for Public Policy Studies, University of Chicago.

Mehra, Rajnish, and Edward C. Prescott. 1985. "The equity premium: A puzzle." *Journal of Monetary Economics* 15 (March): 145–161.

Montier, James. 2002. *Behavioural finance: Insights into irrational minds and markets.* West Sussex, England: John Wiley & Sons.

Montier, James. 2002. "Equity research." Research report, Dresdner Kleinwort Wasserstein.

Montier, James. 2003. "Irrational pessimism and the road to revulsion." Research report, Dresdner Kleinwort Wasserstein, February.

Morse, Adair, and Sophie Shive. 2011. "Patriotism in your portfolio." *Journal of Financial Markets* 14: 411–440, 438.

Lichtenstein, Sarah, Baruch Fischhoff, and L. D. Phillips. 1982. "Calibration of probabilities: The state of the art to 1980." In *Judgment under uncertainty: Heuristics and biases,* eds. David Kahneman, Paul Slovic, and Amos Tversky. New York: Cambridge University Press, 306–334.

Nevins, Daniel. 2004. "Goals-based investing: Integrating traditional and behavioral finance," *Journal of Wealth Management* (Spring): 8–23.

Northcraft, Gregory, and Margaret Neale. 1987. "Experts, amateurs, and real estate: An anchoring-and-adjustment perspective on property pricing decisions." *Organizational Behavior and Human Decision Processes* 39: 84–97.

Odean, Terrance. 1999. "Do investors trade too much?" *American Economic Review* 89(5) (December): 1279–1298.

Posner, Richard. 1998. "Rational choice, behavioral economics, and the law." *Stanford Law Review* 50: 1551–1575.

Prechter, Robert J. 1997. *At the crest of the tidal wave: A forecast for the great bear market.* New York: John Wiley & Sons.

Prelec, Drazen, and Duncan Simester. "Always leave home without it: A further investigation of the credit card effect on willingness to pay." *Marketing Letters* 12, no. 1: 5–12.

Park, C. Whan, Bernard J. Jaworski, and Deborah J. MacInnis. 1986. "Strategic brand concept-image management." *Journal of Marketing* 50: 135–145.

Samuelson, William, and Richard Zeckhauser, "Status Quo Bias in Decisions Making," *Journal of Risk and Uncertainty* 1(1): 7–59. With kind permission of Springer Science and Business Media.

Santa-Clara, Pedro, and Rossen Valkanov. 2003. "The presidential puzzle: Political cycles and the stock market." *Journal of Finance* 58(5) (October): 1841–1872.

Shefrin, Hersh, and Meir Statman. 1985. "The disposition to sell winners too early and ride losers too long: Theory and evidence." *Journal of Finance* 40: 77–90.

Shefrin, Hersh, and Meir Statman. 1984. "Explaining investor preference for cash dividends," *Journal of Financial Economics* 13 (June): 253–282. Reprinted in *Advances in behavioral finance*, ed. Richard H. Thaler. New York: Russell Sage Foundation.

Sirgy, Joseph M. 1991. "Value-expressive versus utilitarian advertising appeals: When and why to use which appeal." *Journal of Advertising* 20 (3): 23–33.

Slovic, Paul, Baruch Fischoff, and Sarah Lichtenstein. 1982. "Facts versus fiction: Understanding public fears." In *Judgment under uncertainty: Heuristics and biases*, eds. Daniel Kahneman, Paul Slovic, and Amos Tversky. New York: Cambridge University Press, 463–491.

Snyder, Mark, and Kenneth G. DeBono. 1985. "Appeals to image and claims about quality: Understanding the psychology of advertising." *Journal of Personality and Social Psychology*, 49 (3): 586–597.

Statman, Meir, and Kenneth L. Fisher. 2000. "Cognitive biases and market forecasts." *Journal of Portfolio Management* (Fall).

Thaler, Richard H. "Mental accounting matters," *Journal of Behavioral Decision Making* 12, no. 3: 183–206.

Thaler, Richard H. 1980. "Towards a positive theory of consumer choice," *Journal of Economic Behavior and Organization* 1: 39–60.

Thaler, Richard H., and Shlomo Benartzi. "Save more tomorrow: Using behavioral economics to increase employee saving." *Journal of Political Economy* 112(1): 5164–5187.

Thaler, Richard H., and Hersh M. Shefrin. 1988. "The behavioral life-cycle hypothesis." *Economic Inquiry* 26(4): 609–643.

Thornton, Russ. 2008. "*Quantitative analysis of investor behavior 2008*." Dalbar, Inc.: 1–12. Accessed March 11, 2011. www.scribd.com/doc/13096471/DALBAR-QAIB-2008.

Tversky, Amos, and Daniel Kahneman. 1986. "Rational choice and the framing of decisions." *Journal of Business* 59: S251–S278.

Walster, Elaine. 1966. "Assignment of responsibility for an accident." *Journal of Personality and Social Psychology* 3: 73–79.

CHAPTER 17

Client Discovery

C lient discovery is the initial step in the investment consulting process. Investment advisors and consultants must understand exactly whom they serve in order to make appropriate and suitable recommendations. A thorough evaluation of a client's current financial position, risk tolerance, goals and objectives, time horizon, and tax status is required.

This chapter discusses various investment strategies and models with a focus on strategic, tactical, and dynamic asset allocation. Asset allocation strategies are reviewed from a more traditional lens before adding alternative investments to the mix. Active and passive strategies, goals-based and liability driven strategies, scenario analysis, and the importance of economic and capital markets assumptions are all discussed in detail. Spending policy, core and satellite strategies, and total return strategies are also reviewed.

The last reading discusses the taxation of various investments and describes methods to measure tax efficiency before exploring various strategies to minimize or eliminate tax on investment portfolios.

Part I *Investments: Principles of Portfolio and Equity Analysis:* Portfolio Management: An Overview

Learning Objectives

- Discuss the types of investment management clients and the distinctive characteristics and needs of each.
- Describe the steps in the portfolio management process.

Part II *Strategic Risk Management:* Strategic Asset Allocation

Learning Objectives

- Explain strategic asset allocation and list the key steps in developing a portfolio based on this strategy.
- Explain the concept of combining asset classes to form investment portfolios.
- Discuss the dangers of portfolio optimization.
- Define and discuss asset-liability modeling.
- Describe performance measures and evaluation techniques.

Part III *Strategic Risk Management:* Active versus Passive Management

Learning Objectives

- Present arguments for and against active and passive investing.
- Explain the importance of availability and suitability as they relate to active and passive investing.
- Discuss the relevance of asset classes, style, and size when considering whether to invest in active or passive investments.
- Discuss performance evaluation and the predictability of the performance of active managers going forward.

Part IV *The New Science of Asset Allocation: Risk Management in a Multi-Asset World:* Strategic, Tactical, and Dynamic Asset Allocation

Learning Objectives

- Define and differentiate between strategic, tactical, and dynamic asset allocation strategies.
- Describe the methodology of asset allocation optimization models.
- Explain the use of different risk measures in asset allocation models.

Part V *New Science of Asset Allocation: Risk Management in a Multi-Asset World:* Core and Satellite Investment

Learning Objectives

- Describe the concept of "core and satellite" investing.
- Determine appropriate benchmarks and grouping.
- Describe various methods of implementing a "core and satellite" strategy including the positioning of active, passive, and alternative investments.

Part VI *Financial Advice and Investment Decisions: A Manifesto for Change:* Tax Efficient Investing

Learning Objectives

- Identify and explain the application and impact of various tax types that affect investment portfolios and returns including federal income tax, state and local income tax, capital gains tax, and estate and gift tax.
- Describe the various "types" of gains for tax purposes including interest income, qualified dividends, and gains realized from the sale of capital assets.
- Explain the tax treatment of mutual funds.
- Discuss various strategies to eliminate or reduce taxes in investment portfolios.
- Describe various after-tax performance metrics and benchmarks.

Part I Portfolio Management: An Overview

Investment Clients

Portfolio managers are employed or contracted by a wide variety of investment clients. We can group the clients into categories based on their distinctive characteristics and needs. Our initial distinction is between management of the private wealth of individual investors and investment management for institutional investors.

INDIVIDUAL INVESTORS Individual investors have a variety of motives for investing and constructing portfolios. Short-term goals can include providing for children's education, saving for a major purchase (such as a vehicle or a house), or starting a business. The retirement goal—investing to provide for an income in retirement—is a major part of the investment planning of most individuals. Many employees of public and private companies invest for retirement through a **defined contribution** (DC) pension plan. A DC plan is a pension plan in which contributions rather than benefits are specified, such as 401(k) plans in the United States, group personal pension schemes in the United Kingdom, and superannuation plans in Australia. Individuals will invest part of their wages while working, expecting to draw on the accumulated funds to provide income during retirement or to transfer some of their wealth to their heirs. The key to a DC plan is that the employee accepts the investment risk and is responsible for ensuring that there are enough funds in the plan to meet their needs upon retirement.

Some individuals will be investing for growth and will therefore seek assets that have the potential for capital gains. Others, such as retirees, may need to draw an income from their assets and may therefore choose to invest in fixed-income and dividend-paying shares. The investment needs of individuals will depend in part on their broader financial circumstances, such as their employment prospects and whether they own their own residence. They may also need to consider such issues as building up a cash reserve and the purchase of appropriate insurance policies before undertaking longer-term investments.

INSTITUTIONAL INVESTORS There are many different types of institutional investors. Examples include defined benefit pensions plans, university endowments, charitable foundations, banks, insurance companies, investment companies, and sovereign wealth funds (SWFs). Institutional investors are major participants in the investment markets. Investment funds are the largest category, with insurance companies and pension funds not far behind. The relative importance of these categories does vary significantly across the individual OECD countries.

DEFINED BENEFIT PENSION PLANS In a **defined benefit** (DB) pension plan, an employer has an obligation to pay a certain annual amount to its employees when they retire. In other words, the future benefit is defined because the DB plan requires the plan sponsor to specify the obligation stated in terms of the retirement income benefits owed to participants. DB plans need to invest the assets that will provide cash flows that match the timing of the future pension payments (i.e., liabilities). Plans are committed to paying pensions to members, and the assets of these plans are there to fund those payments. Plan managers need to ensure that sufficient assets will be available to pay pension benefits as they come due. The plan may have an indefinitely long time horizon if new plan members are being admitted or a finite time horizon if the plan has been closed to new members. Even a plan closed to new members may still have a time horizon of 70 or 80 years. For example, a plan member aged 25 may not retire for another 40 years and may live 30 years in retirement. Hence, pension plans can be considered long-term investors. In some cases, the plan managers attempt to match the fund's assets to its liabilities by, for example, investing in bonds that will produce cash flows corresponding to expected future pension payments. There may be many different investment philosophies for pension plans, depending on funded status and other variables.

EXAMPLE 17.1   Spending Rules

The following examples of spending rules are from the Yale University endowment (in the United States) and from the Wellcome Trust (in the United Kingdom).

Yale University Endowment

> *The spending rule is at the heart of fiscal discipline for an endowed institution. Spending policies define an institution's compromise between the conflicting goals of providing substantial support for current operations and preserving purchasing power of Endowment assets. The spending rule must be clearly defined and consistently applied for the concept of budget balance to have meaning. Yale's policy is designed to meet two competing objectives. The first goal is to release substantial current income to the operating budget in a stable stream, since large fluctuations in revenues are difficult to accommodate through changes in University activities or programs. The second goal is to protect the value of Endowment assets against inflation, allowing programs to be supported at today's level far into the future. Yale's spending rule attempts to achieve these two objectives by using a long-term spending rate of 5.25 percent combined with a smoothing rule that adjusts spending gradually to changes in Endowment market value. The amount released under the spending rule is based on a weighted average of prior spending adjusted for inflation (80 percent weight) and an amount determined by applying the target rate to the current Endowment market value (20 percent weight) with an adjustment factor based on inflation and the expected growth of the Endowment net of spending. ("2007 Yale Endowment Annual Report," p. 15 [www.yale.edu/investments/Yale_Endowment_07.pdf])*

Wellcome Trust

> *Our overall investment objective is to generate 6 percent real return over the long term. This is to provide for real increases in annual expenditure*

> *while preserving at least the Trust's capital base in real terms in order to balance the needs of both current and future beneficiaries. We use this absolute return strategy because it aligns asset allocation with funding requirements and it provides a competitive framework in which to judge individual investments. (Wellcome Trust, "History and Objectives: Investment Goals" [www.wellcome.ac.uk/Investments/History-and-objectives/index.htm])*

ENDOWMENTS AND FOUNDATIONS   University endowments are established to provide continuing financial support to a university and its students (e.g., scholarships). Endowments vary in size (assets under management), but many are major investors. It is common for U.S. universities to have large endowments, but it is somewhat less common elsewhere in the world. In terms of non-U.S. examples, the University of Oxford, United Kingdom, and its various colleges were estimated to have a total endowment of £4.8 billion as of 2004 and the University of Cambridge, United Kingdom, and its colleges, £5.3 billion. These were by far the largest endowments in the United Kingdom. The third largest, University of Edinburgh, was £156 million.[1] The French business school INSEAD's endowment was valued at €105 million as of 2008.[2]

Charitable foundations invest donations made to them for the purpose of funding grants that are consistent with the charitable foundation's objectives. Similar to university endowments, many charitable foundations are substantial investors. Again, large foundations are most common in the United States, but they also exist elsewhere. For example, the Wellcome Trust is a U.K.-based medical charity that had approximately £13 billion of assets as of 2008.[3] The Li Ka Shing Foundation is a Hong Kong–based education and medical charity with grants, sponsorships, and commitments amounting to HK$10.7 billion.

A typical investment objective of an endowment or a foundation is to maintain the real (inflation-adjusted) capital value of the fund while generating income to fund the objectives of the institution. Most foundations and endowments are established with the intent of having perpetual lives. Example 17.1 describes the US$22 billion Yale University endowment's approach to balancing short-term spending needs with ensuring that future generations also benefit from the endowment, and it also shows the £13 billion Wellcome Trust's approach. The investment approach undertaken considers the objectives and constraints of the institution (for example, no tobacco investments for a medical endowment).

SOVEREIGN WEALTH FUNDS   Sovereign wealth funds (SWFs) are government-owned investment funds, of which many are very sizable. For example, the largest SWF, managed by Abu Dhabi Investment Authority, is funded with oil revenues that amounted to US$627 billion[4] as of March 2009.

---

[1] Acharya and Dimson (2007).

[2] See www.insead.com/campaign/endowment/index.cfm.

[3] See www.wellcome.ac.uk/Investments/History-and-objectives/index.htm.

[4] SWF Institute (www.Swfinstitute.org/funds.php).

Some funds have been established to invest revenues from finite natural resources (e.g., oil) for the benefit of future generations of citizens. Others manage foreign exchange reserves or other assets of the state. Some funds are quite transparent in nature—disclosing their investment returns and their investment holdings—whereas relatively little is known about the investment operations of others.

Table 17.1 summarizes how investment needs vary across client groups. In some cases, generalizations are possible. In others, needs vary by client.

Steps in the Portfolio Management Process

In the previous section we discussed the different types of investment management clients and the distinctive characteristics and needs of each. The following steps in the investment process are critical in the establishment and management of a client's investment portfolio.

- The Planning Step
    - Understanding the client's needs.
    - Preparation of an investment policy statement (IPS).
- The Execution Step
    - Asset allocation.
    - Security analysis.
    - Portfolio construction.
- The Feedback Step
    - Portfolio monitoring and rebalancing.
    - Performance measurement and reporting.

STEP 1: THE PLANNING STEP   The first step in the investment process is to understand the client's needs (objectives and constraints) and develop an investment policy statement (IPS). A portfolio manager is unlikely to achieve appropriate results for a client without a prior understanding of the client's needs. The IPS is a written planning document that describes the client's investment objectives and the constraints that apply to the client's portfolio. The IPS may state a benchmark—such as a particular rate of return or the performance of a particular market index—that can be used in the feedback stage to assess the performance of the investments and whether objectives have been met. The IPS should be reviewed and updated regularly (for example, either every three years or when a major change in a client's objectives, constraints, or circumstances occurs).

STEP 2: THE EXECUTION STEP   The next step is for the portfolio manager to construct a suitable portfolio based on the IPS of the client. The portfolio execution step consists of first deciding on a target asset allocation, which determines the weighting of asset classes to be included in the portfolio. This step is followed by the analysis, selection, and purchase of individual investment securities.

Asset Allocation   The next step in the process is to assess the risk and return characteristics of the available investments. The analyst forms economic and capital market expectations that can be used to form a proposed allocation of asset classes suitable for the client. Decisions that need to be made in the asset allocation of the portfolio

TABLE 17.1 Summary of Investment Needs by Client Type

Client	Time Horizon	Risk Tolerance	Income Needs	Liquidity Needs
Individual investors	Varies by individual	Varies by individual	Varies by individual	Varies by individual
Defined benefit pension plans	Typically long-term	Typically quite high	High for mature funds; low for growing funds	Typically quite low
Endowments and foundations	Very long-term	Typically high	To meet spending commitments	Typically quite low
Banks	Short-term	Quite low	To pay interest on deposits and operational expenses	High to meet repayment of deposits
Insurance companies	Short-term for property and casualty; long-term for life insurance companies	Typically quite low	Typically low	High to meet claims
Investment companies	Varies by fund	Varies by fund	Varies by fund	High to meet redemptions

include the distribution between equities, fixed income securities, and cash; sub-asset classes, such as corporate and government bonds; and geographical weightings within asset classes. Alternative assets—such as real estate, commodities hedge funds, and private equity—may also be included.

Economists and market strategists may set the top down view on economic conditions and broad market trends. The returns on various asset classes are likely to be affected by economic conditions; for example, equities may do well when economic growth has been unexpectedly strong whereas bonds may do poorly if inflation increases. The economists and strategists will attempt to forecast these conditions.

Top down—A top-down analysis begins with consideration of macroeconomic conditions. Based on the current and forecasted economic environment, analysts evaluate markets and industries with the purpose of investing in those that are expected to perform well. Finally, specific companies within these industries are considered for investment.

Bottom up—Rather than emphasizing economic cycles or industry analysis, a bottom-up analysis focuses on company-specific circumstances, such as management quality and business prospects. It is less concerned with broad economic trends than is the case for top down analysis, but instead focuses on company specifics.

SECURITY ANALYSIS   The top-down view can be combined with the bottom up insights of security analysts who are responsible for identifying attractive investments in particular market sectors. They will use their detailed knowledge of the companies and industries they cover to assess the expected level and risk of the cash flows that each security will produce. This knowledge allows the analysts to assign a valuation to the security and identify preferred investments.

PORTFOLIO CONSTRUCTION   The portfolio manager will then construct the portfolio, taking account of the target asset allocation, security analysis, and the client's requirements as set out in the IPS. A key objective will be to achieve the benefits of diversification (i.e., to avoid putting all the eggs in one basket). Decisions need to be taken on asset class weightings, sector weightings within an asset class, and the selection and weighting of individual securities or assets. The relative importance of these decisions on portfolio performance depends at least in part on the investment strategy selected; for example, consider an investor that actively adjusts asset sector weights in relation to forecasts of sector performance and one who does not. Although all decisions have an effect on portfolio performance, the asset allocation decision is commonly viewed as having the greatest impact.

Table 17.2 shows the broad portfolio weights of the endowment funds of Yale University and the University of Virginia as of June 2008. As you can see, the portfolios have a heavy emphasis on such alternative assets as hedge funds, private equity, and real estate—Yale University particularly so.

Risk management is an important part of the portfolio construction process. The client's risk tolerance will be set out in the IPS, and the portfolio manager must make

TABLE 17.2   Endowment Portfolio Weights, June 2008

Asset Class	Yale University Endowment	University of Virginia Endowment
Public equity	25.3%	53.6%
Fixed income	4.0	15.0
Private equity	20.2	19.6
Real assets (e.g., real estate)	29.3	10.1
Absolute return (e.g., hedge funds)	25.1	8.1
Cash	23.9	26.5
Portfolio value	US$22.9bn	US$5.1bn

Note: The negative cash positions indicate that at the point the figures were taken, the funds had net borrowing rather than net cash.
Sources: "2008 Yale Endowment Annual Report" (p. 2): www.yale.edu/investments/Yale_Endowment_08.pdf, "University of Virginia Investment Management Company Annual Report 2008" (p. 16): http://uvm-web.eservices. virginia.edu/public/reports/FinancialStatements_2008.pdf.

sure the portfolio is consistent with it. As noted previously, the manager will take a diversified portfolio perspective: What is important is not the risk of any single investment, but rather how all the investments perform as a portfolio.

The endowments just shown are relatively risk tolerant investors. Contrast the asset allocation of the endowment funds with the portfolio mix of the insurance companies shown in Table 17.3. You will notice that the majority of the insurance assets are invested in fixed income investments, typically of high quality. Note that

TABLE 17.3   Insurance Company Portfolios, December 2008

Asset Classes	MassMutual Portfolio	MetLife Portfolio
Bonds	56.4%	58.7%
Preferred and common shares	2.2	1.0
Mortgages	15.1	15.9
Real estate	1.3	2.4
Policy loans	10.6	3.0
Partnerships	6.4	1.9
Other assets	4.5	5.3
Cash	3.5	11.8

Asset class definitions: Bonds—Debt instruments of corporations and governments as well as various types of mortgage- and asset-backed securities; Preferred and Common Shares—Investments in preferred and common equities; Mortgages—Mortgage loans secured by various types of commercial property as well as residential mortgage whole loan pools; Real Estate—Investments in real estate; Policy Loans—Loans by policyholders that are secured by insurance and annuity contracts; Partnerships—Investments in partnerships and limited liability companies; Cash—Cash, short-term investments, receivables for securities, and derivatives. Cash equivalents have short maturities (less than one year) or are highly liquid and able to be readily sold.
Sources: "MassMutual Financial Group 2008 Annual Report" (p. 26): www.massmutual.com/mmfg/docs/annual_report/index.html, "MetLife 2008 Annual Report" (p. 83): http://investor.metlife.com/phoenix.zhtml?c=121171&p=irol-reportsannual.

the Yale University portfolio has only 4 percent invested in fixed income, with the remainder invested in such growth assets as equity, real estate, and hedge funds. This allocation is in sharp contrast to the Massachusetts Mutual Life Insurance Company (MassMutual) portfolio, which is over 80 percent invested in bonds, mortgages, loans, and cash—reflecting the differing risk tolerance and constraints (life insurers face regulatory constraints on their investments).

The portfolio construction phase also involves trading. Once the portfolio manager has decided which securities to buy and in what amounts, the securities must be purchased. In many investment firms, the portfolio manager will pass the trades to a buy side trader—a colleague who specializes in securities trading—who will contact a stockbroker or dealer to have the trades executed.

STEP 3: THE FEEDBACK STEP   Finally, the feedback step assists the portfolio manager in rebalancing the portfolio due to a change in, for example, market conditions or the circumstances of the client.

Portfolio Monitoring and Rebalancing   Once the portfolio has been constructed, it needs to be monitored and reviewed and the composition revised as the security analysis changes because of changes in security prices and changes in fundamental factors. When security and asset weightings have drifted from the intended levels as a result of market movements, some rebalancing may be required. The portfolio may also need to be revised if it becomes apparent that the client's needs or circumstances have changed.

Performance Measurement and Reporting   Finally, the performance of the portfolio must be measured, which will include assessing whether the client's objectives have been met. For example, the investor will wish to know whether the return requirement has been achieved and how the portfolio has performed relative to any benchmark that has been set. Analysis of performance may suggest that the client's objectives need to be reviewed and perhaps changes made to the IPS. As we will discuss in the next section, there are numerous investment products that clients can use to meet their investment needs. Many of these products are diversified portfolios that an investor can purchase.

Reference

Acharya, Shanta, and Elroy Dimson. 2007. *Endowment Asset Management: Investment Strategies in Oxford and Cambridge.* New York: Oxford University Press.

Part II Strategic Asset Allocation

Strategic asset allocation is the principal determinant of long-term portfolio performance. It lies at the heart of the investment strategy of most institutional investors, such as endowments and pension funds. The practice is also becoming more widely used for private client portfolios and retail investors.

Strategic asset allocation specifies a static mix of asset classes that is intended to be a long-term plan for an investor. It is based on long-run relationships among asset class returns and the behavior of the investor's liabilities.

In their landmark paper, Brinson, Hood, and Beebower (1986) captured the importance of asset allocation policy, concluding that a static strategic asset allocation explained more than 90 percent of the variation of a fund's total return. Active investment decisions—security selection and market timing—were of less significance.

The importance of strategic asset allocation is also underscored by its role as a behavioral discipline. It provides an anchor against the temptation to follow short-term trends in market returns, which may harm the portfolio's long-term desired risk and return characteristics.

In this section, we discuss the theories behind strategic asset allocation, pitfalls, and practical approaches to successfully conducting and establishing a suitable strategic asset allocation.

Guiding Principles

Harry Markowitz is the founder of modern asset allocation principles. His work on portfolio theory—motivated in the 1940s and first published in 1952—set out the mathematics of diversification and demonstrated, both intuitively and analytically, that investors who diversify achieve better long-term investment performance results than those who do not.

Markowitz argued that investors should be concerned with only two elements of their portfolio: its expected return, as measured by the mean rate of return, and its risk, as measured by the standard deviation or variance of the mean rate of return. His model, which is now called modern portfolio theory (MPT) and which would eventually win him a Nobel Prize, provided new insight into why and how diversification works. This, in turn, led to a new understanding of how stocks are priced individually as well as how they are priced relative to a market portfolio.

Two generations of analysts, finance professors, finance students, security advisors, financial planners, and financial marketers have learned and applied the fundamental principle of diversification to modern asset allocation techniques.

The mean-variance model remains at the heart of MPT and over the past 50 years has become the dominant asset allocation approach. The mean-variance model requires three sets of inputs for the asset classes that make up a given opportunity set: returns, standard deviations, and correlations. The model results in an efficient frontier, where each point on the frontier represents the risk and return of an *efficient* asset allocation. Efficient asset allocations maximize expected return for a given level of risk or, equivalently, minimize risk for a given level of return.

Key Steps

The key steps involved in establishing the strategic asset allocation are shown in Figure 17.1 and discussed further. The four key steps involve:

1. **Making capital market assumptions.** This step involves establishing the forward-looking assumptions for the asset classes being considered. Assumptions include return, risk, and correlation expectations. The asset classes of first choice are usually cash, bonds, and stocks.

Type	Risk Type	Decision
Fund	Governance risk	Governance
Strategy	Asset allocation risk	Fund's purpose
		Strategic asset allocation
	Timing risk	Tactical asset allocation
	Structural risk	Asset class structure
Implement	Manager risk	Manager selection
		Security selection
	Implementation risk	Execution
Review	Monitoring risk	Review and monitor

Assumptions	
Candidate portfolios	Traditional assets
	Alternative assets

Asset–liability modeling
Choose portfolio

FIGURE 17.1   Steps Involved in Strategic Asset Allocation

2. **Identifying candidate portfolios.** Given a set of expected returns, standard deviations, and correlations for various asset classes, it is possible to construct various efficient portfolios of differing asset mixes and to measure the risk and return characteristics of each of those portfolios. These efficient portfolios of differing asset mixes are candidate portfolios for consideration in meeting investor objectives.
3. **Modeling assets and liabilities.** This step involves understanding how the investor's liabilities behave and how they interact with various candidate portfolios. This modeling is usually undertaken with simulation techniques, due to potentially complex interactions between assets and liabilities. This modeling exercise is fundamental; it is the process by which investors evaluate the risk and reward of alternative asset portfolios.
4. **Choosing a suitable portfolio.** This step involves evaluating the outcomes of the asset-liability modeling in meeting investor investment objectives. Doing this helps investors evaluate various asset portfolios tailored to meet their obligations. The nature of an investor's objectives will differ from those of others, as will the key metrics used to assess various asset portfolios. For example, endowments and foundations focus on their distribution or spending commitments.

Capital Market Assumptions

Forecasts of asset class returns are important in developing an asset allocation. The key inputs into any asset allocation are the expected returns, risks (or volatilities), and their interrelationship (or correlations). In essence, these forecasts describe an investor's beliefs about the future behavior of the capital markets. These beliefs, along with the investor's attitude about risk and financial situation, determine what asset allocation has the best chance of achieving the investor's investment objectives.

While the exact magnitude of any of the inputs may be subject to argument by different investors, the long-term relationships of the major asset classes are well understood and their long-term properties are known with relative confidence. Most investors would agree with these expectations:

- Equities are expected to have higher returns than bonds. Bonds are expected to have higher returns than cash.
- Equities are more volatile than bonds. Bonds are more volatile than cash.
- Asset class returns are related but not perfectly so. Equities, bonds, and cash are likely to be uncorrelated enough that combinations of any of them will diversify risk at a portfolio level.

ASSET CLASS RETURN RELATIONSHIPS The relationships between the major asset class expectations can be written as follows:

- Cash return = Real expected cash return + Expected inflation rate
- Government bond return = Cash return + Duration risk premium
- Investment-grade bond return = Government bond return + Credit risk premium
- Equity return = Government bond return + Equity risk premium

The time horizon over which returns are required is important. It is usual to assume a 5- to 10-year return horizon in setting capital market assumptions.

Standard deviations and correlations of each asset class are usually estimated from historical data.

GLOBAL ASSET CLASS ASSUMPTIONS A plausible set of long-term global asset class assumptions for a U.S.-based investor may look like that presented next (see Table 17.4). The assumptions presented are broadly in line with the capital market assumptions of several leading investment managers and investment consultants.

- Expected inflation rate of 2.5 percent per annum (p.a.)
- Real expected cash return of 1.5 percent p.a.
- Duration risk premium of 1 percent p.a.
- Credit risk premium of 1 percent p.a.
- Equity risk premium of 3.5 percent p.a.

TABLE 17.4   Long-Term, Global Asset Class Assumptions for U.S.-Based Investor

Asset Class	Expected Return (% p.a.)	Volatility (% p.a.)	Inflation	Cash	Global Government Bonds	Global Aggregate Bonds*	Global Equity
Inflation	2.5	1.5	1.0				
Cash	4.0	2.0	0.7	1.0			
Global government bonds	5.0	4.0	0.4	0.5	1.0		
Global aggregate bonds*	5.5	5.0	0.5	0.6	0.7	1.0	
Global equity	8.5	16.0	0.1	0.2	0.1	0.1	1.0

*Assumed to be an index of government and investment-grade bonds, with a 50/50 mix.

EQUITY RISK PREMIUM   The key parameter in almost every asset allocation study is the equity risk premium. It deserves a detailed treatment, since the choice between equities and bonds is the primary determinant of long-term portfolio performance. The equity risk premium assumption is discussed from both a historical and a fundamental perspective.

Historical Perspective   There has been extensive research into the equity risk premium by academics and practitioners over the past 15 years (see Cornell 1999). The best-known studies of long-term equities returns are those by Ibbotson Associates (2000) in the United States and Barclays Capital (2001) in the United Kingdom. These studies suggest that equities outperformed bonds by 5 percent to 6 percent p.a. However, the most extensive review and interpretation of the historical evidence is the study by Dimson, Marsh, and Staunton (2002). In that study, the authors produced a very comprehensive historical record of equities, bonds, and cash returns for many countries back to 1900. Their findings are summarized next.

- **Company survivorship.** The authors carefully reconstructed the indexes to avoid survivorship bias. Historical records tend to omit the performance of companies that did not survive, yet these companies would have been part of an investor's portfolio, had the investor held the index over that period. The Dimson et al. study suggests that the Ibbotson and Barclays equity risk premium estimates are about 2 percent p.a. too high due to company survivorship bias.
- **Country survivorship.** Long-term historical studies tend to focus on country stock markets that by definition are those that survived. The United States was the most successful economy over the twentieth century. Relying solely on past U.S. equity performance as a guide to the future may overstate expectations for equity returns. The U.S. economy transitioned from emerging to developed over the twentieth century, and this is a one-time effect on historical returns.
- **Starting dates.** The Dimson et al. start date of 1900 for country index returns can be contrasted with Ibbotson's start date of 1926 and Barclays' start date of 1919. The start dates for the latter two studies were when equity markets were relatively low, creating a slight upward bias in their returns.

Dimson et al.'s study concludes that a more reasonable estimate of the equity risk premium should be about 3 percent to 3.5 percent p.a. relative to bonds.

Fundamental Perspective: The Economics of Risk   There are strong prima facie reasons to believe that equities can be expected to outperform bonds. The return on bonds is stable and has a high degree of security. Equity holders have no legally mandated cash flows owed to them. Dividends that are paid are derived from residual earnings after higher calls on a company's income have been met. Shareholders are the lowest rung in the capital structure in the event the company's fortunes decline. It is clearly more risky to hold equities than cash. Rationally, an investor would do this only if a compensating risk premium could be expected.

Companies are willing to pay the premium to investors. Equity capital is valuable for companies. It allows them to undertake long-term, risky projects with a lower chance of bankruptcy. Equity capital is one of the most flexible sources of capital for a company and involves no refinancing risk. As a result, companies would pay for equity capital in the form of a higher return than bonds.

Fundamental Perspective: Academic Research Recent academic research uses a consumption-based approach to estimate what a reasonable level of the equity risk premium should be. The line of thinking is discussed next.

- Investments are made to preserve or increase purchasing power by deferring consumption.
- The risk of investing in an asset can be assessed by how that investment would impact the riskiness of future consumption.
- The more an asset is correlated with consumption, the more risky it is to an investor because it will pay off more when consumption is high and less when consumption is low. Assets that are more correlated with future consumption demand higher premiums to induce investors to hold them.
- By contrast, an asset that has a low, or negative, correlation with future consumption would tend to pay off well when consumption is falling and vice versa. Such assets are less risky to an investor and therefore command lower premiums.
- These academic studies estimate that the equity risk premium should be around 1 percent.

Fundamental Perspective: Fundamental Lens on Historical Data The dividend discount model is a well-established approach to valuing equities and the basis for many recent studies of equity risk premium. Cornell (1999), for example, provides a good explanation and summary of the research.

The implication of the model is that stock values are a function of three factors:

1. Proportion of earnings paid out as dividends
2. Projected real growth rate of company earnings
3. Suitable rate at which the market discounts future dividends (the required real rate of return)

Rearranging the dividend discount model implies that the required real return on stocks should equal the dividend yield plus the expected annual growth of real earnings. This is shown in the next equation.

$$\text{Required real return} = \text{Dividend yield} + \text{Growth of real earnings}$$

To estimate the current required real return, we consider two components: dividend yield and growth of real earnings.

A reliable long-run real earnings growth series is available for the United States. From about 1926 to today, real earnings growth has been volatile but trendless, averaging 3.8 percent p.a. In contrast, the dividend yield has been steadily trending downward over the same period, consistent with a decline in the required real return and resulting equity price increases. Over the same period, the trend dividend yield stood at 2 percent (figures estimated from data available from Professor Robert Shiller at www.econ.yale .edu/~shiller/data.htm).

The sum of the trend values of the dividend yield and real earnings growth is a good measure of the required real return on equity. Therefore, a required real equity return of 2.0 percent + 3.8 percent = 5.8 percent. We round this to 6 percent. Using the required real equity return as the forecast of future real equity return, we can estimate the future nominal equity return. If we assume the long-run inflation rate is 2.5 percent p.a., then the expected future nominal equity return would be 8.5 percent.

Another perspective on the historical record is provided by Bogle (1991, 2011). He analyzed the sources of U.S. equity returns by decomposing returns into two parts: investment return and speculative return. The investment return is the dividend yield (at the beginning of the period) and the annual rate of earnings growth. The speculative return is the change in the price investors are willing to pay for each dollar of earnings—that is, the change in the price-to-earnings (P/E) ratio. Speculative return is sometimes positive—it adds to the investment return—and sometimes negative—detracting from the investment return.

Simply put, the total return is equal to the initial dividend yield plus earnings growth plus the speculative return.

Bogle (2011) shows that in the 11 decades to 2010, the average total annual return on U.S. equities was 9.1 percent p.a. The sources of returns that contributed to this annual average return were:

- Average dividend yield of 4.5 percent
- Average annual earnings growth of 4.3 percent
- Average speculative return of 0.3 percent

The investment return for the 11 decades was 8.8 percent p.a. compared to the total equity return of 9.1 percent. The sources of return are consistent with the returns achieved.

Based on the current estimates for the United States, Bogle (2011) finds that the dividend yield is about 2.3 percent and corporate earnings growth is 6 percent p.a. Using both as estimates of the future, the investment return component of equities is around 8 percent p.a. for the next 10 years. For the speculative return component, equities are trading at about 20 times earnings, slightly higher than the longer-term average of 17 times earnings (using the Shiller 10-year P/E ratio). Bogle assumes the P/E ratio may fall to 18 over the next 10 years. If so, then the price change would be a fall of 10 percent over 10 years, or 1 percent p.a. A reasonable 10-year expected return on equities is about 7 percent p.a.

What about the return on bonds? The 10-year Treasury yield at the time of Bogle's (2011) discussion was 2 percent p.a., and the return on investment-grade bonds was 3.5 percent p.a.

The equity risk premium is expected to be 3.5 percent p.a. over investment-grade bonds and 5 percent p.a. over Treasury bonds for the next decade.

Conclusion   Based on the Dimson et al. (2002) study of global equities and the fundamental approaches of Bogle and the dividend discount model for U.S. equities, a reasonable expectation for the global equity risk premium is about 3 percent to 3.5 percent over government bonds. This assumes the U.S. expected equity risk premium is a good approximation for the global equity risk premium.

BONDS   To understand the differences between an investor's domestic fixed income market and the global fixed income market, it is necessary to know what the sources of return are to fixed income investments.

When a fixed income security is purchased, an investor does so at the current market yield or yield to maturity. This is the interest rate over the life of the security at which future coupon payments and repayment of the face value at maturity are discounted to arrive at the purchase price.

This market yield is made up of several components:

- **Term structure of risk-free rates.** This is the set of cash rates across varying maturities.
- **Premium for duration.** Investing in longer term to maturity securities usually requires a higher yield to compensate for reinvestment risk and the longer time commitment.
- **Premium for credit risk.** Securities vary according to the risk of the borrower defaulting on the promised obligation. This risk should be reflected in the security's credit rating. A higher return is required to compensate an investor for an increase in default risk.

The total return generated by investing in a fixed income market can be seen as a sum of all the preceding components over and above the cash rate for that market.

Accessing foreign fixed income markets involves currency risk. Currency movements can greatly affect the return of foreign bonds to a domestic investor, unless these are hedged. The volatility of returns to a domestic investor holding foreign fixed income securities can be greatly reduced by hedging currency risk.

For simplicity, we assume that the domestic investor is faced with investing in a local fixed income index and a global fixed income index, such as the Barclays Global Aggregate Index (BarCap), hedged into the domestic investor's home currency.

The investor faces two investments:

1. Domestic fixed income return = Domestic cash return + Domestic duration premium
2. Global hedged fixed income return = Domestic cash return + Global duration premium

If corporate credit securities are included, the investor should expect to add the credit premium for those securities in the domestic market and the global market. Differing illiquidity premiums would also be added.

Therefore, the relative expected returns for domestic and global fixed income markets will be affected by the factors just outlined: differences in duration, credit quality, and liquidity. An additional factor when investing in global fixed income markets is the greater diversification offered by the greater number of securities.

Candidate Portfolios

COMBINING ASSET CLASSES TO FORM PORTFOLIOS   The evaluation of candidate portfolios involves the evaluation of alternative asset allocations. It is common to employ mean-variance optimization procedures, an approach developed by Harry Markowitz in 1952. It is the most widely employed approach for two main reasons: its relative simplicity and intuitive appeal.

Mean-variance optimization takes three inputs: expected returns, volatilities, and correlations among all assets considered. Given a set of expected returns, standard deviations, and correlations, it is possible to construct various portfolios of differing asset mixes and to measure the risk and return characteristics of each of those portfolios. The results of this process yield a set of portfolios that differ in terms of risk and return. This set of portfolios, each representing the best possible combination of asset mixes, is called the "efficient frontier." In other words, an efficient frontier shows the combinations of investments with the highest return per unit of risk. Conversely, a portfolio may be considered inefficient if one (or both) of these scenarios exist:

- A higher expected return can be achieved without taking on any additional risk.
- The same expected return can be achieved at a lower level of risk.

Two Asset Classes   In the simplest case, we can consider two asset classes (or assets). If investors expect that the price of equities will fall when the price of bonds increases, they can utilize this knowledge to reduce part of the risk attached to the individual asset through diversification. When the portfolio is divided between equities and bonds, the risk is diversified at the same time. Diversification means that the investor can obtain a larger return per risk unit. An investor can choose either to reduce risk or to obtain increased returns at the same level of risk. Figure 17.2 illustrates this.

By combining the two investment opportunities, investors will be able to obtain all return/risk combinations on the straight line between bonds and equities. But if the markets fluctuate and the development of the two investments is not identical, investors will get a diversification benefit. In the figure, the risk and return level obtained is found in the area to the northwest of all the combinations that would be obtained by making both investments. The extent to which the efficient frontier extends to the northwest is determined by the correlation between the two assets. If

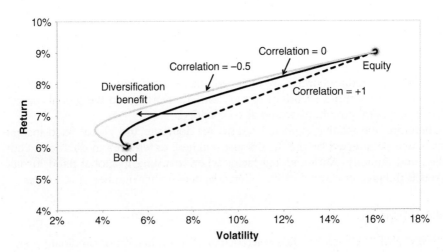

FIGURE 17.2   Efficient Frontier

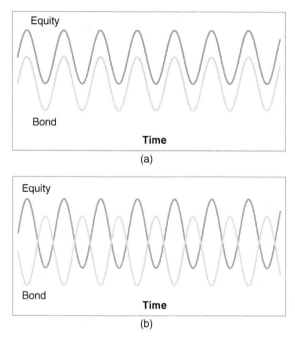

FIGURE 17.3　Correlation of Returns: (a) Positively Correlated; (b) Negatively Correlated

equities and bonds have good and bad returns at the same time, they will be more correlated than when they have good and bad returns at different times. Figure 17.3a and b illustrate this relationship. In Figure 17.3a, bonds and equities have both good and bad performance at the same time; they are positively correlated. In Figure 17.3b, bonds and equities have good and bad performance at different times; they are negatively correlated.

The effect of this correlation on the risk-return trade-off when equities and bonds are combined is shown in Figure 17.2. If both equities and bonds are perfectly positively correlated, the risk-return trade-off is represented by the dashed black line. The more the correlation reduces, the better the possible risk-return trade-off becomes. If both equities and bonds are uncorrelated (a correlation of zero), then the risk-return trade-off is represented by the black solid line. If both equities and bonds are negatively correlated (a correlation of −0.5 in our example), the risk-return trade-off is represented by the gray solid line. The risk-return trade-off would be further improved if the correlation becomes perfectly negatively correlated.

Many Asset Classes　If more than two asset classes are combined, the calculation of the efficient frontier becomes more complex. Markowitz's contribution was the solution to this problem. It is an optimization problem that seeks to maximize the expected return for any given level of risk, given the asset classes' assumptions. Figure 17.4 shows the efficient frontier given five asset classes: U.S. cash, U.S. bonds, international bonds, international equities, and U.S. equities.

The widespread availability of optimization software and cheap computing power have made the calculation of efficient frontiers trivial.

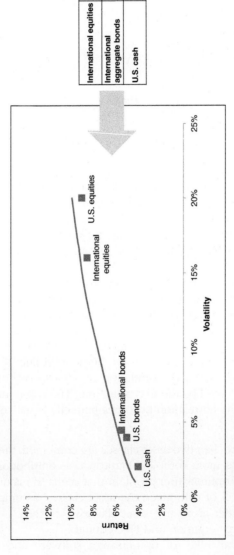

	Expected Return	Volatility	Distribution
International equities	8.5%	16.0%	
International aggregate bonds	5.5%	5.0%	
U.S. cash	4.0%	2.0%	

FIGURE 17.4 Efficient frontier.

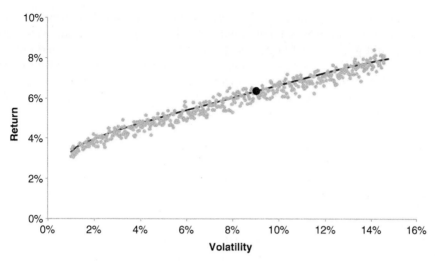

FIGURE 17.5   Efficient Frontier with Parameter Uncertainty

Dangers of Optimization   Even though the efficient frontiers are depicted by thin lines on the figures, they should really be drawn with a thick crayon. The reason is that unless we can predict future returns, a margin of error exists in the estimates of the parameters of assets' return distributions and the correlations between them. Using a solid line conveys a spurious impression of precision. A more realistic depiction is shown in Figure 17.5.

Take the portfolio marked by the solid black circle. It is a portfolio with a unique combination of assets that produces an expected return of 6.35 percent and a standard deviation of returns of 9 percent. A small change to one asset class's expected returns, volatility, and/or correlations with other asset classes can produce a portfolio with a very different mix of assets but a very similar efficient portfolio expected return at the 9 percent standard deviation of returns. To illustrate this further, the exact mix of asset classes of the solid circle is shown in Table 17.5, by the middle column headed "U.S. Equities Expected Return = 8.3%." If we were to estimate the

TABLE 17.5   Efficient Frontier Allocations Based on Small Changes to Inputs

	Optimal Allocation	
Asset Class	U.S. Equities Expected Return = 8.3%	U.S. Equities Expected Return = 8.5%
U.S. equities	23%	28%
International equities	32%	28%
U.S. bonds	22%	22%
International bonds	22%	22%
Cash	0%	0%
Portfolio expected return	6.35%	6.42%
Portfolio standard deviation	9.00%	9.00%

expected return on U.S. equities to be 8.5 percent instead of 8.3 percent, then the allocations to U.S. and international equities would change, leaving the allocations to domestic and international bonds unchanged. The allocation determined by the mean-variance optimizer changes dramatically. At an expected return of 8.3 percent on U.S. equities, the optimal allocation to U.S. and international equities is 23 percent and 32 percent, respectively. However, if the expected return of U.S. equities is 8.5 percent, the optimal allocation to U.S. and international equities becomes 28 percent for each. The change is a shift of 5 percent allocation from international to U.S. equities—a rather substantial shift for a small change in the expected returns.

In practical terms, 8.3 percent versus 8.5 percent expected returns are indistinguishable. In statistical terms, the margin of error on the estimates means they are unlikely to be significantly different from each other. However, the optimizer treats the estimates with precision and allocates accordingly.

The problem faced by an optimizer can be described by way of analogy. Let us say a person is standing on top of a very flat hill and wants to find the peak. It would be hard to say where the peak is since the entire hilltop is the peak. However, if an optimizer were asked to find the peak, it would find the highest blade of grass on the hilltop. If we were to cut that blade of grass, it would find the next highest blade of grass, which may be at the opposite end of the hilltop. It would find two very different locations as a result. Everywhere on the flat hilltop is the peak, but the optimizer is blind to this. In this sense, optimizers are sometimes referred to as error maximizers (Michaud 1998).

Developing an asset allocation policy is an element to developing a long-term investment strategy. However, the use of such policies is viewed with suspicion by both providers, such as consultants, and the ultimate users, the investors who employ their services. Why? Optimization techniques can be and sometimes are misused. To understand this, let us run through the usual process employed (Ilkiw 2003).

- **Suitable asset class assumptions are estimated.** These are inputs into the optimizer. They require expected returns, volatilities, and correlations among asset classes. The typical starting point is historical data combined with a simple assumption that the past will repeat itself, thereby justifying the use of historical data as forecasts. Not all users apply such a simplistic approach. Some rely on financial theory (such as the well-known capital asset pricing model) to ensure the expected returns are derived from that portion of risk that cannot be diversified away.
- **The optimization is run.** The aim is to find the set of weights that provides the highest return at every level of risk. The weights of underlying asset classes combine to provide the "best," or optimal, portfolio at that level of risk. Of course, the optimizers are sensitive to the inputs. If the output is not as desired, the inputs can be changed to suit. Often only small changes are required to deliver the "right" results.

Another, more subtle way of achieving the same outcome is to change the number of assets in the optimization. There is no limit to the number of types of assets that can be optimized. For example, rather than using international equities in the optimization, we can put every country equity market that makes up the international equities asset class into the optimizer. The number of ways (degrees of freedom) to achieve the desired asset allocation mix has increased vastly.

The excessive flexibility in the inputs, number of assets, and outcomes can undermine the usefulness of asset allocation studies only if such studies are used to simply confirm an already desired asset allocation policy.

The real usefulness of asset allocation studies lies in their ability to enable the investor to explore:

- Whether the input assumptions are reasonable and believable in justifying a desired allocation.
- Whether a more complex allocation (which includes active management, hedge funds, private equity, etc.) is expected to perform better than the less complicated alternative comprised of broad market, low-cost market index exposures.

Dealing with Uncertain Inputs The central issue is how best to deal with the uncertainty, or differing degrees of confidence, in the inputs used. There are a number of ways to deal with this, but the two effective ways are discussed next.

1. **Use constraints.** For example, set maximum allocations to any particular asset or asset class, or prevent the use of short selling.
2. **Use resampling techniques.** Such techniques explicitly introduce uncertainty around the estimates of expected return, standard deviation, and correlation into the optimization process using simulation analysis. See Michaud (1998).

These approaches have their own issues, however. The use of constraints implicitly assumes that the user knows what asset allocation is suitable. The answer is known, the constraints are set, and the optimization corresponds to the desired outcome. Constraints can be used to effectively deliver the desired answers.

Resampling techniques, however, are very complicated and elaborate ways of dealing with uncertainty. The degree of expertise required puts these techniques out of reach of many people.

Uncertainty Differs by Investment All estimates of returns and risks for any investments are subject to uncertainty, but some are more prone to risks than others.

For the traditional asset classes, such as equities, bonds, and cash, there is broad consensus about their long-term relationships. They have been studied extensively across many years and countries. Broadly, the long-term relationships can be summarized in this way:

- Equities are expected to outperform bonds, and bonds are expected to outperform cash.
- Equities are more volatile than bonds, and bonds are more volatile than cash.
- The behavior of equities, bonds, and cash is sufficiently uncorrelated to provide diversification.

We are likely to have more confidence in understanding the nature of traditional asset classes and hence the future long-term performance characteristics. Greater confidence should lead to greater weightings into traditional asset classes in any asset allocation mix.

The understanding we can have in many other investment opportunities is less than for the traditional asset classes. Their behavior cannot be modeled with the same degree of confidence. These investment opportunities can be split into two groups:

1. Estimating subasset class characteristics. For example, the decision to overweight or underweight any country within an asset class, relative to market weights, or to over- or underweight growth stocks.
2. Illiquid asset classes where the attractiveness relative to listed counterparts depends in large part on the skill of managers—for example, private equity or hedge funds.

Pragmatic Approach   A more pragmatic approach is suggested and involves three steps (Ilkiw 2003):

1. Determine the allocation between equities and bonds.
2. Establish the domestic versus international equity and fixed income splits.
3. Introduce alternative asset classes into the mix.

In the suggested approach, no optimization is employed, so the pitfalls of optimization are eliminated.

Determine Allocation between Equities and Bonds   Starting with equities and bonds rests on three observations:

1. The equities versus bond decision is the key driver of the risk and return characteristics of a portfolio.
2. The broadest, neutral representation of the opportunity within an asset class is something like a global portfolio of securities of an asset class weighted by the market capitalization of each.
3. While all asset classes are subject to uncertainty around forward-looking parameters, some are more uncertain than others. The major asset classes—equities, bonds, and cash—have been studied for many decades. Their long-term relationships are generally well understood, and their statistical parameters can be estimated with reasonable confidence.

If we consider only equities and bonds, we can dispense with the use of optimization altogether. With only two asset classes, the efficient frontier can be drawn easily by simple altering the allocation to each asset class.

If cash is added to the mix, we could use an optimizer for the three asset classes—equities, bonds, and cash—although this would make a difference only for portfolios on the efficient frontier with low volatilities. To illustrate this, we show the optimized efficient frontier with only these three asset classes in Figure 17.6. If we established 11 portfolios, ranging from 100 percent bond allocation to 100 percent equities allocation, this efficient frontier and the optimized efficient frontier comprised of the three asset classes would be very similar, except for portfolios with

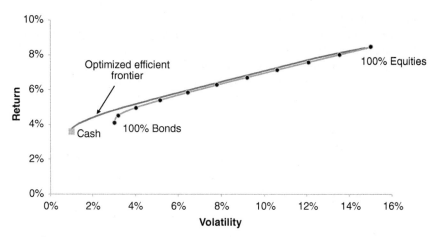

FIGURE 17.6 Efficient Portfolios

low volatilities. In the figure, these portfolios would be those with 90 percent or more allocation to bonds.

Determine Domestic versus International Asset Class Allocations The next step is to determine the domestic versus international split for both the equities and bonds asset classes. The aim is to determine an allocation without the use of current market valuations or investor judgment about the short- to medium-term returns on these asset classes. We suggest an approach next.

Equities The rationale for holdings equities in the first place is to earn the premium they offer over bonds. To improve the chances of earning the equity risk premium, an investor should hold the most diversified exposure to equities. Diversification itself is a strategy, based on risk reduction, and assumes the investor has no foresight about the future returns of any particular market, sector, or country. If, of course, an investor knew with perfect foresight which country or sector would provide the greatest return over a certain time period, then there would be no need to diversify. The investor should simply hold the country or sector that would provide the greatest return.

So what does the most broadly diversified portfolio of equities mean? It is the neutral representation of equities, defined as the market capitalization weight of the global equity market. This holds for all investors, regardless of the domiciled country of their fund.

Market capitalization weighting is a neutral portfolio. Why? The market capitalization of a stock is equal to the price of a stock times the number of shares outstanding. Using this approach assumes that the market has efficiently priced all stocks. The strategic decision is to own stocks according to their market capitalizations. Market capitalization weighting has been criticized for having concentrated holdings in overvalued stocks or markets (see Hsu 2006 and Treynor 2005). The market capitalization weighted index, however, represents the available opportunity set for an equity investor. There are no artificial distortions introduced by the investor's subjective views. Subjective views can still be taken, such as those based on market valuations, although these should be treated as tactical positions and captured as part of the decisions to allocate to active management activities, either security selection or market timing.

Starting with the global market capitalization of equities does not mean investors need hold this equity portfolio in their strategic portfolio. There may be valid reasons for deviating from it and allocating a portion of equities to the domestic market. Some of these reasons are:

- **Taxation differentials.** Differentials may involve different tax treatment of domestic versus international equity investments. For example, there may be withholding taxes on foreign equity investments or preferential dividend tax treatment in the domestic country, such as those with imputation tax systems. Under an imputation tax system, domestic companies are able to pass tax credits to domestic dividends to the extent that the companies have paid corporate tax.
- **Legislation.** There may be legislative restrictions limiting the proportion of international equities that may be held.
- **Cost.** Cost includes the additional transaction, custody, or investment management costs associated with international investment.

Other reasons for holding a domestic allocation to the domestic market, although these are generally noninvestment reasons and are qualitative in nature. Some of these include:

- **Anchoring.** There may be a domestic allocation for historical reasons. This is something of a hangover from previous asset allocations that investors tend to anchor on. Over time, many investors have tended to significantly expand their portfolio internationally, although a domestic bias tends to remain to varying degrees.
- **Home bias.** Investors strongly identify with their own market. Even in markets dominated by a few companies, local investors tend to be biased to their home markets.

Bonds   Investing in any fixed income security is achieved by buying at a particular market yield, or yield to maturity. This is the expected return if the bond is held to maturity, assuming the income (coupon payments) is reinvested at this rate.

Just as for equities, the starting point for bonds is the most diversified fixed income exposure. The BarCap is a widely recognized and good representation of the global fixed income opportunity set.

Any domestic fixed income portfolio would be less diversified than a global fixed income one. As such, the global fixed income portfolio may provide advantages over the domestic fixed income market. Some of these are listed next.

- **Diversification.** There are two main aspects to diversification: greater country choice and a larger universe of issues. The global market provides more than 50 countries to diversify across. The increase in the number of issues for investment will depend on the domicile of the investors. For example, an investor based in the United States would have less improvement in the universe of fixed income by investing internationally than an Australian-based investor. This is because the U.S. fixed income universe is a far greater proportion of the global fixed income universe than Australia's fixed income market.

- **Security selection.** The larger global fixed income universe compared to any domestic universe provides greater opportunities for an active manager to add value.
- **Volatility.** The global fixed income portfolio may actually be less volatile than the domestic portfolio. This is due to the diversification benefits of investing globally, even if the duration of global fixed income is longer than for the domestic market.

When determining the split between global and domestic fixed income, the global fixed income sector should be preferred. Global fixed income is more attractive because of the lower volatility of returns, a larger investment universe, and greater opportunities to add value.

Adding Alternatives to the Mix Alternative asset classes are generally considered to be private equity, private real estate, infrastructure, and hedge funds. They contrast with traditional well-known asset classes, such as listed equities and bonds, in three ways:

1. **Continuous market pricing.** Listed equities and bonds are continuously and freely traded in formal capital markets. Alternative asset classes, however, tend to be illiquid and their assets subject to infrequent pricing. It is usual for pricing to be based on some model-based asset evaluation rather than on an actual trade. Some asset classes, such as real estate, tend to be subject to appraisal-based pricing (which is not based on actual trades) while others, such as venture capital, rely on liquidation-based pricing.
2. **Good-quality historic performance data.** Listed equities and bonds tend to have good-quality, long-term historical data available. (For an example of long-term equities and bond data across many countries, refer to Dimson et al. 2002.) Such data can be the basis to support quantitative analysis of risk and return. Alternative asset classes tend to suffer from shorter data series that do not cover the full range of investments that can constitute the asset class or strategy. Therefore, the reliability of data for risk and return estimates of alternative asset classes tends to be of lower quality than for listed equities and bonds. For example, there are a few data series for the timber asset class. Some extend back to the early 1970s, such as the Hancock U.S. timber series, and others back to the late 1980s, such as the timberland component of the National Council of Real Estate Investment Fiduciaries index. Both series differ in the composition of assets they track.
3. **High-quality benchmarks.** For listed equities and bonds, high-quality benchmarks exist. Good-quality benchmarks display several desirable characteristics:
   - The benchmark represents a strategy an investor can replicate and therefore achieve the returns of the benchmark.
   - The benchmark should include all opportunities that are realistically available to market participants. That is, it should be a good representation of the universe of investments in that asset class.

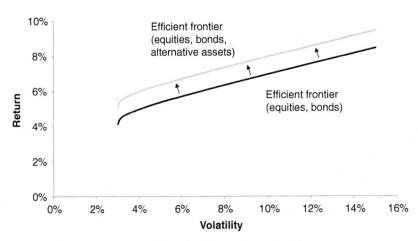

FIGURE 17.7   Efficient Frontiers with and without Alternative Assets

- The benchmark must be constructed in an objective manner such that it has clear, published rules and an open governance structure.
- It should be well recognized and well regarded by market participants and be compiled on an objective basis by an institution of high standing in the market.

Listed asset classes tend to stack up well against these criteria. Alternative assets tend to have benchmarks that represent a portion of the available universe of investments, since investors sometimes voluntarily supply the data. Further, the benchmarks are not reliable for performance reporting purposes. Many are subject to smoothing effects in their performance due in part to the appraisal-based or model-based asset values and in part to index construction methodologies that average these valuations across time. Figure 17.7 shows efficient frontiers with and without alternative assets.

When considering an allocation to alternative investments, the aim is to enhance the efficiency of the portfolio—that is, to improve the trade-off between the risk and expected return of a portfolio. Figure 17.7 shows that efficiency is unequivocally enhanced if substitution of alternative investments for traditional exposures moves a portfolio upward and/or to the left of its existing risk-return position. In other words, efficiency is improved if:

- The expected return is enhanced without increasing risk.
- Risk is mitigated without sacrificing expected return.
- Return is enhanced and risk is reduced.

If introducing alternative investments improves the risk-return trade-off of a portfolio overall, it is worthwhile.

ASSET-LIABILITY MODELING   Asset-liability modeling is a technique for analyzing uncertainty in asset and liability structures simultaneously. It brings together all

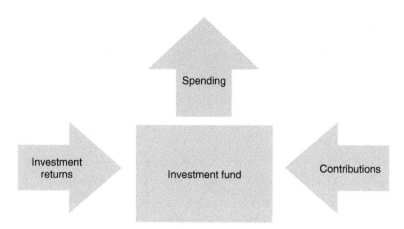

FIGURE 17.8   Fund Revenues and Spending

aspects of the fund's revenue sources and ties them to spending, or distribution, requirements. Figure 17.8 shows this diagrammatically.

The figure illustrates that there are only two revenue sources for funds: contributions raised externally and investment returns generated in the capital markets.

The spending requirements for an institutional fund are tied closely to the fund's purpose. This is where the interests of the beneficiaries are defined, such as the entitlements of the beneficiaries, the competing interests of different types of beneficiaries, and so on.

The investment returns are an important source of revenues for many funds and often dominate the contributions over the fund's life. Therefore, decisions about the investment strategy tend to be the most important decisions for most funds.

Contributions are provided externally. In some funds, the contributions may be prespecified, as with a defined contribution pension plan; in other cases, contributions are one-time only, such as with endowments.

Contributions and investment strategy will tend to interact. For example, with a defined benefit pension plan, the sponsor faces the choice of whether to make contributions in a predictable way or to make contributions as early or as late as possible. Asset-liability modeling helps explore the nature of these interactions over time.

Simulating Outcomes   The interaction between a fund's revenues and its liabilities or spending requirements can be complex. A useful approach to help understand the interactions is to use computer simulation. There is no one way to set up the problem, but doing so requires the input of various parties and some experience in working with such approaches. For example, with a defined benefit plan, the actuary understands how the liabilities behave. This is fundamental since it will be a key yardstick against which to measure the risks and rewards of various asset mixes. The asset consultant understands the behavior of returns from capital markets and provides estimates of the risks and expected returns of various asset classes and strategies. The board of directors or trustees of the plan interact with the plan

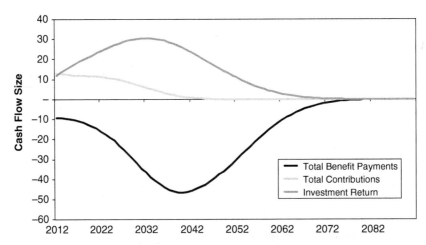

FIGURE 17.9   Hypothetical Pension Plan's Cash Flow Profile

sponsor to understand what contribution rates are realistic and feasible in funding a plan.

Take a hypothetical defined benefit plan's projected cash flow profile, shown in Figure 17.9. The projected benefits payments, employer and employee contributions, and expected investment earnings, based on the plan's current asset mix, are shown every year. There is no risk in the projections—that is, the outcomes that could happen due to investment returns, changes to the liability profile, or changes to the contribution rates that differ from expectations.

Simulations incorporate this risk, or volatility, in the outcomes. Figure 17.10 shows the projected funding ratio over a shorter time frame by the thick black line. The plan starts at an 80 percent funding ratio and is expected to be 110 percent in five years' time. There are other paths the investment returns could take, represented by the other gray lines, based on the current asset mix. At the end of five years, the distribution of outcome can be examined. The distribution is shown to the right, where depth of the distribution shows the frequency of various funding ratios in five years' time.

When evaluating results, it is sometimes easier to visualize the distribution of results using boxplots. Figure 17.11 shows a side-by-side comparison of a boxplot and a probability distribution. The boxplot summarizes the information contained in the probability distribution by showing only five numbers:

1. **95th percentile.** Ninety-five percent of the outcomes lie below this number; 5 percent of the outcomes are equal to or above this number. In the figure 95 percent of the outcomes fall below a funding ratio of 0.97.
2. **75th percentile (upper quartile).** Seventy-five percent of the outcomes lie below this number. In the figure 75 percent of the outcomes fall below a funding ratio of 0.92.
3. **50th percentile (median).** Fifty percent of the outcomes lie below this number. In the figure the median funding ratio is 0.89.

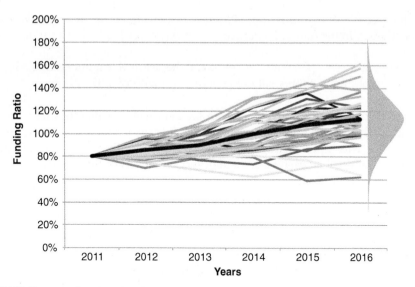

FIGURE 17.10   Simulated Path of Outcomes

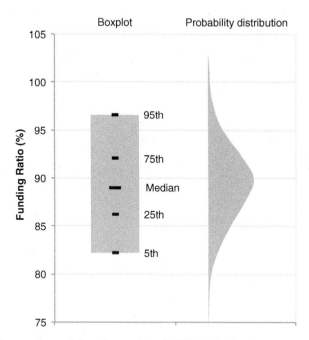

FIGURE 17.11   Comparison of Boxplot and Probability Distribution

4. **25th percentile (lower quartile).** Twenty-five percent of the outcomes lie below this number. In the figure, 25 percent of the outcomes fall below a funding ratio of 0.86.
5. **5th percentile.** Five percent of the outcomes lie below this number. In the figure, 5 percent of the outcomes fall below a funding ratio of 0.82.

The advantage of using boxplots to display information is that they take up less space and are therefore particularly useful for comparing distributions among several groups of data. This is particularly helpful when boards of directors or trustees need to compare a range of alternative asset allocations in terms of the impact of various evaluation criteria that matter.

SELECTING A PORTFOLIO

Performance Measures In order to evaluate the results of an asset-liability study, the relevant performance metrics will need to be established. These metrics should be linked to the investment objectives or may be the investment objectives themselves.

As an example, two commonly used performance measures for defined benefit plans are:

1. **Annualized returns.** The annualized returns expected from different portfolios are the most intuitive evaluation measure for trustees, and even plan members. The limitation of this measure is that it does not provide any information on the liabilities or spending requirements.
2. **Funding ratio.** The ratio of the value of assets to actuarial accrued liabilities is a measure of benefit security in well-funded pension plans. Higher funding ratios result in lower subsequent contributions from the plan sponsor; and low funding ratios trigger increased funding contributions.

Evaluation Horizon It is typical for five-year periods to be used as evaluation horizons. It is not the only horizon used, as the choice depends on the fund being considered and its specific circumstances. Nevertheless, five years have become a common period for trustees and boards both to evaluate fund performance and to conduct their asset allocation studies. Periods less than five years tend to be too short to assess the success or failure of an investment strategy, and longer horizons may become less relevant and sometimes exceed the tenure of trustee and board membership.

Evaluating Results When starting with an investment strategy of traditional equities and bonds, the enhancement to the performance characteristics can be investigated by introducing alternative asset classes and strategies. When introducing lower-confidence alternative assets, a range of plausible investment characteristics for the alternative assets could be explored. It is most useful to consider a base case scenario for the means and volatilities and then evaluate upside and downside scenarios for the estimates.

As an example, we present the results of a hypothetical pension plan and investigate annualized returns and funding ratios over a five-year horizon. (See Figures 17.12 and 17.13.)

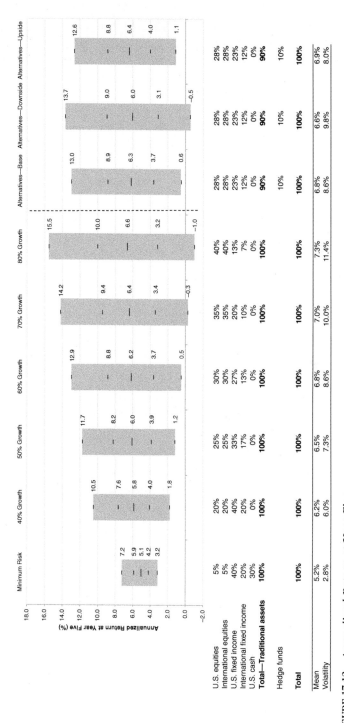

FIGURE 17.12 Annualized Return at Year Five

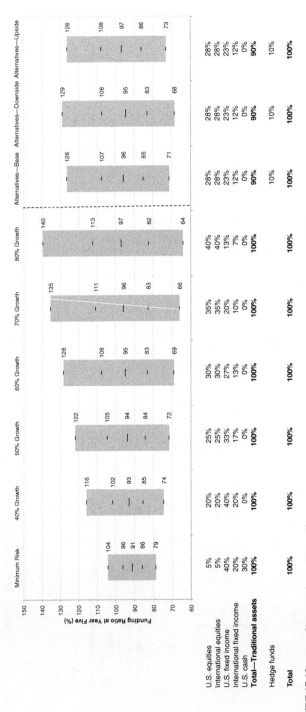

FIGURE 17.13 Funding Ratio at Year Five

Annualized Returns The percentile bars represent five-year annualized returns at the 95th, 75th, 50th, 25th, and 5th percentiles. It is worth noting that the mean is higher than the median as the annualized returns are positively skewed. Below each bar is the asset allocation composition of each portfolio.

The minimum-risk portfolio of 10 percent equity, 60 percent bonds, and 30 percent cash has the narrowest set of returns, ranging from an annualized 3.2 percent return at the 5th percentile to a 7.2 percent return at the 95th percentile. The median is 5.1 percent.

The minimum-risk portfolio is the mix of traditional asset classes that best match the behavior of liabilities.

Minimum-risk portfolios tend to lower the volatility of contributions in the short term at the expense of increasing contributions required in the long term. For this reason, high-return and higher-risk portfolios usually are chosen because they are expected to pay higher long-term returns but at the expense of higher contribution volatility in the short term. For the purpose of this example, we assume that the trustees' level of risk tolerance for shorter-term risk means they opt for the portfolio with 60 percent growth assets.

The choice would be made by evaluating the results of all portfolios composed of traditional assets, from minimum risk to the 80 percent growth assets portfolio.

The 60 percent growth assets portfolio has a higher median return of 6.2 percent. In exchange for the 1.1 percent extra expected return compared to the minimum-risk portfolio, additional risk must be accepted. The minimum-risk portfolio returns range from 3.2 percent to 7.2 percent (5th to 95th percentiles), while the 60 percent growth portfolio returns range from 0.5 percent to 12.9 percent (5th to 95th percentiles). The spread of returns has increased from 4 percent to 12.4 percent.

The consideration of alternative assets would then be assessed relative to the chosen mix of traditional asset classes. That is, alternatives would be added to 60 percent growth portfolio under varying assumptions about their likely future prospects. The degree to which the portfolio is likely to be improved would then be evaluated.

In the example, nondirectional hedge funds are added to the 60 percent growth portfolio. An allocation of 10 percent hedge funds is considered, under three scenarios about how hedge funds are expected to perform in the future. Table 17.6 shows the scenarios for nondirectional hedge fund strategies.

Comparing the base case alternative assets scenario with the 60 percent growth portfolio, there is an improvement in the median return, from 6.2 percent to 6.3 percent, with the same level of risk. The base case scenario is where the implementation of the hedge fund program is fair; manager selection and portfolio construction are assumed to be good but not great. If the performance of hedge funds is better described by the downside case than the base case assumptions, there is a small decrease in median returns over the current portfolio but also an increase in risk. In fact, the risk is closer to the 70 percent growth portfolio with returns expected to be closer to the 50 percent growth portfolio. In other words, good implementation of the hedge fund program is required for the future performance to live up to the base case assumptions. Otherwise the portfolio's performance will be harmed through a combined higher risk and lower return.

If the hedge fund program meets the upside case—assumptions that reflect the historical performance of successful hedge fund programs—the expected improvement in performance is substantial (equivalent to the returns of the 70 percent

TABLE 17.6   Scenarios for Nondirectional Hedge Fund Strategies

Scenario	Expected Excess Return above Cash (after Fees)	Volatility	Correlation with Equities	Correlation with Bonds
Upside case Excellent implementation	Same as equities (3.5%)	Lower than equities (10%)	Zero	Zero
Base case Good implementation	Between equities and bonds (2.5%)	Same as equities (16%)	Low (0.3)	Low (0.3)
Downside case Poor implementation	Same as cash (0%)	Higher than equities (20%)	High (0.7)	High (0.7)

growth assets portfolio but with lower risk than the current 60 percent growth portfolio).

Funding Ratios   The overall pattern of the distribution of outcomes is much the same as the figure of the projected annualized returns. The minimum-risk portfolio has the narrowest outcomes, ranging from 79 percent to 104 percent (5th to 95th percentiles). The 60 percent growth portfolio has a higher median ratio, of 95 percent, with a range of funding ratios from 69 percent to 128 percent (5th to 95th percentiles). Considering the effect of adding hedge funds shifts the distribution of outcomes upward at the base case assumptions, a median funding ratio of 96 percent. The risk of the outcomes is expected to be reduced, ranging from 71 percent to 126 percent (5th to 95th percentiles).

If the performance of hedge funds is better described by the downside case than the base case assumptions, the median funding ratio remains unchanged at 95 percent. However, the risk increases with the range of funding ratios of 68 percent to 129 percent compared to 69 percent to 128 percent (5th to 95th percentiles). It is worth noting the similar 5th and 25th percentile of outcomes between 60 percent growth portfolio and portfolio when adding hedge funds under the downside scenario. This is the result of funding contributions being made, which offset some of the poor investment returns.

If the hedge fund program meets the upside case, the expected improvement in performance is substantial (equivalent to the median funding ratio of the 80 percent growth assets portfolio but with a range of outcomes equivalent to the 50 percent growth portfolio). Very good implementation is expected to materially enhance the funding ratios over a five-year horizon and commensurately lower the pension cost significantly.

Choosing a Suitable Portfolio   The last example serves to illustrate some key points when choosing a suitable portfolio and deciding upon alternative asset classes to incorporate.

- The allocation to growth assets is the most important decision, in terms of risk and return impact, an investor faces. The decision is one that involves deviating from the minimum-risk portfolio. The choice of the proportion to invest in growth assets will depend on the investor's risk tolerance, while considering the likely additional returns and risks that are available.
- The addition of alternative assets, in our example a successful hedge fund program, can enhance the outcomes expected under either the base case or the upside case, with little increase in risk.
- The results from asset-liability modeling can only show that the addition of alternative investments will improve the risk and return characteristics of a portfolio. The modeling exercise cannot prove this will occur. The modeling allows plausible risk and return estimates for alternative investments to be evaluated in terms of the likely impact on the total portfolio. That is, what risk and return expectations are necessary to achieve in order to enhance the overall portfolio.

References

Bogle, J. C. 1991. "Investing in the 1990s." *Journal of Portfolio Management* 17, no. 3 (Spring): 5.

Bogle, J. C. 2011. "The Lessons of History—Endowment and Foundation Investing Today." Presentation of the Vanguard Group before the NMS Investment Management Forum. Washington, DC, September 12. Available at http://johncbogle .com/wordpress/wp-content/uploads/2011/09/NMS-9-12-12.pdf.

Barclays Capital Equity-Gilt Study. 2001. Barclays Capital (ISBN 13: 9780954013509).

Brinson, G., L. Hood, and G. Beebower. 1986. "Determinants of Portfolio Performance." *Financial Analysts Journal* 42, no. 4 (July/August): 39–48.

Cornell, B. 1999. *The Equity Risk Premium.* New York: John Wiley & Sons.

Dimson, E., P. Marsh, and M. Staunton. 2002. *Triumph of the Optimists: 101 Years of Global Investment Returns.* Princeton, NJ: Princeton University Press.

Hsu, J. 2006. "Cap-Weighted Portfolios Are Sub-Optimal Portfolios." *Journal of Investment Management* 4 (3): 44–53.

Ibbotson Associates. 2000. *Stocks, Bonds, Bills and Inflation Year Book.* Chicago: Ibbotson Associates.

Ilkiw, J. H. 2003. "Investment Policies, Processes and Problems in U.S. Public Sector Pension Plans: Some Observations and Solutions from a Practitioner." Presentation to the Public Pension Fund Management World Bank Group. Washington, DC, May 5–7. Available at www1.worldbank.org/finance/assets/images/Ilkiw– investment_policy–doc.pdf.

Markowitz, Harry M. 1952. "Portfolio Selection." *Journal of Finance* 7, no. 1 (March): 77–91.

Michaud, Richard O. 1998. *Efficient Asset Management: A Practical Guide to Stock Portfolio Optimization and Asset Allocation.* Boston: Harvard Business School Press.

Treynor, J. 2005. "Why Market-Valuation-Indifferent Indexing Works." *Financial Analysts Journal* 61 (5): 65–69.

Part III Active versus Passive Management

When structuring an asset class portfolio, the first issue is whether to invest actively or passively. Here we provide a decision framework that discusses active versus passive management as a range of choices available to an investor.

Decision Framework

Table 17.7 provides a number of decisions available to an investor—from passive (index) management through to traditional active management where skilled investment managers are identified to manage securities within an asset class (Ezra and Warren 2010).

Investing in a market-cap-weighted index is the starting point for structuring an asset class. Index products that replicate cap-weighted indexes are usually available at low cost.

MARKET CAPITALIZATION STARTING POINT   William Sharpe, a Nobel Prize–winning financial economist, published an article titled "The Arithmetic of Active Management" (Sharpe 1991). It made a simple point, without any theory or belief in so-called efficient capital markets, that active management is always a zero-sum game. A zero-sum game means the winners win by the amount that the losers lose, before fees. After investment manager fees, brokerage, and other costs are taken into account, active management is a negative-sum game.

For example, consider a portfolio of U.S. common stocks with each stock weighted according to its market capitalization. We call this a cap-weighted market portfolio. A passive investor is anyone whose portfolio of U.S. equities is the cap-weighted market portfolio. An active investor is anyone whose portfolio of U.S. equities is not the cap-weighted portfolio. If we add the portfolio positions of all

TABLE 17.7   Decision Framework

Decision	Action
1. Start with a passive, cap-weighted index.	If reasons for deviating from a cap-weighted index are not suitable, invest in this index.
Reasons to Deviate	
2. **Availability.** Easily replicable index not available.	
3. **Suitability.** Cap-weighted index not consistent with investor objectives.	
4. **Active management believed to outperform.** Types of active management: a. Cap weights are inefficient. b. Market favors active management. c. Skilled managers can be identified.	Alternative to market cap weighting.

Source: Adapted from Ezra and Warren (2010).

passive and active managers in the market, it must be true that this aggregate portfolio is the market portfolio. All passive investors hold the same positions as the market portfolio, so the aggregate positions of all active investors must be the same as the market portfolio.

The implications of this simple point are important.

- Passive investors earn the return on the market portfolio, since this is the portfolio they hold, minus their fees and costs. Active investors, in aggregate, also hold the market portfolio. So they also earn the market return minus their fees and costs. If the fees and costs of active investors are higher than those of passive investors, active investors must in aggregate lose to passive investors. This is the unavoidable arithmetic of active management.
- Appropriate *performance measurement* of active management is essential. The best way to measure a manager's performance is to compare the return to that of a *comparable passive alternative*. That is a benchmark that is a feasible alternative identified *in advance* of the period over which performance is measured. Peer group comparisons are not capitalization weighted and do not represent the full set of active investors.
- The only way to beat the market, apart from luck, is to have special skill. An investor must be much better than all other investors, especially when fees and costs are considered. To win, an investor must, by necessity, take money out of other investors' pockets. This means good or smarter managers will take away from bad managers. Therefore, not everyone can expect to beat the market.

There are, however, three main reasons for considering alternatives to cap-weighted indexes for asset class structuring: availability, suitability, and the ability of active management expected to outperform.

AVAILABILITY   One reason for not investing in a market-capitalization-weighted index for an asset class is where no such index exists. Generally this applies to unlisted asset classes, such as private equity, but some listed asset classes, such as commodities, fit into this category.

For unlisted asset classes, it is common to use peer universes. These are based on surveys of funds in the market and organized by vintage year (year of inception). As these are samples of funds, they do not represent the entire market. Further, the performance metrics rely on appraised value estimates, which are not true market values. It is therefore not possible to create market-capitalization indexes for many unlisted asset classes.

Commodities do not have market capitalizations like equities. However, alternatives exist, such as production-weighted indexes like the S&P Goldman Sachs Commodity Index.

Furthermore, in some asset classes, market-capitalization indexes are available, but replication of the universe of securities in the index is difficult. This includes sub-asset classes, such as emerging market equities and small-cap equities. For example, many of the small-cap equities in the U.S.-based Wilshire 5000 are illiquid. No full-replication index fund exists for the index. A less comprehensive index that is more accessible is needed to enable a manager to buy and sell stocks in the index in adequate volume.

SUITABILITY   Market-capitalization indexes may be inconsistent with an investor's objectives. Three examples, based on Ezra and Warren (2010), are provided next.

1. **Tax reasons.** The tax positions of investors can mean market-capitalization indexes are less than ideal to meet their objectives. For example, investors may be tax advantaged in their home jurisdiction, making a global market-capitalization index potentially inefficient in after-tax risk and return terms. One example is the Australian imputation tax system. Under an imputation tax system, the double taxation of corporate earnings, at the corporate level and then at the personal level, is reduced. This tax benefit makes Australian stocks more attractive than international stocks to Australian investors. A higher weighting to the Australian equities market than implied by a market-capitalization weight in the global index is justified.
2. **Socially responsible investing.** Investors may have objectives that include socially responsible investing. The criteria will be specific to the individual investor and will usually result in specific weights to stocks, sectors, or countries that differ from a market-capitalization-weighted index.
3. **Customized fixed income mandates.** Some investors have specific liabilities, such as the defined liabilities of a pension plan. If the cash flows of those liabilities are explicitly matched, then a broad market-capitalization fixed income index may differ in terms of duration, cash flow patterns, and credit risk. Matching the liabilities is better achieved through bespoke fixed income portfolios.

The suitable alternatives in each case will depend in the investor's specific circumstances and objectives.

ACTIVE MANAGEMENT EXPECTED TO OUTPERFORM   We deal with three possible reasons to expect active management to outperform a passive, market-capitalization-weighted index.

Cap-Weighted Index Considered Inefficient   An investor's beliefs about the suitability of a market-capitalization index and its inefficiency may provide a reason to construct an alternative approach.

Equities   In recent years, alternative approaches to cap-weighting within equities have been proposed. The approaches claim to offer better risk/return characteristics than a cap-weighted index. Many of the approaches are referred to as non-market-capitalization indexes. Some approaches are discussed next.

Low Volatility and Minimum Variance   Investors have recently become interested in low-volatility and minimum-variance strategies because historically they have displayed these characteristics:

- **Lower volatility.** Volatility as measured by the standard deviation of returns is generally around 30 percent lower than the comparable market-capitalization broad market index for a range of risk models and optimization techniques. For example, the MSCI Minimum Variance Index has produced 30 percent lower volatility than the MSCI World Index from 1995 to 2007 (Nielsen and Aylursubramaniar 2008). For U.S. equities, volatility has been 25 percent to 30 percent lower than the broad market index, depending on the minimum variance techniques employed (Clarke, de Silva, and Thorley 2006; Thomas and Shapiro 2009).

■ **Similar returns.** Average returns have been similar to, and sometimes even higher than, the broad market index for both U.S. and global equities.
■ **Lower beta.** The beta relative to the broad market index tends to be around 0.7. The minimum variance strategies tend to outperform in falling markets and underperform in rising markets.

The performance of these portfolios is related to three characteristics of the stocks in the portfolio:

1. They tend to have low market betas.
2. They tend to have low total volatilities or low idiosyncratic volatilities (adjusting for the beta component of returns).
3. They tend to be value stocks (with low price-to-book [P/B] ratios).

All of these characteristics have contributed to the historical average return of the portfolio:

■ Low-beta stocks have delivered superior average risk-adjusted returns and only slightly lower average raw returns than high-beta stocks.
■ Low total and idiosyncratic volatility stocks have delivered slightly higher average risk-adjusted and raw returns than the market. They have delivered much higher average risk-adjusted and raw returns than high total and idiosyncratic volatility stocks (Ang, Hodrick, Xing, and Zhang 2006, 2009).
■ Value stocks have delivered higher average returns than growth stocks.

Fundamental Indexing   Fundamental indexing weights stocks by one of many economic fundamental factors, especially accounting figures, such as sales, earnings, book value, cash flow, and dividends. A key belief behind the fundamental index methodology is that underlying corporate accounting or valuation figures are more accurate estimators of a company's intrinsic value than is the listed market value of the company. That is, one should buy and sell companies in line with their accounting figures rather than according to their current market prices.

The proponents of fundamental indexing claim that the traditional method of capitalization-weighted indexes overweights overvalued stocks and underweights undervalued stocks. That is, they claim that market-capitalization-weighted indexes contain a systematic inefficiency. Weighting by fundamental factors is claimed to avoid the pitfalls of equal weighting while still removing the claimed systematic inefficiency of capitalization weighting.

Fixed Income   Some fixed income indexes suffer a variety of problems that can make them inefficient. Two main problems worth noting are the "bums" problem and the incomplete representation of the universe of issues.

The "bums" problem is where the issuers who go deepest into debt (the biggest bums) have the largest weights in a cap-weighted index. Such an index is unlikely to be efficient in risk-return terms. Such issues would seem to be the most likely to be downgraded or to default. The bums problem applies to countries in an international sovereign bond index and to corporations in a U.S. bond index.

Some standard fixed income indexes are incomplete representations of the available universe. Not only do such indexes not represent the asset class, but there is scope to build a more efficient index by incorporating the excluded securities.

Market Favors Active Management   There may be something about the market or investment environment that favors active management in general. That is, under what market conditions could the average manager beat the market consistently? Some market features, discussed by Ezra and Warren (2010), are provided next.

Investor Differences   Investor differences might result in a group of investors who are willing to accept below-index returns. Some specific examples follow.

- **Different investment horizons.** Differences in investment horizon may lead investors to have different views of risk and return, leading to opportunities for some investors. For example, long-term investors may have the ability to harvest an illiquidity risk premium from private market asset classes, such as private equity; such investors can wait a sufficiently long time to realize such a premium.
- **Liquidity provision.** Some capital providers with less immediate uses for their capital may supply liquidity to those requiring immediacy. This liquidity provision would be done in exchange for adequate compensation.
- **Taking risks others are less able to accept.** Some investors are better able to take on risks than other investors, due either to a higher tolerance for risk or to the ability to diversify these risks in their portfolio. Some examples of such risks from nontraditional asset classes are life settlements, catastrophe bonds, and selling long-dated volatility.

Market Inefficiency   Market inefficiency provides the opportunity for active managers to reliably outperform the index. However, market inefficiency is not sufficient to justify active management. Active managers must be better placed than other investors to exploit the inefficiency. Some market characteristics of an inefficient market are:

- **Segmented markets.** Segmented markets are ones where asset pricing is subject to local factors, such as domestic economic effects and politics. Active managers operating across many markets are capable of taking advantage of these *relative* pricing effects. Emerging markets are an example.
- **Information advantage.** Irrational or less informed investors in a market can provide the basis for market inefficiency, or greater opportunities for mispricing. This type of inefficiency occurs in smaller, less liquid markets, for example small-capitalization equities.

Skilled Managers Identified   It is unlikely that markets are perfectly efficient at pricing information. Some mispricing opportunities must exist to provide an incentive for investors to obtain and process information (Grossman and Stiglitz 1980). However, for an investor to beat the market, market inefficiency is not enough.

Skillful managers must also exist to exploit market inefficiencies. The investor must hold two beliefs in this regard. The first is that skillful managers exist. This is not unreasonable since people, and hence managers, are not created equal. The second is that the investor can identify the skilled managers in advance. This belief comes down to whether the investor has, or has access to, enough manager selection skill to add value.

COST VERSUS BENEFIT OF ALTERNATIVE All costs need to be weighed up against the benefits before selecting the alternative to a market-capitalization index. Costs are usually higher with active management due to manager fees, trading costs, manager monitoring costs and research costs.

Since many of the reasons for deviating from market-cap indexes rely on some form of market inefficiency, we explore this important but often less well understood aspect of capital markets. We break this discussion into two parts: the evidence on market efficiency and the barriers that exist to widespread acceptance of the concept of market efficiency.

Evidence on Market Efficiency

Understanding the concept of market efficiency and evidence on the subject is important. If a person believes in market efficiency, he or she would engage in passive strategies. If a person rejects the concept, he or she should fully understand what market efficiency is. We cover these issues:

- What is market efficiency?
- What is the evidence on market efficiency?

WHAT IS MARKET EFFICIENCY? The concept of market efficiency is a hypothesis developed by Professor Eugene Fama at the University of Chicago. It is commonly referred to as the efficient markets hypothesis (EMH). The hypothesis contends that financial markets are extremely efficient in reflecting information about individual stocks and about the stock market as a whole. When information arrives, the news spreads very quickly and is incorporated into the prices of securities without delay. The conclusion from such a description of financial markets means that neither technical analysis, which is the study of past stock prices in an attempt to predict future prices, nor even fundamental analysis, which is the analysis of financial information such as balance sheets and corporate earnings to help investors identify undervalued stocks, would help an investor to achieve returns greater than those that could be obtained by holding a portfolio of randomly selected stocks, at least not with comparable risk.

The concept of the EMH is closely associated with the idea of a random walk. A random walk means that subsequent price changes are random departures from previous prices. The logic of the random walk is simple. If the flow of information is immediately impounded into stock prices and this flow of information is unimpeded, then tomorrow's news will be unrelated to today's price change. Because news is unpredictable—otherwise it would not be news—price changes that result from that news must by random and unpredictable. The conclusion from this view is that prices reflect all known news, and uninformed investors buying a diversified portfolio of stocks will obtain a rate of return similar to that of the experts.

Burton Malkiel, in his 1973 edition of *A Random Walk Down Wall Street,* described this by saying a blindfolded chimpanzee throwing darts at the *Wall Street Journal* could select a portfolio that would do as well as the professional investment managers. He subsequently explained (Malkiel 2003) that the advice was not to literally throw darts but rather to "throw a towel over the stock pages—that is, to buy a broad-based index fund that bought and held all the stocks in the market and charged very low expenses."

The EMH is an appealing description of competitive market equilibria. In an efficient market, market prices fully reflect available information. Market participants adjust the available supply and aggregate demand in response to publicly available information so as to generate market-clearing prices. It seems plausible that in major stock markets, where millions of dollars are "voting," a rational consensus is reached on the prospects of future cash flows for any company, given available information, and this is best reflected in share prices.

However, even though the EMH may be an elegant economic concept, it may not be true. Prices in securities markets may not fully reflect available information. The early literature on market efficiency was widely interpreted as supportive of the EMH. But by the late 1970s, anomalous evidence was growing. There is now a substantial body of empirical research that casts doubt on the degree of market efficiency. Many who believe in the concept of the EMH are questioning whether share markets are as efficient as once thought.

Markets are not simply either efficient or inefficient. Market efficiency can be viewed as a continuum running from the perfect market to the grossly inefficient market, where excess earning opportunities are abundant. We can therefore think of any market or securities in that market as being characterized by some degree of efficiency. So we may think of the New York Stock Exchange as more efficient than the Brazilian stock market. Likewise, we might regard most actively traded shares are more efficiently priced than thinly traded shares.

A significant risk in any decision on the active versus passive management issue is that the degree of efficiency in markets tends to be significantly understated by market participants, whether investors, investment managers, or corporate executives. Some flatly reject the idea that securities are efficiently priced. In general, the investing community seems to accept mispricing as the norm, both at the aggregate market level and at the individual company level.

WHAT IS THE EVIDENCE ON MARKET EFFICIENCY?   A brief summary of the evidence on market efficient follows (Malkiel 2003).

Behavior of Past Stock Prices

Short-Term Momentum

Early Work   The original studies investigated the correlations of stock prices over successive days and weeks. The general conclusion was that the stock market had no memory. Past price movements were not useful in predicting future price changes.

Recent Work   More recent studies (Lo and MacKinlay 1999; Lo, Mamaysky, and Wang 2000) suggest that there are too many price changes in one direction to be consistent with a random walk. There is also some evidence that technical analysis is slightly predictive, such as head-and-shoulders patterns.

Explanations   Behavioral explanations have been offered for the existence of short-term momentum effects. One such explanation is the "bandwagon effect." A bandwagon effect means the higher the price moves, the more investors "jump onto the bandwagon" by buying and thereby push the price further up, and vice versa. An example is the rise of the U.S. stock market in the late 1990s, or tech-bubble (Shiller 2000). Another explanation is that investors tend to underreact to new information. As investors understand the information more fully, prices adjust and exhibit momentum effects.

Interpreting the Research   Should we conclude that markets are inefficient? Probably not, for three reasons.

1. Researchers find evidence of statistical significance. This is not the same as economic significance. Once transaction costs are accounted for, the strategies are not profitable. Lesmond, Schill, and Zhou (2001) find that trading costs make "relative strength" strategies unprofitable.
2. While the behavioral explanations are conceivable, underreaction does not always occur in stock markets. Underreaction tends to occur as often as overreaction. (See Fama 1998 for a comprehensive survey of event studies.)
3. Momentum effects tend to be inconsistent over time. In other words, they cannot be relied on to generate reliable excess returns. Malkiel (2003) notes that short-term momentum strategies generated positive returns during the late 1990s but large negative returns during the early 2000s. Once predictable patterns in stock prices are published, they tend to disappear soon afterward. This may be due to a genuine profitable opportunity, which, once published, is acted on by investors to the point where the strategy is no longer profitable. One such example is the January effect, where stock prices tended to rise in January. The effect largely disappeared after its discovery. It may also be due to data mining by financial researchers. Positive results may have been found at a particular time period using a particular statistical technique.

Long-Run Return Reversals

Research Findings   Evidence of return reversals appears over longer time periods—typically around three to five years. That is, stocks that have performed poorly over the past three to five years tend to do well over the next three to five years. The reverse also holds (DeBondt and Thaler 1985; Fama and French 1988; Poterba and Summers 1988).

Interpreting the Research   Some explain the return reversals as being due to overreaction. Investors engage in waves of optimism and pessimism, driving stock prices away from fundamental values, which eventually revert. While there is strong support for the return reversal effect, it is not uniform across studies and across time. The return reversal effect may not be evidence of inefficient markets since interest rates tend to mean revert. Stock prices must go up when interest rates decline to be competitive with bond returns. Because interest rates mean revert, so too should stock returns.

Seasonal Patterns

Research Findings Various calendar-based return patterns have been documented. The month of January has tended to produce higher returns than other months, and small-capitalization stocks tend to have higher returns than large-capitalization stocks in January (Keim 1983). Day-of-the-week effects have also been observed. Monday tends to produce higher returns than other days (French 1980). There are also return differences around the turn of the month and holidays (Ariel 1990; Lakonishok and Smidt 1988).

Interpreting the Research The return patterns are not dependable from period to period. Further, the returns tend to not be profitable due to transaction costs involved.

Predictability Based on Financial Metrics

Predicting Returns from Starting Price-Earnings and Dividend Yields

Research Findings Starting price-to-earnings (P/E) ratios appear to predict future returns. Figure 17.14 shows the results of measuring the S&P 500 index P/E ratio each month and the subsequent 10-year return from 1926 until 2012. Ten portfolios were then formed based on the starting P/E ratio; they are shown on the

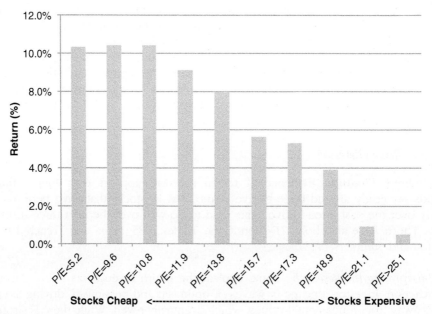

FIGURE 17.14 Future 10-Year Rates of Return When Stocks Are Purchased at Alternative Initial Price-to-Earnings Multiples

Source: Calculated from Shiller's P/E data (1926–2012).

horizontal axis. The figure shows that higher returns were obtained when starting P/Es were low, and vice versa. Starting dividend yield ratios for the whole market show similar predictability as P/E ratios. Higher returns are achieved when starting dividend yield ratios are high.

Interpreting the Research   Dividend yields and interest rates are correlated. Dividend yields tend to be high when interest rates are high. Consequently, the ability of starting dividend yields to predict future returns may simply be the adjustment of the general stock market to economic conditions. Regarding P/E ratios and subsequent returns, Malkiel (2003) notes that the relation is not tight. For example, whereas the P/E ratio of the S&P 500 rose above 20 on June 30, 1987, and the dividend yield fell below 3 percent, predicting low future returns, the average annual return of the S&P 500 during the following 10 years was an extraordinary 16.7 percent. Subsequent research by Fisher and Statman (2006) shows that no trading rules based on initial P/E ratios outperformed a simple buy-and-hold strategy over the period 1871 to 2002.

Predicting Returns Based on Other Financial Metrics

Research Findings   Other financial metrics, such as interest rates, the term structure of interest rates, and spreads between high-grade corporate bonds and short-term interest rates, contain useful information for predicting future stock returns (see Fama and Schwert 1977 on interest rates; Campbell 1987 on term structure of interest rates; and Keim and Stambaugh 1986 on corporate spreads).

Interpreting the Research   The observed predictability may simply reflect the rational time-varying risk premiums for stock investors rather than market inefficiency per se. It is also unclear whether the predictability would result in profitable investment strategies for investors.

Cross-Sectional Predictability   Many patterns have been observed based on various company characteristics. Some of these are summarized next.

Size Effect

Research   Small-company stocks generate larger returns than large-company stocks. On average, small stocks since 1926 in the United States have generated 1 percent per annum higher returns (Keim 1983). Figure 17.15 also shows the size effect from 1963 to 1990, where all stocks are divided into 10 portfolios based on market capitalization. Small stocks produced higher average monthly returns than large stocks (Fama and French 1992).

Interpreting the Research   The essential question is whether small-company stocks allow investors to generate a return above a suitable risk-adjusted return. The problem is obvious. If the measure of expected returns for the higher risk of small-company stocks is incorrect, then small-company stocks may display higher returns than those expected. The conclusion may be that the market inefficiently prices small-company stocks. That conclusion may be wrong, as the assumed expected returns for small-company stocks may be incorrect. This problem is pervasive in

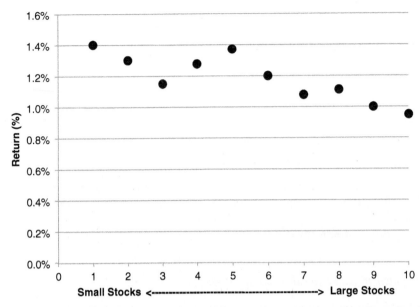

FIGURE 17.15   Average Monthly Returns for Portfolios Formed on Market Capitalization
Source: Adapted from Fama and French (1992).

most empirical research on market efficiency issues. A market inefficiency may simply be the result of an incorrect model of expected returns. Some researchers believe that the observed higher return from small-company stocks reflects higher risk rather than being indicative of market inefficiency. Finally, there are other explanations for the size effect. The computer databases used contain only small companies that survived. If small companies that failed were included, the results may not be positive. Also, since the publication of the size effect, small-company stock returns have not outpaced large stocks. The effect may have been eliminated due to competition or to increased institutional ownership of the market, driving portfolio managers to prefer large-company stocks.

Value Effect

Research   Many studies show value stocks produce higher returns that growth stocks. Common measures of growth and value are P/E ratios and P/B ratios. Stocks with low P/E ratios (or P/B ratios) are referred to as value stocks. Stocks with high P/E ratios are referred to as growth stocks.

Interpreting the Research   One explanation provided for the value effect is that investors are overconfident in projecting high earnings growth and so overprice growth stocks (Kahneman and Riepe 1998). The same cautionary statement noted earlier for small-company stocks applies here. The correctness of the model used to provide expected returns to value and growth stocks must be assessed before concluding that markets are inefficient. P/E ratios and P/B ratios may simply provide better measures of risk than current financial theory predicts. One explanation for the value effect consistent with this view is that companies in financial distress sell for less than book value of equity, and this financial distress factor is not properly captured in current financial theory. Finally, the results of the value effect may simply be time dependent. Eminent financial researchers have argued that the frailty of historical averages means that the observed effects should be treated with suspicion (Sharpe 2005).

SUMMARY Many stock return predictabilities have been researched and published. Malkiel (2003) suggests investors treat the evidence with caution. The patterns are not robust in different time periods, and some patterns may simply reflect a rational pricing of company risk. Malkiel provides a simple argument for why, even if the patterns did persist, they would self-destruct. For example, assume the January effect did persist and proved to be a dependable investment strategy for the first five days of January. Investors would buy stocks on December 31 and sell on January 5. The effect of such investor behavior would be that stocks rise on the last day of December. The strategy would not be as profitable. Investors would need to buy on December 29 instead and sell on January 4. This process continues until the January effect eventually disappears.

The observed predictability may simply be quirks in the data, the result of researchers sifting through the same data for decades looking for positive results to publish.

Finally, the predictability may be unexploitable. Malkiel (2003) provides a quote from a discussion between two well-known financial economists, Robert Shiller and Richard Roll, in which Roll says:

> *I have personally tried to invest money, my client's money and my own, in every single anomaly and predictive device that academics have dreamed up. . . . I have attempted to exploit the so-called year-end anomalies and a whole variety of strategies supposedly documented by academic research. And I have yet to make a nickel on any of these supposed market inefficiencies . . . a true market inefficiency ought to be an exploitable opportunity. If there's nothing investors can exploit in a systematic way, time in and time out, then it's very hard to say that information is not being properly incorporated into stock prices. (p. 72)*

What Barriers Exist to Acceptance of the Concept of Market Efficiency?

Despite the research on the efficiency of markets to date, many investors and market participants do not accept the idea that markets are reasonably efficient. Strong market and behavioral impediments stand in the way of broad acceptance of the market efficiency concept (Bowman and Buchanan 1995). These impediments can be grouped into market impediments and behavioral impediments.

MARKET IMPEDIMENTS Many market factors act against the acceptance of the concept of market efficiency.

No Strong Punishment Mechanism There is no strong mechanism to punish poorly conceived investment strategies. In an efficient market, the risk-adjusted expected return using publicly available information is the same regardless of investment strategy used. This is unlike most other investing activities, such as the investment in operating assets undertaken by companies. Inefficiencies in these activities are expected and well understood, and punishment mechanisms exist. For example, if McDonald's selected operating locations randomly, we would expect its profitability to decline. An efficient market also provides a long-term positive return to investors. Well-diversified portfolios are expected to produce positive returns even if the stock selection procedures are random. Irrational investment strategies that do no harm can persist indefinitely.

We Expect to Observe Winners and Losers   Investment returns are uncertain. Therefore, we expect to see the realized returns of some investors above the average realized return and some below the average realized return of all investors. So observing substantial winners is consistent with market efficiency. We should expect to see extreme winners.

Difficult to Distinguish Skill from Luck   When we see the returns from an investment decision, how do we know whether it is the result of skill or luck? The tendency is to draw a causal link between the investment return and an investment decision-making process rather than luck. The main problem here is that markets are essentially probabilistic in nature and, when combined with a poor understanding of probabilistic events, can result in incorrect inferences being drawn. Compounding the problem is that we often have very few observations of an investment activity. Professional investors may make hundreds of investments each year, but the investment background is continually changing and stock selection models are subject to review. There are really too few genuine observations to evaluate skill. There is a tendency to blame the market rather than the investment strategy.

Vested Interests   The economics of an entire industry depend on an inefficient view of the market. Technical analysts would not be expected to support evidence that stock prices act like random walks. Stockbrokers would not advise their clients to buy and hold, thereby minimizing transaction costs. Investment advisors and investment letters are not expected to educate investors on the latest research proclaiming efficient markets. Bernstein (1992) has commented that "some of the wealthiest people on Wall Street are professionals whose bank accounts have been inflated by a constant flow of investment advisory fees" (p. 17).

The market structure when combined with behavioral factors forms a strong bond to prevent widespread acceptance of the concept of market efficiency.

BEHAVIORAL IMPEDIMENTS   The stock market is often described in emotive terms suggesting irrationality. It is described as having animal spirits or a knee-jerk reaction. Many human traits are better frames of reference and explanations for how we are likely to behave. These are discussed next.

Aversion to Loss Realization   We have a strong tendency to distinguish between paper losses and realized losses. When a stock position is open, the timing of a sale is within our control. A realized loss is considered final, but we often cannot convince ourselves that unrealized losses are unknown. The consequence is to hold losing stock positions too long, hoping that in time losses will be recovered. We may hold a stock at $5 per share for three years and sell at $5 per share. We may say we broke even and conveniently ignore transaction costs, risk undertaken, and the time value of money.

Illusion of Knowledge   We are poor at making statistical inferences and intuitive probabilistic assessments. We also tend to overestimate how much we know about or understand something. Our beliefs about how the market functions are often based on few observations, as noted earlier. Similarly, we often have few observations over which to assess the quality of investment information. Investors who observe five consecutive successful investment recommendations tend to attribute too much to the event. We tend to assume skill of the investment advisor when in fact little weight should be placed on the occurrence. A related behavior is our tendency to overvalue anecdotal information.

Illusion of Control   We exhibit an illusion of control even in chance-based events like coin flipping. When observing a sequence of events, we tend to attribute this to skill or some control being exerted over the outcomes. If we exhibit this behavior with events that we know are chance based, it is no wonder that this behavior is exacerbated when it comes to the complex functioning of the stock market.

Attributing Successes and Failures   We also tend to attribute successes to skill and failures to bad luck. In the context of the stock market, this means we tend to attribute superior investment outcomes to skill and poor outcomes to bad luck.

Thus, in view of these behavioral traits, the biggest risk we face is ourselves. Bowman and Buchanan (1995) describe the combined effect of these behavioral factors:

> *The investor enters this environment with a number of perceptual flaws. The stories of past successes (over few trials) of others are assumed to be replicable rather than fortuitous. We then apply our own particular brand of genius to selecting an investment. If the investment is profitable we ascribe that to our investing acumen. If the investment fares poorly we have a dual strategy. We hold onto the shares, if possible, in hope of a recovery, but if we do realize the loss, we attribute it to bad luck. (p. 163)*

Behavioral research (Luthans and Kreitner 1985) has shown that behavior is best affected through intermittent, unexpected positive reinforcement. Stock markets provide such intermittent reinforcement and therefore encourage engagement in market-beating schemes.

References

Ariel, Robert A. 1990. "High Stock Returns Before Holidays: Existence and Evidence on Possible Causes." *Journal of Finance* 45, no. 5 (December): 1611–1626.

Bernstein, P. L. 1992. *Capital Ideas*. New York: Free Press.

Bowman, Robert G., and J. Buchanan. 1995. "The Efficient Market Hypothesis—A Discussion of Institutional, Agency and Behavioural Issues." *Australian Journal of Management* 20, no. 2 (December): 155–166.

Campbell, John Y. 1987. "Stock Returns and the Term Structure." *Journal of Financial Economics* 18 (June): 373–400.

Clarke, Roger, Harindra de Silva, and Steven Thorley. 2006. "Minimum-Variance Portfolios in the U.S. Equity Market." *Journal of Portfolio Management* 33, no. 1 (Fall): 10–24.

DeBondt, Werner F. M., and Richard Thaler. 1985. "Does the Stock Market Overreact?" *Journal of Finance* 40 (July): 793–805.

Ezra, D., and G. Warren. 2010. "When Should Investors Choose an Alternative to Passively Investing in a Capitalization-Weighted Index?" Working paper, July 15. http://ssrn.com/abstract=1640921.

Fama, Eugene F. 1998. "Market Efficiency, Long-Term Returns, and Behavioral Finance." *Journal of Financial Economics* 49 (3): 283–306.

Fama, Eugene F., and Kenneth R. French. 1988. "Permanent and Temporary Components of Stock Prices." *Journal of Political Economy* 96 (2): 246–273.

Fama, Eugene F., and Kenneth R. French. 1992. "The Cross-Section of Expected Stock Returns." *Journal of Finance* 47 (June): 427–465.

Fama, Eugene F., and G. William Schwert. 1977. "Asset Returns and Inflation." *Journal of Financial Economics* 5, no. 2 (November): 55–69.

French, Kenneth R. 1980. "Stock Returns and the Weekend Effect." *Journal of Financial Economics* 8 (March): 55–69.

Grossman, Sanford J., and Joseph E. Stiglitz. 1980. "On the Impossibility of Informationally Efficient Markets." *American Economic Review* 70 (3): 393–408.

Kahneman, Daniel, and Mark W. Riepe. 1998. "Aspects of Investor Psychology." *Journal of Portfolio Management* 24, no. 4 (Summer): 52–65.

Keim, Donald B. 1983. "Size-Related Anomalies and Stock Return Seasonality: Further Empirical Evidence." *Journal of Financial Economics* 12 (June): 13–32.

Keim, Donald B., and Robert T. Stambaugh. 1986. "Predicting Returns in Stock and Bond Markets." *Journal of Financial Economics* 17 (December): 357–390.

Lakonishok, Josef, and S. Smidt. 1988. "Are Seasonal Anomalies Real? A Ninety-Year Perspective." *Review of Financial Studies* 1, no. 4 (Winter): 403–425.

Lesmond, David, Michael Schill, and Chun-sheng Zhou. 2001. "The Illusory Nature of Momentum Profits." Manuscript, Tulane University.

Lo, Andrew W., and A. Craig MacKinlay. 1999. *A Non-Random Walk Down Wall Street*. Princeton, NJ: Princeton University Press.

Lo, Andrew W., Harry Mamaysky, and Jiang Wang. 2000. "Foundations of Technical Analysis: Computational Algorithms, Statistical Inference, and Empirical Implementation." *Journal of Finance* 55, no. 4 (August): 1705–1765.

Luthans, F., and R. Kreitner. 1985. *Organizational Behavior Modification and Beyond: An Operant and Social Learning Approach*. London: Scott, Foresman.

Malkiel, Burton G. 1973. *A Random Walk Down Wall Street*. New York: Norton.

Malkiel, Burton G. 2003. "The Efficient Market Hypothesis and Its Critics." *Journal of Economic Perspectives* 17, no. 1 (Winter): 59–82.

Nielsen, Frank, and Raman Aylursubramanian. 2008. "Far From the Madding Crowd—Volatility Efficient Indices." MSCI Barra Research Insights.

Poterba, James, and Lawrence Summers. 1988. "Mean Reversion in Stock Returns: Evidence and Implications." *Journal of Financial Economics* 22 (1): 27–59.

Sharpe, William F. 1991. "The Arithmetic of Active Management." *Financial Analysts Journal* 47, no. 1 (January/February): 7–9.

Sharpe, William F. 2005. "Insights from a Pioneer in Portfolio Theory and Practice: A Talk with Nobel Laureate William F. Sharpe, Ph.D." *Journal of Investment Consulting* 7 (2): 10–20.

Shiller, Robert J. 2000. *Irrational Exuberance.* Princeton, NJ: Princeton University Press.

Thomas, Ric, and Robert Shapiro. 2009. "Managed Volatility: A New Approach to Equity Investing." *Journal of Investing* 18, no. 1 (Spring): 1–15.

Part IV Strategic, Tactical, and Dynamic Asset Allocation

One of the limitations of many current asset allocation approaches is that they concentrate primarily on investment in a limited number of assets (stocks, bonds, and real estate). Today, investment in a larger range of investable assets is being addressed through more active asset construction. The increase in potential investment opportunities increases the potential benefit of strategic asset allocation opportunities as well as tactical and dynamic approaches to asset allocation.

The term asset allocation means different things to different people in different contexts. For our purposes we have divided asset allocation decisions into three often-used categories:

1. **Strategic asset allocation** can be characterized as a long-term asset allocation decision. The objective is to determine the long-term normal asset mix that will represent the desirable balance of risk and return. In developing the strategic asset allocation, the investor's return objectives, risk tolerance, and other investment constraints have to be taken into account. Next, the set of asset classes that are permissible under the investor's investment policy statement are used to establish the optimal long-run mix. If the portfolio's performance is evaluated using a specific benchmark, then strategic allocation would correspond to the mix represented by the benchmark. The investment policy statement would need to spell out if and how the strategic allocation should be altered in light of a new economic environment.

2. **Tactical asset allocation (TAA)** represents an active departure from the strategic asset mix. The changes will take place in response to shifts in risk-reward characteristics of different asset classes resulting from changes in the investment environment. Tactical asset allocation is founded on the premise that asset returns are on the average driven by economic fundamentals. There are of course a number of alternative TAA processes. Some rely primarily on economic-based return forecasts, while others are based on historical price movement (e.g., when the asset prices rise rapidly, a tactical asset allocator may tend to sell, and when asset prices fall rapidly, the investor will tend to buy).

3. **Dynamic trading strategies** are designed to change the distribution pattern of the portfolio. The best known of these strategies is the portfolio insurance strategy, which is designed to set a floor for the value of the portfolio.

Historically, asset allocation has centered on long only stock and bond investments, but alternative assets are increasingly being considered in the strategic and tactical areas of asset management as well as underlying assets in various dynamic trading-based structured notes. The unique characteristics of alternative assets also raise a number of issues. For instance, alternative assets are lumpy investments and are typically illiquid, making it difficult to implement typical strategic, tactical, and dynamic strategies. Further, while traditional assets are easily accessible through investable indices, most alternative assets are accessed through selecting active managers, which poses unique issues in asset allocation.

Given the wide range of issues involved in asset allocation, a systematic approach to its use across traditional and alternative asset classes is important for client education, client marketing, and product creation and management. The level of sophistication and detail may differ for each client. For more sophisticated investors, a wider range of asset allocation techniques and approaches are often introduced if for no other reason than to indicate that the firms' modeling processes are competitive in areas such as tracking error, capacity, and liquidity adjustments. At the basic investor level the simple Markowitz mean-variance asset allocation is often used simply because of the clients' background with the methodology. As a consequence, the analysis within this section starts with the use of asset allocation optimization models in portfolio creation and management.

Asset Allocation Optimization Models

Traditional portfolio optimization attempts to find the portfolio with the lowest possible risk (measured by the variance of the return) for a target expected rate of return. More formally, the goal is to find the portfolio weights (note that one can eliminate the usual constraint that weights should add up to one by using returns in excess of a riskless asset) such that:

$$\min_{weights} \quad Var[R_p] \text{ Subject to } E[R_p] = \text{Target and } w_i \geq 0$$

Note that the usual constraint that weights should add up to one can be eliminated by using returns in excess of a riskless asset.

The inputs required to perform the above optimization are:

expected returns
variance-covariance matrix of returns

As mentioned already, the basic premise of portfolio optimization is quite sensible, and under ideal conditions, it should help create portfolios with attractive risk-return profiles. However, in practice a number of problems have to be dealt with before the results of a quantitative portfolio selection model, whether it is a simple mean-variance optimization or a more advanced model, are put to work. The basic principle that one has to remember is that quantitative portfolio construction models need accurate inputs. Further, the output is typically extremely sensitive to some of the inputs, and unfortunately these inputs are typically the ones that cannot be estimated accurately.

A simple example from the real world can demonstrate this. The annualized rate of return on the S&P 500 for the past 14 years has been around 6.5 percent while its annualized standard deviation for the same period has been around 16 percent. Given the long series of returns, one would be tempted to use 6.5 percent as the long-term return on S&P 500. However, you may be surprised to read that statistically that figure is not significantly different from zero. In fact, all we can say is that with 95 percent confidence the mean return is between −2.2 percent and +15 percent. It turns out that the outputs of portfolio optimization methods are highly sensitive to the estimated values of the means. Even if we decide to use 6.5 percent as a good estimate of the mean, we must hope that the future will be similar to the past. In other words, we are assuming that the S&P 500 returns of the past 14 years came from the same distribution that is likely to prevail for the duration of our investment horizon.

While generally the estimation of risk parameters can be improved using high frequency data, no such improvement takes place in estimating expected return. For instance, suppose one has five years of data. If annual returns are used to estimate the variance, the potential estimation error will be very high. However, if we use five years of monthly data to estimate the volatility, one would obtain a more accurate estimate of volatility with a lower estimation error. Nevertheless, it makes absolutely no difference if annual, monthly, or daily data are used to estimate the mean return. They will all give the same estimate with the same estimation error. The only way one can reduce the estimation error is to have a longer series. This means that lack of high frequency data for hedge funds and private equity funds affects our estimates of their risks and not their mean return. On the other hand, not having a long return history severely reduces our confidence in the estimated value of the mean. An additional point needs to be mentioned; that is, the use of any historical time period as a basis for parameter estimation assumes that the period examined represents the expected return and risk characteristics of the future anticipated investment horizon.

ESTIMATING THE INPUTS   The most obvious approach is to use historical averages to estimate expected returns and risk parameters of the investment set. This approach has a number of problems. As discussed previously, one problem often referred to is "maximizing over the errors" because the resulting optimal portfolio maximizes over the errors in estimated parameters.[1] This means that the highest allocation is likely to be made to the investment that has had the highest positive error (e.g., highest realized return or lowest realized volatility). There are five methods for reducing the impact of this problem:

1. **More robust estimation methods:** There are statistical methods that can improve the accuracy of the estimates. However, almost all of these methods deal with estimation of the variance-covariance matrix. Very little can be done to improve the efficiency of the estimated value of the mean.
2. **More robust optimization methods:** There are adjustments that one can make to the classical mean-variance optimization such that the impact of estimation risk is incorporated in the optimization process. These methods require specialized software and typically require specific adjustments to the algorithm to handle some practical problems (e.g., limits on sector exposures or illiquidity of some asset classes).

3. **Bootstrapped or resampled portfolios:** In this case various "versions" of historical data are used to generate various optimal portfolios. Different procedures are available for selecting a representative of simulated portfolios. Though this approach does not yield a unique portfolio, one learns a great deal about the sensitivity of the optimal portfolios to changes in the inputs.

4. **Constraining portfolio weights:** In this case the portfolio manager imposes various constraints on portfolio weights in order to avoid portfolios with extreme weights. This is a rather ad hoc procedure because it is not clear what the constraints should be. However, this simple solution tends to produce portfolios that are sensible, and, according to several studies, they tend to perform well out-of-sample.[2]

5. **Economic model-based estimates:** The most famous version of this approach is the Black-Litterman model. This model takes the weights of a well-diversified portfolio as the starting point. The most appealing aspect of this approach is that it uses an equilibrium economic model to estimate expected returns. If one were to use these estimates as inputs, then the portfolio's mix will be similar to the mix of a well-diversified portfolio, which is typically the portfolio's benchmark. We will have more to say about this approach later in this section.

PREDICTABILITY OF RISK AND RETURN   There is some evidence that risk and returns of major asset classes and trading strategies are predictable. The evidence on the predictability of risk is very strong and there is virtually no disagreement about its strength and significance. The entire academic literature on what is known as ARCH and GARCH models deals with the issue of predictability in risk. It turns out that most of these models perform rather well in predicting short-term changes in risk. For example, it is well known that financial markets display "volatility clustering." This means that when there is a spike in volatility of asset prices, there will be a tendency for that volatility to last several days. However, these models perform rather poorly when it comes to predicting changes in volatility in the long term. Therefore, when it comes to strategic asset allocation, models that predict volatility are not of great use (they could be useful for tactical or dynamic allocation).

To determine if a return series has predictability in its volatility, one could perform a simple test. Suppose we look at daily returns on the Russell 2000 Index, covering January 1, 2006 through December 31, 2008. We run the following simple regression:

$$R_{t,R2K} = a + b \times R_{t-1,R2K} + \varepsilon_t$$

where $R_{t,R2K}$ is the rate of return on Russell 2000 Index on day t. The parameters that have to be estimated are a and b. If the estimated value of slope parameter is -0.10, then there is a small degree of mean reversion in the daily return on Russell 2000, which may not be significant enough to create a profitable trading strategy.

Now, let's try the above experiment again, but instead of using raw returns, we will use returns squared; that is:

$$R_{t,R2K}^2 = a + b \times R_{t-1,R2K}^2 + \varepsilon_t$$

This time if the estimated value of the slope is 0.37. This means that a high volatility day is likely to be followed by a high volatility day. In fact, about 37 percent of the previous day's volatility spills over into the following day's volatility. If the same exercise is performed using monthly data, the estimated value of *b* when raw returns are used may decrease or increase; however, its estimated value when squared returns are used is very likely to decline significantly; that is, long-term volatility is less predictable.

The evidence on the predictability of expected returns is not as strong, and there is a lack of consensus among researchers on whether the apparent predictability is strong enough to be used in asset allocation. During the last several years, a number of studies have demonstrated that a meaningful amount of variation in stock returns be explained by lagged values of variables such as the dividend yield, T-bill yield, and credit risk premium, among others. Unlike predictability in volatility, which is mostly short-term, predictability in stock returns using economic fundamentals is mostly a long-run phenomenon. In this regard, this predictability could be useful for strategic asset allocation.

There is a perception that if returns are predictable, then market efficiency cannot hold. This is not necessarily correct. It is correct to argue that if markets are not efficient, then asset returns are likely to be predictable and one would be able to earn returns not justified by the risk of the position. However, the opposite is not necessarily true. Asset returns could be predictable in a perfectly efficient market. One reason for this is that the risk premiums on various asset classes are not stable and vary through time as the economy moves through various stages of business cycle. This means that to the extent that one can predict changes in the risk premium, then expected returns will be predictable, and this is completely consistent with efficient markets.

OTHER RISK MEASURES   The appropriate measure of risk is dictated by the needs of the investor. Traditionally, variance has been the most common measure of risk in asset allocation programs. Clearly, variance is not an ideal measure of risk in some circumstances. As mentioned above, risk relative to liabilities cannot be captured by variance. Further, in other cases variance may represent only one dimension of the risk. For instance, risk of exposure to unexpected increases in inflation cannot be measured by the variance of the portfolio. Of course, there are many other dimensions to risk (e.g., interest rate risk, credit risk, and currency risk). However, inflation risk poses a special case because it affects real returns; that is, a portfolio with fairly stable nominal return could have a very volatile real return during an inflationary period. In fact, it can be argued that no single variable can ever serve as an accurate measure of total risk.

It is possible to maintain the simple structure of the mean-variance optimization model but instead use measures of risk other than variance. A common approach is to use the semi-standard deviation, which measures the volatility of the portfolio below a target return (e.g., zero). To the degree that return distributions are not symmetric, then the use of semi-standard deviation as a measure of risk could lead to significantly different allocation when compared to classical mean-variance approach.

The next step consists of expanding the classical mean-variance approach to account for multiple measures or sources of risk. For example, suppose one is interested in creating a mean-variance efficient portfolio that would avoid allocation to investments with negative skewness and would favor investments with positive exposure to inflation. Suppose the skewness of the fund is denoted by $S[R_p]$ and the beta of the fund with respect to inflation is denoted by $B[R_p, I]$. Then the classical mean-variance optimization can be changed to the following:

$$\min\{Var[R_p] - a \times S[R] - b \times B[R_p, I]\} \quad \text{Subject to} \quad E[R_p] = \text{Target}, \quad w_i \geq 0$$

Note that the usual constraint that weights should add up to one can be eliminated by using returns in excess of a riskless asset. In this case, the investor minimizes a weighted average of variance, skewness, and beta with respect to inflation, where negative weights are assigned to skewness and inflation beta. The size of a and b are set by the investor. This is where experience and some common sense are needed. Basically, the larger the value of these two parameters, the greater the portfolio's tilt in that direction. This will, of course, come at the expense of a higher variance. After all, there is no free lunch. In a similar fashion, one can incorporate other risk dimensions into the model. However, bear in mind that the more risk dimensions one introduces, the greater the chance that there will be estimation errors in inputs, leading to a portfolio that is only optimal in terms of its allocation to errors.

TRACKING ERROR   As mentioned in the previous section, risk has many dimensions. One of the most common situations in which a multidimensional measure of risk is required is in the area of tracking error. Whatever the primary objective of the portfolio optimizer is, the added objective would be to reduce the tracking error of the portfolio relative to a benchmark, liabilities, or an economic factor. In this case, the objective of the optimizer can be expanded such that reducing the tracking error of the portfolio is included in the optimization process. Similar to what was proposed above in dealing with skewness or inflation, this will require the user to assign a value (a loss function) to the tracking error. In other words, the user has to specify how important the tracking error is and how much performance he is willing to give up for a marginal reduction in tracking error. The resulting efficient frontier will naturally suffer from some inefficiency, but the inclusion of the tracking error will have the beneficial effect of reducing variation in optimal weights through time relative to the chosen index.

OTHER RISK CONCERNS   Even in an ideal world, the investor's degree of risk aversion has to be taken into account. Therefore, a crucial step in the design of any asset allocation program is the determination of the investor's objectives and constraints. Risk aversion affects the level of volatility or beta that the investor is willing to accept in the long run. Through various simulation procedures, one can educate the investor about the potential impacts of assuming various levels of risk. For instance, value at risk could be used to show the impact of high and low volatility strategies.

Risk aversion, especially at the institutional level, may be highly affected by the investor's liabilities. In this context, risk could be measured with respect to liabilities. For instance, a family business that is expected to fund future generations of a family has potential liabilities with long duration and significant exposure to inflation. Therefore, in this context, an optimal portfolio would need to have significant allocation to long duration assets and assets that provide a hedge against inflation. However, if the portfolio is managed on a stand-alone basis, an optimal allocation may have little or no allocation to those assets.

When an optimal portfolio is viewed in relationship to liabilities, one has to pay attention to the cost of not meeting the liabilities. For instance, for a family business the cost of not meeting the obligations is not as significant as it is for a life insurance company. Therefore, if the cost of not meeting its obligations is very high, the investor must take liabilities into account in designing optimal portfolios.

Another constraint on the portfolio is the cash flow requirements of the investor, which is closely related to the time horizon of the investor. In the case of an endowment, the cash flow requirements are fairly predictable and the time horizon is *very* long. This means the endowment can afford to invest in illiquid assets. On the other hand, a casualty insurance company has unpredictable cash flows and the time horizon is somewhat unpredictable as well. Therefore, the insurance fund must maintain significant liquidity.

Strategic Asset Allocation

Strategic asset allocation is a major determinant of variability of a portfolio and, to a lesser degree, its total return. Studies have shown that up to 90 percent of a well-diversified portfolio's return volatility is determined by its strategic allocation. On the other hand, about 20 percent of its mean total return is determined by its strategic allocation.[3] Therefore, no matter how you look at it, the strategic allocation is a major determinant of a portfolio's risk-return profile.

In the previous sections, we discussed various aspects of asset allocation. In this section we present the basic steps that one has to take to implement a strategic asset allocation.

The first step is to identify the investor's objectives and constraints. We have already discussed attitude toward risk and the role of liabilities as being important factors in this area. If liabilities are not important, then the portfolio is managed on a stand-alone basis. Otherwise, the portfolio allocation will need to take liabilities into account.

In the next step, we need to decide if there is a benchmark that will be used to measure the portfolio's performance. This will help us identify the universe of permissible asset classes. Of course, the portfolio may be allowed to invest in asset classes that are not part of the benchmark; but all asset classes that are included in the benchmark should be available to the portfolio.

In step three, we estimate the risk and return characteristics of the permissible asset classes. As indicated already, estimates obtained from historical return series may not always be the best inputs to the strategic allocation model. This is particularly true for expected returns to asset classes. Here, we can use the basic message of equilibrium asset pricing models to obtain internally consistent estimates, which can serve as our starting point. To implement the equilibrium approach we need to create a benchmark that consists of all the asset classes that we are permitted to invest in. Our job will be much easier if the investment committee has already decided on a benchmark. If not, then we need to come up with one or more potential benchmarks. For example, suppose the set of permissible asset classes consists of equity markets that belong to MSCI Global, bond markets that are covered by Barclay's Capital Global Bond Index, commodities that are covered by Goldman Sachs/S&P Commodity Index, and funds of hedge funds.

Given the investor's risk tolerance, we may decide that a benchmark consisting of 40 percent in MSCI Global Index, 30 percent in Barclays Capital Global Bond Index, 10 percent in S&P GSCI Commodity Index, and 20 percent in CISDM Fund of

Funds Index is a sensible benchmark. Using historical data, we estimate the variance-covariance of the returns on these asset classes. Then the expected return on asset class i that is consistent with the above benchmark is given by

$$E[R_i - R_f] = \lambda \times \beta_i$$

where β_i is the beta of asset i with respect to the benchmark portfolio, R_f is the riskless rate, and λ is coefficient measuring the degree of risk aversion. This last parameter may appear to be rather tricky to estimate, and it is. It is given by the investor's attitude toward risk and is rather difficult to estimate. It basically asks how high the return should be to warrant an allocation to the portfolio. Even if one has no estimate of the risk aversion parameter, one can use the above expression to learn what the relative rates of returns should be. The bottom line is that if one were to use the above expected returns in a mean-variance optimization approach, the resulting optimal portfolio would be the same as the benchmark. In practice, the portfolio manager should experiment with various combinations to determine how sensitive expected returns are to changes in the benchmark. It should be noted that the estimates of expected returns obtained through this procedure represent a starting point for our portfolio manager. Next, the manager will adjust these expected returns to reflect her views on the potential performance of various asset classes. For instance, the portfolio manager may decide that because of easy monetary policies of various central banks, inflation is likely to surprise to the upside and thus commodities are likely to perform better than the equilibrium expected return.

Black and Litterman (1992) describe a quantitative procedure to adjust the equilibrium returns so that the portfolio manager's confidence in her forecast is taken into account. A full description of the Black-Litterman approach is beyond the scope of this book. But it must be pointed out that using equilibrium returns to begin the process of estimating expected returns to various asset classes is highly recommended but is rarely followed.

The final step is to use a combination of quantitative and qualitative methods to determine the optimal allocation. Generally speaking, a purely quantitative approach in most cases does not provide a full solution to the investor's problem. For instance, the presence of alternative investments typically complicates a purely quantitative approach because these investments are bulky and illiquid, and they take time to implement. Strategic asset allocation is normally performed on a three- to five-year basis with quarterly rebalancing. If there are major changes in the investor's financial position or the economic environment, the strategic allocation has to be reevaluated.

Tactical Asset Allocation

Tactical asset allocation (TAA) is a dynamic approach to asset allocation where the asset mix is actively adjusted in response to short-term changes in the economic environment. The objective is to adjust the allocation in order to take advantage of temporary pockets of inefficiency. Strategic allocation determines the risk-return of the portfolio while TAA can add value if it is designed correctly and all the potential costs and risks associated with it are taken into account.

Generally, TAA programs are designed to take advantage of temporary changes in market conditions that would favor one asset class over another. The markets, therefore, provide us with the potential opportunity to take advantage of these changing market conditions to improve the performance of a portfolio. It is important to note that the pro forma returns of any tactical asset allocation model are dependent on the actual period of analysis and therefore should be analyzed very carefully in order to decide if the performance is likely to be repeated in the future.

The main source of value derived from a TAA program is the strength and consistency of its signals, which are then used to alter the portfolio mix. The forecasting model of a TAA must possess a number of desirable properties. First, the signals must make economic sense; that is, one should be able to explain in simple terms why the model is able to forecast relative performance of various asset classes. For example, one of the most reliable signals about future performance of equities relative to fixed income instruments has been the slope of the yield curve. An upward sloping yield curve is generally consistent with a period of rising stock prices. The reason behind this is that an upward sloping yield curve is generally observed at the beginning of economic expansion. By examining the economic foundation of the signal, one can avoid using results that have resulted from data mining, that is, the generated signals that are not likely to perform well out of sample.

So what are the economic foundations of a sensible signaling model of a TAA? Clearly, it is difficult to predict risky investment returns. The main reasons are: (1) returns to risky assets are highly volatile and (2) financial markets tend to be highly efficient most of the time. Since the current price of an investment equals the present value of its cash flows discounted by the riskless rate plus a risk premium, the economic model must be able to explain how changes in one or more of these factors are predicted.

TAA models that include a wide variety of assets have more opportunities to identify inefficiencies in various market segments. TAA models benefit from large differences in the alternative asset class choices. The primary problem with TAA modeling is to offer superior return to risk performance while at the same time seeking to avoid allocations that would deviate from the general long-term strategic goals of the investor. One potential problem with many TAA programs is that the client cannot be sure of what possible allocations may be adopted under various scenarios unless the process is constrained so as not to deviate dramatically from the initial strategic asset allocations. In the following, the sample TAA program solution to this problem is achieved to constrain the three alternative portfolios to have somewhat similar stock and bond sensitivities as well as absolute risk.

OUTLINE OF A TAA MODEL   The main features of this program include:

- **Model Portfolios.** Three model portfolios consisting of nine broad asset classes are created for each client. The asset classes are:
    1. Short-term fixed income instruments
    2. Investment grade corporate bonds
    3. Government bonds
    4. High-yield corporate bonds
    5. Large cap equity
    6. Small cap equity
    7. Developed international equity excluding the United States
    8. Emerging markets equity

9. Alternative investments

Other asset classes can be added to or removed from this list depending on the client's needs. The three model portfolios represent a strategic allocation, a conservative tactical allocation, and an aggressive tactical allocation. The strategic allocation represents the long-term, normal portfolio of the client. Conservative tactical allocation will be adopted should the quantitative model indicate that market conditions do not offer attractive risk-return opportunities and therefore a more conservative allocation is warranted. By the same token, the aggressive tactical allocation will be adopted if the model indicates improved return opportunities in equities and other less conservative asset classes. Since this model works with predetermined allocations, the client knows exactly which allocation will be selected, based on certain market conditions.

- **Quantitative Model.** Expected return models are often based on multifactor models. In this case, a four-factor model is used to predict risk and return on each predetermined allocation. The four factors are:
  1. Current level of credit risk premium (CR) compared to its historically normal level
  2. Current level of term premium (TP) compared to its historically normal level
  3. Current level of S&P 500 implied volatility as measured by VIX compared to its historically normal level
  4. Recent return to each allocation

- **Estimation Strategy.** A quantitative approach is adopted to estimate the lead-lag relationship between the performance of each allocation and the factors mentioned above.

$$E[R_{t+1}] = f(CR_t, TP_t, R_t, VIX_t)$$

In this case, five years of monthly returns are used to estimate the model. The estimated relationship is back tested to ensure its robustness and stability.

- **Reallocation Strategy.** Once the quantitative model is estimated, we are prepared to use the model to perform tactical asset allocation. The process is systematic and the role of human judgment is minimal. At the end of each reallocation period (in this case monthly), data on predictive factors are collected and then fed into the model. The output would consist of expected performance of the three model portfolios over the next allocation cycle. The allocation that is likely to perform best for the strategic allocation up to the next reallocation point is selected. In the case that no allocation significantly dominates the other two, the current allocation is maintained.

EXAMPLE This section demonstrates an application of the TAA approach using the following model portfolios. For this example, asset weights are given in Table 17.8. The indices shown in Table 17.9 are employed to represent the historical performance of these asset classes. The performance of asset classes along with the three allocations are presented in Table 17.10.

It can be seen that the three allocations have each had distinct performance in the past. The conservative allocation has demonstrated a relatively stable risk (annual volatility of 6.7 percent) and reasonable return (5 percent per year). As expected,

TABLE 17.8   Hypothetical Weights

	Conservative Allocation	Strategic Allocation	Aggressive Allocation
Short-Term Fixed Income Instruments	29%	15%	5%
Government Bonds	16%	7%	5%
Investment Grade Bonds	8%	8%	5%
High-Yield Corporate Bonds	4%	5%	5%
Large Cap Equity	17%	25%	28%
Small Cap Equity	3%	5%	7%
International Equity Excluding U.S.	10%	17%	18%
Emerging Markets	3%	3%	7%
Alternative Investments	10%	15%	20%
Total	100%	100%	100%

TABLE 17.9   Benchmark Alternatives

Asset Class	Index
Short-Term Fixed Income Instruments	BarCap US. Treasury Bills
Government Bonds	BarCap US Government
Investment Grade Bonds	BarCap US Corporate Investment Grade
High-Yield Corporate Bonds	BarCap US Corporate High-Yield
Large Cap Equity	S&P 500
Small Cap Equity	Russell 2000
International Equity Excluding U.S.	MSCI EAFE
Emerging Markets	MSCI Emerging Markets
Alternative Investments	CISDM EW Hedge Fund Index

TABLE 17.10   Benchmark Performance

12/1996–5/2009	Annualized		Beta with Respect to		
Asset Class	Mean	Std Dev	Government/ Credit Bonds	Large Cap Equity	Information Ratio
Short-Term Fixed Income Instruments	3.7%	0.6%	0.02	0	6.68
Government Bonds	5.7%	5.9%	0.63	−0.04	1.80
Investment Grade Bonds	5.5%	5.9%	1.14	0.09	0.93
High-Yield Corporate Bonds	4.9%	10.3%	0.37	0.37	0.48
Large Cap Equity	3.3%	16.6%	−0.01	1	0.20
Small Cap Equity	4.2%	21.4%	−0.14	1.01	0.20
International Equity Excluding U.S.	1.2%	17.6%	0.13	0.69	0.07
Emerging Markets	4.0%	26.6%	−0.21	1.2	0.15
Alternative Investments	10.0%	8.3%	0.04	0.37	1.21
Conservative	5.0%	6.7%	0.17	0.38	0.75
Strategic	4.9%	9.9%	0.22	0.57	0.50
Aggressive	5.1%	12.2%	0.11	0.69	0.42

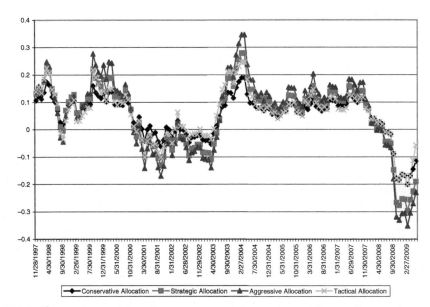

FIGURE 17.16   Twelve-Month Rolling Returns: Risk-Based Portfolios and Tactical
Asset Portfolio

the aggressive allocation has demonstrated the highest performance (5.1 percent per
year) with greatest volatility (12.2 percent per year).

Even though the aggressive allocation has performed better than the other two
allocations over this time period, there have been periods during which the conservative allocation performed better than the other two. Using the procedure discussed
earlier, we estimated the quantitative model using a five-year rolling window starting
with the period between December 1991 and November 1996. The model was used
to perform tactical asset allocation starting in December 1996. The reallocation cycle
was set at one month. The results are presented in Figure 17.16.

Figure 17.16 demonstrates the power of tactical asset allocation. Figure 17.17
demonstrates that the tactical asset allocation model exceeds the performance of the
strategic allocation in the down markets of 2002 and 2008.

These basic features of a tactical asset allocation (TAA) program will adjust strategic allocations to a portfolio of various fund strategies in a predetermined manner.
The approach is systematic and quantitative, leading to a menu of allocations that
have been agreed upon at the beginning of the process. This is the major advantage
of this program when compared to other TAA asset allocation programs offered by
other institutions: the investor knows precisely the changes that will take place in
the strategic allocation based on possible future market conditions.

Dynamic Asset Allocation

In general, dynamic asset allocation programs are targeted at creating a risk-return
profile over time that generally assures a minimum return while preserving the
opportunity for potential gains from the risky assets. In the 1980s various dynamic

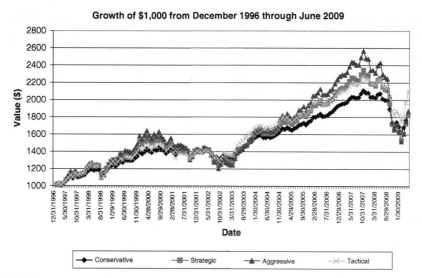

FIGURE 17.17 VAMI: Risk-Based Portfolios and Tactical Asset Portfolio

hedging strategies were created that were known by their general title of portfolio insurance. Portfolio insurance should under optimal conditions create a return profile that is similar to a put-protected investment strategy. Instead of buying a put to protect the portfolio's value, a dynamic asset allocation model adjusts the mix between a risky portfolio and risk-free asset according to a predefined hedge ratio, which adjusts the amount in the two assets as the fund value rises and falls. As an alternative to dynamic portfolio insurance-based strategies, a number of risk management strategies are conducted under the generic concept known as constant proportional portfolio insurance (CPPI). Simply put, under CPPI the exposure to a risky asset is increased as the portfolio rises in value and the exposure to the riskless asset increases as the portfolio value falls. There are a number of constraints in many practical applications of the CPPI, especially in various structured notes or products that have regulatory constraints on what a product can be invested in and how it is invested.

In its simplest form, the CPPI can be represented by the following expression:

$$\text{Size of risky position} = m \times (\text{Portfolio value} - \text{Floor})$$

The portfolio value and floor are typically determined by the client. For example, the floor could be the present value of the portfolio. In this case, the goal is to protect the principal and guarantee a minimum return of zero. The parameter m determines how much risk the investor is willing to accept in terms of violating the floor. For instance, if m is selected to be 5, then the model should work as expected as long as the value of the risk position does not move any more than 20 percent between rebalancing periods (20 percent is equal to 1/5). It can be argued that if the rebalancing period is short, then a diversified portfolio of risky assets should not move by more than 20 percent and the model should work properly. However, it must be borne in mind that there are costs associated with frequent rebalancing and the costs increase rapidly if there are positions in alternative investments. These rebalancing costs and various fees charged by managers of such dynamic allocation products represent a major drag on their performance.

Let's consider a simple example. Suppose a structured note is to be set up where the principal is to be protected. The maturity of the note is 10 years. The underlying assets of the structure are (1) a diversified portfolio of traditional as well alternative assets and (2) U.S. Treasuries. The first step is to calculate the bond floor, which is equal to the present value of the principal discounted using the current term structure of Treasuries. For instance, if the current price of a 10-year zero-coupon Treasury security is .67, this means that for every $100 investment, $67 must be invested in Treasuries to protect the principal. The remaining $33 can be invested in the diversified portfolio. Such a strategy would be free of almost any risk and of course is not likely to provide a meaningful return either.

Alternatively, the investor may be willing to take a small risk and use a CPPI structure to manage the risk. Using a moderate multiplier (e.g., $m = 2$), the investor can have a great deal of confidence that the bond floor will not be violated. In this case, the portfolio manager will invest the following amount in the diversified portfolio:

$$66 = 2 \times (100 - 67)$$

The remaining 34 will be invested in Treasuries. Suppose the bond floor increases to 70, the investment in Treasuries grows 36 and the investment in diversified portfolio grows to 73. The reallocation is determined as follows:

$$78 = 2 \times (36 + 73 - 70)$$

This means that the total investment in diversified portfolio should increase from 73 to 78. The net investment in Treasuries will be $31 = 36 + 73 - 78$. This procedure is followed until the note matures. This simple approach will guarantee that the principal is protected as long as the percentage change in the value of the diversified portfolio between rebalancing does not decline by more 50 percent, which is the inverse of 2.

The multiplier, m, does not have to be constant. In practice, it could change as the volatility of the underlying portfolio changes. Typically, one would want to decrease the value of the multiplier as markets become more volatile. Finally, simulation can be used to obtain distributional properties of the note under various assumptions regarding the behavior of interest rates, underlying assets of the diversified portfolios, fee structures, coupon rates and so on.

What Every Investor Should Remember

- Markowitz-based optimization provides suggested strategy weightings that are sensitive to a wide range of issues related to parameter estimation. For example, asset allocations are sensitive to the differential return forecasts (anticipated weightings may therefore be better determined using forecasted returns) and the measurement interval used in calculating the inputs to the various asset allocation procedures.

> ■ Tactical asset allocations benefit from the consideration of alternative core strategy portfolios that differ in the underlying factors used in determining the tactical rebalancing.
> ■ Dynamic asset allocation processes are by their very nature adjustments based on future unforecastable factors and are liable not only to changes in the underlying factors driving the model but to changes in the business and regulatory environment.

Notes

1. The impact of various optimization models maximizing over errors varies as to the types of assets being considered and the degree to which the errors exist both in return estimation and risk estimation.
2. See Frost and Savarino (1988).
3. For a summary of research in this area, see Tokat, Wicas, and Kinniry (2006).

References

Black, F., and R. Litterman. 1992. "Global Portfolio Optimization." *Financial Analysts Journal* 48, no. 5 (September/October): 28–43.

Frost, P. A., and J. E. Savarino. 1988. "For Better Performance: Constrain Portfolio Weights." *Journal of Portfolio Management* 15, no. 1 (Fall): 29–34.

Tokat, Yesim, Nelson Wicas, and Francis M. Kinniry. 2006. "The Asset Allocation Debate: A Review and Reconciliation." *Journal of Financial Planning* 19 (10): 52–63.

Part V Core and Satellite Investment

Asset allocation consists of a fundamental set of decisions centered on what investments and how much of each investment to buy given an investor's risk preferences. This section provides a traditional basic "core" and "satellite" approach to asset allocation. In so doing, it focuses on the potential impact of moving from more liquid and transparent investment vehicles in each asset class to less liquid and less transparent investment vehicles and the potential change in expected return and risk associated with that movement. To reach this end, the part first defines the concept of core and satellite portfolios and then goes on to discuss the issues associated with benchmarking the different asset classes critical to the implementation of these concepts. Note that the research and data associated with alternative investments is relatively new and must be carefully managed. Next, the part provides examples of an investor's decision making process in moving between and among core and satellite portfolios and offers an overview of sample allocations and expected risk/return scenarios. Finally, this section discusses recent issues in replication theory and how these developments can enhance the value of an investor's decision.

Throughout, the discussion posits that the benefit of diversification is based on the potential for investing in a wide range of assets, each with its own unique return and risk characteristics. A reasoned understanding of the economic and market factors underlying an asset's return and risk profile is critical to the meaningful formulation of investment policies and the exercise of informed judgment.

In a core-satellite approach to traditional stock and bond asset allocation, an investor builds a core consisting mostly of passively managed, liquid, and low cost equity and fixed income assets and adds to this core a set of satellites consisting of actively managed, relatively illiquid, alpha generating assets. The idea is that investors should not spend valuable resources on seeking alpha where it does not exist or is too small to make a difference.

According to Standard & Poor's latest study (Standard & Poor's Indices Versus Active Funds Scorecard, Year End 2008):

- Over the five-year market cycle from 2004 to 2008, the S&P 500 outperformed 71.9 percent of actively managed large cap funds, the S&P MidCap 400 outperformed 79.1 percent of mid cap funds, and the S&P SmallCap 600 outperformed 85.5 percent of small cap funds. These results are similar to that of the previous five-year cycle from 1999 to 2003.
- The belief that bear markets favor active management is a myth. A majority of active funds in eight of the nine domestic equity style boxes were outperformed by indices in the negative markets of 2008. The bear market of 2000 to 2002 showed similar outcomes.
- The difference between the performance of first quartile large cap funds and third quartile large cap funds was 2.73 percent per year from 2003 to 2008. For small cap funds the difference is 4.1 percent.
- Similar results are obtained for fixed income funds and international equity funds.

These results indicate that it does not pay to waste time, money, and effort on finding alpha or top managers in the area of traditional equity and fixed income investments. Not only do most managers fail to beat their benchmarks, even when an investor gets lucky and finds a "good" manager, he fails to outperform other managers by a significant amount.

While the return differential between top and bottom quartile equity and fixed income managers is relatively small, the same cannot be said for alternative investment managers. For instance, according to a report by Yale endowment (Yale Endowment Report, 2005), the return differential between the first quartile venture capital funds and third quartile venture capital funds was 43.2 percent for 1995 to 2005. The result for funds of funds was 7.1 percent. This means it pays to spend time and effort to identify top performing actively managed alternative investments.

Determining the Appropriate Benchmarks and Groupings

As noted, understanding the underlying sources of risk and returns of a given investment or its associated "grouping" is essential to a meaningful asset allocation program. In many programs, noninvestable benchmarks have been used to provide a basis for determining the potential risks and returns of asset classes from traditional stock and bonds to alternative investments such as private equity, real estate, commodities, and hedge funds. The core asset decision should produce an investable portfolio whose return and market risk characteristics reflect those of the noninvestable benchmark portfolio. Due to the desired matching between the noninvestable benchmark portfolio and the investable core portfolio, the core portfolio provides "market returns for market risk." Investors who desire higher potential returns within each asset class must consider investment alternatives that provide higher return potential consistent with higher risk. These investments may be regarded as satellite portfolios to the comparison passive investments within the core asset class.

For a wide range of reasons (academic and commercial), most asset allocation programs have used different approaches to determine the number of core asset classes.[1] While asset allocation for many investors remains dedicated to traditional stock and bond investment, in this section we concentrate on presenting a multi-asset class allocation model that is more suitable for the increasing number of investors who are considering various forms of alternative investment vehicles. For these investors, alternative investments are centered on traditional alternatives such as private equity, real estate, and commodities. For other investors, alternative investments also include various forms of hedge funds and managed futures (often classified as modern alternative investment vehicles). In previous years, most investors were required to find manager based alternative investment products that tracked the performance of the underlying noninvestable benchmarks used in the initial asset allocation analysis. Recently, there has been a growth in various liquid investable products that offer a direct means to access these forms of alternative investment. Today these investable forms include ETFs, strategy-specific algorithmic based trading products, and replication/tracking products that offer the means to invest in liquid transparent vehicles that track the performance of less liquid alternative investment products.

Figure 17.18 proposes a brief schematic that indicates one process for determining the potential strategic portfolio based on a range of noninvestable asset benchmark/indices. It indicates the importance of a systematic investment process in determining an investor's approach to overall asset allocation. As stated, a central part of the strategic management process is to establish a set of core portfolio holdings across a set of predetermined investments that provide the basis for meeting one's long term return to risk. While the underlying core assets that are used to capture the expected return and risk attributes of the strategic portfolio may be passive in nature, the process by which these assets are chosen and managed should be active and include discretionary oversight.

Figure 17.19 reflects a brief taxonomy for reviewing a set of multi-asset investments facing the typical investor. This overview of the investment choices facing the typical investor is similar to that presented in many asset allocation approaches. First, as indicated above, choices must be made as to the series of asset classes considered for investment when determining the strategic portfolio holdings of the investor. Increasing the number of potential asset classes increases both the potential for greater risk management as well as increased return for a predetermined level of risk. As shown in Figure 17.19, while the underlying strategic asset allocation may be based on noninvestable benchmarks, an investor's core portfolio should

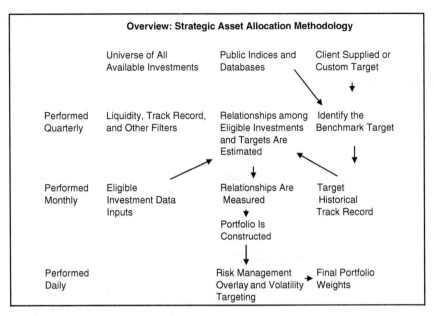

FIGURE 17.18   Benchmark Strategic Asset Allocation Process

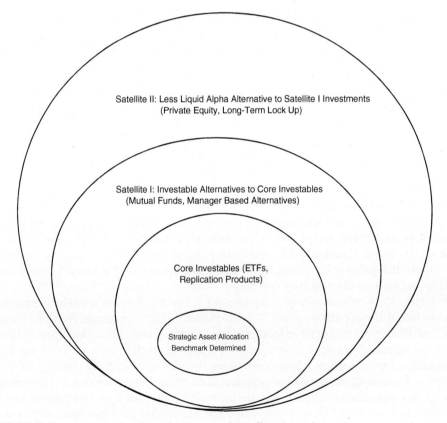

FIGURE 17.19   Strategic Benchmark, Core, and Satellite Groupings

TABLE 17.11 Alternative Asset Classes in Benchmark, Core, and Satellite Groupings

Asset Class	Noninvestable Benchmark	Core	Satellite I	Satellite II
Equity				
Large Cap	Russell 1000	Russell 1000 ETF	Funds	Individual Mgrs.
Small Cap	Russell 2000	Russell 2000 ETF	Funds	Individual Mgrs.
Emerging Mkt.	MSCI Emg. Mkt.	MSCI EM. ETF	Funds	Individual Mgrs.
Non-U.S.-Dev.	MSCI EAFE	MSCI EAFE ETF	Funds	Individual Mgrs.
Fixed Income				
Government/Credit	Barclay Gov.	Barclay Gov. ETF	Funds	Individual Mgrs.
Aggregate	Barclay Agg.	Barclay Agg.ETF	Funds	Individual Mgrs.
High Yield	Barclay HY	Barclay HY ETF	Funds	Individual Mgrs.
Alternative Traditional				
Private Equity	S&P PE Index	S&P PE ETF	Funds	Individual Mgrs.
Real Estate	NAREIT	NAREIT ETF	Funds	Individual Mgrs.
Commoditites	S&P GSCI	SP GSCI ETF	Funds	Individual Mgrs.
Alternative Modern				
Hedge Funds	CISDM EW HF Index	Index Replication	Funds	Individual Mgrs.
Managed Futures	CISDM EW CTA Index	Index Replication	Funds	Individual Mgrs.
		Investment Characteristics		
Higher ⟵	Transparency, Daily Price, Exchange Traded	⟶		Lower
Higher ⟵	Style Consistency, Scalability	⟶		Lower
Lower ⟵	Business and Counterparty Risk	⟶		Higher
Lower ⟵	Alpha	⟶		Higher

contain investable passive investments that capture the underlying returns of the noninvestable benchmarks. If an investor desires to increase their potential return without dramatically changing one's asset class exposure, then, as shown in Figure 17.19, adding additional manager-based investments (Satellite I and Satellite II), which track the passive investable assets but also may contain potential manager alpha, should be considered.

In Table 17.11, the core investment classes have been broken down into equity, fixed income, traditional alternatives, and modern alternatives. Each of these classes of course contains a set of sub-indices (e.g., equity—value and growth, domestic/foreign, small/large) and each of the relevant sub-indices may be combined to achieve a unique risk set consistent with investor needs. In Table 17.11, those potential investments that are both investable and transparent alternatives to the noninvestable asset classes investment vehicles are grouped into the core portfolio. These investments may include a range of investible ETFs as well as closed end funds and/or passive investable tracking programs (hedge fund and CTA tracking products).

For investors who are willing to invest in investments within an asset class which have less liquidity and transparency, a range of investments are listed in Satellite I. These investments include various manager based mutual fund investments as well as investable manager based or managed account benchmark products in the alternative investment area. Satellite II is for those investment products for which liquidity and transparency are lower compared to comparison core products and manager-based products included in Satellite I. In fact, the lower liquidity and lack of transparency

TABLE 17.12　Alternative Product Characteristics in Core through Satellite Products

Investment Sector	Core	Satellite I	Satellite II
Product Characteristics	Index, ETF, Replication	Liquid, Fund Based	Manager Based
Fees	Low	Medium	High
Liquidity	High	Medium	Low
Transparency	High	Medium/High	Low
Required Minimums	Low	Low/Medium	High
Diversified Exposure	High	Medium	Low
Regulatory Oversight	Medium/High	Medium/High	Low
Manager Risk	Low	Medium	High
Style Consistency	High	High	Low
Product Flexibility	High	Low	Low
Valuation Frequency	High	Medium/High	Low
Capacity	Medium/High	Constrained	Constrained
Trading	Systematic	Active	Active
Only Exchange Traded	Yes	No	No

for assets in Satellite II may in some cases form the basis for the excess return for Satellite II products over similar core and Satellite I investment products.

It is important to note that for each product the transition from core to satellite may result in slightly different return and risk characteristics. It is key, however, that these risk characteristics be manager specific and that a portfolio of such assets may provide excess return relative to the core benchmark product but will retain a relatively high correlation with that benchmark. It is essential again to remind investors that the excess return to a particular form of investment within an asset class may not be due solely to price risk but to a range of potential risks consistent with the underlying investment (lack of liquidity, lack of transparency). A range of those potential risks an investor faces when they move from core to satellite groupings is provided in Table 17.12.

Many investors may doubt the ability of various passive investable core products to reflect the return and risk characteristics of various noninvestable asset class benchmarks. Table 17.13 reports the correlations between the noninvestable benchmarks used in portfolio asset allocation determination and the underlying core investments based on investable ETFs, as well as replication indices that track the underlying noninvestable index (the primary period of analysis is 1999–2008, however, for some paired correlations the period of analysis is less). In all cases, the correlations between the noninvestable benchmarks and the investable core are over 0.70. Note again that the use of historical benchmarks in any asset allocation program is based on the assumption that the actual investment mirrors the factor characteristics of the benchmark. In this case, the investable core portfolios are designed to be style pure with consistent expected return and risk characteristics. Satellite I portfolios are generally regarded as additions to the investable core sector portfolio but with the potential for the benefits of active management. Satellite I portfolios as indicated in Figure 17.13 have correlations with the benchmark indices and with the core such that their use should not fundamentally change the market risk characteristics of the benchmark and/or investable core portfolio.

Sample Allocations

The decision that drives the asset allocation process is the underlying risk tolerance of the investor. An investor's risk tolerance may cover a range of desired risk exposures.[2] Typically those ranges have included conservative, moderate, and aggressive risk based portfolios. Within each of these risk tolerance classifications, investors may decide to invest primarily in traditional security investments or they may decide to place additional investments in the alternative investment area without dramatically changing volatility characteristics. These portfolios will reflect an investor's characteristics such as assets, liabilities, time horizon, tax status, and risk tolerance. It is fully expected that increased investment in private equity and hedge funds offer financial consultants the investment products required to provide their clients unique returns that are not available through traditional stocks and bonds; and, just as important, provide financial consultants with a set of assets that enable them to show their unique educational role.

This decision can be broken into the "can" and "will" portion of an investor's asset allocation framework:

- **Can-Risk Capacity:** The investor's objective ability to take financial risks, that is, how much risk the investor is *able* to accept.
  - The investor's ability to take financial risks is externally given by the investor's financial situation. Various academic and practitioner models exist that attempt to map out an investor's current financial situation, their long-term financial needs, and the investor's capacity to take on additional risk.
  - Often various forms of contingent (e.g., minimum asset floor) investment models are used, which permit an investor to feel assured that the minimum investment level is protected while automatically increasing investment and potential return through alternative investments as the minimum investment level is systematically increased and investor wealth or investment levels increase. (Of course, if wealth or investment levels decrease, systematic reductions would also be conducted.)
- **Will-Risk Aversion:** The investor's subjective disposition for taking risks, that is, how much risk the investor is *willing* to accept.[3]
  - Know-how: An investor's understanding of the financial market and its products is a major influence. The better the understanding, the higher the risk level an investor will accept. For instance, even though according to objective measures of risk, hedge funds are less risky than long equity positions, individual investors may avoid any allocation to hedge funds because of their lack of familiarity. An important task of a financial consultant is, therefore, to educate high net worth individuals about the risk-return characteristics of the various private equity opportunities and hedge fund strategies.
  - Positive Experience: Positive experiences with different asset classes in the past increase the willingness to take new risks (i.e., invest in unfamiliar asset classes).
  - Personal Character: Optimism, entrepreneurship, and the discipline of staying with a predefined strategy.

TABLE 17.13 Comparison Correlations for Benchmark, Core, and Satellite Groupings

Benchmark	Russell 1000	Russell 2000	MSCI EAFE	MSCI EM	BarCap US Gov	BarCap US Agg
Core	iShares Russell 1000 Index Fund	iShares Russell 2000 Index Fund	iShares MSCI EAFE	iShares MSCI EM	iShares Barclays Government/ Credit Bond Fund	iShares Barclays Aggregate Bond Fund
Correlations to Benchmark	1.00	1.00	0.98	0.97	0.86	0.95
Satellite 1 Investments	Lipper Lg-Cap Core	Lipper Sm-Cap Core	Lipper Non US Stock	Lipper Emerg Mkt Fd	Lipper A Rated Bnd Fd	Lipper Gen US Govt Fd
Correlations to Benchmark	1.00	0.98	0.93	0.99	0.97	0.94
Satellite 1 Investments	Lipper Lg-Cap Core	Lipper Sm-Cap Core	Lipper Non US Stock	Lipper Emerg Mkt Fd	Lipper A Rated Bnd Fd	Lipper Gen US Govt Fd
Correlations to Core	1.00	0.98	0.95	0.97	0.89	0.87

Core Allocation

Once the risk appetite of the investor is known, decisions can be made as to the core asset allocations as well as the degree to which the investor is willing to hold various satellite portfolios. As noted above, once the underlying strategic asset allocation is determined, the initial problem is to determine which assets to hold that fundamentally track that of the noninvestable assets benchmarks used in the initial strategic asset allocation determination. The economic rationale for investable core traditional and alternative investable products is that while these passive index-based core investment products are designed to generate no alpha, they are designed to provide diversification benefits and help manage underlying risk exposure.

Satellite Investment

Given an investor's desire for greater exposure to manager skill, a series of manager-based products in various satellite portfolios can be considered. Satellite investment products are actively managed and may be a source of risk management or manager alpha. The risk exposures of these products are similar to those of the investable core portfolio and thus can be used without fundamentally changing the core portfolio's risk exposure.[4] Satellite investments are generally regarded as less liquid satellite investments that represent the most likely source of alpha in today's marketplace. The degree of alpha is a function of the liquidity and informational transparency of the investment vehicle.

BarCap US Corporate High-Yield	Private Equity Index	S&P GSCI	FTSE NAREIT ALL REITS	CISDM EW HF Index	CISDM CTA EW Index
SPDR Barclays Capital High Yield Bond ETF	PowerShares Listed Private Equity Portfolio	iShares S&P GSCI Commodity Indexed Trust	iShares FTSE NAREIT Real Estate 50 Index Fund	HF Replication	CTA Replication
0.95 Lipper HI Cur Yld Bd	0.94 Private Equity MF	0.99 Lipper Nat Res Fd IX	0.99 Lipper Real Estate Fd	0.94 HF Investable (Mgr. Based)	0.73 CTA Investable (Mgr. Based)
0.98 Lipper HI Cur Yld Bd	0.68 Private Equity MF	0.63 Lipper Nat Res Fd IX	0.99 Lipper Real Estate Fd	0.90 HF Investable (Mgr. Based)	0.41 CTA Investable (Mgr. Based)
0.90	0.83	0.85	0.98	0.91	0.73

Algorithmic and Discretionary Aspects of Core/Satellite Exposure

Most current research has discussed the algorithmic or discretionary aspects of asset allocation across various core asset classes. However, some research has also addressed various tactical asset allocation processes within a particular asset class. In Table 17.14 we have ranked various Russell 1000 and Russell 2000 growth and value indices on changes in VIX. Results show that decreases in VIX have a more positive impact on Russell Growth than on the Russell Value. In contrast, increases in VIX have a more negative impact on Russell Growth than Russell Value. Investments within a Russell 1000 or Russell 2000 core strategy can thus be dynamically managed to achieve desired risk level within a strategy, however, with a bias toward the underlying equity sector that the investor may think will outperform in the expected market environment.

It is also possible that rather than adjusting between core value and core growth, an investor could simply adjust the weighting within an asset class such that when volatility increases relative to traditional risk levels, dynamic asset allocation will adjust weightings to ensure that an asset's returns reflect historical volatility. For instance, an investor can reduce strategy risk exposure in high volatility markets (therefore reducing exposure to decreasing market return factors) and increase strategy risk exposure in low volatility markets (therefore increasing exposure to increasing market return factors).

The strict use of algorithmic models to manage risk within a core set of strategies or across core and satellite programs may not be sufficient to reach desired goals. In certain cases simple heuristic models of decision making based on a fundamental understanding of the relationship between macroeconomic and market information

TABLE 17.14 Intra-Equity Benchmark Performance: Ranked on Change in VIX

	Low		Medium-Low		Medium-High		High		All Dates
	Min	Max	Min	Max	Min	Max	Min	Max	
Ranking on VIX End-of-Month Change	−15%	−2%	−2%	0%	0%	2%	2%	21%	
Monthly Mean									
VIX End-of-Month Change	−4%		−1%		1%		5%		0%
Russell 1000 Growth	3.53%		2.12%		0.44%		−3.81%		0.65%
Russell 1000 Value	2.82%		1.79%		1.08%		−2.67%		0.82%
Russell 2000 Growth	4.15%		2.63%		0.24%		−4.61%		0.70%
Russell 2000 Value	3.34%		2.41%		0.79%		−2.63%		1.04%

and strategy performance is required. In short, sometimes you simply have to be discretionary in choosing what to hold and when to hold it.

What Every Investor Should Remember

- A central part of the strategic management process is to establish a set of core portfolio holdings across a set of predetermined investments that provide the basis for meeting one's long-term return to risk goals. While the underlying assets may be passive in nature, the process by which these assets are chosen should be active.
- Due to the desired matching between the benchmark portfolio and the core portfolio, the core portfolio is providing "market returns for market risk." Investors who desire higher potential returns within each asset class must consider investment alternatives that provide higher return potential consistent with higher risk. These investments may be regarded as satellite portfolios to the comparison passive investment within the core asset class.
- Little research has discussed the algorithmic or discretionary aspects of asset allocation within a particular core asset class. Investors should be aware of the ability to actively manage security selection within an asset class without fundamentally changing the risk exposure of the core asset.

Notes

1. Different extremes exist. Sharpe (1992) used 12 asset groupings in his analysis of asset allocation. Most of these asset groupings, however, were variants of various equity markets. In contrast, more recent studies on multi-asset allocation use as little as four asset classes (commodities, currencies, equities, fixed income) or as many as eight (equity, fixed income, private equity, real estate, commodities, hedge funds, CTAs). Similarly, within any individual core asset group, various asset allocation models use a wide range of investment strategies that trade securities consistent with the construction of that core asset class (e.g., value/growth and small cap/large cap within a U.S. equity core allocation).
2. Risk aversion, on the other hand, is difficult to determine. Numerous risk-assessment tools developed by banks, brokers, and psychologists try to give investors help in determining their desired level of financial risk. Studies in behavioral finance and decision making under risk have shown that risk aversion is influenced by recent performance (Sewell, 2008).
3. For a discussion of the determinants of risk taking behavior, see Hryshko, Luengo-Prado, and Sorensen (2009).
4. The diversification benefits of less liquid satellite portfolios depend both on the returns drivers of the alternative investments and on the ability of the portfolio to track initial core portfolios (Olan, Sorensen, and Hua, 2009; and Chen, Jiang, and Shu, 2009.

References

Chen, P., G. Jiang, and K. Shu. 2009. "Fund of Funds, Portable Alpha, and Portfolio Optimization." *The Journal of Portfolio Management* 35, no. 3 (Spring): 79–92.

Hryshko, D., M. J. Luengo-Prado, and B. E. Sorensen. 2009. "Childhood Determinants of Risk Aversion." www.ssrn.com.

Olan, E., E. Sorensen, and R. Hua. 2009. "Global Value Investing Delivers Diversification: A Multi-Strategy Perspective." *The Journal of Portfolio Management* 35, no. 2 (Winter): 42–49.

Sewell, Martin. 2008. "Behavioural Finance." University College London (Rev. August). www.behaviouralfinance.net/.

Sharpe, William F. 1992. "Asset Allocation: Management Style and Performance Measurement." *Journal of Portfolio Management* 18 (2): 12–13.

Part VI Tax Efficient Investing

The political process that pushes and pulls on the Internal Revenue Code of the United States has created a monster of complexity. The purpose of this section is to make clearer the principal methods of tax-efficient investing. We discuss context, taxes that affect investment returns, basic tax-efficient principles, and outline after-tax performance measurement.[1]

Context

Historically, the theory and much of the practice of investment management in the United States can be viewed as taking a purely patriotic approach, with too little regard for individual investor circumstances. Investment return after the payment of taxes to the federal government to maintain federal activities and to state and local governments for funding community services has not been an overriding concern. Until recently, the dominant operating philosophy in investment management as conveyed by its leading professionals has been on generating good returns relative to some untaxed market index, and not on any tax consequences. Practitioners and researchers have focused far more on generating alpha by the development of improved asset allocation models that are robust to estimation of input errors or according to better measures of risk, driven by better valuation models, and implemented through more efficient trading strategies. However, as Garland (1987) noted more than 25 years ago:

> Academic literature seems to ignore how taxes affect the portfolios of individual investors and corporations. This omission is understandable, because taxes obscure the already dark and difficult terrain upon which investment theories

---

[1] In this part, we refer to various tax rates. The tax rates mentioned are those that apply to 2013 as set forth in the American Taxpayer Relief Act of 2012 enacted on January 2, 2013. Future tax rates, as well as applicable provisions regarding those tax rates, can be materially different.

are built. It is regrettable, however, because taxes matter so much. Taxes are the biggest expense that most individual investors face—more than commissions, more than investment management fees. (p. 19)

The preponderance of empirical evidence supports Garland's view that taxes are a major drag on performance and, therefore, on the wealth of taxable investors. Many of the practices of investment management for managing the portfolio of tax-exempt investors do not apply to taxable investors. In fact, some principles established to increase the returns of tax-exempt investors actually detract from after-tax returns for taxable investors. Further, Berkin and Ye (2003) conclude:

Our findings show that no matter what market environment occurs in the future, managing a portfolio in a tax-efficient manner gives substantially better after-tax performance than a simple index fund, both before and after liquidation of the portfolio. (p. 91)

In 2000, an annual nationwide telephone survey of 500 U.S. investors conducted by Eaton Vance Management concluded that despite the recognition of the importance of taxes on investment returns and the claim by 80 percent of the survey participants that they examine their investment statements to determine the impact of taxes, there appeared to be little understanding about taxes and investments.[2] For example, 22 percent of the survey participants indicated that they did not know their income tax bracket. Overall the conclusion of the study was that investors exhibit "a significant lack of understanding about the tax implications of investments and a low awareness level of how to approach investing with an eye to tax efficiency." In its 2001 annual survey, the findings were not very different, with the conclusion being the same as in the prior year: "Although most investors recognize the importance of tax considerations, they have only a limited understanding of investment-related tax issues."[3]

However, by the 2005 Eaton Vance survey, the findings were more encouraging. The study concluded not only that "Investors are placing more importance than ever on the tax implications of investing.... While there are indications investors are generally getting smarter about taxes, many remain confused about how to invest for tax-efficiency and retain unrealistic expectations about potential capital gains distributions."[4] The 2008 annual survey, including 1,200 individuals with investments of $50,000 or more, reported that 81 percent of the investors in the survey indicated

---

[2] See "Survey Reveals That Despite Recent Market Correction, Fund Shareholders Don't Pay Attention to Bite Uncle Sam Takes Out of Returns; Low Awareness of How to Minimize Tax Implications of Investments," Eaton Vance 2000 Annual Investor Survey, March 15, 2000, http://corporate.eatonvance.com/Annual-Investor-Surveys.php.

[3] "National Survey: Large Capital Gains Distributions in a Year of Negative Returns Has Mutual Fund Investors More Concerned About Investment Taxes," Eaton Vance 2001 Annual Investor Survey, February 13, 2001.

[4] "Seventh Annual Eaton Vance National Investor Survey Finds: Investors Place Record High Importance on Effect of Taxes on Returns and Support Tax Cut Extensions," Eaton Vance 2005 Annual Investor Survey, December 6, 2005.

that the impact on taxes on their mutual fund return is an important concern and almost half said it is a *very* important concern.[5]

A survey study conducted by the CFA Institute in May 2008, coauthored by Horan and Adler (2009), sheds further light on the adoption of tax-aware investment practices by managers of taxable accounts. Of the 322 participants in the survey study, most indicated that they do incorporate taxes into a client's return requirements and when performing investment policy analysis. However, as explained later in this part, although tax-aware investing has an impact on risk, few participants indicated that they adjust portfolio risk for taxes.

In view of these surveys, it seems that awareness of tax-efficient investing principles is improving, but it still has a long way to go. The two overriding issues of tax efficiency that are critical are:

1. Do investors managing their own investments, or working with a financial advisor to do so, understand the fundamental principles in tax efficient investing?
2. For individual investors with accounts managed by an asset management firm in commingled vehicles such as mutual funds and hedge funds, what are the strategies being used by their management to deal with taxes, and do they fit that particular investor's tax situation?

The principles in this section are applicable within many countries, but our discussion of details is based on U.S. examples. We next briefly review the various U.S. taxes that affect investment returns. This is necessary preparation for understanding tax-efficient investment strategies.

Taxes That Affect Investment Returns

U.S. taxes that most affect investing can be divided into three categories: (1) federal income taxes, (2) state and local income taxes, and (3) federal estate taxes.[6] It is important to realize in looking at the potential impact of taxes on investment returns that the federal and state/local income taxes are not carved in stone. For a variety of reasons, the tax rules and tax rates have changed over time. Future tax regimes in which investment decisions must be made are uncertain, and add another element of risk to investing.

FEDERAL INCOME TAXES   Federal income taxes must be paid on (1) interest income, (2) dividend income, and (3) gains realized from the sale of capital assets.[7]

The highest nominal marginal federal income tax rate in 2013 is approximately 40 percent on investment returns that are classified as ordinary income; this includes most interest and at various times has included dividends. The ordinary income tax rate has varied since the beginning of the twentieth century, reaching a top marginal rate of 90 percent. Even in the last 35 years, the rates have dropped from 70 percent,

[5] "Eaton Vance's 2008 Investor Survey Finds Taxes Top List of Investor Concerns," Eaton Vance 2008 Annual Investor Survey, October 15, 2008.
[6] There are also similar estate taxes imposed by states.
[7] There are different rules for corporations but our focus here is on individual taxpayers.

to 50 percent, and then back to 40 percent. With such instability, predicting long-term rates with certainty seems impossible.

The tax rate can be either higher or lower under the American Taxpayer Relief Act of 2012 because of a new provision (Section 1411) that specifies a 3.8 percent Medicare surtax on what is referred to as "net investment income" (unearned income), which includes dividends, interest, and capital gains. Previously, the Medicare tax did not apply to net investment income. The new provision specifies that the 3.8 percent Medicare surcharge applies to single filers whose income exceeds $200,000 and married couples filing jointly whose income exceeds $250,000.

The effective marginal maximum rate is actually higher for many taxpayers. For example, to derive taxable income, taxpayers are entitled to itemized deduction. Changing the treatment of what expenses are permitted as deductions and limits on the amount that may be taken as an itemized deduction changes the effective maximum tax rate. Several years ago, for example, the elimination of interest deduction for many nonmortgage interest expenses and the imposition of a requirement that itemized deductions must exceed certain percentages of gross income in order to qualify as deductions actually increased the *effective* maximum tax rate despite an announced decline in the *statutory* maximum tax rate from 39.6 percent to 35 percent.

Another example is the increase in the effective marginal tax rate for taxpayers subject to the alternative minimum tax (AMT). Alternative minimum taxable income (AMTI) is a taxpayer's taxable income after certain adjustments for specified tax preferences. It is designed to cause AMTI to approximate economic income and mitigate the benefits associated with what Congress views as excessive deductions. A taxpayer's tax liability is the greater of (1) the tax computed at regular tax rates on taxable income or (2) the tax computed at a lower rate on AMTI. The statutory maximum tax rate for AMTI is 28 percent. AMT raises the income to be taxed. It may indicate either a higher or lower particular taxpayer's tax rate from the regular income tax rate. The product of the applicable income and tax rate determines whether the AMT is an increased total tax and will therefore be applied instead of the regular income tax. This mainly affects taxpayers who have moderately high incomes and extensive tax preferences disallowed by AMT. However, at even higher income levels, the effective marginal ordinary income tax rate is about 40 percent.

Interest Income   Interest received by a taxpayer is included in gross income, unless a specific statutory exemption indicates otherwise. A portion of the income realized from holding a bond may be in the form of capital appreciation rather than interest income. The tax treatment of the income component that represents capital appreciation differs depending on when the bond was issued.

The interest payments received are treated as ordinary income. In addition, income accrued but not paid on bonds where the discount from the maturity value is classified as *original issue discount* (OID) results in taxable income of the accrued interest despite the fact that there has not been a cash payment of interest. The rules dealing with OID are complicated and are not discussed here.

Interest income from bonds issued by state and local governments (referred to as *municipal securities*) may or may not be taxed. The municipal bond market includes taxable and tax-exempt issues. For the latter, the exemption applies only to interest payments received, not to any capital gain.

As mentioned earlier, there are tax preference items that must be included in the determination of AMTI. One of these items is income from certain tax-exempt municipal interest, thereby reducing the benefits associated with these bonds. However, most tax-exempt municipal bonds are not subject to the AMT.

Dividends   For individuals, dividends are taxed in the year they are received (on a cash basis) and were for many years taxable as ordinary income to the recipient. Dividends are classified as ordinary dividends and qualified dividends. For common stock to be classified as qualified dividends, the Internal Revenue Code requires that the investor "must have held the stock for more than 60 days during the 121-day period that begins 60 days before the ex-dividend date." In the case of preferred stock, the requirement is that the investor "must have held the stock more than 90 days during the 181-day period that begins 90 days before the ex-dividend date if the dividends are due to periods totaling more than 366 days." There is favorable tax treatment (i.e., lower tax rate) applicable to qualified dividends. If a dividend does not meet the requirements to be treated as a qualified dividend, it is treated as an ordinary dividend and taxed at ordinary tax rates. The distinction (and differential tax treatment) between ordinary and qualified dividends was scheduled to be phased out in 2013. However, it was retained under the American Taxpayer Relief Act of 2012.

For 2013, under the American Taxpayer Relief Act of 2012, the maximum tax rate applicable to qualified dividends for single filers whose income is at or below $400,000 and married couples filing jointly whose income is at or below $450,000 is 15 percent. However, for investors whose income exceeds those levels, the maximum dividend tax rate is 20 percent. Moreover, there is the 3.8 percent Medicare surcharge on dividends (both qualified and ordinary dividends) for investors in the applicable income levels (single filers exceeding $200,000 and married filing jointly exceeding $250,000). With the AMT, the effective tax rate on qualified dividends may be different.

Income from Sale of Capital Assets   The Internal Revenue Code provides for a special tax treatment on the sale of a capital asset such as stocks and bonds. In order to understand the tax treatment of a capital asset, the *tax basis* of a capital asset must first be defined. In most instances, the *original tax basis* of a capital asset is the taxpayer's total cost on the date of acquisition. The *adjusted tax basis* of a capital asset is its original tax basis increased by capital additions and decreased by capital recoveries (i.e., return of principal). That is,

Adjusted tax basis = Original tax basis + Capital additions − Capital recoveries

As explained later, an important option granted to the investor is the selection of the "lot" that has been sold. For example, if a stock was purchased in lots at different points in time, an investor can identify the specific lot that was sold. The investor can select the one that will be most beneficial from a tax perspective, usually the one with highest purchase cost.

Once the lot is selected, the proceeds received from the sale of a capital asset are compared to the adjusted tax basis to determine if the transaction produced a capital gain or capital loss. If the proceeds exceed the adjusted tax basis, the taxpayer realizes a *capital gain*; a *capital loss* is realized when the adjusted tax basis exceeds the proceeds received by the taxpayer. The rules are summarized as follows:

Situation	Result
Proceeds > Adjusted tax basis	Capital gain
Proceeds < Adjusted tax basis	Capital loss
Proceeds = Adjusted tax basis	No capital gain or loss

Then once a capital gain or capital loss is determined for a capital asset, there are special rules for determining the impact on taxable income. For the 2013 tax year, the maximum long-term capital gains tax rate for individuals depends on the investor's taxable income. For single filers with incomes exceeding $400,000 and married couples filing jointly with incomes exceeding $450,000, the maximum tax rate is 20 percent. For investors below these income levels, the maximum tax rate is 15 percent. However, there is the 3.8 percent Medicare surtax applicable to single filers whose income exceeds $200,000 and married couples filing jointly whose income exceeds $250,000. Consequently, in 2013 the maximum capital gains tax rate is 23.8 percent for investors whose income exceeds $400,000 for single filers and $450,000 for married couples, and 18.8 percent for single filers whose income exceeds $200,000 and married couples filing jointly whose income exceeds $250,000. In our discussion below, we refer to the maximum capital gains tax rate as 23.8 percent.

These tax rates are substantially less than the 40 percent maximum tax rate on ordinary income for those in the higher income level and 35 percent in the lower income level, though with the AMT the effective tax rate slightly differs. However, gains on securities held for a year or less are taxed at the ordinary income rate, and also capital losses are less favorably treated than are ordinary losses. Consequently, a basic understanding of the rather complicated treatment of capital gains and losses is important. The tax treatment for individuals is as follows.

To determine the impact of transactions involving capital assets on taxable income, it is first necessary to ascertain whether the sale resulted in a capital gain or loss that is long term or short term. The classification depends on the length of time the capital asset is held by the taxpayer. The general rule is that if a capital asset is held for one year or less, the gain or loss is a *short-term capital gain* or *short-term capital loss*.[8] A *long-term capital gain* or *long-term capital loss* results when the capital asset is held for one day more than one year, or longer.

Next, all short-term capital gains and losses are combined to produce either a *net short-term capital gain* or a *net short-term capital loss*. The same procedure is followed for long-term capital gains and losses. Either a *net long-term capital gain* or a *net long-term capital loss* will result.

---

[8] An exception to the general rule is a wash sale. A *wash sale* occurs when "substantially identical securities" are acquired within 30 days before or after a sale of securities at a loss. In such cases, the loss is not recognized as a capital loss. Instead, the loss is added to the adjusted tax basis of the securities that caused the loss. The holding period for the new securities in connection with a wash sale then includes the period for which the original securities were held.

Third, an overall *net capital gain* or *net capital loss* is determined by combining the amounts in the previous step. One of the following will occur:

- Overall net short-term capital gain
- Overall net long-term capital gain
- Overall net short-term capital loss
- Overall net long-term capital loss

If an overall net short-term capital gain is realized, the amount is treated as ordinary income and added to taxable income. The tax on the overall net short-term capital gain will be based on the taxpayer's ordinary income tax rate. If an overall net long-term capital gain results, the gain is taxed at the lower of the taxpayer's ordinary income tax rate or the preferential tax rate for capital gains of 23.8 percent. Consequently, a taxpayer facing the maximum marginal tax rate on ordinary income of 40 percent will pay only 23.8 percent of the overall net long-term capital gain.

If an overall net capital loss that is either long-term or short-term results, the loss is deductible from gross income but only to the extent of $3,000 (but $1,500 for married taxpayers filing separate returns). Unused capital losses can be carried over indefinitely until they are all utilized in subsequent tax years. A capital loss carryover maintains its character as long-term or short-term until total gains and losses are netted in future tax years. Notice the asymmetry in the treatment of net capital losses—potential tax reduction from highly taxed realized short-term losses is partially wasted in netting them against more favorably taxed realized long-term gains.[9]

STATE AND LOCAL INCOME TAXES   Most state governments tax both investment income and capital gains, although the rates vary significantly from one jurisdiction to another. Seven states have no state income tax for individuals: Alaska, Florida, Nevada, South Dakota, Texas, Washington, and Wyoming. There are states with a flat rate and states with progressive tax rates based on income, with some states having a maximum tax rate close to 9 percent. There are two states that tax only dividends and interest income and this flat tax rate is quite high: New Hampshire (5 percent) and Tennessee (6 percent). Some local tax authorities tax only dividends.

Consequently, state taxes and, in some cases, local taxes are meaningful. Hence, benefits of gains tax deferral and tax loss harvesting, to be discussed later, get more pronounced when state and local taxes are taken into account.

Each state has its own tax treatment as to how interest income on municipal securities is taxed. The treatment at the state level will be one of the following: (1) exemption of interest from all municipal securities, (2) taxation of interest from all municipal securities, or (3) exemption of interest from municipal securities where the issuer is in the state, but taxation of interest where the issuer is out of state.

ESTATE TAXES   The Unified Gift and Estate Tax is made up of two parts. The *estate tax,* referred to by critics as the "death tax," is the tax imposed on a person's taxable

---

[9] This disadvantageous asymmetric tax treatment further subtracts from the after-tax returns of many actively managed portfolios.

estate upon his or her death. The *gift tax,* designed to prevent the avoidance of the estate tax by reducing the estate's value by gifting assets prior to a person's death, taxes the transfer of assets to a third party. The gift tax will not be discussed further here. The estate tax does not affect most taxpayers because of the significant amount of the estate excluded before the tax is imposed. However for those taxable investors affected, the tax impact is substantial. Note that states also have estate taxes and these create an additional, and not insignificant, tax burden.[10]

The two most important components of the estate tax are the exclusion amount and the maximum estate tax rate. Both the exclusion amount and tax rates have seen changes over time. Historically, since the inception of the estate tax in 1916, the top tax rate has varied from 10 percent to 70 percent. In early 2013, the exclusion amount is $5.12 million per person and the maximum rate is 40 percent. Legislative uncertainty about future estate tax regimes makes, as Horvitz (2008) states: "a source of undiversifiable investment risk for taxable investors."

As Horvitz (2008) notes, there has not been enough attention paid in the investment literature to estate taxes. Instead, the focus has been on the management of assets for institutional accounts that are tax-exempt entities. Even those studies that have examined the issue of tax-efficient investing, little consideration has been given to the impact of estate taxes due to the complex issues associated with such taxes and the frequency with which the tax law dealing with them have been changed by Congress.

Although it is almost always beneficial to defer realization of capital gains, the extent of the benefit may depend on choices that take effect only on the demise of the taxpayer. We cannot begin to do justice here to the range of possibilities opened up through the establishment of various forms of estate planning devices. Horvitz (2008) points out that there is a broad range of possibilities for exposure to the federal estate tax. For this reason, the possibility of the impact of estate taxes, even for those investors whose current net worth may be exempt from such taxes under the prevailing tax rules, must be taken into account in portfolio models used for optimizing after-tax returns. The modeling difficulty arises, as Horvitz states, because the analysis of after-tax expected returns must account for the various factors that will come into play over the investor's life. These factors include, but are not limited to, the amount of the estate tax exemption provided for in the tax code in the year of the investor's death, the forecasted estate tax rate, the estate's value (both publicly traded assets and illiquid assets such as the equity in the investor's home), and the investor's and spouse's actuarial mortality.

Because of these complications, appropriate capital gains tax deferral during one's life is materially different among taxable investors. Overall, consideration of disposition after death enhances the value of tax deferral during one's life. Estate tax law enhances the relevance of the study of very long holding periods before liquidation.

TAX TREATMENT OF MUTUAL FUNDS The tax rules discussed above are for individual investors. Unlike most corporations, mutual funds (or more specifically regulated investment companies, RICs) have special tax rules if certain requirements regarding

---

[10] Some states also have inheritance taxes on amounts received by beneficiaries. Confusingly, sometimes estate taxes are also called *inheritance taxes.*

the sources of gross income, asset composition, and distribution are satisfied. More specifically, at the entity level, mutual funds are not subject to taxation on their income or capital gains if the requirements are met and provided that at least 90 percent of its income (other than net capital gains) is distributed each year. Income that is retained, as well as all capital gains, is taxed at regular corporate tax rates. Moreover, the Internal Revenue Code imposes an excise tax of 4 percent on the "undistributed" amount unless a mutual fund distributes by December 31 at least 98 percent of its ordinary income earned during the calendar year, and 98.2 percent of its net capital gain earned during the 12-month period ending on October 31 of the calendar year. For these tax reasons, mutual funds typically distribute nearly all of their income and capital gains each year to avoid these taxes.

It is the fund investor who is responsible to pay taxes on the ordinary income and capital gains distributed. Dividend distributions are distributions whose source of income is primarily from the interest and dividends earned by the securities in a fund's portfolio and net short-term gains, if any. Long-term capital gains distributions represent a fund's net gains, if any, from the sale of securities held in its portfolio for more than one year.

It should be noted that mutual funds as an investment vehicle have a major drawback from a tax perspective: withdrawals by some fund shareholders can cause taxable realized capital gains (or losses) for the other shareholders who have maintained their positions. Another type of managed fund, one that does not have this adverse tax consequence, is an exchange-traded fund (ETF).

General Principles of After-Tax Investing

The keys to tax-efficient investing are, first, knowing your marginal tax rates and consequently matching investments to your situation, second, recognizing the benefits of tax deferral in reducing effective tax rates, and third, taking advantage of the option value stemming from your ability to choose the timing of taxable events. In that context, and having laid out the main U.S. tax rules, we can now discuss the most important investor strategies, particularly those benefitting from investment tax law's encouragement of saving and long-term equity ownership:

1. Selection of tax-advantaged security types.
2. Lowering effective tax rates through deferral of tax incidence:
    a. Avoiding higher taxes on short-term gains.
    b. Very long holding periods.
    c. Savings vehicles.
    d. Tax loss harvesting to capture option values.
    e. Estate and gift planning.
    f. Legal hazards.
3. After-tax asset allocation and portfolio structure.[11]

SELECTION OF TAX-ADVANTAGED SECURITY TYPES   Taxpayers facing high ordinary income tax rates may benefit from investing in state and municipal bonds exempt

---

[11] Also see Stein (1998).

from federal income taxation. If such bonds are issued in the domicile state of the investor, they are usually exempt from state income taxation as well.

A more widespread benefit accrues to highly taxed investors through the differential advantage conferred by investing in securities whose return comes in the form of capital gains, and, at this time, of dividends, rather than in the form of interest.[12] For these investors, the total tax rate on returns from bonds and bank savings may be almost double that on the returns from common and preferred stock. This in itself is a very substantial incentive to take the higher risks characterized by equity ownership. In addition, the incentive is further amplified by consequent government risk sharing through tax benefits from realized losses.

LOWERING EFFECTIVE TAX RATES THROUGH DEFERRAL OF TAX INCIDENCE *Tax deferral* comes about in several ways. The most obvious are embodied in retirement plans, for example, IRAs and 401(k) plans in the United States. Somewhat less obvious to many investors is the ability to defer the recognition of capital gains on capital assets that are retained in the portfolio. This topic includes valuation of the benefits of tax deferral centering on the relationship between turnover and the holding period, as well as the tax treatment upon final liquidation or upon death, and on just how much tax deferral adds to after-tax wealth.[13] Related is the question of why active management, and particularly the mutual fund industry, seems to perform so dismally when taxes are taken into account. Inevitably, the question of active versus passive management enters into the debate.

Avoiding Short-Term Gains Tax

The simplest way to get a benefit from deferring capital gains taxes in the U.S. under current tax law is to hold securities for more than a year before selling them. This converts a tax at short-term capital gain tax rates, predominately ordinary income tax rates, to the much lower one of long-term capital gains taxes. Suppose, for example, that the federal income tax were 45 percent and the corresponding long-term capital gains tax rate were 30 percent. Assume a 20 percent pretax capital gain after a year. By waiting another day, the after-tax return is converted from 20 percent times 55 percent, or 11 percent, to 20 percent times 70 percent, or 14 percent. An only slightly more complicated way to avoid paying the disadvantageous short-term gain tax is to offset short-term realized gains with short-term losses within the same or earlier tax period.

In our view, very rarely does the investor have sufficient reason to incur the short-term capital gains tax. Those who think they have such reasons are often the victims of overconfidence in their ability to forecast market returns.

Of course, the foregoing is obvious to many investors. But it is perhaps surprising how many investors who try to avoid simple short-term gain realization in conventional stock investing still fail to take into account disadvantageous short-term

---

[12] At the time of this writing, in the United States, dividends are also taxed at a preferentially low rate, but this may change in the future.

[13] See, for example, Garland (1997); Arnott, Berkin, and Ye (2000); Apelfeld, Fowler, and Gordon (1996); Luck (2000); Arnott (1991); Jeffrey and Arnott (1993, 1994); Hertog and Gordon (1994); Mulvahill (2000); and Dickson and Shoven (1993, 1994).

capital gains taxes as applied fully or partially to gains from high turnover mutual funds and hedge funds, and to trades in options, futures, short sales, and foreign exchange. We encourage the investor to seek further information before engaging in such practices.

Very Long Holding Periods The longer we wait to sell a stock after it produces an enduring capital gain, the less is the time-discounted present value of the capital gains tax. But this does not capture the full benefit. If we continue to earn capital gains, then we also earn gains on the amount we have not yet paid in taxes. That is, the benefits are small at the beginning, but they compound at a gradually accelerating rate as unrealized gains are accumulated.

We can understand the effect by considering the case of a single stock purchase held for n years with an annual gain of g. If the capital gains tax rate is T, then for every dollar we invest, we will have at the end:

$$(1 + g)^n (1 - T) + T \text{ dollars}$$

Now consider the hypothetical alternative of selling the stock after each year, and reinvesting the after-tax proceeds in a similar fashion. This time label the tax T^*. The result for every dollar invested would be

$$[1 + g(1 - T^*)]^n \text{ dollars}$$

Set the two expressions equal and solve for T^* to get the effective tax rate.[14] Note that in this case, the average tax rate and the marginal tax rate are the same because the principal is not taxed. This will not be true when we come to the case of savings vehicles such as IRAs.

The table below shows the effective capital gains tax rates assuming an average annual gain for the stock of 5 percent and 8 percent and a 20 percent capital gains tax rate based on the years the stock is held:

Average Annual Gain	Years to Be Held				
	1	10	20	30	40
5%	20%	16.8%	13.9%	11.7%	9.9%
8%	20%	15.2%	11.5%	8.9%	7.1%

Consequently, ignoring variation in the rate of gains over time, a stock with a 5 percent average annual gain held for 20 years and a posted capital gains tax rate of 20 percent would reduce its effective capital gains tax rate to 13.9 percent. Longer holding periods and higher rates of gain amplify this benefit.

One consequent benefit of index funds is their lower annual turnover as compared to actively managed funds, which increases their holding periods and reduces their effective tax rates. Of course, if an index fund has a 5 percent annual turnover, you can do even better with an ETF or a portfolio of individual stocks that has no net realized capital gains until final liquidation. A still greater potential tax reduction for very long holding periods is conferred by U.S. tax law, which does not tax gains on appreciated securities held at the end of the investor's life.

---

[14] See Wilcox and Horvitz (2003).

Savings Vehicles The U.S. federal government provides several types of tax-advantaged savings plans. Examples of such vehicles are tax-deferred retirement accounts—individual retirement accounts (IRAs) and traditional 401(k)s—and tax shelter vehicles such as cash value life insurance policies. These tax-advantaged investments allow the compounding of income without the withdrawal of any proceeds for taxes until retirement.[15] There are also savings plans for educational expenses, the so-called "529 plans," which have their own specialized rules.

Retirement accounts are of two types. The first and more usual type, for example, conventional IRAs and 401(k) plans, allows the investment of pretax dollars from an employee's salary which means that a greater amount can be invested as well as the accumulation of account earnings at a zero tax rate until the funds are withdrawn at retirement. The second type of retirement account, for example, qualified Roth plans, involves investing after-tax dollars but portfolio income is allowed to accrue tax-free. Similarly, cash value life insurance policies are funded with after-tax dollars but the cash buildup in the policy accrues tax free.

These two plan types at first sight are very similar in their final effect, since $(1 + r)(1 + r) \dots (1 + r)(1 - T)$ is identical to $(1 - T)(1 + r) \dots (1 + r)$, where r represents return and T the tax rate. However, one may anticipate the tax rate in retirement to be different from the current tax rate. There are also differences in rule details, such as whether distributions are required (IRA) or not (Roth IRA). Finally, sometimes the investor's ability to match ordinary income losses against the taxes due from initiating a Roth plan may need to be taken into account. In sum, the two types of plans are broadly similar, but which is slightly better for an individual investor can be complicated to determine.

The determination of the effective tax rate to apply to savings plans for the purpose of asset allocation within them is a subject of some controversy.[16] Our view is that the relevant effective tax rate for asset allocation is that which applies to marginal taxes rather than total taxes. Even though when funds are withdrawn from an IRA or 401(k) plan, both the original contributed principal and accumulated gains are taxed, and the tax on the original contribution is irrelevant from this viewpoint. Consequently, the relevant effective tax rate for asset allocation within such a plan is determined in the same way as for the effective capital gains tax rate, with the difference being that the ordinary income tax rate at the time of withdrawal replaces the capital gains tax rate in the calculation.

The following table shows the effective IRA and 401(k) tax rates assuming a 5 percent annual rate of return:

Nominal Rate	Years Yet to Be Held				
	1	10	20	30	40
40%	40%	34.9%	29.9%	25.6%	22.0%
30%	30%	25.7%	21.6%	18.3%	15.6%

---

[15] For a further discussion of tax advantaged savings vehicles and tax shelters, see Ghee and Reichenstein (1996), Shoven and Sialm (1998), Reichenstein (1999, 2000a, 2000b), Shoven (1999), and Lewis and Bowles (2001).

[16] A well-argued view different from ours is provided in Horan and Al Zaman (2008).

Tax Loss Harvesting   Suppose there is a need for some sales, either to raise cash or to invest in new opportunities. *Tax loss harvesting* in this case lengthens the period before capital gains taxes must be paid.[17] Given two similar held securities, one can choose to preferentially sell the security with an unrealized loss and hold the one with a gain. More generally, investors can select to sell tax lots with the highest tax cost basis, and thus the least realized gain, whether or not the transactions represent losses.

The value of tax loss harvesting within a portfolio depends on price dispersion over cost basis. In some ways, this is analogous to the volatility that affects the value of an option and, in fact, the ability of the investor to choose when to sell an investment does confer tax-based option value. Some of the issues studies involving tax loss harvesting have addressed include:

- How much are tax losses worth and how do you calculate that value?
- How often should losses be harvested?
- How much loss does it take before it should be taken?
- How do you weigh the trading and transaction costs against the current value of the tax loss?

In our experience, no simple formula can answer the questions posed above. One has to construct simulations with many randomized outcomes to search for the best strategy, and this will depend on many factors—the investor's preexisting tax situation and the degree of price volatility of the securities being especially important.

Most studies on the academic side focus on designing the optimal strategies for realizing gains and losses. For example, Constantinides (1983, 1984) describes the optimal choice of whether to defer taxes by not selling the security as an option under two tax regimes: a symmetric tax regime when short-term and long-term tax rates are the same and an asymmetric tax regime when they are different. Others have also studied the asymmetric tax regime.[18] These studies find that the optimal strategy is to sell securities when there is a substantial loss *even when there is no other reason to sell,* a practice rather contrary to a strict but probably unenforceable reading of the Internal Revenue Code, and to defer the gains as long as practicable.

Here is some heuristic advice. Don't sell stocks for mainly tax reasons unless losses are material—something like a 30 percent loss is a plausible threshold, and 50 percent may be better. Don't wait until the end of a tax period to sell if you do have a big unrealized loss. Do tilt purchases toward a variety of specific risks, and buy at different times, so as to increase the later dispersion of ratios of price to purchase cost, or cost basis, providing a greater option value to the choice as to when to sell. Finally, when calculating effective tax rates for use in allocation, remember that tax loss harvesting can further reduce the effective capital gains tax rate and provide a reason for somewhat increasing the allocation given to stocks as opposed to bonds within taxable accounts.

---

[17] See Jacob (1995); Gordon and Rosen (2001); Stein, Vadlamudi, and Bouchey (2009); Stein and Narasimhan (1999); Arnott, Berkin, and Ye (2000, 2001); and Berkin and Ye (2003).
[18] See Dammon and Spatt (1996) and Dammon, Spatt, and Zhang (2001).

Estate and Gift Planning   The basic principle of estate and gift planning is to be ever alert for the relatively frequent changes to the Internal Revenue Code as the political process plays out the struggle among valid but conflicting aims. On the one hand, the ability to pass on resources to one's children is a motivator for economic achievement. On the other, there is a societal interest in providing for economic mobility by limiting the unearned advantages of children born to wealthy families. Additionally, there is societal benefit in promoting voluntary charitable giving.

Typical techniques include avoiding actual sale of securities, taking full advantage of gift tax exemptions, and setting up intermediate legal entities such as trusts and limited partnerships that may legally own assets but divide risk taking, principal, and interest in a way so as to permit use of money without triggering gift and estate taxes. As a very simple example, one may donate appreciated securities to a charity or educational institution with the provision that income will be usable by the donor during his or her lifetime, thereby getting a tax deduction for the gift, avoiding triggering a capital gains tax, and getting some use of the funds for the remainder of one's life. This area is replete with arcane and transitory knowledge that requires assistance from competent legal counsel to avoid foolish attempts at exploiting nonexistent tax loopholes.

Tax Hazards   A major concern is that some tax advisors and financial advisors have promoted tax strategies/tax shelters that led not only to adverse tax implications but to investments that produced no economic benefits beyond tax benefits. On top of this, there are interest and penalties imposed by the Internal Revenue Service (IRS). These investment proposals are sold on the basis that the amount of the tax reduction is large relative to the amount that must be invested or that although the cash return from the investment will be less than the amount invested, the tax benefits will well exceed the amount invested.

How can an investor determine if a proposed tax shelter or transaction will be viewed by the IRS as a sham and thereby treated as a transaction that is viewed by the IRS as tax evasion (a criminal act) rather than a tax shelter? One cannot necessarily rely on even highly reputable tax or financial advisors, because as promoters of such transactions they have a vested economic interest in obtaining investors. Getting an opinion letter from an accounting firm or tax attorney that has no vested interest with the promoter of the transaction is the minimum that should be done.[19] The IRS maintains a hotline that taxpayers can call (anonymously if preferred) about abusive tax shelters and transactions. It may turn out that the only true economic benefit of a proposed tax shelter is the informant award provided by the IRS for providing specific and credible information about abusive tax shelters and transactions.

AFTER-TAX ASSET ALLOCATION AND PORTFOLIO STRUCTURE   The topic of asset allocation and portfolio structure for taxable investors is wide ranging. Some studies have dealt with methods of analyzing optimal portfolios and finding efficient frontiers on an after-tax basis. In a series of papers, Reichenstein (2001, 2006) stressed the

---

[19] Some sellers may require an investor to sign a confidentiality agreement so as to discourage the investor from obtaining an independent third-party opinion. This would be a signal that one should avoid the proposed transaction.

importance of determining a high-net-worth investor's asset allocation decision on an after tax-basis. Several authors have proposed after-tax portfolio optimization models and procedures for calculating the necessary inputs.[20] Although these models take somewhat different approaches, they represent a major step forward in the recognition of taxes in the structuring of a taxable investor's portfolio.

Our own advice is to keep in mind the following three major asset allocation principles:

1. Note that a tax on returns affects optimal asset allocations through a differential effect on mean and variance of returns. That is, to a first approximation a tax reduces the mean and standard deviation in equal proportions by multiplying them by $1 - T$, where T is the tax rate. But it affects variance by multiplying it by $(1 - T)$ squared, consequently tilting the optimal asset allocation toward greater tolerance for risk by highly taxed investors.
2. The tax rate affecting the inputs to an optimal asset allocation are the effective *marginal* tax rates, taking into account that deferred tax payments reduce the marginal impact of posted or nominal tax rates.
3. Assets that are subject to different tax rates by virtue of their account location, such as bonds held in a currently taxable account, bonds held in a 401(k) plan, and bonds held in a Roth plan, should be treated as separate asset classes.

Consequently, after-tax optimal asset allocation first involves determining the applicable tax rates (which may be different for interest, dividends, and gains, as well as for the individual investor), then calculating effective marginal tax rates, and then applying these rates to adjust both mean and variance of each after-tax asset class, all before carrying out a Markowitz mean-variance optimal portfolio analysis.

Almost as a by-product, the foregoing procedure answers the location question. That is, several studies have investigated how investors who have the opportunity to invest in both a taxable and tax-deferred accounts should allocate funds. More specifically, two decisions must be resolved simultaneously to be optimal:

1. The asset allocation decision as to how much to allocate to each asset class (i.e., equities, taxable bonds, and tax-exempt bonds).
2. The asset location decision which is how much of each asset class to allocate between taxable and tax-deferred accounts.

Partitioning different tax situations as separate asset classes provides an answer.

In the presence of tax-exempt bonds, several studies have investigated whether it is efficient from a tax perspective to allocate equity to the taxable account and taxable bonds to the tax-deferred account.[21] Dammon, Spatt, and Zhang (2004), argue that even in the presence of tax-exempt bonds and because of the higher tax

---

[20] See Reichenstein (2007a, 2007b); Wilcox, Horvitz, and diBartolomeo (2006); Horan (2007a, 2007b); and Horan and Al Zaman (2008).

[21] See Poterba, Shoven, and Sialm (2004); Shoven (1999); and Shoven and Sialm (2003).

burden imposed on income from taxable bonds relative to equity, there should be a strong preference for holding taxable bonds in the tax-exempt account and equity in the taxable account.[22] As they note:

> The results we derive on the optimal location of asset holdings are in sharp contrast to the financial advice that investors receive in practice. Financial advisors commonly recommend that investors hold a mix of stocks and bonds in both their taxable and tax-deferred accounts, with some financial advisors recommending that investors tilt their tax-deferred accounts toward equity. The asset location decisions made in practice mirror these recommendations, with many investors holding equity in a tax-deferred account and bonds in a taxable account. (p. 1002)

Beyond these broad asset allocation ideas, there have also been studies that considered how to tilt securities within asset classes for taxable investors, such as emphasizing growth over value, small cap over large cap, or minimizing dividends.[23] Other work has looked at tactical asset allocation (e.g., market timing), and how to best accomplish it while minimizing taxes.[24]

Measurement of After-Tax Performance and Benchmarks

The importance of after-tax analysis is made clear by Dickson and Shoven (1993) who studied the ranking of mutual funds performance on a pretax and after-tax basis.[25] They found that the rankings of mutual funds are dramatically different once the impact of income taxes is taken into account.

In the analysis of the investment performance over some specified investment horizon, two critical elements are (1) the measure of investment return over the investment horizon and (2) the benchmark return over the investment horizon. Though performance analysis should be done on an after-tax basis, returns are too often reported on a pretax basis and benchmark returns are always reported in the same manner. The CFA study by Horan and Adler (2009) mentioned earlier in this section found that although the vast majority of taxable account managers had a high level of tax awareness in dealing with portfolio issues, only about 11 percent indicated that they reported tax-adjusted performance numbers to clients. And for those that did, only about half employ an after-tax benchmark.

Minck (1998) argues that a benchmark that takes into account income taxes is different for every investor, a sentiment that was subsequently expressed by others such as Poterba (1999, 2000). The reasons why formulating a performance evaluation

---

[22] This finding was confirmed by Turvey, Basu, and Verhoeven (2011).

[23] See Brunel (1999a, 2000); Yaari and Fabozzi (1985); and Choi, Fabozzi, and Yaari (1991).

[24] See, for example, Meecham, Yoo, and Fong (1995); Brunel (1999); Arnott (1999); Horvitz (2000); Jeffrey (2001); and Leibowitz and Bova (2009).

[25] Bergstresser and Poterba (2002) found that the inflow into equity mutual funds over the period 1993 to 1993 is explained better by after-tax return performance than pretax return performance. Moreover, for those mutual funds that have large unrealized capital gains in their portfolio, there were small inflows compared to funds without such gains.

model and reporting of after-tax performance are challenging is explained by Horan, Lawton, and Johnson (2008):

> Clients' varied tax situations and investment objectives affect the tax implications associated with a manager's investment policy. For example, clients face different rates and have different realized gains and losses outside the portfolio that may offset losses or gains inside the portfolio. Even knowing an investor's anticipated marginal tax rate can be difficult, as it can change over the course of a tax year and from one year to the next. Another challenge of measuring after-tax performance is that two identically managed portfolios with different cost bases will generate different after-tax cash flows. It is difficult to measure the tax obligations arising from a manager's investment activities because tax obligations, like those on capital gains, may accrue in one period but be paid at a later date. (p. 69)

There are simple methodologies for approximating after-tax returns. The more common ones are described by Minck. Two extreme methodologies assume the following. The first is to ignore taxes on realized capital gains and adjust the dividends for taxes in computing the return. At the other extreme is the methodology that assumes that all capital gains are realized and taxed. Using an illustration of the purchase of the S&P 500 in 1985 and for various holding period through 1997, Minck shows these methodologies on a passive index to be "grossly wrong."

Price (1996) was one of the first to propose how to measure after-tax performance where recognition of both the tax implications of a manager's investment decisions and those decisions not under the manager's control attributable to external cash inflows and outflows were taken into account. Rogers (2005, 2006), as well as others, discuss after-tax performance attribution.

The CFA Institute requires after-tax returns be calculated in a specific way as set forth in the *Global Investment Performance Standards (GIPS®) Guidance Statement for Country-Specific Taxation Issues* that went into effect in January 2005. The calculation method requires that a realized basis "preliquidation" calculation methodology be utilized. Although this methodology takes into account any taxes realized during the evaluation period, it ignores any embedded tax consequences within the portfolio such as future tax payments associated with unrealized gains or tax benefits or adverse tax consequences associated with unrealized losses. Another approach in calculating after-tax returns is to immediately take these embedded tax consequences into accounting using a post-liquidation basis. Other proposals for calculating after-tax returns have been proposed by Stein (1995), Price (1996), and Horan (2007b). Horan, Lawton, and Johnson (2008) propose an approach that integrates the Stein and Horan approaches. We won't describe here the drawbacks and advantages of each model. Suffice it to say that despite the differences in the models, all agree that there is a need for reporting after-tax returns.

For mutual funds, the Securities and Exchange Commission (SEC) requires the reporting on a standardized basis after-tax returns for 1-, 5-, and 10-year periods. After-tax returns are presented in two ways:

- After taxes on fund distributions only (preliquidation).
- After taxes on fund distributions and an assumed redemption of fund shares (post-liquidation).

References

Apelfeld, Roberto, Gordon B. Fowler, Jr., and James P. Gordon, Jr. 1996. "Tax Aware Equity Investing." *Journal of Portfolio Management* 22 (2): 18–27.

Arnott, Robert D. 1991. "Tax Consequences of Trading." First Quadrant Corporation, No. 3.

Arnott, Robert D. 1999. "Overlays and Taxation." First Quadrant, L.P.

Arnott, Robert D., Andrew L. Berkin, and Jia Ye. 2000. "How Well Have Taxable Investors Been Served in the 1980s and 1990s?" *Journal of Portfolio Management* 26 (4): 84–93.

Arnott, Robert D., Andrew L. Berkin, and Jia Ye. 2001. "Loss Harvesting: What's It Worth to the Taxable Investor?" *Journal of Wealth Management* 3 (4): 10–18.

Bergstresser, Daniel, and James Poterba. 2002. "Do After-Tax Returns Affect Mutual Fund Inflows?" *Journal of Financial Economics* 63: 381–414.

Berkin, Andrew L., and Jia Ye. 2003. "Tax Management, Loss-Harvesting and HIFO Accounting." *Financial Analysts Journal* 59 (4): 91–102.

Brunel, Jean L. P. 1999a. "Revisiting the Fallacy of Market-Timing in an After-Tax Context." *Journal of Private Portfolio Management* 2 (2): 16–25.

Brunel, Jean L. P. 1999b. "The Role of Alternative Assets in Tax-Efficient Portfolio Construction." *Journal of Private Portfolio Management* 2 (1): 9–25.

Brunel, Jean L. P. 2000. "Active Style Diversification in an After-Tax Context: An Impossible Challenge?" *Journal of Private Portfolio Management* 2 (4): 41–50.

Choi, Jongmoo Jay, Frank J. Fabozzi, and Uzi Yaari. 1991. "How to Diversify the Tax-Sheltered Equity Fund." *Advances in Investment Analysis and Portfolio Management* 1: 117–125.

Constantinides, George M. 1983. "Capital Market Equilibrium with Personal Tax." *Econometrica* 5: 611–636.

Constantinides, George M. 1984. "Optimal Stock Trading with Personal Taxes." *Journal of Financial Economics* 13: 65–89.

Dammon, Robert R., and Chester S. Spatt. 1996. "The Optimal Trading and Pricing of Securities with Asymmetric Capital Gains Taxes and Transaction Costs." *Review of Financial Studies* 9: 921–952.

Dammon, Robert R., Chester S. Spatt, and Harold H. Zhang. 2001. "Optimal Consumption and Investment with Capital Gains Taxes." *Review of Financial Studies* 14: 583–616.

Dammon, Robert R., Chester S. Spatt, and Harold H. Zhang. 2004. "Optimal Asset Location and Allocation with Taxable and Tax-Deferred Investing." *Journal of Finance* 59 (3): 999–1037.

Dickson, Joel M., and John B. Shoven. 1993. "Ranking Mutual Funds on an After-Tax Basis." NBER Working Paper Series, No. w4393.

Dickson, Joel M., and John B. Shoven. 1994. "A Stock Index Mutual Fund without Net Capital Gains Realizations." NBER Working Paper, No. w4717.

Garland, James P. 1987. "Taxable Portfolios: Value and Performance." *Journal of Portfolio Management* 13 (2): 19–24.

Ghee, William, and William Reichenstein. 1996. "The After-Tax Returns from Different Savings Vehicles." *Financial Analysts Journal* 51 (4): 16–19.

Gordon, Robert N., and Jan Rosen, 2001. "The Benefits and Methods of Harvesting Your Losses, and Not Just at Year-End." *Journal of Wealth Management* 4 (2): 60–63.

Hertog, Roger, and Mark R. Gordon. 1994. "Is Your Alpha Big Enough to Cover Its Taxes?: Comment." *Journal of Portfolio Management* 20 (4): 93–95.

Horan, Stephen M. 2007a. "Applying After-Tax Valuation." *Journal of Wealth Management* 10 (2): 84–93.

Horan, Stephen M. 2007b. "An Alternative Approach to After-Tax Valuation." *Financial Services Review* 16 (3): 167–182.

Horan, Stephen M., and David Adler. 2009. "Tax Aware Investment Management Practice." *Journal of Wealth Management* 12 (2): 71–88.

Horan, Stephen M., and Ashraf Al Zaman. 2008. "Tax-Adjusted Portfolio Optimization and Asset Location: Extensions and Synthesis." *Journal of Wealth Management* 11 (3): 56–73.

Horan, Stephen M., Philip N. Lawton, and Robert R. Johnson. 2008. "After-Tax Performance Measurement." *Journal of Wealth Management* 11 (1): 69–83.

Horvitz, Jeffrey E. 2000. "Asset Classes and Asset Allocation: Problems of Classification." *Journal of Private Portfolio Management* 2 (4): 27–32.

Horvitz, Jeffrey E. 2008. "Investment Implications of the Estate Tax." *Journal of Wealth Management* 11 (2): 47–52.

Jacob, Nancy L. 1995. "Tax-Efficient Investing: Reduce the Tax Drag, Improve Asset Growth." *Trusts and Estates* (May): 25–33.

Jeffrey, Robert H. 2001. "Tax Efficient Investing Is Easier Said Than Done." *Journal of Wealth Management* 4 (1): 9–15.

Jeffrey, Robert H., and Robert D. Arnott. 1993. "Is Your Alpha Big Enough to Cover Its Taxes?" *Journal of Portfolio Management* 19 (3): 15–25.

Jeffrey, Robert H., and Robert D. Arnott. 1994. "Is Your Alpha Big Enough to Cover Its Taxes?: Reply to Comment." *Journal of Portfolio Management* 20 (4): 96–97.

Leibowitz, Martin L., and Anthony Bova. 2009. "Risk-Return Ratios under Taxation." *Journal of Portfolio Management* 35 (4): 43–51.

Lewis, W. Cris, and Tyler J. Bowles. 2001. "The Effect of Income Taxes on Optimal Portfolio Selection." *Journal of Wealth Management* 4 (2): 29–35.

Luck, Christopher G. 2000. "Tax-Advantaged Investing." First Quadrant, L.P.

Meecham, James P., Daihyun Yoo, and H. Gifford Fong. 1995. "Taxable Asset Allocation with Varying Market Risk Premiums." *Journal of Portfolio Management* 22 (1): 79–87.

Minck, Jeffrey L. 1998. "Tax Adjusted Equity Benchmarks." *Journal of Private Portfolio Management* 1 (2): 41–50.

Mulvahill, Donald. 2000. "After-Tax Wealth Management." Goldman Sachs & Co., March.

Poterba, James M. 1999. "Unrealized Capital Gains and the Measurement of After-Tax Portfolio Performance." *Journal of Private Portfolio Management* 1 (4): 23–34.

Poterba, James M. 2000. "After-Tax Performance Evaluation." In *Association of Investment Management and Research Conference Proceedings*, 57–67. Charlottesville, VA: Association of Investment Management and Research.

Poterba, James M., John Shoven, and Clemens Sialm. 2004. "Asset Location for Retirement Savers." In *Public Policies and Private Pensions*, edited by William Gale, John Shoven, and Mark Warshawsky, 290–331. Washington, DC: Brookings Institution.

Price, Lee N. 1996. "Calculation and Reporting of After-Tax Performance." *Journal of Performance Measurement* 1 (2): 6–13.

Reichenstein, William. 1999. "Savings Vehicles and the Taxation of Individual Investors." *Journal of Private Portfolio Management* 2 (3): 15–26.

Reichenstein, William. 2000a. "An Analysis of Non-Qualified Tax-Deferred Annuities." *Journal of Investing* 9 (2): 1–12.

Reichenstein, William. 2000b. "Calculating the Asset Allocation." *Journal of Wealth Management* 3 (2): 20–25.

Reichenstein, William. 2001. "Asset Allocation and Asset Location Decisions Revisited." *Journal of Wealth Management* 4 (1): 16–26.

Reichenstein, William. 2007a. "Implications of Principal, Risk, and Returns Sharing Across Savings Vehicles." *Financial Services Review* 16 (1): 1–17.

Reichenstein, William. 2007b. "Note on 'Applying After-Tax Asset Allocation.'" *Journal of Wealth Management* 10 (2): 94–97.

Shoven, John B. 1999. "The Location and Allocation of Assets in Pension and Conventional Savings Accounts." National Bureau of Economic Research. Working Paper No. 7007.

Shoven, John B., and Clemens Sialm. 1998. "Long-Run Asset Allocation for Retirement Savings." *Journal of Private Portfolio Management* 1 (2): 13–26.

Shoven, John B., and Clemens Sialm. 2003. "Asset Location in Tax-Deferred and Conventional Savings Accounts." *Journal of Public Economics* 88: 23–38.

Stein, David M. 1995. "Measuring and Evaluating Portfolio Performance after Taxes." *Journal of Portfolio Management* 24 (2): 117–124.

Stein, David M. 1998. "Investment Management for Taxable Investors." In *The Handbook of Portfolio Management*, edited by Frank J. Fabozzi, 93–106. New York: John Wiley & Sons.

Stein, David M., and Premkumar Narasimhan. 1999. "Of Passive and Active Equity Portfolios in the Presence of Taxes." *Journal of Private Portfolio Management* 2 (2): 55–63.

Stein, David M., Hemambara Vadlamudi, and Paul Bouchey. 2009. "Enhancing Active Tax Management through the Realization of Capital Gains." *Journal of Wealth Management* 10 (4): 9–16.

Turvey, Phillip Ashley, Anup K. Basu, and Peter Verhoeven. 2011. "Embedded Tax Liabilities and Portfolio Choice." Working Paper, Queensland University of Technology.

Wilcox, Jarrod W., and Jeffrey Horvitz. 2003. "Know When to Hold 'em and When to Fold 'em: The Value of Effective Taxable Investment Management." *Journal of Wealth Management* 6 (2): 35–59.

Yaari, Uzi, and Frank J. Fabozzi. 1985. "Why IRA and Keogh Plans Should Avoid Growth Stocks." *Journal of Financial Research* 8 (3): 203–216.

CHAPTER 18

Investment Policy Statement (IPS)

The Investment Policy Statement (IPS) is a critical document for investment advisors and consultants and their clients. It clearly defines the fund objectives, allowable asset classes, target asset allocation and benchmarks (when applicable), risk metrics and constraints, special restrictions, and rebalancing protocol. It also includes a description of the client's risk tolerance, time horizon, tax position, target rate of return (when applicable), liability policy (when applicable), monitoring requirements, capital markets expectations, spending policy, appropriate governance, and additional client constraints. This chapter takes a look at the more common components of the IPS and uses examples to show how investment professionals may analyze unique client situations and build an appropriate IPS under different circumstances.

Investments: Basics of Portfolio Planning and Construction

Learning Objectives

- Explain the reasons for a written investment policy statement (IPS).
- List and explain the major components of an IPS.
- Discuss risk and return objectives, including their preparation.
- Distinguish between the willingness and the ability (capacity) to take risk in analyzing an investor's financial risk tolerance.
- Describe the investment constraints of liquidity, time horizon, tax concerns, legal and regulatory factors, and unique circumstances and their implications for the choice of portfolio assets.

Basics of Portfolio Planning and Construction

To build a suitable portfolio for a client, investment advisers should first seek to understand the client's investment goals, resources, circumstances, and constraints. Investors can be categorized into broad groups based on shared characteristics with respect to these factors (e.g., various types of individual investors and institutional investors). Even investors within a given type, however, will invariably have a number of distinctive requirements. In this chapter, we consider in detail the planning for investment success based on an individualized understanding of the client.

Portfolio Planning

Portfolio planning can be defined as a program developed in advance of constructing a portfolio that is expected to satisfy the client's investment objectives. The written document governing this process is the investment policy statement (IPS).

THE INVESTMENT POLICY STATEMENT   The IPS is the starting point of the portfolio management process. Without a full understanding of the client's situation and requirements, it is unlikely that successful results will be achieved. Success can be defined as a client achieving his or her important investment goals using means that he or she is comfortable with (in terms of risks taken and other concerns). The IPS essentially communicates a plan for achieving investment success.

The IPS will be developed following a fact-finding discussion with the client. This fact-finding discussion can include the use of a questionnaire designed to articulate the client's risk tolerance as well as specific circumstances. In the case of institutional clients, the fact-finding may involve asset–liability management studies, identification of liquidity needs, and a wide range of tax and legal considerations.

The IPS can take a variety of forms. A typical format will include the client's investment objectives and the constraints that apply to the client's portfolio.

The client's objectives are specified in terms of risk tolerance and return requirements. These must be consistent with each other: A client is unlikely to be able to find a portfolio that offers a relatively high expected return without taking on a relatively high level of risk.

The constraints section covers factors that need to be taken into account when constructing a portfolio for the client that meets the objectives. The typical constraint categories are liquidity requirements, time horizon, regulatory requirements, tax status, and unique needs. The constraints may be internal (i.e., set by the client), or external (i.e., set by law or regulation). These are discussed in detail next.

Having a well-constructed IPS for all clients should be standard procedure for a portfolio manager. The portfolio manager should have the IPS close at hand and be able to refer to it to assess the suitability of a particular investment for the client. In some cases, the need for the IPS goes beyond simply being a matter of standard procedure. In some countries, the IPS (or an equivalent document) is a legal or regulatory requirement. For example, U.K. pension schemes must have a statement of investment principles under the Pensions Act 1995 (Section 35), and this statement is in essence an IPS. The U.K. Financial Services Authority also has requirements for investment firms to "know their customers." The European Union's Markets in Financial Instruments Directive (MiFID) requires firms to assign clients to categories, such as professional clients and retail clients.

In the case of an institution, such as a pension plan or university endowment, the IPS may set out the governance arrangements that apply to the investment funds. For example, this information could cover the investment committee's approach to appointing and reviewing investment managers for the portfolio, and the discretion that those managers have. The IPS could also set out the institution's approach to corporate governance, in terms of how it will approach the use of shareholder voting rights and other forms of engagement with corporate management.

The IPS should be reviewed on a regular basis to ensure that it remains consistent with the client's circumstances and requirements. For example, the U.K. Pensions

Regulator suggests that a pension scheme's statements of investment principles—a form of IPS—should be reviewed at least every three years. The IPS should also be reviewed if the manager becomes aware of a material change in the client's circumstances, or on the initiative of the client when his or her objectives, time horizon, or liquidity needs change.

MAJOR COMPONENTS OF AN IPS   There is no single standard format for an IPS. Many IPSs, however, include the following sections:

Introduction. This section describes the client.

Statement of Purpose. This section states the purpose of the IPS.

Statement of Duties and Responsibilities. This section details the duties and responsibilities of the client, the custodian of the client's assets, and the investment managers.

Procedures. This section explains the steps to take to keep the IPS current and the procedures to follow to respond to various contingencies.

Investment Objectives. This section explains the client's objectives in investing.

Investment Constraints. This section presents the factors that constrain the client in seeking to achieve the investment objectives.

Investment Guidelines. This section provides information about how policy should be executed (e.g., on the permissible use of leverage and derivatives) and on specific types of assets excluded from investment, if any.

Evaluation and Review. This section provides guidance on obtaining feedback on investment results.

Appendices: (A) Strategic Asset Allocation (B) Rebalancing Policy. Many investors specify a strategic asset allocation (SAA), also known as the policy portfolio, which is the baseline allocation of portfolio assets to asset classes in view of the investor's investment objectives and the investor's policy with respect to rebalancing asset class weights.

The sections that are most closely linked to the client's distinctive needs, and probably the most important from a planning perspective, are those dealing with investment objectives and constraints. An IPS focusing on these two elements has been called an IPS in an "objectives and constraints" format.

In the following sections, we discuss the investment objectives and constraints format of an IPS beginning with risk and return objectives. We follow a tradition of CFA Institute presentations in discussing risk objectives first. The process of developing the IPS is the basic mechanism for evaluating and trying to improve an investor's overall expected return–risk stance. In a portfolio context, "investors have learned to appreciate that their objective is not to manage reward but to control and manage risk."[1] Stated another way, return objectives and expectations must be tailored to be consistent with risk objectives. The risk and return objectives must also be consistent with the constraints that apply to the portfolio.

---

[1] Maginn and Tuttle (1983), p. 23.

Risk Objectives When constructing a portfolio for a client, it is important to ensure that the risk of the portfolio is suitable for the client. The IPS should state clearly the risk tolerance of the client.

Risk objectives are specifications for portfolio risk that reflect the risk tolerance of the client. Quantitative risk objectives can be absolute or relative or a combination of the two.

Examples of an absolute risk objective would be a desire not to suffer any loss of capital or not to lose more than a given percent of capital in any 12-month period. Note that these objectives are not related to investment market performance, good or bad, and are absolute in the sense of being self-standing. The fulfillment of such objectives could be achieved by not taking any risk; for example, by investing in an insured bank certificate of deposit at a creditworthy bank. If investments in risky assets are undertaken, however, such statements would need to be restated as a probability statement to be operational (i.e., practically useful). For example, the desire to not lose more than 4 percent of capital in any 12-month period might be restated as an objective that with 95 percent probability the portfolio not lose more than 4 percent in any 12-month period. Measures of absolute risk include the variance or standard deviation of returns and value at risk.[2]

Some clients may choose to express relative risk objectives, which relate risk relative to one or more benchmarks perceived to represent appropriate risk standards. For example, investments in large-cap U.K. equities could be benchmarked to an equity market index, such as the FTSE 100 Index. The S&P 500 Index could be used as a benchmark for large-cap U.S. equities, or, for investments with cash-like characteristics, the benchmark could be an interest rate such as LIBOR or a Treasury bill rate. For risk relative to a benchmark, the relevant measure is tracking risk, or tracking error.[3]

EXAMPLE 18.1   Types of Risk Objectives

A Japanese institutional investor has a portfolio valued at ¥10 billion. The investor expresses his first risk objective as a desire not to lose more than ¥1 billion in the coming 12-month period. The investor specifies a second risk objective of achieving returns within 4 percent of the return to the TOPIX stock market index, which is the investor's benchmark. Based on this information, address the following:

Problem 1:

A. Characterize the first risk objective as absolute or relative.
B. Give an example of how the risk objective could be restated in a practical manner.

---

[2] **Value at risk** is a money measure of the minimum value of losses expected during a specified time period at a given level of probability.

[3] **Tracking risk** (sometimes called **tracking error**) is the standard deviation of the differences between a portfolio's returns and its benchmark's returns.

Problem 2:

A. Characterize the second risk objective as absolute or relative.
B. Identify a measure for quantifying the risk objective.

Solution to 1:

A. This is an absolute risk objective.
B. This risk objective could be restated in a practical manner by specifying that the 12-month 95 percent value at risk of the portfolio must not be more than ¥1 billion.

Solution to 2:

A. This is a relative risk objective.
B. This risk objective could be quantified using the tracking risk as a measure. For example, assuming returns follow a normal distribution, an expected tracking risk of 2 percent would imply a return within 4 percent of the index return approximately 95 percent of the time. Remember that tracking risk is stated as a one standard deviation measure.

For institutional clients, the benchmark may be linked to some form of liability the institution has. For example, a pension plan must meet the pension payments as they come due and the risk objective will be to minimize the probability that it will fail to do so. (A related return objective might be to outperform the discount rate used in finding the present value of liabilities over a multiyear time horizon.)

When a policy portfolio (that is, a specified set of long-term asset class weightings) is used, the risk objective may be expressed as a desire for the portfolio return to be within a band of plus or minus X percent of the benchmark return calculated by assigning an index or benchmark to represent each asset class present in the policy portfolio. Again, this objective has to be interpreted as a statement of probability; for example, a 95 percent probability that the portfolio return will be within X percent of the benchmark return over a stated time period. Example 18.1 reviews this material.

A client's overall risk tolerance is a function of the client's ability to bear (accept) risk and his or her "risk attitude," which might be considered as the client's willingness to take risk. For ease of expression, from this point on we will refer to ability to bear risk and willingness to take risk as the two components of risk tolerance. Above-average ability to bear risk and above-average willingness to take risk imply above-average risk tolerance. Below-average ability to bear risk and below-average willingness to take risk imply below-average risk tolerance.

The ability to bear risk is measured mainly in terms of objective factors, such as time horizon, expected income, and the level of wealth relative to liabilities. For example, an investor with a 20-year time horizon can be considered to have a greater ability to bear risk, other things being equal, than an investor with a two-year horizon. This difference is because over 20 years there is more scope for losses to be recovered or other adjustments to circumstances to be made than there is over two years.

Similarly, an investor whose assets are comfortably in excess of their liabilities has more ability to bear risk than an investor whose wealth and expected future expenditure are more closely balanced. For example, a wealthy individual who can sustain a comfortable lifestyle after a very substantial investment loss has a relatively high ability to bear risk. A pension plan that has a large surplus of assets over liabilities has a relatively high ability to bear risk.

Risk attitude, or willingness to take risk, is a more subjective factor based on the client's psychology and perhaps also his or her current circumstances. Although the list of factors that are related to an individual's risk attitude remains open to debate, it is believed that some psychological factors, such as personality type, self-esteem, and inclination to independent thinking, are correlated with risk attitude. Some individuals are comfortable taking financial and investment risk, whereas others find it distressing. Although there is no single agreed-upon method for measuring risk tolerance, a willingness to take risk may be gauged by discussing risk with the client or by asking the client to complete a psychometric questionnaire. For example, financial planning academic John Grable and collaborators have developed 13-item and 5-item risk attitude questionnaires that have undergone some level of technical validation. The five-item questionnaire is shown in Exhibit 18.1.

EXHIBIT 18.1   A Five-Item Risk Assessment Instrument

1. Investing is too difficult to understand.
   A. Strongly agree
   B. Tend to agree
   C. Tend to disagree
   D. Strongly disagree
2. I am more comfortable putting my money in a bank account than in the stock market.
   A. Strongly agree
   B. Tend to agree
   C. Tend to disagree
   D. Strongly disagree
3. When I think of the word "risk" the term "loss" comes to mind immediately.
   A. Strongly agree
   B. Tend to agree
   C. Tend to disagree
   D. Strongly disagree
4. Making money in stocks and bonds is based on luck.
   A. Strongly agree
   B. Tend to agree
   C. Tend to disagree
   D. Strongly disagree
5. In terms of investing, safety is more important than returns.
   A. Strongly agree

> B. Tend to agree
> C. Tend to disagree
> D. Strongly disagree
>
> ―――――――
> *Source:* Grable and Joo (2004).

The responses, (A), (B), (C), and (D), are coded 1, 2, 3, and 4, respectively, and summed. The lowest score is 5 and the highest score is 20, with higher scores indicating greater risk tolerance. For two random samples drawn from the faculty and staff of large U.S. universities ($n = 406$), the mean score was 12.86 with a standard deviation of 3.01 and a median (i.e., most frequently observed) score of 13.

Note that a question, such as the first one in Exhibit 18.1, indicates that risk attitude may be associated with nonpsychological factors (such as level of financial knowledge and understanding and decision-making style) as well as psychological factors.

The adviser needs to examine whether a client's ability to accept risk is consistent with the client's willingness to take risk. For example, a wealthy investor with a 20-year time horizon, who is thus able to take risk, may also be comfortable taking risk; in this case the factors are consistent. If the wealthy investor has a low willingness to take risk, there would be a conflict.

In the institutional context, there could also be conflict between ability and willingness to take risk. In addition, different stakeholders within the institution may take different views. For example, the trustees of a well-funded pension plan may desire a low-risk approach to safeguard the funding of the scheme and beneficiaries of the scheme may take a similar view. The sponsor, however, may wish a higher-risk/higher-return approach in an attempt to reduce future funding costs. When a trustee bears a fiduciary responsibility to pension beneficiaries and the interests of the pension sponsor and the pension beneficiaries conflict, the trustee should act in the best interests of the beneficiaries.

When ability to take risk and willingness to take risk are consistent, the investment adviser's task is the simplest. When ability to take risk is below average and willingness to take risk is above average, the investor's risk tolerance should be assessed as below average overall.

When ability to take risk is above average but willingness is below average, the portfolio manager or adviser may seek to counsel the client and explain the conflict and its implications. For example, the adviser could outline the reasons why the client is considered to have a high ability to take risk and explain the likely consequences, in terms of reduced expected return, of not taking risk. The investment adviser, however, should not aim to change a client's willingness to take risk that is not a result of a miscalculation or misperception. Modification of elements of personality is not within the purview of the investment adviser's role. The prudent approach is to reach a conclusion about risk tolerance consistent with the lower of the two factors (ability and willingness) and to document the decisions made.

Example 18.2 is the first of a set that follows the analysis of a private wealth management client through the preparation of the major elements of an IPS.

EXAMPLE 18.2   The Case of Henri Gascon: Risk Tolerance

Henri Gascon is an energy trader who works for a major French oil company based in Paris. He is 30 years old and married with one son, aged five. Gascon has decided that it is time to review his financial situation and consults a financial adviser. The financial adviser notes the following aspects of Gascon's situation:

> Gascon's annual salary of €250,000 is more than sufficient to cover the family's outgoings.
> Gascon owns his apartment outright and has €1,000,000 of savings.
> Gascon perceives that his job is reasonably secure. Gascon has a good knowledge of financial matters and is confident that equity markets will deliver positive returns over the longer term. In the risk tolerance questionnaire, Gascon strongly disagrees with the statements that "making money in stocks and bonds is based on luck" and that "in terms of investing, safety is more important than returns." Gascon expects that most of his savings will be used to fund his retirement, which he hopes to start at age 50.

Based only on the information given, which of the following statements is *most* accurate?

A. Gascon has a low ability to take risk, but a high willingness to take risk.
B. Gascon has a high ability to take risk, but a low willingness to take risk.
C. Gascon has a high ability to take risk, and a high willingness to take risk.

Solution: C is correct. Gascon has a high income relative to outgoings, a high level of assets, a secure job, and a time horizon of 20 years. This information suggests a high *ability* to take risk. At the same time, Gascon is knowledgeable and confident about financial markets and responds to the questionnaire with answers that suggest risk tolerance. This result suggests he also has a high *willingness* to take risk.

EXAMPLE 18.3   The Case of Jacques Gascon: Risk Tolerance

Henri Gascon is so pleased with the services provided by the financial adviser, that he suggests to his brother Jacques that he should also consult the adviser. Jacques thinks it is a good idea. Jacques is a self-employed computer consultant also based in Paris. He is 40 years old and divorced with four children, aged between 12 and 16. The financial adviser notes the following aspects of Jacques' situation:

> Jacques' consultancy earnings average €40,000 per annum, but are quite volatile.
> Jacques is required to pay €10,000 per year to his ex-wife and children.

Jacques has a mortgage on his apartment of €100,000 and €10,000 of savings.

Jacques has a good knowledge of financial matters and expects that equity markets will deliver very high returns over the longer term.

In the risk tolerance questionnaire, Jacques strongly disagrees with the statements "I am more comfortable putting my money in a bank account than in the stock market" and "When I think of the word "risk" the term "loss" comes to mind immediately."

Jacques expects that most of his savings will be required to support his children at university.

Based on the preceding information, which statement is correct?

A. Jacques has a low ability to take risk, but a high willingness to take risk.
B. Jacques has a high ability to take risk, but a low willingness to take risk.
C. Jacques has a high ability to take risk, and a high willingness to take risk.

Solution: A is correct. Jacques does not have a particularly high income, his income is unstable, and he has reasonably high outgoings for his mortgage and maintenance payments. His investment time horizon is approximately two to six years given the ages of his children and his desire to support them at university. This finely balanced financial situation and short time horizon suggests a low ability to take risk. In contrast, his expectations for financial market returns and risk tolerance questionnaire answers suggest a high willingness to take risk. The financial adviser may wish to explain to Jacques how finely balanced his financial situation is and suggest that, despite his desire to take more risk, a relatively cautious portfolio might be the most appropriate approach to take.

Return Objectives A client's return objectives can be stated in a number of ways. Similar to risk objectives, return objectives may be stated on an absolute or a relative basis.

As an example of an absolute objective, the client may want to achieve a particular percentage rate of return, for example, X percent. This could be a nominal rate of return or be expressed in real (inflation-adjusted) terms.

Alternatively, the return objective can be stated on a relative basis, for example, relative to a benchmark return. The benchmark could be an equity market index, such as the S&P 500 or the FTSE 100, or a cash rate of interest such as LIBOR. LIBOR might be appropriate when the investor has some liability that is linked to that rate; for example, a bank that has a particular cost of funding linked to LIBOR. A relative return objective might be stated as, for example, a desire to outperform the benchmark index by one percentage point per year.

Some institutions also set their return objective relative to a peer group or universe of managers; for example, an endowment aiming for a return that is in the top 50 percent of returns of similar institutions, or a private equity mandate aiming for returns in the top quartile among the private equity universe. This objective can be problematic when limited information is known about the investment strategies or the returns calculation methodology being used by peers, and we must bear in mind the impossibility of *all* institutions being "above average." Furthermore, a good benchmark should be investable—that is, able to be replicated by the investor—and a peer benchmark typically does not meet that criterion.

In each case, the return requirement can be stated before or after fees. Care should be taken that the fee basis used is clear and understood by both the manager and client. The return can also be stated on either a pre- or post-tax basis when the investor is required to pay tax. For a taxable investor, the baseline is to state and analyze returns on an after-tax basis.

The return objective could be a required return—that is, the amount the investor needs to earn to meet a particular future goal—such as a certain level of retirement income.

The manager or adviser must ensure that the return objective is realistic. Care should be taken that client and manager are in agreement on whether the return objective is nominal (which is more convenient for measurement purposes) or real (i.e., inflation-adjusted, which usually relates better to the objective). It must be consistent with the client's risk objective (high expected returns are unlikely to be possible without high levels of risk) and also with the current economic and market environment. For example, 15 percent nominal returns might be possible when inflation is 10 percent, but will be unlikely when inflation is 3 percent.

When a client has unrealistic return expectations, the manager or adviser will need to counsel them about what is achievable in the current market environment and within the client's tolerance for risk.

EXAMPLE 18.4   The Case of Henri Gascon: Return Objectives

Having assessed his risk tolerance, Henri Gascon now begins to discuss his retirement income needs with the financial adviser. He wishes to retire at age 50, which is 20 years from now. His salary meets current and expected future expenditure requirements, but he does not expect to be able to make any additional pension contributions to his fund. Gascon sets aside €100,000 of his savings as an emergency fund to be held in cash. The remaining €900,000 is invested for his retirement.

Gascon estimates that a before-tax amount of €2,000,000 in today's money will be sufficient to fund his retirement income needs. The financial adviser expects inflation to average 2 percent per year over the next 20 years. Pension fund contributions and pension fund returns in France are exempt from tax, but pension fund distributions are taxable upon retirement.

1. Which of the following is closest to the amount of money Gascon will have to accumulate in nominal terms by his retirement date to meet his retirement income objective (i.e., expressed in money of the day in 20 years)?
   A. €900,000
   B. €2,000,000
   C. €3,000,000

---

2. Which of the following is closest to the annual rate of return that Gascon must earn on his pension portfolio to meet his retirement income objective?
A. 2.0 percent
B. 6.2 percent
C. 8.1 percent

Solution to 1: C is correct. At 2 percent annual inflation, €2,000,000 in today's money equates to €2,971,895 in 20 years measured in money of the day [2m × (1 + 2%)^{20}].

Solution to 2: B is correct. €900,000 growing at 6.2 percent per year for 20 years will accumulate to €2,997,318, which is just above the required amount. (The solution of 6.2 percent comes from €2,997,318/€900,000 = (1 + X)^{20}, where X is the required rate of return.)

In the following sections, we analyze five major types of constraints on portfolio selection: liquidity, time horizon, tax concerns, legal and regulatory factors, and unique circumstances.

Liquidity   The IPS should state what the likely requirements are to withdraw funds from the portfolio. Examples for an individual investor would be outlays for covering health care payments or tuition fees. For institutions, it could be spending rules and requirements for endowment funds, the existence of claims coming due in the case of property and casualty insurance, or benefit payments for pension funds and life insurance companies.

When the client does have such a requirement, the manager should allocate part of the portfolio to cover the liability. This part of the portfolio will be invested in assets that are liquid—that is, easily converted to cash—and low risk at the point in time the liquidity need is actually present (e.g., a bond maturing at the time when private education expenses will be incurred), so that their value is known with reasonable certainty. For example, the asset allocation in the insurance portfolios of Finnish insurer Sampo (see Figure 18.1) shows a large allocation to fixed-income investments, some of which are either highly liquid or have a short maturity. These investments enable the company, in the case of property and casualty insurance, to pay out on potentially "lumpy" claims of which the timing is unpredictable, and in the case of life insurance, to pay out on life benefits, the size and timing of which are more predictable and can therefore be matched with the maturity profile of the fixed-income portfolio.

Time Horizon   The IPS should state the time horizon over which the investor is investing. It may be the period over which the portfolio is accumulating before any assets need to be withdrawn; it could also be the period until the client's circumstances are likely to change. For example, a 50-year-old pension plan investor hoping to retire at age 60 has a 10-year horizon. The portfolio may not be liquidated at age 60, but its structure may need to change, for example, as the investor begins to draw an income from the fund.

Panel A. Allocation of Investment Assets,
Sampo Group, 31 December 2008

Sampo Group €16,502 Million

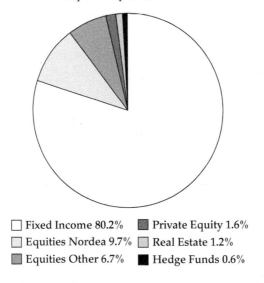

☐ Fixed Income 80.2%   ▨ Private Equity 1.6%
☐ Equities Nordea 9.7%   ☐ Real Estate 1.2%
▨ Equities Other 6.7%   ■ Hedge Funds 0.6%

Panel B. Fixed-Income Investments by Type of Instrument,
Sampo Group, 31 December 2008

Sampo Group €13,214 Million

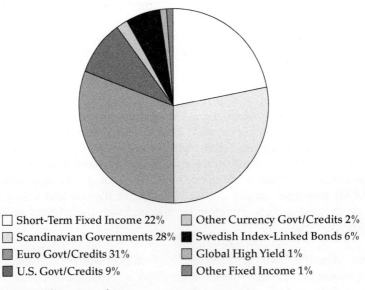

☐ Short-Term Fixed Income 22%   ☐ Other Currency Govt/Credits 2%
☐ Scandinavian Governments 28%   ■ Swedish Index-Linked Bonds 6%
▨ Euro Govt/Credits 31%   ☐ Global High Yield 1%
■ U.S. Govt/Credits 9%   ▨ Other Fixed Income 1%

FIGURE 18.1   Asset Allocation of Sampo
Source: Sampo Group, 2008 Annual Report, pp. 59–61.

The time horizon of the investor will affect the nature of investments used in the portfolio. Illiquid or risky investments may be unsuitable for an investor with a short time horizon because the investor may not have enough time to recover from investment losses, for example. Such investments, however, may be suitable for an investor with a longer horizon, especially if the risky investments are expected to have higher returns.

EXAMPLE 18.5   Investment Time Horizon

1. Frank Johnson is investing for retirement and has a 20-year horizon. He has an average risk tolerance. Which investment is likely to be the *least* suitable for a major allocation in Johnson's portfolio?
   A. Listed equities.
   B. Private equity.
   C. U.S. Treasury bills.
2. Al Smith has to pay a large tax bill in six months and wants to invest the money in the meantime. Which investment is likely to be the *least* suitable for a major allocation in Smith's portfolio?
   A. Listed equities.
   B. Private equity.
   C. U.S. Treasury bills.

Solution to 1: C is correct. With a 20-year horizon and average risk tolerance, Johnson can accept the additional risk of listed equities and private equity compared with U.S. Treasury bills.

Solution to 2: B is correct. Private equity is risky, has no public market, and is the least liquid among the assets mentioned.

TAX CONCERNS   Tax status varies among investors. Some investors will be subject to taxation on investment returns and some will not. For example, in many countries returns to pension funds are exempt from tax. Some investors will face various rates of tax on income (dividends and interest payments) than they do on capital gains (associated with increases in asset prices). Typically, when there is a differential, income is taxed more highly than gains. Gains may be subject to a lower rate of tax or part or all of the gain may be exempt from taxation. Furthermore, income may be taxed as it is earned, whereas gains may be taxed when they are realized. Hence, in such cases there is a time value of money benefit in the deferment of taxation of gains relative to income.

In many cases, the portfolio should reflect the tax status of the client. For example, a taxable investor may wish to hold a portfolio that emphasizes capital gains and receives little income. A taxable investor based in the United States is also likely to consider including U.S. municipal bonds ("munis") in his or her portfolio because interest income from munis, unlike from treasuries and corporate bonds, is exempt from taxes. A tax-exempt investor, such as a pension fund, will be relatively indifferent to the form of returns.

TABLE 18.1   Examples of Pension Fund Investment Restrictions

Country	Listed Equity	Real Estate	Government Bonds	Corporate Bonds	Foreign Assets
Switzerland	50%	50%	No limits	No limits	30%
Russia	65%	Not allowed	No limits	80%	10%
Japan	No limits	Not permitted	No limits	No limits	No limits
India	Minimum 25 percent in central government bonds; minimum 15 percent in state government bonds; minimum 30 percent invested in bonds of public sector enterprises				

Source: OECD Survey of Investment Regulations of Pension Funds, July 2008.

LEGAL AND REGULATORY FACTORS   The IPS should state any legal and regulatory restrictions that constrain how the portfolio is invested.

In some countries, such institutional investors as pension funds are subject to restrictions on the composition of the portfolio. For example, there may be a limit on the proportion of equities or other risky assets in the portfolio, or on the proportion of the portfolio that may be invested overseas. The United States has no limits on pension fund asset allocation but some countries do, examples of which are shown in Table 18.1. Pension funds also often face restrictions on the percentage of assets that can be invested in securities issued by the plan sponsor, so called **self-investment limits**.

When an individual has access to material nonpublic information about a particular security, this situation may also form a constraint. For example, the directors of a public company may need to refrain from trading the company's stock at certain points of the year before financial results are published. The IPS should note this constraint so that the portfolio manager does not inadvertently trade the stock on the client's behalf.

UNIQUE CIRCUMSTANCES   This section of the IPS should cover any other aspect of the client's circumstances that is likely to have a material impact on the composition of the portfolio. A client may have considerations derived from his or her religion or ethical values that could constrain investment choices. For instance, a Muslim investor seeking compliance with Shari'a (the Islamic law) will avoid investing in businesses and financial instruments inconsistent with Shari'a, such as casinos and bonds, because Shari'a prohibits gambling and lending money on interest. Similarly, a Christian investor may wish to avoid investments that he or she believes are inconsistent with their faith.

Whether rooted in religious beliefs or not, a client may have personal objections to certain products (e.g., pornography, weapons, tobacco, gambling) or practices (e.g., environmental impact of business activities, human impact of government policies, labor standards), which could lead to the exclusion of certain companies, countries, or types of securities (e.g., interest-bearing debt) from the investable universe as well as the client's benchmark. Such considerations are often referred to as ESG (environmental, social, governance), and investing in accordance with such considerations is referred to as SRI (socially responsible investing).

EXAMPLE 18.6   Ethical Preferences

The $3 billion F&C Stewardship Growth Fund is designed for investors who wish to have ethical and environmental principles applied to the selection of their investments. The fund's managers apply both positive (characteristics to be emphasized in the portfolio) and negative (characteristics to be avoided in the portfolio) screening criteria:

Positive Criteria

Supplies the basic necessities of life (e.g., healthy food, housing, clothing, water, energy, communication, health care, public transport, safety, personal finance, education).

Offers product choices for ethical and sustainable lifestyles (e.g., fair trade, organic).

Improves quality of life through the responsible use of new technologies.

Shows good environmental management.

Actively addresses climate change (e.g., renewable energy, energy efficiency).

Promotes and protects human rights.

Supports good employment practices.

Provides a positive impact on local communities.

Maintains good relations with customers and suppliers.

Applies effective anticorruption controls.

Uses transparent communication.

Negative Criteria

Tobacco production.

Alcohol production.

Gambling.

Pornography or violent material.

Manufacture and sale of weapons.

Unnecessary exploitation of animals.

Nuclear power generation.

Poor environmental practices.

Human rights abuses.

Poor relations with employees, customers, or suppliers.

Source: Excerpted from F&C documents; www.fandc.com/new/Advisor/Default.aspx ?ID=79620.

When the portfolio represents only part of the client's total wealth, there may be aspects or portions of wealth not under the control of the manager that have implications for the portfolio. For example, an employee of a public company whose labor income and retirement income provision are reliant on that company and who may have substantial investment exposure to the company through employee share options and stock holdings, may decide that their portfolio should not invest additional amounts in that stock. An entrepreneur may be reluctant to see his or her portfolio invested in the shares of competing businesses or in any business that has risk exposures aligned with his or her entrepreneurial venture.

A client's income may rely on a particular industry or asset class. Appropriate diversification requires that industry or asset class to be deemphasized in the client's investments. For example, a stockbroker should consider having a relatively low weighting in equities, as his skills and thus income-generating ability are worth less when equities do not perform well. Employees should similarly be wary of having concentrated share positions in the equity of the company they work for. If the employer encounters difficulties, not only may the employee lose his or her job, but their investment portfolio could also suffer a significant loss of value.

Gathering Client Information   As noted previously, it is important for portfolio managers and investment advisers to know their clients. For example, Dutch securities industry practice requires financial intermediaries to undertake substantial fact finding. This is required not only in the case of full-service wealth management or in the context of an IPS, but also in lighter forms of financial intermediation, such as advisory relationships (in which clients make investment decisions after consultation with their investment adviser or broker) or execution-only relationships (in which the client makes his investment decisions independently).

An exercise in fact-finding about the customer should take place at the beginning of the client relationship. This will involve gathering information about the client's circumstances as well as discussing the client's objectives and requirements.

Important data to gather from a client should cover family and employment situations as well as financial information. If the client is an individual, it may also be necessary to know about the situation and requirements of the client's spouse or other family members. The health of the client and his or her dependents is also relevant information. In an institutional relationship, it will be important to know about key stakeholders in the organization and what their perspective and requirements are. Information gathering may be done in an informal way or may involve structured interviews or questionnaires or analysis of data. Many advisers will capture data electronically and use special systems that record data and produce customized reports.

Good recordkeeping is very important, and may be crucial in a case in which any aspect of the client relationship comes into dispute at a later stage.

EXAMPLE 18.7   Henri Gascon: Description of Constraints

Henri Gascon continues to discuss his investment requirements with the financial adviser. The financial adviser begins to draft the constraints section of the IPS.

Gascon expects that he will continue to work for the oil company and that his relatively high income will continue for the foreseeable future. Gascon and his wife do not plan to have any additional children, but expect that their son will go to a university at age 18. They expect that their son's education costs can be met out of their salary income.

Gascon's emergency reserve of €100,000 is considered to be sufficient as a reserve for unforeseen expenditures and emergencies. His retirement savings of €900,000 has been contributed to his defined-contribution pension plan account to fund his retirement. Under French regulation, pension fund contributions are paid from gross income (i.e., income prior to deduction of tax) and pension fund returns are exempt from tax, but pension payments from a fund to retirees are taxed as income to the retiree.

With respect to Gascon's retirement savings portfolio, refer back to Example 18.3 as needed and address the following:

1. As concerns liquidity,
   A. A maximum of 50 percent of the portfolio should be invested in liquid assets.
   B. The portfolio should be invested entirely in liquid assets because of high spending needs.
   C. The portfolio has no need for liquidity because there are no short-term spending requirements.
2. The investment time horizon is closest to
   A. 5 years.
   B. 20 years.
   C. 40 years.
3. As concerns taxation, the portfolio
   A. Should emphasize capital gains because income is taxable.
   B. Should emphasize income because capital gains are taxable.
   C. Is tax exempt and thus indifferent between income and capital gains.
4. The principle legal and regulatory factors applying to the portfolio are
   A. U.S. Securities laws.
   B. European banking laws.
   C. French pension fund regulations.
5. As concerns unique needs, the portfolio should
   A. Have a high weighting in oil and other commodity stocks.
   B. Be invested only in responsible and sustainable investments.
   C. Not have significant exposure to oil and other commodity stocks.

Solution to 1: C is correct. The assets are for retirement use, which is 20 years away. Any short-term spending needs will be met from other assets or income.

Solution to 2: B is correct. The relevant time horizon is to the retirement date, which is 20 years away. The assets may not be liquidated at that point, but a restructuring of the portfolio is to be expected as Gascon starts to draw an income from it.

Solution to 3: C is correct. Because no tax is paid in the pension fund, it does not matter whether returns come in the form of income or capital gains.

Solution to 4: C is correct. The management of the portfolio will have to comply with any rules relating to the French pension funds.

Solution to 5: C is correct. Gascon's human capital (i.e., future labor income) is affected by the prospects of the oil industry. If his portfolio has significant exposure to oil stocks, he would be increasing a risk exposure he already has.

Example 18.8, the final one based on Henri Gascon, shows how the information obtained from the fact-finding exercises might be incorporated into the objectives and constraints section of an IPS.

EXAMPLE 18.8   Henri Gascon: Outline of an IPS

Following is a simplified excerpt from the IPS the adviser prepares for Henri Gascon, covering objectives and constraints.

Risk Objectives:

The portfolio may take on relatively high amounts of risk in seeking to meet the return requirements. With a 20-year time horizon and significant assets and income, the client has an above-average ability to take risk. The client is a knowledgeable investor, with an above-average willingness to take risk. Hence, the client's risk tolerance is above average, explaining the above portfolio risk objective.

The portfolio should be well diversified with respect to asset classes and concentration of positions within an asset class. Although the client has above-average risk tolerance, his investment assets should be diversified to control the risk of catastrophic loss.

Return Objectives:

The portfolio's long-term return requirement is 6.2 percent per year, in nominal terms and net of fees, to meet the client's retirement income goal.

Constraints:

Liquidity: The portfolio consists of pension fund assets and there is no need for liquidity in the short to medium term.

Time horizon: The portfolio will be invested with a 20-year time horizon. The client intends to retire in 20 years, at which time an income will be drawn from the portfolio.

Tax status: Under French law, contributions to the fund are made gross of tax and returns in the fund are tax-free. Hence, the client is indifferent between income and capital gains in the fund.

> *Legal and regulatory factors:* The management of the portfolio must comply with French pension fund regulations.
>
> *Unique needs:* The client is an executive in the oil industry. The portfolio should strive to minimize additional exposures to oil and related stocks.

References

Grable, John E., and Soo-Hyun Joo. 2004. "Environmental and Biopsychosocial Factors Associated with Financial Risk Tolerance." *Financial Counseling and Planning* 15 (1): 73–82.

Maginn, John L., and Donald L. Tuttle. 1983. "The Portfolio Management Process and Its Dynamics." *Managing Investment Portfolios: A Dynamic Process*. Boston: Warren, Gorham & Lamont.

CHAPTER **19**

Portfolio Risk Management Strategies

I nvestment advisors and consultants must understand the concept, calculations, and applications of risk; but they must also possess the knowledge and skill to manage portfolio risk effectively. This chapter reviews traditional methods for managing risk such as diversification and hedging through insurance and options strategies. The readings also focus on risk budgeting, risk decomposition, and specific strategies such as minimum variance portfolios and risk parity. The authors look at a number of risk factors including: market risk, credit and counterparty risk, liquidity risk, volatility risk, and operational risk; and how they may be adjusted for in the portfolio. The last reading describes risk as it relates to retirement portfolios, and considers a number of theories and strategies built to overcome this important challenge facing retirees and their advisors.

Part I *The New Science of Asset Allocation:* Risk Budgeting and Asset Allocation

Learning Objectives
- Describe the multifactor approach to portfolio risk management.
- Identify various sources of risk that may be identified and managed within a portfolio.
- Discuss the use of volatility as a risk target.
- Explain how risk may be decomposed using value at risk to measure a portfolio's overall risk.
- Describe how risk may be managed using futures and options.

Part II Article from *Wilmott Magazine:* "Dynamic Risk-Based Asset Allocation"

Learning Objectives
- Define the concept of equal risk contribution portfolios.
- Describe the concept and construction of minimum variance portfolios.
- Describe and explain the historical performance of market-cap weighted indexes in comparison to minimum variance equity indexes.

Part III *Portfolio Design:* Investing and Spending in Retirement

Learning Objectives

- Discuss the appropriateness of risk-taking in retirement, particularly as it pertains to equity allocations in a retirement portfolio.
- Describe target date funds.
- Discuss longevity as it relates to life spans and number of years living in retirement.
- Define spending rules and discuss different schools of thought for spending rules in retirement.
- Describe the impact of market returns and the sequence of those returns on retirement portfolios.

Part I Risk Budgeting and Asset Allocation

Asset allocation and risk management are about finding the right balance of risk and return. In this chapter, we focus on several practical techniques that can be used to measure, monitor, and manage the risk of a portfolio. What we want readers to take from this chapter is that asset allocation is the same as risk allocation and that the road to a portfolio that meets an investor's investment goals through time comes from actively monitoring and managing the risk of the portfolio.

The concept of risk-adjusted returns is not easy to explain because there is no consensus on how the "true" risk of a portfolio should be measured and because, as was discussed in previous chapters, risk cannot be measured in isolation—it depends on other assets and liabilities of the investor. While an investor's interest is on the total return generated by a portfolio, good returns are difficult to achieve. The fact that markets are efficient most of the time means that high returns will typically come at the cost of higher risk. The good news is that while managing a portfolio to earn a high rate of return is difficult, managing the risk profile of a portfolio is relatively easy.

Process of Risk Management: Multifactor Approach

Risk management is a process that involves several steps. When it comes to risk management of multiasset portfolios, the first step is to understand the investor. What are her attitudes toward risk, what are her liabilities, and what does she hope to achieve with help of the portfolio? Once this first step is completed, our attention must turn to the portfolio. In this context, first, we need to find out what the sources of portfolio risks are. Next, we must use quantitative and qualitative tools to measure the exposure of the portfolio to these sources of risk. This is important because, in the long run, the major determinants of a portfolio's total return are its exposures to various sources of risk. At this stage, we need to define various sources of risk. These may include:

> **Market risk:** This is the risk associated with unexpected changes in broad asset classes or economic variables. Let's look at some of the major sources of risk that come under market risk:

Equity risk: This is the most well known and best understood source of risk. It results from unexpected changes in global economic prices. Since equity prices are expected have a positive return in the long run, higher exposure to this risk should lead to higher return.

Interest risk: This is also a fairly well understood source of risk and it mostly affects fixed income instruments and equity prices of financial institutions.

Currency risk: Positions denominated in foreign currencies have direct exposure to this source of risk. However, currency risk is not one of those risks that should contribute to a higher return on a portfolio. This means that if the hedging cost is zero, one may consider eliminating this risk.

Commodity risk: Investment in commodities has become an increasingly important asset class in recent years. A portfolio may have exposure to unexpected changes in commodity prices even if it does not have direct investment in commodities; for example, an unexpected increase in oil price may significantly affect several sectors of the economy.

Inflation risk: This risk will manifest itself through changes in interest rates and commodity prices. Further, this is a larger risk for those portfolios where the total return is supposed to fund operations of an entity, cover the cost of living of a family, or pay for the replacement of real assets.

Others: Risks associated with various economic sectors, small capitalization firms, emerging markets, and so on.

Credit and counterparty risk: This risk is caused by the failure of a counterparty or a debtor to meet its legal obligations. It can also be caused by changes in the credit rating of a credit instrument. Counterparty risks arise whenever positions are established in over-the-counter instruments such as credit derivatives, interest swaps, or forward contracts. Higher exposure to credit risk may not always lead to higher return on the portfolio. This is especially correct for counterparty risk, where higher return may come at too high a cost. The reason is that most instruments that are exposed to counterparty risk are purchased for risk management purposes rather than return enhancement. The cost of not having the anticipated protection when it is needed could be quite high.

Liquidity risk: This arises when an investment cannot be converted into cash quickly without paying a significant penalty. For exchange-traded instruments, this risk can be measured using the bid-ask spread. For alternative investments, liquidity risk is difficult to measure. Recent experience with hedge funds imposing restrictions on redemptions shows that liquidity risk is not constant and could arise exactly when liquidity is most valued. Liquidity can be a major source of return for some alternative asset classes (e.g., private equity and some hedge fund strategies). A major difficulty in this area is measuring liquidity risk. Quantitative methods to measure this risk are lacking and therefore common sense and qualitative due diligence should be used to supplement the analysis.

Volatility risk: This risk arises when there are unexpected increases in volatility. This source of risk can be further expanded by looking at volatility of specific segments of the market (e.g., equity, interest rate, commodity prices, and so forth). This risk is particularly important if the portfolio has instruments with nonlinear payoffs (e.g., options) or the portfolio manager is using dynamic trading strategies to replicate the payoff to such instruments. There is some controversy with regard to this risk; that is, do investments that have positive exposure to this risk carn a premium (positive or negative) for exposure to volatility? Available empirical evidence seems to indicate that the market price of risk for volatility is actually negative. This means that those instruments that are positively correlated to changes in volatility offer lower rate of return.

Operational risk: This risk generally arises if the portfolio has allocation to active managers. System failures, lack of adequate control, and fraud are examples of operational risk that could affect a portfolio's performance. As discussed later, there are generally no rewards for exposure to operational risk and therefore it pays to avoid it.

Others: There are several other sources of risk that could affect a portfolio's return. For instance, political risk may be important for a portfolio that has allocation to emerging economies. Changes in regulatory environment and tax codes represent additional sources of risk.

In general, the higher the total risk of a portfolio, the higher its long-term rate of return. This statement is correct in the long-run and during normal periods. However, during periods of market stress, higher risk is typically associated with lower return. The reason is that investors begin to reassess their risk exposures and start selling risky assets during such periods. As a result, higher risk is associated with lower return during periods of market stress. Further, even in the long-run not every risk exposure is going to translate into higher return, or a marginal higher return could come at the cost of much higher risk. Two examples may demonstrate this. First, suppose a portfolio manager is considering allocation to both AAA and BBB rated corporate bonds. In this case, any increased allocation to the BBB rated bond index should increase the long-term return of the portfolio while increasing the portfolio's exposure to credit risk. So depending on the current risk profile of the portfolio and the investor's attitude toward risk, one may decide to increase the allocation to BBB rated bond index in order to generate a higher return over time. Second, consider a portfolio manager who is considering allocation to two hedge funds. One has a state-of–the-art enterprise risk management system and therefore will expose the portfolio manager to very little operational risk. The other manager runs a rather small fund and cannot afford to have all risk management tools in place. In this case, there is no reward to bearing the operational risk of the second manager.

Once the relevant sources of risk are identified, next comes the more difficult task of measuring a portfolio's exposure. The most common approach to measure exposure is to use a multivariate linear regression. These multifactor models can be quite effective as long as one can find a factor that has pure exposure to the desired source of risk. Some risk factors can be identified quite easily while others have to be constructed through a careful process, and some risk factors may be impossible to identify (e.g., liquidity risk factor).

The general form of a multifactor is:

$$R_{it} - R_f = \alpha_i + \beta_{i1}F_{1t} + \beta_{i2}F_{2t} + \ldots + \beta_{iK}F_{Kt} + \varepsilon_{it}$$

where

R_{it} = Total return on asset class i in time period t
R_f = Riskless rate
α_i = Intercept
β_{i1} = Exposure of the investment to factor 1
ε_{it} = Unexplained part of return
F_{kt} = Factor representing the source of risk

The factors must be selected carefully so that they unambiguously represent a unique source of risk. For example, credit risk can be expressed as the difference between the return on a high-yield bond index and the return on a Treasury Bond index with the same duration, or interest rate risk can be measured as the return differential between an index of medium-term Treasuries and short-term Treasuries. Generally, as you can see, one should attempt to represent the factors as excess returns on portfolios.

The goal of risk management in the context of portfolio management is not to eliminate every risk, but to find the right combination of risks that is consistent with the investor's risk preference and at the same time not to expose the portfolio to risks that do not contribute to its long-term performance. Thus, in the next step of the risk management process, the portfolio manager has to decide on the potential reward from various sources of risk. The issues related to estimating risk premiums associated with various factors were discussed in previous chapters. Briefly, for those risk factors that are represented by returns on traded assets, the risk premium associated with risk factors can be estimated by examining the excess return on the corresponding asset. For instance, the mean of the return differential between a high-yield bond index and Treasury index of the same duration is a reasonable estimate of the price of credit risk. If no such an asset can be identified, then create a portfolio with high exposure to the factor and a portfolio with low exposure to the same factor. The mean of the return differential between the two portfolios is a reasonable estimate of the risk premium associated with that factor. For instance, if the mean return for a portfolio with positive exposure to inflation is not different from the mean return on a portfolio with negative exposure to inflation, then inflation risk is not priced by markets. This means that having exposure to inflation is not likely to contribute to the portfolio's performance and therefore should be eliminated, assuming the cost of doing so is zero. However, eliminating exposure to inflation without affecting the entire risk-return profile of a portfolio is a difficult task.

Once market prices of various factors are estimated, and considering the investor's tolerance for risk and her liabilities, the portfolio manager has to decide how much exposure to each risk the portfolio should have. For instance, if the only relevant risk factor were equity risk, then risk management would require the portfolio manager to establish the right equity beta for the portfolio, and then adjust the portfolio's allocation to equity through time to maintain the targeted beta. As stated, the portfolio should have exposures to those sources of risk that contribute to the portfolio's performance, and the exposure should be relatively low for those sources of risk that do not provide a large benefit.

The final step is to construct the portfolio with the appropriate risk attributes and then monitor changes in those risk exposures through time to ensure that the portfolio remains within the parameters set forth in the investment policy statement. Given the factor model that was expressed in the previous equation, the expected return on the portfolio is given by

$$E[R_{it}] - R_f = \alpha_i + \beta_{i1} \times E[F_{1t}] + \beta_{i2} \times E[F_{2t}] + \ldots + \beta_{iK} \times E[F_{Kt}]$$

Therefore, the expected total return on the portfolio is primarily determined by its exposure to various sources of risk. Since the beta of the portfolio with respect to each risk factor is just the weighted average of the risk exposures of the components of the portfolio, the weights should be selected to manage the portfolio's risk exposures. The following quantitative approach can be used to construct the portfolio:

$$\min_w \quad \text{Var}[R_p] \quad \text{Subject to}$$

$$w_i \geq 0$$

$$\sum_{i=1}^{N} w_i \beta_{i1} = \text{Exposure}_1$$

$$\ldots$$

$$\sum_{i=1}^{N} w_i \beta_{iK} = \text{Exposure}_K$$

This means the portfolio is constructed to have minimum volatility subject to various constraints on the portfolio's exposure. This problem can be solved using standard optimization packages such as Microsoft Excel's Solver. Note that one can eliminate the usual constraint that weights should add up to one by using returns in excess of a riskless asset.

Typically, the above analysis is performed using available equity, fixed income, and alternative asset indices. Once the optimal allocations are determined, the portfolio manager has to find the investment products that have the same characteristics as those indices. This task is relatively straightforward for equity and fixed income investments. However, when it comes to alternative asset classes and especially those for which manager skill is rather important, it may be impossible to find managers who have the same exposures as the indices. In some cases, the portfolio manager may need to revise the equity and fixed income exposures of the portfolio in order to rebalance the overall exposure of the portfolio. For instance, if the equity exposures of the hedge fund managers who are selected are higher than the equity exposure of the hedge fund index used in the analysis, the portfolio manager may need to reduce the fund's exposure to equity using the liquid portion of the portfolio.

Process of Risk Management: Volatility Target

A simple and yet effective application of what was discussed above is to adjust a portfolio's overall exposure to markets by adjusting its volatility. Though we have argued that risk is multidimensional and that volatility should not be used as a portfolio's only measure of risk, monitoring a fund's volatility and making appropriate adjustments to the portfolio mix can significantly improve a portfolio's risk-return profile.

TABLE 19.1   Sample Portfolio Allocations

Broad Asset Classes	Allocations
Global Short-Term Fixed Income	5%
Global Long-Term Fixed Income	35%
Developed Markets Equity	20%
Emerging Markers Equity	10%
Funds of Hedge Funds and CTAs	10%
Private Equity	5%
Commodities	5%
Real Estate	10%
Total	100%

The procedure described here is rather simple and inexpensive to implement. Therefore, unless the portfolio manager has implemented a more sophisticated risk management model (e.g., a multifactor model), portfolio rebalancing through volatility balancing is a sensible risk management method.

Here, we present this method through an example. Table 19.1 provides one sample portfolio allocation across multiple asset classes. Consider the case of a family business, which currently has an investment of $200 million in a well-diversified portfolio of traditional global equity and fixed income assets as well as alternative investments.

The five-year historical volatility on the portfolio's pro-forma return has been 10 percent, while during the same period the average implied volatility of U.S. equity market has been around 18 percent. This means that the portfolio's volatility has been about 55 percent of VIX. Once the portfolio is constructed, the portfolio manager will need to monitor the VIX. If there is a significant increase in VIX, the portfolio manager will use index futures to hedge out some of the portfolio's volatility such that its expected volatility remains close to the target. For instance if VIX increases to 24 percent, the expected volatility of the portfolio will be 55 percent × 24 percent = 13.2 percent. Using a relatively small short position in S&P 500 futures, the portfolio manager would be able to bring back the portfolio's expected volatility close to the target. Consider the expression on the following page for the volatility of portfolio plus a position in the futures contract.

$$\text{Target} = \sqrt{\sigma_p^2 + w^2 VIX^2 + 2w VIX^2 \beta_p}$$

where

σ_p = Standard deviation of the portfolio (13.2 percent in this case)
w = Size of futures position relative to the size of the portfolio
β_p = Beta of the portfolio with respect to S&P 500 futures
     (e.g., 0.5 in this case)

Calculation will show that a short position of about 8.5 percent of the portfolio will reduce the expected volatility back to 10 percent. The rebalancing can take place on a regular basis (e.g., monthly) or whenever the expected volatility of the portfolio moves outside a narrow band. This strategy will reduce the portfolio's risk exposure when there is a spike in VIX because of market stress, while it will slowly increase the portfolio's exposure as markets calm down, because changes in VIX are not symmetric; that is, increases in VIX tend to be dramatic when there is market stress, but declines in VIX tend to be gradual as the market returns to normal.

Risk Decomposition of Portfolio

As we have tried to emphasize throughout this book, asset allocation is the process of creating a portfolio with a proper risk-return balance. Further, as we have also argued, the performance of a diversified portfolio is mostly determined by its exposures to various sources of risk. In this section, we use value at risk (VaR) to measure a portfolio's overall risk. Then we show how the VaR of a portfolio can be decomposed so one could know how allocation to each asset class contributes to the total risk of the portfolio. In this way, the portfolio manager can balance the potential return from each allocation by the contribution of the allocation to the total risk of the portfolio.

The VaR of a portfolio measures its potential losses due to market risks. In particular, the daily VaR of a portfolio at the confidence level of α states that the portfolio will not suffer a loss greater than VaR with probability of α. Let $\mathrm{Var}(R_p)$ denote the per-period VaR of a portfolio. Then this measure of total risk can be decomposed as follows:

$$\mathrm{VaR}(R_p) = \mathrm{MVaR}(R_1) \times w_1 + \mathrm{MVaR}(R_2) \times w_2 + \dots + \mathrm{MVaR}(R_N) \times w_N$$

where $\mathrm{MVaR}(R_i)$ is the marginal VaR of asset class i and it measures the contribution of one unit of asset class i to the total VaR of the portfolio. The marginal VaR of investment i is calculated using the following expression:

$$\mathrm{MVaR}(R_i) = \mathrm{VaR}(R_p) \times \beta_i$$

where β_i is the beta of asset class i with respect to the portfolio. This result indicates that an asset class that has a high beta with respect to the portfolio makes a relatively large contribution to the total risk of the portfolio. It is essential that a portfolio manager be fully aware of how much risk each asset class contributes to the total risk of the portfolio. For a portfolio that is properly balanced in terms of risk and return, the expected return from each asset class should be directly related to the marginal contribution of that asset class to the risk of the portfolio. Therefore, if the contribution of an asset class to the total risk of a portfolio, as measured by $\mathrm{MVaR}(R_i) \times w_i$, is twice as high as the marginal contribution of another asset, then the expected contribution of the first asset to the portfolio's performance should be about twice as high as that of the second asset.

Risk Management Using Futures

It is well known that futures provide a means to directly track underlying investment markets as well as to provide risk reduction opportunities. Since futures markets permit individuals to buy or sell financial assets for future delivery at a price set today, futures contracts offer a means to hedge the risk of unexpected price changes. For instance, a commodity, foreign currency, equity, or fixed income hedge is usually caused by buying (selling) a futures contract to initiate a futures position and closing out (offsetting) the position at a later date by selling (buying) the contract in the futures market rather than taking delivery. The hedger benefits to the extent that a gain in the futures position offsets a loss in the spot position. An investor purchasing long-term bonds in September may wish to reduce the risk of interest rate variability by simultaneously selling a December T-Bond futures contract. If interest rates rise during the holding period, the losses in the spot market are reduced by gains in the futures market. Likewise, the foreign currency futures market offers similar protection against unanticipated currency price changes. A U.S. exporter selling goods to a French customer on March 1 but not expecting delivery (payment) until June in euros may wish to sell a June euro futures contract. If the value of the euro falls in the interim, the loss in the spot market is balanced by the gain in the futures position.

It is important to note that opposite price movements result in similar final values as a rise in the value of the euro results in gains on the spot market but losses in the futures market. There is, of course, no guarantee that the spot market gain or loss will be perfectly offset by the futures trade. Since price changes of the cash security and futures contract are often not of the same magnitude, the success of the hedging strategy depends on determining the proper hedge ratio. For many, the proper hedge ratio is determined simply by the relative sensitivity of the return on the spot asset to the return on the futures contract (e.g., beta for stocks, duration for bonds). The actual number of contracts held is determined by the proper hedge ratio times the relative cash value of the spot position times the relative value of the futures contract.[1]

For equities, the minimum risk hedge ratio (X_f^*) is equivalent to the negative of the slope coefficient of regression of cash price changes on futures contract price changes. The higher the correlation between cash and futures price changes, the higher the expected effectiveness of the futures market for hedging purposes. The implementation of this model requires a portfolio manager to regress time series data of historical price changes of the cash instrument to be hedged (ΔP_c) against the price changes of the futures contract (ΔP_f). The optimal hedge ratio (HR) is simply the slope coefficient of:

$$\Delta P_{ct} = \alpha + HR\Delta P_{ft}$$

If an individual holds a $1 million position in a stock index futures market, for an $HR = 0.90$, a $900,000 principal position ($0.9 \times 1 million) would be taken in the stock index futures market. For stock index futures, the contract value depends on the level of the index. For example, if the S&P futures price is 1,006.90, the face value of the futures contract is $251,725 ($1,006.90 \times 250). This would translate into four S&P futures contracts (e.g., $1 million $\div$ $251,725 \times 0.9 = 4$). The regression based model, however, assumes that historical relationships between price changes of the cash security and price changes in the futures contract are stable. However, for fixed income securities, price changes are a function of duration that changes through time. The following duration model attempts to explicitly account for these duration estimates.

For fixed income securities, the minimum risk hedge ratio is often based on the relative durations of the security and the futures contract:

$$HR = \frac{D_i R_i P_i}{D_f R_f P_f}$$

where

R_f = Expected change in yield on the instrument underlying futures contract f

R_i = Expected change in yield on bond i

P_f = Price agreed upon the futures contract f to be paid upon maturity of the futures contract for title to the instrument underlying P_f

P_i = Price of bond i expected to prevail on (1) the planned termination date of the hedge for an anticipatory hedge and (2) today's date for cash hedge

D_i = Duration of bond i expected to prevail on (1) the planned termination date of the hedge for an anticipatory hedge and (2) today's date for cash hedge

D_f = Duration of the instrument underlying futures contract f at the delivery date

The duration of a 3-3/8 percent coupon T-Note with a 9 year 11 months maturity yielding 3.44 percent (price = 99.46) is 8.49 years. The duration of the 7-1/2 percent coupon, 6-year 11-month T-Note yielding 2.83 percent (price = 129.21) underlying the futures contract is 5.70 years. Assume that the relative yield change of the two bonds is the same (i.e., $R_i = R_f$). Using this information, the HR is

$$HR = \frac{(\$99.46)(8.49)}{(\$129.21)(5.70)} = 1.14$$

This means that 1.48 T-Bond contracts should be traded for each $100,000 face value of the cash bond held. If the manager holds $1 million in bonds, he should sell approximately 11 T-Bond futures contracts ($1 million ÷ 100,000 × 1.14). The duration model makes some assumptions about the kind of interest rate changes that will occur. Different models exist for alternative forecasts of yield shifts. The model therefore requires certain assumptions on relative yield curve shifts. Moreover, duration theory itself has been criticized as not adequately measuring bond price movement. The duration model also requires certain forecasts of expected relative yield volatilities. Historical estimates may be used; however, the stability of past yield relationships is often questionable.

There are a multitude of considerations and approaches involved in futures trading or the use of futures in risk and return management. There are also various means to determine the proper hedge ratio and for many assets no direct futures based contracts exist. Notwithstanding the foregoing, futures contracts have been used to both reduce risk exposure and to increase exposure to particular market factors. For instance, futures have been used to create various portable alpha programs in which the market risks of a particular strategy are hedged away, leaving the excess return. Futures have also been used to create benchmark-plus type programs in which futures contracts are added to an existing portfolio in order to create a new portfolio with a correlation closer to the benchmark portfolio and with hopefully a higher return than the benchmark portfolio.

Risk Management Using Options

Options can be used to implement drastic changes in the risk-return profile of an investment. Traditional long only assets offer investors a limited set of choices in terms of directly managing the risk of the underlying spot positions. As discussed earlier, futures contracts offer the ability to reduce or increase the underlying variability of an asset, but futures do not permit one to fundamentally change the risk structure of the asset (e.g., create a skewed distribution). Options (when available) provide the means to purchase (call) or sell (put) a security in the future for a price determined today. Unlike with a futures contract, the purchaser of an option has the right but not the obligation to make or accept delivery. Below we discuss two examples involving using options to manage the risk profile of an investment.

Covered Call

A covered call writing strategy (often referred to as a buy-write) typically entails the writing (selling) of a call on an equity index against a long position in the same underlying equity index. However, the strategy may be implemented on individual equities or other indices that have options written on them. In essence, the sale of the call sacrifices a portion of the upside return distribution of the underlying index in exchange for the collection of a fixed premium. The extent of upside participation depends on the initial moneyness of the written call. The further out-of-the-money the call is when written, the less of the upside that will potentially be sacrificed. On the other hand, the further out-of-the-money the call is when written, the smaller the premium that will be collected. The other factor that must be considered in the choice of calls is the initial time to expiration. Since an option's time value decay rate increases as the option approaches expiration, short-term options tend to decay in value quicker than long-term options, all things being equal. For this reason, many researchers use one-month calls when considering buy-write strategies.

The interest in the use of buy-write strategies for investment purposes has grown significantly in recent years. In light of the growing investment interest, the CBOE has recently introduced a number of buy-write indices based on a variety of equity indices such as the S&P 500, the Dow Jones Industrial Average, the NASDAQ 100 and the Russell 2000. In addition, a number of funds based on a buy-write strategy have been introduced over the last five years.[2] As illustrated in Kapadia and Szado (2007), the excess risk-adjusted performance of the passive buy-write strategy is primarily derived from selling calls at an implied volatility that exceeds the subsequently realized volatility. In fact, they find that if the calls were sold at the Black-Scholes price corresponding with the realized volatility, the buy-write strategy would underperform the underlying index. In this sense, the buy-write is providing something more than a simple return distribution truncation; it is also providing an additional source of returns—the option volatility risk premium. While Kapadia and Szado (2007) consider a variety of implementations of a buy-write strategy on the Russell 2000, Table 19.2 provides summary statistics for the one-month call buy-write for their period of analysis.

Over this 10-year period, the buy-write strategy provided similar returns to the underlying Russell 2000 at far lower standard deviations and drawdowns. In addition, they break the 10-year period into two periods, one that is decidedly unfavorable for the buy-write (relative to a buy-and-hold strategy on the underlying) as well as a favorable period. Since the buy-write sacrifices potential upside for guaranteed premium collection and the size of premiums are based on expected volatility levels, one would expect the buy-write to perform poorly relative to the underlying in sustained low volatility markets with strong upward trends. Kapadia and Szado

TABLE 19.2 Performance Statistics for Comparison Spot and Buy-Write: Summary Statistics for the One-Month to Expiration Russell 2000 Buy-Write (January 18, 1996–November 16, 2006)

	Russell 2000	2% OTM	ATM	2% ITM
Annualized Return	10.7%	10.6%	9.2%	9.60%
Annualized Standard Deviation	20.5%	14.9%	13.4%	11.98%
Maximum Drawdown	−34.7%	−27.2%	−17.5%	21.36%

Source: Kapadia and Szado (2007).

(2007) chose the subperiod from February 20, 2003, to November 16, 2006, to represent such an unfavorable market environment.[3] Interestingly, the results suggest that even in this unfavorable market environment, the buy-write strategy achieved over two-thirds of the return of the index at about half its volatility. Not surprisingly, in the earlier (favorable) period of January 1996 to February 2003, the buy-write strategy had a higher annualized return than the index (5.06 percent, versus the 3.84 percent). It is interesting to note that this higher return was achieved at a significantly lower volatility of 15.41 percent compared with the index volatility of 22.69 percent.

The results of the study certainly suggest that the buy-write strategy is capable of enhancing return and providing some loss mitigation if applied in the right market environment. While the buy-write strategy is often referred to in the literature as a hedging or downside protection strategy, it would be more accurate to think of it as a return enhancing strategy. The small returns typically generated month to month from the option volatility risk premium tend to provide a cushion in market down moves and a return enhancement in sideways markets.

Long Collar

One of the limiting factors of the use of the buy-write is that, while it typically provides a return enhancement that can help cushion losses, it leaves one exposed to the full downside of the underlying's return distribution. The collar strategy can address this shortcoming. The long collar essentially combines a buy-write strategy with a protective put. In general, a long collar strategy involves the purchase of a put against a long position in the underlying, combined with the writing of a call on the same underlying. The purpose of the put is to provide protection against a downside move of the long underlying position.

The call is written to at least partially cover the cost of the purchase of the put, at the expense of limiting the strategy's participation in upside moves of the underlying. A collar strategy is particularly appealing for investors who are seeking some protection from a potential downside move, or a reduction in the market exposure of their portfolio. Ultimately, the collar strategy is expected to offer investors an opportunity to significantly reduce the volatility of their returns, relative to a long position in the underlying index. This is due to the fact that the payoff of the long put reduces the losses of the long index position in downward market moves, while the short call reduces the gains of the long index position in upward market moves.[4] The long collar provides a great deal of flexibility. At one extreme, a very wide collar using far out-of-the-money options is essentially equivalent to a long position in the underlying, with no protection from downside market moves, and full participation in upside moves. At the other extreme, an at-the-money collar is essentially equivalent to a cash or money market position, insulated from market movements when held to expiration. Relative to a long position in the underlying index, the collar strategy has the highest advantage when the market experiences a strong downward trend and has the highest relative disadvantage during sustained strong upward trends.

To take advantage of the faster decay of short-term options, the collar can be implemented using six-month puts and one-month calls. In this way, the long six-month put decays relatively slowly, while each sequential one-month short call decays quickly. Table 19.3 provides results that suggest that a one-month call/six-month put 2 percent OTM collar strategies on the QQQ (NASDAQ 100 ETF) significantly outperformed the underlying QQQ in the period from April 1999 to May 2009. The returns for the collar were far higher at about one-third the volatility.

Ultimately, the risk of the collar strategy relative to holding the underlying is an opportunity cost risk. This risk is common to any hedging program. If the underlying performs extremely well, then a portion of the potential returns will be lost on the short call position (which is written to fund the purchase of the put's downside protection). Likewise, the ultimate relative benefit of the collar is equivalent to the protection provided by a standard insurance contract or hedge; that is, if the market experiences a significant downward move, losses are largely eliminated.

TABLE 19.3   Performance Statistics for Underlying and Long Collar April 1999–May 2009

April 1999–May 2009	QQQ TR	QQQ 2% OTM Collar 1 Mo. Put/1 Mo. Call.	QQQ 2% OTM Collar 6 Mo. Put/1 Mo. Call.
Annualized Return	−3.6%	−0.3%	9.3%
Annualized Std. Dev.	30.4%	6.3%	11.0%
Stutzer Index	−0.07	−0.50	0.59
Maximum Drawdown	−81.1%	−22.9%	−17.9%
April 1999–Sept. 2002			
Annualized Return	−23.3%	−3.5%	21.2%
Annualized Std. Dev.	42.4%	6.4%	13.7%
Stutzer Index	−0.51	−1.18	1.21
Maximum Drawdown	−81.1%	−22.7%	−7.5%
Sept. 2002–Sept. 2007			
Annualized Return	20.4%	3.5%	5.2%
Annualized Std. Dev.	17.5%	5.8%	7.9%
Stutzer Index	1.01	0.14	0.32
Maximum Drawdown	−12.4%	−6.7%	−14.0%
Sept. 2007–May 2009			
Annualized Return	−19.8%	−4.7%	−1.4%
Annualized Std. Dev.	29.2%	7.2%	11.6%
Stutzer Index	−0.67	−0.85	−0.20
Maximum Drawdown	−49.7%	−14.4%	−17.9%

Source: Szado and Schneeweis (2009).

What Every Investor Should Remember

Application of risk management tools in the context of portfolio management does not mean elimination of risks. It means that the portfolio has the right balance of risk and return from the viewpoint of the investor.

Risk management requires that a portfolio's exposures to various risks be measured and monitored over time.

Only those risks that contribute to the performance of the portfolio should be assumed and the others should be eliminated, assuming the cost of doing so is close to zero.

Decomposition of total risk as measured by VaR enables the portfolio manager to understand the contribution of each asset class to the total risk of a portfolio.

Risk contribution of an asset class should be closely related to the contribution of that asset class to the performance of the portfolio.

Futures and options provide direct means both to reduce or enhance an asset's standard deviation (futures) or to fundamentally change the characteristics of the distribution (options).

Dynamically managing the exposure of an asset relative to various measures of volatility may help limit an assets drawdown in periods of extreme negative market returns.

Notes

1. For more detail on the use of financial futures as a risk management tool, see www.cmegroup.com.
2. Academic and industry research papers have consistently found that the buy-write strategy on major equity indices such as the Russell 2000 and the S&P 500 typically outperform the underlying indices on a risk-adjusted basis. For example, see Kapadia and Szado (2007) and Hill, Balasubramanian, Gregory, and Tierens (2006).
3. The favorable and unfavorable periods refer to the performance of the buy-write strategy in comparisons to a buy and hold Russell 2000 investment. The annualized return for the Russell in the unfavorable period (February 20, 2003, to November 16, 2006) and favorable periods (January 1996 to February 2003) was 24.82 percent and 3.84 percent, respectively. The volatility in the unfavorable period was 15.34 percent compared with 22.69 percent for the favorable period.
4. Madoff's investment strategy was primarily a long collar strategy.

References

Hill, J. M., V. Balasubramanian, K. Gregory, and I. Tierens. 2006. "Finding Alpha via Covered Index Writing." *Financial Analysts Journal* 62, no. 5 (September/October): 29–46.

Kapadia, N., and E. Szado. 2007. "The Risk and Return Characteristics of the Buy-Write Strategy on the Russell 2000 Index." *The Journal of Alternative Investments* 9, no. 4 (Spring): 39–56.

Szado, E., and T. Schneeweis. 2009. "Loosening the Collar." CISDM Working Paper.

Part II Dynamic Risk-Based Asset Allocation

Introduction

Already in 1980, Merton emphasized the relative difficulty of forecasting properly expected returns, versus forecasting risk. Optimization techniques are well known to be sensitive to differences in expected returns and as a consequence, portfolio weights are dominated by the asset classes for which the estimation error in the expected returns is the largest (e.g., Best and Grauer, 1991). In contrast, risk is highly predictable, explaining the recent shift in the investment paradigm from return-based to risk-based portfolio allocation techniques and optimization models.

Risk-based portfolio solutions are portfolio allocation techniques that do not require explicit modeling of expected returns. Because of the time variation in risk and the dependence across stock returns, optimal risk-based portfolios are rebalanced frequently, such that the ex-post risk profile does not drift away from the investment objectives. Examples are the minimum risk portfolio, the 60/40 portfolio, and the equal risk contribution portfolio.

In the context of a bond–equity portfolio, invested in the market capitalization-weighted equity index, this leads typically to portfolios that have very high allocations to bonds, and given today's low interest rate regime and high bond prices, relatively low expected returns. For this reason, American fund managers have advocated to overlay the equal risk contribution portfolio with leverage. Such a leverage risk-diversified portfolio is commonly referred to as a risk-parity strategy.

This paper emphasizes that a more risk-controlled way of increasing the allocation to equity is to invest in a low-risk equity subset when targeting a portfolio where all asset classes are weighted according to an equal risk contribution objective.

A more direct way of increasing the equity portion in the portfolio is to tactically decide to switch from the equal risk contribution objective to a 60/40 risk allocation objective. In contrast to the 60/40 weight allocation portfolio, the 60/40 risk allocation portfolio loads automatically less on the more risky asset and has therefore still a low overall risk.

In what follows, we first review the main theoretical aspects of equal risk contribution portfolios. Then the empirical properties of low-risk equity portfolios are compared with those of market capitalization-weighted indices, both in a standalone case as in the context of bond–equity portfolio allocation.

Review of Equal Risk Contribution Portfolios

A major advantage of a portfolio invested in multiple asset classes is that the portfolio risk can be diversified across the different asset risk factors. As such, portfolio drawdowns are reduced compared with a portfolio that is invested in the most risky asset, while attractive upward return potential is created, compared with investing in the asset class with the lowest risk. The highest diversification of risk is obtained by the equal risk contribution (ERC) portfolio, in which all assets contribute equally to portfolio risk.

The risk contribution of an asset is formally defined as the simple product of its portfolio weight and its marginal contribution to risk. For simplicity in exposition, we focus here on the portfolio standard deviation as risk measure.[1] Qian (2006) illustrates that for many common cases these risk contributions can be linked directly to the asset's loss contribution. Furthermore, the volatility risk contribution has a simple explicit expression. More precisely, let Σ denote the covariance matrix for the return over the reference period. Then the risk contribution of the ith asset in a portfolio with weight w is given by:

$$RC_i = w_i \Sigma w / \sqrt{w'\Sigma w}$$

Because of the 1-homogeneity of standard deviation as a risk measure, Euler's theorem on homogeneous functions implies that the sum of the component risk contributions is the portfolio volatility:

$$\sum_{i=1}^{N} RC_i = \sqrt{w'\Sigma w}$$

where N denotes the number of portfolio components.

Note that, in the general case, the ERC portfolio allocation depends on the relative differences in volatility and correlation of the portfolio components. In fact, as shown by Lee (2011), the higher the volatility and/or the correlation of an asset with other assets, the lower its weight in the ERC portfolio.

In a two-asset framework, such as the bond–equity portfolio, the correlation cancels out in the ERC constraint $RC_{BONDS} = RC_{EQUITY}$ and the allocation to equity is exactly equal to the ratio of bond volatility to the sum of equity and bond volatility:

$$w^*_{EQUITY} = \sigma_{EQUITY} / (\sigma_{EQUITY} + \sigma_{BONDS})$$

This is a key equation, since it translates directly the volatility of the equity part of the portfolio into the portfolio weight. When stock volatility is twice that of bonds, one-third of the portfolio will be allocated to stocks.

The ERC criterion is thus an explicit rule for deciding how to rebalance the portfolio in response to changes in the covariance matrix. This is a distinctive factor of the allocation strategies with respect to the more traditional asset allocation strategies that rebalance the portfolio in response to changing market conditions.[2]

The ERC bond–equity portfolio is characterized by a 50/50 risk allocation to equity and bonds. There is *a priori* no economic reason why the 50/50 allocation is optimal. We feel that, in today's market of low interest rates and high durations, a

---

[1] See Boudt et al. (2011) for an extension to downside risk measures.
[2] Constant-proportion portfolio insurance (CPPI) and option-based portfolio insurance (OBPI) are examples of strategies that sell stocks as the market falls and buy stocks as the market rises. Constant-mix strategies buy stocks as the market falls and sell them as it rises (see, e.g., Perold and Sharpe, 1988).

tactical shift toward a higher risk allocation to equity is desirable in many regards. We define such risk allocation portfolios using the percentage risk contributions:

$$\%RC_i = RC_i / \sqrt{w'\Sigma w},$$

In analogy with the 60/40 equity–bond weighted allocation, we relax the 50/50 constraint of the ERC portfolio and study below also the 60/40 risk allocation portfolio, where the weight of equity is determined such that equity contributes 60 percent of the portfolio volatility.

Illustration

The performance of the ERC portfolio depends clearly on the choice of the underlying equity subportfolio. The most common way of implementing the ERC portfolio is to invest in market capitalization-weighted indices. However, in equities, it has been shown by various authors that over the past decades a higher return and a lower risk was achieved by dynamically selecting stocks based on their low-risk characteristic rather than their market capitalization. For example, Clarke et al. (2006) find that minimum variance portfolios based on the 1,000 largest U.S. stocks over the 1968–2005 period achieve a volatility reduction of about 25 percent while delivering comparable or even higher average returns than the market portfolio.

For the ERC bond–equity portfolio, a direct consequence of investing in a low-risk equity subportfolio rather than a market capitalization-weighted portfolio is that the budget allocation to equity increases. Next we illustrate this for a market capitalization-weighted and minimum variance index invested in a broad world-wide universe.[3] The cumulative value of 100 EUR invested in each of these indices is shown in Figure 19.1.

Consistent with the literature on the low-volatility anomaly (e.g., Baker et al., 2011; Boudt and Peeters, 2012), the minimum variance index offers over January 2002–May 2012 a higher return (6 percent versus 5 percent) and a lower standard deviation (9 percent versus 13 percent). Over the same period, a buy-and-hold investment strategy in the Barclays global treasuries bond index yielded an annualized compound return of 4 percent, with an annualized standard deviation of 3 percent.

A dynamic equal risk contribution portfolio involves estimating on a rolling basis the volatilities of the bond and equity subportfolios, and adjusting the portfolio weights such that they contribute equally to the overall portfolio risk. In our example, we measure volatility using a rolling one-year historical volatility estimate computed from daily returns over the period January 2002–May 2012 and assume a monthly rebalancing frequency.[4] The rolling volatility estimates are plotted in Figure 19.2.

---

[3] We choose these indices for illustrative purposes only. The minimum variance index has only a partial approach to risk, as it minimizes only the variance of the equity portfolio. Because of the non-normality of the return distribution, a truly low-risk portfolio requires taking into account the whole return distribution. See Danielsson (2011) for more theoretical details and Boudt and Peeters (2012) for the practical application. Because of the time-variation in risk, the minimum variance portfolio is rebalanced on a regular basis.

[4] Such a simple risk estimate was chosen for expositional purposes and also because of the short horizon. More accurate estimates of long-term bond risk can be constructed using the bond duration and potentially also the volatility of credit default swaps, as in Bruder et al. (2011).

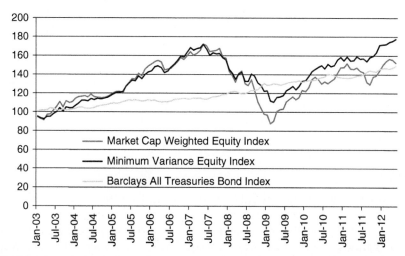

FIGURE 19.1 Cumulative Value of a Buy-and-Hold Strategy Invested in the Market Cap-Weighted Equity Index, the Minimum Variance Equity Index, and the Hedged Barclays Global Treasuries Bond Index

Figure 19.3 shows the sensitivity of the equity weights to the dynamic asset allocation rule. The blue line is the reference line corresponding to the weight of equity in the ERC portfolio, when the equity subportfolio is allocated as a function of the market capitalization of stocks. By design, the weight of equity in the portfolio increases when the relative volatility of equity decreases and vice versa. Over the whole period, the volatility of the market capitalization-weighted index was between 4 and 10 times the volatility of the bond index, leading to equity weights in the ERC

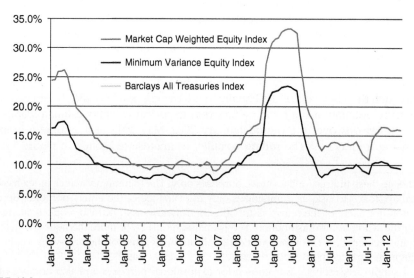

FIGURE 19.2 One-Year Rolling Volatility Estimates for the Market Cap-Weighted and Minimum Variance Equity Index, and the Hedged Barclays Global Treasuries Index

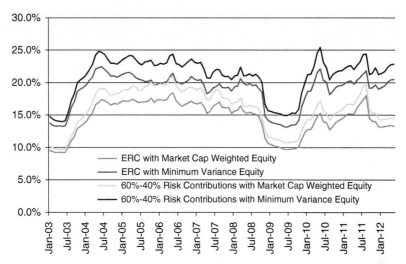

FIGURE 19.3 Weight of Equity in the ERC and 60/40 Risk Allocation Portfolio. The Equity Portion Is Either Invested in the World Market Cap-Weighted Index or the Minimum Variance Index

portfolio that vary between 9 percent and 18 percent, with an average value of 15 percent.

Over that same period, the minimum variance equity has a substantially lower volatility than the market capitalization-weighted index. Consequently, substituting the market cap index with the minimum variance index leads to a significant upward shift of the equity allocation in the ERC portfolio. When invested in the minimum variance equity index, the allocation of equity varies between 13 percent and 23 percent, with an average value of 19 percent.

Figure 19.3 shows also the sensitivity of the equity weights to changing the equal risk contribution constraint to a 60/40 equity–bonds risk allocation constraint. When the market capitalization-weighted index is used, this leads to an increase in the average equity weight from 15 percent to 16 percent. For the minimum variance index, the average weight increases from 19 percent to 21 percent.

In Table 19.4 we analyze the impact on the monthly returns of switching from a single asset class strategy to a dynamic risk allocation-based strategy.

We observe that, for both the market capitalization-weighted and minimum variance indices, the dynamic ERC or 60/40 risk allocation strategy improves substantially the risk-adjusted performance of the portfolio. This is not the case for the constant-mix 60 percent equity, 40 percent bonds portfolio, for which the Sharpe ratio and maximum drawdown are significantly worse than for investment in the bond index.

Over the 2003–2012 evaluation period, the minimum variance index had the highest return, at the price of a significantly higher risk compared with investing in bonds. An attractive compromise of both is obtained by combining the minimum variance equity and bond index in the ERC or 60/40 risk-weighted portfolios. Because of the combination with bonds, the maximum drawdown of the ERC and 60/40 risk-weighted portfolios is reduced from 35.7 percent to less than 3 percent (compared with 49 percent for the market capitalization-weighted index).

TABLE 19.4   Monthly Returns Analysis of Portfolios Invested in the World Market Capitalization Weighted Index and Minimum Variance Index, as Well as the Hedged Barclays All Treasuries Bond Index

	Annualized Return	Annualized Standard Deviation	Sharpe Ratio ($RF = 0$)	Maximum Drawdown
Single Asset Class Strategies				
Hedged Barclays all treasuries bond index	4.3%	2.9%	1.486	−3%
Market cap-weighted equity	4.6%	13.2%	0.345	−49.0%
Minimum variance equity	6.3%	9.4%	0.668	−35.7%
Dynamically Rebalanced Portfolios				
ERC with market cap-weighted equity	4.4%	2.5%	1.777	−2.4%
ERC with minimum variance equity	4.9%	2.7%	1.805	−2.6%
60% equity risk contribution, 40% bond risk contribution with market cap-weighted equity	4.4%	2.6%	1.712	−2.5%
60% equity risk contribution, 40% bond risk contribution with minimum variance equity	5.0%	2.8%	1.804	−2.9%
Constant-mix portfolio with 60% market cap-weighted equity, 40% bonds	4.7%	7.6%	0.628	−29.1%
Constant-mix portfolio with 60% minimum variance equity, 40% bonds	5.6%	5.6%	1.015	−18.6%

References

Baker, M., B. Bradley, and J. Wurgler. 2011. "Benchmarks as Limits to Arbitrage: Understanding the Low Volatility Anomaly." *Financial Analysts Journal* 67: 40–54.

Best, M. J., and R. Grauer. 1991. "On the Sensitivity of Mean-Variance Efficient Portfolios to Changes in Asset Means: Some Analytical and Computational Results." *Review of Financial Studies* 4: 315–342.

Boudt, K., P. Carl, and B. Peterson. 2013. "Asset Allocation with Conditional Value at Risk Budgets." *Journal of Risk* 15: 39–68.

Boudt, K., and B. Peters. 2012. "Risk-Optimised Investing in Equity Markets." Finvex White Paper, April.

Bruder, B., P. Heriel, and T. Roncalli. 2011. "Managing Sovereign Credit Risk in Bond Portfolios." *Journal of Indexes Europe* 4: 20–27.

Clarke, R., H. de Silve, and S. Thorley. 2006. "Minimum Variance Portfolios in the U.S. Equity Market." *Journal of Portfolio Management* (Fall): 10–24.

Danielsson, J. 2011. *Financial Risk Forecasting: The Theory and Practice of Forecasting Market Risk with Implementation in R and Matlab.* Chichester, UK: John Wiley & Sons.

Lee, W. 2011. "Risk-Based Asset Allocation: A New Answer to an Old Question?" *Journal of Portfolio Management* (Summer): 11–28.

Merton, R. 1980. "On Estimating the Expected Return on the Market." *Journal of Financial Economics* 8: 323–361.

Perold, A. F., and W. F. Sharpe. 1988. "Dynamic Strategies for Asset Allocation." *Financial Analysts Journal* 44: 16–27.

Qian, E. 2006. "On the Financial Interpretation of Risk Contribution: Risk Budgets Do Add Up." *Journal of Investment Management* 4 (4): 1–11.

Part III Investing and Spending in Retirement

After a foundation chooses its asset allocation, it should be able to leave that allocation unchanged for the indefinite future. A foundation can set up a spending plan and choose a long-run strategic asset allocation to support it. Unless there is major distress in the markets, the foundation should be able to carry out its plans without making changes to its allocation. It will hire and fire managers, but the overall investment plan should remain unchanged. Some foundations, of course, will pursue *tactical* asset allocation in an attempt to take advantage of short-term opportunities to overweight or underweight specific asset classes. But usually the tactical asset shifts are relative to a *strategic* (i.e., long-run) asset allocation that remains unchanged.

Individual investors are different. Most individual investors have one major investment goal—to save enough for retirement. Spending out of their portfolio is usually minimal in the years when they are working. Then spending becomes essential at the time of retirement. For this reason, there is a *life-cycle* to investing. In the years when wealth is being accumulated, asset allocation is much more aggressive than when the investor nears retirement.

In the past few years, investment firms have begun to formalize this process by which asset allocation changes over time. These firms have created *target retirement funds* that change continuously as the investor gets closer to retirement. The funds are usually defined relative to the year of retirement. So in 2010 a 52-year-old might invest in a 2025 retirement fund because that investor intends to retire at 67 years of age (for full Social Security benefits).[1] Consider the 2025 target retirement fund offered by Vanguard as shown in Figure 19.4. The 52-year-old is initially invested in a 75/25 stock/bond portfolio (diversified between domestic and foreign stocks). By the time of retirement 15 years later, this investor will have only 50 percent invested in stocks and 50 percent invested in bonds with a 10 percent allocation in inflation-protected bonds (to help protect against inflation in retirement).

Target retirement funds are designed to model the life cycle of investing beginning with the early years of working when very aggressive allocations are called for. Figure 19.5 shows the evolution over time of the Vanguard allocations in their 2035 target retirement fund. Until the investor reaches 25 years before retirement, Vanguard chooses a 90/10 stock/bond allocation. Then the fund begins to increase its allocation to bonds until the investor finally reaches the retirement age (denoted R in the figure). Even after retirement, the allocation continues to shift. Five years after retirement, the stock/bond allocation is at 36/64. Experts can debate whether these specific allocations are optimal, but the figure shows clearly how the proportion of riskier assets depends on the distance from the age of retirement.

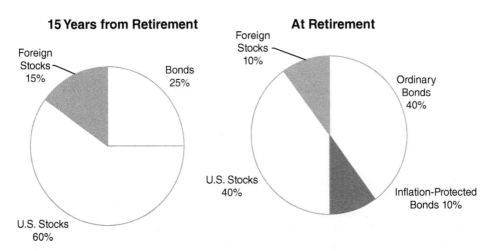

FIGURE 19.4   Portfolios for Investors 15 Years Prior to and at Retirement (Vanguard 2025 Target Retirement Fund)

Source: www.vanguard.com.

Vanguard is only one of the firms that offer such target retirement funds. Figure 19.6 shows the allocation chosen by four major firms for an investor in 2010 planning to retire in 2025.[2] The stock/bond ratio varies from 68/32 in the Fidelity program to 79/21 in the T. Rowe Price program. And the percent of stocks invested in foreign markets varies from 30 percent in the Schwab program to 20 percent in the Vanguard program. Figure 19.6 shows that experts can disagree about the

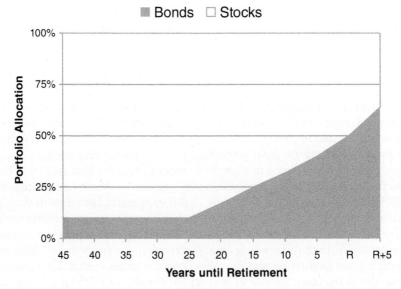

FIGURE 19.5   Vanguard's Target Portfolio Allocations Determined by Years until Retirement

Source: www.vanguard.com.

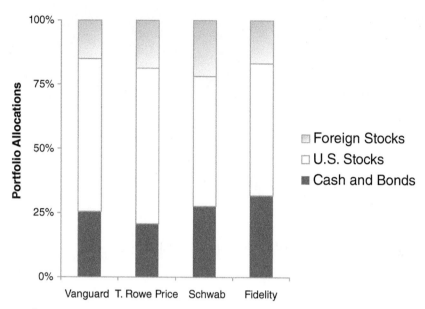

FIGURE 19.6   2010 Asset Allocations for Four Target 2025 Funds

Sources: Websites of firms—www.vanguard.com, http://corporate.troweprice.com/ccw/
home.do, https://www.schwab.com/, https://www.fidelity.com/?imm_pid=3&immid=007
85&imm_eid=e39121977&buf=999999.

specific asset allocation. But it's clear that for all such programs, the asset allocation
is governed by savings and spending decisions for retirement.

Longevity

Many Americans don't really understand how long their retirement may be. Life
expectancy has increased steadily over the last 50 years at the same time that the
age of retirement has fallen. According to the Labor Department, the median age of
retirement for both men and women is about 62 years of age.[3] That's down from
an average age between 66 and 67 in the 1950s. Americans at 62 can often look
forward to 20 or even 30 more years of life in retirement. Yet few Americans have
a coherent plan to make sure their resources will last that long. Savings are often
inadequate and spending is often too high to be sustainable. Investment decisions,
moreover, are often inconsistent with spending rates.

Some Americans are fortunate enough to have guaranteed pensions that provide
them with a steady income throughout their retirements. These are the old-style
defined benefit pensions that were once quite common in corporate America (and
are still provided by many state and local governments). The pensions provide a
guaranteed income to the employee and often to the employee's spouse in the event
of the death of the employee. Sometimes the income is indexed to inflation, rising
with the cost of living during retirement. Today, the balance has shifted away from
defined benefit pension plans to *defined contribution* pension plans, like the 401(k)
plan, where workers contribute part of their salaries to the plan, with firms often

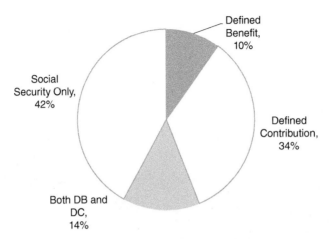

FIGURE 19.7   Pensions of Full-Time Employees in Private Industry in 2003, U.S. Department of Labor

Source: Wiatrowski, 2004.

matching or supplementing the employee contributions. According to a Department of Labor study summarized in Figure 19.7, in 2003 only 24 percent of Americans in the private sector still had defined benefit pensions compared with 48 percent that had defined contribution plans.[4] Employees with the latter type of pension plan are, in a sense, responsible for their own retirement. If they save enough during their careers and invest wisely, they can enjoy a comfortable retirement.

How much is enough? That depends on how much they hope to spend in retirement and how much income they can derive from their portfolios. This chapter will explore both investing and spending in retirement. Decisions that Americans make about investing and spending can make a big difference in determining how financially secure they are in retirement.

In considering these issues, it will be helpful to know just how long our savings must last. Figure 19.8 presents some estimates of how long current 62-year-olds are likely to live.[5] For a 62-year-old man today, the median age of death is estimated to be 85 years, with 25 percent of his cohort likely to live to be 92 years old. For a 62-year-old woman, the median age is 88 and the 25 percent point is reached at 94 years. For a married couple at 62 years old, the relevant statistic is the life expectancy of the *surviving* spouse. The median age of death for the surviving spouse is 92 years of age! So the nest egg accumulated for retirement must last a long time.

With lifetimes this long, investment horizons must be just as long. In fact, they need to be longer because you may live longer than the average person your age. Yet Americans entering retirement often choose portfolios appropriate for retirees of their grandparents' generation who typically lived only a few years after they retired. Retirees of that generation used to invest in bonds during retirement. Investing in bonds surely seems the safe thing to do. It helps us to sleep at night if we avoid stocks and other volatile investments. That's all well and good for emotional well-being, but does the average American realize how little can be spent if a portfolio is weighted heavily toward bonds?

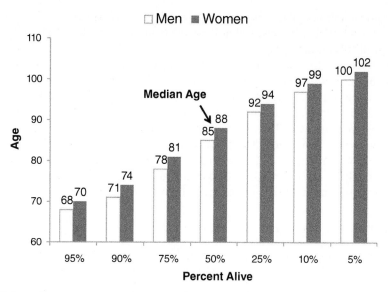

FIGURE 19.8   Life Expectancies of Today's 62-Year-Olds

Source: Financeware®.

Spending Rules for Retirement

There is a key concept in retirement planning that most Americans have not even heard of. That is the concept of a *spending rule*, a rate of spending in retirement that can be sustained through time. As explained in the last chapter, foundations have spending rules that guide their activities through time. So must retirees, since they also must live off of their endowment—the wealth they have accumulated for retirement. If the retiree has a *defined benefit* retirement plan, spending can be tied to the income from that plan (plus Social Security). Most of us are not fortunate enough to have such a plan. For the many Americans with only *defined contribution* retirement plans, there is no guaranteed income from those plans, and retirement spending must depend on returns from accumulated wealth. So a spending plan is necessary.

Like foundations, some retirees base their spending in retirement on the *income* from their bonds and stocks. They choose their portfolios so as to maximize the coupons from their bond portfolios and dividends from their stock portfolios. This strategy may or may not be ideal as an investment strategy, but it should not be the basis of a spending rule. Retirees should be willing to use both income and principal from their portfolio *if the spending can be sustained.*

Like foundations, retirees have to worry about the volatility of their portfolio returns. We can measure that volatility using standard deviations, but somehow that doesn't fully capture investment risk as perceived by retirees. After all, a foundation can go out of business if it draws bad returns. A retiree must struggle on. The timing of returns certainly matter. Bad returns may occur early in retirement. A bear market like that experienced in 2001 or 2008 can cripple a retirement. To take into account such bad scenarios, we use simulation methods where a large range of different outcomes can be examined. By considering many trials drawn from a sample with given average returns and volatilities, we can try to model the investment uncertainties facing retirees. Each trial will consist of at least 1,000 simulations drawn randomly from a statistical distribution.

Returns are not the only source of uncertainty for the retiree. Central to investing and spending in retirement is *longevity risk*. If we knew for certain when we were to die, we could have a strategy for using up our capital before death. This is the principal behind annuities that guarantee income up until death (see discussion that follows). To properly model spending rules, it's important to incorporate longevity risk directly into the simulation. The simulation software we will use, *Financeware®*, does just that. Whenever a simulation is run, it draws from the mortality distributions developed by the Society of Actuaries. So in any given simulation, the man or woman may die early in retirement or live long past the median age of death for that cohort.

Portfolios of Stocks and Bonds

By the time of retirement, the investor should have reduced the proportion of stocks in the portfolio way below that chosen during earlier working years. As discussed above, the Vanguard Target Retirement Fund shifts the investor from a 90 percent stock portfolio when the investor is 25 years from retirement to a 50/50 portfolio at retirement. The 50/50 retirement portfolio is a common one chosen, at least early in retirement.

Because risk is central to the success or failure of spending rules, we will try to reduce risk by diversifying the portfolio just as in the previous chapter on foundations. In the case of bonds, the bond returns are based on the Barclays Aggregate index. In the case of stocks, both foreign and domestic stocks are included, with foreign stocks being one fifth of the total stock allocation (as in the Vanguard Fund). Foreign stocks are represented by the Morgan Stanley EAFE index, while U.S. stocks are represented by the Russell 3000 index. So a 50/50 bond/stock portfolio consists of 50 percent in the Barclays Aggregate index, 40 percent in the Russell 3000, and 10 percent in the MSCI EAFE indexes.

The returns on these three indexes are obtained using the premium method. The premiums are then applied to the historical returns on the basic capital market assets, the S&P 500 and medium-term Treasury bond measured over the period since 1951. The compound *real* returns on these assets were 2.4 percent for the Treasury bond and 6.7 percent for the S&P 500.[6] The premiums are the same as in the previous chapter: 0.3 percent for the Barclays Aggregate and MSCI EAFE indexes and 0 percent for the Russell 3000 index. Standard deviations and correlations were calculated over the 1979 to 2009 sample period.

Baseline Case: Can Two Live More Cheaply Than One?

We begin with two sets of simulations that will investigate differences between spending rules for single individuals and married couples. The first simulation will be for a 62-year-old man who has just retired. The second simulation will be for a 62-year-old married couple also newly retired.

At retirement, the 62-year-old man is assumed to choose a spending rule that is to rise with inflation. For example, a 5 percent spending rule for a retiree with $1 million will permit the retiree to spend $50,000 (before tax) the first year. With a

2.5 percent inflation rate, spending will rise to $51,250 the second year, and so on. Later simulations will allow part of the spending to fluctuate with the size of the portfolio rather than being a set dollar amount (adjusted for inflation).

The 62-year-old is assumed to want to use his wealth to support his retirement. That is, he has no plans to leave a bequest, so his wealth can be used up during his lifetime. This will allow him to raise his rate of spending higher than in the case where his aim is to keep a given wealth level intact. Later simulations will allow for a specific bequest. Of course, he does not know his age of death ahead of time, so the challenge will be to adopt a spending rule that will keep his wealth positive throughout the remainder of his life.

The retiree must choose a spending rule low enough so that he does not *run out of money before death*. In the presence of uncertainty, however, it is difficult to eliminate all possibility of running out of money. So the aim is to choose a spending rule low enough so that the probability of running out of money (failure) is low. So we will be asking the following question: What is the probability of failure if a specific spending rule is adopted?

Simulations are run for spending rules ranging from 4 percent to 6 percent of initial wealth. The results for a single man at 62 are moderately encouraging. A spending rule of 4.5 percent has only a 4 percent probability of failure. That is, in 4 percent of the simulations, the 62-year-old man runs out of money before his death. A 5 percent spending rule raises the failure rate only to 10 percent.

Consider how these results are changed if the family consists of a married couple rather than a single man. The results will be different for two reasons. First, there are two lives to worry about rather than one, so the median age of death of the surviving retiree will generally be later than that of a single retiree. Second, the second person involved is a woman with a longer life expectancy. The results of both sets of simulations are reported in Figure 19.9.

Consider first a 5 percent spending rule. The probability of failure for the couple is 19 percent rather than the 10 percent found for a single man. If the spending rule is lowered to 4.5 percent, the probability of failure becomes 9 percent rather than 4 percent. The moral of the story seems to be: *reduce your spending in order to enjoy marital bliss*. Isn't it true that two can live more cheaply than one?

Effects of Bequests and Variable Spending Rules

There are two features of the simulations discussed above that need to be investigated. First, the simulations assume the retirees are willing to use up wealth during their lifetimes. Some retirees may want to leave a bequest to charity or to their heirs. By introducing a planned bequest, the retiree also provides a cutoff point for the spending plan before wealth is more seriously depleted by market events. After all, not many retirees will adhere to a spending plan that completely impoverishes them. Second, the simulations assume that the retirees will keep spending at a given rate regardless of how high or low their investment returns are. We will investigate changing both features.

Consider first the bequest motive. The simulations might be designed so that the *target* level of wealth at death is some fraction of the original wealth level (adjusted for inflation). The retirees may choose this target for two different reasons. As stated above, the higher target will provide a bequest after death. But the higher target

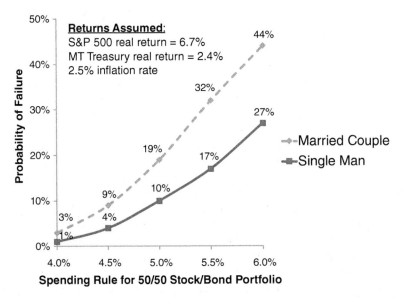

FIGURE 19.9   Spending Rules and Failure Rates for Single Man and Married Couple

may also be chosen because retirees regard a decline in the portfolio anywhere near 100 percent as a disaster. Instead of a target level of zero wealth at death, suppose we assume that the retirees have a target level equal to 50 percent of the initial wealth.

Raising the target level of wealth will raise the probability of failure, since now failure is defined as having initial wealth fall below 50 percent of the initial wealth. So it's important to find some other way to mitigate the effects of a bad sequence of returns. Realistically, retirees are not going to keep spending the same amount if their wealth has fallen drastically. And they are not likely to keep their spending constant if they have had a whole string of good returns. So the second modification we will make is to have spending vary with current wealth.

It may not make sense for all spending to vary with wealth. (A proportional spending rule of 5 percent would cut the dollar amount spent in half, adjusted for inflation, if wealth falls by 50 percent). Perhaps a reasonable plan is to make half of the spending vary with wealth and to make half of it fixed (in real terms) over time. We will consider a plan where wealth is allowed to drop to 50 percent of its initial level and where half of the spending is tied to current wealth. So, for example, a 5 percent spending rule for retirees with $1 million will be split into $25,000 that is held fixed over time (adjusted for inflation) and 2.5 percent that will vary with the level of wealth. (The fixed allocation might be designed to cover fixed expenses). This flexibility in the spending rule will make it easier to keep wealth above the target level.

Figure 19.10 shows the results of these simulations. These simulations are once again for 62-year-old married couples who are newly retired. For comparison purposes, the simulations based on no bequest are shown again. The results are quite distressing. Spending rules of 5 percent are downright dangerous with a 31 percent failure rate. (Would you want a nearly one-third chance of dropping 50 percent

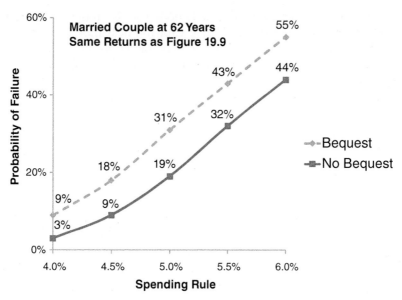

FIGURE 19.10   Effects of Bequest and Flexible Spending

below your initial wealth?) Spending rules of 4.5 percent result in an 18 percent failure rate (compared with 9 percent when no bequest is made). The bottom line is that spending rates as low as 4.5 percent appear to be problematic if the retirees want to make sure that the portfolio stays at least 50 percent intact.

Do retirees have portfolios large enough to live on less than 4.5 percent of wealth? Some do, of course. But for many American families, retirement in this new age of defined contribution plans may be bleak.

How Can I Turn a Defined Contribution Plan into a Defined Benefit Plan?

Many retirees relying on their savings to finance a retirement envy the financial security of those with defined benefit plans. Such plans guarantee an income flow for the rest of the retiree's life. In some cases, the income flows are indexed to inflation. The great advantage of such plans is that they insure against the most important risk in retirement—longevity risk.

Retirees relying on defined contribution plans can try to create a defined benefit plan *ex post*. This income stream is obtained by investing a portion of the initial wealth in an *immediate fixed annuity*. The annuity works by pooling a large group of retirees of the same age in the same pool. Some will die early and will end up not capturing as much income as the average member of the pool. Others will die much later and will capture much more than the average member of the pool. By joining a pool of other retirees of the same age, retirees can guarantee that they never run out of money.

Why does that increase income in retirement? The reason is that the wealth invested in the annuity can be deliberately exhausted before death. It's always possible to increase the income on a bond portfolio if we are willing to use up the capital in that portfolio. The immediate fixed annuity does just that. Individual retirees cannot take the chance of using up all of their capital unless they know the date of their death in advance! But a pool of retirees can jointly use up their capital since actuaries can predict fairly accurately the longevity of a large pool of retirees. To further protect the individual retiree, an insurance company not only organizes the pool but guarantees annuity payments in the event that the actuaries underestimate annuity commitments.[7]

There is one big drawback of many annuities offered to retirees. They do not protect against inflation. For the same reason that we base spending rules on real returns so that nominal spending can rise with inflation, we should want to invest in annuities that are indexed to inflation. The income from these inflation-indexed annuities will naturally be lower than in the case of a nominal annuity. But investing in an inflation-indexed annuity will protect against two major risks in retirement—longevity risk and inflation risk. This is exactly what the current social security system does. It provides us lifetime income that is indexed to the CPI.

It's not really necessary to run new simulations to illustrate outcomes if such annuities are purchased. Consider a retiree who decides to invest a third of the portfolio in immediate annuities indexed to inflation. That annuity will provide a floor on retirement income very much like Social Security does. Given that floor, the retiree can consider simulations like those already analyzed, but where disaster leaves the retiree with some floor level of income.

Concluding Comments—Postpone Retirement?

Americans are retiring in their early 60s and living long lives in retirement. Many of these Americans lack the luxury of a defined benefit plan providing them income in retirement. They might have accumulated wealth to carry them through the retirement years, but many do not understand how to invest that wealth and how to make sure that it lasts a lifetime. That's why it is so important to address the issue of spending rules in retirement.

No set of simulations can give you a spending rule that is the correct one. So let's summarize the key issues that those contemplating retirement must address. First, you need to focus on the risk that really matters in retirement, the risk of running out of money. Second, you need to base your spending rate on the returns you expect to earn on your portfolio *after inflation has been taken out*. Third, the spending rate has to be lower than the expected real, or inflation-adjusted, return because otherwise your risk of failure will be too high. Fourth, you have to recognize that we are not sure about what average real returns will be in the future, so we may have to be even more conservative than past returns would indicate.

If investors want to raise spending in retirement beyond the spending rules analyzed above, then it makes sense to annuitize some of the retirement portfolio. But there is one other suggestion that may make sense to investors—postpone retirement. The benefits of working a few more years are multiple. First, Social Security benefits increase each year that retirement is postponed. A 62-year-old gains an extra 7 percent or more per year in benefits by delaying retirement until 66 (the normal retirement age for those nearing retirement). Second, the investor has a few more years to save for retirement. Third, the investor can allow the portfolio to grow further before beginning to draw it down with retirement spending. Fourth, when the

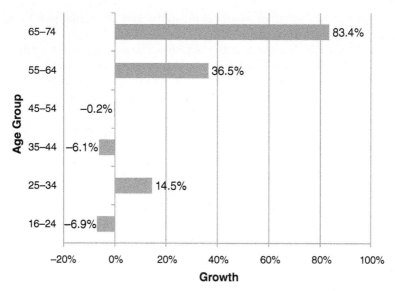

FIGURE 19.11   U.S. Labor Force by Age Percent Change from 2006 to 2016
Source: U.S. Department of Labor (Toossi, 2007).

investor finally does retire, annuities will provide even better returns than before. That's because the annuity tables work in favor of older investors.

With all of these reasons to postpone retirement, more Americans are deciding to work longer. In fact, the fastest-growing part of the labor force is the cohort aged 65 years or older which the U.S. Department of Labor projects will grow by more than 80 percent between 2006 and 2016.[8] That percentage is applied to only 4.4 million Americans in 2006, but that's still an extra 3.5 million or so to be added to the labor force by 2016. (This projection was made before the financial crisis and the loss of more than eight million jobs. But the portfolio losses associated with this crisis have put even more pressure on those nearing retirement to work longer). As Figure 19.11 shows, the only other segment of the labor force likely to grow substantially over this 10-year period is the cohort aged 55 to 64 years of age. So much for early retirement and endless days of golf!

No spending rule and investment plan can eliminate the financial uncertainties of retirement, but sensible planning can help to stretch wealth through the retirement years. For this to happen, retirees must be much more deliberate in their financial decision-making in retirement. And that starts with sensible spending rules and investment allocations.

Notes

1. The full retirement age for a 52-year-old in 2010 is actually 66 years and 8 months. See http://ssa.gov/pubs/ageincrease.htm.
2. Each firm maintains websites with specific allocations for a 2025 target date fund. Fidelity's website, for example, is found at www.fidelity.com. The data was

drawn from the four websites in July 2010, so the investor at that point was about 15 years from retirement.

3. According to the U.S. Bureau of Labor Statistics, the median age of retirement for the years 1995 to 2000 was 62.0 for men and 61.4 for women (see Gendell, 2001).

4. Fourteen percent of these had both types of pensions, so 34 percent of them had only defined contribution plans. See Wiatrowski (Department of Labor, August 2004).

5. The estimates are from Financeware® based on mortality tables from the Society of Actuaries.

6. This chapter will not investigate the effects of even lower stock returns based on earnings growth rather than capital gains. Though the results that follow are depressing enough, the alternative stock return estimates considered in the last chapter would lower spending rules even further.

7. The financial crisis reminded us that annuities carry the risk of an insurance company default. So a prudent investor should try to diversify that risk by arranging annuities with several insurance firms.

8. See Toosi (Department of Labor, November 2007).

References

Gendell, Murray. 2001. "Retirement Age Declines Again in 1990s." *Monthly Labor Review* (Department of Labor), October.

Wiatrowski, William J. 2004. "Medical and Retirement Plan Coverage: Exploring the Decline in Recent Years." *Monthly Labor Review* (U.S. Department of Labor), August.

Toossi, Mitra. 2007. "Labor Force Projections to 2016: More Workers in Their Golden Years." *Monthly Labor Review* (U.S. Department of Labor), November.

CHAPTER 20

Manager Search, Selection, and Monitoring

M anager search and selection is important to investment advisors and consultants who integrate active management into the portfolios they manage. This process of evaluation and analysis is, however, also important for those who use smart-beta strategies (strategies that intersect active and passive management) as well. The first reading in this chapter will review a more traditional, formal method for reviewing and choosing investment managers including an analysis of the manager's philosophy, people, plans, processes, progress, price, and performance. The second reading dives into the challenging task of measuring alpha and determining which managers have created it and whether or not they can be expected to outperform consistently going forward.

Part I *Strategic Risk Management:* Manager Selection

Learning Objectives

- Discuss the importance of asset class structure as it relates to choosing investment managers.
- List and describe the various methods of collecting information from prospective investment managers.
- Describe manager evaluation techniques including analysis of the organization, people, process, portfolio, and performance.
- Discuss the advantages and disadvantages of and the process of firing managers.
- Discuss the importance of fees in the manager selection process including performance or incentive–based management fees.

Part II *The New Science of Asset Allocation:* Alpha and Beta, and the Search for a True Measure of Manager Value

Learning Objectives

- Define and calculate alpha.
- Differentiate between alpha and beta.
- List and describe characteristics of the Fama-French four-factor model.
- Describe the challenges in measuring consistent alpha.

- Explain the role of regression models in determining alpha.
- Discuss the importance of choosing the right benchmark or index in the search for alpha.

Part I Manager Selection

Hiring and firing investment managers is an important task facing many funds. This is because investment managers are entrusted with managing the assets of a fund and delivering on its investment objectives. The process of manager selection requires good research, constant manager monitoring, and an appropriate governance structure so the fund can respond appropriately and hastily when required. These manager selection tasks require a significant commitment of resources and time to undertake effectively. In this chapter, we outline the key to good processes that will aid in making effective manager hiring and firing decisions.

Hiring Managers

Manager selection is not always an easy task. Even the best manager selection processes and manager evaluations can result in poor outcomes. Luck plays a role in the outcome. This does not mean that selecting managers by throwing darts at a list of manager names is the answer. Rather, a disciplined approach to manager evaluation and selection will have a better chance of producing superior outcomes over time. Increasing the chances of hiring and keeping good managers requires three things:

1. An asset class structure
2. Collecting information
3. Evaluating managers

ASSET CLASS STRUCTURE   Having a predefined asset class structure is necessary before manager selection can be undertaken. Asset class structures assist with manager selection in these ways:

- They refine the manager search universe. If a small-cap manager is required, there is no point searching for a growth manager.
- They help focus the investor's attention on managers that fit the portfolio structure rather than choosing managers on the basis of good recent performance.
- They can prevent early manager termination. An asset class structure can help the investor distinguish between underperformance due to the manager's style and underperformance due to a failure of a manager's skill to add value.

COLLECTING INFORMATION   Collecting information on investment managers takes time. The purpose is to gain insights into the manager and add value to the selection process. There are a number of ways of obtaining this information, including:

- Using advisors
- Via questionnaires

- Marketing visits
- Manager interviews

Using Advisors The advisory industry on manager research has grown rapidly over the years. Advisors usually have a large database of performance information and manager research opinions on a select group of the universe of managers.

Questionnaires Information can be gathered by sending a questionnaire to a number of investment organizations. The approaches taken by managers in their responses can vary a lot. Increasingly, managers will submit pre-prepared, or stock, responses for similar but not identical questions the manager has received from another investor in the past. The investor should be sure to outline the investment structure and approach the potential manager would be part of. This may help managers tailor their responses.

Marketing Visits Investment managers will visit potential investors, but this will depend on the size of the firm and the amount of assets under management. Larger firms usually have well-resourced marketing teams. In smaller firms, owners often make the visits.

The degree of experience a fund has with investment processes will largely determine the type of managers encountered and the depth of the discussions. More sophisticated funds tend to explore firms with new concepts or those using the latest investment approaches. Less sophisticated funds may wish to meet with a wide range of managers to increase their understanding of the state of the industry and to get a feel for the type of investment processes available.

Manager Interviews Interviewing managers is simply a process of obtaining qualitative information as input into subjective assessments about the quality and suitability of managers to manage assets. A structured approach to interviews is necessary to ensure that the right information is extracted and there is consistent treatment across managers. Specifics of the interviews are discussed next.

Aim of Interview The main aim of interviews is to choose managers who can add value. Adding value will involve taking risks. The interview should result in a good understanding of the investment process, identification of the risks the manager takes in adding value, and assessment of the resources (staff, systems, and organizational support) to support the risks taken.

Interviews should ideally be conducted face-to-face and take place over a period of time. A single meeting will not be sufficient to obtain a deep understanding of the firm. Further meetings with different people from the manager's firm will allow for better access to the manager's insights and enable the formation of a well-rounded opinion.

Focus of Interview Qualitative insights require focusing on four key areas of the investment manager: investment staff (people), investment philosophy and approach (process), structure of the portfolio over time (portfolio), and historical performance over market cycles (performance). Each aspect will allow a detailed understanding of the manager's risk taking and provide comfort that past performance can be repeated in the future.

The main focus of a manager interview should be on people and process, the qualitative aspects of the manager evaluation. The qualitative impressions assembled from manager interviews can be supported or called into question by quantitative evaluation of the portfolio and performance.

Some key interview questions follow. There are no right or wrong questions; these are just a starting point.

Equity Manager Questions

- What is the investment philosophy and how has it changed over time?
- Why will the investment philosophy be successful in the future? What evidence supports the belief?
- What valuation approaches are used in evaluating countries and stocks?
- What specific fundamental factors (P/B, earnings, growth, sales margins) are integral to the stock selection process? What is the relative importance of these factors?
- What factors drive the sell decision?
- How is diversification defined and what role does it play in portfolio construction?
- How many stocks are contained in the portfolio?
- How are individual country and stock weightings determined?
- What mistakes, if any, have been made and what lessons have been learned?

Fixed Income Manager Questions

- Describe the approach to managing the fixed income portfolio (duration, credit selection).
- What market anomaly or inefficiency is being captured?
- Why will the anomaly or inefficiency be expected to persist in the future? What evidence supports the claim?
- How is the portfolio positioned?
- Discuss the qualitative and quantitative processes used.
- What credit rating services are used and how?
- How is diversification defined and reflected in the portfolio construction?
- Describe how the following factors contribute to the value-add and risk expected over time:
  - Security selection
  - Sector bets
  - Duration management
  - Yield curve management

Organizational Questions

- Are leaders of the organization generally promoted from their positions from within the organization or brought in from the outside?
- Is the leaders' prior experience in business management or portfolio management?
- What does it take to be successful and how is success defined?

TABLE 20.1   Evaluation Criteria

Organization	People	Process	Portfolio	Performance
Goals and philosophy	Proven expertise	Coherent and understandable	Consistency with investment philosophy	Competitive results versus benchmark and peers
Incentives	Staff continuity	Disciplined philosophy	Corroborate the investment process	Demonstrated success in different environments consistent with process
Stability	Tenure and experience	Generates a portfolio consistent with philosophy	Indicates an understanding of risks taken	
Ownership	Experience in unfavorable environments	Enduring		
Integrity/ professionalism	Desire to excel			
Client list				
Succession/ contingency				

- What is the vision for the firm? How is it determined and communicated?
- What are the firm's comparative advantages and competitive pressures?
- What new business lines, distribution channels, and products will be added?
- How does the firm plan on ensuring that future growth does not compromise the integrity of its existing investment process and products?
- What is the ownership structure of the firm? If it has changed, or is likely to change, why?

MANAGER EVALUATION   There are broadly five main criteria across which a manager should be evaluated. These are summarized in Table 20.1.

In arriving at a final ranking for each manager, a weighting scheme of the importance of each type of criterion will need to be established.

Organization   Issues around organizational stability and effectiveness need to be evaluated. Important areas include the extent to which the leadership within the firm is sound, effective, and capable of ensuring continued, long-term business success as well as investment success.

Areas to Evaluate
- The consistency between the business growth goals and the firm's investment philosophy
- How investment professionals are motivated and compensated
- Likelihood that the investment team will stay together in the future.
- Be aware of any of these signs of organizational problems:
  - Business focus on asset gathering rather than value added
  - Unclear succession planning
  - Ownership problems
  - Conflicting business and investment philosophies
  - Poor leadership
- Does the firm have sufficient size and depth to provide the necessary level of client service?

Good Signs
- Leaders who motivate the firm's professionals toward a common goal.
- Has been in existence for a sufficiently long enough period to ensure a high chance of continued success.
- Size and depth of firm sufficient to ensure quality decision making and client servicing.
- Staff members act with integrity and professionalism.
- Growth goals are reasonable and consistent with value adding rather than asset gathering.
- No recent ownership changes.

People   Superior investment management performance relies on good staff and an appropriate management structure. When it comes to investment staff, the key aspect to focus on is how their experience and skills are used. This involves an assessment of how key investment decisions are made and includes:

- Determining which companies are candidates for research and inclusion in the portfolio.
- What emphasis is placed on views about markets and sectors versus company-specific views.
- The approach to deciding allocations to companies and how the portfolio is structured.
- The factors used to determine when companies are sold.
- When and how the portfolio is reviewed. This includes how whether views about companies have changed and how this manifests in changes to the portfolio.

After the assessment about how investment decisions are made, the next step is identifying who is responsible for each decision and the degree of organizational support. This involves assessing the extent to which key investment staff are involved in research functions, participate at the investment committee, and receive administrative and technology support from the organization.

Areas to Evaluate
- The prior experience of investment professionals and applicability of that experience to current responsibilities
- Whether investment experience was obtained from a previous firm; if so, whether that firm shared the same investment philosophy as the current firm
- The degree to which the experience of the investment professionals is complementary and how well they work together

Good Signs
- Experience
  - Investment professionals have had portfolio management experience in both favorable and difficult market conditions
  - High-quality education and experience
  - Investment professionals have diverse backgrounds
  - A strong desire to generate superior performance

- Staff continuity
  - The investment track record has been produced by current investment professionals
  - Minimum professional staff turnover
  - Good administrative and technology support from the organization

Process An extensive understanding of the investment process is necessary to identify what risks are being taken to generate superior performance. Doing this usually involves understanding the investment strategy, the investment philosophy that underpins that strategy, and understanding how much risk is taken and when.

Areas to Evaluate In assessing the investment strategy, the key focus is to evaluate whether the manager appreciates the nature and extent of the risk being taken in the investment strategy, so that there is confidence good investment decisions are likely to be made in the future. Good investment performance by itself simply means that the manager took the right type of risk at the right time.

In assessing whether the manager appreciates and understands the risks, two areas should be focused on:

1. **Portfolio risks.** Portfolio risks are likely to be driven by several factors. These include:
   - The extent of diversification across company holdings
   - Whether, and how, cash is employed to manage portfolio volatility
   - The extent to which the overall portfolio is affected by the volatility of individual companies, sectors, or country exposures
   - The extent to which industry dynamics and macro-economic views drive portfolio structure and how often such views are taken
2. **Company risks.** Company risks cover the extent to which the manager understands the company-specific factors that drive valuation. It also includes whether the manager appreciates the extent to which the market has priced in the manager's view of intrinsic value.

After the assessment of the investment strategy and the extent to which risks are understood, the next step is to evaluate how the manager decided on the amount of risk to take. Deciding how much risk to take is essential to good portfolio construction and to ensure the desired performance eventuates. Ideally, the approach should be clearly articulated and supported by a defendable rationale. Managers vary in their approaches. Some rely on quantitative methods in determining how much risk to take on. The portfolio construction process tends to be more objective and simpler to evaluate. Others rely on subjective judgment, in which case evaluation of key investment staff plays a greater role.

Once the investment risk taking approach is understood, the organizational support should be evaluated. These include:

- **Internal resources.** Portfolio managers, research analysts, computer and data support.

■ **External resources.** The extent to which information from research brokerage firms is obtained and utilized. The quality and accuracy of investment ideas received from brokerage firms and the commissions paid should be understood.

When evaluating historical performance, it is important to assess whether the investment process and key staff that produced the performance have changed. It is important to understand the impact of the growth in assets on historical performance. Growth in assets may affect the manager's ability to generate superior performance in the future.

The evaluation should cover these issues:

■ The potential returns and risks implementing the investment strategy successfully.
■ The manager's competence in consistently implementing the investment strategy over time.
■ Whether the resources are adequate to support the strategy.
■ The impact of poor implementation of the investment strategy.

The assessment requires a deep insight into the manager's process and is highly subjective. It is usual to conduct the assessment over a sufficiently long period of time.

Good Signs
■ Investment philosophy
  ■ Coherent and understandable investment philosophy.
  ■ Philosophy adaptable and suitable for all market environments.
■ Decision-making process
  ■ Identifiable member of the team with ultimate responsibility at each decision-making stage.
  ■ Timely decision-making process.
  ■ Research and portfolio management roles clearly distinguished and understood by team members.
■ Stock selection
  ■ Comprehensive and coherent process for selecting stocks.
  ■ Clearly identifiable buy and sell disciplines.
  ■ Complete investment research coverage.

Portfolio   Assessment of the manager's portfolio should focus on its structure. The portfolio structure should reveal how successfully the manager has implemented the investment strategy. The assessment corroborates whether the investment risks claimed to be the basis of the investment strategy actually have contributed to past performance.

Areas to Evaluate   Analysis of portfolio structure aids in understanding the investment philosophy, strategy, and its implementation. It is typical to use quantitative tools to analyze a representative portfolio at distinct points in time. The points in time should cover varying market conditions. As an example, with equity managers, an assessment of the consistency of investment risks taken can be investigated by focusing on portfolio characteristics such as: price-to-earnings (P/E) ratio, price-to-book (P/B) ratio, return on equity (ROE), earnings growth, distribution of companies by size and style, and cash levels.

Both qualitative and quantitative assessment is required to form a comprehensive understanding of the manager's process and investment approach. This should lead to a good understanding of the types of risk taken by the manager in generating added value.

- Portfolio structure
  - Clear, articulate criteria for how the portfolio is structured, which reflects an awareness of the risks taken.
  - Understandable rationale for company, sector, or country biases.
- Risk
  - Manager thoroughly understands risks that are taken.
  - Risks taken are reasonable in generating potential returns.

Performance   The final step in evaluating a manager is consideration of past performance. Past performance can only be competently analyzed and understood once a good understanding of people, process, and portfolio structure has been established.

Areas to Evaluate   The focus should be on two key issues:

1. Is the return history—the pattern of returns, highs, and lows—consistent with the manager's investment strategy?

   Managers that employ investment styles, such as value or growth investing, will generate superior performance when their style performs well. Their return patterns should be measured against a suitable style index to assess value added. Managers with lower-risk strategies will tend to produce smaller deviations from the appropriate benchmark.
2. How does performance compare with other managers that employ a similar investment approach?

   This assessment requires comparison with a group of peer managers with the same investment strategy. Unless a manager's results correctly adjusts for their investment approach that manager may be inappropriately terminated and a wrong manager may be hired as a replacement.

Good Signs
- Performance exceeds a passive benchmark with appropriate adjustment for the investment strategy and fees.
- Proven ability to add value over a market cycle adjusted for risk, as demonstrated against a peer group.

Firing Managers

At some point, something changes with an investment manager firm. It may be the people, the investment process, or the structure of the portfolio, which may affect the performance results. Senior management may leave and/or new investment staff may join; there may be a change in the investment philosophy (during the tech boom of the late 1990s, some value managers became growth managers); the ownership structure may change, resulting in different incentives for investment staff; and the edge provided by the investment process or efficiency of portfolio implementation may deteriorate.

Any of these changes may affect confidence in the manager's ability to deliver expected performance. Firing and replacing the manager would then be necessary. Changing managers, however, is costly. The costs include search costs of finding a new manager and legal, administrative, and brokerage costs in moving the portfolio to a new manager.

An evaluation of the costs and benefits of changing managers must be undertaken.

TRADE-OFF An investor may consider changing a manager for reasons other than changes with the manager. For example, the objectives of the fund may change; the risk tolerance of the trustees may change; or the asset class structure may change, requiring a new lineup of managers.

When deciding whether to change managers, an investor faces this choice: Retain the incumbent manager and receive the returns of the manager, or change the manager and incur the certain costs of transitioning the manager and the returns of the new manager.

The trade-off involves a simple decision: Does the change in uncertain future returns exceed the certain costs?

The benefits cover:

- The change in the expected returns of the managers.
- The change in the characteristics of the return pattern, for example, whether the manager is a value manager.
- How the new manager fits in the overall portfolio structure. Correlation of the manager's return with other managers.

The costs include:

- Search costs in finding a new manager
- Appointment costs (legal, administrative)
- Transition costs

BENEFITS The benefit of changing managers is the expected improvement in the future returns of the new manager compared to the existing manager. This requires assessments about the expected return and risk (dispersion of returns around the expectation).

Expected Returns There are many ways of forming performance expectations. One way is to look at the typical ranges of performance outcomes for managers in the market similar to the incumbent manager. The investor can then calibrate the changes using the typical range of performance outcomes as a guide.

For example, Table 20.2 and Figure 20.1 show 10-year historical performance data of various managers up to December 31, 2009.

TABLE 20.2   Index Returns Compared to Median, Top, and Bottom Funds (10 Years Ended December 31, 2009)

Asset Class	10-Year Index Return	Top Decile	Top Quartile	Median	Bottom Quartile	Bottom Decile
U.S. intermediate bond	6.3%	6.8%	6.2%	5.8%	5.3%	4.6%
U.S. high-yield bond	7.1%	6.6%	6.1%	5.4%	4.2%	3.3%
International bond	10.3%	9.7%	8.3%	7.1%	6.1%	5.0%
U.S. large-cap value	2.5%	5.5%	4.4%	3.0%	1.7%	0.5%
U.S. large-cap core	−0.9%	3.7%	1.8%	−0.4%	−1.3%	−2.1%
U.S. large-cap growth	−4.0%	1.7%	0.1%	−1.8%	−3.4%	−5.3%
U.S. mid-cap value	7.6%	10.6%	8.7%	7.0%	6.3%	1.8%
U.S. mid-cap core	5.0%	8.6%	6.6%	5.4%	2.9%	1.4%
U.S. mid-cap growth	−0.5%	6.4%	3.9%	0.7%	−1.9%	−4.3%
U.S. small-cap value	8.3%	11.6%	10.3%	8.4%	7.4%	6.5%
U.S. small-cap core	3.5%	10.8%	8.5%	6.3%	4.2%	1.9%
U.S. small-cap growth	−1.4%	6.4%	3.9%	0.7%	−1.8%	−4.8%
U.S. real estate	10.6%	11.5%	10.9%	10.1%	9.6%	8.4%
International value	4.0%	6.7%	5.8%	4.1%	2.1%	1.0%
International core	1.6%	4.1%	2.3%	0.6%	−0.5%	−1.9%
International growth	−1.0%	3.9%	2.4%	0.6%	−1.1%	−2.4%
Emerging markets	10.1%	12.6%	11.6%	9.3%	7.8%	6.5%

Source: Adapted from Rice and Strotman (2010).

The index returns are marked by the black triangle alongside each gray box—the longer horizontal line represents the median manager, the next horizontal line on either side of the median manager marks the top and bottom quartile manager, and the highest and lowest horizontal lines represent the top and bottom decile managers, respectively.

There are various ways to use the information in the table and figure. If it is believed a manager will produce returns in a particular quartile or decile in the future, the historical information could be used for forming these expectations. An example using a U.S. large-cap core manager follows.

- Let us say the incumbent manager was believed to be in the top quartile of managers in the U.S. large-cap core space. Now, due to the manager's changed circumstances, it is believed that the manager has fallen into the middle of the pack. The historical performance of U.S. large-cap core managers shows that this *fall* in returns should be about 2.2 percent per annum (p.a.), from 1.8 percent to −0.4 percent. If the new manager is expected to be in the top quartile, the expected return benefit from a manager change will be 2.2 percent p.a.
- However, if the manager's change is extreme, say because the investment team has departed for another firm, the manager's future performance may be in the bottom quartile of managers or perhaps worse, in the bottom decile. The historical performance shows that the return expectation should *fall* by 3.1 percent p.a. (from 1.8 percent to −1.3 percent) if the manager becomes a bottom-quartile manager. If a new manager is believed to be in the top quartile, then 3.1 percent p.a. would be the expected benefit, in return terms, of changing managers.

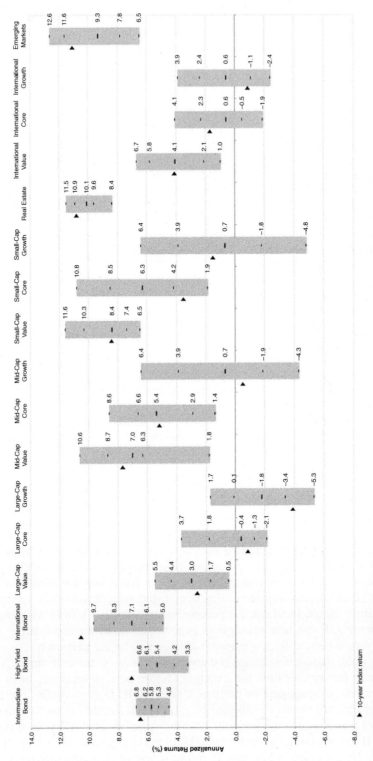

FIGURE 20.1 Index Returns Compared to Median, Top, and Bottom Funds (10 Years Ended December 31, 2009).

Source: Adapted from Rice and Strotman (2010).

■ It would also be possible to have the assets managed passively instead of replacing the manager with another active manager. In this case, if it is believed the manager has fallen to the bottom quartile, the return benefit of this change would be 0.4 percent p.a. (index returns of −0.9 percent compared with bottom-quartile manager of −1.3 percent).

It is important to ensure that the level of risk of the candidate manager is similar to that of the incumbent manager. This will provide a better basis for relying on historical return estimates for establishing future return expectations. Historical returns will not perfectly apply for future outcomes, but they are a useful starting point.

Diversification Benefit   Let us say an investor has employed two managers with complementary investment styles—one growth and one value manager—and the value manager changes style to growth. This may be cause for termination.

Diversification across styles can be very effective. If it is believed that there is not a material expected return difference between value and growth investment styles, then style diversification will reduce tracking error without impacting the expected return. Therefore, if a manager employed within the asset class changes style, the risk of the portfolio would increase.

In our example, if the value manager becomes a growth manager, the total risk of the equities asset class would increase, as would the total portfolio risk.

This is represented in a stylized way in Figure 20.2a and b.

In the figures, the value manager is shown before and after changing investment style. The figures plot the style of each manager relative to the index on two dimensions: company size and growth versus value. Figure 20.2 shows the two-manager, style-neutral structure: a value manager and a growth manager, and neither manager has a size bias relative to the index. The combined manager structure is shown by the black circle marked A. The combined structure has neither a growth-value bias nor a size bias.

In Figure 20.2, the value manager changes style and becomes a growth manager, with a slight large-cap bias. The combined structure is now represented by the black circle marked B. The portfolio now has a significant growth bias and a slight large-cap bias. The resulting portfolio would now have more tracking error than before the style change.

This is represented in Figure 20.3 in alpha (expected excess returns) and tracking error terms. Point A shows the alpha/tracking error position of the style-neutral portfolio before the manager's style change. After the style change, the portfolio's alpha/tracking error is shown by point B. It is assumed that the alpha of the portfolio does not change. That is, the value manager's alpha does not change with the shift in style.

The new portfolio, marked by point B in Figure 20.3, is now less efficient than before; the alpha of the portfolio per unit of tracking error has declined because of the increased tracking error of the portfolio. How much does an investor care about the reduced efficiency? At the very least, an investor should expect the alpha of the portfolio to be at point C. This is the alpha that an investor could achieve with a style-neutral portfolio at the same level of tracking error as portfolio B. However, since the investor actually prefers the level of risk at point A, the investor may require a higher level of compensation than the expected return difference between points B and C.

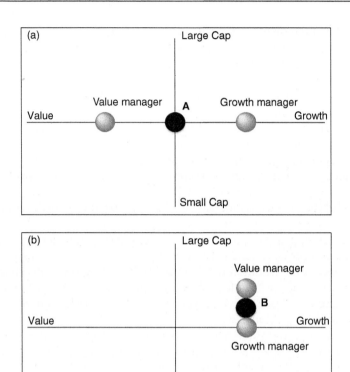

FIGURE 20.2   Manager Changing Investment Style: (a) Before; (b) After

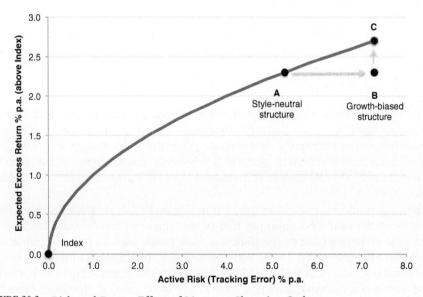

FIGURE 20.3   Risk and Return Effect of Manager Changing Style

It can be said that the diversification benefit of having a new value manager replace the value-manager-turned-growth-manager is worth at least the return difference between points B and C.

COSTS The costs of change will depend on the investor's specific portfolio. The three main costs of change are the search costs of finding a new manager, the costs of moving the portfolio, and the costs of appointing a new manager.

Search Costs The costs in finding a new manager can be broken down into direct and indirect costs.

Direct costs include the additional fees paid to various service providers needed to find a new manager—asset consultants and travel costs for internal staff members to review managers. The costs increase with the complexity of the search and location of managers. Travel and accommodation costs will increase if overseas manager research trips are conducted.

Indirect costs include the cost of staff and trustee time devoted to the search— time that could otherwise be spent on other activities. Typically the search time can average around two weeks full time.

Another important indirect cost is the implementation slippage that arises from delay in implementing a recommended manager change. Costs of delay are often overlooked but can be substantial. There are no simple measures to assess the costs of such delays.

Moving the Portfolio Costs Replacing a manager is an expensive exercise. The normal direct costs of transition include bid/offer spreads, commissions, and, in some markets, official charges. These costs, however, form only one part of the total costs of the portfolio restructuring that occurs when a new manager is substituted for an old one. A larger element of costs arises because neither the outgoing nor the incoming fund manager is aligned with the investor's objective, which is to maximize the proceeds of securities being sold and to minimize the cost of acquiring new securities. The new manager will not want all of the securities of the outgoing manager; therefore, unwanted securities must be sold.

A number of options are available to the investor when it comes to executing the trades.

- A specialist "transition broker" could be employed to do all the dealing.
- An agency broker could be used for the transactions, capturing some part of the usual agency fee for the client.
- Crossing networks could be used to liquidate some or all of the portfolio.

Appointing New Manager Costs The costs of appointing a new manager include writing contracts and investment mandates with the new investment firm. Legal costs are usually low as a proportion of the assets subject to the investment management arrangement. If the investor has a custodian, there are additional account setup costs involved with the custodian.

The indirect costs involved can be substantial—the costs of trustees' time and internal staff time in negotiating legal terms and establishing the investment mandate.

TABLE 20.3   Cost-Benefit Trade-Off

Benefit		2.0% p.a.
Change in the risk-adjusted expected return (from B to C, Figure 20.3)	2.0% p.a.	
Total cost		2.0% p.a.
Search cost	0.1%	
Hiring cost	0.1%	
Moving the portfolio cost	1.8%	

OVERALL TRADE-OFF   The trade-off is a simple one of asking whether the benefits outweigh the costs. An investor would estimate the costs and benefits of a manager change specific to his or her circumstances. Given that costs are certain and the benefits are uncertain, it would be sensible for the benefits to exceed the costs by a reasonable margin. The reasonableness of the margin in turn would depend on the level of confidence the investor would have in the benefits.

EXAMPLE   A U.S. equity team that had a strong value investment philosophy has decided to shift away from that style. As a result, it is expected that the patterns of returns will be more marketlike. The other manager is a growth manager, and the team has a project-based relationship with an asset consultant for discretionary manager search services. The value manager's total account size is $70 million.

The transition will depend on whether the benefits exceed the costs. The benefits are mainly from hiring a manager with desired value style. The estimates arrived at are presented in Table 20.3.

In this example, the costs and benefits are similar.

Fees

Investment management fees are a major expense of many funds. Fees are generally negotiated at the time of manager appointment, usually starting from standard fee schedules published by the managers. Some managers are willing to negotiate fees; others will not budge from their stated fee schedules under any circumstances. These managers are often concerned about the flow-on effects if their other clients find out about fee reductions.

STATED FEE SCHEDULES   As a starting point for fee negotiations, it is useful to refer to stated fee schedules of a wide range of managers in a particular asset class. Some asset consultants collect stated fee schedules of managers as part of their manager research process. These fee schedules can then be aggregated within an asset class without giving reference to any particular manager. Such fee universe comparisons are useful for undertaking a review of fees as well as for negotiating a new mandate.

In Table 20.4, the fee schedule of a hypothetical international fixed income manager (Manager A) is shown.

The manager has three fee breakpoints. For assets up to $50 million, the fee is 35 basis points (bps); for assets from $50 million to $100 million, the fee is 33 bps; and for assets greater than $100 million, a flat fee of 22 bps is charged.

Assuming an investor has a portfolio of $300 million invested with the manager, the effective fee would be 26 bps. Figure 20.4 compares Manager A's fees with the fees of other international fixed income managers.

TABLE 20.4   Manager A International Fixed Income Fee Schedule

Fee Schedule		Portfolio Value as of September 31, 2012	Effective Fee
First $50m	0.35%	$300m	0.26%
Next $50m	0.33%		
Balance	0.22%		

The comparison shows the effective fees payable using the actual fee scales of Manager A and the stated fee schedules for a representative sample of international fixed income managers. Stated fee schedules do not necessarily represent the fees that actually would be paid to managers, as some are willing to negotiate.

The figure shows percentiles of fees charged by international fixed income managers. If the data are arranged in ascending order, the 5th percentile is the value 5 percent of the way through the list, the 25th percentile is the value 25 percent of the way through the list, and so on.

The graph shows the 5th, 25th, 50th (median), 75th, and 95th percentiles of the distribution being shown for portfolio sizes of $50 million, $100 million, $200 million, and $300 million. The effective fees that would be payable to Manager A for each of these portfolio sizes are then plotted beside these ranges (as marked by the solid black triangles). The data represented are indicative only.

Manager A's fees are most competitive for small to intermediate-size mandates, those below $100 million. For large mandates, the fees still remain competitive, around the 75th percentile.

Fees schedules are most typical among investment managers in public markets. Hedge funds tend to employ a combination of base fees plus performance-related fee schedules, as do many private market managers.

Performance-/Incentive-Based Investment Management Fees

The typical base fees charged by investment managers on the assets under management are sometimes criticized as not providing effective alignment between investors and managers. Some argue for performance-linked fees to reward managers on the basis of the excess returns they deliver to investors. We next explore the typical kinds of performance fees used and look at their impact on incentive alignment between manager and investor next.

Typical Base Fee   A base fee charged on the assets under management is the typical manager fee structure. For example a manager's fee may be expressed as 30 bps of the total assets under advice. Regardless of the value added, the manager is paid the same fee.

Types Of Performance Fees   We will explore two potential types of performance-related fees:

1. Performance fee plus a base fee
2. Performance fee with a cap and floor, plus a base fee

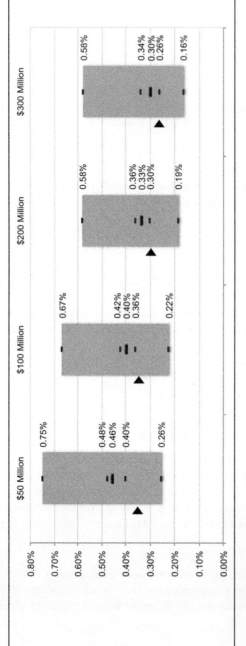

	$50 Million	$100 Million	$200 Million	$300 Million
5th Percentile	0.26%	0.22%	0.19%	0.16%
25th Percentile	0.40%	0.36%	0.30%	0.26%
Median	0.46%	0.40%	0.33%	0.30%
75th Percentile	0.48%	0.42%	0.36%	0.34%
95th Percentile	0.75%	0.67%	0.58%	0.58%
Manager A	0.35%	0.34%	0.30%	0.26%

FIGURE 20.4   Fee Schedule Universe of International Fixed Income Managers

Performance Fee Plus a Base Fee The fixed base fee is usually smaller when a performance fee element is introduced than when no performance fee exists. The performance fee is designed to share the value added between the manager and the investor. Since value added is shared, the interests of the manager and investor are usually more aligned. However, the performance fee has downside potential for the manager. If the manager has a period of poor performance, the performance fee can be significantly negative. The manager's business could be at risk. This performance fee effectively reduces the investor's exposure to active risk and shifts it to the manager.

Performance Fee with a Floor and Cap Managers are more likely to accept a performance fee with a floor because of the business risk associated. Under this arrangement, the manager receives an increased fee for producing positive value-add up to a point (since upside is capped) but does not share in the downside. Such a fee arrangement is not without its problems.

- If the manager realizes a very large value-add toward the end of a performance-fee calculation period, he or she is strongly motivated to reduce the active risk taken in the portfolio. This way the manager locks in the value added until the end of the fee calculation period.
- If the manager realizes a large negative value-add toward the end of the calculation period, it is in his or her best interest to increase the active risk of the portfolio. The manager would increase the active positions; there is little to lose, because of the floor, and everything to gain.

This fee arrangement incentivizes the manager to "game the benchmark" at the expense of the investor. The cap on performance reduces this incentive but does not completely remove it.

Even with a cap and a floor on performance fees, the manager has an incentive to keep the active risk of the portfolio, and hence the value added, within the bounds of the floor and cap. The investor is, however, better off when both active risk and value added are high. The level of active risk that is good for the manager is not necessarily good for the investor and vice versa. But since the manager controls the level of active risk, there is a divergence of interests between the manager and investor about this level of risk.

Are Typical Base Fees Already a Performance Fee Contract? Berk (2005) argues that the typical base fee arrangement is already a performance fee contract. Better managers manage larger funds, and so fund size is some, albeit noisy, measure of manager skill. When a manager does well and outperforms the benchmark, assets will tend to flow into that manager. The manager's compensation will rise since the fees are charged on a proportion of assets under management. However, when the manager does poorly, assets will flow out of the manager's funds, and his or her compensation will fall.

Conclusion

Fees are certain, but performance is not. Understanding the competitiveness of a manager's fees and the suitability of the fee arrangement to an investor is essential to ensure the best outcome is achieved for investors.

References

Berk, J. B. 2005. "Five Myths of Active Portfolio Management." *Journal of Portfolio Management* 31 (3): 27–31.

Rice, M., and G. Strotman. 2010. "The Next Chapter in the Active versus Passive Debate (2010 Update)." DiMeo Schneider & Associates, L.L.C. White paper, March.

Part II Alpha and Beta, and the Search for a True Measure of Manager Value

While asset allocation is basically the process by which an investor allocates assets between investments based on expected risk and return, much of investment analysis is centered on the determination of which individual investments, portfolios, or asset classes may offer superior returns to other comparable securities, portfolios, or asset classes. We show that even in the simple world of single-factor risk models (standard deviation, skewness, market beta) as well as in more complex models of risk and return determination, the risk models themselves may get in the way of understanding the fundamental risks we face.

In short, there is hidden risk in assuming that we know how to define risk. There is also what we term model risk imbedded in the actual models that we use for risk estimation or manager alpha determination. For instance, we show that most single-factor risk–based models provide only a limited means of exploring asset risk or of determining true manager alpha. As an alternative, we explore the use of multifactor as well as simple replication/tracking approaches to determine the additional value that a manager may bring to the investment process.

What Is Alpha?

In most investment seminars and conferences, manager after manager remains intent on proving their ability to produce something they refer to as "alpha," or the excess return relative to a comparable nonmanager–based investment of comparable risk. This alpha therefore represents the additional return a manager may add to the investment process that does not impact the underlying risk of the portfolio. Each manager and investor has their own unique take on what alpha is and how it should be measured. It should come as no surprise that academics and practitioners have also weighed in on the central questions of this issue:

What is alpha?

Since alpha is often measured in terms of beta, what is the best way to measure the beta of an investment strategy?

Since beta is not an all-encompassing measure of risk, what are its benefits and what are its limitations?

As one moves from single-factor risk models such as beta, what benefits exist from more multifactor models of return estimation?

In recent years, there has been an increase in the use of systematic algorithmic-based tracking strategies to capture the expected return process of individual strategies. Is this the future?

In the world of academics, an active manager's performance alpha is generally defined as the excess return to active management adjusted for risk. A better definition of alpha would be the return adjusted for the return of a comparably risky investable "nonactively managed" asset or portfolio. The expected return on a comparably risky nonactively managed investment strategy is often either derived from academic theory or statistically derived from historical pricing relationships. The primary issue, of course, remains how to create a comparably risky investable nonactively managed asset. Even when one believes in the use of ex ante equilibrium (e.g., CAPM) or arbitrage (e.g., APT) models of expected return, problems in empirically estimating the required parameters usually results in alpha being determined using statistical models based on the underlying theoretical model.

As generally measured in a statistical sense, the term alpha is often derived from a linear regression in which the equation that relates an observed variable y (asset return) to some other factor x (market index) is written as:

$$y = \alpha + \beta x + \varepsilon$$

The first term, α (alpha) represents the intercept; β (beta) represents the slope; and ε (epsilon) represents a random error term. In finance, the above equation is often known as the market model. The alpha term is important in finance because it represents the return that the investor would receive even if the benchmark had a zero return or the beta of the investment is zero. Rearranging the above equation (and ignoring the error term for now), we can restate the equation to focus on the alpha:

$$\alpha = y - \beta x$$

Alpha measured using raw returns rather than excess returns is not strictly correct because it assumes that the cost of leverage is zero. Therefore, the return in excess of the risk-free return is the proper estimate of alpha (whether it is single-factor or multifactor)

$$\alpha = (E(R_i) - R_f) - \beta(E(R_m) - R_f)$$

where

$E(R_i)$ = Expected return on investment i
R_f = Riskless rate of return
$E(R_m)$ = Rate of return on benchmark

Given the knowledge that R_m may not adequately measure the market portfolio, the equation has been expanded to cover a number of additional risk factors that impact expected return.

$$\alpha_i = (E(R_i) - R_f) - \beta_{i1}(E(B_1) - R_f) - \beta_{i2}(E(B_2) - R_f) - \dots$$

where

$E(B_j)$ = Expected rate of return on investable benchmark j

Finally, the multifactor model can be expanded by allowing the betas to change through time. For example, if a manager has market timing skill, then she could increase (decrease) the beta if she anticipates a relatively high (low) rate of return on the market. In some cases the beta may change because of changes in the market environment. For example, to the degree that fund flows increase when markets are rising, cash holdings of fund managers may initially increase during rising markets. The reason is that it may take the fund manager several days to invest the new funds. Under such a circumstance, the beta of the fund will initially decline because of increased cash holdings. This type of conditional model can be estimated as follows (we are going to use the CAPM as an example):

$$R_{it} - R_f = \alpha_i + \beta_{it} \times (R_{mt} - R_f) + \varepsilon_{it}$$

where

R_{it} = Rate of return on investment i at time t
R_{mt} = Rate of return on the market at time t
β_{it} = Beta of the investment with respect to the market at time t.

Next, we need to model the beta. Suppose we believe that a fund manager uses VIX to adjust the beta of her portfolio. Then the beta can be modeled as:

$$\beta_{it} = a + b \times VIX_{t-1}$$

where a and b are parameters of the "beta model" that we need to estimate. Note that the beta is assumed to depend on the lagged value of the VIX. This means we are assuming that the manager looks at the lagged value of VIX to change the beta. On the other hand, if we believe that the manager has some skill in predicting the future value of VIX, we may use the current value of VIX. In its present form the final expression for alpha would look like this:

$$\alpha_i = E(R_i) - R_f - (a_i E(R_m - R_f) + b_i VIX_{t-1} E(R_m - R_f))$$

The same idea can be used to present the conditional version of the multifactor model. Of course, the key is to identify the relevant factors. For many actively managed portfolios, it may be impossible to determine what the relevant factors are because they represent the skill that the manager is bringing to the table.

While simple or conditional multifactor models are preferred by the academic community, the problem remains that practitioners prefer to use their own model. This means different investment managers and consultants offer an estimate of alpha that may not be easily comparable across investment managers. Various alternatives used by practitioners are given in Table 20.5.

The equations are all correct under very limited circumstances. However, a few points about measurement of investment performance may be of value:

The risk-free rate benchmark is typically used by edge fund and assumes that the fund has zero beta and that investors do not demand a premium for volatility.

The problems with the CAPM-based benchmark have already been discussed. It assumes that market risk is the only relevant source of risk.

The Sharpe Ratio–based model assumes in part that there exists a known market portfolio Sharpe Ratio (e.g., .70).

TABLE 20.5   Alpha Determination: Alternative Risk-Adjusted Benchmarks

Alpha Benchmark Model	Alpha Determination	Alpha
T-Bill	$E(R_i) - R_f$	5.26%
CAPM	$\alpha = (E(R_i) - R_f) - (\beta(E(R_m) - R_f))$	4.42%
Sharpe Ratio	$\alpha = (E(R_i) - R_f) - \left(\dfrac{E(R_m) - R_f}{\sigma_m} \times \sigma_i \right)$	.68%
Multifactor	$\alpha_i = (E(R_i) - R_f) - (\beta_{i1}(E(B_1) - R_f) + \beta_{i2}(E(B_2) - R_f) - \ldots)$	−0.97%

In the case of multifactor models, identifying the factors is the most serious problem.

More modern variants of these models (e.g., the conditional version) pose other problems. For example, because more risk parameters have to be estimated, the estimation error of the parameters will increase unless sufficient return data are available. For instance, since the average life of hedge funds is about five years, most of these models cannot be applied to this asset class.

When considering the benefit of adding an asset to an existing portfolio, an alternative approach known as the breakeven analysis is often used. Modern pricing theory emphasizes the risk of an asset as its marginal contribution to the risk of an investor's portfolio. Breakeven analysis is often used to test for the potential contribution of an asset to the risk/return profile of an existing stand-alone portfolio. The breakeven (R_c) and excess breakeven rate of return (EBK) is often computed as follows:

$$E(R_c) = \left(\frac{E(R_p) - R_f}{\sigma_p} \right) (\rho_{cp}) \sigma_c + R_f$$

$$EBK = R_c - \left[\left(\frac{E(R_p) - R_f}{\sigma_p} \right) (\rho_{cp}) \sigma_c + R_f \right]$$

where

$E(R_c)$ = Breakeven rate of return required for the asset to improve the Sharpe Ratio of alternative index p
R_c = Rate of return on asset c
R_f = Riskless rate of return
$E(R_p)$ = Rate of return on alternative index p
ρ_{cp} = Correlation coefficient between asset c and alternative benchmark p
σ_c = Standard deviation of asset c
σ_p = Standard deviation of alternative index p

First, it is important to realize that the above expression is based on the assumption that only mean and variance matter in evaluating the risk-return profile of a portfolio. Second, one must be familiar with the potential problems that can arise in using this expression. For example, if there is a period of high historical R_f, then almost any asset would fail to have a return (R_c) in excess of its EBK. Further, the EBK is dependent on the measurement of correlation. Some investment managers emphasize the noncorrelation of their strategy with the S&P 500 and then turn around and offer a comparison of their Sharpe Ratio with that of the S&P 500 to indicate superior alpha performance. Even in this case, the comparison will not indicate its potential alpha benefit relative to other, nontested, active manager portfolios; nor does it provide an indication of whether another like investment will have produced a similar or even greater increase in the Sharpe Ratio of the newly constructed portfolio. In short, the ability of a manager to achieve alpha is based on the ability to achieve a return via an active strategy, that is, greater than what could be achieved using a passive strategy designed to capture the same risks and hence the same expected returns of the active strategy. If that strategy fits into the existing portfolio and helps the investor achieve his/her unique goals, it should be added to the portfolio as an additional investment in contrast to a similar passive strategy.[1]

As mentioned previously, multifactor models of alpha determination should be used whenever an investor is concerned with dimensions of risk not covered by the market risk. One of the most common and simplest methods that can be used to build multifactor models is to use portfolios that represent returns to various factors (they are called factor mimicking portfolios).

In general, these factor portfolios are used for two purposes. First, to measure the exposure of a portfolio or an asset to the factor that is represented by the factor portfolio. For example, by running a regression of the excess return of a manager's return against the return to the factor portfolio that represents the size factor, we measure the manager's exposure to this risk: Does the manager have a significant exposure to the performance of small cap stocks? Second, the factor portfolio can be used to measure the return to the factor. For example, the mean return to the factor portfolio representing the size factor can be used to measure the expected return to this factor. If the return to this factor is deemed to be attractive, an investor may decide to shift to a portfolio that has a relatively large exposure to small cap stocks. This can then be used to measure a manager's return from this source.

There are several methods for creating factor portfolios. The most common approach is to rank a large of number of securities according to a characteristic that we wish to represent by a factor portfolio. For example, suppose we wish to create a factor portfolio that represents the inflation factor or risk. Suppose the universe of assets we wish to consider is the U.S. stock market. First, we calculate the beta of all stocks with respect to inflation rate (this can be done using a simple regression). Second, we rank all the stocks according to size of their betas. Next, we create two equally weighted portfolios. The first one will consist of the 25 percent of the firms with highest exposure to inflation and the second will consist of the 25 percent of the firms with lowest exposure to inflation. Finally, we "go short" the low inflation exposure portfolio and "go long" the high inflation exposure portfolio. The return to this position, which requires no investment in theory, represents the return to the factor portfolio representing inflation risk. If the average return on this portfolio is positive, then we may conclude that expected return to inflation exposure is positive. In the same manner one can create factor portfolios representing size, value/growth, P/E, momentum, industry, and others.

One of the most commonly used factor models is the Fama-French four-factor model. The four factors are:

1. Excess return to the market
2. High book value minus low book value (HML)
3. Small minus big (SMB)
4. Up minus down (UMD)

That is, HML represents returns to a long/short portfolio sorted on book-to-market, with high book-to-market stocks long and low book- to-market stocks short. SMB represents returns to a long/short portfolio, with small cap stocks long and large cap stocks short. UMD represents returns to a long/short portfolio, with past winners long and past losers short.

For our hedge fund indices we estimate the following regression model:

$$R_{it} - R_f = a_i + b_i(R_{mt} - R_f) + h_i \times HML_t + s_i \times SMB_t + u_i \times UMD_t + \varepsilon_{it}$$

That is, we regress the excess returns of our investment, $R_{it} - R_f$, on the excess returns of the market, $R_{mt} - R_f$, and returns on a three-factor portfolio: HML_t, SMB_t, and UMD_t. The residual ε_{it} captures any other variation in excess returns that cannot be explained by the factors.

Again, careful use of the results of these models is required. For instance, returns to some of the factors may not be significant all the time and even the sign may change. Everyone remembers how growth stocks outperformed value stocks during the Internet bubble of 1999 to 2000 and then how value stocks significantly outperformed growth stocks during the post-bubble period of 2001 to 2003.

Issues in Alpha and Beta Determination

Extensive academic and practitioner literature exists on asset pricing and return generating models. In general, these expected return models are based on an expected relationship between expected returns and the underlying risk factors driving those expected returns. To the extent that returns to those risk factors can be predicted, then that knowledge can be used to determine asset weighting between various asset classes.[2] Unfortunately, academic research has generally concluded that it is not possible to obtain accurate estimates of future returns to macroeconomic factors such that, as a result, future expected returns are often based on subjective estimates related to long term historical returns to risk factors.

In the investment area one of the primary, if not the essential, questions is the value of active management relative to manager–based or security/market factor passive investable indices. Most investors are aware of the number of articles as well as books that attempt to address the value of active versus passive management. For years, this discussion was primarily limited to the traditional stock and bond area as informational and trading costs limited its use in the traditional alternative investments (commodities and private equity) area as well as in the area of modern alternatives (hedge funds and CTAs). Today, as new trading instruments become available, a number of new passive products (ETFs and replication products) have become available that attempt to mimic the performance of various active traditional

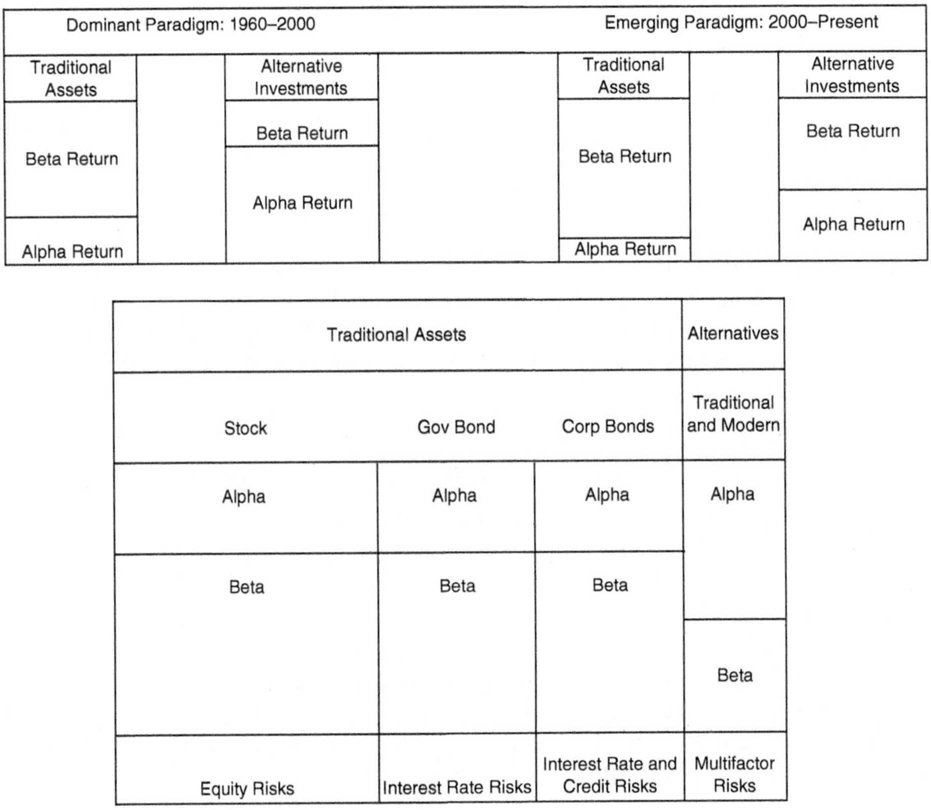

Dominant Paradigm: 1960–2000				Emerging Paradigm: 2000–Present		
Traditional Assets		Alternative Investments		Traditional Assets		Alternative Investments
Beta Return		Beta Return		Beta Return		Beta Return
		Alpha Return				Alpha Return
Alpha Return				Alpha Return		

Traditional Assets			Alternatives
Stock	Gov Bond	Corp Bonds	Traditional and Modern
Alpha	Alpha	Alpha	Alpha
Beta	Beta	Beta	
			Beta
Equity Risks	Interest Rate Risks	Interest Rate and Credit Risks	Multifactor Risks

FIGURE 20.5 Changing Importance of Alpha and Beta in Return Estimation

as well as alternative investment strategies. Figure 20.5 displays changes in the market perception of both traditional and alternative assets as more academic research regarding the value added by active management has become available.

In *Alice in Wonderland*, Alice asks the Cheshire Cat what path to take. The cat asks in return: Where do you want to go? Alice replies that she has no idea. The cat responds: Then it really doesn't matter which path you take. For managers, however, it does matter which path they take. Is alpha to be used as a marketing device, or as a measure of comparable risk/return performance? If managers wish to define alpha to fit their own marketing purposes and use alpha to sell a product, it is understandable from a product management viewpoint, if not desirable from an academic or investor focus. However, when faced with an alpha estimate in a product marketing document, an investor should never mistake this "marketing alpha" for perhaps a more theoretically defensible "performance alpha."

In sum, if the manager can choose asset positions with a higher return (but the same ex ante risk) to some comparable naive passive investment position, then that person can be said to achieve a positive performance alpha. But performance alpha is all about properly measured return relative to a benchmark. For traditional portfolios such as mutual funds, the multifactor models discussed above tend to do a reasonable job. Of course, the set of factors may be expanded to include factor portfolios representing risks such as inflation, interest rate, or currency risks.

Unfortunately, when it comes to actively managed portfolios that have broad mandates (e.g., hedge funds or CTAs), we have no simple method for establishing this benchmark except under very restrictive situations. But at the very least, we do know that investment decisions involve some risk and that even similar investment strategies often entail different risk exposures (e.g., leverage), so the riskless rate is probably not appropriate as a performance benchmark for hedge funds. How much return should be added and what method should be used to determine the incremental return to add to the risk-free rate to obtain the appropriate return comparison remains open for discussion. For instance, in a recent study (Fernandez, 2009b), the average Market Risk Premium (6.3 percent) used in 2008 by finance professors in the United States was higher than the one (5.3 percent) used by their colleagues in Europe. Fernandez also reports statistics for 18 countries, which show that the average MRP used in 2008 ranges from 4.1 percent (Belgium) to 10.5 percent (India). Similarly wide ranges exist in estimates of beta. For example, Fernandez (2009a) reports that among various web and database sources the minimum and maximum reported betas for Coca-Cola ranged from a high of 0.80 to a low of 0.31. Similar beta ranges existed for a wide range of other well-known firms.

Problems in Alpha and Beta Determination

Perceived wisdom suggests that the growth of the asset management industry is substantially due to the superior returns offered by fund managers. Investors should realize that there is neither consensus on exactly what constitutes "superior" returns, nor is there a methodology to identify and describe such returns on a quantitative basis. To the typical industry participant, "alpha" means the incremental return attributable to a manager relative to a specified benchmark, and as such, attempts to measure that incremental return on an ex post basis by estimating a least squares regression of manager performance against the specified benchmark. The key is that the benchmark must be well specified in measuring the risk of the investment portfolio. To illustrate potential problems in using a benchmark that is not well specified, note that one can write a fund's and benchmark's alphas as a function of average excess returns to each other, their respective volatilities, and their correlation.

As the following equation shows, we are using a benchmark to measure the alpha of the fund and then use the fund to measure the alpha of the benchmark. It may seem odd to use a fund as the benchmark for estimating the alpha of a passively managed portfolio such as the S&P 500. However, you may be surprised to know that if these two equations are estimated for a large set of hedge funds, and you will find that a large number of funds have positive alpha with respect to a benchmark while at the same time the benchmark may have an alpha with respect to the same funds.

$$\alpha_{fund} = E(R_{fund} - R_f) - Corr(R_{fund}, R_{bench}) \times \frac{\sigma_{fund}}{\sigma_{bench}} E(R_{bench} - R_f)$$

$$\alpha_{bench} = E(R_{bench} - R_f) - Corr(R_{fund}, R_{bench}) \times \frac{\sigma_{bench}}{\sigma_{fund}} E(R_{fund} - R_f)$$

Such a result should not be obtained if the benchmark was well specified. We can see that a low correlation could lead to a positive alpha and the low correlation could work in both directions: giving the fund an alpha with respect to the benchmark

TABLE 20.6   Relative Directional Move of Asset and Benchmark Alpha

Period	+/+	-/+	+/-	-/-
1998–9/2005	22%	3%	76%	0%
1998–2000	35%	43%	22%	0%
2001–9/2005	11%	5%	84%	0%

Source: Martin (2005).

and giving the benchmark an alpha with respect to the fund. We can investigate the validity of the prevailing economic intuition of alpha as incremental value added by conducting a simple analysis in which we first estimate alpha of a fund relative to a benchmark, and then the converse—the alpha of the benchmark relative to the fund. Characteristic of each of these concepts is the implicit idea that if a hedge fund exhibits alpha relative to a benchmark, then that benchmark should not add alpha relative to the hedge fund. However, for low correlation, and positive excess returns to the fund and the benchmark, fund alpha and benchmark alpha may both be positive. Table 20.6 offers the results of regressing excess returns to 37 hedge fund indices (HFR indices) on the S&P 500, and vice versa, for the periods indicated. The respective columns count the percentage of indices with corresponding signs of their alphas. Thus "+/+" (which we term "weak alpha") means index's alpha with respect to the S&P 500 is positive while at the same time S&P 500's alpha with respect to the index is positive as well. On the other hand, "+/−" (which we may term "strong alpha") means that index's alpha is positive while the S&P 500's alpha with respect to the index is negative—the conventional interpretation of alpha.

The same misspecification could create a problem with regard to ranking of portfolios; that is, suppose Fund A has a positive alpha with respect to a benchmark and Fund B has a larger positive alpha with respect to the same benchmark. Does this mean that Fund B has a positive alpha with respect to Fund A? The answer is no. Indeed, it is possible for Fund B to have a negative alpha with respect to Fund A. So who has the skill? Clearly, in the absence of a well-specified benchmark, any estimate of alpha should be viewed with a great deal of skepticism.

An additional issue within alpha and beta determination deals with the notion of convexity of portfolio returns relative to a benchmark (see Figure 20.6). Academics and practitioners have long recognized that a key feature of active portfolio management is the ability to assume nonlinear exposures to market factors, either from dynamic allocation of exposure to market factors or from the selection of assets with nonlinear payoffs relative to the market in order to deliver improved risk-adjusted returns. In its advantageous form, this dynamic exposure is hypothesized to take the form of increased factor exposure during periods when market factors deliver positive returns, and correspondingly, decreased exposure during downturns in market factors. This payoff profile is generically referred to as "market timing"; however, given the fact that this result may be due either to market timing via dynamic asset allocation, or due to security selection, such terminology is potentially misleading. Early attempts to measure this convexity included a quadratic term in the conventional linear model of performance measurement. In general, we believe that convexity is a more powerful measure of active portfolio management since it is more difficult to manufacture than a linear measure of alpha. As is discussed later in this

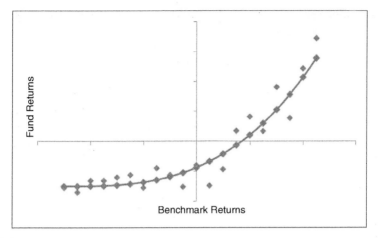

FIGURE 20.6   Return Convexity

book, various dynamic and option–based approaches to risk management may provide such convexity patterns but not without underlying costs (e.g., insurance).

Multifactor Return Estimation: An Example

Simple use of average historical returns has been shown to be a poor indicator of future returns. As an alternative, research has shown that underlying market factors (e.g., credit spreads, term structure) are important in determining performance of equity, fixed income, and alternative investment strategies. This means that not only multifactor models can be used to examine the performance of a portfolio on an ex post basis (to measure its alpha), they can also be used to forecast returns to major asset classes. While a quantitative model is used as a primary basis for strategy return forecasts, actual returns may differ from estimated returns for a variety of reasons, including model misspecification. Strict use of return estimation models at the portfolio level could lead to portfolios that are highly exposed to certain risk factors and inconsistent with current economic conditions to the degree that qualitative factors cannot be incorporated into the model. Qualitative judgments can be used to make marginal adjustments to forecast returns if it is determined that the quantitative model is not capable of incorporating certain aspects of the prevailing economic condition. Simple use of these return estimations without an understanding of the complexities of investment return estimation is not recommended.

In this section, we use a multifactor regression model to develop estimates of returns. There are many additional approaches to return estimation. In this example, estimated return can be modeled as:

$$R_t = \alpha + \beta_1 \times F_{1,t-1} + \beta_2 \times F_{2,t-1} + \ldots + \varepsilon_t,$$

where

R_t	=	Investment strategy return
α	=	Intercept
$F_{1,t-1}$	=	Lagged value of a relevant factor (e.g., credit spread, term spread, etc.)
β_1	=	Coefficient of independent variable 1

It is very important to point out that, unlike previous multifactor models, factors that appear on the right-hand side of the equation do not have to represent excess returns on investable portfolios. Next, the variables on the right-hand side are lagged one period because they are used to predict return on the asset class. Finally, it is typically better to use several lagged values of a factor rather than change in the factor. For instance, if credit risk premium is one of the factors, then it may be better to use two lagged values of the credit risk premium rather than the change in the premium. If the contemporaneous values of the factors are used in the above regression, then the idea is that it is easier to forecast factor values than the return on the investment directly. Indeed, in some cases it may be easier to use past experience and professional judgment to forecast certain factors than directly forecasting the return on an asset class.

For example, regression coefficients from an explanatory model for the S&P 500 regressed on credit spread, term spread, and growth in corporate earnings can be used with forecasted values of the independent variables to obtain a forecast of returns for the S&P 500. Similar models have been designed to provide an estimate for expected returns for various strategies depending on the economic environment. We believe these factor estimates reflect current economic conditions; however, other qualitative/quantitative approaches to factor estimation can be used. The factors included in the current model are T-Bill rate (Bloomberg Generic Treasury Three-Month Rate), Credit Spread (Moody's Baa–Moody's Aaa), Term Spread (Bloomberg Treasury 10-Year Rate–Bloomberg Treasury Six-Month Rate), and Growth in Corporate Earnings (corporate profits with inventory valuation and capital consumption adjustments).

Table 20.7 presents an example of forecasted returns for the S&P 500 index. In these examples, historical returns are used to estimate the coefficients. Then using

TABLE 20.7   Factor Inputs in Regression Model

S&P 500

Variable	Exposure
Intercept	0.04
T-Bill TR	1.61
Credit Spread	−4.81
Term Spread	0.19
Growth in Corp Earnings	0.34

Forecasted Independent Variable

Variable	Exposure
T-Bill TR	1.03%
Credit Spread	0.83%
Term Spread	1.53%
Growth in Corp Earnings	2.18%

S&P 500 Forecast

Lower	Mean	Upper
4.29%	11.38%	18.47%

our professional judgment as well as other quantitative models we have obtained forecasts for future values of the factors. Then these forecasted values are used to obtain estimates for expected returns on the S&P 500. Further, instead of using a point estimate for forecasted factors, we used a range of values and this leads to a range of forecasts for the performance of the S&P 500.

Further improvements can be made to make this multifactor model more realistic. For instance, we may suspect that the response of the S&P 500 index to changes in the level of risk premium is a function of the level of volatility in the interest rates. Similar to the procedure that was highlighted before, we can assume that the coefficient of one or more factors is related to other factors. For example, the coefficient of the first factor may be expressed as

$$\beta_{1t} = a + b \times Vol_t$$

where Vol_t is an estimate of the volatility of interest rates at time t. This would allow us to estimate the impact of interaction between volatility of interest rates and changes in the credit risk premium.

These are just some examples of what practitioners can do with models of risk and return that account for many factors. There is extensive academic and practitioner literature that discusses expected asset returns as conditioned on a range of factors that may change over time. One important issue that has to be remembered is that more sophisticated models require more data and, if enough data are not available, the estimated parameters will be subject to severe estimation errors. Further, even if enough data are available, the estimated values of the parameters may significantly change if a new factor is added or a factor is dropped from the model.

It should be noted that short run changes in asset values are affected primarily by unexpected changes in information affecting asset values. For instance, the U.S. stock market has been shown to lead future economic conditions; that is, if the markets correctly estimate that economic conditions will improve, then the stock market may immediately rise in anticipation of those expected future improvements in economic conditions. It is also true that other asset classes that have economic risks similar to equity (e.g., high-yield debt) may also increase in value before actual changes in economic conditions. As a result, academic research has focused on certain macroeconomic factors that may represent current and future shifts in economic activity. As indicated previously, economic conditions may impact the expected return process; therefore, each of them may be viewed as a risk factor underlying the expected return process of a particular investment class sensitive to that information.

Previous research on conditional performance evaluation has concentrated on the traditional segment of the asset management industry such as equity and fixed income funds. (See Ferson and Khang 2002, and Ferson, Kisgen, and Henry 2003.) More recent studies have extended this research to alternative strategies such as hedge funds (Kazemi, Tu, and Li 2008). In addition, this research has examined whether a conditional performance model that uses a dynamically adjusted portfolio as a benchmark reaches significantly different conclusions compared to those reached by an unconditional linear model.

Tracking Alternatives in Alpha Determination

Various investment benchmarks are often utilized to measure the effectiveness and skill with which a manager selects securities. Thus, as an alternative to single- or multifactor models of return determination, the relative outperformance of a manager in comparison to a predefined benchmark index is often used as a basis for measuring a manager's alpha. One of the principal issues in benchmark determination is the degree to which the comparison benchmark is fully investable. For a manager's alpha to be truly measureable it must be compared to a non-manager-based (e.g., passive) investible asset of equal risk. Here, in order to provide a meaningful analysis of the manager and the comparison benchmark the managers fees must be net of all expenses and the fees and expenses associated with directly investing in the benchmark must also be considered. This can be a particularly thorny issue in dealing with alternatives such as private equity, commodities, hedge funds, or real estate, where there are few commonly accepted investable benchmark surrogates. In contrast, there exists a wide range of publicly available investment vehicles (that have been vetted over time) for equity and fixed income that provide access to the returns reflected in their associated benchmarks.

The use of investable benchmark alternatives (futures contracts, ETFs) as vehicles to derive manager alpha has been discussed in a wide range of practitioner and academic studies. In this section, we illustrate the creation of an investable tracking index to provide an investable alternative to the corresponding actively managed investment. One approach is to use investable forms of the risk factors used to describe asset returns in the previous section on multifactor return estimation. To the degree that these risk factors are investable and capture the underlying risk of the manager's security holdings, the risk factor weightings can be used to create a passive investment alternative. This approach is of course susceptible to the basic issues surrounding any multifactor return estimation model. In addition, a multi-factor risk model–based approach may not capture the unique strategy aspects of an individual manager's approach. An alternative approach reflects the use of ETFs with an algorithmic-based model to track the comparison noninvestable index or comparison fund.

In Table 20.8, a range of investable ETFs are used to create a tracking portfolio that reflects the performance of the CISDM Fund of Fund Hedge Fund index. In this case the correlation between the CISDM Fund of Fund Hedge Fund index and its tracker is over .90. Research (Kazemi and Schneeweis, 2009) has shown investable alternatives can be created from a series of ETFs that offer an investable

TABLE 20.8 Performance: CISDM Fund of Fund Tracker

Tracking Example (CISDM Fund of Funds)	CISDM Fund of Fund (Tracker)	CISDM Fund of Fund	S&P 500	BarCap U.S. Aggregate
Annualized Returns	0.7%	−7.6%	−26.8%	5.2%
Annualized Standard Deviation	6.4%	7.8%	18.5%	4.9%
Information Ratio	0.10	(0.97)	(1.45)	1.06
Maximum Drawdown	−9.7%	−17.7%	−45.1%	−3.8%
Correlation with CISDM Fund of Funds	0.99	1.00	0.62	0.13
Correlation with S&P 500	0.83	0.62	1.00	0.30
Correlation with BarCap US Agg	0.36	0.13	0.30	1.00

Summary Statistics: May 2007 to Jan 2009.

non-manager-based benchmark to the number of noninvestable as well as investable manager–based indices. There exist, of course, a range of issues in the creation of systematic algorithmic–based tracker benchmarks, including the fact that the tracker fund is often based on matching the performance of manager or product over a past historical period, while the current manager portfolio or product may reflect more current asset allocation or security decisions. Finally, there exist a number of algorithmic–based trading products that attempt to recreate, at a passive systematic level, the underlying strategy of a particular manager. For example, while each individual manager may regard themselves as unique, most managers within a particular strategy often trade in a similar fashion. These approaches may be regarded as more bottom up strategy-tracking-based approaches.

What Every Investor Should Remember

- An active manager's performance alpha is generally defined as the excess return to active management adjusted for risk, that is, the return adjusted for the return of a comparable investable nonactively managed risky asset position or portfolio. The question is, therefore, how to define the expected risk of the manager's investment and how to obtain the return on that investment.
- Use of a single-index model assumes that the single market factor in the model replicates the fundamental risk factor driving the return of the strategy. If not, a multifactor model should be used to describe the various market factors that drive the return strategy. One of the basic tenets of statistical regression says it is better to over specify a model (include more sources of systematic risk than the fund is exposed to) than under specify (include fewer factors).
- Economic conditions may impact the expected return process and may be viewed as a risk factor underlying the expected return process of a particular investment class sensitive to that information. Research has indicated that a conditional performance model that uses a dynamically adjusted portfolio as a benchmark reaches significantly different conclusions compared to those reached by an unconditional linear model.
- The ability to assume nonlinear exposures to market factors, either from dynamic allocation of exposure to market factors or from the selection of assets with nonlinear payoffs relative to market, may deliver improved risk-adjusted returns.

Notes

1. There is extensive literature on Sharpe Ratios and alternative relative risk comparison measures (e.g., the Jensen and the Treynor indices). See Bodie, Kane, and Marcus (2008). There have also been additional papers recently on the use of various volatility comparison performance measures in which the volatility of the asset is directly adjusted to equal the benchmark (e.g., Modigliani and Modigliani 1997 and Graham and Harvey 1996). In addition, the use of any average realized

return/risk comparison model may not capture manager skill if managers follow conditional risk models (Bansal and Harvey 1996). Lastly, for portfolios in which the underlying return distribution is fundamentally different from the assumed benchmark or when investors value those parameters in ways different from the assumed theoretical model's derived benchmark, the use of a corresponding naive benchmark may not capture for investors the relative return benefits of active manager choices.

2. In addition to macroeconomic factors driving asset class returns, considerable research exists on microeconomic or firm related factors driving returns on individual assets or asset classes. This brief review does not address issues such as unexpected changes in earnings per share as a basis for individual security valuation.

References

Bansal, R., and C. R. Harvey. 1996. "Performance Evaluation in the Presence of Dynamic Trading Strategies." Duke University, Working Paper.

Bodie, Z., A. Kane, and A. Marcus. 2008. *Investments*. New York: McGraw-Hill.

Fernandez, P. 2009a. "Betas Used by Professors: A Survey with 2,500 Answers." University of Navarra, IESE Business School, May.

Fernandez, P. 2009b. "Market Risk Premia Used in 2008 by Professors: A Survey with 1,400 Answers." University of Navarra, IESE Business School, April.

Ferson, W. E., and K. Khang. 2002. "Conditional Performance Measurement Using Portfolio Weights: Evidence for Pension Funds." NBER Working Paper No. W8790, February.

Ferson, W. E., D. Kisgen, and T. Henry. 2003. "Evaluating Fixed Income Fund Performance with Stochastic Discount Factors." EFA 2003 Annual Conference Paper No. 486, April.

Graham, J., and C. Harvey. 1996. "Market Timing Ability and Volatility Implied in Investment Newsletters' Asset Allocation Recommendations." *Journal of Financial Economics* 42, no. 3 (November): 397–421.

Kazemi, H., and T. Schneeweis. 2009. "Conditional Performance of Hedge Funds." CISDM Working Paper.

Kazemi, H., F. Tu, and Y. Li. 2008. "Replication and Benchmarking of Hedge Funds." *The Journal of Alternative Investments* 11, no. 2 (Fall): 40–59.

Martin, G. 2005. "Alpha and Pseudo-Alpha in Hedge Fund Returns: A Note on Admissible Measures of Portfolio Performance." CISDM.

Modigliani, F., and L. Modigliani. 1997. "Risk-Adjusted Performance." *Journal of Portfolio Management* 23, no. 2 (Winter): 45–54.

CHAPTER 21

Perform Portfolio Review
and Revisions Process

R egular monitoring, analyzing, and revising a portfolio and the investment policy statement (IPS) are key responsibilities in investment management. Investment advisors and consultants must periodically review client goals, time horizon, circumstances, and constraints. The first reading in this chapter looks at the importance of rebalancing and considers the implications of rebalancing during different times in a market cycle as opposed to not rebalancing at all. The second reading focuses on rebalancing approaches and practical considerations such as costs, taxes, and portfolio constraints. This reading will then consider the costs of, challenges of, and options for firing and replacing investment managers within the portfolio. The last reading discusses the importance of portfolio and performance reporting and analysis. Style drift, absolute and relative evaluation, peer groups and benchmarks will all be discussed as they relate to ongoing portfolio management.

Part I *Portfolio Design:* The Discipline of Asset Allocation—Rebalancing

Learning Objectives

- ▪ Differentiate between market timing and portfolio rebalancing.
- ▪ Describe the significance of rebalancing during market upswings and bull markets.
- ▪ Describe the significance of rebalancing during market downturns and bear markets.
- ▪ Explain the ramifications of not rebalancing a portfolio.

Part II *Strategic Risk Management:* Execution

Learning Objectives

- ▪ Define rebalancing.
- ▪ Discuss allocation drift and its impact on a portfolio.
- ▪ Explain how rebalancing is accomplished (i.e., how rebalancing is carried out).
- ▪ Describe three common rebalancing approaches and determine which is most appropriate.

- List and explain several practical considerations of rebalancing including transaction costs, taxes, and allocation limitations.
- Discuss the importance and ramifications of replacing investment managers within a portfolio.
- Explain why changing investment managers is so costly.
- Describe five process options for replacing investment managers.

Part III *Strategic Risk Management:* Review and Monitoring

Learning Objectives
- Describe the three primary levels of performance reporting including: fund level, asset class level, and manager level.
- Discuss potential sample reports and the items included within each.
- Explain the importance of and differentiate between absolute and relative performance.
- Describe style drift.
- Discuss peer-relative comparison and issues with peer universes.
- List and explain the primary focus and significance of regular portfolio monitoring and reviews.

Part I The Discipline of Asset Allocation: Rebalancing

Investing is not easy. It takes a lot of discipline for an investor to choose an appropriate asset allocation and then stick to it. How many investors abandoned their stock allocations after the NASDAQ collapsed in 2000 or after the financial crisis drove down stocks in 2008?

Many investors believe that they can *time the market*. It's not just the aggressive investors who have an investment philosophy built around entry and exit from the market. A much larger group of investors are willing to adopt a long-run asset allocation strategy *as long as markets behave themselves*. But when the stock market swoons, as it periodically does, these investors will abandon that strategy. And having done that, it will be very difficult for them to wade back into the market. After a sharp downturn like we experienced recently, it's seldom clear when to reenter the market. And by the time the rally is in full swing, the investor has missed most of the rebound. Chapter 1 discussed investor experience during the nine recessions since 1951. On all but one occasion, the market reached bottom before the end of the recession. And in all nine recessions, the rise in the market was very rapid once it reached bottom. Few investors react quickly enough if they time the market.

Investors also abandon asset allocation in boom times. When unusual investment opportunities present themselves, as in the case of the NASDAQ bubble in the late 1990s or the real estate bubble earlier this decade, investors will often jump into the bubble blindly. If they do it soon enough, they will make some money and perhaps feel confident enough to double up again. But investors are often late to the party. In the NASDAQ boom of the late 1990s, many investors piled into tech stocks or into venture capital partnerships only after substantial gains had already been made. And in the recent real estate boom, investor enthusiasm peaked shortly before prices started to turn down.

Rebalancing Defined

Rebalancing is the term used to describe the periodic adjustment of a portfolio to restore a strategic asset allocation. Rebalancing sounds so sensible in theory. You rebalance in order to keep investments in line with your original allocation. In practice it is very difficult to carry out. Consider the experience of investors in 1999 as shown in Figure 21.1. In 1999 growth stocks had soared, while value stocks just lumbered on. The Russell 1000 Growth Index registered a 33.2 percent return while the Russell 2000 Growth Index gave a return 10 percent higher than its large cap counterpart. An investor who believed in asset allocation should have rebalanced away from these growth investments into the value sector even though the Russell 1000 Value Index had returned only 7.3 percent in 1999. But given the splendid performance of the growth sector, how many investors were willing to *sell their winners and buy their losers?* It takes an awful lot of discipline to rebalance when one type of investment is doing so well. Besides, the investor assured himself that *this time it is different.* The world had changed and growth stocks, tech stocks in particular, no longer had to follow ordinary rules.

Little did the investor know that the tide was about to change. In the following year, growth stocks plunged. The large-cap and small-cap growth indexes both lost more than 22 percent in that year. In the meantime, large-cap value earned another 7 percent return. This turnaround in fortune for growth stocks is admittedly unusual. But it should nonetheless not be surprising.

Notice how challenging it was to evaluate investment managers during this two-year period. Unless the investor used a benchmark to evaluate each manager, it would be difficult for a value manager to survive in 1999. After all, why would you keep a manager with a 7 percent return when you could shift money to a manager earning a 30 percent-plus return?

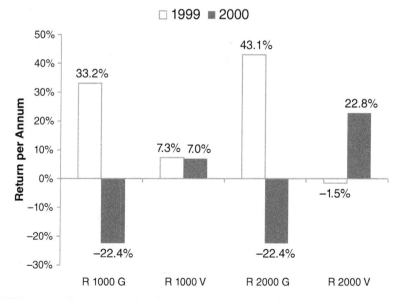

FIGURE 21.1   Russell Growth and Value Returns in 1999 and 2000
Source: Russell®.

The experience of investors in 1999 and 2000 suggests how difficult it is to stick to an asset allocation in practice. The failure to do so, however, will undermine investment strategy.

Rebalancing When Times Are Good

Rebalancing is difficult when times are good or bad. Consider the experience of investors in the five-year period from October 2002 (the trough of the market) through October 2007.[1] Normally, stock markets bottom out prior to the end of a recession. But in the recession following the NASDAQ collapse, stock markets were still falling when the recession ended in November 2001. It was only in October 2002 that markets finally reached bottom.

Suppose that in October 2002, an investor chose a portfolio with 30 percent invested in bonds and 70 percent in stocks. Let's diversify the stock market investments so that we have 40 percent in U.S. stocks (represented by the Russell 3000 Index), 15 percent in the MSCI EAFE Index, 5 percent in MSCI Emerging Markets, and 10 percent in REITS. The bond investment is tracked using the Barclays Capital Aggregate Index. Figure 21.2 summarizes the allocation.

Over the next five years, stock markets boomed. EAFE rose 189.8 percent while the MSCI EM index rose 443.9 percent and the FTSE NAREIT index rose 181.3 percent. Bonds, in contrast, limped along with a 24.1 percent total return over five years. An investor who never rebalanced would find that the portfolio had drifted to a much riskier allocation. Figure 21.3 shows the drift of this portfolio. Even though the investor left the portfolio alone, the bond allocation drifts down from 30 percent in bonds to 17.2 percent by October 2007. Where did the money go? The rise in stock markets lifted the emerging market allocation from 5 percent to 12.6 percent, lifted the foreign stock allocation from 15 percent to 20.1 percent, and lifted the REIT allocation from 10 percent to 13 percent. Investors ended up with a lot more risk than they bargained for.

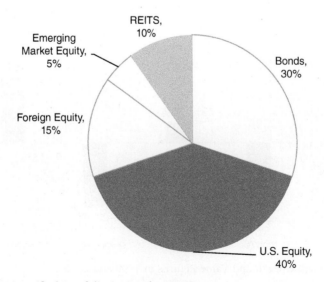

FIGURE 21.2   Diversified Portfolio in October 2002

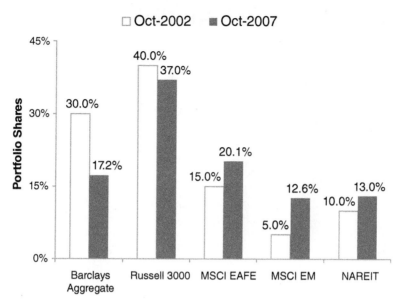

FIGURE 21.3   Drift of Portfolio Shares in Boom Barclays Capital, Russell®, MSCI, and ©FTSE

In the case of a booming market, the failure to rebalance increases the risk profile of the asset allocation unnecessarily. Some investors like to ride a good wave. That may be really enjoyable for a while.

Rebalancing When Times Are Bad

If it seems difficult to rebalance when markets are soaring, it is even more difficult to do so when markets are tumbling. Consider the experience of investors during the bust from October 2007 through March 2009.[2] During that period, the S&P 500 fell by almost 47 percent as did the Russell 3000. Foreign stocks fell even more, EAFE by 53.6 percent and MSCI Emerging Markets by 55.9 percent. REITS topped them all by falling 63.4 percent.

Figure 21.4 shows how these sharp losses distorted the asset allocation. The bond allocation drifted upward from 30 percent of the portfolio to 48.7 percent. The U.S. stock allocation plummeted by 8 percent, foreign stocks by 4.5 percent. REITS fell from 10 percent of the portfolio to 5.5 percent.

What should the investor have done in that bleak winter of 2008 and 2009? If the investor followed a disciplined approach to asset allocation, the portfolio should have been rebalanced at the trough or, perhaps more realistically, early in 2009 when annual returns were reported for 2008. But what tremendous discipline would have been required! The United States and the world as a whole had just gone through the worst financial crisis since the 1930s depression. Several major financial institutions had failed or had been saved by mergers and government bailouts. The economy was already in one of the deepest recessions since World War II. It takes a hardy soul to rebalance in such circumstances.

Yet consider the cost of not rebalancing. An investor who had meant to have 70 percent allocated to stocks has a little more than 50 percent in stocks as the market

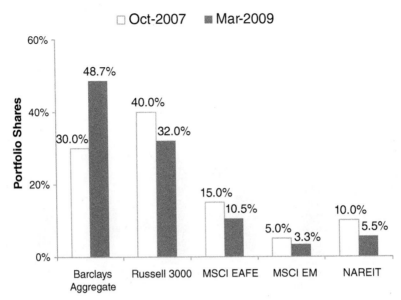

FIGURE 21.4   Drift of Portfolio Shares in Bust
Data Sources: Barclays Capital, Russell®, MSCI, and ©FTSE

starts to rebound. And the shortfall is due to inaction, not to deliberate investment policy. This just illustrates how hard it is to follow a consistent asset allocation strategy. And that is why, at the end of the day, an investor has to really believe in asset allocation to match the long-term returns that have been reported in this book.

Notes

1. The trough for the S&P 500 occurred on October 9, 2002. It reached a peak five years later on October 9, 2007.
2. The S&P 500 peaked on October 9, 2007 and reached bottom on March 9, 2009.

Part II   Execution

Execution involves implementing the investment program efficiently. Doing this may involve developing investment manager guidelines and implementing changes across and within asset classes (rebalancing and transitioning between managers). This chapter deals with rebalancing and transitioning assets between managers.

Rebalancing

"Rebalancing" means periodically adjusting a portfolio's asset allocation back to its benchmark, or strategic, asset allocation.

WHY IS REBALANCING NECESSARY?   The fund's strategic asset allocation represents the portfolio that the governing body determines best meets the objectives of the fund,

TABLE 21.1   Example of Portfolio Drift

Asset Class	Benchmark Allocation	Amount Invested	Return for Month	Amount at Month-End	Allocation Month-End
Equities	40%	$400	10%	$440	43%
Fixed income	40%	$400	−6%	$376	37%
Cash	20%	$200	2%	$204	20%
Total	100%	$1,000	2%	$1,020	100%

given the risk–return trade-off. The strategic asset allocation is often referred to as the fund's benchmark asset allocation.

Over time, however, the returns to each asset class will differ, and, even if the fund's asset allocation was initially exactly at benchmark, the actual asset allocation will drift away from the benchmark.

For example, suppose that the benchmark was 40 percent equities, 40 percent fixed interest, and 20 percent cash and that we invested $1,000 in this benchmark asset allocation at the start of the month. Performance during the month is as shown in Table 21.1.

During the month, each asset class performed differently. Equities returned 10 percent, fixed income fell by 6 percent, and cash increased by 2 percent. At the end of the month the asset allocation had drifted from the benchmark asset allocation. If the benchmark asset allocation represents the best portfolio for the fund, then after one month, the actual portfolio is no longer the best portfolio.

When the actual asset allocation drifts away from the benchmark, investment performance is adversely affected in two ways:

1. The portfolio may be subject to a higher level of risk than necessary for the returns it can be expected to provide.
2. The risk–return trade-off may no longer be suitable to meet the fund's objectives.

To address these problems, the portfolio must be rebalanced back to the benchmark asset allocation.

The benefit of rebalancing is that it will tend to buy low/sell high. Over time, a disciplined rebalancing policy will sell appreciating assets when markets have risen, as the asset proportion would have exceeded the benchmark weight, and buy assets when markets have fallen, when their relative performance causes their asset proportion to fall below benchmark weight.

PRINCIPLES OF REBALANCING   In the absence of costs, continuously rebalancing would be the most appropriate action. However, costs of rebalancing can be significant. Therefore, there is a trade-off between the frequency of rebalancing, to maintain the desired asset allocation, and the costs of rebalancing.

- Rebalancing too frequently will result in many small positions being traded. The benefits of rebalancing would be quickly offset by the costs of trading.

- A small amount of drift does not move the portfolio's risk–return profile significantly away from the benchmark profile.

HOW IS REBALANCING ACCOMPLISHED?   Rebalancing can be carried out in two ways.

1. **Cash flows.** Many assets produce cash dividends and coupon payments that themselves require reinvestment. These cash flows can be directed to under weight asset classes so as to mitigate the need for explicit rebalancing activities. Some funds may receive regular contributions that may be sufficient to meet all or part of the rebalancing requirements.
2. **Sales and purchases.** Assets can be sold in over weight asset classes and the funds used to purchase under weight asset classes.

WHAT SORT OF REBALANCING APPROACH IS APPROPRIATE?   Jaconetti, Francis, and Zilbering (2010) compare three rebalancing rules:

1. No rebalancing
2. Periodic rebalancing (monthly, quarterly, and annually)
3. Rebalancing when one or more asset classes reach trigger points, such as 1 percent, 5 percent, or 10 percent deviations from benchmark

The study shows that choosing not to rebalance portfolios is the least effective approach (i.e., portfolio efficiency is adversely affected). There is no appreciable difference between periodic rebalancing policies and trigger-point rebalancing policies, although the costs of rebalancing rise dramatically the shorter the rebalancing period. Overall, an effective balance between risk–reward and frequency of rebalancing seems to occur with equity rebalancing ranges of about 5 percent.

PRACTICAL CONSIDERATIONS   In designing an appropriate rebalancing policy, it is worth taking into account these points:

- The greater the transaction cost for rebalancing a particular asset class, the wider the rebalancing range should be.
- The actual differences between rebalancing policies tend to be small.
- The rebalancing focus should be on the significantly different asset classes, such as equities and bonds. Getting this mix right is more important than the domestic/international allocations.
- Rebalancing ranges should consider the volatility of the asset class as well as transaction costs. For example, domestic/international allocations within an asset class tend to have similar volatilities. The domestic/international rebalancing range should be smaller than the equities/bonds rebalancing range.
- The lowest-cost methods of rebalancing should be used.
  - Net cash, from dividends, coupons, or net contributions, should be used first.
  - Next, futures should be used where possible to effect rebalancing rather than selling or buying physical assets. Futures allow moves to be made more quickly and do not disturb underlying portfolios. The use of futures permits investors to adopt narrower rebalancing triggers.
  - Last, physical transactions to rebalance should be performed.

TABLE 21.2   Sample Rebalancing Ranges

Asset Class	Benchmark	Drift Range	Rebalancing Range
Domestic equities	30%	±3%	27%–33%
International equities	20%	±3%	17%–23%
Total equity	50%	±5%	45%–55%
Domestic fixed income	30%	±3%	27%–33%
International fixed income	20%	±3%	17%–23%
Cash	0%	±3%	0%–3%

EXAMPLE   The example in Table 21.2 demonstrates what a rebalancing policy could look like.

DISCIPLINE IS ESSENTIAL   Strict adherence to rebalancing policy is essential. In a similar vein, the only way that a rebalancing policy can be beneficial is for it to be applied diligently and objectively. Doing this requires regular assessment of a portfolio's actual asset allocation against the benchmark, with consequential trading decisions being taken on the basis of well-defined rules rather than subjective views about the future return prospects of asset classes. In other words, rebalancing policy should not be used as a tool for taking a tactical approach to asset allocation. These decisions should at least be separated. This does not mean, however, that practical considerations not captured by the rebalancing model (e.g., one-time cash flows for such purposes as tax) should not be taken into account as part of the rebalancing process.

Transitioning Managers

Replacing a portfolio manager is an expensive exercise. Just how expensive is not widely appreciated. If the broad structure of the portfolio remains unchanged after the replacement, costs are likely to be around 1 percent to 2 percent. If significant restructuring takes place and the securities are of limited liquidity, the costs could be greater than 5 percent.

Whatever the reason for the change, two key principles should be observed.

1. The potential costs and potential benefits of the change should be evaluated in advance.
2. The transition of assets between managers should be managed carefully to minimize the costs of the transition.

Furthermore, exposure to market movements should be managed during the transition. If the investor's portfolio is held in cash during the transition and the market rises, the opportunity cost to the investor may exceed the transition costs being saved.

WHY IS CHANGE COSTLY?   The costs of a transition are broadly twofold. First are normal costs of trading the portfolio, and second is the potential lack of alignment between the investor and both the outgoing (or old) and incoming (or new) manager.

The normal costs of trading are associated with buying and selling securities. These include commissions and bid/offer spreads, and, in some markets, official charges.

The lack of alignment issue tends to be more significant than the normal costs of trading. The investor's objective is to ensure the maximum proceeds for the securities being sold and to minimize the costs of acquiring new securities. However, the old manager, having been terminated, gains very little benefit from acting in the investor's best interests. It is usual to therefore exclude the old manager from the transition process. This occurs by preventing the old manager from making any further changes to the investor's portfolio and having the list of current portfolio holdings passed on to the investor. The investor may pass the list of holdings to the new manager. The new manager may then be instructed to sell securities the manager does not wish to retain and reinvest the proceeds in the securities the manager wishes to obtain. It is rare for the old manager to participate in the buying and selling process involved in restructuring the portfolio.

Why would the new manager not act in the investor's best interests in restructuring the portfolio? There are several reasons.

The new manager may not be familiar with the securities held by the old manager. This can occur when the old manager held securities that are not well researched or tend not to be widely held by other managers. For example, if the old manager specializes in small-capitalization securities and the new manager focuses on large-capitalization securities, then the new manager will have little experience and expertise in small-capitalization securities. The risk is the unwanted securities are sold by a seller that does not understand the trading and valuation dynamics of the market in which trading takes place.

The investor may think the new manager has an incentive to ensure the unwanted securities are sold carefully, since the sale proceeds will determine the starting portfolio value of the new manager. The portfolio will affect the ongoing performance and hence the management fee earned by the manager. The new manager has to balance the impact on the potential management fees from poor transitioning with the resources needed to research the old manager's portfolio.

In practice, the new manager knows there is a honeymoon period with new investor portfolios—the period during which the new manager restructures the portfolio and during which poor performance is often accepted by the investor. Some investors recognize the honeymoon period and agree to measure performance of the new manager after the portfolio has been restructured.

The knowledge of the honeymoon period had two main effects. First, new managers are keen to ensure the incoming portfolio matches their desired portfolio as quickly as possible. The new manager feels little obligation to understand the market for the unwanted securities. If the size of the position in unwanted securities is large relative to the market's normal dealing size, the new manager's indifference can have a substantial negative effect on the sale price. Poor sales proceeds can also be blamed on the old manager, knowing that many investors monitor the trading process with great diligence. Second, expensive transitions can also be blamed on the restructuring process, knowing that the period of poor performance will not be attributed to the new manager. Even if no explicit honeymoon period is agreed on between the investor and the new manager, the new manager will explain away poor performance as being the costs of restructuring the portfolio, hoping that investors will give the new manager the benefit of the doubt.

Transition costs are unavoidable but not uncontrollable. The remainder of this chapter considers ways in which the investor can ensure that transition costs are minimized.

PROCESS IN CHANGING MANAGERS   The usual procedure used for making a manager change has been described. The old manager is prevented from making any further changes to the portfolio, and is asked to deliver a list of the current portfolio holdings. That list is then given to the new manager, who then decides which securities to retain and which to sell.

The process assumes a new manager has been identified. There may be circumstances where the old manager must be terminated immediately: fraud, or serious breach of investment guidelines. In these circumstances the portfolio could be held in suspense until a new manager is identified. A custodian bank can usually manage the mechanical aspects of a portfolio in suspense, but responsibility for decisions about the securities held in the portfolio rest with the investor.

In conducting a transition the following five options are available—each with their advantages and disadvantages.

1. The new manager could implement all the required trades.
2. Both the new and old managers could work together.
3. The old manager could be instructed to sell the unwanted securities and pass the sale proceeds to the new manager. The new manager would purchase the desired securities.
4. The investor could implement the transition with the help of a broker.
5. Appoint a dedicated transition manager.

SELECTING THE APPROPRIATE OPTION   There is no single answer to which option is best. Judgments will need to be made on several criteria, the most important of which are:

- The number and liquidity of shares held
- The degree to which the investor is willing to be involved in the process
- The decision to employ a dedicated transition manager
- The new manager's expertise in managing the securities held by the old manager
- The ability and willingness of the investor's other managers to purchase or accept unwanted securities
- The timeframe over which the transition must be completed

In practice, many investors prefer to use dedicated transition managers. A transition manager offers dedicated transition management services tailored to the specific requirements involved in moving a portfolio of assets from one manager to another and executing the required trades on the investor's behalf. The transition manager can take over the assets from the old manager, sell the securities that need to be sold and buy securities to build a portfolio based on the new manager's advice. The transition manager then delivers the portfolio to the new manager. The advantage of a transition manager, compared to the investor-conducted transition, is the specialist expertise and resources devoted to administration involved in the transition, dedicated risk and trading systems to minimize costs and reporting services which are particularly necessary for complex transitions.

Reference

Jaconetti, C. M., M. K. Francis, and Y. Zilbering. 2010. "Best Practices for Portfolio Rebalancing." Vanguard. July.

Part III Review and Monitoring

Reporting back to the board or investment committee is essential to effectively manage monitoring risk. Every aspect of the governance arrangement and investment process should be monitored and appropriately evaluated. Good investment reports are necessary to communicate essential information so that any issues can be clearly identified and effective solutions reached.

Levels of Performance Reporting

Any fund's portfolio can usually be split into three levels performance reporting: fund level, asset class level, and manager level. These are represented diagrammatically in Figure 21.5.

FUND LEVEL   At this level the total fund return is measured and compared to the fund's return objective and strategic asset allocation, or benchmark, return. In the case of a defined benefit plan, the funding discount rate (that is used in the actuarial funding valuation) would also be presented.

ASSET CLASS LEVEL   At the asset class level, the performance of different investment strategies for each asset class is measured. A variety of manager structures may be employed. For a single-manager structure, the performance of the manager's portfolio is measured relative to the manager's benchmark return. The separate effects of the manager's security selection decisions can be accounted for at this level. The asset allocation timing decisions would be reflected in the difference between the actual asset class allocations and the benchmark asset class allocations.

Reporting Level	Decision	Description				
Fund Level	Governance	Who does what				
	Fund's purpose	Goals and objectives				
Asset Class Level	Strategic asset allocation	Equities			Bonds	
	Tactical asset allocation	Short-term deviations from strategic asset allocation				
	Asset class structure	Value	Core	Growth	Broad	Extended
Manager Level	Manager selection	A	B	C	D	E

FIGURE 21.5   Levels of Reporting

MANAGER LEVEL The manager level of reporting captures the performance of the individual managers relative to a benchmark that reflects their strategy or style. For example, an investor may express the global equities asset class in terms of a value and a growth style. The combined value and growth manager performance is measured against the MSCI World Index, for example. The individual manager performance would be measured against the appropriate style index. The growth manager may be benchmarked against the MSCI World Growth Index, while the value manager may be benchmarked against the MSCI World Value Index. Each level of reporting is explored in greater detail with examples.

Sample Reports

FUND LEVEL At the fund level, the performance report usually addresses three key areas:

1. **Earnings.** How has the fund performed against its total return expectation?
2. **Spending.** How has the actual spending of the fund compared to expectations? For charitable trusts or endowments this addresses the distribution levels of the fund.
3. **Value-added.** Have the investments produced superior returns due to active management decisions? The main sources of value-add are can be split into asset allocation timing and security selection decisions.

We present an example for a charitable trust in Table 21.3.
The trustees of the charitable trust can get a snapshot of the state of the fund.

- The trust expects to earn 8 percent per annum (p.a.) over the long term. It has exceeded this by 4 percent since inception of the fund (excess return).

TABLE 21.3 Charitable Trust Performance Report, Year Ended September 31, 2012

Investment Performance	Quarter	Year to Date	Since Inception (May 1, 2003) (% p.a.)	
Nominal fund return	1.0%	5.0%	12.0%	(1)
Benchmark fund return	0.6%	3.5%	10.0%	(2)
Expected nominal return		8.0%	8.0%	(3)
Excess return		−3.0%	4.0%	(4)
Spending rate				
Expected spending rate		3.5%	3.0%	(5)
Actual spending rate		3.7%	2.8%	(6)
Active management				
Value added (1–2)	0.4%	1.5%	2.0%	(7)
Attribution				
Asset allocation timing	0.2%	0.2%	−0.3%	(8)
Security selection	0.2%	1.3%	2.3%	(9)

- The targeted spending rate is 3 percent p.a. over the long term. However, since inception, the excess return has meant the trust can afford a higher spending rate in the future. The trust has adjusted up its expected spending rate to 3.5 percent p.a. Actual spending rates, however, have turned out to be lower than expected.
- The trust has benefited from its active management activities. Since inception, the trust has earned 2.0 percent p.a. more than passive management, after fees. The value added is broken down as 2.3 percent p.a. from security selection and −0.3 percent from asset allocation timing. The trust does not engage in tactical asset allocation; the asset allocation timing represents the deviation of the actual fund's asset allocation against the strategic asset allocation, which is tolerated under the trust's rebalancing policy. Rebalancing sometimes generates a positive return and sometimes a negative return, but is not expected to be significant in the long term. More recently, the value added from active management has declined. This decline should prompt the trustees to investigate the reasons. Some issues to be addressed are: Is the confidence in the active managers still present? Has something changed with the managers' processes? Are the return outcomes within the typical variation expected when the active managers were hired?

ASSET CLASS LEVEL At the asset class level, the aggregate performance of all strategies within that asset class is measured. For example, if a multiple-manager structure is employed within an asset class, the returns across all managers in the structure are aggregated and compared to the appropriate benchmark index and peer universe. For instance, international equities strategies are usually evaluated against the MSCI World Index (excluding the domestic country if there is a separate domestic equities allocation) while U.S. equities strategies are usually compared against the S&P 500 or Russell 1000 index returns.

If balanced fund managers are used, then the performance evaluation would be against the manager's benchmark return, which is usually the same as the fund's strategic asset allocation benchmark.

Tables 21.4 and 21.5 shows a typical performance summary at the asset class level. The examples assume a specialist manager structure is employed. Table 21.4

TABLE 21.4   Summary of Manager and Asset Class Allocation, September 31, 2012

	Domestic Equities	International Equities	Domestic Fixed Income	International Fixed Income	Global Real Estate	Domestic Cash	Manager Total
Manager A	8.3%		4.6%			37.5%	50.4%
Manager B	2.8%				5.3%		8.0%
Manager C		16.1%		7.8%			23.9%
Manager D		17.7%					17.7%
Asset class total	11.0%	33.8%	4.6%	7.8%	5.3%	37.5%	100.0%
Strategic asset allocation	12.0%	32.9%	4.2%	8.6%	5.2%	37.2%	100.0%

TABLE 21.5 Performance Summary by Manager and Asset Class, September 31, 2012

	Market Values $ millions	Latest Quarter		Latest Year		Since May 03 (%)	
		Actual	Index	Actual	Index	Actual	Index
Domestic equities	27.5	10.0%	9.2%	19.9%	23.5%	19.8%	22.3%
Manager A	20.6	10.3%	9.2%	20.3%	23.5%	19.6%	22.3%
Manager B	6.9	9.2%	9.2%	18.6%	23.5%	20.3%	22.3%
International equities	84.5	14.3%	15.0%	19.9%	19.9%	7.1%	7.5%
Manager C (growth)	40.2	16.3%	19.6%	18.6%	20.6%	7.3%	8.5%
Manager D (market oriented)	44.3	12.2%	10.3%	21.2%	19.1%	6.9%	6.5%
Domestic fixed income	11.5	3.6%	3.3%	9.6%	8.3%	5.5%	4.9%
Manager A	11.5	3.6%	3.3%	9.6%	8.3%	5.5%	4.9%
International fixed income	19.5	2.3%	2.6%	7.6%	6.8%	5.6%	6.5%
Manager C	19.5	2.3%	2.6%	7.6%	6.8%	5.6%	6.5%
Global real estate	13.1	12.8%	13.5%	17.9%	17.9%	6.4%	6.8%
Manager B	13.1	12.8%	13.5%	17.9%	17.9%	6.4%	6.8%
Domestic cash	93.8	0.5%	0.4%	1.2%	1.5%	3.5%	3.7%
Manager A	93.8	0.5%	0.4%	1.2%	1.5%	3.5%	3.7%
TOTAL	250	7.1%	7.3%	11.3%	11.7%	6.9%	7.5%

provides a summary of the asset values by manager and asset class. In the sample report, Manager C manages two specialty mandates: one for international fixed income and one for international equities. Manager B also manages two mandates: domestic equities and global real estate. The fund's actual allocation across asset classes against the policy portfolio is shown in the last two rows. The actual allocation is close to the policy benchmark, indicating no need to rebalance the portfolio.

Table 21.5 shows a performance summary of each asset class, and managers within each asset class, against the relevant benchmarks. The asset class benchmarks should match those chosen when the asset allocation policy was established.

MANAGER LEVEL Active managers are hired in the expectation they will generate superior returns above a simple, passive index. However, active managers will not always beat their benchmark. Temporary periods of underperformance should be expected. Good reporting, at the manager level, should help an investor identify the cause of underperformance, and address issues such as whether: it is due to a change in the manager's investment process? It is due to the manager's investment style? Whether the performance is typical variation, expected when the manager was hired?

The following areas should be addressed:

- How the manager's expected value-add (alpha) and active risk (tracking error) compares to expectations
- How the manager's style has drifted over time
- How the manager compares to other managers of similar investment style

Figure 21.6 addresses all three areas, while Figures 21.7 and 21.8 deal with the second and third areas, respectively.

Relative Performance Expectations Figure 21.6 provides a comprehensive way to monitor the risks in active strategies.

Manager D is a market-oriented international equities manager expected to outperform the MSCI World Index by 1 percent p.a. over the long term with 2 percent tracking error. This means that Manager D is expected to outperform the index by 1 percent p.a. and underperform the index in 40 percent of quarters, 31 percent of calendar years, and 20 percent of three-year periods.

Panels B, C, and D show the manager's excess returns, tracking error, and information ratio (excess returns relative to tracking error). In panel B, the dotted line is the expected value added, of 1 percent p.a., and the black line is the rolling annualized value added.

Panel C shows the manager tracking error, the amount of benchmark relative risk, produced over rolling annual periods. The manager's tracking error has been below expectations, of 2 percent p.a. over 2009 through 2011. However, in the past year, tracking error has risen dramatically and been close to 6 percent p.a.

Panel D shows the information ratio—the ratio of excess returns to tracking error. Over rolling annual periods, the information ratio has been very high over the 2009 to 2011 periods, relative to an expectation of 0.5. Excess returns were well above benchmark, and tracking error risk very low. However, given both the decline

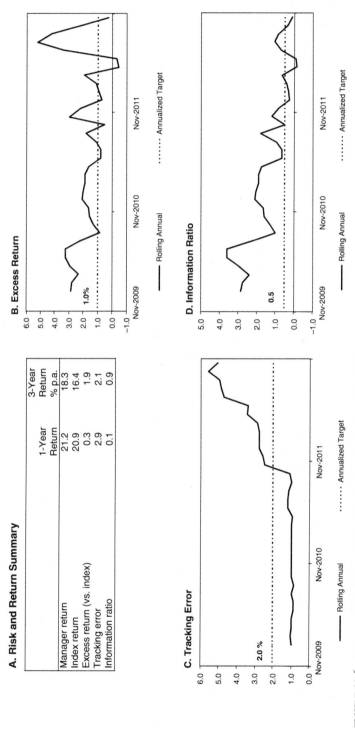

A. Risk and Return Summary

	1-Year Return	3-Year Return % p.a.
Manager return	21.2	18.3
Index return	20.9	16.4
Excess return (vs. index)	0.3	1.9
Tracking error	2.9	2.1
Information ratio	0.1	0.9

B. Excess Return

C. Tracking Error

D. Information Ratio

FIGURE 21.6 Manager D's Value Added; Period to September 31, 2012

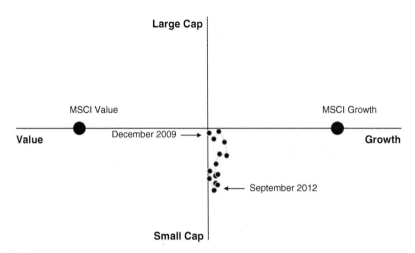

FIGURE 21.7   Style over Time; Period to September 31, 2012

in excess returns and the remarkable increase in tracking error, the information ratio has plummeted.

The significant rise in tracking error should be cause for concern, despite the excess returns being well within reasonable expectations.

Further investigation would be warranted. Some issues that would be addressed are: Has the manager's style drifted over time, and how has the manager performed relative to other similar managers in the universe?

STYLE DRIFT   Figure 21.7 shows Manager D's style relative to the index, the MSCI World Index. The center of the figure represents the MSCI World Index. The MSCI style indexes, value, and growth, are marked by the solid black circles. The manager's style and capitalization bias is shown for each quarter from December 2009 to September 2012 by the black dots linked by the gray line. Manager D's portfolio has shown significant size drift over that period, from being in line with the benchmark to having a significant small-capitalization bias.

The drift toward smaller-capitalization stocks partly explains the significant increase in tracking error risk observed in the past year. This shift should be cause for concern, as the manager no longer suits the asset class strategy for which he or she was employed. Further discussions with the manager would help in understanding the reasons for the drift.

PEER-RELATIVE COMPARISON   Figure 21.8 compares the manager's performance to the peer universe of market-oriented international equities managers.

The figure shows the universe of peer managers over one, two, and three years, in annualized performance. The number of managers in the universe is shown and includes 120 in the one-year performance numbers, 100 in the two-year performance numbers, and 75 in the three-year performance numbers. Over a one-year period, Manager D produced returns in the top decile, although the median manager underperformed the benchmark. Over a two-year period, Manager D produced returns in the bottom quartile. Over a three-year period, Manager D produced returns in the top

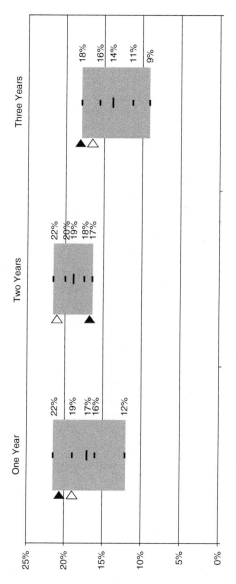

	One Year Return	Two Years Return	Three Years Return
95th Percentile	22	22	18
75th Percentile	19	20	15.6
Median	17	19	13.9
25th Percentile	16	17.5	11.3
5th Percentile	12	16.5	9.1
Number of Portfolios	120	100	75
Manager D ▲	21.2	17.5	18.3
MSCI World Index △	19.1	21	16.8

FIGURE 21.8 Performance against Peers; Period to September 31, 2012

5 percent of peer managers, and the median manager significantly underperformed the benchmark.

While the manager's performance over three years is in the top 5 percent and in the top decile in the past year, it has been produced with an excessive level of tracking error risk driven by a strong bias to smaller-capitalization stocks. In other words, the peer comparison becomes less relevant since the manager's performance is more likely to be due to smaller-capitalization stocks outperforming than due to the manager's stock selection capabilities.

ISSUES WITH PEER UNIVERSES The example with Manager D illustrates some limitations of the use of peer universe comparative performance. While peer manager universes are a useful part of the manager evaluation process, they can be dangerous when used for investment decision-making purposes. Some reasons are provided next.

- Peer universes tend to differ across various data providers. It is possible that an investor's manager may be above the median manager in one peer universe but below the median in another.
- The benchmark is investable, the median manager is not. The median manager is known only after the fact.
- Peer universes will display a survivorship bias over time. Persistently poor managers tend to terminate their businesses and will be removed from peer universes. Better managers will remain resulting in an upward bias in the median manager's return. A good manager will struggle to beat this upward bias and could be unjustifiably fired if compared to the median manager's performance over time.

Similar care should be adhered to when undertaking total fund performance comparisons. Many investors compare their total fund performance to the total fund performance of other investors. Such comparisons may encourage investors to chase the strategic asset allocation of peer funds, based on their past performance. The costs of performance chasing behavior are twofold: the opportunity cost of the investor's original strategic asset allocation, and the transaction costs of changing the portfolio. Maintaining the investor's initial strategic asset allocation is often the best course of action, as it is the most suitable to meet the investor's objectives.

Conclusion

Performance evaluation is essential to the review process and for managing and monitoring risk. Good performance reporting helps the investor highlight where any performance issues exist. Performance reports should identify investment strategies that add value and assist the investor in taking appropriate action on strategies that subtract value. The end result should be to improve the quality and effectiveness of investment decisions taken by the investor.

IMCA

Investment Management Consultants Association® (IMCA®) was established in 1985 as the standard-bearer of ethics, education, and credentialing for investment consultants and private wealth advisors. IMCA delivers premier investment and wealth management credentials and world-class education to practitioners who want to distinguish their expertise in a global and highly sophisticated marketplace.

The Certified Investment Management Analyst® (CIMA®) certification is the only financial services credential in the United States to meet the international standard for personnel certification (ISO 17024) and earn accreditation by American National Standards Institute (ANSI). CIMA professionals integrate a complex body of investment knowledge, ethically contributing to prudent investment decisions by providing objective advice and guidance to individual investors and institutional investors.

The Certified Private Wealth Advisor® (CPWA®) certification is an advanced wealth management competency for advisors committed to serving the needs of clients with a net worth of more than $5 million. Those who earn this certification have learned to identify and analyze challenges facing high-net-worth clients and how to develop strategies to minimize taxes, monetize and protect assets, maximize growth, and transfer wealth.

IMCA Membership is open to any professional primarily engaged in investment consulting or wealth management. IMCA members receive discounted rates for world-class educational offerings, subscriptions to leading-edge publications including *Investments & Wealth Monitor* and the *Journal of Investment Consulting*, and 24-hour access to powerful online resources and networking opportunities.

IMCA is dedicated to the advanced education of investment and wealth management professionals. IMCA's conferences and seminars host more than 4,000 attendees per year. In addition to conference offerings, IMCA provides a variety of online webinars, self-study programs, an online Resource Center for CIMA Candidates, and several other publications for advisors.

IMCA members set the standard for quality and trusted investment advice. Each certified professional and all IMCA members must adhere to IMCA's rigorous *Code of Professional Responsibility*.

IMCA.org

About the Author

Jim Dobbs, CIMA®, CFP®, CPWA®
President, Dobbs Education, LLC
    Financial Education & Certification Programs Consultant
President, Dobbs Wealth Management Group, LLC
    Fee-only Financial Planning and Investment Management

Jim Dobbs specializes in designing, developing, and managing financial training and certification programs. He has served as consultant to several universities and certification associations, working regularly with organization directors, executives, board members, committees, task forces, staff, and volunteers. Jim has written numerous program feasibility studies and business plans. Mr. Dobbs has designed the structure, content, and delivery of various certification and designation programs; taught in and directed training programs; and helped organizations market and position these programs. He developed and currently serves as program director of MIT Sloan's online registered education program for CIMA certification.

Mr. Dobbs served the Investment Management Consultants Association (IMCA) as director of education, where he helped create the Certified Private Wealth Advisor® certification program. The CPWA registered education program is delivered through the University of Chicago's Booth School of Business, where he serves as program director. He also helped develop the Advanced Investment Strategist program in portfolio risk management; led a project to help update and revise the Certified Investment Management Analyst® (CIMA) certification program curriculum; and currently serves as chair of IMCA's Technical Advisory Board. Mr. Dobbs founded and managed the CFP Board registered financial planning certificate programs at Southern Methodist University in Dallas and The University of Texas at Austin, where he was program director. Later he served Certified Financial Planner Board of Standards, Inc., as director of education.

Mr. Dobbs is president of Dobbs Wealth Management Group, LLC, a registered investment advisory practice offering financial planning and investment management services since 1998. Before founding Dobbs Wealth, he worked for several financial services firms, including Mercer; IDS (now Ameriprise); Harris, Webb & Garrison (now SMH Group); and Citigroup. In addition to serving clients at each firm, Jim held various managerial positions.

Mr. Dobbs earned an Executive MBA from Carnegie Mellon University's Tepper School of Business (with a specialization in asset and wealth management) and holds a master's degree from the University of Lausanne (Switzerland), in partnership with Swiss Finance Institute. He earned a Post-Baccalaureate Award in Taxation from UCLA Extension and is a graduate of the Management Development for

1105

Entrepreneurs (MDE) Program offered through UCLA's Anderson School of Management. He earned a bachelor's degree in Business Administration (majoring in financial services and planning) from the Hankamer School of Business at Baylor University.

Jim resides with his wife Sandi and their three children, Erika, Dylan, and Drew, in the foothills of Colorado.

Index